D1476456

MAYFLOWER Source Records

From The New England Historical and Genealogical Register

MAYFLOWER
Source Records

Primary Data Concerning Southeastern Massachusetts, Cape Cod, and the Islands of Nantucket and Martha's Vineyard

From The New England Historical and Genealogical Register

Selected and Introduced by
GARY BOYD ROBERTS

GENEALOGICAL PUBLISHING CO., INC.
Baltimore 1986

Excerpted and reprinted from *The New England Historical and Genealogical Register* ©
with added Introduction, Table of Contents, and Index, by
Genealogical Publishing Co., Inc., Baltimore, 1986.

Library of Congress Catalogue Card Number 85-82063
International Standard Book Number 0-8063-1145-2
Made in the United States of America

Introduction

IN THE more than 150 years between the landing of the ship *Mayflower* (1620) and the outbreak of the American Revolution (1775) descendants of the *Mayflower* Pilgrims spread throughout the southeastern Massachusetts counties of Plymouth, Bristol, and Barnstable (Cape Cod). By the 1790s *Mayflower* descendants were also in Rhode Island and Connecticut, Long Island and New Jersey, North Carolina, Maine, and Nova Scotia; movement had begun as well into upstate New York. Throughout the colonial period, however, their geographical center had remained Plymouth, Bristol, and Barnstable counties, formed in 1685, a few years before the parent Plymouth Colony was absorbed by Massachusetts Bay. Although other ships and possibly a thousand or so other colonists arrived in Plymouth in the 1620s and later, the generally somewhat older *Mayflower* Pilgrims were so prolific—John Howland, Edward Doty, John Alden, Richard Warren, and George Soule alone left 250 or more grandchildren who themselves left issue—that by 1750 or so perhaps half of the inhabitants of Plymouth and Bristol counties, and of Cape Cod, were descendants of the twenty-three *Mayflower* sires who left American progeny.

Plymouth, Bristol, and Barnstable counties are thus "*Mayflower* country." Following considerable Quaker conversion and settlement on Cape Cod in the 1660s and later, various *Mayflower* scions, especially Gorham great- and great-great-grandchildren of John Howland, settled on Nantucket. Spouses of these early Nantucket Gorhams included one or more Bunkers, Coffins, Folgers, Gardners, Macys, Starbucks, Swains, and Worths. By the early nineteenth century a very large number of Nantucket natives were thus also *Mayflower* descendants—via Gorhams or other Cape Cod families especially. In addition various Plymouth, Cape Cod, or Nantucket *Mayflower* families moved also to Martha's Vineyard. Elizabeth Hawes, another great-granddaughter of John Howland through the Gorhams, married Thomas^3 Daggett in 1683/4; their children's Vineyard spouses included three Butlers, another Daggett, a Norton, and a Pease. A generation earlier Lydia Snow, a granddaughter of Richard Warren, married Stephen Skiffe of Sandwich and left two daughters who settled on the Vineyard; sons-in-law of these daughters included two Luces, two Wests, and a Skiffe of Chilmark. Although "*Mayflower* country" does not encompass Nantucket or Martha's Vineyard, many families in both have been *Mayflower* descendants for many generations.

Given the commonality, even preponderance, of *Mayflower* descent for their colonial and later residents, a volume of primary data covering southeastern Massachusetts, Cape Cod, Nantucket, and Martha's Vineyard becomes then a collection of *Mayflower Source Records*. Included herein is all such material—largely vital, church, and ministerial records, probate abstracts, and cemetery inscriptions—published in the nation's oldest genealogical journal, *The New England Historical and Genealogical Register,* between 1847 and 1983. Two recent articles, "Lists of Baptists in Rehoboth, Massachusetts, in the 1700s," by H. L. Peter Rounds (*Register* 138[1984]:24-31) and "Swansea, Massachusetts Baptist Church Records," edited by Robert Charles Anderson (139[1985]:21-49), appeared after this present volume was assembled. Also omitted were all articles covering the Plymouth Colony towns of Bristol and Little Compton, annexed to Rhode Island in 1747, and all primary data, mostly Bible records, concerning single families of *Mayflower* descent. Bristol and Little Compton articles will be included in any future consolidation of Connecticut and Rhode Island source materials, and all Bible records from the *Register,* plus all items that are in effect Bible records, may be consolidated into a future volume as well. Other single-family primary source items omitted from this collection include "Extract of a Letter dated St. George's, at the Eastward, May 22, 1758" (14[1860]: 222, concerning the death or Indian capture of several Bradfords), "Atkinson, King, Obern, Winslow" (29[1875]:110, taken from a 1744 record book of Joshua Winslow), "Letter of Jonathan Alden of Marshfield, 1722" (48[1894]:310-311), "Col. John Gorham's 'Wast Book.' Fac-similes" (52[1898]:186-192), and "Petition of Desire Gorham" (52:229).

Mayflower Source Records contains vital, church, ministerial, cemetery or other records for all but three of the Plymouth Colony towns that composed early Plymouth, Bristol, and Barnstable counties and were *not* later annexed by Rhode Island. So represented herein then are Barnstable, Bridgewater, Dartmouth, Eastham, Freetown, Marshfield, Middleboro, Plymouth, Rehoboth, Sandwich, Scituate, Taunton, and Yarmouth—plus Nantucket and the three original towns of the Vineyard (Chilmark, Edgartown, and Tisbury). Omitted are Duxbury, Rochester, and Swansea. For convenient maps of these towns circa 1690 and today see the front and back inside covers of *Plymouth Colony Probate Guide: Where to Find Wills and Related Data for 800 People of Plymouth Colony, 1620-1691,* compiled by Ruth Wilder Sherman and Robert S. Wakefield (1983). Included also in *Mayflower Source Records* is data from almost a dozen later towns of the three mainland counties —Chatham, Dennis, Falmouth, Kingston, Norwell, Orleans, Pembroke, Provincetown, Raynham, Seekonk, and Wareham. Most extensively covered are Bridgewater, Chilmark, Edgartown, Nantucket, Norwell, Pembroke, Raynham, Scituate, and Yarmouth. Often this town data considerably amplifies information in the published Massachusetts vital records, or covers towns not yet included in that series. For a listing of all such printed volumes through 1983, and all journal article or known manuscript copies of pre-1850 Massachusetts town vital records, see the bibliography by Edward W. Hanson in *Genealogical Research in New England,* ed. Ralph J. Crandall (1984), pp. 97-108, 113-114.

Finally of note among the specific articles herein are the almost sixty pages of "Abstracts from the First Book of Bristol County Probate Records" by Lucy Hall Greenlaw, and almost forty pages of "Abstracts of the First Wills in the Probate Office, Plymouth," by Justin Winsor. The Plymouth abstracts cover the years 1633-1671, or the bulk of the Plymouth *Colony* period. The Bristol County abstracts, covering the 1690s, are a continuation of Mrs. Greenlaw's earlier Bristol County probate series in Volumes 3 and 4 of *The Genealogical Advertiser: A Quarterly Magazine of Family History* (1900-1901). This journal, which also contains a series of Plymouth *County* abstracts covering the decade 1686-1695, was issued in only four volumes and reprinted in one by Genealogical Publishing Company (GPC) in Baltimore in 1974. Other GPC reprints of *Mayflower*-related source material include George Ernest Bowman, *The Mayflower Reader: A Selection of Articles from the Mayflower Descendant* [1899-1905] (1978), *Plymouth Church Records, 1620-1858,* 2 vols. (1975), and Nathaniel Bradstreet Shurtleff, *Records of Plymouth Colony: Births, Marriages, Deaths, Burials, and Other Records, 1633-1689* (1976).

Mayflower Source Records stands by itself as a major compendium of primary data covering "*Mayflower* country," southeastern Massachusetts, Nantucket, and Martha's Vineyard. It is also, however, a companion volume to *Genealogies of Mayflower Families from The New England Historical and Genealogical Register,* 3 vols. (1985), and the second in a possible series of source record volumes from the *Register*—the first was *Suffolk County Wills: Abstracts of the Earliest Wills Upon Record in the County of Suffolk, Massachusetts* (1984). *Mayflower Source Records* should help many genealogists trace their *Mayflower* line or southeastern Massachusetts ancestry. It is much to be hoped also that its general reception will encourage the reprinting or transcribing of many other volumes of New England primary sources.

Gary Boyd Roberts

Contents

MAYFLOWER
Source Records

From The New England Historical
and Genealogical Register

MARRIAGES IN THE NORTH PARISH OF BRIDGEWATER (NOW NORTH BRIDGEWATER), FROM JANUARY 1, 1742, TO JANUARY, 1780.

BY REV. JOHN PORTER.

[Communicated by BRADFORD KINGMAN, Esq., Brookline, Mass.]

Daniel Ames and Hannah Keith, Jan. 28, 1742.
Joseph Richards and Mary Hamlin, Sept. 28, 1742.
Jacob Packard and Dorothy Perkins, Nov. 24, 1742.
James Powel and Alice Harris, Jan. 12, 1743.
Henry Kingman and Abigail Copeland, March 15, 1743.
Thomas Henry and Ann Miller, March 21, 1743.
*Thomas Mitchell and Rebecca Colly, March 8, 1744.
Jedediah Jordan and Sarah French, June 4, 1744.
Elias Monk and Elizabeth Buck, June 28, 1744.
William Shurtleff and Sarah Kingman, Feb. 7, 1745.
Isaac Allen and Joanna Packard, Feb. 20, 1745.
Joseph Petengill and Mary Edson, Feb. 25, 1745.
John Alden and Rebecca Nightengale, March 15, 1745.
Peter Edson and Sarah Southworth, March 28, 1745.
Isaac Packard and Abigail Porter, March 28, 1745.
*Amos Cordner and Abigail Colly, April 18, 1745.
David Edson and Susanna Emmett, Jan. 1, 1746.
Ebenezer Packard and Sarah Perkins, Feb. 25, 1746.
Nathan Keith and Hannah Snell, Aug. 26, 1746.
Nathan Hartwell and Susanna Field, Oct. 16, 1746.
Joseph Petengill and Lydia Phillips, Dec. 25, 1746.
Josiah Packard and Sarah Ames, Jan. 12, 1747.
Joseph Crossman and Mary Cary, Feb. 18, 1747.
Benjamin Petengill and Mary Kingman, April 30, 1747.
Zebulon Cary and Mehitable Gannett, Oct. 8, 1747.
Ebenezer Warren and Mary Nightengale, Oct. 19, 1747.
Jonathan Cary and Mary Curtis, Dec. 30, 1747.
William Strowbridge and Jennet Samson, June 16, 1748.
Thomas Reynolds and Elisabeth Turner, Nov. 3, 1748.
William Morrison and Sarah Montgomery, Nov. 10, 1748.
Nehemiah Lincoln and Keziah Packard, Nov. 24, 1748.
Simeon Brett and Mehitable Packard, Jan. 31, 1749.
Samuel Noyes and Mary Field, March 16, 1749.
Capt. John Phillips and Widow Bridget Southworth, April 19, 1749.
Abijah Hill and Sarah Lawson, May 12, 1749.
Jonathan Randall and Abigail Allen, July 27, 1749.

* Blacks.

Luke Perkins and Rebecca Packard, Aug. 24, 1749.
John Battles and Hannah Curtis, Nov. 16, 1749.
Ebenezer Hayward and Elizabeth Hanmer, Dec. 13, 1750.
Edward Southworth and Abia Packard, Dec. 16, 1750.
David Howard, jr. and Kezia Ames, Feb. 5, 1751.
Noah Tinkham and Sarah Porter, June 16, 1751.
David French and Abigail Owen, July 4, 1751.
Ebenezer Edson and Lucy Packard, Nov. 7, 1751.
William Curtis and Deborah Wales, Jan. 2, 1752.
*Moses Sash and Sarah Colley, May 1, 1752.
Elias Monk and Elisabeth Wright, May 27, 1752.
Samuel Cole and Sarah Packard, Nov. 16, 1752.
*Segnio Scott and Peggy Howland, Dec. 13, 1752.
John Allen and Sarah Campbell, July 12, 1753.
*Cuff Robin and Mary Robin, Nov. 3, 1753.
Zachariah Gurney and Mary Ames, Jan. 9, 1754.
Jesse Edson and Lydia Packard, March 26, 1754.
Isaac Perkins and Joanna Edson, May 2, 1754.
Simeon Cary and Mary Howard, June 27, 1754.
William Edson and Martha Howard, Nov. 27, 1754.
John McBride and Jane Wilson, Jan. 16, 1755.
Daniel Petengill, jr. and Sarah Gannett, April 9, 1755.
Barnabas Howard and Mehitable Packard, July 2, 1755.
Josiah Perkins and Abigail Edson, Aug. 17, 1755.
Matthew Kingman and Jane Packard, Nov. 6, 1755.
Isaac Alden and Martha Packard, Nov. 6, 1755.
Nathaniel Tilden and Susanna Brett, Nov. 11, 1755.
Jacob Dunbar and Hannah Randall, July 8, 1756.
Nathaniel Littlefield and Hannah Curtis, March 3, 1756.
Andrew Gammel and Betty Sampson, Oct. 27, 1756.
Joshua Packard, jr. and Martha Hartwell, Oct. 28, 1756.
David Edson and Sarah Edson, Dec. 8, 1756.
Thomas West and Mercy Packard, Dec. 9, 1756.
Edmund Soper and Eunice Curtis, Dec. 30, 1756.
Robert Howard and Abigail Snell, May 5, 1757.
Lemuel Southworth and Patience West, Nov. 6, 1757.
Joseph Cole and Betty Southworth, Dec. 8, 1757.
Simon Griffin and Widow Jennet Brown, Jan. 5, 1758.
Ephraim Willis and Elisabeth Gurnsey, April 13, 1758.
Frederick Pope and Mary Cole, June 8, 1758.
Abia Packard and Phebe Pain, Dec. 30, 1758.
Jacob Edson and Betty Packard, May 14, 1759.
Aaron Hammond and Mary Hammond, June 25, 1759.
Adam Howard and Mary Keith, June 25, 1759.
Reuben Packard and Anna Perkins, Oct. 3, 1759.
Jonathan Orcutt and Experience Washburn, Nov. 5, 1759.
Levi Keith and Jemima Perkins, Nov. 8, 1759.
Elisha Gurney and Jane Kingman, March 13, 1760.
Adam Kingman and Ruth White, March 27, 1760.
Solomon Packard and Widow Dorothy Perkins, Oct. 5, 1760.
Edmund Petengill and Sarah Curtis, Jan. 15, 1761.
Robert Morrison and widow Mary Dorman, Jan. 22, 1761.
Ezekiel Southworth and Mary Newman, April 7, 1761.

Zebedee Snell and Martha Howard, April 9, 1761.
Simeon Packard and Mary Perkins, July 6, 1761.
Zachariah Watkins and Abigail Keith, Sept. 4, 1761.
Seth Dunbar and Deborah Belcher, Dec. 3, 1761.
Daniel Littlefield and Catharine Cole, Feb. 11, 1762.
Solomon Smith and Elisabeth Cole, Feb. 11, 1762.
Nathaniel Southworth and Catherine Howard, Aug. 27, 1762.
Ephraim Thayer and Phebe Porter, Dec. 23, 1762.
Benjamin Packard and Ruth Leach, Feb. 13, 1763.
Capt. Eliphalet Phillips and Mary Howard, March 3, 1763.
Benjamin Southworth and Mary Smith, March 3, 1763.
Josiah Hayden and Silence Howard, March 15, 1763.
John Packard and Sarah Hammond, March 17, 1763.
Simeon Alden and Mary Packard, May 23, 1763.
Samuel Briggs, jr. and Rhoda Juree, Sept. 3, 1763.
Joseph Petengill, jr. and widow Hepzibah Townsend, Feb. 20, 1764.
Ebenezer Snell and Sarah Packard, April 5, 1764.
Job Bryant and Mary Turner, May 3, 1764.
Samuel Porter and Widow Ruth Reed, May 31, 1764.
*Bennet O. Batton and Abigail Cordner, Nov. 8, 1764.
*Pompey and Mehitable Colly, Nov. 8, 1764.
*Plato and Rachel Colly, Nov. 8, 1764.
Mark Ford and Hannah Brett, Nov. 22, 1764.
Levi French and Amy Packard, Nov. 29, 1764.
David Packard and Joanna Jackson, Dec. 27, 1764.
Isaac Brett and Priscilla Jackson, Jan. 17, 1765.
Dependence French and Rebecca Hammond, Feb. 7, 1765.
Seth Bryant and Elisabeth French, Feb. 7, 1765.
Micah Gurney and Hopestill Jackson, April 25, 1765.
Jonathan Lawrence and Rachel Smith, May 22, 1765.
Enoch Thayer and Rebecca Curtis, July 4, 1765.
Daniel Packard and Hannah Perkins, July 14, 1765.
Daniel Edson and Olive Fuller, Oct. 21, 1765.
Phillip Reynolds and Hannah Packard, Oct. 29, 1765.
Simeon Leach and Betty Curtis, Dec. 31, 1765.
Theophilus Curtis and Mehitable Keith, Feb. 13, 1766.
George Packard and Abigail Packard, May 15, 1766.
John Morrison and Elisabeth Griffin, Oct. 27, 1766.
Robert Fulton and Agnes Thompson, July 23, 1767.
Hosea Dunbar and Jennet Hendry, Oct. 22, 1767.
David Packard and Dorothy Bassett, Dec. 31, 1767.
Jeremiah Beal and Mary French, June 20, 1768.
Dominicus Record and Martha Dailey, Aug. 19, 1768.
Isaiah Fuller and Mary Keyzer, Sept. 30, 1768.
Joshua Beals and Susanna Edson, Oct. 17, 1768.
Joseph Hayward and Olive Manly, Oct. 20, 1768.
Eliab Packard and Alice Packard, May 14, 1769.
Jesse Perkins and Susanna Field, June 5, 1769.
William Packard and Hannah Reynolds, June 8, 1769.
Eleazer Cole and Lucy Shurtleff, July 11, 1769.
Samuel Sturtevant and Sarah Packard, Sept. 14, 1769.
Thomas Burgall and Elisabeth Pain, Dec. 3, 1769.
Capt. Moses Curtis and Hannah Belcher, Dec. 14, 1769.

James Carkis Woodwis and Hannah Washburn, Feb. 12, 1770.
*Henry Traveller and Violet Powell, Feb. 27, 1770.
*Ashley Curtis and Susanna Fuller, April 12, 1770.
Thomas Hammond and Betty Mallet, April 18, 1770.
Benjamin Robinson and Eve Packard, May 29, 1770.
Japhet Beal and Patience Keith, Feb. 7, 1771.
John Montgomery and Margaret Hendry, Feb. 28, 1771.
Daniel Dunbar and Abigail Kingman, May 2, 1771.
John Ames, jr. and Martha Park, May 9, 1771.
Abijah Stowell and Rhoda Packard, Oct. 17, 1771.
Zachariah Sylvester and Mehitable Cary, Nov. 14, 1771.
John Kingman and Widow Ann Petengill, Feb. 13, 1772.
Edward Bass and Bathsheba Keith, Feb. 27, 1772.
Edward Bartlett and Zilpah Cole, May 7, 1772.
Rev. Samuel Niles and Mrs. Mary Dodge, June 8, 1772.
Silas Dunbar and Amy Reynolds, July 2, 1772.
Joseph Reynolds and Jemima Perkins, Sept. 17, 1772.
Samuel Dike and Lois Fuller, Nov. 12, 1772.
Isaac Buck and Sarah Hayward, Feb. 4, 1773.
Benjamin Ford and Sarah Brett, Feb. 18, 1773.
Moses Cary and Susanna Field, April 13, 1773.
William Shaw and Dorcas Smith, June 24, 1773.
Daniel Howard and Vesta Howard, June 29, 1773.
William French and Mary Perkins, July 8, 1773.
William French and Alice Washburn, Aug. 12, 1773.
Ephraim Packard and Sarah Packard, Sept. 1, 1773.
Edward Spear and Catherine Dorman, Dec. 7, 1773.
Ebenezer Howard and Silence Snell, Dec. 23, 1773.
John Freelove and Sarah Wood, Jan. 4, 1774.
Ebenezer Packard and Mary Reynolds, March 31, 1774.
Jacob Packard 3d and Rebecca French, May 5, 1774.
Barnabas Curtis and Esther Finney, June 6, 1774.
Abiel Harris and Susanna Snell, Nov. 17, 1774.
Mark Packard and Hannah Shaw, Dec. 15, 1774.
Simeon Keith and Molly Cary, June 15, 1775.
Benjamin Packard and Lurania Finney, Aug. 22, 1775.
Amaziah Cole and Rebecca Cole, Sept. 8, 1775.
Rufus Brett and Susanna Cary, Sept. 28, 1775.
Benjamin Clark and Mehitable Edson, Dec. 21, 1775.
Seth Harris and Susanna Warren, April 2, 1776.
Ebenezer Warren and Eunice Warren, May 9, 1776.
*Elias Sewell and Amy Dunbar, Oct. 28, 1776.
Seth Wentworth and Jane Warren, Nov. 7, 1776.
John Noyes and Zibia Brett, Nov. 7, 1776.
Samuel Linfield and Elizabeth Porter, Dec. 5, 1776.
Daniel Howard and Abigail Packard, Dec. 22, 1776.
Nathaniel Hammond and Elisabeth Wales, Jan. 13, 1777.
John Gurney and Mehitable Southworth, Jan. 29, 1777.
Nathaniel Southworth and Jenny Brett, March 18, 1777.
Daniel Dickerman and Ruth Tuel, March 20, 1777.
Josiah Edson 2d and Reliance Fuller, April 2, 1777.
Nathaniel Reynolds, jr. and Bethia Keith, April 20, 1777.
Capt. Zebedee Snell and Mary Hayward, July 2, 1777.

Thaddeus Pratt and Rachel Churchill, July 23, 1777.
Jonathan Keith and Hannah Snell, Aug. 28, 1777.
Benjamin Fuller and Sarah Ames, Sept. 8, 1777.
Jonas Packard and Mehitable Brett, Sept. 11, 1777.
Noah Pratt and Desire Cole, Sept. 25, 1777.
Oliver Packard and Relief Edson, Nov. 20, 1777.
Ephraim Cole and Silence Webb, Dec. 18, 1777.
Benjamin Hayward and Abigail Perkins, Dec. 25, 1777.
Simeon Brett and Susanna Perkins, Dec. 25, 1777.
Elisha Hayward, jr. and Molly Blanchard, Jan. 13, 1778.
*Boston Foye and Betty Cordner, Feb. 26, 1778.
Samuel Brett, jr. and Molly Packard, March 18, 1778.
*Cajar Easton and Eunice Sewell, May 19, 1778.
Seth Keith and Widow Hannah Keith, April 2, 1778.
*Luther Jotham and Mary Mitchell, April 8, 1778.
Parmenas Packard and Martha Reynolds, April 9, 1778.
Charles Snell and Mary Kingman, April 26, 1778.
Daniel Cary and Mehitable Brett, May 14, 1778.
Nathan Edson and Susanna Allen, May 28, 1778.
*Cuffee Wright and Anna Cordner, Aug. 6, 1778.
Nathan Billings and Sarah Warren, Aug. 19, 1778.
James Packard, jr. and Jemima Churchill, Aug. 27, 1778.
Noah Ames and Ruhamah French, Oct. 5, 1778.
Archippas Taylor and Hannah Warren, Oct. 27, 1778.
Seth Snow and Mary Snow, Nov. 17, 1778.
Timothy Ames and Abigail Howard, Nov. 19, 1778.
John French and Damaris Howard, Jan. 20, 1779.
Abijah Thayer and Betty Howard, March 16, 1779.
Cary Hayward and Mary Thompson, April 29, 1779.
Oliver Wentworth and Sarah Leach, June 15, 1779.
Zephaniah Lathrop and Sarah Packard, Sept. 2, 1779.
Ebenezer Thayer and Lydia West, Sept. 23, 1779.
Ephraim Willis, jr. and Eunice Egerton, Sept. 23, 1779.
Israel Burr and Hannah Ames, Oct. 26, 1779.
Silas Hayward and Mary Thayer, Dec. 9, 1779.

MARRIAGES IN THE TOWN OF BRIDGEWATER PREVIOUS TO ITS DIVISION.*

[Communicated by BRADFORD KINGMAN, Esq., Brookline, Mass.]

JOHN CARY, Jr. and Abigail Allen, Dec. 7, 1670.
Nicholas Byram, Jr. and Mary Edson, Sept. 20, 1676.
John Washburn, Jr. and Rebecca Lapham, April 16, 1679.
James Cary and Mary Shaw, Jan. 4, 1681.
Nathaniel Brett and Sarah Hayward, Nov. 21, 1683.
Samuel Allen, Jr. and Rebecca Cary, Dec. 2, 1685.
Isaac Alden and Mehitabel Allen, Dec. 2, 1685.
John Whitman and Hannah Pratt, June 10, 1686.
Joseph Edson and Mary ———, Nov. 2, 1686.
William Snow and Naomi Whitman, Nov. 30, 1686.
James Dunbar and Jane Harris, 1683.
Jacob Mitchell and Deliverance Kingman, Jan. 1, 1696.
Thomas Mitchell and Elizabeth Kingman, Jan. 1, 1696.
Samuel Kingman and Mary Mitchell, Jan. 1, 1696.
James Harris and Elizabeth Fry, March 11, 1696.
Jeremiah Newland and Susannah Harris, April 7, 1696.
Nathaniel Allen and Bethia Conant, Dec. 14, 1696.
Job Ames and Sarah Washburn, Jan. 12, 1697.
Daniel Hudson and Mary Orcutt, May 19, 1697.
Clement Briggs and Elizabeth Field, Nov. 3, 1697.
John Field and Elizabeth Ames, —— 1697.
William Uyyohart and Hannah Smith, Sept. 21, 1698.
Ebenezer Allen and Rebecca Scate, Oct. 11, 1698.
John Kingman and Bethia Newcomb, Dec. 1, 1698.
William Ames and Mary Hayward, Dec. 13, 1698.
David Perkins and Martha Howard, Feb. 1, 1699.
Josiah Leonard and Marjoram Washburn, Nov. 2, 1699.
Ebenezer Whitman and Abigail Burnam, Nov. 17, 1699.
Chilton Latham and Susanna Kingman, Dec. 6, 1699.
Caleb Chard and Eleanor Waters, April 23, 1700.
Amos Snell and Mary Packard, May 2, 1700.
Joseph Hayward and Mehitable Dunham, May 30, 1700.
Peter Cornet and Priscilla Howland, Oct. 30, 1700.
Nicholas Whitman and Sarah Vining, Nov. 19, 1700.
Samuel Washburn and Deliverance Leonard, Jan. 9, 1701.
Israel Randall and Mary Willis, Jan. 21, 1701.
Isaac Leonard and Mary Randall, April 16, 1701.
Josiah Conant and Elizabeth Washburn, Sept. 1, 1701.
Thomas Manly and Lydia Field, Oct. 2, 1701.
Elisha Allen and Mehitabel Byram, Dec. 3, 1701.

* The ancient town of Bridgewater was the first interior settlement in the County of Plymouth, and was incorporated in 1656, and embraced within its limits the four towns now known as *North Bridgewater*, *East Bridgewater*, *West Bridgewater*, and the present town of Bridgewater. The town was formerly divided into five *Parishes* or *Precincts*, viz., *North*, *East*, *West*, *South*, and *Titicut*. The North Parish was incorporated into a Town June 15, 1821—the West in 1822—the East in 1823—the South Parish retaining the original name of Bridgewater, which also includes *Titicut Parish*.

Joseph Joslyn and Sarah Ford, March 5, 1702.
Elnathan Bassett and Mary Hill, June 19, 1702.
Benjamin Leach and Hepzibah Washburn, Sept. 8, 1702.
Thomas Hayward and Susanna Hayward, Nov. 11, 1702.
Nathaniel Ames and Susannah Howard, Dec. 2, 1702.
Josiah Keith and Mary Lathrop, Jan. 6, 1703.
Samuel Keith and Bethia Fobes, Jan. 20, 1703.
William Bassett and Sarah Bump, June 23, 1703.
John Barden and Mary Parlow, Aug. 23, 1703.
Joseph Hayward, Jr. and Sarah Crossman, Sept. 9, 1703.
James Hogg and Ruth Hill, Jan. 23, 1704.
Samuel Cary and Mary Pool, April 25, 1704.
Joseph Edson and Lydia Cary, June 1, 1704.
Josiah Edson and Sarah Packard, July 27, 1704.
John Fobes and Abigail Robinson, Nov. 14, 1704.
Samuel Staples and Elizabeth Pratt, Dec. 25, 1704.
Ephraim Marble and Susanna Burnham, Feb. 8, 1705.
Samuel Packard and Elizabeth Edson, May 24, 1705.
Samuel Reed and Mary Davis, Oct. 1, 1705.
Benjamin Snow and Sarah Cary, Oct. 25, 1705.
Richard Field and Susanna Waldo, Jan. 17, 1706.
Enoch Leonard and Elizabeth Hooper, Feb. 12, 1706.
Thomas Ames and Mary Hayward, Feb. 27, 1706.
Daniel Field and Sarah Ames, March 6, 1706.
Samuel Willis and Margaret Brett, March 19, 1706.
Thomas Howard and Bethia Brett, June 5, 1706.
John Heiford and Lydia Pierce, July 3, 1706.
Andrew Ford and Mercy Whitman, Nov. 27, 1706.
——— Sash and Mary Cornish, Dec. 1, 1706.
Elihu Brett and Susanna Hayward, Dec. 17, 1706.
John Hayward and Sarah Willis, Dec. 24, 1706.
Nehemiah Allen and Sarah Wormal, Jan. 8, 1707.
Joshua Willis and Experience Barber, Feb. 4, 1707.
Joseph Trufant and Mercy Pierce, May 15, 1707.
David Hearsey and Esther Read, Aug. 6, 1707.
Isaac Reynolds and Dorothy Leeker, Nov. 24, 1707.
William Cleaves and Eleanor Hacket, Dec. 1, 1707.
Josiah Allen and Mary Read, Dec. 25, 1707.
Nathaniel Woodward and Elizabeth Willis, April 16, 1708.
Thomas Washburn and Sarah Leonard, July 28, 1708.
Nicholas Byram and Anne Snell, Aug. 3, 1708.
John Hutchinson and Hepzibah Washburn, Oct. 29, 1708.
Israel Washburn and Waitstill Sumner, Nov. 3, 1708.
Francis Cuff and Fidelia ———, Nov. 24, 1708.
Samuel Bennett and Ruth Perry, Jan. 6, 1709.
Elisha Hayward and Experience Harvey, Jan. 20, 1709.
Ephraim Cary and Hannah Waldo, Feb. 3, 1709.
William Terrill and Deborah Hearsey, April 27, 1709.
John Haines and Hannah Shaw, Aug. 11, 1709.
Nathan Perkins and Martha Leonard, Nov. 9, 1709.
Francis Wood and Sarah Hooper, Jan. 5, 1710.
Samuel Harris and Abigail Harding, Jan. 10, 1710.
John Bolton and Ruth Hooper, Jan. 25, 1710.

Noah Washburn and Elizabeth Shaw, Jan. 25, 1710.
James Howard and Elizabeth Wallis, Jan. 26, 1710.
Edward Hayford and Ruth Bryant, Jan. 27, 1710.
John Cole and Patience Barber, Jan. 27, 1710.
Timothy Keith and Hannah Fobes, Feb. 1, 1710.
John Washburn and Margaret Packard, Feb. 16, 1710.
Nathaniel Hill and Hannah Conant, May 30, 1710.
John Tobey and Mary Jennings, Aug. 30, 1710.
Samuel Lathrop and Abiel Lazell, Nov. 14, 1710.
John Benson and Elizabeth Washburn, Dec. 4, 1710.
Samuel Perry and Sarah Leonard, Dec. 14, 1710.
Benjamin Richards and Mehitable Alden, Jan. 1, 1711.
Edward Howard and Mary Byram, Feb. 7, 1711.
Thomas Latham and Deborah Harden, March 19, 1711.
John Keith and Hannah Washburn, April 18, 1711.
Thomas Washburn and Abigail Heiford, July 24, 1711.
Joshua Fobes and Abigail Dunbar, Dec. 4, 1711.
Nathaniel Whitaker and Abigail Read, Dec. 20, 1711.
Recompense Cary and Mary Crossman, Dec. 25, 1711.
Hezekiah King and Sarah Read, May 14, 1712.
Jonathan Randall and Bethia Howard, Aug. 12, 1712.
Andrew Lovell and Lydia Conant, Sept. 14, 1712.
Seth Pratt and Sarah Alden, Oct. 13, 1712.
Richard Whitman and Lydia Ford, Oct 15, 1712.
Joseph Leonard and Hannah Jennings, Nov. 19, 1712.
Joseph Snell and Hannah Williams, Dec. 3, 1712.
Joseph Pratt and Lydia Leonard, Dec. 9, 1712.
David Packard and Hannah Ames, Dec. 17, 1712.
Thomas Buck and Elizabeth Howard, Dec. 18, 1712.
Jonathan Willis and Abigail Stoughton, Jan. 14, 1713.
John Pierce and Susanna Newland, Jan. 26, 1713.
Hezekiah Ford and Ruth Whitmarsh, March 19, 1713.
Nehemiah Washburn and Jane Howard, March 26, 1713.
David Thurston and Mercy Cary, April 28, 1713.
Daniel Packard and Mary Harris, Dec. 2, 1713.
Josiah Williams and Martha Howard, Jan. 26, 1714.
Benjamin Washburn and Bethia Kingman, Feb. 11, 1714.
Stephen Read and Mary Whitmarsh, March 12, 1714.
Ebenezer Hill and Susannah Leonard, March 22, 1714.
Ephraim Fobes and Martha Snell, April 22, 1714.
Shubael Ewers and Rebecca Conant, June 15, 1714.
Edward Hobart and Abigail Whitman, Nov. 12, 1714.
Ebenezer Byram and Hannah Hayward, Dec. 9, 1714.
John Snell and Susanna Packard, Feb. 1, 1715.
Nathaniel Harden and Susanna Latham, Feb. 17, 1715.
Nicholas Wade and Anne Latham, Feb. 17, 1715.
William Washburn and Experience Mann, June 13, 1715.
Benjamin Edson and Joanna Orcutt, July 14, 1715.
Josiah Hayward and Sarah Kingsley, July 19, 1715.
Benjamin Leonard and Hannah Phillips, Aug. 15, 1715.
Nicholas Whitman and Mary Cary, Sept. 14, 1715.
Solomon Packard and Sarah Lathrop, Nov. 16, 1715.
John Lathrop and Mary Edson, May 23, 1716.
Nathaniel Hayward and Mary Harvey, June 21, 1716.

Jacob Bump and Catharine Aldrich, Nov. 7, 1716.
Nathaniel Conant and Elizabeth Harris, Dec. 17, 1716.
Thomas Willis and Mary Kingsley, Dec. 18, 1716.
Ebenezer Pratt and Anna Dyar, Jan. 10, 1717.
Ebenezer French and Elizabeth Orcutt, Jan. 31, 1717.
Thomas Perkins and Mary Washburn, Feb. 20, 1717.
Isaac Harris and Elizabeth Washburn, July 22, 1717.
Benoni Hayward and Hannah Gould, Sept. 11, 1717.
Josiah Leonard and Abigail Washburn, Nov. 21, 1717.
Jonathan Cary and Susanna Keith, Dec. 11, 1717.
Israel Alger and Susanna Snow, Dec. 25, 1717.
Daniel Alden and Abigail Shaw, Dec. 25, 1717.
William Phillips and Hannah Pryor, Jan. 16, 1718.
Joseph Lathrop and Mary Snow, Jan. 17, 1718.
John Leach and Susannah White, Feb. 20, 1718.
Jeremy Howell and Lydia Packard, April 7, 1718.
Samuel Hall and Mercy Willis, April 15, 1718.
John Cavener and Anne Jennings, July 7, 1718.
David Johnson and Rebecca Washburn, Jan. 7, 1719.
Solomon Pratt and Sarah Johnson, Jan. 27, 1719.
Timothy Edson and Mary Alden, Feb. 10, 1719.
Ephraim Jennings and Deliverance Washburn, Feb. 18, 1719.
William Bassett and Mary Mahurin, Feb. 19, 1719.
Benjamin Pratt and Sarah Kingman, June 24, 1719.
Jonathan Howard and Sarah Field, July 30, 1719.
George Vaughan and Faithful Packard, Aug. 13, 1719.
Joseph Alger and Mary Ames, Sept. 3, 1719.
Isaac Lazell and Mary Hudson, Oct. 29, 1719.
Nicholas Whitman and Mary Conant, Nov. 17, 1719.
Benjamin Willis and Mary Leonard, Nov. 27, 1719.
Jonathan Cary and Experience Carver, Dec. 10, 1719.
Jonathan Packard and Susanna Hayward, Dec. 24, 1719.
Elisha Hayward and Bethia Snow, Feb. 1, 1720.
William Orcutt and Sarah Leonard, Feb. 27, 1720.
Eleazer Alden and Martha Shaw, May 11, 1720.
Josiah Sears and Judith Gilbert, Aug. 18, 1720.
John Webb and Mary Alden, Oct. 6, 1720.
Benjamin Webb and Mehitabel Williams, Oct. 20, 1720.
James Washburn and Elizabeth Leonard, Nov. 23, 1720.
Ebenezer Pratt and Waitstill Washburn, Dec. 15, 1720.
Benjamin Williams and Susanna Howard, Dec. 22, 1720.
Thomas Hooper and Sarah Packard, Jan. 18, 1721.
James Dunbar and Experience Hayward, Jan. 31, 1721.
Samuel Edson and Mehitabel Brett, March 30, 1721.
Benjamin Fobes and Martha Hunt, May 3, 1721.
David Turner and Sarah Howard, May 4, 1721.
John Orcutt and Desire Kingman, June 27, 1721.
William Ames and Elizabeth Jennings, June 29, 1721.
Joseph Leonard and Mary Packard, Sept. 14, 1721.
Joseph Keith and Susanna Field, Oct. 3, 1721.
Josiah Winslow and Sarah Hayward, Jan. 10, 1722.
James Cary and Mary Shaw, Feb. 8, 1722.
Benjamin Snow and Jemima Snell, March 7, 1722.
Mark Lathrop and Hannah Alden, March 29, 1722.

RECORD OF MARRIAGES SOLEMNIZED IN THE EAST PARISH OF BRIDGEWATER, MASS.

From March 4, 1725, to August 3, 1803,

By the Rev. John Angier* (settled 1724, died April 14, 1787), and the Rev. Samuel Angier,† his son and colleague (settled 1767, died Jan. 18, 1805).

Communicated by the Rev. Henry F. Jenks, A.M., of Canton, Mass., from the original manuscript in the possession of Miss Mary H. Rust, of East Bridgewater, great-great-grand-daughter of the Rev. John Angier.

March 4th 1725—I marry'd Samuel Beale and Mary Bassett.
June 30th 1725—I marry'd Mr. Theodosius Moore, and Mrs. Sarah Pryer.
Janry 5th 1725-6—I marry'd Daniel Johnson and Betty Lathum.

* Rev. John Angier was born in Watertown, July 1, 1701, graduated Harvard College 1720, married Nov. 23, 1732, Mary, daughter of Ezra Bourne of Sandwich.

† Rev. Samuel Angier was born March 20, 1743, graduated Harvard College 1763, married 1796, Judith, daughter of Rev. Joshua Smith of Pembroke.

Novembr 29th 1726—I marry'd Henry Kingman junr. and Mary Allen.

Janry. 17th 1726–7—I marry'd Deacon Recompense Cary and Sarah Brett.

Novemr. 1 1727—I marry'd John Thomas of Pembroke and Mary Cowet of Bridgewater, both Indians.

Novemr. 22d 1727—I marry'd Thomas Whitman and Jemima Alden, and at the same time
I marry'd John Alden and Hannah Kingman.

May 15th 1728—I marry'd Isaac Hayward and the widow Martha Perkins.

Octobr. 15th 1729—I marry'd Christopher Askins and Susanna Robinson.

NOTE.—C. Erskin from Ireland m. S., dau. of Gain Robinson, 1729.—See Mitchell's Hist. of Bridgewater.

Novembr. 10th 1729—I marry'd John Whitman and Elizabeth Cary.

Novembr. 13th 1729—I marry'd Caleb Brand and Damaris James both Indians.

Decemr. 31st 1729—I marry'd Samuel Pratt and Bethiah Byram.

Jany. 1st 1729—I marry'd Benjamin Allen and Mehitabel Cary.

Jany. 23 1729—I marry'd Zechariah Whitmarsh of Weymouth and Hannah Washburn.

NOTE.—1729 in the last two entries should probably be written 1729–30, as Mitchell's Hist. of Bridgewater gives 1730.

April 16th 1730—I marry'd William Davenport and Sarah Richards.

Novembr. 12th 1730—I marry'd Timothy Hayward and the widow Mary Read; and the same night I marry'd Arthur Harris and Mehetabel Rickard.

October 21st 1731—I marry'd John Johnson and Peggie Holman.

Decembr. 13th 1732—I marry'd Joseph Newel and Hannah Pierce.

Febry. 1st 1732–3—I marry'd Arthur Lathum and Alice Allen.

Aprl 24th 1733—I marry'd Samuel Allen and Susanna Perkins.

June 14th 1733—I marry'd Ebenezer Shaw and Mary Read.

July 5th 1733—I marry'd John Allen and Lydia Kingman.

Augst 5th 1733—I marry'd John Cary and Susanna Allen.

Octobr. 18th 1733—I marry'd Jonathan Pitcher of Norwich and Mehetabel Patingal of Bridgwater.

Decembr 11th 1733—I marry'd David Hill and Mary Buck.

Janry 15th 1733–4—I marry'd Nathaniel Pratt and Sarah Allen.

June 20th 1734—I marry'd John Holman and Ann Harris.

July 11th 1734—I marry'd Joseph Newel and Rachel Sylvester of Pembroke.

Augst 22d 1734—I marry'd Chin the negro man that belongs to John Johnson, and Rose, the negro woman that belongs to Sam'l Beale.

Octobr. 8th 1734—I marry'd John Cary and Sarah Drake.

Decmbr 18th 1734—I marry'd Matthew Allen and Sarah Harden.

July 22d 1735—I marry'd Thomas Kiff and Mary Bunton.

Novembr 11th 1735—I marry'd Matthew Allen jun'r. and Sarah Brett.

Novembr. 19th 1735—I marry'd Seth Allen & Rebecca Rickard of Plympton.

June 24th 1736—I marry'd Gideon Ramsdel of Hanover and Sarah Farrington.

July 15th 1736—I marry'd Andrew Bearse of Halifax and Margaret Dawes of Bridgwater.

Feby. 3d 1736-7—I marry'd Benjamin Vickery and Mary Allen.
Feby. 8th 1736-7—I marry'd Ezra Cary and Mary Holman.
Feby. 23d 1736-7—I marry'd Micah Allen and Hannah Edson.
Jany. 17th 1737-8—I marry'd Jonathan Perkins & Bethya Hayward.
Jany. 31st 1737-8—I marry'd David Pratt and Ann Leonard.
Feby. 2d 1737-8—I marry'd Samuel Robbin & Bathsheba Wompom Indians.
July 13th 1738—I marry'd David Whitman and Susanna Hayward.
Oct. 11th 1738— I marry'd Josiah Hayward & the Widow Sarah Moore.
Novr 22d 1738—I marry'd Eleazar Washburn and Anna Alden
Ephraim Cary and Susanna Alden,
Ebenazer Byram to Abigail Alden, and also
Benaiah Smith of Easton & Mary Hill of (this?) Town.
Decembr 21st 1738—I marry'd Seth Mitchell and Anne Lathum.
Decembr 26th 1738—I marry'd James Radsford and Margaret Balls.
March 27th 1739—I marry'd Jonathan Allen of Braintree, and the widow Alice Lathum.
May 16th 1739—I marry'd Samuel Harden and Elizabeth Wade.
Novr 20th 1739—I marry'd Bridgwater & Kate, Col. Holman's negroes.
Decr 10th 1739—I marry'd Charles Cushman and Mary Harvey.
Decembr. 21st 1739—I marry'd Benjamin Vickery and Mary Kingman.
December 25th 1739—I marry'd John Buck of Bridgwater and Mary Eames of (Norton?).
September 16th 1740—I marry'd Daniel Richards and Mary Packard, and at the same time I marry'd William Packard and Sarah Richards.
April 28th 1741—I marry'd Josiah Allen and Sarah Orcutt.
May 20th 1741—I marry'd Arthur Harris and Bethiah Hayward.
June 23d 1741—I marry'd Seth Whitman and Ruth Read.
Nov. 11th 1741—I marry'd Jonathan Bass junr. and Susanna Byram.
Decr. 3d 1741—I marry'd Ichabod Cary and Hannah Gannett.
Jany. 6th 1741-2—I marry'd Benjamin Hayward and Sarah Cary.
Jany. 28th 1741-2—I marry'd Daniel Cary and Martha Cary.
June 30th 1742—I marry'd Jesse Byram and Abigail Thurston
Aug. 4th 1742—I marry'd Hugh Orr and Mary Bass.
Nov. 9th 1742—I marry'd Eleazar Whitman and Abigail Alden.
Novem. 10th 1742—I marry'd James Allen and the widow Ann Pryor.
Novem. 11th 1742—I marry'd Zachariah Cary and Susanna Bass.
Decem. 13th 1742—I marry'd Japhet Byram and Sarah Allen.
Decem. 16th 1742—I marry'd Joseph Allen and Susannah Packard.
March 16th 1743—I marry'd John Whitman and the widow Hannah Snow.
Novem. 30th 1743—I marry'd Nathan Allen and Rebecca Read.
Jan. 18th 1743-4—I marry'd Daniel Howell and Deliverance Latham.
Feb. 7th 1743-4—I marry'd John Edson and Mary Gannet.
May 28th 1744—I marry'd Robert Dawes and Lydia Harden.
June 7th 1744—I marry'd Joseph Gannet junr. and Betty Latham.
Sept. 27th 1744—I marry'd Naphtali Byram and Hannah Pratt.
Octob. 17th 1745—I marry'd Samuel Beale and Elisabeth Blackman.
Octob. 24th 1745—I marry'd Elisha Allen and Rebecca Pratt.
Decem. 17th 1745—I marry'd Joseph Byram & Mary Bowditch of Braintree.

RECORD OF MARRIAGES SOLEMNIZED IN THE EAST PARISH OF BRIDGEWATER, MASS.

From March 4, 1725, to August 3, 1803.

By the Rev. John Angier (settled 1724, died April 14, 1787), and the Rev. Samuel Angier, his son and colleague (settled 1767, died Jan. 18, 1805).

Communicated by the Rev. Henry F. Jenks, A.M., of Canton, Mass., from the original manuscript in the possession of Miss Mary H. Rust, of East Bridgewater, great-great-grand daughter of the Rev. John Angier.

June 30th 1746—I marry'd Doctor Otis and Mehetabel Bass.
Octob. 7th 1746—I marry'd Joseph Keith jun'r. and Ann Turner.
Octob. 10th 1746—I marry'd Joseph Robinson and Abigail Keith.
Novem. 26th 1746—I marry'd Thomas Wade & Susanna Lathum.
Nov'r 27th 1746—I marry'd John Egerton and Abigail Snow.
Jan'y. 5th 1746-7—I marry'd Daniel Alden jun'r. and Jane Turner.
Sept. 29th 1747—I marry'd Abijah Edson and Susanna Snow.
Octob. 7th 1747—I marry'd Josiah Whitman and Elisabeth Smith.
Novem. 3d 1747—I marry'd Jonathan Whitman and Elisabeth Harvey.
Decemb. 25th 1747—I marry'd Thomas Phillips & ye widow Hannah Allen.
Jany. 29th 1747—I marry'd David Conant junr. & Rhoda Lathum.
March 2d 1747-8—I marry'd Anthony Pierce & the Widow Martha Petingal.
March 23d 1747-8—I marry'd Job Burgess & Patience Thomas—Indians.
Feb. 7th 1748-9—I marry'd Stephen Leach and Sarah Hooper.

April 27th 1749—I marry'd Theophilus Byram and Elisabeth Beale.
May 3d 1749—I marry'd Henry Cary and Martha Byram.
May 11th 1749—I marry'd James Edson and Esther Allen.
Octob. 5th 1749—I marry'd John Smith and Mary Hanmer.
Novr. 28th 1749—I marry'd Zebulun Cary and Lydia Phillips.
Jany. 16th 1749-50—I marry'd Nathan Alden and Mary Hudson.
Mar. 16th 1749-50—I marry'd Simeon Whitman and Martha Snow.
April 3d 1750—I marry'd Daniel Beale and Mehetabel Byram.
April 9th 1750—I marry'd Matthew Gannet & Martha Byram.
August 22d 1750—I marry'd Ignatius Loring and Bathsheba Bass.
Nov. 5th 1750—I marry'd William Holmes & Elisabeth Hamblin.
Dec. 20th 1750—I marry'd Benjamin Gannet and Mary Copeland.
Feb. 14th 1750-51—I marry'd Elijah Hayward and Silence Snell.
May 2d 1751—I marry'd Samuel Bisbe of Pembrook, and Martha Snell.
Augst. 28th 1751—I marry'd John Pratt of Pembrooke and Sarah Pierce.
Septr. 19th 1751—I marry'd John Wade and Hannah Kingman.
Nov. 27th 1751—I marry'd John Richards and Kezia Bailey.
Decr. 18th 1751—I marry'd Benjamin Harris and Sarah Snow.
Decr. 19th 1751—I marry'd William Barrel and Sarah Cary.
Janry. 13th 1751-2— I marry'd Ezra Warren and Mary Phillips.
June 18th 1752—I marry'd Peter Whitman and Susanna Keith.
June 30th 1752—I marry'd Eleazar Hamblen and Lydia Bonne.
August 5th 1752—I marry'd David Kingman, junr. and Abigail Hall.
Octobr. 26th 1752 N. S.—I marry'd James Keith and Sarah Holman.
Nov. 3d 1752 N. S.—I marry'd John Orcutt junr. and Jerusha Hanmer.
Nov. 22d 1752 N. S.—I marry'd John Young and Eunice Bass.
Dec. 28th 1752 N. S.—I marry'd John Howard jur. and Abigail Hudson.
Jany. 10th 1753—I marry'd Nathaniel Ramsdel and Mary Pratt.
Octobr. 31st 1753—I marry'd George Bradley and Susanna Pierce.
Janry 15th 1754—I marry'd Hezekiah Egerton and Mary Hegbone.
Octobr. 2d 1754—I marry'd David Keith and Jemima Whitman.
Novembr. 7th 1754—I marry'd Seth Gannet and Susanna Allen.
Novembr. 26th 1754—I marry'd Samuel Kingman and Deborah Loring.
Novembr. 28th 1754—I marry'd James Lovel and Dorcas Pratt.
Jany. 1st 1755—I marry'd Samuel Dawes and Abigail Kingman.
March 18th 1755—I marry'd Sam'l Bowditch and Rebecca Byram,
and also Jonathan Allen and Sarah Bass.
June 19th 1755—I marry'd Thomas Phillips, Jur. and Mary Hatch.
Octobr. 30th 1755—I marry'd Thomas Snell, Jur. and Bithiah Allen.
Feby. 12th 1756—I marry'd John Churchill of Plympton and Joanna Bisby.
April 20th 1756—I marry'd John Barrel and Judith Snow.
August 19th 1756—I marry'd William Allen and Katharine Demseh.
Sept. 23d 1756—I marry'd Benjamin Chamberlane of Pembroke and Hannah Snell.
Novr. 23d 1756—I marry'd Samuel Billing of Stoughton & Reliance Hudson.
Feby. 3d 1757—I marry'd Benjamin Whitman & Mary Lathum.
April 6th 1757—I marry'd Benjamin Byram and Ann Holman.
Novembr. 17th 1757—I marry'd Richard Bartlett and Mary Robinson.
Decembr. 15th 1757—I marry'd Judah Wood of Halifax, and Hannah Porter of Bridgwater.
Novembr. 16th 1758—I marry'd Samuel Allen and Hannah Pratt, both of Bridgwater.
Feby. 7th 1759—I marry'd Joseph Snow and Ruth Shaw, both of Bridgwater.

Febry, 21st 1759—I marry'd James Bradly and Catharine Moore both of Bridgwater.
March 29th 1759—I marry'd Nathanael Edson and Joanna Snow.
June 12th 1759—I marry'd Jonathan Conant and Jane Lathum.
Octobr. 25th 1759—I marry'd Joseph Robinson and Hannah Snow.
Febry 21st 1760—I marry'd Seth Mitchell and Mary Wade.
April 10th 1760—I marry'd Benjamin Byram and Rachel Baily.
Sept. 11th 1760—I marry'd Eleazar Keith and Elisabeth Mitchel.
Octr. 9th 1760—I marry'd John Hanmer and Martha Pryer.
Novr. 20th 1760—I marry'd Solomon Packard, jur. and Hannah Baily.
Febry. 19th 1761—I marry'd Jepthae Byram of Mendham in New Jersey, and Susannah Washburn of Bridgwater.
March 19th 1761—I marry'd Nathan Whitman and Betty Allen.
April 23d 1761—I marry'd Ezra Allen and Phebe Cary.
May 26th 1761—I marry'd William Whitman and Mary Studley.
Sept. 17th 1761—I marry'd Consider Bearce of Hallifax, & Elizabeth Perkins of Bridgwater.
October 15th 1761—I marry'd Archibald Thompson and Martha Robinson, both of Bridgwater.
Decr. 8th 1761—I marry'd Jonathan Snow and Betty Packard, both of Bridgwater.
Febry 17th 1762—I marry'd Ephraim Groves and Bathsheba Bowditch, both of Bridgwater.
April 29th 1762—I marry'd Nathaniel Lowden of Duxborough and Experience Pratt of Bridgwater.
May 27th 1762—I marry'd Obadiah Bates and Ruth Pratt both of Bridgwater.
Sept. 30th 1762—I marry'd Edward Mitchell jur. and Jane Lathum both of Bridgwater.
Decr. 7th 1762—I marry'd Jacob Allen and Abigail Baily, both of Bridgwater.
Jany. 26th 1763—I marry'd Jacob Mitchel and Rebecca Loring both of Bridgwater.
March 24th 1763—I marry'd Winslow Richardson and Rhode Johnson, both of Bridgwater.
June 16th 1763—I marry'd John Keith and Alice Mitchel, both of Bridgwater.
Octobr. 26th 1763—I marry'd Joseph Keith and the Widow Baily, both of Bridgwater.
Decembr. 8th 1763—I marry'd Lot Dwellee of Hanover and Sarah Allen of Bridgwater.
March 15th 1764—I marry'd Zebulun Packard and Rebecca Richardson, both of Bridgwater.
August 28th 1764—I marry'd Abner Pratt and the Widow Martha Cary both of Bridgwater.
Sept. 13th 1764—I marry'd Samuel Darby and Sarah Atwood, both of Bridgwater.
Novr. 22d 1764—I marry'd Amos Whitman and Anna Washburn both of Bridgwater.
Decembr. 27th 1764—I marry'd Seth Keith and Abigail Holman, both of Bridgwater.
Janry. 10th 1765—I marry'd Zachariah Whitmarsh of Weymouth and the Widow Mary Pinkney of Bridgwater.

Sept. 26th 1765—I marry'd Cushing Mitchel and Jennit Orr, both of Bridgwater.

Octobr. 17th 1765—I marry'd Arthur Lathum and Margaret Bearse both of Bridgwater.

Novemr. 14th 1765—I marry'd James Thompson and Abigail Allen both of Bridgwater.

Decembr. 5th 1765—I marry'd John Hubbard of Abington and Mary Allen of Bridgwater.

Decembr. 9th 1765—I marry'd Samuel Staples of Hanover and Betty Washburn of Bridgwater.

Jany 9th 1766—I marry'd Joseph Noyes of Abington and Mercy Hatch of Bridgwater.

April 14th 1766—I marry'd William Bonney and Phebe Allen both of Bridgwater.

May 29th 1766—I marry'd Amos Foord of Duxborough and the Widow Sarah Patingale of Bridgwater.

June 5th 1766—I marry'd William Britton of Raynham and Mary Latham of Bridgwater.

August 18th 1766—I marry'd Samuel Nickels of Norton and Silence Bleen of Bridgwater.

Sept. 23d 1766—I marry'd Jonathan Orcutt and Thankfull Cary both of Bridgwater.

October 6th 1766—I marry'd Robert Orr and Hannah Kingman, both of Bridgwater.

Novembr. 6th 1766—I marry'd Josiah Fobes, jur. and Sarah Pryor both of Bridgwater.

Novembr. 27th 1766—I marry'd Polycarpus Snell & Susanna Shaw both of Bridgwater.

Decr. 4th 1766—I marry'd Josiah Hathaway jur. of Halifax & Hanah Latham of Bridgwater.

Jany. 29th 1767—I marry'd Deacon Thomas Whitman and the Widow Rebecca Allen.

Mar. 19th 1767—I marry'd Nathaniel Chamberlain and Deliverance Snell.

April 23d 1767—I marry'd Stephen Whitman and Mary Orr both of Bridgwater.

October 12th 1767—I marry'd Lemuel Leach and Rebecca Washburn both of Bridgwater, and at the same time John Sprague and Rebecca Alden of Bridgwater.

Octobr. 15th 1767—I marry'd Mr. Ephraim Hyde of Rehoboth and Mrs. Mary Angier* of Bridgwater.

Nov. 26th 1767—I marry'd Nathan Hudson and Betty Gannet, both of Bridgwater.

April 27th 1768—I marry'd Winslow Richardson and Elisabeth Byram, both of Bridgwater.

April 28th 1768—I marry'd Elijah Dean and Susanna Bass, both of Bridgwater.

May 12th 1768—I marry'd Zadok Hayward of Plymouth and Experience Bearse of Bridgwater.

Sept. 29th 1768—I marry'd George Keith and Deborah Cleft, both of Bridgwater.

* The unmarried daughter of Rev. John Angier. Young ladies were then called "Misstress," the term "Miss" being used for children under ten.

RECORD OF MARRIAGES SOLEMNIZED IN THE EAST PARISH OF BRIDGEWATER, MASS.

FROM MARCH 4, 1725, TO AUGUST 3, 1803.

By the Rev. John Angier (settled 1724, died April 14, 1787), and the Rev. Samuel Angier,* his son and colleague (settled 1767, died Jan. 18, 1805).

Communicated by the Rev. HENRY F. JENKS, A.M., of Canton, Mass., from the original manuscript in the possession of Miss Mary H. Rust, of East Bridgewater, great-great-granddaughter of the Rev. John Angier.

Janry. 30th. 1769—I marry'd Eleazar Hill and Anna Field, both of Bridgwater.

May 18th. 1769—Abraham Josselyn, Junr. of Pembrook, and Eunice Hill of Bridgwater were marry'd by Saml. Angier of Bridgwater.

July 6th. 1769—Joseph Ford and Betty Howard, both of Bridgwater were marry'd by Samuel Angier.

Octobr 2d. 1769—John Hudson and Bethiah Otis, both of Bridgwr were marry'd by Saml. Angier.

Novr. 15th 1769—Seth Brett, Jur. and Susanna Lathum, both of Bridgwater were marry'd by Samuel Angier.

Novr. 23d. 1769—Joshua Barrel Jur. and Olive Bass, both of Bridgwater were marry'd by John Angier, and Moses Symmons and Lois Hayward, both of Bridgwater, were marry'd by Samuel Angier.

Decembr. 4th 1769—Isaac Kingman, Jur. and Content Packard, both of Bridgwater, were marry'd by Samuel Angier.

Jany. 31st. 1770—James Loring and Jane Kingman were marry'd by John Angier.

March 15th. 1770—Isaac Kingman and the widow Ruth Loring were marry'd by J. Angier.

Mar. 29th. 1770—Nehemiah Washburn and Ruth Egerton, both of Bridgwater were marry'd by Samuel Angier.

(Returnd to the Clerk April 6th. 1770.)

April 12th 1770—Obadiah Reed of Abington and Elisabeth Shaw of Bridgwater were marry'd by Saml Angier.

May 3d. 1770—John Edson and Judith Shaw were marry'd by Saml. Angier.

May 17th. 1770—James Hendrey and Mehetabel Hall, both of Bridgwater were marry'd by Samuel Angier.

Novembr. 20th. 1770—Stephen Washburn and Sarah Faxon, both of Bridgwater, were marry'd by Samuel Angier.

Decembr. 4th 1770—Joseph Symmonds of Pembroke and Elisabeth Chamberlain of Bridgwater, were marry'd by Samuel Angier.

Febry. 5th 1771—Joseph Allen and Mehetabel Cary, both of Bridgwater were marry'd by Samuel Angier.

(Returnd to the Clerk, Septr. 30th. 1771.)

* Rev. Samuel Angier's wife Judith was daughter of the Rev. Thomas Smith of Pembroke, not Joshua as stated in the note on page 12 in the January number. Thomas Smith** was a graduate of Harvard College of the Class of 1725. See Barry's History of Hanover, Mass., p. 375.

**p. 10, this volume.

Octobr. 16th. 1771—Hugh Orr of the Nine Partners in New York Government, and Agnis Corbett of Bridgwater were marry'd by Saml. Angier.
Octobr. 17th. 1771—Christopher Sever and Hannah Harden, both of Bridgwer, were marry'd by Saml. Angier.
Decembr. 25th. 1771—Ephraim Cary, Jur. and Jane Holman, both of Bridgwater, were marry'd by Samuel Angier.
Jany. 2d. 1772—Thomas White of Bridgwater and Hannah Green of Abington, were marry'd by Samuel Angier.
Febry. 6th. 1772—Cuph Ashpot, Nathan Mitchel's Negro man was marry'd to Elisabeth Quay, a Molatto girl brought up by Anthony Winslow; they were marry'd by Saml. Angier.
Novembr. 27th. 1772—Josiah Otis and Susanna Orr were marry'd by Saml. Angier.
Decr. 2d. 1772—Robert Robinson and Bethya Kingman were marry'd by S. Angier.
Janry. 20th. 1773—Pompey Freeman of Bedford and Lois Hill of Bridgwater, Free Negroes, were marry'd by John Angier.
Febry. 27th. 1773—Eleazar Barow of Rochester and Jane Sherman of Bridgwater, were married by Samuel Angier.
March 17th 1773—Solomon Washburn and Ann Mitchel, both of Bridgwater were marry'd by Samuel Angier.
March 25th. 1773—Seth Reed of Number 5 in the Massachusetts Bay, and Thankful Whitmarsh of Bridgwater were marry'd by Saml. Angier.
April 29th. 1773—Scipio Ponus, David Keith's Negro Man, and Elisabeth Cesar a free Negro Woman, both of Bridgwater, were marry'd by Saml. Angier.
August 5th. 1773—John Whitman, ye third & Abigail Whitman, both of Bridgwater, were marry'd by Samuel Angier.
Sept. 6th. 1773—Richard Smith of Taunton & Rhoda Reed of Bridgwater were marry'd by Samuel Angier.
Decembr. 14th. 1773—Joseph Wesley & Margaret Robinson both of Bridgwater were marry'd by Samuel Angier.
April 21st. 1774—John Keith of Hardwick & Ann Belcher of Bridgwater were marry'd by Samuel Angier.

These marriages returned to ye Clerk May 5th. 1774.

June 21st. 1774—Asa Keith and Susanna Cary, both of Bridgwater, were marry'd by Samuel Angier.
June 30th. 1774—Abram Packard and Freelove Dyer, both of Bridgwater, were marry'd by Samuel Angier.
Sept. 22d. 1774—William Vinton & Susanna Robinson, both of Bridgwater, were marry'd by Samuel Angier.
Sept. 30th. 1774—Joseph Vinton of Braintree & Anna Hill of Bridgwater were marry'd by Samuel Angier.
Novembr. 22d 1774—Levi Washburn & Molly Allen, both of Bridgwater, were marry'd by Samuel Angier.
Novembr. 24. 1774—Silas Kinsley of Easton & Rebecca Packard of Bridgwater, were marry'd by Samuel Angier.
Febry. 2d. 1775—Elisha Records of Pembroke & Ruth Chamberlain of Bridgwater, were married by John Angier.
August 3d. 1775—Peleg Stutson of Abington & Ruth Gurney of Bridgwater, were marry'd by Samuel Angier.
August 31st. 1775—Peter Whitman & Sarah Wright, both of Bridgwater, were marry'd by Samuel Angier.

October 30th. 1775—Sylvanus Lazel & Abigail Robinson both of Bridgwater, were marry'd by John Angier.
Novebr. 16th. 1775—Nehemiah Shaw & Molly Hill, both of Bridgwater, were marry'd by Samuel Angier.
January 24th. 1776—Nathan Alden, Junr. & Sarah Barrel were marry'd by Samuel Angier, both of Bridgwater.
April 18th. 1776—William Snow and Jerusha Hill, both of Bridgwater, were marry'd by Samuel Angier.
May 21st. 1776—Isaac Allen, Junr. & Sylvia Brett, both of Bridgwater were marry'd by Samuel Angier.
June 12th. 1776—Seth Reed of Number Five in the County of Hampshire & Mary Lazell of Bridgwater were marry'd by Saml. Angier.
June 13th. 1776—Josiah Newton of Brookfield & Hannah Sherman of Bridgwater were marry'd by Samuel Angier.
June 25th. 1776—Alexander Munro & Mary Hutchinson, both of Bridgwater, were marry'd by John Angier.
August 8th. 1776—Azariah Beal & Bathsheba Bisbe, both of Bridgwater, were marry'd by Samuel Angier.
October 3d. 1776—Mr. Adam Porter of Abington & Mrs. Deborah Gannett* of Bridgwater, were marry'd by Samuel Angier.
Decembr. 31st. 1776—Robert Young & Molly Kingman, both of Bridgwater, were marry'd by Samuel Angier.
January 13th. 1777—Adna Winslow Cliff & Bethia Orr, both of Bridgwater, were marry'd by Saml. Angier.
Febry. 19th. 1777—Pelatiah Gilbert of Brookfield & Sarah Whitman of Bridgwater were marry'd by John Angier.
Febry. 20th. 1777—Eliab Washburn & Molly Lazel, both of Bridgwater, were marry'd by Samuel Angier.
April 17th. 1777—Obadiah Hearsey of Abington & Naomi Reed of Bridgwater were marry'd by Saml. Angier.
May 8th. 1777—James Richards of Newtown & Dorothy Packard of Bridgwater were marry'd by S. Angier.
These marriages returned to ye Clerk July 7th. 1777.

RECORD OF MARRIAGES SOLEMNIZED IN THE EAST PARISH OF BRIDGEWATER, MASS.

From March 4, 1725, to August 3, 1803.

By the Rev. John Angier (settled 1724, died April 14, 1787), and the Rev. Samuel Angier, his son and colleague (settled 1767, died Jan. 18, 1805).

Communicated by the Rev. Henry F. Jenks, A.M., of Canton, Mass., from the original manuscript in the possession of Miss Mary H. Rust, of East Bridgewater, great-great-granddaughter of the Rev. John Angier.

August 19th. 1777—Sylvanus Packard of Bridgwater & Elisabeth Marston of Boston were marry'd by S. Angier.
October 7th. 1777—Zacharias Shaw & Hannah Bisbee, both of Bridgwater, were marry'd by S. Angier.
Novembr. 6th. 1777—Francis Gray of Boston & Sarah Harris of Bridgwater were marry'd by S. Angier.

* Daughter of Capt. Joseph Gannett.

Decembr. 4th. 1777—Jonathan Alden & Hannah White, both of Bridgwater, were marry'd by S. Angier.
March 12th 1778—Ebenezer Bisbee & Mehitabel Shaw both of Bridgwater; and also John Thomson & Gennet Allen, both of Bridgwater, were marry'd by S. Angier.
March 26th. 1778—Jacob Harden of Abington & Mehetable Gannett of Bridgwater, were marry'd by S. Angier.
May 28th. 1778—Pero Jeffery, Negro Man of Dr. Isaac Otis, & Crely Williams, Negro Woman living with Seth Mitchel, both of Bridgwater, were marry'd by S. Angier.
July 27th. 1778—George Vining & Abigail Alden, both of Bridgwater, were marry'd by S. Angier.
Sept. 17th. 1778—Joseph Whitten [Whiting] & Nabby Alden both of Bridgwater, were marry'd by S. Angier.
October 1st. 1778—William Shaw, Junr. & Deliverance Washburn, both of Bridgwater, were marry'd by S. Angier.
Novbr. 18th. 1778—Robert Latham & Jerusha Hooper, both of Bridgwater, were marry'd by S. Angier.
Novbr 23d. 1778—James Allen & Polly Whitman, both of Bridgwater were marry'd by S. Angier.
Decembr. 17th. 1778—Anthony Pearce & Sile Pratt, both of Bridgwater, were marry'd by S. Angier.
March 11th. 1779—John Bisbee & Huldah Shaw, both of Bridgwater, were marry'd by S. Angier.
May 19th 1779—Edward Hayford & Lenity Kingman, both of Bridgwater, were marry'd by John Angier.
June 10th 1779—Isaac Lazel & Jenny Byram, both of Bridgwater, were marry'd by S. Angier.
June 23d. 1779—Solomon Packard & the Widow Sarah Stetson, both of Bridgwater, were marry'd by S. Angier.
July 1st. 1779—John Smith & Ruth Cornish, both of Bridgwater, were marry'd by S. Angier.
Sept. 16th. 1779—Josiah Hill & Abigail Beal, both of Bridgwater, were marry'd by S. Angier.
These marriages return'd to ye Clerk Sept. 21, 1779.
Novbr. 8th. 1779—William Johnson & Jane Robinson, both of Bridgwater, were marry'd by S. Angier.
Decembr. 9th 1779—John Harden Junr. of Abington & Lydia Hersey of Bridgwater, were marry'd by S. Angier.
Decembr. 20th. 1779—Matthew Ramsdel & Mary Allen, both of Bridgwater, were marry'd by S. Angier.
Febry. 17th. 1780—Ichabod Howland of Pembroke & Mary Hatch of Bridgwater, were marry'd by S. Angier.
March 15th. 1780—Cushing Mitchel & Hannah Newton, both of Bridgwater, were marry'd by S. Angier.
March 23d. 1780—Ephraim Snell & Anna Keith, both of Bridgwater, were marry'd by S. Angier.
May 4th. 1780—James Keith, Junr. & Molly Mitchel, both of Bridgwater, were marry'd by John Angier.
June 14th. 1780—George Keith & Elisabeth Ford, both of Bridgwater, were marry'd by S. Angier.
Sept. 7th. 1780—Joseph Whitman & Mary Phillips, both of Bridgwater, were marry'd by S. Angier.

Sept. 7th. 1780—Elijah Snow & Sarah Shaw, both of Bridgwater, were marry'd by S. Angier.

October 5th. 1780—Walter Hatch & Eunice Kingman, both of Bridgwater, were marry'd by S. Angier.

Octobr. 17th. 1780—Ichabod Packard of Lebanon in ye County of Grafton in ye New-hamshire grant, & Rachel Chamberlain of Bridgwater in ye County of Plymouth were marry'd by S. Angier.

Novbr. 2d. 1780—Job Bearce & Sarah Keith, both of Bridgwater, were marry'd by S. Angier.

Novbr. 7th. 1780—Jonathan Beal & ye Widow Abigail Egerton, both of Bridgwater, were marry'd by S. Angier.

Novr. 9th. 1780—William Robinson & Hannah Egerton, both of Bridgwater were marry'd by S. Angier.

Decembr. 12th. 1780—Benjamin White, Junr. of Hanover & Mary Chamberlain of Bridgwater were marry'd by S. Angier.

Decembr. 28th. 1780—Joseph Sampson & Hannah Gurney, both of Bridgwater, were marry'd by S. Angier.

These marriages return'd to ye Clerk Janry. 8th. 1781.

Janry. 18th. 1781—Isaac Mehuren & Mary Allen, both of Bridgwater, were marry'd by S. Angier.

Febry. 1st. 1781—William Donham of Plymouth & ye Widow Deborah Hooper of Bridgwater, were marry'd by S. Angier.

Feb. 6th. 1781—Isaac Washburn & Huldah Allen, both of Bridgwater, were marry'd by S. Angier.

March 1st. 1781—Oliver Washburn & Hannah Gannet, both of Bridgwater, were marry'd by S. Angier.

May 14th. 1781—Isaac Alden & Mary Russel, both of Bridgwater, were marry'd by S. Angier.

June 14th. 1781—Arthur Harris & Celia Mitchel, both of Bridgwater, were marry'd by S. Angier.

Sept. 24th. 1781—John Mitchel & Anna Byram, both of Bridgwater, were marry'd by S. Angier.

Novbr. 22d. 1781—Thomas Whitman & Lydia Sherman, both of Bridgwater, were marry'd by S. Angier.

Novbr. 26th. 1781—Seth Whitman & Eunice Bass, both of Bridgwater, were marry'd by S. Angier.

Returned to ye Clerk Janry. 28th. 1782.

RECORD OF MARRIAGES SOLEMNIZED IN THE EAST PARISH OF BRIDGEWATER, MASS.

From March 4, 1725, to August 3, 1803,

By the Rev. John Angier (settled 1724, died April 14, 1787), and the Rev. Samuel Angier, his son and colleague (settled 1767, died Jan. 18, 1805).

Communicated by the Rev. Henry F. Jenks, A.M., of Canton, Mass., from the original manuscript in the possession of Miss Mary H. Rust, of East Bridgewater, great-great-granddaughter of the Rev. John Angier.

Janry. 29th 1782—Eliphalet Baily & Martha Robinson, both of Bridgwater, were marry'd by S. Angier.

March 26th 1782—Joshua Bowen of Roxbury & Abigail Smith of Bridgwater, were marry'd by S. Angier.

July 18th. 1782—Reuben Harden of Pembroke & Rebecca Harden of Bridgwater were marry'd by S. Angier.

August 7th. 1782—Seth Hobart & Esther Allen, both of Bridgwater were marry'd by S. Angier.

August 29th. 1782—Josiah Torry & Olive Pratt, both of Bridgwater were marry'd by S. Angier.

Sept. 25th. 1782—Benjamin Richards & Polly Bartlett, both of Bridgwater, were marry'd by S. Angier.

Novbr. 14th. 1782—Ezra Kingman & Susannah Whitman, both of Bridgwater, were marry'd by S. Angier.

Novbr. 28th 1782—Robert Packard & Ruth Barrel, both of Bridgwater, were marry'd by S. Angier.
Decembr. 5th. 1782—William Brett & Molly Allen, both of Bridgwater, were marry'd by John Angier.
Returned to ye Town Clerk. Janry 20, 1783.
Janry. 23d. 1783—Charles Ramsdel of Pembroke & Betty Terril of Bridgwater, were marry'd by S. Angier.
March 20th. 1783—Matthew Gannett of Abington & Alice Latham of Bridgwater, were marry'd, by S. Angier.
April 3d. 1783—Rotheus Mitchel & Hepza Hayward, both of Bridgwater, were marry'd by S. Angier.
April 15th. 1783—Solomon Inglee of Halifax & Bathsheba Orr of Bridgwater, were marry'd by S. Angier.
July 17th. 1783—David Snell & Molly Baker, both of Bridgwater, were marry'd by S. Angier.
August 11th. 1783—Joshua Pool of Abington & Lucenda Latham of Bridgwater, were marry'd by S. Angier.
Sept. 4th. 1783—Jacob Mitchel & ye Widow Sally Whitman both of Bridgwater, were marry'd by S. Angier.
Octobr. 23d. 1783—Reuben Mitchel & Anne Wade, both of Bridgwater, were marry'd by S. Angier.
Octobr. 30th. 1783—Joshua Pratt & Mary Pratt, both of Bridgwater, & also Thomas Phillips & Martha Whitman both of Bridgwater, were marry'd by S. Angier.
Novbr. 6th. 1783—Capt. Simeon Whitman & ye Widow Sarah Byram, both of Bridgwater, were marry'd by S. Angier.
Decembr. 11th. 1783—Samuel Faxon & Priscilla Thomas, both of Bridgwater, were marry'd by S. Angier.
Returned to ye Clerk, Janry. 1st. 1784.
Janry. 1st. 1784—James Reed of Abington & Ruth Porter of Bridgwater, were marry'd by S. Angier.
March 4th. 1784—Reed Erskine of Abington & Mary Whitmarsh of Bridgwater, were marry'd by S. Angier.
April 22d. 1784—Jacob Whitmarsh, Junr. & Anna Pool, both of Bridgwater, were marry'd by S. Angier.
April 29th 1784—Isaiah Whitman & Chloe Phillips, both of Bridgwater, were marry'd by S. Angier.
May 20th. 1784—Revd. William Reed of Easton & Olive Pool of Bridgwater, were marry'd by S. Angier.
May 25th. 1784—Isaac Keith, & Betty Keith, both of Bridgwater, were marry'd by S. Angier.
June 10th. 1784—George Erskine & Huldah Whitmarsh, both of Bridgwater, were marry'd by S. Angier.
June 17th. 1784—Spencer Forrest of Halifax & Abigail Wade of Bridgwater, were marry'd by S. Angier.
Sept. 30th. 1784—John Ramsdel of Pembroke & Hannah Allen of Bridgwater, were marry'd by S. Angier.
Octobr. 21st. 1784—John Phillips & Jennet Young, both of Bridgwater, were marry'd by S. Angier.
Novbr. 16th. 1784—Daniel Orcutt & Olive Whitman, both of Bridgwater, were marry'd by S. Angier.
Novbr. 23d. 1784—Josiah Johnson, Junr. & Eunice Allen both of Bridgwater, were marry'd by S. Angier.

Novbr. 25th. 1784—Jacob Allen & Susanna Alden, both of Bridgwater, were marry'd by S. Angier.

Decembr. 16th. 1784—Thomas Osburne & Hannah Wade both of Bridgwater, were marry'd by S. Angier.

Decembr. 22d. 1784—Joseph Chamberlain & Sarah Bass, both of Bridgwater, were marry'd by S. Angier.

Returned to ye Clerk Febry. 21. 1785.

The following is an account of marriages consummated by me, Samuel Angier.

Janry. 13th 1785—I marry'd Samuel Harden of Abington & Relief Spear of Bridgwater.

Janry. 27th. 1785—I marry'd Benjamin Darling of Pembroke & Sarah Lowden of Bridgwater.

Febry. 3d. 1785—I marry'd Thomas Chamberlain & Molly Whitman both of Bridgwater.

Febry. 17th. 1785—I marry'd Peter Salmon of Hanover & ye Widow Eunice Whitman of Bridgwater.

March 8th. 1785—I marry'd Holman Keith & Sylvia Keith both of Bridgwater.

March 9th. 1785—I marry'd Hugh Orr, Jun'r. & Sylvia Mitchel both of Bridgwater.

March 10th. 1785—I marry'd Samuel Dunbar, a transient mulatto Fellow & Hannah James of Bridgwater.

March 15th. 1785—I marry'd John Edson ye 3d. & Susanna Orcutt both of Bridgwater

May 26th 1785—I marry'd Simeon Allen & Huldah Cary, both of Bridg- [water.

June 2d. 1785—I marry'd Capt. Isaac Whitman & Bathsheba Allen both of Bridgwater.

July 14th. 1785—I marry'd James Lovell & Jemima Leach, both of Bridg- [water.

Sept. 15th. 1785—I marry'd James Barrell & Betsey Russell both of Bridgwater.

Novbr. 17th. 1785—I marry'd James Ramsdel & Eunice Allen both of Bridgwater.

Decembr. 1st. 1785—I marry'd Daniel Kinsley & Molly Keith both of Bridgwater.

These marriages returned to ye Town Clerk, March 11th. 1786.

The following is an Account of the Persons marry'd by me, Samuel Angier, with ye time when they were marry'd,

1786.

Febry. 7th—Byram Allen of Bridgwater & Elisabeth Child of Roxbury.

Febry. 9th—Thomas Blanchard, Jun'r. of Abington & Susanna Latham of Bridgwater.

Febry. 9th—Levi Keith the 2d & Huldah Keith, both of Bridgwater.

March 2d—Samuel Pool, Jun'r. & Abigail Porter, both of Bridgwater.

May 25—Nathaniel Dammon of Marshfield & Molly Allen of Bridgwater.

May 25th—Roger Sutman & Phillis Suel, both of Bridgwater, Negroes.

August 24th—Henry Jackson & Mehitabel Alden, both of Bridgwater.

Sept. 26th—James Willis & Sarah Jackson, both of Bridgwater.

Decembr. 21st—Matthew Allen ye 2d. & Jane Keen, both of Bridgwater.

Returned to ye Clerk Janry. 1st. 1787.

RECORD OF MARRIAGES SOLEMNIZED IN THE EAST PARISH OF BRIDGEWATER, MASS.

FROM MARCH 4, 1725, TO AUGUST 3, 1803,

By the Rev. John Angier (settled 1724, died April 14, 1787), and the Rev. Samuel Angier, his son and colleague (settled 1767, died Jan. 18, 1805).

Communicated by the Rev. HENRY F. JENKS, A.M., of Canton, Mass., from the original manuscript in the possession of Miss Mary H. Rust, of East Bridgewater, great-great-granddaughter of the Rev. John Angier.

1787.

Febry. 15th.—Joseph Keith ye 2d & Betsey Sherman, both of Bridgwater.
Febry. 20th.—Asa Forrest of Halifax & Susa Mitchell of Bridgwater.
March 1st.—Ephraim Tinkham of Middleborough & Molly Gurney of Bridgwater. [water.
March 20th.—Samuel Whitman, Junr. & Hannah Egerton, both of Bridg-
April 3d.—Turner Phillips & Huldah Whitman, both of Bridgwater.
April 5th.—Benjamin Tayler & Martha Childs, both of Bridgwater.
May 17th.—Oliver Pratt & Susanna Lowden, both of Bridgwater.
June 21st.—Dyer Robinson & Abigail Stetson, both of Bridgwater.
August 23d.—Jacob Pool, Junr. of Abington & Zeruiah Whitmarsh of Bridgwater.
September 20th.—Jonah Besse & Eunice Washburn, both of Bridgwater.
Novbr. 1st.—Seth Allen Whitman & Philebert Whitman, both of Bridgwater.
Novbr. 15th.—Benjamin Pinchin & Molly Stetson, both of Bridgwater.
Novbr. 22d.—Daniel Cushing & Zeruiah Chamberlain, both of Bridgwater.
Carry'd to the Town Clerk to be recorded, Janry. 8th. 1788.

1788.

Janry. 10th.—Seth Gurney and Rebecca Packard, both of Bridgwater.
Febry. 20th.—James Lincoln of Cohasset in the County of Suffolk & Nabby Mitchel of Bridgwater.
March 17th,—Alexander Terril & Lydia Bryant, both of Bridgwater.
March 27th.—Nathan Whitman & Mercy Byram, both of Bridgwater.
April 3d.—Timothy Allen & Celia Whitman, both of Bridgwater.
May 14th.—William Harris & Alice Mitchel, both of Bridgwater.
July 10th.—Isaac Allen of Bridgwater & ye Widow Susanna Allen of Brookfield. [water.
July 23d.—Josiah Parris of Pembroke & Experience Lowden of Bridg-
Octob'r 7th.—Ebenezer Whitman, Junr. & Lydia Whitman, both of Bridgwater.
Octob'r. 16.—George Byram & Phebe Randal, both of Bridgwater.
Octob'r. 22d.—Solomon Johnson & Sally Robinson, both of Bridgwater.
Novbr. 25.—Israel Cowing of Scituate & Rebecca Wade of Bridgwater.
Carry'd to ye Town Clerk to be recorded, April 7. 1789.

1789.

April 2d.—Joel Edson & Hannah Packard, both of Bridgwater.
April 16th.—Benjamin Strowbridge of Middleborough, & Elisabeth Whitman of Bridgwater.

April 23d.—Mark Phillips, Junr. & Celia Chamberlain, both of Bridgwater.
Sept. 10th.—Nathan Bates of Abington & Betty Allen of Bridgwater.
Sept. 24th.—Daniel Bryant of Watertown & Jennit Mitchell of Bridgwater.
Octob'r. 20th.—William Keith, Junr. & Abigail Russel, both of Bridgwater.
Novbr. 5th.—Noah Hobart of Abington & Deborah Winslow Thomas of Bridgwater.
Decembr. 31st.—Israel Bailey & Lucy Whitman, both of Bridgwater.
Carry'd to ye Town Clerk to be recorded, April 19th, 1790.

1790.

May 13th.—Noah Packard of Dartmouth & Polly Packard of Bridgwater.
June 10th.—Noah Ramsdale of Abington & Hittie Whitmarsh of Bridgwater.
June 16th.—Oakes Whitman & Susanna Barrell, both of Bridgwater.
August 9th.—Samuel Rogers & Betty Allen, both of Bridgwater.
Sept. 13th.—Luther Hatch of Hanover & Molly Whitman of Bridgwater.
Novbr. 23d.—Winslow Thomas & Polly Cole, both of Bridgwater.
Decembr. 9th.—John Porter 2d & Susa Groves, both of Bridgwater.

1791.

Janry. 25th.—William Soul of Halifax & Rachel Dillingham of Bridgwater. [water.
Janry. 27th.—Benjamin Harris, Junr. & Sarah Mitchel, both of Bridg-
March 22d.—Reuben Tomson & Eunice Whitman, both of Bridgwater.
March 24th.—Barzee Kingman & Molly Phillips, both of Bridgwater.
April 14th.—Jacob Mitchel & the Widow Jerusha Latham, both of Bridgwater.
Carry'd to the Town Clerk, to be recorded April 23d, 1791.
June 13th.—Oliver Mitchel & Armelia Gannett, both of Bridgwater.
August 1st.—Seth Byram & Matilda Whitman, both of Bridgwater.
Sept. 29th.—David Byram & Lucy Randal, both of Bridgwater.
Octobe'r 26th.—George Briggs of Norton & Elisabeth Whitman of Bridgwater.
Novbr. 14th.—David Howard & Rebecca Whitman, both of Bridgwater.
and also Timothy Allen & ye Widow Betty Keith, both of Bridgwater.
Novbr. 17th.—Zenas Whitman & Sally Allen, both of Bridgwater.

1792.

March 12th.—Henry Thornberry Smith & Priscilla Brown, both of Bridgwater.
March 16th.—Libeus Washburn of Plymton & Alice Keith of Bridgwater.
Carry'd to ye Town Clerk to be recorded, April 26th, 1792.
May 3d.—Thomas Snell & Susanna Allen, both of Bridgwater.
May 17th.—Daniel French & Rhoda Tribou, both of Bridgwater.
July 4th.—Josiah Keen & Hannah Whitman, both of Bridgwater.
Octob'r. 22d.—John Boyd of New York & Jane Orr of Bridgwater.
Novbr. 1st.—Zenas Keith & Jane Cary, both of Bridgwater.
Novembr. 29th.—John Quincy Keith & Mary Hudson, both of Bridgwater.

1793.

Janry. 21st.—Josiah Johnson, Junr. & Olive Orcutt, both of Bridgwater.
Febry. 7th.—Thomas Hearsey of Abington & Deborah Pool of Bridgwater.

Febry. 19th.—Jonathan Kingman, Junr. & Mehitabel Hudson, both of Bridgwater.

Carry'd to ye Town Clerk to be recorded, April 27th, 1793.

August 22d.—John Lowden & Susanna Clark, both of Bridgwater.

August 27th.—Bela Reed & Polly Beal, both of Bridgwater.

Sept. 12th.—Seth Keith & Molly Keith, both of Bridgwater.

Sept. 26th.—Byram Lazell & Jennit Wesley, both of Bridgwater.

1794.

Janry 1st.—Lot Ramsdel & Lucinda Gannet, both of Bridgwater.

Febry. 24th.—Jarib White of Amherst in ye County of Hamshire & Ruth Shearman of Bridgwater, in ye County of Plymouth.

Carry'd to ye Town Clerk to be recorded, May 2d, 1794.

May 29th.—Silas Shaw of Rindge in New Hampshire & Lucy White of Bridgwater.

June 4th.—John Terril Junr. & Rhoda Smith, both of Bridgwater.

June 11th.—Mr. Nahum Mitchell & Nabby Lazell, both of Bridgwater.

July 3d.—Calvin Keith & Bethia Stetson, both of Bridgwater.

July 17th.—Southworth Washburn & Rebecca Bisbee, both of Bridgwater.

August 11th.—Rodolphus Kinsley of Stoughton & Salome Cary of Bridgwater.

also Asahel Allen & Rhoda Tilson, both of Bridgwater.

Sept. 30th.—John Loring of Turner & Jennett Barrell of Bridgwater.

Octobr. 20th.—James Lamberton of Ware in ye County of Hamshire, & Hannah Chamberlain of Bridgwater.

Novbr. 6th.—Isaac Alden ye 2d & Ruth Byram, both of Bridgwater.

Decbr. 4th.—Jacob Louden & Susanna Phillips, both of Bridgwater.

1795.

March 5th.—Ezra Whitman, Junr. & Eunice Allen, both of Bridgwater.

March 17th.—Zebulon Allen & Priscilla Attwood, both of Bridgwater.

Carry'd to the Town Clerk, April 3d, 1795.

April 29th.—John Harris & Eunice Young, both of Bridgwater.

Sept. 1st.—Harlow Harden & Sarah Stetson, both of Bridgwater.

Sept. 3d.—William Pool of Bridgwater & Sarah Packard of Abington.

Novbr. 12th.—Eleazar Keith & ye widow Susanna Keith, both of Bridgwater.

Novbr. 19th.—Joseph Thayer of Stoughton & Sarah Richards of Bridg-[water.

Decembr. 31st.—Ebenezer Noyes of Abington & Betty Ramsdel of Bridgwater.

1796.

Janry. 21st.—Abel Delano of Pembroke & Deborah Pinchin of Bridgwater.

Janry. 26th.—David Allen & Rachel Dunbar, both of Bridgwater.

also William Bonney & Molly Dunbar, both of Bridgwater.

Febry. 9th.—Stephen Snell & Patty Cole, both of Bridgwater.

March 3d.—Whitcom Stetson of Abington & Lucy Snell of Bridgwater.

March 10th.—Allen Latham of Bridgwater & Jannett Dunbar of Halifax.

March 24th.—Timothy Bailey & Anna Whitman, both of Bridgwater.

March 30th.—Isaac Allen & Metilda Pratt, both of Bridgwater.

Return'd to ye Clerk, April 23d, 1796.

July 18th.—Abishai Stetson & Alice Allen, both of Bridgwater.

Sept. 8th.—Barza Allen & Johanna Bonney, both of Bridgwater.

Novbr. 7th.—Ezra Whitman & Thankful Freelove, both of Bridgwater.
Decembr. 15th.—Zenas Mitchell & Nabby Washburn, both of Bridgwater.

1797.
March 15th.—Cyrus Edson & Hannah Hudson, both of Bridgwater.
April 4th.—Josiah James & Jenny Pegin, both of Bridgwater—Indians.
N.B. I marry'd the above named Josiah James & Jenny Pegin in ye Presence of two white People, & a number of Negroes & Indians.
April 18th.—Jacob Washburn & Ruth Shaw, both of Bridgwater.
Returned to ye Clerk, April 28th, 1797.
June 1st.—David Churchell, Junr. & Molly Hearsey, both of Bridgwater.
June 28th.—David French & Rachel Hanks, both of Bridgwater.
July 3d.—Lieut. Ebenezer Cutler of Western in ye County of Worcester, & Mrss. Cynthia Sylvester Bonney of Bridgwater in ye County of Plymouth.
August 31st.—Oliver Hayward & Anna Washburn, both of Bridgwater.
Sept. 28th.—Sylvester Briggs of Norton & Leah Whitman of Bridgwater.
Novbr. 30th.—William Vinton & Mary Alden, both of Bridgwater.
Decembr. 25th.—Mr. John Skinner of Boston & Miss Rebecca McClench of Bridgwater.

1798. [water.
Janry. 29th.—Benjamin Pinchin Junr. & Polly Whitting, both of Bridg-
March 1st.—Isaac Lothrop, Junr. of Easton & Celia Keith of Bridgwater.
April 16th.—John Alden & Debby Robinson, both of Bridgwater.
Return'd to ye Clerk, June 4th, 1798.
May 31st.—David Snow Whitman of Bridgwater & Ruth Stetson of Pembroke. [water.
August 30th.—Eli Blanchard of Abington & Deborah Harden of Bridg-
October 22d.—Theodore Mitchel & Ruhama Newton, both of Bridgwater.
October 24th.—Ezra Alden & Abigail Vinton, both of Bridgwater.
Novbr. 22d.—James Johnson, Junr. & Sally Washburn, both of Bridgwater. [water.
Decembr. 20th.—John Crooker of Pembroke & Polly Smith of Bridg-
Return'd to ye Clerk, March 26th, 1799.

1799.
May 2d.—Uriah Brett & Nanny Robinson, both of Bridgwater.
July 16th.—Seth Beals of Pembroke & Thirza Hatch of Bridgwater.
July 25th.—Nathaniel Clift & Abigail Byram, both of Bridgwater.
August 29th.—Joseph Hearsey, Junr. of Abington & Sarah White of Bridgwater.
Sept. 17th.—John Willet of Abington & Lovisa Hatch of Bridgwater.
Sept. 19th.—Levi Churchill of Plymton & Cynthia Packard of Bridgwater.
Novbr. 14th.—Rev'd. William Briggs of Kittery & Miss Betsy Hudson of Bridgwater.
Novbr. 14th.—Joseph Smith, Junr. & Eunice Muxam, both of Bridgwater.
Novbr. 14th.—Achish Pool & Susanna Hearsey, both of Bridgwater.

1800.
Janry. 8th.—Henry Munro, Junr. of Halifax & Deborah Delano of Bridgwater.
Febry 24th.—Zephaniah Howard & Jennet Latham, both of Bridgwater.
April 14th.—Seth Latham & ye Widow Elisabeth Hanks, both of Bridgwater.
Return'd to ye Clerk, May 6th, 1800.

Sept. 9th.—John Keith, Junr. & Mehitable Keith, both of Bridgwater.
Sept. 24th.—John Winnet of Abington & Susanna Brown of Bridgwater.
Decembr. 11th.—Levi Thomas of Pembroke & Lydia Thomas of Bridgwater.

1801.
May 21st.—Melvin Holmes of Halifax & Hannah Wade of Bridgwater.
June 4th.—William Barrel, Junr. & Huldah Bisbee, both of Bridgwater.
July 1st.—David Keith, Junr. & Lydia Alden, both of Bridgwater.
Sept. 30th.—Samuel Wood & Debby Sherly, both of Bridgwater.
Octob'r. 6th.—Nehemiah Latham & Hannah Allen, both of Bridgwater.
Octob'r. 27th.—Samuel Pratt French & Olive Read, both of Bridgwater.
Novembr. 9th.—Leiut. Bradford Mitchell & Meribah Keen, both of Bridgwater.
Novembr. 26th.—Mr. Bartholomew Brown & Miss Betsey Lazell, both of Bridgwater.

1802.
Janry. 13th.—Solomon Hearsey, Junr. & Sylvia Gurney, both of Bridgwater.
Febry. 10th.—Alpheus Orcutt of Bridgwater & Mercy Pratt of Pembroke.
Febry. 17th.—Barza Allen & Lucy Baldwin, both of Bridgwater.
March 4th.—Comfort Carpenter Dresser of Chester in ye State of Vermont, & Celia Wade of Bridgwater.
Returned to ye Clerk, April 26th, 1802.

1801.
N. B. The marriages consummated by me for this year, being few in Number were not returned to ye Town Clerk, until April 26th in ye year 1802; & were then return'd with ye marriages consummated by me in 1802, prior to that date, April 26th.

1802.
April 28th.—Ichabod Keith & Susanna Robinson, both of Bridgwater.
July 9th.—Elihu Stephens & Susa Foy, both of Bridgwater; mulatto people.
August 16th.—Charles Keen & Celia Mitchell, both of Bridgwater.
Sept. 16th.—Mr. Moses Noyes of Providence & Miss Hannah Whitman of Bridgwater.
Novbr. 4th.—Mr. Daniel Howard, 3d, & Miss Susanna Kingman, both of Bridgwater.
Novbr. 13th.—Cyrus Cary of Claremont & Nabby Keith of Bridgwater.
Novbr. 25th.—Leiut. Galen Latham & Susanna Keith, both of Bridgwater.

1803.
March 7th.—Simeon Jones of Pembroke & Susanna Washburn of Bridgwater.
March 24th.—Bartholomew Trow & Mary Washburn, both of Bridgwater.
April 4th.—William Vinton & Nabby Otis, both of Bridgwater.
April 14th.—Isaac Read & Sally Stetson, both of Bridgwater.
June 23d—John Harden, Junr. & Jenny Stetson, both of Bridgwater.
Return'd to ye Clerk, June 29th, 1803.
August 3d.—Jacob Bicknel, Junr. of Abington & Hitty White of Bridgwater.
Return'd to ye Clerk, Oct. 4th, 1804.

EXTRACTS FROM THE EARLY PROBATE RECORDS OF BRISTOL COUNTY, WITH NOTES FROM THE REGISTRY OF DEEDS AND TOWN RECORDS.

[By Gen. EBENEZER W. PEIRCE, of Freetown.]

1687. August 8th.—Letters of Administration were granted to Samuel Howland, upon the estate of his brother John Howland, deceased.

[Samuel, John and Zoeth, were sons of Henry Howland, of Duxbury, said Henry being one of the 26 original proprietors of Freetown. Henry Howland died in 1670, and Mary his wife died June 16, 1674. Zoeth had a son Nathaniel, who divided his grand-father's lot (the 6th in Freetown) with uncle Samuel, Feb. 13, 1687. In this division Samuel Howland also received 32 acres of land in Swansea. Nathaniel Howland, of Dartmouth, in consideration of 60 pounds, sold Henry Brightman, of Portsmouth, R. I., half a freeman's share in Freetown, and half a freeman's share in the meadows at Sippacan, December 8, 1691. Zoeth was the ancestor of the New Bedford branch of the Howland family.]

1705. March 6th.—Benjamin Chase appointed "guardian unto his grand-daughter Sarah Makepeace."

[This was Benjamin Chase, the cooper, who was the earliest of the Chase family who settled at Freetown. Sarah Makepeace married, February 22d, 1711, Isaac Hathaway, of Freetown. The very numerous family of Chase in Plymouth and Bristol counties are descended from Benjamin Chase, the cooper.]

1704. June 8th.—Mr. John Rogers, Lieut. James Leonard, of Taunton, Lt. Job Winslow and Lieut. Josiah Winslow, both of Freetown, divided the estate of Lieut. Thomas Terry, of Freetown, deceased.

"Thomas the N. E. half part of the 17-lot 51 rods and 6 feet in breadth. Two acres at Brants neck, called the broad meadow at the westerly end to be measured with an 18 foot pole, 6 pole from a rock at the head of Shepherds cove. If a bridge and way be made through this 2 acres then Thomas to be allowed for it in meadow adjoining.

"Widow Anna to have the remainder of said meadow by estimation 6 acres during her life. One half the upland at Briants neck to Thomas, and the other half to John and Benjamin Terry. Thomas to pay the widow 10 shillings per year.

"In the 17-lot Benjamin to have next to Thomas 12 rods 9 feet and a half in breadth, so far as the 100 acres bought of Osborn extends, and above that 25 rods in breadth.

"The remainder of 17-lot to John Terry."

[Lieut. Thomas Terry was one of the first board of selectmen of Freetown, elected June 2d, 1685, and he was re-elected in 1686–1689 and 1690. He was commissioned Lieut., June 4th, 1686; Representative to the General Court in 1689.

Thomas, the son, was commissioned a Justice of Peace for the County of Bristol in 1720. He was Representative to the General Court in 1725, a Selectman of Freetown 24 years, Assessor 17 years, Treasurer 7 years, and Moderator of the annual town meeting 9 years.]

1715. Feb. 15th.—Samuel Howland, of Freetown, Yeoman, made his will and gave "to wife Mary, 2 cows, White mare and ye colt, one warming-pan, one bason and my chamber pot and bed I commonly lie upon and the bedding belonging to it, also one sheet and a box and all therein at the time of my decease.

"To daughter Mary Rounsevill one cow. To daughter Content Sanford more than she has had one pound. To sons Samuel, John, Abraham, Joshua and Gershom, more than they have had in other things one shilling each. To grand daughter Mary Morton one shilling, and to each of son Isaac's children one pound in money."

This will was presented and proved in the court of Probate May 7th, 1716.

[Besides the above enumerated gifts, Samuel Howland had conveyed to his sons by deed as follows. "1711, April 13th. To son Joshua of Taunton, one quarter of the sixth lot, one quarter part in width and upon the north side. 1712, Dec. 16th, to son Joshua who is now said to be of Freetown, one quarter part in bredth of the sixth lot from Taunton river to the great fresh pond. 1712, Dec. 16th, to sons Samuel and Gershom of Freetown a part of the northerly half of sixth lot."

Samuel Howland, the parent, was elected one of the Selectmen of Freetown May 12, 1690, and an Assessor Nov. 24th, 1697. He is undoubtedly the Samuel Howland who resided in Duxbury in 1662, and was fined 10 shillings or be whipt for carrying on the Lord's day a grist from mill; and he was also charged with *"discharging a fowling peece on the body of William Howse,"* of Sandwich, while gunning at the *"high pyne on Salthouse beach.* A verdict was given by the jury, *not guilty* of *willful murder, yett we find that the said Howse received his deadly wound by Samuel Howland's gun* goeing off, *as it lay on his shoulder."* Mary, the daughter of Samuel Howland, is supposed to have been the wife of Philip Rounsevill and mother of the entire Rounsevill family in this country.]

1726. June 22d.—James Barnaby, of Freetown, cordwainer, made a will, and gave his daughter Lydia Perry 30 pounds. To son Ambrose all his real estate. Ambrose, sole executor.

[James Barnaby died July 5th, 1726, in the 56th year of his age. His wife, Joanna *Harlow,* died Sept. 4th, 1725, aged about 56 years. The real estate given Ambrose Barnaby in his father's will was the farm purchased of Lieut. Nichols Morey in Feb., 1725, for 1300 pounds, and still owned by the Barnaby family.]

1729. March.—James Cudworth, of Freetown, made a will, and gave "to son David the land bought of Mr. Timothy Lindall where David's dwelling house stands and also 5 acres of land on ye west side of the road next to Mr. Lindall's lot, and to begin at the road and run to the brook which bounds out Lindall's land into the meadows. Give and bequeath all the rest of my lands and buildings in Freetown and else where to my two sons David and James. To daughter Bathiah Jones 26 pounds in bills. To daughter Lydia 40 pounds in bills. To daughter Abagail the looms she now useth and all the Slays and harness. To daughter Mary 40 pounds. To daughter

Zuriah 40 pounds. To daughters all my house hold goods and utensils in doors."

[James, the parent, married Betty Hatch, who bore him children as follows: David, who married Phebe Drinkwater; James, born Jan. 16, 1697, m. Sybil Chase, March 19, 1735; Abagail, born March 9th, 1699, m. Benjamin Smith; Mary, born Nov. 14, 1702, married Benjamin Leonard, of Dighton, June 13, 1734; Zeruiah, born April 1st, 1704, m. Nathaniel Potter, of Dartmouth, March 10, 1726; Jessee, born Jan. 11, 1706.]

1731. July.—The will of Benjamin Chace, the cooper, was proved in the Court of Probate. "To sons Benjamin and Walter all my lands in Freetown purchase. To grand son Benjamin Grinnell one 40 acre lot of land in No. 23, and also the 7th share in 3d lot, it being a cedar swamp lot in Middleboro'. To daughter Barthiah Dunham one half of the 14th lot near Baiting Brook in Middleboro' and one cow. To son Benjamin the fifth share of the aforesaid third lot in Middleborough purchase. To sons Benjamin and Walter all the rest of my lands in Middleborough. To daughter Philip Hathaway, and son in law Jacob Hathaway, all my land from and adjoining the land that my son Jacob Hathaway bought of my son Benjamin Chase and shall be a quarter Share in breadth and extending in leangth down to the river, always excepting 3 rods square which is to be reserved for a burying place and is to be in the south west corner. Also to daughter Philip 20 pounds, and all my moveable furnature that I have removed to my son Jacob Hathaway's house. To grand daughter Sarah the wife of Isaac Hathaway one cow. To grand child Daniel Grinell 5 shillings. Son Walter, sole executor."

[The grand children Grinell were the children of Benjamin Chase's daughter Mary. Sarah, the wife of Isaac Hathaway, was the daughter of his daughter Sarah, the wife of Thomas Makepeace. Benjamin Chase, the parent, was a Selectman of Freetown in 1698–99 and 1708; Assessor in 1691.]

1757. May 5th.—George Winslow made a will and gave "to son George south half of the 16th lot in Freetown up to the mill brook that is to extend one quarter of a share in bredth from Captain Ambrose Barnaby's land Northerly from road to the brook, and also my 5 acre lot eastward of the salt meadow and one quarter acre lot in the south side of the landing place on the said 16th lot at the river, also my salt meadows in the town ship of Swansea from Labor in vain Creek north up toward Taunton on the west side of Taunton River. Also half of my quarter of a share of land in said Freetown, lying above the mill brook in said 16th lot, and one eighth part of the mills on said mill brook with all the priviledges to said 8th part belonging. Also, one half that salt marsh given me by my brother William late of said Freetown, and also half of 3 acres given me by said William. Also my best anvil and half my smiths and carpenters tools, except my Steel anvil which I gave to my son Barnabas. Son George to pay legacies. To daughter Phebe 3 pounds 7 shillings in house hold goods. To daug. Elizabeth Strange 7 pounds in house hold goods.

"To son Barnabas the northerly half of homestead and buildings, except a part of house yard and garden given to wife. To son Barnabas half my quarter share of land above mill brook. Also to son

Barnabas one eighth the mills and priviledge and half my smiths and carpenters tools, and all the land above the mill brook given me by my brother William, and half the 3 acre lot and half my salt marsh. Barnabas to pay to daughter Elizabeth Strange 2 pounds 12 shillings lawful money, and to Rebecca Winslow 9 pounds and 12 shillings, or value in house hold goods. To daughter Hopestill Cook, to be paid by my two sons beside what I have already given her, five shillings. Sons to pay wife Elizabeth annually 8 pounds. Wife Elizabeth to have half the house and half the wood yard and garden, and after her to go to son Barnabas. Son George to be sole executor."

1747. July 7th.—Letters of Administration were granted to the widow Philip Paine, upon the estate of her late husband John Paine, Jr., of Freetown, deceased. The inventory showed the estate to consist of a house and 30 acres of land.

[Philip, the widow, was a daughter of Lieut. Lot Strange. After the decease of John Paine, Jr., she married Seth Chase, of Freetown, whom she also survived, and then married John Crandon, of Dartmouth. Her children by John Paine, Jr., were : John, who married Barbery Rice, of Warwick, R. I. ; Ebenezer, born 1740, married Wait Freeborn, May 20th, 1769, and Widow Hannah Randall 1792, and died Feb. 8, 1826 ; Abagail, who married Edward Chase, of F., Jan. 26, 1764 ; Mary, who married Jesse Cudworth, of F., January 30th, 1761. Her children by Seth Chase, were : Augustus, born in 1753, married Olive Chase, of F., Nov. 18, 1782, and died June 28, 1839 ; Philip, born 1760, married Polly Read, of F., 1782, and died Oct. 6th, 1818.]

1748. May 5th.—Thomas Terry, Esq. made a will, and disposed of his estate as follows : " To wife Abagail one third of my dwelling house during life. Also twenty pounds old tenor to be paid to her annually, and She also to have the Service, government, and improvement of my negro maid Jemima. Son Abial to find wife fire wood for one fire. To wife Abagail two beds and furniture belonging to them, and as much house hold goods as shall be necessary for her use during life, and after her decease to go to my executor, except one bed. Executor to provide food suitable for wife both in sickness and in health, and also for the negro maid.

" To son Thomas all that tract of land and buildings and fences I bought of Josiah Winslow, Jr., of Freetown, it being a part of the 24th lot in said town. I give him also that tract of salt meadows and flats and inlet flats I bought of Joseph Holloway, and lying in Dighton at a place called Timothy's neck. If Thomas dies without lawful issue, then my will is that what I have given my son Thomas, Abial shall have, and in case son Abial die, then his heirs to have the same. To daughter Lydia Jones beside what I have given her one Hundred pounds old tenor. Son Abiel to have all the rest of my property. Son Abial to be guardian to son Thomas until Thomas understanding be restored to him again. Son Abial Executor." This will proved in the Court of Probate for county of Bristol, June 15th, 1757.

1756. Aug. 30th. — Joanna Weaver, widow, granted letter of administration on the estate of Capt. Benjamin Weaver, Junr. of Swansea, deceased.

1757. Nov. 1st.—Joanna Weaver, of Freetown, widow, appointed guardian to her son Benjamin Weaver.

[Joanna Weaver was a daughter of Capt. Ambrose Barnaby and

Elizabeth Gardner his wife. Joanna was born at Freetown, June 26, 1733, and married Capt. Benjamin Weaver, Jr., of Swansea, Nov 4, 1753. Benjamin, their only child, was born June 25, 1755, and entered the Patriot army in the war of the revolution as a 5th Sergeant, from which he was promoted to captain, and from captain to Lieut. Colonel, in a Regt. of which George Claghorn (afterwards master builder of the frigate Constitution) was Colonel, and Robert Earl, of Westport, Major. Col. Weaver was a Selectman and Assessor of Freetown, and Treasurer of that town, 29 years. As a Judge of an inferior court he left the record of three thousand cases that had been tried before him. Joanna Weaver, the widow, for a 2d husband married Colonel Sylvester Childs, of Warren, R. I., in 1758. Colonel Childs commanded a Regt. under the King before the war of the Revolution. He was appointed Colonel in 1764 ; Thomas Church being his Lieut. Colonel, and N. Cogswell, Major.]

ABSTRACTS FROM THE FIRST BOOK OF BRISTOL COUNTY PROBATE RECORDS.

Copied by Mrs. Lucy Hall Greenlaw.

The following Probate Abstracts are a continuation of the series which, from page ½ to 49 of the original book, appeared in *The Genealogical Advertiser*, vols. 3 and 4, edited by Mrs. Greenlaw and now discontinued. The Register has been able to arrange with Mrs. Greenlaw for this valuable material.

---

[50] Will of William Witherell Senr of Taunton, dated Aug. 15, 1691, he "being Very ſicke". "I Commit * * * my Body to the Earth to be Decently Entered by my Children". To my two sons, William and John, my half a North Purchase to be equally divided between them. To son William my five acres of upland lying up at Timothy meadow. To Jerimiah the son of my son William all that land comprehended in a deed I made to my son Ephraim, "who being Deceaſed: Left into my Diſpoſe again". To my daughter Dorithy Wood, ten acres of land lying on the south side of the pond by my house, to begin at the place where the house stood which William Wood lived in, and so run southward from it. Having already disposed of my other lands to my sons, my will is that they should enjoy them severally. What my wife brought with her to be wholly at her "Diſpoſs", according to agreement between us before marriage, also my sons to pay her annually what was promised her by said agreement, also she shall enjoy my stock of cattle and household stuff during her widowhood and bearing my name. After her decease or marriage, what is left to be equally divided between my sons. Sons William and John to be executors. Witnessed by Giles Gilbert, Joseph X Gray and Samuel Danforth, who all made oath to said will Dec. 4, 1691, before Thomas Leonard, County Magistrate. Will entered by Jno Cary, Regist^r, Sept. 18, 1694.

[51] Jacob Barney of Rehoboth yeoman "being weak of Body" and "aged & Deſeaſsed", made his will July 30, 1692, making null and void all former wills made by me either by writing or word of mouth. To "my truely Loueing Son (being my Eldeſt) John Barney as a toaken of my loue" £20, I having formerly given him about £70 or £80 in money, which completes his portion. To my four sons, Joseph, Israell, Jonathan and Samuel Barney all my housing and lands divided or undivided in the bounds of Rehoboth with all implements of husbandry, to be equally divided between them at the death of my wife Ann Barney, "or at her mariage to another man." If any of my four sons die before the age of twenty-one, his portion to be equally divided among the survivors. To my daughter Sarah Hampton £10 in money; to my daughter Ruth Barney, same; to my daughter Dorcas Throope, same; to my daughter Abigail Marshall a Bible, which with £15 formerly given her by me is her full share; to my daughter Hannah Barney £10 in money to be paid to her at the age of twenty-one or at her marriage whichever shall first happen. If she dies "before Either of them happen," her share to be equally divided between my four daughters above. Wife Ann Barney to be sole executrix

until such time as said son Joseph Barney shall come to age of twenty-one, when he shall join with his mother as executors in joint partnership, they to pay all debts and legacies. Wife Ann to have all goods, chattels, buildings and lands until her death or remarriage. My "truely Loueing freinds" Thomas Estabrooks Senr, Capt Timothy Brooks and Samuell Bullock to be overseers. Witnessed by the three above and Richard Smith, who were all sworn Jan. 10, 1692. Entered by John Cary, Register, Feb. 20, 1693–4.

[52] Inventory of the estate of "Goodman" Witherill dec'd, taken Nov. 13, 1691, by "goodman Nuland", Joseph White and Giles Gilbert. Amount, £136. 16. 0. Signed by Giles Gilberte, Joseph White and Anthony X Newland, and sworn to by William Witherill, executor to the will of his father Wm Witherill dec'd, Dec. 16, 1691, before John Walley, Assis^{t}. Entered Sept. 18, 1694 by John Cary, Regist^{r}.

Account of the estate of "m: s" Anna Miles late of Swansey dec'd dated Feb. 5, 1694 and rendered by Joseph Kent, administrator. Items: Business done for her before her death "as I was her atturney", viz: one day to fetch a warrant from m^{r} Pecks; one day to fetch another warrant from Justice Saffins; one day going to Bristol to implead Nicholas Lange, Junr; to the charge of her funeral, viz: "for Rum Spice Suger & Nailes for the Coffin & alſo Sider & graue Digging &c:" to John Ingolls 20s. towards Rates; "paid to John Ingolls Senr: for m^{s}: Milees Diatt & attendance". Amount, £8. 1. 04. Account allowed by John Saffin Proba^{r}:, Feb. 5, 1694. Entered Feb. 6, 1694–5 by Jno Cary Regist^{r}.

[53] Receipt given by Mary Tucker, daughter of Abraham Tucker in the town of Dartmouth to her uncle, John Tucker, executor of the will of her grandfather Henry Tucker dec'd, which was dated the first day of the first month 1693, for ten pounds in money given her by her said grandfather. Receipt dated thirteenth day of the ninth month 1700, and witnessed by Abraham Tucker and Hannah X Tucker. Entered Nov. 11, 1708 by John Cary, Regist^{r}.

"Receiued the ———— in the year of our Lord 1705 by me Patience Tucker Daughter of Abraham Tucker which his wife Mary Tucker bare unto him, of my Vnkle John Tucker, Executor of my Grandfather Henry Tucker his Laſt will and Teſtament bearing date the firſt day of the firſt month: 1693:" the sum of ten pounds in money being a legacy given me by the said Henry Tucker. Dated May 4, 1705 and witnessed by Amos White, Joseph Woodell and Meribath Slocum. Entered Nov. 11, 1708, by John Cary, Reg^{r}.

[54] Henry Tucker of Dartmouth gave receipt dated "the 4 day of the 2^{d} month Anno Dom̄ 1702" to "my Vnkle John Tucker Executor of my Grandfather his Laſt will & Teſtoment bareing date the firſt day of the firſt month 1693", for twenty pounds in money and cattle being a legacy left me by my said grandfather Henry Tucker. Entered Nov. 11, 1708, by John Cary, Regist^{r}.

Martha Tucker of Dartmouth gave receipt dated "the 30th day of the 2^{d} month 1708", to my uncle John Tucker for ten pounds in cattle being a legacy left me by my grandfather Henry Tucker in his will. Entered Nov. 11, 1708, by John Cary, Regist^{r}.

Abigail Tucker of Dartmouth gave receipt dated "the 7th day of the 7th

month Anno: 1708" to my uncle John Tucker executor, for a legacy of ten pounds in money given me by my grandfather Henry Tucker in his will. Entered by John Cary, Register, Nov. 11, 1708.

[55] Will of John Smith of Dartmouth dated June 8, 1691. "In the firſt place I Deſire my Soule may return to god that gaue it me & I reſt with him for Euer". To "my well beloued wife Ruhamah Smith" all my stock and moveables "untill the Day of her Deceaſe"; also my two sons Judah Smith and Gershom Smith shall maintain said stock with the produce of the land that I have given them. To my daughter Hassadiah, wife of Jonathan Russell, one cow and two ewe sheep; to my daughter Mehitabell, wife of John Russell, same; to my daughter Hannah Smith one cow, one bed and bedding together with what I have already given her; to my daughter Sarah Smith one cow, two ewe sheep together with what I have given her already; to my daughter Deborah Smith, same. "I Giue my ſon Eliazer Smith his Son James Smith & unto Jonathan Ruſſell his ſon James Ruſſell Equally between them that Twenty accers of land that lyeth at the head of my aforeſ^{d} ſon Eliezers Smith his land" * * said land to remain to the aforesaid James Smith and James Russell. To my two sons Judah Smith and Gershom Smith that two acres of salt marsh that I have by exchange with my son in law John Russell. Wife Reuhamah Smith to be "ſole Executrix together with ſon Deliuerance Smith Executor". Legacies to be paid after death of said executrix or before, and all undivided lands in the town of Dartmouth, I divide unto my six sons, except ten acres which I give unto my grandson Mical Smith, the son of Hezekiah Smith, and I have given to every one of them lands by deed, which is sufficient for them. "I Deſire my truſty & well beloued freinds Seth pope & my brother in law Recompence Carby them to my ouerſeers of this my laſt will & teſtament and to be aſsiſtant unto my ſaid Executrix and Executor". Witnessed by Benjamin Howland and "uallantine hudelſton". I also give to my two sons Hezekiah Smith and Deliverance Smith all my acre and three quarters of meadow that I had by exchange with my son Deliverance, lying on the northwest corner of Heze-ziah Smith's land. The two witnesses made oath to the said will, Nov. 12, 1692, before Seth Pope, justice of the peace, also made oath before John Saffin (no date). Entered Jan. 26, 1693-4 by John Cary, Regist^{r}.

[56] Will of Anthony Low, dated Aug. 6, 1692. To my loving wife the house she now lives in during her life, and after her decease to my son Samuel Low and his heirs. To my eldest son John Low all my right and title at Warick. To my son Samuel "my ſloop Dulphin which now I am in, my wife & my ſon Samuel takeing Care to maintain my Daughter Elezabeth Dureing her life So Reſting with Dear loue to all my friends this I leaue as my laſt will and Teſtament". I also bequeath my plantation at Swanzey to my son Simon Davis and all the rest that is mine to my wife and son Samuel as aforesaid. Witnessed by Richard Dean and John James. I certify the above written to be a true copy of the original examined and registered By me Francis Rawle Deputy Reg^{r}. Entered July 1, 1693, by John Cary Reg^{r}.

John Low of Warick in the Colony of Rhode Island and Providence Plantations do quitclaim unto my brother Samuel Low of Swanzey yeoman all my right to estate that belonged to my honored father Anthony Low deceased, in the town of Swanzey. Dated Nov. 10, 1692, and witnessed by William Brenton, Jerimiah X Osborn and Richard Smith. Entered July 1, 1693 by John Cary Reg^r^.

[57] Mary Sison of Dartmouth widow, made her will "the fifteenth day of the fecond month Caled aprill" 1690, "being uery ill in body". To my loving son Georg Sison £35 in money and a Bible. To my two grandchildren John and Mary Sison, children of my son John Sison £35 in money to be divided equally between them, to be paid to my son Georg Sison for the use of said two grandchildren. All my brafs, pewter, iron, linen and woolen, milk vessels and pails shall be divided into three equal parts. One part I give to my daughter Elizabeth wife of Caleb Allin, also £5.. 10. in money, one chest and a wheel. Another part I give to my daughter Ann wife of Peleg Tripp, also £5.. 10 in money, a chest and a wheel. The other part I give to my granddaughter Mary Sison daughter of my son George Sison, also £5 in money. I hereby acknowledge that I have received of my son James Sison in full for all estate left me by my husband Richard Sison in his will, and acquit him of the same. Said son James to be sole executor. Witnessed by Joseph Tripp, George Cadman and Jn° Anthony, of whom the first two made oath at Bristol Dec. 1, 1692, before John Saffin. Attest Stephen Burton Regist^r^. Entered Sept. 1, 1693 by John Cary Regist^r^.

[58] Inventory of the estate of widow Mary Sison taken by George Cadman, James Trip and Valentine Hudestun, Sept. 22, 1692, and sworn to at Bristol, Dec. 1, 1692 before John Saffin Prob^r^, by James Sison executor of her will. Attest Stephen Burton Regist^r^. Entered Sept. 1, 1693 by John Cary Regist^r^.

[59] Peter Hunt of Rehoboth, "being Weak in body & not knowing how Soon I may be remoued out of this world", made his will June 19, 1689. To my eldest son Enoch Hunt all that land which I bought of m^r^ Paine, which he purchased of John Woodcock Senr., upon part of which said Enoch's house now standeth, also 30 acres of swamp and upland on the Neck side, and the salt meadow butting up to the highway, and the meadows on both sides of the river I had of "ffather Bowen", except a small piece of fresh meadow and swamp I have already given to my son John Hunt, and a hundred pounds estate of Commonage in the town of Rehoboth as expressed in a deed of gift bearing date June 9, 1687. To my son John Hunt one half my uplands where said John Hunt's house now stands, one half my uplands and meadows on the east side of Palmers River and the Newmeadow River on both sides of the Rocky River, 4 acres of salt meadow on the neck side, a small piece of swamp and meadow that was formerly ffather Bowen's and a hundred pounds estate of Commonage in the town of Rehoboth as expressed in a deed of gift dated June 9, 1687. Also ten acres of upland joining Nathaniel Paine's land where Daniel Shepperson lately lived. To my son Ephraim Hunt one half of all the uplands adjoining my salt meadows where the dwelling houses of my sons John and Ephraim Hunt now stand, lying on both sides of the highway that goeth from Bowen's bridge to the hundred acre Run, one half my meadow and upland lying on the east side of Palmers River upon the Newmeadow River on both sides of Rocky river, a piece of meadow and swamp, and a hundred pounds estate of Commonage in the bounds of Rehoboth as expressed in a deed of gift to said son Ephraim, dated June 9, 1687. To my son Benjamin Hunt my now dwelling house, barn, orchard,

home lot, shop and tools, piece of salt meadow at the hundred acres called the Governors Meadow, seventy acres on the neck at a place commonly called Sharpers tree, and a hundred and thirty pounds estate of commonage in the town of Rehoboth, to him said Benjamin Hunt after decease of myself and wife. To my daughter Judeth Williams and to her two sons Nathaniel Cooper and Thomas Cooper that lot of salt marsh at Belchers Creek, and £20 to be paid within one year after my decease. To my son in law Samuel Peck five shillings; to my son in [60] law James Willett one shilling; to my granddaughter Ann Paine five pounds; to my granddaughter Sarah Pecke twenty pounds. All the rest of my land, viz: my whole share on the north side, all my fresh meadow at m^r Browns pond and at Palmers River, my land in the neck by Jerimiah Wheatten, my lot and orchard at William Carpenters, my lot I bought of Thomas Barns, the salt marsh I bought of m^r Brown, a piece of marsh called three mens mow, a piece of marsh I bought of John Woodcock Senr, fifteen acres I bought of Rice Leonard and all other lands in Rehoboth, Swanzey or elsewhere and all personal estate I give to my wife Elizabeth (who is to be sole executrix) during her life, all real estate then remaining to be equally divided between my four sons, Enoch, John, Ephraim and Benjamin Hunt. Further my will is that son Benjamin shall have two oxen, two cows, a horse and a "mair." Witnessed by Daniel Smith, Samuel Newman and Stephen Paine. This may certify that I said Peter Hunt have already given my grandchild Sarah Peck ten pounds in bedding and cattle which is to be deducted from her legacy above expressed. Samuel Newman and Stephen Paine made oath to said will, Dec. 26, 1692. Entered May 10, 1694 by John Cary Regist^r.

Agreement made between those concerned in the estate of Richard Briggs of Taunton dec'd. William Briggs, eldest son, is to have the twelve acre lot expressed in the inventory, John Briggs is to have the new house and the land belonging thereto, and is to maintain his mother, widow of said Richard Briggs, "ſo long as She bears his fathers Name", also he is to take care for the bringing up of the young children. Also we have agreed that the four youngest sons are to have the home lot, and the three daughters six pounds each. Agreement dated Dec. 13, 1692 and signed by Rebecah X Briggs, Williams Briggs, John Brigs and Nathaniel Thayer. Witnessed by Jonah X Linkon and James X Woodward who made oath to the same Dec. 15, 1692 before John Saffin Jus^t: Entered Mar. 16, 1694 by John Cary Regist^r.

[61] Will of William Hoar, baker, of Bristol dated July 23, 1697, he "being weak in Body and Labouring Vnder ſuch & ſo great infirmityes as giues Juſt occaſion to Expect my Speedy Deſolution. Yet at the writing hereof am of a ſound Memory and as Good Vnderſtand as Euer I had". "Imp^r. I Commend my Spirit to that God from whom I did Receiue it. through my Deareſt Lord Jeſus Chriſt that hath ſo Dearly Bought it as wth no leſs then his Deareſt heart Blood and to the Euer Bleſſed Spirit of Grace that hath been Concerned for my Saluation Euer Since I was Borne. Item—I Committ my Body to the Earth of wch. it was made there to Reſt in Jeſus till the Reſurection and I will that it may haue Decent Buriall, Naturall Affections Cannot be Reſtrained when Near Relation Dye Lett thoſe be Improued for themſelues, not for me. Therefore would haue no Moads of Mourning worn for me. Nor ſigne of the Ground where I was Buried.

for as I ſlighted the world when I was in it. I do much more ſo now." To my "Beloued wife Hannah who is the wife of my Youth & the Naturall Mother of all the Children that Euer I had in the world Not willing ſhe ſhould be forced to goe to her Cradle for Comfort, The whole of what I ſhall be Poſſeſſed off at my Death" during her widowhood, of which she can sell, with the consent of the overseers, any part of the real estate, for necessity only. At her decease estate to be divided among my surviving children, "without Reſpect to to age or Sex", wife to give any or all children whole or part of their portions if she sees fit. If wife marrys, she shall have her thirds by law. Wife Hannah to be sole executrix and "my Very Good freinds Decon John Cary John Birge & Nathaniel Blagroue" to be overseers "praying them to Deale as becometh faithfull Chriſtians". Witnessed by John Cary, Thomas Walker and Nath: Blagrove, who all made oath to the above in Bristol, Dec. 27, 1698, before John Saffin Esqr Judge of Probate. John Cary Regist^{r}. Entered Dec. 29, 1698 by John Cary Regist^{r}.

[62, 63 and 64, blank].

ABSTRACTS FROM THE FIRST BOOK OF BRISTOL COUNTY PROBATE RECORDS.

Copied by Mrs. Lucy Hall Greenlaw.

[65] Agreement between John Allen of Bristol and Thomas Read of Rehoboth, overseers of the will of Isacce Allen late of Rehoboth, dec'd, of the one part, and Daniel Jencks of Attleborough on the other part. Whereas there was obtained of Katheren Allen late widow of Isacce Allen aforesaid deceased, a deed of gift to her son Nehemiah Allen, dated June 30, 1693, which is judged by the parties concerned to be not proper, it is agreed that said Daniel Jencks, husband to the above said Kathern shall take care of all the children of the said Isacce Allen, and cause them to be instructed in reading English, Nehemiah Allen, only son of the deceased, to be taught reading, writing and the trade of a blacksmith, " the which he Now Vſeth ", provided said Nehemiah be bound to said Jencks until he is twenty one years old. On this condition performed by said Jencks, John Allen and Thomas Reed as overseers and with the consent of said Katheren promise not to molest said Jencks or said Katheren his now wife or make any claim or challenge of them upon the virtue of said deed (which is now cancelled) made by said Katherine in favor of her son. Dated May 8, 1695 and witnessed by Stephen Paine, Joseph Brown and John Cary, and acknowledged same day by Daniel Jencks and John Allen before Jn° Saffin Justice & Probation^{r}. Entered May 28, 1695 by John Cary Regist^{r}.

[66] " In Rehoboth in the Coloney of Newplimouth—Iſace Allen being ſick & week in body but ſound in Vnderſtanding & haueing his perfect fence ſaw Cauſe to ſett his houſe in order & to make his will ", which is dated Oct. 3, 1692. To my eldest daughter Katherine my ten acres of salt meadow in Swanzey on a place called the tongue, thirty acres in Rehoboth lying by the Broad Cove path, and all my rights in Commons in Rehoboth, she paying to her sister Sarah when she comes to age, ten pounds in money. To my daughter Bethiah fifty acres of upland which I purchased of Thomas Man, belonging to the North Shares, one half my meadow belonging to that farm and one half the Commons in said shares. To my daughter Deborah fifty acres of upland in the North Shares and the other half of my meadows and commons in said shares. To my only son Nehemiah my dwelling house and farm I now live on, one half when he cometh to age, the other half after the death of his mother, he paying to his sister Sarah, when she comes to age, five pounds in money. To my wife Katharine my dwelling house and half my farm I now live on during her life, she paying her daughter Sarah five pounds when she cometh to age, also all chattels and goods for the bringing up of my children, she to be executrix. My " truſty & well beloued Brother John Allen & my beloued freind Thomas Reed " to be overseers. Witnessed by Jonathan Sprague, John Allen and Bethiah Allen. " Thus Entered by John Cary after m^{r} Burtons Deceaſe ".

Account of the charges arising upon the division of the lands in partnership between the heirs of Isacce Allen late of Rehoboth dec'd and Anthony Sprague of same town. Persons named: John Allen, Thomas Read, Daniel Jenckes, Joseph Buckland. Account allowed by Jn° Saffin Proba^{r}. John Cary Regist^{r}. Entered May 8, 1695 by John Cary Regist^{r}.

[67] Joseph Buckland Senr, m^{r} John Allen of Swansey and "Infigne" Thomas Reed of Rehoboth are impowered to make a division of lands now undivided between Anthony Sprague and the children of Isacce Allen late of Rehoboth dec'd, Jan. 5, 1693, by Jno Saffin Proba^{r}. Entered Jan. 5, 1693 by John Cary Reg^{r}.

Memorandum. m^{r} [*blank*] Joseph Buckland Senr: & Daniel Jencks all of Rehoboth are joined in Commission with the abovesaid Jno Allen and Thomas Read overseers to make an equal division of the aforesaid lands between Anthony Sprague and his partners and [*sic*] the children of Isacce Allen late of Rehoboth dec'd. Dated Dec. 24, 1694. John Saffin Probater.

Inventory of the estate of Thomas Brentnall dec'd taken Oct. 14, 1692 by John Ware and Thomas Skiner Senr. and sworn to by Ester Brentnall his widow, Feb. 6, 1693 before Jno Saffin Proba^{r}. Amount £126..15..02. Entered Feb. 6, 1693 by John Cary Regist^{r}.

[68] Inventory of the estate of Elizabeth Janson widow "who Deceaced the Thirty firft Day of may one thoufand Six hundred Ninety four", taken by William Salisbuery and James Wheeller. Amount £37..14..00. Sworn to by Elisha Davis administrator of the estate of Elizabeth Janson late of Swansey dec'd, July 10, 1694 before John Saffin Judge of Probate. John Cary Regist^{r}. Entered July 10, 1694 by John Cary Regist^{r}.

Division of the lands and meadows lying in partnership between Isaace Allen late of Rehoboth deceased, and Anthony Sprague of the same town, made by John Allen and Thomas Read, overseers to the children of said Isaace Allen, and Joseph Buckland Senr and Daniel Jencks, July 16, 1694, and approved by Jno Saffin, Prob^{r}: John Cary Reg^{r}. May 7, 1695. Recorded by John Cary Reg^{r}. Jan. 7, 1698–9.

[69] Inventory of the estate of Peter Pitts dec'd taken by John Pollerd and Henry Hodges, Jan. 9, 1692. "By virtue of an order of John Saffin Esqr. I Thomas Leonard Efquire * * haue this Day (being the ninth of January) Adminiftred an Oath unto Mary pitts Widdow a uery antient & infirm Woman not being able to trauile" to this effect that the said inventory was a true account of the estate of her late husband Peter Pitts dec'd. Entered Nov. 28, 1693 by John Cary Regist^{r}.

[70] Will of Peter Pitts of Taunton he "being Sick of body", dated June 9, 1692. To my son Samuell Pitts that parcel of land by the Mill River that he hath already in possession, being part of that late joining Samuell Waldron his now dwelling house, and twenty acres on the other side of Browns Brook so called, only the privilege of fire wood shall belong to those that inherit my now dwelling house, also I give him all that meadow between that which I have already fenced toward Muddy Cove, and half a purchase right, he paying five pounds to his sister Alce his mother having the use thereof during her life. To my son Peter the other part of that land, barn and orchard joining to Samuell Waldron, the other part of the land on the other side of the highway joining to John Hodges, six acres of land at the head of the aforesaid lot and all my land at Weniconett, and half a purchase right, his mother having the use thereof during her life. To my son Ebenezer my now dwelling house and the home lot belonging to it, being six acres, and the meadow at the South purchase at Secreegancet belonging to the house aforesaid and a half purchase right, he paying five pounds to his sister Alce, his mother having the use thereof during her life. To my daughter Mary, she having received something

already, ten pounds more. To my daughter Sarah that land called the paddock and forty acres more belonging thereto as yet not laid out, and a quarter purchase right and a half share of two silver cups, her mother having the use thereof during her life. To my daughter Alce my half share in the old Iron works, a North purchase right, a half share in two silver cups and ten pounds to be paid by her brothers Samuell and Ebenezer. Rest of estate to wife Mary Pitts, whom I make sole executrix, revoking all other wills by me heretofore made. I desire that John Hodges and Henry Hodges be overseers. Witnessed by John Pollord, Sam^ll^ X Thresher and Sam^ll^ Waldron, of whom Sam^ll^ Thresher and Sam^ll^ Waldron made oath "in the prefence of their Maj^ties^ Juftices of the peace for the County of Briftoll (m^r^ Stephen Burton being fick & abfent)" before John Saffin at Bristol, Jan. 12, 1692, that said testator was of sound mind, and that said Jno Polord did sign as a witness. Entered Sept. 22, 1693 by John Cary Regist^r^.

[71] Georg Sison "of Road Ifland in the Collony of Road Ifland and prouidence plantations" has received of my brother James Sison of Dartmouth the money and goods given me by my mother Mary Sison by her will. Dated "the feuenteeth of ye 10th m^th^ Cald December 1692", and witnessed by Valentine Hudelstun and Richard Allen. Entered Oct. 10, 1693 by John Cary Regist^r^.

George Sisson of Road Island gave receipt to my brother James Sisson of Dartmouth for £35 in money that my mother Mary Sisson gave by will to my brother John Sisson's two children. Dated Dec. 17, 1692, and witnessed by Valentine Hudelstun and Richard Allen. Entered Oct. 10, 1693 by John Cary Regist^r^.

Elizabeth Allen wife of Caleb Allen of Sandwich, Barnstable Co., has received of my brother James Sisson of Dartmouth the money and goods given me by my mother Mary Sisson in her will. Dated Dec. 17, 1692, and witnessed by Vallentine Hudlestun and Deliverance Smith. Entered Oct. 10, 1693 by John Cary Regist^r^.

[72] Ann Tripp wife of Peleg Tripp "of the Colleny of Road Ifland & prouidence plantations" has received of my brother James Sisson of Dartmouth, the money and goods given me by my mother Mary Sisson in her will. Dated Dec. 17, 1692 and witnessed by Vallentine Hudlestun and Richard Allen.

Mary Sisson daughter of George Sisson "of Road Ifland Colleny & prouidence plantations" has received of my uncle James Sisson of Dartmouth all the money and goods given me by my grandmother Mary Sisson in her will. Dated Dec. 17, 1692 and witnessed by Valentine Hudlestun and Deliverance Smith.

An agreement made Dec. 7, 1687. Robert Crosman of Taunton promises to give to Martha Eatton of Bristol widow during her life "(fhe being forthwith to be my maried wiffe)" all that lands I bought of Capt Foster of Dorchester with all buildings "that is or fhall be on ye Same", with half a purchase right, all situate in Taunton lying between land of John Dean and the widow Andross, also I give her all goods and chattels during her life, one half to be at her absolute dispose at her death. Witnessed by Edmond Ranger and Richard Smith. Acknowledged by said Robert Crosman Nov. 18, 1690 before Daniel Smith Asst. Recorded Jan. 16, 1693–4 by Cary Regist^r^

[73] Inventory of the estate of Robert Crossman senior of Taunton dec'd, taken Oct. 27, 1692 by James Leonard and Thomas Dean. Amount,

£35..19..01. "Here followeth what the widow brought with her when ſhe maried her huſband Robt Croſman above named", amounting to £3 17 00. The appraisement of the housing and home land made Nov. 24, 1692 by Thomas Harvy and Moses Knape. More, including "ſome hay to John Threſher" appraised Jan. 23, 1692 by Philip King and Ezra Dean. John Saffin "being informed that the widdow Croſman is aged and infirm not in a Capaſsity to Come to briſtoll to make oath to the Inuentory of her Deceaſed huſbands Eſtat" requested Capt. Leonard to administer the oath to her and send it with the inventory to "m^{r} Burton the Regiſter" to be recorded. Order dated Nov. 26, 1692. Martha Crosman, therefore, took said oath before Thomas Leonard Justice of the peace in Taunton, Jan. 23, 1692–3. Entered by John Cary Register, Nov. 7, 1693.

[74] Inventory of the estate of Philipe Tabor of Dartmouth dec'd, taken Mar. 4, 1692–3, by Thomas Taber and Joseph Tripp, who with Mary Davice (all of Dartmouth) made oath to said inventory "this laſt of augſt 1693." Amount £230..12..06. More to be added, £1 02 00. John Cary Register.

[75] John Briant of Taunton, "Being week of body" made his will, Feb. 10, 1684. To "my Dear & welbeloued wife Elizabeth" during her life, my now dwelling house and barn with all lands belonging to same on the west side of the river, and the lot of land on the east side of the river, opposite that on the west side, also all goods and cattle "to her own diſpoſe as god ſhall dirictt her". Rest of lands in township of Taunton to my son John Briant, also my meadows in or about "affonate Bay" and my North purchase of land, and the reversion of my housing and lands after my wife's decease. Wife Elizabeth to be executrix, and all former wills to be utterly void. Witnessed by John Macumber sen^{r}. Joseph Wilbore and John Richmond, of whom John Richmond made oath to said will at Bristol, Aug. 31, 1693 before Jno Saffin Proba^{r}. Attest Jno Cary Regist^{r}. Entered Sept. 2, 1693 by Jno Cary Regist^{r}.

[76] Inventory of the estate of John Briant of Taunton, "who dyed the Eleuenth day of Auguſt 1693", taken by John Richmond, Samuell Williams and Robert Crosman, Aug. 21, 1693. Amount, £229..17..06. More, £2 2 00, "and as to what is due to: or from the eſtate in Reſpt of Debtes Cannot well be known. as yet: there being no books: to directt". Elizabeth, relict to John Briant of Taunton dec'd, made oath to same before John Saffin Prob^{r}., John Cary Register. Entered Sept. 2, 1693 by John Cary Regist^{r}.

[77] Will of George Macey of Taunton, dated June 20, 1693, he "being weak of body". To my daughter Elizabeth Hodges my division of land lying in the South purchase both divided and undivided, also two acres of meadow lying "in affonatt againſt the Bay. John Deans Meadow on the one ſid: and the meadow of Joſhua Tiſdall on the other ſide". To my grandchild Samuell Hodges one half a purchase right in the township of Taunton, also two little lots lying on the south side of the Three mile river being part of the South purchase. To my daughter Elizabeth Hodges fifty acres of land in the North purchase. To my daughter Sarah Black forty-two acres of land near Bristol way, bounded on the west near the land that formerly belonged to William Harvy, and by lands of Giles Gilbert on the east, also nine acres of a thirty acre lot division, also seven acres where my son in law Samuell Blacks house now standeth, also two acres at the head of my home lot where I now dwell, also two

acres of meadow at "wenicunit", also half a purchase right in the township of Taunton. To my daughter Mary Williams fifty acres of land lying in the south side of the Neck plain so called, near Thomas Leonards land, also two acres of meadow at a place called Browns farm. To my daughter Rebeccah Williams threescore acres of land at "Lockaty: allis water feild" which is three Rumford divisions viz. twenty acres on my right, twenty acres on m[r] Bishopes Right which I bought of him, and twenty acres I bought of John Cobb sen[r] which was his Rumford division. To my daughter Deborah after the death of my wife Susannah my dwelling house and lands adjacent viz.: my house lot on which my house now standeth, my pasture on the west side of the mill river, also about twenty acres on the west side of the Ridge so called, also a parcel of meadow at "weniconite", bounded by the meadow I gave my daughter Sarah, also my purchase rights in the township of Taunton, also "my goods in my Parlor as Bedfteads table Cheftes and all other timber goods belonig to that Rome". [78] To wife Susanah rest of lands undisposed of and all goods and chattels, she to be sole executrix and to pay debts and funeral charges. "I defire my Loueing freinds John Hall and Jofeph willis to be helpfull to my Beloued wife". Witnessed by Samuell Danforth, John Hoskines and Shadrach Wilbore, who, all of Taunton, made oath Sept. 5, 1693 before John Saffin Proba[r]. John Cary Regist[r], that they did see Capt. George Macey late of Taunton now dec'd, sign above. Entered Sept. 7, 1693 by John Cary Regist[r].

[79] Richard Williams "aged about Eighty being in Competent health", made his will May 5, 1686. To my eldest son Samuell my two lots which I purchased of Timothy Holloway, now in possession of said son Samuell, also the rights to future divisions of lands belonging to that lot formerly in the occupation of Anthony Slokam. To my son Nathaniell the land, house and barn which now he possesseth being part of the lot which I bought of Henry Uxley containing half an acre, with rights to future divisions thereto belonging, also seven acres lying between the great lots of Nicholas White and Hezekiah Hoare, also sixteen acres which I had for my great lot bounded on the west by Walter Deans land, also three acres of swamp at pale Brook, one half my meadow at little worth and three acres of land allowed me by the town in satisfaction for a highway through said seven acres. To my son Joseph the land, house and barn now in his possession, and rights to future divisions belonging to the lot heretofore of John Gingell now in the possession of my son Samuell, also eight acres on the south side of the great river by the land of m[r] John Pooll, also two acres of salt marsh at Assonat between the land of Leiften[t] George Macey and the next Creek westerly. To my son Thomas the westerly part of my dwelling house with six acres of land being the westerly part of the lot on which said part of my dwelling house stands, also one half my division of land at "Weefquobonoonfuk" with one half my meadow adjoining thereto and one quarter of meadow at Littleworth, also one half my fifty acres "about Stonie ware on the great Riuer", also my twenty two acre division on the Three mile river, he to keep one cow for his mother during her pleasure. To my son Benjamin my share of land in the North purchase, the other half of my division of lands at "Weefquobonoonfuk", the other half of my said meadow thereto adjoining, the other half my fifty acres at "Stonnie ware", one quarter my meadow at Littleworth, also my Tan yard with the stock thereof, and after my wifes decease the easterly part of my dwelling house and the remainder of the house lot not disposed of to said Thomas,

also one bed with its furniture, he to pay my wife annually four pounds in money and keep one cow for her during pleasure. To my daughter Elizabeth sixty acres at "goofbery" meadow with two acres of meadow I bought of James Philips. To my daughter Hannah my whole share of land in the South purchase. To my two sons Thomas and Benjamin my pasture with my barn thereon to be equally divided between them. To "my beloued wife ffrauncis" during her life, the easterly part of my dwelling house with the garden, lands at Assonat & meadow not disposed of, with fifteen pounds annually and the keeping of two cows during pleasure, also I give her two cows and all household goods forever. [80] If my wife's necessity require it, the land at Assonate and share in the Iron works shall be sold for her supply, if not, I give it after her decease to sons, Samuell, Nathanell, Joseph, Thomas and Benjamin. The above sons to be joint executors and to pay annually to my wife during her life eleven pounds besides the four pounds before assigned to be paid by son Benjamin. "I alfo will them to tack Care of her their faid mother in all things Neceffary for her Comfort to their abillitie". I make null and void all former wills made by me. Witnessed by James Walker, Thomas Leonard and James X Leonard Junr. Oct. 10, 1693, Capt. Thomas Leonard and James Leonard both of Taunton made oath before Jno Saffin Prob^tr^. John Cary Regis^t^. that they saw Richard Williams late of Taunton dec'd sign said will and saw James Walker late of Taunton sign as a witness. Entered by John Cary Reg^t^ Oct. 11, 1694.

Will of Mary Walker of Rehoboth dated May 15, 1694, she "being uery Sick & weake". To my three brothers Samuell Walker, Philip Walker and Ebenezer Walker all my lands, divided or undivided, to be equally divided between them. To my sister Elizabeth Sweet all my apparell, both linen and woolen, and all my other linen. To my "Cozen Ann Perren a Book Caled the Cordiall Comforts, and Cozen Abraham Peren a book Caled Secreet Thoughts in Dyeing times". To "my Cozen Sarah Peren my Bible". "I Giue to my Sifter martha walker my Cheft And Glafs Bottles and her Daughter Patience my box". I give my pewter to my brother Samuel's and brother Philip's children to be equally divided between them. To my "Dearly beloued mother Jane Polles" my silk hood. Brother Samuell Walker to be sole executor. After charges are paid what money I have to be equally distributed among my Cozens. Witnessed by Joseph Dogget, John Butterworth and William Carpenter who all made oath at Rehoboth, May 28, 1694, before John Saffin Proba^r^. John Cary Register. Entered May 30, 1694 by Jno Cary Regist^r^.

[81] Inventory of the estate of Mary Walker late of Rehoboth dec'd taken May 25, 1694. Amount, £44..15..03.

Inventory of the estate of John Peren late of Rehoboth dec'd taken May 23, 1694 by Sam^ll^ Peck, Thomas Reed and William Carpenter, and sworn to at Rehoboth May 28, 1694 by Sarah Peren widow of said John Peren, before John Saffin Proba^r^. John Cary Register. Amount £145..15..00, plus a Steel trap appraised at 12s. Recorded May 30, 1694 by Jno Cary Register.

[82] Will of Thomas Willmouth Senr, dated Rehoboth, Dec. 10, 1678. To wife Rachell my now dwelling house & orchard, one half my home lot, and my salt meadow and creek that lyeth at the "Narrow Pafsage", during her life, also one third of all live stock and one third moveable goods for her dispose. To my two daughters Elizabeth and Mary the other two

for wages" ; "to John Titus for Cart wheels & Barrills" ; "to Jarrett I'graham" ; "to my father Perens Eftat Due"; to William Carpenter about division of the estate; to "Sa'll Peck" same; to Ensign Read same; "Due Vpon A Bill to the town Committee toward the Settlement of mr Greenwood". "A Steel Trape Since Come to Light to be now aded the Inuentory". Sarah Peren relict of John Peren Junr late of Rehoboth made oath that the above was a true account of the debts paid out of the estate of her said late husband, before John Saffin Probr: John Cary Registr:, at Bristol, Aug. 7, 1694. Entered Aug. 8, 1694 by Jno Cary Registr.

Samuel Peck, Will Carpentr, Thomas Read, Samll Walker and Nicolas Ide all of Rehoboth, commissioned May 28, 1694 by John Saffin Esqr Judge of Probate to make a division of the estate of John Peren Senr late of Rehoboth, "who deceafed at Rocksbery", between his surviving children, divided the same "Amonft his Seauen Children". "To Samll Peren wch he hath already in his hands"; to Noah Peren second son surviving and Susanah Peren the youngest daughter, that part of the dwelling house and half barn that the said John Peren did reserve for himself when he disposed of the other to his son John Peren now deceased, with one half his house lot and one half a parcel of land at the lower end of the house lot, a parcel of land and meadow at Mantoms neck, a piece of meadow lying between the meadows of Timo Ide and Samll Millerd, [95] also one third of their commons. Said Noah to have all the above lands and to pay to his sister Susanah when she comes to the age of eighteen, sixteen pounds four shillings, and to the administrators of his father's estate, two pounds six shillings with which they shall make up Susanah's portion to eighteen pounds, ten shillings; if he refuse or neglect to do this, Susanah to have her proportion of the lands. To Daniell Peren third son surviving, one half his father's fresh meadow and swamp at the Mile Run, one half the salt meadow near to Jonath Bosworth, twenty five acres on the North purchased lands near Snake hill, eleven acres of upland in Wachamokett Neck; a third of the commons, and four acres in the second division, between the lands of the heirs of Abraham Peren and Capt Saunders, Samuell Peren to pay unto Daniel Peren ten shillings he now hath in his hands, and a gun and sword. To David Peren the fourth son surviving, one half the salt meadow near to Jonathan Bozworth adjoining to John Ficthes, one half the fresh meadow and swamp on the Mile Run, fifteen acres in the pine lot at the north end of the great plain, and the north meadow, fourteen acres lying on both sides of the Rocky River at a place called Zachariah pen, one third of the commons, and two plain lots on the east side of the highway, Samuell Peren to pay his brother David Peren £1..15 that he hath now in his hands. To Mary Peren, eldest daughter, £17 in goods and chattels, and one half of eight acres near mr Brown's Pond. [96] To Mehettabell Peren, second daughter, £10 in household goods and sheep, also one half of eight acres near mr Brown's Pond, Samuel Peren to pay to Mehettabell £1..16 which he hath in his hands. The remainder of her portion to make it up to eighteen pounds ten shillings to be paid her at eighteen years of age by "her Vnkle Infigne Thomas Read". The above division made Aug. 3, 1694 and signed by William Carpentr:, Samuell Peck, Thomas Read, Samuell Walker and Nicholas Ide, and sworn to Aug. 7, 1694 by Thomas Read, Samuel Walker and Nicholas Ide before Jno Saffin, Judge of Probate. Ordered to be recorded, John Saffin. John Cary Registrm:

thirds of my moveables. To my three sons, Thomas John and Jonathan, and my two daughters Elizabeth and Mary the remainder of my live stock to be equally divided between them. My three sons are to pay my debt "at old Goodman Paines" for which I give them my farthest share of meadow on the North side and that hundred acres of land laid out to me on the North side. They shall also have all the rest of my lands, are to be executors and are to "Difcharge & make good my obligation to my wiues Children as of all other Debts". I also desire that "my beloued Brethren in Law Sarjant Jonathan Blifs and Sarjant Thomas Read" be overseers. Witnessed by Daniel Smith and Joshua X Smith. Rehoboth, May 28, 1694, Joshua Smith made oath before John Saffin Probatr. John Cary Registr, that he saw Thomas Willmott sign said will and that mr Daniell Smith did subscribe as a witness, and that Thomas Read was present at the same time. Entered May 31, 1694 by Jno Cary Registr.

[83] Inventory of the estate of "Enfigne Thomas willmath" late of Rehoboth deceased, taken May 26, 1694 by William Carpenter and John Butterworth, and sworn to May 28, 1694 by Rachel Willmouth, widow of said Thomas, John Willmath and Jonathan Willmath before Jno Saffin Probar. John Cary Register. Amount £204..04..00. Entered June 11, 1694 by John Cary Registr.

[84] Inventory of the estate of Abraham Perin late of Rehoboth taken May 24, 1694 by Samuell Peck, William Carpenter and Nicholas Ide, and sworn to before John Saffin Probar: John Cary Registr, Aug. 7, 1694 by Tho Read and Saml Walker administrators of said estate. Amount £230.. 14..06. Entered Aug. 7, 1694 by John Cary Registr.

[85] Will of Henry Tucker of Dartmouth dated "the firft Day of the firft Month 169¾". "ffirft I Defire my foule may returne to god who gaue it me & Reft with him for Euer". To my wife Martha Tucker twelve pounds yearly during her life, also one feather bed and what clothing doth belong thereto. To my daughter Sarah Tucker threescore pounds "in as much as She hath had no portion as yet". To my son Abraham Tucker £30 in money. To my grandchild Henry Tucker son of Abraham Tucker one half of all my lands, when he comes to age of twenty one, but if my wife is living he shall not possess the same until her death, also I give him twenty pounds, because I have given him no part of my house or orchard. To the four daughters of my son Abraham Tucker "which his firft wife Mary Tucker bare Vnto him" viz. Mary, Patience, Martha and Abigail, ten pounds each when they come to age of sixteen years. If any of said daughters die, her legacy to be equally divided among the survivors. To my son in law Nathaniel Slocum twenty pounds in money or goods. To son in law Samuel Perry twenty pounds in money. "I giue to the Church in Chrift and people of god in fcorne Caled Quakers on Road Ifland" five pounds. Rest of estate to son John Tucker, he to be sole executor. Witnessed by John Akin, Thomas X Briggs and Eliazar Smith. The three above witnesses, all living at Dartmouth, made oath to above will before Jno Saffin, John Cary Registr, at Bristol, July 3, 1694. Entered July 4, 1694 by Jno Cary Registr.

[86] Inventory of the estate of Henry Tucker late of Dartmouth taken May 1, 1694 by Jonathan Russell and Thomas X Briggs and [87] sworn to by John Tucker of Dartmouth before John Saffin Esqr at Bristol, July 3, 1694. John Cary Registr Recorded July 5, 1694 by John Cary Registr. Amount £362..09..02.

ABSTRACTS FROM THE FIRST BOOK OF BRISTOL COUNTY PROBATE RECORDS.

Copied by Mrs. Lucy Hall Greenlaw.

[88] Joseph French Senr of Taunton, "being Very weak & Ill", made his will, Apr. 24, 1694. To son Joseph that piece of land where he is now building a dwelling house, beginning near the path that goeth to the great meadow, bounding with land formerly in the possession of Richard Burt Senr, which tract of land is a thirty acre division which I formerly bought of John Smith, and part of a thirty acre division which I bought of Malichi Holloway, also one half a great swamp lying towards the north-east of a plain called a valley, which swamp I bought of John Richmond, Samuel Williams and Samuel Thresher, also one half a tract of land lying on the north side of a great swamp which we call the old plain, also a pair of oxen and two cows. To my son John a tract of land lying southerly from my home lot where he is now building a dwelling house, extending from a path which leadeth towards Elkanah Bobbitts—the line of James Philips mentioned—five acres of which said land is not yet laid out, being granted to me on the right of Nicholas White senior's fifty acre division, taking in a pond commonly called half way pond, also I give him a pair of steers and one cow. To my son Nathaniel a tract of land on the east side of the aforesaid great meadow path, which said path parts the land of Joseph and Nathaniel, also one half the said swamp joining said plain which said swamp is bounded by a "mark tree" marked with J F, which said tree is the bounds between my swamp and the swamp of "Jno macumber Cooper, . . which ſd line was agreed Vpon by the ſaid Jno macumber & I", said tract of land I bought mostly of the aforesaid John Richmond, Sam^{ll} Williams and Samuel Thresher, also half that tract of land lying on the north side of the said great swamp which we call the old plain, bounded on the east by lands of Jno Macumber, cooper, and on the west by land of Jno Tesdale. To son Jacob a tract of land lying southerly from Joseph's land, the path that goeth towards Elkanah Bobbitt's mentioned. [89] To Ebenezer and Jonathan equally after the death of my wife Experience French, my home lot bounded on the east by the aforesaid highway which goeth towards Elkanah Bobbitt's and from said path to the "Cōtry Road which goeth towards Rood Island" and along said highway till it comes to the land of James Philips, taking in a pond "made by Drowning" which we call the upper pond. Wife Experience to be sole executrix and to have cattle and moveables undisposed of. My "loueing freinds Deacon Henry Hodges & John Smith both of Taunton" to be overseers. To my daughter Elizabeth wife of James Philips six pounds out of the moveables after death of my wife, or sooner if she can spare it. I impower my executrix to divide among my children my land in Billrica, 100 acres lying by heath swamp and 10 acres of meadow in heath swamp meadow, also lands in Taunton not mentioned. Witnessed by John Smith, John Spur, Thomas Richmond and Samuel Danforth, of whom John Smith Senr and Thomas Richmond, both of Taunton, made oath to said will at Bristol, July 3, 1694, before Jno Saffin Proba^r: John Cary Regist^{rm}, and John Spur made oath before the same July 7, 1694. Will recorded July 5, 1694 by Jno Cary Regist^r.

[90] Inventory of the estate of Joseph French late of Taunton dec'd taken May 18, 1694, by John Smith, Henry Hodges and John Pollard and sworn to by Experience French, executrix of said Joseph's will, July 3, 1694, before John Saffin Proba^r John Cary Regist^{rm}. Amount £350..19..00. Entered July 5, 1694 by John Cary Regist^{rm}.

We, Rachel Wilmoth relict of Ensign Thomas Wilmoth, Jonathan Fuller in behalf of my wife Elizabeth, eldest daughter to said Ensign Wilmoth, and Mary Gilbert younger daughter of same, being heirs by the will of Ensign Thomas Wilmoth have received our portions of the moveables according to the will, and do discharge John Wilmoth and Jonathan Wilmoth of the same. Receipt dated June 4, 1694 and signed by Rachel × Welmoth, Jonathan Fuller and Mary × Gilbert in the presence of Thomas Read and Thomas Read Junr. Acknowledged same day by the three signers before Nicolas Peck Justice of the peace, and allowed by John Saffin Esqr "Judge of Probats of wills within this County" July 3, 1694. Recorded July 5, 1694 by John Cary Reg^r.

[91] We, Mary Wilmoth relict of Thomas Wilmoth dec'd, eldest son to Ensign Thomas Willmoth of Rehoboth late dec'd, allowed guardian unto the orphans of my husband dec'd, and George Robbinson allowed assistant, have divided the lands and meadows with John Wilmoth and Jonathan Wilmoth, each of them equal by the will of the dec'd Ensign Thomas Wilmoth, and also have received the children's part of the stock, June 4 1694. Signed by Mary × Wilmoth and Georg Robinson Junr and wi nessed by Thomas Read and Jonathan Fuller. Acknowledged June 1694 before Nicolas Pecke Justice of the peace, and allowed by Jo Saffin Esqr Judge of Probate, July 3, 1694. John Cary Regist^{rm}. Ente July 6, 1694 by Jno Cary Regist^{rm}.

Whereas John Rogers of Bristol, administrator to the "smale Ef Left by Jethro Negro of Swanſey Deci^d", hath made administration t upon, the estate being insolvent, so far as it will extend among the cred that appeared before the "Commiſſioner Captaine John Browne", therefore discharged from the administration by John Saffin Proba^r: 21, 1694. John Cary Regist^{rm}: Recorded July 21, 1694 by John Regist^{rm}:

[92] Inventory of the estate of John Medbery, appraised by N Tanner and Thomas Barns. "This land was prized by Vs being Medberyes land befor mariage which ſhe ſcruples to put into the tory" at £70..00..00. Dated May 15, 1694. Sarah Medbery relict Medbery late of Swansey dec'd made oath at Bristol July 3, 169 inventory before John Saffin Prob^r: John Cary Regist^{rm}: Ente 9, 1694 by John Cary Regist^{rm}:

[93] Inventory of the estate of Ephraim Hunt late of Rehob taken by Sam^{ll} Peck William Carpent^r and Thomas Read Ju and sworn to by Rebeccah Hunt of Rehoboth late wife of sai dec'd, July 31, 1694 before John Saffin. John Cary Regist July 31, 1694 by John Cary Regist^{rm}:

[94] An account of the widow Sarah Peren, relict and a of estate of John Peren Junr late of Rehoboth, for debts Items: to James Sabin; "to the Docter for phiſick for he "to Mehetable Peren our maide for wages"; "to Rebecca P

Account of the administrators of John Peren Senr. Paid "for Rent & Repair at Rocksbury Due from ye Eſtate of Jno Peren Senr: to the Eſtate of John Polle late of Rocksbery Dec:d"; "Giuen with the youngeſt Child of John Peren Senr: being about Six years old when Diſpoſed of"—£2; for a Journey of Thomas Read to Rocksbery for business respecting the estate; to Samuel Peck for helping managing business at Rocksbery one day. Above account sworn to, Aug. 7, 1694, by Thomas Read one of the administrators before Jno Saffin Esqr Judge of Probate. John Cary Reg-ist^rm. Recorded Aug. 7, 1694.

[97] Samuel Peck, William Carpenter, Thomas Read, Sam^ll Walker and Nicolas Ide all of Rehoboth were appointed by Jno Saffin, Judge of Probate, May 28, 1694 to make a division of the lands that were in partnership between Jno Peren Senr, Jno Peren Junr and Abraham Peren all late of Rehoboth dec'd. June 12, 1694 they divided the north side meadow, lying between the meadows of the heirs of Sam^ll Carpent^r and the meadow of John Smith, lying upon the ten mile River, and set up stakes and cast lots, "& the heirs of John Peren Senr: fell Vp stream & the heires of Abraham Peren Down Stream"; also divided sixteen acres near m^r Browns Pond between the same, also four small plain lots, thirty acres called the pine lot, and nine acres of land in the second division in which the heirs of John Peren Senr: fell upon the southward side next to Capt Saunder's land, and heirs of Abraham Peren next to James Sabin's land. June 16, 1694 they divided between the same, a piece of salt meadow lying between the meadow of Samuel Millard and Timothy Ide, another piece of salt meadow between the meadows of Jno Ficth and Richard Bowen Senr, an upland lot containing thirty four acres, lying on both sides of the Rocky River at a place called Zacheriah's pen and a fifty acre lot in the North Purchased lands near Diomon Hill, divided across the run that comes out of Buckland's meadow. [98] July 19, 1694 they divided between the same, a lot in Wachamoket containing twenty two acres, lying between the lands laid out to "Decon Newman" and those laid out to "Decon Walker" and the meadow and swamp on both sides of the mile Run. July 20, 1694, they divided between the same, five acres and a quarter at the end of their house lots, a parcel of land in Mantums Neck of which the southern end next to "Georg kinriks" lot fell to the heirs of John Peren Senr, also a strip of meadow in Mantums Neck. June 16, 1694, they divided between the heirs of Abraham Peren and the widow and heir of John Peren Junr, twenty two acres of upland on the east side of the mile Run, of which the northernmost side next m^r Sweetings fell to the heirs of Abraham Peren, also a piece of salt marsh adjoining the upland in the New Meadow Neck, also two small lots of fresh meadow, containing an acre each, in Bushy meadow "& laid to Abraham Perens heirs that lot that is Adjoyning to their own wch was firſt Decon walkers".

[99] July 20, 1694, they divided between the heirs of John Peren Senr and the widow and heir of John Peren Junr the house lot being eight acres "& the Diuiding line is from the middle of the Leantoo Door of the Dwelling Houſe to an Aple tree markt", also one half the land at the end of the house lot. The same day, they divided between the heirs of Abraham Peren, and the widow and heir of John Peren Jr., an eight acre lot in the second division, adjoining to the "Schole maſters lott", also an acre of fresh mead in Rose meadow. Said division dated Aug. 3, 1694, and signed by the five commissioners, of whom Thomas Read, Samuel Walker and

Nicholas Ide made oath to the same, Aug. 7, 1694, before Jn° Saffin Probar: who allowed the same, and ordered it to be recorded, which was done the same day by John Cary Registrm.

[100] Division of the estate of Philip Taber late of Dartmouth dec'd, made by Thomas Taber, Jonathan Delano, Joseph Tripp, Joseph Taber and George Cadman all of Dartmouth, Nov. 27, 1693. To his relict, one third of estate both real and personal, viz. the lower room in the new house and the cellar, and the south end of the land and meadow with the orchard upon it; it is bounded on the south side by the lands of Mary Timberleg. To eldest son Philip Taber, upland, one half the marsh lying before said part of land, and one half of all the undivided lands formerly belonging to said Philip Taber dec'd, also the other two thirds of the housing, the whole amounting to £50, he to pay to his sister Hester Taber, £14..7..4 when she comes to the age of eighteen, or at the day of her marriage if it happen before. To son John Taber the remainder of the divided land, with the other half of the marsh lying at the north end of his brother Philip's marsh, and the other half of the undivided land, the whole amounting to £30, he to pay to his sister Bethiah Taber £12..3..8 when she is eighteen, or at marriage. To his five daughters, viz. Sarah, Lidiah, Abigail, Easter and Bethiah £17..16..4 each. [101] To daughter Mary Earle £7..16..4 to make up her portion equal to the rest. Above division sworn to by the above five commissioners, Sept. 13, 1694 before Jn° Saffin Probar John Cary Registrm: Entered Sept. 14, 1694 by Jn° Cary Registrm:

Inventory of the estate of John Peren Senr dec'd taken Nov. 4, 1692, by Thomas Read, and Abraham Peren, and sworn to Jan. 10, 1692 by Jn° Peren, to whom administration is granted May 2, 1693. Amount, £147..17..00. Entered Oct. 4, 1694 by Jn° Cary Register.

[102] I, Lidiah Taber, daughter of Phillip Taber late of Dartmouth dec'd, have received of my mother Mary Davis, administratrix of the estate of my father aforesaid, £17..16..4 in full payment of my just part thereof. Dated Dec. 13, 1693. Entered Nov. 16, 1694 by John Cary Registr.

Sarah Taber, daughter of Phillip Taber late of Dartmouth dec'd, gave receipt to her mother Mary Davis, administratrix of the estate of her father aforesaid, for £17..16..4, being her share of said estate. Dated Dec. 13, 1693. Entered Nov. 16, 1694 by John Cary Registr.

We, Thomas Earl and wife Mary Earl, daughter of Philip Taber late of Dartmouth dec'd have received of our mother Mary Davis administratrix of the estate of said Philip Taber, £7..16..4 to make up what we had formerly received of our father, equal to the other children's shares. Receipt dated Dec. 16, 1693, and entered Nov. 16, 1694 by Jn° Cary Registr.

[103] "I John Green of the town of Newport in the Colloney of Road Ifland & Prouidence Plantations: Marinr being Very Sick & week But of perfect Vnderftanding Blefsed be god Doe this fourth Day of September one Thoufand Six hundred Ninety & four mak my Laft will & Teftament". To Elizabeth Allen of Boston, living at the south end of the town, forty pounds in silver money. To Nathaniel Allen five pounds, also five pounds to the father of Nathaniel and Elizabeth Allen, and five pounds to Sarah Allen, the aforesaid fifty five pounds to be paid by Stephen Squire of Cambridge, which was paid to him for part of a sloop wherein I was con-

cerned. To Dr. James Collins £15 in money. To Benjamin Palmer and his sister Elizabeth one half of what is in my chest which is at Benjamin Palmer's. To William Beho, £20. To my landlord Childs, £20, likewise £10 to the children of m^{r} Childs. The other half of what is in my chest, after legacies and funeral charges are paid, I give unto my fellow soldiers. I give "my Pied Horſs" to Thomas Lanford, and the black horse to him that keeps the pasture. My two rings I give to m^{r} Nicolas Peck and his wife. To "Doctor huges" two gold buttons, to Dr. James Collins two gold buttons. I "apoint Thomas Way to ſe me Decently Buried". To Dr. Huges twenty pieces of gold; My arms and wearing apparel to Benjamin Palmer, likewise my wearing apparel that is with me to Dr. Collins. "Mr Allen I pray pay to m^{s} Gold ſome ſmale matter that I owe her". To Thomas Way one of the largest bars of gold in my chest, he to be sole executor. The "Coppy of this will was taken By Doctor James Collins from m^{r} John Greens mouth before Nicolas Peck Eſq^{r}: & his wife & m^{rs} Childs And when this will was Drawn & Read to him & to the beſt underſtanding of the perſons preſent was willing to haue Signed & ſealed it But was Sudenly taken in a fitt & ſo uncapable to ſigne & ſeale it & Deceaſed in the fitt, whereof we Do teſtify & haue hereunto ſett our hands this fourth of September 1694". Signed John × Manchester, Joseph Cross and William Carpenter, of whom Jno Manchester and Joseph Cross made oath to the above will Oct. 4, 1694 before Jno Saffin Proba^{r}. [104] The next day "Came alſo Nicolas Peck Eſq^{r} and m^{r} Willi Carpenter and ms Martha Child" who testified to the truth of said will before Jno Saffin Proba^{r}: Entered Oct. 10, 1694, by John Cary Regist^{rm}.

[105] Will of Joseph Chaffee of Swansey dated Sept. 22, 1694, he "being Sick & weake in Body". To my beloved wife all my household goods for her to dispose of to herself or her children at her discretion, also the improvement of my dwelling house and one half of my upland and meadow ground in Swansey during her life, after which it shall be equally divided between my two sons John and Joseph Chaffee. To two said sons, the other half of my upland and meadow ground in Swansey, when they come to the age of twenty one years, to be equally divided between them, also my tools and my gun. To son John a heifer of three years old. To son Joseph the Great Bible that was my father's and my sword and sickle and a heifer that I had of Joseph. After my wife's decease, when my two sons come to possess the upland and meadow ground that I have given her during her life, they shall pay three pounds apiece to my daughters as a legacy which I give to them. Other estate, as my stock and debts due to me, I give to my wife for her to give my daughters according to her discretion. My beloved wife to be executrix and my two sons John and Joseph to be executors, and I hereby make void all former wills. Witnessed by John Martin, Bamfeild Capron and Nathaell Chaffee, who all made oath to said will before Jno Saffin Proba^{r}: John Cary Regist^{r}: at Bristol, Nov. 13, 1694. Entered Nov. 13, 1694 by Jno Cary Regist^{rm}. [106] Inventory of the estate of Joseph Chaffee dec'd of Swansey taken Nov. 9, 1694 by John Peck, Israel Peck and John Ormsby. Total amount, £237..01..00. Item: "Tract of Land Lyeing between Decon John Butterworth & the land y^{t} was Jno meadberyes". Nov. 13, 1694, Ann Chaffee the executrix and Jno and Joseph Chaffee executors made oath to said inventory before Jno Saffin Proba^{r}: John Cary Regist^{rm}. Entered Nov. 13, 1694 by John Cary Regist^{rm}.

[107] Thomas Barns, Israel Peck, John Paine and Nath[ll] Pecke all of Swansey and John Cary of Bristol, being commissioned by John Saffin Esq[r] Judge of Probate, made a division of the estate of Jn[o] Meadbery late of Swansey dec'd, between the widow and children, Oct. 15, 1694. To the widow thirty pounds of the moveables, and half the house and half the home lot being twenty five acres in the whole lot, bounded south on land belonging to the heirs of John Dixi late of Swansey dec'd, and north on land belonging to John Allen, also half of two acres of meadow at the head of Long Beach so called, also the use of the whole above mentioned until her son John Meadbery comes to the age of twenty one. To John Meadbery, eldest son, his father's gun, half the house and half the home lot, with half the two acres of meadow at the head of Long Beach, he to come into possession of the above when he comes to the age of twenty one, in full of his double portion, and after his mother's decease, he shall possess the whole of the said house, upland and meadow, provided he pays his brother Thomas £10 and his brother Nathaniel £17..2..10, when they reach twenty one. To second son Benjamin, twenty acres in Swansey, bounded south by lands of Deacon Butterworth, west by land of Israel Peck, and joining on the north to lands of Joseph Chaffee, his mother to have the use thereof until Benjamin is of lawful age, also he is to have his father's sword. [108] Thomas, third son of the dec'd, shall receive from his mother when he reaches twenty one years, £7..2..10, and from his brother Jn[o] Meadbery, £10, and Nath[ll], youngest son, shall receive from his brother John Meadbery when he comes to age of twenty one, £17..2..10, and Hannah and Sarah, daughters of the dec'd, shall receive from their mother, £17..2..10 each. Signed by Sarah Meadbery (widow of said John dec'd) and the five commissioners, who all made oath before John Saffin Judge of Probate, Nov. 6, 1694, who allowed the same. Entered Nov. 6, 1694 by John Cary Regist[rm]:

Account of the estate of Henery Annadown late of Rehoboth dec'd. Dec. 27, 1695, amount of the inventory, £13..02..04. Items of account: "five pounds pd to his Sifter Dec[r]: 31 as by her Receipt in full"; "Ballance Reft w[ch]: (the Debt all pd) Belongs to Philip Annadown his Brother". Philip Annadown made oath to the truth of this account before John Saffin Esq[r]. Judge of Probate, Jan. 3, 1695, John Cary Regist[r].

[109] Inventory of the estate of Noah Sabin dec'd, taken by William Carpent[r]: and Thomas Cooper Sen[r]: Nov. 13, and sworn to in court Nov. 18, 1691, by James Sabin administrator. Items: "Noahs wages for Twenty weeks of which there is in Johns Hands 1..6..7"; "A Sword loft in Cannady by Noah"; "ffresh meadow at m[r] Browns Pond". Total amount, £40..15..9.

An inventory of the lands of Hezikiah Sabin dec'd, taken by William Carpent[r] Sen[r] and Thomas Cooper Sen[r]: (no date). Amount, £23..10..00. Entered Dec. 4, 1694 by John Cary Regist[rm].

[110] Inventory of the goods chattels and lands of Hezekiah Sabin dec'd taken July 3, 1693 by William Carpenter and Thomas Read, and sworn to by James Sabin of Rehoboth, brother of Hezekiah, before John Saffin Esq[r] Judge of Probate, John Cary Regist[r]. Items: "A maire and an Inkhorn & Catouch box in James Sabins hands"; "About Thirty Sheep w[ch] my mother Difpofed fome off y[m] to my Sifters & the Reft my Brother John had"; "three yearling heifers two of which my Brother

Jno Sabin had & one my mother had"; "A maire & a Coulte and a Gun y^{t} my Brother Jno Sabin had". Total sum, £37..15..00. Entered Dec. 4, 1694 by Jno Cary Regist^{rm}:

Inventory of the estate of John Green dec'd, taken Sept. 10, 1694 by Robert Little and Tho: Brooks. Amount, £442..11..00. Items: "peices $\frac{8}{8}$ 180 Lyon Dollers 1320 & other Siluer all amounting to 352=14=00"; "37 peices of gold att 11^{s} p^{r} peice & other Brocken Gold amounting to £049=00=00"; "A Bagg of arabian peices". Inventory sworn to at Bristol, Jan. 1, 1694 by Thomas Way of Newport, executor of the will of Jno Green late of Newport dec'd, before Jno Saffin Probat^{r} John Cary Regist^{r}. Recorded Jan. 2, 1694.

[111] Inventory of the goods and chattels of John Hall Senr dec'd of Taunton, taken Oct. 2, 1693 by Henry Hodges, Jonathan X Pratt and Shadrach Wilbore Senr. and sworn to in court by the administrators Oct. 12, 1693 before Jno Saffin Probat^{r}: Jno Cary Regist^{rm}: Amount, £447.. 00..10. Item: "his half Share in the old Iron works in Taunton". Entered Jan 29, 1694–5 by John Cary Regist^{rm}.

ABSTRACTS FROM THE FIRST BOOK OF BRISTOL COUNTY PROBATE RECORDS

Copied by MRS. LUCY HALL GREENLAW

[112] Inventory of the estate of Joseph Bozworth late of Rehoboth dec'd taken by William Carpent^{r} and Enoch Hunt, Jan. 2, 1694–5. Items: "A Gun & Sword & Belt"; "the one halph of a Looking Glafs"; "an old great Bible"; "In fider & a tobacco Box". Amount, £104..19..00. Said inventory sworn to Jan. 28, 1694 by Hester Boszworth, relict of said Joseph, before Jno Saffin Proba^{r}: John Cary Regist^{r}: Entered Jan. 30, 1694–5 by Jno Cary Regist^{rm}

[113] Inventory of the estate of John Russell late of Dartmouth dec'd taken Feb. 21, 1694–5 by John Shareman and Thomas Taber. Amount, £186..08..00. "This Inuentory was by John Rufsell attefted Vpon oath in the prefence of Almighty God", April 2, 1695, before Jno Saffin Proba^{r} Jno Cary Regist^{r}: Entered April 2, 1695 by John Cary Regist^{r}:

[114] Will of John Russell "of Dartmouth in the County of Briftoll in New England in America", dated Jan. 19, 1687–8, "I being at this time in fome bodily health & my memory & Vnderftanding being yet good & Sound". To my eldest son John Russell my home dwelling house with all the land thereto belonging in the township of Dartmouth. Whereas my son Jonathan Russell, besides his quarter share of land which I gave him by deed, hath had of me some upland and some meadow land near the place called Coxseeset, my will is, that to that shall be added enough to make three acres of meadow land and fifty acres of upland, all of which fifty acres of upland and three acres of meadow land, I give to my grandson Jonathan Russell, son of my said son Jonathan Russell. To my grandson John Russell, son of my son Joseph Russell, fifty acres of upland and three acres of meadow land to be laid out to him by my son John Russell, when he comes to the age of twenty-one. My sheep, household goods, cart and plow tackling to son John Russell, and my cattle and horses to be divided by my executor equally among all my grandchildren "So Near as Conveinientiy he Can Diuid them". My loving son John Russell to be sole executor. Witnessed by Robert X Dennis, Mary X Gatchell and William Wodell. Mary Wodell, formerly Mary Gatchel, made oath April 2, 1695, before Jno Saffin Proba^{r}: Jno Cary Regist^{r}: that she saw said John Russell sign said will, also that "fhe Did fee Robert Dennis & william wodell (Sence Deceafed) Signe as witnefses at ye fame time together with her felf". Entered April 2, 1695 by John Cary Regist^{r}.

[115] Inventory of the estate of John Stevenson "who Deceafed the Sixteenth of Septembe^{r}. 1695" taken Oct. 11, 1695 by David Freeman and Samuell Robinson. Amount, £57..05..02. Items: "his Gun his Cutlafh his Catuch Bux"; "his Goofe & Sheires". Sworn to at Bristol, Oct. 16, 1695 before Jno Saffin Proba^{r}: John Cary Regist^{r}: by James Stevenson of Springfield, brother of said John Stevenson. Entered Oct. 16, 1695 by Jno Cary Regist^{r}.

[116] The account of Thomas Way of Newport, R. I., executor of the will of John Green lately deceased at Rehoboth, of legacies paid out as follows:

"to Elezabeth Brooks in Spetia as Bequeathed"
"To Robert Little Vpon the account of Benjamin Palmer"
"To Henry Brightman Vpon the account of ye Allens at Bofton"
"To Jerimiah Childs of Rehoboth & his Children"
"To Doctr william Hughs of Boftcn"
"To Robert Gardner of Road Iland for william Beho"
"To Elizabeth Collins wife of Doctr: Collins of Bofton"
"To Nicolas Peck Efqr"
"To Thomas Langford of Road Ifland"
"To John Dave of Road Ifland"
"To Benjamin Palmer a Gun & Piftolls". Amount of legacies, £333..08..08.

Account sworn to April 8, 1695, by Thomas Way before John Saffin Probar; "There being only Remaineing one Hundred and Nine pounds Eleuen fhilling & four pence of the faid Eftate according to the Inventory which was Bequeathed By the faid Teftatr. to his ffellow Soldiers whereof the faid Executor is one the Reft unnamed which the faid Executr. Thomas Way hath Giuen Bond to Sattisfy when Demanded Vpon which mr Jabez Howland is fully Difcharged that was his Surty". Recorded April 8, 1695 by John Cary Registr:

Thomas Brooks of Newport, R. I., mariner, gave receipt to Thomas Way of Newport, R. I., for a legacy of £68 "in Spetia", bequeathed to "my Daughter Elizabeth Brooks" by the late dec'd John Green in his will dated Sept. 4, 1694, and agrees to refund her proportion of said legacy to pay any debt, now unknown that may arise. Receipt, to which said Elizabeth Brooks gave consent, dated Jan. 3, 1694, and witnessed by John Pocock and Arnold Collins. Entered April 8, 1695 by Jno Cary Regist.

[117] Robert Little of Newport R. I. gave receipt to Thomas Way for £63..10 in full for all silver, gold, crowned money and plate given by John Green "which Dyed at Secunk laft September 1694" to Benjamin Palmer, which was purchased by said Little of said Palmer, and he also engages to pay his proportion of any future debt. Receipt dated April 8, 1695, and entered the same day by Jno Cary Registr.

Henry Brightman gave receipt to Thomas Way for £55, being for four legacies given to Daniel Allen and his children by John Green, who died at Secunk in Sept. 1694, he also engaging to bear his proportion of any arising debt. Dated April 8, 1695 and entered by John Cary Registr: the same day.

Received of Thomas Way executor of the will of John Green dec'd bearing date Sept. 4, 1694, a legacy of £20 in silver bequeathed to me, Jeremiah Child and "Ten pounds to his Children, in all thirty three pounds fifteen fhillings in Spetia Bequeathed Vnto him as in faid will Spetifyed", he also promising to return his proportion of any debt. Dated Mar. 1, 1694–5, witnessed by Nicolas Peck and Benjamin × Whight, and entered April 8, 1695 by John Cary Registr.

William Hewes of Boston has received of Thomas Way, executor of the will of Jno Green, bearing date Sept. 4, 1694, £11 in full payment of his legacy, and agrees to return his proportion of any unknown debt. Dated Mar. 16, 1694–5 and witnessed by Henry Franklin and Abraham Smith. Entered April 1695 by Jno Cary Registr:

[118] Receipt given by Robert Gardner to Thomas Way for £20, being the amount given William Beho for a legacy left him by John Green. Dated at Newport, R. I., Feb. 27, 1694–5, and entered April 8, 1695 by John Cary Registr.

Received of Thomas Way £15, in full of a legacy left my husband James Collins by John Green dec'd. Dated Boston, Jan. 30, 1694-5 and signed by Elizabeth Collins, by the order of her husband. Entered April 8, 1695 by Jn° Cary Regist^{r}:

Mar. 4, 1694-5, received of Thomas Way two gold rings being a legacy left to me and my wife by John Green dec'd. Signed Nicholas Peck, and entered April 8, 1695 by John Cary Regist^{r}:

John Davy of Newport, R. I. has received of Thomas Way one black horse as a legacy bequeathed to me by the will of John Green. Dated April 15, 1695, and entered May 10, 1695 by John Cary Regist^{rm}

Thomas Langford of Newport, R. I. has received of Thomas Way "one pyebald horſs", being a legacy bequeathed to me by John Green dec'd. Dated April 15, 1695, and entered May 10, 1695 by John Cary Regist^{r}.

[119] Inventory of the estate of Richard Marten late of Rehoboth dec'd, taken by Samuel Newman, John Peck and William Carpenter. Item: "An old great Bible". Total, £22..18..08. Sworn to at Rehoboth, May 7, 1695, by John Marten son of said Richard Marten dec'd, before Jn° Saffin Proba^{r}: John Cary Regist^{r}: Entered May 9, 1695 by John Cary Regist^{rm}:

A bill of charges of John Marten against his father's estate. Items: "I Paid in the firſt Indian war for his Rate in Siluer money in the year 1676"; "for Six years Dieting of my ffather and Tendance"; "for ffunerall Charges Drink Coffin & Graue"; "A Debt Chalenged by my Siſter Annis Chaffe being part of her portion yet Vnpaid". The above named John Marten son and executor of the will of his father Richard Marten late of Rehoboth dec'd made oath to the above before Jn° Saffin Proba^{r}: who allowed the same. John Cary Regist^{rm}: Entered May 9, 1695 by John Cary Regist^{rm}

[120] Will of Richard Marten of Rehoboth, dated June 2, 1686, he "being Aged and Not Knowing the Day of my Death". To my son Richard "which is Now in old England", two houses with a barn and malt house (being those houses which I formerly willed to him and my son John) also three acres of land. To "my ſonne ffraunces which is Now in old England a Houſe orchard & Garden: which I formerly Intended to Giue Vnto Annis. Lyeing Next to m^{r} ffrenches". To the two sons my son Francis, two thirds of my lands in the North Purchased lands belonging to Rehoboth, "if my ſaid GranChildren Come ouer to New England to Improue & make Vſe of them". The other third part of above lands I give to my grandchild John Marten my son Richard's eldest son, "if my ſaid Granchild come ouer to New England to Improue it". My grandchild John Ormsby, my daughter Grace's eldest son, shall improve said lands "Vntill my Granchildren in Old England Come ouer to make Vſe of them, & if they Neuer Come ouer: &c: the ſaid John ormsby to haue hold & Enjoy them for Euer". To my son John Martin "that is Now with me", my house, orchard and all other lands. My household goods to be divided among my three children that are in New England, viz: John, Grace and Annis, son John to have one half, the other half to be equally divided between Grace and Annis. My cattle to be equally divided between son John and daughter Grace Ormsby and Annis Chaffee. Son John to be sole executor and loving friends Deacon Samuel Newman and William Carpenter to be overseers. Witnessed by William Carpenter, Thomas Read and Stephen Paine, who all made oath to the above, at Rehoboth, May 7, 1695, before Jn° Saffin Proba^{r}: John Cary Regist^{r}: Entered May 9, 1695 by Jn° Cary Regist^{r}:

[121] Inventory of the estate of Mathew Allen "Planter of Dartmouth", dec'd, taken "the firft Day of the Third month Commonly Caled may" 1695, by John Sharman and John Tucker, and sworn to by Sarah Allen, relict and executrix of the will of said Mathew Allen, before Jn° Saffin Proba^{r}: John Cary Regist^{r}: Amount, £127..02..00. Entered May 23, 1695 by Jn° Cary Regist^{rm}

[122] Mathew Allen of Dartmouth, "being Sick & weak in Body", made his will Feb. 7, 1688. To John Calvin, my son in law, and Dorothy his wife, that £13 in money due to me by a bond dated Feb. 15, 1683. My wife Sarah Allen to have house room and a suitable maintenance out of my estate during her widowhood, and at her marriage to forego the same and then to receive two cattle. To son Samuel Allen one half of all my lands in Dartmouth, and to son Mathew Allen the other half of all my uplands and meadow in the said town, Samuel to deliver said land to his brother Mathew when he is twenty one. To daughter Mirriam Easton one cow; to daughter Deborah Allen the same; to daughter Mary Allen the same; to daughter Hassadyah Allen the same when she is eighteen; to son Mathew Allen the same when he is twenty one. Rest of personal estate to my loving wife Sarah Allen, who is to be sole executrix. I desire Henry Tucker John Russel and Nathaniel Howland to be overseers, "and to afsiftant to my faid Executrixs where & when fhe ftands in Need". Witnessed by John Russell, Thomas Taber and Val Hudleston, who all made oath to the above will, May 23, 1695 before Jn° Saffin Proba^{r}: John Cary Regist^{r}: Entered May 23, 1695 by John Cary Record^{r}

[123] Bristol, July 2, 1695. Account of John Tucker, executor of the will of Henry Tucker late of Dartmouth dec'd, of the legacies paid out, as follows: "To Sarah Tucker, Since married & Now Known by the Name of Sarah Horffee"; to Nathaniel Slocum; to Samuel Perry; to Abraham Tucker; to "John Eafton of Newport, in behalfe of a fofietty Cald Quakers, & for the Vfe of faid Sofietty". Above account allowed by John Saffin, Judge of Probate. "The Legacies Giuen by will of the faid Henry Dec^{d}: = to his Grand Children being Not Due till they Come off age And fo at p^{r}fent Remains in the hands of the above faid Executor". Entered July 3, 1695 by John Cary Regist^{rm}:

Sarah Horssee of Sandwich in the County of Barnstable gave receipt to my brother, John Tucker, executor of my father Henry Tucker's will, bearing date the first day of the first month 1693, for sixty pounds being a legacy given me by my said father. Receipt dated "the 4th of the firft mth in the year of our lord 1694/5". Signed Sarah × Haxse, Joseph Haxse. Entered July 3, 1695 by Jn° Cary Regist^{r}:

"Receiued the Twelueth of the firft month in the year of o^{r} lord 1695: by me Nathaniel Slocum fhr[u?]sberry within the County of Monmouth In Eaft New jerfy" of my brother John Tucker, executor of the will of my father Henry Tucker dec'd, dated first day of the first month 1693, twenty pounds being a legacy given me by my father in law, said Henry Tucker. Witnessed by Sarah Reape and William Reape. Recorded July 3, 1695 by Jn° Cary Regist^{rm}:

[124] Samuel Perry of Sandwich in the County of Barnstable gave receipt to my brother John Tucker, executor of the will of my father Henry Tucker, which was dated first of the first month 1693, for £20 being a legacy bequeathed to me by my father in law, said Henry Tucker. Dated the 4th of the first month 1694–5. Entered July 3, 1695 by Jn° Cary Regist^{rm}:

I Abraham Tucker of Dartmouth have received of my brother John

Tucker, executor of my father Henry Tucker's will, a legacy of £30 given me by my said father. Dated first day of the first month 1695 and witnessed by William X Shearman. Entered July 3, 1695 by John Cary Regist^{rm}

We "in the behalfe of the Reſt of the people in Scorn Called Quakers have Receiued of John Tucker Execut^{r} to his father Henry Tucker the ſum of fiue pounds Currantt Money of New England it being a leegacie bequeathed to Vs by ſaid Henry Tucker in his laſt will & Teſtament beareing Date the firſt day of the firſt mth: Called march in the year 1693 & Receiued the ſecond Day of the Ninth month Called Nouember in the year 1694 and is ſigned by us Vnderwritten of Road Iſland &c the 27 of ye 6th: mth: Called Auguſt 1695". Signed Walter Clarke, John Easton, Jacob Mott, Daniel Gould and John Gould. Entered July 17, 1697 by Jno Cary Regist^{rm}

[125] Account exhibited July 2, 1695 by Experience French executrix of the will of her late husband Joseph French late of Taunton dec'd. She has paid the legacies, consisting chiefly of lands, bequeathed by her said husband to his sons, Joseph, John and Nathaniel, as may appear by their receipt dated Mar. 7, 1694–5. The legacy given his son Jacob French "(who is of age and about to Chuſe his Gardian)" is "to be Receiued accordingly wch none Can hinder". "The other two Sons Viz^{t} Ebenezer & Jonathan ffrench are yet Vnder the Tuition of their Mother the Executrix" whose portions are not to be enjoyed till after their mother's decease. Said account allowed by John Saffin Judge of Probate. John Cary Register.

Taunton, Mar. 7, 1694–5. We Joseph French, Jno French and Nathaniel French have received of our honored mother Experience French, executrix of the will of our honored father dec'd, our whole portion of his estate as bequeathed to us. Witnessed by John Smith, Henry Hodges and Robert Crosman, and allowed by John Saffin Proba^{r}: at Bristol, July 2, 1695. John Cary Register. Entered July 3, 1695 by John Cary Regist^{r}

[126] Debts paid by the said executrix as follows: to John Foster of Marshfield; to William Horskins of Taunton; to Joseph Wood of same; to Ebenezer Burt of same; to the widow Linkhorn of same; to William Makepeace of Freetown. "There is yet Remaineing Due from ſaid Eſtate to her Brother John ffoster Ralph Thacher & Jno Wadsworth Eſq^{r}". The debts due to said estate are from William Wood and Francis Cary, and a bond under the hand of Benjamin Duttun. Said executrix is obliged to pay six pounds out of the movables to her daughter Elizabeth the wife of James Phillips of Taunton. Sworn to by said Experience French before John Saffin Proba^{r}: John Cary Regist^{rm}: Entered July 3, 1695 by Jno Cary Regist^{r}:

Citation issued by John Saffin, Judge of Probate, to Joseph Woodbery and Isaace Woodbery of Beverly. Whereas I am informed by m^{r} Hugh Woodbery of Bristol, administrator of the estate of Isaace Woodbery late of Salem dec'd, that there are lands in Freetown which are shortly to be divided between the persons concerned by law, "& that yo^{r}ſelues haue ſome Intereſt in the Right of yor father Mr Nicolas Woodbery Dec^{d}: in part of thoſe lands formerly pertaining to the ſd Nicolas & Iſace woodbery Dec^{d}: as yet Vndivided". You are hereby cited to appear at a probate court to be held at Bristol, Oct. 20, 1697, to make claim to and assist in dividing said lands. Dated Aug. 30, 1697. Entered Sept. 3, 1697 by John Cary Regist^{r}:

[127] Division of the estate of Joseph Williams late of Taunton dec'd made July 5, 1695 by Thomas Leonard Esq[r], Shadrach Wilbore, John Richmond, Henry Hodges and Samuel Williams, all of Taunton, being so commissioned April 13, 1695 by Jn[o] Saffin Esq[r]., Judge of Probate, between Elizabeth Williams, administratrix of said estate and the children. To the widow, said administratrix, £17..08..11 out of the moveables after debts are paid, also we set out to her during her life, the share in the Iron works, and the dwelling house and the land about it, the benefit of one fifth of the Purchase Right to herbage &c. and the improvement of all the lands appointed to the children until they successively reach age. To eldest son, Joseph Williams, the share in the North Purchase, the rest of the land at home and the barn, he to pay 10 shillings 6 pence to the administratrix. To second son Benjamin the twenty acre and the fifty acre division at three Mile River, and to pay 19 shillings 5 pence to the administratrix. To third son Ebenezer the land at Shallow water bought of Thomas Dean, eight acres more between that and m[r] Pooles land, the meadow at lilley Pond, and three acres of swamp, he to pay 4 shillings 5 pence to the administratrix. To fourth son Richard, thirty acres "Between Road Iland Path and Skunk hill", two acres of salt meadow at Assonate and seven pence out of the movables. To Mahettabell Robbinson, the eldest daughter, £19..00..07 out of the movables. To youngest daughter Phebe, the share "in the Drowned Dead Swamp", six acres on Shallow water plain and £14..10..7 out of the moveables. The Purchase Right to commonage, and the late division of Cedar Swamp to the four sons abovenamed equally, except that set out to the widow. [128] Signed by the five commissioners and witnessed by Stephen Marick, Benjamin Dean and Edward Richmond and allowed by Jn[o] Saffin, July 12, 1695. Entered July 18, 1695 by John Cary Regist[rm]:

June 6, 1695. I Gilbert Brook of Rehoboth, "being aged & Vnder prefent weaknes and Expecting my Chainge", do make my will. To beloved wife Sarah my dwelling house, orchard and homelot, my feather bed with its furniture, my chest with a lock and key to it and what other household stuff she may desire for her need, "Dureing the time of her Widowhood and Bearing my Name", she to give in security that the tenement and fences shall be kept in repair and that no waste be made of said estate, but that it shall upon her decease or marriage be delivered to my executors "Vnlefs by unaVoydable Cafsualty the faid houfe or goods fhould be Damnifyed or Deftroyed". Also I give her six sheep, one cow, half my swine and half my provision in my house, half my flax and yarn and a quarter of my wool in my house, also a "Barell of Sider"; "in Case god taks me away when the Croop is on the ground", said wife to have the whole crop, and six bushels of corn until harvest, otherwise sixteen bushels of corn, ten of Indian and six of rye. To Benony Wigin my grandson, land, and a quarter part of my commons, on the North Side, "my Bed he Vfeth to lye on & Bofster one blanket & one Coverlit and a pair of fheets in his hands", and my old Iron Pot. To Zachariah Carpenter that lives with me, forty shillings, my sword that I bought last, with half my ammunition and an axe that was his fathers. To my nine daughters an equal share of my estate, only my daughter Rachel's share I give to my grandson Benony Wigen. If any of my children be dead, their share to go to their surviving children, that is to say with what some of them have had already as may appear on the other side of the leaf with my hand to it. "My Beloued fons in law Robert Crofsman & william Manle" to be executors.

[129] To my grandchild Basheba Walker twenty shillings "if fhe liue with me". To my grandson Brook Thresher twenty shillings. To Zachariah Carpenter a coverlid. Witnessed by Samuel Newman, Richard Bowen and Nathaniel Chaffee who, all of Rehoboth, made oath to said will at Bristol, July 5, 1695 before John Saffin Proba[r]. Jn[o] Cary Regist[r]: Entered Oct. 5, 1695 by John Cary Regist[r]:

Inventory of the estate of Gilbert Brooks of Rehoboth, "who Deceafed the thirteenth Day of June 1695", taken [130] July 4, 1695 by Nicolas Peck and Richard Bowen, and sworn to at Bristol, July 5, 1695 by Robert Crossman and William Manley, the executors. Amount, £84..00..00. "An appendix to the will of M[r]: Gilbert Brooks late of Rehoboth Deceafed—That which I haue Payd my Children or Grand Children as follows

to Mary Coleborn a Cow a Mare & a horfe

to Hannah Crofman a Cow

to Bethiah Threfher a Cow

Rebeccah Horfkins fhall haue no more of my Eftate haueing Receiued fome other things with a warming Pan already

Efter Stephens hafs had her whole Share"

Signed Gilbert X Brook. Entered Oct. 5, 1695 by Jn[o] Cary Regist[r]:

[131] Thomas Brintnall's account of what he paid and did for Thomas Platts and his orders, during his residing on his farm. Items: Pd for bringing up of four cattle from Roxbery; Pd by Harlakinden Simons; Pd for "Hanging the Signe"; Pd by Richard Middleton; Pd for "Entertaineing Cap[t] Prentice Negro in your Seruis"; Pd for Joseph Skiner's diet; for "Money Pay[d] to Doct[r] Toothaccer"; Pd for "Aarthur Hailes Diat while Stoneing the fd Celler"; Pd for "Drink at the Raifeing of the Houfe"; Pd to Thomas Thurston; Pd to Timothy Foster; [132] Pd in rates to Danel Preston; Pd to John Minott for rates; Pd to Samuell Leads for rates. Total sum, £110..10..11. "Itt befids for mending the Bridge in Sir Edmunds time". Sworn to May 5, 1690 by Thomas Brintnall before Daniel Smith Assist. Recorded Dec. 27, 1695 by John Cary Regist[r]:

Account of Ann Chaffee widow and executrix of the will of Joseph Chaffee late of Swansey dec'd, together with her sons John and Joseph, executors, sworn to before Jn[o] Saffin at Bristol, Dec. 18, 1695, and allowed by him. Items: Paid to Thomas Barnes, to Enoch Hunt, to James Adams, to John Marten. Entered Jan. 7, 1695 by John Cary Record[r]:

[133] Will of Robert Wheaten of Rehoboth, he "being weake & aged", dated Oct. 2, 1687. To my eldest son Joseph twenty acres that was last laid out on the east side of Palmers River, a parcel of salt marsh at the hundred acres, and ten pounds estate of Commons in Rehoboth. If son Joseph die without issue all said lands given him (allowing the thirds to his wife for her lifetime) shall descend to my son Samuel's children. To son Jerimiah my lot last laid out in wachamoket Neck, my meadow at Bushy meadow and ten pounds estate of Commons in Rehoboth. To son John ten pounds estate of Commons in Rehoboth. To son Obadiah the rest of my lands in the North purchased lands which I have not given to my sons Ephraim and Benjamin by deed. To son Ephraim twenty acres at Palmers River, a piece of meadow at same place joining to Rice Leonard's, a third part of the undivided land on the North Side, and ten pounds of Commons in Rehoboth, all which I have given him by deed of gift. To son Benjamin one half my fifty acre lot and my share of meadow on the North Side and

one third of my undivided lands in the North Purchase, all which I have given him by deed of gift. To my son Samuel's children ten pounds estate of Commons in Rehoboth. To my three daughters, Bethiah, Hannah and Mary twelve pence each. To my beloved wife Alice, my house, lands and meadows, household goods and stock not otherwise disposed of, she to be sole executrix. If my wife decease before me, what estate I have given her shall be equally divided among all my children, son Joseph to have my house and home lot upon an indifferent appraisal, and to pay the value above his share to his brothers and sisters. Witnessed by John Peck, William Carpenter and John Butterworth, who all made oath to the same at Rehoboth, Feb. 24, 1695–6 before Jn° Saffin Esq[r]. Judge of Probate. John Cary Regist[r]. Recorded Mar. 2, 1695–6.

[134] Inventory of above estate taken Jan. 11, 1695–6 by William Carpenter and Samuel Millard, and sworn to by Alice, widow and executrix of the will of Robert Wheaton abovenamed, Feb. 24, 1695 before John Saffin Proba[r]: Jn° Cary Regist[r]: Entered Mar. 2, 1695–6 by John Cary Regist[r]:

ABSTRACTS FROM THE FIRST BOOK OF BRISTOL COUNTY PROBATE RECORDS.

Copied by Mrs. Lucy Hall Greenlaw

Will of Thomas Read of Rehoboth, Tanner, dated June 23, 1695, he "Being in a Low & weeke Condition". To my eldest son James Read twenty-three acres of upland and swamp upon the "Raged plaine" lying between my own lands and Josiah Carpenter's, and thirty acres lying in the fork of the river "where the Damm was"; also nineteen acres by the side of Red Earth hill, ten acres on both sides of Rocky river, two acres of fresh meadow upon the Hundred acres Tongue, a share of fresh meadow on the east side of the Mill River, [135] forty pounds estate of commonage in the old bounds of Rehoboth, one half a share of undivided land in the North purchase, and my lot on the great plain. As for other estate I have already given him to the value of £24. To my beloved wife Hannah Read fifty pounds of stock and moveables to be at her own dispose, one room of the house which she shall choose, and a privilege in the cellar, during her widowhood, likewise the improvement of the rest of my housing and lands, tan fats and orchards not disposed of, until my son Thomas comes to the age of twenty-one, then my wife and my son Thomas are to improve it together until my son Nathaniel is twenty-one, then my wife shall resign up all said lands and housing to my two said sons, except the room and cellar privilege, they to provide her with corn, meat, malt, wood and clothing, to provide for two cows for her during her widowhood, and help if need require, and some fruit of the orchard. To my two sons Thomas and Nathaniel, (upon the above condition, to provide for their mother), my dwelling house, barn, orchard, tan fats and house lot, twelve acres in the Ragged plain, four acres more, lying between the land of James Read and Nathaniel Carpenter, fifty acres in the fork of the river upon the Mill River, two shares of meadow ground and the ponds on the east side of the river adjacent to the lands, ten acres nearest to the aforesaid lands in the fork of the river, ten acres in the second division and my meadow in the forty acres, four acres of salt meadow at the hundred acres, likewise ten acres of land at the northerly end of the great plain (unless David Peren continues with them until he comes to the age of twenty-one years, if he does then they shall deliver said ten acres to him), also sixty pounds estate of commonage within the old bounds of Rehoboth, and three quarters of a share of undivided lands in the North Purchase. They are to be possessed of abovesaid housing and lands and to pay all legacies and debts remaining unpaid, when they come of age, said housing and lands to be equally divided between them. To my daughter Sarah, one half of a fifty acre lot upon Red Earth Hill which I purchased of John Allen, and one half of my meadow ground on the west side of Abbots Run and an eighth part of a share of undivided land in the North Purchase, also ten pounds to be paid out of my other estate. To my daughter Elizabeth twenty-five acres of land being the southerly end of my lot on Red Earth Hill on the east side of the hill, [136] also a piece of meadow and swamp on the side of Abbotts Run, and an eighth part of a share of undivided lands in the North Purchase, she having received the other part of her portion at her marriage. To my daughter Mary the other half of a fifty acre lot on Red Earth Hill which I purchased of John Allen, one half of my meadow and swamp on the west side of Abbotts Run, an eighth part of a share of undivided land in the North Purchase and thirteen pounds out of my other estate. To my daughter Hannah nineteen acres of land on the east side of Abbotts Run which I purchased of Stephen Paine, my part of meadow ground near Snake Hill, one eighth of a share of undivided land in the North Purchase, and ten pounds out of my other estate. To my daughter Mehittabell twenty acres of land on the fork of the river, a piece of swamp on the Seven Mile river, one eighth of a share of undivided land in the North Purchase and ten pounds out of my other estate. To my daughter Martha twenty acres in the fork of the river, one eighth of a share of undivided land in the North Purchase, ten pounds out of my other estate and a piece of swamp upon the Seven Mile river. My well beloved wife to be executrix and my sons Thomas and Nathaniel executors of this my last will, likewise "I Doe appoint & Conftitute My beloued Brothers william Carpenter Mofes Reed & Daniel Read" to be overseers of my will and guardians of my sons Thomas and Nathaniel until they come to the age of 21. I hereby revoke any former will or wills made by me. It is my will that the fifty pounds before given to my wife at her dispose is to be understood if she marry, but if she marry not, then twenty pounds, and the thirty to be improved towards her maintenance during her life. Witnessed by Moses Read, John Wilmath and William Carpenter who all appeared before John Saffin Esqr Judge of Probate of wills, at a court held at Rehoboth, Feb. 24, 1695–6 and made oath to the above. John Cary Regist^r: Entered March 6, 1695–6 by Jno Cary Regist^r:

[137] Inventory of the estate of "Infigne Thomas Read" late of Rehoboth dec'd taken Feb. 12, 1695–6 by Capt Nicolas Peck Esqr., "Decon" Samuel Peck and Lieu^t Preserved Abell, the amount being £390..14..9. Sworn to Feb. 24, 1695 by Hannah Read widow and executrix before Jno Saffin Proba^r: John Cary Regist^r: Entered March 6, 1695–6 by John Cary Regist^r.

[138] Susanah Macey's account of debts and legacies paid by her as executrix of the last will of her beloved husband George Macey late of Taunton dec'd, according to said will, viz. To Elizabeth Hodges, to Samuel Hodges, to Sarah Blacke, to Rebecca Williams, to Mary Williams, to Deborah Macey, also a debt to Mr John Pool of Boston. The rest of the estate remains with me only forty-six acres of land are to go to Israel

Woodward for services done partly before my said husband's decease and partly since. Sworn to by said Susannah Macey April 16, 1696, and allowed by John Saffin Esqr Judge of probate. John Cary Regist^r: Entered April 16, 1696 by John Cary Regist^r.

[139] Will of John Cook of Dartmouth dated Nov. 9, 1694, he "being weake of Body". To my son in law Arthur Hathaway and his wife Sarah my daughter, all my land in the point at or near the burying place in Dartmouth, which I bought of John Russell. To my son in law Stephen West and his wife Mercey my daughter, one third of a share of lands in Dartmouth, with all my housing and orchards thereto belonging, they to possess the same after the decease of my wife Sarah. To Jonathan Delano one third of a share of meadow called the Freemens meadow lying in the township of Rochester. To my grandson Thomas Taber my little island called Ram Island lying in Cushnat River in Dartmouth, with one third of my share in Freemens Meadow in Rochester, also my gun and sword. To my granddaughter Hester Perry one feather bed and bolster. Rest of estate to my loving wife Sarah to dispose of as she sees good, she to be sole executrix. Witnessed by Aaron X Savory and Thomas Taber who both made oath to the above before John Saffin Esqr. April 16, 1696. John Cary Regist^r: Entered May 8, 1696 by Jno Cary Regist^r:

[140] Inventory of above estate taken Dec. 7, 1696 [*sic*] by Aarther Hathaway and Thomas Tabar and sworn to April 10, 1696 by widow Sarah Cooke before Seth Pope, Justice of peace. Amount, £299..19..00. "The aboue Named Sarah Cooke being a Very Antient woman and Vnable to trauile far, it was Neceffary that her Depofition fhould be Taken as aboue Said", the which I do allow, Apr. 16, 1696. Jno Saffin Proba^r: Jno Cary Regist^r: Recorded May 19, 1696 by Jno Cary Regist^r:

[141] John Russell of Dartmouth being of sound mind made his will March 20, 1695–6. To "my Brother Jonathan: fon Jonathan" one sixteenth and one thirty-second parts of a share of land in the township of Dartmouth, excepting the six hundred acres to a share already laid out. To my brother Joseph's son John, the same. To my loving wife my dwelling house and all my lot of land thereto belonging, during her life, then to go to my son John Russell. To my said son the remainder of my lands in Dartmouth, also twenty pounds in silver money to be paid him when he is twenty-one, by my executrix. To my wife the rest of my estate, goods and chattels, she to be sole executrix. Witnessed by John Sharman, Robert Havens and Thomas Taber who all made oath before John Saffin Esqr. April 16, 1696. John Cary Regist^r: Entered May 12, 1696 by John Cary Regist^r:

[142] Inventory of said estate, amounting to £407..07..08, taken March 30, 1696 by John Sharman and Thomas Taber, and sworn to April 16, 1696 by Mehettabell Russell relict of said deceased before John Saffin Judge of probate. John Cary Regist^r: Recorded May 12, 1696 by John Cary Regist^rm:

[143] Inventory of the estate of Samuel Wilbore late of Taunton deceased taken Jan. 21, 1695–6 by Stephen Marick, Israel Thresher and Shadrach Willbore Senr. Amount, £161..08..00. April 15, 1696 Sarah Willbore relict and administratrix of the estate of the above named Samuel Willbore made oath to the truth of said inventory "Except three hundred foot of Bords therein Entered by miftake as fhall appear", before Jno

Saffin Proba[r]. Jn° Cary Regist[r]: Entered April 22, 1696 by Jn° Cary Regist[rm]

[144] Inventory of the estate of Thomas Briggs of the North purchase who deceased "the firft of Aprill in the year 1696", taken April 9, 1696 by Jn° Witherel, Eliazer Carver, Uriah Leonard and Sam[l] Brentnal. Amount £144..01..04. May 5, 1696, Samuel Briggs youngest son of the said Thomas Briggs and administrator of said estate "(the other two Elder Sons Refufeing the same)" made oath to said inventory before John Saffin Proba[r]: John Cary Regist[r]: "the land giuen by the Dec[d]:, by Deed of gift to two of the fons, as yet Vndiuided, being included herein". Recorded May 5, 1696 by Jn° Cary Regist[rm]:

[145] Inventory of the goods and chattels of Samuel Pitts of Taunton dec'd taken Feb. 6, 1695–6, by Richard Godfree and Edward Bobbit. Items: 25 acres of land lying near a hill by Nathaniel Hoars; one South Purchase with a little strap of meadow and meadowish land lying between the fence of Ebenezer Pitts his meadow and Muddy Cove; part of an orchard and one acre of meadow and meadowish land on the southerly side of the Mill River near the land of Peter Pitts; "Memorandum, befides the lands aboue mentioned in this Inventory there are fome other lands w[ch] f[d] Samuel Pitts Claimed by Defent being y[e] Eldeft Son of Peter Pitts of Tanton Dec[d]: Namely fuch lands as his f[d] father Did omit, or not mention in y[t] writting Caled his laft will & Teftament and f[d] lands are thofe which follow Namely 40 accers of out land in 3 perticular planes w[ch] was in peter pitts his Inventory prifed at ten pounds"; one bill of five pounds money due from W[m]: Briggs. Total, £177..03..00. Sarah Pitts relict and administratrix of the estate of the above named Samuel Pitts made oath to the above, April 15, 1696 before Jn° Saffin Proba[r]: Jn° Cary Regist[rm] Entered April 16, 1696 by John Cary Regist[r]:

[146] Inventory of the estate of John Eddy dec'd of Taunton, taken Dec. 11, 1695 by Henry Hodges, Uriah Leonard and Eliazer Carver. Items: his 2 acres of M[r] Shoves of meadowish ground; his 20 acres of land and 2 acres of meadowish land of Increase Robinson; his 20 acres of land and 2 acres of meadowish land of Benjamin Leonard; his 20 acres of land & 2 acres of meadowish land of Thomas Gilbert; his 5 acres of meadowish land of William Witherel at Scadins. Total, £215..10..00. Sworn to by Deliverance Eddy relict of John Eddy dec'd before Jn° Saffin Proba[r]: John Cary Regist[r]: at Bristol Jan 14, 1695. Recorded May 22, 1696 by John Cary Regist[r]

[147–50] Inventory of the estate of "Cap[t] Nathan Hayman Marin[r] late of Briftoll in New England Deceafed" taken Feb. 3, 1689 by Jn° Saffin and John Walley. Items: two house lots by Gladings; three lots by John Smiths; [debts due from] M[r]. Jn° Nellson, M[r]. Benja: Davis, M[r] Richard Harris, M[r] Anthony Low, M[r] Russell and Cap[t] Byfield;
" $\frac{2}{3}$ of Briganteen John & mary with the Cargoe
$\frac{1}{6}$ of Ketch Betty Phillip Knell Mas[t]:
$\frac{1}{4}$ Pink Kathirine Pullin maf[t]:
$\frac{1}{16}$ Pink & Effects Brackenbery mas[t]:
$\frac{1}{16}$ Ship michael williams Mas[t]";
"Left in England of the produce of m[r] woodberys Cargoe"; Negro woman. Total amount £2965..16.

May 1, 1696, "Mr Nathaniel Blagroue of Briftoll marchant & Elizabeth his wife, Relect of Mr Nathan Hayman late of Briftoll aforef^d Dec^d:" made oath to the above inventory before Jno. Saffin, Jno Cary Regist^r: Entered June 3, 1696 by Jno Cary Regist^r

[151] Thomas Leonard, Esqr., Philip King, Henry Hodges and James Leonard all of Taunton, being commissioned by John Saffin Judge of Probate to make an equal division of the estate left by Robert Crossman late of Taunton deceased, between his sons and daughters, divided the same June 29, 1696 as follows: To John Crossman the eldest son, half a south purchase which he had in his possession before his father's decease, six acres of land near Taunton Training place between the lands of Thomas Harvey Senr and Richard Stephens which was his father's Purchase lot, two acres on the west side of the three mile river, four acres on the northeastward side of the Great Pine Swamp, £12..13..09 in money and 37 shillings 9 pence out of the moveables. To Robert Crossman the second son, half a South Purchase which he had in his possession before his father's decease, six acres of land on the great plain, six acres over the great river, four acres on the northeastward side of the great pine swamp, £4..00..01 in money and 37 shillings 8 pence in moveables. To Sarah Woodward the eldest daughter and to Mary Gould the second daughter, the meadow called Bobbetts meadow towards Rehoboth and twelve acres of land joining to it, five acres of low land on the south of Prospect Hill Pond, eight acres on the northeastward side of the great Pine Swamp, these lands to be equally divided between them, also said Sarah Woodward shall have £6..15..09 in money and 47 shillings in moveables, and Mary Gould shall have £6..19..09 in money and 43 shillings in moveables. To Elizabeth Hayward the third daughter, so much of the Rumford Division so called as shall amount to £5..10, also £6..17..09 in money and 20 shillings in moveables.

[152] To the children of Joseph Crossman dec'd, the third son, so much of the Rumford Division as amounts to 40 shillings, also eighteen acres of land on the northeastward side of the great pine swamp, £6..17..09 in money and 20 shillings out of the moveables. To Samuel Crossman the youngest son and to Marcey Thresher the youngest daughter, the purchase right in the old township of Taunton and fifteen acres yet due to said right by the late fifty acre division, and eight acres on the northeastward side of the great Pine Swamp, all to be equally divided between them. Samuel also is to have £7..12..01 in money and 40 shillings 8 pence in moveables, and Mercey is to have £7..12..06 in money and 40 shillings 3 pence in moveables. Said Elizabeth Hayward is also to have four acres of land on the northeastward side of the Pine Swamp as the rest of the children have. Signed by the four above named commissioners and John Hathway, and witnessed by Isaace Hathway and Mary X Hathway. Allowed by John Saffin Esqr, Judge of Probate, July 25, 1696. John Cary Regist^r: Entered same day by John Cary Regist^r.

[153] An account of the funeral charges and debts paid by Robert Crosman and William Manley executors of the will of "Mr Gilbert Brooks who Dec^d: 30th Day of June 1695", paid July 6, 1695 and since; Items:

"to money william Manley layed out for father at Bofton"
"to Capt Peck for helping take the Inventory"
"to Abiah Carpenter for hurdles & other work"
"to Samuel Carpenter for his Boyes work"

"to m^r william Carpenter"
"to hunts wife & the Taylor"
"to John Redawayes wife for her Boyes work"
"to Nath^ll Chaffee for his Euidence to ye will & Smiths work"
"to James Carpenter the weaver"
"to Deacon Newman for his Evidence to the will"
"to Sam^ll Haskins"
"to James Walker & ffrances Stevens"
"to Sam^ll Thresher"
"to Mr Jarate Ingraham for work"
"to Richard Bowen Doct^r:"
"to Mr Sweeting the fuller"
"to Mr Richard Bowen for Inventorying & Euidencing to y^e will"
"to Sarah Perry for linnen Cloath"
"to Nuson the Taylor"

"There is yet a Debt to pay Richard Bowen Junr: of Rehoboth 10 or 12^s: we know not Juſt what for want of opportunity to Recon".

"The Eſtate Credit from Jonathan Carpenter" 3^s. "and one & Nine pence Due from John Marten=and about 3^s from Joſeph Doget which yet we cannot come at". Said account presented to John Saffin Esqr Judge of probate by Robert Crosman one of the executors, July 15, 1696, and allowed by him. John Cary Regist^r:

[154] An account of the legacies paid July 6 and since by Robert Crosman and William Manley executors of the will of Mr Gilbert Brooks as follows: To the widow; to Zachariah Carpenter; to "Bononi wigins"; to Brooks Thresher; "A warming Pann to Rebecca Huſkins in her poſseſsion at the time of the Death of the Teſtator with other things not perticularly mentioned and therefore No sum to them but all her Due by will".

"Here follows an accompt of what portions we haue payd to the Children=
"To Bathsheba walker"
"to Bethiah Threſher"
"to Sarah lyon"
"to Elizabeth Steuenes Children"

"and as to Rachel another Daughter being at long Island we haue as yet No opportunity to pay her any thing

Mary Colebond as yet will not Receiue any portion but rather Shows Diſlike of the will

And as to the lands we haue Not yet oportunity to Divide y^m Our Mother, the widow haueing the houſe & home lott Dureing her widowhood, by will". Recorded Oct. 30, 1696 by John Cary Regist^rm:

[155] Will of John Shaw of Swanzey dated Sept. 24, 1696, he being "Very Sick & weake in Body". My will is that the house and land that I have lately purchased at Boston of James Hawkins bricklayer be speedily put into repair and made tennantable by my wife Hannah out of the first payment of money due to me by bill from Thomas Earle of Dartmouth, and so to be kept in good repair until my son John Shaw shall come to the age of twenty-one, or capable of choosing a guardian, when said house and land shall be his. My wife's daughter Hannah Mare shall have all the household stuff that was her mother's before I married her, also one good milch cow. To my loving wife Hannah Shaw remainder of estate, she to maintain my son John Shaw until he shall reach the age of twenty-one, he "to be well Entered by ſcouleing and in the fear of god and at that age of Twenty one years to Deliuer him poſseſsion of ſaid Houſe & land in

good Repaire & Tennantable and himfelf to be futtably Cloathed". My said wife shall deliver unto Thomas Earle of Dartmouth on or before Oct. 15 next, lawful possession of my late dwelling house in Swanzey with the land thereto belonging, which said house and land I have sold to said Earle as by deed of sale bearing equal date with this testament. My trusty and well beloved wife to be sole executrix. Witnessed by John Simmons, Ralph × Earle, Martha × Simmons, Thomas Earle and Sam[ll] Gardn[r]: of whom Samuel Gardner, Thomas Earle and Ralph Earle made oath to said will before Jn[o] Saffin, Oct. 12, 1696. John Cary Regist[r]: Registered Oct. 21, 1696 by John Cary Regist[r]

[156] Inventory of above estate taken Oct. 8, 1696 by John Hathway, James × Bell and Nicholas Moorey. Items: "to Leather at home and at William Slades"; "to 5 pound Rec[d] of John Hathaway"; "to what m[r] Thomas Earle is to pay for Houfe & land". Total £279..18..09. Said inventory sworn to by Hannah Shaw late wife of said dec'd, Oct. 12, 1696 before John Saffin Probat[r] John Cary Regist[r]: Entered Oct. 21, 1696 by John Cary Regist[r].

[157] Samuel Peck, William Carpenter, Samuel Newman, Stephen Paine and Enoch Hunt being commissioned by John Saffin Esq. Judge of probate, to divide the estate of Ephraim Hunt late of Rehoboth dec'd between his widow Rebecca Hunt and the children, and whereas said Ephraim Hunt had lands in partnership with his brother John Hunt, said commissioners made division between said widow and children and said John Hunt, May 21 and 22, 1696. To John Hunt 22½ acres on the northerly side of Rocky River adjoining to Nathaniel Paine's land and likewise the salt meadow adjoining to Nathaniel Paine's, also the southermost part of the upland on the south side of Rocky River from the highway that goeth between the lands of Benjamin Paine and John Hunt, likewise the small neck of salt meadow adjoining to said upland, also 13 acres joining his own land near his house and adjoining to Enoch Hunt's lands, together with a parcel of swamp. To Rebecca Hunt and her children 19 acres of upland and swamp on the north side of Rocky River being all the lands on both sides the great highway and the highway that goeth to the Mill and the land of Obadiah Bowen Jun[r], also a parcel of salt meadow, also land on the south side of Rocky River joining to John Hunt's land, the great neck of Salt meadow on the south side of Rocky River, 3 acres due them to be laid out, [158] 5 acres of upland joining to the southerly side of their home lot that is fenced in, a piece of swamp, and 8 acres of upland and swamp. Said division allowed by John Saffin Judge of probate Aug. 4, 1696, upon which day John Hunt acknowledged his satisfaction therewith. John Cary Regist[r]. Entered Nov. 18, 1696 by John Cary Regist[r].

Division of the estate of Ephraim Hunt deceased made May 25, 1696 between the widow Rebecca Hunt and her four children as follows: To the widow Rebecca Hunt her third part, viz. one half of the dwelling house, barn, orchards, homestead lands, and the lands on the north side of the highway before the house, and one third of the commonage belonging to the said estate. To Daniel Hunt eldest son, the other half of the dwelling house, barn, orchard, house lot and meadow adjoining and the lands before the house, also nineteen acres of upland and swamp, and a parcel of salt marsh on the northerly side of Rocky River, three acres of land yet to be laid out and fifty pounds estate of commonage, likewise the biggest gun and little trap, he to pay to his sister Hannah when she comes of age £3..10. [159] To John Hunt the youngest son, nine acres of land on the southerly side of Rocky River, the great neck of salt meadow joining said lands, fifty pounds estate of commons and a small gun and great trap, he to pay to his sister Sarah £1..7 and to his sister Hannah £1..3, when they come of age. To Sarah Hunt one half of her father's wearing apparel, cattle, household goods, books, and the amount to be paid by her brother John, all amounting to £23. To Hannah Hunt, the other half of her father's wearing apparel, cattle, household goods, books, money to be paid by her brothers Daniel and John, all amounting to £23. Above division presented by Rebecca Hunt said widow, to John Saffin Esq[r] Judge of Probate Aug. 4, 1696, who allowed the same. John Cary Regist[r]: Entered Nov. 18, 1696 by John Cary Regist[r]:

[160] Account of Rebecca Hunt administratrix of the estate of Ephraim Hunt late of Rehoboth dec'd, of debts paid: Items:

"Paide Vpon a Bill for m[r] Greenwoods Settlement"

"Payd to m[r] Sweeting for fulling"

"Payde to william Carpenter"

"Payd a Debt to David Carpenter"

"Payd to Nicolas Lang"

"Payd to David Carpenter when his time was out"

"Payd to David Carpenter in Cloathing before & at the Expireing of his time".

An account of the widow's thirds and children's portions out of the moveables, viz: to the widow, to Sarah eldest daughter, to Hannah youngest daughter. An account of the division of the lands, viz: to the widow, to Daniel Hunt eldest son, to John Hunt second son. Said accounts presented by said Rebecca Hunt and allowed by John Saffin Judge of Probate Oct. 23, 1696. John Cary Regist[r]: Recorded Nov. 18, 1696 by John Cary Regist[r].

[161] Account of the moveables of the estate of John Smith late of Dartmouth dec'd rendered Dec. 1, 1696, by Deliverance Smith in behalf of himself executor and his mother Ruhamah Smith executrix, according to the inventory of said estate which was given into the Registry Dec. 19, 1693. They have paid out the following legacies according to the will, viz: To Hassadiah wife of Jonathan Russell, to Meahittabell wife of John Russell, to Hannah Smith and to Sarah Smith, Deborah Smith not being of age to receive her legacy. Above account allowed by John Saffin Judge of probate. John Cary Regist[r]: Entered Dec. 2, 1696 by John Cary Regist[r]:

Whereas John Smith of Dartmouth in his will dated June 8, 1691 did bequeath to his daughter Hassadiah Russell wife of Jonathan Russell one cow and two ewe sheep to be paid at or before the decease of his wife Ruhamah Smith, and did appoint his said wife Ruhamah Smith and his son Deliverance Smith his sole executrix and executor, said Jonathan Russell and Hassadiah his wife having received said legacy hereby acknowledge receipt thereof and discharge said Ruhamah Smith and Deliverance Smith in all respects concerning said legacy. Receipt dated Jan. 10, 1693-4 and witnessed by Joseph Ripley and Ichabod Damon. Recorded Dec. 2, 1696 by J. C.

[162] Similar receipt given same day by John Russell and his wife Mehittabell, a daughter of said John Smith, for one cow and two ewe sheep.

Similar receipt given same day by Hannah Smith, a daughter of said John Smith, for one cow and one bed and bedding.

Similar receipt given same day by Sarah Smith, a daughter of said John Smith, for one cow and two ewe sheep.

ABSTRACTS FROM THE FIRST BOOK OF BRISTOL COUNTY PROBATE RECORDS

Copied by MRS. LUCY HALL GREENLAW

[163] "Whereas Jerimy Newland of Taunton about fifteen yeares Since Dyed inteſtat Leaueing Kathirine his widow with four ſmale Children wth Very little to Maintaine them Viz^{t}: a poor Houſe with about ſix accers of mean land Scituate lyeing & being in Taunton afforeſd & now in the Poſſeſsion & Occupation of the ſaid widow with a few other things of ſmale Value * * * And whereas the ſaid widow through Ignorance & Extreame poverty as ſhe ſaith could not goe ſo farr as Plimouth to take adminiſt^{on}: on the ſaid Little Eſtate as the law Directs But hath all this time by Gods Bleſsing and her owne Induſtry & hard labour, with the Charity of good people made a ſhift to liue, pay her Huſbands Debts & bring Vp her ſaid Children to Ripeneſs of years which hath Coſt her much more then the ſaid Eſtate amounts to, and ſhe being Now grown ancient and not able to work as ſhe hath done Prays that the ſaid Houſe & land (ſuch as it is) with thoſe few Moueables that Remaine May be Granted & Confirmed to her", which accordingly is hereby granted to the said widow Katharine by me John Saffin Esqr. Judge of probate, July 12, 1695. Entered May 28, 1697 by John Cary Regist^{r}:

[164] Little Compton, Dec. 5, 1696. We, being chosen by the children of Capt Edward Richmond to apprise his goods and estate, have valued them at £326..06..00. Items: "3 Indians Peter awaſhuick", "Amos", "John ahame". Signed by Danl: Eaton and Will Foabs. Said inventory presented by Edward Richmond eldest son of Edward Richmond late of Little Compton dec'd, and administer of his estate, Dec. 8, 1696 and sworn to before John Saffin Esqr. Judge of probate. John Cary Regist^{r}: Entered Dec. 8, 1696 by John Cary Regist^{r}.

[165] Will of Remember Briggs of Taunton dated April 22, 1696, he "being By the Providence of God Vnder Bodyly weakneſs & Not Knowing How it may pleaſe god to Diſpoſe of me". Whereas I am bound by obligation for the payment of fifty pounds, which money I took upon interest "of a perſon in Boſton whoſe Name hath ſlipt my memory at the preſent", for the payment of which, Maj^{r} Ephraim Hunt and Mr Joseph Green both of Weymouth are bound with me, and I having received of the said Joseph Green thirty pounds in money which was in part to pay for sixteen acres of land and meadow lying in Weymouth, which I sold him on condition that he pay the aforesaid fifty pounds which with the thirty paid myself amounts to eighty pounds which (if complied with) I do order my executrix to deliver a deed of sale to the said Joseph Green for the said sixteen acres. What other estate I have at Taunton or elsewhere shall be disposed of to my wife and children as the law directs when a person dies intestate. My true and well beloved wife Mary Briggs to be sole executrix and "I Do alſo Deſire & apoint my Very worthy ffreinds Maj^{r} Ephraim Hunt of weymouth and John Staple of Taunton to be my Overſeers of this my ſd will and Teſtament". I revoke all former wills made by me. Witnessed by Peter Reynold, Priscilla Reynold and Nath^{ll}. Paine who all made oath at Bristol Jan. 13, 1696–7 before John Saffin Esqr. Judge of Probate.

John Cary Regist^{r}. Recorded Feb. 3, 1696–7 by John Cary Reg^{r}:

[166] Inventory of above estate taken May 22, 1696 by Henry Andrews and Joseph Richmond. Item: "Carpenters tools". Bristol, Jan. 13, 1696–7, "Then Mary Staple late widow & Relect of Remember Briggs late of Taunton Deceaſed" made oath to said inventory before John Saffin. John Cary Regist^{r}: Entered Feb. 5, 1696–7 by Jno Cary Regist^{r}:

[167] Inventory of the estate of William Wood Senr of Dartmouth late dec'd taken Jan. 4, 1696 by Aron Davis, Wm Macumber, Jonathan Devil and Increase Allen. Item: "Shoemakers working Geer". Amount, £411.. 13 . . 02. [168] Also "A Sixth part of one halfe share of Vndivided land in Dartmouth priſed and Brought into the office ffebruary 3^{d}. 169$\frac{6}{7}$". Above inventory sworn to at Bristol, Feb. 3, 1696–7 by William Wood and George Wood sons of said William Wood dec'd, before John Saffin Judge of probate. John Cary Regist^{r}. Entered Feb. 24, 1696–7 by John Cary Regist^{r}:

Additional inventory of goods apprised at £4.. 13.. 06 by George Sisson and Peleg Shearman, entered March 30, 1697 by John Cary Regist^{r}. Houses and lands of above deceased apprised April 14, 1697 at £226, by William Fobes, Joseph Taber and Christop^{r}: Allen.

[169] Inventory of the estate of Samuel Gardner late of Swanzey "who deceaſed ye 8th of Decemb^{r}: 1696" taken Feb. 15, 1697 by Hezekiah Luther, Ralph Chapman and James Cole. Amount, £1046 .. 15 .. 00. Sworn to Feb. 17, 1696–7, at Bristol, by Elizabeth Gardner widow of Lieu^{t} Samuel Gardner late of Swanzey dec'd before John Saffin. John Cary Regist^{r}. Entered Feb. 26, 1696–7 by John Cary Regist^{r}:

[170 blank]

[171] "Whereas Hezekiah Sabin & Noah Sabin Sons to William Sabin late of Rehoboth Dec^{d}., had lands & Chattels Giuen them by their ſaid father as fully appeares by the Laſt will & Teſtament of the ſaid William Sabin. And the ſaid Hezekiah and Noah Sabin Deceaſed without Iſsue & Made No will. And James Sabin Eldeſt Brother of the Whole Blood takeing of Adminiſtration of Both Eſtates, in order to a Diviſsion of their ſaid Brother Eſtats To Divide between the Brothers and Siſters of the whole Blood as the law Directs, In purſuance hereof. the ſaid Brothers and Siſters Mett together the Tweluelth Day of march one Thouſand Six hundred Ninety & fiue. Six: (Viz^{t}) James Sabin & John Sabin & Leu^{t}: Preferued Abel in the behalfe of Margaret Sabin youngeſt Siſter to the ſ^{d} Deceaſed, being her Gardian, and Joſeph Buckland Junr in the behalfe of his wife Mehetabel Eldeſt Siſter of the whole Blood. and Mary Sabin. and Sarah Sabin, ſecond & Third Siſters to the Dec^{d}: for themſelues being of age", and made a full division as follows: To James Sabin the salt meadow upon the Hundred acre Tongue that was his brother Hezekiah's. To John Sabin all the land that was his brother Noah's, as appears by their father's will, except two tracts of fresh meadow at the place called Mr Browns Pond, one of them adjoining to Stephen Paine's meadow, the other lying between "Mr Blacks Medow and the Dogets Medow", also he shall have ten acres at Palmers River near the Dam. To Mehitabel Buckland her part already paid her by her brother James, one half the fresh meadow at Palmers River that was Hezekiah's, £25 estate of commonage in Rehoboth and 16 shillings, 4 pence to be paid her by James. To Mary

Sabin her part already paid her by her brother James, 22 acres at Palmers River lying next to the Widow Man's, £25 commonage in Rehoboth and £1..06..04 to be paid by James. To Sarah Sabin her part already paid her by her brother James, one half the meadow at Palmers River that was Hezekiah's, the remainder of the lot by the dam at Palmer's river and £1..01..04 to be paid by James. [172] To Margaret Sabin two pieces of meadow ground at Mr Browns pond, one adjoining to "Stephens Meadow [*sic*] & the other between Mr Blaks Meadow and the Dogets Meadow" that was Noah's, and £1..12..04 to be paid her by her brother John. Said division signed March 15, 1695 by James Sabin, John Sabin, Preserved Abel, Joseph Bucklon, Mary × Sabin and Sarah × Sabin, and acknowledged Oct. 13, 1696 by James and John Sabin before John Saffin Judge of probate, John Cary Regist^r^., and by Preserved Abel, Joseph Bucklen, Mary Sabin and Sarah Sabin before the same Dec. 1, 1696. Entered March 1, 1696–7 by John Cary Regist^r^.

Account of the estate of Henry Annadown late of Rehoboth deceased. Dec. 27, 1694, to the inventory. Items of account: "fiue pounds pay^d^ to his Sifter Dec^br^: 31"; "Ballence Reft w^ch^ (the Debts all pd) belongs to Philip Annadown his Brother". Account sworn to Jan 3, [*sic*] before John Saffin Esqr Judge of probate. John Cary Regist^r^: Entered Jan. 3, 1695 by John Cary Regist^r^:

[173] Inventory of the estate of Richard Briggs of Taunton dec'd taken July 8, 1696 by Henry Hodges, Richard Stephens and Sam^ll^ Dean, and sworn to July 15, 1696 by Rebecca Briggs widow of said deceased before Jno Saffin Proba^r^. John Cary Regist^r^ Entered March 26, 1697 by John Cary Regist^rm^:

Phillip King, Robert Crosman and Abell Burt all of Taunton and Lieu^t^ Joseph Tripp and Aron Davis of Dartmouth being commissioned by John Saffin Esq. Judge of probate, April 16, 1697, to make an equal division of some land in Little Compton, being one equal purchase, between John Irish now of said Compton and Rebecca now the wife of Jonathan Greenel of said Compton, said Rebecca being the daughter of Elias Irish of Taunton deceased and said lands appertaining to said Rebecca in the right of her father said Elias Irish, said Philip King, Robert Crosman, Abell [174] Burt and Joseph Tripp met together in the town of Little Compton, April 29, 1697, and having divers writings presented to us both by said John Irish and William Foabs of said Compton guardian to said Rebecca, we plainly find that said Elias Irish had an equal share and half part of said lands, and the other half part belongs to the abovesaid John Irish, and as there is already laid to said equal purchase, 320 acres of land, we set off to the aforesaid John Irish, the great lot where his now dwelling house is, being the 16th lot in number, about 3 acres of meadow in Saconet Neck being the 11th in number, also the 24 acre lot, being the 31st in number, a ten acre lot being the 66th in number in the third division of house lots, also a 20 acre lot in that part of Saconet called Cokeset being the first in number, about three quarters of an acre on the west side of Wm Hilliard's lands being the 12th in number and 3 acres of a ten acre lot at Cokesett, being the 27th in number. Secondly we divide unto Rebecca Greenel sole daughter of abovesaid Elias Irish, the fifty acre lot being part of the 11th and 12th lots, an eighteen acre lot being the 15th in number lying in Saconet Neck, an eleven acre lot being the 22nd in number, the thirty acre lot being the 9th in number lying near the quick sand ponds, a sixteen acre lot being the 14th in number lying among the sixteen acre lots, a ten acre lot being the 4th in number lying in the first division of house lots, also a fifteen acre lot being the 33rd in number lying at Cokesett, also about half an acre laid out in that 50 acre lot formerly laid out to Mr Joseph Church being the 9th in number, a piece of meadow in Barkers Neck so called of about two acres being the 16th in number, and seven acres of a ten acre lot lying at Cokeset being the 27th in number. Both parties are to have an equal share in all the undivided lands belonging to said share. Dated April 29, 1697 and signed by the four above named commissioners. Allowed by John Saffin, May 4, 1697. John Cary Regist^{r}: Entered May 7, 1697 by John Cary Record^{r}

[175] Edward Richmond administrator of the estate of his father Capt Edward Richmond late of Little Compton dec'd exhibited an account May 19, 1697 of debts "which I haue payde, and ſtand Engaged to pay Since his Deceaſe". Items: Paid

"to Doct^{r}: Arnold for his help in my fathers Sickneſs"
"for Drinke at the funerall"
"to M^{r} william foabs & Daniel Eatton for taken an Inventory"
"Payde Weſton Clarke"
"to Saml Crandall for Keepeing a payr of oxen"
"for three quarts of Rum when we DiVided the Eſtat"
"to Daniel Howland"
„ "Twiſe Goeing to Briſtoll and Chriſtop^{r}: Charges"
„ "Joſeph Blackman for three paire of ſhoose"
„ "Eſeck Carr for Triming of Caſke"
„ "m^{r} Jones in money which was Due by him by Bond"
„ "Simon Rouſe for mending a Gunn lock"
„ "John Iriſh for half a C of Clabords"
„ "John Peckham for Mowing"
„ "Daniel Greenel for Expence when the land was lotted"
„ "Daniel Greenel for fathers Expence"
„ "Daniel Eatton for fathers Expence"
„ "Tom the Indian for Digging the Graue & a Debt due to him before"
„ "John Briggs for Keeping of Rams and 5^{s}: for boot for Horſs"
„ "John Smith the Taylor for work Done"
„ "Brother Henry & Ann"
„ "m^{r} pabodie for the allotment & going with us"
„ "Ebenezer Allen"
„ "Thomas waite"
„ "Doct^{r} Talmon for Cureing Amos his Legg"
„ "william Simmons for Smith worke"
„ "Zachariah Allin"
„ "m^{r} Natha [*sic*] Payde for a Debt upon Booke"
„ "m^{r} Collings for Rent of Sheep"
„ "m^{r} Codington for Book Debt"
„ "Daniel Thirſton for money lent & Book D^{t}:"
„ "m^{r} Homsbye for Expence"
„ "m^{r} Pabodye & m^{r} foabs for laying out land"
„ "Jonathan Danford for makeing a Coff"
„ "Aunt Northway for a winding ſheet"
„ "Joſeph Church Junr"

to "mr william foabs 8s: wch he pd for father for the purchafs of land"
" "Aron Davis: for Keeping a calfe & one Board lent"

[176] "And for feuerall parts of ye fd Eftat Deliuered to the feveral Children". Total £351..19..10. Above account sworn to May 19, 1697 by said Edward Richmond administrator before John Saffin who discharged him from said administration. John Cary Registr Recorded same day by John Cary Registr:

An agreement of the division of the estate of Capt Edward Richmond late deceased among his children as followeth, who do acquit and discharge each other: Edward Richmond, John Richmond "in his own Right & the Right of his Sifter abigail Rementon", William Palmer, John Palmer, [177] Silvester Richmond, Sarah Richmond, and Thomas Burge. Signed by the seven above, and exhibited and allowed by John Saffin Esqr Judge of probate, May 19, 1697. John Cary Registr: Entered same day by Jno Cary Recordr:

April 14, 1697, Majr Benjamin Church, Mr Joseph Church, Capt Wm Southworth, Mr Christopher Allene and Mr Wm: Foabs, together with several Indians, namely Jannootas and Sue Codomuck, brother and sister of one Stephen an Indian well known at Little Compton, and other Indians being present, it was declared before me John Saffin Esqr Judge of Probate that said Stephen the Indian owned one half of a certain neck of land in Little Compton commonly called by the Indians Monunkaest and by the English Stephens Neck, and that when said Stephen was sick of a disease of which he died, "which was on the 19th Xb:r 1696" he gave to said Sue his sister one half his part of said neck and to his said brother Jannootas the other half, and that when she died the other half of his part of said neck should be divided among the sons and daughters of Suncanawash brother of said Stephen, "Viz Hezekiah James Sampfon Efter Rebecca", and the other half of said Neck did appertaine to Richard Decd and his heirs "Viz. Josiah and Sampfon Borfon & Zacheus the fon of fam and Sam Pauchachux". All of which was declared to be the right and just propriety of the whole of said neck of land to the satisfaction of all the said Indians present viz: Capt Howdee, Wm Simons, Daniel Hinckley, David Tockamana, Sam Church, Robin Muchcakett, and the English men above named. Acknowledged before John Saffin Probar: John Cary Registr: Entered May 28, 1697 by John Cary Registr

[178] Joseph Tripp, William Foabs and Joseph Taber, being appointed by Mr John Saffin Esqr Judge of probate to make a division of the estate of William Wood of Dartmouth deceased find that after debts are paid there remains £370 .. 4 .. 4, which "being Divided amonft ten Children & the Eldeft fon haueing a Dubble fhare, Makes to Each Share Thirty three pounds thirteen shillings". To William Wood, who "being ye Eldeft fon had two fhares", the house and 100 acres and meadow already laid out, also one fourth of the half share of land after 300 acres are laid out to George Wood, also two guns, the whole amounting to £168 .. 10 .. 00, said William Wood to pay to Josiah Wood, Daniel Wood and John Wood, each £33 .. 13 .. 00. To George Wood 300 acres to be laid out, also three quarters of the undivided lands belonging to the half share of land, one loom and one small bed, the whole amounting to £67 .. 06 .. 00, he to pay to Joseph Wood £33 .. 13 .. 00. To "mr Mallett wife a Bed at Mariage" with cattle and household goods amounting to £33 .. 13 .. 00. To Sarah Wood, cattle and

household goods amounting to £33 .. 13 .. 00. To Margaret Wood, the same. [179] To Rebecca Wood the same. Above division was exhibited to John Saffin and allowed by him April 14, 1697. John Cary Regist^{r}: Recorded same day by Jno Cary Regist^{r}.

[180] "Whereas it hath pleafed Almighty God in his Providence to Call me to Jepardize a frail life at Sea where the Dangers at this Juncture of time by Enemises are increafed, I william Stone of Briftoll in the Teritory of New England Marrin^{r} being of found Memory Do Make this my Laft will & Teftament". I give "My Body to the Duft whence it was Taken, by fuch a Burial, as Gods Allwife Difpofeing providence fhall fee Beft Subordinatly hereto: to My Executrix hereafter Mentioned. thereof I leaue the Mannagment". After debts are discharged, "I will to Each of my Dear Children Namely. Hannah & Abigail. a peice of Eight". Remainder of estate to my dear wife Hannah to be at her absolute disposal, she to be sole executrix. Dated July 22, 1692, and witnessed by Rebecca Blackman, Mary Jones and Edward Mills, of whom Edward Mills and Mary Jones made oath to above will, May 29, 1697 before Jno Saffin. John Cary Regist^{r}: Entered June 22, 1697 by John Cary Regist^{rm}:

Inventory of above estate taken at Bristol, Nov. 14, 1696 by Hugh Woodberree, John X Glading Junr. and John Cary. Amount £121 .. 06 .. 06.

[181] Inventory of the goods and chattels of William Stone late of Bristol "what of his Eftate is Now in Taunton" taken Nov. 21, 1696 by Shadrach Wilbore and Henry Hodges. Amount £256 .. 16 .. 02. Total amount of said estate, £378 .. 2 .. 8. Above inventories presented at a court at Bristol, June 22, 1697 by Hannah Stone widow, and sworn to before Jno Saffin Proba^{r}: John Cary Regist^{r}: Entered same day by John Cary Regist^{r}:

[182] Account of James Stevenson of Springfield administrator of the estate of John Stevenson late of Rehoboth deceased. Items: "By Israel Read Rec^{d}"; "By Davide ffreeman"; "payd to william Carpenter Senr"; "payd to Mofes Read"; "payd to Doct^{r} Bowen"; "payd to Capt Brown in a prefsing Iron"; "to John ficth"; "To Capt peck"; To David whipple"; "To John Redway"; "To Mofes Read"; "To william Carpenter". Above account sworn to June 13, 1697 by said James Stevenson before John Saffin Judge. John Cary Regist^{r}. Entered June 30, 1697 by John Cary Regist^{r}:

[183] Thomas Dean of Taunton "being at prefent Sick & weak of Body" made his will Aug. 7, 1690. "I Giue . . . my Body to the Graue to be Buried by my Surviueing freind as becometh Chriftians". I make my wife Katharine sole executrix of this my last will and also I leave her all my estate "for to Bring Vp my fmale Children", the estate to be at her disposing as long as she continues my widow, and after her decease or marriage I give all my lands to my only son Thomas Dean, except my two south purchases and my twenty acres at or near Scadings and my meadow at wenecunnet all in the township of Taunton, which lands thus excepted I leave with my wife to dispose of to my children at her discretion or to sell if necessary for the bringing up of my children. My will is that my wife pay out of my moveable estate to each of my daughters viz. Hannah, Deborah, Katherine, Lidiah, Mercey and Elizabeth five pounds each as they come of age or at their marriage, the rest of my moveable estate to be disposed of to my children at her discretion, my son to have as good a part thereof as any of my daughters. After the death or marriage of my wife

my son shall have my part in the Iron Works. I desire my two brothers John Dean and Isaace Dean to be overseers of this my will. Witnessed by Thomas Leonard, John Dean and Isaace Dean, of whom Thomas Leonard Esq[r] and Isaace Dean made oath to above will July 15, 1697 before Jn[o] Saffin, John Cary Regist[r]: they testifying that the said John Dean also signed as a witness with them. Recorded July 21, 1697 by John Cary Regist[r]

[184] Inventory of above estate taken June 30, 1697 by Thomas Leonard, John Dean, Richard Stephens and Isaace Dean. Items: "halfe the lott that was M[r] Andrews"; "the Eight accres of land that was Cafses great lott"; "the great lott of Twenty accers Bought of John Dean"; "the Houfe Orchard & Eight accers of land Bought of Joans"; "two lotts of land at Squabinanfit giuen him by his father"; "Twenty accers of land Bought of John Hall at Squabinanfit"; "the Meaddow his father Gaue him"; "the little Neck fo called which his father Bought of James Bates & gaue to him"; [185] Said inventory sworn to July 15, 1697 by Katherine Dean widow before John Saffin Proba[r]: John Cary Regist[r]: Recorded July 23, 1697 by John Cary Regist[r]

An agreement bearing date of July 13, 1697 made between Katherine Dean widow of Thomas Dean late of Taunton deceased and executrix of his will on the one party and Thomas Dean only son of said Thomas Dean dec'd on the other party. It is agreed first that Katharine Dean is to accept the office of executrix. Second, that whereas by said will of said Thomas Dean the improvement of the whole estate was left to his widow during her widowhood, nevertheless under the conditions hereafter mentioned said Katherine Deane doth agree that her son Thomas Deane shall possess the easterly end of the dwelling house, that part in which said Thomas Dean now dwells, also that lot called Jones lot and house thereon, the land at Pale Brook and at Squabbanansett forthwith, and that that part of the lot bought of Jn[o] Dean, between the river & the highway is to come under his improvement the next spring after the date hereof. Third, said Thomas Dean agrees with his mother Katherine Deane that she shall and may pay to her daughters Hannah, Deborah, Katharine, Lidia, Mercey and Elizabeth five pounds each out of the moveables as expressed in his father's will [186] and that the rest of the moveables be divided among the children by said executrix as in the will expressed and that the land at Scadings and wenicunnet given to the said daughters by will shall belong to them, and whereas the two south purchases mentioned in said will to be given to said daughters, were sold by said Thomas Dean dec'd before his decease, and the estate of the said Thomas Dean is found to be considerably increased since the date of his will, said Thomas Dean doth agree with his said mother Katharine Dean that she shall dispose of the three North purchases unto her said daughters, also that he will pay to said Katherine or such of her said daughters as she shall appoint, £70 in money at the rate of £10 per annum, and the first payment to be made when that estate (that is, lands) which his mother now lives on, shall come into his possession, which according to said will is after the decease of his said mother or the expiration of her widowhood. Witnessed by Thomas Leonard, Isaace Deane and Samuel Blake, and sworn to July 15, 1697 by Katherine Deane and Thomas Deane before John Saffin who allowed the same. John Cary Regist[r]: Entered July 23, 1697 by John Cary Regist[r]:

ABSTRACTS FROM THE FIRST BOOK OF BRISTOL COUNTY PROBATE RECORDS

Copied by Mrs. Lucy Hall Greenlaw

[187] Account of Thomas Leonard of Taunton, administrator of the estate of his "Honrd: ffather Mr James Leonard" late of Taunton deceased. Paid: "to his Mother in law M^{s}. Margaret Leonard"; to his brother James Leonard; "his two Brothers Jofeph and Uriah Leonard they & Jofephs Executrix Pofsefs what they were to haue"; to his brother Benjamin Leonard; to his brother and sister John and Abigail Kinsley; to his brother and sister Isaace and Rebecca Chapman; his brother and sister Isaac and Hannah Dean have received their due. Debts and other charges have been paid to the following persons: Ensigne John Hall, Nathaniel French, Eliazer Carver, Joseph Willis Senr., Mr Danforth [for] Rate, Samuel Waldron, Isace Dean, William Hoskins, Thomas Dean, Benjamin Dean, Nathaniel Bun for Jno Macomber Cooper, John Crane, Philip King, Richard Burt, Sam^{ll} Hall Senr., John Macumber Junr., John Crane for Jno Echee, Nath. William's widow, John Thresher, Mr Pool for goods in Taunton and Boston, Mr Burton clerk,—Cary clerk. Dated Aug. 24, 1697 and exhibited same day before John Saffin Judge of probate, who allowed the same. John Cary Regist^{rm}: Recorded Sept. 4, 1697 by John Cary Regist^{rm}:

[188] Account of Thomas Leonard of Taunton, administrator on the estate of John Smith late of Taunton deceased, dated Aug. 24, 1694. Items, debts due: from Samuel Smith of Medfield, from me for 3 years' rent of the land Mr Pool hired, from Stephen Casswel for 3 years' rent of land he hired, to several tracts of land mentioned in the inventory which by the will are not to be divided until John Smith, son of said John Smith, comes of age. The estate is debtor to: Mr Daniel Smith late of Rehoboth for coming to Bristol, to Mr Burton when the will was proved Jan. 12, 1691–2, to Mr Cary the clerk for himself and Mr Saffin, to Richard Godfry, to William Paul, to the widow Makepeace, "to John Hofkins Conftable the arrears of ye Minifters Rate in 1690 & 1691"; to "the Town Rate to Benja: Williams Conftable in 1691"; "to Ditto Conftable the Rate Called Hugh Brigges his Rate in 1691"; to the wife of Joseph Grey Senr.; "to Thomas Gilbert to procure a Deed for Nicolas his land," to Maj^{r}. Bradford; "allowed to Samuel Smith of Meadfeild for bringing back a Runaway"; to Nathaniel Parker towards his wife's Due; "Due to Jno Hathway Senr."; to Mr Stephen Marick. "Nicholas Joanes Alias Smith produced proff that his father Smith Gaue him one of the Breeding Mares & her increafe & one of the heifers and he had them". The land about the house Mr Marick improves and pays the rent to the widow as her thirds of the profits of the lands; "one of the heifers was Goared wth a beaft & Dyed thereof". [189] The balance of this account to be fully accomplished "when the heires Comes of age", according to the will. Sworn to Aug. 24, 1697 before John Saffin Judge of probate, John Cary Regist^{rm}: Entered Sept. 4, 1697 by John Cary Regist^{rm}.

In consideration of the mean and low condition that Mary Chaplin widow of William Chaplin late of Swanzey deceased is left in, there being no house or land and the estate in moveables so very small and the estate insolvent, I John Saffin Judge of probate do assign to the said widow a bed and furniture thereunto belonging, also one iron pot and hooks and a spinning wheel "as her Paraphenalia". Dated Dec. 10, 1697. John Cary Regist[r]. Entered same day by John Cary Regist[r]:

[190] The inventory "of the widow Bartrams Eftate" taken by Hezekiah Luther and Zachariah Eddy amounted to £60 .. 15 .. 05, and was sworn to by William Hammon, Nov. 6, 1694 before John Saffin Proba[r]: John Cary Regist[r]: Entered Sept. 26, 1697 by John Cary Regist[r]:

[191] Will of William Wodell "of Pocafset" who is "Very Ill of body" made "the Eight day of the feuenth Month Called September" 1692, "for the preventing future trouble among my Children & Grand Children". To my granddaughter Sarah Wodell £15 in money to be paid within two years after my decease. To Priscila and Isabell Gatchel £10 each in money "to be payd to Each of them at the age of Sixteen years. Sifters of the faid Sarah wodell". To my daughter Mary Greenell wife of Daniel Greenel £5 in money within three years after my decease. To my grandson Richard Greenel the same. To my grandsons William and Samuel Sanfords, each the same. To my grandson John Anthony son of my daughter Frances 40 shillings in money within two years after my decease. To my grandson Joseph Anthony son of my daughter Frances £5 in money within three years after my decease. To my grandson William Anthony son of my daughter Frances the same. To my granddaughter Susannah daughter of my daughter Frances the same. To my granddaughters Elizabeth and Alice Anthony daughters of my daughter Frances each 50 shillings to be paid them at the age of fifteen. To my grandson William Wodell 1 shilling. To my daughter Alice Anthony 1 shilling. To my loving friend John Green of Warwick 20 shillings. To my grandson Richard Wodell £5 within one year after my decease. To my grandson Return Wodell the same. To my grandson Gershom Wodell, for him to pay the above legacies and my debts, my northermost share of land being the 12th share, and also my southermost share of land whereon my house standeth being the 13th share, only my will is that his mother shall have equal privileges with him in said 13th share during her life. To my granddaughter Sarah Woodell my best feather bed and bolster. To Priscilla Gatchell a feather bed and bolster. To Isabel Gatchel the same. To my grandson-in-law Robert Lawton "two Books Gadberry and wing". To John Potter of Warwick and the rest of the present free inhabitants of that town and their successors for an enlargement of the commons of said township, one half of all my right to [192] land mentioned in the original deed of the Grand Purchase of that land out of which the said township of Warwick was granted, and the other half of said land I give to my loving friend Major John Green of Warwick. "And whereas it hath been faid by feueral perfons that I with fome others Did goe about to wrong the town of Portfmouth in Purchafeing of Hog Ifland of an Indian Sachem Called Mocecup. I am fo far from doing any wrong therein that I do giue Vnto the free Inhabitants of the faid Town of Portfmouth * * all the land on the faid Hog Ifland that doth * * to me belong by Vertue of faid Purchafs. And whereas it hath been faid by feverall perfons y[t] I with

fome others Did Goe about to wrong the ffree Inhabitants of Road Ifland in Purchafeing the Revertion and Remainder of Road Ifland. of an Indian Sachem Called Mocecup: I am fo far from Doing any wrong therein that I doe giue vnto the free Inhabitants of the faid Road Ifland as of Right it fhould belong, and their Succefsors * * all the land on the faid Road Ifland that doth of Right to me belong by Vertue of said purchafe". It is my will that my grandson Gershom Woddell and his mother "Do take Care & fee this my laft will & Teftament performed fullfilled & Kept". I "Defire Nominate & appoint my loueing Neighbors Samfon & Samuel Shearman to be the overfeers of this my laft will & Teftament Defireing them to Counfell & afsift my Executrix fo far as they Can". Witnessed by Joshua Rawlins, Ichabod Rogers and Thristram Bowerman, who all made oath to above will May 2, 1693 before Jn° Saffin Proba^r: Stephen Burton Regist^r:

Above will was proved and Gershom Wodell and Mary Wodell his mother were appointed administrators of the estate of William Wodell "late of Little compton. alias. Pocafset", May 2, 1693, by John Saffin Proba^r: Burton Regist^r: at a court held at Bristol. Entered Oct. 26, 1697 by John Cary Regist^rm:

[193] Account of above estate presented to John Saffin Judge of probate Oct. 8, 1697 by Gershom Wodell executor and Mary Wodell executrix, and allowed by him. John Cary Regist^r: Items: "By a Legacie to william Anthony fon of John Anthony" £5; "to Jofeph Anthony according to will" £5; "To Sufanah Anthony" £5; "To Daniel Greenel & Mary Greenel" £5; "To william & Samuel Sanford Sons vnto Samuel Sandford of Portfmouth ten pounds to fattisfaction as by their fathers Samuel Sanford his Receipt Dated Nouemb^r: fecond 1695"; "To John Green of warwick". Debts paid as follows to: John Kees of Portsmouth, Gershom Wodell, Thomas Hicky, Job Manchester, Richard Wodell, Samuel Shearman, Sarah Denny, Samson Sherman, Robert Layton, John Anthony Senr., Robert Fish and Job Layton. The balance of the estate chiefly consists of lands and some moveables, which by the will are bequeathed to Gershom Wodell and Mary the executrix and there are yet remaining four legacies viz. to Prisilla Gatchel and Isabel Gatchel each ten pounds and a bed and bolster, and to Elizabeth Anthony and Alice Anthony daughters of John Anthony of Portsmouth five pounds to be divided equally between them. Sworn to Oct. 8, 1697 by Gershom Wodell heir to William Wodell deceased and Mary Wodell executrix of his will before John Saffin Proba^r: John Cary Regist^r: Entered Oct. 26, 1697 by John Cary Regist^r:

[194] Bristol, Oct. 21, 1697. Whereas there is a certain tract of land lying within the townships of Freetown and Swanzey, together with some meadows lying at a place called Cippican (being a whole freeman's share), belonging to Nicolas Woodbery late of Beverly and Isacce Woodbery late of Salem deceased (equally between them) and the said Isacce Woodbery dying intestate, administration was granted to Hugh Woodbery of Bristol by John Saffin Judge of probate, and some of the children of Nicolas Woodbery being cited by the said Judge to appear at Bristol on the 20th of this instant before him to make their claims unto the estate of the said Isacce Woodbery dec'd, "And Ifacce woodbery fonne to the faid Nicolas woodbery being prefent and m^r Thomas west and m^r Philip ffowles Atturnys to the Reft of the Children of the faid Nicolas woodbery Dec^d: Viz^t: Mary woodbery Relict of Nicolas woodbery Son to the faid Nicolas woodbery:

(Allſo Deceaſed) Joſeph woodbery Emma woodbery Relict to Andrew woodbery late of Beaverly allſo ſon to the ſaid Nicolas Deceaſed and Benjamin woodbery" it is agreed that the said half of the lands and meadows belonging to Isacce Woodbery above said shall be equally divided between Hugh Woodberry abovesaid and the children of Nicolas Woodbery particularly above named according to the bounds of said lands in a certain deed signed by Richard Moor dated Aug. 30, 1673. Debts due from the estate of said Isacce Woodberry shall be equally borne by each party. Signed by Hugh Woodbere, Isacce Woodbery, Thomas West and Philip Foules attorney, and allowed by John Saffin Judge of probate same day. John Cary Regist[r] Entered Oct. 21, 1697 by John Cary Regist[rm]:

Memorandum. It is understood by the above that Hugh Woodbery is to have one moiety or half part of the half share of land above, and the above named children the other part of said half share of land to be equally divided between them. John Saffin Judge of Probate. John Cary Regist[r]. Entered Dec. 23, 1699 by John Cary Regist[r].

[195] Account of Hannah Shaw widow and executrix of the will of John Shaw late of Swanzey deceased rendered Oct. 23, 1697. Items: paid to Lidia Moor due to her for money lent to the deceased a little before his death; to Samuel Pool carpenter for repairing the house in Boston according to the will; to William Webster for work done about said house; to paid "for Clearing of the Drean & Seller" of said house; to charge of removing from Swanzey to Boston; to Doct[r] Talmon for charges in coming to Bristol to finish administration. Sworn to by said Hannah Shaw at a court held at Bristol Oct. 23, 1697 before John Saffin. John Cary Regist[r]: Entered Oct. 23, 1697 by John Cary Regist[rm]

[196] Will of Thomas Casewell Senr. of Taunton dated Sept. 28, 1691. To my eldest son Stephen Casswell the land whereon his house now standeth and my land at Skunk Hill. To my second son Thomas Casswell six acres of land in the great plain, other lands of mine now in his possession and one half quarter part of my share in the North purchase. To my third son Peter Casswell sixteen acres on the south side of the highway opposite where his house now standeth. To my fourth son John Caswell "a pond Called the ſtage pound" also one half quarter part of my share in the North purchase. To my fifth son William Caswell the land whereon his house now standeth and the land called the Neck, also ten acres of land at "Thinn Swamp" and three acres of swamp at the old Beaver Dam. To my sixth son Samuel Caswell my house wherein I now dwell with my orchard, meadow and other land, all my land on the north side of the highway as far as James Bell's land, except a little piece where my son Peter Caswell's house stands which I formerly gave to my said son Peter. Also I give to said Samuel forty-six acres of my fifty acre division lying at Cotly between the land of Isacce Dean and Shadrach Wilbor's land. To my loving wife Mary one quarter of my share in the North purchase, the use of all my moveables within my house, and the westerly lower room in my house during her widowhood. My son Samuel Caswell to be sole executor, he to take care of and provide for his mother and maintain her during her widowhood. To my daughters Mary, Sarah, Hannah, Elizabeth, Abigail and Hester the one half of my share in the North purchase to be equally divided among them. To my daughter Hannah wife of Daniel Ramsdell one heifer of a year old. Witnessed by Shadrach Wilbore, Samuel Wilbore and Joseph Wilbore. "Poſcript" dated March 15, 1696–7: Where-

as my share in the North purchase has since been sold for the sum of £12, which money my son Samuel made use of, my will is that he pay the [197] sum of £12 to those of my children to whom said share was given, in proportion as expressed in the will. Codicil witnessed by Elizabeth X Briant, Isaak X Leonard and Samuel Danforth. Joseph Wilbore one of the witnesses made oath to said will at Bristol, Sept. 14, 1697 and Shadrach Wilbore another witness "Did * * make oath to the Ton^e: and Effect of Jofeph wilbore his oath: and that Samuel wilbore was p^r efent and Did Signe as a witnefs at the fame time: Since Deceafed", at Taunton, Oct. 9, 1697. The same day Mr Samuel Danforth and Elizabeth Briant testifyed to the truth of the above will before John Saffin Judge of probate. John Cary Regist^r: Entered Oct. 30, 1697 by John Cary Regist^r:

Inventory of above estate taken March 30, 1696–7 [198] by Israel Thresher, Josep Richmond and Henry Andrews, and presented at court at Taunton Oct. 9, 1697 by Samuel Caswell executor before Jno Saffin, John Cary Regist^r: Entered Oct. 30, 1697 by John Cary Regist^rm: Amount of inventory, £306 .. 09 .. 06.

Receipt given Feb. 12, 1697–8 by Thomas Mallett of Newport, R. I. to William Wood of Dartmouth executor of the will of William Wood of Dartmouth deceased for £67 .. 06, being a legacy given to Daniel Wood and John Wood by said William Wood in his will, said Thomas Mallet being guardian of said Daniel and John. Witnessed by Isacce Martindale and Richard X Evins. Entered May 12, 1698 by John Cary Regist^r:

An account of the estate of John Fitch late of Rehoboth deceased rendered by Mary Fitch Executrix; "those lands that were Bequeathed to ye four Daughters by the will to be prefently divided between them. Are all divided. as appeares by an Inftrument Vnder hands & feales". Items, paid to: Tho: Omsby Junr., Benja Robbinson, Phillip Walker, Jarrard Ingraham, Henry Sweeting. Received of: Israel Read, Gilbert Grant, Sam Walker, Leu^t Joseph Brown, Mr Jeremiah Childs, Moses Read. Sworn to by said Mary Fitch at Rehoboth April 21, 1699 before John Saffin. John Cary Reg^r. Entered same day by John Cary Reg^r.

[199] Will of Samuel Williams of Taunton dated Aug. 6, 1697, he "being Vnd^r. Bodily Infirmity & pain". To my eldest son Seth Williams my land on the southeast side of Taunton great river containing eight or nine acres, thirty acres on the south side of the path going from "ware Bridge" toward Plymouth, bounded by John Macumber's land on the south side and parted by a path from Richard Haskin's land. My son Seth Williams to improve my dwelling house, homestead and barn until my son Daniel reaches age, then it shall be his. One half of a purchase right to lands in Taunton I give to my son Seth Williams, one quarter to my son Samuel Williams and the other quarter to my son Daniel Williams. To my son Samuel Williams my South purchase, the meadow land I purchased of Hezekiah Hoar "Near the Needles" and my Rumford Division. To my three daughters Sarah Dean, Mary Andros and Hannah Bun eight pounds each. My moveables I give to my executor for payment of debts and legacies to my daughters, only the cow and calf, mare and colt which my son Samuel calls his, I give to him, and the two heifers which my son Daniel calls his I give to him. I give my wife liberty to live with my son Seth in my house a twelve month time after my decease if she wishes, "but if fhe rather Chufe to Return home again to her own before winter" I give

her six bushels of corn and a hog, also what she desires of the linen cloth in the house and the woolen cloth now at the weaver's. Son Seth to be sole executor. Witnessed by John Richmond, Thomas Gilbert and Abigail × Richmond who all appeared before John Saffin Esq[r]. Judge of Probate and made oath to above will, Oct. 9, 1697. John Cary Regist[r]: Entered Nov. 1697 by John Cary Regist[r].

[200] Inventory of the estate of Samuel Williams of Taunton late dec'd taken Aug. 31, 1697, by John Richmond, Thomas Gilbert and Thomas Williams. Amount, £340 .. 03 .. 00. Sworn to Oct. 9, 1697 by Seth Williams executor of the will of the above named Samuel Williams before John Saffin Proba[r]: Jn[o] Cary Regist[r]: Entered Nov. 2, 1697 by John Cary Regist[r].

Bristol, Jan. 3, 1698–9, "this Refers to Margaret Sabins Inventory. Recorded foliou 203". Account of the administrator allowed by Jn[o] Saffin Proba[r]. Entered same day by John Cary Register.

[201] Whereas our honored mother M[s] Ann Barney has a right in the estate of our late honored father Jacob Barney late of Rehoboth dec'd during her life or until her marriage, as appears by his will, and whereas the said Ann Barney "hath Condefcended that the faid Houfeing and lands ſhould be Divided Vnto her * * fons," we, Joseph Barney, Israel Barney, Jonathan Barney and Samuel Barney all of Rehoboth, all sons of M[r] Jacob Barney agree with our mother as follows: first, that we pay to her yearly £10 .. 10 in money to be paid quarterly; second that we provide a good and comfortable room of about twelve or fourteen feet square with a good and convenient chimney, for her comfortable living and lodging therein, to be built and finished with all convenient speed to be set up at the west end of Israel Barney's house, and the said Joseph Barney doth promise his mother the use of the fruit on one apple tree yearly which she shall choose each year, also she shall not hereby be cut off from reasonable privileges in the now dwelling house "& Efpetially till f[d] Room be built", also said sons agree to find her firewood. Dated Dec. 8, 1697 and signed by Joseph Barney and Israel Barney for themselves, Solomon Curtice as guardian to Jonathan Barney, and Samuel Bullock as guardian unto Samuel Barney. Witnessed by Nath[ll] Paine, John West and John Cary, and acknowledged before Jn[o] Saffin Esq[r]., Dec. 8, 1697. Recorded Jan. 8, 1697–8 by Jn[o] Cary Regist[r].

[202] We, being commissioned by M[r] John Saffin Esq[r]., Judge of Probate, to make an equal division of the housing and lands left by M[r] Jacob Barnee late of Rehoboth dec'd between his four sons according to his will saving to Ann Barnee his relict her due rights, have divided the estate as follows: Joseph Barney's share is the northermost lot of land and meadow, bounded northerly on Samuel Bullock, and he is to pay £21 in money to the other three brothers on the account of equality. The second allotment being Jonathan Barney's is bounded northerly on Joseph Barney's land. The third allotment being for Samuel Barney is bounded northerly on the land of Jonathan Barney. The fourth allotment being Israel Barney's is bounded northerly of the land of Samuel Barney, easterly on Samuel Peck's meadow and his own meadow. Said Israel Barney's meadow is bounded northerly on the meadow of Samuel Barney and southerly on Samuel Peck's meadow. Each is to have at all times a convenient highway through each other's lot to his meadows. Said Joseph Barney is to pay to Jonathan

Barney £5 .. 10 in money, to Israel Barney £4 .. 10 and to Samuel Barney £11, and said Israel Barney is to have the old house. Dated Dec. 8, 1697 and signed by Sam[ll] Bullock, Tho: Omsbe, John West, Solomon Curtis and James Therber. Said division presented to John Saffin Esq[r]. Judge of Probate and allowed by him same day. Entered Jan. 8, 1697–8 by John Cary Regist[r]

[203] Inventory of the estate of Peter Pampillo dec'd taken Nov. 26, 1697 by Vzal Wardall and Jabez Gorham, and sworn to at Bristol, Dec. 7, 1697 by M[s] Joan Papillio, widow of said deceased, before John Saffin Esq[r]. John Cary Regist[r]: Amount £343 .. 17 .. 00. Entered Dec. 7, 1697 by John Cary Regist[r]:

Inventory of the estate of Margaret Sabin dec'd taken by William Carpenter and Samuel Peck, Dec. 6, 1697, the amount being £8 .. 15 .. 00. Items: two pieces of meadow ground at m[r] Browns Pond; a debt due to her estate from John Sabin. Said inventory sworn to by James Sabin Dec. 7, 1697, before John Saffin Probat[r]: John Cary Regist[r]:

Debts due from the estate of Margaret Sabin dec'd: "Payd to Doct Arnold for phiſike and a journey"; "Payd to Doct[r]: Bowen for Phizike & his trouble about her"; "for a months Tendance of James Sabin at his houſe w[hen] she was Diſtrated"; "Her funeral Charges in Drink Coffin & the Graue Diging", "for Charge to the Crowner Vnleſs he will abate". Entered Dec. 7, 1697 by John Cary Regist[r]:

The account of James Sabin administrator of the estate of Margaret Sabin was allowed and entered in this book folio 200, Jan. 3, 1698 By John Cary Reg[r]

ABSTRACTS FROM THE FIRST BOOK OF BRISTOL COUNTY PROBATE RECORDS

Copied by Mrs. Lucy Hall Greenlaw

[204] We, being desired by Mr Ebenezer Brenton to apprize the eighth part of the "Ship ſeaflower. whereof william Brenton was late Maſt^{r}: as ſhe Came home from Barbadus", the said eighth part (and other things) belonging to the said William Brenton dec'd, do hereby declare that said eighth part of the ship Seaflower is worth £75, and we also apprize about 180 gallons of rum at 3 shillings 6 pence per gallon, and about 200 gallons of "Malleſsus" at 20 pence per gallon, together with other personal estate. Dated Apr. 1, 1697 and signed by Benjamin Funell, Jno Jenkins and Sam^{ll} Pelton. Also John Cary, John Wilkins and Jabez Howland being requested by Ebenezer Brenton administrator of the estate of his brother William Brenton deceased to apprize a dwelling house in Bristol belonging to said estate with land belonging to said house as much as hath been improved formerly by the said Brenton dec'd do value said house and land at £90. Total inventory of said estate amounted to £288..04..08, and was sworn to at Bristol, Feb. 19, 1697–8 by Mr Ebenezer Brenton administrator before John Saffin Esqr Judge of Probate, John Cary Regist^{r}: Recorded same day by John Cary Regist^{rm}

[205] "An account of the Debts of william Brenton of Briſtoll Contracted in his life and what became Due after he Deceaſed is as follows: Videlleſit:"

"To what the Eighth part of the ſeaflower was Debt^{r} to Ebenezer Brenton before ſhe went out to Barbadus & afterw^{d} whileſt ſhe was the ſ^{d} Wm Brentons"
"To Caſh Bor^{d} of Ebenezer Brenton to be pd in Barbadus & not pd"
"To thouſand of ſhingles ſent to Barbadus & ſold for three p^{d} net"
"To Caſh pd Mr Richard Jenkins for m^{r} Parkinſon: Money Bor^{d}:"
"To Caſh pd ſ^{d} Jenkins for Money Bor^{d}: of M^{s} Elizabeth Eliot"
"To Caſh payd ſ^{d} Jenkins for his Commiſſion for s^{d} Eighth"
"To Mr Pool for money pd for ſ^{d} william Brenton at antogue"
"To m^{r} Natha^{ll} Paine Money Due by Bill"
"To Caſh paid Mr Birge for work done"
"To Mr Rowland Robbinſon for a horſs"
"To Edward Adams for ſhoues"
"to Georg waldron for Glaſs"
"To Caſh pd Mr Thomas Durffee"
"To Caſh pd Mr Throop"
"To Caſh pd Capt Gallup"
"to James Adams for Sho^{s}"
"To Cloathing the Children ſince their father Dec^{d}."
"To m^{r} Jerimiah Osborn for Neceſsarys for Jahleel"

Above account sworn to Feb. 22, 1697–8 by Mr Ebenezer Brenton administrator before John Saffin Esqr. Judge of Probate, and allowed by him. John Cary Regist^{r}: Entered same day by John Cary Regist^{r}.

[206] Sept. 1, 1696, the estate of William Brenton of Bristol is debted to Ebenezer to sundry goods delivered to the children as follows: To Wil-

liam Brenton, Jr., to Sam[ll] Brenton, to Benjamin Brenton, [207] to Jahleel Brenton. An account of money paid to several persons "y[t] was Due before W[m] Brenton went to Barbadus", viz:
"Payd to Edward Adams for ſhoes & Leather"
"Payde to James Adams for Shoes"
"Payd to M[r] John Birge for work"
Entered Feb. 22, 1697-8 by John Cary Regist[r]

Will of John Titus of Rehoboth dated Nov. 1, 1697, he "being Very ſick & weake". To my Beloved wife Sarah my new dwelling house and barn, one half of my cellar in the old house, one half of the house lot my house stands on, one half of the homestead that I purchased of John Carpenter, one half of my pasture, one half of my meadow at Rose Meadow and Bushy Meadow and my plain lot, one half of my second division lot, one half of my Neck lot, one half of my meadow at Palmers River which I purchased of Joseph Peck Sen[r], William Sabin and John Carpenter, one half of a nine acre lot at the farther side of homes Plain, one half of a ten acre lot that is to be laid out in the thousand acre division, one half of my meadow at the forty acres purchased of John Carpenter, one half of a plain lot, £40 estate of commonage in the old bounds of Rehoboth, and one half of my salt meadow. All the above I bequeath unto my wife "Dureing her Widowhood whilſt ſhe Bares my Name", and at her marriage or decease I give it to my eldest son John Titus. I give to my wife at her own dispose my cart and plow, chains, yokes and other utensils for husbandry, and all my household goods, sheep, cattle, horses [208] and swine (except what I shall particularly dispose of to my children) all debts due to me and corn and provision towards house keeping. To my eldest son John Titus my old house, excepting that part of the cellar I have given to his mother, and my shop, also the other half part of above lands bequeathed to her, also £40 estate of commonage in the old bounds of Rehoboth, all to be possessed by him when he comes to the age of twenty-one, also I give him a set of tools for a cooper, "a Broad ax and a Burz, a pair of Chiſels and an Inch & half and Inch & quarter Borcior anarow ax & Square a feather bed & beding a Iron pot and two platter and one Cow & Six Sheep I giue my ſonne John a ſett of Hops & Boxes for a pare of wheeles". To my son Samuel the dwelling house and house lot that was my father's, seven acres of land in the second division, the meadow ground of wrights meadow and the meadow at forty acres which I purchased of Richard Bowen, likewise a bed and bed clothes, a narrow axe and £17 estate of commonage in Rehoboth, to be possessed of said lands when he comes of age. To my son Robert fifty acres at Stonny Bottom, a share of meadow at the great meadow, a narrow axe, and my half share of undivided lands in the North purchase, to be possessed when he comes of age. To my son Timothy my land and swamp upon the Mile River at M[r] Browns Pond, my meadow at M[r] Browns Pond and £17 estate of Commons in Rehoboth and a narrow axe to be possessed of them when he comes of age. To my daughter Lidya twenty acres of land that is to be laid out in the two thousand acre division, "a feather Bed which was her mothers and a pott & two platters that was her mothers, Marckt with her maiden Name". To "my Daughter" Hannah and Sarah twenty acres of land on the east side of Palmers River to be equally divided between them, and their mother is to pay to each of them a cow when they come to the age of eighteen years. To "my Daughter" Elizabeth and Abygail each of them a cow when they come to the age of eighteen years to be paid to them by their mother, also seven acres of land at Beveredge hill in the field. To "my Cozen John ffuller" twenty acres of land lying upon the Mill River by the way that leads to Kenrick Run, also "I giue him a fett of Tools for a Cooper & a Broad ax & a Square that was his Grandfather titus". I hereby engage my wife and my son John to fulfil all my engagements which I am under to "my Mother Abigail Palm^r Dureing her Mariage ftate and likewife if god fhould order it that my mother fhould be left a widow that they take the Care of her according to my Ingagments". If my wife should marry again and the house and land which I have given her during her widowhood return to my son John, then she shall be clear of any engagement to my mother, and my son John shall fulfil the same. [209] I do appoint my wife Sarah Titus executrix and my son John Titus executor of this my will. I give to my son Samuel "the Loames & flayes & harnefs & other Vtenfels for a weaver to be pofsefsed by him when he comes of age of Twenty one years. I do Defire & appoint my Loueing friends Brother Samuel Millard and my Brother Leonard Newfum to be my overfeers of this my laft will to be helpfull to my wife & fonne in the Managment of their Bufines". Witnessed by Richard Bowen Senr, Richard Bowen, Samuel Carpenter and William Carpenter, of whom the first three all of Rehoboth made oath to above will before John Saffin Esqr. Judge of Probate, Jan. 10, 1697–8, John Cary Regist^r. Entered same day by John Cary Regist^r:

Inventory of above estate taken Dec. 8, 1697 by [210] Jonah Palmer, William Carpenter and Samuel Millerd, and sworn to at Bristol Jan. 10, 1697–8 by Sarah Titus executrix and John Titus executor of above will before John Saffin Esqr Judge of Probate, John Cary Regist^r: Entered same day by John Cary Record^r: Amount, £293..12..06

[211] John Fitch of Rehoboth, "Being Aged & weak of Body and of found & perfect Memory praife be giuen to Almighty God" made his will June 20, 1693. To my beloved wife Mary my dwelling house, barn, orchard and house lot, all my lands at Mantoms Neck, my nearest lot in wachameket lot, being eight acres, all my meadow grounds both salt and fresh in Rehoboth, and my commons for her "livelyhood" during her life, and at her decease all above house and lands are to be equally divided between my four daughters, Mary, Rebecca, Sarah and Hannah if they be living, or if any of them be deceased to the heirs of their body. To my four above named daughters all the rest of my lands to be equally divided. Rest of personal estate and chattels I give to my wife Mary, whom I appoint sole executrix. What is left of my personal estate at my wife's decease, she shall have power with the advice of my overseers to dispose of among my children at her discretion to those that may be most helpful to her. I desire my loving friends Nicolas Peck Esquire and Abraham Peren to be overseers of this my will. I likewise revoke all former wills made by me. Witnessed by Nicolas Peck, Christop^r Sanders and William Carpenter, of whom Nicolas Peck Esqr. and William Carpenter made oath to above will at Rehoboth, Feb. 23, 1697–8 before Jno Saffin Esqr. Judge of Probate, John Cary Regist^r., they testifying [212] that Christop^r Sanders was present and set his name as a witness at the same time. Entered Feb. 23, 1697–8 by John Cary Regist^rm:

Inventory of above estate taken Feb. 1, 1697–8, by Capt Nicolas Peck, Richard Bowen Senr., William Carpenter and Samuel Millerd. Amount, £357..05..03. Said inventory sworn to at Rehoboth, Feb. 23, 1697–8 by

Mary Fitch widow of said John Fitch before John Saffin Esq[r] Judge of Probate, John Cary Regist[r]. Entered same day by John Cary Regist[r].

[213] Will of Shadrach Willbore Sen[r] of Taunton dated Sept. 12, 1696, he "being weake of Body". To my loving wife Hannah £30 in money, two good cows, "and allſo free Liberty to take all the Eſtate (that was hers) that ſhe brought to me from Brantree, what of it is in being at my Deceaſe, that is Provided y[t] my ſ[d] wife Hannah haue a Deſire to Return againe to her Children at Brantree, But if my ſaid wife Hannah will pleaſe to ſtay with my Children & be as a Mother to them, Then my will is, that ſhe ſhall haue y[e] Vſe of the Beſt Room in my Houſe ſo long as ſhe ſhall Continue here, and Bare my Name, She ſhall be Maintained out of my Eſtate, as my wife, * * as Concerning my Eldeſt Son Samuel wilbore (Deceaſed) Conſidering that I did not in his Life time, Giue vnto him my ſaid Son Samuel wilbore any aſsurance by writting of what he Enjoyed, Therefore Now I do Rattify & confirme what he he [*sic*] Did Enjoy to belong to his wife & Children as it is on the Inventory of his Eſtate which was taken by Stephen Merick & Iſrael Threſher". To my son Joseph Wilbore a parcel of land at the head of my home lot with the house standing on it on the east side of the highway, also six acres on the west side of said highway, my lot at Rumford of twenty acres of upland and two of meadow, twenty acres lying northerly from Prospect Hill, and about three or four acres of land that I bought of Daniel Makeny, provided that said son Joseph Willbore shall pay to his brother John Willbore five pounds "towards the Building of him a Houſe". To my son Shadrach Wilbore the southerly side of the land that I bought of James Bell, with the house and barn standing on it, also six acres in the plain lying on the northerly side of the six acres that I gave to my son Joseph Wilbore, twenty acres of upland and two of meadow, that I bought of Moses Knap and Thomas Briggs lying at Rumford, and twenty acres lying northerly from Prospect Hill, provided said son Shadrach Wilbore shall pay unto his brother Eliazer Wilbore £10 towards the building of a house and a convenient cartway across his land to the common highway. To my son John Willbore a parcel of land at the head of the lots of John Farwell and John Cobb which I bought of the widow Mary Andrews and her son Henry Andrews, also twenty-three acres of land lying northerly from Prospect Hill, "Joyning to y[e] land y[t] his Vnkle Joſeph Willbore Gaue to him", also one half of my share in the Dead Swamp. To my son Eliazer Willbore the northerly side of that land I bought of James Bell, twenty acres of land [214] lying northerly from Prospect Hill "Joyneing to y[e] land that his Vnkle Joſeph willbore gaue to my ſon Eliezer willbore", also one half of my share in Dead Swamp. To my son Benjamin Wilbore my house in which I now dwell, the barn and lots on which they stand, my meadow and swamp on the easterly side of the great River opposite to my house, twenty acres of land lying northerly from Prospect Hill, also my little orchard so called, always excepting what I have granted to my wife Hannah if she please to stay and make use of it. To my daughter Sarah, the now wife of Nathanil Hoar, £10 sterling besides what she hath had formerly. To my daughter Rebecah, the now wife of Abraham Hathway, the same. To my sons Joseph, Shadrach, Eliazer and Benjamin Wilbors and to my grandson Samuel Willbore all my purchase right in the old township of Taunton to be equally divided among them. I appoint my son Joseph and Shadrach Willbore executors of this my will, to whom I bequeath £5 in silver money. Any land remaining undisposed of to be equally divided among my five

sons, Joseph, Shadrach, John, Eliazer and Benjamin. Notwithstanding all that I have bequeathed above to my children, it shall not cut off or disannul any thing that I have engaged or promised to my wife Hannah, but she shall be provided for out of my whole estate if she "do ftay here wth my Children and take a Motherly Care: of them & Continue in my Name". Legacies to be paid and then rest of my moveables to be equally divided among my five sons. My son Joseph Wilbore "fhall take the Charge & Care of all my writtings & Books of account". Witnessed by Henry Hodges, Israel Thresher and John Heskins, of whom Deacon Henry Hodges and John Heskins made oath to above will at Bristol, March 1, 1697–8 before John Saffin Esqr. Judge of Probate, John Cary Regist^{r}, testifying "that they allfoe fee Ifrael Threfher figne as a witnefs at the fame time" Entered Mar. 1, 1697–8 by John Cary Regist^{r}:

[215] Inventory of above estate taken Feb. 23, 1697–8 by Thomas Lenard, Henry Hodges, Stephen Merick and John Heskins, and, amounting to £772..00..09, [216] was presented and sworn to by Joseph Wilbore and Shadrach Wilbore both of Taunton, sons unto Shadrach Wilbore late of Taunton dec'd. before Jno Saffin Esqr Judge of Probate, Jno Cary Register, March 1, 1697–8. Entered same day by John Cary Regist^{r}.

An account exhibited by William Wood and George Wood, administrators of the estate left by William Wood late of Dartmouth dec'd, dated Mar. 10, 1697–8. Items:

"To william wood his Dubble portion Eldeft fon"

"To Georg wood Adm^{r}: with william wood abouefaid"

"To Jofeph wood payd in lands Next Brother"

"To thefe three Brethren aboue Named the lands were Divided And farther the Adm^{rs} hath payd thefe following Legaties To Daniel wood payd to his Gaurdian as p^{r} his Receipt"

"To Jno wood as p^{r} Receipt Signed by Thomas Mallet"

"To Jofiah wood payd his Gaurdian David Lake"

"To m^{s} Mary Mallet p^{r} Receipt figned by Mallet"

"To Sarah wood as p^{r} her Recept payd"

"To Margaret wood her Gaurdian David Lake pd as by his Receipt"

"To Rebecah wood payd her Gaurdian David Lake as by his Receipt".

Above account allowed by John Saffin Esq. Judge of Probate Mar. 10, 1697–8. John Cary Register. Entered May 12, 1698 by Jno Cary Regist^{r}.

[217] Receipt dated Mar. 14, 1697–8, given by David Lake of Tiverton guardian of Joseph Wood, son of William Wood late of Dartmouth, to George Wood, joint administrator with his brother William Wood of the estate left by their father William Wood dec'd, for £33..13 in full for that part of abovesaid estate divided unto said Joseph Wood, to whom I am guardian. Entered May 12, 1698 by John Cary Regist^{rm}:

David Lake of Tiverton, guardian of Margaret Wood and Rebeccah Wood, has received of William Wood and George Wood of Dartmouth, £67..06. Receipt dated May 10, 1697, and entered May 12, 1698 by John Cary Regist^{r}

David Lake has received of William Wood of Dartmouth on the account of Josiah Wood son of the late deceased William Wood of Dartmouth £33.. 13. Receipt dated Feb. 8, 1697–8 and witnessed by Zacheas Butt and Increase Allen. Entered May 12, 1698 by John Cary Regist^{r}

Sarah Wood, daughter of Wm Wood of Dartmouth dec'd, has received from William Wood and George Wood, administrators of the estate of William Wood of Dartmouth dec'd, the sum of £33..13. Receipt dated Apr. 14,

1697 and entered May 12, 1698 by John Cary Record[r]

Thomas Mallett "of Newport on Roads Ifland Linnen Draper" has received from William Wood and George Wood administrators of the estate of William Wood of Dartmouth dec'd, the sum of £33..13 "Vpon the account of his wiues Portion Mary Mallet". Dated Apr. 14, 1697 and entered May 12, 1698 by John Cary Regist[r]:

[218] William Wood and George Wood sons of and administrators of the estate of their father William Wood late of Dartmouth deceased, having finished their administration are hereby discharged from the same by John Saffin Judge of Probate for Bristol County, Mar. 10, 1697–8. John Cary Regist[r]: Entered May 12, 1698 by John Cary Regist[r]

Will of Benjamin Paine who is "Now Refident in Briftoll . . . being Sick of Body . . . And Calling to mind the vncertain Eftate of this Life and that all flefh muft yeild vnto Death, when it fhall pleafe God to Call", dated April 18, 1698; "whereas my Brother John Paine of Swanzey hath by y[e] Providence of God been long Exerfifed with Sicknefs" I order that £20 be paid him before there is any division of my estate. "I do Giue to m[s] Jones my Lanlady who hath been Very tender of mee in this my prefent Secknes fiue pounds to be payd her as a Token of my Thankfullnes to her". All my estate, after legacies are paid, to be equally divided among all my brothers and sisters, "hereby Not Excluding my Brother John but that he allfo haue an Equall part with them Notwithftanding the abouefd Twenty pounds Giuen him And laftly I doe hereby Nominate & appoint my well beloued Brother Stephen Paine & my Brother in law Deacon Samuel Peck" my executors. [219] Witnessed by Benjamin Jones, Tristrem Bowerman and Nath[ll] Paine, who all appeared before John Saffin Esq[r] Judge of Probate and made oath to above will, May 3, 1698. John Cary Regist[r] Entered same day by John Cary Regist[r]:

Inventory of above estate taken by Hugh Woodbery and Nathaniel Paine, May 3, 1698. Items: "To a Bond from Samuel Moulton of Palmers River"; "Ditto a bond from Ephraim Peirce fen[r]: & Eriakim Peirce of Swanzey with the Intereft at 6 p[r] Cent"; "Ditto a Bond from will Ingraham Jun[r] of Briftoll with y[e] Intereft one year"; "To Money in Henry Brags hands". Amount, £261..16..00. Above inventory presented and sworn to at Bristol, May 3, 1698 by M[r] Stephen Paine and Deacon Samuel Peck, executors, before John Saffin Esq. Judge of Probate. John Cary Regist[r]. Entered May 3, 1698 by John Cary Regist[r] Additional inventory taken Apr. 21, 1699 by Capt Peck and W[m] Carpent[r]: to be added to above.

[220] Little Compton, Apr. 20, 1698. Inventory of the estate of Mary Price "of late Dec[d]." taken by Christopher Allen and William Foabs. Amount, £392..15..02. Above inventory sworn to by John Price, administrator of the estate of his mother, Mary Price late of Little Compton dec'd, before John Saffin Esq[r]. Judge of Probate, John Cary Regist[r]. May 3, 1698. Entered same day by John Cary Regist[r]:

[221] "I Jofeph wood of taunton . . . being of found mind & Memory but very weak of Body" do make my last will, Feb. 12, 1697–8; "my will is that my Beloued wife Abigale fhall haue that Eftate which fhe brought with her and one third of the Reft of moueable Eftate". Rest of estate both lands and moveables to be divided among all my children, "Viz, Jofeph & John & Ephraim and that Childe faid wife is with Child off, be

it a ſon or be it a Daughter allways ſo as my ſon Joſeph haue a Dubble portion". If any of my children die before they are married, such share to be divided among my surviving children; "my wife ſhall haue the vſe of my feather Bed Vntill my ſon John ſhall come to be Twenty one years old and then he to haue that Bed and a Childs red Blanket as part of his Portion Allſo I do hereby make my Beloued Brother in law Joſeph Deane my ſole Executor * * I allſo Deſire my Beloued Brothers, in law Peter walker & John Paul to be ouerſeers to this my laſt will & Teſtament, and to be helpfull wth their Councill & Advice to my Dear wife & Children whom I leaue behind". Witnessed by Thomas Leonard, Silvanus × Camball and Elkanah Leonard of whom Silvanus Camball and Elkanah Leonard made oath to above will in Bristol, May 19, 1698 before John Saffin Esq[r] Judge of Probate, John Cary Regist[r], stating that Cap[t] Thomas Leonard did sign as a witness at the same time. Entered May 19, 1698 by John Cary Regist[r]:

[222] Inventory of the estate of Joseph Wood of Taunton, "who Deceaſed in the month of february the 12th day 169$\frac{7}{8}$" taken Apr. 30, 1698 by Abell Burt, John Crossman and Robert Crossman. Amount, £214..02..07. Said inventory sworn to at Bristol, May 19, 1698, by Joseph Dean executor of above will before John Saffin Proba[r]: John Cary Regist[r]. Entered same day by John Cary Regist[r]:

[223] We, the subscribers, viz: Thomas Leonard, James Leonard, Henry Hodges, John Richmond Sen[r]: and Thomas Williams, all of Taunton, being commissioned by John Saffin Esq[r] Judge of Probate, to made an equal division of the estate of Nathaniel Williams late of said Taunton dec'd, "Between Elizabeth Williams the Relect & Adminiſtratrix with John Williams ſon of the ſaid Dec[d]: Between her & his Children" do divide said estate as follows: To the widow the west end of the dwelling house, the west end of the barn, a third part of the yearly income of the lands set out to her sons John and Nathaniel Williams during her life, and one third of the moveables forever. To John Williams eldest son of said dec'd, the dwelling house, barn, orchard, the land at home, the ten acre lot in the great lots, the seven acre lot in the great lots, the three acres of land near John Thresher's, the North Purchase, the eight acres of land in the Little woods so called, half a purchase right in the old township, the meadow at Littleworth, three acres of land at Pale Brook, the share in the Dead Swamp, the rest of the land lately taken up or yet due to said Purchase right in the old township to be equally divided between said John Williams and his brother Nathaniel Williams, said John Williams also to have £56 out of the moveables and to pay his Grandmother Williams 6 shillings 8 pence per annum during her life. To Nathaniel Williams second son of said dec'd, his father's fifty acre division and his thirty acre division in said township, six acres of land on the Neck plain so called, the South Purchase, half a Purchase Right in the old township, the division of land called the Rumford division, the meadow and upland at the Neck, three acres of swamp at Pale Brook and the part of the Cedar Swamp bought of John Thresher, also what is to be divided between him and his brother John as abovesaid, and £7..16..8 out of the moveables, he to pay his Grandmother Williams 3 shillings 4 pence per annum during her life. To Elizabeth the only daughter of said deceased £60.:10 in money at the time of her marriage or when she comes to eighteen years of age. Dated July 25, 1698, signed by the five above named commissioners and witnessed by Philip

King and John Smith. Said division presented [224] to John Saffin Judge of Probate by Thomas Leonard Esqr one of the above subscribers and allowed by said Judge Oct. 11, 1698. John Cary Regist^{r} Entered Oct. 14, 1698 by John Cary Regist^{r}.

Inventory of the estate of Samuel Smith of Taunton dec'd taken Aug. 25, 1698 by Robert Crosman and Richard Stevens and sworn to by his son Samuel Smith of Taunton at Bristol, Oct. 13, 1698 before John Saffin Proba^{r}: John Cary Regist^{r} Recorded Oct. 17, 1698 by John Cary Regist^{r}.

"March the tenth 169$\frac{8}{9}$ Then brought in & prefented to the Judg John Saffin Efq^{r}. by Jofeph willbore one of the Exe^{rs} to the laft will & teftam^{t} of his ffather Shadrach wilbore thefe perticulars following Omitted & not put into the Inventory which is Entered in y^{e} 215 page of this Book", amounting to £4..11..06, which were prized in 1698 by Henry Hodges and Stephen Marick. Dec. 9, 1701, Joseph Willbore, executor, brought in these particulars to be added to his late father's inventory, viz: "A Debt oweing from Captain Negus"; "more from John Dean Junr:" Total amount of above, £5..19..00.

[225] An account of the funeral charges and debts paid "Due from the Eftate of Thomas Brentnall Deceafed 1692, giuen in this 27th: of December 1695 by Samuel Brentnall and Nathaniel Brentnall fonnes to the Deceafed, & Bondsmen with their Mother Eafter Brentnall is as followeth". Items: "for the goeing to John Richmond & the Staying for the writting of a Deed 3 dayes man & Horfs"; "To Cafh payd John Richmond for to Signe faid Deed"; Paid Steven Arnold, Leu^{t} Preferued Abell, Robert Avery of Dedham, "John Ware of Wrenham Senr:", Samuel Brentnall, "Thomancheft^{r}", Thomas Read, Wm Carpenter Senr, John Willmath, Will: Carpent^{r}. Junr, Ric^{d}: George, William Ireland.
This account was given into the Register's office at Bristol by Samuel Brentnall and Nathaniel Brentnall sons of said dec'd, and sworn to by them as a true account to their certain knowledge particularly acted by each of them except the payments to Preserved Abell, William Carpenter Jr. and William Ireland, "which they are informed was Tranfacted by their faid mother", before Jno Saffin Proba^{r}: John Cary Reg^{r}: Dec. 27, 1695. On Sept. 10, 1697 the within named Hester Brentnall made oath to the truth of above account before John Saffin Proba^{r}: John Cary Reg^{r}: The inventory of the estate of Thomas Brentnall late of Taunton dec'd given by the administratrix Hester Brentnall did amount to £126..15..02. Entered Oct. 1, 1697 by John Cary Regist^{r}:

[226] "Bofton february the 5th: 1701 Receiued of m^{rs}. Eafter Smith Adminiftratrix to her Hufband Thomas Brentnall of Wading Riuer Receiued of m^{r} Samuel Brentner the fum of three pounds fix fhillings of m^{r} Samuel Brentner by her order & is in full of all acc^{ts}. whatfoeuer for the Acc^{t} of m^{r} John Jolliff dec^{d} I fay Receiued by me Jarvis Ballard Executor to m^{r} John Jolliff". Signed Jarvis Ballard.

[227–229 blank]

[230] I John Saffin of Bristol "Out of meer loue to & for the Incoragment of my Negro man Adam to goe on Chearfully in his Bufines and Imployment by me Now put into the Coftadie Seruis and Command of

Thomas Sheapard my tennant on Bound feild farme in Briftoll Aforefaid for and Dureing the tearm of Seauen years from the Twenty fifth Day of march laft paft 1694". At the close of that time I do "Enfranchife, Clear and mak free my faid Negro man Named Adam to be fully at his own Difpofe and Liberty as other freemen are or ought to be * * Always Prouided that the faid Adam my fervant Doe in the mean time goe on Cherfully Quiettly and Indufterouf ly in the Lawfull bufinefs that Either my felf or my afsignes fhall from time to time Reafonably fett him about or Imploy him in and Doe behaue & abare himfelf as an honeft true & faithfull Saruant ought to Doe Dureing the terme of feuen years as aforefaid". Witnessed by Rachell × Brown, Richard Smith and Samuel Galop. Entered Nov. 15, 1694 by John Cary Record[r]

[End of Volume I]

CHATHAM, MASS., GRAVESTONE INSCRIPTIONS.—In a field northwest of the Old Burying Ground, and northwest of the house late of Samuel Clifford, and south of the road that leads from the late Stephen Smith's to East Harwich, just west of an old fence, are a number of graves, probably eight in all, of which four have headstones, the inscriptions on which are here given in their order from south to north; the fourth headstone being separated by a considerable interval from the other three:

"Here lies buried Mrs. Bershebe Smith widow of Mr. Stephen Smith who Dec[d] in Ye 57th year of her age with the small pox. She Dec[d] Jany. ye 16th 1766.

Here Lies buried Mr. Stephen Smith A Deacon who Dec[d] Jany. ye 13th 1766 in ye 60th year of his age with the small pox.

Here Lies buried Mr. Stephen Rider Dec[d] Jany. ye 18th 1766 in ye 49th year of his age with the Small pox."

The following inscription is from the separated stone, in a field belonging to the late Rufus Smith, north of the above graves and of the road last mentioned:

"Here Lies buried Mr. Paul Crowell son to Deacon Paul Crowell & Mrs. Rebecca his Wife who Dec[d] with the Small pox Nov[r] ye 23rd 1765. in ye 21st year of his age.

At the foot of this grave Lyes 2 Infant Children Dec[d] December ye 12th 1766."

On a hill in Chathamport,* east of the late Rufus Smith's and south of the late Christopher Ryder's, are three headstones among graves of the Ryder family with whom the small pox epidemic of 1766 is said to have originated, of which the following are not complete literal transcripts, but are correct copies of names, dates and ages:

"Zenas Rider died with the smallpox Jan. 1766 in his 4[*illegible*]* th year.

Elizabeth, wife of Zenas Rider, died with the smallpox Jan. 1766 in her 39th year.

John Rider died Jan. 10, 1766, with the smalpox in his 76th year."

South of the West Chatham school house, by the side of two rocks on land now belonging to Richard Young (deceased's grandnephew) and close to the fence that separates that land from land on the east now belonging to Sparrow Harding, is the following stone which is broken and has fallen down, but the inscription is legible:

"Mr. Richard Young† he died July ye 29 1798 in his 23[d] year."

* Josiah Paine, Esq., of Harwich, informs me that his notes of a visit to this hill some fifty years ago show a stone then standing to Ebenezer Eldredge, who died Feb. 25, 1797, aged 90 years; and also one to Ebenezer's wife Deliverance (Nickerson) Eldredge, but he has no note of the inscription on this one.

Zenas Rider he says died in his fortieth year.

† The family tradition is that he died of smallpox, and the character of the burial place confirms it.

North of the late Samuel Clifford's, on the east side of the road that leads to the late Rufus Smith's, is part of a stone:

"[Ebenezer Paine, who died Jan. 22, 1766,]* in the 38th year of his age."

South of the road, a little west of the South Chatham depot, is one inscribed:

"Abigail, wife of David Eldredge, died Dec. 5, 1849, æ. 51 years.
David Eldredge died Aug. 8, 1845, æ. 61 years."

35 Nassau St., New York City. JAMES W. HAWES.

DEATHS IN CHATHAM, MASS.—Among some 100 MSS. sermons that I own of the late Rev. John Adams Vinton, D.D., the well-known genealogist, I found the enclosed MS., which may be of some interest to the readers of the REGISTER.

A Bill of mortality in the Town of Chatham AD 1836
march 16th miss Patia Basset
march 19th A Child of David Howes
April 1st the Wife of mr Benson mayo
April 1st mr Joshua N Ryder
april 19th mr Sylvanus mayo
april 22d mr Mulford Hamilton
may 4th a Child of Christopher Taylor
may 19th mr Isaiah Nye
July 12th a Child of David Howes
July 13th a Child of James Oldson
July 14th David G Atwood Drowned July 17th. mr David Ryder on Grand Bank
July 16th miss Ann Nickerson
August 12th the wife of mr Isaiah Harding. Henry Sudan
Septemr 4th the Wife of mr Joseph Taylor
September 5th a Child of mr John Emery
Septr 12th a Child of Capt Elisha Small. Sept 12th a Child of Samll Anable Jur
Septr 19th the wife of Samuel Anable Jur
Septr 19th a Child of Joshua Eldredge
Septemr 26th the wife of mr Paul Hamilton
October 5th a Child of David Howes
Octr 19th mrs Keziah Nye
Octr 12th Basset Gill and Ethan Gould. Vessel Sunk
Octr 19th a Child of mr Isaac Hardy Jur
Octr 21st a Child of Samuel C Howes
November 8th a Child Capt Joseph Reed
Novr 12th the wife of mr Charles Higgens
December 21st Widow Tamzin Harding 30 Deaths

103 Hammond St., Cambridge, Mass. WILLIAM L. PALMER.

CHATHAM, MASS., GRAVESTONE INSCRIPTIONS (*ante*, page 203).—Between the* record of Stephen Smith and that of Stephen Rider should be inserted the following:

"Here Lies buried Mrs. Mercy Doane the wife of Mr. Joseph Doane Jur She Decd with the Small pox Jany. ye 16th 1766. in ye 23rd year of her age."

And in the line following the record of Mr. Stephen Rider, the words "from the separated stone" should read "from a stone."

New York City. JAMES W. HAWES.

*p. 93, this volume.

DIARY OF REV. WILLIAM HOMES OF CHILMARK, MARTHA'S VINEYARD, 1689–1746.

Contributed by Dr. CHARLES EDWARD BANKS, U. S. Marine Hospital Service, Portland, Me.

IN the library of the Maine Historical Society there is a manuscript volume of 96 pp., of the size known as quarto, bound in contemporary leather and containing the notes of births, marriages, deaths, and important events occurring within the personal knowledge of the diarist. It is closely written from cover to cover, even the fly leaves and insides of the covers being utilized by the original owner or its subsequent possessors. It is the diary or note book of the Reverend William Homes, a native of the North of Ireland,* sometime pastor of Strabane, and from 1715 to his death the settled minister of Chilmark on Martha's Vineyard. Mr. Homes was born in 1663, and when a young man came to the Vineyard where he taught school for three years, 1686–9.—(Allen, Biographical Dictionary, 463). He returned to Ireland, where in 1692 he was ordained over the parish of Strabane, and next year, September 26,

* His father was buried at Donachmore, according to the Diary, which may give a clue to the origin of the family.

1693, he married Katherine, daughter of Reverend Robert Craghead of Londonderry. The first child of this marriage was born in Stragolun, and the others in Strabane. He continued as pastor of this church till 1714–5, when with his wife and nine children he crossed the ocean and made his future home in Chilmark, where he was ordained pastor September 15, 1715. He kept this relationship to the day of his death, June 20, 1746, a period of over thirty years. He published several sermons and religious works.

The greater portion of the diary is made up of weekly entries dated "Lord's day," detailing his texts and sermon, of which the following is a sample of the whole:

xber 7 1718 being Lords day I preached before noon from 1 pet 24 to whom coming as unto a living stone and after sermon administered the sacrament of the Lords supper afternoon I preached from Col: 1. 13. Who hath delivered us from the power of darkness in all which I hope I was assisted the Lord follow my poor labours with a rich blessing to edification and salvation of souls.

These weekly entries are usually followed by some note of a death, "remarkable providence," birth, baptism, admission to church membership, state of weather or such kindred items. The first few leaves of the book contain his family record, sons, daughters and grandchildren, with a list of marriages and deaths in the town of Chilmark during his residence. These entries I have transcribed and they follow this introduction:

Mr John Mayhew of Chilmark died feb^{r} 3^{d} 168$\frac{8}{9}$ about two of the clock in the morning: and was buryed feb^{r} 4th His distemper was a pain in the stomacke, shortness of breath and a faintness his distemper continued from the last of september till the time abovesaid.

Mr Rich: Airy of Edgartown departed this life feb^{r} 14th 168$\frac{8}{9}$ about 10 before noon. His distemper was a violent pain in his small gutts attended with a continual vomiting. By the application of fried oats &c The pain removed from his Body to his stomacke: no means that were made use of for his recovery proved useful to him. He was burryed the fifteenth day about two afternoon.

The truly virtuous gentlewoman Mrs Mary Mayhew Spouse to the Honoured Matthew Mayhew Esqr of Edgartstown, departed this life May 1st 1690 about 9 at night. Her distemper was a Milignant fever. It continued from the 29th day of April in the morning till the time of her Comfortable departure. She was burryed the next day towards night.

My brother John Homes was killed by Thunder and lightening in the Parishe of Raphe, Maij 20th 1692 about two afternoon. He was burryed next day toward night in his fathers grave in the Churchyard of Donachmore, he left behind him five children, viz: Margaret, John, Johnet, Jane and Rebecca.

Mr William Homes [the diarist] and Katheren Craghead were Marryed September 26th 1693 by the Revd Mr Robert Craghead of Londonderry in his own house about 8 at night in the presence of Mr Thomas Craghead, Mr James Hamilton, John Wilson, James Smith and his spouse, and those of Mr Cragheads own family. It was upon Tuesday.

My son Robert Homes was born July the 23^{d} 1694 being Munday at 12 of the clock in the day time. In Stragolan and was baptized the Wednesday following in my own house by m^{r} Robert Craghead his grandfather.

My Daughter Margaret was born Feb^{r} 28 $169\frac{5}{6}$ being friday at 11 before noon And was baptized the 5 of march following in the meeting house of Straban, by the Revd Mr Sam: Hallyday.

My Son William was born March 24th $169\frac{6}{7}$ being Wednesday about one of the clock in the Morning. He was baptized in the meeting house of Straban March 31st 1697 By the Revd James Pringle.

My Daughter Katherin was born March 20th $169\frac{8}{9}$ being Munday about three in the morning And was baptized by the Revd Mr Thomas Craghead in the meeting house of Straban March 22^{d} being Wednesday

My Son William departed this life feb^{r} 18, 1699 alias 1700 about 1 morning he sickened the 7th Day of ^{sd} moneth on the Saturday following we perceived severale purple spots upon him, on the Thursday following he bleed excessively at the nose from 9 night till near 12. By the application of the Joyce of Nettles his bleeding stoped, the Thursday following his feet began to swell and on friday his whole body. His heat was excessively great from frieday till the time of his death during which time he continued speechless. He was burryed the 19 of feb^{r} towards night in the church yeard of Straban.

My Son John was born July 30 1700 being Tuesday about 7 morning. He was baptized in the meeting house of Straban July 31st by the Rev^{d} m^{r} Sam: Hallyday.

My Daughter Jane was born Aughst 30 1701 being Saturday about 11 night. She was baptized in the meeting house of Straban September 3^{d} by the Rev^{d} m^{r} William Homes of Urney.

My Daughter Agnes was born May 31 1704 being Wednesday at 4 morning she was baptized in the meeting house of Straban by the Rev^{d} m^{r} William Homes of Urney.

My Daughter Elizabeth was born September 15th 1706 about 8 night she was baptized in the meeting house of Straban by the Rev^{d} mr William Homes of Urney.

My Daughter Hanna was born Jany 31. $170\frac{8}{9}$ about 2 morning being munday. She was baptized the frieday following in the meeting house of Straban By the Rev^{d} m^{r} Thomas Craghead.

My Daughter Margery was born Jany 23^{d} $17\frac{10}{11}$ at 1 morning. She was baptized the Thursday following in my own house by the Rev^{d} m^{r} Thomas Craghead. She was born on the Lords day.

My Sister Maryan departed this life feb^{r} 24th 1705 being Lords day about 5 morning. Her distemper was a pain in her body and stomake attended with frequent vomiting.

My Son Robert was Marryed in Boston to m^{rs} Mary Franklin April 3^{d} 1716 at 9 at night by the Rev^{d} m^{r} Eben^{r} Pemberton.

My Grand Son William Homes was born Jany 10 $17\frac{16}{17}$ at 2 afternoon. He was baptized in the old north church by Dr Increase Mather the 13th day of the same month.

Mr John Allen and my Daughter Margaret Homes were marryed March the 1° $17\frac{15}{16}$ I Joyned them in marreage.

My grand Daughter Katherin and Rebeccah Allen were born feb^{r} 26 $17\frac{16}{17}$ And were baptized march . . . . following.

My great grand daughter Susanna Allen was born November 5 about noon Anno 1738.

My grandson William Dagget was born 9ber 18 1738 about 3 afternoon was baptized the next day.

My grand son Eleazer Allen was born June 10 1739 at 6 in the morning being the Lords day.

My grand daughter Katherin Smith departed this life August 4: 1740 being munday about 6 afternoon. She was when she died 15 years of age and 3 months wanting two days; the distemper that was the occasion of her death was y^{t} called the throat distemper. In her last sickness she gave evidences of a pious disposition.

My great grand daughter Susan Allen departed this life July 1 1740 being about a year and 8 months old.

My son in law Joshua Allen departed this life May 30 1730 he died in Nutfield of the small pox, he sickened the 12 day and died ye 30th in his last sickness he expressed himselfe very christianly and as one that had good hope thro grace as I am informed. I forgot to insert this in its proper place.

My grandson William Dagget departed this life 7ber 14 1740 being Lords day he was when he died two years old wanting two months and 4 days.

My grandson Eleazer Allen departed this life 8ber 2 1740 at 5 morning being one year old and four months wanting 8 days.

My grandson Timothy Dagget was born Jany 31 $174\frac{0}{1}$.

My grand son $Will^{m}$ Homes had a daughter born March 5 $174\frac{0}{1}$ called Ma[ry?].

My great grand son Nathan Mayhew was born May 18. 1741 about sun rising being Munday.

My grand daughter Katherin Moor departed this life June 6 about 5 afternoon she died of an Epileptick fit she was born feb 26 $171\frac{6}{7}$ She was when she died 24 years 3 months and near 8 days.

My grand daughter Hanna Allen was born July 23^{d} about 5 in y^{e} morning 1741 she departed this life August 30 about 7 at night being 38 days old.

My grand son Timothy Dagget departed this life Feb^{ry} 3 $174\frac{1}{2}$ he was when he died a year and two days old.

My great grandson John Wass died Jany 10 1744 at 10 night.

My grand daughter mary Peckham departed this life 7ber 1 1745, was born 7ber $172\frac{4}{5}$.

An Account of y^{e} persons I Married since my Setlement in Chilmark which was 7ber 15 1715 and some others.

John Allen and Margaret Homes were Married March 1° $17\frac{15}{16}$
Benjamin Smith & Mary Basset were Married 9ber 28 1716
Solomon Atheaon & Sarah Skiffe were Married July 24 1717
William Hunt & Jane Tilton were Married June 2 1718
Jethro Athearn & Mary Mayhew were Married 7ber 8 1720
$Capt^{n}$ Samuel Smith & Kathren Homes were Married May 30 1721
Thomas Smith & Elisabeth Basset were Marred 9ber 9 1721
Nicolas Nickerson & Deborah Chipman were Married May 2 1722
Benjamin Skiffe & Abigail Peese were Married 7ber 13 1722
Jonathan Hilman & Bethiah lovel were Married Feb^{r} 5 $172\frac{2}{3}$
Shubal Smith Junr & Martha Mayhew were Married Jany 23 $172\frac{3}{4}$

Pain Mayhew and Dina Norton were marryed
xber 5° by Captn Mayhew 1724

Elisha Elisha [*sic*] & Mary Steel were marryed Jany 7 $172\frac{4}{5}$

Silvanus Allen & Jane Homes were marryed July 1° 1725

Mr Barnabas Taylor and Martha allen were married 9ber 4 1725

Thomas Tilton and Jemimah Mayhew were married xber 9 1725

Joshua Allen and Agnes Homes were Married xber 14th 1725

Elnathan Wing and Hanna Allen were maryed 8ber 7th 1726

John Mills and Bathsheba Allen were Married 8ber 31st 1726

Thoma McGee and Mary Blaire were Married 8ber 10th 1726

Abishar Folger & Sarah Mayhew were Married 9ber 8 1727

Prince Coffine and Marey Skiffe were married 9ber 10 1727

John Sturges and Abigail Allen were Married 7ber 5 1728

Beriah Tilton and Mary Mayhew were married xber 12 1728

Eliashib Adams and Reliance Mayhew were married feb 15 $172\frac{8}{9}$

Jonathan Lock and Mary Norton were Married Jany 1° $17\frac{29}{30}$

Benjamin Allen and Abia Mahew were maried Jany 8 $17\frac{29}{30}$

Ja: Hutchison and Elizabeth Homes were Married Feb 5 $17\frac{29}{30}$
They were married in Boston by m^{r} Prince

Matthias Roggers and Sarah Hilman were Married 8ber 28 1730

Ebenezer Tisdale and Hope Basset were married 9ber 12 1730

Timothy Mayhew & Abia Mayhew were married Jany 14 $17\frac{30}{31}$

Captn John Gould and Sarah Clarke were married June 18 1731

Jacob Norton & Bethiah Mayhew were married Feb^{r} 30 $173\frac{1}{2}$

Thomas Mayhew and Lidia Lothrop were married July 27 1732

Thomas Claghorn of Edgartown and Susanna Gibbs of Chilmark were married November 2 1732

Wilmot Wass and Rebecah Allen were married March 22 $173\frac{2}{3}$

Jonathan Allen and Abigail Mayhew were married 9ber 16 1733

Doctor Thomas Little and Lucy Mayhew were married November 13 1733

Benjamin Dagget and Margery Homes were Married June 11 1734

John Thatcher and Content Norton were Married 9ber 28 1734

Benjamin Lumbert & Bathsheba Mayhew were Maried Jany 16 $173\frac{4}{5}$

Thomas Sturges & Rebeccah Norton were Married Feby 27 $173\frac{4}{5}$

John Basset and Jane Mayhew were married July 31 1735

Thomas Hamilton and Jane McClean were married 8ber 16 1735

Zephaniah Mayhew and Hannah Mayhew were married 8ber 23 1735

Dick and Mereah Negroes belonging to Sam Norton Esq^{ur} were married Feby 27 $173\frac{5}{6}$

Moses Belcher Junr and Eunice Mayhew were married March 15 $173\frac{5}{6}$

Jethro Allen and Dinah Mayhew were married March 25 1736

Matthias King and Mary Lock were married 8ber 28 1736

Joseph Tilton and Ruth Mayhew were married 9ber 4 1736

William Allen and Sarah Mayhew were married 9ber 3 1737

Joseph Hilman and Kezia Norton were married 9ber 24 1737

Beriah Tilton and Jedidah Mayhew were Married March 16 $173\frac{7}{8}$

Captn David Moor & Kathren Allen were married August 3 1738

Zachariah Mayhew & Elizabeth Allen were married 9ber 21 1738

John Peese and Abigail Burgess were married May 24 1739

Samuel Mayhew and Lois Norton were married xber 27 1739

Handly Chipman and Jane Allen were married April 24 1740

Stephen Skiffe and Bathshebah Tilton were married Augst 26 1742

Mr Bosworth and Eliz Mayhew were Married Augst 15 1745

A list of ye grown persons that have died in this town since I came to it.

1715 July 21 died Thomas Mathew Esqu^{r}

1716 8ber 13 It is supposed that Isaac Chase died at sea in a violent storm

1717 8ber 8 An Indian belonging to John Allen Esqu^{r} called Andrew was killed by the cart coming from Holmes Hole

1717 Augs^{t} 30 Mr Ben Mayhew departed this life

$171\frac{7}{8}$ Feb 17 Ben Skiffe Esqu^{r} departed this life

1618 June 7 Mrs Abigail Smith died

1718 August John McClelland was Drowned at Sandy point

1720 Ap 11 Old m^{r} Tilton died

1720 May 7 Mrs Hunt Senr died

$172\frac{1}{2}$ Feb^{r} 23 Sam Tilton Junr died

$172\frac{1}{2}$ Feb 25 Moses Allen died

$172\frac{1}{2}$ March 2 Mrs Mayhew spouse to m^{r} Experience Mayhew died

$172\frac{1}{2}$ March 15 Shubel Cotle died

1722 May 20 Mrs Mary Allen departed this life

1722 Augst 7 Mrs Allen Senr died

1722 7ber 20 James Steel was drowned at Cancer

1723 Augst Andrew [. . .]ton was drowned at Canser

1723 8ber 27 Thomas Blair died

$172\frac{3}{4}$ Feb^{r} 14 Ja. Allen died

1724 June 6 James Skiffe died

1724 June 19 Mrs Skiffe spouse to Nathan Skiffe died

$172\frac{5}{6}$ Jany 29 Mrs Chipman died

$172\frac{5}{6}$ Feby 9 Mr Nathan Skiffe died

1726 May 2 Susanna Blair was drowned in one of the tan pitts

$172\frac{6}{7}$ Jany 9 Mr Hunt Senr died

1727 June 11 Sam Hilman died

1727 June 21 Bertha and Mary Hilman died

1727 8ber 9 Sam Merry died

$172\frac{7}{8}$ March 6 John Mills and John Skiffe died

1728 March 28 John Clifford died

1728 Apr. 16 Jo Hilman Junr died

1728 April 28 Daniel Luke died

1729 July 16 Mrs Allen spouse to Ichabod Allen died

$17\frac{29}{30}$ Jany 8 Mrs Reliance Adams

1730 August 19 Mrs Jedidah Little died

1731 9ber 29 m^{r} Samuel Tilton Senr died in the 94 year of his age

1731 July 12 Pain Mayhew Junr was drowned his corps came on shore at gay head July 22

1732 October 19 Jane Hunt died

1732 October 20 Captn Tho Butler died

$173\frac{2}{3}$ Jany 29 Eliz: Merry died

1733 May 24 Eben Allen Esqu^{r} died

1733 8ber 14 m^{r} Nathan Mayhew died aged 21 years

1733 9ber 20 Zeph. Mayhew died

1733 9ber 27 Jonathan Allen died in y^{e} 21 year of his age

1734 Apr 24 Mr Shubael Smith Senr died aged 81

Sarah Folger of Nantucket, daughter to Major Pain Mayhew of Chilmark and wife of Abigail Folger departed this life July 13. 1734 about 12 in the day time aged about 25 years she left behind her 4 children and had been married 7 years lacking 2 months 26 days

1734 December 30 about 11 before noon died Elijah Mayhew Taylor aged about

$173\frac{4}{5}$ Feb^{r} 22 died Mrs Bethiah Clark being about fifty years of age she was a church member and daughter to Major Mayhew

1735 May 5 in the morning died Daniel Butler of Chekomy of a fluxus hepaticus, he seemed to be religiously inclined

1735 Mr Eleazer Allen departed this life 9ber 7 about 6 in the morning in the 30th year of his life he was high sherife when he died

$173\frac{5}{6}$ John Mayhew Senr departed this life March 3^{d} in the morning in y^{e} 60 year of his age was buried the next day

$173\frac{8}{9}$ Samuel Hatch departed this life Jan^{r} 13 in the morning his distemper was a high fever he was much out of his head in his ilness

$173\frac{8}{9}$ Mrs Abigail Skiff departed this life March 4 in the morning of a consumption. She gave evidence of a gracious disposition in her sickness. She had been for some time a member of this church

1739 Mrs Content Norton spouse to Sam Norton Esqr died Aug 1 about 7 in y^{e} 63 year of her age

Susanna Allen daughter to William Allen departed this life July the first 1740 a child of about a year and eight months old

Abigail Hilman departed this life July 2 in the morning 1740 she was daughter to Richard Hilman. a young woman going on the 16 year of her age

Ruth Tilton Wife to Joseph Tilton and m^{r} Ben: Mayhews daughter departed this life December 5 about 2 in the morning

Mrs Sarah Mayhew formerly wife to Thomas Mayhew Esqr of Chilmark departed this life December 30, in the night, she was very ancient being some years above ninety—as I am informed. She was in 96 year when she died. She was a gentlewoman of meeke and quiet spirit, and very inoffensive in her deportment. She was a member of the church in this place and behaved her selfe as becomes the gospel, her memory failed her greatly for several years before she died.

1743 Rich. Hilman departed this life suddenly March 26. He was agreable and industrious in life wel stricken in years being some moneths above 63

1743 Jethro Norton departed this life May 12 about 3 after noon He had been long in a bad state of health, being consumptive, he was never married. He was when he died about 32 years of age

1742 The night between ye 22 and 23 of June Sarah Tilton daughter to William Tilton departed this life

1743 9ber 8 about 6 in the morning Mrs Mary Basset spouse to m^{r} Nathan Basset departed this life in the 71 year of her age. She was a peacable, industrious and pious woman.

1743 9ber 16 about 7 afternoon Nathan Basset departed this life in the 77 y^{r} of his age he had been long afflicted with a palsie he was one that feared God and was peaceable and industrious

Dr Thomas Little departed this life March 30 1744 before noon His distemper was a fever that prevailed in the town

Ben Hilman departed this life April 22 1745 towards the evening

May 26 1745 Thomas Mayhew son to Zachary Mayhew Esqr departed this life about 9 afternoon he was about twenty when he died

Elisha Elisha [*sic*] and his daughter Abia were drowned in the pond May 12 1746 She about 9 years of age when she died and he about 40

[Mr. Homes died June 20, 1746, about six weeks after the last entry above given.—C. E. B.]

DIARY OF REV. WILLIAM HOMES OF CHILMARK, MARTHA'S VINEYARD, 1689–1746.

II.

Contributed by Dr. CHARLES EDWARD BANKS, U. S. Marine Hospital Service, Portland, Me.

IN a previous issue of the REGISTER (xlviii., 446), may be found* a transcript of some entries found in the diary of Rev. William Homes, contributed by myself, and I have extracted these which follow from the body of the book, as previously described. They were all which I found to be of a general interest, and were interspersed among the usual entries of his texts, sermons and religious reflections.

On the twenty first of July Anno 1715 being Thursday about two of the clock in the morning Thomas Mayhew Esqu[r] of Chilmarke departed this life he had been for several yeares troubled with the distemper called the kings evil by which he was brought neere the gates of Death but by some applications made to him by an Indian doctor he recovered so far that he was able to rid about and look after his affairs, but in the latter end of the spring or begining of summer this year he was suddenly taken with a stopag

*p. 95, this volume.

of his urine and a violent pain in his right leg, after some time his left leg swelled pretty much yet the paine continued in the other leg, by the use of means the stopag of his urine was removed, yet the other symptoms continued. After some time there came a doctor to the Island that thought the swelling and pain in his legs might be removed by bathing and sweathing, which preceded accordingly in some measure, but after some time the swelling proceeded upwardly and he was siesed with an inwerd fever and shortness of breth which prevaild upon him till it carried him off. His nostril and throat grew so sore some days before he died that he could not speak so as to be understood, he was a man of good sense considering his education and seemed to be piously inclined tho he did entertain some singulare opinions in religion.

On the fifteenth of 7ber [1715] I was installed in the pastorate office in the congregation of Chilmarke there were then but two members of that church that wer men, viz Nathan Skiffe and Benjamin Mayhew that day Mr Experience Mayhew who was formerly a member of the Indian church upon this Island having obtained his dismission from thence was joyned to this church. On the second of October Mr Nathan Basset & M^r^ Ja: Allen were added to ye church here and were both baptized that day.

On the 9th of 8ber 1715 were baptized six of m^r^ James Allen his children viz Silvanus, Bathshebah, Joshua, Mary, Unice & Timothy Allen

On the 22d of Augst old stile or the first of september new stile anno 1715 about 8 in ye morning died the French king Lewis the 14th at versailes.

In March 25th 1716 m^r^ Symon Mayhew was added to the church here and he and two of his children were baptized the following Lords day

8ber ye 13th 1716. [a violent storm of wind and rain described] Isaac Chase was lost this day being in a sloop was cast away.

November ye 15. 1716 [another storm described].

November the 29th 1716 there were several whale boats belonging to Bilingsgate had been at permet upon a whaleing designe the s^d^ day they set all out with a designe to return Home but after they had rowed a little way they were discouraged finding the wind very high so that they all returned to permet shore except one boat only this boat held on its way having the wind faire, when they came to Bilingsgate shore there were but three men in the boat of which one was dead the othere two at the point of death: and died very soon after they were brought on shore the boat was let so full of watter, they had neither oar nor craft on board they were full manned when they went from Permet and had their oars and craft compleat.

February the 18 [1716–17]. A violent storm of snow and sleet is described, lasting several days, during which "many sheep were burryed under this snow"

On the 22 [of March] I found some sheep that had been burried under the snow that fell Feb 21 one of wch was still alive. She was taken out the 23d of March alive and continued to live for severall days she had continued under the snow without any food about 31 days. This storm did much damage in the country the snow was said to be in the woods where it did not drive about 3 feet and a halfe deep generally on the maine land

July 13. 1717 Mr Ben: Mayhew set out for Rod Island about 3 or 4 of the clock afternoon in a whalle boat in company of one Indian man one boy and two squaws he was then and had been for a long time much indisposed and went that he might be near his doctor.

July 22 I joyned Solomon Athearn and Sarah Skiffe in marriage. We had pretty much rain this weeke we began to reap our barly on Thursday the 25th day.

Aug[st] 8th 1717

Mr John Allen sent his Indian boy called Andrew with his cart to bring up some goods from Holmes hole (wch he had from Boston) in company with several othere carts, and went himselfe to see the cart loaded, and after all the carts were loaded and sent off the gentlemen to whom they did belong tarryed behind, for some time and then took their horses to return home. Cap[tn] Mayhew rid foremost and when he came near Newtown he perceived m[r] John Allens boy lying in the path, and when he came near to him he found him dead; it seems he had fallen before the wheels and could not recover himselfe till the cart went over him. they found that the wheel had gone over the hinder part of his head, had broken his skull and pressed his face in the ground. he had bled very much. it is supposed that he was Drunk for he had a gimblet in his pocket wherewith he had mad a hole in a barrel of roome that was in the cart and had put a pine in it. He was a young man much given to drunkenness and stealing and seemed to have little or no regard for religion.

Friday the 9th of August mr Ben: Mayhew returned home from Rod Island and supposed himselfe much better than when he went abroad in severall respects: on the Lords day following he attended the publick worship of God in the forenoon but could not stay till afternoon exercise; he looked very pale and seemed to be under much bodyly indisposition.

1717 I was Informed that July 31 one Deacon Wadsworth of Milton brother to Rev[d] Ben: Wadsworth Pastour of the old Church in Boston went out that morning with a designe to rake together some Hay, and that some time after he was found lying upon his back with the racke cross his breast stone dead. this man was esteemed truely pious.

Augst 18th; pain Mayhew Esq[ur] and his wife were taken into the fellowship of the church and were both baptized this afternoon and Jane Homes was propounded

August 30th; I attended the funerall of m[r] Ben: Mayhew he was a man of much straightness, of a generous temper and of a cheerful disposition. He fell under an Ill habit of body, above a year agone and dayly declined to the last. he had the advice of Doctor Talmond who was of oppinion that he might recover, and by the medecine he gave him he seemed to recover a little, but after some time his distempers recurred and indeed many of the most dangerous symptoms did abate as his great shortness of breath and spiting of blood &c yet he continued under a habituall fever and a bad concoction, with great restlessness. Some time agoe he went to Rod Island and continued with his doctor several days, when he returned home he seemed to be much revived. * * * * * * * He left five children behind him a pretty handsome estate he died much lamented and finished well He was born September 11th 1679 He died aged 38 years wanting 12 days.

September 20th. 1717 Brother Craghead came to the Island but brought no news only told us his Children are [illegible]. he stayed here till Tuesday on the lords day he preached both before and after noon. he spoke also of going to Barmudas but with what view I know not our converse was free without any heat or misunderstanding; we settled accounts between us.

September 29th 1717 One Mr Walter Stewart came here Saturday about three afternoon to see me and stayed till nine this morning and then went to the ship to which he belonged which lay at Homes hole bound for Virginia

November 3^{d} 1717 John McClellan and James Jamison came to my house. Mr Bethiah Mayhew spouse to Mr Zephaniah Mayhew was received into the communion of the church this Lords day

9ber 9 This day I was Informed that Captn Belcher of Boston merchant died lately and Captn Sewalls lady not long before and that it is a very sickly time in Boston.

9ber 10 1717 Mrs Reliance Mayhew was received in to the communion

9ber 15th 1717 this day being Friday I was informed that one Samuel Dagget servant and relation to Captain Smith a youth being in perfect health on Thursday morning and died the next day before noon. I was likewise informed that majo^{r} general Winthrop Doctor Cutler, one m^{r} fiske Captn Sendall all of Boston died lately of the same distemper and that the season continues sickly there.

November 17. I was informed that m^{rs} Thatcher who formerly lived in this town is dead.

November 24. 1717 John Mayhew was received into the Church and baptized This day I received several letters twofrom Doctor Cotton Mather one from severall gentlemen proprietors of lands at or near to Casco Bay.

December 1. 1717. Mr Zephania Mayhew was propounded to the church

December 8. 1717 William Hunt was propounded to the church

December 22^{d} 1717 Mr Zephania Mayhew was received into the communion of the church and he and all his chlldren were Baptized her children were Abiah, Zephaniah and Jerusha

February 2^{d} 17$\frac{17}{18}$ Mr Ichabod Allen was taken off from attending the publike worship in burying one of his children viz the youngest being a twine the othere was buried last weeke I observed that m^{r} Smith and his wife were very melancholy this day they had heard on Friday last of the death of one of their daughters who died Thursday was Sevennight being the 23^{d} day of Jany in the evening

Feb^{r} 16th 17$\frac{17}{18}$ I heard last night that two persons died at old Town last weeke viz Matt: Pease and Thomas Traps wife the one viz the first of a Malignant fever the other of an Astma

Feb^{r} 17th 17$\frac{17}{18}$ This day between 9 and 10 In the morning Maj^{r} Benjamin Skiffe of Chilmarke Esqr departed this life. He was a man of about 63 years of age of good sense considering his education, straight and upright in his dealings. He was Majo^{r} of the militia of the county, Judge of Probate, Judge of the Common please, Justice of the peace, and representative for the whole Island in the great and generall court when he died.

March 2^{d} 17$\frac{17}{18}$ Mrs Hanna Skiffe was received into the communion of this church and Mrs Abigail Smith was propounded.

March 23. Samuel Hilman was received into the church and Pain Mayhew Esqre his children were Baptized viz Mary Pain Martha Sarah Thomas Bethia and Hanna

May 4. 1718 I was informed that m^{r} Hamlin died yesterday afternoon and is to be buried tomorrow.

DIARY OF REV. WILLIAM HOMES OF CHILMARK, MARTHA'S VINEYARD, 1689–1746.

Contributed by Dr. CHARLES E. BANKS, U. S. Marine Hospital Service, Washington, D. C.

May 18, 1718. * * * After sermon I baptized a child of Mr Experience Mayhew called Zachariah

June 8, 1718. * * * Mrs Abigail Smith departed this life last night about 9 of the clock. She was a peaceable, prudent, pious woman. * * * On Tuesday last in the afternoon she had a fever with a pain in her head, Shortness of breath, with a great defluction yet though she had a small cough she raised nothing. I visited her Friday and Saturday. She seemed to have a good hope and well grounded of her future well being.

June 9, 1718. This day being Munday I attended the funeral of Mrs Abigail Smith, wife of Mr Shubael Smith of Chilmark.

June 15, 1718. Capt Zaccheus Mayhew and his wife were propounded to the church this day

June 29. 1718. * * * After sermon I baptized a child of Mr John Mayhew called Zilpha

July 6. 1718. * * * After sermon we received into the church of Christ Capt Zaccheus Mayhew and his wife.

July 13. 1718. * * * After sermon I baptized Capt Zacheus three children viz: Susanna Lucy and Elizabeth.

August 10. 1718. * * * Mrs Mary Allen was received into the church this day

August 15. 1718. * * * This day about two of the clock after noon several children particularly Ben: Ward and Thomas Allen having got a shot gun and some powder were diverting themselves near John Allen's barn, where were a considerable quantity of English grain and hay, some in the barn and some near it in stacks. Ben: Ward having a brand of fire in his hand, seeing his uncle Captn Mayhew riding by to sermon, threw the brand out of his hands, that his uncle might not see it. It chanced to fall near some English grain, which presently took fire, and consumed the barn and all the English grain to ashes in a very short time. All or most of the men in town presently came with an intent to extinguish the flames, but they did not effect anything.

7ber 7th 1718. * * * I heard some days ago that John McLelland son to James McLelland being engaged in a fishing designe, under took to wade over a creek at Sandy Point where the vessel wherein he was was riding at an anchor, and the day being foggy, he perished in the waters

8ber 19. 1718. On Monday last the house of Mr Zephaniah Mayhew was burnt to the ground by an accidental fire and much of his household stuff and wearing clothes were consumed in the flames. On Thursday James McLelland came here to look after his sons effects and went last week to Nantucket on that designe

9ber 9. 1718. * * * After sermon I baptized two children of Justice Allen, viz: Joseph and Benjamin. They were born on Monday morning at one o'clock

Dec. 16. 1718. This evening about 8 of the clock. Capt Zaccheus Mayhew his barn catched fire. How is not certainly known, and burned down to the ground, together with all his hay, except one load.

Febru. 15. $17\frac{18}{19}$. * * * After sermon Mrs Bethia Clarke was received into the church.

Feb. 22. $17\frac{18}{19}$. * * * Mrs Bethia Clarke was baptized after sermon.

March 1. $17\frac{18}{19}$. * * * Capt Zaccheus Mayhew had a child baptized this day called Sarah

March 15. $17\frac{18}{19}$. * * * Poor Mrs Skiffe is and hath been for several days past in a despairing condition.

March 22. $17\frac{18}{19}$. * * * Afternoon Mr Experience Mayhew preached from Cant. 1. 2. The sermon was well compressed but he was at some loss in reading of it.

Son John came home to see us yesternight

April 12. 17$\frac{18}{19}$. * * * After sermon I baptized a grandson called William Allen.

Apl. 19. 17$\frac{18}{19}$. * * * I baptized a child of Zeph[h] Mayhew called Jedidah.

May 31. 1719. Deacon [James] Skiffe and his daughter were at sermon to day. I mean his daughter [Hannah] Daggett, [wife of Jacob], and another stranger.

June 21. 1719. Mr Experience Mayhew preached afternoon from Cant. 1. 3. The matter of the discourse was not despisable but his delivery was flat and dull.

July 5. 1719. * * * After sermon I baptized William Hunts first born child called Abia

Sept. 11. 1719. Mary Steel had a child baptized called Martha.

9ber. 29. 1719. I baptized a child this day to Simon Mayhew called Simon.

Jany. 10 17$\frac{19}{20}$. The week past hath been very cold especially Thursday last. Mr Bryce Blair by a fall yesterday in the evening broke his left arm above the elbow.

March 13. 17$\frac{19}{20}$. On Wed. last Sam: Barrett was wonderfully saved from drowning, for working upon a whale he was struck overboard by her and fell upon the whale, and his feet were entangled in the warp, so that she carryed him under water, and held him there for some time, but he got himself free from the warp. and some in the boat throwing him an oar he escaped the danger and received no considerable hurt.

April 10. 1720. Old Mrs Tilton was taken ill on Friday morning last with a convulsion of the nerves, and a dead pulse, and on Saturday evening she became speechless, and seems now to be near her end.

April 17. 1720. Mrs Tilton departed this life Munday last about one in the morning. * * * Old Mrs Allen is become very fraile. and is apprehendsive that the time of her departure out of this world draws near.

May 1. 1720. * * * Between Thursday and Friday last week died Matthew Mayhew of Edgartown eldest son of Matthew Mayhew Esq[r] of the same town deceased. A son also of Justice Norton died the same week.

May 8. 1720. * * * Mrs Hunt sen[r] departed this life yesterday about five of the clock afternoon and was burryed this evening.

June 5. 1720. * * * Mrs Jane Hunt was received into the church this day.

July 10. 1720. * * * M[r] Benjamin Smith of Edgartown died last week. He died suddenly July 4. 1720, being a Munday.

7ber 4. 1720. * * * Our house was raised on Tuesday of this week being the 6th day.

7ber 11. 1720. * * * I married Jethro Athearn and Mary Mayhew on Thursday last being y[e] 8th day.

9ber 13. 1720. Capt Mayhew's son Nathaniel died this morning.

Xber 25. 1720. * * * Our people here. some of them, brought a drift whale ashore at Squibnocket on friday and cut her up on Saturday.

July 23. 1721. * * * Justice Allen had a daughter born yesterday about half an hour afternoon and baptized today called Rebekah.

Xber 3. 1721. * * * The small pox I hear prevails at Sandwich.

Xber 10. 1721. Mr Clark had a child baptized today called Mary.

Jan. 26, 17$\frac{21}{22}$. Thomas Chase died friday the 22[d] of December last.

Feby 25. 17$\frac{21}{22}$. On friday morning last died Samuel Tilton son to Will: Tilton, and this morning died Moses Allen, both of this town.

Mch 4. 17$\frac{21}{22}$. On friday last between five and six afternoon died Mrs Mayhew spouse to Mr Experience Mayhew.

March 18. 17$\frac{21}{22}$. * * * I understand that Shubael Cottle of [Cape pogue?] departed this life on thursday night last. He was a young man, son to James Cottle. He died of a distemper that has affiicted several people last winter and this spring, and hath carreed off several persons.

May 27. 1722. Mrs Mary Allen departed this life last Lords day about 7 of the clock afternoon and was buryed the evening of next day. She was a pious virtuous gentlewoman.

July 8. 1722. Poor Mrs Bassett is exceedingly tossed and harassed by grievous temptation, Satan taking advantage of the distemper of her body.

July 15. 1722. Poor Mrs Bassett continues still under great uneasiness by reason of the disquietment of her mind, occasioned by a melancholy which hath prevailed upon her gradually since the beginning of winter.

August 12. 1722. * * * Old Mrs Allen died Tuesday last being the 7th inst about 10 at night.

8ber 28. 1722. I had a letter from son John dated 7ber 29 wherein he writes that on the 20th day of said month James Steel fell overboard and was drowned.

March 31. 1723. * * * I had an account that Mr Newcomb died lately, he was taken suddenly while was in the cellar drawing molasses, either with an apoplectic fit or a lethargy.

April 7. 1723. Mr Little of Old town died lately

April 21. 1723. Mrs Mayhew of old town widow of Matthew Mayhew deceased died on Wednesday last

May 19. 1723. * * * I baptized a child of Captn Mayhew called Zaccheus, this day. I have been informed that this is a sickly mortal time in Newbury, Rowley and Marblehead.

May 26. 1723. I have heard that Mr Medcalfe minister of Saccones-sett departed this life on Friday last. He sickened as I am told on Mon-day and died on friday. He was a young man. Left behind 8 children and perhaps no very plentiful estate to support them. He was a man, it is said of considerable worth.

August 18. 1723. * * * I baptized a child of William Hunts called Jane.

August 25. 1723. I was credibly informed that Andrew Stratton was drowned some time ago at Canso.

1723. 8ber 27. * * * This night about 10 of the clock Thomas Blair departed this life. He had gone some time ago to the Jarsies and came home with a fever and ague upon him.

8ber 8. 1723. * * * Mrs Bacon died on Thursday last and Mr Torrey on Saturday morning, her distemper was a consumption. Mr Tor-rey had been for some time under a bad habit of body. About a month agoe he was taken sick with the jaundice and voiding of blood from all the passages of his body, as I have been told, and then he was taken with a dropsie and flux. It was said that of late he had drunk too freely and too frequently of spirits. He was buryed on the evening of y^{e} Lords day. He was pastor of the church of Tisbury, had been a preacher about 20 years and died in y^{e} 43^{d} year of his age.

Feby 14. 17$\frac{23}{24}$ being friday about $\frac{1}{2}$ an hour after 2 afternoon, James Allen departed this life. His distemper was a putrid fever with cough.

He died the 26th day of his sickness. He was a pious sober man, and one of a publick spirit, well esteemed by his neighbours. He was buryed on Saturday about 5 afternoon.

June 7. 1724. * * * Mr James Skiffe died yesterday afternoon.

June 14. 1724. * * * I understand that Mr Worth departed this life this morning and that there was an Indian killed at Menamsha yesterday.

June 21. 1724. * * * Mrs Skiffe, spouse to Mr Nathan Skiffe departed this life on Friday last about noon.

July 12. 1724. * * * On friday last we raised our new meeting house. Gershom Cathcart, a young man belonging to New town fell from the third story, and was very much bruised. His recovery is uncertain [his] reason seems not to be impaired by his fall. Lord make the providence a wakening to others!

August 23. 1724. * * * I took occasion to reprove some young folk publickly for their irreverent and profane deportment in the time of Gods publick worship

August 30. 1724. * * * After sermon we received Jabez Athearn into the church and baptized him.

7ber 13. 1724. * * * Mr Clark had a child baptized today called Thankful.

7ber 20. 1724. My daughter Allen was delivered of a daughter Thursday last about one afternoon, being the 17th day of the month.

7ber 27. 1724. * * * This day my two daughters Agnes and Elizabeth were received into the church

8ber 4. 1724. I had an account today that John Manter's wife of New town departed this life yesterday

8ber 25. 1724. * * * I am informed that 7 Indians belonging to Gay Head coming from Rhod Island home in a whale boat were all lost, as is generally thought. It is said they were in drink when they went on board.

Jan: 10. $17\frac{24}{25}$. * * * Last Monday son Allen carryed two men prisoners to Boston, viz: Capt Lane and Mr McGowan:

May 30. 1725. * * * Yesterday William Case of Tisbury, weaver, departed this life. He was a man between 30 and 40 years of age as I think.

June 27. 1725. * * * James Hamilton's wife of Old town died Thursday night last.

8ber 31. 1725. * * * I understand that Jonathan Hillmans child died suddenly last night.

Xber 5. 1725. * * * Last week a sloop came ashore on the south side of the island, the men and cargo were saved, the master having been long sick died Friday night last and was buryed this day. His name was Cash. the sloop belonged to Rhod Island.

Feb. 6. $17\frac{25}{26}$. * * * Mrs Chipman departed this life last Saturday night, about midnight. She died in Dartmouth at Capt Popes. She was a pious good woman and died well, with a rational assurance of her future well being. She had long been in a languishing condition. She went in the fall to visit $Capt^n$ Pope and sickened there. She was buryed the Tuesday following in Dartmouth.

Feb. 13. $17\frac{25}{26}$. On Wednesday morning last, being the 9th instant Mr Nathan Skiffe departed this life. He was, I hope, a good man and died well. He had been some months in a languishing condition and died in the 68th year of his age.

March 13. 17$\frac{25}{26}$. * * * The snow which has continued for most part since some time in November is now almost gone.

May 1. 1726. * * * Baptized a child of Mr Clarks this after noon called Jane.

May 8. 1726. On Monday last, in the evening, a child of widow Blairs of this town called Susanna dropt into a tanpit near her own house, but was taken out alive yet died about ten of the clock that night and was buryed next day.

June 8. 1726. * * * Baptized four children one to Jabez Athearn named Abigail, one to Hammet, named Abigail, one to John Cottle called Elizabeth, and one to Israel Butler named Nathaniel.

July 10. 1726. * * * I baptized two children to William Hunt, born some time ago, called Hanna and Sarah.

August 7. 1726. * * * I baptized a child belong to Mr Barnabas Taylor called Nathaniel.

August 14. 1726. * * * daughter Allen had a young child buryed on Saturday last.

August 28. 1726. * * * On Thursday last Capt Thomas Daggett of Old town departed this life. He had been ill several weeks. He was a peaceable man and well inclined and of good understanding.

Jany 8. 17$\frac{26}{27}$. Last night before sundown Old William Hunt departed this life, he was a man of good age, had been long fraile. He died suddenly, none of his family knowing when he died. [Aged about 73 years. grave stone]

Jany 15. 17$\frac{26}{27}$. * * * I heard that Mrs Ward mother to Capt Mayhews wife died lately, and a daughter of Captain Daggett.

March 19. 17$\frac{26}{27}$. * * * Joseph Allen hath been for some time in a dangerous condition thro' vomiting etc

March 26. 1727. Mr Joseph Allen of Tisbury departed this life Munday night last. The distemper that carryed him off seems to have been the iliac passion; he continued ill several days, was much out of his head at times, continued vomiting. He was a man of about 60 years of age, of good understanding, peaceable and industrious. I do not remember to have heard any evil report of him.

April 2. 1727. On Friday last one Thomas Lues of Tisbury helping to get off a vessel that had been forced on shore by a late storm, the pries not being well fixed, came down on his head, bruised his skull very much so that his recovery is despaired of by many. I am informed that the said Thomas Lewes departed this life Saturday night last. He was a poor man, and left a numerous family of small children behind him, and his wife a poor helpless woman.

May 7. 1727. * * * I understand that Hester Cottle departed this life lately.

June 11. 1727. * * * Samuel Hillman departed this life this morning, as I am informed. He was a church member, but became slack and negligent in his attending upon publick ordinances some time before his death.

June 18. 1727. Bethia and Mary Hillman departed this life June 21. 1727 in the afternoon. They died almost at one time and were burried together. Their distemper was a pleurisy fever.

July 23. 1727. * * * Mr Handcock is to be ordained pastor of the church in Tisbury on Wednesday next.

July 30 1727. Being Lords day Mr Handcock preached both before and afternoon from James 2. 23 And he was called the friend of God: the discourse was not very animate yet hope it may be useful. Lord follow thy word and ordinances with a blessing. The day was fair clear and hot. On Wednesday last, being the 26th instant, Mr. Handcock was ordained Pastor of the Church in Tisbury. I preached the ordination sermon and Mr Russell and I imposed hands on him, for there was none other minister there. Mr Russell made the first prayer and I gave the Charge and made the second prayer, and Mr Russell gave him the right hand of fellowship.

August 27. 1727. We had an account last week that King George died June 11th last past in Germany on his journey to Hanover, and that his son the prince of Wales was proclaimed King under the title of George 2.

7ber 10 1727. * * * Last friday morning Joseph Smith departed this life. He was a sober temporate Indian a young man about 26 years of age: he was so well as to be at meeting last Lords day.

Oct 15. 1727. Sam: Merry departed this life on Munday last was buried on Tuesday. Son John and Betty returned home Thursday last from Rhod Island.

October 22. 1727. * * * I heard the melancholy news of son Roberts death, but had no account of the circumstances of it.

9ber 5. 1727. Last Lords day, in the afternoon, about 11 of the clock we had a shock of an earthquake, that continued above a minute: it was considerably great, but seemed to be greater in some places than others, whether it hath been felt all the country over or not I have not yet heard.

9ber 12. 1727. I understand that the earthquake was much more severe easterly than in these parts.

9ber 19. 1727. This morning between eight and nine of the clock my daughter Jane was safely delivered of a daughter.

9ber 25, 1727. I baptized a grandchild of mine this day called Kathren daughter to Silvanus Allen.

Xber 31. 1727. We had a public fast on Wednesday last on account of y^e^ earthquake.

Jany 21. $17\frac{27}{28}$. I heard today that Peter Rea died at Old town last week, he was formerly an inhabitant there, but had removed to Boston some time before he died.

Feb 25. $17\frac{27}{28}$. I have heard that Thomas Weste died lately at Rhod Island. He had some time ago undertaken to pilot a vessel to Boston and was forced off the coast by a storm and driven to Martinico, and either by the fatigue of the voyage or by some distemper contracted in that island he was brought very low before he arrived at Rhod Island, and not long after he came on shore he died. His friends concluded he had been lost in the storm. I have also good intelligence that Dr Cotton Mather of Boston departed this life on Tuesday the 13th instant between 8 and 9 of the clock before noon, and was buried the 19th day. He was a man of superior parts and learning. He was when he died 65 years of age and some hours. The Lord prepare me for my great change.

March 10. $17\frac{27}{28}$. On Wednesday last John Skiffe and Mr John Mills departed this life: the former about five after noon and the other about ten. John Skiffe was a young man about 23 years of age, son to Nathan Skiffe, late of this town: the other was born in England, but had lived in this town several years, and marryed above a year ago a daughter of Mr James Allen late of this town, but after marriage removed to Newtown and died there: he followed merchandizing

March 31. 1728. About three of the clock on Thursday morning, John Clifford a young man belonging to this town, departed this life, and it is said he died well. He died at Mr Cobbs of Newtown. I understand that John Campbell Esqr of Boston died the fourth of this month.

April 7. 1728. My daughter Margaret was safely delivered of a daughter Wednesday last, being the third day of the month, between 9 and 10 of the clock before noon.

April 21. 1728. John Hillman Junr died last Tuesday between nine and ten at night. His distemper was a malignant fever. He was often delirious. He died the eighth day of his sickness.

April 28. 1728. About one of the clock this morning Daniel Luke a young man, who was apprentice to Mr Bassett departed this life. He was out of his head most part of the time of his sickness: his distemper was a malignant fever.

May 19. 1728. On Munday last being ye 13th instant Jacob Robinson of Newtown departed this life.

June 2, 1728. I heard today that Isaac Robinson of Newton departed this life last evening. He was a man of an inoffensive conversation * * * * There were 18 days between the death of the two brothers, viz Jacob and Isaac Robinson.

July 7. 1728. We appointed Wednesday last to be observed as a publick fast, but we had a plentiful rain on Tuesday, which occasioned our changing the fast into a thanksgiving.

August 11. 1728. I heard that old Mr Newcome of Old town died lately.

8ber 17. 1728. I was informed that John Smith of Edgartown departed this life yesterday morning.

9ber 3 1728. I had a letter Saturday last from Mr Nathan Bassett informing that his brother Barachiah died lately in South Carolina.

Xber 29. 1728. I am informed that Justice Parker of Barnstable departed this life some day last week.

Jany 5. $17\frac{28}{29}$. I was informed last week that Mrs Harlock and Joseph Norton's wife died lately, both of them belonged to the Old town and had been long indisposed.

Jany 26. $17\frac{28}{29}$. Mr Draper of Boston died lately: he was a pious understanding man, and well stricken in years.

June 8. 1729. I baptized a negro of Captn Mayhew called Ceasar this day.

July 6. 1729. I was informed this day that Rev^{d} Mr Cotton departed this life last week; he was minister of a church in Bristol: he was at the council in Sandwich that met the 18th of June last. On Saturday following as I was told, he was somewhat disordered in mind. On the Lords day his disorder increased upon him, yet he did attend the publick worship of God very composedly, and did preach to a considerable number of persons: in the evening on Munday his disorder increased so that all were sensible of it, and so it continued to do on Tuesday and Wednesday. He died July 3^{d} about 2 P. M.

July 13. 1729. Ichabod Allen's wife departed this life about midnight, between the 16th and 17th day of this month. She had been long in languishing circumstances, being a consumptive. She seemed to be pious and orderly in her conversation.

August 24, 1729. I understand that the poor in Ireland are in great distress thro' a famine of bread. Since, by a letter from daughter Betty we have the news of Abra Homes death confirmed. She died the third of this month. [She was daughter of William Homes of Boston, and granddaughter of the diarist].

August 31. 1729. I understand that it is a sickly time in Boston, but the sickness not very mortal.

October 5, 1729. Old Mrs Russell of Barnstable departed this life last Lords day after a short illness. She was a daughter of Rev^{d} Mr Moody, and widow to the Rev^{d} Mr Russell. She was a discreet pious gentlewoman. She died aged about 67 years.

8ber 26, 1729. I was informed today that Ben. Hillmans eldest son was lately dead, and that Sarah Hillman is dangerously ill.

9ber 23, 1729. I baptized today a child of Captn Mayhew's called Martha.

Xber 7, 1729. I baptized a child of Silvanus Allens named Mary

Xber 21. 1729. I understand that Mr Taylor is to be ordained pastor of a church in Bristol Wednesday night.

Jany 4, 17$\frac{29}{30}$. I baptized a child of Mr Adams this day called Mayhew.

Jany 11, 17$\frac{29}{30}$. I understand that Judge Sewall died lately in Boston, viz: on the 3^{d} day of the month in y^{e} 78th year of his age. On the eighth day of this month, about 3 in the morning Mrs Relyance Adams of this town departed this life. She was lately safely delivered of a child, but was soon after taken with a fever which carryed her off. She was a pious prudent woman of blameless conversation.

Jany 25, 17$\frac{29}{30}$. I am informed that the Rev^{d} Mr Samuel Hunt pastor of a church in Dartmouth departed this life on Wednesday last which was the 21st instant and was buried on the Friday following.

Feby 8, 17$\frac{29}{30}$. I am informed that Joseph Russells wife of Barnstable died lately in child-bed.

April 2. 1730. I have heard that the small pox prevails much in Boston. They have gone very much into the practice of communicating the distemper by inoculation, and many of those that take it, both in the natural way and by inoculation die.

May 17. 1730. I baptized this day a grandson called John Allen.

May 24. 1730. Mr Presbury of Old town died last Lords Day, and a child of William Hunts on Tuesday last.

June 14, 1730. I had an account by letters from good hands last week that my son in law Joshua Allen departed this life at Medfield the 30th day of May. His distemper was the small pox.

8ber 25, 1730. I have heard that it is a sickly time on the Mainland in several places.

July 12. 1731. Pam Mayhew Jr was drowned near the West Chop of Holmes Hole. He had been to Nantucket and was coming home and being steering the whale boat, the strap broke and he went overboard and was lost. It was in the evening. His corps came on Shore July 22 toward night at Gay Head, and he was buried the next day towards night in the burying place in Chilmark. My daughter Betty Hutchinson set out on her journey to Holmeshole with designe to take passage for Boston and from thence to Pennsylvania on Wednesday August 25, 1731.

7ber 6 1731. I am informed that the day abovesaid four men viz: Mr Taylor Mr Mood. Russell, John Sturges and the mentioned above called called also John Sturges [of Barnstable] took a whaleboat and went over to a point of land with a designe to kill some small birds, where they stayed so long that the tide left their boat dry, which they went about to carry to place where it might swim, but this Sturges complained that it was too heavy for him, so that he would not help to carry it any further and so left them, as they thought he intended to go to a place where they behooved to come after they got off the boat in their passage home, but he continued to move towards the sloop till he was drowned.

November 29, 1731. About midnight Mr. Samuel Tilton departed this life in the 94th year of his age: he was a man of good understanding, was an antipedobaptist in his judgment, but pious and regular in his conversation. He was against swearing and usery.

I was informed 9ber 9 1733 that John Cunningham of Edgar-Town died there yesterday somewhat suddenly and much out of his head.

Rachel Lumbert wife to Jonathan Lumbart the thirteenth day of February 17$\frac{33}{34}$ about 8 at night, being in her ordinary health she went up stairs in her own house and dropt down in an apoplectic fit, and never spake. She continued till 2 of the clock afternoon of the next day, being the 14th day.

July 9 [1737] and the night after it, we had excessive rains which raised the rivers upon this island to such a degree that the dams of the water mills were carryed away by them, and the mowing ground near the rivers was very much damnified, to the great loss of several of the inhabitants.

August 11, 1737. The sky towards the N. and N.W. appeared with an unusual redness, which continued for some time extending itself more and more easterly. About 11 the red was mixed with white streaks that were very luminous, being broad below and gradual growing narrower till they ended in a point. About midnight there appeared a bow reaching from east to west in the form of a rainbow, only there was no diversity of colors, the whole bow was luminous so that the air was lighter than it is at full moon, tho' it was 2 or 3 days before the change [of] the moon. It did rather resemble day light before the sun rises than moonlight.

Xber 7, 1737. About 10 at night there was felt by several persons on the island, Martha's Vineyard, the shock of an earthquake.

Xber 13. 1737. About 5 weeks ago there came a vessel to the old town from Philadelphia that had the small pox on board and several persons there were infected with the distemper, of which I was informed that Doct Mathuz[?] died of it yesterday morning and Ezra Covel died last night. There have died of the same distemper five grown persons, in all seven grown persons, and several are sick of it there.

Xber 26. 1737. Some affirm that they felt the shock of an earth quake about 12 at night Xber 30. Last night David Dunham's wife died of small pox, as I am informed.

Jany 6. [17$\frac{37}{38}$]. I am informed that Samuel Smith of old town died Saturday night last of the small pox.

Jany 10. 173$\frac{7}{8}$. I understand that Mrs Pease and a mulatto woman in the old town lately died of the small pox. A considerable shock of an earth quake was felt by some Jany 2. 173$\frac{7}{8}$ about midnight.

I am informed Jany 13 that there have been 35 persons sick of the small pox this season in Edgartown, out of which number 14 have died. By the best information I can get concerning the way and manner how the people in Edgartown were taken with the small pox the last fall, it was as followeth: Several persons belonging to the town were in Mr Hamiltons that kept a tavern the 18th of 9ber last; there was nobody sick of that distemper in that family: there was indeed a vessel in the harbour that had the small pox on board, but none of them that were sick lodged on shore:

those who took the distemper were all taken in one day. None of those that were in Hamiltons the day before nor afterward were infected.

November 21. 1738. There came a ship ashore on the South side of this island, belonging to New York. She came last from Jamaica: the lading and mens lives were saved, but it is supposed the ship cannot be got off again.

The 27th day of February 173$\frac{8}{9}$ I was informed that a flash of lightning we had the 25th day fell upon a house in Edgartown belonging to this island, where one Abram Ripley dwelt, and damaged it: yet none of the inhabitants were killed by it.

March 4. 17$\frac{38}{39}$. I was informed that Abigail Skiffe departed this life this morning. She had long languished under a consumption.

July 13. 1740. While I was at prayer in the morning I fainted away in the pulpit and fell down, so that I was rendered incapable of performing any further publick service that day, for which I desire to be deeply humbled. [This note conveys the premonitory sign of a failure in health from which he never entirely recovered, and accounts for the paucity of entries in his diary, of a public interest, from the date until his death, six years later.]

August 3, 1740. My grand daughter Kath: Smith hath been sick the most part of last week and continues so still.

1740 August 10. After sermon, Tim: Mayhew and wife were received into the church and she and the four children were baptized, viz: Reliance, Rachel, Hannah and Bathshebah. The first that was seized with that called the throat distemper in this town was Susan Allen; the next was Abigail Hillman, both these died. The next Katharine Smith, she also died. Next Mrs Little, she is in a fair way of recovery. Next Sam: Bassett's daughter, she also is in a hopeful way: next Bethia Clark and my grand daughter Mary Allen

August 17. 1740. After sermon received into communion of the church Josiah Crocker and Jonathan Mayhew.

August 24. 1740. After sermon Jane Hunt was received into the church as a member in full communion.

7ber 7. 1740. A child of Gunino Finla, of about 9 years of age died on Friday last of throat distemper, and three in my son Sylvanus Allen's family are under the distemper.

7ber 14. 1740. John Bassett and his wife were received into the church and their two children baptized, viz. Elizabeth and Ruth.

7ber 15. 1740. I had the uncomfortable news that my grandson William Daggett departed this life the day before.

7ber 17. 1740. Was observed through the island as a day of fasting and prayer to beg mercy of God that the distemper that has prevailed among us for some time might be removed and health restored*. . . . A child of Zach: Hatch died of the throat distemper this night.

7ber 28 1740. At 5 o'clock on Thursday morning in this week my grandson Eleazer Allen departed this life.

* This was an epidemic disease, known then as the "throat distemper," probably diphtheria, which broke out at Kingston, N. H., in the Spring of 1735 and gradually spread over New England during the next few years and later extended over all the colonies. The disease was very fatal and several thousand deaths of young people in New England are chargeable to its ravages. It lingered for several years, and the appearance of it on the Vineyard in 1740 may be traced to the general dissemination of the contagion over the New England colonies by that time. C. E. B.

8ber 19. 1740. After sermon William Bassett and his wife, Abigail Allen and Hannah Clark were received into the church and Mrs Bassett and her six children were baptized, viz: Nathaniel, Barachiah, Nathan, Anna and Susanna.

9ber 2. 1740. Received into the church Ruth Mayhew and Susanna Hatch and baptized a child of the Rev. Mr. Taylor, called Eleazer and another of John Tiltons called Mary

9ber 16. 1740. After sermon Zephaniah Mayhew and his wife were received into the church and their two children viz Jehoiadah and Lucinda were baptized and a child of Ja^{s} Foster called Hanna was baptized also.

9ber 23. 1740. Received into the church Rebecca Allen in full communion.

Feby 22. $17\frac{40}{41}$. This day Mr. Saml Allen and his daughter Mariah were received into the church as members in full communion.

March 15. $174\frac{0}{1}$. Mary Mayhew was received into the church.

March 22 $174\frac{0}{1}$. Jedidah Allen was received into the church and was baptized.

April 5, 1741. This day Shubal Hawes was propounded to the church.

May 2. 1741. This day Mrs. Abigail Pees departed this life in the 80 year of her age. She was of a quiet inoffensive deportment. She died about 12 o'clock this day.

7ber 6, 1741. We had this summer a drought that hurt both the grass and the Indian corn very much. This was accompanied with an unusual number of grasshoppers that devoured both grass and corn.

9ber 12. 1741. We had a general Thanksgiving appointed by our Governour, William Shirley Esqr.

August 15. 1742. This morning Mrs Gold had withdrawn herself to some obscure place which put the family into disorder.

7ber 12. 1742. I baptized a child of Mr Taylors to-day called Elizabeth.

Oct. 19. 1742. About three afternoon the chimney in the room where I commonly stay catched fire, and being very foul, burned very fiercely, which put the whole house in no small danger. It continued to burn till within the night. It was a day time and the wind very high, yet through the mercy of God we received no great damage, only the mantle tree catched fire and is part damnified. Several of our neighbors came to our assistance seasonably. I desire to bless God for our preservation.

June 19. 1743. I went to the place of Gods public worship as usual, but was so faint that I fainted away in the time of the first prayer, and was carried home by my friends. I found myself very ill all morning and the most of the preceding week. About 3 years before I had such a fit in the pulpit and in the time of prayer too. Lord prepare me for my great change.

April 29. 1744. I received into the church Jonathan Hillman and his wife and baptized them and their children, and a child of John Cottles.

[The remainder of the diary, until June 22, 1746, when the last entry was made, is entirely composed of notes of the Sunday services; the name of the preacher who occupied his pulpit, for he was too feeble to continue work after the above entry was made, and the texts chosen by the preachers, usually followed by some pious ejaculation. As stated in the first installment the diarest died June 20, 1746. C. E. B.]

RECORDS OF THE CONGREGATIONAL CHURCH OF CHILMARK, MASS. 1787–1820.

Communicated by WILLIAM J. ROTCH, Esq., of West Tisbury, Mass.

THESE recently discovered church records of Chilmark, Island of Martha's Vineyard, add much to the published vital records of the town.*

The church called Rev. Jonathan Smith to settle with them in the work of the gospel ministry, Wednesday, Aug. 22, 1787.

The Town concurred Aug. 30, 1787, & voted an annual salary of £110.

The acceptance of the call dated Dec. 1, 1787.

Ordination — Jan. 23, 1788.

Rev. Jonathan Smith was ordained to the pastoral care of the Church of Christ in Chilmark on the twenty third day of January one thousand seven hundred and eighty eight

The following persons belonged to the Church at the time of the ordination.

Mr Zechariah Mayhew & Elizabeth his wife
Matthew Mayhew Esq.
Dea. James Allen & Martha his wife
John Bassett & Jane his wife
John Cottle & Zerviah his wife
John Mayhew
Jeremiah Mayhew & Fear his wife
Robert Allen & Desire his wife
William Steward & Deborah his wife
Nathan Mayhew & Abigail his wife
Hannah Homes
Widow Anna Allen
" Deborah Allen
" Remember Skiff
" Mary Tilton
" Mary Tilton
Zilpha, wife to Joseph Tilton
Beulah, wife to Samuel Tilton
Abigail, wife to Reuben Tilton
Rebecca, wife to Stephen Tilton
Hannah, wife to Elijah Smith
Mercy, wife to Seth Mayhew
Mary, wife to John Allen Esq
Zerviah, wife to Ezra Hilman
Ruth, wife to Timothy Mayhew
Elizabeth, wife to Josiah Tilton
Widow Rebecca Norton
" Elizabeth Butler
" Peggy Mayhew
Mehitable Mayhew
Mary Hunt

* See VITAL RECORDS OF CHILMARK, MASSACHUSETTS, TO THE YEAR 1850. Published by the New-England Historic Genealogical Society, at the charge of the Eddy Town-Record Fund. Boston, Mass. 1904. 8vo. Cloth. pp. 96.

Margaret Allen
Hannah Wyer
Catherine Boardman
Eleanor Mayhew
Jerusha Mayhew
Bethia Mayhew
Ruhamah Tilton
Widow Thankful Pitts
Elizabeth wife of Josiah Tilton Esq

1788 April 6 Samuel Allen adult by baptism
Reuben Tilton adult " "
Matthew Tilton & Sarah his wife
Love Allen wife of Wm Allen
Apl 10 Matthew Mayhew & Rebecca his wife members of the Church at Edgartow were admitted into the Church.
" " Ezra Allen, Lois wife of Jona. Allen Jr & Desire Allen members of Tisb. Church were also incl. into this Ch.
Apl 12. Samuel Norton & Elizabeth his wife
Benjamin Hillman & Mary his wife
Jonathan Mayhew
Robert Allen Jr
Apl 20. Widow Lydia Bassett by baptism
27 Samuel Bassett & Anna his wife
May 4 Hannah Cottle
June 8 Nathaniel Bassett
Nathan Bassett & Mary his wife
Rebecca Hillman wife to Robert Hillman
Prudence Mayhew
Martha Allen
Widow Sarah Bassett by baptism
Athearn Butler " "
Perez Bassett " "
June 15 Parnell Mayhew
June 29 Widow Hannah Butler
July 6 Seth Mayhew
Widow Abigail Hillman
Sarah Flanders wife to John Flanders by baptism
Nancy Mayhew wife to Wilmot Mayhew
Elizabeth Boardman
Jemima Tilton
July 13 Silas Hillman
Jane Daggett wife to Solomon Daggett
Jedidah Bassett
Solomon Daggett by baptism
Rebecca Cottle wife of John Cottle " "
Jerusha Cottle wife of Silas Cottle " "
July 20 James Butler
Prince Look
Bathsheba Allen wife of Josiah Allen
Sarah Look, wife of Prince Look by baptism
Aug 10 Elijah Tilton & Eunice his wife
Aug 31 Widow Abigail Nickerson by baptism
" Mary Hillman " "

Parnell wife to Thomas Mayhew by baptism
Rebecca Mayhew
Sept 14 Silas Cottle
Sept 28 Wilmot Mayhew
Richard Hillman by baptism
Jane Hillman wife of Richard Hillman
1789 March 1 Lydda wife of Sylvester Norton
Mch 29 Sylvanus Boardman
Apl 19 Widow Abigail Burgess
May 10 Anna Bassett wife of John Bassett by baptism
May 17 Rachel Tilton by baptism
July 12 Jedidah Allen
Beulah Allen
Aug[t] 6 Puella, wife of James Butler } Members of the church at Tisbury were received under the inspection of this church
Eunice, wife of Silas Hillman
Sept 20 Daniel Jones & Polly who had owned the covenant, upon expressing their wishes partook of the sacrament & considered as members in full communion.
Sep 27 Lois Mayhew wife of Samuel Mayhew by baptism
Oct. 18. William Wimpenny partook of the sacrament
Nov. 1. Robert Hillman
Tryphena Hatch by baptism
1790 March 21. Zebulon Allen
Apl 11 Anna Smith wife of Jonathan Smith
admitted by a recommendation from the church in Sandwich
Oct 6. William Poole & Mary his wife by baptism
1791 Apl 10. Ransom Norton by baptism
Susanna wife of Ransom Norton
1792 Apl 8 Joseph Bassett
Mary wife of Joseph Bassett.
July 8 Jane wife of Walter Boardman by baptism
Sept 2 William Allen
1793 Mch 3 Simon Mayhew
Nov 5 Widow Abigail Allen by baptism
1794 May 5 William Armstrong
July 2 Samuel Mayhew.
1795 Oct 29 Ruhamah Mayhew by baptism
1796 Feb 13 Sarah Pease wife of Abishai Pease by baptism
Mar 27 Deidamia wife of Joseph Tilton Jr.
July 3 Joseph Tilton at his own house by baptism
Sep 25 Mary Ferguson wife of John Ferguson
Oct 30 Hebron & Deborah Mayhew
1797 Mch 19 Thankful Mayhew by baptism
July 2 Josiah Allen
Aug 23 Thomas Tilton by baptism aged 95.
1798 Apl 15 Beulah, wife of Ezra Allen
1799 Apl 14 Widow Sarah Lothrop
1800 July 20 Allen Mayhew & Eunice his wife
Oct 5 Samuel Hillman
Tristram Allen & Clarissa his wife
1801 Jan 11 Nathan Skiffe

1803 Oct 31 Sarah wife of Thomas West by baptism
1804 May 20 William Tilton Jr " "
Peggy wife of Wm Tilton Jr
May 27 William & Phebe Mayhew rec'd the communion
July 8 Abiah Luce by baptism
Aug 5 Sukey Hillman wife of Silas Hillman Jr
Aug 19 Betsey Hancock
Aug 19 Betsey Mayhew wife of Seth Mayhew
Lucy & Clara Mayhew
Love Norton rec'd the communion
Sep 23. Parnell Mayhew
1805 Oct 6 Lucy wife of Maltiah Mayhew
Feb 13 Abishai Mayhew
1807 June 21 Jedidah Stewart
Sep 29 Ephraim Mayhew at his own house
1808 May 8 Elijah Smith
Matilda his wife by baptism
Sept 11 Widow Jedidah Mayhew
1809 Aug 6 S—— Tilton by baptism
Oct 22 Eunice Tilton wife of Oliver Tilton by baptism
Albert Tilton
Nov 26 Peggy Tilton
Rebecca Mayhew
1810 Mar 26 Oliver Mayhew & Anna Mayhew by baptism
Jane, wife of Oliver Mayhew
Stephen Tilton
1811 Oct 30 Elizabeth Pease wife of Fortunatus Pease by baptism.

The above is the complete entry as made in the Church Records

1788 June 26 Mr Nathan Mayhew chosen deacon
1791 Aug 12 Mr Reuben Tilton chosen deacon
1806. Apl 18 { Zebulon Allen, Oliver Mayhew } chosen deacons.

Chilmark Church Records.

Deaths in Chilmark.

1788 Jan 1. Uriah Tilton ae 74 consumption
Mch 31. Jedidah, widow of Uriah ae 69 " "
Apl 7. Sarson Lathrop at sea ae 20
May 30 Elijah Mayhew ae 19 nervous fever
Oct 25 son of Elijah & Hannah Smith ae 1. consumption
Sep 20 Richard son of John & Sarah Flanders, ae 14, at sea
Nov 11. Remember wife of Cyreno Tilton ae 86
1790 Jan 16 John Mayhew ae 89
Feb. 18 Child of Edward Hillman
Mch 20 Mrs Mayhew wife of Rev. Zechariah Mayhew ae 69 pleurisy & consumption.
Mch 30 Josiah Tilton Esq.
Apl 10–14 Jerusha dau. of Silas Cottle ae 11 mos.
Jun 14 Capt. Jeremiah Mayhew ae 85
Jun 23 Hannah wife of Elijah Smith ae 42 consumption
July 9 Dau. of Thomas West ae 14 months

1789	Mar	18	Mary Hunt ae 68 bilious fever
	May	22	Jerusha wife of Silas Cottle
1790	July	11	Child of Zebulon Allen
			still born child of Francis Mayhew
	Oct	7	William Poole ae 49 atrophy
	Nov	2	Martha wife of Nathan Bassett ae 34–2 Delirium & lunacy: lived 16¼ days without swallowing anything: seldom spoke & kept her mouth almost always closed.
	Nov.	21	son of Salathiel & Lucy Allen ae 6 days
	Dec	27.	Jane, dau. of John & Sarah Flanders ae 13 putrid fever
	Dec	29	Nathan Weeks ae 78 atrophy
1791	Jan	14	Child of Nathl Russell Esq ae 3 days
	Feb	24	Cyrano Tilton ae 91
	Mar	25	Dea. Nathan Mayhew
	Mar	21	Child of Thomas & Ruth Hillman 1 day
	July	12	John Bassett ae 85
	Sept	6	Elizabeth wife of Samuel Norton. consumption
	Sept	9	Twins of Walter & Jane Boardman
	Oct.		George Allen
1792	Jan	15	Nathan Bassett ae 54 pleurisy
1792	Mch	27	Mehitable Mayhew ae 85
	June	13	Desire Allen wife of Robert Allen
	Nov	23	Abiah wife of Simon Mayhew ae 65 apoplexy.
	Oct	28	Child of Thomas Hillman
1793	Feb	23.	Jerusha Mayhew ae 75
	Apl	—	child of Wm Tilton Jr ae 4 days
	Apl	13	Jacob Norton coming from Bedford
	Aug	20	Davis Allen ae 15, mortification, son to Eph^{m} Allen
	Aug	31	{ Nabby ae 4 yrs & William aged 2 yrs. ch.^{d} of W^{m} & Bathsheba Stewart, dysentery
	Oct	18	Lucy wife of Salathiel Allen
1794	Jan'y	18	Child of Sylvanus Allen ae 12 hours
	Mch	10	Hannah Homes ae 85
	June	3	Anna Allen ae 67
	Nov	17	Lucy dau. of Tryphena Hatch. diabetes
1795	Jan	4.	Child of Sylvanus Allen just born
	Apl	15.	Child of Fortunatus Pease ae 8 weeks
	Sept	21.	Peggy Mayhew wife of Capt. Jeremiah Mayhew
1796	May	11	Bethiah Mayhew
	July		child of Jno Mayhew
	Aug	12	child of Fortunatus Pease ae 9 weeks
	Sep	3	Joseph Tilton ae 85
	Sep	5	Child of Nathl & Elizabeth Pease ae 4 weeks
	"	13	Child of Ward & Betsey Tilton, ae a few hours
			Isaiah Hillman lost at sea
			Oliver Mayhew
			Perez Bassett in England
1797	June	22	Child of Sylvanus Allen ae 6 weeks
	July	23	Solomon Daggett ae 81
	Sep	15	Walter Hillman, lost at sea
	Nov	5	Israel Luce ae 73 dysentery
	Nov	6	Patience wife of Matthew Allen ae 20 fever
	"	10	Sarah wife of Abishai Pease ae 63. dropsy

		18	Hannah Cottle ae 54
1798	Mch	7	Catherine wife of N Bassett Esq ae 46 apoplexy
	Aug	4	—— wife of Fort: Pease Jr. consunption
	Aug	21.	Henry Hillman, yellow fever
	Oct	2.	Widow—Burgess ae 82 pleurisy
	Oct	6	Thomas Pease
	Oct	11	Shubael Burgess ae 81 palsy
			Capt Thomas Lathrop at Martinico
	Oct	27	Twins of William Stewart
1799	Apl	19	Matty Skiff ae 44. consumption
	"	30	Josias Mayhew
	May	20	Lydia Tilton ae 23
	July	12	Widow Mary Bassett consumption
			Clement Bassett at sea
			Benjamin Pool at sea
1800	Feb.	2.	Child of Jno Mayhew ae 1 month
	"	5.	Child of Wm Norton ae 17 mo
	Ap	7	Samuel Mayhew ae 88
	"	18	Sarah wife of Prince Look ae 36 consumption
	July	2	Eliza Burgess
	"	26	Capt Nathan Mayhew ae 34 convulsions
	"	31	Capt James Adams ae 44 Savanna fever
	Sep	12	Mary wife of Seth Mayhew 59 dysentery
	Sept	20	Seth Mayhew ae 60 dysentery
1801	Jan	27	Samuel Hillman cancer
	Apl	3.	Thomas Tilton ae 98 – 5
	"	13	Jesse Weeks ae 87
		17	Clement Bassett son to Wm Norton ae 6 mo
	Jun	4	Child of Ezra Tilton ae 18 mo
	"	19	Robert Allen ae 69
			Simon Mayhew
	July	10	Abigail wife of Dr Tillton ae 59 consumption
	Dec	14	Hannah wife of Jno Mayhew 35 childbed
			Thomas Cox, at sea
1802	——	1	Elizabeth Butler ae 93
	Feb	13	Widow Abigail Nickerson 82 palsy
	Mch	1	William Norton 32 consumption
	Feb	25	William Armstrong
	May		Prince Hillman, at sea
	Oc	22	Hannah Wyer
	May	7	Widow Lois Mayhew
1803	Jan	2.	Matty wife of David Tilton consumption
	Apl	17	Widow Elizabeth Tilton ae 77
	"	19	Widow Jane Bassett ae 89
	Jan	9	Child of Nathl Pease
	Sept	13	Widow Mary Tilton ae 87
1804	Feb		John Cottle ae 97
	May	7	Samuel Norton
	"	13	Nathl Bassett Esq
	Aug	15	James Hancock ae 37
1805	Feb	7	Matthew Tilton Jr ae 25 consumption
	Mch	5	Beulah wife of Samuel Allen ae 83
	——		Rebecca Norton ae 87 dropsy

	—		——— Hatch , delivery
	July	2	Sarah wife of Matthew Tilton
	Aug	10	Dr Matthew Mayhew ae 85
	Sept	4	Child of Mayhew Smith ae 1
	Dec	16	Jonathan Mayhew ae 51 consumption
			Matthew Poole at sea
1806	——		Frederick son to Henry & Sophia Allen ae 1—9mo
	Mch	6	Rev. Zechariah Mayhew ae 89
	May	28	Beulah Allen
	July	15	Patty Mayhew ae 17 consumption
	Aug	30	Polly wife of Ephraim Pool ae 26
	Sep	29	Harriet Mayhew ae 19
	Oct	16	Jethro Mayhew ae 55
	Oct		Child of Samuel Manter
	July	12	Widow Abigail Allen
	Nov		Polly Pease dysentery
	Dec	22	Child of Oliver Tilton ae 14 mos
1807	Apl		Salathiel Tilton at sea
	Oct	4	Ephraim Mayhew ae 62 mortification
	"	26	Anna Smith —— to Jeremi Smith 48
	"	29	Pardon Hillman ae 20
			Thomas West at sea
1808	Feb	10	Parnell wid. of Jona. Mayhew 47 consunption
	June	4	Thomas W Mayhew ae 52 consumption
	Oct	25	Samuel Allen ae 88
	Oct	25	Nabby Bassett ae 23 consumption
	Dec	4	Hannah dau. of McCollum ae 2, 7mo quinsy
	Sep	24	Abiah Tilton ae 35 consumption
1809	Feb	3	Jane Daggett
	Mar	29	Child of —— Mayhew
	Jun	12	Ruth Norton dropsy
1810	Feb	18.	Widow Zilpha Tilton ae 89
	Mch	13	Jemima Tilton wife to Isaac 32 consumption
	Apl	6	Mary wife of John Ferguson ae 50
	Aug	2	Ezra Hillman ae 69 consumption
	Sep	20	Child of McCollum ae 3 weeks
	Aug		Tristram Mayhew of Liverpool—small pox
1811	Feb.	27	Levina Tilton 35 dropsical consumption
	Apl	6	James Norton ae 57 consumption
	Jun	5	Molly Dunham
	April		Nathan Tilton at sea
	July	5	Bathsheba Tilton ae 49 inflam. of brain
	Dec		Child of Zephaniah Mayhew ae 18 wh. cough
1812	——		Sally Allen —— ——
	Mch	16	Zipporah Bassett apoplexy
	"	21	Thankful Pitts pleurisy
	"	23	Parnell Mayhew cancer
			George Look at sea
1813	Mar	25	Polly Norton consumption
	May	9	Stephen Tilton
	June		Child of Cap. Saml Hancock
	Dec	7	Child of William Adams
1814	Jan	20	Albert Tilton typhus fever

	Feb.	9	Mark Mayhew ae 66 dropsy
	July	23	James Norton consumption
	Dec		Child of William Clark
1815	Jan.		Child of Wm Adams
	Feb	10.	Thomas Lumbert ae 49 lethargy
	May	23	Remember Skiff ae 100. 9^{m} dropsy
	Aug	2	—— Hawkes ae 77 consumption
	Oc	8	Jane Nickerson ae 50 "
	Oct	15.	—— Skiff ae 54 dropsy
	"	31	Rebecca Hillman 70 consumption
	Nov	3	Dea. James Allen ae 84 influenza
	Dec	6	Silas Hillman ae 84 consumption
	"	17	Ruth Mayhew ae 94 influenza
	"	28	Isaac Tilton ae 83 mortification
1816	Jan	20	Daniel Jones ae 77
	Feb		Sarah wife of Thomas West consumption
	May		Molly Hillman "
	Apl	9	Levinthia Tilton "
	Sep	12	William Tilton 77 "
	Aug	4	Twins of Samuel Norton
1817	Jan	15	Child of Wm B. Mayhew
	Jany		Moses Tilton at sea
	May		Nathan Skiff ae 89 consumption
	Aug	2	Child of David Tilton ae 2 yrs worm fever
	Sept	1	Elizabeth Pease ae 79 consumption
	Sept		Child of Ebenezer Luce
	Nov	4	Zeno Tilton at sea ae 18
	Aug	11	Hilliard Mayhew ae 25. apoplexy
1818	Mch	6.	Daniel Tilton dropsy
	July		Susan wife of Pain Tilton fever
	Sept	4	Wife of David Luce
	"	22	Betsey Norton consumption
	Dec	18	Mrs N—— ae 94
1819	Feb	7.	Child of —— Pool
	Jun	1	Deborah wife of Hayden Lumbert
	Aug	2	Moses Lumbert
	"	18	James Hillman
	Sept	6	Prudence Lumbert
	Oct	30	Nathan Tilton
	Oct	15	Child of David Mayhew

RECORDS OF THE CONGREGATIONAL CHURCH OF CHILMARK, MASS. 1787–1820.

Communicated by William J. Rotch, Esq., of West Tisbury, Mass.

Marriages in Chilmark.

1788

May 1. Nathaniel Bassett Esq & Catherine Boardman
Sep 25 Capt Wm Worth, Edgartown & Martha Allen Jr
Oct 2 Athearn Butler & Desire Allen Jr
Nov 6 Jeremiah Steward & Mary Lumbert
28 Fortunatus Pease Jr & Rose Gifford
Dec 25 Joseph Tilton Jr & Deidamia Davis

1789

Feb 17 John Gray, Tisbury & Mary Tilton 3rd, Chilmk
May 7 Zebulon Allen & Prudence Mayhew
Sep 17 Wm Stewart Jr & Bathsheba Tilton
Nov 5 Nicholas Butler & Lucy Norton
Dec 3 Reuben Hatch & Lucy Tilton

1790

Dec 4 Walter Boardman *m* Jane Hillman
" 9 Henry Hillman *m* Jane Mayhew

1791

Jan 9 Anderson Taylor, Hallowell *m* Persis Pease, Chilmk
23 Oliver Tilton *m* Eunice Tilton
Mch 24 Benj. Richardson, Unity, *m* Sylvia Hawkes
27 Ransom Norton *m* Susanna Mayhew

1791

Apl 14 Jonathan Crowell, Tisbury *m* Remember Tilton, Chil.
" Wm Churchill 3rd, Plympton *m* Peggy Tilton, Chil.

Ap 21 Samuel Athearn, Tisbury *m* Susanna Adams, Chil.
Aug 14 Benj Luce Jr *m* Prudence Pease
" 28 Elijah Smith *m* Matilda Mayhew
Sept 1 Cyrus Hatch *m* Betsy Flanders
" 22 Norton Bassett *m* Clarissa Stewart
Oc 30 Thomas Lumbert *m* Parnell Hillman
Dec 1 Benj. Hammett, Tisbury *m* Olive Hillman, Chil.
Nov 10 Wm Norton & Polly Bassett

1792

Apl 20 Cornelius Robinson & Fear Gifford
Sep 12 Rev. Moses Halleck, Plainfield N J *m* Peggy Allen, Chil.
" Solomon Butler *m* Rebecca Allen
Sep 20 Hebron Mayhew *m* Rebecca Stewart
Oc 25 Jonathan Mayhew *m* Parnell Mayhew
26 Cap. Jeremiah Mayhew, New Bedford *m* Peggy Mayhew
Dec 23 John Flanders Jr *m* Hannah Tilton

1793

Aug 22 Benj Smith *m* Ruhamah Mayhew Jr
Oct 24 John Cole, New Bedford *m* Peggy Ryan, Chil.
Nov 11 Moses Nye, Sandwich *m* Rhoda Butler, Chil.
21 Robert Allen *m* Mary Tilton

1794

Mar 20 Shadrack Hillman *m* Prudence Butler
Sep 11 Moses Hillman *m* Lydia Chase
Nov 16 Wm Bassett *m* Olivia Tilton
Dec 4 Rufus Davis, Edgartoun *m* Rebecca Mayhew, Chil.

1795

Mch 19 Silas Cottle *m* Jemima Tilton
Aug 23 Abel Baker, New Sharon *m* Deborah Mayhew
Dec 17 Tristram Allen *m* Clarissa Mayhew
18 Dr Allen Mayhew *m* Miss Eunice Allen

1796

Feb 21 Nathl Pease *m* Elizabeth Gifford
Oc 23 Jos. Mayhew, Falmouth *m* Polly Cottle, Chil.
" 27 George West *m* Prudence Lumbert

1797

July 6 Mayhew Norton of Tisbury *m* Hannah Luce of Chil.
oct 19 Warren Luce of Tisbury *m* Sally West of Chil^k
Dec 21 Uriel Hillman *m* Betsey Adams

1798

May 17 Wm Pool *m* Bathsheba Lumbert
Oct 11 Freeman Gray of Tisbury *m* Betsey Nichols of Chil.
" 25 Silas Hillman Jr *m* Sukey Jones
Nov 29 Matthew Allen, Chilmk *m* Temperance Allen of Tisbury

1799

Feb 21 Matthew Coffin, Edgartown *m* Betsey Allen, Chil.
Sept 8 Peleg Peabody, Dartmouth *m* Sally Pease, Chil.
Nov 1 Richard Fisher, Edgartow *m* Lydia West, Chil.

1800

Feb 27 Daniel Tilton *m* Matty Skiff
Apl 24 Archibald McCollum *m* Patty Godfrey

Oc 2 Ephraim Smith, New Sharon *m* Mary Mayhew
Nov 6 Wm B Mayhew *m* Prudence Allen
" 19 Jona. Lumbert, Chilmk *m* Love Manter, Tisbury
" 20 Isaac Winslow, Tisbury *m* Deborah Lambert, Chil.
" 27 George Look, Tisbury *m* Persis Allen

1801

July 18 Prince Hillman *m* Nancy Hillman
Nov 5 Wm Lawrence, Falmouth *m* Hannah Allen, Chil.
Feb 19 Henry Allen, Chilmark *m* Sophia Spalding, Tisbury
Mch 19 Asa Tilton *m* Sally Smith
June 4 Seth Mayhew & Betsey Cottle
" 23 Eleazer Dunham, Tisbury *m* Dinah Hillman, Chil.

1802

Apl 22 Rev [Nymphas] Hatch *m* Nancy [Abigail ?] Allen
Nov 25 Jabez Luce, Tisbury *m* Reliance Nichols, ch.

1803

June 9 Shubael Cottle Esq, Tisbury *m* Mary Allen, Chil.
Oct 27 Mayhew Smith *m* Sarah Cottle
Nov 15 James Allen 2nd *m* Cynthia Cottle
Dec 7 Jeruel West of Tisbury *m* Belinda Lumbert

1804

Sept 30 Lot Cottle, Tisbury *m* Catherine Smith
Oct 7 Daniel Look, Addison Me *m* Lois Hillman
" 18 Ephraim Pool *m* Polly Mayhew
Dec 13 Mayhew Cottle *m* Sarah Tilton

1805

Feb. 14 Ephraim Mayhew Jr & Susanna Pease
May 17 Thomas Tilton *m* Fear Hawkes
Dec 26 Lathrop Merry, Tisbury *m* Abigail Pease

1806

Jan 23 Wm Cottle *m* Anna B. Williams
Apl 1 Matthew Tilton *m* Polly* Dunham
April 24 Stephen Hillman *m* Bathsheba Skiff
Sept 25 David Tilton *m* Jedidah Robinson
Oct 26 Thomas Norton, Edgartown *m* Louisa Adams

1807

July 9 ——— Knowles of ——— *m* Prudence Hillman
" 25 John Robinson *m* Jane Allen
Nov 5 Abner Mayhew *m* Eunice Smith

1808

Mar 27 Samuel Look, Tisbury *m* Nancy Hillman

1809

Mar 23 William West of Tisbury *m* Polly Pool, Chil.
Dec 6 Joshua Johnson *m* Anna Cole (colored)
" 21 Matthew Vincent, Edgartown *m* Sophia Tilton

1810

Jany 18 Ephraim Poole *m* Lucinda Tilton
Sep 13 Shubael Smith *m* Deidamia Tilton
Dec 23 Thomas W. Mayhew *m* Lucy Allen

* She was a Mayhew and widow of Wm Dunham son of David Dunham.

1811

Jun 6 Wm Lumbert, Tisbury *m* Laura Lumbert
July 28 Frederick Mayhew *m* Zelinda Tilton
Dec 26 Hebron Tilton *m* Prudence Tilton

1812

Sept 13 Francis Tilton *m* Parnell Tilton
Oct 16 Ward Tilton Jr *m* Anna Robinson
Nov 26 Joshua Skiff *m* Rebecca West

1813

July 4 Joseph Green, Falmouth *m* Rebecca Cottle
Sep 26 Pain Tilton Jr *m* Persis Mayhew
Oct 21 Capt Saml Coffin *m* Lucy Sprage [Sprague] both of Edgartown
Nov. 25 Tristram Norton *m* Polly B. Tilton

1814

Nov 24 Josiah Tilton *m* Polly Norton

1815

Mar 8 Wm Packard of Plymouth *m* Rebecca Hilman
Nov 9 Samuel Tilton *m* Rebecca Tilton
Dec 12 Nathaniel Mayhew *m* Nancy Allen

1816

Oct 3 Thomas Nickerson *m* Peggy Mayhew
Nov 21 Cornelius Tilton *m* Elmira Flanders

1817

Jan 9 Capt Richard Luce *m* Hepsibah Allen
Aug 15 Capt Samuel Nickerson *m* Rebecca Mayhew
" 25 George Mayhew *m* Clarissa Mayhew
Sept 13 Beriah Tilton *m* Juliana Hancock
" 18 Wm Tilton Jr *m* Mary Stewart
" 28 Tristram Hillman *m* Nabby Stewart
Dec 4 Jeremiah Mayhew *m* Martha B. Tilton

1818

Nov. 26. Hayden Lumbert *m* Deborah Lumbert
Dec 9 John Johnson, Tisbury *m* Philura Hancock

1819

May 26. Cap. Josiah B Andrews of Salem *m* Jane K. Withington, Chilmk.
Sept 22 Warren Bullen, Farmington *m* Sally Mayhew

1820

Jan 26 Benjamin Skiff *m* Betsey Mayhew
Nov 16 Moses McKinstry *m* Louisa Robinson
" 23 Dea Wm Mayhew, Edgartown *m* Parnell Mayhew, Chil.
Dec 14 Harrison P. Mayhew *m* Susan Mayhew

The above are all the marriages in the Church Records excepting those of colored people.

Births in Chilmark.

1788

Feb.	12	William Tilton & Margaret—	daughter
Mch	28	Beriah Tilton & Lydia—	son
Apl	9	Nathan Bassett & Martha	son
May	9	Benj. Luce & Damaris	daughter
"	25	Matthew Mayhew & Rebecca	daughter

Jun	27	Nathl Mayhew & Mary	son
July	5	Daniel Jones & Mary	son
Aug		Timothy Mayhew & Ruth	——
Sept	6	Thomas Hillman & Ruth	dau
"	22	Ephraim Mayhew & Jedidah	son
Oct	15	John Cottle & Rebecca	dau
Nov	29	Ward Tilton & Elizabeth	son
"	23	Nathl Nickerson & Lydia	son
——		Joseph Bassett & Mary	son
		Edward Hillman & Lydia	——
		Zaccheus Mayhew & Pamela	——
		Pain Tilton & Susanna	——
		1789	
Jan	29	Prince Look & Sarah	son
Mch	1	Abishai Pease Jr & Mary	dau
	23	Matthew Tilton & Sarah	son
Apl	14	Ezra Hillman & Zerviah	dau
	27	Samuel Bassett & Anna	"
May	7	Thos. Wade Mayhew & Parnell	"
	17	Silas Cottle & Jerusha	"
June	3	Nath[l] Bassett & Catharine	son
	4	Joseph Tilton Jr & Deidamia	dau
	7	Thomas West & Sarah	"
	14	Shubael Luce & Hannah	son
	19	John Pease & Hannah	dau
July	21	Athearn Butler & Desire	"
Sep	3	Benj. Bassett & Abigail	"
Oct		Thomas Cox & Sarah	——
	15	Dea Nathan Mayhew & Abigail	son
	29	W[m] Stewart & Bathsheba	dau
		1790	
Jan	8	John Allen Esq & Mary	dau
May	16	William Allen & Love	"
		Zebulon Allen & Prudence	still born
		Benj. Mayhew	——
		Francis Mayhew	still born
July	11	Joseph Bassett & Mary	son
Aug	2	Reuben Hatch & Lucy	dau
	12	Nathan Bassett & Martha	son
Sep	24	Beriah Tilton & Lydia	dau
Oct	5	Saml Nickerson & Jane	son
	16	Zaccheus Mayhew & Pamela	"
	29	William Tilton & Peggy	"
	25	Ward Tilton & Elizabeth	dau
Nov	13	Salathiel Allen & Lucy	son
"	10	Benj. Hillman & Mary	dau
"	14	Ebenezer Bassett	——
		1791	
Jan	7	Prince Look & Sarah	son
	11	Nath[l] Bassett Esq & Catherine	dau
	13	Jonathan Smith & Anna	——
	16	Pain Tilton & Susanna	"

	27	John Mayhew & Hannah	——
Feb	17	Matt. Mayhew & Rebecca	son
"	23	Matthew Tilton & Sarah	dau
"	28	Zebulon Allen & Prudence	——
Mch	18	Ephraim Mayhew & Jedidah twins	sons
	20	Thomas Hillman & Ruth	son
Apl	3	Lot Look & Susanna	——
	12	Fortunatus Pease Jr	dau
	27	Edward Hillman & Lydia	son
May	6	Athearn Butler & Desire	dau
	11	Nath'l Nickerson & Lydia	——
June	10	Nicholos Butler & Lucy	son
Aug		Alsberry Luce & Sarah	"
"	26	Walter Boardman & Jane twins	son & dau
"	30	Jeremiah Stewart & Mary	son
Aug		Francis Mayhew & Susanna	son
Sep	6	Isaac & Jemima Tilton	dau
Sep	7	Anderson Taylor & Persis	son
	9	Widow Abigail Mayhew	"
	30	John Cottle & Rebecca	dau
Nov.	6	Benjamin & Lydia Mayhew	son
	13	Thomas Cox & Sarah	dau
	20	Wm Stewart & Bathsheba	son
		Shubael Norton & Love	"
Dec	4	Oliver Tilton & Eunice	son

1792

Mch	18	Beriah Tilton & Lydia	dau
	22	Benj. Bassett Esq & Abigail	son
Apl	12	Nath[l] Mayhew & Mary	dau
	26	William Allen & Love	son
May	12	Salathiel Allen & Lucy	dau
	28	Cyrus Hatch & Betsey	——
Aug	28	Norton Bassett & Clarissa	dau
Sep	7	Thomas Lumbert & Parnell	"
	22	Joseph Bassett & Mary	son
Oct	11	Fortunatus Pease Jr &	——
	18	Thomas Hillman & Ruth	son
	31	Ebenezer Skiff & Deborah	son
In Jan or Feb.		Ebenezer Bassett	——
"	"	Reuben Hatch	——
Dec	29	William Norton & Polly	dau

1793

Jan	20	Thos. Wade Mayhew & Parnell	dau
Mch	28	Reuben Hatch & Lucy	son
——		Timothy Green & Hannah?	dau
Apl	3	Ezra Hillman & Zerviah	son
	4	W[m]. Tilton Jr & Peggy	"
July	5	Hebron Mayhew & Deborah	"
	14	Prince Look & Sarah	dau
	28	Benj Mayhew & Lydia	son
	8	John Mayhew & Hannah	"
	9	Ezra Tilton	——
	—	Nicholas Butler & Lucy	——

	—	Joseph Tilton Jr	—
Nov		Jonathan Smith & Anna	son
Dec	4	Daniel Tilton & Lavina	son
		1794	
Jan	6	Isaac Tilton & Jemima	dau
	16	Ebenezer Jones & Sukey	dau
	17	Sylvanus Allen & Catherine	—
Feb	9	Wm Stewart & Bathsheba	son
	18	Matthew Tilton & Sarah	dau
Apl	12	Wm Tilton & Peggy	"
	14	Cyrus Hatch & Betsey	son
May	15	Ebenezer Skiff & Deborah	son
—		Job Look	—
—		James Hancock	—
June	27	Jeremiah Cottle & Rebecca	son
July		Ephraim Mayhew & Jedidah	dau
Aug		Vinal Skiff	—
Sept	22	Beriah Tilton & Lydia	son
		Matthew Mayhew Jr & Rebecca	"
"	25	Zebulon Allen & Prudence	dau
Oct	6	Nathl Mayhew & Mary	son
Nov		Wm Ferguson	—
—		Ebenezer Bassett	—
—		John Flanders	son
—		Zephaniah Luce	—
Dec	17	William Norton & Polly	son
	22	Thomas Wade Mayhew & Parnell	son
		1795	
Jan	2	Oliver Tilton & Eunice	dau
	4	Sylvanus Allen & Catherine	—
	28	Thomas Cox	son
Mch	25	N. Bassett Esq & Catherine	dau
Feb	18	Fortunatus Pease & Rose	son
Apl	8	Thomas Lumbert & Parnell	son
May	31	Shubael Norton & Love	dau
Jun	18	Jonathan Mayhew & Parnell	dau
	26	Thos. Hillman & Ruth	"
Aug	5	William Bassett & Olivia	son
	14	Moses Hillman & Lydia	son
Sept.		Joseph Tilton	—
Oct	17	John Flanders & Hannah	—
	8	Hebron Mayhew & Deborah	—
Nov	8[?]	William Mayhew & Phebe	dau
Oct	30	Prince Look & Sarah	—
Dec	22	Sylvanus Allen & Catherine	dau
—		Benjamin Mayhew Esq & Lydia	—
		1796	
		Ebenezer Bassett	—
Mch	1	Wm. Stewart & Bathsheba	—
	18	Thomas West	—
	—	Jeremiah Stewart & Polly	dau
May	9	Fortunatus Pease & Rose	son
—		Isaac Tilton & Jemima	son

——		James Hancock		——
June		John Mayhew		——
Aug	7	Nath[1] Pease & Elizabeth		dau
	9	Beriah Tilton & Lydia		——
	10	Shubael Norton & Love		dau
	18	Matthew Tilton & Sarah		son
	"	Oliver Tilton & Eunice		son
Sept	12	Ward Tilton & Elizabeth		——
Oct	7	Tristram Allen & Clarissa		son
Nov		Nathl Mayhew & Polly		dau
		William Norton & Polly		"
Oct		Wm Ferguson		——
—		Zepaniah Mayhew		——
—		William Adams		——
		1797		
Jan	3	Dr Allen Mayhew & Eunice		son
Ap	2	Moses Hillman & Lydia		son
Apl		Jonathan Mayhew & Parnell		son
Jan	26	Ebenezer Skiff & Deborah		son
Ap	28	Wm Tilton & Peggy		dau
May	10	Daniel Tilton & Levina		son
	11	Sylvanus Allen & Catherine		son
	11	Fortunatus Pease & Rose		——
	17	Thomas Lumbert & Parnell		dau
June	1	William Bassett & Olivia		——
	7	Owen Hillman & Polly		——
	—	John Flanders & Hannah		——
	—	Joseph Tilton & Deidamia		dau
July	10	Zebulon Allen & Prudence		dau
	13	Ephraim Mayhew & Jedidah		son
	22	Matthew Mayhew & Rebecca	twins	dau dau
Sept	14	Nathl Pease & Elizabeth		dau
Oct	20	Matthew Allen & Patience		dau
Nov	20	George West & Prudence		son
Nov	26	John Mayhew & Hannah		dau
June	30	Ebenezer Bassett		——
		1798		
Jan		John Cottle & Rebecca		——
Mch	11	Shubael Norton & Love		son
	14	William Mayhew & Phebe		son
Ap	8	Hebron Mayhew & Deborah		dau
	12	Oliver Tilton & Eunice		——
July	8	James Hancock		dau
	14	Uriel Hillman & Betsey		"
Aug		Sylvanus Allen & Catherine		son
Sept.		William Norton & Polly		"
Oc	27	Wm Stewart & Bathsheba		twins dead
—		Beriah Tilton & Lydia		——
Dec	5	Owen Hillman & Polly		son
Sept	5	Moses Hillman & Lydia		——
—		Abishai Lumbert		——

RECORDS OF THE CONGREGATIONAL CHURCH OF CHILMARK, MASS. 1787–1820.

Communicated by WILLIAM J. ROTCH, Esq., of West Tisbury, Mass.

1799

		Tristram Allen & Clarissa	son
		Nath[l] Mayhew & Polly	son
Apl	15	John Flanders & Hannah	——
May	6	W[m] Ferguson	——
June		Nicholas Butler	——
Aug	25	Nath[l] Pease	——
Sep	16	Matthew Allen & Temperance	son
	23	William Tilton & Peggy	——
	—	Francis Lumbert	——
Oct	12	Sylvanus Allen & Patience	dau
—		Shubael Norton & Love	——
—		Moses Adams & Martha	——
July		Benjamin Mayhew Esq & Lydia	dau
Oct		William Pool & Bathsheba	——
—		Daniel Tilton & Lavina	——
—		James Adams	——
Dec	20	Ezra Tilton	——
—		Joseph Tilton & Deidamia	son

1800

Jan	3	William Adams	——
	13	John Mayhew	——
	29	Thomas Cox	——
Mch	9	W[m] Stewart & Bathsheba	dau
	10	Zebulon Allen & Prudence	son
May		Ward Tilton & Elizabeth	son
"	15	George West & Prudence	dau
July	11	Archibald McCollum & Polly	son
Aug	7	Susanna Johnson	——
	8	Oliver Tilton & Eunice	dau
	19	James Hancock	——
	25	Jonathan Mayhew & Parnell	son
Sep	11	Hebron Mayhew & Deborah	son
	30	Ezra Allen & Beulah	dau
—		W[m] Norton & Polly	son
Oct	13	Polly, Stewart	son
	26	William Mayhew & Phebe	——
Mch		Matthew Coffin & Betsey	——
—		Uriel Hillman	——
Sept	4	Dr Allen Mayhew & Eunice	dau

1801

Jan	5	Moses Hillman & Lydia	dau
	24	David Tilton & Matty	"
Mch	27	Fortunatus Pease	——

Ap	26	Zephaniah Mayhew	——
Jun	30	Nathl Mayhew & Polly	dau
Aug	9	W^m B Mayhew & Prudence	"
	16	Wm Bassett & Olivia	"
—		Shubael Norton & Love	
Nov	9	John Flanders	
—		Nathl Pease	
June		Abishai Lumbert	

1802

Jan	1.	Thos. Lumbert & Parnell	dau
	12	Tristram Allen & Clarissa	"
	—	Henry Allen & Sophia	son
Ap	3	Beriah Tilton & Lydia	dau
	24	Seth Mayhew & Betsey	son
—		Benjamin Mayhew Esq	——
Mch	29	Wm Ferguson	dau
Ap	23	Wm Tilton & Peggy	dau
Apl	27	Ezra Tilton	dau
	28?	William Adams	"
May	23	Archibald McCollum	son
Mch	12	Mattheu Allen	dau
May	27	Prince Hillman & Nancy	"
July	25	Daniel Tilton & Lavina	"
Nov	10	Sylvanus Allen & Catharine	"
	20	Samuel Manter	"
Dec	6	James Hancock	son
	14	Rebecca Hillman	dau

1803

Jan	2	Wm Stewart & Bathsheba	son
	7	Moses Hillman & Lydia	dau
	15	Fortunatus Pease	son
Feb	15	Experience Douglass	son
Jun	4	Hebron Mayhew & Deborah	son
	8	Nathl Pease & Elizabeth	——
	23	W^m B Mayhew & Prudence	son
July	8	Wm Bassett & Olivia	dau
Aug	1	Archibald McCollum & Polly	son
Sep	2	Samuel Nickerson & Jane	son
Sep	25	Shubael Norton & Love	dau
Oct	23	William Mayhew & Phebe	son
Dec	19	Nathl Mayhew & Polly	son

1804

Feb	22	Jeremiah Pease	dau
Mch	15	Henry Allen & Sophia	son
	29	John Flanders & Hannah	son
Apl	3	William Ferguson	——
	13	George West & Prudence	dau
	23	Seth Mayhew & Betsy	"
June	8	Beriah Tilton & Lydia	"
	27	Nathl Pease & Elizabeth	son

Aug	3	James Allen & Cynthia	son
Sep	1	Mayhew Smith & Sally	dau
	5	Tristram Allen & Clarissa	son
	7	Zebulon Allen & Prudence	son
Oct	1	Joseph Mayhew & Jedidah	dau
	14	Thomas Lumbert & Parnell	son
Nov	14	Zephaniah Mayhew & Eunice	son
Dec	8	Moses Hillman & Lydia	dau

1805

Jan	30	Benjamin Mayhew & Lydia	son
Mch	1	Samuel Manter & Sally	"
Apl	22	Betsey Hancock	"
May	13	Sylvanus Allen & Catherine	dau
Jun	22	William Adams & Thankful	son
Sep	14	Thomas Tilton & Fear	son
	21	Hebron Mayhew & Deborah	dau
Oc	14	Oliver Tilton & Eunice	son
	22	Mayhew Cottle & Sally	dau
—		George Look & Persis	——

1806

Jan	10	Fortunatus Pease & Rose	dau
	18	Daniel Luce & Abigail	son
Feb	3	Horace Gould & Polly	dau
	23	James Allen & Cynthia	"
Mch	10	Wm B Mayhew & Prudence	son
Apl	5	Moses Hillman & Lydia	dau
	27	Ephraim Pease & Sukey	"
	28	Archibald McCollum & Patty	"
May	12	Wm Stewart & Bathsheba	"
Jun	29	John Flanders & Hannah	dau
July	18	Ephraim Pool & Polly	"
Aug	17	William Mayhew & Phebe	"
Sep	7	Seth Mayhew & Betsey	"
Oct	1	Mayhew Smith & Sally	"
	4	Henry Allen & Sophia	"
Nov	6	David Mayhew & Patty	"
	27	George West & Prudence	"

1807

Jan	21	Tristram Allen & Clarissa	dau
Feb	19	George Look & Persis	"
May	21	Daniel Luce & Abigail	son
	27	Benjamin Mayhew & Lydia	"
Jun	27	Mayhew Cottle & Sally	dau
July	7	Joseph Mayhew & Jedidah	"
Aug	25	William Tilton & Peggy	"
Sep	15	Thomas Norton & Lavina	son
Oct	12	Nathl Pease & Elizabeth	"
	21	Samuel Hancock	dau
	27	Thomas Tilton & Fear	son
Nov	25	Zebulon Allen & Prudence	dau

1808

Jan	17	Thomas Lumbert & Parnell	dau
Apl	19	Archibald McCollum & Patty	"
	27	Mayhew Smith & Sally	son
July	8	William Adams & Thankful	son
	18	Abner Mayhew & Eunice	dau
Aug	8	John Robinson & Jane	dau
Sep	1	Moses Hillman & Lydia	son
	7	William Cottle & Anne	"
	11	David Mayhew & Patty	"
	14	George Look & Persis	dau
	17	Ephraim Mayhew & Sukey	son
Nov	8	Moses Adams & Martha	dau
Dec	5	Daniel Luce & Abigail	son

1809

Jan	18	Jeremiah Pease	dau
	27	James Allen & Cynthia	son
	30	William Mayhew & Phebe	dau
Feb	3	Seth Mayhew & Betsey	dau
	8	Wm Stewart & Bathsheba	son
	20	W^m B Mayhew & Prudence	dau
Mch		Benjamin Mayhew & Lydia	dau
Apl		George West	dau
May	27	Mayhew Cottle & Sally	dau
Jun	4	John Flanders & Hannah	son
—		Daniel Tilton & Lavina	dau
July	31	Stephen Hillman & Bathsheba	dau
Oct	4	Mayhew Smith & Sally	dau
Nov	22	Nathaniel Vincent	son
—		Ephraim Allen Jr	dau
Dec	12	Samuel Hancock	dau

1810

Apl	4	Nathl Pease & Elizabeth	dau
—		Thomas Tilton & Fear	dau
	15	Ephraim Mayhew & Susannah	dau
	27	Abner Mayhew & Eunice	dau
	30	George Look & Persis	dau
Jun	21	Zephaniah Mayhew	son
July	17	William Adams & Thankful	son
Aug	18	Ephraim Pool & Lucinda	son
	28	Daniel Luce & Abigail	son
Sep	13	Archibald McCollum	dau
	22	Henry Allen & Sophia	son
Oct	14	William Cottle	son
	18	David Mayhew	son
—		Moses Hillman & Lydia	son
—		Jeremiah Pease	——

1811

—		Mayhew Smith & Sally	dau
Ap	21	Owen Hillman & Polly	dau

May	11	Seth Mayhew & Betsey	son
July	3	David Tilton & Jedidah	son
Aug	10	W^m B Mayhew & Prudence	dau
	26	Tristram Allen & Clarissa	son
	29	Ephraim Allen & Rebecca	dau
Sep	7	Moses Adams & Martha	son
	9	James Allen & Cynthia	dau
Oct	4	William Mayhew & Phebe	son
—		Stephen Skiff & Bathsheba	——
Nov	29	Benjamin Bassett & Prudence	dau
Dec	7	George West & Prudence	son
	10	Thomas W Mayhew & Lucy	son

1812

Jany	12	John Flanders & Hannah	son
	21	Daniel Luce & Abigail	dau
Feb	25	Abner Mayhew & Eunice	dau
	26	Serano Tilton	son
Mch	10	Wm Stewart & Bathsheba	dau
Apl	13	Joseph Mayhew & Jedidah	son
	21	Ephraim Pool & Lucinda	dau
	26	Samuel Norton	son
July	11	William Adams & Thankful	dau
	14	Archibald McCollum & Patty	dau
Sep	23	George West & Prudence	dau
Dec	11	Francis Tilton & Parnell	dau
	25	David Mayhew & Polly	dau

1813

Feby	—	Nath'l Pease & Elizabeth	twins { son dau
	16	Jethro Robinson & Jane	dau
	23	Owen Hillman & Polly	dau
	26	Frederick Mayhew & Ethelinda [Zelinda?]	dau
Mar	24	Wm Cottle & Anne	dau
	26	Mayhew Cottle & Sally	son
Jun	7	Thomas Tilton & Fear	son
	15	Samuel Hancock & Fanny	son
July	8	Hebron Tilton & Deidamia	son
	16	Ephraim Allen Jr	dau
Aug	3	Ephraim Pool & Lucinda	son
	22	Mayhew Cottle & Sally	dau
Dec	4	Zephaniah Mayhew	son
	12	Benjamin Bassett & Prudence	son
	26	Paine Tilton & Persis	son
—		David Tilton	
	31	Wade Mayhew & Lucy	son

1814

Jan	16	Malatiah Mayhew	son
	26	Samuel Crowell	son
Feb	2	W^m B Mayhew & Prudence	dau
	26	Tristram Allen & Clarissa	dau

Mch	2	Ward Tilton Jr	dau
	15	Moses Hillman & Lydia	son
May	2	Francis Tilton & Parnell	son
	5	Henry Allen & Sophia	dau
	18	George West & Prudence	son
July	15	Abner Mayhew & Eunice	dau
	24	William Mayhew & Phebe	son
Sept	20	Hebron and Prudence —— [Tilton?]	son
Oct	24	Moses Adams & Matty	dau
Nov	2	William Clark	dau
Dec	12	John Hancock	dau
	24	John Robinson & Jane	son
June	25	Nathl Pease & Elizabeth	dau

1815

Jan	14	William Adams & Thankful	son
Mch	13	Jeremiah Pease & Nancy	son
	14	Stephen Skiff & Bathsheba	son
Apl	5	Archibald McCollum & Patty	son
	10	Owen Hillman & Polly	dau
May	16	Ephraim Mayhew & Susan	dau
Jun	1	Ward Tilton & Anna	son
	3	David Mayhew & Patty	dau
	15	Wm Packard & Rebecca	twins { son, son
July	24	Ephraim Pool & Lucinda	son
	31	Francis Tilton & Parnell	son
Oct	26	Pain Tilton & Persis	dau
Nov	17	Ephraim Allen & Rebecca	son
	25	Mayhew Cottle & Sally	dau
Dec	8	David Tilton & Jedidah	dau
	14	Hebron Tilton & Prudence	son

1816

Jany	21	Josiah Tilton & Polly	son
Mch	14	Mayhew & Sally —— [Cottle?]	son
Apl	3	Joseph Mayhew	son
May	4	Aaron Look	dau
July	23	Thomas Tilton & Fear	son
Aug	3	Samuel Norton	twins { son, dau
Sept	4	Thos Wade Mayhew & Lucy	dau
Oct	20	Zephaniah ———	son
Nov		Henry Allen & Sophia	son
Dec	11	John Robinson & Jane	son

1817

Jan	8	Wm B Mayhew & Prudence	son
	27	George West & Prudence	son
	28	Shubael Smith & Deidamia	dau
	29	William Mayhew & Phebe	dau
Feb	3	Archibald McCollum & Patty	dau
Mch	11	Asa Johnson & Prudence	son

Apl	27	Ebenezer Luce	dau
May	23	Cornelius Tilton & Elmira	son
Jun	6	David Mayhew & Patty	dau
	13	Ephraim Pool & Lucinda	dau
July	21	John Hancock	dau
Aug	4	Abishai Lumbert	"
Oct	3	David & Jedidah —— [Tilton?]	son
	4	Owen Hillman	dau
Oct	—	Jeremiah Pease	——
Nov	20	Pain Tilton & Persis	son

1818

Jany	19	Ephraim Allen	dau
Mch	31	Melatiah Mayhew	son
Apl	5	Love West	dau
Jun	17	Wm Tilton Jr	"
July	15	Samuel Tilton & Rebecca	"
	26	Mayhew & Sally Smith	son
Sept	2	Joseph Mayhew	son
Oct	9	John Lewis	dau
	19	W^m^ B Mayhew	son
	27	William Adams	dau
Nov	8	George Mayhew	son
Dec	4	Josias Tilton	dau
	16	Ebenezer Luce	dau
	3	Abner Mayhew	son
	20	Mayhew Cottle & Sally	dau
	28	Stephen Skiff	son

1819

Feb.	8.	Cornelius Tilton & Elmira	dau
Mch	17.	Ephraim Pool & Lucinda	"
	28	Asa Johnson & Prudence	dau
May	13	Thos W Mayhew & Lucy	son
Sept	8	John Robinson & Jane	son
	15	William Mayhew & Phebe	son
Oct	6	Jeremiah Manter & Elizabeth	son
	14	David Mayhew & Martha	dau
Nov	13	George West & Prudence	son
Dec	2	Mayhew Smith & Sally	dau
	13	Pain Tilton & Persis	son

1820

Mch	7	Ephraim Allen	son
	26	David Tilton	son
Aug	18	Cornelius Tilton	dau
Sep	27	Davis Mayhew	dau
Oct	26	John Thaxter	son
Dec	18	Joseph Mayhew	son
—		David Luce	——
—		Beriah Tilton	——

Finis

Truman Cottle b. June 27, 1794.

BIRTHS, MARRIAGES AND DEATHS, FROM THE RECORDS OF THE ANCIENT TOWN OF DARTMOUTH,* MASS.

[Transcribed by JAMES B. CONGDON, Esq., of New Bedford, and communicated for the Register.]

Morton, Ruth, d. of Manasseh	Feb. 8, 1713–14
Morton, Seth, s. of Manasseh and Mary	Jan. 20, 1721–2
Michell, Hannah, d. of James and Hannah	Aug. 22, 1743
Morton, Sarah, d. of Seth and Elizabeth	July 3, 1748
Morton, Hannah, d. of " "	April 16, 1750
Morton, Ruth, d. of " "	June 3, 1752
Morton, Timothy, s. of " "	March 3, 1754
Summerton, Thomas, s. of Thomas	April 15, 1711
" Daniel, s. of "	Nov. 15, 1713
Smith, William, s. of David and Jean	Dec. 3, 1740
" Thomas, s. of " "	March 6, 1741
" Hannah, d. of " "	Feb. 27, 1743
" Barnabas, s. of " "	May 6, 1745
" David, s. of " "	Jan. 1, 1753
" James, s. of " "	Dec. 30, 1755
" Ruth, d. of " "	Aug. 27, 1757
Lapham, Thomas, s. of John	Sept. 30, 1682
Pope, Hannah, d. of Seth 2d [son of Elnathan] and Sarah	July 2, 17—
Pope, Hannah, d. of Seth 2d and Sarah	March 8, 1755
Slocum, ——— d. of Peleg	Oct. 29, 1682
" Deliverance, d. of "	Feb. 10, 1684
" Content, d. of "	July 2, 1687
" Elizabeth, d. of "	Feb. 3, 1689
" Peleg, s. of "	March 24, 1692
" Giles, s. of "	Feb. 21, 169$\frac{4}{5}$
" Holder, s. of "	June 14, 1697
Tucker, James, s. of John	Aug. 27, 1691
" John, s. of "	Oct. 25, 1693
" Joseph, s. of "	Nov. 7, 1696
" Rebecca, d. of Abraham, jr. and Elizabeth	Dec. 18, 1722
" James, s. of " " "	Sept. 23, 1724
Smith, Jeremiah, s. of Daniel [Humphrey's son] and Rebecca	June 4, 1766
" Humphrey, s. of Daniel and Rebecca	Jan. 10, 1767
" Elizabeth, d. of " " "	Nov. 12, 1768
" James, s. of " " "	July 20, 1770
" . . . & Abigail, s. & d. " " "	April — 1773
" s " " "	July 23, 1775
Russell, ——— d. of Joseph, jr., by his first wife	May 24, 1702
" Mary, d. of " " second "	June 1, 1704

* At the time these records were made, Dartmouth included Westport, New Bedford, Fairhaven and Acushnet.

Russell, Abraham, s. of	Joseph, jr.	March 19, 170$\frac{5}{6}$
" William, s. of	"	Dec. 20, 1708
" Abigail, d. of	"	March 19, 1711
" Caleb, s. of	"	Aug, 9, 1713
" Martha, d. of	"	June 24, 1716
" Joseph, s. of	"	Oct. 8, 1719
" Mary, d. of	"	Dec. 20, 1723
" Patience, d. of	"	Oct. 8, 1727
" Abigail, d. of	Abraham and Dinah	Jan. 26, 17$\frac{29}{30}$
" Barnabas, s. of	Joseph, jr., and Judith	May 26, 1745
" Rebecca, d. of	"	April 30, 1747
" Patience, d. of	"	March 10, 174$\frac{8}{9}$
" Martha, d. of	"	April 14, 1751
Ricketson, Rebecca, d. of	William	May 4, 1681
" John, s. of	"	Feb. 11, 1683
" Elizabeth, d. of	"	Sept. 1, 1684
" William, s. of	"	Feb. 26, 1686
" Jonathan, s. of	"	April 7, 1688
" Timothy, s. of	"	Jan. 22, 1690
Wing, Joseph, s. of	Matthew	Feb. 20, 169$\frac{6}{7}$
" Benjamin, s. of	"	Feb. 1, 1698
" Abigail, d. of	"	Feb. 1, 170$\frac{1}{2}$
Tucker, Henry, son of	Abraham	Oct. 30, 1680
" Mary, d. of	"	Feb. 1, 1683
" Martha, d. of	"	Nov. 28, 168–
" Patience, d. of	"	Nov. 28, 1686
" Abigail, d. of	"	Dec. 21, 1688
" Elizabeth, d. of	"	Aug. 24, 1691
" Sarah, d. of	"	April 23, 1693
" Content, d. of	"	March 12, 1695
" Abraham, s. of	"	March 5, 1697
" Joanna, d. of	"	Oct. 14, 1699
" Ruth, d. of	"	Jan. 16, 1701
" Hannah, d. of	"	April 22, 1704
Macomber, Matthew, s. of	William	Dec. 19, 1698
" Joseph, s. of	"	April 23, 1700
" William, s. of	"	March 29, 1702
" Hannah, d. of	"	Nov. 8, 1703
" Elizabeth, d. of	"	Sept. 4, 1705
" Samuel, s. of	"	July 8, 1707
" Sarah, d. of	"	March 13, 1709
" Timothy, s. of	"	Oct. 8, 1711
" Ruth, d. of	"	Oct. 28, 1714
" Margaret, d. of	"	Jan. 16, 1719
Mosher, Thomas and Philip, sons of	Benjamin and Phebe	June 17, 1755
" Desire, d. of	Benjamin and Phebe	March 12, 1757
" Richard, s. of	" "	May 4, 1759
" Phebe, d. of	" "	May 19, 1761
" Stephen, s. of	" "	July 22, 1763
" Lydia, d. of	" "	March 9, 1765
" James, s. of	" "	Nov. 3, 1766
" Jonathan, s. of	" "	April 18, 1768

Smith, George, s. of Deliverance	Aug. 27, 1701
" Hope, d. of "	Jan. 28, 1703
Potter, Isabel, d. of Stoak	Oct. 19, 1703
" Margaret, d. of "	June 30, 1705
" Hannah, d. of "	May 3, 1707
" Nathaniel, s. of "	Jan. 7, $170\frac{8}{9}$
" Benjamin, s. of "	June 21, 1711
" Dorothy, d. of "	Feb. 2, 1713 or 14
" Lydia, d. of Nathaniel (son of Stoak and Mary)	Dec. 7, 1727
" Desire, d. of Nathaniel	Sept. 12, 1729
" Stoak & Elizabeth, s. & d. "	Dec. 10, 1731
" Joseph, s. of "	July 31, 1735
" Bathsheba, d. of "	May 19, 1737
" Cornelius, s. of "	May 20, 1739
" Stephen, s. of "	March 5, 1741
" Mary, d. of "	Oct. 1, 1743
" Hannah, d. of "	Oct. 25, 1747
Sisson, Susannah, d. of Richard	Oct. 24, 1703
" Richard, s. of "	July 17, 1705
" Thomas, s. of "	April 22, 1707
" George, s. of "	March 26, 1711
" Ledijah, d. of "	Sept. 8, 1714
" James, s. of "	July 11, 1716
" Lemuel, s. of "	Sept. 21, 1725
Mosher, Hope, d. of Jonathan and Ann	April 17, 1757
" Gardner, s. of " "	Aug. 30, 1752
" Elizabeth, d. of " "	November, 1754
Wilcocks, Susannah, d. of Stephen	Feb. 14, 169–
" Daniel, s. of "	Dec. 29, 1699
" Thomas, s. of "	Oct. 12, 1701
" Elizabeth, d. of "	Jan. 18, 1704
" Stephen, s. of "	Jan. 10, 1708
Soul, Martha, d. of Benjamin and Meribeh	Oct. 1, 1743
" Patience, d. of " "	Jan. 30, 1745
Howland, Gideon, s. of Benj^a. & Mary	May 11, 1750
" Silvia, d. of " "	Feb. 12, 175–
" Benjamin, s. of " "	Oct. 12, 1754
Tripp, Abigail, d. of Joseph	Aug. 11, 1710
" Ruth, d. of "	Nov. 6, 1712
" Price, s. of "	May 15, 1715
" Dinah, d. of "	November, 1716
" Philip, s. of "	April 3, 1725
" Hannah, d. of "	Aug. 13, 1728
Russell, Meribah, d. of Seth & Mary	March 24, 1760
" Dinah, d. of " "	Sept. 10, 1761
" Seth, s. of " & Keziah	Sept. 25, 1766
" Charles, s. of " "	Nov. 22, 1768
" James, s. of Jonathan	May 7, 1687
" William, s. of "	Oct. 28, 1691
Allin, Rebecah, d. of Benjamin	April 28, 1705
Born [Bourne?] William, s. of William	Oct. 3, 1704
Huddlestone, Peleg, s. of Henry	Jan. 2, 1702

Huddlestone, Elizabeth, d. of Henry	Oct. 1, 1704
Merehaw, [Merrihew ?] John, s. of Jonathan	March 14, 1695
" Thomas, s. of "	Jan. 1, 1697
" Timothy, s. of "	Aug. 11, 1702
" Elias, s. of "	Sept. 6, 1704
Talman, Mary, d. of Jonathan	May 3, 1695
" Nathaniel, s. of "	Jan. 14, 1696
" James, s. of "	Feb. 7, 1698
" Darius, s. of "	Feb. 3, 1690
" Sirus [Cyrus?] s. of "	Nov. 26, 1702
" Timothy, s. of "	Feb. 24, 1704
Russell, Elizabeth, d. of John	April 19, 1705
Lake, Alice, d. of Thomas	Dec. 6, 1677
" Thomas, s. of "	Nov. 13, 1680
" John, s. of "	Aug. 23, 1683
" Joseph, s. of "	July 17, 1686
" Mary, d. of "	Sept. 19, 1689
" Benjamin, s. of "	May 29, 1697
Smith, John, s. of Eliezer	June 23, 1681
" Eliphal, s. of "	May 28, 1683
" Thomas, s. of "	May 19, 1685
" Rebecah, d. of "	June 21, 1688
" James, s. of "	Feb. 8, 1689
" Desire, d. of "	Dec. 13, 1692
" Joseph, s. of "	Oct. 26, 169–
Hathaway, Sarah, d. of John	Feb. 24, $168\frac{3}{4}$
" Joannah, d. of "	Jan. 28, 1685
" John, s. of "	March 18, 1687
" s. of "	April 3, 1690
" Hannah, d. of "	Feb. 16, 1692
" Mary, d. of "	June 11, 1694
Sisson, Richard, s. of James	Feb. 19, 1692
" Mary, d. of "	Feb. 26, $168\frac{4}{5}$
Russell, John, s. of John [and Mehitable]	June 16, 1686
Hathaway, Jonathan, s. of John	June 23, 1697
" Richard, s. of "	May 21, 1699
" Thomas, s. of "	Feb. 5, 1700

MARRIAGES.

Tucker, Abraham, Junr.	Russell, Elizabeth	March 1, 1721
Burrel, James	Russell, Mehetabel	March 14, $170\frac{4}{5}$
Eson, Peter, of R. I.	Slocum, Content	April 17, 1705
Spooner, Jonathan	Gidloo, Annes,	April 17, 1705
Perry, Edward, of Sandwich	Smith, Elizabeth	Oct. 16, 1705
Wood, Daniel,	Ricketson, Elizabeth	Oct. 17, 1705
Briggs, Thomas, Junr.	Allen, Mary, dau. of Ebenezer	April 25, 1706
Tripp, Aial	Davis, Anne	Jan. 25, $17\frac{10}{11}$
Wate, Thomas	Tripp, Mary	Jan. 25, $17\frac{10}{11}$
Elles, Joel	Gatchell, ——	May 25, 1715
Mosher, Hugh	Devil, Sarah	April 25, 1717
Manchester, Thomas	Maccomber, Mary	Oct. 18, 1717
Goddard, Daniel, of Jamestown	Tripp, Mary	Nov. 21, 1717

Mosher, Joseph	Smith, Mehetebel	Oct. 23, 1718
Mott, Adam	Hathaway, Apphia	Dec. 18, 1718
Brown, William, of Portsmouth	Earl, Hannah	Aug. 27, 1718
Mosher, Jonathan	Potter, Isabel	Jan. 7, 171$\frac{19}{20}$
Wait, Reuben	Elizabeth	Aug. 2, 1720
Weden, Daniel, of Jamestown	Slocum, Joanna	March 2, 1720-1
Allen, Increase, Jr.	Allen, Lydia	June 29, 1721
Borden, Thomas, of Tivertown	Gifford, Mary	Aug. 3, 1721
Allen, Joseph	Ray, [?] Jeneatte	Nov. 17, 1721
Jenins, Joseph	Mosher, Hannah	Dec. 28, 1721
Tucker, Abraham, Jr.	Russell, Elizabeth	March 1, 1721
Brownell, George	Devil, ———	June 22, 1716
Pope, Elnathan	Pope, Mary	March 14, 17$\frac{15}{16}$
Howland, Henry	Briggs, Elizabeth	Dec. 27, 1722
Wing, Matthew	Ricketson, Elizabeth	Sept. 4, 1696
Tucker, Abraham, s. of Henry, deceased	Slocum, Mary, of R. I.	Oct. 30, 1679
Tucker, Abraham	Mott, Hannah, of R.I.	Nov. 26, 1690
Wilcocks, Stephen	Briggs, Susannah	Feb. 9, 169-
Tripp, Joseph	Smith, Elizabeth	Oct. 13, 1709
Russell, John	Rebeccah	April 25, 1704
Smith, Eliezer	Sprague, Ruth	Aug. 12, 1680
Hathaway, John	Joannah	March 15, 1682
Russell, John	Mahitable	July 17, 16—
Hathaway, John	Patience	Sept. 29, 1696

Deaths.

Summerton, Thomas	October 1, 1736
Smith, Barnabas, s. of David and Jane	" 12, 1765
Soule, George	May 12, ——
Soule, John	" 11, 1704
Man, Frances, w. of William	Feb. 26, 1699 or 1700
Lapham, William	Aug. 8, 1702
Lapham, Thomas	May 8, 1704
H—— Robert	April 1, 1708
Cadmon, George	Nov. 24, 1718
Tripp, Joseph	Nov. 17, 1718
Pickham, Stephen	April 23, 1721
Huddlestone, Volintine (99 years old)	June 8, 1727
Jenney, John	April 10, 1727
Pope, Seth	March 17, 172$\frac{7}{6}$
Pope, Hannah, d. of Seth 2d	Aug. 9, 1753
Tucker, John, Jr.	June 14, 1730
Tucker, Elizabeth, w. of Abraham, Jr.	Oct. 9, 1724
Russell, Joseph	April 13, 1748
Tucker, Mary, w. of Abraham	Sept. 25, 1689
Wilcox, Stephen	Nov. 13, 1736
Howland, Benjamin	Oct. 8, 1755
Russell, Mary, w. of Seth	July 22, 1764

BIRTHS, MARRIAGES AND DEATHS, FROM THE RECORDS OF THE ANCIENT TOWN OF DARTMOUTH, MASS.

[Transcribed by JAMES B. CONGDON, Esq., of New Bedford, for the Register.]

MARRIAGES.

Tripp, Peleg [second wife]	Cornell, Elizabeth, dau. of Stephen	Jan. 29, 1712
Waite, Joseph	Wolf, Elizabeth	Nov. 30, 1715
Barker, James	Tucker, Elizabeth	Dec. 31, 1715
Devil, Jeremiah	Allen, Sarah,	May 24, 1711
Cannon, John	Hathaway, Sarah, dau. of John	Oct. 11, 1709
Earl, Ralph, s. of Ralph	Dillingham, Dorcas, dau. of Henry	1692
Tripp, Joseph	Fish, Mehitable	Aug. 6, 1667
Maxfeld, Timothy	Sherman, Lediah	Jan. 15, 1707
Howland, Henry	Briggs, Deborah	June 3, 1698
Howland, Henry	Northup, Elizab'h	Feb. 17, 1713–14
Taber, Thomas	Rebeccah,	July 4, 1700
Howland, Benjamin	Sampson, Judith	April 3, 1684
Mosher, James	Daniel, Mercy	May 6, 1714
Tripp, John	Spooner, Rebec.	Jan. 13, 1712–13
Tripp, John	Daniel, Hannah	Oct. 24, 1737
Taber, Thomas	Harlow, Rebeccah, d. of Samuel of Plymouth [See Savage.]	July 4, 1700
Soule, Jacob	Gifford, Rebecca	Jan. 22, 1709–10
Howland, Benjamin	Johnson, ? ——	Jan. 3, 1684
Russell, Jonathan	Smith, Hasadiah	Feb., 1678
Lapham, John	Russell, Mary dau. of Joseph	April 3, 1700
Howland, Henry	Briggs, Deborah	June, 1698
Delano, Jonathan, Jr.	Hatch, Anne	June 20, 170–

"July y^e 20th, 1708. Then Joyned in maryedg $Leiu^t$. nathaniel Soul and meribah Gifforord Into the true bonds of matre mony as Lawfull Lawfull man and wife witnes my hand the day above written.

WILLIAM ARNOLD, Justtis."

Delano, Jonathan	Hathaway, Anne	
Taber, Joseph	Elizabeth	Jan. 28, 170½
Smith, Gershom	Ripley, Rebecca	June 6, 1695
Cornell, Thomas	Potter, Katharinah	—— 5, ——
Russell, Jonathan	Sampson, Judah [Judith ?]	May 6, 1707
Delano, Jabez	——, Mary	Feb. 8, 1709–10
Hathaway, Jonathan	Pope, Susanna, d. of Capt. Seth	Dec. 31, 1701

Hathaway, John	Pope, Joanna, dau. of Thomas	Mar. 15, $168\frac{2}{3}$
" John	——, Patience,	Sept. 19, 1696

Deaths.

Smith, Rebecca, dau. of Peleg, jr. and Mary	April 12, 1770
Hunt, Samuel, Rev. at his own house [the first ordained minister at Dartmouth.]	Jan. 21, 1729–30
" Dorothy, w. of Ephraim	Jan. 17, 1743
Tripp, James	May 30, 1730
Hart, Thomas, s. of William	Nov. 8, 1729
Lewis, John	Jan. 24, $17\frac{12}{11}$
Cannon, John, s. of John	Sept. 11, 1726
" John	March 28, 1750
Maxfeld, Edmund, s. of Timothy	Nov. 23, 1708
Davil, [Devil or Devol ?] Jeremi'all	Nov. 29, 1753
Howland, Edward, s. of Henry	Feb. 9, 1701
" Abigail, d. of Henry	July, 1708
" Deborah, w. of Henry	Jan. 25, 1712
Russell, Dorathy, w. of John	Dec. 18, 1687
" John, Jr.	Feb. 13, 1694–5
Cook, John	Nov. 23, 1695
Russell, John	March 20, 1695
Hathaway, Joanna, w. of John	Dec. 25, 1695
Ricketson, William	March 1, 1691
" John	Jan. 9, 1704
Sog, Rebecca, w. of John	Oct. 2, 1752
Tripp, Rebecca, w. of John	March 9, 1728–9
Taber, Samuel, s. of Thomas	Oct. 9, 1718
" Thomas	July 14, 1748
Akin, John, aged 83	June 13, 1746
Taber, Tucker, s. of Philip and Susannah	June 25, 1749
Gifford, Stephen, s. of Stephen	Feb. 23, 1711–12
Soule, Oliver, s. of Jacob and Rebecca	Jan. 4, 1714–15
Wood, Sarah, w. of Luthan	July 25, 1771
Howland, Benjamin	Feb. 12, 1726–7
Mosher, Diana, d. of John and Hannah	5 mo. 30, 1743
Howland, Edward, s. of Henry	Feb. 9, 1701
West, Bartholomew, s. of Bartholomew and Ann	between 1753 & 1756
Hix, Benjamin, s. of Joseph	Nov. 10, 1708
Hix, Joseph	Aug. 6, 1709
" Constant, s. of William	Aug. 22, 1752
Howland, Nathaniel	March 3, 1723
Smith, Gershom, s. of Gershom	Oct. 11, 171–
" Gershom	April 3, 1718
" Deliverance	June 30, 1729
" Hezekiah	Feb. 28, 1726–7
Havens, Ruth	Sept. 26, 1742
Russell, Jonathan, Jr.	Sept. 20, 1730
" Deborah, d. of Jonathan and Judah [Judith ?]	Oct. 27, 1731
" Judah, w. of Jonathan	Aug. 27, 1752
" Judah, d. of Benjamin and Hannah	March 15, 1771

Delano, Jabez	Dec. 23, 1735
Hathaway, Elizabeth, d. of Jonathan and Susanna	April 29, 1703
" Paul, s. of Jona. and Susanna	Jan. 2, 1722-3
" Jonathan, Sen.	Sept. 17, 1727
" Joanna, w. of John	Oct. 25, 1695

BIRTHS.

Fish, John, s. of John	Jan. 14, 1707-8
Spooner, James, s. of John and Elizabeth	Sept. 5, 1739
" Elizabeth, d. of " "	June 1, 1741
" John, s. of " "	Dec. 29, 1745
Shaw, Mary, d. of William and Sussana	Sept. 14, 1745
" Content, d. of " "	Feb. 9, 1747-8
" Susanna, d. of " "	Aug. 27, 1749
" John, s. of " "	April 30, 1751
" William, s. of " "	Aug. 27, 1754
Smith, Lowry, s. of Peleg, Jr. and Mary	Feb. 13, 1763
" Rebecca, d. of " "	June 20, 1765
" Elizabeth, d. of " "	Oct. 24, 1766
" Elihu, s. of " "	April 17, 1768
" John, s. of " "	May 30, 1770
" Christopher, s. of " "	Feb. 7, 1772
Pope, Abigail, d. of Isaac	Dec. 23, 1687
" Margaret, d. of "	June 30, 1690
" Deborah, d. of "	April 25, 1693
" Thomas, s. of "	April 6, 1695
" Isaac. s. of "	Sept. 10, 1697
" Joanna, d. of "	March 31, 1700
" Elnathan, s. of "	Aug. 14, 1703
Hunt, Deborah, d. of Samuel	March 8, 17$\frac{10}{11}$
" Ephraim, s. of "	Jan. 14, 17$\frac{13}{14}$
" Joanna, d. of "	July 27, 1716
" Rebecca, d. of "	April 23, 1719
" Sarah, d. of "	July 28, 1722
" Sarah, d. of Ephraim and Dorothy	May 23, 1742
" Samuel, s. of " "	Jan. 12, 1743
Mitchell, Seth, s. of William and Sarah	Dec. 11, 1738-9
" Bette, d. of " "	March 22, 1741
" David, s. of William, Jr. and Pernal	Jan. 20, 1748-9
" Ruth, d. of " "	Oct. 10, 1752
Hazzard, Lucretia, d. of Oliver and Abigail	May 13, 1769
" Phebe, d. of " "	July 6, 1770
Anthony, Thomas, s. of Thomas and Ruth	Sept. 25, 1754
" Abraham, s. of " "	Sept. 26, 1756
" Jacob, s. of " "	Oct. 30, 1759
" Richard, s. of " "	April 27, 1762
" Daniel, s. of " "	Jan. 26, 1765
" Sarah, d. of " "	Jan. 22, 1768
Allen, Barbara, d. of William	Feb. 10, 1703-4
" Noah, s. of "	July 24, 1707
" George, s. of "	Nov. 10, 1709
" Josiah, s. of "	Oct. 29, 1711

Allen, Sarah, d. of	William		March 21, 1714
" Marmaduke, s. of	"		Aug. 23, 1716
" Mary, d. of	"		July 9, 1718
" Joseph, s. of	"		May 23, 1721
" William, s. of	"		Aug. 18, 1723
" Elizabeth, d. of	"		Dec. 1, 1725
" Elizabeth, d. of	Noah and Rebecca		Feb. 6, 1727
" Jonathan, s. of	"	"	Aug. 3, 1729
" Sylvanus, s. of	"	"	Dec. 30, 1730
" Noah, s. of	"	"	May 6, 1732
" John, s. of	"	"	Feb. 8, 1733
" Rebecca, d. of	Sylvanus and Mary		Nov. 10, 1755
Spooner, William, s. of	Samuel		Feb. 13, 1688
" Mary, d. of	"		Jan. 4, 1690
" Samuel, s. of	"		Feb. 4, 1692
" Seth, s. of	"		Jan. 31, 1694
" Hannah, d. of	"		Jan. 27, 1696
" Joseph, s. of	"		Nov. 13, 1698
" Anna, d. of	"		April 18, 1700
" Experience, d. of	"		June 19, 1702
" Bulah, d. of	"		June 27, 1705
" Daniel, s. of	"		Feb. 28, 1693
Macomber, Elizabeth, d. of	William		March 17, 1673
" William, s. of	"		Dec. 26, 1674
" Thomas, s. of	"		June 3, 1679
" Abiel, s. of	"		Jan. 12, 1685
" John, s. of	"		July 11, 1687
" Ephraim, s. of	"		Feb 11, 1692
" Mary, d. of	"		Feb. 15, 1695
Jene, Lydia, d. of	Samuel, s. of John		Jan. 19, 1703
" John, s. of	"		July 11, 1705
Spooner, Wing, s. of	Samuel		April 30,
Smith, Jonathan, s. of	Gersham		May 15,
Tripp, s. of	James		Nov. 8, 1685
" Elizabeth, d. of	"		Nov. 21, 1687
" Robert, s. of	"		May 15, 1691
" James, s. of	"		July 17, 1694
" Mary, d. of	"		Jan. 9, 1700
" Francis, s. of	"		June 3, 1705
Havens, Robert, s. of	Robert		1686
" Ruth, d. of	"		Dec. 14, 1690
" Elizabeth, d. of	"		Feb. 1, 1694
" William, s. of	"		June, 1698
" George, s. of	"		March 24, 1700
" Joseph, s. of	"		June 9, 1705
Wait, Thomas, s. of	Reuben		April 23, 1683
" Eleazer, d. of	"		Jan. 4, 1688
" Benjamin, s. of	"		Jan. 12, 1690
" Joseph and s. of / Abigail d. of	"		June 24, 1693
" Reuben and s. of / Tabitha, d. of	"		Jan. 15, 1695
" Jeremiah, s. of	"		Jan. 16, 1698

Mosher, Robert, s. of	John	Oct. 12, 1693
" Hannah, d. of	"	Nov. 9, 1697
" Patience, d. of	"	March 30, 1698
" Abigail, d. of	"	Sept. 21, 1699
" John, s. of	"	March 12, 1703
Tripp, Lydia, d. of	James	April 30, 1707
" Thankful, d. of	"	March 8, 1708-9
" Stephen, s. of	"	Sept. 30, 1710
" Isabel, d. of	"	Dec. 31, 1713
" Israel, s. of	"	March 22, 1716

BIRTHS, MARRIAGES AND DEATHS, FROM THE RECORDS OF THE ANCIENT TOWN OF DARTMOUTH, MASS.

[Transcribed by JAMES B. CONGDON, Esq., of New Bedford, for the Register.]

BIRTHS.

Hart, Hannah, d. of William and Sarah	June 9, 1713
" Mary, d. of " "	Nov. 7, 1715
" Deborah, d. of Archepas and Sarah	March 24, 1727–8
" Hart, d. of " "	July 6, 1730
" Mary, d. of " "	May 22, 1738
" Lydia, d. of " "	Feb. 25, 1742
Luis, Archelaus, s. of John	Feb. 7, 1707
" John, s. of "	Oct. 1, 1708
" Elizabeth, d. of "	April 12, 1712
Soule, Mary, d. of George	July 30, 1695
Little, Barker, s. of Nathaniel and Lydia	Oct. 24, 1747
Howland, Abigail, d. of Stephen and Mary	Sept. 1, 1744
" Elizabeth, d. of " "	March 7, 1748
" Prince, s. of " "	Nov. 29, 1749
Wood, Zilpha, d. of George and Sarah	May 19, 1745
" George, s. of " "	May 29, 1747
" Sarah, d. of " "	March 3, 1748–9
" Phebe, d. of " "	Oct. 8, 1750
" Anne, d. of " "	July 17, 1753
" Stephen, s. of " "	April 17, 1755
" Martha and Rebecca, ds. of George and Sarah	Nov. 22, 1761
Babcock, Mary, d. of Return	Oct. 16, 1683
" Dorothy, d. of "	Jan. 19, 1684
" Sarah, d. of "	Jan. 31, 1686
" Elizabeth, d. of "	April 5, 1689
" William, s. of "	Feb. 27, 1689–?
" George, s. of "	June 21, 1692
" Benjamin, s. of "	Nov. 12, 1696
" Joseph, s. of "	Dec. 29, 1698
" Return, s. of "	Dec. 23, 1700
" James, s. of "	June 22, 1703
" Abner, s. of "	March 19, 1706
" Hannah, d. of "	Aug. 4, 1708
Hathaway, Simon, s. of Arthur	Dec. 26, 1711
" Joanna, d. of "	Nov. 5, 1713
Spooner, Paul, s. of Cornelius and Elizabeth	May 22, 1758
" Silas, s. of " "	Dec. 26, 1760
" David, s. of " "	April 9, 1763
" Elizabeth, d. of " "	June 14, 1764
Cannon, Cornelius, s. of John	July 18, 1711
" John, s. of "	Aug. 11, 1714
" Elizabeth, d. of "	March 20, $17\frac{16}{17}$
" Mary, d. of "	April 3, 1719

Cannon, Philip,	s. of John	Sept. 11, 1721
" Joanna,	d. of "	March 27, 1728
Devil, Christopher,	s. of Joseph	Jan. 7, 1700
" Lydia,	d. of "	April 3, 1701
" Joseph,	s. of "	Jan. 15, 1702
" Mary,	d. of "	July 14, 1705
Tripp, John,	s. of James	Nov. 3, 1685
" Elizabeth,	d. of "	Nov. 21, 1687
" Robert,	s. of "	May 15, 1691
" James,	s. of "	July 17, 1694
" Mary,	d. of "	Jan. 9, 1700
" Francis,	s. of "	June 3, 1705
Lapham, Mary,	d. of John	Oct. 5, 1686
" Nicholas,	s. of "	April 1, 1689
Earl, Deborah,	d. of Ralph	Sept. 27, 1693
" Barnabas,	s. of "	Feb. 3, 1698
" Hannah,	d. of "	Dec. 21, 1701
" Meribah,	d. of "	Jan. 29, 1703
Colvin, Anna,	d. of John	March 26, 1679
" John,	s. of "	April 19, 1681
" Stephen,	s. of "	Sept. 24, 1683
" Abigail,	d. of "	July 28, 1686
" Samuel,	s. of "	Dec. 10, 1688
" Anne,	d. of "	Oct. 31, 1690
" Deborah,	d. of "	May 28, 1693
" James,	s. of "	Nov. 24, 1695
" Josiah,	s. of "	June 6, 1700
Franklin, James,	s. of James	July 8, 1682
" Lydia,	d. of "	June 18, 1688
" Abel,	s. of "	May 18, 1690
Willcocks, Jeremiah,	s. of Samuel	Sept. 24, 1683
" William,	s. of "	Feb. 2, 1685
" Mary,	d. of "	Feb. 14, 1688
Earl, John,	s. of John	Aug. 7, 1688
" John,	s. of John and Mary	Aug. 7, 1687
Howland, Rebekah,	d. of Nathaniel	Aug. 12, 1685
" John,	s. of "	April 14, 1687
" Thomas,	s. of "	Feb. 18, 1689
" Sarah,	d. of "	Nov. 15, 1690
" George.	s. of "	Dec. 11, 1693
" Mary,	d. of "	
Spooner, Benjamin,	s. of William	March 31, 1690
" Joseph,	s. of "	Feb. 18, 1692
" Joshua,	s. of "	March 16, 1694
" Sarah,	d. of "	Oct. 6, 1700
" Abagail,	d. of "	Dec. 6, 1702
Tripp, John,	s. of Joseph	July 6, 1668
" Thomas,	s. of "	March 28, 1670
" Jonathan,	s. of "	Oct. 5, 1671
" Peleg,	s. of "	Nov. 5, 1673
" Ebenezer,	s. of "	Dec. 17, 1675
" James,	s. of "	Jan. 12, 1677
" Alice,	d. of "	Feb. 1, 1679

Tripp, Abiel, s. of Joseph Jan. 8, 1681
" Mehitable, d. of " Oct. 9, 1683
" Joseph, s. of " Aug. 24, 1685
" Jabez, s. of " Nov. 3, 1687
" Mary, d. of " Aug. 22, 1689
" Daniel, s. of " Nov. 3, 1691
Peckcom, [Peckham] Stephen, s. of Stephen Feb. 23, 1683
" Samuel, s. of " Aug. 17, 1685
" Eleanor, d. of " Jan. 12, 1686
" William, s. of " Oct. 27, 1688
" Mary, d. of " Aug. 17, 1690
" Hannah, d. of " Jan. 28, 1691
" John, s. of " Jan. 15, 1697
" Deborah, d. of " June 18, 1699
" Joseph, s. of " Feb. 2, 1700-1
" Jean, d. of " Jan, 23, 1702-3
" Isaiah, s. of " Sept. 14, 1705
Jene, Sarah, d. of John May 21, 1672
" Mehitable, d. of " Sept. 26, 1673
" Elizabeth, d. of " Feb. 5, 1676
" Samuel, s. of " Feb. 4, 1678
" Lydia, d. of " March 6, 1682
" John, s. of " April 18, 1684
Russell, Rebecca, d. of Joseph Jan. 3, 1688
" Benjamin, s. of " March 17, 1691
" Seth, s. of " April 7, 1696
West, Katharine, d. of Stephen Sept. 9, 1684
" Sarah, d. of " Aug. 1, 1686
" Ann, d. of " July 9, 1688
" Bartholomew, s. of " July 31, 1690
" Amy, d. of " May 22, 1693
" Stephen, s. of " May 19, 1695
" John, s. of " April 27, 1697
" Eunice, d. of " June 21, 1699
" Lois, d. of " April 12, 1701
Porter, Mary, d. of Nathaniel March 25, 1702
Tripp, Lydia, d. of Benjamin Oct. 31, 1714
" Rebecca, d. of " May 1, 1717
" Elizabeth, d. of " May 6, 1722
" Stoak, s. of " May 13, 1725
Howland, Lydia, d. of David and Levina May 24, 1754
" Henry, s. of " " Jan. 3, 1757
" Rebecca, d. of " " Jan. 24, 1760
Maxfeld, Edmund, s. of Timothy Sept. 12, 1708
" Timothy, s. of " Sept. 12, 1708
" Abagail, d. of " Aug. 17, 1710
" Elizabeth, d. of " Aug. 13, 1713
" Mary, d. of " Aug. 22, 1716
" Dorcas, d. of " Aug. 30, 1719
" Lydia, d. of " Oct. 27, 1721
" John, s. of " Aug. 16, 1726
" Nathaniel, s. of John and Dinah Sept. 5, 1756
" Abraham, s. of " " Aug. 5, 1759

Maxfeld, Mary, d. of John and Mehitabel	Aug. 11, 1772
" Dorcas, d. of " "	May 3, 1774
" Mehitable, d. of " "	April 23, 1776
Daniel, Reuben, s. of Jeremiah	July 24, 1712
" Timothy, s. of "	Jan. 1, 1713
Akin, Susannah, d. of Benjamin, Jr., and Mary	Nov. 9, 1759
" Eunice, d. of " "	July 11, 1762
Taber, Meribah, d. of John and Mary	Sept. 27, 1753
[John T. was minister Philip's son]	
" John, s. of John and Mary	Jan. 12, 1756
Howland, Edward, s. of Henry	Aug. 10, 1698
" Zoheth, s. of "	Nov. 2, 1701
" Henry, s. of "	April 3, 1703
" Mary, d. of "	March 27, 1706
" Abagail, d. of "	May 9, 1708
" Thomas, s. of "	June 6, 1709
" Hannah, d. of "	Sept. 17, 1711
" Stephen, s. of "	May 14, 1716
" Deborah, d. of "	March 17, 1717
" William, s. of "	May 30, 1720
Pope, John, s. of Seth	Oct. 23, 1675
" Thomas, s. of "	Sept. 1, 1677
" Susannah, d. of "	July 31, 1681
" Sarah, d. of "	Feb. 16, 1683
" Maty d. of "	Sept. 11, 1686
" Seth, s. of "	April 5, 1689
" Elnathan, s. of "	Aug. 15, 1694
" Hannah, d. of "	Dec. 14, 1693
" Lemuel, s. of "	Feb. 21, 1696
Taber, Precillah, d. of Thomas	Jan. 28, 1701–2
" Jonathan, s. of "	Feb. 24, 1702–3
" Amaziah, s. of "	July 9, 1704
Allen, Mary, d. of Ebenezer	Oct. 2, 1682
" Philip, s. of "	Feb. 28, 1684
" Zebulon, s. of "	May 26, 1687
" Ebenezer, s. of "	Jan. 16, 1690
" Sarah, d. of "	June 9, 1692
" James, s. of "	Nov. 30, 1695
" Hannah, d. of "	Aug. 10, 1697
Allen, Abagail, d. of Ebenezer	Dec. 16, 1705
Howland, Abagail, d. of Benjamin	Nov. 30, 1686
" Benjamin, s. of "	Nov. 16, 1688
" Isaac, s. of "	Jan. 30, 1694
" Desire, d. of "	Aug. 29, 1696
" Barnabas, s. of "	Sept. 16, 1699
" Lydia, d. of "	Oct. 10, 1701
Smith, John, s. of Deliverance	July 11, 1693
" Deborah, d. of "	July 13, 1695
" Ann, d. of "	Dec. 16, 1696
" Alice, d. of "	Oct. 29, 1698
" Peleg, s. of "	May 27, 1700
" George, s. of "	Jan. 23,

BIRTHS, MARRIAGES AND DEATHS, FROM THE RECORDS OF THE ANCIENT TOWN OF DARTMOUTH, MASS.

Transcribed for the REGISTER by JAMES B. CONGDEN, Esq., of New-Bedford.

BIRTHS.

Spooner, Simson,	s. of Isaac	Jan. 12, 1699
" Edward,	s. of "	Dec. 27, 1701
" Mercy,	d. of "	April 22, 1707
Waite, John,	s. of Thomas	Nov. 30, 171–
" Reuben,	s. of "	Feb. 7, 1713
" Thomas,	s. of "	Feb, 29, 1715–16
" Mary,	d. of "	April 5, 1718
" Meribah,	d. of "	July 20, 1720
" Mehitable,	d. of "	Nov. 18, 1722
" Martha,	d. of "	April 6, 1725
Slade, Ruth,	d. of Joseph and Deborah	April 14, 1762
Pequit, Thomas,	s. of James and Alice	June 23, 1773
" Lydia,	d. of " "	Aug. 17, 1775
Claghorn, Prince,	s. of Joseph and Elizabeth	Aug. 22, 1752
" Elizabeth	d. of " "	May 4, 1754
Mosher, William,	s. of James	March 24, 1715
" Timothy,	s. of "	Oct. 27, 1716
" Jonathan,	s. of "	May 9, 1718
" David,	s. of "	March 29, 1720
" Jeremiah,	s. of "	June 16, 1722
Sog Sarah,	d. of John and Rebecca	April 25, 1729
" Thomas,	s. of " "	Feb. 25, 1730–31
" Hannah,	d. of " "	June 6, 1733
" Mary,	d. of " "	Oct. 26, 1735
" Timothy,	s. of " "	Oct. 23, 1738
Tripp, George,	s. of John	June 16, 1716
" Timothy,	s. of "	Feb. 22, 1717
" Ruth,	d. of "	April 4, 1720
" Elizabeth,	d. of "	Aug. 23, 1722
" Rebeccah,	d. of "	July 27, 1724
" Hannah,	d. of " and Hannah	Aug. 25, 1738
" Mary,	d. of " "	March 20, 1741
Gifford, Silas,	s. of Adam and Ann	Nov. 4, 1747
" Peace,	d. of " "	Oct. 25, 1750
" William,	s. of " "	July 28, 1755

Name	Relation	Parent	Date
Tripp, Thomas,	s. of	James	Oct. 9, 1710
" William,	s. of	"	Feb. 27, 1712–13
" Timothy,	s. of	"	Oct. 22, 1716
" Mary,	d. of	"	Oct. 14, 1720
" Isaac,	s. of	"	Jan. 2, 1726–7
Taber, Jonathan, Grandson to Philip Taber, of Coaksit, minister,	s. of	Jonathan and Robey	March 20, 1735
Taber, Margaret,	d. of	Jonathan and Robey	July 10, 1740
" Gardner,	s. of	" "	May 20, 1742
" Benjamin,	s. of	" "	Feb. 20, 1747
" Peleg,	s. of	" "	Jan. 27, 1751
" Eseck,	s. of	" "	Nov. 5, 1755

[Note.—With each of these records the fact is connected that they were grand children of Philip Taber, of Coaksit, or Acoaksit, minister.]

Name	Relation	Parent	Date
Taber, Thomas,	s. of	* * Taber	Oct. 22, 1668
" Esther,	d. of	"	April 17, 1671
" Lydia,	d. of	"	Aug. 8, 1673
" Mary,	d. of	"	March 18, 1677
" Joseph,	s. of	"	March 7, 1679
" John,	s. of	"	Feb. 22, 1681
" Jacob,	s. of	"	July 26, 1683
" Jonathan,	s. of	"	Sept. 22, 1685
" Bethiah,	d. of	"	Sept. 3, 1687
" Philip,	s. of	"	Feb. 1689
" Abigail,	d. of	"	May 1693
" Sarah,	d. of	"	Jan. 1674

[Note by recorder—the 4th is last by mistake.]

[The record is so worn that the name of the father of the foregoing twelve children cannot be ascertained. The name of the first (?) child is obliterated, but the entry that follows the above gives Thomas Taber the son of Thomas *above.*]

Name	Relation	Parent	Date
Taber, Pricilia,	d. of	Thomas	June 28, 1701
" Jonathan,	s. of	"	Feb. 24, 1702–3
" Amaziah,	s. of	"	July 9, 1704
" Esther,	d. of	"	March 6, 1709–10
" Mary,	d. of	"	Nov. 12, 1711
" Samuel,	s. of	"	Dec. 4, 1714
" Seth,	s. of	"	July 5, 1719
" Peace,	d. of	Thomas (son of Joseph) & Ruth	Nov. 5, 1745
" Ruth,	d. of	" "	May 7, 1748
Akin, Davin (?)	s. of	John	Sept. 1689
" Susan,	d. of	"	Jan. 1, 1691
" Deborah,	d. of	"	Dec. 30, 1692
" Timothy,	s. of	"	Jan. 1, 1694
" Mary,	d. of	"	Jan. 23, 1697
" Hannah,	d. of	"	March 12, 1699
" Thomas,	s. of	"	March 29, 1702
" Elizabeth,	d. of	"	May 23, 1704

Aken, James,	s. of John		Aug. 1, 1706
" Judith,	d. of "		Oct. 17, 1708
" Benjamin,	s. of "		May 18, 1715
" Ebenezer,	s. of "		Dec. 2, 1717
" Susanna,	d. of John and Hannah		Sept. 27, 1718
" Elihu,	s. of " "		Aug. 6, 1720
Spooner, Jemima,	d. of William		Dec. 7, 1700
" Jane,	d. of "		May 12, 1703
" Elizabeth,	d. of "		May 22, 1705
" Micah,	s. of "		April 2, 1707

BIRTHS, MARRIAGES AND DEATHS FROM THE RECORDS OF THE ANCIENT TOWN OF DARTMOUTH, MASS.

Transcribed for the REGISTER by JAMES B. CONGDON, Esq., of New Bedford.

BIRTHS.

Spooner, Nathaniel,	s. of William	April 21, 1709
" Rebecca,	d. of "	Nov. 17, 1710
" Sarah,	d. of "	Jan. 18, 1711 or 12
" Mercy [or Mary],	d. of William	Jan. 8, 1713–14
" Isaac,	s. of William	Jan. 9, 1715–16
" Alice [?],	d. of "	March 27, 1718
" William,	s. of "	Jan. 29, 1719–20
" Ebenezer,	s. of "	May 29, 1724
Delano, Thomas, s. & " Rebeccah, d.	of Nathan & Sarah	Oct. 18, 1754
Smith, William,	s. of Jonathan & Phebe	Aug. 14, 1733
" Gideon,	s. of William & Elizabeth	Dec. 28, 1753
" Zadoc,	s. of " "	Dec. 8, 1755
" Judith,	d. of " "	July 14, 1757
" Rebecca,	d. of " "	June 7, 1759
" Catharine,	d. of " "	July 29, 1761
" Caleb,	s. of " "	Nov. 5, 1763
" Noah,	s. of " "	March 29, 1765
" Anne,	d. of " "	May 4, 1768
" Elizabeth,	d. of " "	Nov. 26, 1770
Tabor, Richard,	s. of Philip & Susannah	Nov. 25, 1711
" Thomas,	s. of " "	Nov. 18, 1713
" Zephaniah,	s. of " "	Oct. 1, 1715

BIRTHS, MARRIAGES AND DEATHS FROM THE RECORDS OF THE ANCIENT TOWN OF DARTMOUTH, MASS.

Transcribed for the REGISTER by JAMES B. CONGDON, Esq., of New Bedford.

BIRTHS.

Taber, Tucker,	s. of	Philip & Susannah	Oct. 10, 1717
" Jesse,	s. of	" "	Nov. 21, 1719
" Peace	d. of	" "	Feb. 22, 1722
" Huldah,	d. of	" "	March, 1724
" Noah,	s. of	" "	July 7, 1727
" Philip,	s. of	" "	Oct. 31, 1730
Hathway [Hathaway] Charles,	s. of	Daniel & Ruth	July 2, 1758
" Charlotte,	d. of	" "	July 25, 1760
" Nicholas,	s. of	" "	May 23, 1762
" Osman,	s. of	" "	May 13, 1765
" Zerviah,	d. of	" "	April 16, 1767
" Isaac,	s. of	" "	July 26, 1769
Ricketson, Timothy,	s. of	Jonathan	Feb. 18, 1710–11
" Mary,	d. of	"	Oct. 28, 1712
" Rebecca,	d. of	"	Feby 6, 1714–15
" Benjamin,	s. of	"	March 7, 1716–17
" Abigail,	d. of	"	April 5, 1719
Tripp, Edmond,	s. of	Philip & Sarah	June 1, 1755
" Deborah,	d. of	" "	Feb. 3, 1757
Mosher, Allen,	s. of	Joseph (Jonathan's son) & Meribah	Sept. 25, 1755
Gifford, Stephen,	s. of	Stephen & Mary	Jan. 30, 1711–12
" Patience,	d. of	" "	Dec. 16, 1712
" Hananiah,	s. of	" "	Aug. 20, 1714
" Susannah,	d. of	" "	May 24, 1716
" Pricilla,	d. of	" "	June 17, 1718
" Keziah,	d. of	" "	Feb. 27, 1720
" Abigail,	d. of	" "	Nov. 4, 1721
" Mary,	d. of	" "	Aug. 12, 1723
" Ruth,	d. of	" "	Oct. 5, 1725
" Benjamin,	s. of	" "	Feb. 2, 1727–8
" Simeon,	s. of	Job & Martha	Nov. 18, 1750
" Stephen,	s. of	" "	July 25, 1753
" Susanna,	d. of	" "	April 29, 1756
" Abraham,	s. of	" "	Jan. 7, 1759
" Thomas,	s. of	" "	May 6, 1765
" Martha,	d. of	" "	Dec. 26, 1771
Soule, William,	s. of	William	Augt. 28, 16—
" Hannah,	d. of	"	June 1, 1694
" George,	s. of	"	Oct. 5, 1695
" Benjamin,	s. of	"	May 14, 1698
" Mary,	d. of	"	Jan. 23, 1698–9
" Joseph,	s. of	"	Nov. 8, 1701
" Sarah,	d. of	"	Nov. 8, 1703

BIRTHS, MARRIAGES AND DEATHS FROM THE RECORDS OF THE ANCIENT TOWN OF DARTMOUTH, MASS.

Transcribed for the REGISTER by the late JAMES B. CONGDON, Esq., of New Bedford.

BIRTHS.

Soule,	Ealce,	d. of William		Feb. 15, 1705
"	Samuel,	s. of "		June 26, 1708
"	Jonathan,	s. of "		Dec. 15, 1710
"	Deborah,	d. of "		Feb. 1, 1712–13
Tripp,	Constant,	s. of David & Rebecca		May 25, 1721
"	Thomas,	s. of " "		May 19, 1734
Soule,	Joseph,	s. of Jacob & Rebecca		Feb. 16, 1710–11
"	Elizabeth,	d. of " "		Nov. 14, 1712
"	Oliver,	s. of " "		Sept. 7, 1714
"	Rebecca,	d. of " "		Dec. 18, 1715
"	Nathaniel,	s. of " "		Jan. 23, 1717–18
"	Benjamin,	s. of " "		Nov. 18, 1719
"	Rosamond,	d. of " "		July 28, 1723
"	Stephen,	s. of " "		Jan. 1, 1726–7
"	Isaac,	s. of Nathaniel & Jane		Aug. 22, 1742
Smith,	Abner,	s. of George (George's son) & Phebe		Sept. 19, 1767
"	Ruth,	d. of " "		Feb. 20, 1769
"	Robe,	d. of " "		Dec. 2, 1770
"	* * *	d. of Judah		3 mo. 1697
"	Susannah,	d. of "		12 mo. 28, 1699
"	Richard,	s. of "		3 mo. 7, 1702
"	William,	s. of "		8 mo. 10, 1705
"	Miribah,	d. of "		7 mo. 5, 1706
"	Michael,	s. of "		12 mo. 26, 1708–9
Taber,	Eleanor,	d. of William		Jan. 24, 1752
Wood,	Mary,	d. of Luthan & Sarah		Oct. 2, 176
"	Rebecca,	d. of " "		May 13, 17
"	Mulborough,	s. of " "		Feb. 25, 176
"	Osman,	s. of Luthan & Susannah		Sept. 12, 1775
"	Sarah,	d. of " "		May 15, 1776
Howland,	Abagail,	d. of Benjamin		Nov. 30, 1686
"	Benjamin,	s. of "		Nov. 30, 1688
"	Isaac,	s. of "		Jan. 1694
"	Desire,	d. of "		Aug. 20, 1696
"	Barnabas,	s. of "		Sept. 16, 1699
"	Lydia,	d. of "		Oct. 8, 1701
Mosher,	John,	s. of [no parents given]		1 mo. 12, 1703
"	Hannah,	d. of [same]		1 mo. 13, 1712
"	Obadiah,	s. of John & Hannah		10 mo. 1, 1734
"	Diana,	d. of " "		11 mo. 1, 1733–4
"	Abigail,	d. of " "		12 mo. 21, 1735–6
"	Peace,	d. of " "		1 mo. 12, 1738

BIRTHS, MARRIAGES AND DEATHS FROM THE RECORDS OF THE ANCIENT TOWN OF DARTMOUTH, MASS.

Transcribed for the REGISTER by the late JAMES B. CONGDON, Esq., of New Bedford.

BIRTHS.

Mosher,	Paul,	s. of John and Hannah		4 mo. 15, 1740
"	Hannah,	d. of " "		10 mo. 21, 1743
"	Keziah,	d. of " "		2 mo. 1, 17
"	Sarah	d. of " "		4 mo. 16, 1751
Taber,	Thomas,	s. of Thomas		Octo. 22, 1668
"	Esther,	d. of "		April 17, 1671
"	Lydia,	d. of "		Aug. 8,
Butts,	Moses,	s. of Thomas		July 30, 1673
		d. of John		
Taber,	Sarah,	d. of Thomas		Jany 28, 16
"	Mary,	d. of "		March 18, 1677
"	Joseph,	s. of "		March 7, 1679
Russell,	Joseph,	s. of Joseph	twins	November 22, 167
"	John,	s. of "	twins	Nov. 22, 167
"	William,	s. of "		May 6, 1681
"	Mary,	d. of "		July 10, 1683
"	Joshua,	s. of "		Jany 26, 1686
"	Jonathan,	s. of Jonathan		Nov. 13, 1679
"	Deborah,	d. of "		Jany 10, 1681
"	Dorothy,	d. of "		May 21, 1684
Taber,	John,	s. of Thomas		Feby 22, 1681
"	Jacob,	s. of "		July 26, 1683
"	Jonathan,	s. of "		Sept. 22, 1685
"	Bethiah,	d. of "		Sept. 3, 168
"	Philip,	s. of "		Feby 7, 1689
"	Abigail,	d. of "		May 2, 1693

NOTE.—The *twenty-three* foregoing names are found upon what I consider the oldest existing page of Dartmouth records. It is, as many other of the loose sheets of these records are, very much dilapidated, and it should be borne in mind that whenever an omission is found it is owing to this fact. No one need look at the records with any hope of finding any more than is here given.

Taber,	Mary,	d. of Philip	Jany 28, 1668
"	Sarah,	d. of "	March 26, 1671
"	Lydia,	d. of "	Sept. 28, 1673
"	Philip,	s. of "	Feby 29, 1675
"	Abigail,	d. of "	Oct. 27, 1678
"	Esther,	d. of "	Feby 23, 1680
"	John,	s. of "	July 18, 1684
"	Bethiah,	d. of "	April 18, 1689
Badcock [Babcock]	Mary,	d. of return	Oct. 16, 1683
"	Dorothy,	d. of "	Jany 19, 1684

Badcock, Sarah,	d. of return	Jany 31, 1686
" Elizabeth,	d. of "	April 5, 1689
" George,	s. of "	June 21, 1692
" Benjamin,	s. of "	Nov. 12, 1696
" Joseph,	s. of "	Dec. 29, 1698
" Return,	s. of "	Dec. 23, 1700
" James,	s. of "	June 22, 1703

[The 17 next preceding names are from one of the earliest pages of the record. All the Babcocks are marked "transcribed."]

Lapham, Elizabeth,	d. of John and Mary	July 29, 1701
" John,	s. of " "	Oct. 2, 1703
Briggs, Mary,	d. of Thomas	Augt 9, 1671
" Susanna,	d. of "	March 14, 1672
" Deborah,	d. of "	Oct. 16, 1674
" Hannah,	d. of "	May 1, 1676
" John	s. of "	Oct. 2, 1678
" Thomas,	s. of "	April 27, 1684
" Weston,	s. of John	Nov. 4, 1702
" Thomas,	s. of "	Jany. 10, 1704
Slocumb, Meribah,	d. of Eleazer	April 28, 1689
" Mary,	d. of "	Augt. 12, 1691
" Eleazer,	s. of "	Jany 20, 1693–4
" John,	s. of "	Jany 20, 1696–7
" Benjamin,	s. of "	Dec. 14, 1699
" Joanna,	d. of "	July 15, 1702
Soule, William,	s. of William	Augt 28, 1692
" Keziah [see REG. xxxiv. 198]		June 1, 1694
" George,	s. of William	Oct. 5, 1695
" Benjamin,	s. of "	May 14, 1698
" Mary,	d. of "	Jany 22, 1698–9
" Joseph,	s. of "	Nov. 8, 1701
" Sarah,	d. of "	Nov. 8, 1703
Cummings, Mary,	d. of Philip	Jany 3, 1686
" Sarah,	d. of "	Oct. 15, 1688
" John,	s. of "	May 14, 1691
" James,	s. of "	Nov. 9, 1693
" Abigail,	d. of "	Nov. 20, 1698
" Elizabeth,	d. of "	Nov. 22, 1701
" David,	s. of "	Sept. 25, 1704
" Benjamin,	s. of "	Sept. 6, 1695
Howland, Edward,	s. of Henry	Augt 10, 1698
" Zohuth,	s. of "	Nov. 2, 1701
" * * *	s. of "	April 3, 1703
Delano, Sarah,	d. of Jonathan, Jun.	March 18, 17**
" Jane,	d. of "	Dec. 16

MARRIAGES AND MARRIAGE INTENTIONS, 1795-1844
TOWN OF EASTHAM, MASSACHUSETTS

Contributed by VERNON R. NICKERSON, of Taunton, Mass.

The following records were lately discovered by Mrs. Horace Lowe, Historian of the Town of Eastham, Massachusetts, while searching through some old books. A book labeled "Bills of Sale" was found to contain the records of marriages and publishments from October 1795 through 1844. The book is now in the possession of the Town Clerk of the Eastham Town Hall.

Record of Marriages in Eastham by Mr. Shaw

Thomas Pain and Asenath Higgins Oct. 6, 1795.
Uriah Mayo and Bethiah Knowles May 19, 1796.
Seth Smith and Susannah Foster June 6, 1796.
Thomas Cobb and Abigail Freeman Oct. 23, 1796.
John Doane and Mercy Pepper Nov. 15, 1796.
Joseph Linkhornew [Lincoln] and Phebe Walker Nov. 24, 1796.
John Brown and Sally Pepper Dec. 24, 1796.
Stephen Cole and Bethiah Nickerson Jan. 5, 1797.
John Mayo Jr. and Hannah Knowles Doane Jan. 26, 1797.
David Smith and Experience Cook Feb. 2, 1797.
Isaac Doane Jr. and Thankful Mayo March 2, 1797.
Phillip Smith and Experience Snow April 18, 1797.
Heman Smith and Ruth Doane April 27, 1797.
Thomas Dill and Ruth Linkarnew [Lincoln] June 8, 1797.
Daniel Pepper and Bethiah Freeman Aug. 31, 1797.
Ezekiel Doane and Rachel Atwood Feb. 17, 1798.
Joseph Bassett and Ruth Knowles Feb. 27, 1798.
Henry Mayo and Dorothy Collins March 9, 1798.
Joseph Linkhornew and Sarah Remick May 22, 1798.
David Gill and Mercy Mayo October 1798.
Timothy Mayo and Betty Lumbard December 1798.
Henry Wily and Polly Parker June 1798.
Samuel Doane and Polly Lumbard July 7, 1798.
Joshua Higgins and Eunice Mayo November 1798.
Henry Mayo and Bethiah Knowles Feb. 19, 1799.
Myrick Doane and Rebecca Doane Feb. 17, 1799.
Samuel Mayo and Betty Knowles Feb. 26, 1799.
Myrick Doane and Alice Freeman Feb. 24, 1799.
Timothy Cole and Azuba Nickerson April 7, 1799.

Seth Rider and Hannah Doane April 7, 1799.
Treat Moores and Mercy Briggs October 1799.
Barnabas Atwood and Lidia Gill December 1799.
Nathaniel Cole and Bethiah Cole August 1801.
Elisha Holbrook and Lucy Mayo December 11, 1801.
Samuel Knowles and Hannah Pepper Nov. 11, 1801.
Benjamin Knowles and Alice Doane Dec. 3, 1801.
Nehemiah Smith and Polly Knowles Dec. 27, 1801.
Abraham Smith and Polly Hickman February 1802.
Solomon Taylor and Hannah Dier March 9, 1802.
Samuel Cook and Priscilla Higgins March 21, 1802.
Simeon Doane and Zilpha Pepper Nov. 25, 1802.
Harding Knowles and Margery Knowles Feb. 2, 1803.
David Snow and Susanna Gill Feb. 10, 1803.
Joshua Higgins and Mercy Gill March 13, 1803.
Ephriam Cole and Jedidah Nickerson 1803.
Elisha Holbrook and Sarah Brown October 1803.
Doane Linkhornew [Lincoln] and Ruth Ward Dec. 1, 1803.
Jesse Myrick and Eliza Knowles December 1803.
Seymore Bangs and Bethiah Mayo Sept. 9, 1804.
Stephen Chipman and Betsy Mayo Sept. 1804.
Myrick Doane and Temperance Knowles October 1804.
Edward Brewer and Hitty Mayo Oct. 14, 1804.
Joshua Knowles and Lydia Knowles Dec. 23, 1804.
Elijah Knowles and Betsy A. Collins February 1805.
Ezekiel Ward and Ruth S. Cook May 1805.
Samuel Braket and Mercy Cobb November 1805.
Nathaniel Gould and Hannah Knowles October 1806.
Francis Kragman and Mary Pepper October 1806.
Dawson Linkhorn [Lincoln] and Rachel Doane Oct. 28, 1806.
David Whipple and Abigail Pepper November 1806.
Heman Doane and Mehitable Butters January 1807.
Ephriam Smith and Hannah Smith November 1806.
Eldad Dill and Roxanna Knowles May 1807.
Capt. Benjamin Seabury and Palina Collins July 1807.
Abigail Gill and Tabitha Mayo December 1807.
Scotto Cobb and Phebe Knowles February 1808.
Capt. Jesse Doane and Ruth Mayo March 1808.
Doane Collings and Ruth Clark March 1808.
Timothy Mayo and Lydia Doane April 1808.
Azanath Smith and Lydia Hopkins August 1808.
Stephen Brown and Joanna Gill August 1808.
Myrick Smith and Sally Myrick September 1808.
Samuel Mayo and Rebecca Knowles November 1808.
Ezekiel Dill and Mary Hickman December 1808.
Samuel Horton and Zerviah Hickman December 1808.
Freeman Horton and Phebe Atwood February 1809.
Josiah Doane and Abigail Hatch February 1809.
Richard Sparrow and Susan Knowles February 1809.
Samuel Myrick and Ruth Smith November 1809.
Freeman Smith and Phebe Gill December 1809.
James Mayo Jr. and Lydia Mayo March 1810.
Reuben Chapman and Susan Paine April 1810.
Nehemiah Doane and Hannah Crowel August 1810.
Lot Doane and Eliza Mayo October 1810.
Elkanah Cole and Sally Gould June 1809.
Timothy Rogers and Reliance Cobb December 1810.
Moses Wiley and Pedia Smith December 1810.
Jesse Knowles and Polly F. Doane April 1811.
Goel Snow and Phebe Snow May 1811.
Parker Brown and Rachel Atwood May 1811.
John Jarvis and Thankful Mayo July 1811.

Simeon Mayo and Patty Doane August 1811.
Aaron Higgins and Apphia Gill October 1811.
David C. Atwood and Abigail Horton October 1812.
Moses Lewis and Mehitable Pepper August 1812.
Heman Snow and Lydia Knowles December 1812.
Thomas Dill and Susan Hatch January 1813.
Edward Knowles and Abbie Knowles March 1813.
Reuben Nickerson and Kezia Smith March 1813.
Foster Brown and Polly Higgins March 1813.
Ichabod Collins and Zilah Doane September 1813.
George Clark and Betsy Collins November 1813.
Edward Freeman and Hannah Cole November 1813.
Freeman Knowles and Patty Mayo December 1813.
Harding Myrick and Rebecca Higgins February 1813.
David Cook and Susanah Mayo March 1814.
Elkanah Linnel and Sarah Walker March 1814.
John Gould and Betty Mayo April 1814.
Josiah Mayo and Betsey Atwood April 1814.
Theophilus Knowles and Hannah Doane November 1814.
Barnabas Doane and Thankful Knowles November 1814.
Dean S. Snow and Mercy Paine March 1815.
Joshua P. Atwood and Sally Knowles March 1815.
Higgins Brown and Bethiah Cook May 1815.
Daniel Cole and Priscilla Newcomb December 1815.
Ezekiel Knowles and Betsy Gill 1815.
Josiah A. Gill and Nabby Knowles February 1816.
Samuel Snow and Phebe Snow April 1816.
Elkanah Hopkins and Sally Mayo April 1816.
Josiah Doane and Sarah Smith July 1816.
Abigail Paine and Joseph Linkhorn [Lincoln] September 1816.
Allen Rogers and Polly Doane September 1816.
Harding Knowles and Betsy Knowles October 1816.
Edward C. Clark and Jerusha Cobb December 1816.
Barnabas F. Knowles and Lucy Mayo January 1817.
David Brown and Diana Walker January 1817.
Thomas Cobb and Betsey Chipman January 1817.
Samuel Sparrow and Hapsey Paine January 1817.
John Brown and Hannah Mayo February 1817.
Benjamin Higgins and Hannah Walker February 1817.
Freeman Doane and Eunice Smith February 1817.
Freeman Hatch and Abigail Mayo March 1817.
Michael Collins Jr. and Dorcas D. Cobb April 1817.
Myrick Doane and Lydia Atwood July 1817.
Capt. Joseph Collins and Hannah Mayo August 1817.
John Cook Jr. and Sally Cobb November 1817.
William Brown Jr. and Dorcas Doane March 1818.
Joshua B. Cook and Abigail Doane March 1818.
Heman Linnel and Hannah C. Walker March 1818.
Josiah Higgins and Anna Doane November 1818.
Carri Higgins and Sally Walker January 1819.
Dean Smith and Eliza Harding November 1818.
James Knowles and Ruth Doane Knowles December 1818.
Simeon Higgins and Paulina Collins December 1818.
Prince Doane and Sabrina Doane December 1818.
Samuel Nickerson and Joanna Mayo December 1818.
Josiah Smith and Rachel Cook February 1819.
John Hopkins and Diana Stubs March 1819.
Obed Knowles and Bethiah Bangs April 1819.
Freeman Doane and Zilla Mayo May 1819.
Nathan F. Cobb and Nancy Doane August 1819.
Ibanny Hatch and Sally Dill December 1819.
Abraham Davis and Mercy Doane September 1819.

James Garrt and Ruth Paine October 1819.
Jobel Nickerson and Sally Paine December 1819.
Elijah Gaut and Joanna Atwood March 1820.
Reuben Higgins and Abigail Walker February 1820.
E——— (?) Hinkley and Jimima Clark March 1820.
Josiah Mayo and Ruth Cole February 1820.
Samuel Freeman and Sally Cobb November 1821.
Benjamin A. Atwood and Polly C. Harding September 1820.
Timothy Cole and Rebecca Brown 1821.
Ichabod Linkroenew [Lincoln] and Maria Freeman 1821.
Prince Harding and Nancy Knowles September 1821.
Noah Doane and Caroline Crosby September 1821.
Barnabas Higgins and Anner Higgins October 1821.
Ebenezer Ward and Phebe Briggs January 1822.
John Harden and Eliza Gent April 1822.
Theophilus Smith and Parmelia (Grey ?) 1822.
David Smith and Ann Brown July 1822.
Daniel Dill and Jerusha Knowles October 1822.
Daniel Gill and Polly C. Horton October 1822.
Asa Gill and Rebecca Mayo October 1822.
Whitfield Willard and Phebe Doane November 1822.
Simeon Snow and Anna Knowles 1823.
Timothy Smith and Ruth F. Knowles November 1823.
William Myrick and Polly Cobb 1823.
Pain Smith and Olive Knowles 1823.
Jonathan Sherman and Mehitable Knowles January 1824.*
James Lincoln and Mercy Mayo January 1824.
Jonathan Sherman and Mehitable Knowles January 1824.*
Uriah Nickerson and Rebecca Covel February 1824.
John Atwood and Rebecca Gill February 1824.
Joshua Paine and Deborah Sherman February 1824.

Marriages in Eastham by Nathan Paine

Mr. Samuel Stinson of Boston to Miss Lydia M. Chipman of Eastham December 1823.
Davis Smith and Miss Olive Knowles, both of Eastham Nov 1823.
Mr. Knowles Doane and Miss Lucindia Cobb Apr. 8, 1824.
Mr. Joshua Young of Orleans and Miss Ruth Doane of Eastham January 1824.

Married in Eastham by Mr. Ephriam K. Avery

Mr. Crowell Doane Jr. and Miss Abigail D. Knowles, both of Eastham January 24, 1826.

Married in Eastham by Rev. B. Thatcher

Mr. Nathaniel Wiley of Welfleet and Miss Matilda Mayo of Eastham December 7, 1826.

Mr. Barnabas Cook and Miss Sophrinia Doane, both of Eastham July 20, 1826.

Married in Eastham by Rev. Frederick Upham

Mr. Seymore Bangs and Miss Anna M. Cobb, both of Eastham April 27, 1829.

Mr. Daniel Pennaman and Miss Betty Mayo, both of Eastham April 30, 1829.

Married in Eastham by Rev. Hector Brownson

Mr. Thomas Cobb 2d and Miss Priscilla M. Doane, both of Eastham June 20, 1831.

Mr. Freeman Cobb and Miss Thankful M. Doane, both of Eastham October 12, 1831.

Mr. Freeman Knowles and Miss Hannah D. Dill, both of Eastham Nov. 8, 1831.

Mr. James Chapman of Barnstable and Miss Ann P. D. Higgins of Eastham Dec. 18, 1831.

*This entry is given twice.

Mr. Leantes Lincoln and Miss Sarah D. Dill, both of Eastham 22 Dec. 1831.

Mr. Nathaniel Baker of Welfleet and Miss Evelina Smith of Eastham Feb. 5, 1832.

Mr. Joseph Emery and Miss Almira Horton, both of Eastham Jan. 3, 1833.

Mr. Elnathan Snow of Orleans and Miss Naomi Mayo of Eastham Feb. 21, 1833.

Mr. George Ward Jr. of Welfleet and Miss Mercy Smith of Eastham Dec. 4, 1832.

Mr. Myrick C. Horton and Miss Sarah T. Knowles married June 1833.

Married in Eastham by the Rev. Mr. Shaw

1824 Joshua Cole and Clarissa Smith.
1825 Heman Doane and Paulina Freeman.
1825 Joel Sparrow and Mary Crosby.
1825 Stephen C. Smith and Ruth Brown.
1825 Jonathan Snow and Bethiah Doane.
1826 Freeman D. Mayo and Bathsheba Smith.
1826 William F. Knowles and Betsy Doane.
1826 William Gill and Hannah K. Collins.
1826 Joseph M. Dill and Tamson Lincoln.
1826 Leonard Higgins and Betsy P. Gould.
1826 Jabez C. Moses and Mehitable Dill.
1826 Elisha Cobb and Thankful Doane.
1827 Samuel Higgins and Luvania Paine.
1828 James G. Smith and Alice F. Doane.
1828 John Atwood and Lucy Holbrook.
1828 Barnabas Freeman and Eliza Knowles.
1828 Samuel Sherman and Ruth Snow.
1829 Elkanah C. Braket and Sally Holbrook.
1829 Elisha Holbrook Jr. and Mehitable Smith.
1829 Harvey Snow and Thankful Knowles.
1830 Joshua W. Nickerson and Menoy Walker.
1830 Thomas Elis and Abigail Ward.
1830 Nathan Gill and Tamson Gould.
1830 Nathan Horton and Paulina Doane.
1830 Seth Paine and Rebekah Knowles.
1831 William Smith and Ruth Walker.
1831 Elkanah W. Paine and Mehitable P. Knowles.
1832 Edward Brewer and Lydia Ward.
1832 Henry Newcomb and Almania Knowles.
Nov. 29, 1830 Thomas S. Snow of Welfleet and Mary Cole of Eastham.
1833 William Bracket and Almania Brown.
1833 James Brewer and Hannah R. Snow.
1833 Whitfield Witherel and Hannah Knowles.
1833 Calvin Chapman and Mary K. Smith.
1833 Silvanus Smith and Polly A. Smith.
1833 Timothy Lincoln and Sally Smith.
1833 Curtis Hopkins and Betsey A. Brown.
1833 Benjamin Snow and Emeline Cole.
1831 Michael Sherman and Paulina Knowles.
1831 Warren Lincoln and Mary B. Freeman.
1831 Russell Doane and Martha Crosby.
1831 Joseph Cummins and Clarissa Paine.
1831 Elisha Snow and Mary P. Doane.
1832 Timothy D. Whitherel and Betsy Smith.
1832 Knowles Doane and Mary Knowles.
1832 Samuel Brackett and Patty Doane.
Feb. 1834 Josiah P. Witherell and Rebekah Smith.

Married in Eastham by the Rev. Lemuel Hanlone

Sept. 1833 Mr. Barnabas Mayo and Miss Lydia Knowles.
1833 Josiah Knowles and Martha B. Wiley.
1833 Timothy Dagget and Tabitha M. Gill.

1833 Curtis Doane and Polly Higgins.
1833 Percy C. Horton and Chloe Gill.
1834 Alpheus Baker and Bethiah Bangs.

Married in Eastham by the Rev. Mr. Shaw

1834 Josiah R. Witherel and Rebekah Smith.
1834 Frederick Prence and Phebe Lincoln.
1834 Elisha Cobb and Rebekah Gill.
1834 Lewis Smith and Mehitable Smith.
1834 Joseph Cummings and Hannah H. Knowles.
Nov. 27, 1834 Joseph Baker and Eunice S. Harding.
1834 William C. Cobb and Susan Knowles.

Married by Rev. Ezekiel Vose

Dec. 1834 Joseph Silver and Amelia Gill.

Married by the Rev. Thomas G. Brown

Nov. 27 1834 Sylvanus Collins and Palina Atwood.
April 23, 1835 Joseph Twain of Orleans and Azenath [?] of Eastham.
1835 John W. Higgins of Eastham and Mary Payton of Welfleet.
1835 Joshua Higgins and Maria H. Cobb, both of Eastham.
1835 Asa Newcomb of Welfleet and Lucindea Wiley of Eastham.
1835 Samuel S. Taylor of Welfleet and Phebe H. Higgins of Eastham.
April 30, 1836 Mr. Elkanah W. Stubs of Welfleet to Miss Pamela Horton of Eastham.
May 29, 1836 Mr. Joel Brewer and Miss Thankful M. Cobb, both of Eastham.
Dec. 26, 1836 Mr. Edward B. Sprague of Boston and Miss Catherine Briggs of Eastham, married by the Rev. Frederick Upham.

Married by the Rev. Hadden Emerson

Abijah Mayo and Miss Phebe K. Cobb, both of Eastham Oct. 18, 1836.
Henry Horton and Miss Abigail Mayo, both of Eastham Dec. 1, 1836.
Joel Snow Jr. and Miss Ruth C. Collins, both of Eastham Dec. 29, 1836.
Zenas Gray of Dennis and Miss Mary Knowles of Eastham, Jan. 10, 1837.
Josiah Doane and Miss Temperance Knowles, both of Eastham Feb. 23, 1837.

Married by the Rev. Thomas G. Brown

Mr. Albert Smith of Eastham and Miss Betsey Doane of Orleans, Feb. 16, 1837.
Capt. Thomas Knowles to Miss Rachel Horton, both of Eastham the 4 May 1837 by Rev. Warren Emerson.
Mr. Joseph Snow of Orleans to Miss Phebe Ann Smith of Eastham Nov. 5, 1837 married by Rev. Thomas G. Brown.

Married in Eastham by the Rev. Warren Emerson

Nov. 7, 1837 William Williams of Provincetown and Phebe B. Knowles of Eastham.
Nov. 28, 1837 Solomon Doane and Betsy F. Snow, both of Eastham.
Nov. 30, 1837 Bethuel Hurd of Orleans and Lovy M. Brewer of Eastham.
Jan. 23, 1838 Joshua Knowles and Lucindia Doane, both of Eastham.

Married in Eastham by the Rev. Josiah Litch

Aug. 7, 1839 Mr. William Swain of Orleans and Miss Sarah Higgins of Eastham.
Nov. 21, 1839 Mr. Freeman Dill and Miss Elizabeth Collins of Eastham.
Nov. 28, 1839 Mr. Moses Wiley Jr. and Miss Julia A. Clark, both of Eastham.
Jan. 21, 1840 Mr. Henry Doane and Miss Rebecca H. Cobb, both of Eastham.
Oct. 29, 1840 Mr. Edward Knowles Jr. of Welfleet and Miss Mary A. Horton.
Nov. 5, 1840 Mr. Winslow Snow of Orleans and Miss Alice K. Mayo of Eastham.
Dec. 17, 1840 Mr. Knowles Smith of Orleans and Miss Bethiah C. Mayo of Eastham.
March 4, 1841 Abigail Baker of Orleans and Miss Abigail M. Knowles of Eastham.

April 30, 1841 Mr. Seth T. Doane of Orleans and Miss Sally S. Smith of Eastham.
March 18, 1841 Mr. Dean Sparrow and Miss Kazilla Snow, both of Eastham.
May 18, 1841 Mr. Freeman Horton Jr. and Miss Dorcas D. Cobb both of Eastham.

Married by E. H. Jackson

Aug. 22, 1841 Mr. Zephamiah Hosea of Boston and Miss Hannah A. Dill of Eastham.
Dec. 15, 1841 Mr. Lincoln F. Cobb and Miss Mercy Doane, both of Eastham.
Oct. 14, 1841 by Rev. Solomon Hardy Mr. David Jewell of Natick to Miss Eliza J. Atwood of Eastham.
March 2, 1843 by the Rev. James G. Burt Mr. Elijah E. Knowles to Miss Tabitha G. Holbrook of Eastham.
Nov. 25, 1842 by the Rev. Jacob White Mr. Charles Brown to Miss Louisa Doane, both of Eastham.
June 16, 1843 in Orleans Mr. Richard Smith Jr. of Eastham to Miss Achsah S. Crosby of Orleans.
Sept. 19, 1842 by the Rev. Mr. Robbins Mr. Charles B. Lothrop of Boston and Miss Elizabeth R. Whelden of Eastham.
Nov. 15, 1842 Mr. Thomas Knowles and Miss Catherine P. Ingraham, both of Eastham.
Sept. 15, 1843 Married in Boston Mr. Lewis G. Smith of Eastham and Miss Caroline S. Moulton of Cambridgeport.
July 27, 1843 Mr. Otis Bradford of Duxbury to Miss Jane A. Collins of Eastham.
Sept. 5, 1843 Mr. Henry Bailey of Boston and Miss Mary F. Cobb of Eastham.
April 11, 1844 Mr. Eldridge F. Smith of Provincetown and Miss Rachel A. Horton of Eastham.

The above persons were married by Rev. O. Robbins, minister of the Methodist Episcopal Church of Eastham.

July 25, 1844 Mr. Cushing Horton Jr. and Miss Mary F. Higgins by Rev. Enoch Pratt of Brewster.
Nov. 3, 1844 Mr. Solomon H. Mayo and Miss Phebe Gould, both of Eastham were married by the Rev. Jacob White of Orleans.
Nov. 28, 1844 Mr. Nicholas R. Knowles and Miss Harriet B. Nickerson, both of Eastham were married by the Rev. Jacob White.

Record of Certificates of Publishments 1827:

Mr. Randal Doane of Eastham and Miss Eliza Sellers of Dear. (Island ?) April 7, 1827.
Mr. David Higgins of Eastham and Miss Sally Twain of Orleans, April 11, 1827.
Mr. Oliver Smith of Eastham and Miss Mary D. Pike of Scarborough, Sept. 4, 1827.
Capt. Herman Doane 3d and Mrs. Pamela Smith, both of Eastham, Sept. 28, 1827.
Mr. Joshua W. Lincoln of Eastham and Miss Mercy Chipman of Welfleet, Oct. 30, 1827.
John Atwood of Welfleet and Miss Lucy Holbrook of Eastham, Dec. 3, 1827.
Mr. Dawson W. Lincoln of Eastham and Miss Hannah Baker of Welfleet, Dec. 19, 1827.
Mr. Ephriam Higgins of Eastham and Miss Deborah P. Young of Orleans Feb. 11, 1828.
Mr. James G. Smith and Miss Allice F. Doan, both of Eastham, March 11, 1828.
Mr. Nehemiah Doane and Mrs. Polly F. Knowles, both of Eastham, April 6, 1828.
Mr. Ben Higgins of Eastham and Miss Hannah Higgins of Welfleet, July 23, 1828.
Mr. Elisha Cobb of Eastham and Miss Sophia Kenrick of Orleans, Oct. 28, 1828.
Mr. John Knowles of Eastham and Miss Zerviah Atkins of Truro, Nov. 17, 1828.
Mr. John Brown of Eastham and Miss Hannah Knowles of Orleans, Nov. 24, 1828.
Mr. Samuel Sherman and Mrs. Ruth Snow of Eastham, Dec. 22, 1828.
Mr. Barnabas Freeman and Miss Eliza Knowles, both of Eastham, Dec. 22, 1828.
Mr. Elisha Holbrook and Miss Mehitable Smith, both of Eastham, Jan. 12, 1829.

Mr. Elkanah C. Bracket of Welfleet and Miss Sally Holbrook of Eastham, Jan. 12, 1829.
Mr. Nathan S. Knowles and Miss Betsy C. Mayo, both of Eastham, Feb. 16, 1829.
Mr. Daniel Peniman and Miss Betsey Mayo, both of Eastham, April 25, 1829.
Mr. Seymour Bangs and Miss Anna M. Cobb, both of Eastham, April 25, 1829.
Mr. Harvey Snow and Miss Thankful Knowles, both of Eastham, June 15, 1829.
Mr. John Y. Jacobs of Welfleet and Miss Polly Clark of Eastham, July 13, 1829.
Mr. Joseph C. Mayo of Eastham and Miss Harriet Snow of Orleans, Oct. 24, 1829.
Mr. Andre W. Higgins of Eastham and Miss Rebecca B. Atkins of Orleans, Nov. 9, 1829.
Mr. Franklin Knowles of Eastham and Miss Caroline Brown of Welfleet, Dec. 24, 1929.
Mr. John K. Higgins of Welfleet and Miss Ruth Wiley of Eastham, Jan. 18, 1830.
Mr. Joshua W. Nickerson and Miss Mercy Walker, both of Eastham, May 10, 1830.
Mr. John P. Knowles of Eastham and Miss Susanna Crosby of Orleans, Sept. 10, 1830.
Mr. Daniel F. Marshal and Miss Hannah H. Knowles, both of Eastham, Sept. 10, 1830.
Mr. Nathan A. Gill and Miss Tamson Gould, both of Eastham, Sept. 20, 1830.
Mr. Thomas S. Ellis and Miss Abigail M. Ward, both of Eastham, Nov. 22, 1830.
Mr. Abram Horton and Miss Patina Doane, both of Eastham, Nov. 22, 1830.
Mr. Seth Paine and Miss Rebecca Knowles, both of Eastham, Nov. 29, 1830.
Mr. Timothy Crosby of Orleans and Miss Louisa Smith of Eastham, Nov. 29, 1830.
Mr. Nathan Mayo and Miss Martha B. Snow, both of Eastham, Dec. 6, 1830.
Mr. Nathaniel Snow of Welfleet and Miss Betsy R. Lincoln of Eastham, Dec. 27, 1830.
Mr. William Smith and Miss Ruth A. Walker, both of Eastham, Feb. 28, 1831.
Mr. Oliver Smith of Eastham and Mrs. Mary P. Doane of Orleans, March 29, 1831.
Mr. Elkanah K. Paine and Miss Mehitable P. Knowles, both of Eastham, April 25, 1831.
Mr. Freeman Cobb and Miss Thankful M. Doane, both of Eastham, May 21, 1831.
Mr. Thomas Cobb 2d and Miss Priscilla M. Doane, both of Eastham, May 21, 1831.
Mr. Elkanah W. Stubbs of Welfleet and Miss Susanna Collins of Eastham, June 4, 1831.
Mr. Joseph Smith and Miss Susana H. Steel, both of Eastham, June 25, 1831.
Mr. Freeman Knowles and Miss Hannah H. Dill, both of Eastham, July 9, 1831.
Mr. Henry Harding and Miss Almira Smith, both of Eastham, Nov. 12, 1831.
Mr. Michael Sherman of Orleans and Miss Palina Knowles of Eastham, Nov. 12, 1831.
Mr. James Chapman of Barnstable and Miss Ann S. D. Higgins of Eastham, Nov. 19, 1831.
Mr. Warren Lincoln of Brewster and Miss Mary B. Freeman of Eastham, Nov. 19, 1831.
Mr. Russel Doane and Miss Martha Crosby, both of Eastham.
Mr. Crowell Doane of Eastham and Miss Hannah Gayns of Beverly, Nov. 26, 1831.
Mr. Leantes Lincoln and Miss Sarah D. Dill, both of Eastham, Nov. 26, 1831.
Mr. Joseph Cummings of Orleans and Miss Clarissa Paine of Eastham, Dec. 9, 1831.
Mr. John Walker of Eastham and Miss Hannah Linnell of Orleans, Dec. 10, 1831.
Mr. Nathaniel Baker of Welfleet and Miss Evelina Smith of Eastham, Dec. 10, 1831.
Mr. Elisha Snow of Orleans and Miss Mary P. Doane of Eastham, Dec. 31, 1831.
Mr. David Smith of Eastham and Mrs. Anna Bush of Truro, Jan. 28, 1832.
Mr. Timothy D. Witherell of Welfleet and Miss Betsy Smith of Eastham, Feb. 4, 1832.
Mr. Peter Walker of Eastham and Miss Susanna Thomas of Truro, April 4, 1832.
Mr. Knowles Doane and Miss Mary Knowles, both of Eastham, Aug. 25, 1832.
Mr. George Ward of Welfleet and Miss Mercy Smith of Eastham, Sept. 22, 1832.

MARRIAGES AND MARRIAGE INTENTIONS, 1796-1844
TOWN OF EASTHAM, MASSACHUSETTS

Contributed by VERNON R. NICKERSON, of Taunton, Mass.

Mr. Joseph Emory and Miss Almira Horton, both of Eastham, Sept. 29, 1832.
Mr. Heman S. Dill and Miss Caroline Gill, both of Eastham, Sept. 29, 1832.
Mr. Henry Newcomb of Welfleet and Miss Almira Knowles of Eastham, Oct. 13, 1832.
Mr. Reuben Nickerson of Eastham and Miss Mehitable Doane of Orleans, Oct. 13, 1832.
Mr. Thomas Snow of Welfleet and Miss Mary Cole of Eastham, Oct. 20, 1832.
Mr. Edward Brewer and Miss Lydia Ward, both of Eastham, Oct. 20, 1832.
Mr. Samuel Bracket of Welfleet and Miss Patty Doane of Eastham, Nov. 3, 1832.
Mr. Elnathan Snow of Orleans and Miss Naomi Mayo of Eastham, Jan. 26, 1833.
Mr. Myrick C. Horton and Miss Sarah B. Knowles, both of Eastham, May 18, 1833.
Mr. Barnabas K. Mayo and Miss Lydia Knowles, both of Eastham, June 27, 1833.
Mr. Josiah Knowles of Welfleet and Miss Martha B. Wiley of Eastham, July 27, 1833.
Mr. Lincoln Rogers of Orleans and Miss Azubeth Knowles of Eastham, March 1, 1834.
Mr. Fredrick Hance of Orleans and Miss Phebe Lincoln of Eastham, March 22, 1834.
Mr. Jonathan Doane of Welfleet and Miss Eliza F. Horton of Eastham, May 3, 1834.
Mr. Elisha Cobb and Miss Rebekah Gill, both of Eastham, May 3, 1834.
Mr. Lewis Smith of Orleans and Miss Mehitable Smith of Eastham, Sept. 6, 1834.
Mr. Silvanus Collins and Miss Palina Atwood, both of Eastham, Sept. 20, 1834.
Capt. Joseph Comings of Orleans and Miss Hannah H. Knowles of Eastham, Nov. 4, 1834.
Mr. Joseph Baker of Welfleet and Miss Eunice S. Harding, Nov. 15, 1834.
Mr. Joseph Silver of Orleans and Miss Amelia Gill of Eastham, Nov. 27, 1834.
Mr. William C. Cobb and Miss Susan Knowles, both of Eastham, Nov. 29, 1834.
Mr. Warren Higgens of Orleans and Miss Hannah Brown of Eastham, Dec. 6, 1834.
Mr. Clarington Smith of Eastham and Miss Apphia Rogers of Orleans, Dec. 20, 1834.
Mr. Rolin Doane of Eastham and Miss Sarah E. Rich of Lynn, March 7, 1835.
Mr. Elkanah C. Bracket of Eastham and Miss Paulina Cole of Welfleet, March 21, 1835.
Mr. Timothy Cole and Mrs. Patty Crosby, both of Eastham, March 28, 1835.
Mr. Edward Sprague of Provincetown and Miss Catherine C. Briggs of Eastham, April 4, 1835.
Mr. Joseph Swaine of Orleans and Miss Asenath Higgins of Eastham, April 4, 1835.
Mr. John W. Higgins of Eastham and Miss Mary Taylor of Welfleet, Sept. 5, 1835.
Mr. Myrick Doane and Miss Joanna Lewis, both of Eastham, Sept. 26, 1835.
Mr. Franklin Smith and Miss Mercy Higgins, both of Eastham, Oct. 10, 1835.
Mr. Asa Newcomb of Welfleet and Miss Lucindia Wiley of Eastham, Oct. 17, 1835.
Mr. Joshua Higgins and Miss Maria H. Cobb, both of Eastham, Oct. 31, 1835.
Mr. Sullivan Freeman of Orleans and Miss Phebe Smith of Eastham, Nov. 14, 1835.
Mr. Nathaniel Smith and Miss Hannah Cole, both of Eastham, Nov. 14, 1835.
Mr. Stephen S. Moses of Eastham and Miss Sophrona Hurd of Orleans, Nov. 21, 1835.
Mr. Samuel S. Taylor of Welfleet and Miss Phebe H. Higgins of Eastham, Nov. 28, 1835.
Mr. John Crosby of Eastham and Miss Harriet Sears of Brewster, Dec. 2, 1835.
Mr. Elkanah W. Stubbs of Welfleet and Miss Pamela Horton of Eastham, Feb. 20, 1836.

Mr. Josiah Higgins and Mrs. Anna Snow, both of Eastham, March 2, 1836.
Mr. Simeon Doane and Miss Hannah Clark, both of Eastham, March 19, 1836.
Mr. Joel Brewer and Miss Thankful M. Cobb, both of Eastham, May 10, 1836.
Mr. Francis Smith of Eastham and Miss Harriet H. Crosby of Orleans, June 11, 1836.
Mr. Abijah Mayo and Miss Phebe K. Cobb, both of Eastham, Oct. 12, 1836.
Mr. Henry Horton and Miss Abigail K. Mayo, both of Eastham, Nov. 12, 1836.
Mr. Isaac Doane of Eastham and Miss Phebe Myrick of Orleans, Nov. 5, 1836.
Mr. Edward B. Sprague of Boston and Miss Catherine C. Briggs of Eastham, Nov. 12, 1836.
Mr. Elijah Doane and Miss Lydia Smith, both of Eastham, Nov. 19, 1836.
Mr. Allen H. Knowles of Eastham and Miss Mary E. Howe of Orleans, Nov. 17, 1836.
Mr. Zenus Gray of Dennis and Miss Mary Knowles of Eastham, Nov. 26, 1836.
Mr. Joel Snow and Miss Ruth C. Collins, both of Eastham, Dec. 10, 1836.
Mr. Timothy Jarves of Orleans and Miss Lucinda Knowles of Eastham, Jan. 14, 1837.
Mr. Josiah Doane and Miss Temperance Knowles, both of Eastham, Jan. 21, 1837.
Mr. Albert Smith of Eastham and Miss Betsey Doane of Orleans, Jan. 28, 1837.
Capt. Thomas Knowles and Miss Rachel Horton, both of Eastham, Feb. 25, 1837.
Mr. William Williams of Provincetown and Miss Phebe B. Knowles of Eastham, Aug. 26, 1837.
Mr. Solomon Doane and Miss Betsey Snow, both of Eastham, Sept. 2, 1837.
Mr. Joseph Pierce of Eastham and Miss Betsey H. Horton of Welfleet, Sept. 16, 1837.
Mr. Reuben Nikerson Jr. of Eastham and Miss Elizabeth Doane of Orleans, Sept. 16, 1837.
Mr. Jonathan Kenrick of Harwich and Miss Mary H. Dill of Eastham, Sept. 30, 1837.
Mr. Joseph Snow of Orleans and Miss Phebe A. Smith of Eastham, Sept. 30, 1837.
Mr. Berthel Hurd of Orleans and Miss Lovey Brewer of Eastham, Nov. 4, 1837.
Mr. Joseph C. Silver of Orleans and Miss Deborah H. Burgess of Eastham, Nov. 4, 1837.
Mr. Travius Kragman and Miss Sarah Snow, both of Eastham, Nov. 18, 1837.
Mr. Caleb Hopkins of Orleans and Miss Sarah Doane of Eastham, Nov. 25, 1837.
Mr. Joshua Knowles and Miss Lucindia Doane, both of Eastham, Jan. 8, 1838.
Capt. Alexander C. Childs of Barnstable and Miss Lucy C. Shaw of Eastham, Jan. 22, 1838.
Mr. Asa Hopkins, Jr. of Eastham and Miss Catherine F. Kragman of Eastham, Feb. 26, 1838.
Mr. Noah Doane and Miss Sephronia Doane, both of Eastham, Feb. 26, 1838.
Mr. Mark Crosby of Eastham and Miss Margaret S. Kockwood (Lockwood ?) of Holliston, April 10, 1838.
Mr. Jesse G. Baker of Welfleet and Miss Terrisa Doane of Eastham, July 14, 1838.
Capt. Henry Knowles and Miss Tempy S. Hopkins, both of Eastham, July 14, 1838.
Mr. Joseph Holbrook of Eastham and Miss Priscilla Cole of Welfleet, July 21, 1838.
Mr. Luther Hurd Jr. of Orleans and Miss Polly M. Smith of Eastham, Sept. 15, 1838.
Mr. Parker Brown Jr. and Miss Hannah D. Mayo, both of Eastham, Nov. 12, 1838.
Mr. Luther G. Northrop of Orleans and Miss Elizaann Nekerson of Eastham, Nov. 26, 1838.
Mr. John Doane and Miss Abegal F. Cobb, both of Eastham, Dec. 14, 1838.
Mr. William F. Clapp of Boston and Miss Hannah Knowles of Eastham, Feb. 23, 1839.
Mr. Calvin Snow of Orleans and Miss Matilda Cole of Eastham, March 25, 1839.
Mr. Robert Mayo and Miss Lydia Cole, both of Eastham, April 29, 1839.
Mr. Godfrey Sparrow and Miss Lucia Knowles, both of Eastham, May 20, 1839.
Mr. Nehemiah Smith of Eastham and Miss Patty K. Mayo of Orleans, Oct. 15, 1839.
Mr. Freeman Dill and Miss Elizabeth A. Collins of Eastham, Nov. 4, 1839.

Mr. Silvanus Doane and Mrs. Jerusha Sparrow, both of Eastham, Nov. 25, 1839.
Mr. Moses Wiley Jr. and Miss Julian Clark, both of Eastham, Dec. 2, 1839.
Mr. William Swane of Orleans and Miss Sarah Higgins of Eastham, July 20, 1839.
Mr. Heman Smith of Eastham and Miss Hannah S. Newcomb of Welfleet, Jan. 14, 1840.
Mr. Henry Doane and Miss Rebecca H. Cobb, both of Eastham, Jan. 20, 1840.
Mr. Josiah Cole Jr. of Welfleet and Miss Rachel Doane of Eastham, Feb. 18, 1840.
Mr. Daniel H. Babcock of Eastham and Miss Amenda Avery of Andover, March 7, 1840.
Mr. William Dill and Miss Philena Smith, both of Eastham, Sept. 28, 1840.
Mr. Edward Knowles of Welfleet and Miss Maryann Horton of Eastham, Oct. 26, 1840.
Mr. Winsor Snow of Orleans and Miss Alice Mayo of Eastham, Oct. 26, 1840.
Mr. Samuel K. Smith of Eastham and Miss Sally Hatch of Orleans, Nov. 16, 1840.
Mr. Knowles Smith of Orleans and Miss Bethiah C. Mayo of Eastham, Dec. 10, 1840.
Mr. Abijah Baker of Orleans and Miss Abigail M. Knowles of Eastham, Feb. 22, 1841.
Mr. Dean Sparrow and Miss Kazilba Snow, both of Eastham, March 15, 1841.
Mr. Seth P. Doane of Orleans and Miss Sally S. Smith of Eastham, April 17, 1841.
Mr. Freeman Harden Jr. and Miss Dorcas D. Cobb, both of Eastham, May 17, 1841.
Mr. Elijah E. Knowles of Eastham and Miss Mercy A. Myrick of New Salem, July 5, 1841.
Mr. Simeon Childs of Barnstable and Miss Druzilla D. Cook of Eastham, Aug. 15, 1841.
Mr. Zephaniah Haza (or Hoza ?) of Boston and Miss Hannah A. Dill of Eastham, July 23, 1841.
Mr. Lueva Benny and Miss Rachel D. Smith, both of Eastham, Sept. 25, 1841.
Mr. David Jewell of Natick and Miss Eliza Atwood of Eastham, Sept. 25, 1841.
Mr. Jesse W. Snow of Eastham and Miss Sarah T. Howes of Chatham, Oct. 25, 1841.
Mr. Abner Freeman of Orleans and Miss Lucy Harding of Eastham, Nov. 22, 1841.
Mr. Lincoln F. Cobb and Miss Mercy Doane, both of Eastham, Dec. 6, 1841.
Mr. Daniel Atwood of Welfleet and Miss Mehitable Holbrook of Eastham, Dec. 17, 1841.
Mr. Simeon Doane of Eastham and Miss Priscilla F. Young of Orleans, Dec. 17, 1841.
Mr. Thomas S. Knowles and Miss Catherine Ingham, both of Eastham, Feb. 5, 1842.
Mr. Barnabas Snow and Miss Zubella L. Ingham, both of Eastham, Feb. 19, 1842.
Mr. Timothy Sparrow and Miss Mary M. Seabury, both of Eastham, April 16, 1842.
Mr. Nathan Stone of Dennis and Miss Sarah Knowles of Eastham, May 27, 1842.
Mr. Charles Brown and Miss Louisa Doane, both of Eastham, Oct. 18, 1842.
Mr. Joseph M. Cobb of Eastham and Miss Jane Wixon of Harwich, Oct. 22, 1842.
Mr. Elijah Hamilton of Eastham & Mercy P. Linnell of Orleans, October 22, 1842.
Mr. Josiah Myrick of Orleans & Miss Susan Mayo of Eastham, Nov. 27, 1842.
Mr. James H. Knowles of Eastham & Miss Sally Freeman of Brewster, Jan. 16, 1843.
Mr. Richard Smith of Eastham & Miss Achsah S. Crosby of Orleans, Jan. 21, 1843.
Mr. Elijah E. Knowles and Miss Tabitha Holbrook, both of Eastham, Feb. 13, 1843.
Mr. Willard Rogers of Eastham and Miss Sally W. Goute of Orleans, April 29, 1843.
Mr. Lewis G. Smith of Eastham and Miss Caroline S. Moulton of Cambridgeport, May 27, 1843.
Mr. Henry Bailey of Boston and Miss Mary F. Cobb of Eastham, Sept. 2, 1843.
Mr. Otis Bradford of Duxbury and Miss Jane A. Collins of Eastham, Sept. 2, 1843.
Mr. Alvin Rogers Jr. of Eastham and Miss Eliza N. Crosby of Orleans, Oct. 14, 1843.
Mr. Ezekiel Brown of Eastham and Miss Hannah Cole of Wellfleet, Nov. 18, 1843.

Mr. Joel Sparrow of Eastham and Miss Caroline Snow of Orleans, Dec. 29, 1843.
Mr. Samuel Horton of Eastham and Miss Olive L. Hurd of Orleans, Jan. 27, 1844.
Mr. Eldridge F. Smith of Provincetown and Miss Rachel A. Horton of Eastham, April 1, 1844.
Mr. Ephriam S. Hopkins and Miss Mary P. Horton, both of Eastham, April 6, 1844.
Mr. Robert R. Jennison of Natick and Miss Phebe A. Snow of Eastham, April 27, 1844.
Mr. James Lincoln of Eastham and Miss Hannah H. Knowles of Truro, July 6, 1844.
Mr. Cushing Horton, Jr., and Miss Mary F. Higgins, both of Eastham, June 22, 1844.
Mr. Simeon Smith of Eastham and Miss Sarah A. Crosby of Orleans, Aug. 3, 1844.
Mr. Joseph Pierce and Miss Rhoda Atwood, both of Eastham, Aug. 25, 1844.
Mr. Solomon H. Mayo and Miss Phebe Gould, both of Eastham, Sept. 14, 1844.
Mr. Prince Freeman of Provincetown and Miss Eliza A. Horton of Eastham, Sept. 28, 1844.
Mr. Sidney Phillips of Boston and Miss Abby Atwood of Eastham, Oct. 5, 1844.
Mr. Nickalus R. Knowles and Miss Harriet B. Nickerson, both of Eastham, Oct. 12, 1844.
Mr. Nathan Hopkins Jr. of Eastham and Miss Mary A. Dearborn of Boscawen, N.H., Oct. 19, 1844.
Mr. Benjamin Smith of Provincetown and Miss Sarah Smith of Eastham, Oct. 26, 1844.
Mr. James H. Knowles and Miss Martha Bracket, both of Eastham, Dec. 7, 1844.
Mr. Joshua H. Dill of Wellfleet and Miss Polina Hopkins of Eastham, Dec. 14, 1844.
Mr. Lewis Lombard of Wellfleet and Miss Lucinda C. Collins of Eastham, Dec. 14, 1844.
Mr. Leonard Young of Orleans and Miss Mariah Doane of Eastham, Dec. 21, 1844.
Mr. Luther Hurd and Miss Elizabeth S. Harding, both of Eastham, Dec. 28, 1844.
Mr. Timothy Mayo and Miss Lydia Knowles, both of Eastham, Feb. 15, 1845.
Mr. Isaac Higgins of Wellfleet and Miss Lydia Hopkins of Eastham, Feb. 15, 1845.
Mr. Enoch S. Hamilton of Truro and Miss Almira S. Rogers of Eastham, March 15, 1845.
Mr. Asa Smith, Jr., and Miss Bachuel M. Smith, both of Eastham, March 15, 1845.
Mr. Moses F. Eaton of Boston and Miss Lydia C. S. Doane of Eastham, April 19, 1845.
Mr. Lewis A. Guild (Gill or Gould ?) of Eastham and Miss Rebeccah Smith of Orleans, July 5, 1845.
Mr. Abner Snow Jr. of Orleans and Miss Keziah N. Smith of Eastham, July 26, 1845.
Mr. Abijah Gill of Eastham and Miss Lucy F. Cook of Provincetown, August 2, 1845.
Mr. Freeman Smith of Eastham and Miss Rosanna S. Crosby of Orleans, Oct. 18, 1845.
Mr. Thomas Collins of Wellfleet and Miss Louesa Horton of Eastham, Oct. 25, 1845.
Mr. Henry A. Cook of Boston and Miss Caroline Smith of Eastham, Oct. 25, 1845.
Mr. Jonathan Sparrow and Miss Mary A. Smith, both of Eastham, Nov. 1, 1845.
Mr. Simeon Doane of Eastham and Miss Ann P. Young of Orleans, Jan. 3, 1846.
Mr. Benjamin Doane of Eastham and Miss Sarah C. Bracket of Wellfleet, Jan. 3, 1846.
Mr. James S. Hatch and Miss Susan F. Clark, both of Eastham, Feb. 7, 1846.
Mr. Freeman Hatch and Miss Lydia Hopkins, both of Eastham, April 25, 1846.
Mr. Thomas P. Nickerson and Miss Abigail Gould, both of Eastham, Aug. 1, 1846.
Mr. Warren A. Dill of Eastham and Miss Julia Maria Linnell of Orleans, Sept. 19, 1846.
Mr. Joseph Kragman of Eastham and Miss Abigail Higgins of Wellfleet, Sept. 26, 1846.
Mr. Stephen Snow of Orleans and Miss Mary B. Harding of Eastham, Sept. 26, 1846.

Mr. Theodore Brown of Wellfleet and Miss Mercy S. Sparrow of Eastham, Oct. 3, 1846.
Mr. Henry Y. Hatch and Miss Sophia Horton, both of Eastham, Oct. 10, 1846.
Mr. Abijah Gill and Mrs. Priscilla Doane, both of Eastham, Oct. 10, 1846.
Mr. Martin Manuel of Provincetown and Miss Rebecca F. Mayo of Eastham, Oct. 24, 1846.
Mr. Joseph Collins of Eastham and Miss Harriet N. Dill of Wellfleet, Oct. 24, 1846.
Mr. Joshua Sparrow of Eastham and Miss Mary R. Higgins of Wellfleet, Oct. 31, 1846.
Mr. Jonathan Knowles and Miss Caroline Gill, both of Eastham, Dec. 26, 1846.
Mr. Reuben Brewer of Eastham and Miss Ruth Snow of Orleans, Dec. 26, 1846.
Mr. Thomas Gould of Eastham and Miss Martha Snow of Orleans, Feb. 6, 1847.
Mr. Issachour Berry of Brewster and Miss Lydda Mayo of Eastham, Feb. 20, 1847.
Mr. Joshua Snow of Eastham and Miss Rebeca K. Collins of Truro, Feb. 20, 1847.
Mr. Edward B. Hinckley of Osterville and Miss Ruth F. Smith of Eastham, March 6, 1847.
Mr. Lorenzo Dow Dill and Miss Catherine Broocks, both of Eastham, March 4, 1847.
Mr. Elkanah Cole Jr. and Miss Polly Gould, both of Eastham, March 17, 1847.
Capt. Jesse Collins of Springfield and Mrs. Sarah Atwood of Eastham, May 15, 1847.
Mr. Oliver Mayo and Miss Rebecah F. Knowles, both of Eastham, Oct. 16, 1847.
Mr. Avery A. Brown of Eastham and Miss Martha M. Green of Boston, Nov. 6, 1847.
Mr. Nathaniel Cole of Eastham and Miss Mary W. Dill of Wellfleet, Nov. 16, 1847.
Mr. Dean Smith of Eastham and Miss Rebekah C. Cole of Eastham, Jan. 1, 1848.
Mr. Isaac Lincoln of Eastham and Miss Mercy Russel of Truro, Feb. 12, 1848.
Mr. Jesse Lincoln of Eastham and Miss Hannah Woodward of Bowdoin, Maine, Feb. 19, 1848.
Mr. Freeman Knowles and Miss Joanna F. Smith, both of Eastham, March 18, 1848.
Mr. James Rogers, Jr., of Orleans and Miss Hannah L. Knowles of Eastham, March 25, 1848.
Mr. Daniel Sparrow and Miss Elvira T. Hatch, both of Eastham, April 8, 1848.
Mr. John Phillips, M.D., and Mrs. Mehitable Mores, both of Eastham, Sept. 9, 1848.
Mr. Joseph M. Higgins and Miss Olive W. Doane, both of Eastham, Oct. 14, 1848.
Mr. William Higgins of Wellfleet and Miss Mary K. Doane of Eastham, Nov. 18, 1848.
Mr. Allen F. Smith and Miss Elisa A. Hopkins, both of Eastham, Dec. 2, 1848.
Mr. Treat Moore of Eastham and Miss Rebecca D. Hurd of Orleans, Feb. 3, 1849.
Mr. Samuel Nickerson, Jr., and Miss Ruth Lincoln, both of Eastham, Feb. 22, 1849.
Mr. Freeman Horton and Miss Rebecca Doane, both of Eastham, March 31, 1849.
Mr. John C. Brown of Orleans and Miss Mary F. Snow of Eastham, Sept. 15, 1849.
Mr. Abel Shattuck of Orleans and Miss Abby B. Nickerson of Eastham, Feb. 29, 1849.
Mr. James S. Brown of Wellfleet and Miss Ruth A. Mayo of Eastham, Oct. 20, 1849.
Mr. Henry K. Cobb and Miss Mary A. Walker, both of Eastham, Nov. 17, 1849.
Capt. Francis Kragman and Miss Lydia Smith, both of Eastham, Dec. 1, 1849.
Mr. Elkanah Hopkins Jr. of Eastham and Miss Sabra A. Doane of Chatham, Dec. 6, 1849.
Capt. Harding K. Cobb of Eastham and Miss Amanda Burnham of Boston, Dec. 18, 1849.
Mr. Eben P. Chapman of Brewster and Miss Harriet Knowles of Eastham, Jan. 1, 1850.
Mr. Joseph Snow of Eastham and Miss Sarah P. Snow of Orleans, Jan. 4, 1850.
Mr. Isaiah A. Freeman of Wellfleet and Mrs. Polina Collins of Eastham, Jan. 10, 1850.
Mr. Josiah M. Knowles and Miss Susan Snow, both of Eastham, March 9, 1850.

Mr. Nathan B. Nickerson and Miss Phebe Horton, both of Eastham, March 23, 1850.
Mr. Samuel Snow Jr. of Eastham and Miss Lydia N. Darling of Orleans, April 6, 1850.
Mr. Barnabas Doane Jr. and Mrs. Mary P. Hopkins, both of Eastham, April 20, 1850.
Mr. Sylvanus D. Knowles of Eastham and Miss Emerline S. Nickerson of Eastham, May 10, 1856 (1850 ?).
Mr. Eldad A. Dill and Miss Ruth S. Gould, both of Eastham, Sept. 25, 1850.
Mr. Josiah M. Cole and Miss Elsey F. Snow, both of Eastham, Dec. 2, 1850.
Mr. James Hurd of Orleans and Miss Bethiah Cole of Eastham, Dec. 19, 1850.
Mr. William Knowles and Miss Betsey C. Atwood, both of Eastham, Dec. 31, 1850.
Mr. Lorenzo D. Young of Orleans and Miss Mary E. Crosby of Eastham, Jan. 12, 1851.
Mr. Calvin Sears of Dennis and Miss Phebe Cole of Eastham, Jan. 12, 1851.
Mr. James S. Hatch and Miss Jerusha C. Clark, both of Eastham, April 5, 1851.
Mr. Reuben Nickerson of Eastham and Miss Sarah Doane of Orleans, March 31, 1851.
Mr. Crowell Doane of Eastham and Miss Abby C. Dill of Eastham, April 29, 1851.
Mr. Robert Still of Walpole, N.H., and Miss Joann Sparrow of Eastham, May 14, 1851.
Mr. Daniel Robbins of Eastham and Miss Eliza Doane of Eastham, July 10, 1851.
Mr. James F. Holbrook of Wellfleet and Miss Betsey Dill of Eastham, Nov. 22, 1851.
Mr. Columbus Dill and Mrs. Tamsin Dill, all of Eastham, Nov. 22, 1851.
Mr. Benaiah G. Higgins and Miss Hannah T. Dill, all of Eastham, Nov. 26, 1851.
Mr. Henry F. Lewis and Miss Mary A. Hopkins, both of Eastham, Nov. 29, 1851.
Mr. Henry Harding of Eastham and Mrs. Susan Eldridge of Chatham, Dec. 2, 1851.
Mr. John Myrick of Truro and Miss Mercy Lincoln of Eastham, Dec. 9, 1851.
Mr. Hinckley Lincoln and Miss Lillah D. Rogers, both of Eastham, Dec. 14, 1851.
Mr. Elijah E.K. Cobb and Miss Laura P. Horton, both of Eastham, Dec. 17, 1851.
Mr. John H. Bangs and Miss Abigail F. Cobb, both of Eastham, Dec. 17, 1851.
Capt. James Prince of Truro and Miss Betsey F. Higgins of Eastham, Jan. 26, 1852.
Mr. Benjamin Doane of Eastham and Miss Elizabeth Leonard of Chatham, Feb. 9, 1852.
Mr. Franklin D. Snow of Somerville, Ms. and Miss Harriet N. Horton of Eastham, March, 1852.
Mr. Lelotez Rogers of Eastham and Miss Louisa A. Crosby of Eastham, April 17, 1852.
Mr. Ebenezer W. Holway of Provincetown and Mrs. Mary Jane Horton of Eastham, May 17, 1852.
Mr. William M. Smith of Eastham and Miss Lucinda F. Knowles of Orleans, June 29, 1852.
Mr. Asa G. Nickerson and Miss Rebecca C. Gould, both of Eastham, July 7, 1852.
Mr. Seth Knowles and Miss Abigail W. Kragman, both of Eastham, Aug. 9, 1852.
Mr. Abner Doane and Miss Thankful F. Cobb, both of Eastham, Oct. 28, 1852.
Mr. Charles L. Harding of Wellfleet and Miss Betsey Atwood of Eastham, Nov. 11, 1852.
Mr. Nathan M. Hatch and Miss Mary Jane Higgins of Eastham, Nov. 20, 1852.
Mr. Joshua G. Doane of Eastham and Miss Mercy S. Freeman of Orleans, Nov. 19, 1852.
Mr. Dean S. Smith of Orleans and Miss Olive D. Dill of Eastham, Nov. 25, 1852.
Mr. James Smith of Eastham and Miss Thankful S. Hopkins of Orleans, Dec. 2, 1852.
Mr. Asa S. Nickerson of Eastham and Miss Laura A. Gould of Orleans, Dec. 16, 1852.
Mr. James Savage and Miss Hannah R. Higgins, all of Eastham, Dec. 23, 1852.
Mr. Owen Higgins of Eastham and Miss Eliza J. Smith of Orleans, Jan. 21, 1853.
Capt. Barnabas Chipman of Wellfleet and Miss Sarah M. Hatch, Jan. 22, 1853.
Mr. Lewis Doane of Orleans and Mrs. Elizabeth Smith of Eastham, Feb. 14, 1853.

Mr. Joshua S. Paine of Eastham and Miss Minerva Hatch of Wellfleet, March 9, 1853.
Mr. Nathaniel Wiley of Wellfleet and Miss Huldah A. Snow of Eastham, March 15, 1853.
Mr. Charles Cole and Miss Mercy A. Moore, both of Eastham, April 23, 1853.
Mr. John N.M. Hopkins and Miss Thankful M. Knowles, both of Eastham, May 9, 1853.
Mr. Josiah M. Knowles and Miss Rebecca F. Knowles, both of Eastham, July 30, 1853.
Mr. Charles H. Youlden of Boston and Miss Hannah J. Walker of Eastham, Sept. 5, 1853.
Capt. Henry Rich of Malden and Miss Thankful Smith of Eastham, Sept. 19, 1853.
Mr. Stephen C. Smith and Miss Mary H. Horton, both of Eastham, Oct. 14, 1853.
Mr. Elisha Y. Mayo of Orleans and Miss Thankful Smith of Eastham, Nov. 22, 1853.
Mr. Edmund F. Knowles and Miss Pamela Smith, both of Eastham, Dec. 10, 1853.
Mr. Archibald MacCurdy of Provincetown and Miss Hannah M. Doane of Eastham, Dec. 30, 1853.
Mr. Elijah S. Young of Cambridge and Miss Mercy A. Higgins of Eastham, Feb. 10, 1854.
Mr. Noah Rich of Truro and Miss Tamzin D. Dill of Eastham, May 16, 1854.
Mr. James W. Graham of Wellfleet and Miss Abby D. Hatch of Eastham, Oct. 21, 1854.
Mr. Rowland Doane and Miss Deborah Sealy of Eastham, Nov. 2, 1854.
Mr. Uriah Nickerson and Miss Priscilla P. Hopkins, all of Eastham, Nov. 7, 1854.
Mr. Frederick Lewis of Boston and Miss Mary C.B. Bangs of Eastham, Nov. 29, 1854.
Mr. Joseph Hope of Bellingham and Miss Stephonia N. Atwood of Eastham, Feb. 1, 1855.
Mr. Micah S. Paine of Eastham and Miss Hannah N. Crosby of Orleans, March 15, 1855.
Mr. Benjamin Knowles and Miss Betsey C. Higgins, both of Eastham, Dec. 3, 1855.
Mr. William Doyle and Miss Lusania H. Nickerson, both of Eastham, Dec. 8, 1855.
Mr. Sylvanus Freeman of Orleans and Miss Sarah H. Walker of Eastham, Dec. 17, 1855.
Mr. Josiah M. Cole and Miss Mary E. Doane, both of Eastham, Dec. 18, 1855.
Mr. Warren D. Mayo and Miss Dianry B. Smith, both of Eastham, Dec. 24, 1855.
Mr. Isaac Smith Jr. of Orleans, and Miss Elizabeth A. Dill of Eastham, Jan. 15, 1856.
Rev. George S. Alexander of Cumberland, R.I., and Miss Abby S. Smith of Eastham, March 11, 1856.
Mr. Jabez Sparrow of Eastham and Miss Esther Mayo of Orleans, June 12, 1856.
Mr. Heman S. Gill and Miss Mary J. Brewer, Nov. 8, 1856.
Mr. Joshua Cole, Jr., and Miss Sophia K. Cobb, both of Eastham, Nov. 20, 1856.
Mr. Freeman Doane and Miss Sarah Paine, both of Eastham, Nov. 28, 1856.
Mr. Timothy M. Hatch and Miss Sarah A. Bracket, both of Eastham, Dec. 6, 1856.
Mr. Thomas Mayo and Miss Melinda F. Collins, both of Eastham, Dec. 20, 1856.
Mr. George Leonard and Miss Lydia D. Knowles, both of Eastham, March 2, 1857.
Mr. John Doane 2nd and Miss Sarah K. Doane, both of Eastham, May 18, 1857.
Mr. Henry A. Higgins of Eastham and Miss Christania Whitney of Hamden, Maine, August 27, 1857.

COPY OF A RECORD OF DEATHS KEPT BY THE REV. SAMUEL KINGSBURY, MINISTER OF THE GOSPEL AT EDGARTOWN, MASS.

Communicated by Miss HARRIET M. PEASE, Genealogist, of Edgartown, Mass.

"*Deaths in ye Town of Edgartown.*"

			No.
1761			
	Enoch Coffin Esqr Æt. *fortasse*	83	1
	Two children		2, 3
	Capt. Killy	70	4
	Widow Cleavland	70	5
	Cornelius Merchant	40	6
	ye Wife of Peter Riply	39	7
1762	ye Widow clachorn	75	8
	James Coval	75	9
	Seth Merchant	26	10
	ye wife of Thos Peas	30	11
	a child of Seth Donham		12
	ye wife of Nicholas Butler	45	13
	2 children of Atsat		14, 15
	a child of Nath. Vinson		16
	Son of Enoch Norton	20	17
1763	a child of Stephen Peas		18
	Mr. Joseph Jenkins	43	19
	a child who lived at Mr. Jno. Coffin's	7	20
	Mrs. Jane Butler	40	21
June	ye Wife of Sam[l] Smith	50	22
	Joseph Vinson	65	23
	Tho[s] Neal	50	24
	Mrs. Jenkins	40	25
	a child of Jethro Coval		26
	Widow Norton		27
	John Cuningham	60	28
	John Newman Es q[r]	43	29
1764	a child of Stephen Peas		30
	a child of Mr. Norton		31
	a child of Tho[s] Cooke		32
	a child of Edy Coffin		33
	a child of Silas Merchant		34
	a child of Jos. Huxford		35
	ye Wife of Sam[l] Cottle	50	36
	a child of John Homes		37
	a child of Jos. Cleavland		38
	a child of Eben[r] Donham		39

	ye wife of Tho[s] Vinson		40	40
	a child of W[m] Norton			41
	ye wife of John Merchant		72	42
1765				
Jany 15	Tho[s] Peas		70	43
———	Son of Jos. Peas	at sea	20	44
Feb 24	Sam[l] Butler		82	45
	ye Widow Killy		66	46
	Gamaliel Butler		74	47
	W[m] Cole		76	48
Aug 31	Henry Norton		27	49
	a child of Henry Norton			50
	ye Widow Cole		80	51
Nov 1	John Cozens		70	52
Do 23	Isaac Norton		85	53
1766				
Feb 8	Benaj[h] Donham		80	54
April	Asa Donham was killed by a fall from a Mast		23	55
	ye Wife of John Peas		42	56
	ye Wife of Abraham Peas		30	57
Oct	a child of ye Widow Mears			58
Dec[r]	a child of Tho[s] Cooke			59
1767				
Feb 9	John Merchant		87	60
March 22	ye Wife of Eph. Peas		29	61
April 9	ye Widow Dagget		80	62
April 26	ye Wife of Abner Butler		35	63
	a child of Obed Peas			64
August 17	Hannah Peas, Midwife		72	65
	a child of Tho[s] Pease			66
Oct	ye wife of Dan[l] Coffin		40	67
Do	ye Wife of Edy Coffin		24	68
	ye Wife of Jn[o] Peas		42	69
	This year there were about 18 persons Lost at sea			
1768				
May 13	Lemuel Peas		26	70
	a child of Joseph Donham			71
June 3	ye Widow Sara Peas		79	72
	a child of Wm Norton			73
June 19	Enoch Norton		68	74
August 2	Tim[y] Norton		58	75
Oct	ye Widow Peas		58	76
Oct	ye Wife of Jethro Coval		40	77
	2 persons lost at sea			78, 79
1769				
Feb 4	ye Wife of Mr. Ichabod Wiswall		61	80
Feb 28	ye Widow Butler	Æt.	82	81
March 7	ye Widow Cosens		66	82
April 11	Eben[r] Norton Esqr		78	83

April	a child of Lot Norton	1	84
May 2	ye Widow Hepz^{h} Norton	90	85
July 17	ye Wife of David Norton	35	86
August 30, 31	2 children of Nathl Vinson	3 & 5	87, 88
Sep 29	Jane Parmer	35	89
Do	a child of John Butler	1	90
October 2	Weeks, by a wound received from a whale	35	91
October 3	ye Wife of Benaj^{h} Donham Jr	55	92
Oct 5	Joseph Peas	70	93
1770			
March 5	Lydia Luce	22	94
Do 21	a child of Thos Lawson	1	95
May	a child of Jo^{s} Barret Drowned	4	96
June 15	a child of Seth Donham Drowned	8	97
June 15	Isaac Butler killed by ye accidental discharge of a gun	22	98
1771			
March 21	Saml Huxford	88	99
May 31	ye Wife of Prince Peas	39	100
June 6	a child of Abner Norton	1	101
June 30	ye Widow Abia Peas	79	102
August 11	a child of Nathl Fish	1	103
Do 17	a child of Prince Peas	1	104
Sep 18	a child of David Donham	3	105
Oct 15	Eben^{r} Smith Esqr	71	106
Decr 14	a child of Henry Butler	1	107
	a child of Bayes Norton Jr.	1	108
Decr 28	Eben^{r} Joy	55	109
1772			
	a child of Shobal Davis	1	110
Jany 10	the son of Prince Daggett killed with a gun	18	111
Jany 28	Nicholas Butler	94	112
	a child of Obed Norton		113
	a child of Eben^{r} Butler		114
	a child of Benj Butler		115
	a child of Matt Butler	3	116
April	an apprentis David Reynolds	17	117
	Joseph Dagget	68	118
July 5	ye Wife of Wm Russel	30	119
July 9	ye Wife of Matthew Butler	36	120
July 29	ye wife of Judah Norton	42	121
Do	a child of Thomas Beetle	2	122
Do	a child of Robt Hamet		123
July 31	a child of Thos Clachorn	2	124
	Died at Sea { Huxford Merchant by sickness		125
	Died at Sea { Richard Sprague by a whale		126
	Died at Sea { Edwd Ranger by a fall		127
Oct 5	a child of Jona^{n} Cottle	2	128
	a child of Wm Vinson		129
	a child of Thos Smith		130
Oct 13	a child of Timothy Vinson	3	131

Do	29	a child of Prince Dagget by a scald	5	132
		a child of Abraham Luce		133
Dec[r]	2	the Widow Deborah Norton	93	134
Do	4	a child of Marshal Jenkins	2	135

NOTES IN EXPLANATION, BY HARRIET M. PEASE.

No. 4 was Donken (Duncan) Kelley.
" 7 was Damaris (Chase), daughter of Joseph. She died Dec. 6, æ. 37.
" 11 was the first wife Lydia (———). She died June 21, æ. 26, 2, 27.
" 22 was Eunice (Vincent). She was the second wife of this Samuel Smith, who, being the second of the name, was called Samuel Smith, Jr., although he was not the son of Samuel, Senior. Samuel, Jr., had four wives.
" 25 was Abigail (Little), widow of Joseph Jenkins.
" 32 was Temple Philip, who died Feb. 7, æ. 13 days.
" 40 was the first wife Jean (Norton). She died Oct. 11, 1764, æ. 41, 2, 4.
" 46 was Jean (Sarson), widow of Duncan Kelley. He was her third husband.
" 51 was, probably, Mary (Trapp), daughter of Thomas Trapp and widow of William Cole.
" 57 was the first wife Hannah (———).
" 61 was Hannah (Harper), his first wife.
" 67 was his first wife Mary (Harlock).
" 68 was the first wife Sarah (Martin).
" 80 was Jerusha (Norton).
" 82 was Jemimah (———), the widow of John Cosens.
" 86 was Anna (Pease), his first wife.
" 92 was Lydia (Pease), the first wife.
" 100 was Martha (Marchant).
" 119 was Lydia (Mayhew).
" 120 was Elizabeth (Osborn).
" 121 was Jerusha (Vincent).
" 134 was Deborah (Mayhew), widow of Ebenezer Norton.

MISS PEASE'S DESCRIPTION OF THE BOOK FROM WHICH THESE RECORDS ARE COPIED.

When in Boston some weeks since, I spoke to you of a certain little book belonging to my father's collection of valuable papers. This little book contains a record of upwards of one thousand deaths in the town of Edgartown. It was kept by the Rev. Samuel Kingsbury and by the Rev. Joseph Thaxter, and covers a period of sixty-seven years, beginning in 1761 and ending in 1827. I speak of it as the Thaxter Record of Deaths as most of it is in his hand.

Under date December 18, 1851, my father, Richard L. Pease, says of it: "These records were kept by Rev. Joseph Thaxter, in a small memorandum Book, which more than 20 years after his death, I found in a garret, with other old papers. In the Town Records only a few scattering Records of death were kept prior to 1821, when Isaiah D. Pease, Esq., was chosen Town Clerk." "The original mem[o] Book is now in my possession. That book and this," — referring to a copy he had just taken — "contain the only record of deaths from 1761 to 1821."

The value of this little book can hardly be estimated, containing as it does the *sole* record of death of many of the former inhabitants of this town. Realizing its value and foreseeing the loss it would be if any accident should wipe it out of existence, I became convinced that it should be duplicated and preserved in some more enduring form, so asked if you would like to have it to print. With this I send the first instalment — 243 deaths — the record kept by the Rev. Mr. Kingsbury.

I enclose some notes which may be used or not—just as you please. As the preservation of this little record is due to my father's thoughtfulness and care, I would be glad if you would mention him in connection with it.

COPY OF A RECORD OF DEATHS KEPT BY THE REV. SAMUEL KINGSBURY, MINISTER OF THE GOSPEL AT EDGARTOWN, MASS.

Communicated by Miss HARRIET M. PEASE, Genealogist, of Edgartown, Mass.

" *Deaths in ye Town of Edgartown.*"

1773				No.
Jan^y	11	the wife of Lem^l Jenkins	28	136
Do	29	the Wife of Jona^n Peas	25	137
Feb.		a child of Nathl Fish		138
March	13	The wife of Hez. Donham	33	139
		also his child		140
April	7	ye Wife of Eb^n Butler	40	141
Do	19	ye Widow Love Norton	74	142
May	6	ye wife of Eliphelet Leach	22	143
		a child of Jonathan Cottle		144
May	9	a child of Barzillai Peas	3	145
Do		a child of Benj Butler		146
Do	11	Thos Vinson	94	147
July		a child of Joseph Covel		148
Aug	24	a Daughter of Mel. Peas	16	149
Oct	1	Phebe Mayhew	21	150
		a child of Grey		151
1774				
Feb	17	ye wife of Saml Smith	46	152
March	29	Widow Trask	70	153
April	10	ye Wife of Enoch Coffin Esqr	59	154
Do	23	a child of Timothy Smith		155

May	5	a child of John Wass			156
Do	23	a child of Nath Vinson Jr			157
July	21	Capt. Thomas Arey Junr		30(?)	158
August	7	a child of Joseph Norton			159
Nov	29	Rebecca ye wife of Benjamin Pease		67	160

[These lines refer to number 29.—H. M. PEASE.]

Stay reader for a moment stay
Newman is gone! he's left his Clay
Beneath this stone entombed it lies
Till God himself shall bid it rise
On earth he grew in wealth and Power
Untill the grand decisive hour
When wealth nor Pow'r could shield his hart
From the force of Death's alconquering Dart
But at Gods call he must depart
Then Reader know yt earth's a Toy
And seek for more Substantial Joy
That when you die & then arise
You may ascend above the skies.

Dec^r	11	Mary ye wife of Marshall Jenkins		27	161
Dec^r	23	Reuben Vinson		89	162
1775					
May		a child of Pelatiah Russel		3	163
June	10	a child of James Baning		5	164
June	14	the Wife of Timothy Norton		50	165
Aug	25	a child of Adams		4	166
Sep.	15	a child of Grays		2	167
Sep.	17	Capt. Timothy Dagget		85	168
Oct	12	a child of Henry Fish		1	169
Do	13	a child of Benjamin Smith		2	170
Oct	17	a child of Cornelius Merchant		3	171
1776					
March		a child of Nathl Vinson		3	172
April		ye Wife of Wm Vinson		33	173
Do		Abigail Donham		21	174
Do		a son of Robt Hammet		20	175
Do		a child of Peter Peas		8	176
June	22	a child of Edy Coffin			177
Do	24	a son of John Norton		16	178
Do	27	ye Wife of Jonathan Peas		23	179
July		ye Wife of Lem^l Jenkins		22	180
		Pelatiah Russel Junr	at sea	18	181
Sep.	3	the Widow Huxford		76	182
Dec^r		a child of David Reynolds			183
Dec^r	16	the Widow Abigail Peas		99	184
		Seth Crossman		23	185
1777					
March	12	a child of Cheney Look			186
May	13	Mary Frederick		31	187
May	22	John Smith		61	188
May	31	the wife of Eben^r Smith Esq		39	189
Oct	20	John Worth Junr	Drowned	27	190
Nov		Thomas Atsatt		27	191
Nov	18	Silas Merchant		55	192

1778				
Jan^{y}		Jonathan Peas	74	193
Feb		Jonathan Butler	23	194
June	6	Sylvanus Peas	50	195
June	21	a child of Thos Jernegan	2	196
June	24	a child of Thos Jernegan	4	197
June	25	a child of John Davis	2	198
June	18	a child of Eliakim Norton	1	199
July		a child of James Coffin		200
August	13	ye Wife of Peter Ripley Jr	40	201
Do	16	ye Widow Donham	85	202
Do		a child of Jonathan Peas		203
Do		a child of Prat		204
Oct		the wife of Isaac Norton	58	205
Do		Thankfull Lawson	28	206
Do		a child of John Davis		207
Nov	28	Daniel Stuart	67	208
Dec^{r}	5	Dea^{n} Matthew Norton	84	209
		(Another handwriting here.)		
Decem	14	Mary Norton D^{ns} Wife Aet.	82	210
	29	Mary the wife of Bro^{ton} Daggett Esqr	48	211
Decem	30	Rev. Mr. Kingsbury	43	212
		Mr Kingsbury 42 years & two days old		
1779				
Jan	1	Jonathan Bunker	50	213
Feb	4	Love the wife of Eph^{m} Pease	35	214
		an infant of Eph^{m} Pease		215
March		an infant of John Harper Pease		216
		a child of Obediah Pease	4	217
		an infant of Barzillai Pease		218
April	5	Mary the Wife of Joseph Cleavland	63	219
Jan	25	Sarah Wife of Thomas Vinson	93	220
March	24	a child of Thomas Vinson	3	221
Jan^{y}	3	Jonathan Cottle		222
Jan	10	Tim^{o} Smith drowned	53	223
Oct		Bulah the Wife of Thomas Arey	61	224
		Rebeckah the Wife of James Preston		225
		Saml Vinson		226
		a child of Thos Ripley		227
		a child of Abraham Ripley		228
		a child of Zephaniah Butler		229
		a child of James Skiff		230
		a child of Cornelius Merchant		231
Decem		an infant of Barzillai Pease		232
		a child of Peter Champ's		233
		a child of Saml Fish		234
		a child of Jethro Dunham		235
		Reuben Pease		236
		a child of Silas Butler		237
		Tristram Pease		238
		a child of Jonathan Pease		239
		a child of James Banning		240
		a child of Henry Fish		241
		Isaac Lockwood drowned		242

1780
March Hannah the wife of Melatiah Pease 243

Notes in Explanation, by Harriet M. Pease.

No. 136 was Elizabeth (Butler), his first wife.
" 137 was Beulah (Coffin), the first wife.
" 139 was Jean (Stuart), daughter of Daniel.
" 143 was Jedidah (Stuart), daughter of Samuel.
" 152 was born Deborah Pease, and married, 1st, —— Instance. She was the third wife of Samuel Smith, Jr.
" 154 was Jean (Claghorn) Whellen.
" 160 was Rebecca (Dunham).
" 161 was Mary (Pease), the first wife of Marshall Jenkins. These were the grandparents of Maj.-Gen. William Jenkins Worth.
" 173 was Lydia (Marchant), the first wife.
" 179 was Hannah (Coffin), 2d wife, and daughter of Daniel Coffin.
" 180 was Elizabeth (Mayhew, daughter of Zaccheus), and the 2d wife of Lemuel Jenkins.
" 184 was Abigail (Vincent), widow of Nathaniel Pease.
" 189 was Jean (Marchant), the first wife of Ebenezer Smith.
" 206 was Thankful (Hammet), wife of Thomas Lawson.
" 214 was Love (Harper), the second wife of Ephraim Pease.

DEATHS AT EDGARTOWN, MASS.

Communicated by Miss HARRIET M. PEASE, Genealogist, of Edgartown, Mass.

Deaths in Edgartown from the Time of my coming to this Place May 26, 1780.

JOS. THAXTER.

Date		Name	Cause	Age	No.
1780					
Nov.	2	a child of Thomas Jernegan	infant	Ætatis	1
Decem	16	a child of Lem^l Kelley		10 months	2
1781					
Jan:	15	Mary the Grand Daughter of Thos Arey	consump.	Æt 11	3
April	14	Joseph Thaxter a child of Thomas Cookes		3 month	4
	21	Anna the Wife of John Butler	puerperal Fev.	Æt 29	5
	27	The Widdow Elizabeth Norton	Fev.	73	6
June	19	John Marchant	Fev.	74	7
		a child of James Beetle		10 months	8
Aug	29	John Ward Son of the Widdow Hannah Ward	Billious Chollick & mortif. of Bowels	Æt 18	9
Sept	25	Polly Norton the Daughter of Beriah Norton	choaked to Death by a Bean in her Wind Pipe	7	10
		Mary Weeks Daughter of Widdow Jane	consu^n	18	11
Oct	4	The Widdow Mary Daggett	old age	88	12
Nov.	27	Sarah Cottle Sister of Thos Cottle H. H.	dissent:	9	13
1782					
Jan	17	Matthew Butler	They all perished the 14th	46	14
		Saml Wiswall	in a ship cast away at Gay	44	15
		Baze Norton	Head. Baze Norton & Isaac	38	16
		Saml Fish	Bunker were not found the	40	17
		Jethro Norton	Rest were brought to the	21	18
		Isaac Bunker	Meeting House & buried	20	19

in the New Burying Place which were the first laid there. They left Four Widdows & Twenty Four Fatherless children & Mrs. Butler near her Time of lying in—9 of our People were saved & Three that belonged to the Ship. the Rest 8 perished—
Baze Norton & Isaac Bunker were found afterwards & buried at Chilmark.

Date		Name	Cause	Age	No.
1782					
Feb	25	Daniel Son of Elijah Stewart:	mortific	Æt 3	20
April	1	A still born Infant of Thos Cooke Esqr The Eleventh Son & never had a Daughter			21

April	5	Dinah the Widdow of Saml Fish	Drop	41	22
	7	an Infant of Stephen Pease Jun. that was born blind			23
	15	Richmond Son of Benja Daggett Jun.	Inf.		24
	27	an Infant of Saml Fish late deceased			25
	28	an Infant of Immanuel Salvara			26
May	24	Lois the Wife of Nathaniel Vinson	Ner: Fev	46	27
	28	a child of Nicholas Norton scalded to Death in a Tub of boiling Lye		2	28
June	17	Mr. Ichabod Wiswall A.M.	Cancer	78	29
July	23	Betsey the Daughter of Ebenr Smith Esqr	Fev:	12	30
Aug	15	a child son of Joseph Swasey Jr. at Chapaquid:		5	31
	23	Hepsibah the wife of Antoy Flagg	Ner. Fev:	43	32
	26	Hepsibah the Wife of John Coffin Esqr	Numb Palsey	71	33
Oct	18	Peter Ripley with an Hypo ropus[?] on his Heart		70	34
Nov	18	Love, the Daughter of Zachariah Pease	Sore Throat	4	35
1783					
Jan	2	an Infant of David Reynolds			36
	3	an Infant of John Spragues			37
	6	James Norton at Quampachee	Billious	29	38
	20	Lot Norton's Twins lived but a few Hours			39 40
Feb	8	John Hollie	Strang.	70	41
March	17	the Widdow Mehitabel Vinson	old age	93	42
	22	Lyddia the Wife of Leml Pease West side Holmes Hole was burried from her Father's Elijah Smith's	Cholick	44	
April	18	an Infant of Stephen Pease Jr born blind			43
	21	the Widdow Bethiah Jones	old age	82	44
May	3	the Widdow Ann Hollie	Scurvy & Dropsy	63	45
	7	Thos Daggett He left a Widdow Æt 81 they had lived together 60 years	old age	83	46
	13	Brotherton Daggett Esqr	Het: & scorbut	59	47
	31	Margery the Wife of Dea. Benj. Daggett	Fit	73	48
June	7	Robart Norton Baptist	Schirrous Liver	27	49
July		The Wife of Timothy Butler died Fev. at Chilmark	fortasse	25	50
		James Skiff died in the West Indies	fortasse	30	
Sept	28	an Infant of Nathl Vinsons			51
Oct	23	The Wid: Jerusha Daggett	consump	46	52
		an Infant of David Smiths			53
Sept	6	the Widdow Daggett Homes Hole	old age	89	54

1784					
Jan	28	Stephen Pease	Dysent	66	55
	29	one Hill a Stranger			
Feb	6	a Child of Zach: Pease		2	56
	10	Thos Claghorn Homes Hole	old age	93	57
March	22	a Child of Saml Norton Homes Hole	fits	2	58
May	29	Barna Cousins Norton killed on board a Ship in letting go the Anchor he was caught in the Cable		24	59
June		a Child of James Beetle Homes Hole		2	60
Aug	31	a Child of Elijah Butler Jun H. Hole	Inf.		61
Sept	3	a Child of Benja Pease Senior		3	62
	14	an Infant of Immanuel Silvara's			63
	30	Lemuel Kelley who was drowned Twelve Days ago was taken up & buried		20	64
1784					
Oct	30	an Infant of Leml Jenkins			65
Nov	17	a Child of John Harper Pease	worms	2	66
	22	Mary the Daughter of Thos Vinson		13	67
1785					
Jan	28	Easter Fish the Wife of Jos Fish	lying in Fev.		68
Feb	23	a Child of Silas Butlers	by a burn	2	69
March	3	Benjn Norton of Quampechee	old age	89	70
July	4	Josiah Pease son of Seth Pease	Fits	27	71
July	11	Betsey Noise Daught of Wid Cottle	cons:	Æt 19	72
July	23	Joseph Swasey Jur Chapaquiddick	Bleeding at the Mouth from a Hurt	35	73
Aug.	12	Sarah Noise Daughter of Wid. Cottle	Nervous Fever	25	74
Sept	19	The Wd Mary Pease	Scurvey & dropsy	80	75
Oct.	23	The Wd of Fish	old age	84	76
		James Stewart died on his Passage from the West Indies		19	77
Oct.	25	a Child of Jabez Norton	scalded to Death		78
	25	Avis Norton	consumption fortasse	53	78
Decem	14	Naomi the Wife of Seth Dunham	with a Pain in her breast: died sudden	70	79
1786					
May	11	Stephen Cham a Stranger said to be an Englishman, a man of University Education			
	13	an Infant of Elijah Arey			80
June	20	Shubael Davis's Son	drowned	7	81
	21	Andrew Macartney Ryan	consumption of the Lungs fortasse	30	82
Aug.	27	Anna the Wife of Wm Covel	Child Bed	31	83
Sept	27	Elizabeth Martin	Universal Decay	67	84
	29	John Pease	old age	80	85
Nov	27	The Widdow Susanna Claghorn	pul: fever	76	86

Nov		an Infant of Stephen Pease	born blind		87
Decem	7	Susanna the Wife of Richard Bunker	consump	23	88
	12	Obed Norton & his Son		37	89
		both fell thro the Ice & were drowned		14	90
	15	The Wife of Silvanus Norton	paral.	67	91
	5	Jonathan Smith } Two Sons of		27	92
		Cornelius Smith } Eben^{r} Smith Esqr		24	
		perished being cast away at Marsfiel near the North River			93
1787					
Jan	16	Anthony Flag	consumption	42	94
Feb	2	The Widdow Matilda Vinson	old age	84	95
March	8	Abiah the Wife of Thomas Pease	mortifi.	54	96
April	27	Anna the Wife Benjn Pease Ju^{r}			97
May	8	The Widdow Smith H. Hole	gout in Stom.	84	98
	24	a Child of John Butler Ju^{r}	Rickets	2	99
June	14	Thos Arey	pulmonary Consump	71	100
July	13	Sarah the Wife of David Smith	hect: Decay	29	101
Aug	4	Timothy Norton	Pul: Comsump	71	102
Aug	5	an Infant of Francis Butlers		3 days	103
Aug	13	Mary the Wife of Jethro Worth	Paralit	28	104
Sept	10	Anna Butler	Hect: Decay	20	105
Sept	26	Female Infant of John Daggett Ju^{r}	Inf. Bow	1	106
Oct	26	Female Inf^{t} of Wm Beetle	Hoop Cough	10 mo	107
Nov.		Female Inf^{t} of Simeon Hatch	Hoop Cough	6 mo	108
Decem	7	Wid Jane Ryan Daug^{t} of Mr Cottle	Hec^{t} Decay	23	109
	16	Clarissa Daugh^{t} of Joseph Swasey	Hoop Cough	13 days	110
1788					
Jan	19	Polly Daughter of Enoch Coffin	Worms	5	111
	31	Benj^{a} Pease	Hernia & Scorb	83	112
March	17	Wid Deborah Vinson	Slow Fever	83	113
April	16	Anna Wife of John Pease Ju^{r}	Inf. Bowels	26	114
May	4	Infant of John Marchant	overlaid	3 mo	115
	22	an Infant of Benjn Stewart	Female nep:	4 mo	116
June	5	an Infant of James Fish Jn^{r}	overlaid	25 Days	117
July	19	a Child of Eman^{l} Silvara Sen	consump	9 months	118
Nov	25	Phebe the Wife of Matth^{w} Mayhew	billious	70	119
1789					
Jan	5	a Male Infant of John Daggett	sore mouth	17 days	120
	9	Susanna Wife of Abisha Marchant	Hec^{t} Decay	47	121
	16	Sarah Covel Daugh^{t} of Joseph	Hectick Decay	30	122
Feb	23	Elizabeth Dunham Daug^{t} of Eben^{r}	mortif.	18	123

Mar	7	Ephraim Pease	appoplexy	52	124
April	7	Elijah Butler	Chollick	77	125
May	14	a Male Infant of Voluntine Peases		8 days	126
	24	Hannah Wife of Jonn Harper	old age	86	127
July	5	Elizabeth Philips	Hec^{t}: Decay	22	128
	22	Henry Cooke Son of Thos Cooke E^{sq}	drowned	16	129
	24	Daniel Coffin	Consumption	69	130
Aug	23	Male Infant of Thos Jernegan	Sore Mouth	6½ weeks	131
Sep^{t}	19	a Male Infant of James Fish Ju^{r}		9 weeks	132
		——— Survash		45 perhaps	133
		Ansel Daggett Son of Prince	drowned at the Straits	20	134
Oct	4	Wid: Love Daggett	Infam Fever	88	135
	"	Wid Mehitable Dunham	Cold	88	136
Decem	23	Isaac Norton	Pain in Stomach	80	137
1790					
March	10	a Male Infant of Benj^{m} Davis	sore mouth	21 Days	148
	25	Michael Stuart	Billious Fev.	25	149
April	24	Sarrah Daught of Zachariah Pease	Bil: Fev.	18	150
May	22	Wid Sarah Dunham	Scurvy	69	150
June	7	Jane the Wife of Jo^{s} Holly	Scurvy	25	151
Oct.	17	an Infant of James Fish Ju^{r}		8 days	152
Nov	2	Mercy Wife of Wm Norton	a Schirrous Tumor in her Breast	49	153
Decem	6	Deborah Pease	old age	94	154
	7	a Male Infant Zachariah Nortons	Fits	12 days	155
	13	Hannah Beetle	Universal Decay	25	156
	23	Wid: Meriam Marchant	old age	85	157
		Thos Butler Son of Silas Butler	died in Suriam	24	158
1791					
Jan	26	Jane Stuart	Pul Cons^{tn}	75	1[illegible]
Feb	16	John Harper	inflam: Fever	91	160
April	2	Male Infant John Sprague	Cons:	1 yr 5 days	161
	24	The W^{d} of Stephen Pease	sudden	72	162
June	5	Love the Wife of Prince Norton		66	163
		Eben^{r} Talcut	at Surrinam, fortasse	35	163
		Lemuel Weeks	in West Indies	23	164
	16	Jeremiah Son of James Banning		4	165
	26	a Male Infant of Corn^{s} Marchant		2 Hours	166
July	18	Melatiah Pease	appoplexy	84	167
	21	Judith Covil Daug^{t} of Joseph	Hectick	25	168
Sep^{t}	10	Ephraim Pease Butler Son of Francis Butler	Dissent Inf^{t}		169
Decem	31	John Coffin Esqr		82	170
		Benjamin Daggett a Deacon of the Chh in this Place a man of eminent Piety & Virtue removed from this Place to Fox Island where he died of a Cancer		Æ 90	

Date	Name	Remarks	Æt	No.
	Foundered at Sea in the year 1781.		Æt	
	Joseph Hammet		28	1
	Prat		26	2
	Henry Coffin 1781		22	3
	Lawson		17	4
	Gamaliel Marchant 1783	the Ages of these I am not certain of	38	5
	James Shaw		50	6
	Benj[a] Claghorn		20	7
	Thos Claghorn		18	8
	Bazillai Butler		16	9
	John Neal		25	10
	Died in Prison Ships & at Sea.			
	Henry Butler		36	11
	Ebenezer Shaw		26	12
	Enoch Coffin Son of Enoch Coffin	foundered at Sea	28	13
	Simeon Coffin		30	14
1785	Tristram Coffin	foundered at Sea	32	15
1792			Æt	
Jan 23	Jane the Wife of Rob: Hammett	Paralit	64	171
Feb 5	Peter Norton Esqr a Deacon of the Baptist Chh at Homes's Hole	Scurvey	74	172
March 5	Philip Smith	Drowned at the East Chop the Father & Son	46	173
	Oliver Smith		20	174
Sep[t]	Henry Marchant	in Virginia	24	175
Oct	Pelatiah Willis	in Carolina	15	176
Nov	A Male Infant of Dexters	mortif:	10 months	177
Decem 25	A Female Infant of Peter Coffin		4 days	178
1793				
Feb 20	Hepsibah Holly Daug[t] of John Holley non Compos the most miserable object always in Pain & Distress & for four Weeks did not take one Pint of anything		19 months	179
March 7	a Female Inf[t] of Francis Meeders	consum	11m. 23D.	180
13	Bulah Covil	Hect: Decay		181
April 29	the Widdow Russell	Consump	65	182
Feb	Abraham Smith killed in the West Indies by a fall from mast		23	183
	Frederick Norton son of Beriah	died at Sea of a Fever	22	184

NOTES IN EXPLANATION, BY HARRIET M. PEASE.

No. 12 was Mary (Smith), widow of Capt. Timothy Daggett.
" 22 was Dinah (Vincent), daughter of Joseph Vincent.
" 27 was Lois (Smith), the first wife of Nathaniel Vincent, Jr.
" 32 was Hepsibah (Ripley), daughter of Abraham Ripley.
" 33 was Hepsibah (Lambert), second wife of John Coffin.
" 42 was Mehitabel (Pease), widow of Reuben Vincent.
" 45 was Anna (Pease), widow of John Holley.
" 52 was Jerusha (Pease), second wife of Maj. Brotherton Daggett.

No. 54 supposed to be Thankful (Daggett), widow of Brotherton Daggett, Sen.

" 75 was Mary (Newcomb), widow of Jonathan Pease.

" 76 was Ruth (Butler), daughter of Henry Butler, and widow of Thomas Fish.

" 84 was Elizabeth (Butler), daughter of Samuel Butler, and widow of Peter Martin.

" 86 was Susannah (Gibbs), second wife, and widow of Thomas Claghorn.

" 91 was Hannah Norton before marriage.

" 95 was Matilda (Dunham), widow of Joseph Vincent.

" 96 was Abiah (Smith) Shaw, second wife of Thomas Pease, Jr.

" 98 was probably Thankful (———), widow of Ebenezer Smith, who died in 1771.

" 101 was Sarah (Skiff), the first wife of David Smith.

" 109 was Jane (Noise), widow of Andrew Macartney Ryan, and daughter of Sarah (Daggett), Noyes, who afterwards married Jonathan Cottle.

" 113 was Deborah (Stuart), widow of Nathaniel Vincent, Sen.

" 127 was Hannah Sprowell before marriage.

" 135 was Love (Coffin), widow of Thomas Daggett.

" 136 was Mehitable (Vincent), widow of Jethro Dunham.

" 151 was Jane (Russell), first wife of Capt. Joseph Holley.

" 154 was Deborah (———), widow of Thomas Pease, Jr.

" 157 was Miriam (Cleveland), widow of John Marchant, Jr.

" 159 was Jean (Vincent), widow of Daniel Stuart.

" 162 was Jemimah (Vincent).

" 182 was Jane (Pease), widow of Pelatiah Russell.

No. 1. Joseph Hammett was the son of Robert and Jean (Butler) Hammett.

" 2. ——— Pratt. Probably the brother-in-la of Joseph Hammett, the husband of his sister Anna, whose Chris name is unknown to me.

" 3. Henry Coffin, b. March 16, 1756, was the s of Enoch and Jane (Claghorn) Coffin.

" 4. ——— Lawson may have been a son of Th s Lawson, who married in 1768 (perhaps a second wife) Thankful Hammett, a sister of Joseph.

" 5. Gamaliel Marchant, born in October, 1740, was the son of John and Miriam (Cleveland) Marchant, and is said to have been lost at sea in 1782.

" 6. James Shaw served in the war of the Revolution as lieutenant in Capt. Benjamin Smith's company, stationed on the island of Martha's Vineyard. He married an Edgartown woman, but his birthplace is unknown to me. He may have come from Plympton.

" 7. Benjamin Claghorn } were in all probability the sons of Thomas, Jr.,
" 8. Thomas Claghorn } and Mary (Huxford) Claghorn.

" 9. Barzillai Butler, b. Aug. 14, 1669, was the son of Henry and Elizabeth (Ripley) Butler. He died Nov. —, 1784.

" 10. John Neal, baptized in 1754, was the son of Thomas and Lois (Stewart) Neal.

" 11. Henry Butler, baptized Oct. 25, 1741, was the son of Nicholas and second wife Thankful (Marchant) Butler. He served in the war of the Revolution as private in Capt. Benjamin Smith's company, stationed on Martha's Vineyard in defense of the sea coast.

" 12. Ebenezer Shaw, b. Sept. 27, 1756, was the son of Jonathan Shaw of Plympton, who married March —, 1754, Abiah Smith of Edgartown. Ebenezer married in March, 1779, Keturah Pease, who, in 1783, married a second husband. Ebenezer Shaw served in the war of the Revolution as private in Capt. Benjamin Smith's company, in the regiment for Dukes County.

" 13. Enoch Coffin, born Oct. 25, 1750, was the son of Enoch and Jane (Claghorn) Coffin.

" 14. Simeon Coffin was the son of Samuel and Elizabeth (Gardner) Coffin.

" 15. Tristram Coffin, born April 5, 1755, was the son of Samuel and Elizabeth (Gardner) Coffin.

DEATHS AT EDGARTOWN, MASS.

Communicated by Miss Harriet M. Pease, of Edgartown, Mass.

1793					No.
May	15	Samuel Stuart	Confump.	71	185
		occasioned by a Wound by overfetting a Cart upon him.			
June	13	a Female Infant Benj[n] Davis Son of Malt.		5 weeks	186

	15	Molly wife of Benjn Davis	Dyst	36	187
July	12	Priscilla Snow	Consump	56	188
	20	Sarſon Kelly	Consump	27	189
Aug.	20	a Female Infant of John Benjn Downs:	Col morb	4 weeks	190
Sept	9	a Male Child of Zepha^{h} Butlers	Dyſent	2 y. 2 m	191
	12	a Male Child of Wm Norton J^{nr}	Dyſt	1 year 1	192
	22	a Female Inf^{t} of Noah Norton	worms	10 m	193
Oct.	3	Benj^{a} Coffin	Dyſent	76	194
		a Male Inf^{t} Thos Ripley	Dyſt	20 mo	195
Oct	15	John Coffin Son of Daniel Coffin by a Fall from a Ships Yrd		20	196
Nov	9	a Son of Imman^{l} Silvara	Quinſey	5	197
Decem	9	John Butler	Schir: Liver	60	198
		Nathan Daggett of the Small Pox in the Weſt Indies ſome Time in October	Fortaſse	30	199
		a Child of James Beetle	male	6 m	200
1794				Æt	
Jan	11	Love Cunningham	Hect: Decay	38	201
	13	Thos Peaſe	Paralit	66	202
Feb.	3	Mary Wife of Wm Jernigan Esqr		62	203
	5	Mary Wife of Litlton Cooke	Hect:	21	204
March	6	Lucy Mayhew Daug^{t} of Deacon Mayhew	Hect:	17	205
	23	Lydia Arey		33	206
Feb		Abraham Whaley	died in West Indies	22	207
		Robert Fiſh	died in West Indies	20	208
		John Survaſh	died in West Indies	16	209
April	2	a Female Infant of Noah Norton		7 days	210
		William Waſs	in Virginia	25	211
		Cornelius Butler	in West Indies	60	212
		Robartus Peaſe	in West Indies	24	213
May	26	Eben^{r} Smith Esqr	Mortif: Bow:	60	214
June		a Daugh^{t} of Jaſen Luce		9 mos.	215
Aug^{t}		Sarah Daggett	old age	85	216
		William Rawson	died at Sea Georgia Fever	18	217
		James Banning Ju^{r}	died at Sea Georgia Fever	18	218
Sept	4	Bartlett Butler — These Three were together with Capt. Thos Coffin	ſame Fever	14	219
Sept		John Harper Peaſe	in Jamaica	39	220
Oct	9	Clement Pease	Southern Fever	23	221
Aug^{t}		Luke Gray	in New Jerſey	49	222
		Huxford Marchant	in Weſt Indies	20	223
		Silas Butler Ju^{r}	Weſt Indies	21	224
		Daniel Norton	Weſt Indies	15	225
Oct		Isaac Daggett	Virginia	25	226
Sept		Richard Hall	in Carolina	24	227
		Seba Peaſe	in Weſt Indies	25	228

Note. Just here Parson Thaxter says:
"There is a miſtake in the Number in 1790 they were 137 & from that to 1795 147 ſo that the true Number is 218."

As mistakes of this kind occur further on I will hereafter give my own numbering, calling 219, as he gives it, 229 to avoid confusion in looking up the references.

H. M. Pease.

Month	Day	Name	Cause / Place	Age	No.
1795					
Jan	6	Meriam Wife of Thos Vinſon		54	229
	13	Prince Daggett		71	230
April	6	a male Inf^{t} of Bartlet Claghorn		8 weeks	231
	11	Richard Grove Hoſmer of Middletown Connecticut			
May		Dorcas Stizacre	fortaſse	75	232
		Peter Cleavland	at Jamaica	16	233
July	10	a Male Infant of Dan: Fiſh	H. C.	4 mo	234
	16	Hannah Wife of Cornelius Marchant Ju^{r}	mort: Bow:	25	235
Aug^{t}	12	Christopher Luce	Rheum^{m}	76	236
	19	A Female child	worms		237
	24	a male Inft of Cornel^{s} Ripley, Ju^{r}.	worms	11 months	238
Sep^{t}	20	a Female Inf^{t} of Wm. Dunham	conf	4 m	239
		Zebediah Vinſon	Weſt Ind: Fever	22	240
Dec	10	a Male Inf^{t} of Sanford Davis		6 days	241
		a male of James Beetle			242
Aug		a male of John Harper Pease	worms	3	243
1796					
Jan	11	a Daugh^{t} of Thos Stuart	canker Rash	4	244
Feb	5	Widdow Thankful Pease		89	245
March	12	Joſeph Dunham	Gout in Stom	56	246
April	10	Ruhamah Peaſe Daugh^{t} of Noah Pease	Conſumption	17	247
	19	Harrison Son of Noah Peaſe	Ner Fev.	13	248
	28	a Female Child of Triſtram Norton	worms	4	249
May		Serena Peaſe Daugh^{t} of Seth	Both }	22	250
		Rachel Peaſe Do	Ner. Fev. }	28	251
June	16	Saml Smith	Decay	84	252
		a Female child of Corn^{l} Huxford	Cramps	5	253
		John Worth, Son of Jethro	Jamaica	17	254
		Francis Butler on his Paſsage from the Weſt Indies		37	255
		Bartlett Norton	in Weſt Indies	24	256
Sept	4	an Infant of Jaſon Luce		10 weeks	257
	7	a Son of Francis Butler	Dy	15 months	258
	8	a Daugh^{t} of Thos Jernigan an Ideot it took not more than a Spoonful a Day for 11 weeks		5 yrs & 5 mo	259
	11	Sarah Wife of Jo^{s} Peaſe	mortif:		260
	28	Abiah Vinſon	Hect: Decay	32	261
		Freeman Peaſe son of John	Conſump^{n}	22	262
Oct	22	Jedidah widdow of Tim^{o} Norton	Conf	59	263
	27	Saml Smith Esqr	Schirrous Liver	69	264
Nov	18	a Male Inf^{t} of Jona^{n} Worth	Fits	6 m	265
		Benjn Ripley	in Carolina	26	266
		Littleton Cooke	in Weſt Indies	26	267
		Thomas Coffin	in Georgia	49	268
Decem	25	Joſeph Cleavland	Gravel	82	269

1797					
March	22	Peggy Fiſh Daug^{t} of Jona^{n}	cancer	12	270
July	29	Sarah the wife of Benjn Vinſon	conſs	54	271
Aug	11	Isaac Norton	cancer	71	272
	12	Lemuel Kelley	appoplexy	61	273
		George Pease Lost at Sea 1796		32	274
Sept	3	Sarah wife of Jona^{n} Worth	conſump	39	275
	2	Timothy Vinſon died a Weſt Port	Dyſ^{y}		276
Oct	12	Nathan Danham	Drowned in Harb	62	277
	14	Sarah Daugh^{t} of Wm Norton Ju^{r}	Dyſent	2	278
Nov.	2	Lucy the Wife of Dea^{n} Wm Mayhew	Conſ	46	279
		James Coffin Ju^{r} in Baltimore	conſ	22	280
		Homes Waſs Struck overboard by the Boom on his Paſsage to Philadel^{a}			281
Dec.	12	a Female Infant of David Smith	worms	20 months	282
	30	Abner Vinson	abſces in side	59	283
1798					
Jan	31	Eunice Stewart	cancer	53	284
May		Isaiah Dunham	Jamaica	32	285
		Isaac Lockwood	Jamaica	20	286
June	31	Sprowel Peaſe	putrid Fever	21	287
July	31	Abraham Norton son of Jo^{s}	drowned	23	288
Oct	8	Thos Peaſe	col. morb. fortaſse	45	289
Oct		Ephraim Peaſe Ju^{r}	in Weſt Indies fort	22	290
	31	William Peaſe	scurvy	64	292
Nov.	26	Wid Hannah Croſman	Decay	77	291
		Wid Luce	fortaſse	75	293
1799					
Jan		Two Spaniards died at Ezra Cleavlands being badly froze the 1st died in twelve Hours owing wholly to the froſt & ill uſage on board the Vessel in which he came to this Place the 2 with the Lock Jaw occasioned by the frost in his Feet.			294, 295
March	5	Eben^{r} Dunham		74	296
	28	John Boder of Marblehead		26	297
May	2	Sarah wife of Seth Peaſe	Diar.	65	298
	17	Edy Coffin Ju^{r} died at Sea on his Paſsage from Florida	Yellow Fever	23	299
June	26	Nathan Smith at Boston with Yellow Fever taken on board a veſsel from the Havannah		40	300
July	1	John Worth Son of Jethro Worth	Duſent	14 m	301
Augt	23	Seth Dunham	old age	85	302
Oct	11	Matth^{w} Mayhew	conſump^{t}		303
Nov.	9	Martha the wife of Ichabod Cleavland	cancer in Breast		304
1800					
April	1	Sally Fiſh wife of Daniel Fiſh	in Travail	33	305
	7	Henry Fiſh	Hect: Decay fortaſse	75	306
		Ellis Fiſh Son of James Fiſh Ju^{n} Drowned in coming into to Waqua his Father attempted to swim on Shore			307

Month	Day	Entry	Age	No.
		with him on his back he was washed of and seen no more an early Blossom ſoon cut down.		
		Jared Worth the Son of Jethro Worth		
		Henry Osborn Son of Henry Osborn age about	18	308
		both died at the Havannah about July 1799		309
June	3	Suſanna the wife of John Daggett Pul: Conf	38	310
July	13	Jonathan Daggett with the Yellow Fever in Georgia	24	311
	23	an Infant of Gray's a Daught	4m	312
Aug^{t}	11	a Male Infant Danl Vinſon	5w	313
	13	Betſey Stewart with Fits that attaced her from 4th years old	41	314
Sept	22	Lydia Fiſh the wife of Richard Fiſh child bed	22	315
		William Maning Mayhew Son of Deacon Mayhew	20	316
		William Ripley these two died at Baltimore of the Yellow Fever fortaſse	24	317
Oct	17	Stephen Norton Languiſ^{mt}	73	318
1801.				
Jan	28	Cornelius Ripley conſump fortaſe	35	319
Feb	21	Wid. Mercy Butler conſm	85	320
		Oliver Butler son of Daniel and	24	321
		Joseph Gray son of Luke were foundered at Sea the last year	16	322
March	9	Sarah the Wife of Jo^{s} Kelley conſump^{t}	25	323
		Abraham Cleavland Son of Ichabod Cleavland was loſt at Sea Nov 8 1800	19	324
April	11	Silvanus Norton Old Age	83	325
	28	Joseph Vinson Infla^{m} Bowells	69	326
		a male Infant of Richard Fiſher	7m	327
June	17	Littleton Cooke Son of Thomas Cooke Ju^{r} Fits	3	328
July	12	Nabby Beetle Daug^{t} of Wm Beetle Fever nervous	19	329
	17	Polly Marchant Wife of Ephraim Marchant Hec^{t} Decay	22	330
		Gamaliel Fiſh } were lost at Sea in April		331
		William Dunham } They both left Wives in a State of Pregnancy Dunham's Wife was delivered of Twins July 15 both boys		332
Sept	12	W^{d} Jane Folgier the mother of Thos Cooke Esq. by a former Husband	90	333
Oct	6	Mary Pease the Wife of Peter Pease ſudently in a Fit	73	334
	10	a Male Infant & Twin of William Dunham late deceased	3m	335
		Richard Beetle Son of Wm Beetle Died at Bedford in Sept 20 of the Yellow Fever	22	336
		Christopher Beetle Son of Wm Beetle Died in Virginia Sept 11 of Yellow Fever	24	337

	21	A male Infant of Wm Dunham late defeafed a Twin	3m	338
		Enoch Coffin Jur Died his Passage from West Indies	44	339
Nov	5	Hugh Vinfon Dyfent	24	340
	23	Samuel Norton Strang:	59	341
		The 2d of Sept George Corlis Peafe the Deaf & Dumb Son of Wm Pease late defeased fell over board & was drowned in the Englifh Channel	32	342

NOTES IN EXPLANATION, BY HARRIET M. PEASE.

No. 187 was Molly (Daggett), born August 8, 1757, daughter of Major Brotherton and Mary (Tucker) Daggett, and first wife of Benj. Davis.
" 188 was the daughter of Thomas and Priscilla (Butler) Snow.
" 189 was John Sarson Kelley, son of Lemuel and Bathsheba (Harper) Kelley.
" 201 was Love (Daggett), daughter of Prince Daggett and widow of Thomas Cunningham.
" 203 was Mary (Osborn), daughter of Samuel and Keziah (Butler) Osborn, and the first wife of William Jernegan, Esq.
" 204 was Mary (Swasey), dau. of Joseph and Susannah (Pease) Swasey.
" 205 was the daughter of Dea. William Mayhew and Lucy (Mayhew), his first wife.
" 206 was the daughter of Thomas and Beulah (Trapp) Arey.
" 208 was the son of Jonathan and Eunice (Holley) Fisher.
" 211 was the son of Homes and Sarah (Mayhew) Wass.
" 213 was the son of Benjamin and Anne (Butler) Pease.
" 216 was in all probability Sarah, widow of John Daggett and the mother of Prince.
" 217 was the son of John and Elizabeth (Cleveland) Rawson.
" 218 was the son of James and Mercy (Coffin) Banning.
" 219 was the son of Zephaniah and Hannah (Ripley) Butler.
" 221 was the son of Obedh and Rachel (Coffin) Pease.
" 223 was the son of Abishai Marchant and his first wife, Susannah Harper.
" 226 was the son of Brotherton and Mary (Tucker) Daggett.
" 228 was the son of John Pease and Mary Norton his 4th wife.
" 229 was Miriam (Norton), the second wife. She was the daughter of Phinehas and Patience (Cleveland) Norton.
" 232 was the wife—or widow—of William Stizacre.
" 233 was the son of Ichabod and Martha (Dunham) Cleveland.
" 235 was Hannah (Young), his first wife.
" 240 was the son of William Vinson (or Vincent) and Lydia Marchant, his first wife.
" 252 was the son of John and Hannah (Pease) Smith.
Being the second of the name he was called Samuel Smith, Jr.
" 260 was Sarah (Smith), the first wife of Joseph Pease, Jr., and daughter of Samuel Smith, Jr., and Eunice Vincent, his second wife.
" 263 was Jedidiah Allen, the second wife of Timothy Norton.
" 264 was the son of Capt. Samuel Smith and Katherine Homes, his second wife. Until the death of his father he was called Samuel Smith, Tertius, being the third of the name. Samuel, son of John, being older, was called Samuel Smith, Jr.
" 271 was Sarah (Luce), daughter of Christopher and Sarah (Arey) Luce.
" 275 was Sarah (Mayhew), the first wife. She was the daughter of Dr. Matthew and Mary (Allen) Mayhew.
" 279 was Lucy (Mayhew), his first wife and the daughter of Zaccheus and Rebecca (Pope) Mayhew.
" 284 was the daughter of Samuel and Sarah (——) Stewart.
" 286 was the son of Isaac and Elizabeth (Fisher) Lockwood.
" 287 was the son of Noah and Hannah (Dunham) Pease.

No. 292 was the widow of Seth Crossman. Her maiden name is unknown. It may have been Arnold, as a grandson bore that name. Think she came from Rhode Island. Her children were Hannah, Abigail, Seth and Peleg—and perhaps Anthony. Hannah and Peleg married and died in Edgartown. Son Seth also died there.

" 293 was probably Hannah (Chase) Ferguson, daughter of Abraham Chase and Abigail Barnard, his first wife, widow of John Ferguson and second wife and widow of Christopher Luce.

" 298 was Sarah (Chase), daughter of Joseph and Lydia (Coffin) Chase.

" 304 was Martha (Dunham), parentage not determined.

" 305 was Sally (Fish) daughter of John and Sarah (Fish) Fish and the first wife of Daniel.

" 310 was Susannah (Stewart), his first wife and daughter of Daniel and Jean (Vincent) Stewart.

" 314 was the daughter of Daniel and Jean (Vincent) Stewart.

" 315 was Lydia (West).

" 320 was Mercy (Dunham), second wife and widow of Gamaliel Butler and daughter of Benajah and Sarah (Covel) Dunham.

" 323 was Sarah (Vincent), daughter of Joseph Vincent, Jr., and Thankful (Dunham) Stewart, his wife.

" 330 was Polly (Coffin), his first wife, and daughter of James and Huldah (Allen) Coffin.

" 333 was Jane (Daggett), daughter of Israel and Ruth (Norton) Daggett. She was three times a widow. Her first husband was Temple Philip Cooke. She married next a Crittenden or Cruttenden, perhaps Dr. Thomas, of Guildford, Conn. The third was a Folger, given name not known.

" 334 was Mary (Beetle), daughter of Christopher and Mary (Norton) Beetle.

" 339 was Enoch Coffin, 3d, and Jr., son of Daniel and Mary (Harlock) Coffin. He was called Enoch Coffin, 3d, until the death of his cousin Enoch.

" 340 was the son of William Vinson and Anna Stewart, his second wife.

DEATHS AT EDGARTOWN, MASS.

Communicated by Miss HARRIET M. PEASE, of Edgartown, Mass.

1802				Æt	No.
Jan	27	Benajah Donham	old age	93	343
		This man has been the oldeft in this Town for 10 Years in which Time 170 have died younger than he was			
Feb	7	a Female Infant		18 days	344
	10	Elijah Smith	appoplex:	89	345
March	3	Thankful Peafe	Decay	72	346
March	23	Enoch Coffin Esqr	old age	90	347
April	5	Molly Thaxter wife of Revd Jofeph Thaxter with an abfcess in her Side		45	348
	26	Robert Hammet	mort:	80	349
May	6	a Daugh^t of Harlow Crofby	Decay	11	350
	9	The Wid: Hannah Ward	Decay	72	351
July	1	a Female Inf^t of Wm Vinfon Ju^r	worms and meazles	2	352
		John Worth Esqr a Deacon of the Chh. a Pillar in the Chh. An Honour to his Profefsion an Ifraelite in Deed in whom was no Guile		77	353
	4	Lucy Coffin Daugh^t of James Coffin	Hect.	21	354
		Ephraim Marchants wife who died laft year was his Daugh^t They were remarkable for their Sprightlinefs while in Health. a			

Month	Day	Name	Age	No.
		Sicked bed and long sickness calmed(?) them & they died in Peace & Good Hope		
	4	a Child of Lydia Butler, ſon.	4 mon	355
Aug^{t}	16	Hepſibah Fiſher wife of Obed Fiſher in Child-Bed a peculiar case Palpitation of the Heart & Spasms on the Diaphram	25	356
		Triſtram Cleaveland loſt at Sea in Feb fell overboard and was eaten by an Alligator in the Harbour of Batavia.	31	357
Sep^{t}		Alexander Peaſe in Weſt Indies	17	358
Oct	3	a Female Inf^{t} of James Tupper	13 mo	359
Decem	20	Sarah Peaſe Wife of Peter Peaſe	65	360
		She had burried two Huſbands & Four Children which was all she had. She was a midwife very useful and much beloved		
	28	Seth Peaſe Having a Multiplication of Disorders	73	361
1803				
Jan	5	a Male Infant of Jab Rowley	3 days	362
	22	Jethro Covel	79	363
	25	Ama Norton Daugh^{t} of Jo^{s} Influenza	30	364
	27	Lois Neal she had been a member of the Chh. upwards of 60 Years	89	365
Feb	19	Bethiah Smith W^{d} of Elijah Smith	85	366
March	5	Ann Smith W^{d} of Saml Smith Esqr a woman of diſtinguiſhed Piety	70	367
	6	Thomas Beetle billious Fever	63	368
	7	Hiram an Inf^{t} of Benjn Worth	9 weeks	369
	30	Jane the wife of Abisha Marchant	64	370
April	15	Ralph Ripley Son of Joſeph Ripley	16	371
		He with Bartlett Fiſher & Coatny were fiſhing, they were driven by the wind & Tide under Squibnockett where they lay in an open Boat in a violent Gale of Wind & Storm all Night the next morning drifted to Nomans Land where Ripley was drowned but the others saved.		
Oct	29	The Widdow Eunice Coffin cancer	68	372
Nov	24	The W^{d} Anna Butler Suddent	70	373
Decem	8	Hannah the Wife of Zephaniah Butler Inf^{n} of Liver		374
1804				
Feb	12	Jedidah the wife of Elijah Stewart	49	375
	26	W^{d} Sarah Coffin Daniels W^{d}	77	376
March	21	Benjn Weeks Dropſy	39	377
May	1	Peggy Norton wife of Dennis(?) Norton She was from Baltimore Conſump^{n}	29	378
May	5	Thomas Fiſher The Family of Fiſh have changed their Name to Fisher	80	379
June	27	Abner Butler he had been totally Helpleſs for many Years with the Rheumatiſm	71	380
		deiſtical & died in awful Horrors of Conſcience.		

July	12	Joseph Saunders formerly of Cape Ann	Col: Morb.		381
	24	Lydia Coffin Daugh^{t} of Wm Coffin a Quaker.		25	382
	27	Sarah Peafe w^{d} of Benjn Peafe			383
	29	a Male Inf^{t} of Wm Jernegan Ju^{r} lived $\frac{1}{2}$ an Hour			384
		John Peafe Ju^{r}	appoplexy	44	385
July	12	Jerufha Wife of John Peafe Esqr		69	386
		January 1 1804 Henry Coffin the Son of James Coffin was struck over board & drowned in his Pafsage to Europe		20	387
Sep^{t}	4	Anna Wife of Wm Vincent	Conf	58	388
	8	Sarah Norton w^{d} of Peter Norton Esq.		86	389
Decm	6	John Sprague was struck overboard about a mile from Nantuckett Bar & drowned. found the laft of May 1805 on Nantuckett Point & burried there.		55	390
1805					
March	5	Robert Thaxter Son of Jofeph Thaxter at Six Years & a half old he loft his sight by Nervous Pain in his Head. at 9 Years he had a severe shock of the Palsy & died of the Lock Jaw		12	391
April	7	Obediah an Infant of Marfhall Peafe		5 Days	392
		a Child of Rufus Davis			393
		a Child of Bartlett Claghorn			394
		I know not the Day nor Age they being Baptifts of Homes Hole did not let me know alfo a Female Infant born blind			
	16	Charles Peafe Son of Thomas Peafe j^{r} Struck overboard in the Streights of Gibralter & drowned		22	395
	20	a Female Child of Eben^{r} Smith	Can. Rafh	20 mo	396
May	20	a Child of Bartlet Claghorn			397
	29	Thomas Vincent		85	398
	28	William Jenkins	Confumption	36	399
June	30	Robinfon a stranger			
		Jethro Norton son of David on his Pafsage from Weft Indies			400
July	18	Hope Norton wife of Shubael Norton	Can	71	401
	27	a Male Infant of John Smith J^{r}		3 mo	402
Sep^{t}	23	a Female Infant of Seth Vincents	Col	15 mo	403
Oc^{t}	4	Anna Peafe Daugh^{t} of Salathiel Peafe		16	404
	5	a Infant of Jafon Luce's			405
	26	Patience Norton w^{d} of Baze Norton She had been a member of the Church 63 Years		92	406
Nov	8	Sarah Worth w^{d} of Dea^{n} John Worth		85	407
	16	Carr Barker of Drefden Kennebeck			
	21	Sarah Daugh^{t} of Salathiel Peafe		13	408
		Coffin Fifher Son of Amaz^{h} died in the Weft Indies			409
Decem	9	Olive Daugh^{t} of Henry Ofborn		17	410
		His Daught Lydia who married Kendrick died at the same Time at Rochefter		21	

	4	Ann the Daugh^{t} of John Sprague on a viſit to her Sister died at Albany		17	411
1806					
Jan	14	A Female Infan^{t} of Wm Jernegan Ju^{r}		4½ mo	412
March	8	Prince Norton	Pauper old	78	413
April	1	a Male Infan^{t} of Sukey Colt		18 days	414
	2	Wid^{w} Jane Claghorn	Homes Hole	70	415
		Benjn Worth died at Sea			416
May	23	Daniel Vincent	bleeding at mouth	46	417
	26	a Son of Ruben Beetle	Consn	8	418
	28	a Male Inf^{t} of Beriah Weeks	H. Cough	7 weeks	419
		Some Time in March 1805 Enoch Coffin Grand Son of Enoch Coffin Esqr &		27	420
		Fraſier Banning son of James Banning periſhed at Sea in their Paſsage from England		20	421
July	10	Elijah Arey	Conſumption		422
Aug^{t}	15	Widdow Mary Paint	Suddently	60	423
Oct	6	George Waſhington Peaſe Son of Peter Peaſe Ju^{r}	Dyſen^{t}	7	424
	9	Fanny Smith Daught of Benjn	Conf	27	425
		John Whelden died in March while on a whailing Voiage in the India Seas	fortaſse	43	426
Nov	4	Mary the wife of Thomas Claghorn	gout in Stomach	72	427
	6	Enoch Peaſe an Idiot	fortaſse	50	428
	14	David Norton	Conſumption	72	429
Decem	3	Joſeph Randal son of Joſeph	fits	15 days	430
	23	John Sprague Butler son of Walter Butler	fits	11 days	431
1807					
Jan	1	Thomas Beetle	Conſu^{n}	34	432
	24	Daniel Butler	years & conf.	70	433
	25	Anna Arey Wi^{d} of Elijah Arey She had been confined to her Bed for about 24 years in which Time she had three Sons, (not at one Birth) all of them large healthy Children & one now living the laſt. Three Months of her Life her diſtreſs of Body was very great which She indured with Patience.		52	434
Feb	26	Matthew Norton Son of Beriah Norton Esqr He had been in a state of mental derangment for upwards of 25 years for the laſt 15 he very sildom went to bed or even laid down he sildom suffered any of his Clothes to be Shifted often than twice or Three Times a Year He eat but once in 24 Hours The last six months he never lay down He suffered himself to sleep but very little		44	435
March	7	Joſeph Swaſey	appoplexy	64	436
Feb	15	James Paint was struck over board and drowned			437
		(There is a Mistake of 20 The true Number is I think			427)

Month	Day	Name	Cause	Age	No.
April	7	a Male Inf^{t} of Timothy Pease's		5 days	438
	21	John Beetle	Consump^{n}	28	439
	28	A Male Grand Child of Immanuel Silvara	Quinsy	4	440
May	8	Lucy Coffin Crocker Daugh^{t} of Silvanus Crocker & Eliza his Wife		7 weeks	441
	25	The W^{d} Drufilla Mayhew	Conf^{n}	32	442
June	2	Simeon Coffin	Pulmo^{n} Fever	27	443
July	8	William Norton jun^{r}	Fever	49	444
	18	William Norton senior	Dropfy		445
		A Male Infant of Jofeph Linton			446
Aug^{t}	14	John Vincent	Cholick	76	447
		He was a Bachelor & lived alone for near Twenty Years extreme poor a Weakly Mind an honest Heart he suffered becaufe he would not beg & could not be prevailed upon to go into any Family preferring his Solitary den where he had neither Bed nor bedding to protect him from the cold often nothing but a neft of Straw in this way he lived contented & died in Peace			
	19	David Dunham	Dropfy	83	448
		Sprowel Dunham was drowned at the Straits some Time in June		22	449
Sep^{t}	10	Abifhai Marchant	Influenza	69	450
	29	John Thomas Beetle the Son of John Beetle late deceafed	Conf^{n}	8 mo	451
Oct	7	Fanny Peafe Daugh^{t} of Noah Peafe	Fever	18	452
	26	Eunice Jernegan wife of Hon^{bl} Wm Jernegan Esqr	broken Heart	55	453
Nov	29	Lydia Fifher W^{d} of Thomas	old age	85	454
Decem	12	a Female Inf^{t} of John Smith ju^{r}		4 mo	455
	24	a male Infant of Elihu Marchant		7 days	456
1808					
Jan	12	a male Inf^{t} of Eph^{r} Marchant	fits	8 days	457
Feb	5	Henry Ofborn	Fiftula in ano	58	458
	23	Nicholas Norton in Piloting a vessel was struck overboard the Back of Cape Cod & drowned		60	459
	26	Ebenezer Butler	old age	85	460
		The Dates previous to this Time were the Day of the Funeral from this Time they will be the Day of their Death			
	29	Thomas Smith	Confump	68	461
May	27	Phebe Beetle Wid^{w} of Thomas Beetle	Confumption	62	462
June	22	Thomas Gilbert Worth son of Thomas Worth	worms	5	463
July	18	a male Child of Uriah Morfe a twin	fits	18 mo	464
	24	a male Child of Uriah Morfe the other twin	worms	18 mo	465

Month	Day	Name	Cause	Age	No.
Aug^t	7	Edgar son of George Marchant	Diar:	18 mo	466
	15	Thomas Son of Peter Coffin	Diar^h:	22 mo	467
Sep^t	1	an Infant of Uriah Coffin		1 day	468
Oct	9	Abner Cottle	Sudden	60	469
Nov	14	Sarah Silvara wife of Immanuel Silvara	Lethergy	54	470
1809					
March	21	Jane Smith wi^d of Eben^r Smith Esqr	appop	70	471
	22	Dorcas Worth	Decay	80	472
May	21	Seth Cleavland	Languish^t	68	473
Nov	17	Cornelius Marchant	Conf^n	66	474
1810					
Jan	28	Elizabeth Coffin relict of Benj Coffin		83	475
March	16	Grace C. Coffin Daug^t of Timothy		19	476
April		Fordam Peafe died in New York	fortafse	44	477
May	1	Sarah Coffin Wife of Uriah Coffin	Confump	41	478
July	4	Edward son of Jethro Worth Esqr			479
	23	Sufan Coffin Daug^t of Thos Coffin late Deceased	Confumption	26	480
Sept	4	William Cleavland	Bil. Fever	26	481
	6	Sufan Swafey Worth Daugh^t of Thos Worth	Infant in Fits		482
	8	Hilyard Norton he came from Charlefton S. Carolina died very suddently supposed	Malig. Fever	28	483
Oct	10	Prifcilla wi^d of David Dunham		80	484
	19	A male Inf^t of Saml Nortons		4 days	485
Nov		Sarah wife of Jona^n Peafe	Mortif.	60	486
Oct	27	Shubael Norton	Cancer		487
Decem	18	Katy the wife of Lot Cottle in confequence of a Fright by Abraham Kelley which produced a miscarriage		27	488
	23	Wi^d Sarah Stewart wi^d of Saml Stuart		84	489
1811					
Feb	9	Wi^d Matilda Dunham	Suddent	85	490
March	14	George Norton	Fev.		491
May	7	John Clarke	Apoplex	69	492
Aug^t	13	Edmund Lewis Twenty Nine Years & Two Days	Scirrous Liver	29	493
Sep^t	19	a Male Infant of Barzillai Luce		3 days	494
Oct	5	Jane Daug^t of Thos Cooke Esqr	Nervous Fever about 28 Days	27	495
Nov	14	Rebecca Crofby wife of John Crofby	brilliant Fever	36	496
	17	Timothy Butler		58	497
	18	A Female Inf^t of Silvanus Crocker		6 days	498
Decem	25	John Fifher He went to bed well as ufual and was dead by the side of his wife in the morning		85	499
1812					
Jan	2	Matt^w Vincent had Twins born one died on the 4 the other on the 5 day		4 days 5 days	500 501

7 Chriftopher Vincent Cancer 40 502
19 Bulah Coffin old age 86 503
Feb 6 Jofeph Cleavland Inflamation under Right Breaft 38 504
March 6 Lot Norton Paralit. & Confump 69 505
Jonathan S. Smith son of Benj^{a} Smith Esqr was loft at Sea the laft Year 506
Temple P. Cooke son of Thos Cooke Esqr died the laft Year in Virginia 507
May 29 Thos Worth Confumption 47 508
July 3 David Allen Confump fortafse 73 509
9 Barnabas Vincent Conf^{n} 87 510
Decem 29 Lydia Covel old age 87 511

1813
April 9 Eunice Smith she had been in a low state bereaved of her Reafon for a Number of Years her Body so drawn that she could not be straightened 63 512
20 Bathsheba Killey wid^{w} of Leml Kelley 74 513
May 8 Hannah the wife of Noah Peafe Schop(?) 57 514
13 Thos Claghorn Dropfy fortafse 83 515
15 Naomi the Wife of George Daggett Conf^{n} 66 516
July 8 a Male Child of Mr. Alley who married Thos Fifhers Daught Occationed by a Scald on the Stomach
Augt 2 a Female child of Edmond Bradley 18 mo 517
19 Betfey Ripley Daug^{t} of Jos Conf 21 518
24 a Daug^{t} of Danl Fifher putrid malignant Fever died the 7th Day the firft Fever known in this Place except a few Inftances of thofe who took on board Vefsels 6 519
Sep^{t} 3 Judah Norton old age 89 520
The laft Thirty Years he had led a penfive Life did no Business converfed but little I never could get to speak of things serious he was kindly treated by his son Thos Martin Norton
27 Thomas son of Saml Huxford 5 521
Oc^{t} 6 Jedidah Clarke wife of John she died suddently in a Fit in the Night probably Epilep 49 522
13 Eunice Preble Confump^{n} 50 523
She was Daug^{t} of Benj Peafe. Frost the Methodift attended.
July 18 John Marchant died at Siera Leone He went out on a Privateering Cruife & was taken & carried
$\frac{1}{3}$ of the Crew died, 28 out of 86 55 524
Oc^{t} 26 A male of Lot Norton 3 525
29 a Female Child of Anna Smiths 4 526
31 Francis Fifher by the prevailing Fever. he is the firft out of 70 a very long & diftrefsing Fever has been prevalent from Augt 15. fortafse 27 527

Nov	2	a male Child of Wm Croſman		2	528
Dec^{r}	3	John Peaſe Esqr	old age	82	529
	21	James Mayhew son of Mat^{w}		12	530
1814					
Jan	1	Dorcas Norton a Daug^{t} of Prince Norton She followed Itenerant Preacher got deranged & died in a Miſerable Condition		52	531
	22	Thankful Smith Wi^{d} of Thomas		70	532
	25	Triſtram Peaſe had been unwell for some Time fell into mental Derangment & languish about 5 Weeks		34	533
Feb	21	Wi^{d} Sarah Fiſher	old age	83	534
		Saml Cleveland loſt a child			535
March	25	Benjn Peaſe Methodiſt	old	83	536
May	9	Marshall Peaſe He languiſhed a few months & died with Bleeding at the Nose. Left 8 children		45	537
June	3	W^{d} Thankful Vincent A woman of Eminent Piety & Virtue.	Decay		538
July	17	John Norton he had been blind for about 12 Years he left a widdow in her 93^{d} year		84	539
	29	Mary w^{d} of John Norton	old age	93	540
Nov		A male child of Benjn Dunham		1	541
		Joſeph Swaſey } lost at Sea 1813			542
		Edmund Norton } lost at Sea 1813			543
		In 1812 Gamaliel Marchant son of George Marchant was loſt at sea		15	544
		Also a son of Richard Bunkers wife	fortaſse	15	545
1815					
Feb	3	Joſeph Thaxter ju^{r} He was drowned on the South Side of Nantuckett By the Care of the Rev^{d} Mr. Swift he was kept till the 19 & then brought Home & burried the 20th Bleſsed God I bow thy will is done.		28	546
March	8	a Male Inf^{t} of George Lawrence		10 days	547
	15	a Female of Lot Norton Twin		16 mo	548
	16	a male Inf^{t} of Gamaliel Fiſher		4 weeks	549
	17	Frederick son of Rufus Fiſher	Quinſy	32 mo	550
April	9	Huldah Norton W^{d} of W^{m}	Conſump	59	551
	10	W^{d} Hannah Peaſe	Conſump	79	552
	18	Annis Norton Daug^{t} of Hul^{h} Norton She died of Mortification in Conſequence of a Cold taken suddenly		17	553
	14	Rebecca Norton Daug^{t} of Wm Junr died at the Factory in Taunton		27	554
July	9	Cornelius Ripley	old age fort	75	555
	19	a Female Infant of Daniel Fellows		3 mo	556
Sept	3	Elihu Marchant	Fever	45	557
	25	A Male Inf^{t} of Joſeph Dunham		3 mo	558
Oct	20	Lydia Baſsett Daug^{t} of Peter Norton Esq^{e}	Conſumpt	68	559
Nov		Rebecca Wiſe of Rufus Davis	Conſ^{n}	53	560

1816					
Feb	21	Eliza Beetle Daug^{t} of W^{m}	Conſum	22	561
		Eliza Wife of Silvanus Crocker		30	562
	25	Dolly the Wife of Harlow Croſby	Conſ^{n}	45	563
May	4	Martha Norton Daug^{t} of Peter Norton Esq^{e} Her Parents turned Baptiſt both her Siſters & moſt of her Brothers much Pains was taken to Convert her She remained firm & unſhaken and was Diſtinguiſhed for her Piety and Virtue.		72	564
	26	James Fiſher He had lain in a helpleſs Condition a long Time & died suddently He had lived with his Wife 51 Years & not a Death in his Family He left 13 Children 51 Grand Children 6 G^{t} G^{d} Children		77	565
June	19	Benjn Vincent	Palſy	85	566
		same Time laſt Week the Widdow Davis of Homes Hole	fortaſse	83	567
July	19	Zephaniah Butler	Languiſhment	67	568
Aug^{t}	13	Suſanna the Wife of Jo^{s} Dunham	Conſ^{n}	34	569
	26	Henry Son of Saml Coffin	Inflam of Bowels	13 mo	570
	30	a male Inf^{t} of Beriah Weeks Baptiſt			571
Sep^{t}	16	a male Infant of Henry P. Worth	Fits	8 days	572
Oct	16	Jane the Wife of Dea^{n} Wm Mayhew		53	573
		about this Time Benjn Luce an old man & Baptiſt died		73	574
Sep^{t}	15	about this Time Dinah Norton the Daug^{t} of Shubael Norton died a Baptist	fortaſse	58	575
Nov	15	Bays Norton	Cancer		576
Decem	11	Nancy Fiſher Convulſ Fits	fortaſse	24	577
		& the child born gaſped & died			578
	29	Catharine Smith w^{d} of Saml	Conf	83	579
1817					
April	1	The Wife of Joſeph Norton		70	580
	4	Sally the Infant Daughter of Daniel Fellows		5 mo	581
May	16	The Wid^{w} Thankful Ripley She turned Methodiſt in her old age. Bart: Peaſe attended.		83	582
		The beginning of this month Ebenezer Smith Son of Benj^{a} Smith Jun died in the State of New York		15	583
	31	Deacon Jonathan Worth A man of Correct Principles, rational Piety & upright Life. He died as he lived in Peace		62	584
June		William Cooke Son of Thos Cooke Esqr died in Boston		41	585
July	26	Honble William Jernegan Esqr he was left an orphan had but little Education, but good natural Talents quick Penitration sound Judgment & retentive memory he served in all Town office, represented the Town in the general (court) & served one Year in the Senate		89 wanting a few days	586

Month	Day	Name	Cause	Age	No.
	28	a Female of Abifha Norton		3	587
Aug^{t}	5	Hannah Butler Daug^{t} of Eben^{r} Butler a Pauper	Confum	61	588
Sep^{t}	16	Rebeccah the Wife of Elifha Dunham	Confump	75	589
	22	Margret Wife of Thos Mayhew sad, sad, sad,	Dyfent. fortafse	37	590
Oct^{r}	23	John Cooke Convulfion Fits They had followed him some Years.	fortafse	45	591
Nov	9	a Male Infant Aaron Norton	Fits	6 weeks	592
	18	A Son of Bartlett Claghorn He by Sickness had for some Years been deprived of his means in a great meafure & was a miferable object		20	593
	25	Matilda Marchant w^{d} of John She was on the Town suffered much & Languifhed		56	594

Notes in Explanation, by Harriet M. Pease.

No. 346 was the daughter of Nathan and Sarah (Vincent) Pease.

" 348 was Mary (Allen), daughter of Robert and Desire (Norton) Allen, and the first wife of Rev. Mr. Thaxter.

" 351 was Hannah (Cooke), daughter of Temple Philip and Jane (Daggett) Cooke, and widow of John Ward.

" 356 was Hepsibah (Butler), daughter of Silas and Mary (Neal) Butler, and first wife of Obed Fisher.

" 358 was the son of Prince and Desire (Coffin) Pease.

" 360 was Sarah (Daggett), daughter of Samuel and Sarah (Chase) Daggett. She married James Noise in 1758, Jonathan Cottle in 1770, and Peter Pease in 1802.

" 365 was Lois (Stewart), daughter of Charles and Margaret (———) Stewart. She was the widow of Thomas Hewes and of Thomas Neal.

" 366 was Bethiah (Harlock), daughter of Thomas and Hannah (———) Harlock.

" 367 was Anna (Wass), daughter of Wilmot and Rebecca (Allen) Wass.

" 370 was Jane Weeks, a widow, when she married Abishai Marchant. She was his second wite — her maiden name not known.

" 372 was Eunice (Gardner), widow of Timothy Coffin, and daughter of Tristram and Deborah (Coffin) Gardner.

" 373 was Anna (Dunham), widow of John Butler and daughter of Jethro and Mehitable (Vincent) Dunham.

" 374 was Hannah (Ripley), daughter of Peter and Damaris (Chase) Ripley.

" 375 was Jedidah (Butler), first wife of Elijah Stewart, and daughter of Gamaliel Butler and Mercy Dunham, his second wife.

" 376 was Sarah (Ripley), second wife of Daniel Coffin and daughter of Abraham and Elizabeth (Marchant) Ripley.

" 383 was Sarah (Pease), daughter of David and Sarah (Dunham) Pease, and second wife of Benjamin Pease.

" 386 was Jerusha (Norton), daughter of Matthew and Mary (Daggett) Norton.

" 388 was Anna (Stewart), daughter of Daniel and Jean (Vincent) Stewart.

" 389 was Sarah (Bassett), daughter of Samuel and Martha (———) Bassett.

" 401 was Hope (Norton), daughter of Bayes and Mary (Merry) Norton.

" 406 was Patience (Cleveland), daughter of Ebenezer and Mary (Vincent) Cleveland, widow of Phinehas Norton, and the second wife and widow of Baze Norton.

" 407 was Sarah (Athearn), daughter of Jethro and Mary (Mayhew) Athearn.

" 415 was probably Jean (Bartlett), widow of Matthew Claghorn.

" 420 was the son of Enoch, Jr., and Deborah (Pease) Coffin.

No. 423 was Mary (Stewart), daughter of Samuel and Sarah (Smith?) Stewart.
" 427 was Mary (Huxford), daughter of Samuel Huxford and Temperance (Daggett), his second wife.
" 434 was Anna (Pease), daughter of Benjamin Pease and Anne (Butler), his first wife.
" 442 was Drusilla (Dunham), widow of Matthew Mayhew, and daughter of David Dunham, Jr., and Priscilla (Butler), his second wife.
" 453 was Eunice (Coffin), second wife of William Jernegan, and daughter of Benjamin and Elizabeth (Norton) Coffin. Her first husband was Simeon Coffin.
" 454 was "Lydia (Fisher) of Falmouth."
" 470 was Sarah (Fisher), daughter of Thomas and Lydia (Fisher) Fisher.
" 471 was Jane (Claghorn) Mears, daughter of Thomas Claghorn and Susannah Gibbs, his second wife, widow of Garrison Mears, and second wife and widow of Ebenezer Smith, Esq.
" 472 was the daughter of John Worth and Dorcas (Smith) Hawes, his third wife.
" 475 was Elizabeth (Norton), daughter of Matthew and Mary (Daggett) Norton.
" 478 was Sarah (Beetle), his first wife, and the daughter of Thomas and Phebe (   ) Beetle.
" 484 was Priscilla (Butler), daughter of Nicholas Butler and Thankful Marchant, his second wife.
" 486 was Sarah (Mayhew) Wass, daughter of Matthew and Phebe (Manning) Mayhew, widow of Homes Wass, and third wife of Jonathan Pease.
" 488 was Catherine (Smith), daughter of Philip and Eunice (Manter) Smith.
" 490 was Matilda (Vincent), widow of Nathan Dunham, and daughter of Joseph and Matilda (Dunham) Vincent.
" 496 was Rebecca (Merry) Smith Pease, wife of John Crosby, Jr., widow of Nathan Smith and of John Pease, Jr.
" 503 was the daughter of Enoch Coffin, Jr., and Jane (Claghorn) Whellen, his wife.
" 508 was the father of Maj.-Gen. William Jenkins Worth.
" 511 was Lydia (Vincent), wife of Jethro Covel and daughter of Reuben and Mehitable (Pease) Vincent.
" 512 was the daughter of Samuel Smith, Jr., and Eunice (Vincent), his second wife.
" 513 was Bathsheba (Harper), daughter of John and Hannah (Sprowel) Harper.
" 514 was Hannah (Dunham), daughter of Elijah and Sarah (Vincent) Dunham.
" 516 was *Ethannah* — not "Naomi"* — (Dunham), daughter of Seth and Naomi (Marchant) Dunham.
" 522 was Jedidah (Fish), daughter of John and Sarah (Fish) Fish.
" 523 was the widow of Abraham Preble, Jr.
" 532 was Thankful (Norton), daughter of Isaac, Jr., and Hannah (Norton) Norton.
" 534 was Sarah (Fish), daughter of Thomas and Ruth (Butler) Fish, and widow of John Fish (er).
" 538 was Thankful (Dunham) Stewart, widow of Timothy Stewart and of Joseph Vincent, and daughter of Daniel and Sarah (Huxford) Dunham.
" 540 was Mary (Norton),— parents not known.
" 542 was the son of Capt. Joseph and Susannah (Pease) Swasey.
" 543 was the son of Oliver and Harriet (Holley) Norton.
" 551 was Huldah (Daggett), widow of Job Norton and of William Norton, senior.
" 552 was probably Hannah (Luce), widow of Daniel Pease, and daughter of John and Jemimah (Luce) Luce.

* There is a mistake in the name. The wife of George Daggett was Ethannah Dunham. She had a sister Naomi and a daughter Naomi, as well as a mother of that name. This perhaps may account for the mistake made by Rev. Mr. Thaxter.

No. 553 was the daughter of Wm. Norton, senior, and Huldah (Daggett), his second wife.

" 554 was the daughter of William Norton, Jr., and Hannah (Daggett), his wife.

" 559 was Lydia (Norton), daughter of Major Peter and Sarah (Bassett) Norton, and wife of Nathan Bassett.

" 560 was Rebecca (Mayhew), daughter of Zaccheus and Rebecca (Pope) Mayhew.

" 562 was Eliza (Coffin), daughter of James and Huldah (Allen) Coffin.

" 563 was Dolly (Norton).

" 567 was Sarah (Cosens), widow of Capt. David Davis, and daughter of John and Jemimah (Norton) Cosens.

" 569 was Susannah (Stewart), daughter of Elijah Stewart and Jedidah (Butler), his first wife.

" 573 was Jane (Kelley), daughter of Lemuel and Bathsheba (Harper) Kelley, third wife and widow of Ephraim Pease, and second wife of Dea^{n} William Mayhew.

" 579 was Katherine (Harper), fourth wife and widow of Samuel Smith, Jr., and the daughter of John and Hannah (Sprowel) Harper.

" 582 was Thankful (Pease), widow of Cornelius Ripley, and daughter of Benjamin Pease and Abiah (Vincent), his second wife.

" 589 was Rebecca (Vincent), first wife of Elisha Dunham, and daughter of Joseph and Matilda (Dunham) Vincent.

" 590 was Margaret (Latham), and came from Hudson, N. Y. She was the first wife of Thomas Mayhew.

" 594 was Matilda (Dunham), daughter of Nathan and Matilda (Vincent) Dunham.

EDGARTOWN DEATHS.—In the REGISTER, vol. 59, page 303, in the article entitled "Deaths at Edgartown," it is stated (page 307) that the Beulah Coffin who * died Jan. 19, 1812, age 86, was the daughter of Enoch and Jane (Claghorn) (Whellen) Coffin. The contributor has made a mistake, as the Beulah, daughter of above, was born Oct. 10, 1748, married, Jan. 5, 1769, Jonathan Pease, and died Jan. 29, 1773. The Beulah who died Jan. 19, 1812, was the daughter of Enoch and Beulah (Eddy) Coffin. C. H. C.

Philadelphia, Penn.

*p. 209, this volume.

DEATHS AT EDGARTOWN, MASS.

Communicated by Miss HARRIET M. PEASE, of Edgartown, Mass.

1818				Æt	No.
May	5	Jonathan Peafe	Dropfy	74	595
June	8	W[d] Mehitable Norton	suddenly	75	596
	9	a Child of Tho[s] Norton		3 mo	597
	14	a Male Infant of Sufan Worth w[d] of Tho[s] Worth	overlaid & stifled	5 weeks	598
	27	Mary Butler wife of Silas Butler A Woman Diftinguished for good senfe, for her Piety & Religion. She languifhed under great Pain & Diftrefs totally Helplefs for Two Years with out a murmur.		74	599
	27	Benj[a] Fitch a Town Pauper he had a shock of the Palfey 14 Years ago He had been helplefs a Bed rid for a long Time & had no Reafon.		67	600
July	4	a male Inft of Shubal Norton	Twins	9 days	601
	8	a male Inft of Shubael Norton	Twins	13 days	602
	18	a male Child of Tho[s] Milton a poor Thing torn out of Shape by the Ricketts		23 mo	603
	21	a male of Sam[l] Huxford	Hoop Coug	7 mo	604
	25	Electa Fellows Daughter of Daniel Fellows The 5 Daug[t] which they have loft		6 mo	605
Aug[t].	1	James Coffin Esq[r]	Confump	72	606
	15	a male of Nathan[l] Vincent Ju[r]		5	607
		The 3[d] Day of April Charles Norton Son of W[m] Norton was drowned. A whale stove the Boat & before Relief could get him he sunk		25	608
		The 30th of May John Crofman son of Peleg was on a whaling Voiage, he fell from the main Top maft Yard into the sea & was drowned		23	609
Sept	22	Ofborn Fifher. He had been Georgia, come Home Sick after about 10 Days a Dyfentery took Place of which he Died		27	610
Nov	19	a Female Infant of Aaron Norton		15 days	611

Month	Day	Entry	Age	No.
Nov	27	Dennis Davis son of Melatiah died diſtracted in chains & Hand Cufs He was a Baptiſt they sent for James Croſby a very ignorant man to attend Fun.	42	612
Decem	18	Ruben Beetle Hect. Decay	54	613
1819				
May	3	Bartlett son of Jesse Peaſe in consequence of a burn by falling into the Fire	8 mo	614
June	3	Puella Wife of John Gray. She had for some Years had an Anuriſm on the Right carotid it burſt and she expired in a few moments.		615
July	1	John Coffin he had been rendered very feeble by a paralitick shock for Years he had failed for some months was attacked with a Dyſentery & languiſhed for Ten Days	73	616
		Cornelius Ripley died on his Paſsage from the Weſt Indies the 20th of June	19	617
Sept	4	Triſtram Mayhew son of Matt^{w} a suddent diſsontion of Blood & Mortification	15	618
	21	a Male Child of William Fiſhers	13 mo	619
Aug^{t}		Benjn Weeks died in New Orleans	23	620
Nov	14	a Female Infant of Thos Coffin Eldridge a Baptiſt attended Funeral	4 mo	621
Decem^{r}	20	W^{d} Anna Dunham	92	622
	30	Ann Frances Norton Wife of Col. Beriah Norton She had declined for a number of Years and was helpleſs	83	623
1820				
Jan.	1	The Wid^{w} Hannah Beetle a worthy Chriſtian she had for several Years been deprived of her Reaſon	95	624
		The Wid: Abigail Fiſher she had been helpleſs by a shock of the Palſy a Town Pauper	73	625
	13	The Wi^{d} Jedidah Cleavland She was a humble Chriſtian She languiſhed for a number of Years her sufferings were very great I fear some through Neglect She was a Town Pauper & lived with her Daug^{t} Matta Cleavland	71	626
	23	Edmund Bradley's Twins both mails died the Day of their Birth	1 day	627 628
Feb	18	Wi^{d} Jane Vincent She had lived a W^{d} 41 Years. She was very weakly & pious Woman	88	629
	20	Mary Norton w^{d} of Samuel Norton she was siſter to the Davises who are zealous Baptiſts they could never shake her Faith She was a member of this Chh she languiſhed for several Years	77	630
March	9	Elizabeth wife of Leonard Jernegan. in Child Bed	43	631
	20	Received the News that Leonard Jernegan was loſt in the Gulph Stream. The Schooner		

		upset & he with Forty Three Pafsengers & crew perished on the 6th of March. his mate & one seaman were taken from the wreck on the 8th		35	632
	25	Naomi wife of Wm Brown		45	633
	26	Anthony Chadwick Universal Decay He was a Portugee a State Pauper		67	634
April	9	Amaziah Fifher Ju^{r} He had been married 4 months			635
May	8	a Son of Saml Coffins		2	636
Aug^{t}	2	a Female Child of Eb^{r} Smiths		1	637
	26	Levy Fifher	Palfy	30	638
Sept	2	Jafon Luce			639
Oct	4	a male of Thos Smith	suddent	6	640
	24	a male of John Marchant		2	641
Nov	14	Sarah wife of Elijah Dunham		90½	642
	20	Lemuel Clarke	untimely	46	643
Decem	2	Thomas Cooke Efq^{r}	Languifhment	82	644
		Rebeccah wife of Elisha Dunham Ju^{r}	Conf		645
	4	Beriah Norton Efq^{r}	old age	86	646
	7	Freeborn Fifher son of Amaz^{h}	Fever	17	647
1821					
Jan	13	Elijah Dunham	old age	87	648
	30	Rebeccah wife of Saml Butler	in Child Bed	26	649
Feb	4	a Female Child of Nathaniel Vincent		16 mo	650
	23	Wi^{d} Sufan Cleavland. She had pafsed thro a Sea of Trouble & diftrefs for many Years		55	651
	23	Lydia Norton a poor miferable object with a canser which eat for several Years till her Nofe was entirely gone	fortafse	68	652
March	9	Sarah Marchant She was a Town Pauper. Her sufferings were beyond defcription Subject to mental Derangements but when in the Exercife of her Reafon strictly virtuous and pious		62	653
April	9	Ann Thaxter wife of Jofeph	dropfy	60	654
May	5	Benjamin Smith Efq^{r} He was a man of the firft abilities and I believe of strict integrity There is a miftake in the Number it is 660		82	655
	15	Henry Ofborn Fellows son Danl Ju^{r}		9	656
July	6	Polly Arey	Child Bed	39	657
		She had Twins about a fortnight ago they gafped & died	1 male		658
			1 Female		659
Sept		Mr. Nathan Shearman Read of New Haven died of a Paralitic shock on his Head on board of Capt. Catlin sloop, & was buried he had been a Clergyman but difmifsed for his Imprudence. He left a w^{d} but no children. His parents are living			660
Oct.	15	Melatiah Davis He was a Baptift a mixed character unhappy in his Temper weak & avaricious		72	661

Oct. 23 a male child of Thos Smith Burnt to Death
by its clothes Taking Fire 3 3 mo 662
27 Abigail Jernegan Dropſey 26 663
A pious & Virtuous young Woman
Nov 5 Eraſtus Beecher a Native of Connect^{t} fortaſse 60 674
He has lived here a number of Years & left
a w^{d} & Five Daughters poor.
Decem 21 Mary the Wife of Edmund Bradley 37 665
a Female of Thomas Mayhew Ju^{r} in Fits
in conſequence of a scald 2 666

1822
March 5 Sarah wife of Andrew Fiſher child Bed 31 667
a Female of Saml Huxford non compos 3 668
Samuel Norris at Homes Hole I knew not
his age. He called himſelf a Baptiſt 669
30 Received the News of the Death of Triſtram
Cleavland drowned in the Pacific Ocean.
He was the son of Joſeph & Matta Cleavland 19 670
May 5 a male of William Fiſher. This is the 3^{d} he
has loſt. The two firſt while he lived at
Homes Hole. 19 mo 671
8 Received the News of the Death of Peter Peaſe
3^{d}. He died at Port au Prince Island of
St Domingo 672
30 Nathaniel Vincent old age 97 673
He was a meek & humble Chriſtian prudent,
Diſcreet, upright & honeſt "an Iſraelite indeed in whom was no guile." He retained
his reaſon to the laſt moment
June 24 Jane Beetle wife of William Beetle conſump 62 674
a woman of exemplary Piety & Virtue
July 25 Huldah wife of Thomas Jernigan a Woman
diſtinguiſhed for her remarkable Piety from
early Life 72 675
Augt 29 Eliſha Dunham Mortification occationed by
a Cut on his Leg with a Scyth 73 676
last of Sept. Oliver Davis a Baptiſt at H. Hole The Ty-
pus Fever has prevailed at Homes Hole occationed I believe by putrid menhaden in
Davis Corn Field. Wm Butlers Family &
Eben^{n} Smith have several of them & others
had it thro the Goodness of God it has not
proved mortal 33 677
9 We received the News of the Death of Henry
Cooke son of Littleton Cooke who died in
Batavia 678
10 Betſey Dunham Daug^{t} of Benajah Dunham
& Mary his Wife He went & died abroad
about 30 Years ago. She had been helpleſs
& a publick charge for many Years 35 679
Oct 27 Ezra Cleavland turned Baptiſt but never was
diped he was not happy in his Family his
Wife & Children it is believed was the Cause 76 680

Decem 17 Mary Shaw Norris bapt. H. Hole 24 681
26 An Infant of Arnold Butlers still born 682

1823

Jan 3 a male Infant of Uriah Coffin a little thing 4 weeks 683
Feb 14 a male of Matthew Fifhers 14 mo 684
April 29 Jofeph Fifher angina Pect 67 685
Jan 2 Martin Arey died at Valparizo South America master of the sloop Apollo 32 686
July 24 Thomas Stewart an exemplary Chriftian an Honest man a good citizen. His family had turned Methodift and for a Number of Years treated him very ill. He bore it with Patience in his laft sickness which was long & diftrefsing he was treated with kindness 80 687
Augt 8 Zoraida Coffin Daug^{t} of Timothy Coffin Confump 23 688
Sep^{t} 26 Elijah Daggett suddent He fell dead out at the Door he had been lingering some Time fortafse 38 689
19 Peleg Norton Cancer in his Face 72 690
20 Anna Smith wife of Harrifon Smith Consump 36 691
she was the Daug^{t} of William Beetle a Pious & Virtuous Woman
Oct 12 Capt Melatiah Peafe old age 90 692
A worthy character He left a W^{d} with whom he had lived 68 & upward of 100 Descendents
27 Ichabod Cleavland 75 693
Nov 16 Love Smith W^{d} of Benjn late Deceafed old 82 694
Decem 1 Frederick Coffin Son of Tim^{o} Confump 29 695
17 a male Infant of David Coffin 3 days 696
Ann Frances Norton Daug^{t} of Col Norton 47 697
21 a Child of Saml Paints Deformed lived a few hours 698
25 a male Infant of Ephraim Marchant 3 days 699

1824

Feb 9 Francis Peafe Methodift 67 700
March 18 Rachel wife of Obediah Peafe She was distinguifhed for Piety Virtue & Prudence. 82 701
22 Received the News of the Death of William Fellows son of Daniel Fellows J^{r}. He was in the Almira Capt I. Daggett Pacific Ocean 21 702
29 a Female Inft of Freeman Ripley 4 days 703
April 25 Hepsibah Stewart wife of Elijah Stewart Efq^{r} 704
seting at Dinner fell back & expired without a Groan She had Four Children by her formar Hufband They all died some Years ago She pafsed thro much Tribulation & I truft entered into the Kingom of Heaven.
April 2 Priam Peafe son of Capt Melatiah Peafe late Dyc^{d} died in New York 705
May 3 Dorcas Norton wid of Bays Norton who was drowned at Gay Head Jan ye 14th 1782 She

		was left with Six Children the youngeft at her Breaft a Houfe & small Garden was all she had She brought up her family honourably & virtuoufly without beging. She was a Shining Example of the Chriftian Virtues & died in good Hope of eternal Life	77	706
May	13	Sufanna Swafey w^{d} of Jofeph Swafey. She was a Professor of Religion she pafsed thro great Tribulation with her Family she was long confined to her bed underwent great Pain but pofsefed a Calm & steady mind	81	707
June	29	Hiram Fellows son of Daniel Fellows Ju^{r} Efq^{r} This is the Ninth Child he has loft. He had been to Carolina & taken the Southern Fever under which he languifhed a long Time. He was an amiable & virtuous Youth. He has but one left a feeble son	18	708
July	17	A male Infant of Mrs. Raymond	3 days	709
July	26	Elizabeth wife of Henry Fifher fortafse	68	710
Aug^{t}	21	a male Infant of Homes Smith	3 mo	711
Sept	26	a Female of Isaiah Mills	1 year	712
	28	a male Inf^{t} of Abner Peafe	6 weeks	713
Oct	20	We heard of the Death of Capt Thomas Worth	31	714
		and William Beetle his mate in the ship Globe of Nantuckett they were murdered by the Crew one Comftock a Native of Nantuckett was at the Head of the mutineers fell out among themselves and killed Comftock Gilbert Smith a son of John Smith Ju^{r} when the mutineers were on shore cut the Cable put to Sea with Six of the Crew & got safe to Valparizo. The mutineers when they killed Worth & Beetle threw a son of Abishai Lambert of Chilmark overboard & drowned	28	715
				716
		him. N. B & a son of Amaziah Fifher's		717
Nov	28	Abner Fifher. Town Paup. He had pafsed thro a vaft Scene of Diftrefs	57	718
	29	a Male Inf^{t} of Francis Smith	5 weeks	719
	30	a Female Inf^{t} of Jofeph Mayhew	2 weeks	720
Decem		We received the News of the Death of Silas Butler son of Zephaniah drowned in Pacifick ocean fortafse	27	721
Oct^{r}		Julia Ann Clarke died at a Factory in the State of Rhodifland	19	722
1825				
Jan	3	Daniel Smith remar^{ble} for Induf'^{y}	58	723
Feb	22	Peleg Crofsman a poor laborer very induftrious & a strictly honeft man	73	724
March	2	Charles son of Charles Butler	16 mo	725
April	11	Bartlett Fifher was struck overboard by the steering Oar coming in at Wafhqua & drowned. he had only an Indian Boy in the Boat. He was a remarkable steady virtuous		

		young man his Father Gamaliel Fiſher		
		periſhed at Sea many Years ago	27	726
April	18	I now record the following Fordham Peaſe son	22	727
		of Valentine Charles Coffin son of Peter	19	728
		They sailed in the Ship Lady Adams. She		
		has long been diſpaired of it is thought they		
		were loſt about mid Sumer 1823 they were		
		very Promiſing young men		
May	10	A Male of Mary Cornels Spaſms	3	729
June	30	Charles son of Joſeph & Nancy Mayhew	6	730
July	14	Love Luce Daug^{t} of Chriſtopher Luce a Sin-		
		gle aged Woman at N Weſt Part of the		
		Town Jeſse Peaſe attended the funeral	73	731
Aug^{t}	4	a Child of Saml Huxford a poor helpless thing		
		weighed 8^{lbs}	2 y. & 8 days	732
	15	a Child male of Ira Darrow of Waterford State		
		of Connecticut on a viſit to her Father Capt		
		Matt^{w} Norton aged	3 mo	733
	29	Phebe McKensy wife of Capt McKensy came		
		home She had Twins one died in June the		
		other This Day. She calls herſelf a Baptiſt.		734
		Henry Marchant attended Funeral		735
Aug^{t}	30	W^{d} Patience Dunham	84	736
Sept	4	a male of Zadock Nortons Methodiſt	18 mo	737
	7	a Female of Frederick Baylies Ju^{r} a Baptiſt	9 mo	738
		I attended both these Funerals		
Aug^{t}	28	About this Time John Godfrey died on Staten		
		Iſland. He had been to Savannah Malig-		
		nant Fever He was a Pruſsian by birth		
		left a W^{d} with a Family of Children very		
		poor	45	739
	18	A male Child of Math^{w} Peaſe Methodeſt	17 mo	740
		I attended the Funeral		
Oct	4	Hannah Butler W^{d} of Daniel old age & Decay		
		buried 6th corpse putrid	78	741
Nov	18	Hepſibah Norton wife Joſeph Norton She		
		went to bed well he awoke about 10 oclck		
		& lay by his side dead	65	742
Decem	4	Hannah the Wife of Benjamin Norton. She		
		was one of the firſt that turned Baptist on		
		the Iſland	70	743
	22	John Oliver of Yorkshire in England fortaſse	28	744
		He had complained & turned into his Cabin		
		they gave him some hot coffee He appeared		
		to fall a sleep but was in a short Time found		
		dead. The Brig belonged to Beverly		
	27	a Male Infant a Twin of Saml Cleavland's		
		Daughter illeg about	6 weeks	745
		The Widd^{w} Lydia Marchant old age	83	746
		She died rejoicing in the Hope of that Glory		
		which is to be revealed.		
Decem	27	The W^{d} Suſannah Fiſher She had passed		
		thro the moſt painful scene for 12 Years with		

		a gathering of Water in her Womb which burst every Night with as severe Pain as bringing a Child into the world. The Fun^{l} of Mrs. Marchant & Mrs. Fifher was attended at the Meeting House the 29	93	747
1826				
Feb	5	a Female Inf^{t} of Jonathan Fifher, Jr	3	748
	6	Emeline Arey Daug^{t} of George W Arey Confumption	17	749
	24	Molly wife of Jethro Norton She was not a Baptift but her Parents Zach Peafe would not be satisfied for me to attend. She was carried to the Baptift Meeting House & her Brother Jefse performed &c	52	750
	25	A male Infant the other Twin of Saml Cleavland's Daughter illeg	3 mo	751
March	4	Abraham Vincent a Criple from his Birth walked on his knees. A Town Pauper idiot	53	752
	8	George Daggett Town-Pauper	91	753
	8	Violet Wafs Negro Eminent for her Piety & Virtue Town Pauper	90	754
	15	A male Inft of Eliza Courtney illeg	5 mo	755
April	2	Richard Norton. He had gone thro great Hardfhip at Sea his Conftitution was worn down a mortification took Place in his Leg I attended the Fun^{l} there was a large Collection The family are divided as soon as I clofed my Difcourse Henry Marchant began to harrangue, one Thilly a Stranger Bap^{t} made a prayer	41	756
	8	Molly W^{d} of Frank Peafe	67	757
	14	Lydia Clarke Town Pauper	88	758
May	9	a male Inf^{t} of James W. Black	6 hours	759
	20	An Infant taken with Inftruments from Julia Whelden illegitimate never had we so many Inftances till of late		760
July	8	Almira wife of George Osborn Daug^{t} of Jethro Daggett She was from her Childhood very feeble & often under mental Derangement		761
July	31	a male Inf^{t} of Frederick Baylies the 3^{d} out of 4 which has died	4½ mo	762
Aug^{t}	7	Thomas Benson of Tifbury. He had lived here a few months	28	763
	19	Sukey the wife of Uriah Coffin. She had turned Baptift	44	764
Sept	16	Female child of John Peafe	2	765
	25	William Vincent old age	94	766
Oct	21	Anna Fitch Asthma Pauper	76	767
Nov	2	Katherine Vincent	85	768
	7	Thomas Fifher Decay	70	769
	9	James Banning Universal Decay He lacked but 18 Days of	80	770
	13	Huldah Coffin w^{d} of James Coffin	73	771

	15	Martha w^{d} of the late Melatiah Peaſe a virtuous Woman	94	772
Decem	3	a male child of Danl Stewart Vincents. gave an Exhortation	22 mo	773
	24	Mary wife of Danl Butler She was put to bed with Twins the 23. Jeſse Peaſe attended the Fun^{l}	36	774
1827				
Jan	3	a female Infant of Danl Butlers Twins		775
	10	We had News of the Death of George Luce he was drowned on his Passage with Capt Henry Osborn bound to Charleſton South Carolina He was a Native of Nantuckett		776
	13	a male Inft of W^{m} Fiſhers. This is the fourth male He has two Females	14 mo	777
	23	we received the News that Capt Thomas Fiſher died on his Passage from the Weſt Indies		778
	25	Sarah the Wife of Capt Timothy Daggett with a Dropſy her sufferings were great. She bore them with the Patience of a Chriſtian & died in the lively Hope of a happy Immor^{ty}	51	779
Feb	5	Had News of the Death of James W. Black of Charleſtown South Carolina. He fell on board a Steam Boat & was killed. He married Suſan Oſborn of this Town	34 fortaſse	780
	18	Ruth Fiſher she had laboured under great Infirmity for more than 20 Yrs. She was I believe a pious and virtuous woman	66	781
March	17	W^{d} Ruth Luce a poor diſtreſsed object she received after her situation was known every benevolent attention. She was a peculiar body a profeſsed Methodist Henry Marchant attended. John Adams being abſent.	62	782
May	11	Lyman Burton of Taſhua in Connecticut died on board a Vessel from Bridge Port. I attended his Fun^{l} at the Meeting Houſe	40	783
June		Saml Oſborn a female Inf^{t}	3 mo	784
June	7	Love Courtney. Conſump. She was the Daug^{t} of Benj Vincent a poor laborer. She married an Irishman who turned out a poor intemperate man. She met with great Trials but by my Benevolence she supported her Children. Four Sons & a Daug^{t} They are hired Three in this Town one in Connecticut. Leonard I brought him to Years of Age My Daug^{t} Thayer brought Eliza. Eliza & Leonard now live with us. Smart active industrious & Prudent.		

[NOTE. — Here the record ends, with an indication of failing powers. Rev. Joseph Thaxter died July 18, 1827, aged 83 years, 2 months, and 14 days.]

Notes in Explanation, by Harriet M. Pease.

No. 596 was Mehitable (Pease), daughter of Stephen and Jemimah (Vincent) Pease, and widow of Obed Norton.

" 599 was Mary (Neal), daughter of Thomas and Lois (Stewart) Neal.

" 615 was Puella (Butler), daughter of Matthew Butler and Jean (Vinson or Vincent), his second wife.

" 620 was Benjamin Osborn Weeks, son of Benjamin and Lydia (Pease) Weeks.

" 622 was Anna (Harper), daughter of John and Hannah (Sprowel) Harper, widow of Cornelius Marchant and second wife and widow of Benajah Dunham, Jr.

" 623 was Ann Frances (Cosens), daughter of John and Jemimah (Norton) Cosens.

" 624 was Hannah (Butler), widow of Christopher Beetle, Jr., and daughter of Simeon and Hannah (Cheney) Butler.

" 625 was Abigail (Osborn), daughter of Samuel and Keziah (Butler) Osborn, and widow of James Fish(er).

" 626 was Jedidah (Claghorn), widow of Seth Cleveland, and daughter of Shubael and Martha (Hillman) Claghorn.

" 629 was Jane (Pease), widow of Samuel Vincent, and daughter of Benjamin Pease and Abiah (Vincent), his second wife.

" 630 was Mary (Davis), daughter of Col. Malatiah and Jemimah (Dunham) Davis, widow of Henry Norton and of Samuel Norton.

" 631 was Elizabeth, or "Betsey" (Pease), daughter of Thomas Pease, Jr., and Hepsibah (Pease), his wife.

" 633 was Naomi (Daggett), daughter of George and Ethannah (Dunham) Daggett, and first wife of William Brown.

" 642 was Sarah (Vincent), daughter of Joseph and Matilda (Dunham) Vincent.

" 645 was Rebecca (Ripley), first wife of Elisha Dunham, Jr., and daughter of Joseph and Lydia (Ripley) Ripley.

" 649 was Rebecca (Smith), daughter of Samuel Smith, Esq., and Love Pease, his wife.

" 651 was Susan (Daggett), daughter of Major Brotherton and Mary (Tucker) Daggett, and widow of Tristram Cleveland.

" 653 was probably the daughter of Seth and Lydia (Dunham) Marchant.

" 654 was Anna (Smith), second wife of Rev. Joseph Thaxter, and daughter of Samuel Smith, Esq., and Anna Wass, his wife.

" 657 was the daughter of Elijah and Anna (Pease) Arey.

" 663 was the daughter of William and Abigail (Mayhew) Jernegan.

" 665 was Mary (Beetle), first wife of Edmund Bradley, and daughter of William and Jane (Coffin) Beetle.

" 667 was Sarah (Butler), first wife of Andrew Fisher.

" 672 was the son of Peter and Keziah (Fitch) Pease. He died Mch. 15, 1822. in his 29th year.

" 674 was Jane (Coffin), daughter of Richard and Mary (Cooke) Coffin.

" 675 was Huldah (Coffin), daughter of Benjamin and Elizabeth (Norton) Coffin.

" 681 was probably a daughter of Samuel and Lucy (Shaw) Norris.

" 686 was the son of Elijah and Anna (Pease) Arey.

" 691 was Anna (Beetle), daughter of William and Jane (Coffin) Beetle.

" 694 was Love Coffin, daughter of Enoch Coffin, Jr., and Jane (Claghorn) Whellen, his wife.

" 697 was the daughter of Col. Beriah and Ann Frances (Cosens) Norton.

" 701 was Rachel (Coffin), daughter of John Coffin and Hepsibah Lambert, his second wife.

" 704 was Hepsibah (Pease), daughter of John Pease, Jr., and Jerusha Norton, his wife, widow of Thomas Pease, Jr., and second wife of Elijah Stewart.

" 706 was Dorcas (Pease), daughter of John and Abigail (Burgess) Pease.

" 707 was Susannah (Pease), daughter of John and Hepsibah (Ripley) Pease.

" 710 was Elizabeth (Whippey), wife of Henry Fisher, Jr.

No. 734 } were twin daughters of Capt. Daniel and Phebe Mayhew (Smith)
" 735 } McKenzie. Adeline died in June and Mary in August.

" 736 was Patience (Hathaway), widow of Joseph Dunham, and daughter of Benjamin and Elizabeth (Richmond) Hathaway.

" 741 was Hannah (Crossman), daughter of Seth and Hannah.

" 742 was Hepsibah (Claghorn), second wife of Joseph Norton, and probably a daughter of Thomas Claghorn, Jr., and Mary Huford, his wife.

" 743 was Hannah (Norton), parents not known.

" 746 was Lydia (Ripley), widow of Gamaliel Marchant, and daughter of Peter Ripley and Damaris Chase, his first wife.

" 747 was Susannah (Vincent), widow of Henry Fish(er) Senior, and daughter of Joseph and Matilda (Dunham) Vincent.

" 750 was Mary (Pease), the first wife of Jethro Norton, and daughter of Zachariah and Lydia (Crowell) Pease.

" 752 was a son of Barnabas and Mehitable (Dunham) Vincent.

" 758 was Lydia (Dunham), daughter of Benajah Dunham, Jr., and Lydia Pease, his first wife, and widow of Seth Marchant and of John Clark, senior.

" 764 was Susan (Nye), first wife of Uriah Coffin, and daughter of John and Tamar (Weeks) Nye.

" 767 was Anna (Osborn), widow of Benjamin Fitch, and daughter of Samuel and Keziah (Butler) Osborn.

" 768 was Katharine (Smith), widow of Jonathan Vincent, and daughter of Samuel Smith, Jr., and Eunice Vincent, his second wife.

" 771 was Huldah (Allen), daughter of Robert and Desire (Norton) Allen.

" 772 was Martha (Harper), daughter of Capt. John and Hannah (Sprowel) Harper.

" 774 was Mary (Norton), first wife of Daniel Butler, Jr., and daughter of Tristram and Jane (Marchant) Norton.

" 779 was Sarah (Jernegan), first wife of Timothy Daggett, and daughter of Hon. William Jernegan and Mary Osborn, his first wife.

" 781 was the daughter of Henry and Susannah (Vincent) Fish(er).

" 782 was Ruth (Norton), second wife of Jason Luce.

" 787 was Lovia (Vincent), wife of Barcus Courtney, and daughter of Benjamin and Sarah (Luce) Vincent.

Additional Notes in Explanation. Vol. 52, page 230.*

No. 6 was Mary (Vincent), widow of Ebenezer Cleveland, and daughter of Thomas and Sarah (Post) Vincent.

" 8 was Mercy (Norton), widow of James Claghorn, and daughter of Isaac and Ruth (Bayes) Norton.

" 13 was Thankful (Marchant), the second wife of Nicholas Butler, and daughter of John and Hepsibah (Huxford) Marchant.

" 21 was Jane Butler, daughter of John and Elizabeth (Daggett) Butler. Her brother John Butler was appointed administrator on her estate June 27, 1763.

" 36 was his second wife, Sarah Pease, perhaps a daughter of Nathan and Sarah (Vincent) Pease.

" 42 was Elizabeth (Daggett), his second wife, and daughter of Joseph and Amy (Eddy) Daggett.

" 56 was Abigail (Norton), second wife of John Pease, senior.

" 63 was Abigail (Ripley), daughter of Abraham and Elizabeth (Marchant) Ripley.

" 65 was probably Hannah (Pease), daughter of Thomas and Bathsheba (Merry) Pease, and widow of John Smith and of Nathaniel Pease.

" 69 was Sarah (Norton), third wife of John Pease, senior.

" 72 was Sarah (Vincent), widow of Nathan Pease, and daughter of Thomas and Sarah (Post) Vincent.

" 75 was the son of Nicholas and Martha (Daggett) Norton.

" 76 was perhaps Keziah (Butler), widow of Samuel Osborn and of Matthew Pease, and daughter of John and Elizabeth (Daggett) Butler.

*p. 177, this volume.

No. 81 was probably Hannah (Cheney), widow of Simeon Butler, and daughter of Thomas and Hannah (Woodie) Cheney.
" 85 was Hepsibah (Skiffe), widow of Thomas Norton and daughter of Nathan Skiffe and his first wife, Hepsibah Codman.
" 102 was Abiah (Vincent), second wife and widow of Benjamin Pease, senior, and daughter of Thomas and Sarah (Post) Vincent.

Vol. 52, page 368.*

No. 141 was Bethiah (——), second wife of Ebenezer Butler. (Perhaps a daughter of Capt. John and Sarah Clarke Gould.)
" 153 was the mother of Dr. Benjamin Trask.
" 165 was Amy (Daggett), first wife of Timothy Norton, son of Bayes, and daughter of John and Sarah Daggett.
" 182 was Temperance (Daggett), second wife and widow of Samuel Huxford, and daughter of Joseph and Amy (Eddy) Daggett.
" 187 was the daughter of John and Mary (——) Frederick.
" 201 was Elizabeth (Norton), daughter of Enoch and Hepsibah (Daggett) Norton.
" 205 was Hannah (Norton), first wife of Isaac, and daughter of Nicholas and Martha (Daggett) Norton.
" 210 was Mary (Daggett), daughter of Capt. Thomas and Elizabeth (Hawes) Daggett.
" 211 was Mary (Tucker), first wife of Maj. Brotherton Daggett.
" 219 was Mary (Covel), first wife of Joseph Cleveland, and daughter of James and Mary (Dunham) Covel.
" 220 was Sarah (Martin.)
" 224 was Beulah (Trapp), daughter of Jabez and Hepsibah (Daggett) Trapp.
" 243 was Hannah (Jenkins), daughter of Joseph and Hannah (——) Jenkins.

Vol. 53, page 102. **

No. 6 was Elizabeth (Marchant), widow of Abraham Ripley, second wife and widow of Enoch Norton, and daughter of John and Hepsibah (Huxford) Marchant.
" 44 was the widow of Philip Jones.
" 48 was Margery (Homes), daughter of Rev. William and Katherine (Craighead) Homes.
" 50 was Jedidah (Tilton), his first wife, and daughter of Uriah and Jedidah (Mayhew) Tilton.
" 54 was *not* "Thankful Daggett, widow of Brotherton Daggett, senior," for *she* married a third husband, Jabez Athearn.
" 68 was Esther (Dunham), first wife of Joseph Fish, and daughter of Ebenezer and Abigail (Vincent) Dunham.
" 75 was probably Mary (Stewart), widow of Joseph Pease, and daughter of John and Margaret Stewart.
" 78 was the daughter of Nicholas and Martha (Daggett) Norton.
" 79 was Naomi (Marchant), daughter of John and Hepzibah (Huxford) Marchant.
" 83 was Anna (Butler), his first wife.
" 97 was Anna (Butler), first wife of Benjamin Pease, Jr., and daughter of Gamaliel Butler and Anna (Vincent), his first wife.
" 102 was the son of Bayes and Mary (Merry) Norton.
" 104 was Mary (Jernegan), first wife of Jethro Worth, and daughter of Hon. Wm. Jernegan and Mary Osborn, his first wife.
" 114 was Anna (Mayhew), first wife of John Pease, Jr., and daughter of Matthew and Phebe (Manning) Mayhew.
" 119 was Phebe (Manning), daughter of William and Hannah (Gorham) Manning.
" 121 was Susannah (Harper), first wife of Abishai Marchant, and daughter of John and Hannah (Sprowell) Harper.
" 128 was the daughter of William (or John) and Lucinda (Holley) Philips.
" 153 was Mercy (Osborn), daughter of Samuel and Keziah (Butler) Osborn, and first wife of William Norton, senior.
" 171 was Jane (Butler), daughter of Joseph and Thankful (Isum) Butler.

*p. 181, this volume. **p. 185, this volume.

INSCRIPTIONS AT EDGARTOWN, MARTHA'S VINEYARD, MASS.

Communicated by Miss HARRIET M. PEASE, Genealogist, of Edgartown, Mass.

THIS list of the gravestones in the Old Burying Ground near Tower Hill, in Edgartown, Martha's Vineyard, Mass., was taken by Richard L. Pease of Edgartown, historian and genealogist, in April, 1849, and found among his papers. This copy is furnished for publication in the New-England Historical and Genealogical REGISTER by his daughter.

John Cooke, son of Thos and Abigail, d. Dec. 26, 1766, æ. 20 days.

Temple Philip, son of Thos and Abigail, d. Feb. 7, 1764, æ. 13 days.

Jane Vinson, wife of Thos Vinson, Jr., d. Oct. 11, 1764, æ. 41. 2. 4.

Joseph Jenkins, d. May 8, 1763, æ. 46. 0. 1.

Abigail, his widow, d. Aug. 17, 1763, æ. 43. 10.

Wm Jenkins, son of Marshal, d. May 28, 1805, 36th yr.

Mary Jenkins, wife of Marshall, d. Dec. 11, 1774, 29th yr.

Elizabeth Jenkins, wife of Lemuel, d. July 27, 1776, 21st yr.

Elizabeth Jenkins, wife of Lemuel, d. Jan. 11, 1772, 29th yr.

Mary Jenkins, daughter of Marshal and Mary, d. Dec. 2, 1772, æ. 1. 0. 13.

James Claghorn, d. Jan. 18, 1749, æ. 60. 5.

Mary Newman, mother of Rev. John Newman, pastor of the Church of Christ in this town, d. Sept. 28, 1755, 71st yr.

John Newman, Esq., d. Dec. 1st, 1763, 43rd yr.

"Here lies buried ye body of ye Rev. Mr. Samuel Wiswall, late Pastor of the Church of Christ in this Town, who departed this life Dec. 23d, A.D. 1746, æ. 67 yrs. 3 months, 21 days."

Brotherton Daggett, d. March 5, 1740, æ. 53.

Jos Chase, d. May 1, 1749, æ. 60. 2. 20.

Lydia, his widow, d. July 17, 1749, æ. 52. 2. 11.

Thos Harlock, Esq., d. June 9, 1744, 86th yr.

Timothy Smith, d. Jan. 10, 1779, 53rd yr.

John Smith, d. May 21, 1777, 56th yr.

Mary Smith, only child of John and Mary, d. Jan. 7, 1755, 8th yr.

Hepsibah Coffin, wife of John, d. Dec. 30, 1736, æ. 25. 10.

Hepsibah Coffin, daughter of John and Hepsibah, d. Feb. 28, 1736–7, æ. 0. 2. 0.

Seth Cleveland d. Sept. 30, 1734, æ. 22. 11. 19. [He was son of Eben ezer and Mary Vincent Cleveland.]

Zephaniah Butler, d. Sept. 15, 1721, æ. — years.

Abiah Claghorn, wife of Thos, d. Feb. 10, 1730, æ. 31. 7. —.

Dorcas Worth, wife of John Worth, Esq., d. Aug. 4, 1730, 33rd year (?53rd yr.).

Jedidah Smith, wife to Benj. Smith, Esq., d. Jan. 6, 1736, 80th yr.

Benj. Smith, Esq., d. July 4, 1720, 65th yr. (63?).

Benjamin Sumner, son of John and Jedidah, d. Nov. 7, 1739, æ. 0. 3. —.

Susannah Sumner, daughter of John and Susannah, d. Sept. 28, 1740, 11th yr.

Benjamin Smith, Esq., d. Dec. 18, 1737, 46th yr of his age.

Shubael Hawes, son of Benj. and Dorcas, d. March 12, 1722, æ. 1. 7. —.

Mehetable Lothrop, wife of Thomas, d. July 31, 1733, æ. 60 yrs.

John Stanbridge, son of Saml and Elizabeth, d. Dec. 12, 1730, æ. 21. 10. 10.

John Worth, Esq., d. Feb. 1, 1732, 65th yr of his age.

Ann Worth, his wife, d. June 14, 1724, æ. 53. 3. 15.

John Worth, Jr., son of John and Sarah, drowned Oct. 20, 1777, æ. 26. 4. —.

Damaris Ripley, wife of Peter, d. Dec. 6, 1761, æ. 37. 7. 4.

Hepsibah Flagg, wife of Anthony, d. Aug. 22, 1782, æ. 42. 2. 4.

Anthony Flagg, d. Jan. 14, 1787, 41st yr.

1769. L. D. Rough stone.

1742. ? "

1766. B. P. 83 "

Asa Dunham, son of Benajah and Lydia, d. April 3, 1766; fell from a vessel's mast head; æ. 22. 11. 8.

Mary Norton, daughter of Beriah and Ann Frances, d. Sept. 23, 1781, æ. 6. 11. 8.

Capt. Timothy Daggett, d. Sept. 17, 1775, 85th yr.

Mary Daggett, his wife, d. Oct. 2, 1781, 87th yr.

"Here lies y^{e} body of y^{e} Rev. Mr. Jonathan Donham, who died $Decem^{br}$ 18, Anno. Dom. 1717, aged about 85 yrs. Pastor of y^{e} church of Christ at Edgartown.

With Toil and Pains at first He Tell'd y^{e} Ground,
Call'd to Dress God's Vineyard and w^{s} faithful Found;
Full thirty Years y^{e} Gospel he Did Despense,
His Work Being Done, Christ Jesus cal'd Him Hence."

"In memory of the Rev. Samuel Kingsbury, who died of the small pox Dec. 30, 1778, æ. 42, 0. 2.

He did in virtue and in meakness shine,
A learned scholar and a good Divine."

"Here lyes y^{e} body of Thomas Trapp aged 85 years. died $Octo^{r}$ the 15th, 1719.

All you that comes my grave to see
Such as I am so must you be.
Flee sin therefor, live godly still,
Then welcome death come when it will."

Lemuel Little, d. March 21, 1723.

Mary Little, daughter of Thos and Jedidah, d. Jan. 25, 1726–7, æ. 0. 6. 22.

Abigail Trapp, wife of Thomas, d. Feb. 14, 1717, æ. 29. 5. —

Sarah Trapp, wife of John, d. June 18, 1718, æ. 35. 4. 14.

John Trapp, d. Feb. 3, 1717–18, æ. 42.

Ebenezer Norton, Esq., d. April 11, 1769, 79th yr.

Deborah Norton, his widow, d. Dec. 3, 1772, 92nd yr.

"Shade-like my days decline away
And like the withered grass I fall;
But Lord Thou dost abide for aye
Thy mem'ry eke to ages all."

Susanna Swasey, daughter of Joseph and Susanna, d. Sept. 7, 1773, æ. 29. 0. 9.

Joseph Norton, Esq., d. Jan. 30, 1741-2, æ. 89. 10. —.

John Coffin, d. Sept. 5, 1711, æ. about 64 yrs.

Mr. John Logan, d. May 22, 1730, æ. 36. 3. 0.

James Pees, d. March 27, 1719, æ. 82. 0. 12.

Henry Butler, son of Henry and Sarah, d. Dec. 17, 1737, 27th yr.

Dea. Matthew Norton, d. Dec. 5, 1779, æ. 82. 7. 13.

Mary, his wife, d. Dec. 13, 1779, æ. 80. 4. —.

Miss Mary Norton, d. 1781.

John Norton, one of his majesties coroners, d. Dec. 6, 1730, æ. about 56 years.

Mary Beetle, wife of Christopher, d. Jan. 15, 1746, 46th yr.

Anna Butler, wife of Thomas, d. Oct. 1, 1733, æ. about 51 yrs.

Mary Norton, daughter of John and Hepsibah, d. Nov. 21, 1740, æ. 6. 0. 4.

Robert Stone, Senr, d. March 12, 1689-90, æ. 65 yrs.

Jeremiah Pease, ye only son of Nathaniel Pease, by Hannah his wife, d. July 3, 1749, 20th yr of his age.

Bayes Norton, d. March 1, 1785, 87th yr of his age.

Mary Norton, his wife, d. March 13, 1754, æ. 58 yrs.

The foregoing are *all* that now remain on the gravestones of the Old Burying Ground, April, 1849.—R. L. PEASE.

NOTE.—This list of stones was taken by my father for his own use and not for publication, hence the words "In memory of," "Here lyes ye body of," and "departed this life," do not appear, and only a few of the epitaphs. These stones are of dark blue slate. Only one, that of Wm Jenkins, is of white marble. The epitaph of Elizabeth, 2d wife of Lemuel Jenkins and daughter of Zaccheus Mayhen, reads as follows;

"Could blooming Years and modesty
And all thats pleasing to the eye
Against grim death ben a defence
Elizabeth had not gone hence
The God that gave her called her home
Whose pow'r divine shall burst this tomb
Then Pheonex like from Parent dust
She'l soar on high to God most just."

One other stone, probably placed there after the list was made, reads as follows: "Mr. Benajah Dunhan died April—, 1799, æ 94 yrs. Erected by Joseph Dunham, his great grandson, 1849." This does not, however, agree with the date given in the Rev. Joseph Thaxter's Diary of Deaths. Parson Thaxter says: "Benajah Dunham died January 27, 1802, of old age, aged about 93" and adds: "This man has been the oldest in this Town for 10 years in which Time 170 have died younger than he was." The date given, Jan. 27, was the date of the funeral and not of death which was probably the day before.

The three graves marked by "rough stones" are doubtless those of members of the Dunham family. "1769, L.D." was probably intended for Lydia Dunham, first wife of the above named Benajah Dunham. She died, or was buried, Oct. 3, 1769, aged about 55 years. "1766, B. P. (*?D.*) 83" no doubt was intended for Benajah Dunham, who died Feb. 8, 1766, aged about 80. "1742," the stone between the other two, and on which the letters cannot be deciphered, may mark the grave of Sarah [Covel], the wife of Benajah Dunham the elder, and of whose death we have no record.

The stone of Robert Stone, sen., was replaced by another of white marble by the same hands and reads as follows: "Here lyes buried ye Body of Robert Stone, senr. æ. 65 yrs. departed this life 12 day of March 1689. This is in place of the oldest grave stone on Martha's Vinyard. Erected by Joseph Dunham, 1863. The old stone lies here defaced. Sixty rods south east from this grave may be seen the ruins of the cellar of the House of the first white settlers, who came to the Island 1630."

This stone too, now lies on the ground broken. Several have disappeared entirely, and some are broken into bits. Of these are the stones of Lemuel Little and Mary Little. One fragment lying on the ground has the letters "ittle" upon it.

HARRIET M. PEASE.—*Genealogist.*

RECORDS OF THE SECOND CHURCH, FALMOUTH, MASS., KNOWN AS THE EAST END MEETING HOUSE

Abstracted by MRS. MARJORIE DRAKE (RHOADES) ROSS, of Boston

The Second Church was formed from the First Congregational Church of Falmouth in 1821, when the group which had built the East End Meeting House in 1797 established itself as a separate society. It is still a Congregational Church associated with the United Church of Christ. It faces the Sandwich Road, having been turned about 90° clockwise from its original position in 1841, when the steeple and bell were added. The late Shubael Lawrence bequeathed $10,000 to the Society, the income to be used for preaching only. The Restoration Committee is trying to raise $50,000 to complete the restoration of the Meeting House which is now in process.

These records are published by the consent of the Board through the courtesy of Henry Jensen and Winthrop Lawrence, the Chairman of the Committee.

MEMBERS 4 APRIL 1821, FROM AN ORIGINAL RECORD BOOK

Prudence Weeks
Rosamond Swift
Sofia Eldridge
Susannah Jenkins
Hannah Snow
Love Stickney
Rachel Hatch, Jr.
Zipporah Fish
Keziah Robinson
Susnna Phinney
Polly Phinney
Mercy Childs
Rebua Jenkins
Lydia Jenkins
Hannah Jenkins
Ana Green
Tabitha Hatch
Betsy Hatch
Olive Phinney
Benjamin Hatch
Stephen [ ]
David Bourn
Jethrow Swift
Benjamin Nye
Benjamin Fish
Nathan D. Fish
Seth Robinson
Abner Jenkins
Silvanus Hatch
Peter Phinney
Anthony Smally
Nathaniel Phinney
Charles Robinson
Philip Jenkins
Benjamin Green
Nathaniel Shiverick
Reiuben Hatch
Isaiah Hatch
Esther Robinson
Patty Bourne
Bethia Jenkins
Susanna Snow
Sarah Hatch
Love Phinney
Fear Chadwick
Chloe Lumbert
[ ]is Phinney
Reliance Phinney
Mary Eldridge
Cloay Childs
Mary Jenkins
Mary Smally
Phebe Jenkins
Salome Shiverick
Lucy Hatch
Sarah Chadwick
Lydia Fuller
Philip Phinney
John Swift
Jonathan Phinney
Ebenezer Nye
Simon Eldred
Simon Harding
Silas Weeks
Eli Jenkins
John Nye, Jr.
Freeman Fish
Asa Phinney
William Phinney
Benjamin Parker
Daniel Jenkins
Abisher Green
Calvin Childs
Nathaniel Hatch
Abner Phinney
Asenath Phinney

MARRIAGES—SOLEMNIZED BY SILAS SHORES

1822

Mr. Uriah R. Swift & Miss Hannah Chadwick—both of Falmouth—December 1st

1823

Mr. John Bourne & Miss Martha Swift—both of Falmouth—January 30th
Mr. Ellis H. Fish, of Sandwich & Miss Hannah B. Nye of Falmouth—April 10th
Mr. William B. Bunker & Miss Cloe Baker—both of Falmouth—May 11th
Mr. Andrew Baker & Emira Davis—both of Falmouth—May 22nd
Capt. Henry Weeks of Dartmouth & Miss Terzah Phinney of Falmouth—August 21st
Mr. Robinson Snow & Miss Rebecca Phinney—both of Falmouth—Sept. 4th
Mr. Jonathan Hatch & Miss Lucy P. Swift—both of Falmouth—Sept 30th
Mr. Rufus Tobey & Miss Roxanna Hatch—both of Falmouth—October 19th
Mr. Ezera Jones of Sandwich & Miss Eliza Fish of Falmouth—October 20th
Mr. Obidiah Baker & Miss Tabitha Hatch—both of Falmouth—November 5th
Mr. Thomas Lewis & Miss Rebecca Bourne—both of Falmouth—November 6th
Mr. Mark M. Hatch & Miss Priscilla Fuller—both of Falmouth—December 2nd
Mr. Nathan Fish & Miss Ruth C. Baker—both of this Town—December 18th

1824

Capt. Seth Hamblin & Miss Rebecca Grew—both of Falmouth—March 9th
Mr. Charles Fisher & Miss Sabry Fisher—both of Falmouth—April 12th
Mr. Daniel Fuller of Falmouth & Miss Mehitable Jones of Sandwich—September 29th
Mr. Charles Dimmick & Miss Frances Manwaring—both of Falmouth—September 29th
Mr. Reuben Eldred & Miss Hannah Jenkins—both of Falmouth—Oct. 14th
Mr. Lot C. Fish & Miss Chloe Hamblin—both of Falmouth—December 16th
Mr. Elijah Swift, Jr. & Miss Love Phinney—both of Falmouth—December 9th

1825

Mr. Elnathan Eldridge, Jr. & Miss Sophia Eldridge—both of Falmouth—August 11th
Capt. Isaac H. Hamblin & Miss Chloe P. Swift—both of Falmouth—September 15th
Mr. Moses Robinson & Miss Susan Chadwick—both of Falmouth—October 6th
Mr. James Davis & Miss Emaline Davis—both of Falmouth—October 24th
Mr. Timothy Fish & Mrs. Cynthia Baker—both of Falmouth—December 20th

1826

Mr. Arnold Smalley & Miss Lucretia Hamblin—both of Falmouth—February 12th
Mr. Frederick Davis & Miss Lucy S. Robinson—both of Falmouth—April 30th
Mr. Benjamin Hamblin, Jr. & Miss Betsey Baxter—both of Falmouth—June 1st
Capt. Nathan Hamblin & Miss Cynthia Eldridge—both of Falmouth—July 23rd
Capt. Crocker Davis & Miss Roxanna Swift—both of Falmouth—August 1st
Mr. Elias B. Herrington & Miss Lydia Fuller—both of Falmouth—August 20th
Mr. Russell Crocker of Barnstable & Miss Caroline Fish of Falmouth—September 7th
Mr. Henry Fish of Sandwich & Miss Olive Hinckley of Falmouth—September 14th

1827

Mr. Freeman Robinson & Miss Temperance Hatch—both of Falmouth—May 15th
Mr. Joseph Swift & Miss Keziah Sturgis—both of Falmouth—May 18th
Mr. William Layland & Miss Lucinda Bourne—both of Falmouth—June 14th
Mr. Judah Bowerman & Miss Anna Fuller—both of Falmouth—September 11th
Mr. James H. Hatch & Miss Deborah N. Gifford—both of Falmouth—November 28th
Mr. Alvan Wing of Sandwich & Miss Mary Ellis of Falmouth—December 27th
Mr. Elijah Dimmick of Barnstable & Miss Sarah L. Phinney of Falmouth—November 22nd

1828

Dr. Isaiah D. Edgerly of Barnstable & Miss Metilda T. Bourne of Falmouth—March 26th

Marriages—Solemnized by Timothy Davis

1835

Mr. Allen Green of Falmouth & Miss Jane Lovell of Sandwich—July 5th
Mr. Nathaniel Hatch & Miss Mary P. Chadwick—both of Falmouth—September 28th
Mr. Henry Hilman of New Bedford & Miss Tabitha Hatch of Falmouth—November 10th
Mr. Reuben Fuller & Miss Lucy H. Fuller—both of Falmouth—November 12th

1836

Mr. Peter B. Blossom of Barnstable & Miss Emma H. Childs of Falmouth—January 21st
Mr. Henry S. Crocker of Barnstable & Miss Hannah P. Crocker of Falmouth—June 6th

Marriages—Solemnized by William Harlow

1837

Mr. John Welch of Boston & Miss Martha J. Edmonds of Falmouth—October 4th
Capt. Solomon G. Bourne & Rebeca Snow—both of Falmouth—December 26th

1838

Mr. Elisha Howland of Sandwich & Miss Martha Ann Fisher of Falmouth—January 4th
Mr. Charles H. Eldredge & Miss Susan Ewer—both of Falmouth—January 23rd
Mr. Seth Swift of Wareham & Miss Mehitable Bourne of Falmouth—April 12th
Mr. Rositer Gifford & Miss Sarah Jenkins—both of Falmouth—June 19th

Marriages—Solemnized by James D. Lewis

1840

Mr. William Baker & Miss Chloe S. Crowell—both of Falmouth—December 19th

1841

Mr. William S. Benson of Falmouth & Miss Lydia Reed of Tillston Maine—April 19th
Mr. Reuben Smith & Miss Lucy L. Robinson—of Falmouth—May 3rd
Mr. Esra L. Bourne & Miss Mercy C. Hatch—of Falmouth—August 2nd
Mr. Edward S. Barnard of Nantucket & Miss Lucy N. Hatch of Falmouth—September 22nd

1842

Mr. Washington Smalley to Miss Phebe G. Hilliard—both of Falmouth—February 4th
Mr. Josiah Tobey of Sandwich to Miss Sarah Lewis of Falmouth—February 8th
Mr. Edmond C. Hatch to Miss Sylvina N. Gifford—both of Falmouth—March 11
Mr. Elijah Hinckley, Jr. to Miss Lucy Fish—both of Falmouth—October 18th
Mr. Daniel N. Taber of Fair Haven to Sarah A. Parker of Falmouth—October 7th

1843

Solomon C. Howland of Sandwich to Adelia Hatch—January 1
Hiram Hamblin of Falmouth to Louisa Hamblin of Barnstable—January 16th

Names of adults who were baptised

1821—Amanda Hatch—daughter of Isaac Hatch—November 25th
1825—Mary Phinney—wife of Ebenezer Phinney—September 11th
1826—Rhoda Crocker—wife of Henry Crocker—September 17th

Adults Baptised by N. G. Wheeler

1830—Mr. Henry Weeks—July 18th
Mrs. Henry Weeks—July 18th

Mr. Thomas Eldred—July 18th
Mrs. Lucy Ewer—July 18th
Mr. Joshua Nye—November 21
Mr. Barnabas Chadwick—November 21

ADULTS BAPTIZED BY REV. TIMOTHY DAVIS

1834—Mercy Eldridge—October 12
Isaac Hatch & Rhoda his wife—July 10
Temperance Robinson
Lucy Fuller

ADULTS BAPTISED BY REV. WILLIAM HARLOW

1838—Lucy E. Phinney—October 14th
Julia Ann Parker

NAMES OF CHILDREN BAPTISED TOGETHER WITH THE NAMES OF PARENTS

1821

Mary Ann—daughter of Brother Stephen Nye—November 25th
Harriot Frances—daughter of Brother John Swift—November 25th

1822

Southward Potter—son of Brother Isaiah Hatch—August 18th
Arsah—daughter of Brother Nathaniel Shiverick—August 25th
Sophronia—daughter of Brother Ebenezer Hatch—October 6th

1823

Adelia and Phebe—daughters of Brother Sylvanus Hatch—July 13th
Ebenezer—son of Brother Ebenezer Nye—July 20th
Rebecca—daughter of Brother Abisha Green—December 3rd

1824

Oliver Holmes & Barnabas—sons of Mr. Bomas Childs—January 7th
Thomas & Peter Eldredge—sons of Mr. Thomas Childs—January 7th
David—son of Silas Shores—May 9th
Salome—daughter of Brother Nathaniel Shiverick, Jr.—September 26th
Philander, Peter & Benjamin—sons of Brother Henry Crocker—October 5th
Unie, Blossom & Celia—daughters of Brother Henry Crocker—October 5th

1826

Charles & William P. sons of Sister Mary Phinney, wife of Capt. Ebenezer Phinney
Mary & Susan—daughters of Sister Mary Phinney, wife of Capt. Ebenezer Phinney Jan. 24th
Clarissa, daughter of Brother Silvanus Hatch—May 21
Harriot N.—daughter of Brother Isaiah Hatch—June 11

1827

Evelina daughter of Brother Abishai Green—July 20th
Henry Robinson son of Brother Henry Crocker—October 11th
William & Susanna Childs—children of Sister Lydia Childs wife of Thomas Childs —October 11th
James Merchant Childs, son of Sister Chloe Childs the wife of Barnabas Childs— October 11th

1828

Mary Price; William Wendal;
Elizabeth, Jane & Eunice Townsend children of Sister Anna the wife of Thatcher Chadwick Apr. 22nd

NAMES OF CHILDREN BAPTISED BY N. G. WHEELER

1830

Josse Hatch, Joseph Henry children of Elias Harrington—November 6th

Chloe Hatch—daughter of Sylvanus Hatch—November 21st
Elizabeth Fearing; Elihu; Alexander Gibbs; Achsah Bourne; Philena Darwen—children of Joshua Nye—December 19
Nathaniel Shiverick, son of Nathaniel Shiverick—December 19

Baptised by Rev. John Hyde

1833

Silas—son of Silvanus Hatch—August 11th
Elijah, Peter Lewis & Enas Ewer sons of Brother Barnabas Brown—Oct. or Nov.
Elizabeth Jane & Lucy Goodspeed daughters of Henry Crocker and Rhoda Crocker—Oct. or Nov.

Persons baptised by Revd Timothy Davis

1834

Widow Mercy Eldridge—October 12th

1835

Ephraim Allen Swift, Rebeccah, Alexander and William Henry—children of Alexander Crocker—July 12th
Isaac Hatch & Rhoda his wife
Temperance Robinson, wife of Freeman Robinson
Esther Freeman, Fanny Lincoln, & Love Francis—their children
Lucy Fuller wife of Coleman Fuller; Noah & Charles Hamlin their sons—July 12th

Names of children baptised by William Harlow

1837

Seth R.—son of Brother Thomas & Mary B. Hatch—October 8th

1838

Sarah Harding Childs, adopted daughter of Brother Simeon Harding—October 14th

1840

Freeman Peale son of Timothy & M. B. Hatch—August 2nd by H. B. Hoocker

1841

Betsey Freeman daughter of Timothy Fish—February by James D. Lewis

Members received after the 25 of November 1821

Mrs. Betsey Hatch—recommended from the first Church in this Town—May 30, 1822
Mr. Silas Shores—recommended from the First Church in Taunton—July 31, 1822
Mrs. Celia Nye—recommended from the first Church in Sandwich—August 4, 1822
Mrs. Mehitable Bourne—recommended from the first Church in Falmouth—August 4, 1822
Mrs. Lydia Child & Mrs. Martha Swift—recommended from the first Church in Falmouth—August 11th 1822
Widow Martha Hambelton—April 4, 1824
Mrs. Mary Phinney—September 11, 1825
Mrs. Rhoda Crocker—September 17, 1826
Mrs. Hannah Eldred—April 4th, 1827
She obtained a dismissal and recommendation from the Church in Barnstable
Mr. William Hamblin was appropriated by a vote of the Church & propounded, but not formally received on account of his ill health. Deceased
Mr. Abner Phinney recommended from the first church of Falmouth—February 28, 1830
Mr. Timothy Fish & Cinthy Fish his wife—August 28, 1831
Mrs. Bethany Lewis—January 9th, 1833

OLD COLONY INSCRIPTIONS.

LAKEVILLE, [formerly a part of Middleborough] Nov. 14, 1853.

To the Editor of the N. E. Hist. Gen. Register. Sir,—I have had the pleasure to become somewhat acquainted with your work entitled the New England Historical and Genealogical Register, and highly approve of its object, and sincerely wish that it was in my power to do you essential service in carrying on so good a work.

The following inscriptions are from stones in an old burial ground near the Old Forge, so called, in Freetown, and were taken from the stones and carefully preserved several years since. Freetown was my native place, and these are the oldest that I have found in that town.

In memory of Mrs. Hannah wife of Col. Ebenezer Hathaway who died Dec. ye 20th 1727 in ye 34th year of her age.

Soon must the rising dead appear
Soon the decisive Sentence hear.

In memory of Shadrach Hathaway M. A. died Decembr ye 3 1749 in ye 33 year of his Age.

[Shadrach Hathaway, I am told, was the first college educated man at Freetown who was raised or rather born and bred there.]

In memory of Col. Ebenezer Hathaway who died Feb. ye 16th 1768 in ye 79th Year of his age.

Under these silent clods I sleep
In CHRIST may I arise
And when the angel Gabriel sounds
Meet JESUS in the skies.

In Memory of Mrs. Elizabeth Hathaway wife of Mr. Gilbert Hathaway died Feb^{r} ye 2d 1779 in ye 29th year of her age.

In Memory of Capt. Eben^{r} Hathaway who died June 16th 1791 in ye 73d year of his age.

This is the end of all that live
This is my dark long home
Jesus himself lay in the grave
The house whence all must come.

[These stones are slate and handsomely executed. I was careful to copy capitals where they were used on the stones.

The following is the oldest to be found in the oldest burial ground near the first Christian chapel in Freetown, slate stone considerably ornamented :—]

In memory of Isaac Hathaway died June ye 7th 1749 in the 45th year of his age.

There are more persons in Freetown bearing the name Hathaway than any other, and has been for years past, and next to the Hathaways come the Chases.

From the ancient burial ground near the old muster field in Berkley. No labor bestowed on the stones except to cut the letters, which are all capitals, with a dot or period between the words :—

Here lies the body of William Paul aged 80 year died November the 9 day in the year 1704.

Here lies the body of William Phillips aged 35 died in the year 1705 June 12.

Here lies the body of Thomas Richmond aged 47 died the 14 day Desember in the year 1705.

Here lies the body of James Tisdale aged 71 died in the year 1715 January 15.

Here lies the body of John Paul aged 56 died in the year 1718 March the 23.

Here lies the Body of Ruth the daughter of Ephraim Pray aged 3 died in the year 1719 October the 7.

Here lies the body of Hannah Phillips the wife of William Phillips aged 28 died in the year 1705 June 6.

Here lies the body of Ebenezer Tisdale aged 22 died in the year 1705 November the 11.

Here lies the body of Mary the wife of James Tisdale Aged 66 died in the year 1713 September 9.

Here lise the body of Judeth Pray aged 3 year died in the year 1715 January the 28.

Here lies the body of Mary Paul the wife of William Paul aged 76 died October ye 3 in the year 1715.

Here lies the body of Lidia the daughter of Ephraim Pray aged one year died January 20 1716.

Here lies the body of Sara Blackman aged 24 died in the year 1717 May the 13.

Here lies the body of Ephraim the son of Ephraim Pray aged 6 died October 11 in the year 1719.

Here lies the body of Lidia the wife of Theophilus Wetherell aged 67 died in the year 1719 September 7.

The following are from stones in the old burial ground of the Precincts Congregational society of Lakeville and Taunton. The stones are not smoother than the hand of Nature made them, and all the letters are capitals, very similar to those at Berkley :—

Here lies a child of Elkanah Leonard died in the year 1711.

Here lise the body of Elkanah Leonard aged 38 died in the year 1714 December ye 29.

Henry Leonard born and died in the 1714.

Thomas Leona

Very respectfully and truly yours,
EBENEZER W. PEIRCE.

INSCRIPTIONS FROM FREETOWN, MASS.

[Communicated by EBENEZER W. PEIRCE, of Freetown.]

The following are copies of inscriptions to be found in the old burial ground in Fall River, (near the line of Freetown), upon the land that Samuel Lynde, of Boston, gave the inhabitants of the town of Freetown, about the year 1730, and where the first meeting-house in Freetown was erected. In the division of Freetown in 1803, this lot of land fell within the limits of Troy, now Fall River.

Here lieth ye Body of Capt. Constant Church, died March ye 9th 1726–7, aged 49.

Here lieth Nathaniel, ye son of Constant & Patience Church, died Decem^br^ 14, 1726, aged 4 mo. 2 days.

Here lies the body of Capt. Charles Church, died March ye 9th, 1727, aged about 42 years.

IN MEMORY of Capt. Charles Church, who died May 6th, A. D. 1762, aged 52 years.

Here lies the body of James Barnaby, died July ye 5th, 1726, in the 56 year of his age.

Here lies the body of Johannah, wife of James Barnaby, died Sept. ye 4, 1725, aged about 36 years.

In Memory of Capt. Ambrose Barnaby, he died April ye 18th, 1775, in the 69th year of his age.

In Memory of Mrs. Elizabeth, the wife of Capt. Ambrose Barnaby, she died Jany. 28, 1788.

In Memory of Mr. Ambrose Barnaby, who departed this life June 8th, A. D. 1802, in the 57th year of His Age.

In Memory of Mrs. Elizabeth, wife of Mr. Ambrose Barnaby, she died December ye 23^d^, 1775, in the 32^d^ year of her age.

In Memory of Mrs. Philena, wife of Mr. Ambrose Barnaby. She died Oct. 3^d^ 1790, in the 32d year of her age.

In Memory of Capt. Ambrose Barnaby, who died May 26, 1820, in the 36 year of his age.

In Memory of Lydia, ye wife of Mr. Nathan Simmons, died June ye 10, 1747, Aged 29 years.

Remember me as you pass by,
For as you are so once was I;
But as I am now so must you be,
Therefore prepare to follow me.

In Memory of Abraham Simmons, died May ye 22^d^, 1749, in ye 70th year of his age.

In Memory of Experience, the wife of Jeremiah Simmons, died January, 1756, in ye 25 year of her age.

In Memory of Capt. NATHAN SIMMONS, who died June ye 26th, 1774, in the 65th year of his age.

O Death, thou hast Conquered me,
I by thy dart am slain;
But Jesus Christ has Conquered the,
And I shall Rise again.

Inscriptions from stones found in the Evans burial ground in Freetown:

Here lieth Ebenezer, ye son of Ebenezer & Sarah Rumreill, died Feb. 1732–3, aged 3 years and 11 Mo.

Here lieth Abagail, ye Daughter of Ebenezer & Sarah Rumreill, died Octo. ye 26, 1733, aged 6 months.

In Memory of Baly Evins, died June ye 12, 1748, in ye 37 year of his age.

In Memory of Marey, Daughter of David & Sarah Evins, died June ye 21st, 1748, in ye 48 year of her age.

In Memory of Mrs. MARY PARSONS, Wife of Capt. David Parsons, she died Nov. 24th, 1783, aged 58.

In all the foregoing, care was taken to copy capital letters where they were used upon the stones, and the same is true of the following, the oldest to be found in the old burial ground, near the First Christian Chapel in Assonet Village.

In memory of Isaac Hathaway, died June ye 7th, 1749, in the 45th year of his age.

In Memory of Bettey, ye Wife of Barnabas Canady, died Nov. 6, 1758, in ye 21 year of her Age.

In Memory of Betty H., dautr of Zephr. & Mrs. Hope Terry, she died May 17th, 1779 aged 5 years, 2 mts & 8 days.

Memento Mori. In Memory of Capt. Jael Hatheway, Obiit Jan. 10th, 1811, in his 92d year.

Rejoice in Glorious hope
Jesus the Judge will come,
And take his Servants up
To their Eternal home.

In memory of Mrs. Rebeckah wife of Capt. Jael Hatheway, who died Jan. 24th, 1785, in ye 69th Year of her age.

My children dear, this place draw near,
A mothers grave to see;
Not long ago I was with you,
And soon yo ll be with me.

In memory of Mrs. Elizabeth, Wife of Mr. Jule Hathaway, Who died May 1st, 1816, aged 65 years.

Capt. Russel Hathaway, of Fall River, is a son of Capt. Jael Hathaway, and Capt. Jael was the youngest son of Jacob Hathaway, of Freetown. Capt. Jael was a workman in the forge owned in part by Jacob, and in old deeds is called Jael Hatheway, Bloomer. Tradition tells us that in the war of the Revolution, Capt. Jael took sides with the mother country, and was a *very strong Tory*. An armed force being sent to arrest him, he shut the door of his house against them, and as they entered, stood in the attitude of defence armed with a broad axe, which he threw with violence among them. The exasperated soldiers seized him and dragged him out of the house by the heels, and to silence his cries crammed his mouth with dirt and filth.

INSCRIPTIONS COPIED FROM THE BURYING GROUND AT KINGSTON, MASS.

KINGSTON, Sept. 20, 1855.

S. G. DRAKE, ESQ.—DEAR SIR:—I beg leave to hand you inclosed "Notes from a Grave Yard," which I have made during my researches among the old tomb-stones at Kingston, Mass., for facts concerning the genealogy of the Holmes'. The list is not as full as I could wish, not having the time to spare to attempt to copy but a few of the most dilapidated ones; but if I have an opportunity before returning to your city, will avail myself of it, to make further copies from the yard at this place, or at Duxbury—and remain, very truly yours, D. W. HOLMES.

"Notes from a Grave Yard."

In memory of Mr Ebenezer Cobb who Died Dec^{br} 8th 1801. Aged 107 Years 8 months 6 days.

Here lyes buried Mrs. Lydia, ye wife of Mr Ebenezer Cobb who Dec^{d} Sept^{br} ye 10th 1745 in ye 47th year of her Age.

In memory of Mr^{s} Joanna Cobb wife of Mr Ebenezer Cobb who died January ye 15th 1791 in ye 87th year of her age.

In memory of Deac^{n} Wrastling Brewster, who dec^{d} Jany ye 21st 1761 aged 72 years 4 months 28 days.

In memory of Mr^{s} Hannah Brewster, Widow of Deac^{n} Wrastling Brewster, who died Augs^{t} y^{e} 20– 1788– aged 90 Years, wanting 21 days.

Here lyes the body of Mary Partridge, wife to Mr John Partridge. She Dec^{d} Nov^{br} ye 12th 1742– aged 80 Years 11 m & 29 Days.

Here lyes ye Body of James Stubbs* Who dec^{d} Jany y^{e} 20th 173$\frac{1}{2}$ in y^{e} 30th year of his age.

Mary Dau^{tr} to Mr Joshua & Bethiah Cushing his Wife, Dec^{d} April y^{e} 6th 1741 aged 4 years 4 months & six days.

In memory of Mr^{s} Patience, Widow of Mr Samuel Gray, she died April y^{e} 23– 1782, in y^{e} 76th year of her age.

Eliza^{bth} Dau^{tr} To Mr Samuell & Mr^{s} Patience Gra† who died Nov^{br} ye 4th day 1740 aged 6 years 6 m^{n} & 6 days.

Mary Dau^{tr} To Samuel & Patience Gray, His wife Dec^{d} Sept ye 10– 1728 aged 5 weeks.

Thomas Gray son of Co^{l} John Gray & Mrs Dezire his wife—Died Decem^{br} 24 1707—7 yrs & 8 m.

In memory of Mr Benjamin Bradford who died Nov ye 16, 1783 aged 78 years.

In memory of Zeresh Bradford the wife of Mr Benjamin Bradford dec^{d} April ye 6th 1763 in ye 51st year of her age.

Here lies buried Mr. Israel Bradford who died March ye 26–1760 in ye 83^{d} year of his age.

Here lies buried Mr^{s} Sarah ye widow to Mr Israel Bradford who dec^{d} April ye 3rd 1761 in ye 80th year of her age.

In memory of Mr Abner Bradford who died June ye 18–1784 in ye 78th year of his age.

Priscilla Croade dau to Thomas and Rachel Croade aged 1 month 18 days, dec^{d} Feby 18th 1724-5.

Rachel dau to Mr Thomas and Mr^{s} Rachel Croade his wife, dec April 2^{d} 1726-7.

---

* Not *perfectly* legible.

† There was not room to put on the Y, so they left it off, I suppose.

John son to Mr Thomas & Mrs Rachel Croade his Wife, decd Jany 30th 1725-6 aged 15 days.

Thomas Croade son to Mr Thomas & Mrs Rachel Croade Born 3d 1722 died July 9–1729.

In Memory of Mr John Holmes who died January 23d 1748 in ye 66th year of his age.

Here lyes 2 daughtrs To Mr William and Mrs Johannah Goumer, his wife—Priscilla Decd April ye 14th 1726 age 3 Weeks—Rebeckah, Decd Septbr ye 3d 1728—18 months.

Here lyes ye body of Mrs Priscilla Wiswall widow of the Revd Mr Ichabod Wiswall Obt June ye 3rd 1724—age 71.

Here lyes body of Mrs Elizabeth Bradford wife to Lnt Ephraim Bradord decd Decbr 5th 1741 in ye 51st year.

Deborah Bradford dau to Lieut Ephraim & Elizabeth Bradford his wife, Dec June 10–1752 aged 19 years 11 m & 20 Days.

In memory of Mr Nathan Bradford who died Oct ye 14–1787 aged 65 years.

In memory of Mrs Elizabeth ye wife of Mr Nathan Bradford who Decd April ye 30th 1773 age 42 yrs 11 mos 19 days.

In memory of Mrs Mercy Fuller widow of Mr Jabez Fuller . . . (not readable) . . . 5th 1782 in the 79th year age.

MARSHFIELD INSCRIPTIONS.

FROM THE BURIAL-GROUND ON THE HILL, SOMETIMES CALLED WINSLOW BURIAL-GROUND.

[Communicated by MISS M. A. THOMAS, of Marshfield.]

In Memory of Mrs Mary Bourn, wife to Mr. Jedediah Bourn, who Deceased June ye 28, 1743, in ye 44th year of her age.

Here Lyes Buried Mr Jedediah Bourn, who Dyed Oct ye 18th, 1743, in ye 74th year of his age.

Thomas Bourn, son of Thomas and Deborah Bourn, died Sept ye 14th 1723 aged 7 years 3 months and 3 days.

Ebenezar Bourn, son of Thomas and Deborah Bourn, died Sept ye 20th, 1723, aged 3 years 5 months and 16 days.

Deborah Bourn, daugh^ter^ of Thomas and Deborah Bourn, died Oct ye 2nd, 1723 aged 1 year 7 months and 15 days.

In Memory of Capt Rouse Bourn, who died June 21st, 1763, in ye 29th year of his age.

In Memory of Miss Lucy Bourn, who died December 14th, 1788, aged 19 years 11 months and 12 days.

Nathaniel, son of Dea Rouse & Mrs Hannah Bourn, died Sept 17, 1810, aged 3 months.

In Memory of Mrs Bradford, wife of Andrew Bradford Esq, who died June 10, 1825, ÆT 73.

Ask what a daughter, wife and friend should be,
In this imperfect state, and that was she.

In Memory of Mrs Lucy Delano, wife of Mr Joseph Delano, who died Aug 24th, 1789, in the 53rd year of her age.

This Stone is Erected in Memory of Dea Thomas Dingley, who departed this life Sept. 15, 1806, aged 74 years. He was Deacon of the first Church in Marshfield 26 years, to the great satisfaction of the Church.

This stone is Erected in Memory of Mr John Dingley, son of Dea Thomas Dingley and Mrs Anna his wife who departed this life May 10, 1806, aged 41 years.

ERECTED to the memory of Thomas Dingley, born May 22, 1761, died Feb 2, 1827, and his wife Ruth S. Winslow, born Dec 1778, died Oct 10, 1846.

Here Lyes ye Body of Dea John Foster, who died May ye 13th, 1732, aged 91 years.

Here Lyes the Body of Mrs Sarah Foster, wife to Dea John Foster, who dyed May ye 26th, 1731.

Here Lyes Buried the Body of Deborah Foster, who dyed Nov ye 4th, 1732, in ye 42 year of her age.

Here Lyes Buried the Body of Mr. Solomon Hewet, aged 45 years and 10 days, who Deceased December ye 5th, 1715.

Here Lyes Buried the Body of Mr Winter Hewet, who Decd March ye 3rd, 1717–18, in ye 39th year of his age.

In Memory of Capt Joseph Kent, who died Jan 1st, 1801, aged 83 years and 10 days.

In Memory of Mrs Lydia Kent, widow of Capt Joseph Kent, who died April 9, 1810, aged 89 years.

Here Lyes Buried the Body of Isaac Little Esq. aged about 53 years, dyed December ye 29th, 1699.

Here Lyes the Body of Mrs Bethiah Little, wife to Asquir Isaac Little, who dyed Sept ye 3rd, 1718, aged — years.

Marcy Little, daughter to Capt Isaac Little Esq. dyed July ye 23rd, 1729, aged 9 years.

In Memory of Mr John Moorehead, who died June 15, 1836, aged 76 years.

Arthur Moorehead, died March 14, 1840, aged 10 months and 24 days.

John Moorehead, born Oct 8, 1821, died Dec 27, 1847.

Here the weary are at rest.

Here Lyes Interred the Body of Mrs Elizabeth Pelham, who dyed April ye 1st, 1706, in ye 84th year of her age.

Here Lyes the Body of John Rouse, Sen, aged 74 years, dyed Oct 1717.

Here Lyes the Body of John Rouse aged 26 years dyed May ye 26th, 1704.

Here Lyeth the Ashes of ye Reverend Edward Tompson, Pastor of ye Church of Marshfield who suddenly departed this life March ye 10th, 1705, Anno ÆTATIS SUAE 40.

Here in a tyrant's hand doth captive lie
A rare synopsis of divinity.
Old patriarchs, phrophets, gospel bishops meet
Under deep silence, in their winding-sheet;
All rest awhile, in hopes, and full intent,
When their King calls to sit in parliament.

Here Lyes what Remains of William Thomas, Esq, one of the Founders of New Plymouth Colony, who dyed in ye month of August, 1651, about ye 78th year of his age.

Here Lyes the Remains of Nathaniel Thomas Gentm, who Decd ye 13th day of February 1674, about ye 68th year of his age.

Here Lyes interred the Body of William Thomas Gentm, who Decd March ye 30th, 1718, in ye 80th year of his age.

Here Lyes Buried ye Body of ye Honorable Nathaniel Thomas Esq, who Decd Oct ye 22, 1718, in ye 75th year of his age.

Deborah ye wife of Nathaniel Thomas, Esq., decd June ye 17, 1696, in ye 53d year of her age.

Here Lyes ye Body of Mrs. Elizth Thomas, wife to Nathaniel Thomas, Esq., formerly wife to Capt. William Condy, decd Oct. ye 11th, 1713, in ye 61st year of her age.

Here Lyes Buried ye Body of Mrs. Mary Thomas, wife to Nathaniel Thomas, Esq., who Decd Oct. ye 7th, 1727, in ye 54th year of her age.

Here Lyes interred the Body of Mrs Mary Thomas, wife to John Thomas Esq, Dyed May ye 3rd, 1737, in ye 35th year of her age.

Here Lyes Buried the Body of Alice Thomas, wife of Nathan Thomas, aged 25 years Dyed June ye 14th, 1715.

Here Lyes the Body of Abiah Thomas, wife of Nathan Thomas, aged 26 years Decd Feb ye 1st 1717 | 18.

Here Lyes the Body of Mr Samuel Thomas, aged 65 years deceased Sept ye 2nd, 1720.

Here Lyes Buried the Body of Mrs Marcy Thomas, widow of Mr Samuel Thomas, who Decd Sept, 1741, aged 79 years.

Ann Thomas, daughter of John and Lydia Thomas dyed Decemˢber 7th, 1723, in ye 6th year of her age.

Here Lyes the Body of Kezie, Daughter of Mr John and Mrs Lydia Thomas, who Dyed Decemher ye 11th, 1751, aged 21 years 1 month and 4 days.

Here Lyes ye Body of Mrs Lydia Thomas, wife to Mr John Thomas who died Jany ye 17th, 1750, aged 60 years and 11 months.

Here Lyes the Body of Mr John Thomas, who departed this life April the 14th, 1770, in the 86th year of his age.

In Memory of Col Anthony Thomas, who died July the 14th, 1781, aged 62 years 3 months and 20 days.

John Thomas, son of Mr Anthony and Mrs Abigail Thomas, died Nov 11th, 1748, aged 5 years.

Sacred to the Memory of Mrs Lucy Thomas, wife of Capt John Thomas, she died August 30, 1804, aged 40 years, 11 months and 8 days.

In Memory of Capt John Thomas, Born August 30, 1764, Died July 27, 1737.

Erected to the memory of Mrs Lucy Thomas, wife of John Thomas, who died March 15, 1849, aged 78 years.

My Mother.

Beneath this rest the ashes of Nathaniel Ray Thomas, son of John and Lucy Thomas, Born at Marshfield June 9, 1812, Died at Washington D.C. March 17, 1840, aged 27 years.

Here Lyes the Body of Mr. Joshua Taylor, who dyed Sept y[e] 13th 1727, aged 67 years.

Here Lyes the body of Mr Joseph Waterman, Junr, dyed Dec[r] 23rd, 1715, in y[e] 39th year of his age.

Here Lyes the body of Mr Anthony Waterman, who dyed April y[e] 23rd, 1715, in the 31st year of his age.

Here Lyes the body of Mr Joseph Waterman, aged 69 years dyed Jany

Here Lyes buried the body of Mrs Sarah Waterman, widow of Mr Joseph Waterman who Dec[d] Sept 1741, aged 90 years and 3 months.

In Memory of Mr Daniel Wright, who died May 6, 1829, ÆT 76 years.

Mrs Sarah Wright, wife of Mr Daniel Wright, died March 16, 1822, ÆT 65 years.

Here Lyes buried the Body of Capt. Nathaniel Winslow, who Dec[d] Decem[br] 1st, 1709, in y[e] 81st year of his age.

Here Lyes Buried the Body of Mrs Faith Winslow, wife to Capt Nathaniel Winslow, who Dec[d] Nov 9, Anno Domini 1729, in y[e] 85th year of her age.

Here Lyes Buried the Body of Kenelm Winslow Esq, of Marshfield, who departed this life June the 1st 1757, aged 82 years.

Here Lyes Buried the Body of Mrs Abigail Winslow, wife to Mr Kenelm Winslow, who Dec[d] August y[e] 18th, Anno Domini 1729, aged 47 years 7 months and 15 days.

Here Lyes Buried the Body of Nath[l] Winslow, he was drowned in North River May y[e] 24th, 1734, aged 25 years and 11 months.

Eleanor Winslow, daughter of Mr. Kenelm Winslow Dec[d] April y[e] 12th, 1719, aged 9 months and 25 days.

Here Lyes Buried the body of Nathaniel, son of Mr John Winslow, who dyed March y[e] 26, 1723, aged 10.

Here Lyes Buried the body of John Winslow, son of Mr John Winslow, who dyed August y[e] 8th 1724, aged 18 years.

Here Lies interred Abigail Winslow, Daughter of the Hon. Silvanus Bourn Esq of Barnstable, and the late wife of Kenelm Winslow Esq, Born the first of June, 1729, Died at Marshfield 21st Dec, 1761, aged 32 years.

In Memory of Kenelm Winslow Esq. who died May 13, 1780, in the 63rd year of his age.

Mary Winslow, widow of Seth Winslow, died March 23rd, 1827, aged 49 years.

FROM THE WINSLOW TOMBSTONE.

The HON[ble] Josiah Winslow, Gou[r] of New Plymouth Dyed December ye 18, 1680, ÆTatis 52.

Penelope, ye widdow of Gou[r] Winslow, Dyed December ye 7, 1703, ÆTatis 73.

The HON[ble] Isaac Winslow Esq. dyed December ye 14, 1738, Ætatis 67.

Hon John Winslow Esq. died April 17, 1774, ÆT 72.

Isaac Winslow MD, died Oct 24, 1814, aged 80.

John Winslow Esq, died at Natchez August 24, 1822, aged 48.

Pelham Winslow, died August 19, 1832, aged 23.

MARRIAGES FROM THE EARLY RECORDS OF MARSHFIELD, MASS.

[Communicated by Miss M. A. THOMAS.]

[The following list comprises all the marriages found recorded in the Town Books of Marshfield, from the first organization of the town, in 1642, to the year 1729. In some instances, it will be seen, there were no marriages recorded for two or three consecutive years; and from 1702 to 1709 there is a deficiency of over six years. The transcriber, whose accuracy is proverbial in the Old Colony, made her collection from tattered and scattered pages of the record, and therefore the facts are placed in the order in which they were found, and are not so chronologically arranged as she otherwise would have desired. Some of the earliest are copied in full, to show the manner of the original registrations; others are contracted for convenience. Where she *knew* the females to be *widows*, she has so noted by adding the word "widow" in brackets. The names of the magistrates and clergymen before whom the marriages were solemnized, are generally added; those which took place after 1709 were chiefly by Rev. Mr. Gardner.

N. B. S.]

Ralph Chapman and Lydia Wills were maried 23 November, 1642.

John Bourne and Alis Besbege, was married ye 18 July, 1645.

John Thomas and Sarah Pitney was maryed the 21 December, 1648.

Jeremiah Burrowes and —— Hewet were maried May, 1651.

George Vaughn and Elizabeth Hincksman was maried —— 1652.

John Branch and Mary —— was maried 6 Dec. 1652.

Timothy Williamson and Mary Howland were maried 6 June, 1653.

Joseph Rose and Elizabeth Bumpus was maried first Monday in June, 1654.

John Phillips and Grace Holloway [widow] was maried 6 July, 1654.

Thomas Dogget and Joane Chillingsworth [widow] was maried 17 August, 1654.

John Walker and Lydia Read was married 20 October, 1654.

Josias Standish and Mary Dingley married 19 Dec. 1654.

John Adams and Jane James, m. 27 Dec. 1654.

Samuel Baker and Ellen Winslow m. 29 Dec. 1656.

William fford, Jun., and Sarah Dingley m. 4 Nov. 1658.

John Carver and Mellicent fford m. 4 Nov. 1658.

Thomas Durram and Sarah Bumpus m. March, 1659.

Justice Eames and Mehetabell Chillingsworth, 20 May, 1661.

Nathaniel Thomas and Deborah Jacob m. Jan. 1663.

Thomas Tilden and Mary Holmes, m. 24 Jan. 1664.

Richard Childs and Mary Truant m. 24 Jan. 1664.

Nathaniel Winslow and Faith Miller, m. 3 Aug. 1664.

—— —colme and Edith Maycomber, m. Nov. 1664.

John Sawyer and Mercy Little m. Nov. 1666.

Josiah Bent and Elizabeth Bourn m. 30 June, 1666.

Josiah Read and Grace Holloway m. Nov. 1666.

Arthur Howland and Mrs. Elizabeth Prince m. 9 Dec. 1667.
Michael fford and Abigail Snow m. 12 Dec. 1667.
William Sherman and Desire Dotey m. 25 Dec. 1667.
John Hewet and Martha Winter m ——, 1668.
John Tracy and Mary Winslow m. 10 June, 1670.
Josiah Snow and Rebekah Baker m. —— ——
Joseph Hammon and Bethiah Tulb m. 24 June, 1674.
Walter Hatch and —— —stable m. 5 Aug. 1674.
Daniel White and Hannah Hunt m. 19 Aug. 1674.
James Clement and Martha Deane m. 28 Dec. 1674.
Joseph Truant and Hannah Barnes m. 6 Jan. 1674.
John Rouse and Elizabeth Dotey, m. 13 Jan. 1674.
Thomas Maycumber and Sarah Crooker m. 20 Jan. 1676.
Robert Batson and Ann Winter m. 13 July, 1676.
Mr. Ralph Powell and Martha Clement m. 30 Oct. 1676.
Samuel Baker and Patience Simmons m. 21 ffeb. 1677.
John Phillips and Ann Torry, m. 3 April, 1677.
John Baily and Ann Bourn, m. 9 May. 1677.
John Sherman and Jane Hatch were married at Boston the 25 of October, 1677.
William Sherman, Jun. and Desire Dotey, m. 26 Dec. 1677.
Valentine Decrow and Martha Bourne, m. 26 ffeb. 1678.
Josiah Slawson and Mary Williamson, Jun. m. 12 Mar. 1678-9.
Israel Holmes and Anna Rouse, m. April, 1678.
Robert Stanford and Mary Williamson, [widow] 22 Jan. 1679.
Mellicent Carver [wid.] and Thomas Drake m. 9 March, 1680-1.
Samuel Thomas and Mercy fford m. 27 May, 1680.
Benjamin Phillips and Sarah Thomas, 12 Jan. 1681.
Thomas Bourne and Elizabeth Rouse m. 18 April, 1681.
Israel Holmes and Desire Sherman m. 24 Nov. 1681.
Jonathan Eames and Hannah Truant m. 11 Jan. 1682.
Daniel Crooker and Mary Bumpus m. 20 Jan. 1682.
William Carver and Elizabeth ffoster m. 18 Jan. 1682.
Samuel Doget and Mary Roggers m. 24 Jan. 1682.
Samuel Little and Sarah Grey were married before Mr. Alden the 18 of May, 1682.
Michael fford and Bethiah Hatch m. 29 March, 1683.
William ffisher and Lydia Walker m. 17 March, 1684.
Joseph Taylour and Experience Williamson, m. 25 April, 1684.
Mr. Stephen Burton and Mrs. Elizabeth Winslow m. 4 Sept. 1684.
Anthony Eames and Mercy Sawyer m. 2 Dec. 1686.
Samuel Doggett and Bathsheba Holmes m. 21 Jan. 1691.
Joseph Otis and Dorothy Thomas were maried the 20th day of Nov. 1688, by Mr. Mighill, minister.
John Doget and Mehitabell Trouant m. 3 Sept. 1691.
Nathaniel Winslow and Lydia Snow m. ——, 1692.
Mr. John Croad and Deborah Thomas were married the first day of Dec. 1692, by Mr. Samuel Arnold, minister.
Mr. Nathaniel Thomas and Mrs. Mary Appleton were married June the 20th, 1694, by Mr. John Rogers, minister.
John Sawyer and Rebekah Snow [widow] were conjoined in marriage, Nov. 23, 1694, by Mr. Weld, minister.

Nathaniel Thomas, Esq. and Mrs. Elizabeth Dolbery were married Nov. 3rd, 1696, by Mr. Cotton Mather.

John Hatch and Mary ffoster, m. Dec. 30, 1696, by A. Thomas.

William Sherman and Mercy White m. ffeb. 3, 1697, by E. Tompson.

John Jones & Ellenor Winslow, m. ffeb. 17, 1697, by E. Tompson.

Thomas Fish and Margarett Woodworth m. Jan. 10, 1697, by A. Thomas.

Thomas Doggett and Experience fford m. Jan. 18, 1698, by E. Tompson.

Gilbert Winslow and Mercy Snow m. ffeb. 7, 1698, by E. Tompson.

Israel Thomas and Bethiah Sherman, m. ffeb. 23, 1698, by E. Tompson.

James Ford and Hannah Dingly, m. ffeb. 28, 1698, by E. Tompson.

Daniel Thomas and Experience Tilden, m. April 26, 1698, by E. Tompson.

Samuel Witherell and Anna Rogers, m. May 26, 1698, by E. Tompson.

Samuel Little and Mary Mayhew, m. Dec. 5, 1698, by E. Tompson.

Joshua Cushing and Mary Bacon, m. March 31, 1699, by E. Tompson.

Ichabod Bartlett and Elizabeth Waterman, m. Dec. 28, 1699, by E. Tompson.

Samuel Baker and Sarah Snow, m. —— 1699, by E. Tompson.

John White and Susanna Sherman, m. ffeb. 18, 1700, by E. Tompson.

Isaac Winslow and Sarah Wensley, m. July 11, 1700, by Cotton Mather.

Samuel Silvester and Lucretia Joyce, m. Oct. 9, 1700, by E. Tompson.

John Rogers and Hannah Sprague, m. Dec. 11, 1700, by E. Tompson.

John Blackmore and Anna Branch, m. Dec. 19, 1700, by E. Tompson.

Joseph Tilden and Joanna Bouls, m. Jan. 23, 1701, by E. Tompson.

Thomas Joyce and Elizabeth Bent, m. Oct. 11, 1701, by E. Tompson.

Samuel Lapham and Hannah Rogers, m. Nov. 19, 1701, by E. Tompson.

Ebenezer Sherman and Margaret Decro, m. Sept. 18, 1702, by E. Tompson.

Thomas Bourne and Elizabeth Holmes, m. Nov. 23, 1702, by E. Tompson.

John Foster and Sarah Thomas, (wid.) m. Dec. 30, 1702, by E. Tompson.

By the Rev. JAMES GARDNER.

Joseph Waterman and Susanna Snow, m. June 16, 1709.
John Porter and Margaret fford, m. Dec. 6, 1709.
John Carver and ——— Rogers, m. Dec. 22, 1709.
John Allen and Sarah Dogget, m. Jan. 12, 1710.
John Phillips and Patience Stevens, m. ffeb. 16, 1710.
Samuel Dogget and Bethiah Waterman, m. ffeb. 20, 1710.
John Holmes and Joanna Sprague, m. May 11, 1710.
Joseph Phillips and Mary Eames, m. July 19, 1711.
James Macaul and Rachel Turner, m. Nov. 15, 1711.
William Carver and Abigail Branch, m. ffeb. 28, 1711–12.
John Sherman and Sarah Baker, m. March 26, 1711–12.
—— Thorp and Sarah Silvester, m. May 26, 1712.
Thomas Rogers and Bethiah Ewell, m. June 6, 1712, before Joseph Otis.
Isaac Walker and Bethiah N—, m. Oct. 31, 1713, before Joseph Otis.
David Sampson and Mary Chaffin, m. June 5, 1712.
Ebenezer White and Mary Dogget, m. Sept. 29, 1712.
Hezekiah Heredon and Anna Tranton, m. Nov. 10, 1712.
David Briant and Elizabeth Bo——, m. Dec. 16, 1712.
Ephraim Norcut and Elizabeth Bonney, m. Jan 30, 1712–13.
Joseph Lapham and Hannah Eames, m. ffeb. 5, 1712–13.
Elnathan ffish and Sarah Dingley, m. ffeb. 25, 1712–13.
Ebenezer White and Hanna Dogget, m. March 9, 1712–13.
George Bourn and Elizabeth Chandler, m. May 21, 1713.
Nathan Thomas and Alice Baker, m. March 1, 1712–13.
Nathaniel Torry and Hannah Tilden, m. Nov. 26, 1713.
John Barker and Bethiah Foord, m. Jan. 5, 1714, by I. Winslow.
Ralph Norcutt and Mary Remington, m. March 17, 1714–15.
Thomas Bourne and Deborah Trasey, m. April 5, 1714.
Caleb Tilden and Lidia Hewit, m. May 26, 1714.
Ezekiel Smith of M. and Dinah May of Roxbury, m. June 29, 1714, by. I. Winslow.
Jonathan Crooker and Sarah Allen, m. Nov. 11, 1714.
Benjamin White and ffaith Oakman, m. Dec. 2, 1714.
John Thomas and Lidia Waterman, m. Dec. 23, 1714.
John Tilden and Susanna ffoord, m. Jan. 13, 1714.
Nathan Thomas and Abiah Snow, m. Jan. 2, 1716–17.
Benjamin Phillips and Eleanor Baker, m. Jan. 16, 1716–17.
Arthur Low and Elizabeth Crooker, m. Jan. 24, 1716–17.
Philip Delleno and Elizabeth Dingley, m. Jan. 31, 1716–17.
James Sprague and Hannah Black, m. Nov. 19, 1717.
Jonathan Alden and Elizabeth Waterman [wid.] m. Jan. 17, 1717–18.
James Macaul and Hannah Green, m. Jan. 28, 1717–18.
Thomas Standish and Mary Carver, m. Jan. 30, 1717–18.
Lawrence Cane and Elizabeth Childs, m. July 31, 1718.
Joseph Thomas and Lidia Winslow, m. Dec. 10, 1718.
Richard Loudon and Elizabeth ffoord, m. Dec. 11, 1718.
Shubael Tinkham and Priscilla Childs, m. Dec. 17, 1718.

William Carver and Elizabeth Rouse, m. Jan. 28, 1718–19.
James Thomas and Deborah Sherman, m. ffeb. 12, 1718–19.
John Kent and Bathsheba Dogget, m. Sept. 17, 1719.
William Sherman and Mary Eames, m. Oct. 8, 1719.
John Doggett of Rochester and Margery Eames of M., m. Nov. 5, 1719.
Nathaniel Eames of M. and Abigail Oldham of Scituate, m. Jan. 2, 1720.
Elisha fford and Elizabeth Oakman, m. Jan. 11, 1719–20.
Jedediah Bourn and Mary Croad, m. Jan. 15, 1719–20.
Roger Perry and Ann Hamedon, m. April 10, 1720.
Joshua Tilden and Mary Norcutt, m. May 26, 1720.
Joseph Rider of Plimouth and Hanna Stephens of M., m. June 15, 1720.
John Holmes and Sarah Thomas, m. Sept. 8, 1720.
John ffullinton of M. and Ruth Sampson of Duxbury, m. Oct. 13, 1720.
Gideon Thomas and Abigail Baker, m. ffeb. 9, 1720–21.
Josiah Holmes of Rochester and Hannah Sherman of M., m. May 12, 1721.
David Hercey of Pembroke and Elizabeth Joyce, m. May 12, 1721.
Samuel Taylor and Elizabeth Carver, m. Nov. 16, 1721.
Arthur Howland and Abigail Eames, m. Nov. 30, 1721.
William fford and Hannah Truant, m. Dec. 7, 1721.
Josiah Johnson of Scituate and Abigail Phillips of M., m. Feb. 8, 1721–22.
Benjamin Randall and Sarah Oakman, m. May 1, 1722.
Nicholas Porter of Abington and Ruth Rogers of M., m. Dec. 19, 1722.
Josiah Bartlett of M. and Mercy Chandler of Duxbury, m. Jan. 3, 1722–23.
Robert Atkins and Thankful Sherman, m. Jan. 3, 1722–23.
Samuel Hills of Duxbury and Hannah Turner of M., m. Nov. 28, 1722.
Ebenezer Howland and Sarah Green, m. March 28, 1723.
James Dexter of Rochester and Lois Sherman, m. May 29, 1723.
Thomas Tracy and Susanna Waterman, m. June 3, 1723.
Benjamin Kent and Persis Dogget, m. Oct. 31, 1723.
John Logan and Margaret Car, m. Jan. 7, 1723–24.
Joshua Rose and Elizabeth Gibson, m. Jan. 30, 1723–24.
James Warren of Plimouth and Penelope Winslow, m. Jan. 30, 1723–24.
Francis Crooker and Patience Childs, m. March 11, 1723–24.
Samuel Sherman and Mary Williamson, m. ffeb. 17, 1723–24.
Benjamin Hanks and Mary White, m. April 23, 1724.
Joshua Sampson and Mary Oakman, m. May 23, 1724.
Thomas Stockbridge and Hannah Rogers, m. July 8, 1724.
Mr. John Thomas and Mrs. Mary Ray, m. Oct. 8, 1724.
William Stephens and Patience Jones, m. Oct. 9, 1724.
Caleb Oldham of Scituate and Bethiah Stephens, m. Oct. 21, 1724.

Anthony Eames and Grace Oldham of Scituate, m. Dec. 11, 1724.
Sylvanus Hall of Plymouth and Elizabeth Doggett, m. Jan. 13, 1725.
Thomas Phillips and Mary Sherman, m. ffeb. 23, 1725.
Adam Hall and Sarah Sherman, m. Jan. 6, 1725.
Anthony Eames and Anna Barker, m. March 25, 1725.
John Winslow of Plimouth and Mary Little, m. ffeb. 16, 1725.
Ichabod Washburn of Plimouth and Bethiah Phillips, m. June 2, 1725.
William Lucas of Plimouth and Sarah Thomas, m. Oct. 21, 1725.
Nathaniel Keen of Pembroke and Thankful Winslow, m. Oct. 27, 1725.
William Hammilton and Jean Hopkins, m. Oct. 27, 1725.
Ebenezer Damon of Scituate and Abigail Thomas, m. Oct. 27, 1725.
John Poland and Thankful Atkins [wid.] m. May 26, 1726.
Josiah Phinney of Plimouth and Mercy Thomas, m. Sept. 14, 1726.
Samuel Baker and Hannah fford, m. Nov. 9, 1726.
Seth Joyce and Rachel Sherman, m. Nov. 9, 1726.
Ebenezer Taylor and Sarah Carver, m. Jan. 11, 1727.
Stephen Stoddard of Hingham and Rebecka King, m. Jan. 24, 1727.
Isaac Phillips and Sarah White, m. Jan. 25, 1727.
John Carver and Mary Truant, m. April 5, 1727.
Thomas Oldham of Scituate and Desire Waterman, m. May 8, 1727.
Robert Waterman of Plimpton and Abigail Dingley, m. June 18, 1727.
Ebenezer Jones and Jane King, m. March 19, 1727–28.
Bezaleel Palmer of Scituate, and Anna Jones, m. March 19, 1727–28.
Isaac Taylor of Pembroke and Jerusha Tilden, m. May 28, 1728.
Joshua Carver and Martha fford, m. July 4, 1728.
Tobias Paine of Boston and Sarah Winslow, m. Oct. 14, 1728.
William ffoord and Hannah Barstow, m. Oct. 30, 1728.
Snow Winslow and Deborah Briant, m. Nov. 6, 1728.
Samuel Kent and Desire Barker, m. Nov. 14, 1728.
John Magoon of Scituate and Abigail Waterman, Nov. 18, 1728.
Thomas Dogget and Joanna ffuller, m. Dec. 11, 1728.
Joseph Hewet and Sarah Dingley, m. Dec. 19, 1728.
Joshua Eames and Abigail Dogget, m. —— 18, 1728.
Samuel ffoord, and Sarah Rogers, m. —— 16, 1728.

DEATHS AND BURIALS FROM THE EARLY RECORDS OF MARSHFIELD, Ms.

[Communicated by Miss M. A. THOMAS.]

1649.

Lydia dau. of Ralph Chapman	dyed Nov. 26, 1649.
Mr. William Thomas	" Aug. —, 1651.
Robert Waterman	buried Sept. 10, 1652.

Ralph son of Ralph Chapman	dyed	July 29, 1653.
John son of Mr. Edward Bulkly	buried	Feb. 26, 1655.
Mary wife of Josiah Standish of Duxborough dyed and was buried at Duxborough		July 1, 1665.
John son of John Dingley	buried	July 9, 1665.
Elizabeth dau. of Thomas Chillingsworth	dyed	Sept. 28, 1665.
John Granger dyed and was buried at Scituate		Oct. 4, 1655.
Dorothy dau. of John Russell	buried	Jan. 13, 1657.
John Adams a dau.	"	Feb. 19, 1657.
Maj. Winslow a dau.	"	Mar. 14, 1658.
John Dingly	"	1658.
Christian wife of Robert Carver	"	July 23, 1658.
Elizabeth wife of Thomas Bourn aged 70	"	" 18, 1660.
John Walker	"	Dec. 11, 1663.
Mr. Thomas Bourn dyed and was being then aged 83.	"	May 11, 1664,
Elizabeth wife of Thomas Tilden	"	Dec. 12, 1663.
Killed by Lightning. Grace wife of John Phillips	buried	June 24, 1666.
Killed by Lightning. William Shirtley (Shurtleff)	"	June 24, 1666.
Killed by Lightning. Jeremiah Phillips	"	
Edward son of Maj. Josias Winslow	"	Dec. 11, 1667.
Susanna dau. of Clement King	"	June 19, 1669.
—— White Jun.	"	Mar. 27, 1670.
—— wife of Resolved White	"	Apl. 3, 1670.
Thomas Little	"	Mar. 12, 1671.
Joseph Beadle	dyed	Sept. 1, 1672.
Kenelm Winslow dyed at Salem and was buried there		Sept. 13, 1672.
Richard Beare	buried	—— 1673.
John Thomas	"	June 26, 1673.
James Clement	"	Feb. 10, 1674.
Capt. Nathl Thomas	"	Feb. 16, 1674.
Mr. Josias Winslow being in the 69th year of his age.	"	Dec. 1, 1674,
Ephraim Little a dau	"	June 14, 1675.
Arthur Howland Sen.	"	Oct. 30, 1675.
Faith wife of John Phillips	"	Dec. 21, 1675.
John the son of John Branch was slayne with Capt Pearce near Rehoboth & there buried the latter end of		March, 1676.
Timothy Williamson	buried	Aug. 6, 1676.
Ellen wife of Samuel Baker	"	Aug. 27, 1676.
Jonathan Winslow being 38 years old	"	Sept. 8, 1676,
William Ford sen aged 72	"	Sept. 23, 1676.
George son of John Rouse	"	Dec. 13, 1676.
Mary dau of Simon Rouse	"	Dec. 21, 1676.
William Holmes being 86 years old	"	Nov. 9, 1678,
Mehitable dau of John Carver	"	Apl. 19, 1679.
John Carver sen being 42 years old	"	June 23, 1679,

DEATHS AND BURIALS FROM THE EARLY RECORDS OF MARSHFIELD, Ms.

[Communicated by Miss M. A. THOMAS.]

William Sherman sen.	buried	Oct. 25, 1679.
James Emerson a dau.	"	Feb. 28, 1680.
Bathsheba dau. of Wm Ford	"	Mar. 12, 1680.
Robert Carver being 86 years old	"	Apl. —, 1680,
Sarah wife of Samuel Sherman	"	July —, 1680.
—nah wife of Edward	"	Oct. 1, 1680.
Gov Josiah Winslow	"	Dec. 23, 1680.
Deborah dau. of Josiah Snow	"	Oct. 31, 1681.
Ellen widow of Kenelm Winslow being 83 years old	"	Dec. 5, 1661,
Samuel son of Richard Childs	"	Dec. 10, 1681.
Sarah wife of John Thomas sen.	"	Jan. 2, 1682.
George son of John Rouse Jun.	"	Feb. 26, 1682.
Josiah son of Nath[l] Winslow	"	May 16, 1682.
Abigail dau. of Michael Ford	"	June 26, 1682.
Anne dau. of John Sawyer	"	Sept. 1, 1682.
Timothy Williamson	"	Sept. 18, 1682.
Margaret widow of Arthur Howland Sen.	"	Oct. 23, 1683.
Michael Ford had two dau.	"	Nov. 17, 1683.
Isaac Little a dau.	"	Dec. 17, 1683.
Christopher Winter	"	Dec. 22, 1683.
Joseph Trouant and Israel Holmes were cast away sailing into Plymouth harbor and drowned, buried at Plymouth		Feb. 24, 1684.
Anna widow of Wm. Ford sen.	"	Sept. 1, 1684.
Joane wife of Thomas Dogget	"	Sept. 4, 1684.
Susanna dau. of Thomas Tilden	"	Sept. 9, 1684.
Persis wife of John Dogget	"	— — 168–.
John Rousse	"	Sept. 16, 1684.
Mr. John Bourn	"	Dec. 8, 1684.
John son of Thomas Tilden	deceased	Apl. 20, 1685.
Morris Truant	"	Apl. 21, 1685.
Alice late wife of Mr. John Bowrn	buried	May 9, 1686.
Elizabeth dau. of Thomas Bowrn	deceased	Apl. 14, 1689.
Bethiah dau. of Isaac Little	"	— — 1689.
Mary wife of Samuel Dogget	"	Apl. —, 1690.
Elizabeth widow of Wm Holmes in the 86 year of her age	"	Feb. 17, 1689.
Elizabeth wife of Abram Holmes	"	May —, 1690.
Joseph Thomas	"	July 13, 1690.
The wife of Samel Waterman	"	July —, 16–0.
Martha wife of John Hewet	"	June 22, 1691.
Alice dau. of Josiah ——	"	Aug. —, 1691.
Jacob Dingley	"	Aug. 18, 1691.
Daniel Crooker	"	Feb. 5, 1692.
Anthony Snow	"	Aug. —, 1692.

Josias Snow	deceased	Aug. —, 1692.
Thomas Doggett	"	May 18, 1692.
Edward Bumpus	"	Feb. 3, 1693.
Isaac son of John Doggett	buried	Sept. 21, 1692.
Mercy wife of John Sawyer	"	Feb. 10, 1693.
Hannah widow of old Edward Bumpus	deceased	Feb. 12, 1693.
The wife of Francis Crooker	"	Mar. —, 1692–3.
James Maccall	"	May 9, 1693.
Mr. Samuel Arnold	"	Sept. 1, 1603.
William Norcutt	"	Sept. 18, 1693.
William White	"	Jan. 24, 1695.
Elizabeth Carver	"	Apl. 4, 1694.
William son of Josiah Ford	"	Aug. —, 1696.
Lydia wife of Experience Branch	"	Nov. 5, 1697.
Experience Branch	"	Nov. 14, 1697.
Christopher son of Jonathan Crooker	"	Feb. 1, 1699.
William son of Thomas Doggett	"	Feb. 16, 1699.
Susanna wife of Clement King	"	June 19, 1699.
Lieu. Isaac Little	"	Nov. 24, 1699.
John Thomas and John Bayley drowned going out of Green's harbor in a canoe	"	May 24, 1699.
Elizabeth wife of Thomas Bourn	"	Apl. 2, 1707.
Sarah dau. of Dea. John Foster	"	Apl. 7, 1702.
Mary wife of Dea. John Foster	"	Sept. 25, 1702.
Mrs. Penelope Winslow widow of Gov. Josiah Winslow aged 73	"	Dec. 7, 1703.
John Rose Jun.	"	May 27, 1704.
Church Records. } Rev. Mr. Edward Thompson	dyed	Mar. 16, 1704–5.
Capt. Peregrine White	deceased	July 20, 1704.
Mrs. Elizabeth Velham	"	Apl. 1, 1706.
Josiah son of Wm. Stephens Jun.	"	Jan. —, 1707.
Mr. Joseph Waterman	"	Jan. —, 1707–8.
Elizabeth wife of Ichabod Bartlett	"	Oct. —, 1708.
Abigail dau. of Solomon Hewet	"	Dec. 8, 1709.
Mrs. Sarah White (widow of Peregrin White)	"	Jan. 22, 1711.
Elizabeth wife of Anthony Eames Jun.	"	Feb. 18, 1711.
Rebecka wife of John Sawyer	"	Apl. 28, 1711.
Hannah wife of Joseph Rose Jun.	"	Sept. 30, 1711.
Joseph son of Joseph Rose Jun.	"	Sept. 30, 1711.
Hannah wife of John Barker	"	June 30, 1713.
Joseph son of Joseph Waterman	"	Mar. 28, 1715.
Mary Childs	"	Apl. 10, 1715.
Rebecka dau. of Samuel Baker	"	Apl. 20, 1715.
Anthony Waterman	deceased	Apl. 3, 1715.
Joseph Waterman	"	Nov. 23, 1715.
Ralph Norcutt	"	Dec. 2, 1715.
Solomon Hewet	"	Dec. 5, 1715.
Lidia wife of Nath[l] Winslow	"	Apl. 8, 1716.
Grace dau. of Joseph Childs	"	Apl. 22, 1716.
Rachel wife of James Maccall	"	Dec. 8, 1716.
Joseph Childs	"	Mar. 11, 1717–8.
John Rogers in the 85th year of his age.	"	May 7, 1717.

Elizabeth Dingly (wid. of Jacob Dingley)	deceased	Mar. 30, 1718.
Mr. William Thomas	"	Mar. 21, 1718.
Nathaniel Thomas Esq.	"	Oct. 2, 1718.
Mr. Samuel Thomas	"	Sept. 2, 1720.
Dea. William Foord	"	Feb. 7. 1721.
William Clift	"	Oct. 17, 1722.
Anna dau. of Isaac and Sarah Winslow deceased at Boston	"	Sept. 16, 1723
Lydia dau. of Gilbert Winslow	"	Oct. 5, 1723.
Martha wife of Valentine Decrow	"	Mar. 25, 1724.
Rebekah Wills	"	Mar. 30, 1724.

May 1724.

The Dispensations of Divine Providence were very awful towards the town of Marshfield in removing several of its inhabitants by Death.

Capt. Josiah Winslow eldest son of Isaac Winslow and Sarah his wife dyed May 1724 being killed in an engagement with the Indian on George's River at the Eastward.

Mr. Daniel White dyed May 6, 1724, in the 70th year of his age.

Henry Gulliford dyed May 9, 1724, being about 40 years of age.

Theodosius Foord son of Josiah Foord and Sarah his wife Deceased at Sandwich May 10, 1724. in the 25th year of his age.

Nathaniel Winslow had a child dyed May 12, 1724, in the 1st year of its age.

Benjamin White dyed May 13, 1724, in the 33rd year of his age.

Josiah Johnson dyed May 18, 1724, in the 25th year of his age.

Robert Atkins dyed May 19, 1724, in the 35th year of his age.

Jonathan Barker son of Mr. John Barker and Hannah his former wife dyed May 25, 1724, in the 18th year of his age.

William Sherman dyed May 26, 1724, in the 30th year of his age.

Mr. Jonathan Eames dyed May 31st, 1724, in the 69th year of his age.

Josiah Baker son of Samuel Baker and Sarah his wife dyed at Lebanon, Connecticut Government, Nov. 20, 1726.

EARLY RECORDS OF MIDDLEBOROUGH.

[Communicated by Mr. Cyrus Orcutt.]

Joseph son of Joseph Bumpas	born	Aug	25	1674
Rebekah daughter of Joseph Bumpas	"	Dec	17	1677
James son of Joseph Bumpas	"	Dec	25	1679
Penelope daughter of Joseph Bumpas	"	Dec	21	1681
Mary daughter of Joseph Bumpas	"	Aug	12	1684
Mehetabel daughter of Joseph Bumpas	"	Jan	21	169$\frac{1}{2}$
Francis son of John Miller	"	Jan	11	170$\frac{2}{3}$
John son of John Miller	"	Oct	28	1704
Hannah daughter of Jonathan Thomas	"	Sept	24	1704
Jacob son of John Tomson	"	June	24	1703
Abigail daughter of Thomas Pratt	"	June	23	1701
Hepsibah daughter of Thomas Pratt	"	April	22	1705
Joseph son of Samuel Chard	"	July	18	1705
John son of John Bardon	"	May	1	1704
William son of John Raymont Junior	"	Dec	20	1704
Thomas son of Thomas Darling	"	Sept	7	1704
David son of John Alden	"	May	18	1702
Priscilla daughter of John Alden	"	March	2	170$\frac{3}{4}$
Priscilla daughter of Samuel Warren	"	Dec	12	1704
John son of Ensign Joseph Vaughn	"	Sept	8	1692
Mary daughter of Ensign Joseph Vaughn	"	Oct	6	1694
Josiah son of Ensign Joseph Vaughn	"	Feb	2	169$\frac{8}{9}$
Joanna daughter of Ensign Joseph Vaughn	"	Jan	26	170$\frac{1}{2}$
Ephraim son of Electiaus Renolds	"	Feb	14	170$\frac{4}{5}$
John son of John Hascol Junior	"	Feb	20	170$\frac{3}{4}$
Sqier son of John Hascol	"	June	1	1706
Ruth daughter of Thomas Nelson	"	Feb	25	170$\frac{5}{6}$
Samuel son of Samuel Richmond (b. in Taunton)	"	Oct	16	1695
Oliver son of Samuel Richmond (b. in Taunton)	"	Aug	25	1697
Thomas son of Sam'l Richmond (b. in Midleboro)	"	Sept	10	1700
Hannah daughter of Samuel Richmond	"	Aug	29	1702
Lydia daughter of Samuel Richmond	"	May	14	1704
Ignatius son of Rodolphus Elmes	"	April	8	1706
Esther daughter of Jacob Tomson	"	Feb	18	170$\frac{6}{7}$
Ichabod son of John Barden	"	Dec	18	1705
Electiaus son of Electiaus Renolds	"	Feb	21	170$\frac{6}{7}$
Jonathan son of Jonathan Morse Junior	"	Aug	18	1705
David son of Jonathan Morse Junior	"	Oct	13	1707
Jabez son of Samuel Warren	"	Feb	3	170$\frac{5}{6}$
Samuel son of Samuel Warren	"	Aug	9	1707
Martha daughter of John Soul	"	April	11	1702
Sarah daughter of John Soul	"	Oct	8	1703
John son of John Soul	"	April	13	1705
Esther daughter of John Soul	"	April	16	1707
Sarah daughter of Ebenezer Bonnet	"	March	27	1707
Ebenezer son of Samuel Barrows	"	July	27	1702
Coombs son of Samuel Barrows	"	Dec	15	1704
William son of Ebenezer Roddin	"	Nov	7	1706
Susanna daughter of Peter Bonnet	"	July	10	1709
Peter son of Peter Bonnet	"	March	16	1711

Joseph son of Elkanah Leonard	born	April	9	1705
Rebekah daughter of Elkanah Leonard	"	Feb	24	$170\frac{5}{6}$
Abiah daughter of Elkanah Leonard	"	April	30	1707
Rachel daughter of Ebenezer Richmond	"	May	6	1707
Elizabeth daughter of Ebenezer Richmond	"	Sept	1	1708
Samuel son of Mrs. Thomas Palmer	"	Aug	8	1707
William son of Samuel Chard	"	Nov	16	1708
Sarah daughter of Stephen Borden	"	April	30	1695
William son of Stephen Borden	"	March	25	1697
Abigail daughter of Stephen Borden	"	March	3	$169\frac{8}{9}$
Stephen son of Stephen Borden	"	May	1	1701
Timothy son of Stephen Borden	"	Jan	3	$170\frac{3}{4}$
Mercy daughter of Stephen Borden	"	Oct	27	1705
Hannah daughter of Stephen Borden	"	March	13	$170\frac{7}{8}$
Bethiah daughter of Nathaniel Allen	"	Jan	25	$170\frac{7}{8}$
Anna daughter of Jonathan Morse	"	April	1	1709
Elnathan son of Abiel Wood	"	April	14	1686
Abijah daughter of Abiel Wood	"	Feb	20	$168\frac{8}{9}$
Abiel son of Abiel Wood	"	March	19	$169\frac{0}{1}$
Timothy son of Abiel Wood	"	Oct	13	1693
Jerusha daughter of Abiel Wood	"	Nov	11	1695
Ebenezer son of Abiel Wood	"	Aug	4	1697
Judah son of Abiel Wood	"	July	28	1700
Thomas son of Abiel Wood	"	Jan	30	$170\frac{2}{3}$
Chipman son of Samuel Cob	"	March	5	$170\frac{8}{9}$
Nathan son of Samuel Prat	"	June	20	1703
Sarah daughter of Samuel Prat	"	Aug	18	1705
Hannah daughter of Samuel Prat	"	May	17	1708
Sarah daughter of John Hascol	"	March	21	1708
Meriam daughter of Edward Thomas	"	Dec	28	1694
Edward son of Edward Thomas	"	May	20	1699
Mary daughter of Edward Thomas	"	July	21	1701
Nathan son of Edward Thomas	"	Sept	12	1707
Mary daughter of John Soul	"	March	14	1709
David son of John Miller	"	April	17	1708
John son of Thomas Palmer	"	July	30	1709
Jonathan son of John Hascol	"	June	25	1710
Fear daughter of Nathaniel Southworth	"	Feb	3	1709
Nathaniel son of Jeremiah Thomas	"	Jan	2	1686
Sarah daughter of Jeremiah Thomas	"	Dec	25	1687
Jeremiah son of Jeremiah Thomas	"	Feb	14	$168\frac{8}{9}$
Elizabeth daughter of Jeremiah Thomas	"	Nov	19	1690
Mary daughter of Jeremiah Thomas	"	June	5	1692
Lydia daughter of Jeremiah Thomas	"	March	26	1694
Thankful daughter of Jeremiah Thomas	"	June	30	1695
Jedediah son of Jeremiah Thomas	"	Aug	19	1698
Bethiah daughter of Jeremiah Thomas	"	March	27	1701
Ebenezer son of Jeremiah Thomas	"	Nov	1	1703
Priscilla daughter of Jeremiah Thomas	"	Oct	13	1705

A RECORD OF BIRTHS, DEATHS, AND MARRIAGES ON NANTUCKET, BEGINNING IN 1662.

[Communicated by WM. C. FOLGER, of Nantucket, Corresponding Member of the N. Eng. H. G. Soc.]

Jean ye Wife of Richard Swaine Departed this life ye 31st Octobr 1662
Mary ye daughter of Nathanl Starbuck was born ye 30 March 1663
Jethro ye son of Edward Starbuck died ye 27th of May 1663
John the son of John Rolfe was born ye 5 March 1663–4
John ye son of John Swaine born the 1st of September 1664
William Worth and Sarah Macy were married ye 11 April 1665
Elizabeth ye daughter of Nathaniel Starbuck was born ye 9 Sept. 1665
John son of Humphrey Varny was born ye 5 Sept. 1664
Samuel ye son of John Rolfe was born ye 8 March 1665
John ye son of William Worth was born ye 19 May 1666
Stephen ye son of John Swaine was born ye 21 November 1666
John ye son of John Coleman was born ye 2 day of August 1667
Abiah ye daughter of Peter Folger was born ye 15 August 1667
Sarah ye daughter of John Rolfe was born ye 2d of December 1667
Nathaniel ye son of Nathl Starbuck was born ye 9 of August 1668
John Barnard and Bethiah ffolger were married ye 25th of Feby. 1668
William Bunker and Mary Macy were married ye 11th of April 1669
Lydia ye daughter of John Coffin was born ye 1st June 1669
Mary ye daughter of Nathaniel Barnard was born ye 24th of Feb. 1667
John Barnard and Bethiah his wife and Isaac Coleman ended their days ye 6th of June 1669 being drown'd out of a canoe between Nantucket and ye Vineyard, at the same time Eleazer Folger was preserved.
Hannah the daughter of Nathaniel Barnard was born 19 July 1669
Thomas ye son of John Coleman was born ye 17 of October 1669
Joseph Gardner and Bethiah Macy were married 30 March 1670
Hope ye daughter of Richard Gardner was born ye 16 of Nov. 1669
Joseph ye son of John Rolfe was born ye 12th of March 1669
John ye son of Nathl Barnard was born ye 24 of Feby. 1670
Judith ye daughter of Edward Cottell was born ye 13 April 1670
Sarah ye daughter of John Swaine was born ye 13 Julie 1670
George the son of William Bunker was born ye 22d of April 1671
Peter the son of John Coffin was born ye 5th of August 1671
Dinah ye daughter of Stephen Coffin was born ye 21 of Sept. 1671
Jethro ye son of Nathaniel Starbuck was born ye 14th of Dec. 1671
Hannah ye daughter of John Rolfe was born ye 5 of February 1671
Samuel ye son of Nathanl Holland was born ye 6 February 1671
Isaac ye son of John Coleman was born ye 6th of February 1671
Elizabeth ye dau. of Saml Bickford was born ye 16 Feb. 1671
Nathaniel the son of Nathl Barnard was born 24 of Nov. 1672.
Lydia ye Daughter of Edward Cottel was born ye 17th of May 1672
Love ye Daughter of Richard Gardner Senr was born ye 2 May 1672
Anne the dau. of Edward Cottle was born ye 3 March 1672–3
Eleazer ye Son of Eleazer Folger was born ye 2d Julie 1672
Sarah ye dau. of Joseph Gardner was born ye 23 October 1672
Experience ye dau. of Thomas Look was born 22 Novem. 1672
Susanna dau. of John Saviges wife was born ye 23 Mar. 1673
Joseph the Son of John Swaine was born 17 July 1673

John ye son of William Bunker was born ye 23 July 1673
Damaris ye dau. of William Gayer was born ye 24 Oct. 1673
Peter ye son of Stephen Coffin was born ye 14 November 1673
Experience ye Daughter of Willm Rogers was born ye 23 Julie 1673
Deborah ye dau. of Saml Bickford was born ye 5 of Feby. 1673
John ye son of John Coffin was born Feby 10. 1673
Eunice ye dau. of Nathl Starbuck was born ye 1 April 1674
Richard Gardner & Mary Austin were married ye 17 May 1674
Phebe the dau. of John Coleman was born ye 15 of June 1674
John ye son of John Savige was born ye 24 June 1674
Damaris ye dau. of Joseph Gardner was born ye 16 Feb. 1674
Stephen ye son of Nathaniel Barnard was born 16 Feb. 1674
Elizabeth ye dau. of Thomas Look was born ye 28 Aug. 1675
Peter ye son of Eleazer Folger was born ye 28 Aug. 1674
Dorcas ye Daughter of Willian Gayer was born ye 29 Aug. 1675
Anne the dau. of Joseph Coleman was born ye 10 Novem. 1675
Patience ye dau. of Richard Gardner Jr. was born June 29. 1675
Mehitable ye dau. of John Gardner was born Nov. 24. 1674
John ye son of Edward Cottle was born ye 7th of Septm. 1675
Mary ye Dau. of Joseph Prat was born ye 16 of Sep. 1675.
William ye Son of Willm Gayer was born ye 3^{d} of June 1677
Thomas Macy Jr. died ye third day of December 1675
Stephen ye Son of Stephen Coffin was born ye 20 Feby. 1675
Ebenezer ye Son of Willm Rogers was born ye 5 of Jany. 1675
Stephen Hussey & Martha Bunker were married Oct. 8 1676
Love ye dau. of John Coffin was born ye 23^{d} of April 1676
Elizabeth ye dau. of John Swain was born May 17th 1676
Deborah ye Dau. of Tobias Coleman was born May 25 1676
Bethiah ye dau. of Joseph Gardner was born Aug. 13. 1676.
Sarah ye dau. of Eleazer Folger was born Aug. 24. 1676.
Jonathan ye son of Willm Bunker was born Feby. 25. 1674
Peleg ye son of Willm Bunker was born ye 1 Dec. 1676
Benjamin ye son of John Coleman was born Jany 17. 1676
Ruth ye Daughter of John Gardner was born Jan. 26 1676
Joseph ye son of Richard Gardner was born May ye 8. 1677
Ebenezer ye son of James Coffin was born March 30, 1678
Sampson ye Son of Edward Cartwright was born Jany 26. 1677
Jabez ye Son of Willm Bunker was born Nov. ye 7th 1678
Tabitha ye Dau. of John Trot was born March y 2^{d} 1679
Sarah ye Dau. of John Macy was born April ye 3^{d} 1677
Puella ye dau. of Stephen Hussey was born Oct. 10th 1677
Abigail ye Dau. of Stephen Hussey was born Dec^{e} 22^{d} 1679
Deborah ye dau. of John Macy was born Mar. 3^{d} 1679
Benjamin ye Son of John Swaine was born ye 5 July 1679
Betty ye dau. of Denis Manning was born July ye 10. 1679
Sarah ye dau. of Nathl Barnard was born Mar. 23^{d} 1677
Eleanor ye dau. of Nathl Barnard was born June 18. 1679
Joseph ye son of James Coffin was born Feby ye 4th 1679
Susanna y^{c} dau. of Edward Cartwright was born Feb. 16. 1680
Jane dau. of Thos Look was born Dec. 24th 1680
Joseph ye son of John Trott was born Mar. 10th 1680
Nath^{ll} Wire Senr died March ye 1st — — 1680–1

A RECORD OF BIRTHS, DEATHS, AND MARRIAGES ON NANTUCKET, BEGINNING IN 1662.

[Communicated by Wm. C. Folger, of Nantucket, Corresponding Member of the N. Eng. H. G. Soc.]

Solomon ye son of Richard Gardner Jr. was born July 1. 1680.
Mary ye dau. of Willm. Parkman was born Feby 25th. 1680
Dorothy Cottle died ye first day of October—1681
Mr. Tristram Coffin Died ye 2 Day of October 1681.
Richard Swaine Senior Died ye 14th of Aprill 1682
Mr. Thomas Macy Departed this Life Aprill ye 19th 1682
Thomas ye Son of Willm Bunker was yorn ye 8th of Aprell 1680
Hephsibah the Daughter of Nathll. Starbuck was born ye 2d of April 1680
James ye Son of Dennis Manning was born ye 20th of January 1680
Silvanus ye Son of Stephen Hussey was born May ye 13th Day 1682
Peter ye Son of Jeremiah Coleman was born ye 6th of ye 2d m 1716
David ye Son of Dennis Manning was born ye 2d of April 1683
Benjamin ye Son of Richard Gardner was born July ye 20th 1683
Rachel ye Daughter of John Trot was born August ye 23d 1683
John Worth and Miriam Gardner were Married the 22d of Septm. 1684
Benjamin ye Son of Willm. Bunker was born May ye 28th 1683
Edward ye Son of Edward Cartwright, was born May ye 5 1683
Mr. Thomas Macy Departed this life ye 19th of Aprill 1682
Bethiah ye Daughter of John Macy was born April ye 8th 1681
Benjamin ye Son of James Coffin was born August ye 28th 1683
Deborah ye Daughter of Joseph Gardner was born March ye 30: 1681
Hope ye Daughter of Joseph Garner was born January ye 7th 1683
Miriam ye Daughter of Richard Gardner was born July ye 14th 1685
Jonathan ye Son of John Worth was born ye 31st of October 1685
Abigail ye Daughter of Richard Swaine was born February ye 7, 1683
Jonathan ye Son of Richard Swaine was born ye 23d of December 1685
Tristram ye Son of Peter Coffin Junr was born ye 26 Aprill 1685
Nathll. ye Son of John Worth was born September ye 8th 1687
William ye Son of John Swaine Jr. was born October ye 2d, 1688
Lidia ye Daughter of Richard Gardner Junr. was born June ye 16, 1687
Mr. Richard Gardner Departed this Life January ye 23d 1688
Lidia ye Daughter of Richard Gardner Jr. Departed this Life february th 8th 1688
Peter Coffin & Elizabeth Starbuck were married August the 15th 1682
Abigail ye Daughter of Mr. Peter Coffin Jr. was born July ye 9th 1683
Nathaniel ye Son of Mr. Peter Coffin was born ye 26th of March 1687
Lamuell ye Son of Mr. Peter Coffin was born ye 26th of february 1689
Barnabas ye Son of Mr. Peter Coffin Jr. was born february ye 12th 1690
Mary ye Daughter of Edward Cartwright was born June ye 29th 1687
Edward Starbuck Departed this Life ye 4th of ye 12mo. 1690, aged 86 yr.
Ishmael the Son of Betty Servant to Willm. Worth born at Boston May 1688
Judith ye Daughter of Jno. Worth was born December ye 22d 1689
Richard ye Son of John Worth was born ye 27th of May 1692
William ye Son of John Worth was born ye 27 of November 1694
Lidia ye Daughter of Peter Coffin Son of Mr. John Coffin was born the 23d Day of November 1697

Mary ye Daughter of Eleazer folger was born february 14th 1684
Batchlour the Son of Stephen Hussey was born february ye 18th 1684–5
Daniel ye Son of Stephen Hussey was born ye 20th of October 1687
Mary ye Daughter of Stephen Hussey was born March ye 24th 1689–90
George ye Son of Stephen Hussey was born ye 21st of June 1694
Theodata ye Daughter of Stephn Hussey was born September ye 15th 1700
Margaret ye Daughter of Jethro Coffin was born June ye 10th 1689
Precilla ye Daughter of Jethro Coffin was born December ye 26th 1691
John ye Son of Jethro Coffin was born ye 12th of Aprill 1694
Josia ye Son of Jethro Coffin was born ye 28 of July 1698
Abigaile ye Daughter of Jethro Coffin was born ye 12 Day of 12mo 1700–1
Joseph Paddack and Sarah Gardner were married March ye 5th 1696
Richard ye Son of John Helman was born October 7th 1682.
Robert ye Son of Jethro Coffin was born ye 21 of ye 2d mo 1704
Peter ye Son of Joseph Swaine was born ye 22dof June 1697
Richard ye Son of Joseph Swaine was born ye 16th of August 1698
Edward Cartwright Died ye 2d Day of ye 7mo 1705
Nicholas Cartwright Died ye 10 Day of the 7 mo 1706
Alice ye Daughter of Sampson Cartwright was born September ye 21 1702
Caleb ye Son of William Stretton was born ye 3d Day of ye 10mo 1708
Mary ye Daughter of William Stretton was born 1 Day 8mo 1710
Elizabeth ye Daughter of Willm Stretton was born ye: 14: Day: 8mo 1712
Deborah ye Daughter of Willm. Stretton was born ye 21st of ye 10mo 1714
Hagar Daughter to Betty Willm Worth Servant born August ye 7th 1696
Daniel ye Son of George Bunker was born August ye 16 Day 1696
Seth the Son of Joseph Paddack was born July ye 9th Day 1699
Dorcas ye Daughter of Nathll Coffin was born July ye 22d 1693
Christian ye Daughter of Nathll Coffin was born Aprill ye 8: 1695
Lydia ye Daughter of Nathll Coffin was born May ye 16th 1697
William ye Son of Nathll Coffin was born: December ye 1st: 1699
John Macy Departed this Life October ye 14th 1693
Thomas Howse & Abigaile Hussey were married April ye 5th: 1700
Thomas Howse ye Son of Thomas Howse was born March ye 6: 1701–2
Micha ye Son of Joseph Coffin was born ye 6th of July 1705
Nathaniell Coffin and Damaris Gayer were married 17th: of ye 8th mo: 1692: by me Willm Worth Justice of ye Peace.
Jethro Starbuck & Dorcas Gayer were married ye 6th Day of ye 10: mo 1694: by me Willm Worth Justice of the Peace.
Mary ye Daughter of Edward Allin was born ye 25: day of August 1698
Joseph ye Son of Edward Allin was born ye 10 day of October 1695 & deceased ye 4: 5 mo 1706.
Benjamin ye Son of Edward Allin was borne ye 22 day of March 1697
Nathll. ye Son of Edward Allin was borne february ye 24th 1700
Daniel ye Son of Edward Allin was born ye 23: day of ye 2 mo 1704
Benjamin ye Son of John Ingraham was borne ye 23: of January 1703
Judith ye Daughter of Peleg Bunker was borne ye 21 of September 1701
Prissilla ye Daughter of Peleg Bunker was borne ye 8th of December 1703
Dinah ye Daughter of Peleg Bunker was borne January ye 25th 1705
Paul ye Son of Stephen Coffin Senior was borne ye 15 of April 1695
Silvanus ye Son of Edward Allin was borne ye 6 day of ye 3mo 1706
Thomas ye Son of Matthew Genkins was born ye 29: day of ye 9mo 1707

Christopher ye Son of Bachelor Hussey was borne ye 10 day of ye 2mo 1706.

Mary ye Daughter of Bachelor Hussey was borne ye 9 day of ye 12 mo 1707

Jedidah ye Daughter of Bachelor Hussey was borne ye 27 day of ye 7mo 1708

Eunice Daughter of Peter Coffin was borne Sept 23: 1693

Jonathan ye Son of Richard Pinkham was borne ye 12 day of ye 9mo 1684

Shubal ye Son of Richard Pinkham was born ye 7 day of ye 4 mo 1691

Nathaniel ye Son of Richard Pinkham was borne ye 22: day of ye 11 mo 1692

Deborah ye Daughter of Richard Pinkham was borne ye 28 day of ye 12 mo 1694

Daniel ye Son of Richard Pinkham was borne ye 8 day of ye 10mo 1697

Barnabas ye Son of Richard Pinkham was borne ye 3 day of ye 11 mo 1699

Peleg ye Son of Richard Pinkham was borne ye 5 day of ye 12mo 1701

Theophilus ye Son of Richard Pinkham was borne ye 14 day of ye first month 1705

James ye Son of Richard Pinkham was borne ye 19 day of ye 12mo 1707–8

John ye Son of Jonathan Pinkham was borne ye 15 day of ye 8mo 1707

Jonath. Coffin ye Son of James Coffin & Mary his wiffe was borne ye 28 of ye 6mo 1692

Anthony odar ye Son of Nicholas odar of Newport in ye Ile of White in ye County of hampsheer in old England, was married to Sarah folger ye Daughter of Eleazer folger of Nantucket in New England on ye 10 day of March 1702–3 by Will-worth Justis of peace on Nantucket.

Elizabeth Daughter of Anthony odar & Sarah his wiffee was borne ye 16: day of December 1703

John ye Son of Bachelor Hussey was borne ye 6: day of ye 8 mo 1710

John Swaine ye third & Patience Skiffe were married ye 3: of October 1706 by me Will-Worth

Sarah ye Daughter of Nicholas Cartwright was born ye 13: day of ye 8 mo 1695

Elenor ye Daughter of Nicholas Cartwright was borne ye 14 day of ye 8mo 1697

Hope ye Daughter of Nicholas Cartwright was borne ye 27 day of ye 6 mo 1699

Lydia ye Daughter of Nicholas Cartwright was borne ye 15 day of ye 10 mo 1701

Nicholas ye Son of Nicholas Cartwright was borne ye 4 day of ye 11 mo 1705

Abigail ye Daughter of Morris Phariss was borne ye 8 day of ye 2mo 1709

Tabitha ye Daughter of John Trott was born ye 2: day of ye first mo 1679

Joseph ye Son of John Trott was borne ye 10 day of ye 2 mo 1681

John ye Son of John Trott was borne ye 28: day of ye 6 mo 1683

Benjamin ye Son of John Trott was borne ye 8: day of ye 9 mo 1685

James ye Son of John Trott was borne ye 20: day of ye 11 mo 1687

Mary ye Daughter of John Trott was born ye 31: day of ye 8 mo 1690

Abigail ye Daughter of John Trott was ye 8: day of ye 4 mo 1693

Prissilla ye daughter of John Trott was born ye 11 day of ye first month 1697

Mary ye Daughter of Jedediah fitch was borne ye 22: day of ye 6mo 1708

Hannah ye Daughter of Nathll. Gardner was borne ye 6: day of ye 5 mo 1686

Ebenezer ye Son of Nathaniel Gardner was borne ye 27 day of ye 8 mo 1688

Peleg ye Son of Nathaniel Gardner was borne ye 22: day of ye 5 mo 1691

Judith ye Daughter of Nathll Gardner was borne ye 28 day of ye 8 mo 1693

Margaret ye Daughter of Nathll Gardner was borne ye 28 day of ye 11 mo 1695

Nathll ye Son of Nathll Gardner was born ye 14 day of ye 10 mo 1697

Andrew ye Son of Nathll Gardner was borne ye 26 day of ye 10 mo 1699

Abel ye Son of Nathaniel Gardner was borne ye 6 day of ye 6 mo 1702

Susannah ye Daughter of Nathaniel Gardner was borne ye 4 day of ye 6 mo 1706

Abigaile ye wiffe of Nathaniel Gardner Died on ye 15: day of ye 3 mo 1709

Jemima ye Daughter of John Barnard was borne ye 14: day of ye 9 mo 1699

Robert ye Son of John Barnard was borne ye 14 day of ye 11 mo 1702

Matthew ye Son of John Barnard was borne ye 7 day of ye 9 mo 1705

Lamuel ye Son of John Barnard was born ye 3: day of ye 7 mo 1707

Nathll Starbuck ye Son of Nathll Starbuck & Dinah Coffin ye Daughter of James Coffin were married ye 20: day of November 1690 p. John Gardner Justice

Mary ye Daughter of Nathll Starbuck Jr. was borne ye 31 day of Decembr. 1692

Paul ye Son of Nathll Starbuck Jr. was borne ye 29 day of Octobr. 1694

Prissilla ye Daughter of Nathll Starbuck Jr. was borne ye 25 day of Octobr 1696

Elizabeth ye Daughter of Nathll Starbuck Jr. was borne ye 27 day of. Novembr. 1698

Hephzibah ye daughter of Nathll Starbuck, Jr. was borne ye 8th day of November, 1700

Abigail ye Daughter of Nathll Starbuck Jr. was borne ye 28 day of ye 6 mo 1704

Benjamin ye Son of Nathll Starbuck Jr. was borne ye 16 day of ye 7 mo 1707

Tristram ye Son of Nathll Starbuck Jr. was borne ye 18 day of ye 6 mo 1709

Ruth ye Daughter of Nathll Starbuck Jr. was borne ye 24 day of ye 12 mo 1714–5

Anna ye Daughter of Nathll Starbuck Jr. was born ye 12 day of ye 10 mo 1716

Jethro Starbuck & Dorcas Gayer were married ye 6 day of ye 10 mo 1694 by me William Worth Justice of Peace

George Bunker & Deborah Coffin were married ye 10 day of ye 8mo 1695

James Coffin Jr. & Ruth Gardner were married ye 19 day of ye 3 mo 1692

George ye Son of James Coffin Jr. was borne ye 22: day of ye 2 mo 1693

A RECORD OF BIRTHS, DEATHS, AND MARRIAGES ON NANTUCKET, BEGINNING IN 1662.

[Communicated by Wm. C. Folger, of Nantucket, Corresponding Member of the N. Eng. H. G. Soc.]

Sarah ye Daughter of James Coffin Jr. was borne ye 9 day of ye first month 1695

Nathan ye Son of James Coffin Jr. was borne ye 13: day of ye 9 mo 1696

Elisha ye Son of James Coffin Jr. was borne ye 10: day of ye 6 mo 1699

Joshua ye Son of James Coffin Jr. was born ye 16: day of ye 7 mo 1701

Elizabeth ye Daughter of James Coffin Jr. was borne ye 27: day of ye 8 mo 1703

Prissilla ye Daughter of James Coffin Jr. was borne ye 3 day of ye 4 mo 1708

Mary ye Daughter of James Coffin Jr. was borne ye 29: day of ye 5 mo 1710

James ye Son of James Coffin Jr. was borne ye 10: day of ye 4 mo 1713

Rachel ye Daughter of Edward Allin was born ye 31: day of ye 12 mo 1709

Bachelor Hussey & Abigail Halle were married ye 11 day of October 1704 by William Worth Justice of ye Peace

Stephen Coffin Jr. & Experience Look were married ye 21: day of ye 9 mo 1693

Shubal ye Son of Stephen Coffin Jr. was born ye 2 day of ye 12 mo 1694

Zephaniah ye Son of Stephen Coffin Jr. was borne ye 28 day of ye 8 mo 1699

Mary ye Daughter of Stephen Coffin Jr. was borne ye 31: day of ye 3 mo 1705

Hephzibah ye Daughter of Stephen Coffin Jr. was borne ye 20 of ye 10 mo 1708

Dinah ye Daughter of Stephen Coffin Jr. was borne ye 23 day of ye 5 mo 1713

Nathan Folger & Sarah Church were married ye 29 day of Dec. 1699

Ebenezer Coffin was married to Elenor Barnard: ye 12: day of Dec. 1700

Thomas Clark was married to Mary Church ye 13 day of Dec. 1700

Peleg Bunker was married to Susanna Coffin ye 9 day of January 1700

These are to Signifie to al yt it may Concerne yt Stephen Goarham & Elizabeth Gardner: were married ye 25: day of December, 1703 by me William Worth Justice of ye Peace.

These are to Signifie unto those whome it may Concerne yt Ambross Dawes Jr. & Mehetable Gardner were married by me ye 14 day of August 1704. William Worth Justice of Peace.

Persis ye Daughter of John Coleman Jr. was borne ye 7 day of December 1695

Nathaniel Coleman ye Son of John Coleman Jr. was borne ye 20 day of December 1697

Elihu Coleman ye Son of John Coleman Jr. was borne ye 12 day of february 1699

Barnabas Coleman ye Son of John Coleman Jr. was borne ye 24: of April 1704

Sarah Starbuck ye Daughter of Jethro Starbuck was borne ye 20 day of December 1696

William Starbuck ye Son of Jethro Starbuck was borne ye 22: day of July 1699

Eunice Starbuck ye Daughter of Jethro Starbuck was borne ye 4 day of february 1701

Lydia Starbuck ye Daughter of Jethro Starbuck was borne ye 15 day of September 1704

Thomas Starbuck ye Son of Jethro Starbuck was borne ye 12: day of ye 10 mo 1706

Dorcas ye Daughter of Jethro Starbuck was borne ye 13: day of ye 2 mo 1710

Ye above Dorcas Daughter of Jethro Starbuck died in ye 10 mo following

Jemima Daughter of Jethro Starbuck was born ye 2: day of ye 5 mo 1712

Mary ye Daughter of Jethro Starbuck was born ye 8: day of ye 7 mo 1715

Thomas Howes of Yarmouth was Drowned between Nantucket & ye Maine: ye 1 day: 6 mo 1700

Patience ye Daughter of Joseph Marshall was borne ye 29 day of november 1699

Margret ye Daughter of Joseph Marshall was borne ye 8: day of December 1702

Ruth ye Daughter of Joseph Marshall was born ye 21 day of August 1704

Benjamin ye Son of Joseph Marshall was born ye 21 day ye 8 mo 1706

Hawkins ye Son of Joseph Marshall was born ye 8 day of ye 7 mo 1710

Jerusha ye Daughter of Thomas Clark was born ye 2 day of ye 5 mo 1702

David & Jonathan ye Sons of Thomas Clark were borne at a birth ye 18 of ye 5 mo 1704

Peter ye Son of Thomas Clark was born ye 29: of ye 4 mo 1707

Siman ye Son of Thomas Clark was born ye 21: day of ye first month 1709

Amos ye Son of Thomas Clark was born ye 16 day of ye 9 mo 1711

Josiah ye Son of Thomas Clark was born ye 30: day of ye 9 mo 1712

Abigail ye Daughter of Thomas Clark was born ye 20 day of ye 6 mo 1714

Patience ye Second Daughter of Joseph Marshall was born ye 11 day of ye 5 mo 1708

John ye Son of George Bunker was born ye 27: day of ye 10 mo 1697

Caleb ye Son of George Bunker was born ye 2: day of ye 9 mo 1699

John Arthur & Mary folger were married ye 27: day of ye 12 mo 1704–5

Eunice ye Daughter of John Arthur was borne ye 29 day of ye 6 mo 1706

Rhoda ye Daughter of John Arthur was borne ye 26 day of ye 9 mo 1708

Persis ye Daughter of John Arthur was borne ye 17 day of ye 9 mo 1710

Susanna ye Daughter of Jonathan Coffin was borne ye 30 day of ye 10 mo 1712

Hennery ye Son of Jonathan Coffin was borne ye 23 day of ye 1 mo 1716

Daniel ye Son of Jonathan Coffin was borne ye 22 day of ye 12 mo 1718

Nathl Paddack & Ann Bunker were married before William Worth ye 15 day 10 mo 1706

Matthew Jenkins & Mary Gardner were married before William Worth Justice of Peace ye 9 day of ye 8 mo 1706

EXTRACTS FROM NANTUCKET RECORDS.

We received, last spring, from Daniel S. Durrie, Esq., of Madison, Wis., Librarian of the State Historical Society of Wisconsin, a copy of some interesting extracts from the Records of Nantucket, which he found in the "Independent Chronicle," published in Boston in 1782. We enclosed the copy to William C. Folger, Esq., of Nantucket, for the purpose of having it corrected by the original, which he had consented to do. Mr. Folger sent us a new transcript, remarking that he could more easily imitate the original by a new copy than by altering the one sent, although that was a tolerably correct transcript. He has added an item or two of extracts from the Records, to those published in the "Chronicle." "Some few words," he writes, "are hard to make out, as the records are much worn; and some words are worn off."

Whale Fishing, &c.

[From Records of Nantucket, Book 1st, page 30.]

"5: 4: James Loper doth Ingage to carry on a Designe of whale
72 catching on this Iland of nantucket that is the sayd James Ingages to be a therd in al Respeckes And some of the Town Ingages to be on the other Two Therds with him, in like maner, the Town doth also consent that first one company shal begin, and afterwards, the Rest of the freholders or any of them, have liberty to set up an other Company, provided that they make a tender to those Freholders that have no share in the first company, And if any refuse, the rest may go on themselves, And the Town do Also Ingage that no other company shal be allowed hereafter, Also whosoever kil any whale of the company or companys aforesaid, they are to pay to the Town for every such whale five shillings,———

And for the Incourragement of the sayd James Loper the town doth grant him Ten Akers of Land, in some conveneant place that he may chuse in (woodland exepted) and also liberty for the commonage of Thre Cows, and Twenty Sheepe, and one horse, with nessesary wood & warter for his use, on condition, that he follow the trad of whalling on this Iland, Tow yeares, In al the seasons thereof, begining the first of march next Insuing, also he is to build upon his land, and when he leaves Inhabiting upon this Iland, then he is first to ofer his land to the Town at a valluable price, and if the town do not buy it, Then he may sel it to whome he please, The commonage is granted only for the tim of his staying here—

5. 4: The Town hath granted unto John Savidge Ten Akers of land to
72 build upon, and commonage for Three Cows, Twenty Sheepe, and one horse, as also Liberty of wood for firing, and fencing stuf, and any stuf for his Trad, (his house lot is to be in the most conveneant place that is comon) on condition that he build and Inhabit on this Iland before the first of march next, and not depart by removing for the space of Thre years, and also to Follow his Trade of a Cooper upon this Iland as the Town, or whale company Shal have need to Imploy him—his commonage is granted for so long tim as he stay heere, also when he Remove from the Iland he is to tender his Land to the Town at a valluable price, and if the town do not buy it then he may sel it to whome he please.

[Page 31, July 5, 72.] ordered that mr. Edward Starbuk and peter foulger are to vew what stroy may be in the Indians corne to Judg it, and they ar to be pay^{d} for their time of the owneres of the catle orderd by the Town that no Inhabitant shal in any Case, either sel or lend, any Sheep or lamb to any Indian upon the penalty of Twenty Shillings for Every Sheepe or lamb so lent or given.

[Page 31.] August 5. 72: A grant was made by the Town (the freeholders Inhabitants purchasers and associates) now Inhabiting on this Iland) unto mr. John Gardner of Salim mariner, A seamans Accommodation, with all Appurtinances belonging unto it as fully as the other Seamen and Tradsmen have in ther former grants, upon condition that he com to Inhabit and to set up the Trade of fishing with a sufficient vessal fit for the taking of Codfish, and that any of the Inhabitants shall have liberty to Jeyne him in such a vessall with him, That is to say an eight part or a quarter part or more or less, And the aforesayd John Gardner shall use his best Endevour to prosecute the fishing Trade to efect in the fit Seasons of the year, and if he see cause to depart from the Iland within thre years after the time that he shall com to Inhabit, that then the Land shall Return into the hands of the aforesayd Grantters, they paying for al nessesary building or fencing that ar upon it, as it shal be Judged worth, also the say[d] John Gardner is to be here with his famely at or before the last Day of Aprill: 74. or else this grant to be voyd."

Indian Claims.

[Book Second of Records, Page 1.]

" the 8th Agust 78 " mr Haray complayneth against Spotso for keeping and withholdinge from hem his land, which is on halfe of the Land that Spotso Is posest of.

mr. Harry was cast in his cause by the maior part of the Court * * mr Harry appeald in the presents of ye court. wannack mamack saith that nickanosse his father gave Spotso's father and harry father land.

wannach mameck went to mount hope with nickanoses father to Assomecking and he desired him that those 2 men & Spotso father and harry father should have that land no longer but desired that wanack mameck might have it and the sachem was willing.

Some time after harry father com to him and desired he might have the land againe and he did not grant it them: afterward there was a great hunting meetting at manna and a great many Endians were there and harrys father was not there then. Spattsos father came to wanack mameck and desired him he would let have the land he had before and he did so.

after this he wannack mameck told nickanosse his father the have the land they had before.

Nickanosse saith a loung time agoe at dadaduchaconset was a great metting and then the Sachem his father did give to Spotso father and nanasoket or harrys father takpockcamock and Shuahkemmuck after this thes toe men ware to doo some murther and thare land was taken from them. after this nanasoket father did come to wanackmaket father and asked his for the land that he had before but wanach mameck saith nothing too him: but after that at a great metting at mana Spotso did desier wanackmameck to let him have the land that he had before and he gave hem this answer you shall have the land you had before, that is tappocommoo and Shouahkommock and after that he told my father I have given them the land they had before that is tuppockcommoo and Showahkemmack

The testimony of old tahtahcummumuck he saith there was a great mettinge and nickanosse his father was there and some greatmen and they ware in the house and they went out to smock it and when those great men cum in again they said that they did put in to the hands of Cuscuttogens father tappockcommoo and Shouahcommo and he gave it to nana Sockets father and Spattso father

The Testimony of Petotaquan & womhomon who saith only Spotso father had the land and the other had not the land

The testimony of old Gentelman saith upon his knowledg that Spotso father had only the Land and no other with him.

The Testimony of myoack who saith that Spotsos father had only a Sachem Right

The Testimony of old uttasheme who saith the land was only given to Spottso father

the Testimony of Agnas who saith he was at the meting that was Spoken of in the other Evidence and Saith the land was only given to Spotsos father

The testimony of Safede who saith that harry father and Spotso father said thankky when nickanosses father gave them the land.

The testimony of Reastocky who saith he hath heard so much confirming it that he Judgeth that he will ly that saith that only on hath the Land

The testimony of Sahtahcommo who saith that he was with them when Nickanosse gave Spotso father the land only"

On a leaf at the other end of the same Vol. 2, I find the following:

" Will sasapanna hath p^d m^r. Harry six pound for his land given to him by the Sachems and the General Court as written by my hand.

Witness W^m. Worth"

" At a General Court held at nantucket July 19. 1673

Y^e town complaineth against wawinet and his father Neckanoose for defameing the title of the English to the neck called pakamaquok, the case was heard and witnesses examined with the deeds, al being examined and duly considered, the sentence of the Court is that the titel of the land is good with the Case of the Court.

[Book II., page 2.] Sherburne upon nantukket July 21. 1673

Peter Foulger is chosen and appoynted by the General Court to the Office of a Clark of the writte and also Recordor to the Court In the name of the Court signed by

Thomas Mayhew
Rich. Gardner'

MARRIAGES IN NANTUCKET. 1717–1777.

Communicated by Otis G. Hammond, Esq., of Concord, N. H.

I send herewith, for publication in the Register, a copy of some ancient marriage records of Nantucket, Mass., which I have taken from an old account book now in possession of the New Hampshire Historical Society. This book was presented to the society by Rev. Howard F. Hill, of Concord, N. H., June 14, 1871. It was kept by George and Caleb Bunker, of Nantucket, during the greater part of the 18th century, and is filled principally with ordinary merchants' accounts of no particular value. But the two Bunkers were also justices of the peace and recorded the marriages performed by them in the same book with their accounts.

George Bunker's entries begin March 5, 1717, and continue until Nov. 22, 1741, a period of twenty-four years and a little more than eight months, during which time he performed and recorded sixty-four marriages. From the last date until Jan. 2, 1765, there are no records. Then Caleb Bunker's entries begin and continue until June 8, 1777, a period of twelve years and five months, during which time fifty marriages are recorded. So that the whole time actually covered by these records is thirty-seven years, and the total number of marriage records found is one hundred and fourteen.

The book also contains judicial proceedings before George Bunker, as justice of the peace, from Aug. 7, 1718, to April 7, 1726, and before Caleb Bunker from Oct. 13, 1763, to Jan. 18, 1775. These records consist principally of trials for petty misdemeanors and the administering of oaths of office to town officers of Nantucket.

I send you these records for publication, as I know they must be of great value to the people of Nantucket and to all who trace their genealogy back to that ancient and honorable town; and because in Vol. 7 of the REGISTER there are already published some Nantucket births, marriages, and deaths ante-dating these entries, among which* are recorded the births of many of the people whom George and Caleb Bunker joined in matrimony, and whose names are entered in this old account book.

The credit for the re-discovery of these records belongs to Hon. Ezra S. Stearns, Secretary of the State of New Hampshire, who called my attention to them a few months ago, while we, as members of a committee, were examining the manuscripts belonging to the Historical Society.

A RECORD OF MARIEGES.

These are to Certifie to all whome it may Concern that Nathan Cofin & Lydia Bunker boeth of the Island of Nantuket ware Lawfully Maried before me the subscriber being one of his Majesties Justices of the peace for Nantucket ye fifth Day of March in ye yeare 1717: p^{r} me Geor^{e} Bunker Justice peace

These are to Certifie to all whome it Doeth Concern y^{t} Samuel Long & Lydia Coffin boeth of ye Island of Nantucket ware Lawfully Maried ye fortenth Day of March in the year 1717 by me Geor^{e} Buncker Justice of peace

These are to Certifie to all whom it Doeth Concern y^{t} Roberd Wotson & Jane Bunker both of the Island of Nantuket ware Lawfulli maried before me ye twentifirst Day of march in ye yeare 1717 by me Geor^{e} Bunker Justice of peace

These are to Certifie to whome it may Concern that Eliakim Swain & Elizabath Arther boeth of the Island of Nantucket ware Lawfully maried ye Eightenth Day of April in ye year 1717 by me George Buncker Justice of peace for Nantucket

These are to Certifie to all whome it Doeth Concern y^{t} Eleazer folger and Mary marshall boeth of the Island of Nantucket ware Maried acording to Law ye twentiefifth day of September in the year 1717 by me Geor^{e} Bunker Justice of peace

These are to Certifie to all whome it Doeth Concern y^{t} George Coffin & Ruth Swain Boeth of ye Island of Nantucket ware Maried Lawfully ye fortenth Day of november in ye year 1717 by me Geor^{e} Bunker Justice of peace for the Island of nantucket

These are to Certifie to all whome it doeth Concern y^{t} Daniel Bunker & Prissilla Swain boeth of the Island of nantucket ware Lawfully maried ye fortenth day of november in ye year 1717 by me George Buncker Justice of Peace for ye Island of nantucket

These are to Certifie to all whome it doeth Concern y^{t} John Gorton & Elizabeth Peirce ware maried acording to law the sevententh Day of november 1717 being boeth of the Island of nantucket by me Geor^{e} Buncker one of his majestyes Justyces of ye Peace for nantucket

These are to Certifie to all whom it doeth Concern that Jonathan upham and Ruth Peese (boeth Inhabitants of the Island of Nantuket) ware maried Lafully the 19th Day of December in the year 1717 by me George Buncker Justice of the peace for Nantucket

*p. 254, this volume.

These are to Certifie to all whom it may Concern y^{t} Thomas Carr and Martha Grindey Boath of ye Island of nantuket ware Lawfully Married by me George Bunker on of his Majesties Justices of ye peace for ye Island of Nantucket this 28th daie of April 1718

nantucket ss november ye 18: 1718.

Nathaniel Folger & Prisilla Chase ware maried in November ye 18: 1718 by me George Bunker Justice of peace

Richard Coffin & Ruth Bunker wase maried in November ye 20th 1718 by me George Bunker Justice of peace

Barnebas Gardner & mary wheler ware maried in December ye 11th 1718 by me George Bunker Justice of peace

Barttlet Coffin & Judeth Bunker ware maried ye first day of January in the yeare 1718 by me George Bunker Justice of peace

Peter Swain & Elizabath Ellis ware maried ye 16th day of December 1719 by me Geor^{e} Bunker Justice of peace for nantucket

Joseph mott of Rhoad Island & Rebekah maning ware maried in December ye 19th day 1719 by me Geor^{e} Bunker Justice of peace

william Gardner Hephzibath Gardner ware maried in January ye 20th day 1719 by me George Bunker Justice of peace

Ebinezer Gardner & Judeth Coffin ware maried on ye 27th day of January in ye year 1719/20 by me George Bunker Justice of peace

Ebinezer Ellis & Charity Swain ware maried on ye 10th day of February in ye year 1719/20 by me George Bunker Justice of peace

Thomas Crook and Hope Cartwright ware maried on ye 24th day of march in ye year 1719/20 by me George Bunker Justice of peace

Thomas Commet & margrett hallowell wase maried in Jun ye 28: day: 1720 by me George Bunker Justice of peace

Elisha Coffin & Dinah Bunker ware maried on ye 3^{d} day of Aprill in ye year 1721: before me George Bunker Justice of peace

These are to Certifie to all whom it may Concern y^{t} petey Pinkham and Elizabath Swain boath of Nantucket ware maried Twentieth day of Jun in 1722 before me George Bunker Justice of peace for s^{d} County

Nantucket July ye 5: 1720

Robert wier & Katharin Swain ware maried ye 7th day of July in 1720 by me George Bunker Justice of peace

will^{m} Baxter & margret Cook boath of nantucket ware maried ye 11th day of August 1720 by me George Bunker Justice of peace

Manuel & Elizabath Ellit ware maried ye 18th day of August in 1720 by me George Bunker Justice of peace

Joseph worth & Lediah Goarham ware maried ye 8th day of September: 1720 by me George Bunker Justice of peace

Josiah Coffin & Elizibath Coffin ware maried ye 5th day of october in ye year 1720 by me George Bunker Justice of peace

Barnabas pinkham & Prisillah Gardner ware maried ye 8 day of December 1720 by me George Bunker Justice of peace

Elisha Coffin & Dinah Bunker ware maried ye 3^{d} day of Aprill: 1721 by me George Bunker Justice of peace

Nantucket ss These are to Certifie to all to whom it may Concern that John way & Mary Long Boath of ye Nantucket ware Maried acording to law ye 23rd day of November 1721 p^{r} me Geor^{e} Bunker Justice of peace

Nantucket ss Ebinez^{r} Coleman & Sarah Smith boath of Nantucket ware lawfully Maried ye thirtieth day of November in ye yeare 1721 p^{r} me Geor^{e} Bunker Justice of peace

Nantucket ss humphery Ellis & mary hamlington boath of Nantucket ware lawfully Maried the first Day of December 1721 p^r me George Bunker Justice of peace

These are to Certifie to all to whom it may Concern that John ungust & Sarah Mitchel boath of nantucket ware lawfully maried ye 14 day of December 1721 p^r me George Bunker Justice of peace

These are to Certifie all whom it may Concern y^t Mardecai Ellis and margret Swain boath of nantucket ware Maried ye 19 day of march in 1722 before me George Bunker Justice of peace

Nantucket ss These are to Certifie all whom it may Concern y^t Richerd folger & Sarah Peas boath of Nantucket ware Maried ye 20th day of Jun in 1722 before me George Bunker Justice of peace

Nantucket ss These are to Certifie to all whom it may Concern y^t Stephen Swain and Ellener Ellis boath of nantucket ware maried ye 24th day of november in 1723 before me George Bunker Justice of peace

Nantucket ss These are Certifie all whom it may Concern that James williams and Dinah Coffin boath of the Island of Nantucket being publeshed as ye law directs ware Maried ye 31st day of December 1724 by me George Bunker Justice of peace

MARRIAGES IN NANTUCKET. 1717–1777.

Communicated by Otis G. Hammond, Esq., of Concord, N. H.

Nantucket ss these are to Certifie all whome it may Consern y^t Thomas Green and mary hussey boath of nantucket being publeshed as ye law Directs were Maried Jenuary ye 30th 1725/6 by me George Bunker Justice of peace

Nantucket ss These are to Certifie all whome it may Concern y^t John Bunker and mary Coffin boath of nantucket being publeshed as ye Law Directs ware maried ye 13th day of february 1725/6 by me George Bunker Justice of peace

Nantucket ss These ar to Certefie to all whom it may Concern y^t John willn and Elezabath Sibley being publeshed as ye Law directs ware maried by me George Bunker Justice of peace in ye 24 of may 1726

Nantucket ss these are to Certifie to all whom it may Concern y^t Eliphelit Smith and Hephzibath Bunker boath of nantucket being published as ye Law directs ware maried october ye 3^d day 1726 by me George Bunker Justice of peace

Nantucket ss These are to Certifie all whom it may Concern that Calib Bunker and Prissilla Coffin Boath of Nantucket being Published as ye Law directs ware Maried in october ye 3rd 1725 [1726] by me George Bunker Justice of ye peace for Nantucket

Nantucket ss These are to certifie all whom it may Concern that Andrew Newell and Eunice Coffin boath of Nantucket being published as ye Law directs ware Maried ye 6th day of November in 1726 by me George Bunker Justice of ye peace

Nantucket these are certifie all whom it may Concern y^t Seth Paddok & Leah Gardner boath of nantucket being publeshed as ye Law diricts ware maried ye 22nd day of november 1727 by me George Bunker Justice of peace

Nantucket ss these may certifie all whom it may Concern that James whipper & Patiance Long being publeshed as ye law Directs ware maried in october 31: 1727 by me—George Bunker Justice of peace

Nantucket ss These may certifie all whome it may Consern y[t] Isaac myrick & Deborah Pinkham of nantucket ware mared (being publeshed as y[e] law Directes) y[e] 9th day of January 1728/9 by me Geor[e] Bunker Justice of peace

Nantucket ss These may certifie all whom it may Consern y[t] Thomas Jenkins & Judeth Folger boath of nantucket being publeshed as y[e] Law directs ware Maried in January 22: day 1728/9 by me George Bunker Justice peace

Nantucket ss These may certefie all whome it may Concern y[t] Andrew Myrick & Jedidah pinkham of nantucket being publeshed as y[e] Law diricts ware maried January y[e] 23[d] 1728/9 by me George Bunker Justice of peace

Daniel allin & Elezabath Bunker boath of nantucket ware Lafully publeshed & maryed by me on January y[e] 26th 1737/8 George Bunker Justice of peace

Thomas Jenkins & Judeth Folger boath of nantucket being Lafully publeshed ware maried by me 22nd Day of January 1728/9 George Bunker Justice peace

April 23[d] 1731 peter Folger & Christian Swain boath of nantucket being Lafully publeshed ware then maried by me George Bunker Justice of peace

october y[e] 30th 1736 John meeder & Hannah Stewart being Lawfully publeshed ware maried by me George Bunker Justice of y[e] peace for nantucket

December y[e] 27th 1733 Charlse Gardner and Anna Pinkham ware Lafully published being boath of Nantucket and maried by me George Bunker Justice of peace

Sherborn January y[e] 23: 1728/9 Andrew Myrick & Jedidah pinkham boath of nantucket ware Lafully published and maried by me—George Bunker Justice of y[e] peace for nantucket

Sherborn September y[e] 14: 1731 then John Ellis & Dinah williams boath of nantucket being Lafully publeshed ware married by me—George Bunker Justice of peace

November y[e] 29: 1734 then Stephen Swain & Katharin Heath boath of nantucket being publeshed as y[e] Law Directs ware married by me—George Bunker Justice of peace

August y[e] 7th 1735 John Long & Jane Luce boath of Sherborn on nantucket being Legualley Publeshed was then maryed by me—George Bunker Justice of peace

April y[e] 3[d] 1735: then Stephen Kidder and mercy Godfery boath of nantucket being Lawfully Published ware maried by me George Bunker Justice of peace

Nantucket ss october y[e] 28th 1738 then wase Uriah Bunker and Zerviah Pinkham boath of nantucket being lawfully publeshed ware maried by me George Bunker Justice of peace for s[d] County

Nantucket August y[e] 16: 1733

These are Certifie all whome it may Consern y[t] Benjamin Thistin residant on nantucket and Hepzibath Smith of nantucket ware maried being boath Published on nantucket as y[e] Law Diricts—p[r] me George Bunker Justice of peace

August y[e] 16: 1733 James Sheffield and Frances Sanford boat Declared being boath of Road Island y[t] they Did not know y[t] Benjemin thistin had promised marige to any woman or made Sute to any woman there Directly or Indirectly and ware accordingly maried by me George Bunker Justice of peace agust 16: 1733

April ye 27th 1738 then Uriah Gardner and Ruth Bunker boath of Sherborn on nantucket ware maried by me George Bunker Justice of peace

1741 June ye 29th Then Daniel Bunker & Margret Davice boath of Nantucket being lafully publesht ware maried by me George Bunker Justice of peace

1741: November 22 then william oldridg & Abigail pinkham boath of Sherborn on Nantucket being Lafully publeshed ware Maried by me—George Bunker Justice of ye peace for S^{d} County

Nantucket January: 3: y^{t} 1765 Christopher Bunker & Abigail Worth both of Sherborn on Nantucket being Lawfully Published ware married by me Caleb Bunker Justice of the Peace

Nantucket April: 24: y^{t} 1765 Andrew Brock and Eunice Arthur both of Sherborn on Nantucket being Lawfully Published ware marred by me Caleb Bunker Justice of the Peace

Nantucket July: 6 y^{t} 1766 Thomas Andreus residant on Nantucket & mary Burrige of Nantucket ware marred by me being both Published on Nantucket three publick days marrid by me Caleb Bunker Justice of the Peace

Nantucket march: 1^{yt} 1767 Henry Hood & Judith Cattle both of Sherborn on Nantucket being Lawfully Published ware marred by me Caleb Bunker Justice of the Peace

Nantucket March ye 5: 1767 William Mingo & Esther Homeneck both of Sherborn on Nantucket being Lawfully Publiched ware marred by me—Caleb Bunker Justice of the Peace

Nantucket December: 4^{yt} 1767 Reuben Barnard & Phebe Coleman both of Sherborn on Nantucket being Published Six days three of them publick days ware marred by me—Caleb Bunker Justice of the Peace

Nantucket August: 21^{yt} 1768 Jeames Burrage & Rebekah Godfrey both of Sherborn on Nantucket being Published according to Lawfully ware marred by me Caleb Bunker Justice of the Peace

Nantucket December: 28^{yt} 1768 Reuben Morton and Mary Worth both of Sherborn on Nantucket being Published according to Law ware marrid by me Caleb Bunker Justice of the Peace

Nantucket Jenuary: 19th ye 1769 Eliphalet Smith and Deborah Bunker both of Sherborn on Nantucket being Lawfully Publish ware married by me Caleb Bunker Justice of the Peace

Nantucket Apriel: 2^{yt} 1769 Micajah Swain and Eunies Bunker both of Sherborn on Nantucket being Lawfully Publish ware marrid by me Caleb Bunker Justice of the Peace

Nantucket october: 30^{yt} 1769 Jethro Coffin and Margaret Brock both of Sherborn on Nantucket being Lawfully Publish ware Married by me Caleb Bunker Justice of the Peace

Nantucket Jenuary: ye 3^{d} ye 1770 Lot Cattle and Ruth Colman both of Sherborn on Nantucket being Lawfully Publish ware marrid by me Caleb Bunker Justice of the Peace

Nantucket March: 22^{yt} 1770 Zaccheus Coffin and Thankfull Joy both of Sherborn on Nantucket being Lawfully Publish ware marrid by me Caleb Bunker Justice of the Peace

Nantucket November: 30^{yt} 1770 Daniel Smith and Abigail Gorham both of Sherborn on Nantucket being Lawfuly Publish ware marrid by me Caleb Bunker Justic of the Peace

Nantucket December: 17^{yt} 1770 Ebenezer Hussey and Mehetabel Smith both of Sherborn on Nantucket being Lawfuly Publish ware marrid by me Caleb Bunker Justic of the Peace

Nantucket December: 20yt 1770 Elisha Bunker and Margaret Garner both of Sherborn on Nantucket being Lawfuly Publish ware maried by me Caleb Bunker Justic of the Peace

Nantucket May: 12yt 1771

Peleg Coffin and Hephesibah Pinkham both of Sherborn on Nantucket being Lawfully Published ware marred by me Caleb Bunker Justice of the Peace

Nantucket June: 16yt 1771 William Bunker and Abigail Gardner both of Sherborn hath been Published according to Law ware marred by me Caleb Bunker Justice of the Peace

Nantucket october: 15yt 1771 William Ramsdell and Ruth Gardner both of Sherborn on Nantucket hath been Published three Days ware marred by me Caleb Bunker Justic of the Peace

Nantucket October: 20yt 1771 Shubal Gardner and Hephzibah Gardner both of Sherborn on Nantucket hath been published Seven Days ware marred by me Caleb Bunker Justice of the peace

Nantucket October: 27yt 1771 Solomon Bunker and Abigail Coffin both of Sherborn on Nantucket hath been published Seven days ware marred by Caleb Bunker Justice of the peace

Nantucket November 24yt 1771 Grindal Gardner and Judith Hinpenny both of Sherborn on Nantucket hath been Published according to Law ware marred by me Caleb Bunker Justice of the Peace

Nantucket December: 5yt 1771 Soloman Coffin and Eunies Macy both of Sherborn on Nantucket hath been Published according to Law ware marred by me Caleb Bunker Justice of the Peace

Nantucket January: 16yt 1772 Peleg Bunker and Deborah Gorham both of Sherborn on Nantucket hath been published Twelve days ware marred by me Caleb Bunker Justice of the Peace

Nantucket November: 8yt 1772 Edward Lloyd Whittemore and Prissilla Bunker both of Sherborn on Nantucket hath been published according to Law ware marred by me Caleb Bunker Justice of the Peace

Nantucket December: 7yt 1772 William Homes and Lydia Bourage both of Sherborn on Nantucket hath ben Published a Cordin to Law ware marred by me Caleb Bunker Jestic of the Peace

Nantucket June: 14yt 1773 Peter herry and Sarah Dugan to Indians of this Town have been Published ACording to Law ware marred by me Caleb Bunker Justic of the Peace

Nantucket August: 22yt 1773 Bachelor Bunker and Abigail Hussey harth been published according to Law ware marred by me Caleb Bunker Justic of the Peace

Nantucket Sepetember: 5yt 1773 John Worth and Jemima Swain harth been published according to Law ware marred by me. Caleb Bunker Justic of the Peace

Nantucket September: 19yt 1773 Peleg Bunker and Lydia Gardner hath been published according to Law ware marred by me Caleb Bunker Justic of the Peace

Nantucket October: 18yt 1773 Peter Coffin & Marriam Perry hath been published according to Law ware Marred by me Caleb Bunker Justic of the Peace

Nantucket December: 30yt 1773 William Swain and Eunies Barnard hath been published according to Law ware marred by me Caleb Bunker Justice of the Peace

Nantucket July 7^{yt} 1774 Manuel Joseph & Eunies Coffin hath been published according to Law ware marred by me Caleb Bunker Justice of the Peace

Nantucket Sepetember: 29:^{yt} 1774 John Noblee and Eunice Worth hath been published according to Law ware marred by me Caleb Bunker Jestice of the Peace

Nantucket october: 15^{yt} 1774 Charles West & Hephzibah Barnard hath been published according to Law ware marred by me Caleb Bunker Jestice of the Peace

Nantucket october: 27^{yt} 1774 Timothy Swain and Dinah Gardner hath been published acording to Law ware marred by me—Caleb Bunker Jestic of the Peace

Nantucket March: 5^{yt} 1775 Isaiah Maxy and Ruth Bunker hath been published acording to Law ware marred by me Caleb Bunker Jestic of the Peace

Nantucket Apriel: 2^{yt}: 1775 Shubael Gardner and Deborah Ellis hath ben published acording to Law ware marred by me Caleb Bunker Jestic of the Peace

Nantucket June 1 day: 1775 John Wolf and Phebe Godfrey hath been published acording to Law ware marred by me Caleb Bunker Jestic of the Peace

Nantucket: July: 27:^{yt} 1775 William Abrams & Mary Coffin hath been published acording to Law ware marred by me Caleb Bunker Jestic of the Peace

Nantucket August: 3^{yt} 1775 Elihu Miller and Patience Coffin hath been published Acording to Law ware marred by me Caleb Bunker Jestic of the Peace

Nantucket Sepetember: 2^{yt} 1775 Benjamin Bunker & Rebekah Folger hath been published acording to Law ware marred by me Caleb Bunker Jestic of the Peace

Nantucket Sepetember: 7^{yt} 1775 Ebenezer Bunker and Mary Maxy hath been published acording to Law ware marred by me Caleb Bunker Jestic of the Peace

Nantucket Sepetember: 7^{yt} 1775 Elisha Ellis and Anna Swain hath been published acording to Law ware marred by me Caleb Bunker Jestic of the Peace

Nantucket December: 24^{yt} 1775 Abner Coffin and Desire Benthall hath been Lawfully published ware marred by me Caleb Bunker Jestic of the Peace

Nantucket February: 22^{yt} 1776 Nathan Waldron and Patience Coffin both of Sherborn on Nantucket hath been Published according to Law was marred by me Caleb Bunker Justic of the Peace

Nantucket September 1^{dy} y 1776 Paul Paddack and Anna Starbuck hath been Published according to Law was marred by me Caleb Bunker Jestic of the Peace

Nantucket September: 7^{yt} 1776 Barnabas Coleman and Abiel Clark hath been published according to Law was Marred by me Caleb Bunker Jestic of the Peace

Nantucket November: 16^{yt} 1776 John Cartueright and Mary Starbuck hath been published according to Law was marred by me Caleb Bunker Jestic of the Peace

Nantucket June: 8^{yt} 1777 Francis Brown and Deborah Clark hath been published according to Law was marred by me Caleb Bunker Jestic of the Peac

NANTUCKET SUPPLEMENTARY RECORDS

Contributed by MRS. SETH AMES LEWIS of Springfield, Mass.

The following death records were copied from an old book kept by Isaac Coffin of Nantucket, born in 1764, died in 1842. He was a prominent man and was selectman, a state senator and judge of probate.

The book came from the Joseph Hatch Starbuck collection of

Nantucket and is now in the possession of Dr. Amber A. Starbuck of Springfield, Mass., a great-great-granddaughter of the said Isaac Coffin.

These records disclose new names and additional information not found in the printed Vital Records of Nantucket.

DEATHS

1821–1834

ABBEY, Samuel, drowned round Cape Horn, 1834, ae. 24.

ADAMS, ———, ch. of Edmund, Sept. 27, 1833, ae. 1 y. 2 m.

ADAN, Samuel, of Machias, drowned off Nantucket, Mar. 22, 1829.

ADLINGTON, Mary Elizabeth, ch. George, Oct. 26, 1831, ae. 1 y. 1 m.

ALDRICH, ALDRIDGE, Elizabeth, Oct. 28, 1821, ae. 86 y. 3 m.
Ishabod, Oct. 25, 1821, ae. 88 y. 5 m.
John, drowned off Nantucket, from Brig Packet of Providence, R. I., Dec. 3, 1828.
Obed, s. Valentine, Oct. 27, 1833, ae. 3 y. 7 m.
Polly, wid. Obed, in Baltimore, Aug. 22, 1822, ae. 53 y. 3 m.

ALEBAT, Mehitable, Aug. 27, 1822, ae. 19 y. 1 m.

ALLEN, Caleb, s. Daniel, drowned, May, 1824, ae. 44 y. 7 m.
Catharine, w. Silvanus, Sept. 14, 1827, ae. 54 y. 3 m.
Charles Frederick, s. George, Aug. 13, 1831, ae. 3 y. 3 m.
David Meader, s. David, Jr., Sept. 13, 1833, ae. 3 y. 6 m.
Edward, ch. Shubael, Apr. 13, 1822, ae. 1 y. 6 m.
Frederick, s. David, May 24, 1823, ae. 16 y. 7 m.
James Henry, ch. Reuben, Sept. 4, 1825, ae. 1 y. 1 m.
John, Feb. 5, 1822, ae. 67 y. 7 m.
John Nobles, at sea, 1826, ae. 30 y.
Love, w. Caleb, in Baltimore, Sept. 27, 1823, ae. 42 y. 11 m.
Lydia, w. Howard, Jan. 7, 1822, ae. 55 y. 1 m.
Lydia, w. John, in Baltimore, Oct. 23, 1824, ae. 41 y. 4 m.
Naomi, w. Job, in New Bedford, May 20, 1822, ae. 45 y.
Paul, in Baltimore, Aug. 19, 1826, ae. 52 y.
Sarah, dau. Reuben, Aug. 28, 1828, ae. 3 y. 1 m.
Shubael, s. Shubael, Feb. 15, 1833, ae. 1 y. 6 m.
Susan, dau. William & gr. dau. Seth Coleman, in Dartmouth, County of Halifax, Nova Scotia, Jan., 1828, ae. 12 y. 1 m.
Susanna, w. David, Dec. 27, 1822, ae. 56 y. 9 m.
William Howard, s. Howard, killed by Pirates in West Indies, Aug. 15, 1822, ae. 31 y. 6 m.
———, ch. of Benjamin, June 6, 1826, ae. 1 y.
———, s. of George, Aug. 20, 1828, ae. 1 y. 2 m.
———, ch. of David, June 4, 1829, ae. 4 m.
———, s. of Shubael, Sept. 27, 1829, ae. 2 y. 2 m.
———, ch. of Walter, Aug. 19, 1830, ae. 1 y. 6 m.
———, ch. (twin) of George, Mar. 6, 1831, ae. abt. 4 weeks.

ALLEY, Eunice, w. Jacob, July 24, 1823, ae. 85 y. 2 m.
Jacob, Nov. 16, 1823, ae. 83 y. 7 m.
Martha, w. Richard, Dec. 5, 1823, ae. 62 y.
Susanna, 2d, w. Reuben & dau. Brown Coffin, Apr. 9, 1827, ae. 48 y. 11 m.
———, ch. of John, Aug. 4, 1822.
———, dau. of late Capt. Charles, Oct. 6, 1828, ae. 1 y. 3 m.

AMES, Polly, w. Nathan of Barnstable, at Seth Clark's house, Sept. 5, 1831, ae. 24 y. 3 m.
———, wid. Benjamin, Feb. 7, 1824, ae. 89 y. 8 m.

———, the Widow, mother of Samuel & Allen Ames, Aug. 25, 1834, ae. 80 y. 9 m.

ANDREWS, Isaac, s. late Jacob, Dec. 13, 1825, ae. 14 y. 2 m.
Jacob, drowned, July 20, 1823, ae. 52 y. 10 m.
Mary, wid. Abraham, Aug. 22, 1832, ae. 85 y. 11 m.

AREY, George W., in Edgartown, Jan. 14, 1828, ae. 45 y. 1 m.
Capt. Martin, in Pacific Ocean, 1823, ae. 42 y.

ARMINGTON, Abby, dau. Lydia & gr. dau. William Googins, 1832, ae. 2 y. 1 m.
Lydia, dau. William Googins, late of Nantucket, June 5, 1832, ae. abt. 34 y.

ASPINWALL, Hon. William, Apr. 16, 1823, ae. 80 y. 6 m., Surgeon & Physician.

ATWOOD, Samuel, Mar. 4, 1824, ae. 32 y. 11 m.
———, ch. Nathaniel, Sept. —, 1822, ae. 7 m.
———, ch. Nathaniel, June 22, 1825.

AUSTIN, Daniel, s. Jeremiah, in City of Mexico, June 21, 1831, ae. 43 y.
Edward, s. Daniel, on ship board round Cape Horn, 1831, ae. 16 y. 2 m.
Edward, s. George & gr. s. Edward Creasy, on coast of Japan, Oct., 1831, ae. 20 y. 6 m.
George Folger, s. Benjamin, at Saint Jago de Cuba, July 31, 1827, ae. 29 y.
Joseph, s. Daniel, Mar. 22, 1823, ae. 9 y. 9 m.
Phebe, dau. Benjamin, a single woman, Feb. 2, 1832, ae. 71 y.
Susanna, wid. Benjamin, Jan. 14, 1824, ae. 88 y. 8 m.
———, ch. of George Folger, Feb. 8, 1830, ae. 2 y.

AVEREL, AVERELL, Ebenezer Wild, s. Isaac, drowned at Barnstable, buried July 31, 1821, ae. 8 y. 3 m.
Helen Loisa, dau. Isaac, Mar. 17, 1834, ae. 1 y. 6 m.

BACKMORE, James, lost at sea, May 21, 1832.

BACKUS, Alexander M., s. Thomas, Nov. 20, 1833, ae. 1 m.
William H., s. Crocker, Sept. 8, 1827, ae. 4 y. 2 m.
———, ch. of Crocker, Aug. —, 1827, ae. 8 m.

BAILEY, Benjamin, Aug. 20, 1822, ae. 56 y. 5 m.
John of Hanover, Jan. 23, 1823, ae. 71 y. 4 m. Member of the Quaker Society, a Preacher.
John, lost at sea, May 21, 1832.
Sarah G., dau. Rev. Stephen, Nov. 27, 1822, ae. 1 y. 8 m.
Tabitha, wid. John, Jan. 14, 1828, ae. 75 y. 4 m.

BAKER, Abner, s. Lemuel & Abiel, drowned in New York Harbour, Oct. 7, 1829, ae. 25 y.
Eliza, dau. Prince & gr. dau. Isaiah Macey, Sept. 4, 1834, ae. 28 y. 6 m.
Isaac, drowned Feb. 27, 1826, ae. 40 y. 9 m.
Lemuel, h. Abiel Pinkham, d. in Halifax, Nova Scotia, June 22, 1827, ae. 67 y. 3 m.
Ruth, of Bass River, Oct. 13, 1824, ae. 76 y. 1 m.
Thomas, lost overboard on way to Norfolk, Va., Jan., 1828, ae. 21 y. 11 m.
———, ch. of Jesse, Apr. 13, 1833, ae. 1 m.

BALCH, ———, ch. of Simeon, Aug. 4, 1826, ae. 10 m.

BALDWIN, Elijah, Feb. 3, 1825, ae. 42 y. 1 m.
Harriet Chandler, dau. Elijah, Oct. 6, 1825, ae. 1 y. 3 m.

BANNING, Charles Lawrence, s. Jeremiah, at Edgartown while on a visit, Aug. 14, 1834, ae. 10 m.

BARKER, Isaac Parker, s. Samuel, killed by Spaniards at Oreco, South America, 1823, ae. 22 y.
Latham, May 2, 1824, ae. 70 y. 2 m.

Robert, s. Jacob, of New York, d. on passage to Buenos Ayres, Dec. 24, 1830, ae. 26 y. 10 m.
William Coffin, s. James, merchant of New York, Feb. 26, 1824, ae. 33 y. 5 m.

BARNARD, Albert Wyer, ch. Charles H., Oct. 6, 1823, ae. 1 y. 4 m.
Anna, w. Valentine, d. in New York, some years before 1824, ae. 68 y. 9 m. (some years before her husband's death in 1824).
Benjamin, s. Benjamin, Dec. 3, 1830, ae. 49 y. 1 m.
Charles Hussey, s. Obed, d. in Cincinnati, Feb. —, 1831, ae. 39 y. 5 m.
Capt. David, late of Nantucket, d. near Lake Champlain, in Vermont, June —, 1827, ae. 75 y. 9 m.
Edward, shot in the South, Apr. —, 1823, ae. 35 y. 2 m.
Elizabeth, wid. Robert & dau. late Zebulon Whippey, July 9, 1825, ae. 20 y. 1 m.
Eunice, w. Zacheus & dau. William Abrahams, d. at Ohio, July, 1825, ae. 36 y. 4 m.
Eunice, wid. Libni, d. at New Garden, N. C., Jan. 7, 1833, ae. 60 y. 1 m., dau. Paul Coffin of Nantucket.
Henry the Second, s. Josiah, drowned round Cape Horn, Mar. —, 1833, ae. 24 y. 6 m.
John, s. James, Feb. (or Mar.) 4, 1832, ae. 25 y. 1 m.
Libni, s. Jonathan, June 29, 1823, ae. 58 y. 3 m.
Mary, w. Benjamin the Third, dau. Peter Paddock, Apr. 20, 1824, ae. 21 y. 7 m.
Mary Coffin, ch. of Charles, Aug. 17, 1834, ae. 1 y. 6 m.
Peter, of Hudson, N. Y., formerly of Nantucket, Mar. —, 1830, ae. 83 y. 4 m.
Reuben, formerly of Nantucket, at De Ruyter, May 11, 1825, ae. 82 y. 11 m., s. Francis, the old Governor.
Reuben, in ——, N. Y., 1827, ae. 83 y.
Robert, s. Shubael, gr. s. Robert Barnard Lewis, dec'd, gr. s. Widow Nancy Carr of Dunkirk in French Flanders, drowned in New Orleans, Jan. 1, 1825, ae. 24 y. 7 m.
Ruth, wid. Shubael, Mar. 14, 1823, ae. 82 y. 6 m.
Ruth, in Cincinnati, Apr. 1, 1823, ae. 72 y.
Sally, dau. Thomas, Nov. 8, 1821, ae. 19 y. 8 m.
Shubael, June 7, 1822, ae. 92 y. 2 m. 15 d.
Solomon, Nov. 1, 1829, ae. 21 y.
Timothy, s. Mary Barnard & gr. s. John, dec'd, in New York, Jan. 20, 1828, ae. 40 y. 3 m.
Valentine, in New York, Jan. —, 1824, ae. 74 y. 1 m.
Zaccheus, s. Thomas, in Cincinnati, O., formerly of Nantucket, 1833, ae. 53 y.
———, ch. of Shubael, Jr., June 26, 1821, ae. 8 m.
———, ch. of Frederick, July 10, 1827, ae. 8 m.
———, ch. of Edwin, Dec. 5, 1832, ae. 1 y. 10 m.
———, ch. of Edwin, 1833, ae. 10 m.

BARNEY, Ann, w. Peter, at New Bedford, Sept. 19, 1828, ae. 66 y.
Daniel, Jr., s. Daniel, at Mobile, May 20, 1829, ae. 27 y. 10 m.
Jethro Starbuck, s. Nathaniel, Aug. 7, 1832, ae. 9 m.
Rebecca, 2d, w. Paul & dau. Cornelius Howland, at New Bedford, Jan. 18, 1825, ae. 35 y. 10 m.
Thomas Folger, s. Thomas, Sept. 26, 1833, ae. 4 y. 6 m.
William, s. Charles, Dec. 7, 1824, ae. 2 y. 2 m.
———, ch. of Nathaniel, Aug. 22, 1822.
———, w. of David, d. in England, 1824, ae. 38 y. 9 m.
———, ch. of William, Aug. 12, 1826, ae. 1 y.

BARRETT, Benjamin Gardner, s. Peter, Dec. 28, 1823, ae. 4 y. 2 m.
Edward, s. John, on board ship Washington around Cape Horn, 1828, ae. 20 y. 1 m., Feb. —, 1828.
George, on coast of Japan, Nov. 15, 1821, ae. 48 y. 7 m., Master of Ship Independence.

John, around Cape Horn, 1833.
William, s. John, around Cape Horn, 1833, ae. 21 y.

BARTLETT, Mary Lamson, dau. Oliver C., Sept. 19, 1825, ae. 1 m.

BARTON, Mary, dau. Absolam F., July 16, 1831, ae. 1 y. 1 m.

BEARD, William Henry, s. John Barrett, drowned at sea, Mar. 27, 1827, ae. 15 y. 7 m.

BEARSE, Prince, at Hyannis, Aug. 30, 1831, ae. 38 y. 4 m.

BEAUCHAMP, William, at Paoli, Ill., formerly of Nantucket, Nov. 8, 1824, ae. 56 y. A Methodist Preacher.

BEEBEE, Ezra, Oct. 31, 1821, ae. 26 y. 5 m.

BEERS, ———, ch. of Henry, Aug. 9, 1828, ae. 6 m.

BENNARD, Senato, drowned off Nantucket from Brig Packet of R. I., Dec. 3, 1828.

BENNETT, Cynthia, dau. Stephen, June 27, 1823, ae. 36 y. 9 m.
———, ch. of Hiram, Sept. 20, 1833, ae. 1 y. 1 m.

BERRY, John, drowned Jan. 1, 1823, ae. 40 y.

BINGHAM, Martha, of Connecticut, Mar. 11, 1822, ae. 63 y.

BIZZEL, Abigail or Nabby, wid. William & dau. of late Batchelor Swain, Aug. 21, 1830, ae. 56 y. 2 m.

BLACK, Betsey, w. Clovis, Jan. 23, 1831, ae. 55 y. 7 m.
Timothy Coffin, s. Clovis, round Cape Horn, June —, 1823, ae. 24 y.

BLACKWELL, Hannah, w. Benjamin, July 7, 1823, ae. 21 y. 4 m. (in child bed).
Jane, w. Samuel, Apr. 12, 1832, ae. 47 y. 9 m.
Mary, wid. Rowland, Jan. 27, 1825, ae. 84 y. 11 m.

BLANKENSHIP, Betsey, w. Capt. George, in Rochester, May 17, 1833, ae. 70 y.

BLISH, ———, ch. of Abraham, May 1, 1830, ae. 2 m.

BLOOD, George, at sea, 1824, ae. 18 y. 9 m.

BLOSSOM, Samuel, of New Bedford, drowned there, Apr. 14, 1828, ae. 21 y.

BOGGS, Phebe, dau. Francis, Mar. 8, 1831, ae. 18 y.

BONZON, Martin, a Dutchman, June 21, 1828, ae. 60 y. 9 m.

BORDEN, BOURDEN, Edward, May 14, 1822, ae. abt. 45 y.
Elizabeth, wid. Simon, Mar. 21, 1832, ae. 62 y. 7 m.
Susanna, dau. Simon, Jan. 5, 1823, ae. 19 y. 1 m.

BOSTON, John C., s. Charles F., Nov. 26, 1832, ae. 1 y. 7 m.

BOURGOIN, Lewis, lost at sea, May 21, 1832.

BOURNE, Capt. Silas, lost overboard, from Falmouth to Norfolk, 1828, ae. 51 y. 1 m.

BRAYTON, George, s. Robert, in New Bedford, Dec. —, 1827, ae. 27 y. 3 m.
George, s. of the late George & gr. s. Paul Mitchell, May 2, 1828, ae. 1 y. 3 m.
Sarah, wid. Isaac & dau. Paul Hussey & Hannah, suddenly, in Boston, Apr. 16, 1834, ae. 68 y. 2 m.
———, ch. of the late Alexander, Mar. 24, 1832, ae. 1 y. 10 m.

BREED, Harriet, ch. Nathaniel, Sept. 3, 1825, ae. 2 y. 1 m.
Horace Augustus, s. Nathaniel, Sept. 11, 1833, ae. 2 y. 2 m.
Nathaniel, July 1, 1834, ae. 42 y. 2 m., he married Freeman Sherman's daughter.

BRIGGS, Cyrus Peirce, ch. of ——— Briggs, Nov. 8, 1821, ae. 2 y. 6 m.
William C., round Cape Horn, Oct. —, 1831, ae. 36 y. 7 m.

BROCK, Eunice, wid. Andrew, Feb. 21, 1825, ae. 83 y. 1 m.
Frederick, s. John, in the Havanna, July 13, 1828, ae. 25 y. 4 m. Mate of a Brig.
Thomas, Jr., in a mutiny at sea, Mar. 21, 1825, ae. 47 y.
———, ch. of Thomas, Jr., Sept. —, 1821.
———, ch. of Thomas, Jr., May 12, 1825, ae. 1 y. 3 m.
———, ch. of Peleg, Sept. 8, 1825, ae. 1 y.
———, dau. of Priam, Nov. 20, 1831, ae. 6 y. 6 m.

BROOKS, ———, ch. of William, June 10, 1826, ae. abt. 6 m.

BROWN, George, Jr., s. George, on Ship Fabine, abt. Nov. 20, 1830, ae. 16 y. 2 m.
Margaret, dau. George, July 13, 1833, ae. 9 m.
Ruth, Oct. 26, 1831, ae. 1 y., dau. John & gr. dau. William Brown. John married Ruth Folger, dau. Isaac.
Samuel, s. John & gr. s. Freeman Ellis, d. round Cape Horn, Mar. —, 1833, ae. 33 y. 1 m.
Shubael, Nov. 18, 1820, ae. 40 y. 6 m.
William, in Easton, Nov. —, 1821, ae. 80 y. 9 m.
William, s. John & gr. s. Freeman Ellis, killed by a whale on the Brazil Bank, Jan. —, 1828, ae. 23 y. 6 m.
———, ch. of Timothy Coffin, July 9, 1825, ae. abt. 1 y. 4 m.
———, dau. of George, Apr. 24, 1828, ae. 5 m.
———, dau. of Thomas & gr. dau. Isaac Folger, May 7, 1830, ae. 1 y. 8 m.

BRUFF, Jane, wid. Samuel & dau. Nathaniel Whippey, Dec. 31, 1823, ae. 63 y. 4 m.
Rebecca, dau. George, June 8, 1824, ae. 15 y. 11 m.

BULL, Eliza Brown Cartwright, dau. John Brown, July 18, 1833, ae. 21 y. 3 m.

BUNKER, Abigail, dau. Joseph, May 3, 1822, ae. 65 y. 3 m.
Abigail, w. Elijah, in Hudson, N. Y., Apr. 24, 1823, ae. 58 y. 4 m., formerly of Nantucket, dau. Christopher Folger, Sr., dec'd.
Ann, dau. Charles, Sept. 18, 1833, ae. 4 y. 7 m.
Barzillai, in Hudson, N. Y., Aug. —, 1830, ae. 76 y.
Barzillai Burdett, s. Gorham, lost overboard off Cape Horn, May 9, 1825, ae. 15 y. 6 m.
Betsey, wid. John & dau. of late Dr. Samuel Gelston, in Wareham, Jan. 12, 1834, ae. 49 y. 8 m.
Elihu, s. Samuel, at Hudson, where he lived many years, July 6, 1822, ae. 74 y. 6 m.
Elihu Marshall, s. George M., July 1, 1833, ae. 3 y. 6 m.
Emily A., dau. Frederick F., July 6, 1835, ae. 3 y. 2 m.
George, s. William & bro. of Benjamin, at West Chester, N. Y., Sept. 5, 1829, ae. 70 y.
George the 4th, s. Nathaniel, off Shore Ground, Feb. 24, 1822, ae. 28 y. 4 m. Capt. of Ship John Adams.
George C., s. Timothy, June 25, 1828, ae. 12 y. 7 m.
Franklin, s. Owen, in West Indies, Aug. —, 1823, ae. 19 y. 7 m.
James, s. Shubael, in New Bedford, June 25, 1829, ae. 44 y. 6 m.
James Colesworthy, s. Andrew, Sept. 3, 1825, ae. 7 y. 10 m.
John, s. Elijah, of Hudson, formerly of Nantucket, Oct. —, 1821, ae. 30 y. A sailor on a Whaling Voyage round Cape Horn; his mother was Abigail Folger & she was gr. dau. of David Joy, Sr.
John C., at sea round Cape Horn, Sept. —, 1823, ae. 40 y. 9 m.
Josephine, dau. Thomas, May —, 1834, ae. 6 y. 9 m., d. in N. Y.
Lydia, dau. Latham, Aug. 2, 1824, ae. 30 y. 7 m.
Lydia, w. Nathaniel, Apr. 5, 1825, ae. 64 y. 10 m.
Lydia, w. Barzillai, in Hudson, N. Y., Oct. 14, 1826, ae. 69 y. 2 m
Lydia, wid. Shubael, Jr., in New Bedford, June 20, 1833, ae. 76 y., formerly of Nantucket.
Matthew, Aug. 23, 1824, ae. 86 y.

Miriam, w. David, in Hudson, N. Y., abt. two yrs. ago, ae. 76 y. (entry follows one of July 19, 1826).
Miriam, w. Elihu S., formerly of Nantucket, Sept. 14, 1833, ae. 58 y. 4 m.
Nathaniel, s. John, in Hospital, Staten Island, N. Y., Sept. 11, 1824, ae. 31 y. 11 m.
Nathaniel, Jr., at Pensacola, July —, 1826, ae. 34 y. 7 m.; a Lieutenant in United States Service.
Priscilla, ch. Thomas, Oct. 2, 1825, ae. 3 y. 4 m.
Capt. Richard, at Martha's Vineyard, Aug. 27, 1834, ae. 80 y. 4 m.
Robert Folger, s. Samuel, Aug. 19, 1826, ae. 1 y. 5 m.
Sarah Ann, dau. Henry C., at Falmouth, Aug. 18, 1832, ae. 6 y.
Thomas, s. Thomas, Mar. 13, 1827, ae. 2 y. 2 m.
William, Jr., s. William, in West Indies, July —, 1825, ae. 26 y. 1 m.
William Henry, ch. Capt. Samuel, Oct. 1, 1833, ae. 5 y. 3 m.
William P., lost overboard, Apr. 28, 1832, ae. 21 y.
———, ch. of George F., Nov. 13, 1821, ae. 3 y.
———, ch. of Henry C., Jan. 20, 1824, ae. 1 y. 3 m.
———, ch. of Joshua, Aug. 9, 1829, ae. 5 m.
———, ch. of Obed, Nov. 5, 1831, ae. 7 m.
———, ch. of Capt. Samuel, Aug. 27, 1833, ae. 1 y. 7 m.
———, son of Thomas, in New York, May —, 1834, ae. 1 y. 6 m.

BURDETT, Edward, s. Reuben, drowned in Pacific Ocean, Nov. 15, 1833, ae. 28 y.
Hannah, w. William, Jan. 21, 1824, ae. 25 y. 11 m.

BURGES, BURGESS, Lemuel, drowned Nov. 20, 1828, ae. 53 y.
Rosilla, dau. Nathaniel, Oct. 2, 1828, ae. 18 y. 1 m.
———, ch. of Weston, Oct. 24, 1833, ae. 2 y.

BURNELL, Eliza Myrick, oldest ch. of Jonathan, Nov. 13, 1823, ae. 4 y.

BURRELL, Deborah Moreton, dau. Judith & gr. dau. Taber Moreton, Jan. 17, 1832, ae. 70 y. 4 m.

BURROWS, Deborah, w. James Davis & dau. George Manter, Dec. 25, 1833, ae. 33 y. 3 m.

BUTLER, Elizabeth, wid. Zebulon, formerly of Nantucket, now of Amherst, N. H., Mar. —, 1822, ae. 64 y.
Silas, 1825, ae. 22 y., around Cape Horn.
———, ch. of Thomas, Sept. 6, 1843, ae. 9 m.

CALDER, Charles, s. Robert, May —, 1824, ae. 29 y. 9 m.
James, s. Thomas, July 14, 1822, ae. 3 y. 4 m.

CALLOWAY, Robert, h. of Anna Holmes, Nov. 22, 1829, ae. 47 y. 6 m.

CAMPBELL, Loisa, w. William, at Sydney, Co. Kennebeck, Oct. 11, 1832, ae. 25 y. 8 m.

CANNON, Mary Ann, dau. Humphrey, Dec. 31, 1832, ae. 14 y. 6 m.

CARLOT, Lewis, son-in-law to Elijah Swift of Falmouth, drowned, Jan. 28, 1825, ae. 31 y. 7 m.

CARNES, Thomas, drowned from Sloop Meteor, on passage from here to New Orleans, Mar. —, 1831, ae. 35 y. 9 m.
———, ch. of Thomas, Apr. 27, 1828, ae. 5 m.

CARPENTER, Dr. Amos, in Gent, N. Y., Aug. 14, 1832, 78 y. 9 m., he has several daus. married in Nantucket.

CARR, James W., Oct. 10, 1831, ae. 28 y. 2 m., d. at the North Shore.
Joseph, s. Moses, July 19, 1826, ae. 2 y. 1 m.
Mary Ann B., dau. Moses, 1831, ae. 3 y.
Warren, Oct. 10, 1831, ae. 26 y.
———, ch. of Obed S., Sept. 11, 1828, ae. 4 m.

CARTER, Dorcas, w. John, Oct. 31, 1824, ae. 41 y. 4 m.

CARTWRIGHT, Charles W., s. Charles W., & gr. s. of John, Aug. 19, 1830, ae. 16 y., in Boston.
Elizabeth, wid. Thomas, at New Haven, June 17, 1831, ae. 50 y. 3 m.; she lived there with her son David.
———, ch. of Joseph B., Oct. 11, 1826, ae. 3 m.

CARY, Charles, s. Edward, Sr., Mar. —, 1829, ae. 39 y. 6 m., on passage from New Orleans to New York.

CASWELL, John R., 1824, ae. 36 y. 9 m., on coast of Japan.

CATHCART, Alexander C., s. Arial, Aug. 9, 1833, ae. 4 y. 3 m.
Ann Eliza, dau. Ariel & Eliza, Aug. 21, 1834, ae. 3 m.
Frederick B., s. Ariel, Aug. 24, 1833, ae. 1 y. 6 m.
Hephzibah, dau. Ariel, June 10, 1826, ae. 5 m.
Hugh, of Martha's Vineyard, July 10, 1824, ae. 78 y. 9 m.
Joseph, Feb. 3, 1823, ae. 75 y. 8 m.
Leander, Apr. 2, 1823, ae. 15 y. 5 m., off cost of Chile.
Peggy, w. Jonathan & dau. Bryant Gall & gr. dau. Molly Quinn, Apr. 16, 1834, ae. 62 y. 4 m., in Fall River.
Robert, s. Gershom & h. of Polly Swain, dau. of David Swain, June 20, 1833, ae. 55 y. 10 m., in Boston.
William, at Mobile, Aug. 27, 1822, ae. 45 y. 4 m.
William Jenkins, s. George, Aug. 16, 1830, ae. 10 m.
———, ch. of Zimri, Oct. 12, 1822, ae. 1 y. 4 m.
———, ch. of Obed, Aug. 10, 1827, ae. 6 m.
———, ch. of Zimri, July 30, 1828, ae. 9 m.
———, ch. of Robert, June 25, 1829, ae. 3 m.
———, ch. of George, Aug. 27, 1830, ae. 10 m.
———, ch. of William, Jan. 21, 1832, ae. 5 weeks.
———, ch. of William H., Jan. 24, 1832, ae. 2 m.

CENTER, ———, ch. of Edward H., July 14, 1826, ae. 5 m.

CHADWICK, Alexander Baker, s. David, Oct. 7, 1825, ae. 6 y. 6 m.
Anna, wid. Antonio & mother of Antonio, Oct. 18, 1823, ae. 62 y. 3 m.
Benjamin, s. Wickliffe, Mar. 8, 1832, ae. 52 y., drowned in Boston.
David, Feb. 13, 1827, on coast of Africa.
George, s. Wickerlief, 1822, ae. 30 y. 4 m., lost off coast of Ireland.
Joseph, s. David, 1829, ae. 40 y. 4 m., round Cape Horn.
Lydia, wid. John, July 4, 1823, ae. 78 y. 11 m., at Falmouth.
———, ch. of David, Jr., Jan. 29, 1831, ae. 3 y.
———, ch. of Oliver, Aug. 2, 1834, ae. 1 y.

CHASE, Benjamin, s. Jonathan, Jan. —, 1822, ae. 37 y. 2 m.
Benjamin, s. Jonathan, 1830, ae. 46 y., at sea.
Betsey, dau. Joseph, Jr., Mar. 18, 1822, ae. 18 y. 1 m.
Charles Frederick, s. Capt. Paul, Nov. 4, 1833, ae. 3 wks.
Eliza, dau. George Brown Chase, formerly of Nantucket, d. in Auburn, July 16, 1834, ae. 20 y. 8 m.
Elizabeth, w. Charles of Lynn & sister to Dr. Paul Swift & Seth Swift, June 21, 1832, ae. 30 y., at Sandwich.
Eunice, w. Benjamin Coffin Chase & dau. Peter Paddock, Mar. 18, 1828, ae. 28 y. 7 m., at Sidney, Maine.
Franklin B., s. Urial, Sept. 2, 1832, ae. 32 y., in New Bedford.
Frederick S., s. Capt. Owen, Aug. 19, 1829, ae. 1 y.
George Franklin, s. Paul, Oct. 23, 1828, ae. 1 y. 6 m.
George Parker, s. Henry, Oct. 23, 1833, ae. 4 y. 9 m.
George Washington, s. Paul, Sept. 28, 1830, ae. 3 m.
Hephzibah, w. Capt. Shubael, Aug. 3, 1824, ae. 33 y. 6 m.
Capt. Isaac, Jan. 3, 1831, ae. 25 y. 6 m. Capt. of Brig Moscow.
Jonathan, Nov. 13, 1821, ae. 68 y. 4 m.
Mary, dau. Thomas, Sept. 4, 1822, ae. 58 y. 10 m.

Capt. Paul, s. Francis, Sr., Nov. —, 1833, ae. 50 y. 3 m., formerly of Nantucket, d. in New Orleans.
Peter Gardner, s. Reuben, Feb. 18, 1821, ae. 33 y.
Rowland B., s. late Peter G., 1832, ae. 21 y., d. on Charles Island, one of the Gallipogos Islands.
———, ch. of Benjamin Wheelwright, Nov. 10, 1821, ae. 2 y. 6 m.
———, dau. of Reuben, Apr. 16, 1828, ae. 6 m.
———, ch. of Joseph, Sept. 11, 1828, ae. 10 m.
———, ch. of Shubael, Jan. 24, 1831, ae. abt. 3 y.

CHILDS, Mary, wid., Aug. 29, 1831, ae. 83 y. 3 m., in Barnstable.
William D., Feb. 1, 1824, ae. 43 y. 4 m., in Portsmouth, N. H.
———, wife of James, dau. of Alvin Crocker, Apr. 29, 1828, ae. 48 y. 9 m., in Barnstable.

CLAPP, ———, ch. of Timothy, Sept. 17, 1829, ae. 1 y. 6 m.

CLARK, Benjamin, s. Uriah, 1827, ae. 24 y. 9 m., round Cape Horn.
Charles, Aug. 31, 1823, ae. 32 y. 6 m. Master of a Ship from New Orleans.
Charles, s. William of Chilmark, stabbed on board ship John Jay of Nantucket, Jan. 28, 1828, lived 17 days, ae. 24 y. 6 m. Married at the Vineyard, left one child.
Daniel, Apr. 15, 1823, ae. 78 y. 3 m., in Hudson.
Eliza, w. Henry & dau. Tristram Folger, Sept. 19, 1825, ae. 26 y., in Cincinnati, Ohio.
George H., s. George, Aug. 19, 1823, ae. 17 y. 11 m.
Mary (Molly), dau. William, 1826, ae. abt. 63 y. 6 m.
Stephen, s. Albert, June —, 1825, ae. 18 y. 6 m.
Thomas, drowned, June —, 1825, ae. 22 y.
Thomas A., s. Thomas M. & Eliza G., Oct. 9, 1833, ae. 1 y. 2 m.
———, s. Alexander, June 10, 1830, ae. 3 y. 2 m., drowned at E. Falmouth.
———, ch. of Charles, Aug. 5, 1831, ae. 6 m.
———, ch. of John & Betsey (Wing), Jan. 31, 1834, ae. 3 y. 6 m.

CLASBY, Charles, July 17, 1821, ae. 46 y., in Cincinnati.
Charles Wesley, s. Benjamin, May 8, 1831, ae. 2 y. 2 m.
Frederick, s. Joseph, dec'd, 1832, ae. 40 y., carried away with a whale line, between New York and Cape Verd Islands.
James, s. Benjamin, Apr. 20, 1831, ae. 6 y. 1 m., in New Bedford.
Louiza, dau. Reuben, Feb. 12, 1825, ae. 20 y. 1 m.
Loviza, dau. Reuben, Jan. 16, 1825, ae. 19 y.
Nancy Myrick, ch. William, June 6, 1828, ae. 10 m.

CLEAVES, ———, ch. of Benjamin Mack, Jan. 24, 1822, ae. abt. 2 y.

CLISBY, Elizabeth, w. Seth, July 11, 1824, ae. 33 y.
Nancy, dau. William & Hephzibah, Mar. 1, 1827, ae. 45 y. 6 m.

COBB, George, s. William, Jr., Aug. —, 1828, ae. 15 y., on Brazil Bank.
Leander, s. Nathaniel, Dec. 7, 1828, ae. 8 m.

COD, Coffin, s. Peggy, 1833, ae. 24 y. Around Cape Horn.
Nicholas Coffin, 1833, around Cape Horn.

COFFIN, Abigail, wid. Elias, Sept. 29, 1823, ae. 80 y. 9 m.; she d. in Boston where she lived with her dau. Peggy Cod, who was dau. Maj. Josiah Coffin, Esq.
Abigail, wid., Mar. 29, 1828, ae. 77 y. 9 m., in Boston.
Abigail, w. Capt. Seth, July 9, 1833, ae. 31 y. 7 m., near Cape Sable.
Alexander S., s. Benjamin F., gr. s. Capt. Jonathan, in West Indies or Gibraltar Bay, Mar. —, 1822, ae. 27 y. 10 m.
Andrew Jackson, s. John Foster & gr. s. Isaac, Dec. 27, 1827, ae. 6 y. 7 m.
Anna, wid. Thomas, May —, 1827, having come here from Philadelphia for a visit.
Avis A., dau. George B., 1831, ae. 17, in Hudson, N. Y.
Caleb S., s. Shubael, June 4, 1829, ae. 62 y., in Athens, N. Y.

Caroline, dau. John Foster, Aug. 31, 1827, ae. 1 y. 1 m. 24 days, in New York.
Charles, Oct. 26, 1821, ae. 17 y. 8 m.
Charles Frederick, s. Alexander, Nov. 19, 1833, ae. 5 y. 3 m.
Charles H., s. James G., Jan. 15, 1832, ae. 1 y. 4 m.
Charles J., s. Job, June —, 1829, ae. 19 y., in Hudson, N. Y.
Cromwell, s. Philip, killed by a Spermaceti whale on coast of Japan, Mar. —, 1823, ae. 26 y. 1 m.
Capt. Daniel, s. Daniel, murdered by his vessel's crew, Feb. or Mar., 1827, ae. 35 y. 6 m.
Capt. David, s. John, Aug. 23, 1833, ae. 50 y., in Springfield, O.
Deborah, w. Timothy, Nov. 9, 1824, ae. 35 y. 1 m., in New York.
Delia Maria, dau. Capt. Joshua, Dec. 18, 1833, ae. 1 y. 4 m.
Capt. Eddy, late Master of Ship Richard Mitchell of Nantucket, d. at Edgartown, Mar. 21, 1829, ae. 29 y. 6 m.
Elenor, w. Dr. Nathaniel, Sept. 10, 1822, ae. 70 y., at Portland, Me.
Elihu, s. Benjamin, June 30, 1825, ae. 78 y. 7 m., at Biddeford, Me.
Eliza, dau. Silvanus & Judith, gr. dau. Barzillai Macy, great-gr. dau. Caleb Macey, dec'd, Oct. 10, 1825, ae. 18 y. 1 m.
Elizabeth, w. Latham, Oct. 18, 1822, ae. 57 y. 11 m.
Elizabeth, wid. Joseph the Painter, Oct. 8, 1829, ae. 81 y. 3 m.
Francis, s. Francis, gr. s. Richard, May —, 1828, ae. 60 y., in New York City
Francis, s. Capt. Francis, lost at sea, 1831.
Frederick, Dec. 4, 1823, ae. 29 y. 3 m., at Martha's Vineyard.
Frederick Henry (or Frederick William), s. Capt. Alexander, Mar. 17, 1832, ae. 59 y., in Extreville, S. C., formerly of Nantucket.
Frederick William, s. Benjamin, Esq., Aug. 22, 1821, ae. 12 y. 3 m.

NANTUCKET SUPPLEMENTARY RECORDS

Contributed by MRS. SETH AMES LEWIS of Springfield, Mass.

DEATHS

COFFIN, George Fearing, s. Timothy G., Feb. 2, 1828, ae. 1 m., at New Bedford.
George Folger, s. of the late Benjamin, May 15, 1828, ae. 25 y. 9 m.
George Gardner, s. Barnabas, Mar. 24, 1825, ae. abt. 6 m
George Gorham, s. Simeon, June 29, 1822, ae. 33 y. 1 m.
Gideon, s. Barnabas, July 29, 1825, ae. 2 y. 10 m.
Hannah, dau. Shubael, July 29, 1824, ae. 29 y. 2 m., in Providence, R. I., late of Nantucket.
Hephzibah, w. Zephaniah & dau. Jonathan Bunker, Mar. 15, 1828, ae. 78 y. 7 m., at Ghent, N. Y.
Jacob, s. William of Easton, abt. 1827, ae. 63 y., at Lysander, N. Y.
Jared, Apr. 10, 1831, ae. 77 y., in Hudson, N. Y.
Job, s. Jethro, May 8, 1832, ae. 57 y. 11 m.
John Hussey, s. Daniel, Esq., Oct. 22, 1821, ae. 23 y. 1 m.
Joseph, a Cannaccak Indian, June 16, 1832, ae. 24 y.
Judith, w. Capt. David, Nov. 17, 1827, ae. 50 y. 2 m., in Galliopolis, Ohio.
Judith, wid. Silvanus & dau. Barzillai Macey, Jan. 22, 1829, ae. 41 y. 1 m.
Kezia, dau. Timothy, Nov. 30, 1822, ae. 7 y. 4 m.
Lydia, dau. Reuben, Jan. 11, 1828, ae. 15 y. 6 m.
Lydia Beard, dau. William Russell, Sept. 23, 1832, ae. 2 y
Mary, w. or wid. Stephen, Oct. 12, 1822, ae. 86 y.
Mary, dau. Zimri, Sept. 10, 1825, ae. 18 y. 11 m.
Mary, w. Uriel & dau. Daniel Pinkham, Sept. 11, 1829, ae. 58 y. 6 m., in New Britain, formerly of Nantucket.
Mary Ann, dau. Alfred, Sept. —, 1821.
Mary Foster, dau. John Foster, June 26, 1825, ae. 2 y. 1 m. 13 d., in New York.
Matilda, wid. Matthew, sometime past, ae. 77 y. 4 m., in Pennsylvania (Feb. 1830, date of entry).
Noah, s. Stephen, July 3, 1825, ae. 63 y. 8 m., in Cooperstown, N. Y., formerly of Nantucket.
Obadiah, lost at sea, Sept. 26, 1821.
Obed, s. Samuel, June 4, 1832, ae. 75 y., at Martha's Vineyard.
Pardon Cook, s. William, Feb. 13, 1827, ae. 23 y. 8 m., on coast of Africa.
Paul, s. Zephaniah, June —, 1829, ae. 86 y. at Oblang [?].
Peter Fosdick, s. Henry, July 11, 1823, ae. 42 y. 8 m.
Phebe, dau. Nathaniel, Jan. 2, 1824, ae. 51 y. 4 m.
Polly, w. Job, Oct. 20, 1821, ae. 44 y. 10 m.
Reuben, s. John, dec'd, Aug. 13, 1825, ae. 1 y. 3 m.
Reuben, s. Capt. Francis, lost at sea, 1831.
Reuben Swain, s. Jared, June 20, 1824, ae. 1 y. 5 m.
Robert Inat, s. Absolam, 1826, ae. 24 y., round Cape Horn.

Robert Jenkins, s. Job B. & gr. s. Stephen, Feb. 3, 1828, ae. 22 y. 3 m., in Hudson.
Rowland C., s. John Foster, Apr. 22, 1834, ae. 1 y. 4 m.
Sally, wid. Thomas C., May 8, 1833, ae. 75 y. 6 m., in Edgartown.
Sarah, dau. Thomas, Jr., Apr. 26, 1824, ae. 33 y., in Philadelphia (fell down stairs).
Sarah, w. Benjamin Franklin & dau. Capt. David Harris, Feb. 27, 1827, ae. 24 y. 10 m.
Seth, s. Gideon, Oct. 15, 1829, ae. 21 y. 4 m., in Cuba.
Seth Macy, s. Barzillai, May —, 1824, ae. 21 y. 3 m.
Shubael, Nov. 7, 1821, ae. 68 y. 9 m.
Sophia Whitfield, dau. Jethro, Sept. 20, 1832, ae. 3 y. 1 m.
Susan, ch. Jesse, Nov. 8, 1821, ae. 2 y.
Susan, w. Uriah of Edgartown, Aug. 25, 1826, ae. 42 y. 7 m.
Susanna, w. Paul, June —, 1829, ae. 83 y., at Oblang.
Thomas, s. Gilbert, Aug. 20, 1825, ae. 2 y. 6 m.
Uriah, Sept. 23, 1823, ae. 72 y. 6 m., at Hudson, formerly of this place.
Uriah, s. Hezekiah, Feb. 14, 1830, ae. 78 y. 6 m., at New Paltz, formerly of Nantucket.
Uriel, s. Paul, Feb. 21, 1831, ae. 64 y. 4 m., in Chatham near Hudson, late of Nantucket. He married Mary Pinkham, dau. Daniel of Hudson.
Valentine Cook, s. William, Jan. 30, 1825, ae. 40 y., in Charleston, S. C., on way to West Indies.
William, s. William, Jr., Sept. 26, 1827, ae. 2 m.
Capt. William, great-gr. s. Tristram Coffin, May 23, 1828, ae. 26 y. 9 m., in Portsmouth.
William Allen, s. George Bunker, 1831, ae. 24 y., in Hudson, N. Y.
William Henry, s. Valentine & gr. s. William, drowned near New Bedford river, Nov. 20, 1828, ae. 14 y.
William P., s. James Josiah, July —, 1822, ae. 34 y. 6 m., at Batavia; Master of a Ship.
Zenas, s. Charles G., June 3, 1829, ae. 4 m.
Zephaniah, s. Zephaniah, June 4, 1829, ae. 82 y.
Zoraide N., dau. Timothy, Aug. —. 1823, ae. 23 y. 4 m., at Edgartown
———, ch. of Edward, Oct. —, 1821.
———, ch. of William Barnard, Aug. 7, 1821, ae. abt. 8 m.
———, ch. of Reuben, Aug. 26, 1822, ae. 2 y.
———, ch. of Job C., Oct. 9, 1822, ae. 1 y. 5 m.
———, ch. of William Russell, July 24, 1823, ae. 1 y. 8 m.
———, ch. of Caleb, Oct. 11, 1823, ae. 2 y. 1 m.
———, ch. of Barnabas, Mar. 23, 1825, ae. 5 m.
———, ch. of Barnabas, July 29, 1825, ae. 2 y. 10 m.
———, ch. of Iriah, Aug. 17, 1825, ae. 8 m.
———, ch. of Gorham, Sept. 26, 1825, ae. 10 m.
———, ch. of Job C., Jan. —, 1826, ae. 1 y.
———, ch. of William Henry, June 6, 1828, ae. 4 m.
———, ch. of Prince, June 21, 1828, ae. 1 y. 2 m.
———, ch. of William Russell, Apr. 18, 1829, ae. 1 m.
———, ch. of Asa, Aug. 11, 1832, ae. 2 y.
———, ch. of Elijah, Sept. 21, 1833, ae. 2 y. 1 m.
———, ch. of James Munroe, Apr. 15, 1834, ae. 9 m.

COGGESHALL, Caleb, in New York sometime past, ae. 65 y. (entry dated Jan., 1824).
James, s. Gideon of New Bedford, Nov. 25, 1833, ae. 32 y.

COLBURN, Frederick Riddell, s. Samuel, Nov. 5, 1827, ae. 2 y.

COLEMAN, Abdeel, Nov. 16, 1824, ae. 42 y. 9 m., a Methodist Preacher.
Alexander, s. Barnabas, lost at sea, 1825–6.
Alexander, s. Barnabas C., not heard from since he sailed July 9, 1825, ae. 32 y.
Barnabas, Apr. 26, 1822, ae. 71 y. 10 m.
Betsey, dau. Gardner, Jan. 6, 1832, ae. 29 y. 11 m., she was a Quaker.

Charles, s. Jethro, Nov. 12, 1821, ae. 74 y.
Charles, s. David, Apr. 10, 1824, ae. 40 y. 11 m., in Cuba.
Christopher, Oct. —, 1824, ae. 69 y. 7 m., round Cape Horn.
Edward, s. Gardner, Sept. 11, 1825, ae. 11 y. 1 m.
Edwin S., s. Frederick William, lost at sea 1830, ae. 18 y. 4 m.
Eliza Collins, d. Samuel, Apr. 9, 1831, ae. 30 y. 6 m., at Hopkinton, R. I.
Elizabeth, wid. Elihu, July —, 1825, ae. 83 y. 4 m., in Hudson.
Elizabeth, w. Zebulon & dau. of late Edward Creasy, Apr. 27, 1829, ae. 26 y. 10 m.
Eunice Coffin, dau. Frederick Brown & gr. dau. Isaac Coffin, Apr. 18, 1829, ae. 3 m.
Capt. John, s. Ebenezer, Dec. 2, 1822, ae. 39 y. 2 m., in Tampico, Fla., or Bay of Mexico.
Phebe, dau. Capt. Samuel, late of Nantucket, Nov. 18, 1833, ae. 28 y. 4 m., in Ghent, N. Y.
Robert B., s. Samuel B., Aug. 23, 1834, ae. 6 m.
Samuel, s. Tristram, Sept. —, 1824, ae. 4 y. 2 m.
Samuel, Mar. 12, 1825, ae. 52 y. 6 m., in Chatham, N. Y.
Sarah, w. Prince, Jan. 28, 1824, ae. 66 y.
Seth, Mar. 26, 1822, ae. 77 y. 9 m.
Sukey or Susanna, wid. Henry & dau. Jonathan Harris, Mar. 6, 1823, ae. 51 y. 3 m.; her mother was James Whippey's daughter.
Susan Bunker, dau. George S. & gr. dau. James Bunker & John Coleman, Aug. 22, 1832, ae. 4 y. 8 m.
William Myrick, ch. of Tristram & Eunice (Coffin), Sept. 4, 1833, ae. 2 y.
William, Sr., Jan. 7, 1823, ae. 74 y. 5 m.
———, ch. of Gorham, Sept. —, 1822, ae. 1 y. 7 m.
———, ch. of Job 2d, Oct. 14, 1822, ae. 3 m.
———, s. of Job, May 15, 1828, ae. 3 m.
———, one of the twins of Tristram, June 9, 1828, ae. 6 m.
———, ch. of Zenas, Oct. 16, 1828, ae. 1 y. 1 m.
———, ch. of Benjamin Allen, July 21, 1829, ae. 6 m.
———, ch. of John Franklin, Aug. 29, 1829, ae. 4 y. 2 m.

COLESWORTHY, Alexander Gardner, s. Jonathan, lost overboard from Brig Napolian, Oct. 1, 1830, ae. 28 y. 2 m.
Charles, Nov. —, 1827, ae. 40 y. 9 m., on passage from Mobile to New York.
Hephzibah, wid. Jonathan, Jan. 19, 1827, ae. 79 y. 1 m.
Louisa, w. Hiram of Nantucket, Mar. 13, 1831, ae. 23 y. 2 m., in New York.
Thomas M., s. John, lost at sea, May 21, 1832, ae. 23 y. 7 m.
———, ch. of Hiram, Aug. 13, 1831, ae. 10 m.

COLLINGWOOD, ———, ch. of William, Oct. 7, 1821, ae. abt. 18 m.

COLLINS, John, Apr. 2, 1823, off coast of Chile.
Phebe, w. Stephen, in Dartmouth, Nova Scotia, 1831, dau. Reuben Coffin, s. of Tristram who d. in North Carolina.
Stephen, in Dartmouth, Nova Scotia, 1831.
William, Apr. 29, 1831, ae. 34 y. 3 m., son-in-law of Samuel Coleman.
———, ch. of William, June —, 1823, ae. 1 y. 3 m.

CONE, Eliza, drowned on board sloop Iris, Sept. 29, 1823, ae. 20 y. 3 m., she belonged to East Haddam, Conn.

CONGDON, Caleb, June —, 1852, ae. 65 y. 6 m., in New Bedford.

COOMBS, Daniel Myrick, s. Daniel & Lydia, gr. ch. Lydia Adlington, July 21, 1829, ae. 2 y. 2 m.

COON, ———, ch. of William, June 27, 1824, ae. abt. 3 weeks.

CORNELL, Lydia, w. William, May 25, 1828, ae. 51 y. 8 m., in Cincinnati.

COTTLE, Frederick William, s. Shubael, Sept. 9, 1825, ae. 2 y. 1 m.
Ruth, wid. Lot, Sept. 18, 1824, ae. 74 y. 3 m.

COTTON, Josiah, Feb. 5, 1822, ae. 42 y. 9 m., in Plymouth.
———, ch. of John, gr. ch. Samuel Burrell, Jan. 24, 1832, ae. 6 m.

COVEL, Obed, drowned Apr. 1, 1825, ae. 20 y. 9 m.

CROCKER, Abiah, mother of Nailer, June —, 1823, ae. 78 y. 4 m., in Barnstable.
Cynthia, w. Zeno & dau. William Bennett, lately of Sandwich, Aug. 23, 1833, ae. 26 y. 9 m.
Fear, w. Joshua, Sept. 14, 1833, ae. 75 y. 1 m., at Cotuit.
Joseph, Nov. 21, 1824, ae. 68 y., in the Southern States.
Miss Rhoda, Aug. 26, 1831, ae. 25 y. 3 m., in Falmouth.
Robinson, Nov. 21, 1824, ae. 51 y., of Falmouth, d. in the Southern States.
Seth, s. Isaiah, Aug. —, 1833, ae. 31 y., in New Orleans.
Timothy, Nov. 8, 1827, ae. 41 y.
———, ch. of Luther, June 20, 1831, ae. 1 m.
———, ch. of Luther & gr. ch. Capt. Isaac Hodges, Dec. 21, 1831, ae. 1 y. 6 m.

CROSBY, Charlottee E., w. George L., June 30, 1834, ae. 25 y. 11 m., formerly of Nantucket, d. in Pittsburg, Pa.
———, ch. of John & ——— (Coleman), Sept. 5, 1833, ae. 6 m.

CURTIS, ———, ch. of Edward H., Feb. 5, 1825, ae. 9 m.

CUSHMAN, Benjamin, s. Caleb, Sept. 1, 1823, ae. 11 m.
Nancy, first wife of Jabez, Oct. 7, 1831, ae. 45 y. 5 m.
Sally, dau. Caleb, Sept. 3, 1823, ae. 4 y. 5 m.
Sarah, w. Caleb & dau. John Green, Apr. 8, 1824, ae. 24 y. 3 m.
———, s. of Caleb, Apr. 23, 1833, ae. 3 y.

DAGGETT, Jethro, Jan. 22, 1832, ae. 70 y. 4 m., at Rye, N. Y.
Silas, drowned in Vineyard Sound, Nov. —, 1825, ae. 70 y.

DAVIS, Amasa, Quarter Master General, Feb. 2, 1825, ae. 75 y. 2 m., in Boston.
Catharine T., dau. Job C., Sept. 9, 1825, ae. 23 y. 9 m.
James, Jan. 18, 1825, ae. 80 y. 11 m., a Quaker Preacher, d. in New Bedford.
James Newton, s. Lathrop, Nov. —, 1826, ae. 3 m., in Barnstable.
John, Judge of Probate in Barnstable, Mar. 27, 1825, ae. 81 y. 3 m.
Oliver, Oct. 7, 1822, ae. 33 y. 2 m., at Edgartown.

DAYTON, Charles, s. Nehemiah, Aug. 4, 1822, ae. 12 y.
———, ch. of Nehemiah, Aug. 29, 1821.

DELANO, Capt. Abishai, s. Thomas, Oct. 10, 1831, ae. 67 y. 6 m., in Charlestown, N. H.

DERRICK, John, Aug. 4, 1824, ae. 57 y. 3 m., a Flemish cooper.

DEXTER, Gideon (and his brother), frozen to death, in Buzzard's Bay, Feb. —, 1827, ae. 42 y. 9 m., brother, ae. 40 y. 4 m.

DICKINSON, Thomas, May —, 1827, ae. 71 y. 6 m., in North Carolina.

DIMMICK, Hon. Joseph, Sept. 28, 1822, ae. 88 y. 9 m., in Falmouth.

DIXON, Robert, May 29, 1824, ae. abt. 49 y. 6 m.

DORRANCE, Lewis, May 18, 1834, ae. 22 y.

DOUGHLAS, Sabrina, Dec. 19, 1825.

DOW, Reuben, Feb. 16, 1822, ae. 47 y. 8 m.
———, ch. of Alexander, Sept. 28, 1825.

DREW, George, s. Benjamin, 1825, ae. 31 y., around Cape Horn.

DUNHAM, Maria, w. George, 1823, ae. 22 y. 6 m.
———, ch. of Daniel, Dec. 31, 1821, ae. abt. 3 weeks.
———, s. Harrison Gray Otis, Sept. 27, 1825, ae. 1 y. 7 m.

DUNNEMAN, Mercy, w. Daniel, Apr. 22, 1823, ae. 32 y. 9 m.

EASTON, Charles Starbuck, s. Charles, Feb. 16, 1823, ae. 3 y. 3 m.
David, s. Peleg, lost at sea, Sept. —, 1829, ae. 39 y. 4 m.
Harriet R., dau. William R., Nov. 30, 1833, ae. 3 y.
Mary H., dau. George, Dec. 28, 1824, ae. 5 y. 11 m.
Matthew Barnard, s. Peleg, Aug. 16, 1833, ae. 13 y. 6 m.
Reuben Starbuck, s. Frederick, Sept. —, 1822, ae. 6 y. 2 m.
———, ch. of Charles, Nov. 25, 1823, ae. 1 y. 6 m.
———, ch. of Frederick, May 22, 1827, ae. 4 m.
———, ch. of James, Oct. 10, 1831, ae. 2 y.

EDDY, Caleb, a stranger, Apr. 2, 1823, off the coast of Chile.

EDWARDS, Samuel, s. Dea. Joseph of Mattapoisett, Dec. 20, 1831, ae. 18 y. 4 m., in Valparaiso.
Sarah Perry, w. Lewis & dau. Samuel Perry, Apr. 11, 1827, ae. 38 y. 7 m., in Washington.
———, ch. of Joseph, Nov. 18, 1826, ae. 3 y. 6 m.

ELDRIDGE, Edmund, s. Polly, June —, 1826, ae. 18 y.
James, a Seaman, lost overboard coming from Boston, May 31, 1830, ae. 33 y. 1 m.
Thomson, Sept. 5, 1822, ae. 23 y.

ELKINS, ELLKINS, Amiel, at sea, 1832, ae. 49 y.
Barker Burnell, s. Ammiel, Jan. 3, 1826, ae. 21 y., around Cape Horn.
Daniel, Nov. 1, 1823, ae. 34 y. 1 m., in Savannah.
Joseph, s. John, late of Nantucket, Mar. —, 1829, ae. 48 y. 2 m., off Cape Horn in vessel of U. S. Navy.

ELLIS, Benjamin, s. Heman, drowned Sept. 23, 1827, ae. 17 y. 11 m.
Betsey, w. Moses & dau. J. Stubbs, Feb. 28, 1822, ae. 41 y. 9 m., in Brookfield, N. Y.
Deborah, wid. Simeon, June 17, 1824, ae. 63 y. 8 m.
Lurana, w. William, Dec. 4, 1821, ae. 75 y. 2 m.
Rebecca, wid. Henry (also Tweedy's widow) & dau. of Thomas James, Oct. 30, 1824, ae. 46 y.

ELLIS, Ruth, wid. Freeman & dau. late James Perry, Sept. 21, 1828, ae. 84 y. 1 m.
William, Sr., Jan. 7, 1822, ae. 84 y. 2 m.

EMMETT, John, in Barnstable, some time past, ae. 48 y. 10 m., dated Jan. 1824.
Thomas Addis, Nov. 8, 1827, ae. 55 y. 4 m., in New York City.

ENOS, Joseph, drowned round Cape Horn, 1834.
———, s. Manuel, June 9, 1833, ae. 5 y.

EVANS, Commodore Samuel, of the *Constitution*, June 7, 1824, ae. 54 y. 7 m.

EWER, Alvin, 1826, ae. 30 y., round Cape Horn.
Eunice, w. Peter F., Aug. 21, 1822, ae. 22 y. 9 m.
———, ch. of George Washington, June 25, 1828, ae. 11 m.

FANNING, David Swain, s. Barkley, Mar. 11, 1826, ae. 4 y. 3 m., in Poughkepsie.
Edmund, Aug. 5, 1822, ae. 34 y. 9 m., shot himself in Coguimbo, South America.
Edmund, the Second, 1824.
Capt. Thomas, s. Phineas, Oct. —, 1829, ae. 43 y. 2 m.
Thomas, s. Phinehas, lost at sea, 1833, ae. 47 y.
———, s. William C., 1824.

FARNUM, Eliza Ann, Oct. 28, 1826, ae. 18 y., in Boston, originally of Nantucket.
Sally, wid. William & dau. late Isaac Myrick, Aug. 19, 1832, ae. 60 y. 6 m.

FARRIS, John, s. Thomas, May 21, 1834, ae. 7 y. 3 m.

FAYE (FOYE), ———, ch. of Joseph, Oct. 11, 1825, ae. 1 m.

FIEFIELD, Abednego, Oct. 19, 1832, ae. 40 y., from Stratham, N. H.

FIELD, ——— s. Edward, Sept. 9, 1831, ae. 4 y.

FILLMORE, ———, ch. of Daniel, Oct. 11, 1826, ae. 1 y. 3 m.

FISH, Asa, Feb. 5, 1822, ae. 52 y., in Sandwich.
Hannah, w. Reuben & dau. Philip Coffin, Apr. 5, 1824, ae. 22 y. 9 m.
Simeon, Nov. 4, 1833, ae. 75 y. 9 m.
———, ch. of Theodore, Mar. 6, 1825, ae. 1 y. 4 m.
———, ch. of Nathan, Aug. 29, 1831, ae. 2 y. 1 m.

FISHER, Abiah, fall of 1827, ae. 50 y. 4 m., at the Vineyard.
Delia B., dau. Nehemiah, Mar. 19, 1833, ae. 8 m.
Henry, at Edgartown, Mar. 10, 1829, ae. 76 y.
James Harry, s. Henry, lost at sea, May 21, 1833.
Jonathan, bro. of Maltiah Fisher, May 28, 1834, ae. 30 y., in New Bedford.
Leonard, Jan. —, 1826.
Zebediah, on ship board at the Northward of the Gulf Stream, Sept. —, 1834, ae., 45 y. 2 m.
———, ch. of Zebediah, Aug. 7, 1825, ae. 2 y. 2 m.

FITCH, Anna, wid. Benjamin, Oct. 27, 1826, ae. 76 y. 6 m., at Edgartown.
Beriah, s. Jonathan Gorham, Mar. 7, 1825, ae. 53 y. 3 m., at Charlestown, N. H.
Charles Frederick Augustus, s. Jonathan Gorham, Jr., Nov. 4, 1827, ae. 18 y. 6 m., round Cape Horn, buried at Saint Francisco, South Sea Islands.

FITZGERALD, FITTZ GERRALD, FITTZ GERROLD, Eliza, w. David, Mar. 2, 1822, ae. 17 y. 2 m.
Hannah, w. James & dau. Nathaniel Whippey, burned to death, Apr. 9, 1828, ae. 50 y. 9 m.
Jonathan, Mar. 28, 1830, ae. 80 y. 2 m.
———, ch. of Nathaniel, Sept. 21, 1825, ae. 1 y. 3 m.

FLING, Darius Perry, s. Hephzibah, at sea, 1830, ae. 37 y. 9 m.
Hephzibah, wid. Michael, Feb. 24, 1830, ae. 76 y. 6 m.

FOLGER, Adaline C., dau. Charles Austin & gr. dau. Barzillai Burdett, Sept. 18, 1833, ae. 4 y.
Albert, s. Albert, dec'd, drowned round Cape Horn, 1824, ae. 24 y. 3 m.
Anna, w. Seth, Oct. 17, 1822, ae. 71 y. 3 m.
Charles C., s. Barnabas, killed by a whale round Cape Horn, July —, 1829, ae. 23 y. 4 m.
Charles Franklin, s. Benjamin, Sept. 17, 1833, ae. 6 m.
Christopher Columbus, s. Isaiah, Oct. 9, 1830, ae. 4 y. 3 m.
Daniel, s. Elisha, June 19, 1829, ae. 51 y., at New Orleans.
David, s. David & gr. s. Richard, June 1, 1833, ae. 74 y. 6 m., near Cincinnati, O.
Edmund, s. Walter, Nov. 3, 1825, ae. 1 y. 1 m.
Edward Clark, s. Thomas, Sept. 18, 1825, ae. 2 y. 2 m.
Edward J., s. Timothy, Sept. 10, 1831, ae. 32 y. 7 m., in Boston.
Elisha, s. Daniel, of Fort Ann, New York, May 17, 1824, ae. 65 y. 4 m.
George Franklin, s. Isaiah, Sept. 26, 1833, ae. 4 y. 6 m.
George Gorham, s. Mark, Aug. 25, 1834, ae. 2 weeks.
Gilbert, Mar. 22, 1824, ae. 79 y. 3 m.
Hephzibah, wid. Timothy & dau. Richard Chadwick, Jun., July —, 1825, ae. 62 y. 10 m., at Ohio.
James Hinckley, s. Benjamin Franklin, Nov. 28, 1833, ae. 6 y. 1 m.
Jethro, s. Elihu, May 19, 1833, ae. 38 y. 3 m., formerly of Nantucket, d. in New Orleans.
Capt. Joshua, s. late Capt. Obed, Aug. 6, 1827, ae. 40 y. 3 m., in New York.
Latham, s. Reuben, Oct. 9, 1833, ae. 3 y. 4 m., formerly of Nantucket, d. in Union County, Ind.
Lucretia, Oct. 22, 1824.
Lydia, dau. Nathaniel, Nov. —, 1824, ae. 63 y. 4 m., in Hudson.

Margaret, wid. Silvanus & dau. Daniel Russell, Aug. —, 1833, ae. 69 y. 2 m., at Cincinnati, O.
Martha, dau. Charles, Oct. 7, 1828, ae. 1 y. 3 m.
Mary, w. Richard & dau. Peleg Bunker, Jan. 30, 1833, ae. 51 y. 9 m., at Cincinnati, O.
Mayhew, Sept. 4, 1828, ae. 54 y. 6 m., at Massilon, Starks Co., Ohio.
Obadiah, Oct. 25, 1821, ae. 65 y. 10 m.
Owen, July 17, 1821, ae. 85 y. 6 m.
Richard, of Cincinnati, O., Feb. 1, 1825, ae. 49 y. 11 m., from the bite of a spider.
Richard Russell, s. Richard, formerly of Nantucket, d. in Cincinnati, O., Feb. 13, 1834, ae. 18 y. 3 m.
Robert, 1827, ae. 82 y., in Hudson, N. Y.
Sarah, w. Timothy, July 5, 1823, ae. 53 y. 11 m.
Silvanus, of Cincinnati, Apr. 25, 1822, ae. 59 y. 8 m.
Susanna, wid. Silas & dau. Samuel Foy, dec'd, May 21, 1832, ae. 69 y. 6 m.
Timothy, of Cincinnati, formerly of this town, Mar. 27, 1825, ae. abt. 65 y.
Tristram Coffin, s. Tristram, late of Cincinnati, d. in New Orleans, Apr. 28, 1832, ae. 37 y. 2 m., formerly of Nantucket.
William, s. Henry, killed by a whale round Cape Horn, July 5, 1823, ae. 16 y.
William Frederick, s. Timothy, Mar. 23, 1824, ae. 29 y. 9 m., in New York.
———, ch. of Samuel Brown, Mar. 29, 1822, ae. abt. 2 m.
———, w. Reuben Coffin, dau. Robert Macy, of Chatham, County of Columbia, N. Y., Aug. 2, 1823, ae. 33 y., d. in N. Y.
———, ch. of Daniel, Feb. 1, 1824, ae. 3 days.
———, ch. of Frederick, May 1, 1824, ae. 5 m.
———, ch. of Isaiah, July 21, 1825, ae. 4 m.
———, s. Rowland, Sept. 23, 1826, ae. 10 m.
———, s. Moses, Sept. 14, 1830, ae. 1 y. 4 m.
———, s. Isaiah, Oct. 9, 1830, ae. 4 y. 3 m.
———, ch. of Edward, gr. ch. Charles, Aug. 26, 1833, ae. 2 y.
———, ch. of Benjamin, Sept. 11, 1833, ae. 9 m.
———, ch. of Benjamin, Sept. 29, 1833, ae. 2 y. 6 m.

FOLSOM, Eliza B., dau. Joseph, Jan. 31, 1834, ae. 1 y.

FOSDICK, Anna, dau. Benjamin, Apr. 23, 1834, ae. 76 y. 1 m., a Single Sister.
Charlotte Ann, ch. Peter G., Sept. 12, 1823, ae. 14 m.
Margaret, dau. Peter, Aug. —, 1825.

FOSTER, Thomas F., in Cincinnati, O., Nov. 13, 1825, ae. 30 y., he married Eliza Coffin, dau. Isaiah.

FOX, William, a Quaker, drowned in New York Harbour, May 3, 1823, ae. 71 y.

FOYE, Charles, s. Obed, May 3, 1822, ae. 27 y.

FREEMAN, Elizabeth, w. John, of Sandwich, Feb. 1, 1825, ae. 62 y.
William, gr. s. Timothy Myrick, lost at sea between Boston and Philadelphia, 1830, ae. 27 y.

FRIEZE, Lydia, dau. Silas Gardner, w. George Gorham Coffin & w. ——— Frieze, Apr. 21 1833, ae. 36 y., in Baltimore.

FROBISHER, ———, ch. of Joseph, gr. ch. of George Cannon, Oct. 26, 1831, ae. 1 y. 1 m.

FROST, Huldah, w. Leonard, the Minister, Nov. 6, 1824, ae. 35 y.

FRYE, Martha Ann, dau. William Gray, Aug. 20, 1833, ae. 1 y. 2 m.

FULLER, Nancy, dau. Capt. Allen, Jan. 17, 1834, ae. 17 y. 1 m.
———, ch. of Allen, Oct. 9, 1830, ae. 1 y. 1 m.

GALE, ———, ch. of Edmund's widow, June —, 1825, ae. 1 yr. 8 m.

GALLAGHER, John, Dec. 17, 1833, ae. 36 y. 3 m.
William, an Irishman, drowned Mar. 7, 1833, ae. 30 y.

GARDNER, Abigail, w. Peleg, Sept. 8, 1833, ae. 46 y. 4 m., at Fall River.
Ann Maria, dau. George Ellis, Feb. 3, 1834, ae. 4 m.

GARDNER, Benjamin, s. Levi, Feb. 10, 1825, ae. 40 y. 3 m., in Harve-de-Grass.
Benjamin, Sept. 1, 1828, ae. 31 y. 9 m., in Pernambuco.
Charles, s. Alexander, Jr., Apr. —, 1825, ae. 35 y.
Charles, s. Joseph, Feb. 10, 1827, ae. 44 y.
Charles Lee, s. Albert, Jan. 14, 1825, ae. 33 y. 1 m., on voyage out of New York.
Daniel, s. Silas, Jan. 8, 1825, ae. 37 y., on board ship.
Edmund, s. Silas, Jan. —, 1828, ae. 37 y. 1 m., on trip from West Indies, d. at Charleston, N. C.
Edward Barnard, s. Uriah, Aug. 15, 1824, ae. 1 y. 2 m.
Elijah, s. Silvanus, Oct. —, 1830, ae. 50 y. 1 m., at Chatham.
Elizabeth, wid. Reuben, Mar. 18, 1826, ae. 80 y. 8 m.
Emmaline Coffin, dau. Timothy Myrick, Sept. 17, 1828, ae. 1 y. 10 m.
Eunice, dau. Jared, Dec. 31, 1821, ae. 8 y. 6 m.
Franklin, s. Jared, 2d, carried away with a Whale line, round Cape Horn, Jan. 20, 1821, ae. 21 y. 10 m.
Frederick, s. Frederick, gr. s. Levi, great gr. s. Elihu, lost overboard round Cape Horn, Mar. —, 1826, ae. 17 y.
Gilbert, s. Gilbert of Hudson, gr. s. Samuel Gardner, lost at sea, fall of 1830, ae. 39 y.
Henry C., s. Jared, Feb. —, 1826, ae. 18 y. 6 m.
Joshua, s. Silvanus, lost at sea, 1831–2, ae. 37 y.
Judith, wid. Shubael, Jan. 20, 1822, ae. 77 y.
Lucretia, wid. Francis & dau. Paul Paddack, Mar. —, 1830, ae. 84 y. 2 m., in Newport, R. I.
Lydia Andrews, dau. Jethro, Nov. 24, 1833, ae. 3 y.
Margaret, wid. Grispus, Sept. 27, 1823, ae. 80 y. 5 m.
Margaret, w. Timothy, Jr., & dau. Capt. Joshua Bunker, d. in Baltimore, Nov. —, 1825, ae. 64 y. 2 m., formerly of Nantucket.
Martha Ann, dau. George C., Nov. 7, 1833, ae. 1 y.
Merab, w. Paul, Dec. 30, 1821, ae. 54 y. 1 m.
Mercy, w. Jethro, July 1, 1827, ae. 27 y. 1 m.
Peleg, s. George, July 18, 1829, ae. 1 y. 3 m.
Peter, s. Richard, Dec. —, 1832, ae. 63 y. 11 m., in Ohio, he married Lurana Giles.
Rowland, s. Latham, Sept. 1, 1825, ae. 39 y. 6 m., in Albany or Saratoga Springs.
Ruth, wid. Ebenezer, Jan. 29, 1823, ae. 88 y. 2 m., dau. John Beard.
Shubael, Sr., Nov. 15, 1823, ae. 78 y. 4 m.
Silas, s. Grafton, May 13, 1826, ae. 73 y. 1 m., in Kennebunk, Maine.
Silvanus, Oct. —, 1830, ae. 91 y. 3 m., at Chatham, N. Y., formerly of Nantucket.
Simeon, s. Simeon, June —, 1829, ae. 46 y. 9 m., in Yarmouth, Nova Scotia.
Thomas B., s. Edward Pollard, July 19, 1832, ae. 1 y. 2 m.
Timothy, s. Timothy, Dec. 3, 1830, ae. 73 y. 1 m., in Baltimore.
William, s. Grindal, Aug. —, 1832, ae. 48 y., in London.
William H., s. Tristram, Dec. —, 1824, ae. 25 y. 2 m., in the West Indies.
———, ch. of Eliza Ann, Feb. 3, 1822, ae. 2 m.
———, ch. of Henry, 3d, June 24, 1822, ae. 1 y. 3 m.
———, ch. of Jesse, Mar. 20, 1825, ae. 9 m.
———, ch. of Uriah, May 7, 1825, ae. 6 m.
———, ch. of Henry, 3d, June 20, 1825.
———, ch. of Silas, Aug. 7, 1825, ae. 8 m.
———, ch. of Timothy M., July 23, 1826, ae. 1 y. 10 m.
———, ch. of John, Sept. 14, 1828, ae. 1 y. 6 m.
———, ch. of Edward, Nov. 20, 1831, ae. 1 y. 6 m.
———, ch. of William Henry, Sept. 9, 1832, ae. 5 m.

———, ch. of Josiah, June 22, 1833, ae. 1 y. 4 m.
———, ch. of Thomas A., Sept. 21, 1833, ae. 4 weeks.
———, ch. of William Henry, Dec. —, 1833, ae. 1 y. 7 m.

GATES, Andrew, of Phil., committed suicide, Aug. 20. 1832, ae. abt. 27 y.

GEHTON, Samuel, Aug. 15, 1823, ae. 37 y. 9 m., on passage from Mobile.

GERALD, ———, ch. of Timothy, Oct. 7, 1821, ae. abt. 18 m.

GIBBS, Elnathan, June 11, 1825, at Wareham, he married Judith, dau. Job Chase.
Hannah, w. Silvanus, June —, 1832, ae. 78 y. 9 m., in Sandwich.
Henry, s. Samuel, lost at sea, 1826–7, ae. 28 y. 9 m.
John, the old Smoker, May 11, 1825, ae. 77 y. in Sandwich.
Martha, w. James, July 24, 1831, ae. 45 y. 7 m.
Thomas, May 18, 1822, ae. 67 y. 9 m., in Sandwich.
William, Nov. —, 1821, ae. 19 y., fell from aloft on board Ship at Edgartown.

GIFFORD, Ruth, wid. Robert, July 6, 1823, ae. 41 y. 8 m.

GILES, George Barnard, s. David, dec'd, scalded to death on board steam boat at Missouri, Feb. 20, 1830, ae. 28 y. 6 m.
Mary, dau. late David Upham, Aug. 27, 1829, ae. 23 y. 7 m., in Staten Island, N. Y.
Paul, Mar. 5, 1824, ae. 84 y. 2 m.

GLOVER, Elizabeth, w. Reuben, Aug. —, 1832, ae. 56 y. 4 m., in New York.

GODFREY, Betsey, wid. John & dau. William Gardner, Jan 14, 1832, ae. 48 y. 4 m.

GOFF, Deborah, wid., Apr. 3, 1829, ae. 70, in New York, dau. late Isaac Myrick, of Nantucket.
Eliza, dau. Mrs. Deborah & gr. dau. late Isaac Myrick of Nantucket, May 29, 1823, ae. 23 y.

GOODRICH, Julianna, w. James T., May 5, 1824, ae. 21 y.

GOODSPEED, ———, ch. of Timothy, May 10, 1825, ae. 1 y. 2 m.
———, w. Walley, Nov. 4, 1825, ae. 69 y. 9 m.

GOOGINS, Alexander, d. away from Nantucket, Dec. —, 1826, ae. 28 y. 1 m.
Elizabeth, wid. William, dau. late Henry Dow, Aug. 30, 1832, ae. 62 y., formerly of Nantucket, d. in Oxford.
William, June 7, 1832, ae. 64, in Oxford.
———, ch. of Alexander, Sept. 24, 1825, ae. 2 y.
———, ch. of Alexander, Sept. 28, 1825.

GORHAM, Henry W., s. Davis, July 7, 1831, ae. 11 y. 1 m.
John Butler, s. John, May 6, 1834, ae. 12 y. 6 m.
Josiah, s. James, Feb. 21, 1824, ae. 9 y. 6 m.
———, ch. of John, Nov. 8, 1821, ae. abt. 1 y.
———, ch. of John, Aug. 12, 1826, ae. 1 y. 9 m.
———, ch. of James, Oct. 7, 1832, ae. 3 m.

GRANGER, Hannah, w. Calvin, d. in Boston, ae. 40 y. (entry dated Jan., 1824).

GRANT, ———, ch. of James, Aug. 26, 1830, ae. 6 m.

GRAY, Elizabeth, w. William, Esq., Sept. 29, 1823, ae. 71 y., in Boston.

GREEN, Benjamin, s. John, lost overboard, June, 1825, ae. 23 y.
Caleb, Jan. 16, 1824, ae. 73 y. 4 m., in New Bedford.
Sarah G., w. Welcome of Providence & dau. Zenas Gardner, Oct. 30, 1833, ae. 26 y. 2 m.

GREW, Samuel B., s. Barzillai, June 1, 1834, ae. 2 y. 2 m.
———, ch. of Jervis, Oct. 26, 1821.
———, ch. of Barzillai, July 12, 1830, ae. 2 m.

GRIFFITH, Frederick W., of the Ship Planter of Nantucket, killed by the Spanish Indians round Cape Horn, 1823, ae. 30 y.

GROVES, Joseph, drowned off Nantucket, Dec. 3, 1828, from Brig Packet of Providence, R. I.

GURNEY, Mary Jane, dau. James, the Minister, Aug. 20, 1823, ae. 3 y. 2 m.
———, dau. of Ephraim, Sept. —, 1822, ae. 9 y. 3 m.

GURRELL, Hannah, w. Capt. John, Junior, Feb. 5, 1829, ae. 25 y. 6 m., in New York.
Hannah Mariah, dau. William, Sept. 30, 1831, ae. 3 y. 1 m.
John, drowned, Feb. 3, 1826, ae. 27 y.
John, Jr., July 6, 1831, ae. 35 y. 7 m., in Petersburg, Russia.

GWINN, Zebdial, June 7, 1824, ae. 71 y. 3 m.

HAGADARN, Mary Dame, dau. Jacob & gr. dau. James Gerrold, Sept. 16, 1833 ae. 1 y. 8 m.

HAGGETT, William S., killed by a whale around Cape Horn, 1834, ae. 25 y. He married Lucy Ann Sayward, dau. Polly.

HALL, David of Nantucket, May 26, 1834, ae. 27 y. 1 m., in Albany, N. Y.
Frederick Andrew, s. Isaac & gr. s. Paul Mitchell, of Nantucket, Sept. —, 1833, ae. 21 y. 3 m., in New York.

HALLETT, Eliza Ann, dau. Capt. Thomas, Aug. 21, 1826, ae. 1 m.
Rachel, mother of Edward Macy's wife, of Yarmouth, May 8, 1823, ae. 53 y. 1 m.
Thomas, Oct. 26, 1827, ae. 25 y. 2 m., in the Hospital on Staten Island.

HALLIDAY, James, lost at sea, May 21, 1832.

HALSEY, Peggy, wid. John, Sept. 16, 1822, ae. 55 y. 11 m.

HAMBLIN, ———, ch. of Ansel, Nov. 11, 1832, ae. 2 y.

HAMMATT, Benjamin, s. William, killed by a Malay, Oct. —, 1821, ae. 30 y. 1 m.

HAMMOND, Barzillai, from New Bedford, July 29, 1824, ae. 61 y. 6 m., he married Sally Trenton, an English girl.

HANDY, Rebecca, wid., June 21, 1826, ae. 60 y. 10 m.

HARPS, Eunice, wid. John, Dec. 29, 1824, ae. 43 y. 2 m.

NANTUCKET SUPPLEMENTARY RECORDS

Contributed by MRS. SETH AMES LEWIS of Springfield, Mass.

DEATHS

HARPS, John, a Dutchman, July 9, 1823, ae. 40 y. 7 m.
Nathaniel Chadwick, June —, 1824, ae. 1 y. 5 m.

HARRIS, David of Vasalborough, County of Kennebeck, late of Nantucket, Mar. 1, 1830, ae. 59 y. 9 m.
George, drowned off South side of Nantucket, Dec. 3, 1828, from Brig Packet of Providence, R. I.
Joseph, Feb. 2, 1823, ae. 75 y., in Smithfield.

HARTSHORN, Davis, s. Harvey, Aug. 12, 1834, ae. 5 m.

HASKILL, Benjamin Franklin, gr. s. Benjamin Worth, lost at sea, May 21, 1832, ae. 19 y. 3 m.
Sarah, ae. 24 y. and her infant child, 1 week, April 13, 1823.

HATCH, Elizabeth, w. William, J., Jan. 30, 1828, ae. 68 y. 10 m., in New Bedford.
Gibbs, Apr. 23, 1823, ae. 36 y. 4 m., brother-in-law of Elisha Raymond.
Shubael, Jan. 16, 1824, ae. 78 y. 2 m., in Falmouth.

HATHAWAY, Anna, w. Nathaniel, formerly of Nantucket, Sept. 3, 1833, ae. 36 y. 4 m., in Dartmouth or New Bedford.
Benjamin, an inhabitant of Nantucket, in Barrington, R. I., Jan. 20, 1830, ae. 84 y. 3 m.
Elizabeth, dau. Nathaniel, Oct. 27, 1825, ae. 6 y. 3 m.

HAYDEN, Abigail, sister of Zopher, an Irish Woman, Feb. 3, 1822, ae. 41 y.
Mary Gorham, dau. Prince, May 24, 1829, ae. 5 y. 6 m.

HEDGE, Mary, wid. Capt. Elisha, Oct. 20, 1828, ae. 90 y. 3 m. at Yarmouth.

HENDERSON, Thomas, drowned Mar. —, 1829, ae. 24 y.

HIGGINS, Charlotte, dau. George, Oct. 24, 1825, ae. 6 m.
———, ch. of George, Dec. 7, 1828, ae. 1 y. 6 m.

HILBURN, George Barney, s. Thomas, Nov. 15, 1829, ae. 2 m.

HILL, Edward, July 15, 1833, ae. 35 y. 4 m., at Hingham; he married Phebe Coffin, dau. Elial Coffin.
William, Oct. 23, 1832, ae. 37 y. 9 m., in New York; he married Amelia, dau. Peter Hussey, and Peggy Pinkham, dau. Shubael Coffin.

HILLAR, George, of Barnstable, Dec. 13, 1825.

HILLMAN, ———, ch. of Reuben, Oct. 28, 1826, ae. 1 y. 3 m. Reuben has buried his wife and 3 children at New Bedford within one year.

HINCKLEY, A . . . bella O . . . steen, dau. Isaac, Aug. 22, 1826, ae. 11 m.
Edward, Apr. 2, 1823, at sea off coast of Chile.
Isaac, lived at Nantucket, in Barnstable, Oct. 30, 1828, ae. 31 y. 4 m.
Isaac Newton, ch. of late Isaac Hinckley and gr. ch. of Jesse Crosby, July 28, 1829, ae. 10 m.
Maria, dau. Elisha, Feb. 10, 1830, ae. 32 y. 3 m., in New York.

HOAG, ———, ch. of Frederick, May 28, 1822, ae. 3 y.
———, s. Frederick, Aug. 4, 1826, ae. 2 y. 4 m.

HOBBS, Jane, dau. William, Nov. 8, 1833, ae. 6 y. 7 m.

HOBSON, George, Dec. 6, 1830, ae. 53 y. 6 m., in Baltimore.

HODGES, Hercules, s. Isaac, Apr. 29, 1831, ae. 35 y. 6 m., at Pensacola, keeper of the Light House.

HOLLAND, Joanna, Oct. 14, 1833, ae. 24 y. 4 m., an Indian woman.

HOLLEY (HAWLEY), Polly, w. William, Apr. 21, 1822, ae. 35 y. 6 m.
Zaccheus, s. William, Sept. 21, 1823, ae. 5 y. 3 m.
———, ch. of William, Aug. 23, 1821.
———, infant of William, Apr. 19, 1822, buried with his wife.
———, ch. of William, Sept. 4, 1833, ae. 9 m.

HOLMES, Allen Gorham, s. Watson & ——— (Bennett), Oct. 5, 1833, ae. 1 y. 11 m.
Bartlett, drowned in Barnstable Harbour, Monday, Mar. 27, 1826, ae. 64 y. 3 m.
Harriot, dau. Benjamin, Nov. 2, 1833, ae. 4 y. 2 m.
Capt. John, lost at sea, 1825–6.
Mary, dau. Thomas, May 2, 1834, ae. 17 y. 10 m.
Phebe, w. Thomas & dau. Jesse Parlow of Wareham or Rochester, Jan. 10, 1832, ae. 41 y. 1 m.
Phebe, ch. of John, Dec. 6, 1833, ae. 9 y.
———, ch. of Charles, Feb. 2, 1828, ae. 2 m.
———, ch. of Robert, Feb. 2, 1828, ae. 1 m.
———, w. Watson, dau. of William Bennett the Second, Sept. 4, 1833, ae. 29 y.

HOLWAY, ——— twin ch. of William, Mar. 3, 1830, ae. 7 m., the other twin died some time past.

HOMANS, Benjamin, Esq., Chief Clerk in the Navy Department, Dec. 7, 1823, ae. 59 y., at George Town, District of Columbia.

HOMER, Benjamin, Dec. 13, 1825, ae. 55 y.

HOOTAN, Sarah, Sept. 23, 1822, ae. 87 y.

HOPKINS, Richard, Aug. 17, 1822, ae. 29 y. 3 m., a partner of William Barker, Merchants in New York, Barker & Hopkins.

HORSFIELD, Timothy, Jan. 22, 1826.

HORSFORD, Molly, w. Joseph, Apr. 15, 1828, ae. 82 y., at Edgartown.

HOSIER, William Giles, Mar. 31, 1822, ae. 25 y. 6 m.

HOUSE, William, s. Hephzibah, drowned in Delaware River, May —, 1825, ae. 26 y.

HOW, ———, Mrs., w. Samuel, May 4, 1832, ae. 45 y.

HOWLAND, Deborah, wid. Philip H., Jan. 12, 1826, ae. 61 y., in Dartmouth.

HULL, Phebe, June 5, 1822, ae. 62 y. 4 m.
William, s. Thomas, on ship board round Cape Horn, 1831 ae. 24 y. 7 m.

HUMPHREY, ———, ch. of Augustus, Aug. 26, 1822, ae. 3 y.

HUNTINGTON, Lydia Ellingwood, dau. David, Nov. 20, 1833, ae. 6 y.
Sarah Bunker, dau. David, Nov. 22, 1833, ae. 3 y. 8 m.

HUNTOON, Jonathan, h. Lucretia Bennett, dau. of William, at sea, fall of 1831, ae. 35 y.

HUSHING, John, Sept. 29, 1833, ae. 26 y. 6 m.

HUSSEY, Andrew, Peter, Feb. 14, 1824, ae. 2 y. 4 m.
Ann Cartwright, dau. Frederick, Jan. 12, 1827, ae. 3 y. 2 m.
Anna, wid. Thomas, May 25, 1824, ae. 57 y. 6 m.
Benjamin Franklin, s. Capt. Benjamin, Mar. 25, 1829, ae. 2 y. 3 m.
Benjamin Franklin, 1830, of Ship Dauphin, lost at Cape of Good Hope.
Daniel, s. Albert the second, Apr. —, 1824, ae. 19 y. 2 d., lost on Brazil Coast.
Daniel J., at sea, July, 1831, ae. 15 y. 6 m., son of Susanna J. Gelston. (She was formerly wife of Daniel Hussey.)
Edward, s. Isaiah, of New York, Aug. 17, 1824, ae. 22 y. 7 m., at New Orleans.
Elizabeth, wid. Seth, Apr. 30, 1831, ae. 56 y. 6 m., at Falmouth while on a visit to her daughter, the wife of Alexander Clark the 3rd.
Hannah Ballard, dau. Frederick, Jan. 9, 1825, ae. 5 y. 2 m.
Hephzibah, wid. Daniel, Feb. 22, 1822, ae. 80 y. 1 m., at Hudson.
James, s. William C., May 21, 1833, ae. 7 y.
John Butler, s. Cyrus, Nov. 4, 1832, ae. 32 y. 8 m., in Cincinnati, O.
Lydia C., w. Frederick & dau. John Cartwright, Feb. 13, 1828, ae. 44 y. 5 m.
Mary Abby, dau. Capt. Benjamin Russell, Sept. 28, 1833, ae. 8 m.
Peter, Oct. 10, 1825, ae. 25 y. 4 m., at Saint Michaels.
Samuel, s. Samuel, Sept. 5, 1822, ae. 24 y., in Wilmington, N. C., late of Hallowell but formerly of Nantucket.
Stephen, s. Thomas, Dec. 31, 1823, ae. 22 y. 4 m.
Tristram, Oct. 10, 1822, ae. 69 y. 8 m.
———, ch. of Charles 2d, July 3, 1821, ae. abt. 18 m.
———, ch. of Frederick, Dec. 26, 1822, ae. 1 y. 6 m.
———, ch. of Thomas, Jan. 12, 1824, ae. 1 y.
———, s. Albert the Second, Jan. 13, 1824, ae. 1 y. 3 m.
———, ch. of Francis F., Sept. 8, 1824, ae. 1 y. 1 m.
———, d. Henry, Sept. 7, 1825, ae. 4 m.
———, ch. of Francis Folger, Oct. 11, 1825, ae. 10 m.
———, ch. of Alexander S., May 4, 1828, ae. 8 m.
———, ch. of Edward Barnard, Aug. 19, 1830, ae. 1 y. 6 m.
———, ch. of John, Jr., & gr. ch. of Isaac Myrick, Dec. 31, 1832, ae. 2 y.
———, ch. of William C., May 24, 1834, ae. 1 m.

IMBERT, Harriet Myrick, ch. Lewis B., Aug. 29, 1829, ae. 2 y. 2 m.
Harriot, dau. Lewis, Dec. —, 1825, ae. 3 y. 1 m.
———, ch. of Lewis, July 14, 1826, ae. 1 y. 1 m.

INNIS, Stephen, Oct. 20, 1831, ae. 69 y. 1 m.

JACKSON, Abigail, wid. John & dau. Ebenezer Cleaveland, Feb. 20, 1832, ae. 81 y.
Elizabeth, wid. of John of Connecticut & mother of Sally Kelley (dau. of Joseph), Feb. 6, 1825, ae. 71 y. 3 m.

JAMES, Daniel N., s. Joseph, Jan. 4, 1834, ae. 1 y. 5 m.
Francis, s. Francis, Dec. 20, 1823, ae. 28 y. 9 m.
Phebe Ann., dau. Edwin, Dec. 27, 1833, ae. 1 y. 8 m.
Rowland B., s. Edwin, Oct. 7, 1832, ae. 2 y. 3 m.
———, ch. of Jonathan, Dec. 6, 1821.
———, s. Charles, Oct. 3, 1828, ae. 5 y.
———, ch. of Jonathan, Oct. 7, 1832, ae. 2 y. 8 m.
———, ch. of Edwin, Dec. 21, 1833, ae. 2 y. 6 m.
———, ch. of Edwin, Sept. 6, 1834, ae. 6 m.
———, ch. of Edwin, Sept. 20, 1834, ae. 1 y. 2 m.

JANE, Nancy, w. ——— Jane & dau. of John Adlington, Jan. 9, 1834, ae. 45 y. 9 m.

JENKINS, Barnabas E., drowned round Cape Horn, Jan. 3, 1823, ae. 26 y. 2 m.
Barzillai, s. Charles, Sept. —, 1823, ae. 46 y., in Hudson.
Joseph, Dec. —, 1832, ae. 69 y. 1 m., in Barnstable.
Matthew, Dec. 19, 1830, ae. 50 y. 3 m., in Brooklin, Long Island.
Seth, formerly of Nantucket, s. Seth, the Mayor of Hudson, at Columbia Villa, N. Y., Aug. 15, 1831, ae. 51 y. 4 m.
———, ch. of John, Oct. 16, 1826, ae. 1 y. 3 m.
———, ch. of William, Aug. —, 1830.

JENKS, Abigail, wid. late Capt. Samuel, Jan. 14, 1828, ae. 84 y. 3 m., at Medford, near Boston.
Isaac Coffin, s. Robert W. & Eunice (Coffin), Feb. 29, 1824.
Samuel, the Town Crier, Jan. 20, 1833, ae. 66 y. 10 m.
———, ch. of Samuel H., Aug. 1, 1825, ae. 1 y. 8 m.

JENNY, Judith, 1821, in Alexandria, ae. 44 y. 6 m., formerly Judith Lawrence, wid. George Lawrence, Jr., & dau. of Oliver Spencer.

JETHRO, Abigail, an Indian Squaw, Jan. 19, 1822, ae. 69 y.

JOHNSON, Cloa, Indian woman, Aug. 19, 1832, ae. 27 y.
Joseph H., at sea, Jan. 1, 1830, ae. 22 y. 9 m.
Nelson, drowned off South side of Nantucket, Dec. 3, 1828, from Brig Packet of Providence, R. I.
Thomas Jefferson, of Machias, drowned off Nantucket, Mar. 22, 1829.

JONES, Edward, 1825, in Philadelphia.
Harriet Ann, dau. George Macy Jones, Nov. 6, 1833, ae. 1 y. 6 m.
Judith, Jr., dau. Capt. Silas, July 19, 1832, ae. 48 y. 4 m.
Miriam, w. Edward, 1825, in Philadelphia.
Sally, wid. Barzillai, found hanged in her cellar, Apr. 26, 1822, ae. 38 y. 9 m.
Sarah A., dau. William, Sept. 6, 1827, ae. 7 y. 1 m.
William, lost at sea, May 21, 1832.
———, ch. of Daniel, Sept. —, 1821.
———, ch. of William, Sept. 10, 1827, ae. 2 y.

JOSLIN, Isaac, drowned at New Bedford, July 31, 1821, ae. 21 y.

JOY, Benjamin Cartwright, s. Obed, June 1, 1825, ae. 30 y. 3 m., in Brookline, near city of New York, Long Island.
David, Sept. 30, 1826, ae. 51 y. 6 m., suddenly at Pirth Amboy.
Francis, Aug. 30, 1822, ae. 83 y. 6 m.
Gilbert, killed by a whale, Mar. —, 1823.
Harriot, dau. Nancy & Matthew, July 2, 1821, ae. 1 y. 3 m.
Lydia, dau. William, Dec. 23, 1821, ae. 19 y. 2 m.
Lydia Cartwright, dau. Samuel, Aug. 22, 1833, ae. 1 y. 7 m.
Phebe, dau. late Thaddeus & Judith, Aug. 1, 1834, ae. 33 y. 7 m.

KELLEY, Abbey Bates, dau. Joseph, July 15, 1821, ae. 9 y. 4 m.
Emeline, Nov. 20, 1824, ae. 16 y. 9 m.
John, of Yarmouth, Jan. —, 1826, ae. 80 y. 9 m.
John, s. John, lost at sea, Mar. —, 1827, ae. 39 y.
Rebecca, w. Allen, late of Nantucket, July 21, 1832, ae. 33 y. 3 m., in Fair Haven.

KNAPP, Horatio, a sailor, July 11, 1823, ae. 25 y., he belonged to Bridgetown, Maine.

KNOWLES, John, Nov. 30, 1826, ae. 31 y. 7 m., round Cape Horn.
———, d. John, May 13, 1827, ae. 6 y.

LA HOMMEDIEU, Ann Amelia, dau. Benjamin, June 11, 1828, ae. 3 y.
Lucy Cable, dau. Benjamin, May 18, 1828, ae. 9 m.
———, ch. of Benjamin, Apr. 27, 1828, ae. 8 m.

LAVELL, Anber, s. Lazarus, July 2, 1831, ae. 31 y. 4 m., at Barnstable.

LAWRENCE, Betsey G., dau. Francis S., Dec. 21, 1833, ae. 4 m.
William, a seaman, Mar. 4, 1832, ae. 28 y. 4 m.
———, ch. of Charles, Aug. 1, 1830, ae. 2 y.

LEWIS, Francis, of Tisbury, Jan. 20, 1823, ae. 93 y. 3 m.; he was dressed like a woman his first thirty-two years.
Levi, of Oyster Island, drowned on passage from Norfolk, Va., to Nantucket, Oct. —, 1829, ae. 35 y. 4 m.
Nancy, dau. Joseph West, formerly of Nantucket, July 15, 1834, ae. 30 y. 11 m., in Providence, R. I.
Mariner Peter, killed himself, Nov. 19, 1823, ae. 27 y.

LONG, ———, ch. of Valentine, Nov. 16, 1826, ae. 3 y. 2 m.

LOVELL, Benjamin, of Sandwich, Dec. 13, 1825.
———, ch. of Richard L., Feb. 11, 1827, ae. 4 m.

LUCE, Rebecca B., ch. of Obed, Feb. 15, 1833, ae. 2 y. 6 m.
———, ch. of David, Oct. 27, 1825, ae. 11 m.
———, ch. of David, July 20, 1827, ae. 8 m.
———, ch. of Obed, June 21, 1829, ae. 10 m.
———, ch. of Elijah, Aug. 19, 1832, ae. 4 y.

LUMBERT, Abishai Hayden, Apr. 12, 1828, Martha's Vineyard.

LUTHER, William, from Summerfield, drowned Aug. 4, 1826, ae. 30 y.

MACE, Mary C., dau. John Coffin, Dec. 6, 1821, ae. 27 y., in Baltimore.

MACEY, MACY, Alexander, s. Gorham, Sept. 6, 1829, ae. 12 y. 8 m.
Almira, dau. Daniel, Oct. 8, 1821, ae. abt. 8 y. 6 m.
Anna, w. Job, May 19, 1824, ae. 52 y. 10 m.
Augustus J., s. John R., Nov. 3, 1829, ae. 4 y. 6 m.
Charles, ch. of Josiah, July 3, 1821, ae. abt. 3 y.
Charles Henry, s. Paul Bunker, Mar. 20, 1834, ae. 3 m.
Eunice Gardner, dau. Peter, Nov. 5, 1833, ae. 4 y. 1 m.
Harriet, dau. Capt. John, May 15, 1822, ae. 5 y.
Jedidah, dau. Shubael, Sept. 10, 1824, ae. 57 y.
Margaret B., dau. Peter, June 22, 1825, ae. 4 y. 2 m.
Mary, dau. Obed, Aug. 22, 1822, ae. 23 y. 3 m.
Nathaniel, Nov. 5, 1821, ae. 67 y. 9 m.
Sally, w. John Wendell & dau. Thomas Swain, dec'd., Mar. 13, 1824, ae. 33 y. 8 m.
Stephen, Feb. 8, 1822, ae. 80 y. 8 m.
Stephen, s. Stephen, Jan. —, 1825, ae. 63 y. 3 m., in West Indies.
Susannam, dau. Daniel, May 10, 1825, ae. 8 y. 7 m.
———, ch. of William W., July 30, 1821, ae. abt. 2 y.
———, ch. of Thomas W., Dec. 6, 1821.
———, ch. of Frederick, Dec. 28, 1822, ae. 3 m.
———, ch. of William W., Oct. 10, 1823, ae. 1 y. 5 m.
———, ch. of Paul, Sept. 20, 1824, ae. 6 m.
———, ch. of John, Aug. 10, 1825, ae. abt. 2 y. 3 m.
———, ch. of John R., Oct. 1, 1829, ae. 1 y. 6 m.
———, ch. of Peleg, Nov. 25, 1829, ae. 3 m.
———, ch. of Charles & gr. ch. of John Nerboth, Nov. 4, 1832, ae. 2 y. 6 m.
———, ch. of Paul Bunker & gr. ch. of Paul Macey, Aug. 11, 1833, ae. 3 m.
———, ch. of Zaccheus, Oct. 8, 1833, ae. 11 m.

MACK CLEAVE, Benjamin, Sept. 22, 1823, ae. 30 y. 10 m.

MACK GILL, McGILL, Joseph, Nov. —, 1832, ae. 24 y. 9 m.; he married Lydia Ellis, dau. Simeon, moved to Kennebeck.

MALLARD, John W. P., drowned off coast of Japan, June 3, 1828, ae. 28 y. 9 m.

MANCRESTER, John, supposed to be murdered, Aug. 5, 1821, ae. 60 y.

MANSFIELD, ———, ch. of Lyman, Jan. 26, 1832, ae. 3 m.

MANTER, Lucinda, w. Benjamin, Mar. 27, 1834, ae. 62 y. 7 m.
Seth, s. Reuben, July —, 1833, ae. 2 y. 6 m.
———, ch. of George 2d, Sept. —, 1822, ae. 1 y. 1 m.

MARDEN, Daniel Nicher, s. John B. & Deborah C., July 10, 1834, ae. 1 y.

MARSH, Roswell, h. Ichabod Paddock's dau., Jan. —, 1829, ae. 49 y., in E. Greenwich, R. I.

MARSHALL, David, s. Josiah, Oct. 10, 1830, ae. 51 y. 3 m., in Philadelphia.
Reuben, s. Josiah, lost off the coast of Ireland, 1822, ae. 35 y. 5 m.
———, ch. of Obed, July, 1827, ae. 3 m.
———, ch. of Obed, July —, 1826, ae. 8 m.

MARTIN, Alexander, a Sailor, washed overboard between here and Providence, Apr. 3, 1831, ae. 49 y. 6 m.

MATTHEWS, Arthur, Sept. —, 1823, in the Western Country.
William, drowned off the South side of Nantucket, from the Brig Packet of Providence, R. I., Dec. 3, 1828.

MAYO, Eliza, wid. Capt. Obed, Feb. 17, 1829, ae. 44 y., in Ogdensburg, N. Y.

MEAD, William H., Aug. 2, 1829, ae. 30 y., on the coast of Japan.

MEADER, MEEDER, Alexander, ch. of George, June 24, 1822, ae. 7 y. 4 m.
Benjamin, Aug. 1, 1821, ae. 46 y., at City Point, James River, Va. Was Capt. of ship Governor Griswold of New York, lived in Hudson.
Deborah, wid. Robert, Apr. 1, 1826, ae. 80 y. 2 m., on the Banks of the Mohawk River or German Flats.
Rachel Paddock, dau. Samuel, Oct. 15, 1833, ae. 11 y. 6 m.
———, ch. of George, Oct. 8, 1825, ae. 2 y. 2 m.

MEIGS, Amelia, w. Joseph, Oct. 16, 1827, ae. 45 y. 9 m., at Mattapoiset.

MENDINGHALL, Judith, dau. Stephen Gardner, July —, 1831, ae. 77 y. 4 m., in Guilfor Co., N. C.

MERCHANT, Sarah Parr, dau. Benjamin, May 17, 1823, ae. 66 y. 7 m.

MERRY, Samuel, drowned on Brazil Bank, Mar. —, 1825, ae. 30 y. 1 m.

MILLER, Charles H., Dec. —, 1824, ae. 60 y., in Cuba.
John, Aug. 9, 1829, ae. 48 y. 4 m., in New York.
Mrs. Phebe, dau. late William Ray, Jr., Feb. —, 1830, ae. 45 y. 4 m., in Montgomery, Ohio.

MINOR, Jared L., July 30, 1827, ae. 45 y. 6 m.

MITCHELL, Albert, s. David, Dec. 2, 1830, ae. 32 y. 7 m.
Ariana, dau. James, Dec. 12, 1833, ae. 2 y. 3 m.
George Gorham, s. Paul, Oct. 7, 1831, ae. 33 y. 6 m.
Henry, s. Jethro, Oct. 9, 1832, ae. 26 y. 3 m., in Cincinnati, O.
Hephzibah, wid. Richard, Feb. 11, 1822, ae. 85 y. 9 m.
Jethro, Esq., late of Nantucket, Jan. 24, 1833, ae. 49 y., in Cincinnati, O.
John R., s. David, Sept. 22, 1828, ae. 27 y. 3 m., at Edgartown, buried in Nantucket.
Mary, dau. Jethro, Jan. 21, 1827, ae. 17 y. 10 m., in New York.
Phebe, w. Charles & dau. Solomon Coffin, Aug. 19, 1830, ae. 42 y. 10 m., at Auburn.
———, ch. of Seth, Oct. 17, 1822, ae. 1 y. 7 m.
———, ch. of George, Mar. 28, 1824, ae. abt. 6 m.
———, ch. of Samuel, Feb. 22, 1825, ae. 7 m.
———, dau. Samuel, Dec. 15, 1826, ae. 11 m.
———, ch. of Seth, Feb. 15, 1830, ae. 1 y. 5 m.

MITCHELL, ch. of Samuel, May 13, 1831, ae. 1 y.
———, w. Isaac, Oct. 8, 1831, ae. 28 y. 4 m.
———, ch. of George Gorham, Jan. 7, 1832, ae. 3 m. (the child was born the next day after her father's death).

MODLEY, Thomas, Apr. 8, 1826, ae. 49 y. 7 m., an Englishman who married Rebecca Marchant.

MONTGOMERY, Jacob, Mar. —, 1823, ae. 40 y., at Cincinnati, Ohio.

MOODY, William, Sheriff of County of York & Representative in General Court many years, Mar. 21, 1822, ae. 54 y. 8 m.

MOOERS, Benjamin, drowned in Delaware River, Philadelphia, 1830, ae. 31 y.
Robert, drowned in Delaware River, Philadelphia, 1830, ae. 70 y.
Samuel, s. Jonathan, lost overboard between Baltimore and New York, May 19, 1831, ae. 46 y. 9 m.
William Coffin, s. William, drowned Dec. 30, 1821, ae. 14 y. 6 m.

MOREY, Thomas, Apr. 2, 1823, at sea, off coast of Chile.

MORGAN, Charles West, s. Dudley, Aug. 18, 1831, ae. 1 y. 3 m.
Dudley, son-in-law of Peleg West, lost at sea, 1831–2, ae. 40 y.

MORRIS, Alexander Gardner, s. William, Oct. 10, 1829, ae. 5 m.
Alexander Pollard, Jan. 1, 1831, ae. 31 y. 3 m., in West Indies.
Eliza, w. William & dau. Anson Gardner, dec'd., July 20, 1829, ae. 32 y. 2 m.
John P., s. Jacob, May —, 1825, ae. 22 y. 6 m., around Cape Horn.
Jonathan B., late of Nantucket, Jan. 25, 1833, ae. 50 y. 20 days, in Cincinnati, O.
Polly, dau. Jacob, May 12, 1829, ae. 65 y. 10 m.
William, lost at sea, 1829, ae. 36 y. 4 m.; he m. Eliza Childs, wid. William.
———, ch. of Charles, Jan. 12, 1824.

MORSE, Ammi C., s. Solomon B., Aug. 20, 1825, ae. 8 y. 5 m.
Lydia, w. James, Aug. 7, 1824, ae. 37 y.
William, July 3, 1834, ae. 48 y.
William M., Nov. 22, 1831, ae. 37 y. 8 m., s. Stephen & gr. s. Isaac Myrick.

MORSELANDER, MORSLANDER, Cornelius, Jan. 13, 1828, ae. 87 y. 8 m.
Hephzibah, w. Cornelius, May 15, 1823, ae. 85 y. 4 m.
Mary Barnard, dau. Zebulon, Nov. 6, 1833, ae. 1 y. 9 m.
———, s. Cornelius, Dec. —, 1825, in Rio Janaria.

MURPHY, George Charles Henry, s. George, Sept. 15, 1823, ae. 2 y.
Josiah Fitch, s. Charles, Aug. 5, 1833, ae. 3 y. 6 m.
William, s. George, Aug. 11, 1833, ae. 2 y. 8 m.

MURREY, John, June 9, 1824, ae. 59 y. 8 m., in Baltimore, a Counsellor at Law.

MYRICK, Andrew, s. Andrew, Dec. 6, 1830, ae. 61 y. 9 m.
Avis, w. Isaac, Feb. 8, 1824, ae. 37 y. 11 m.
Charles B., s. Peter Coffin, Apr. 9, 1834, ae. 20 y. 2 m., round Cape Horn.
Edward Coffin, s. Peter Coffin, Dec. 10, 1827, ae. 20 y. 6 m., round Cape Horn.
John C., s. James & gr. s. Capt. Benjamin Cartwright, May 17, 1828, ae. 20 y. 4 m., in New York.
Priscilla, w. Jonathan & dau. of late Francis Brown, Sr., Dec. 7, 1831, ae. 73 y. 4 m., in Hudson, N. Y.
Sally, dau. James, Feb. 15, 1831, ae. 29 y. 7 m.
Seth G., Apr. 2, 1823, ae. 27 y., at sea, off coast of Chile.
———, ch. of Charles C., Sept. 8, 1825, ae. 15 days.

NARBOTH, John, Jr., Feb. —, 1827, ae. 25 y., round Cape Horn.

NEWBEGIN, Phebe, wid. James, Feb. 23, 1825, ae. 94 y. 7 m.

NEWELL, Daniel, June 10, 1830, ae. 24 y. 3 m.; he m. Winslow Waldron's daughter and was originally from Kennebeck.
———, ch. of Daniel & gr. ch. of Winslow Waldron, May 5, 1832, ae. 2 y.

NICHOLS, Charles, s. William, Nov. 25, 1830, ae. 38 y. 11 m.
Love, w. Horatio & dau. of Job Myrick, Sept. 23, 1829, ae. 54 y. 10 m.
Sarah Swain, w. Charles & dau. of Elihu Folger, Mar. 30, 1829, ae. 36 y. 9 m., in Providence, R. I.
———, ch. of Charles, July 14, 1826, ae. 1 y. 3 m.

NICHOLSON, Elijah, Aug. 19, 1823, ae. 74 y. 6 m.
Isaiah, s. Isaiah, Sept. 26, 1827, ae. 6 m.
———, ch. of Benoni, Apr. 20, 1822, ae. abt. 2 y. 2 m.
———, ch. of Isaiah, Aug. 13, 1825, ae. 4 m.

NORTON, James, Oct. 9, 1822, ae. 37 y. 9 m.
Lydia, dau. Peter, Sept. 28, 1827, ae. 16 y. 6 m., at Edgartown.
Susan, dau. Thomas, June —, 1825, ae. 1 y. 4 m.

NYE, John, Nov. 8, 1826, ae. 66 y. 9 m. in New Bedford.
Nathan, drowned at Falmouth, July —, 1829, ae. 40 y. 1 m.
——, ch. of George Warren, Aug. 25, 1831, ae. 11 m.

O'CONNER, Peter, lost at sea, May 21, 1832, ae. 20 y.

OLEN, OLIN, ———, ch. of John, Jan. 26, 1832, ae. 9 m.
———, ch. of John W., Jan. 24, 1833, ae. 1 y.

O'NEAL, John, Nov. 27, 1827, ae. 47 y. 6 m.

ORPIN, John Barnard, Sept. —, 1832, ae. 60 y. 6 m., at Siasconsett, a native of Nova Scotia; he m. Susannah Gardner, dau. Silvanus.
Rhoda, wid. Isaac & dau. Nathaniel Fisher, Dec. 8, 1833, ae. 57 y. 6 m.

PACKARD, Deborah Marsh, Dec. 12, 1821, ae. abt. 9 y.

PADDACK, PADDOCK, Aaron, drowned on Brazil Bank, May —, 1824, ae. 40 y. 3 m.
Abigail, wid. Barnabas, June 17, 1823, ae. 79 y. 1 m.
Ann, dau. Seth, June 18, 1824, ae. 7 y. 8 m.
Benjamin, Apr. 30, 1832, ae. 69 y. 11 m., near Cincinnati.
Charles Coffin, s. Laban, Sept. 10, 1825, ae. 28 y. 9 m., in Hudson.
Daniel, s. Obed, killed by a whale Feb. 1, 1830, ae. 18, Fairfield, at Kennebeck.
David S., s. David, Sept. 19, 1834, ae. 20 y. 4 m.
George, June 14, 1821, ae. 29 y., in Baltimore.
Gorham, Sept. 10, 1825, ae. 40 y., in Hudson.
Jemima, w. Benjamin, July 23, 1831, ae. 71 y. 9 m., in Ohio.
Judah, s. Stephen of Hudson, Aug. 14, 1825, ae. 55 y. 11 m.
Lucy, dau. David, Feb. 13, 1825, ae. 18 y. 1 m.
Lydia Clark, dau. Edward & Mary, & gr. dau. Jedidah Lawrence, Sept. 19, 1834, ae. 10 m.
Obed, Jan. 17, 1834, ae. 71 y. 9 m., in Kennebec; his wife died some time before.
Sarah, w. John, Sept. 2, 1823, ae. 22 y. 6 m.
William Coleman, s. William, July 21, 1832, ae. 31 y. 2 m., in Dartmouth.
———, ch. of John, Aug. 4, 1822.
———, ch. of Seth, Aug. 31, 1822.
———, ch. of John, Sept. 26, 1824, ae. 1 y. 3 m.

PALMER, Charles Bunker, ch. of Lot, Jan. 17, 1830, ae. 1 y. 1 m.

PARKER, Betsey, w. Jesse, June 29, 1825, ae. 45 y. 3 m.
Charles F., s. Joseph, Sept. 9, 1832, ae. 8 y.
Joshua H., s. Joshua H., Sept. 28, 1833, ae. 2 m.
Lydia, dau. Isaac, July 19, 1829, ae. 16 y. 4 m.
Lydia, dau. Silas, July 13, 1834, ae. 59 y. 4 m., single, formerly of Nantucket, d. in New Bedford.
Mary, w. Nathan, Mar. 8, 1825, ae. 79 y. 2 m.
Mary, w. William H., Jan. 14, 1828, ae. 31 y. 2 m.
Nathan, Dec. 22, 1827, ae. 86 y. 2 m.

PARKER, Silas, formerly of Nantucket, lately of New Bedford, Feb. 20, 1823, ae. 80 y. 3 m.
William, brother of Robert F., lost overboard, Sept. 10, 1832, ae. 37 y. 6 m.
———, ch, twin, of Joseph, Jan. —, 1826, ae. 9 m.
———, ch. of Jonathan, Sept. 26, 1833, ae. 4 y. 2 m.

PARKMAN, Samuel, of Boston, June 7, 1824, ae. 72 y. 6 m.

PARROTTIN, Nancy B., w. William & dau. Cyrus Hussey, Sept. 9, 1833, ae. 35 y. 6 m., in Dayton, O.

PARSONS, Samuel, of Nantucket, carried away with a whale line, Jan. 10, 1832, ae. 24 y. 6 m.
Theodocius, Aug. 17, 1829, ae. 73 y. 9 m., formerly Post Master at Hames Hole, Martha's Vineyard, a Revolutionary Soldier.

PATTEN, ———, ch. of Joshua, Sept. 10, 1821, ae. 2 m.
———, ch. of Joshua, Sept. —, 1821, at Mary Worth's.

PEASE, Abishai, July —, 1829, ae. 95 y. 4 m., in Chilmark.
Alexander, s. Abraham, Sept. 17, 1823, ae. 4 y. 8 m.
Coffin, s. Matthew, Sept. 24, 1825, ae. 9 m.
Fortunatus, Feb. 3, 1828, ae. 26 y. 9 m., at Chilmark.
Peter, of Edgartown, d. there, Jan. 14, 1829, ae. 93 y. 9 m.
Rebecca Folger, dau. John Harper & Mary (Bunker) Pease, & gr. dau. Gen. Benjamin Bunker, July 26, 1834, ae. 2 y.

PELHAM, Capt. Peter, at Pensacola, Aug. 12, 1826, ae. 33 y.; he m. Martha Coffin, dau. Thomas.

PELL, Benjamin, Feb. —, 1828, ae. 75 y. 6 m., in city of New York; h. Susanna Folger.

PERKINS, William, Mar. 10, 1822, ae. 57 y., suddenly.

PERRY, Jonathan, May 7, 1823, ae. 77 y. 5 m.
Susanna, w. James, June 1, 1831.
William, s. Deborah, Dec. —, 1822, ae. 24 y., formerly of Nantucket, d. in Charlestown, N. H.

PHINNEY, Eli, drowned at Coquimbo, Ship Phoenix, Mar. 25, 1824, ae. 25 y. 6 m.
Joseph, of Barnstable, drowned Nov. 4, 1827, ae. 24 y.

NANTUCKET SUPPLEMENTARY RECORDS

Contributed by MRS. SETH AMES LEWIS of Springfield, Mass.

PIERCE, James, s. Samuel, drowned in New Bedford, May 25, 1833, ae. 8 y. 4 m.

PINCKNEY, Charles Cotesworth, of Charleston, South Carolina, Aug. 16, 1825, ae. 80 y.

PINKHAM, Abiel, w. Abisha & dau. of the late Peleg Bunker of Nantucket, June 29, 1822, ae. 62 y, in Hudson, N. Y.
Celia, w. Alexander & dau. Zaccheus Fuller, July 14, 1823, ae. 22 y. 2 m.
David Coffin, s. Jonathan, Apr. 11, 1833, ae. 36 y. 10 m, mortally wounded in a Duel at Key West.
Eunice, wid. Daniel, Aug. 14, 1823, ae. 88 y. 3 m.

PINKHAM, Henry, s. Jonathan, son-in-law of Barnabas Swain, Mar. 6, 1830, ae. 55 y. 9 m, in Boston.
Hephzibah, wid. Shubael, Feb. 14, 1824, ae. 54 y. 3 m.
Jemima, wid. Jonathan, Oct. 8, 1822, ae. 89 y. 6 m.
John, second s. Tristram, killed by a whale round Cape Horn, Aug. —, 1823, ae. 36 y. 1 m.
Peggy, w. Hezekiah & dau. William Slade, July 1, 1822, ae. 44 y. 5 m, in Hudson, N. Y.
Rebecca, wid. Obed, July 13, 1827, ae. 33 y. 4 m, formerly of Nantucket, d. in Olive Township, Morgan County, Ohio.
Richard, s. Richard, 1832, ae. 77 y, in Barrington, Nova Scotia.
William C., s. George C., Mar. 29, 1824, ae. 4 y. 11 m.
———, ch. of Reuben Gardner, Sept. 28, 1825, ae. 7 m.

PINKNEY, Thomas of Charleston, S. C., Nov. 2, 1828, ae. 84 y. 1 m; he was President of the Cincinnati Societies, brother to late Charles Cartworth Pinkney.

PITMAN, Mary Elizabeth, ch. of Benjamin, Oct. 8, 1825, ae. 5 y. 6 m, in Boston.
William C., July 8, 1825, ae. 30 y. 7 m.

PITTS, Silvanus, Sept. 20, 1832, ae. 58 y. 4 m, late of Nantucket, d. at Bloomfield Co., Kennebeck.

POLLARD, Peter, Esq., Justice of the Peace, in summer of 1820, ae. 54 y. 9 m, at or near New Orleans.
———, ch. of Alexander, Sept. 19, 1829, ae. 6 m.

POMPEY, George, s. John, June 3, 1827, ae. 31 y. 1 m, in Marine Hospital, Chelsea.
Sally, wid. John, Jr., Sept. 26, 1830, ae. 45 y.
Samuel, drowned some time past, ae. 19 y. 11 m. (entry dated Apr. 22, 1828).
———, s. of George, June 9, 1824, ae. 4 y.

POTTER, Hephzibah, dau. Thomas, Aug. 22, 1833, ae. 1 y. 7 m.

PRATT, Betsey, w. Joseph, May 25, 1824, ae. 40 y. 10 m.

PRICHARD, Anna, wid. William, Apr. 4, 1834, ae. 32 y. 2 m.

PRINCE, Catharine, dau. Capt. George, May 7, 1833, ae. 1 y. 6 m.

PROUT, Jane, w. Jacob & dau. Essex Boston, Apr. 17, 1822, ae. 50 y. 6 m.

PUTNAM, Gen. Rufus, June —, 1824, ae. 87 y. 4 m, in Marietta, Ohio.

QUILL, ———, ch. of Joseph Antonio, July 9, 1823, ae. 4 y. 5 m.

RAMSDELL, Eunice, wid. George, Mar. —, 1829, ae. 75 y., at Parnalborough in Me.
Frederick William, s. James, lost from Ship Fame, Jan. —, 1832, ae. 21 y. 7 m.
Obed, ch. of William & Clarinda, Oct. 17, 1833, ae. 2 y. 6 m.
William Myrick, s. William M., Oct. 14, 1833, ae. 4 y. 8 m.
———, ch. of Charles, Oct. 17, 1832, ae. 2 y. 6 m.
———, ch. of John S., Oct. 17, 1832, ae. 3 weeks.
———, ch. of John, Sept. 3, 1833, ae. 10 m.
———, ch. of Joseph Marshall, Sept. 4, 1833, ae. 11 m.

RAND, Eliza C., dau. Thomas, Oct. 13, 1829, ae. abt. 10 m.
George Clark, s. Thomas, Nov. 13, 1828, ae. 2 y.
Dr. Isaac, of Boston, Dec. 11, 1822, ae. 81 y. 1 m.
———, ch. of William B., Feb. 15, 1831, ae. 2 y.

RANDALL, Alexander Pinkham, s. George, Apr. 29, 1831, ae. 11 m., in New Bedford.
Capt. Gideon, May 17, 1833, ae. 66 y. 6 m., formerly of Nantucket, d. in New Bedford.
John Jay, s. William, Sept. 22, 1829, ae. 3 y.

RAWSON, ———, ch. of Charles, Dec. 6, 1823, ae. abt. 1 y.
———, s. Reuel, May 11, 1825, ae. abt. 3 y. 8 m.
———, ch. of Asa, Sept. 17, 1827, ae. 6 m.
———, ch. of Asa, Sept. 16, 1834, ae. 10 m.

RAY, Barzillai Wilber, s. David, Sept. 9, 1825, ae. 1 y. 4 m.
David, Jr., s. David, Dec. 10, 1829, ae. 3 y. 3 m.
Mary Swain, dau. Obed & Anna, July 4, 1833, ae. 7 y. 2 m.
Matilda, dau. Alexander, July 19, 1822, ae. 55 y. 9 m.
Miriam, wid. Benjamin & dau. Stephen Chase, Aug. 18, 1828, ae. 82 y. 6 m., at Hudson. Stephen Chase of Nantucket.
Phebe, w. Isaiah & dau. Stephen Coffin, Nov. 4, 1826, ae. 57 y. 10 m., at Stonington, Conn.
Samuel, s. John, drowned at sea, June 18, 1824, ae. 33 y. 9 m.
———, ch. of Alexander 2d, Dec. 12, 1821, ae. abt. 3 y.
———, ch. of Reuben, Jr., Oct. 2, 1828, ae. abt. 3 weeks.

RAYMOND, Charles Henry, ch. of Charles, Feb. 4, 1834, ae. 3 y. 6 m.
Harriet, dau. Alexander, Oct. 19, 1826, ae. 2 y. 6 m.
Henry Folger, s. William Henry & Mary Ann, Sept. 4, 1834, ae. 6 m.
John, 1823, ae. 33 y. 3 m., round Cape Horn, Master of a Ship from France.
Capt. John, Dec. 24, 1825, ae. 41 y., in New Bedford.
Mary, w. Alexander, Sept. 20, 1824, ae. 25 y. 1 m.
Sarah, w. Thomas, in New York, Feb. 10, 1830, ae. 32 y. 3 m., and child, ae. 6 m.
Thomas Butler, s. Alexander, Dec. 22, 1828, ae. 3 m.

REEVES, Tapping, Esq., Barrister at Law & Judge of the County Court, Dec. 19, 1823, ae. 79 y. 9 m.

REMSEN, William, s. Arnold, drowned July 12, 1822, ae. 22 y. 7 m.

RICE, Sally, w. Stephen & dau. John House, Aug. 5, 1821, ae. 22 y. 8 m.
Capt. William, son-in-law of Gideon Worth, on board Brig Dromo, Feb. 23, 1829, ae. 34 y. 4 m.
———, ch. of Stephen, Sept. —, 1821.
———, ch. of late Capt. William & gr. ch. of Gideon Worth, Sept. 19, 1829, ae. 6 m.

RIDDELL, Josiah Hussey, Sept. 5, 1832, ae. 39 y. 6 m., in New York.
Nancy Folger, dau. Josiah, Aug. 4, 1822, ae. 3 m.
Samuel, Sr., Oct. 21, 1823, ae. 74 y. 10 m.
———, ch. of Josiah H., Nov. 4, 1824, ae. 2 y. 3 m., in New York.
———, ch. of John, Dec. 28, 1824, ae. 8 m.
———, s. John, Mar. 3, 1827, ae. 11 m.

ROBBINS, Charles, Oct. 8, 1831, ae. 33 y. 1 m.
Charles R., s. late Capt. Charles & Nabby, Sept. 8, 1833, ae. 2 y.
James, drowned near Falmouth, Feb. 11, 1829, ae. 22 y. 4 m.
Jennet, w. Charles & dau. Thomas Townsend, July 28, 1822, ae. 23 y.

ROBINSON, Abby, a native of Nantucket, dau. late Capt. Philip & gr. dau. Capt Daniel Smith, d. in Wilmington, Del., July —, 1833, ae. 23 y. 6 m.
Charles, s. James, July 5, 1823, ae. 18 y., round Cape Horn.
Charles H., Jan. —, 1826.
John, 1834, ae. 23 y., round Cape Horn.
Philip, from Charleston, S. C., May 10, 1828, ae. 30 y. 3 m., h. Mary Smith, dau. of Daniel late of Kennebeck, formerly of Nantucket.
William P., s. Philip, formerly of Nantucket, in Wilmington, Del., Aug. 11, 1834, ae. 19 y. 4 m.
———, ch. of Judith, Dec. 1, 1821, ae. 3 y. 1 m.
———, ch. of Benjamin, Jan. 31, 1831, ae. 1 y.

RODNEY, Cesar Alexander, June 10, 1824, ae. 66 y. 7 m.; Minister at Buenes Ayres.

ROGERS, Martha, dau. Capt. Warren N., Nov. 17, 1833, ae. 3 y. 2 m.
Nabby, wid. Joseph & dau. Moses & Sally Montcalm, Oct. 27, 1829, ae. 24 y.
———, ch. of Warren, Jan. 31, 1834, ae. 2 y. 6 m.

ROSE, ———, ch. of Joseph & Amy (Jones), Sept. 5, 1833, ae. 3 m.

ROSS, Margaret, w. Isaac, June 29, 1822, ae. abt. 70 y. 5 m.

ROTCH, Charity, wid. Thomas, Aug. 1, 1824, ae. 56 y. 4 m., in Ohio.
Thomas, at Mount Pleasant, Ohio, July 30, 1823, ae. 57 y. 3 m.; lived in Kendall, Ohio, formerly of Nantucket.
William B., Oct. 11, 1826, ae. 32 y. 11 m., at New Bedford.

RUDEBURG, Anna Mariah, dau. George, Nov. 10, 1833, ae. 2 y. 2 m.

RUGGLES, Charles Rawson, s. Dr. Nathaniel, May 30, 1828, ae. 1 y. 1 m.

RUSSELL, Alexander, 1825, ae. 20 y., round Cape Horn.
Alexander, second s. George, carried off with a Whale Line on Brazil Bank, Mar. 20, 1830, ae. abt. 29 y.
Bradford, at sea, round Cape Horn, 1832, ae. 24 y.
Charles, lost at Cape of Good Hope, 1830, of the Ship Dauphin.
Charles Pinkham, s. Elihu, at Liberia, coast of Africa, Apr. 4, 1832, ae. 37 y. 3 m.
David, Dec. 4, 1823, ae. 31 y. 11 m.
Elizabeth, wid. Jan. 5, 1832, ae. 102 y., in Dartmouth.
George Meader, s. Charles, Jan. 17, 1830, ae. 2 y. 2 m.
James, s. Samuel, shot at Oreco, on coast of Chili, Mar. 13, 1822.
James, s. Daniel, Sept. 8, 1827, ae. 4 y.
John Davis, s. William, Nov. —, 1830, ae. 18 y. 6 m., on Ship Sarah, near Cape Horn.
Judith, wid. Nathaniel, July 7, 1823, ae. 77 y. 7 m.
Lydia, w. Benjamin, Aug. 11, 1823, ae. 78 y. 6 m., in Hudson.
Mary Gardner, dau. Charles, Jan. 28, 1828, ae. 3 y. 1 m.
Nancy, ch. of Benjamin Franklin, Sept. 11, 1831, ae. 1 m.
Owen, s. Seth, Sept. 15, 1823, ae. 31 y.
Philip, s. Elihu, of New Bedford, killed by a whale round Cape Horn, May 26, 1828, ae. 25 y.
Samuel, Jan. 12, 1824, ae. 89 y. 2 m.
Seth, s. Seth, Apr. 14, 1834, ae. 45 y., at U. S. Hospital, Staten Island; he was in Merchant Service from New York.
William, Jr., s. William, Feb. 14, 1833, ae. 68 y., in New Bedford.
———, ch. of Charles & Louisa (Perry), Apr. 25, 1827, ae. 1 y. 8 m.
———, ch. of Charles, Sept. 13, 1828, ae. 9 m.

SAMPSON, Josiah, Esq., July 14, 1829, ae. 76 y., at Cotuit.

SANDFORD, ———, ch. of Edward, Apr. 26, 1832, ae. 1 y. 1 m.

SANDSBURY, Harriet Perkins, ch. of James, Oct. 28, 1825, ae. 2 y. 3 m.

SCUDDER, Ebenezer, s. Capt. James Delap, Feb. 20, 1829, ae. 13 y.
James, Jr., Feb. 20, 1829, ae. 20 y., s. Capt. James Delap.

SEARS, Howes, drowned in the Harbour, Sept. 14, 1831, ae. 35 y. 11 m.; he m. Avis, dau. of Z. Coffin.

SHAW, John, Sept. 22, 1823, ae. 50 y., in Philadelphia.

SHEFFIELD, Thomas Gardner, s. Josiah, Jan. —, 1825, ae. 20 y., on ship board.

SHEPHERD, Allen, Sept. 30, 1825, ae. 52 y., in New York.

SHERMAN, Abigail, w. John Junior & dau. Charles Chase of Nantucket, Mar. 6, 1831, ae. 64 y. 7 m., in New Bedford.
———, ch. of Freeman, Jan. 21, 1824, ae. 1 m.
———, ch. of Samuel, Aug. 15, 1829, ae. 4 y. 6 m.
———, ch. of Samuel, Feb. 28, 1833, ae. 9 m.

SILVESTER, ———, ch. of Joseph, Sept. 8, 1831, ae. 3 m.

SILVIA, John, July 17, 1830, ae. 35 y. 3 m., in New York City.

SIMPSON, Clarissa, w. John, Aug. 10, 1821, ae. 34 y. 8 m.
Sally, w. William J. & dau. Henry Riddell, June 18, 1824, ae. 29 y. 4 m., in New Bedford.

SLADE, Benjamin, Aug. 10, 1833, ae. 34 y. 8 m.
Charlotte, w. William, Aug. —, 1832, ae. 40 y. 4 m., in New York.
William, 1827, ae. 82 y., in Hudon, N. Y.
William, s. Benjamin of Nantucket, Aug. —, 1832, ae. 42 y. 8 m., in New York.

SLOCUM, Abigail, wid. Holder, Apr. 13, 1831, ae. 80 y., in Dartmouth.

SMALLWOOD, James, at sea, 1829, ae. 48 y.
Martha, dau. James, Sept. 19, 1825, ae. 14 y., at New Bedford (ae. 15 y. 9 m.).

SMITH, Abby Weatherel, dau. James, Jan. 14, 1834, ae. 4 y. 3 m.
Albert, of Hanover, late Sheriff of Plymouth, June 9, 1823, ae. 60 y. 9 m.
Benjamin, s. Eliphalet, at sea, 1830, ae. 50 y.
Betsey, wid., Dec. 27, 1833, ae. 60 y. 1 m., in Barnstable.
David, s. Eliphalet, at sea, 1830, ae. 44 y.
Deborah, w. Job, Apr. 21, 1822, ae. 58 y. 9 m.
Edward Francis, s. Edward, Oct. 7, 1833, ae. 2 y. 2 m.
Elisha, s. Daniel, Sr., Aug. —, 1823, ae. 69 y. 3 m., in North Carolina.
Francis Baxter, s. Job, Oct. 19, 1831, ae. 32 y.
Henry, ch. of Shubael, June 24, 1826, ae. 4 y. 2 m.
Reuben, s. Alfred, July —, 1826, ae. 1 y. 2 m.
Capt. Robert, of Ship Caledonia, killed by a whale, Feb. —, 1829, ae. 31 y. 11 m.
———, ch. of Armstrong, Apr. 2, 1831, ae. 3 m.
———, ch. of Elisha & Nancy Meader Smith, July 27, 1833, ae. 3 m.

SNOW, Andrew Jackson, s. Gideon, Feb. 12, 1833, ae.10 m.
Charlotte, dau. Gidian, May 13, 1833, ae. 2 y.
David, ch. of Samuel (he m. Uriah Swain's dau.), Oct. 10, 1833, ae. 1 y. 8 m.
Desiah or Elenore, wid. Joseph, July 28, 1830, ae. 71 y. 10 m.
Mary, w. Joseph of Falmouth, Sept. 17, 1830, ae. 76 y. 9 m.
———, ch. of Aaron, Jan. 20, 1825, ae. 2 m.
———, ch. of Aaron, Dec. 27, 1832, ae. 4 m.

SOULE, Allen, killed by a whale, Jan. 13, 1834, ae. 35 y. 2 m.
Sylvia T., dau. Stephen, Nov. 4, 1833, ae. 2 y. 6 m.

SPENCER, John, killed by a whale round Cape Horn, Nov. 1, 1829, ae. 20 y.

SPOONER, Calvin of Nantucket, Oct. 12, 1821, ae. 32 y. 9 m., in New Bedford.
Jeremiah, s. Merab & gr. s. John Coffin, Oct. 12, 1829, ae. 23 y.

SPRAGUE, ———, ch. of George, Aug. 2, 1822, ae. 6 weeks.

SPRINGER, Rebecca, w. John & dau. Shubael Macey, Feb. 17, 1832, ae. 63 y. 3 m., in Hallowell, Me.

SPROAT, James, Nov. 12, 1825, ae. 68 y. 1 m., in Taunton.

STANFORD, Thomas, Nov. 8, 1827, ae. 28 y. 1 m., a brother of Allen Kelley's wife.

STARBUCK, Anna, ch. of Thomas the 2d, Aug. 21, 1822, ae. 2 y. 3 m.
Charles, drowned in Brazil Bank, Jan. 10, 1825, ae. 24 y. 3 m.
Charles, Mar. 20, 1825, ae. 39 y. 1 m., of the Grand Ship Timalion.
David Joy, ch. of Charles, Sept. 20, 1833, ae. 9 m.
Dinah, w. Thomas, Apr. 18, 1824, ae. 81 y. 7 m.
Elizabeth Gardner, dau. Albert Norton, Oct. 18, 1833, ae. 10 m.
Frederick, drowned at sea, June 18, 1824.
Hezekiah, formerly of Nantucket, June 10, 1830, ae. 81 y., in Clinton County, Ohio.

STARBUCK, Josiah, ch. Charles, July 20, 1821, ae. 8 m., a twin.
Mary, wid. Thaddeus & dau. William Brock, July 24, 1822, ae. 63 y. 2 m.
Susanna, Oct. 22, 1824.
Susanna, ch. of Charles, Aug. —, 1825, ae. 8 m.
Thomas the 2d, July 21, 1823, ae. 39 y. 4 m.
———, ch. of Josiah, Sept. 24, 1825, ae. 1 m.
———, ch. of Thomas, Sept. 24, 1825, ae. 2 y. 6 m.; the father & mother both d. before it.
———, dau. of Henry, June 22, 1828, ae. 5 y. 3 m.

STEPHENS, STEVENS, Ann, w. William of Savannah, & dau. Hon. Thomas Hazard, Oct. 4, 1823, ae. 43 y. 9 m.
Calvin, killed by a whale, in the George Porter, Oct. —, 1822, ae. 25 y. 6 m.
———, ch. of Joseph, Oct. 4, 1825, ae. 2 y. 1 m.

STETSON, Lydia Barnard, dau. Capt. John, Nov. 3, 1833, ae. 3 y. 8 m.
Nancy, dau. Barzillai, Mar. 21, 1824, ae. 19 y. 11 m.

STEWART, David, s. Joseph, Nov. 23, 1833, ae. 9 m.
Hephzibah, w. Elijah, May 4, 1824, ae. 64 y. 1 m., in Edgartown.
William, of Martha's Vineyard, Jan. —, 1824, ae. 94 y. 6 m.
William, late of Nantucket, Apr. 14, 1829, ae. 60 y. 6 m., at Edgartown.

STIGNEY, Isaac, drowned off South side of Nantucket, from Brig Packet of Providence, R. I., Dec. 3, 1828.

STONE, Daniel drowned at Falmouth, July —, 1829, ae. 40 y. 4 m.

STUBBS, Eliza, w. William, late of Nantucket, Jan. —, 1830, ae. 41 y., in Portland.
———, ch. of William, Dec. 6, 1826, ae. 1 y.

STURTEVANT, Josiah, a Congregational Minister in Barnstable, Jan. 14, 1825, ae. 46 y. 9 m.

SUMMERFIELD, John, a Methodist Preacher, June, 1825, ae. 27 y.

SWAIN, Abigail, w. or wid. Nathan, Feb. 3, 1823, ae. 74 y. 8 m.
Abigail, wid. Valentine 2d, Oct. 25, 1823, ae. 44 y. 7 m.
Albert G., s. Moses, at sea, Sept. —, 1828, ae. 33 y. 6 m.
Andrew F., s. Barnabas, Oct. 1, 1828, ae. 30 y. 5 m., in Providence.
Barzilla Cottle, s. Elihu, Nov. 11, 1828, ae. 1 y. 6 m.
Benjamin, Dec. 20, 1821, ae. 39 y. 8 m., Mate of the Golden Farmer.
Charles Gorham, s. Peleg, Aug. 31, 1823, abt. 6 m.
Charles Hussey, s. Thaddeus, May 9, 1826, ae. 26 y. 9 m., in Fair Haven.
Edward, s. Moses of N. Bedford, formerly of Nantucket, 1833, ae. 36 y. 7 m., round Cape Horn.
Edwin, ch. of David, Aug. 28, 1828, ae. 3 m.
Eunice D., dau. Alexander, Dec. 2, 1832, ae. 7 y. 1 m.
Hephzibah, w. Lewis & dau. Micajah Swain, Jan. 6, 1825, ae. 51 y. 1 m.
Isaiah, s. Freeman, lost at sea, 1825–6.
James C., s. Samuel, Jan. 3, 1832, ae. 37 y., at Crosetts Islands, buried there.
Jerusha, wid. Charles, Jr., & dau. Solomon Gardner, Dec. 8, 1824, ae. 67 y. 9 m., in Cambridge.
Joseph, Esq., killed Dec. 15, 1821, ae. 69 y. 2 m.
Love, dau. Job, Apr. 25, 1822, ae. 37 y. 9 m.
Margaret, wid. Jonathan, Feb. 2, 1822, ae. 92 y. 2 m.
Mary, w. Thomas & dau. Thomas Townsend, Sept. 4, 1823, ae. 18 y. 2 m.
Mary, w. Abner, Mar. 17, 1824, ae. 40 y.
Mary, w. William & dau. of late Henry Coffin, May 25, 1828, ae. 75 y. 4 m., at Easton, N. Y.
Mary Lewis, dau. David 2d, Feb. 3, 1823, ae. 11 m.
Mary Lewis, dau. David 2d, Oct. 20, 1830, ae. 1 y. 3 m.
Peleg Barrett, s. Micajah, Aug. 4, 1824, ae. 2 y. 3 m.

SWAIN, Priscilla, wid. Benjamin, Jr., & dau. Samuel Robinson of the Kings Evil, July 20, 1822, ae. 39 y. 9 m.
Rowland, s. Job, May —, 1822, ae. 30 y. 4 m., in West Indies.
Samuel, Aug. 29, 1823, ae. 53 y. 3 m., at Galliopolis, O.
Samuel L., s. Frederick & Ann, July 31, 1834, ae. 6 m.
Samuel Tuck, twin s. Frederick Coffin, Apr. 1, 1833, ae. 1 m.
Sarah, dau. Jonathan 2d, Mar. 29, 1822, ae. 8 y.
Sarah W., dau. Job, Feb. 1, 1824, ae. 16 y. 5 m.
Shubael, s. Joshua, lost at sea, 1831.
Solomon, Aug. 4, 1825, ae. 55 y. 4 m., at Cincinnati, Ohio.
Stephen, s. Samuel, Sept. —, 1823, ae. 28 y. 9 m., near Alexandria.
Susan, dau. George, Jr., Sept. 25, 1833, ae. 7 y. 2 m.
Susanna, wid. Abishai 2d, Nov. 12, 1821, ae. 64 y., in Hudson.
Susanna H., ch. of Reuben, Sept. 26, 1833, ae. 6 y. 4 m.
William Samuel, s. William & gr. s. Grafton Swain, Jan. 7, 1834, ae. 11 y. 3 m.
William Tuck, twin s. Frederick Coffin, Apr. 1, 1833, ae. 1 m.
Zaccheus, s. Charles, Oct. —, 1830, ae. abt. 67 y., in New Garden, N. Carolina.
———, ch. of Laban, Jan. —, 1824, ae. abt. 2 y.
———, ch. of Richard, Dec. 24, 1824, ae. 6 m.
———, ch. of Abraham, Oct. 4, 1825, ae. 1 y. 2 m.
———, ch. of Obed B., Oct. 11, 1825, ae. 1 m.
———, ch. of Jonathan, July 22, 1826, ae. 11 m.
———, ch. of Barzillai, July —, 1826, ae. 6 m.
———, ch. of Daniel, Oct. 20, 1826, ae. 1 y. 6 m.
———, ch. of William C., July 4, 1829, ae. 2 y. 2 m.
———, w. Richard, Dec. 2, 1830, ae. 30 y., in New York.
———, ch. of Edward, May 21, 1832, ae. 6 m.
———, ch. of Frederick Folger, Aug. 13, 1832, ae. 1 y. 10 m.

SWAZEY, David, s. Jonathan, June 29, 1830, ae. 9 y.

SWIFT, Hannah, w. Ezekiel E., Nov. 9, 1833, ae. 35 y. 3 m.
Joseph, formerly from Sandwich, Aug. 14, 1832, ae. 70 y. 7 m.
Sarah Brown, dau. Henry, July 9, 1825, ae. 5 y. 4 m., in Boston.
———, ch. of Seth F., the Minister, Aug. 4, 1822.
———, ch. of Alexander Swain, Apr. 27, 1828, ae. 8 m.
———, ch. of Alexander S., Aug. 19, 1830, ae. 2 m.
———, s. Henry, Feb. 4, 1833, ae. 3 y.
———, ch. of Dr. Paul, Aug. 31, 1833, ae. 4 m.

TABER, James Henry, ch. of John, Jan. 20, 1823, ae. 1 y. 6 m.
———, ch. of William, Mar. 6, 1831, ae. 1 m.
———, ch. of William, May 25, 1834, ae. 2 m.

TALLANT, James Madison, only s. Nathaniel, July 3, 1828, ae. 1 y., in Hallowell.

TASHAMY, Sarah, an Indian Woman, Oct. 27, 1821, ae. 75 y.

TAYLOR, Thomas, lost at sea, May 21, 1832.

TEMPLE, Mary, w. Solomon & dau. Thomas Coffin, Jr., in fall of 1824, ae. 24 y., in Philadelphia.

THATCHER, Lewis, of Barnstable, Sept. 19, 1825, ae. 44 y. 9 m.

THOMAS, Rebecca, w. Nathan, Mar. 8, 1832, ae. 58 y. She was a Holmes of Barnstable.

THOMPSON, Benjamin, drowned off South side of Nantucket, from Brig Packet of Providence, R. I., Dec. 3, 1828.
Isaiah or Isaac C., s. Dea. Isaac, Feb. 11, 1834, ae. 5 y. 2 m.
Dr. John, Sept. 10, 1824, ae. 22 y. 1 m., in New York.
William, drowned off South side of Nantucket, from Brig Packet of Providence, R. I., Dec. 3, 1828.
———, ch. of James, July 4, 1821, ae. abt. 4 m., at Poadpess.

TOBEY, Amira, dau. Tristram, Oct. 11, 1825, ae. 1 y. 4 m.
Charles, lost at sea, 1826.
Nancy, w. William, June 20, 1833, ae. 54 y. 11 m., formerly of Nantucket, d. in Boston. She came from Sandwich.
Samuel, Esq., of Berkley, d. last month, ae. 80 y. 9 m. (Entry dated Jan. —, 1824.)
William, May 12, 1833, ae. 64 y., in Boston, formerly of Nantucket.
———, ch. of Ansel, Sept. —, 1831, ae. 2 m.

TRACY, Eliza G., dau. Henry, Mar. 10, 1833, ae. 56 y. 8 m., in New Bedford.
Elizabeth, wid. Henry & dau. Zaccheus Gardner, Feb. 11, 1832, ae. 82 y. 2 m., at New Bedford, formerly of Nantucket.

TRAFTON, Samuel Gardner, 1823, ae. 28 y. 2 m., at Savannah.
———, ch. of Samuel Gardner, Sept. 28, 1822, ae. 1 y. 6 m., at Providence.

TUCKER, Hannah, w. Abraham, Feb. 17, 1833, ae. 66 y. 3 m., in Dartmouth.

TURNER, Edmund, Jan. 10, 1825, ae. 24 y. 3 m., on ship board, a sailor from Kentucky.

TYLER, Charlottee, wid. Philip, Aug. 22, 1834, ae. 63 y. 4 m.
Capt. Solomon, drowned off South side of Nantucket, Dec. 3, 1828, from Brig Packet of Providence, R. I.

UPHAM, Jonathan, July 26, 1822, ae. 68 y. 9 m.

VAN DYKE, Sarah, wid. Capt. & dau. Capt. Jared Gardner, May —, 1827, ae. 27 y. 9 m., in Albany. Her husband lost at sea.

VARNUM, James M., s. Joseph Bradley, Sept. 11, 1821, ae. 36 y., at Washington City.
Joseph Bradley, Sept. 18, 1821, ae. 72 y. 9 m., at his Seat in Dracut, Middlesex.

VILLIERS, Henry, an Englishman, Oct. 7, 1833, ae. 45 y. 6 m.

VINCENT, Nathaniel, Sr., of Edgartown, Martha's Vineyard, June 5, 1822, ae. 97 y. 4 m., the oldest man on the Vineyard.
Nathaniel, Nov. 7, 1824, ae. 26 y. 7 m., in Charleston.

WADE, Elizabeth, dau. Henry, May 3, 1833, ae. 3 y. 2 m.

WALDRON, Reuben, Aug. 20, 1828, ae. 42 y. 1 m., in Cincinnati, Ohio.

WALKER, Margaret, w. Silas, Mar. 25, 1826, ae. 36 y. 1 m.

WALLACE, Mary, wid., dau. of late Charles West, Nov. 21, 1828, ae. 67 y. 9 m., near Hudson, N. Y.

WARD, Rhoda, w. Josiah & dau. Richard Pinkham, Apr. —, 1830, ae. 71 y., in Hudson.

WARREN, Benjamin, of Nantucket, Apr. 12, 1828, ae. 28 y. 6 m., in Marine Hospital, Chelsea.

WASHBURN, Benjamin, s. Amaziah, Mar. 22, 1823, ae. 5 y. 2 m.

WATERMAN, John, s. Thaddeus, July —, 1833, ae. 42 y. 2 m., in New Orleans.
Mary Ann, w. Jotham, Jan. 10, 1833, ae. 24 y. 3 m., in New Bedford.
Stephen, 1827, ae. 61 y., in Hudson, N. Y.
Thaddeus, Sr., Jan. 22, 1824, ae. 78 y. 9 m.

WATSON, ———, ch. of Henry, Aug. 8, 1832, ae. 1 y.

WEBSTER, Grace, w. Daniel, Esq., Jan. 21, 1828, ae. 40 y. 1 m., in New York.
Martha H., dau. John, Nov. 22, 1831, ae. 17 y., formerly of Nantucket, d. in New Bedford.

WEED, Obadiah, of Deer Island, drowned off Nantucket, Mar. 22, 1829.

WEEKS, Elizabeth, w. Dr. Francis, Oct. 24, 1829, ae. 60 y., in Falmouth.
Sophronia, w. James, June 19, 1830, ae. 39 y. 8 m.
———, ch. of James, Sept. 16, 1822, ae. 1 y. 1 m.

WEIDERHOLD, WIEDERHOLD, Ann Myrick, dau. John, Jr., Oct. 13, 1822, ae. 8 m.
———, ch. of Isaac Myrick, July 26, 1827, ae. 2 y. 1 m.
———, ch. of John, Jr., Oct. 10, 1831, ae. 2 y.

WENTWORTH, Jeremiah, a seaman, lost overboard from Schooner Louisa, Dec. 22, 1830, ae. 24 y.

WESSELLS, William, a sailor, Apr. 30, 1828, ae. 39 y. 6 m.

WEST, Ira M. W., lost at sea, 1831–2, ae. 35 y.
Pardon H., June —, 1831, ae. 25 y., round Cape Horn.
Silas, killed by a whale, Feb. 10, 1822, ae. 40 y. 5 m. Master of a Ship from London.
Dr. Silas, Jan. 18, 1825, ae. 42 y. 8 m., in Tisbury.

WESTGATE, ———, ch. of Daniel, June 2, 1828, ae. abt. 2 m. or 6 weeks.

WHEELWRIGHT, Sally G., w. Samuel & dau. of Reuben Gardner, Jr., July 1, 1833, ae. 54 y. 6 m., in Boston, formerly of Nantucket.
Sarah, w. Samuel, Dec. 18, 1822, ae. 44 y., in Boston.

WHIPPEY, Alexander, s. Josiah & Kezia, drowned round Cape Horn, some time past, ae. 23 y. (Entry dated Feb. —, 1834.)
George, Sr., Apr. 7, 1823, ae. 78 y. 1 m., at New Bedford.
Henry C., ch. of Frederick F., Aug. 19, 1833, ae. 8 m.
John, s. Davis, Oct. 13, 1832, ae. 30 y. 1 m., in Cincinnati, O.
Love, dau. Nathaniel, Apr. 7, 1822, ae. 56 y. 10 m.
Martha, wid. James, Jan. 27, 1830, ae. 77 y. 2 m.
Mary, dau. Benjamin, Nov. 6, 1821, ae. 44 y. 7 m.
Susanna, wid. Zebulon, Dec. 29, 1822, ae. 43 y. 7 m.

WHITE, Ardon, drowned round Cape Horn, 1827–8, ae. 25 y.
David, June 10, 1832, ae. 57 y., in Cincinnatti, O., formerly of Nantucket.

WHITEUS, Reuben, s. James, Jr., 1829, ae. 38 y. 4 m., around Cape Horn.
Susanna, w. Ambrose, Nov. 24, 1830, ae. 48 y. 1 m.

WHITFORD, George L., s. George B., Mar. 4, 1833, ae. 3 y. 2 m.
George Washington, s. George, Mar. 17, 1833, ae. 1 y. 6 m.

WHITMAN, Isaac Winslow, s. Isaac Winslow & Nancy J., Oct. 11, 1833, ae. 2 y. 2 m., in N. Y.
Jonas, of Barnstable, Doctor, July 29, 1824, ae. 75 y. 3 m.
———, ch. of Isaac W., May 8, 1826, ae. 2 m.

WHITNEY, John, at sea, 1823, ae. 27 y.

WHITWELL, Benjamin, Attorney at Law, Apr. 5, 1825, ae. 41 y. 3 m.

WIDGER, William of MarbleHead, d. here Oct. 8, 1823, ae. 76 y.

WILBER, Briggs, July 24, 1831, ae. 36 y. 11 m.
Jacob, s. Abraham, lost at sea Dec. 20, 1821, ae. 18 y.
John, Jr., s. John, June 2, 1834, ae. 45 y. 9 m., at Marine Hospital, Chelsea.
———, ch. of John, Jr., Aug. 24, 1821, ae. 2 m.
———, ch. of John, Jr., May —, 1826, ae. 1 y. 9 m.
———, ch. of Sandford & gr. ch. of Cyrus Hussey and of John Wilber, Jan. 26, 1830, ae. 2 y. 6 m.

WILLCOX, Judith, Feb. 21, 1825, ae. 73 y. 7 m.

WILLIAMS, Lemuel, of New Bedford, Representative for this District, Nov. 11, 1828, ae. 82 y. 3 m.
William, of East Hartford, Feb. 3, 1828, ae. 76 y. 9 m.
———, w. William of East Hartford, Feb. 3, 1828, ae. 56 y. 8 m.

WILLIS, Eliakim, Mar. —, 1825, ae. 65 y. 8 m., in Charleston, South Carolina, formerly of Nantucket.

WING, Cornelius, Oct. 4, 1823, ae. 59 y. 1 m., in Cincinnati, Ohio, formerly of Sandwich, late of Nantucket; he moved his family there.
Samuel T., s. George, Jan. 3, 1834, ae. 3 y. 5 m.

WINSLOW, Benjamin Franklin, s. Benjamin, Jr., July 14, 1833, ae. 3 m.
George W., s. Samuel H., drowned Nov. 15, 1833, ae. 5 y.
Isabella H., ch. of George & gr. ch. of late Joseph Winslow, Sept. 1, 1834, ae. 6 m.
James Henry, ch. George, July 23, 1834, ae. 9 m.
Joseph, June 20, 1829, ae. 54 y. 5 m.
———, ch. of Oliver Perry, July 9, 1825, ae. abt. 10 m.
———, ch. of George, Dec. 27, 1832, ae. 6 m.

WOOD, WOODS, Daniel, Dec. 22, 1821, ae. 42 y. 7 m.
Jera B., ch. of John Coffin, Oct. 2, 1832, ae. 3 m.
Jonathan, Feb. 24, 1823, ae. 88 y. 4 m.
Mary, w. Dr. William & sister-in-law of Jera B. Wood, May 10, 1823, ae. 55 y. 9 m., in Dighton.
Obadiah, July 18, 1825, ae. 69 y. 5 m.
William Fanning, s. Daniel, Jan. 10, 1828, ae. 25 y. 2 m., in N. Y.
———, s. Jera B., July 9, 1822, ae. 11 m.
———, ch. of Zephaniah, Oct. 9, 1822, ae. 1 y. 1 m.
———, ch. of Jera B., Aug. 12, 1826, ae. 9 m.
———, ch. of David, June 4, 1829, ae. 5 m.
———, ch. of Charles, Oct. 2, 1832, ae. 3 m.

WOODBURY, Nathaniel, July 5, 1823, ae. 94 y. 9 m.

WORTH, Alexander M., s. Capt. Seth, Sept. 20, 1832, ae. 6 m.
Andrew S., Aug. 27, 1823, ae. 48 y. 1 m.
Charles Frederick, ch. of Seth, July 23, 1834, ae. 8 m.
Edward, drowned at Great Point, July —, 1830, ae. 16 y. 5 m.
Edward Starbuck, ch. of Charles 2d, Aug. 29, 1823, ae. 14 days.
Eliza Ann, w. Capt. Cyrus B., of Edgartown, Jan. 2, 1828, ae. 23 y. 6 m.
Jethro, Esq., Mar. 10, 1829, ae. 75 y., at Edgartown.
John Akins, s. Thomas & his 3d wife, ——— Akins, Apr. —, 1827, ae. 46 y. 8 m., in Hudson.
Judith, w. Joseph & dau. William Starbuck, Nov. 11, 1830, ae. 96 y. 4 m., in New Garden, N. C.
Sophia Folger, dau. William, Oct. 15, 1825, ae. 16 y. 1 m.
Susanna Clark, dau. Frederick, Aug. 19, 1830, ae. 3 y.
Thomas, Oct. 27, 1821.
Thomas, s. William, Jan. 12, 1828, ae. 14 y.
Thomas S., s. Shubael, Mar. —, 1831, ae. 29 y. 3 m., on Ship Maria, around Cape Horn.
———, s. Frederick, post master, July 26, 1822, ae. 1 y. 7 m.
———, ch. of William the Second, Aug. 20, 1825, ae. 8 m.
———, dau. Frederick, May —, 1826, ae. 2 m.
———, s. Charles A., Dec. 30, 1832, ae. 3 m.
———, s. George B. & gr. s. Capt. Benjamin Worth, 1832, ae. 10 y. 9 m., in New Bedford.

WRIGHT, Christopher, Aug. 1, 1823, ae. 41 y. 4 m., in Killingworth.
Zilphah, wid. Capt. Thomas, June 14, 1829, ae. 66 y. 8 m.

WYER, Caroline Swift, dau. Christopher, Sept. 11, 1833, ae. 5 y. 6 m.
Caroline T., ch. of Benjamin, Apr. 3, 1834, ae. 1 y. 6 m.
Capt. Obed, Oct. 4, 1822, ae. 53 y., on coast of California.
Pernal, dau. of late John, Mar. 4, 1829, ae. 50 y. 9 m., at Sidney, Me.
———, ch. of Benjamin, June 5, 1822, ae. 3 m.

NEGROES

ANTONIA, Joseph, Apr. 12, 1829, ae. 36 y. 10 m.

BINKS, John, Apr. 4, 1833, ae. 32 y. 6 m.

BOSTAN, Reuben, June 29, 1832, ae. 61 y.

BROWN, Elizabeth, Jan. 22, 1823, ae. 30 y.

BUMPER, Michael, Sept. 22, 1830, ae. 30 y.

CARTER, Nancy, w. John, Feb. 4, 1833, ae. 35 y.

COLEMAN, Henry, 1830, ae. 31 y., round Cape Horn.

COOK, Oliver, May 26, 1834, ae. 22 y. 6 m.

COOPER, Mary, July 6, 1826, ae. 45 y. 1 m.
Sophia, w. John, Sept. 9, 1832, ae. 27 y.

DAVIS, Sophia, dau. Samuel & Patience Harris, Dec. 24, 1831, ae. 29 y. 6 m.

DOUGHLASS, Mary, w. Michael & dau. Tobias Boston, July 4, 1834, ae. 65 y.

FRANCIS, John, Mar. 22, 1829, ae. 30 y.

GARDNER, Almira, w. George Washington, Feb. 28, 1834, ae. 27 y. 1 m.
Anstrep, wid. Daniel, Sept. 18, 1832, ae. 66 y. 2 m.
Dorcas, Oct. 27, 1831, ae. 40 y. 11 m.
———, ch. of Daniel, Dec. 31, 1821, ae. 4 m.
———, ch. of Daniel, May —, 1822, ae. 6 m.

GORDEN, GORDON, John, Sept. 12, 1831, ae. 48 y.
Lettice, w. John & dau. Ceasar Summons, Feb. 23, 1828, ae. 33 y. 5 m.

GREEN, Hannah, Sept. 24, 1824, ae. 40 y. 2 m.

HARRIS, Mary, June 19, 1825, ae. 24 y.

JACKSON, Clark, of Nantucket, Jan. 4, 1830, ae. 25 y., in Boston.

JONES, Cloe, June 20, 1831, ae. 31 y. 1 m.
Lucretia, w. Thomas, Oct. 22, 1823, ae. 28 y. 7 m.
Mary, Apr. 14, 1834, ae. 32 y. 2 m.
William, 1832, ae. 30 y., on board Ship Omega.
———, ch. of Jacob, June 6, 1828, ae. 6 m.

JOURDAN, Samuel, Oct. 31, 1828, ae. 58 y. 4 m.

MAJOR, Francis, Oct. 28, 1831, ae. 36 y. 1 m.

MERINO, Francisco, Aug. —, 1832, ae. 31 y. 11 m.

MOANE, John, drowned July 27, 1823, ae. 40 y. 3 m.

MOORE, Sophrona, w. Henry & dau. Isaac Barlow, July 8, 1834, ae. 25 y.

PETERSON, Lewis, at sea, 1830, ae. 40 y.

POMPEY, Ezekiel, Feb. 5, 1825, ae. 36 y. 1 m.
Rosanna, dau. John, July 4, 1833, ae. 21 y.

RANDOLPH, John, May —, 1823.

ROSS, Martha, dau. James, Aug. 25, 1833, ae. 19 y. 2 m.
Matthew, Aug. 5, 1823, ae. 73 y.

SIMPSON, John, drowned Sept. 8, 1823, ae. 45 y. 2 m.

SMITH, George, drowned June 14, 1823, ae. 34 y. 2 m.

STEWART, James W., late of Nantucket, Nov. 22, 1829, ae. 53 y. 3 m., in Boston.

STORY, Lucy, w. John, June 8, 1822, ae. 30 y. 6 m.

SUMMONS, Cloa, mother of Jeffrey, June 12, 1823, ae. 97 y. 6 m.
Grace, Apr. 18, 1826, ae. 44 y. 1 m.
Jeffrey, Dec. 11, 1831, ae. 75 y. 8 m.
Noah, s. Jeffrey, June 10, 1823, ae. 24 y. 8 m.

SYCKLES, James, Apr. 17, 1833, ae. 39 y. 9 m.

TYLER, Philip, Dec. 25, 1831, ae. 63 y. 6 m.

WAMSLEY, Polly, wid. Benjamin, Sept. 21, 1825, ae. 61 y. 10 m.

WARREN, Joseph, Mar. 30, 1828, ae. about 44 y.

WILLIAMS, George, Mar. 7, 1833, ae. 65 y.; he m. Nancy Hero.
John, May 26, 1834, ae. 37 y. 4 m.

WRIGHT, Phillis, w. Bristol, Feb. 11, 1829, ae. 62 y.

RECORDS OF THE SECOND CHURCH OF SCITUATE, NOW THE FIRST UNITARIAN CHURCH OF NORWELL, MASS.

Communicated by GEORGE C. TURNER, Esq., of Norwell.

BAPTISMS.

A Catalogue of the names of all such as have beene baptized by Guilulmo Wetherell* pastor to ye Church since his election into office in Septbre: 1645.

Anno: 1645.	
Sarah ye daughter of Will Wetherell Hopestill ye sonn of Elisha Besby Thomas ye sonn of Thomas King	Septbr ye 7.
Deborah ye daughter } of George Willard Daniel ye sonne — } Hannah ye daughter of Wll Brook	Sept. 14.
Joseph, Benjamin, Thomas, sons of Robt Studson:	Oct: 5.
Joshua ye sonn of Geo: Willard	Novemb. 2.
Joanna ye daughter of Ephraim Kempton.	Novemb. 9.
Sarah, Joseph, Hanna, ye children of Wll Randall	Novemb. 23.
John ye sonn of Elisha Besby	Decemb. 21.
Samuel ye son of Resolved White Rebecca ye daughter of Tho: Lappham Sarah ye daughter of John Stockbridge	March 15

Anno: 1646	1646
Nathaniel ye sonne of Will: Brook	March 29.
Comfort } ye son & daughter of Thomas Starr Elizabeth }	June: 7
Hanna ye daughter of widdow Hatch	June. 14.

* The earliest records in the pastor's own handwriting give his name as *Wetherell.* Mr. Deane, in his History of Scituate, spells the name *Witherell* in almost every instance. Perhaps the pastor later changed the "e" to "i."

Elizabeth } Sarah } yᵉ daughters of Gilbert Brook	June 21.
Samuel yᵉ son of Robt Studson	July. 12 :
Lydia yᵉ daughter of George Sutton	Sept. 13.
Hanna yᵉ daughter of William Wetherell	Febr. 28.
William yᵉ sonne of James Torry	March. 21.
1647.	**1647.**
Mary and William yᵉ children of Wllm Parker	May—16.
William yᵉ sonn of James Adams	May. 23.
Martha yᵉ daughter of William Parker	June 13.
Hesther yᵉ daughter of John Stockbridge	July—11.
Resolved yᵉ sonn of Resolved White	Novemb. 14
Patience yᵉ daughter of Ephraim Kempton	Novemb. 21.
Mary yᵉ daughter of William Brook	Novemb. 28.
William yᵉ son of William Randall	Jan. 2.
Daniel yᵉ sonn of Thomas King	Febr. 13.
1648	**1648.**
Nathaniel yᵉ sonn of Abraham Prebble	Apr. 9.
John yᵉ sonn of Robt Studson	May. 7.
Mary yᵉ daughter of Elisha Besby	Sept. 10.
Joseph yᵉ sonn of Thomas Lappham	Sept. 24.
Sarah yᵉ daughter of George Sutton	Decemb. 3.
1649.	**1649.**
Joseph yᵉ sonn of James Torry	March. 25.
Joseph yᵉ sonn of Richard Garret	Apr. 1.
Ephraim yᵉ sonne of Ephraim Kempton	Apr. 8.
Jonathan } Joseph } ye sonns of John Turner senior	May
Patience yᵉ daughter of William Parker	May. 6.
Anna yᵉ daughter of James Adams	May 20.
Anna yᵉ daughter of Resolved White	June. 10.
Mary yᵉ daughter of Gilbert Brook	July. 15.
Elizabeth yᵉ daughter of Thomas Courtis	Aug. 19.
John yᵉ sonn of James Baits	Octob. 7.
Margaret yᵉ daughter of George Bastow	Febr. 24.
1650.	**1650.**
Naomi yᵉ daughter of Richard Sylvester	Apr. 14.
John yᵉ sonne of William Randall	Apr. 28.
Eunice yᵉ daughter of Robt Studson	May. 19.
Sarah the daughter of Thomas King } Sarah yᵉ daughter of Wllm Brook }	May. 26.
Rachel yᵉ daughter of Gilbert Brook	July. 7.
Deborah yᵉ daughter of William Bastow	Aug. 18.
Sarah yᵉ daughter of George Sutton	Sept. 15.
Nathaniel yᵉ sonne of Mr Joseph Tilden	Septr. 29.
Ezekiell ye son of John Turner senior	January. 19.
Manasseh yᵉ sonne of Ephraim Kempton	Febr : 9 :
Hannah yᵉ daughter of Walter Hatch	Mar. 23.
John : Hannah : } Sarah Mary the } children of John Bryant	Mar. 23.

1651.	1651.
Richard ye sonne of James Adams	Apr. 27.
Martha ye Daughter of Elisha Besbye	Apr. 27.
Mary, Elizab., Sarah } ye daughters of Henry Adverd	June 29 :
Damaris ye daughter of James Torry	Novemb. 2.
John the sonn of Richard Garrett	Novemb. 30.
Martha ye daughter of John Bryant	March : 7,
Lois ye daughter of Robt Studson	March. 21.

1652.	1652.
Experience ye daughter of Henry Adverd,	Apr : 18.
Jeremiah ye son of Jeremy Burroughs	May. 23.
Miriam ye daughter of William Brooks	June 6.
John ye sonne of Thomas King	June 27.
Anna —, Elizabeth } ye daughters of Richard Courtis	July 4.
Elizabeth ye daughter of Resolved White	July 4.
Phebe ye daughter of Gilbert Brooke	Septbr 5.
Mary ye daughter of Wll Hatch, William ye sonne of Wll Bastow }	Octob : 3.
Elizabeth ye. Daughter of Wll Randall	Octob. 17.
John ye sonne of Mr Joseph Tilden	Jan. 2.
Lydia ye daughter of John Turner senior	Febr : 20.

1653.	1653.
John ye sonne of Humphrey Johnson	May. 8.
George ye sonne of George Bastow (deceased at Cambridge)	June. 12.
Elizabeth ye daughter of Geo Sutton	Aug. 28.
Samuel ye sonne of Walter Hatch	Jan. 1.
Mary ye daughter of James Adams	Febr. 5.
John ye sonne of Richard Courtis	Febr. 5.
Robert ye sonne of Robt Studson	Febr. 26.
Samuel ye sonne of John Bryant	Febr. 26.
Thomas ye sonne of Thomas Robinson	Mar. 5.
John ye sonne of Jeremy Burrouges	Mar. 5.
Phoebe ye daughter of William Hatch	Mar. 19.

1654.	1654.
Hesther ye daughter of Richard Sylvester	Mar. 26.
Nathaniell ye sonn of Richard Garrett	May 11.
Jonathan ye sonn of James Torry, Ruth ye daughter of Ephr: Kempton }	Septbr. 24.
Josiah ye sonne of Resolved White	Octob 14.
John ye sonne of John Turner, Elisha ye sonne of Elisha Besbye }	Octob : 29.
Rebecca ye daughter of Mr Joseph Tilden	Febr 25.
Job ye sonne of William Randall	March 4.
Margaret ye daughter of James Adams	March 18.
Deborah ye daughter of William Brooke	March 18.

1655.	1655.
Nathan ye sonne of Thomas Turner	March ye 25.
Batshebah ye daughter of Gilbert Brooke	April 8.
Martha ye daughter of William Bastow	Apr. 22.
Mary ye daughter of John Stockbridge	April. 29.
Elizabeth ye daughter of James Doughty	May 27.
Elizabeth ye daughter of Jeremy Burroughs	May 27.
Joseph ye sonne of Humfrey Johnson	July 22.
Israell ye sonne of John Turner, junior and grandchild to Humfry Turner	Novemb. 25
Mary ye daughter of Richard Garrett	Decembr 30
Elizabeth, Ruth } ye daughters of Nathaniel Rawlins and grand-children to Rich Sylvester	Febr. 24.
Jane, ye daughter of Walter Hatch	March 9.

1656.	1656
Mary ye daughter of Richard Courtis	Apr. 6.
Miles ye sonn of William Parker	Apr. 6.
Lydia ye daughter of William Parker	Apr. 13.
Daniel grandchild to our sister Spring, and sonne to Daniel Pryor	July 6.
Lydia ye daughter of William Hatch	July 6.
Hannah daughter of Nicholas Wade	August 3d.
Increase sonne to John Whetston, Elizabeth daughter to Thomas Turner	August. 10.
Susannah daughter to Resolved White	Novemb. 9.
Margarite ye daughter of Antony Dodson, Lydia daughter to Nathaniel Rawlins	Novemb. 23.
Hannah daughter to Elisha Besbee	Decembr. 7
Mary ye daughter of John Adams of Marshfield & great grandchild to Widdow James	Decemb. 14.
Joseph ye sonne of Thomas Robinson	March. 8.
Mary ye daughter of James Torry, Sarah ye daughter of Thomas Ingham	March 22.

1657	1657.
Joseph ye sonne of mr Joseph Tilden	March 29.
Mary ye daughter of Jeremiah Burroughes	Apr. 5.
Elisha ye sonne of John Turner senior	Apr. 12.
Rebecca ye daughter of Gilbert Brooke	Apr. 12.
Martha ye daughter of James doughty	Apr. 12.
Benjamin ye sonne of Richard Sylvester	May 17.
Elizabeth, Joseph, Daniell } ye children of George & Elizabeth Vaughan	May 31.
Thomas the sonne of William Brooke	June 28.
John ye sonn of John Rogers junr	Aug. 23.
Benjamin ye sonne of Humfrey Johnson	Sept. 20.
Sarah, the daughter, John, Ralph } the sonnes } of Ralph Chapman	Sept. 27.

Grace, Hannah the daughters, Joseph the sonne — of John Phillips	Octob. 4th
Timothy the sonne of Robt Studson	Octob. 11th.
Benjamin the sonne of William Randall	Novemb: 8th.
Mary ye daughter of Thomas Robinson	Febr. 28.

1658.	1658.
Martha ye daughter of Richard Courtisse	May 2d.
Patience ye daughter of Nathaniell Rawlins	July 4th.
Benjamin the sonne of John Phillips	Aug. 15.
Mary the daughter of Thomas Oldham	Octob. 3d.
John the sonne of Thomas Clappe	Octob. 31.
Mary the daughter of Thomas Turner	Novb 7.
John the sonne of Geo: and Elizab: Vaughan	Novemb: 7.
Antipas the sonne of Walter Hatch	Decemb. 5.
Mary ye daughter of John Turner Senr	Jan: 2d.
Isaack the sonne of William Randall	Jan. 9th.
Josiah ye sonne of James Torry	Jan. 30.

1659.	1659.
Mary ye daughter of Jeremy Hatch; Lydia ye daughter of James Doughty	Apr 10.
Elizabeth ye daughter of Elizabeth Barlow(?)	May 8th.
Miriam ye daughter of John Turner junr; John ye sonne of William Tickner	May 15.
Jonah the sonne of Jonah Pickles	June 5.
Stephen the sonne of Mr Joseph Tilden,	July. 3d.
Hannah ye daughter of John Hanmer.	July 24.
Hannah ye daughter of Gilbert Brook	Octob. 2d.
Johanna ye daughter of Wllm Brook	octob. 16th.
Mary ye daughter of Thomas Robinson	November 6th
Nathaniel ye sonne of Nathaniel Rawlins	Decemb. 11th.
Abigail ye daughter of Thomas Clappe	Febr. 5th.
Daniel the sonne of John Bryant	Febr. 5th.
Margaret the daughter of Humfrey Johnson	Febr. 26.

1660.	1660.
Thomas ye sonne of Rhoda Rogers	Mar. 25.
Thomas ye sonne of Richard Curtisse.	Apr. 22.
William ye son of William Hatch	Apr. 29.
John the son of John Lowell of Boston	June 17th.
Hannah ye daughter of Daniell Wetherell	June 24th
Nicholas ye sonne of Nicholas Wade; Batsheba ye daughter of John Whetstone; Mary ye daughter of Geo & Elizabeth Vaughan; Thomas the sonne of Thomas Lambert	these four were baptized July. 1. July. 1, 1660.
Samuel ye sonne of Mr. Joseph Tilden	Novemb. 4th.
Thomas ye sonne of Joseph Oldham	Jan. 6th.
Kenelm ye sonn of Helen Baker,	Mar. 24
Lydia ye daughter of Hellen Baker Marishfield	Mar. 24.
Sarah, ye daughter of James Torry.	Mar. 24.

RECORDS OF THE SECOND CHURCH OF SCITUATE, NOW THE FIRST UNITARIAN CHURCH OF NORWELL, MASS.

Communicated by Miss SARAH R. DAMON and Miss ELLA BATES, of North Scituate, Mass.

1661		
205	Benjamin ye son of John Turner senior	Apr. 14.
	Abraham	
210	Israel } Sarah	
	Isaack } Rebecca } children of Wllm Homes	Apr. 14
	Josiah } children of William Homes	
	Mary }	Apr. 27th
	Bethaia ye daughter of Walter Hatch	May 12th
	Mercy ye daughter of Jonas Pickles }	May 19th
215	Eunice ye daughter of Thomas Turner }	
	Daniell ye sonne of Daniell Hicks	May 19th
	Samuel ye sonne of John Turner jun^r^.	Aug. 4th
	Joanna ye daughter of Richard Stanley	Septbr 29
	Elizab. ye daughter of Nathaniel Rawlings }	Octob. 13
220	Sarah ye daughter of John Folke }	
	Elizeb. ye daughter of William Homes	Octob. 20
1662	Mary ye daughter of John Bryant	Jan. 19
	Jeremy ye sonne of Jeremy Hatch	Apr. 20 1662
	John ye sonne of John Cushion	May 11th.
225	Deborah ye daughter of William Courtisse	May 18
	Joseph ye sonne of John Lowel of Boston	May 25
	Nathan ye sonne of Jonas Pickles	June 8
	Rhoda ye daughter of Rhoda Rogers	Aug. 3d
	Mercy ye daughter of Robt Sprout	October 19
230	Nathaniel ye son of Nathaniel Rawlins	March 22
	Sarah ye daughter of Thomas Oldham	Apr. 5
1663	Mary ye daughter of Humfery Johnson	Apr. 19
	Ruth ye daughter of John Turner senr. }	
	Anne ye daughter of John Turner jur }	May 17
235	Thomas ye son of Thomas Highland }	
	Joanna ye daughter of James Torrey	May 31
	Patience ye daughter of John Lowel Boston	June 7
	Elizab, ye daughter of Elizab Sutton }	July the 19
240	Elizab. ye daughter of Hellen Baker }	
	Sarah ye daughter of Richard Courtisse }	
	Elizabeth } John }	
245	Mary } } ye children of John Buck }	Octob. 4th.
	Joseph } Hannah }	
	John ye sonne of Thomas Ingham }	
1664	Thomas ye sonne of John Cushion	April 3
	Abigail ye daughter of Elizab. Rogers	Apr. 24
	Thomas Pinchen jun^r^ }	
250	Elizabeth his wife } Hannah Young }	
	Elizabeth his daughter } Thomas Young }	June 12.
	William ye sonn of William Tickner }	June 26.
255	Joseph ye sonne of William Courtis }	
	Hannah ye daughter } of Stephen Tilden	July 31
	Stephen ye sonne }	

	Elizabeth ye daughter of John Lowel of Boston }	Aug. 21
	Susanna ye daughter of John Buck }	
260	Elizabeth ye daughter of Major Winsloe }	Octob. 2d
	Mercy ye daughter of Helene Baker }	
	Joseph ye son of Joseph Sylvester	Feb. 12
1665	Mary ye daughter of Elizabeth Rogers	Apr. 16
	Isaack ye sonn of John Turner senr }	
265	Ephraim ye sonn of Daniel Hick }	Apr. 30
	Hannah ye daughter of Tho. Oldhame }	
	Lydia ye daughter of Mr. Pickles }	
	Mathew ye son of John Cushion	May 14
	Sibil ye daughter of Mary Ray	May 28
270	Elizabeth ye daughter of Mr. Joseph Tilden	June 4
	Margaret ye daughter of Edward Wright	June 11th
	Bethaia ye daughter of Anne Torry	Aug. 27th
	Faith ye daughter of Nathaniel Winslow	Sept. 3d
	Elizabeth ye daughter of Thomas Highland	Sept. 24th
275	Elizabeth ye daughter of John Bryant	October 15th
1666	Sarah ye daughter of John Turner junr	June 10th
	Benjamin ye son of John Buck }	
	Mercy ye daughter of Edwd Wright }	June 10th
	Moses the son of Moses Simmons }	
280	Thomas ye sonne of Thomas Pinchon junr }	June 24th
	Hannah ye daughter of George Young }	
	Elizabeth ye daughter of Mary Jacob of Hingham	July 8th
	Jeremiah ye sonne of John Cushin	July 15th
	Abigail ye daughter of Mr. Thomas Newman Dorchester	July 22
285	Lydia ye daughter of Mr. Joseph Tilden	Sept. 2d
	Abigail ye daughter of Stephen Tilden	Sept. 2d
1667	Andrew ye sonne of William Orcott of Marshfield }	Mar. 21
	Mary ye daughter of Joseph Sylvester }	
	Grace ye daughter of Thomas Oldham }	Apr. 14th
290	Benjamin ye sonne of William Courtisse }	
	Benjamin ye sonne of Benjamin Studson	May 19th
	Joseph ye sonne of Joseph Studson	June 16th
	Patience Russell of Namasakesit aged 17 years	June 23d
	Joseph ye sonne of John Bryant }	July 7th
295	Peter ye sonn of William Blackmore }	
	Susanna ye daughter of Joseph Beerstow }	Aug. 4th
	Hannah ye daughter of Edward Wright }	
	Phebe ye daughter of John Lowel of Rehoboth	Aug. 11th
	Joseph ye sonn of Richard Childe of Marshfield	Oct. 27th
300	John ye sonne of Moses Symmons	March 15th
1668	Joannah ye daughter of John Rogers of Marshfield	Apr. 12th
	Mary ye daughter of Tho: Highland junr	June 21st
	Mary ye daughter of Anthony Collimer	June 21st
	Mary ye daughter of Stephen Tilden }	
305	Joanna ye daughter of Tho. Pinchon junr }	July 12th
	Mary ye daughter of George Young }	
	Grace ye daughter of John Turner Senr	Aug. 2d.

	Kenelm ye son of Kenelm Winslow of Yarmouth	Aug. 9th
1669	Benjamin ye sonne of Mr. Joseph Tilden	Feb. 20th
310	James ye sonne of John Cushion	Mar. 21st
	Matthew ye sonne of Benjamin Studson	
	John ye sonne of William Orcott	Apr. 18th
	Zacheus ye sonne of John Lowell of Rehoboth	May 16th
	Jane ye daughter of Richard Child of Marshfield	
315	Isaack ye son of Thomas Oldham	June 20.
	Benjamin ye sonne of John Bryant	
	William ye sonn of William Courtis	
	Richard ye sonn of Nathaniel Church	
	Anna ye daughter of Joseph Sylvester	
320	Gener(?) daughter of Edward Wright	
	John ye sonn of John Magoon	July 18
	Sarah ye daughter of Thomas Pinchon junr	

1670	Hannah ye daughter of John Ensigne	May 29
	John ye sonne of William Blackmore	
325	Nathaniel ye sonne of Nathaniel Winslow of Marshfield	July 3
	Josiah ye son Kenelm Winslow of Yarmouth	
	David ye sonne of Edward Wright	July 3
	Sarah ye daughter of Moses Simons	
	Judith ye daughter of Stephen Tilden	August 14
330	Samuel ye sonne of Thomas Courtis of York	Septbr 4.
	Jemima ye daughter of Edward King of Marshfield	Septbr 18.
	Bethia ye daughter of John Loy[?] of Marblehead	
	Sarah ye daughter of Thomas King junr	
	Samuel ye sonne of Timothy L.[?]	
335	Joshua ye sonne of John Cushion	Octbr. 16
1671	Sarah ye daughter of Thomas Oldham	April 16
	Joseph ye sonne of John Bryant	
	Deborah ye daughter of John Buck	
	Sarah ye daughter of John Sylvester	
340	Martha ye daughter of William Orcot	April 23
	Daniel ye sone of Richard Stanley	May 28
	Mary ye daughter of Thomas Pinchon	
	Elizabeth ye daughter of George Young	
	Rebecca ye daughter of Thomas Nichols	
345	Amos ye sonne of John Turner Senr	June 4th
	Hannah ye daughter of John Magoon	July 23
	Peter ye sonne of Anthony Collymer	August 6.
	John ye sonne of Thomas Highland	
	Mary ye daughter of John Bumpasse	August 20
350	James ye son of Benjamin Studson	August 27
	Sarah ye daughter of John Cushion	August 27
	Lois[?] ye daughter of Timothy Rogers	
	Edward ye son Edward Wright	Novemb. 19
	Naomi ye daughter of Joseph Sylvester	
355	Jabez ye sonne of John Bryant	May 26
1672	Thomas ye sonne of Thomas King junr	
	Aaron ye son of Moses Simmons	August 4th
	Thomas ye son of Thomas Perry	
	Robert ye son of John Buck	

360	Phebe ye daughter of William Blackmore	Septbr. 22
	Nathaniel ye sonne of Nathaniel Church	Septbr 29
	Hannah ye daughter of Thomas Studson	
	John ye son of John Sylvester	
	Joseph ye son of William Orcott	December 9th.
1673 365	Thomas ye sonne of Kenelm Winsloe	March 3
	Jacob / David ye sons of John Turner junr	Apr. 20
	Caleb ye sons of John Cushion	May 11
	Samuel Benjamin Studson	
370	Ruth ye daughter of John Bryant	June 29.
	Martha ye daughter of Benjamin Chandler	
	Joseph ye sonn of Edward Wright	
	Ruth ye daughter of Thomas Highland	Septbr. 4
	John ye son of John Bumpasse	Septbr. 28
375	Sarah ye daughter of Anthony Collymer	
	Timothy the Sonn of Timothy Rogers	Mar. 31
	Solomon the Sonn of Joseph Sylvester	
	Thomas the Sonn of Thomas Studson	
1674	Joseph the Sonn of John Silvester	
380	Jane the Daughter of Tho: King	
	Job the Sonn of Moses Symons	October 4
	James the Son of Tho: Perry	
	Rachel the daughter of John Buck	
1675	Deborah the daughter of John Cushin	
	Mary / Hannah the daughters of William Orcut	Apr. 11
	William the son of William Blackmore	
	Eliab the son of John Maggoon	July 4th
	Philip the son of John Turner Junr	August 15th
390	Samuell the son of Benjamin Chanler	
	Thomas the son of John Bryant junr	Sept. 19
	Daniell the son of Thomas King junr	
	Israel the son of Israel Sylvester	
	Mary the Daughter of Nathaniel Tilden	October 3.
1676	Samuell the sonn of John Bumpas	Apr. 30
	John the sonn of John Witherell	Octobr 3 [worn]
	Joseph the sonn of Joseph Barsto	
	Samuell the sonn of John Silvester	
	John the sonn of Benjamin Chandler	
400	Mary / Susana the daughters of John Cushin / Thomas Perry	
	Patience the daughter of Patience Simons	Mar. 18
	(In modern hand) wid. of Moses Simons.	
1677	Mehittabell the daughter of William Curlien(?)	Mar. 23
	Daborah / Martha the daughter of John Bryant / Andrew Collimer	July 8
	John / Gershom the sonn of Thomas King Junr / Thomas Studson	July 8
	Margarat the daughter of Joseph Turner	Sept 20
	Thomas the sonn of William Orcut	Oct. 2
410	Eunice the daughter of Timothy Rogers	

1678	Thomas	Thomas Ingham	April 4
	John	the sonn of John James	
	Benjamin	Sarah Bumpas	
	Mary	the daughter of Theophilus Witherell	
415	Joseph the sonn of John Cushin		May 12.
	Silence the daughter of Israel Silvester		
	Nathaniell the sonn of Israell Hubard		May 26
	Rebekah the daughter of Israell Hubard		
	Marcy the daughter of John Whiston		
420	William the sonn of John Witherell		June 16
	James the sonn of John Bumpas		
	John the sonn of John Randall		
	Agatha the daughter of John Bryant		
	Naomy the daughter of Joseph Silvester		June 16
425	Martha the daughter of William Barsto		
	Mary the daughter of Tho: Perry		
	Abigail the wife	of John Studson	July 14
	Abigail the daughter		
	Benjamin the sonn	of John Sutton	July 21
430	Nathaniell the sonn		
	Martha the daughter of Tho: Clark		July 28
	Ruth and Elizabeth the daughters of Tho: Oldham		August 18
	Nathaniell the sonn of Nathaniell Tilden		Sept. 22
	John the sonn of Samuell Clap		Oct. 6
	Mary the daughter of Benjamin Studson		
	Samuell the sonn of Samuell Witherell		Nov. 24
	John the sonn of John Berry		
	Stephen the sonn of William Curtis		Dec. 1
	William Perry sonn of William Perry		Dec. 29
440	Mary the daughter of Benjamin Chandler		Mar 16
	Mary the daughter of John Curtis		1678–79
	Deborah the daughter of Jonathan Turner		Mar. 9
1679	Richard the sonn of Samuell Winslow		Mar. 30
	Mary the daughter of Samuell Winslow		
445	Mary the daughter of Thomas King jun^r		
	Benjamin the sonn of John Cushin		Aprill 6
	Joseph the sonne of Cornelius Bridges		Apr 20
	Mercy the daughter of Jeremia Hatch		May 4
	John the sonn of John Studson		May 4.
450	Richard the sonn of Israel Silvester		
	Sarah the daughter of Tho: Studson		
	Mary the daughter of Tho: Nickells		
	Abigail the wife of Henery Joslin		the 10th of June
	Hannah the wife of Japhet Turner		
455	Joannah ye daughter of Jeremiah Hatch		
	Joseph the sonn of James Briges		
	Abraham the sonn of Henery Joslin		
	Abigail the daughter of Henery Joslin		
	Mary the daughter of Israell Cudworth		
460	Isaac the sonn of Stephen Tilden		July the 6
	Lidia the daughter of John Silvestor		
	Ruth the wife Joseph Barrel		July 2 (worn)
	Elizabeth the daughter of Joseph Barrel		
	Rachel the daughter of of Thomas Clarke		

465	Samuel the sonn of Samuel Hatch	August 4
	Gideon the sonn of Stephen Vinall	
	Josiah the sonn of Josiah Litchfield	
	Nicolas the sonn of Israel Chittenden	
	Tho: Perry junior	Aug 3 (worn)
470	Jacob Bumpas	
	Marah the wife of Samuel Hatch	
	Hanah the daughter of Benjamin Studson	
	Lydia the daughter of Tho. Oldham	
	Elizabeth the daughter of Theopholus Witherel	
475	Sarah the daughter of Thomas Waide	
	Samuel the sonn of Samuell Studson	
	Patience the daughter of John Randall	
1680	Beniamin the son of William Orcut	Mar. 9.
	Jonathan the sonn of John Bryant junior	
	Hanna the daughter of Samuell Witherell	
	Barshua the daughter of Joseph Turner	May 9
	Hanna the daughter of Nathaniell Brooks	
	Anna the daughter of John Briant junior	
	Benjamin the sonn Joseph Barsto	
	Abigall the daughter of Samuel Clap	May 16
	Hannah the daughter of Tho. Jenkins	
	Abigall the daughter of John Whiston	
	Eleanor the daughter of Samuell Baker	
	Josia the sonn of Samuel Hatch[?]	
490	Josia the son of Thomas Man	
	John the son of Thomas Perry	
	Jacob the son of Jacob Bumpas	
	Jael the daughter of Israell Huburd	Sept. 5
	Elizabeth the daughter of Anthony Collimer	
495	Mercy the daughter of Jonathan Badcock	
	Hanna, Sarah } the daughters of Josia Litchfield	
	Sara the daughter of William Curtise	
	Caleb the son of Jonathan Badcocke	Octobr 31
500	Ann the daughter of James Torry	
	William the sonne of William Barsto	November [?]
	Jemymah the daughter of Jonathan Turner	
1681	Zoar the son of John Bumpus	March 27
	Mary the daughter of Theopholus Witherell	
505	——— the daughter of Zoar[?]	April 10.
	Ichabod the sonn of Tho. King junr	Aprii 24
	Beniamin the son of Joseph Silvester	May 15th.
	Mary the daughter of Job Randall	
	Mary the daughter of William Barrell	May 22
510	Thomas the sonn of John Witherell	May 29
	Joshua the son of Thomas Studson	June 19
	Susanna the daughter of Thomas Nickalls	
	Bathsheba the daughter of Thomas Nickalls	
	Lois the daughter of Israell Silvester	
515	Mary the daughter of Jonathan Badcock	June 26
	Hannah the daughter of Robert Sprout	September 18
	Bathsheba the daughter of John Whiston	

Nicolas the son of Josia Lichfield
Hannah the daughter of John Silvester } October 16
520 Mary the daughter of John Bryant junor — Oct 31
Sarah the daughter of Samuell Witherell — Dec 4

RECORDS OF THE SECOND CHURCH OF SCITUATE, NOW THE FIRST UNITARIAN CHURCH OF NORWELL, MASS.

Communicated by Miss SARAH R. DAMON, of North Scituate, Mass.

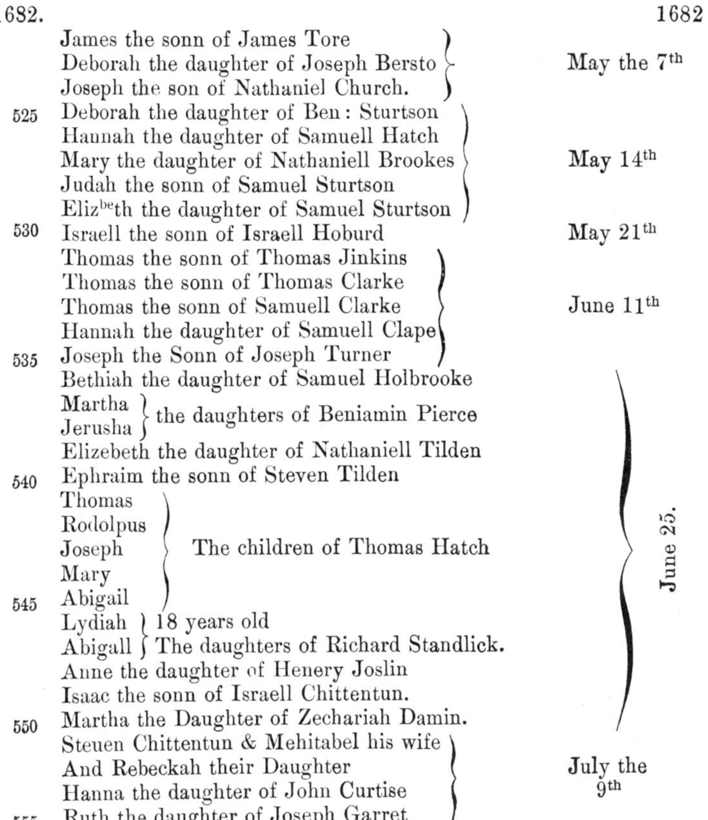

1682. 1682

James the sonn of James Tore
Deborah the daughter of Joseph Bersto
Joseph the son of Nathaniel Church. } May the 7th
525 Deborah the daughter of Ben: Sturtson
Hannah the daughter of Samuell Hatch
Mary the daughter of Nathaniell Brookes
Judah the sonn of Samuel Sturtson
Elizbeth the daughter of Samuel Sturtson } May 14th
530 Israell the sonn of Israell Hoburd — May 21th
Thomas the sonn of Thomas Jinkins
Thomas the sonn of Thomas Clarke
Thomas the sonn of Samuell Clarke
Hannah the daughter of Samuell Clape
535 Joseph the Sonn of Joseph Turner } June 11th
Bethiah the daughter of Samuel Holbrooke
Martha, Jerusha } the daughters of Beniamin Pierce
Elizebeth the daughter of Nathaniell Tilden
540 Ephraim the sonn of Steven Tilden
Thomas, Rodolpus, Joseph, Mary,
545 Abigail } The children of Thomas Hatch
Lydiah } 18 years old
Abigall } The daughters of Richard Standlick.
Anne the daughter of Henery Joslin
Isaac the sonn of Israell Chittentun.
550 Martha the Daughter of Zechariah Damin. } June 25.
Steuen Chittentun & Mehitabel his wife
And Rebeckah their Daughter
Hanna the daughter of John Curtise
555 Ruth the daughter of Joseph Garret } July the 9th

Deborah the wife }
Elizabeth } the children } of Beniamin Woodward } July 16.
Deborah }
Moses } the children of Aaron Simmons
560 Rebecka }
Elizebeth the daughter of Isaace Chittenden }
Susannah } the daughters of Henery Chittenden } July 16th.
Ruth }
Barnabas the sonn of John Sturtson
565 Elizabeth the daughter of William Briant }
Hannah the daughter of William Bersto }
Elizebeth the daughter of William Perry } July the 30th
George the sonn of Thomas King Juner — August 27th
Nathan the Sonn of John Sutten — Novemr 12th

1683. 1683.

570 Isaac the sonn of Jonathan Turner }
Job the sonn of Job Randall } Aperrel 22
William the sonn of William Barrell }
Job the sonn of John Bumpus — Aperrill 29
Beniemen the sonn of Josiah Came [?] }
575 Martha the daughter of Israell Silvester } May the 6th
Sarah } the daughters of Thomas Hatch }
Lidia }
Mary the daughter of Richard Standley } May 20th
Lidia the daughter of Theophilus Wetherell
580 Keturah the daughter of Beniaman Chandeller
Eliazar the sonn of Eliazar Dunham }
Mary the daughter of Mr Thomas Mighill Born and baptised the same day }
Eunice the daughter of Beniamin Sturtson } May the 27th
Caleb the son of Thomas Sturtson
585 Joseph the sonn of John Whetston }
David the sonn of Joseph Siluester — June the 10th
Mary the daughter of James Bridges — June 17th
An the daughter }
Joshua the sonn } of Japhet Turner }
590 Japhet the sonn }
Keturah the daughter } June 24th
Margaret the daughter } of Thomas Hatch
Hannah the daughter } }
Isaac Buck the sonn of Isaac Buck — July 1th
595 Joshua the sonn of Samuel Witherell. — July the 8th
Joshua the sonn of John Witherell }
Ebenezer the sonn of Steven Tilden
Elizebeth the daughter of Jerimya Hatch } Septembr 9th
Mary the daughter of Richard Berry
600 Elizabeth the daughter of Thomas Right }
Mary the daughter of Joseph Garrett }
Edward the sonn of Thomas Jenken } Septembr 24th
William the sonn of James Torey }
Deborah the daughter of William Orcut } October 7th
605 David the sonn of John Briant Juner — November 11th

Sarah the daughter of Samuel Starse [?] — November: 18th
Samuell the sonn of Richard Dwelly — December 2th

$16\frac{83}{84}$ — $16\frac{83}{84}$
608 Abigail the daughter of Israell Hobird March 16th Baptised* by our late pastor M. William Wetherell. [Added, in modern hand, "he died Ap. 9 1684. S. D.," probably by Samuel Deane.]
Those following by our pastor Mr. Thomas Mighell [Mr. Witherell's successor].

1684 — 1684
William the sonn of William Bersto — ffebruary the fifth

$16\frac{84}{85}$ — $16\frac{84}{85}$
Lidia the daughter of William Barrell — March 29th

1685 — 1685
Beniamin the sonn of Benieamin Chandler — Aperrill the 12th
William the sonn of John Curtise
Israell the sonn of Thomas Nickalls
Mary the daughter of Israell Silvester
Mary the daughter of Richard Dwelley Junr — } May the 17th
Baptised May 24th Annah the daughter of Thomas King Juner, aged one year — May 24th
James the sonn of Job Randall
Keziah the daughter Jonathan Turner — } June the 7th
Tabitha the daughter of Thomas Perry — June 21th
William the son of Nathaniell Brookes — July the 5th
Joseph the son of Nathaniell Tilden — September 20th
Samuell the son of William Perry — october 18th
Samuell the son of William Curtice — november 29th
Samuell the son of Mr Thomas Mighell born & Baptized — December [worn]
Elisha the son of Israell Silvester — January the 10
Bethiah the daughter of Robert Woodward — Febuary 28
Marry the daughter of Nathaniell Brookes — Febuary 28th

1686 — 1686
Deborah the daughter of John Briges — Aperrill the 11th
Beniamin the son of Beniamin Silvester — Aprill 25
Elisha the son of Thomas Sturtson — May 23th
Amos the sonn of Joseph Silvester
Nathaniel the son of James Torey — } May the 30th
Isaac the son of Isaac Randall — June 13th
Ebenezer son of Thomas King Junor born Febuary 22th 1685 & baptized June [worn]
Richard the son of Richard Dwelley Junor — July [worn]
Patience the daughter of Thomas Nickalls — August 8th
Joshuah the son } of Thomas Holdum [? Oldham]
Mary the daughter } Junor — August the 8th
Lidia the daughter of Jeremia Hatch — August the 22th
Deborah the daughter of Israell Chittentun — September the 5th
Mary the daughter of William Barrell — September the 12th
Mary the wife of James Bucer [Bowker, in modern hand] — September the 12th

* The word "baptised" is occasionally added to subsequent entries in the records, but will be omitted unless it appears necessary to print it.

Mary the daughter of James Bucer — September the 26th
Lazarus the son of James Bucer — November the 7th
David the sonn of Thomas Perry — November the 21

1687 — 1687

Israell the son of Israel Hubird [? Hobart]
Isaace the son of Samuel Hatch
John the son of John Whetston
Jonathan the son of Jonathan Turner — May the first
Hannah the daughter of John Bayley — May the 8th

1687. — 1687

Icabod the sonn of Jacob Bumpus the 26 of June
Mary the daughter of Samuell Holbrooke the 3 of July.
David the son of Steuen Tilden Seneor July the 17.
John the son of John Bridges [? Briggs] late deceased
Hannah the daughter of Israel Chittentun — August 14
Hannah the Daughter of Mr. Jeremyah Cushin — August 21
James the son of William Barrell — September 24
Joshua the son of John Briant Baptized october the 30th
David the son of James Torey
James the Son of Robert Woodward — 1687/8 March 11th

1688. — 1688

Elisha the sonn of Elisha Turner — March 25
Elijah the sonn of Thomas Sturtson — Aprill the first
Mary the daughter of William Bersto
Abigail the daughter and Margeret the daughter of Isaac Bucke — April 22th
Susannah the daughter of Isaace Randall — Aperill 29th
Susanna the daughter of John Whetston — June the 10th
Elizybeth the daughter of Nathaniell Brooks
Thomas the son of Thomas Brooks
Joseph the son of Beniamen Silvester
Marry the daughter of Nathan Pickles — July the 1.
Nehemiah the son of Job Randall — July 29th
Elizabeth the Daughter of Richard Dwelly Juner — August the 12th
Peter the sonn of Israell Silvester
Lidiah the daughter of John Garret — September 30
Martha the daughter of John Besbe — October 21
Beniamin the sonn of William Perry
Grace the Daughter of Mr. Tho: Mighell — February 10th

1689. — 1689

Samuell the son of John Briant — Aprill the 7th

Number of baptisms to this date. 678 [in modern hand].

In the Book begun by Rev. Nathaniel Eells, in 1704, is the following:

"The Names of those that were in full communion with this church befor I took the charge of it are these viz.:

Deacon Thomas King.	Joseph Bestow
Deacon James Torry.	William Bestow
Capt: Benjamin Stetson	Abraham Shutly
Lieut John Bryan [? Bryant].	Jonathan Turner
William Perry	Joseph Turner

John Turner
Samuel Hatch
Jeremiah Hatch
Robert Sprout
Israel Hobart
John Cushing Senr:
Capt. John Cushing jun^{r}:
Elizabeth Perry
wife to William Perry
Sarah Curtice
Deborah Randal,
Rachel Dwelly
Prudence Stetson,
Bathia Stetson
Mary Bryan
Margaret Stockbridge
Martha Bestow
Johannah Besby
Mary Hatch
Elizabeth Sproute
Deborah King
Sarah Hobart
Susannah Perry
Eunice Torry
Barshua Foster
Mary Hatch
Barshua Turner
Mary Turner
Mercy Turner
Abigail Turner
Elizabeth Turner
Lydia Barrel
Martha Silvester
Miriam Pickles"

"When the Rev^{d}. Mr Lawson forsook this church he left no Catalogue of them that were baptized by him. Neither is there any to be found of those that have been baptized since the death of ye Rev^{d}. Mr Mighell. Therefore I thought fit soon after my ordination to defire Those that have been, And have had their Children baptized Since that time to give in their Names to me, And according to my Request many have done. Whom I have recorded."

John Dwelley Senr baptised by Mr Lawson 1697. John, Rachel and Icabod Dwelly children of John Dwelly by Mr Lawson 1697. Obadiah and Jedidiah 1699. Abuah 1701. Simeon by Mr. Cushing 1702.

Joanna Brooks Daughter of Thomas Brooks by Mr Lawson 1695.

Benjamin and Elizabeth woodward children of Robert Woodward by Mr Lawson 1695 or 96. Joanna 1696. And Mary 1700.

Abigail Collomar Daughter of Peter Coll: by Mr Lawson 1695 Sarah by Mr Jeremiah Cushing 1697. Anthony by Mr Lawson 1699. Peter by Mr Cushing 1701. Mary by Mr Cushing 1703.

Lydia Dwelly Daughter of Richard Dwelly by Mr Lawson 1696

Anthony and Jeremiah Stetson children of Robert Stetson, by Mr Lawson 1695. And Isaac 1700

Deborah And Robert Randal children of Isaac Randal by Mr Lawson 1697. Ruth by Mr Cushing 1699. Gidion by Mr Lawson 1699. Rachel by Mr Cushing 1701.

Elizabeth And Samuel Curtiss children of Sam Curtis, Senr by Mr Cushing 1696 Benjamin by Mr Lawson 1701 Abigail by Mr Cushing 1703.

Margaret Foster Daughter of Hatherly Foster by Mr. Lawson 1699. Joseph by Mr. Cushing 1702.

Mercy Turner Daughter of Jonathan Turner by Mr Gershom Hobart 1691 Ruth by Mr. Lawson 1695. Ignatius by Mr Lawson 1698. Martha by Mr Lawson 1700

Isaac Buck Son of Isaac Buck by Mr Norton of Hingham 1689. Thomas And Ephraim Buck by Mr Lawson 1701

Elizabeth, and Samuel Torry children of Deacon James Torry by M[r] [Hobart?] 1692. Rachel by M[r] Lawson 1693 Joseph by M[r] Lawson 1694 Stephen by M[r] Lawson 1696 Lydia by M[r] Lawson 1698 Eunice by M[r] Cushing 1702

Mary Brock Daughter of Francis Brock by M[r] Lawson 1700 Grace by M[r] Cushing 1704 Barshua by M[r] Cushing 1703

John Besby Elijah Besby, Mary Besby, Moses Besby children of John bosby [? Bisbee] by M[r] Lawson 1696. Elisha by Mr. Lawson 1699 Aron by M[r] Lawson 1700

Mary Torry the Daughter of Josiah Torry by M[r] Norton of Hingham 1686 Josiah by M[r] Norton 1687. Ruth, Caleb, Jeremiah by M[r] Lawson 1700. Kezia by M[r] Cushing 1702

Rebecca Bastow Daughter of William Bestow by M[r] Norton 1676 Benjamin by M[r] Whitman of Hull 1691 Susanna by M[r] Lawson 1694

Sarah Witherill Daughter of Willim Whitheril by M[r] Cushing 1703

Joseph Curtise the Son of Joseph Curtise by M[r] Lawson 1697 Josiah by M[r] Cushing 1698 Rebecca by Mr Lawson 1699 Martha by Mr Lawson 1701

Mary, Benjamin, Ebenezer, Lydia Curtise children of Benjamin Curtise by Mr Lawson 1696 Sarah by Mr Lawson 1699 Ruth by Mr Lawson 1700 Susanna by Mr Cushing 1702

Abigail and Samuel Tilden children of Samuel Tilden by Mr Lawson 1699. Lydia by Mr Làwson 1701. Sarah by Mr Cushing 1703

Mary Turner Daughter of Elisha Turner by Mr Norton of Hingham 1690 Elizabeth by Mr Norton 1692 Jacob by Mr Lawson 1695 Elisha by Mr Lawson 1700

Martha Bryan Daughter of John Bryan was baptized by Mr Lawson 1695

Amos Perry the son of William Perry by M[r] Whitman of Hull 1691. Abigail by M[r] Cushing 1693 William by M[r] Lawson 1694 Hannah by M[r] Lawson 1696 Isaac by M[r] Whitman 1698 Jerusha by M[r] Lawson 1699 Jerimiah by M[r] Caleb Cushing 1701

Abigail Turner Daughter of John Turner by M[r] Willard of Boston 1690 John by M[r] Lawson 1695 Margaret by M[r] Cushing 1696/7 Lydia by M[r] Lawson 1700 Richard by M[r] Cushin 1702

Elizabeth King Daughter of Daniel King by M[r] Cushing 1702

Else [? Alice] Pickles daughter of Nathan Pickles by M[r] Cushing 1692 Miriam by M[r] Cushin 1697 Nathan by M[r] Lawson 1699

Zebulun and Barshua Silvester children of Israel Silvester were baptized by M[r] Lawson 1695. Deborah by M[r] Lawson 1697

Mary, Lydia, Abigail and Benjamin Silvester, children of Benjamin Silvester by M[r] Lawson [no date.]

John Clap Son of Stephen Clap, Temperance his wife, by Mr Lawson
Rachel Clap daughter of Stephen & Temperance Clap, by M[r] Cushing 1701

Ruth Rogers Daughter of Samuel and Jael Rogers of Marshfield by M[r] Lawson 1699.

Elizabeth Rogers Daughter of Sam[ll] and Jael Rogers of Marshfield by M[r] Norton of Hingham 1701

Sarah Stockbridge mary Stockbridge Thomas Stockbridge, Deborah Stockbridge children of Thomas Stockbridge and Sarah his wife by M[r] Torry of Weymouth.

The names of those that I have admitted into full communion with this church, are here sett down.

1 John Hatch, was admitted* Novemb[r] 5, 1704
2 Sarah Tildin the wife of Sam[ll] Tilden of marshfield November 5, 1704
3 Ann Torry Decemb[r] 30 1704 Daughter of Deacon Torry

In the year 1705 these were admitted

1 Daniel King March 18
2 Judith Church wife of Nathanael Church March 18
3 Charles Turner April 8
4 John King of Marshfield May 6th
5 Samuel Curtise and
6 Elizabeth Curtise his wife and } August 5.
7 Joseph Cushing }

1706. In this year these were admitted

1 Stephen Clap and } March 10
2 Temperance Clap his wife }
3 Thomas Stockbridge June 2[d]
4 Mary Torry Daughter of Josiah Torry July 7.
5 Rebecca Wills Wife of Sam[l] Wills August 4
6 Jael Rogers wife of Sam[ll] Rogars of Marshfield, October the 6th

1707. In this year these were admitted

1 Margaret Pratt, Wife of Jonathan Pratt
2 Lydia Lappam Daughter of Thomas Lappam July 6th
3 John Magoone Jun[r] August 3[d] day

1708. In this year was admitted

1 Abigail Lappam wife of Joseph Lappam July 4th

1709. In this year was admitted

1 Grace Stetson Wife of Benjamin Stetson Jun[r] october 2[d]

1710. In this year was admitted

1 Hannah Lappam, wife of Sam[ll] Lappam April 2[d]
2 Benjamin Stetson Jun[r] May 7th
3 Mary Rose, widow of Jabez Rose, August 6th
4 Martha Clark Wife of Thomas Clark Sen[r] October 1st
5 Peter Collomer and
6 Abigail Collomer his wife Nov[r] 5th
7 Thomas Clark Sen[r] Dec. 3[d]

1711.

1—Elizabeth Proute Wife of Edward Proute June 3[d]
2—Ruth Torry daughter of Josiah Torry August 5th

* The word "admitted," which is occasionally added to subsequent entries, will be omitted unless it appears necessary to print it.

RECORDS OF THE SECOND CHURCH OF SCITUATE, NOW THE FIRST UNITARIAN CHURCH OF NORWELL, MASS.

Communicated by WILFORD JACOB LITCHFIELD, M.S., of Southbridge, Mass.

1712.

1 Joseph Stockbridge of Duxborough
2 Philip Turner, June 1st
3 Elizabeth Turner wife of Philip Turner, July 6th
4 Sarah Pinchion Wife of Thomas Pinchion July 6th
5 Joanna Wing wife of Bachelor Wing September 7th 1712
6 Eunice James wife of John James September 7th

1713.

1 Mercy Oldum Wife of Thomas Oldum June 7th
2 Ann Stetson Wife of Gershom Stetson August 2^{d}

1714.

1 Sarah Stockbridge Wife of Thomas Stockbridge, March 7th
2 Lazarus Turner Apprentice to Thomas Stockbridge March 7th
3 Hannah Magoone Wife of John Magoone May 2^{d}
4 Samuel Curtice jun^{r} & } May 2^{d}
5 Anna Curtice his wife } 1714
6 Samuel Tilden of Marshfield June 13
7 Miriam Curtice, August 1st
8 Hannah Brooks wife of Thomas Brooks October 3^{d}
9 Deborah Bryant Wife of John Bryant December 5th
10 Mary Cushing Wife of James Cushing December 5th

1715

1 Mercy Palmer, Wife of Elnathan Palmer, July 10th
Mehithabel oldom,* wife of Joshua Oldum, being a member of ye chh of Christ in Barnstable, and Coming to Live in this town desired to partake with this chh, July 10th 1715. Her dismission from ye chh was read Nov. 1st 1724.
2 Stephen Tilden of Marshfield. August 7th
3 Abigail Bryant wife of Sam^{ll} Bryant August 7th
4 Frances Eells Daughter of John and Frances Eells August: 7th
5 Anna Turner widow of Amasa Turner Sep^{t} 4th 1715
6 Mary Silvester wife of Benj^{m} Silvester november 7th
7 Martha Bryant. Novemb^{r} 6th 1715
8 Hatherly Foster. December 4th 1715

1716

1 Elizabeth Tolman Wife of Benj^{m} Tolman July 1st 1716.
2 Hannah Turner Widow of Japhet Turner. August 5th 1716

* This entry is crossed out in the book. (See later entry in 1724.)

3 Martha Bisby daughter of John Bisby of marshfield. August 5th 1716.
4 George King & his wife } Oct: 7th
5 Deborah King ——— } 1716
6 Edward Prouty Nov 4th 1716.

Anno 1717

1 Nathanael Brooks aged 71 years Jany 6th 1716/17
2 Mary Bryant, wife of Thomas Bryant Aprill 7th 1717

[This last entry is on page 7 of the church book, and is followed by the words: "Carried to fol: 37." The following is therefore continued from the entries on page 37.]

A further List of the names of those yt and admitted into full Comunion with ye Second Chh of Christ in Scittuate. brought from fol: 7th

1717 *Anno* 1717

3 Rebeccah King Wife of John King June 2d 1717
4 Nehemiah Hobart of Hingham was admitted into full Comunion* July 14th 1717
5 John Jacob of Hingham August the 4th 1717
6 Abigail Neal Wife of Joseph Neal october 13. 1717

1718 *Anno* 1718

1 Elizabeth Brooks wife of Gilbert Brooks } March 2d 1717/18
2 Elizabeth Brooks Daughter of Nathanll Brooks }
3 Jemimah Torry Daughter of Josiah Torry }
4 Joseph Nash August. 3d 1718

1719 1719 *Anno.*

1 Ebenezar Goreham. May 3d 1719

1720 *Anno* 1720

1 Lydia Tilden daughter of Samll: Tilden of Marshfield was recievd to Comunion at the Lords Supper January 3d 1719/20.
2 Hannah Lincoln Wife of Solomon Lincoln March 6th 1719/20.
3 Zechariah Dammon. & his wife } were admitted to comunion August 7th 1720.
4 Mehithabel Dammon. }
5 James Briggs }
6 Ruth Silvester wife of Benjm Silr junr }
7 Mary Brooks wife of Nat: Brooks }
8 Sarah Whetstone widow }
9 Hannah Nash, the Wife of Joseph Nash . . . . in this Chh Sept 4th 1720
10 Thomas Toby & } were admitted to Comunion at the Lords Table, October 2d 1720.
11 Mary Toby his wife, }
12 Thomas Merit & }
13 Abigail his wife, }
14 Mary Palmer wife of John Palmer, & }
15 Hannah Briggs wife of James Briggs }
16 John James . . . . wth this Chh: Dec: 4th 1720

* The words "admitted into full Comunion" in subsequent entries will be omitted unless required by the context.

Anno. 1721

1 Daniel Dammon . . . . wth the Chh at the Lords Supper. February 5th 1720/21.
2 Ursellah Randal wife of Job Randal jun^{r} . . . . with the Chh June 4th 1721.
3 Job Randal, & his wife
4 Mary Randal . . . . June 11th 1721

Anno 1722

1 Elijah Cushing . . . . wth the Chh at the Lords Supper. Aprill 1st 1722
2 Samuel Hatch jun^{r} . . . . wth the Chh at ye Lords Supper Aug: 1st 1722
3 Isaac Perry
4 Eliz: Hatch wife of Sam^{ll} Hatch jun^{r}
5 Lydia Stoddard daughter of J: Stoddard
6 Mary Pando, maid Servt to J: Cushing.
} . . . . wth the Chh Sep^{t}: 2^{d} 1722
7 Timothy Symms &
8 Elizabeth his wife
} oct: 7. 1722
9 Sarah House Widow of Sam^{ll} House . . . . wth this Chh December 2^{d}. 1722

Anno 1723

1 Benjamin Perry &
2 Ruth Perry his wife
} February 3^{d} 1722/3
3 Isaac Tailor; and
4 Ruth Tailor his wife . . . . March 10th 1722/3.
5 Ruth Turner wife of Caleb Turner . . . . at ye Lords Supper May 5th 1723.
6 Ruth Stetson Wife of Elijah Stetson, ... at the Lords Table. June 2^{d} 1723

Anno. 1724

1 Elizabeth Cushing wife of John Cushing jun^{r} January. 5th 1723/4.
2 Naomi Chamberlain alias morris Feb: 9th 1723/4
3 Samuel Holbroke, of ye North precinct March 1st:
4 Deborah Brigs wife of Joseph Briggs Senr: April: 5th 1724
5 Abigail Hobart and
6 Desire Hatch
} . . . . April: 5. 1724.
7 Deborah Otis wife of Isaac Otis, ... at the Lords Supper May 3^{d} 1724
8 Desire Silvester wife of Richard Silvester . . . . to the Lords table June 7th 1724.
9 Isaac Buck July 5th 1724.
10 Barshua Torry wife of Saml Torry August 2^{d} 1724.
11 Abigail Brooks wife of Gilbert Brooks August 30th 1724
12 Mehitabel Oldum* Wife of Joshua Oldum being a member of the Chh of Christ in Barnstable had her dismission from y^{t} Chh to this, read in the audience of the Chh: November 1st 1724

* See entry in 1715.

1725

1 Isaack Jones &
2 Hannah Jones his wife &
3 Joanna Rugles wife of John Rugles } .... in this Chh May 2d 1725
4 Hannah Barker wife of Barnabas Barker .... at the Lords table June 6th 1725
5 Jeremiah Hatch .... at the Lords table August 1st 1725
6 Anthony Sisco &
7 Pheby his wife } Negro's .... Dec: 17, 1725

1726

1 Thomas Joslyn June 5th 1726.
2 Fear Turner Nathan Turners widow &
3 Allice Pickles daughter of Nathan Pickles September 4th 1726
4 Sarah lambet wife of James lambet [?Lambert] oct: 9th 1726

Anno 1727

1 Elizabeth Cushing wife of Elijah Cushing of Abington Jan: 1st 1726/7
2 Lydia James wife of John James April 2d 1727
3 Samuel Lappam Sept 3d 1727
4 Samuel Torry oct: 1st 1727
5 Lydia Clift of Marshfield: Octobr 1st 1727
6 Thomas Lambert aged 67.
——— & his wife
7 Joanna Lambert aged 63. Nov 5th 1727
8 Elizabeth Turner wife of Joseph Turner Dec: 3d 1727.

Anno. 1728

1 Thomas Clark &
2 Allice his wife } Jan: 7th 1727/8
3 Joseph Torry. & Deborah
4 his wife, Jan: 7. 1727/8.
5 Joshua Turner
6 Joseph Jacob &
7 Penelipa Hatch } Jan: 7th 1727/8.
8 Desire Tildin wife of Saml Tildin junr of Marshfield .... in this Chh March 3d 1727/8.
9 Mercy Turner wife of Benj'm Turner junr March 3d 1727/8
10 Anna Stetson wife of Anthony Stetson March 31st 1728.
11 Rebecca Curtice wife of Benjamin Curtice March 31st 1728
12 Abigail Turner wife of William Turner March 31. 1728.
13 Grace Hatch wife of John Hatch June 2d 1728.
14 Thomas orcut of Hingham
15 Elizabeth Silvester of Hanover
16 Martha Man of Hanover
17 Jemima Damon Danl D: wife
18 Deborah Stetson Sergt S: S: daughter
19 Silence Dammon a single woman } .... with this Chh. August 4th 1728

20 Thankfull Blossom wife of John Blossom October 6th 1728
21 Lydia Turner Widow of Jonathan Turner October 13th 1728
22 Amy Dwelle widow Oct: 13. 1828.
23 Lydia Simmons wife of Ebenezer Simmons Nov 10th 1728.

Anno 1729

1 Jonah Stetson Feb. 2^{d} 1728/9
2 Elizabeth Butler wife of Israel Butler Feb: 2^{d} 1728/9
3 Mercy Stetson wife of Jonah Stetson April 6th 1729
4 Ruth Perry wife of Amos Perry April 6th 1729
5 Joseph Benson his dismission from the Chh of Christ in Hull to this Chh was read and accepted by a full vote April 4th 1729
6 Benjamin King July 6th 1729, in the 20th year of his age.
7 David Foster August 3^{d} 1729.
8 John Ruggles's dismission from the new north Chh in Boston, was read and accepted by a full vote, oct. 5th 1729.
9 Israel Butler's dismission from the Chh in Tisbury was read to this Chh, and accepted by a full vote oct: 5th 1729 } dismissed to the westerly Chh in Barnstable June twenty fourth 1740. [Later entry]
10 Elizabeth oakman wife of Saml oakman of Marshfield December 7th 1729
11 Rebecca Sprague a Single woman Dec. 7th 1729.

Anno 1730.

1 David Bryant &
2 Hannah his wife } March 1st 1729/30
3 William Barrel &
4 Abigail his wife } March 1st 1729/30.
5 Ephraim Otis: &
6 Joseph Cushing, jun^{r} } March 1st 1729/30.
7 Margret Turner May 10th 1730
8 Robert Woodart (upward of 70 years) June 7th 1730.
9 Rachel Stetson daughter of $Serg^{t}$ Saml Stetson Aug: 2^{d} 1730.
10 Nathan Pickles jun &
11 Richard Turner Sep^{t} 13th 1730
12 Jane Jones wife of Ebenezer Jones of marshfield &.
13 Rebecka Lappam wife of David Lappam of marshfield, &
14 Sarah Tilden daughter of Saml Tilden of Marshfield Sep^{t} 13th 1730
15 $Benj^{m}$ Randal, &
16 Sarah [h]is wife } Nov: 1st 1730
17 Elizabeth Hatch wife of Israel Hatch Nov: 1st 1730
18 Margret Stetson &
19 Leah Stetson —— } daughters of $Benj^{m}$ Stetson Dec: 6th 1730

Anno 1731.

1 Margret Merit wife of Henry Merit January 10th 1730/31.
2 Abigail Foster wife of Joseph Foster March 7th 1730/31
3 Margret Foster daughter of Hatherly Foster April 4th 1731.
4 Lusanna Turner the wife of Hawkins Turner gave to this chh a Letter of recomendation from the chh of christ in Groton in Connecticut wch was accepted by the chh. April 4th 1731

5 Anna Palmer wife of Bazaliel Palmer was baptized & received into full Comunion with this chh. July 25th 1731.
6 Judith Dwelle wife of John Dwelle Aug: 1st 1731.
7 Elizabeth Bryant daughter of David Bryant Sept 5th 1731.
8 Joseph Dunham &
9 Jane Dunham his wife } Oct: 30th 1731

Anno 1732

1 Doctor Isaac Otis Jan: 2d 1731/2
2 John James junr and
3 Lydia Silvester wife of Joseph } March 12th 1731/2
4 William Clift &
5 Judith Clift his wife &
6 John Spooner all of Marshfield } April 2d 1732.
7 Mary Benson wife of Joseph Benson May 14th 1732
8 Nathan Pickels—and
9 Timothy Symms junr } July 2d 1732
10 Mary Neal, wife of John Neal son of Joseph Neal Sept: 3d 1732
11 Benjm Tolman—and
12 Saml Eells &
13 Hannah Eells his wife and
14 Eliz: Dwelle wife of Jedediah Dwelle } Nov: 5th 1732.

Anno 1733

1 Edward Eells Feb. 4th 1732–3.
2 Hannah Barrel daughter of William May 6th 1733.
3 Perciss Stockbridge daughter of Saml Stockbridge June 3d 1733
4 Hannah Bowker wife of James, August 5th 1733.
5 Martin, An Indian man Servant to Mr Hatherly Foster Sept 2d 1733
6 Mary Bowker, aged near 70 years widow Oct: 7th 1733

1734

1 Joseph Clap, and his wife
2 Hannah Clap Feb: 3d 1733/4.
June 9th 1734 after Sacrament the Chh by a manual vote Exprest their willingness that
3 James Chushing;
4 Samuel Stockbridge &
5 Lydia Stockbridge his wife Should be looked upon by all the fraternity as under the watch of this Chh, & Enjoy the priviledge of it as they have done for some years past. Notwithstanding yy have not brought either Letters of dismission or recommendation from the chh into wch they were at first admitted: viz: the 1st chh in Scittuate
6 Rachel Otis wife of Ephraim July 7th 1734.
7 Jurusha Church wife of Nathl Chh junr August 4th 1734
8 Robert Stetson junr Sept 15th 1734
9 Eunice Prouty Sept 15th 1734.
10 Rachel Smith wife of Joseph Smith of Hanover Nov 3d 1734
11 Patience Lamb wife of James Lamb, Judux [?] Nov: 3d 1734.

RECORDS OF THE SECOND CHURCH OF SCITUATE, NOW THE FIRST UNITARIAN CHURCH OF NORWELL, MASS.

Communicated by WILFORD JACOB LITCHFIELD, M.S., of Southbridge, Mass.

Anno. 1735

1 Mary Dwelle wife of Joseph Jan: 12th 1734/5
2 Frances Hatch wife of Jeremiah Hatch Sep^{t} 7th 1735.
3 Mary Cushing wife of John Cushing jun^{r} Esqr Nov: 2^{d} 1735
4 Mehitabel Merit, wife of Jonathan Merit Nov: 9th 1735
5 Mary Toby of about 17 years, daughter of Thomas Dec: 14th 1735.

1736

1 Margret Collomare wife of John Collomar March 7th 1735/6

2 Thomas White of Marshfield and

3 Mary Bryant daughter of David Oct 10th 1736.

1737

1 William Curtice jun^{r} July 3^{d} 1737 dismissed to Pembroke June 24, 1740. [Later entry.]

2 North Eells: Nov: 6th 1737

1738

1 Benjamin Perry jun^{r} Feb 5th 1737/8

2 Mary Silvester wife of Zebulon April 2^{d} 1738.

3 Cesar a Negro Servt of Capt Torrys Augt 6th 1738.

4 Richard, Alias Dick, a negro Servt to Mr Anthony Collomar was received into full comunion wth this chh [no date]

1739

1 Elizabeth Turner (Widow of Benj^{m}) May 6th 1739.

2 Elkanah Tolman &

3 Elizabeth his wife members of the first chh of Christ in Plymouth, had their dissmission & recomendation, Read to & by y^{s} chh, accepted, May 6th 1739.

1740

1 Edward Prouty was received into full Comunion with this chh Sept 14th

1741.

1 Temperance Foster wife of Elisha: May 10th

2 Lemuel Bryant July 5th

3 Ruth Perry, daughter of Benj^{m} Perry Aug. 9th 17,41

1742

1 Anna Lenthal Eells Feb: 7th 1741/2

2 Joseph Copeland, &
3 Elizabeth Copeland his wife } April 4th 1742

4 Joseph Damon &
5 Joseph Palmer &
6 Jane his wife &
7 Mary Williams of Taunton —— } June 6th 1742.

8 Bathsheba Dammon.
9 Jemima Dammon, &
10 Sarah Green } July 4th 1742

11 Sarah Stockbridge wife of Sam^{ll} Stockbridge jun^{r} Augt 1st 1742

12 Bethiah Powers wife of Nicholas Powers Aug 1st 1742

13 Hannah Briggs daughter of Jam^{s} Briggs Augt 1st 1742.

14 Mary Woodart wife of Robert, Aug 29 1742

15 Mary Neal wife of John Neal Augt 29 1742

16 Abigail Lincoln wife of Isaac, Augt 29. 1742

17 William Silvester &
18 Mary his wife } Nov. 7th

19 Abigail Bestow &
20 Mehitabel Northy } Nov. 7, 1742.

21 Mary Buck wife of Isaac Buck jun^{r} Nov: 7th 1742.

22 Samuel Hatch, Son of Jeremiah Hat[c]h Dec: 1st 1742

1743
1 Priscilla Hatch Wife of Micah Hatch February 6th 1742/3
2 Deborah Turner Wife of Israel Turner Feb. 6th 1742/3
3 Edmund Gross and
4 Olive his wife. ——
5 Mary Brook [? Brooks] wife of E [?] m
6 Abigail Marble wife of David
7 Hannah Stetson wife of Ma [?]
} March 6th 1742/3
8 Thomas Bryant junr April 3d 1743.
9 Mary Torry wife of Capt Caleb Torry April 3d 1743
10 Abner Perry Son of Benjm Perry May 1st 1743.
11 Hannnh Collomar Wife of Thomas Collomar June 5th 1743
12 Abigail Turner wife of Jonathan June 5th 1743.
13 Jemima Prouty wife of William Augt 7th
14 Mercy Lincoln wife of Joshua Augt 7th
15 Ruth Eells wife of Nort[h] Augt 7th 1743
16 James Lambert Sept 4th 1743.
17 Capt Nehemiah Randall Oct: 2d 1743
18 Sarah Lambert wife of James Oct: 2d 1743.
19 Michael Turner Nov: 6th 1743

1744
1 Abigail Bowker wife of Lazarus May 13. 1744.
2 Joanna Dammon wife of Joseph June 10th 1744.
{ She is the person yt Compleats the Sum of 295 Since I was ordained, wch was June the 14th 1704. Next thirsday it will be 40 years
3 Isaac Dammon, &
4 Lydia his wife
} July 1st
5 Benimin Stoddard &
6 Mary his wife, &
7 Patience Gorden
} Oct 7th 1744
8 Benjm Curtice Nov. 4th 1744.
9 Cuba, a Negro Servant woman of Mr Isaac Turners Dec: 2d 1744

1745
Leah Foster a free Negro woman Sept 1st 1745.

1746
1 Deborah Turner Daughter of John Turner May 4th 1746.
2 Abiel Benson, widow of Joseph Benson junr Augt 3d 1746
3 Mary Bryant wife of Samuel Bryant junr Nov: 9th 1746.

1747
Grace Church, wife of Joseph Church July 5th 1747.

1748
1 Sarah Wheelright the wife of John Whelelright
2 Jael Whitten a Single woman May 1st 1748.
3 Anna Curtiss a Single woman June 5th 1748
4 Hannah Buck daughter of Isaac Buck aged about 17 yeares Dec: 4th 1748.

1749
1 Sarah House Daughter David House Deceased, a young woman, March 5th 1748/9
2 Mary Northy wife of James July 2d 1749

3 Sarah Ruggles daughter of Brother John Ruggles
4 Sarah Clap the wife of Joseph Clap had her dismiffion from the 2d chirch in Bridgwater to this Church read & accepted Aug^{t}—6 1749.
5 Abigail Bryant wife of Benjamin Sep^{t} 3^{d} 1749.
6 Mary Samfon wife of Charls Samfon Nov: 5th 1749.

Mr Jonathan Dorby's Dismifsion from ye 1st chh: in Hingham was read & he Receiv'd into full Communion with this Church November the 13th: 1754 the morning before He was Ordained

Att^{t} JOSEPH CUSHING JUN^{R}
Clerk of the Church during the Vacancy

The Names* of thofe that I† have baptized in the year 1704 are here set down.

1704.

Ruth Foster daughter of Hatherly Foster. June. 25.
Experience Stock-Bridge, Daughter of Charles Stockbridge. June. 25.
John Stockbridge Son of Joseph Stockbridge July. 2
Deborah Dwelly Daughter of John Dwelly July. 2
Jeffe Turner Son of Jonathan Turner July. 2.
Richard Curtife, Son of Joseph Curtife July. 2.
Edward, and Elizabeth Proutey children of Edward Prouty. July 16,
Deborah Curtife Daughter of Benjamin Curtife July 16.
Richard Silvester Son of Benjamin Silvester July 16.
Daniel King Son of Daniel King. July. 23.
Hopeftil Befby Son of John Befby Auguft. 6.
Thomas Clap, Son of Stephen Clap Auguft. 6.
Caleb Randal, Son of Isaac Randal Auguft 20.
Hawkins Turner, Son of Benjamin Turner September. 3.
Deborah And Aren [? Aaron] Woodward children of Robert Woodward September. 10.
Sarah [?] Turner, Daughter of John Turner September. 17.
Japhet Turner, Son of Japhet Turner September 17,
Abijah and Leah Stetfon children of Benjamin Stetfon Junr: September 24.
Gidion and Elizabeth Rofe Children of Jeremiah Rofe, October. 1.
Mary James, daughter of John James October. 8.
Judith Church, daughter of Nathan^{ll} Church oct^{r}: 8.
Thomas Clark, Son of Thomas Clark jun^{r} october 22.
Hannah and Mary Lappam Children of Samuel Lappam October. 22.
Adult { Elizabeth Jorden aged [*blank*] years, bap^{t}: Novr 5.
Adult { Elizabeth Henchman daughter of Jofeph Henchman aged [*blank*] years bapt: November 5
Judith Bryan, Daughter of Joseph Bryan Novr 5.
William and Amos Stetfon children of Robert Stetson. November. 5.
John Collomar, fon of Peter Collomar. December. 3.
Adult { Joseph Henchman aged [*blank*] years, Dec: 3.
Mary, Thomas, Deborah, Edmond, and Sarah Henchman children of Joseph Henchman were baptized December. 3.

*These baptismal entries begin on page 8 of the Church Book, and continue for 48 pages, into the year 1751.
†Rev. Nathaniel Eells.

1705.

Mary Smith Daughter of Deborah Smith.
March 25

John King fon of John King of Marfhfield, April. 1 [or 3].

Adult { Thomas A Negroe ferv[t] to John Dwelly April. 1 [or 3].

Adult { Thomas Turner aged [*blank*] years. May. 6.

Mary Buker [? Bowker], Elizabeth Buker, Edmund Buker Children of James Buker May. 27.

Adult Experience Pamer [? Palmer] Aged [*blank*] June 17.

Rebeccah Tilden, Daughter of Samuel Tilden of Marshfield June 17

Gorge, And Mary Shove, children of Edward Shove, June. 17.

Lydia Turner, Daughter of Thomas Turner, and martha A his wife. June. 17.

Hannah Witherel Daughter of William Witherel and Sarah his wife July. 15.

John Magoone the fon of John Magoone and Hannah his wife, July 22. 1705

David Magoone, and Mary Magoone Children of Elias and Hannah July 22.

Hannah Henchman Daughter of Joseph Henchman and Mary his wife. July. 29.

Sarah Eells, Daughter of Nathanael and Hannah Eells August. 5. 1705

Keziah Perry daughter of William and Elizabeth Perry. Auguft. 22. 1705

William Curtife, fon of Benjamin Curtife and Mary his wife August. 12.

David Pickles, fon of Nathan Pickles and Miriam his wife, August. 12.

Adult { Mary Joflen aged 21 years, and
Adult { Nathaniel Joflen aged 18 years; August 19.

Adult { Patience Stetfon aged 17. years; daughter of Sam[ll] Stetfon; September. 9th

Ann Clark, Deborah Clark, Charity Clark, Children of Thomas Clark and Martha his wife Sept[r]: 9th.

Nathanael Parker, William Parker Rachel Parker and Miriam, alias Mary Parker, Children of William Parker and Rachel his wife: September. 16.

Charles Turner the Son of Charles turner and his wife September. 30.

Elizabeth Randal Daughter of Ifaac Randal and Deborah his wife; November. 4th.

Adult Mary Beacon, aged 27 years. November 11.

Standly Silvester fon of Benjamin Silvefter and his wife. December 10.

Anno 1706

Jane King daughter of Icabod King and Hannah his Wife. March 3[d].

Timothy Fofter Son of Hatherly Fofter and Barfhua his wife March 10

Benjamin Cufhing fon of John Cufhing and Deborah his wife Aprill 28. 1706

Hannah Turner daughter of Japhet Turner and Hannah his wife. April 28.

Anna Clap daughter of Joseph Clap and Abigail his Wife May. 5

Thomas Clap Son of John Clap and Hannah his Wife May. 5.

David Lappam fon of Sam[ll] Lappan [*sic*]. May. 12.

Adult } { Thomas Stockbridge Aged [*blank*] years May. 19.

Ezekiel Kent Son of John Kent and Sarah his wife. May 26.

Hannah Beacon, Daughter of Mary Beacon. June 16

Samuel And Mary Rogers Children of Samuel Rogers, of Marſhfield and Jael his wife June. 23.

Adult. Lydia Clift Wife of William Clift. July. 14

Lydia Clift, and William Clift, Children of William & Lydia Clift his wife. July. 14.

Joshua Steaples [? Staples] Son of Samuell Steples and Elizabeth His wife July 14.

Elisha Curtice, Son of Joseph Curtice and Rebecca his wife July. 14.

Mary King Daughter of Daniel and Elizabeth King. July. 28

Mary Turner Daughter of Jonathan Turner and Mercy his wife Auguſt. 4.

Rebekah King Daughter of John King and Rebekah his wife Auguſt 25.

[*blank*] Stockbridge daughter of Charles Stockbridge and Abigail his wife Sep^t: 1.

Martha Stetſon Daughter of Robert Stetſon and Mary his wife Sept: 8.

Abiel Turner Son of John Turner and Abigail His Widow October 6th

Adult. Margaret Pratt Wife of Jonathan Pratt October 13.

Abigail Prat, Margret Prat, Martha Pratt Children of Jonathan Prat, and Margarett His Wife October. 13.

Stephen Clap Son of Stephen Clap and Temperance his wife December. 1.

Barſhubah Stockbridge Daughter of Joseph Stockbridge and Margret, his wife, December. 3.

Mary Perry daughter of James Perry and Mary his wife December 1.

James Proute son of Edward Prouty and Elizabeth his wife. Decemb^r: 1.

Miles Parker Son of William Parker and Rachel his wife December, 22.

Anno

1707

Samuel Eells Son of Nathanael & Hannah Eells. February 23. 1706/7

Abigail Kent, Daughter of Ebenezar Kent. Aprill 6.

Deborah Pratt, & Patience Pratt children of Jonathan Pratt & Margaret his wife; May. 4^d

Desire Silveſter, daughters [*sic*] of Richard Silveſter & Desire his wife, May 4^d/

1707.

Bezaleel Palmer Son of Bezaleel & Elizabeth Palmer his Widdow. May 11th.

Ruth Turner Daughter of Thomas Turner and Martha his Wife May. 15th.

Thankfull Dwelly Daughter of John Dwelly & Rachel His Wife May. 25.

Eunice James Daughter of John James & Eunice his Wife May 25.

Rachiel Taylor Daughter of Iſaac Taylor & Sarah his Wife. June. 1st.

Margaret Torry daughter of William Torry & Margaret his Wife June. 1st.

John Mackfarland, Son of John Mackfarland of Duxboroug [Duxbury], and Martha his Wife. June 8th.

Jemima Turner Daughter of Thomas Turner & Hannah his Wife June 15th.

Rachel Silveſter, John Silveſter, & Samuel Silveſter, Children of Samuel Silveſter & Lucretious his wife; of Marshfeild. June. 22.

Isaac Collamare Son of Peter Colomare & Abigail his wife. July 27.

Hannah Lincoln Daughter of Solomon Lincoln, & Hannah his wife, Auguſt 3^d

Joseph Jacob, ſon of David Jacob and Sarah his wife; August 17th.
Mary Clift Daughter of William Clift and Lydia his Wife, Auguſt. 31.
Mary Randal Daughter of Iſaac Randal & Deborah his wife October 26
Amos Silveſter Son of Amoſ Silveſter and Elizabeth his wife. November 16.
Mary Witherell daughter of William Witherell & [*blank*] his wife November. 16.
Miriam Turner daughter of Charls turner, & Mercy his wife November 23.

Anno 1708. Theſe were Baptized viz:

1 Othniel Pratt ſon of Jonathan Pratt and Margaret his wife March. 21.
Joseph King ſon of John King & Rebecca his Wife April: 11th
[*blank*] Church Daughter of Nathanll: Church & Judith his wife, April. 25.
Robert King ſon of Daniel King & Elizabeth his wife. May. 2d.
Mary Roſe, daughter of Jabez Roſe & Mary, his widdow. May 2d
Elias Magoone ſon of Elias Magoone, of Duxborough June. 20.
Joshua Silveſter ſon of Samuel Silveſter of Marshfield, June 27
Thankfull Curtiſe Daughter of Joseph Curtice and Rebecca his wife, June. 27.
Thomas Roſe Son of Jeremiah Roſe an[d] Elizabeth his wife. June. 27.
Adult Hannah Lappam wife of Samuel Lappam
Elizabeth Lappam daughter of Samuel Lappam & Hannah his wife, July. 4t
Barnabas Perry ſon of Henry Perry and [*blank*] his wife July 4th
Eliſha Foſter ſon of Hatherly Foſter and Barshubah His wife July 4th
Samuel Curtice ſon of Samuel Curtice and Anna his wife July 4th.
Adult. John Berstowe, junr: ſon of John Berstowe, & Lydia His wife; July. 18th.
David Curtice ſon of Benjamin Curtice & [*blank*] his Wife; Auguſt 1st.
Jael Rogers daughter of Samll: Rogers & Jael his wife, of Marshfield Auguſt. 8th.
Stephen Good-ſpeed, & Nathanael Goodſpeed, children of Nathanll Goodſpeed & Sarah his Wife; of Rochester. Auguſt. 29.
Mary Dwelly Daughter of John Dwelly & Rachel his wife, Auguſt. 29.
Lydia Hatch daughter of Samuel Hatch, & Elizabeth his wife, Auguſt 29.
Lydia Woodward daughter of Robert Woodward & Bethia His wife. September. 12
Sarah Staples Daughter of Samuel Steples & Elizabeth his wife October 3d.
Magaret Stockbridge Daughter of Joseph Stockbridge and Margaret his wife October. 31.
Mary & Ephraim Cain, Children of Ephraim Cain and Hannah his wife, of Middleborough Decemr: 19

Anno. 1709. theſe were Baptized.

John Eells ſon of Nathanael Eells & Hannah His wife January. 23. 1708/9
Benjamin Stoddard Son of Benjamin Stoddard & Mary his wife March 27.
William Silveſter ſon of Amos Silveſter & Eliſabeth his Wife. March. 27.
Abigail Torry daughter of William Torry & Margaret His wife April. 10.
Faith Silveſter daughter of Richard Silveſter & Deſire his Wife, May. 22.
John James, Son of John James & Eunice his wife June. 5th.

Margret Silvefter Daughter of Joseph Silvefter & Mary his wife of Marshfield June 5th.

Benjamin Dwelly, fon of John Dwelly & Rachel his wife July. 3^{d}.

Richard Prouty fon of Edward Prouty & Eliz: his wife July. 10th.

Nathanael Cufhing fon of John Chufhing & Deborah his wife July. 17th

John Curtice fon of John Curtice & Experience his wife July. 17th

Joseph Church fon of Nathanael Church & Judith his wife July 17th

Gidion Stetfon fon of Robert Stetfon & Mary his Wife July. 24.

Samuel Berstowe fon of Samuel Berstowe & Lidia his Wife July. 24.

Hannah Mackfarland daughter of John Mackfarland & Martha his wife, of Duxborough: Auguft. 7th

Ephraim Spoonner, Servant to Ensign Thomas Stockbridge, Auguft 14th

Ephraim Turner Son of Charls Turner and Mercy his wife; August 28th this child being very fick and at the point of death, was baptized in private.

Deborah Bryant Daughter of John Bryant & Deborah his wife Septr 4th

James Magoone, Thomas Magoone Sarah Magoone, children of James Magoone deceafed, & Sarah his Widow. September. 18th

James Woodworth fon of Robert wodworth October. 2^{d}

Nathanael Clap fon of Stephen Clap & Temperance His wife October. 23.

Elizabeth & Israel Turner children of Philip Turner, & Eliz: his wife oct: 23.

Samuel Clift son of Willm Clift & Lydia his wife, of Marfhfield, October 23.

Charls Stock-bridge fon of Charls Stockbridge & Abigail his wife, March 13. 1709/10 this child being sick, and in danger of death was baptized in private. *i. e.* at his fathers house.

Anno. 1710.

Samuel Staples fon of Sam^{ll} Staples & Elizabeth his wife: April. 2^{d}

Benjamin King Son of John King & Rebekkah his wife, April 16th

Abigail Randall, Daughter of Ifaac & Deborah Randall April. . 30.

Jeffe Curtice Son of Jofeph Curtice and Rebeccah his wife May 7th

Elkanah Totman, fervant to Joseph Turner, May 14

Mehetabel King daughter of Dan^{ll} King & Elizabeth his wife, May. 14.

Ruth Hatch Daughter of Sam^{ll} Hatch jun^{r}: & Elizabeth his wife May. 28.

Ruth Dwelly, Samuel Dwelly, Margrett Dwelly, children of Richard Dwelly Deceafed, and Aimy his Widdow. June 4th 1710

Benjamin Tolman Son of Benja^{in} Tolman & Elizabeth his wife, June 18th

Elizabeth Silvefter daughter of Samuel Silvefter and His wife, of Marfhfield. June 18.

Rachel Prat, daughter of Jonathan Prat & margret his wife July. 16.

Ann Stockbridge Daughter of Thomas Stockbridge & Sarah His wife. July 23.

Thomas Collomar Son of Peter Collomar & Abigail his wife July 30th

Mary Pratt Daughter of Jabez Pratt & [*blank*] His wife of duxborough. September 3^{d}

Robert Stetfon fon of Robert Stetfon and Mary his wife Sept 10.

Ruth church daughter of Richard Chh deceafed. October 1st

David Bryant & Elizabeth Bryant, children of David Bryant and Hannah his wife Oct: 1st

David Clark, Samuel Clark & Mary Clark Children of Thomas Clark & Martha his wife Oct: 8th

Sufannah Rogers daughter of Samuel Rogers & Jael his wife october. 8th

Anna Palmer & Patience Palmer Children of John Palmer and Mary his wife Octr 8th

John Proute, fon of Edward Proute & Elizabeth his Wife, Decemb^{r} 3^{d}

Adult Mary Bryant the wife of Thomas Bryant: December 10th.

Benjamin Bryant the fon of Thomas Bryant & Mary his wife December 10th.

John Alden, fon of John Alden, of Duxborough and Hannah his wife. Dec: 10th.

Adult Isaac Jones aged [*blank*] years son of Isaac & Mary Jones Late of Bofton deceafed Dec: 24th

Peleg Curtice fon of Benjamin Curtice & [*blank*] His wife Dec: 24.

RECORDS OF THE SECOND CHURCH OF SCITUATE, NOW THE FIRST UNITARIAN CHURCH OF NORWELL, MASS.

Communicated by Wilford Jacob Litchfield, M.S., of Southbridge, Mass.

Anno. 1711.

Nathanael Eells Son of Nathanael Eells & Hannah his wife, was baptized February 4th 1710/11

Thomas Turner, Son of Charls Turner & Mercy his wife March 11th 1710/11

Jofeph Silvefter fon of Amos Silvefter & Elizabeth his wife March 11th

Mary Silvefter Daughter of Jofeph Silvefter & Mary his wife of Marshfield March 18th

Joshua Lappam Son of Samuell Lappam & Hannah his wife March 25.

Jofeph houfe, David Houfe, James Houfe, Samuel Houfe, John Houfe, Rebecca Houfe, Elizabeth Houfe children of Samuell Houfe, and Sarah His wife, Aprill 22, 1711

Ann Curtice daughter of Sam^{ll} curtice jun^{r}: & Ann his wife Aprill 22, 1711.

Benjamin James Son of John James & Eunice his wife May. 20th

Mary Stoddard Daughter of Benj^{in} Stoddard & Mary his wife May. 20th

Margaret & Ruth Bryant children of Jonathan Bryant & Elizabeth his wife: May 27th

Deborah King daughter of George King & Deborah his wife may 27th.

Elizabeth Hanks daughter of Benjamin Hanks & Abigail his wife; who live at a place called the Majors Purchafe.

Adult: Elizabeth Wanton of Marfhfield. July. 1st

Thankfull Sprout & Abigail Sprout children of Ebenezar Sprout and [*blank*] His wife July. 22.

Joseph Palmer fon of Sam^{ll} Palmer & Ann his wife. July. 22.

Adult. Sufannah Berstowe. } children of John Ber-
Adult. Abigail Berstowe } stow & & Lydia his
Adult. Lydia Berstowe } wife August. 5th.

Jerufha King Daughter of John King & Rebecca his wife Auguft. 12.

Ruth Palmer, Mary Palmer & John Palmer children of John Palmer & Mary his wife. Sep^{t} 23.

Elizabeth Staples daughter of Sam^{ll} Staples & Elizabeth his wife: Sep^{t} 30.

Mary Bryant daughter of David Bryant & Hannah his wife Sep^{t} 30

Mary Bryant daughter of Thomas Bryant & Mary his wife November 18th

Susannah Stockbridge daughter of Joseph Stockbridge & Margred his wife, of Duxborough: Nov: 25.

Joseph Cufhing Son of Joseph Cufhing & Mercy his wife November. 25. 1711.

Anno. 1712.

John Fofter Son of Hatherly Fofter & Barfheba his wife: Aprill. 6th.

Nehemiah Randal fon of Nehemiah Randall & Mercy his wife. April 13

Joshua Lincoln Son of Solomon Lincoln & Hannah his wife Aprill. 13.

Samuel Tolman fon of Benjamin Tolman & Elizabeth his wife May 4th

Eunice Proutie daughter of Edward Proutie & Eliz: his wife May 4th

Deborah Riply Daughter of John Riply, June 8th

Israel Hatch, David Hatch, Jonathan Hatch, Lidya Hatch Elizabeth Hatch children of Israel Hatch & Elizabeth his wife June 8th

Joseph Smith, brought to baptifm by his uncle Israel And aunt Elizabeth Hatch. June 8th.

Lufanna Dwelle daughter of John Dwelle & Rachel his wife June 15.th

Hannah Symms daughter of Timothy Syms & Elizabeth his Wife: June 29.

Thomas Swift Son of Thomas Swift & Rachel his wife, June 29

Adult: Elifabeth Taylor daughter of John Taylor. July. 20th

Adult: Anna Turner Widow of Amafa turner, and her children viz: Benjamin, Eliab, Anna, & Hannah, July. 20th.

Adult: Deborah Rogers wife of John Rogers jun^{r} and all her children, viz: Daniel, John and one daughter, viz: Elizabeth July 20th.

Cornelius, John, & Mary Briggs children of Joseph Briggs & Deborah his wife, August 10th.

Adult. Lydia Right Wife of John Right. August. 24.

Samuel Collomar Son of Peter Collomar & Abigail his wife August 30th this child being Sick and near unto death as was fuppofed by its parents was Baptized att home.

Adult John Hatch jun^{r}: &
Adult Hannah Hatch wife of John Hatch jun^{r} Sept. 7th.

Agatha Bryant, daughter of John Bryant & Deborah his wife. Sept: 7th.

Adult. Hannah Ewell daughter of Gerfham Ewell. fep^{t} 28.

Mary Houfe daughter of Sam^{ll} Houfe & Sarah his wife: Sep^{t} 28.

Mercy Silvefter daughter of Sam^{ll} Silvefter of Marshfield Sept. 28.

Mercy Newcomb, & Jofhua newcomb, children of Andrew newcomb & mercy his wife, of truerow. Sept.: 28.

Benjamin Tildin Son of Sam^{ll} Tildin & Sarah his wife of Marfhfield October. 5th.

Deborah Bearftow daughter of Sam^{ll}: Berftow & Lydia his wife October. 5th.

Peleg Curtice fon of Joseph Curtice and Rebeckah his wife oct^{r} 12.

Grace Turner daughter of Philip Turner & Elizabeth his wife Octr 12.

Mary Thorne the Adopted daughter of Thomas Pincheon and Sarah his wife. October. 19th.

Sufanna Turner daughter of Isaac Turner & Ruth his wife Dec: 7th

Adult Margret Proute & Adult William Proute Dec: 14th 1712.

Anno. 1713.

Edward Eells Son of Nath[ll]: Eells and Hannah his wife was baptized January 4th 1712/13

Mehetabal Hatch daughter of John hatch jun[r]. and Hannah his wife. Feb: 22. 1712/13

Hincksman Silvefter, fon of Amos Silvefter and Elizabeth his wife march 15th 1712/13

Adult. Jonathan Proute. March 29th

Mary Joflin daughter of Nathan[ll] Joflin & Frances his wife March. 29th

Jonathan Silvefter Son of Jofeph Silvefter of Marfhfield, & mary his wife Aprill 5th

Deborah Briggs daughter of Jofeph Briggs & Deborah his wife April 5th

Grace Randall daughter of Jsaac Randall & Deborah his wife April 12 1713.

Anno 1713.

Samuel Perry, Son of Benjamin Perry & Ruth his wife. May. 10th

Lydia James daughter of John James & Eunice his wife may 17th

Samuel Aldin Son of John Aldin of Duxborouhg & Hannah his wife. May. 17th

Jofhua Bryant Son of Sam[ll] Bryant & Abigail his wife May. 24th

Jofhua Stoddard Son of Hezekiah Stoddard & Lois his wiffe. June 7th

Hannah Dammon daughter of Daniel & Barfheba Dammon. June 14th

Adult. Hope Torry Wife of David Torry June 21.

Stephen Torry & Rachel Torry children of David Torry and Hope his wife. June. 21.

Alexander & Jofhua Parker children of W[m] Parker & Rachel his wife July. 12.

Philip Turner Son of Philip Turner & Elizabeth his wife. July. 12.

Mercy Lappam Daughter of Sam[ll] Lappam & Hannah his wife July. 12.

Deborah White daughter of Jofeph White & Elizabeth his wife, of Marfhfield. Auguft 23

James Randal Son of Nehemiah Randall and Mercy his wife, of Pembrooke Auguft 23.

Thomas King Son of John King and Rebeckkah his Wife, of Marfhfield, Auguft. 23.

Rhoda King daughter of George King & Deborah his wife Aug: 23.

Mercy Right daughter of John & Lydia Right. Auguft 30.

Abner Stetfon Son of Sam[ll] Stetfon & Elizabeth his wife Sep[t]: 6

Martha Curtice Daughter of Sam[ll] Curtice & Anna his wife Sept: 6th

*Anno. 1714**

John Briggs Son of John Briggs and Deborah his wife Oct 25

Ruth Parker Daughter of Charity Parker. Oct: 25

Robert Sproute Son of James Sproute & Elizabeth his wife, November 1st

Adult Lazarus Turner an apprentice to Enfign Stockbridge. Dec: 13 1713

Anno. 1714.

Olieff Silvefter daughter of Zebulem Silvester & Mary his wife Jan: 31st

Seth Bryant Son of Thomas Bryant and Mary his Wife. Feb: 21.

* This should be 1713.

Richard Dwelly Son of Richard & Grace Dwelly, Feb: 21.
Peter Silvefter Son of Peter and Mary Silvefter Feb: 28.
Elizabeth Tolman daughter of Benj^{m} Tolman & Elizabeth his wife. Aprill 25
Adult Hannah Magoone Wife of John Magoone. May 2^{d} 1714.
Miriam Turner Daughter of Charlfe Turner & mercy his wife May 2^{d}
Deborah Rogers Daughter of John & Deborah Rogers May 2^{d}
Timothy Symms, Son to Timothy Symms & Elizab:th his wife May 30.
Sarah houfe, daughter of Sam^{ll} Houfe & Sarah his wife June 13
Jacob Bryant Son of David Bryant and Hannah his wife June 13.
Isaac Lincoln Son of Soloman Lincoln & Hannah his wife June 20.
Caleb Church Son of Nathanaell Church & Judith his wife. June, 27.
Susanna Bryant Daughter of John & Deborah Bryant June. 27.
Hannah Proute Daughter of Edward & Elizabeth Proute July 25th
Content, Deliverance, Ann, and Abigail Bifhop, Children of ftutfon Bifhop, & Abigail his wife. July 25.
Ifrael & Elizabeth Turner, children of Japhet & Hannah Turner were baptifed by me At Pembroke where I occafionally preach'd for Mr Lewes. Auguft 8. 1714.
William Brooks Son of Gilbert, & Elizabeth Brook. Sep^{t} 12. 1714
Jonathan Turner Son of Jsaac & Ruth Turner Sep^{t} 19th 1714
Hannah, Lydia, & William Barrel, Children of William & Elizabeth Barrel. Sep^{t} 26.
Bezaleel & Sufannah Curtice Children of John & Experience Curtice october 10.th 1714.
Adult. Mary Taylor daughter of William Talor. Oct: 24 1714
Adult Defire Oldum, Daughter of Thomas & Mercy Oldum oct: 24. 1714
Ebenezer Rogers Son of Samuel & Jael Rogers of Marfhfield. Oct: 24.
Adult. { Alice Wheaton Daughter of Obediah Wheaton & Sarah his wife: was baptized at Deacon David Jacobs houfe. She being there fick with a Confumption & not Likely to recover. }
Mercy Dwelly daughter of John and Rachel Dwelly Nov: 7th 1714.
John Bifby Son of John Bifby and Mary his wife, of Marfhfield November 7.th 1714.
Job Turner Son of Philip & Elizabeth Turner Dec: 26. 1714

Anno 1715
Hannah Eells Daughter of Nathanael & Hannah Eells was baptized January 30th 1714/15
Jofiah Cufhing Son of John Cufhing, & Sarah His wife was baptized February 13th 1714/15

Anno 1715
George Stetfon Son of Sam^{ll} Stetfon and Elizabeth his wife, Feb: 20. 1714/15
Adult. { Elizabeth Stetfon wife of Samuel Stetfon, was Baptized March 23 1714/15 at home She being fick with a fever & not Likely to Live: }
Elifha James Son of John James & Eunice his wife, April 17th 1715
Micah Stockbridge Son of Thomas Stockbridge & Sarah his wife Aprill 24.
Adult. Sarah Ramfdel Wife of Thomas Ramfdel: and her children whofe names are here Inferted were baptized May 15th 1715.

Mary Ramſdel.
Joſeph Ramsdel
Jemimah Ramſdel
Gidion Ramſdel } Children of Thomas Ramſdel & Sarah, his wife, were Baptized May 15. 1715.

Adult. Frances Joſlin the wife of Nathanaell Joſlin was baptiſed May 29. 1715.

Benjamin Perry Son of Benjamin Perry & Ruth his wife June 12. 1715

{ Benjamin Berſtowe son of Benjamin & Mercy Berſtowe was Baptized the twenty ninth day of June 1715 in the evening, At his fathers houſe, he being Sick, & as was thought not Likely to recover

Adult Mercy Pitcher wife of Joſeph Pitcher were baptized July 3[d] 1715

Jonah Woolſon Son of [blank] Woolſon & [blank] His wife Sometime of watertown July 3[d] 1715

Nathanaell Biſhop Son of Stutſon Biſhop & Abigail his wife July 3. 1715

Thankfull Lappam Daughter of Sam[ll] & Hannah Lappam. July 24. 1715

Robert Thomſon, Son of Robert & Ann Thomſon Auguſt 7th 1715

Samuel Palmer Son of Samuell & Anna Palmer Auguſt 7, 1715

Adult. Mercy Beſtow wife of Benj[m] Beſtow. & Martha Beſtow daughter of Benja[m] & mercy Beſtow, was baptized. Auguſt 14, 1715

Anno 1716*

Mary Sprout daughter of Ebenezar Sprout. Auguſt 14.

Sarah Ramſdel, daughter of Thomas & Sarah Ramſdel August. 14. 1715

Michael Silveſter Son of Amos & Elizabeth Silveſter Auguſt 14. 1715

Mary Clyſt Daughter of W[m] Clift and Lydia his wife, of marſhfield. August 21. 1715

Alice Palmer daughter of [blank] his wife. Auguſt 21.

Sarah Silveſter daughter of Joſeph Silveſter of Marſhfield. Auguſt 21.

Martha Demmon daughter of Zechariah Demmon. Auguſt 21. 1715

Ezekiel Palmer, Samuel Palmer, Sarah Palmer & Deborah Palmer children of Elnathan & mercy Palmer, were baptized Sep[t] 4th 1715.

Anna King Daughter of John & Rebeckah King. Sept 4th 1715.

Grace Turner daughter of John Turner & [blank] His wife, Oct: 9th

Eliſha Stoddard Son of Beniamin & Mary Stoddard Oct: 16. 1715

Joſeph Tolman, ſon of Benjamin and Elizabeth Tolman Nov: 6th

{ Sarah Turner Daughter of Charls & Mercy Turner was Baptiſed Dec: 2[d] 1715. This Child being sick was baptized in Private

Anno 1716

Miriam Curtice daughter of Sam[ll] & Anna Curtice January 1st

Adult. Rachel Thorn (aged about nineteen years. Daughter of Joſeph Thorn of Hingham) was baptized Feb: 19. 1715/16.

Elizabeth Beſtow. Joſeph Beſtow, & James Beſtowe, children of Joſeph & mary Beſtow were Baptiſed, Aprill 8th 1716.

Thomas Bryant Son of Thomas & Mary Bryant Aprill 29. 1716.

Grace Dwelly daughter of Richard Dwelly & Grace his wife, Aprill 29. 1716

Adult James Briggs may 6th 1716.

Elizabeth Brigs the Daughter of James Brigs May 6th 1716

Mary Eells daughter of Nathan[ll] and Hannah Eells, was Baptized May 13th 1716

* This should be 1715.

Hannah Silvefter daughter of Peter & mary Silvefter. may. 27. 1716.
Adult Mary Woodward Wife of Benj^{m} woodward June 3^{d} 1716
Benjamin & Thomas Woodward children of Benj^{m} & mary woodward were baptized June 3^{d} 1716.
Elifha Prouty Son of Edward & Elizabeth Prouty. June 24. 1716
Daniel Dammon Son of Daniel & Barfhebah Dammon. June 24. 1716
Philip Turner Son of Philip and Elizabeth Turner July 1st 1716
Thomas Palmer Son of John Palmer & Mary His wife was Baptized in Private July 8 1716, it being sick and not Likely to recover.
John Bryant Son of John & Deborah Bryant, July 22 1716.
Jofhua Palmer Son of Sam^{ll} Palmer & Anne his wife July 22. 1716
Samuel Bryant Son of Sam^{ll} and Abigail Bryant July 29. 1716
Mehetabel Dammon daughter of Zechariah Dammon, Sep^{t} 2^{d} 1716
Benjamin Beftowe Son of Benj^{m} & Mercy Beftowe Sep^{t} 2^{d} 1716
Samuel Ramfdell } children of Sam^{ll}
Mary Ramfdel } & mary Ramfdel
of Pembroke, were baptized Sept: 2^{d} 1716
Caftle Tuell Son of Benjamin Tuell & Joanna his wife fep^{t} 9th
Anthony Symms fon of Timothy & Elizabeth Symms Sept: 23. 1716.

Anno 1717
{ November 25. 1716.
Being at New Port on
Rhode Ifland, and Preaching,
after Sermon I Baptized }
Elizabeth Tounfand daughter of Nathan & Agatha Tounfand.
Edward & Elizabeth Roffom, children of Edward and Elizabeth Roffom.
John Draper and Elizabeth Draper Children of John Draper &
Thomas Brewer fon Of John Brewer and Ann his wife.
These I Baptifed at Newport, the day and year above mentioned.

1717. Scittuate.
Adult. Henry Joflin aged about twenty years. was Baptized Jan: 27. 1716/17
Adult. Keziah Joflin aged about twenty & one years was Baptized. Jan: 27. 1716/17
Mary Silvester daughter of Amofs & Elizabeth Silvefter April 7th 1717

{ Aprill 14th 1717 Being at
Hingham Coney Haffett & preaching
there; after Sermon I Baptized
Thomas, the Son of Nathan^{ll} and Elizabeth Nicols.
Benjamin the Son of Andrew and Rachel Beals
Samuel the Son of Jezeniah & Rebecca Nicols
Elizabeth the daughter of Hezekiah & Mary Lincoln.
Abigail, the daughter of John and Percis Farrow

Anno 1717
Perez Randal Son of Jsaac and Deborah Randall Baptized Aprill 21, 1717
William Tolman Son of Benjamin & Elizabeth Tolman Baptized Aprill 28 1717
Mercy Cufhing daughter of John Cufhing Efq^{r} & Sarah his wife, Baptized May 19th 1717
Deborah Lincoln daughter of Soloman Lincoln & Hannah his wife; Baptized. May 19th 1717

May 26. 1717. Being at Hingham
and preaching there after Sermon
I Baptized

Stephen Dunbar Son of Joſhuah & Hannah Dunbar.
David Whitten Son of David & Elizabeth Whitten
Benjamin Gilbert Son of Daniel & Judeth Gilbert.

Lydiah Otis daughter of Nathan^{ll} : Otis & Hannah his wife, baptiſed June 2^{d} 1717.

William Gilford Son of Willm & Elizabeth his wife June 2^{d}

Suſannah Gilford daughter of Willm & Eliz : Gilford June 2^{d} 1717

Barnabas Thomſon Son of Robert Thomſon & Anne his wife June 9th 1717

Sarah Rogers daughter of Sam^{ll} & Jael Rogers. June 16 1717

Lydia King Daughter of George King & Deborah his wife June 16. 1717

Adult Jane Right aged about [blank] years was Baptized June 16. 1717

Hezekiah Herrendeen, Son of Hezekiah Herrendeen And His wife, of marſhfield was baptized June 24 1717

Thankful Briggs A Child of Joſeph Briggs & Deborah his wife, was Baptized by me at m^{r} Pitchers meeting houſe: June 30th 1717

Simeon Naſh Son of Joſeph Naſh and Hañah his wife, being Sick was baptiſed at his houſe, July 1st 1717

Lydiah Beſtow daughter of Samuel Bestow & Lydia his wife Baptized July 7th 1717

Isaac Jones Son of Jsaac Jones & Hannah his wife. Baptized July 7th

Mary Beſtow Daughter of Joſeph & Mary Beſtow; Bap^{t}ized July 14th 1717

Peleg Perry Son of Benj^{m} Perry and Ruth his wife July 21. 1717

Joſeph Naſh, John Naſh, Hannah Naſh, Elizabeth Naſh, James Naſh, David Naſh; children of Joſeph Naſh & Hannah his wife were baptized July 28th 1717

Barſheba Bryant daughter of David & Hannah Bryant Baptized July 28. 1717

Eliſha Parker Son of Wm Parker and Rachel his wife of Rocheſter was Baptized July 28. 1717.

Thomas Silveſter, son of Sam^{ll} ſilveſter of marſhfield, baptized, Auguſt 4th 1717

Ruth Foſter Daughter of Hatherly Foſter and Barſhua his wife Auguſt 4th 1717

Elizabeth Torry, Daughter of David Torry & Hope his wife, Bapt^{d} Aug: 11th 1717

Nathanael Beſtow Son of Benj^{m} & Mercy Beſtow Baptized August 11th 1717

Nathanael Turner Son of Philip & Eliz:th Turner, Baptized August 11th 1717

Martha Silvester daughter of Zebulun & mary Silvester Auguſt 11th 1717

Adult Rachel Stetſon Daughter of Serg^{t} Samuel Stetſon was Baptiſed Auguſt 18th 1717

Ziphorah James daughter of John & Eunice James Baptized Sep^{t} 1st 1717

Elizabeth Stetſon daughter of Sam^{ll} Stetſon & Elizabeth his wife, Baptized Sep^{t} 1st 1717

James Warren
Naomy warren
children of John & Naomy Warren, baptized Sept 8th 1717

Mary Harlow, daughter of Sam[ll] Harlow & mary his wife was baptized Sep[r] 8th. 1717

Elifha King Son of John King and Rebeca his wife, of Marfhfield was baptized Oct. 6[th] 1717.

John Briggs Son of James Brigs & Hannah his wife, Oct: 6[th] 1717

Lemuel Dwelly Son of John Dwelly & Rachel his wife, Baptized oct: 13. 1717

Jofhua Silvefter Son of Peter & Mary Silvester, Bap[t]d Nov. 3[d] 1717

Lufanna Bifhop Daughter of Stutfon Bifhop & Abigail His wife Baptized, Nov: 17[th] 1717

Lydiah Pitcher daughter of Joseph & Mercy Pitcher, Baptized november 24[th] 1717

Mehitabel Oldham daughter of Jofhua Oldham and Mehitabel his wife, December 1[st] 1717

1718

John Woodward fon of Benj[m] & mary Woodward, baptized february 23. 1717/18.

Mary Prouty daughter of Edward & Elizabeth Prouty baptifed March 2[d]

March 16th 1717/18

Being at Hingham and Preaching there after Sermon in the afternoon I Baptized severall children.—as—

Jedediah Lincoln Son of Jedediah Lincoln and Bethiah his wife.
Israel Levit, fon of Jsrael & mary Levit;
Margaret Lincoln Daugh[r]: of Israel & margret Lincoln
Dan[ll] Cufhing fon of Dan[ll] & Sarah Cufhing.
Sam[ll] Johnfon fon of Benj[m] & Efter Johnfon
Lydia franklin, Daugh[r] of John & Lydia franklin
Elifabeth Lane Daugh[r] of Jsaac & Hañah Lane.
Deborah Lincoln Daugh[r] of Samuel and Deborah Lincoln.
Dan[ll] Sprague fon of Jofiah & Elifab[eth] Sprague
Thomas Lincoln fon of Thom[s] & Hannah Lincoln.
James Garnet fon of Jam[s] & Jane Garnet
Deborah Loring, of Benj[m] & Debr[r] Loring
Sarah Jones, of Thom[s] & Catherine Jones.
Rachel Mackfarland of James & Sarah mackfarland.

Adult Jonah Stetfon, Son of Sam[ll] Stetfon, was Baptized march 23[d] 1717/18 being of Adult years.

Deborah Curtice, daughter of Sam[ll] & Anna Curtice was baptifed march 23. 1717/18.

Benjamin Curtice Son of Benjamin Curtice jun[r] & Hannah his wife was baptized April 27. 1718

Jael Dammon daughter of Zecheriah & Mehitabel Dammon, was baptifed May 4th 1718

Increafe Whetftone, & John Whetftone children of John Whetftone and [blank] his wife were baptifed May 4th 1718.

Mary Stetfon daughter of Anthony and Anna Stetfon. May 11. 1718

Amafa Turner Son of Amafa & Anna Turner, Baptifed May 18th 1718.

Nathanaell Silvefter Son of Amos & Elizabeth Silvefter, was baptifed July 6th 1718.

Gilbert Brooks Son of Gilbert and Elizabeth Brooks was baptized July 13th 1718.

Timothy Silvefter Son of Joseph Silvefter of marfhfield, baptized July 20th 1718

Peleg Bryant Son of Thomas & Mary Bryant, was Baptifed July 27th 1718

Adult. Mary Buck the wife of Jfaac Buck was Baptized Auguft 3d 1718.

Ifaac Buck the Son of Ifaac & Mary Buck, was baptized August 3d 1718.

James Warren Son of John and Naomy Warren baptized Auguft 3d 1718

Abigail Lathly daughter of Philip Lathly deceafed, was baptized at her mothers requeft, Auguft 17. 1718

Hannah Otis daughter of Nathanll: Otis and Hannah his wife, formerly of this Town but Now of New-London; was Baptized Sept. 7th 1718

North Eells Son of Nathanaell & Hannah Eells, was baptized Sept 28 1718

Amos Lappam Son of Samuel and Hannah Lappam was bapt Sept 28 1718

William Lathly An apprentice Child to John Magoon was baptized Oct: 5 1718

Bartlet Turner, Son of John & mercy Turner. Baptized Oct: 12. 1718.

Mary Church daughter of Nathanll & Judith Chh, was baptized Oct: 26. 1718.

Jofeph Turner Son of Charls & Joanna Turner was Baptized Nov: 2d 1718

Agatha Gilford daughter of Wm Gilford & Elizabeth his wife Nov: 2d 1718

Job Neal Son of Jofep[h] Neal & Abigail his wife was Baptized Nov: 23. 1718

Jfaac Dammon Son of Danll Dammon & Bathfhebah his wife was Bapt Nov. 28 1718

John Bryant Son of Samuell Bryant and Abigail his wife, was Baptized Dec: 21. 1718.

RECORDS OF THE SECOND CHURCH OF SCITUATE, NOW THE FIRST UNITARIAN CHURCH OF NORWELL, MASS.

Communicated by WILFORD JACOB LITCHFIELD, M.S., of Southbridge, Mass.

Anno Domini 1719.

Adult. Allice Clerk, Wife of Thomas clark, being fick & fuppofed to be nigh unto death, defiring baptifm, after some difcourfe with her, & her manifeftation of repentance & faith in Chrift was baptized, in the prefence of Deacon Stephen Clap & fome others of the Chh. March 6th 1719

Adult. Mary Lambert daughter of John Lambert, was Baptized march 8th 1718/19

Mary Jones, daughter of Jfaac Jones and Hannah his wife ; bapt: March 8th 1718/19

Elifha Tollman Son of Benjm Tolman & Elizabeth his wife, was Baptized march 15th 1719

Jfaac Turner, Son of Jsaack & Ruth Turner, baptized Aprill 5th 1719.

John Briggs fon of James & Hannah Brigs, baptized Aprill 5th 1719

Sarah Stockbridge Daughter of Thomas Stockbridge & Sarah his Wife was Baptifed Aprell 26 1719

Mercy Nash, daughter of Jofeph & Hannah his wife was baptized may 3d 1719

Deborah Cufhing daughter of John & Elizabeth cufhing was baptized may 3d 1719

Deborah Tower daughter of Benjm & Bethiah Tower : Baptifed may 3d 1719

John Clerk, mary Clerk, Jofeph Clerk, Seth Clerk, Martha Clerk, Caleb Clerk, children of Thomas Clerk & Allice his wife, were baptifed May 3^d^ 1719

Abiel Perry Son of Benj^m^ & Ruth Perry was baptized in private, it being fick, March 11th 1719

May 17th 1719 I preach'd at Little Hingham, and after Sermon I Baptized Mofes Lincoln the Son of Mofes & Lincoln & Martha his wife. Mary Philips, Daughter of Thomas Philips & Rachel his wife.

John Taylor Son of Jfaac & Ruth Taylor was Baptized May 31. 1719

Tailer Brooks Son of Nathanaell & Mary Brooks, was baptifed May 31. 1719

Sarah King Daughter of George King & Deborah his wife, was baptifed June 7th 1719

Adult. James Bowker jun^r^. was baptifed June 28th 1719

Adult. Hannah Bowker the wife of James Bowker jun^r^. was Baptized June 28. 1719.

Lazarus Bowker Son of James Bowker & Hannah his wife was Baptized June 28th 1719

Thomas Slack Son of Thomas & Ruth Slack of Plympton, was Baptized July 12th 1719

Ann Tomfon daughter of Ann & Robert Tomfon Baptized August 2^d^ 1719

Abigail Tilden daughter of Sam^ll^ and Defire Tilden, of Marfhfield was Baptized Auguft 23. 1719

Auguft 30.th 1719 I preach'd att Little Hingham, and after Sermon I Baptized —

Daniel Lincoln Son of Obadiah and Sufanna Lincoln.

John Stevenfon fon of John & Rachel Stevenfon

Elizabeth Nicols daughter of nathanael and Elizabeth nicols.

Rachel Beal daughter of Andrew & Rachel Beal.

[*blank*] Berftow daughter of Jofeph and Mary Beftow, being An Infant and Sick nigh unto death was Baptized in private Oct: 12 1719

Caleb Silvefter Son of Amofs & Elizabeth Silvefter, was baptifed march 20th 1719/20

Caleb Beftow Son of Benjamin Beftow & Mercy; baptifed march 20th 1719/20

Job Beftow fon of Sam^ll^ & Lydia Beftow was Baptifed April 3^d^ 1720

Content Ramfdel daughter of Samuel & Martha Ramfdel was baptized Aprill 3^d^ 1720

Adult Lydia Wheaten daughter of Obadiah & Sarah wheaten being Sick & Lame at Deacon Jacobs Houfe, & not Likely to recover, was Baptized Aprill 4th 1720.

Abel Curtice, Son of William Curtice & Margret His wife was Baptized Aprill 10th 1720

James Briggs Son of James & Hannah His wife, was baptized Aprill. 24. 1720.

Ifrael & Elifha Silvefter Children of Zebulun Silvefter and Mary his wife, were baptized Aprill 24. 1720.

Sarah Cufhing daughter of John Cufhing jun^r^. & Elizabeth his wife, was Baptifed May 1st 1720.

Benjamin Silvefter Son of Benj^m^ Silvefter & Jerufha his wife was Baptized May 8th 1720

Ruth Silvefter daughter of Benj^m^ & Ruth Silvefter was baptized May 8th 1720.

Elifha Palmer Son of Samuell Palmer & Anna his wife was baptized May 8th 1720

John Tomfon Son of Robert and Anne Tomfon was Baptized may 15th 1720

Elizabeth King daughter of John King & Rebeccah his wife of Marfhfield, was baptized may 29. 1720

Gennet Rogers daughter of William & Gennet Rogers was Baptized May 29. 1720.

June 3d 1720. Elifha Randal Son of Nehemiah Randal & Ruth his wife of Pembroke, was baptized, at his houfe, the child being very fick & not Likely to recover

Simeon Curtice Son of Samll: & Anna Curtice, was Baptized June 5th 1720.

Elijah Stoddard Son of Benjm & Mary Stoddard was Baptized. June 26. 1720

Ruth Randal daughter of Nehem: Randal & Ruth his wife, of Pembroke was Baptized July 10.th 1720

Benjamin Brooks Son of Gilbert and Hannah Brooks was baptized July 31. 1720.

Hannah Bryant daughter Thomas Bryant & mary his wife was Baptized Auguft 7th 1720

Abigail Newcombe Daughter of Andrew newcombe & mercy his wife, of Truro, was baptized Auguft 7th 1720

Ifaac Young Son of Jofeph Young & Anna his wife of Truro was Baptized August 7th 1720.

Lemuel Turner Son of Jsaac Turner & Ruth his wife, was baptifed Aug : 14th 1720

James Buck Son of Jsaac Buck & Mary his wife was Baptized Auguft 14th 1720.

Auguft 21st 1720 I preach'd at Little Hingham, and after Sermon J Baptized —

John Farrow, son of John & Pircif farrow

Daniel Tower son of Daniel and Sarah Tower.

Amos Joy, son of Prince & Abigail joy

Content James, daughter of Thomas & Patience James.

Abigail Brigs Daughter of Jofeph & Deborah Briggs of Scittuate

Silence Nicols, daughter of Jazeniah & Rebeccah Nichols.

Experience Nicols daughter of Roger Nicols & Bethiah.

Adult: Ruth Bates, daughter of Jofeph Bates, was Baptized Auguft 28th 1720

Ezra Clark Son of Thomas & Allice Clarke was baptized Sept 4th 1720

Luke Bifhop Son of Hudfon Bifhop, & his wife of Pembroke. Baptd Sept. 4th 1720

Thomas Curtice Son of Benjamin Curtife junr : & Hannah his wife was Baptized Sept 4th 1720

Adult: Thomas Merit was Baptized Sept 11th 1720 Agatha Merit, Abigail merit, Aimy meret, & mary merit children of Thomas merit & Abigail his wife were Baptized Sept 11th 1720

Nehemiah Turner son of Abner & Aimy Turner, —— & Abner Turner fon of Abner & Aimy Turner, were baptized fept : 11th 1720

John Warren Son of John warren and Aimy his wife Baptized Sept 11. 1720

Hannah Bradford daughter of Elifha Bradford & Barfhua his wife, of Plymouth; was baptized Sept. 18th 1720.

Defire Tilden Daughter of Sam^{ll} Tilden & Defire his wife, of marfhfield was Baptized Sept 18, 1720.

Adult: Thomas Toby and his wife

Adult: Mary Toby were baptized October 2^{d} 1720. and alfo their Children; viz; —— Jane Tobey, Elifha Toby and mary Toby, were baptifed Oct^{t} 2^{d} 1720

Adult. Jfaac Hatch, fon of Jeremiah Hatch was baptized Oct: 2^{d} 1720

Jofhuah Beftow Son of Jofeph Beftow & Elizabeth his wife, was Baptized Dec: 4th 1720

Mary Dammon Daughter of Zech: & mehitabel his wife was Baptized Jan: 1st 1720/21.

Noah Brooks fon of $Nathn^{l}$: & mary his wife was Baptized Jan. 22^{d} 1720/21

Lydia Houfe daughter of Jofeph Houfe & Lydiah his wife was baptifed Feb: 6th 1720/21 at the Houfe of $Benj^{m}$ Curtice, the Child being very sick there.

Adult Abner Turner aged upward of fourty years, being fick and not Likely to recover was baptized at his own houfe Feb: 14th 1720/21

Hannah Silvefter daughter of Jofeph Silvefter of Marfhfield was baptized March 19th 1720/21

Ruth Tolman daughter of Ben: jamin & Elizabeth Tolman was Baptized at Home, Jt being Sick: March 27th 1721.

Adult. Jofeph Joflin fon of Henry Joflin, was baptized may 14th 1721.

Bethiah Tower Daughter of $Benj^{m}$ & Bethiah Tower was baptized may. 14. 1721

Elizabeth Curtice daughter of John Curtice, & Experience his wife was baptized may 28th 1721

Abner Perry Son of $Benj^{m}$ & Ruth Perry was baptized May $28.^{th}$ 1721.

Adult Urfellah Randal wife of Job Randal jun^{r} was baptized & Received in to full Communion wth y^{e} Chh June 4th 1721.

Thomas Randall, Job Randal, Sarah Randal & Mary Randal Children of Job Randal jun^{r} & Urfellah his wife were baptized June 4th 1721.

Thomas Farrow Son of Benjamin farrow & [blank] his wife was baptized June 4th 1721.

James Torry & Sarah Torry } children of James & Sarah Torry of Marfhfield were baptized July 2^{d} 1721

Thomas Church Son of $Nathan^{ll}$ Chh and Jerufha his wife was baptized July 2^{d} 1721

William Clyft Son of William Clift ju^{r} & Judith his wife of marfhfield was baptized July 30th. 1721.

Martha Toby daughter of Thomas Toby & Mary his Wife, was baptized Auguft 13th 1721.

Jofeph Dammon Son of Daniel & Barfhebah his wife was Baptized September 3^{d} 1721.

Benjamin Hatch Son of John Hatch jun^{r} & Grace his wife was baptized Sept 3^{d} 1721

Jsaac Tailer Son of Jsaac Tailer & Ruth his wife was Baptized Sept: 3^{d} 1721

Ruth Perry daughter of Amos & Ruth Perry was Baptized Sep^{t}. 10, 1721.

— Sept 1721. I preach'd at Little Hingham and after Sermon J Baptized Jeffe Stevenfon, Son of John & Rachel Stevenfon

Right Woodart, & Mary Woodart children of Benj[m] & mary woodart were baptized Sep[t] 24 1721

Gerfhom Randal Son of Nehemiah & Ruth his wife. of Pembrok. Baptized Oct 1st 1721

Relief Dammon, (of John Dam̃on & Eliz– his wife of Marfhfield) was Baptized october 1.st 1721

Edmund Silvefter Son of Amof & Eliz: Silvefter was Baptized oct: 8th 1721

Anna Lenthal Eells daughter of Nathanael & Hannah Eells was born october 16th 1721, and baptized october 22.[d] 1721.

Thomas Ruggles Son of John & Joanna Ruggles was Baptized oct: 29. 1721

Seth Briggs Son of James & Hannah Briggs was Baptized oc[t] 29. 1721

Mary Barker daughter of Jsaac Barker & Elizabeth his wife of Rhode Jsland, was Baptized Novemb[r] 1st 1721. at the Houfe of M[r] Jofeph Berftowe. The Child being fick there and not Likely to recover.

Adult Alice Clark wife of Thomas Clark was Baptized nov: 12th 1721

Gael Curtice daughter of W[m] & Margret Curtice was Baptifed nov: 26. 1721

Anno. 1722

Elizabeth Fofter daughter of Hatherly Fofter & Barfhua his wife, Bap[d] Feb: 25.

Lemuel Bryant Son of Thomas and Mary Bryant, Baptized Feb: 25th 1721/22.

Jonah Stetfon Son of Jonah & Mercy Stetfon, Baptized, Feb: 25 1721/22.

Alice Clark daughter of Thom[s] & Allice Clerk Baptized Feb: 25th 1721/22

Luke Curtice Son of Benjamin & Hannah curtice, Baptized March 11th 1722

March 23[d] 1722 Ebenezer Brooks Son of Gilbert Brooks was baptized at his houfe, being not Likely to Live

Mary Silvefter daughter of Peter and Mary, was Baptized March 25

Thomas Thomfon Son of Robert & Ann Thomfon was Baptized May 6, 1722

Stephen Hatch Son of Jsaac Hatch & Sarah his wife was Baptized May 20, 1722.

James Bowker Son of James & Hannah Bowker was Baptized may 20th 1722

Richard Church Son of Richard Church and ——— his wife Baptifed may 20, 1722

Benjamin Ramfdel Son of Jofeph & Mary Ramfdel of Pembroke was Baptifed may 20th 1722

Barfheba Dam̃on daughter of Daniel & Jemima Dammon was baptized June 3[d] 1722

Abigail Neal daughter of Jofeph & Abigail neal Baptized June 17th 1722

Thomas Buck fon of Jsaac Buck and mary his wife Baptized June 17th 1722

James Silvefter Son of Benj[m] & Ruth Silvefter, Baptized June 17th 1722

Elifha Nafh Son of Jofeph & Hannah nafh was Baptized July 8th 1722

Anthony Symms, Son of Timothy & Eliz: Sym̃s, was Baptized July 15th 1722

Patience Jordan; of John Jordan & Patience his wife, Bap^{t} July 15th 1722

Content Cuſhing daughter of James & mary Cuſhing bap^{t} July 22, 1722

Amos Curtice Son of Sam^{ll}: & Anna curtice was baptized July 22. 1722

Joſeph Stetſon ſon of Anthony & Anna Stetſon was Baptized Auguſt 5th 1722

Adult: Deborah Wheaten aged about 23 years was baptized Auguſt 19th 1722

Mercy Beſtow Daughter of Benj^{m} Beſtow & mercy his wife was baptized Auguſt 19, 1722

Benjamin Torry Son of Keziah Torry, was Baptized Aug: 19, 1722

Mercy Tilden Daughter of Sam^{ll} Tilden jun^{r} & deſire his wife of marſhfield, was Bap^{t} ſep^{t} 9th 1722

John Cuſhing Son of John Cuſhing jun^{r} & and his wife Elizabeth, was baptized Sep^{t} 23. 1722

Ezekiel Turner ſon of Jsaac & Ruth Turner, Bap^{t} ſep^{t} 23. 1722

Bradberry daughter of Abner & Sarah Dwelly Bap^{t} ſep^{t} 23. 1722

Nathanael Warren Son of John warren & Naomi His wife was Baptized of Pembroke Sep^{t} 30. 1722.

Iſaac & Joſiah Hatch children of Jsaac Hatch & Lydia his wife were Baptized Sep^{t} 30th 1722.

Joſeph & Alice Stetſon children of ſamuel & Elizabeth Stetſon were baptized Sep^{t} 30th 1722.

Adult: John Lambert ju^{n} was baptized Oct: 21. 1722

John Lambert Son of John Lambert ju^{r} & Ruth his wife was baptized Oct: 21. 1722

Joſeph & Abigail Hanmer children of Benj^{m} & Abigail Hanmer were baptized Oct: 21. 1722

Nathanael Brooks Son of Nathan^{l} & mary Brooks Bap^{t} Oct: 21. 1722.

Hannah Tolman daughter of Benj^{m} & Elizabeth Tolman, being Sick & not Likely to Live to be brought in to Publick, was baptized in Private Oct: 29. 1722

Adult: Deborah Hatch Wife of Jeremiah Hatch ju^{n} was baptized Nov: 4th 1722

Deborah Hatch daughter of Jeremiah Hatch ju^{n} & Deborah his wife was baptized Nov: 4th 1722

Nov: 8th 1722 Job Brigs. ſon of James Brigs & Hannah his wife was Baptized in private, being ſick, and not Likely to Live.

Lydia Church daughter of nathanael & Jeruſha church was baptized Nov: 11th 1722.

Deborah Houſe Daughter of Joſeph Houſe & Lydia his wife was baptized December 16.th 1722

1723

Jan: 8th 1722/3 Ephraim Palmer Son of Saml & Anne Palmer being ſick was Baptized in Private

Mercy Brooks daughter of Gilbert & Abigail Broks, was baptized Feb: 10th

Joſiah Otis ſon of Jsaac, and Deborah Otis, was baptiſed Feb: 24th 1722/3 in private the Child being ſick & not Likely to recover.

Caleb Turner, Rachel Turner Content Turner & Grace Turner Children of Caleb & Rachel Turner were baptized March 24th 1722/3

Adult. Ruth Stetſon wife of Elijah Stetſon was Baptized March 31st 1723, at the ſame time three of her children were baptized; viz:

Nathanael Stetfon, Elifabeth Stetfon & Simeon Stetfon } Children of Elijah & Ruth Stetson were Baptized march 31st 1723

Elijah Stetfon Son of Elijah & Ruth ftetfon was Baptized Aprill 7. 1723.

Adult Elizabeth Prouty Wife of Jfaac Prouty was Baptized Aprill 7th 1723.

Jfaac Prouty, Jacob Prouty, David Prouty, John Prouty, Caleb Prouty, Adam Prouty, & John Prouty Children of Jsaac & Elizabeth Prouty were Baptized April 21. 1723

John Dwelle Son of John & Judith Dwelle was baptized Aprill 21. 1723

Mercy Dammon daughter of John & Elizabeth Damon of Marfhfield was baptized April. 28. 1723

Abigail Beftow daughter of Jofeph & mary Beftow was baptized May 19th 1723

Micael Beftow Son of Saml & Lydia Beftow, was Bapt— may. 19. 1723

Adult Naomi Chamberlain was baptized in Privat at the Houfe of Deacon Jacob. She being fick & not Likely to recover. May 8th 1723

Adult Martha Allen was Baptized may 26, 1723

James Tower Son of Benjm & Bethiah Tower was Baptized May 26. 1723

Hannah Woodart Daughter of Robert woodart junr Bap : may 26. 1722.

Hannah & Sarah Jones Children of Jsaac & Hannah Jones were baptized May 26. 1723

Robert Tomfon Son of Robert Tomfon & Ann his wife, was baptized June 2d 1723

June 9th 1723 This day J preached at weymouth fouth Society ; and after Sermon, J baptized two children *viz:* one for Benjm Orcut, & another for John Kingman.

If J miftake not the name of Benjm Orcut's Child was Lydia, and the name of John Kingman's child was Mary.

Jfaiah Stoddard Son of Benjamin & Mary Stoddard was baptized June 23. 1723.

Adult: Fear Turner wife of nathan Turner was baptized July 14. 1723

Nathan Turner Son of nathan & Leah Turner was baptized July 14th 1723

Hannah Rugles daughter of John & Joanna Rugles was baptized July 14th 1723

Abigail Bryant daughter of Samuel & Abigail Bryant was baptized July 21. 1723.

Job Prouty Son of Jsaac & Eliz : Prouty Baptifed July 28. 1723

Jane Randal, Mary Randall & farah Randal Children of John & Jane Randal were baptized July 28. 1723

Jofeph Young fon of Jofeph & Anna young of Truroe was baptized Auguft 4th 1723

Urfella Randal daughter of Job & urfella Randal was baptized Auguft 4th 1723

Ruth Tailor daughter of Jsaac & Ruth Tailor was baptized Auguft 11th 1723

Ruth Silvefter daughter of Richard Silvefter & Defire his wife, being fick & not Like to Live, was baptized In Private Auguft 22d 1723.

Samuel Hatch Son of Samll Hatch junr. & Elizabeth his wife, was baptized Auguft 25. 1723

Zechariah Dammon fon of Zechariah & Mehitabel Dammon, was baptized Auguft 25.th 1723

William Burdet
Elizabeth Burdet &
Thankfull Burdet— } Children of Henry & Lydia Burdet were baptized Sep[t] 1[t]. 1723

Seth Silvefter & Nehemiah Silvefter Children of Richard Silvefter & Defire his wife, were baptized Sep[t] 8th 1723

Adult Deborah Caffel wife of Timothy Caffel of New-port was baptized October 6th 1723

Prifcilla Perry daughter of Amos & Ruth Perry was baptized oct: 13th 1723

James Buck Son of Jfaac & mary Buck, baptized Nov: 3[d] 1723

{ Ebenezar Tolman fon of Benjamin Tolman & Elifabeth his [wife] was, being dangeroufly fick was Baptized in private, november 21. : 1723.

Adult Jofeph Wheaten was Baptized nov 24th. 1723

Abigail Clark daughter of Thomas & Allice Clark, was baptized Nov: 24. 1723

Ruth Perry daughter of Benj[m] & Ruth Perry was Baptized nov: 24th 1723

Leah Farrow daughter of Benj[m] farrow & Leah his wife was baptized nov: 24th 1723.

George Shaw, Son of John & Abigail Shaw of Plympton was baptized Dec: 29. 1723

RECORDS OF THE SECOND CHURCH OF SCITUATE, NOW THE FIRST UNITARIAN CHURCH OF NORWELL, MASS.

Communicated by Wilford Jacob Litchfield, M.S., of Southbridge, Mass.

1724

Elifha Briggs Son of James & Hannah Brigs was baptized Jan 5th 1723/4

Margret Randal daughter of John & Jane Randal was baptized Jan: 12. 1723/4.

Adult Richard Bowker was baptized Feb: 9th. 1723/4

Adult Jofeph Perry was baptized Feb: 23. 1723/4

Hannah Curtice daughter of Benj^{m} & Hannah Curtice was Baptized March 1st 1724

Adult. Iames Lambert was baptized March 14th 1724 at the Houfe of Henry Joflin, he being Sick there.

Adult Anna Lambert daughter of John Lambert was baptized March 15. 1723/4

Adult. Elizabeth Hammon wife of Jedidiah Hammon was baptized in the evening March 15th 1724. in Private She being dangeroufly Sick.

Barnabas Barker Son of Barnabas & Hannah Barker was baptized in private, being fick with conuulfion, April: 1: 1724.

Mary Silvefter daughter of Amos & Elizabeth filvefter was baptized Apr: 5th.

Levi Silvefter Son of Peter and Mary Silvefter, was baptized April: 5th 1724.

Jane Torry, daughter of Saml & Barfhua Torry was baptized April 5th 1724.

Adult Jofeph Briggs Senr was baptized April: 5th 1724.

Adult: Thomas Joflin fon of Henry Joflin, was Baptized April 5th 1724.

Charles Church Son of Richard Chh and ——— his wife was Baptized April: 19th. 1724

Jemima Damon, daughter of Danl & Jemimah, was baptized May 3d 1724

Adult Judeth Parker was baptized May 3^{d} 1724

Adult: Jedidiah Hammon was Baptized May 17th 1724

Agatha Hammon,
Jofeph Hammon &
Benj^{m} Hammon } Children of Jedidiah Hammon were baptized may 17th 1724.

Jfaac Otis and Deborah Otis children of Jsaac & Deborah otis were Baptized May 17th. 1724

Caleb Lambert Son of John & Ruth Lambert was baptized May 17th 1724

Mary Hatch daughter of John & Grace Hatch was baptized may 17th 1724

Simeon Woodart Son of Benj^{m}: & Mary. Baptiz^{d} May 17. 1724

Adult. Caleb Oldham was baptized May 31. 1724

Anna Stetfon daughter of Anthony & Anna. Bapt: June 7th 1724

Nathanael Church Son of Nathanael Chh jun^{r}. Bapt: June 14

Jofeph Perry, fon of Jofeph Perry. baptifed June 14. 1724

Ebenezar Simmons Son of Ebenezar Simmons, and Lydia his wife Baptized June 28 1724 ——

Adult Anthony Negro Serv[t] to Thomas Rogers of Marſhfield and
Adult Phebe negro ſerv[t] to s[d] Rogers, & wiſe to ſd Anthony, was Baptiſed June 28th 1724

Ruth, Negro daughter of Anthony & Phebie, was baptized June 28 1724

Benjamin Turner Son of Benj[m] Turner jun[r] & Mercy his wife was baptiſed in Private being not likely to Live, June 28. 1724.

Joſeph Torrey Son of Joſeph & Deborah Torry was baptiſed July 5th 1724

William Dwelly Son of Abner & Sarah, was Baptiſed July 5th 1724.

Samuel Curtice Son of Benj[m] & Rebecca Curtice was baptized July 12. 1724.

Mary, the daughter of Ioſeph & Hannah Naſh was Baptized July 19th 1724.

Simeon, the Son of Caleb & Rachel Turner, Baptiſed July 19. 1724

Samuel & Mary, Turner, Children of Nathan & Fear Turner, was bap[d]: July 19 1724

Wills Clyft Son of William & Judeth Clift was baptized July 26th 1724

Joſhua Houſe Son of Joſeph & Lydia Houſe was Baptized Auguſt. 2[d] 1724

William Robinſon: ſervant Child to Col[n] Cuſhing, was baptized Auguſt 2[d] 1724

Nathanael Cuſhing Son of John Cuſhing & Elizabeth his wife, Baptized Auguſt 30th. 1724

Abigail Dammon Daughter of Zechariah & Mehitabel Damon. baptiſed Aug[t] 30 1724

Jacob Silveſter Son of Benj[m] & Ruth, baptized Oct: 4th 1724

Ruth Tilden daughter of Sam[l] & Diſire Tilden of Marſhfield was Baptized Oct: 4th 1724

Jeremiah Roſe, Son of Gidion & Lydia Roſe, baptized Oct: 4 1724

Jſaac Jones Son of Jſaac & Hannah, Baptiz[d] Oct: 11. 1724

Jonathan Tower Son of Benj[m] & Bethiah, was baptized in private, being ſick & not Likely to Live. Nov: 3[d] 1724

William Curtice Son of W[m] Curtice was Baptized Nov: 29. 1724

WaitStill Turner Son of Jsaac & Ruth Turner was baptized nov 29 1724.

Eunice Stetſon Daughter of Jonah & Mercy ſtetson was baptized Nov: 29. 1724

Thomas Moore Son of W[m] More, a Stranger from Jreland, was baptized Nov: 29. 1724.

Simeon Turner Son of Nathan Turner Deceaſed: was baptized Nov: 29. 1724.

Nathanael Bryant Son of Thomas & Mercy Bryant was Baptized Nov: 29 1724 in the Evening, at Thomas Bryants Houſe, being ſick.

Thomas Tobie Son of Thomas & Mary Tobie was baptized Jn private, being ſick; March 23 1724/5

Sarah Cambel daughter of James & Sarah Cambel was baptized April. 4th 1725

Hannah Briggs daughter of James & Hannah was baptized in private, being dangerously Sick. April 10th 1725

John Gilford Son of William & Elizabeth Gilford, an Jnfant Child being Sick was baptized at Benj[m] woodart houſe April 12 1725

Adult Jedediah Hatch was Baptized May 2[d] 1725

Ruth Brooks daughter of Gilbert Brook & Abigail his wife was baptized May 2[d] 1725

Simeon Dwelly Son of John Dwelly & Judith his wife was baptized May 2[d] 1725

Elizabeth Prouty daughter of Jsaac & Elizabeth Prouty was Baptized May 2[d] 1725.

Lydia Lappam daughter of Samuel & Hannah Lappam was Baptized May 9th 1725

Lufanna Chh daughter of Richard Church was baptized May 16th 1725

Elizabeth Gilford daughter of W[m] & Eliz : Gilford was baptized May 16. 1725

Ebenezar & Lucrefia } Twins Children of Jofeph Silvefter of Marfhfield were baptized May 23. 1725

John Bowker Son of James & Hannah Bowker were baptized May 23. 1725

May 30th 1725 J preach'd for M[r] Bourn, and after Sermon J Baptized Seth Man Son of ——— Man.

Jofeph Beftow Son of Sam[l] & Lydia Beftow was Baptifed June 13th 1725

Mary Buck daughter of Jsaac & Mary Buck was Baptized June 13th 1725

Jfaac Shaw, Son of John Shaw & Abigail his wife, of Plympton, was baptized June 27th 1725

Margret Beftow daughter of Benj[m] & Margret Beftow was baptized June 27th 1725

Jfaac Tailor fon of Jfaac & Ruth Tailor was baptized June 27. 1725

Jeremiah Hatch, Son of Jeremiah Hatch & Deborah Hatch was baptized June 27. 1725

Mercy Stockbridge daughter of Charls & Anna Stockbridge was baptized June 27. 1725

Deborah Torry daughter of Jofeph & Deborah Torry was baptized July 4th 1725

Samuel Simmon Son of Ebenezar Simmons was Baptized July. 18 1725

Mary Perry daughter of Amos Perry & Ruth his wife was baptized July 18 1725

{ William Hearfey, Jfaac Hearfey, & Abigail Hearfey Children of William & Abigail Hearfey of Abington, were baptized July 18th 1725

Hannah Rofe, daughter of Jofeph & Elizabeth Rofe of Marfhfield, was Baptized July 25 1725

Thomas Stockbridge Son of Thomas Stockbridge was Baptized in Private being fick Auguft 6th 1725

Jofiah Otis Son of Jfaac & Deborah Otis was baptized Auguft 22.[d] 1725

Adult Hannah Stockbridge Wife of Thomas Stockbridge was Baptized Sep[t] 26. 1725

Hannah Barker daughter of Barnabas Barker & Hannah his wife. Baptized fep : 26 1725

Mary Alias Grace Ruggles daughte[r] of John & Joanna Ruggles, was Baptized fept : 26 : 1725.

Ezekiel Caffel Son of Timothy & Deborah Caffel of New:port on Rhode Jfland, was baptized oct : 17th 1725

William Cufhing fon of John & Elizabeth Cufhing was baptized Oct : 31. 1725

Elijah Cufhing Son of Elijah & Elizabeth Cufhing was baptized Feb : 6th 1725

Penellope Hatch Daughter of Jfaac & Penelope Hatch was Baptized Feb: 20. 1725

Star Turner fon of Jofeph & Elizabeth Turner was baptized March 6th 1725/6.

Richard Dwelle Son of Richard & Margaret Dwelle was baptized March 7th 1725/6. Jn Private, being fick.

Elizabeth Silvefter daughter of Amos & Elizabeth filvefter was Baptized April: 24th 1726

Martha Man daughter Benjamin & Martha Man, was baptifed April 24. 1726.

Elifha Rofe fon of Jofeph Rofe, & Elizabeth his wife of marfhfield, was baptized May 1st 1726.

Caleb Curtice Son of Benjm & Hannah Curtice was baptized May 8th 1726

Abigail Church daughter of Nathanl & Jerufha Chh was baptized may 15th 1726

Job Curtice fon of Benjamin & Rebecca Curtice was Baptized May 15th 1726

Luke Stetfon fon of Elijah & Ruth ftetson was baptized May 15th 1726

Prifcilla Turner daughter of Caleb & Rachel Turner was Baptized May 15th 1726.

Lydia Brooks daughter of Nathanael & Mary Brooks was baptized Jn private may 16th 1726. being fick & not Likely to Recover.

Prince Palmer Son of Samll & Ann Palmer, was baptized May 22d 1726

Sarah Cufhing daughter of James & Mary Cufhing was baptized June 12 1726.

Elizabeth Houfe daughter of Jofeph & Lydia Houfe was baptized June 12. 1726

Sarah Farrow daughter of Benjamin & Leah Farrow was baptized June 19th 1726.

Grace Hatch daughter of John Hatch junr & Grace his wife was baptized June 26th 1726.

Jofhua Burdet Son of Henry Burdet & Lydia his wife was Baptifed June 26th 1726.

John Tolman Son of Benjm. & Elizabeth Tolman was baptized July 10th 1726

Ruth Dwelle daughter of John & Judeth Dwelly was baptized July 10th 1726

Ezekiel Clark fon of Thomas & Allice Clark was baptized July 24th 1726.

William Otis fon of Jsaac & Deborah Otis, was baptized July 24th 1726.

Lydia Shaw daughter of John Shaw & Abigail his wife, of Plympton, was baptized July 31. 1726

Jsaac Perry Son of Benjm & Ruth Perry was baptized Auguft 21. 1726.

Ruben Symmons Son of Ebenezar Symons was baptized Auguft 28 1726

Mehitabel Curtice Daughter of Samuel & Anna Curtice was baptized Sept 11th 1726

Nathanael Clyft Son of William Clift of Marfhfield was baptized Sept 11th 1726

Margaret Randal Daughter of John Randal & Jane his wife was Baptized fept 11th 1726

Sarah Jones daughter of Jfaac & Hannah Jones was baptized Sept 11th 1726

Amos Perry Son of Amos & Ruth Perry was baptized in Private Oct: 11th 1726 it bein[g] fick ——

George Clap Son of John & Mercy Clap was baptifed Oct: 23^{d} 1726
Mary Lucas daughter of Iane Lucas of Marſhfield was baptized Oct: 23. 1726
Deborah Silveſter Daughter of Peter & Mary Silveſter was baptized Nov: 27. 1726

RECORDS OF THE SECOND CHURCH OF SCITUATE, NOW THE FIRST UNITARIAN CHURCH OF NORWELL, MASS.

Communicated by WILFORD JACOB LITCHFIELD, M.S., of Southbridge, Mass.

Nathanael Curtice Son of Benj^{m} Curtice, ju^{r} & Hannah his wife, of Hanover was baptized march 31. 1728

Mary Cocks daughter of W^{m} & Mary Cocks of Hanover was baptiſed March 31. 1728.

Adult. Abigail Barrel wife of Wm Barrel was Baptiſed may 5th 1728.

Abigail & } Children of william & Abigail Barrell were baptized May
James } 5th

Elizabeth Wormwool [or *Wormwoll* or *Wermall*] an adopted Child of Johanna Turner of Marſhfield was baptized May 5th 1728.

William Chh Son of Nathan^{l} & Jeruſha Church was baptized May 5th 1728

Abigail Corniſh daughter of Joſeph & Patience Corniſh of Hanover was baptized May 26. 1728.

Sarah Hatch Daughter of Jsaac Hatch of Hanover was Baptiſed May 26. 1728

Job Stetſon, & } Children of W^{m} & Hannah Stetſon were baptized June
Caleb ſtetſon } 2^{d} 1728.

Nathan Hatch Son of Jeremiah & Frances Hatch was baptized June 30th 1728.

[*Omission*] Daughter of Benj^{m} & Mercy Beſtow was Baptized in private She being ſick & not Likely to Live. July 10th 1728

Anna Warren daughter of John & naomi warren was baptized July 28th

Joſhua Stetſon Son of Elijah & Ruth his wife, was baptiſed July 28 1728.

Adult Silence Damon was baptized Augt 4th 1728

Benj^{m} Curtice Son of Benj^{m} & Rebeccae Curtice was Baptized Augt 18. 1728

Abel Torry Son of Saml & Barſhua Torry was Baptized Aug: 18th 1728

Lucretia Turner daughter of Hawkins Turner was baptized Aug: 18 1728

Francis Burdet Son of Henry Burdet was Baptized Auguſt 18. 1728.

Peleg Simmons Son of Ebenezar Simmons was Baptized Sep^{t} 1st 1728

Hannah Ewel (daughter of Gerſhom Ewel & Submit Ewel his Relict, wife of John Stetſon of Marſhfield) was Baptized In private Sep^{t} 25 1728.

Adult. Thankfull Bloſſom wife of John Bloſſom was baptized Oct: 6th 1728.

Thomas Bloſſom Son of John & Thankfull Broſſom was baptized Oct. 6th 1728.

Adult: Lydia Turner Jonathan Turners widow was Baptized Oct. 13. 1728.

John Clap, Son of John & mercy Clap, was baptized Oct: 13. 1728.

James Blankinſhip (Alias Gordon) Son of Anne Blankinſhip, and apprentice to the widow Rachel Dwelly, was baptized at the defire of fd Dwelle, She being in full Comunion wth this Chh.

Zillah ——— Perry daughter of Benjamin & Ruth Perry was baptized novº 10th 1728.

November 24th 1728

J preach'd at Sandwitch at the houfe of Jofhua Blackwell, after Sermon J baptized feuerall Children viz:

John Swift the Son of Jofiah & Experience Swift.

Deborah Tupper daughter of Eliakim and Joanna Tupper

Jerifha Swift daughter of Thomas and Thankfull Swift.

Sarah Ellis daughter of Jofiah & Sarah Ellis.

Martha Blackwell daughter of Saml : and Mary Blackwell.

Hannah Jones, daughter of Ebenezar & Jane Jones of Marfhfield was baptized Dec : 29th 1728.

1729

Lydiah Clift daughter of Wm Clift of Marfhfield was Baptized Jan: 12th 1728/9.

Ruth Rofe daughter of Jofhua Rofe of Marfhfield was baptized January 12th 1728/9

Sarah Clap daughter of Samuel & Hannah Clap was baptized Jan : 19th 1728/9.

Mary Hearfy Daughter of william Hearfie of Abington was baptized by me at Hanover march 9th 1728/9.

Cornelius Briggs Son of James & Hannah Brigs was baptized march 16th 1728/9

Samuel Randal Son of Nehemiah & Ruth, was baptized march 30th 1729

Defire Barker daughter Barnabas & Hannah was baptized march 30, 1729

Lydia Bowker daughter of James & Hannah was baptized march 30. 1729

John Bourn, Son of John & Abigail Bourn of Marfhfield was Baptized April 13 1729

Abigail Brooks daughter of Gilbert & Abigail, was baptized April. 20th 1729

Adult Martin an Indian man $ferv^{t}$ to Mr Fofter was Baptized April. 4th 1729.

Ruth Prouty daughter of Jsaac & Elizabeth Prouty was Baptized May 11th 1729

Abigail Torry daughter of Jofeph & Bathfheba Torry was baptized June 8th 1729.

Abel Turner Son of william & Abigail Turner was baptized June 8th 1729.

Thomas Lappam Son of David & Rebecca Lappam was baptized June 15th 1729

John Ruggles Son of John & Joanna Ruggles was baptized June 22^{d} : 1729.

Tobias Oakman, Son of Samuel Oakman of Marfhfield, was baptized in private, he being Sick & not Likely to Live. July 1st 1729

Micah Stetfon Son of Jonah & mercy Stetfon being Sick was baptized in private July 4th 1729

Nicolas Daviff Son of Nicholas & Grace Davis of Kingston, was baptized Auguft 3^{d} 1729

Jeffe woodart Son of Benjamin & Mary woodart was baptized Auguft 3^{d} 1729.

Adult Sarah Lambert wife of James Lambert was baptized Auguft 24th 1729

James Lambert & Sarah Lambert Children of James and Sarah Lambert were baptized Auguft 24th 1729

William Perry Son of Amos & Ruth Perry was baptized in Private it being fick & not Likely to Live, Aug[t] 30th

Micael Brooks Son of Nathan[ll] & mary Brook was baptized Oct 5th 1729

Lufanna Merit Daughter of Henry & margret merit being fick was baptized in Private Oct: 8th 1729

Stephen Otis Son of Jsaac & Deborah Otis was baptized Oct: 12. 1729.

October 26th 1729

J preach'd at Sandwitch at the houfe of M[r] Eldad Tupper After Sermon J baptized two Children *viz:* Enoch Tupper Son of Samuel and Hannah Tupper

Mary Blackwell daughter of Samuel & Mary Blackwell.

Anna Toby daughter of Thomas & mary Toby was baptized oct 26 1729 by the Rev[d] m[r] David Turner Paf[tr] of a Chh in Rehoboth

Lemuel Silvefter Son of Jofeph and Lydia Silvefter was baptized nov: 2[d] 1729

Benjamin Dwelly Son of John & Judith Dwelley was baptifed nov 2[d] 1729

Adult. Hannah Randal wife of Caleb Randall was baptized nov: 30th 1729

Stephen Randall Son of Caled [? Caleb] & Hannah was baptized Nov: 30 1729

Elizabeth Dwelle & Deborah Dwelle, children of Jedediah & Elizabeth Dwelle were baptized Nov: 30th 1729.

Thomas Rofe Son of Gidion & Lydia Rofe was baptized Dec: 14th 1729

Eliphalet Northy Son of James Northy & Mary his wife was baptized in Private Dec: 21st in the Evening being Sick & not Likely to recover 1729

Ruth Clap daughter of John & Mercy Clap was baptized Dec: 28th 1729 by the Rev[d] m[r] Bourn

1730

Lydiah Hatch daughter of Jsaac & Penelipa Hatch was Baptized Jan: 4th 1729/30

Adult Jcabod Merit and his Infant Child Jofeph Merit were baptized march 1st 1729/30

David Jacob fon of Jofhua & Mary Jacob was baptized March 1st 1729/30

April 26th J preached at Sandwitch and after Sermon J baptized two Children: Charls Tupper Son of Eliakim & Joanna Tupper.

Micael Ellis Son of Jofiah & Sarah Ellis.

Rebecca Dammon daughter of Zechariah & Mehitabel, was baptized. May 3[d] 1730

Amos Dammon Son of Daniel & Jemimah was Baptized May 3[d] 1730

Eunice Turner daughter of Charls & Eunice Turner was Baptized May 3[d] 1730

Ruth Stetfon Daughter of Elijah & Ruth Stetfon was baptized May 10th 1730

May 17th 1730

I Preach'd at New-port on Rhode Jfland and adminiftred the Sacrament of the Lords Supper; to the 2[d] Congregational Chh there; and Baptized

1. Patience Dodge the wife of Hezakiah Dodge, and
2. Samuel Dodge Son of Hezekiah and Patience Dodge.
3. Thomas Williams Son of lendall & Mehitabel williams.

memorandum
Nathan[l] Tiffany & his wife, members of the Chh in Afhford. & M[rs] Potter a member of the Chh in Briftol, defired the Priviledge of partaking wth y[t] chh; and had it.

Anna Palmer daughter of Sam[l] Palmer & Ann his wife was baptized May 24th 1730

Lufanna Magoone daughter of John & Abigail Magoone was baptized May 24th 1730

David Hatch Son of David & Mary Hatch of Bridgwater was Baptized June 14th

Ezra Stetfon, Son of Anthony & Anna was baptized June 28 1730.

David Lappam Son of David & Rebecca, was baptized July 5th 1730.

Elizabeth Butler daughter of Jsrael & Elizabeth Butler was baptized July 12th 1730.

Elifha Turner Son of Benj[m] & Mercy Turner was baptized July 12. 1730.

Lydia Perry daughter of William Perry of Freetown, & adopted by Elizabeth Tolman wife of Benj[m], was baptized July 19. 1730

Bethiah woodart daughte of Eben: woodart & Bethiah his wife was Baptized July 19. 1730.

Sarah Church Daughter of Nathan[l] Chh jun[r] & Jerufha his wife was baptized July 19 1730.

John Neil, Son of John Neil & ——— his wife (an Jreland man & woman) was baptized July 19. 1730

Adam Stetfon Son of Abijah & Deborah Stetfon was baptized July 19th. 1730.

Mary Bryant daughter of Benj[m] and Abigail his wife; was baptized Auguft 16[th] 1730

David Bryant Son of David Bryant jun[r] & Hannah his wife was baptized Sep[t] 6[th] 1730.

James Prouty Son of Jsaac & Eliz: was baptized Sep[t]: 6[th] 1730

Mary & Abigail twin Children of Barnabas & Hannah Barker were baptized Sep[t]ber by the Rev[d] m[r] Bourn. 1730

Mary Cufhing daughter of John & Mary Cufhing was baptized Sep[t]. 13 1730.

Ruth Bryant daughter of Elizabeth Bryant was baptized Sep[t] 13. 1730

Mary withington daughter of Henry & mary withington of Kingston was Baptized Sep[t] 13 1730

Mary merit daughter of Icabod & Mary Merit was Babtized Oct 11th 1730

Rebecca Curtice daughter of Benjamin & Rebecca his wife was Baptized Oct: 11 1730

Ruth Randall daughter of Caleb & Hannah his wife was baptized Oct: 11th 1730.

Lufanna Dwelle daughter of Jofeph & Mary Dwelly was baptized nov: 8th 1730.

Star Turner Son of Jofeph & Eliz[th]: Turner was baptized Dec: 6th 1730

Dorothy Turner daughter of Hawkins & Lufanna; was bap[t] Dec: 6th 1730

Jael Silvefter daughter of Mary Silvefter was Baptized Dec: 6th 1730

Abigail Iones daughter of Eben[r] Jones & Jane his wife of marfhfield was baptized Dec: 20. 1730

William Witherel Eells Son of Sam[l] & Hannah Eells was baptized Dec: 20.th 1730

1731

Rachel Clap daughter of John & mercy clap was baptifed Feb : 28 1730/1

Hannah Otis daughter of Jsaac & Deborah otis was baptized March 21st 1730/1

Lufanna & Ezekiel Dammon Children of John & Eliz : Dammon of Marfhfield were baptized March 28th 1731

Jofeph Randall, Benjamin Randall Sarah Randal & Ezra Randal Children of Benjm & Sarah Randal were baptized April 4th 1731

Luce Dwelle daughter of Jedidiah & Elizabeth Dwelle was Bapt : April 4th 1731

Ruth Silvefter daughter of Jofeph & Lydia Silvefter, was baptized May 9th 1731

Experience Brooks daughter of Gilbert & Abigail Brooks, was Baptized May 16.th 1731. By the Revd Mr Bourn of the North Society in this town.

John Neal, Son of John & Mary Neal, being Sick & not Likely to Live was baptized in Private May 20th 1731.

Elijah Randal Son of Nehemiah & Ruth was baptized May 23 1731

Abigail Turner daughter of Wm & Abigail was Baptized may 23. 1731

Deborah Bowker daughter of James & Hannah, was baptized may 23. 1731

Luke Lambert Son of James & Sarah Lambert was baptized may 23. 1731

Sarah Ruggles daughter of John & Joanna, was baptized May 30. 1731.

Hannah Perry daughter of Amos & Ruth Perry was Baptized May 31. 1731. in private, being Sick, and as was Supofed in great danger.

Willes Clift Son of Wm & Judith clift of marfhfield was Baptized June 6th 1731

Jofeph Rofe Son of Jofhua & Eliz : Rofe of marfhfield was baptized Jne 6th 1731

Jonathan Bryant Son of David & Hannah, was baptized June 6th 1731

Peter Bourn Son of John & Abigail Bourn of Marfhfield was baptized June 20th 1731

Eleanar Prouty Daughter of Elizabeth Prouty deceafed, was prefented by her Granmother Elizfabeth Prouty to baptifm, & was baptized June 20 1731

John Barker Son of Barnabas and Hannah his wife was Baptized June 27. 1731

Amos Lappam Son of David and Rebecca, was baptized July 11. 1731

Ezekiel Young Son of Jofeph & Lydia, was Baptized July 18.th

John James Son of John James & Rhoda his wife was baptized by the Revd Mr Bourn July 18th 1731.

Mary Moor daughter of John Moor, Of Jreland was baptized by the Revd Mr Bourn July 18. 1731.

Rachel Farrow daughter of Benjm : was baptized by Mr Bourn July 18. 1731.

Bezaliel Palmer & Nathanael Palmer Children of Bezaliel & Anna Palmer, were baptized July 25th 1731.

Adult: Abigail Ruffel was baptized Augst 1st 1731

William Brigs Son of James & Hannah was baptized Auguft 1st 1731.

Mary Barrel daughter William & Abigail was baptized Auguft 1st 1731.

Paul Torry Son of Jofeph & Barfheba his wife was baptized Auguft 24 [?]. 1731.

Malborough Turner Son of Caleb & Rachel was baptized Sept 5th 1731.

Elizbeth Perry daughter of Benj^{m} & Ruth was baptized fept 10th 1731 by the Revd m^{r} Bourn of Scittuate.

Adult: Sep^{t} 17th 1731 Hannah Hatch the wife of Thomas Hatch was baptized in private, fhe being fick, & not Likly to recover.

Sept 26. J preach'd at Hanover, & baptized Jofeph, the Son of Jofeph & mary Curtice

Adult. Jofeph Dunham was Baptized Oct 10. 1731

Jacob, Luke, Zebulun & Nathanael Silvefter, Children of Zebulun & Mary his wife, were baptized Oct: 10th 1731.

Ruth Burded daughter of Henry & Lydia Burdet was baptized nov 7th 1731

Mary Clap daughter of Samuel Clap & Sarah his wife was baptized nov: 14th 1731

Mercy Brooks daughter of Nathan^{l}: & Mary, was baptized Nov 28. 1731.

Zecheriah Dammon Son of Daniel & Jemima was Baptized in private being dangeroufly ill with Convulfions December 6th 1731

RECORDS OF THE SECOND CHURCH OF SCITUATE, NOW THE FIRST UNITARIAN CHURCH OF NORWELL, MASS.

Communicated by Wilford Jacob Litchfield, M.S., of Southbridge, Mass.

1732

Jsaiah Randal Son of Benj^{m} & Sarah his wife was baptized Jan: 2^{d} 1731/2

Robert Lenthall Eells Son of fam^{l} & Hannah Eells was baptized Feb: 13th 1731/2

Ruben Tailor Son of David & Elizabeth was baptized March 19th 1731/2

Luce Bryant daughter of Benj^{m} & Abigail was Baptized March 26. 1732.

Mary Dwelle daughter of Jofeph & Mary was Baptized March 26. 1732.

Benjamin Merit Son of Jcabod & Mary, was baptized April 2^{d} 1732

April 23^{d} 1732 J preached at Marfhfield North meeting houfe And Baptized Several Children their *viz: Mary Hatch* daughter of Jsaac & Penelopia of Scittuate.

Jofeph Dagget, Samuel Dogget noah Dogget & Bethiah dogget Child^{r} of Saml & Bethiah Dogget

Iane Eames, mary Eames, Jedediah Eames, & Penelopia Eames Children of Jedediah & Mary Eames.

Abigail Farrow daughter of Benj^{m} & Leah was baptized by the Revd Mr Bourn April 23. 1732

John Neal, Son of John & Mary neal was baptized in private being fick wth a fore mouth & not Likely to Live April 29th 1732

Lydia Rofe daughter of Gidion & Lydia was baptized April 30th 1732

Jofeph Perry & Elizabeth Perry children of Wm Perry Late of Freetown Deceafed were Baptized June 11th 1732

Israel oakman Son of Saml Oakman of Marſhfield an infant of about afortnigt old, was baptized at his houſe June. 24 1732 this child dyed Soon after it was baptized.

Jeruſha Church daughter of Nathan^{l} Church jun^{r} & Jeruſha his wife was baptized July 9th 1732.

John Stetſon, Son of Abijah & Deborah, was baptized July 9th 1732.

Jane Hatch daughter of Jsrael Hatch jun^{r}: an infant Child being ſick & in danger of dying, was Baptized at his houſe July 11th 1732

Mary Silveſter Daughter of Zebulun & mary was baptized Augt 13. 1732

Waterman Eells son of John & Abiah, was baptized Auguſt 13. 1734

John King Son of John & Mary, of Marſhfield, was bap^{td} Aug 13. 1732.

Mary Jacob, Daughter of Joſhua & Mary was baptized Augt 20th 1732.

Adult Hezekiah Hatch & *Adult* Nehemiah Hatch Brethren were baptized Sep^{t} 10th 1732.

Thomas Hatch Son of Hezekiah & Patience, was Baptized Sep^{t} 10. 1732.

Jane Neal daugher of John Neal Late of Jreland, was Baptized Sep^{t} 10. 1732.

Anna Stetſon daughter of W^{m} & Hannah was baptized Sep^{t} 24 1732

Joſhua Roſe, Son of Joſhua Roſe & —— his wife of Marſhfield was bap^{t} ſep^{t} 24th 1732

Ruben Hatch, son of Nehemiah & Martha was baptized oct 8th 1732

Rachel Tilden daughter of Benj^{m} and Grace Tilden, an infant being ſick & not Likely to recover was baptized in private at the houſe of Serg^{t} Philip Turners oct: 8th 1732

Huldah Palmer daughter of Bezaliel & Anna, was Bapt^{d} Nov 5th 1732

Mary Turner of Joſhua & Elizabeth, was baptized Nov: 12th 1732

Simeon Jones Son of Eben^{z}: & Jane of marſhfield was baptized Dec: 31. 1732

1733

John Clap, Son of John & Mercy Clap, was baptized Jan 14th 1732/3

Abigail Collomare daughter of Anthony collomare, & ——— his wife was baptized Jan: 28th 1732/3

William Cuſhing Son of John Cuſhing jun^{r} Eſq^{r} was baptized March 4th 1732

{ March 12th 1732/3 Luſanna Turner an Infant Child of Caleb & Rachel Turner being ſick was Baptized in Private

Thyne, *alias* Vine Turner Son of Joſeph, & Eliz: was bap^{t}: April 1st 1733

Elizabeth Turner daughter of W^{m} & Abigail, was Bap^{t}: April 1st 1733.

Elizabeth Dunnam Daughter of Joſeph & Jane, was Baptized April 15th 1733

{ April 19th 1733 James Otis, Son of Jsaac & Deborah an infant, being ſick & not Likely to Live, was baptized in private.

Rebecca Lappam daughter of David & Rebecca of Marſhfield was baptized May 6th 1733

Sarah Collomare daughter of John & Margret, was baptized May 6th 1733.

Abigail Magoone daughter of John Magoone jun^{r} & Abigail his wife, was Baptized May 20: 1733.

Mary Lambert daughter of James & Sarah was Baptized June 3^{d}.

Jsaac Prouty Son of Jsaac & Eliz: was Baptized June 3^{d} 1733

Job Briggs Son of James & Hannah was Baptized June 24 1733

Sarah Eells daughter of Sam^{ll} & Hannah of Hanover, was Baptized June 24th. 1733

Edmond Bowker ſon of James [&] Hannah, was Baptized June 24th 1733

Delight Taylor daughter of David & Elizabeth was Bap^{t}. June 24. 1733.

Simeon Brooks Son of Nat^{l} & mary, was Baptized July 1st 1733.

Grace Turner daughter of Hawkins & Luſanna, was Baptized July 1st 1733.

John Moor Son of John more & ——— his wife from Jreland, was baptized July 1st 1733.

Sarah Butler daughter of Jsrael & Elizth was baptized July 15th 1733.

Charls Turner Son of Charles and Eunice, was baptized Augt. 5th 1733

Robert Randal Son of Robert and Dorcaſs was baptized Augt 12. 1733

Benjamin Turner Son of Benj^{m} & Mercy, was Baptized Oct: 23. 1733

Hannah Bryant daughter of David & Hannah was Baptized Nov: 4th 1733

Joſeph Cuſhing ſon of Joſeph And Lydia, was baptized Dec: 2^{d} 1733.

Hannah Randal daughter of Caleb & Hannah was baptized Dec: 9 1733

1734

Charles Stockbridge Brooks Son of Gilbert & Abigail was baptized Jan: 20th.

Hannah Clap daughter of Joſeph & Hannah his wife was baptized Feb: 3 1733/4

Huldah Randal daughter of Benj^{m} & Sarah was Baptized March 3^{d} 1733/4

Amos Perry Son of Amos & Ruth was baptiſed March 17th 1733/4

Abner Dwelly ſon of Jedidiah & Elizabeth was baptized March 17th 1733/4

Druſella Dwelly daughter of Joſeph & Mary was baptized March 17th 1733/4

March 24th 1733/4 Preach[..d] at Hanover and baptized two Children viz: Elizabeth Baſs daughter of the Revd Mr Benj^{m} Baſs; &

Stephen Stockbridge Son of Thomas Stockbridge, of Scittuate.

John Barrel Son of William & Abigail was baptized March 31. 1734.

William Clap Son of Sam^{ll} & Sarah was baptized March 31. 1734

Elizabeth Randal daughter of Capt Nehemiah Randal & Ruth his wife was baptized April 14. 1734

Lydia Barker, of Barnabas & Hannah was baptized Aprl. 21. 1734.

Hannah Eells of John & Abiah, was baptized May 5th 1734

Bathſheba Faunce, of Thomas & Hannah belonging to Plymouth was baptized may 5th 1734.

Jchabod Neal, Son of John & mary an Jnfant being ſick & not Likely to Live was baptized May 10th 1734. Jn private.

Elizabeth Bourn daughter of John & Abigail of Marhſfield was baptized May 12th 1734

William Church Son of Nathan^{l} & Jeruſha was Baptized May 19 1734

Margret Foster daughter of Joſeph & Abigail was Baptized May 26th 1734

Abiel Dammon Son of Danl & Jemima was baptized June 9th 1734

Ephraim Otis Son of Ephraim & Rachel was baptized June 9th 1734

{ Mercy Hatch daughter of Hezekiah & Patience was baptized in Private, ſhe being dangerously Sick with Convulsions, June 15th 1734

Gideon Roſe Son of Gideon & Lydia, was baptized June 16th 1734

Mary Turner daughter of Thomas & Mary his wife was baptized July 7th 1734

Robert Waſon [or Wasson] Son of Thom^{s} & Ann, was baptized July 7th 1734

Eliſha Lappam Son of David & Rebecca of Marſhfield was baptized July 7th 1734.

John Clap, Son of John & Mercy, was baptized July 14th 1734.

Eliſha & Thomas Stetſon Children of Anthony & Anna his wife were Baptized Auguſt 4th 1734

Hannah Merit of Ichabod & Mary was baptized Auguſt 4th 1734

Elizabeth Oakman of Saml & Elizabeth of Marſhfield was baptized August 4th 1734.

Tamar Farrow daughter of Benj^{m} Farrow was Baptized by ye Rev^{d} mr Bourn of this Town Auguſt 11th 1734

Charls Cuſhing ſon of John Cuſhing jun^{r} was baptized Auguſt 18th 1734

Silva, alias *Zilpha*, Clift daughter of Wm Clift of Marſhfield was baptized Auguſt 18th 1734

Abner Turner Son of Caleb, and Rachel was baptized Sep^{t} 1st 1734.

James Curtice Son of Benj^{m} & Rebecca was baptized Sep^{t} 8th 1734

Luſanna Perry daughter of Saml and Elizabeth Perry, was baptized Sep^{t} 8th 1734

Sarah Hatch daughter of Jsaac & Penelopa was Baptized Sep^{t} 15th 1734.

Peter Collomare, son of Jsaac & Thankfull was baptized Oct: 20th 1734

Lydia Woodart daughter of James & Sarah was baptized Oct: 20th 1734.

James Otis, Son of Jsaac & Deborah was baptized October 27. 1734.

Jsaac Smith, Iſrael, Peleg, Levi, Abial, Rachel, & Joſhua Smith, Children of Joſeph & Rachel Smith formerly of Hanover, were baptized November 3^{d} 1734.

Martha Neal daughter of John Neal from Jreland, was baptized Nov: 17th 1734

{ Elizabeth Silveſter, daughter of John and Elizabeth of Marſhfield, being ſick was Baptized in private Nov: 28th 1734.

Lydia Turner an Infant Child of Caleb & Rachel Turner being ſick was Baptized in private Dec: 9th 1734

1735

Joſeph Palmer Son of Joſeph and Jane Palmer was baptized Jan: 5th 1734/5

Bethiah Roſe daughter of Joſhua & Elizabeth Roſe, of Marſhfield was baptized Feb: 16 1734/5

Hannah Lincoln daughter of Joſhua & Mercy was baptized Feb. 23. 1734/5

Mary Bowker daughter of James & Hanah was baptized feb: 23. 1734/5

Content Jones a Child of Eliſha & Sarah Jones of Marſhfield was baptized march 23. 1734/5

{ Ruth Bryant an Jnfant child of David Bryant being ſick was baptized Privatly march 25 1735

Eliſha Jones, Son of Eliſha & Sarah Jones of Marſhfield was baptized May 4th 1735.

May 11th 1735 J preached at Marſhfield north Pariſh, where J Baptized Mary Spooner daughter of John and Hannah Spooner.

Barſhebah Sherman daughter of Ebenezar & Barſhebah.

Obadiah Dammon Son of Ebenezar & Abigail Dammon

Lucretia Silveſter daughter of John & Elizabeth Silveſter.

Adult. Hannah Hat[c]h & her Siſter *Adult.* Zerviah Hatch daughters of Thomas Hatch were baptized May 18th 1735

Mehitabel Curtice daughter of Eliſha & Martha was baptized May 18th 1735

John Jacob Son of Joſhua & Mary was Baptized June 8th 1735

Samuel Eells, son of Samuel & Hannah of Hanover, was baptized June 15th 1735.

Benjamin Bryant, Son of Benjamin & Abigail, was baptized June 22d 1735

Anthony Collomare, Son of Anthony & ——— His wife was baptized. July 13.th 1735.

Elijah Curtice ſon of Samll & Rebecca was Baptized July 20th 1735

Nathanaell Holms, ſon of John Holms of Pembrooke, & adopted ſon of Samuel Lappam, was baptized July 20th 1735.

July 24th 1735.

Adult { Thomas Oldham being ſick and very dangerous; at his earneſt deſire was Baptiſed and his children viz: Thomas & Patience.

Lydiah Lambert daughter of James & Sarah was Baptiſed Augt 17.th 1735

Auguſt 24th 1735 J preached at Marſhfield North meeting houſe baptized—*Adult* Experience Rogers, wife of Saml Rogers junr & Penelopiah & Lydia Rogers children of the above ſaid Saml & Experience Rogers.

Rebecca Prouty daughter of Edward & Rebeccah was baptized Augt 31. 1735.

Adult Ann Hatch daughter of Jeremiah Hatch was baptized Sep: 7th 1735

Eliſha Jacob, Son of Joſeph & Mary was baptized Sept 7th 1735

Ebenezar Jones, ſon of Ebenr & Jane, of Marſhfield was baptized ſept 7th 1735

Eliſha Barrel Son of William and Abigail, was baptiſed Sept 28

Abigail Stetſon daughter of Abijah & Deborah was baptiſed Sept 28: 1735

Catherine Turner of Hawkins & Luſanna, was baptiſed Oct: 5th 1735

Adult { Fortune Gold, and Betty his wife, negro ſervants to Joſeph Hatch were baptized oct: 5th 1735

{ Iames Mullan Son of Arthur & Mary, was Baptized privatly being ſick, Oct: 6th 1735

Iohn Silveſter Son of John & Eliz: of Marſhfield was baptized Oct: 12. 1735.

John Magoone Son of John & Abigail was baptized Oct: 19 1735.

Nov 2d 1735

Sarah Turner, Hannah Turner, Ann Turner & David Turner { Children of Benjamin and Sarah Turner, were baptized, and my Grand-Children.

Adult. Ionathan Merit, and *Adult* Mehitabel merit; & Simeon Merit the ſon of Jonathan & Mehitabel were baptized Nov: 9th 1735.

Lydia Silveſter, daughter of Joſeph & Lydia, was baptized Nov: 9th 1735.

David Marble & Abigail Marble { Children of David & Abigail Marble were baptized Nov. 23 1735.

George Gray Son of Thomas & Sarah his wife from Jreland was baptized nov: 23d 1735.

Eliſha Silveſter Son of Eliſha & Eunice was baptized Nov: 30th 1735.

Mary Collomare daughter of John & Margaret was Baptized Dec: 14th 1735.

Anna Palmer of Bezaliel & Anna was baptized in private being ſick. Dec: 22d 1735.

1736

{ David, & Ziporah Jnfant & Twin children of Barnabas & Hanah Barker were Baptized being ſick, in private January 16th 1735/6

{ Daniel Hatch an Jnfant Child of Bezaliel & Patience being ſick was Baptized in private March 2d 1735/6

{ March 14th J preachd at marſhfield north meeting houſe and then Thomas Rogers Son of Samuel Rogers junr and Experience his wife was baptized

Sarah Taylor daughter of David Taylor & Eliz:th His wife was baptized April 1st 1736 being Great faſt day

{ May 5th 1736 Lydia Powers daughter of Nicalas Powers & Bethiah his wife was baptized in Private.

John Brooks [Son] of Gilferd & Abigail was baptized May 9th 1736

Charls Church of Natll & Jeruſha was baptized May 9th 1736

Nathanael Roſe of Gidion & Elizabeth was baptized may 9th 1736

Elizabeth Lappam of David & Rebecca of marſhfield was baptized at marſhfield Nort[h] meeting houſe may 23. 1736.

Mary Cowing of Job Cowing was baptized by me in the north meeting houſe May 30th 1736.

Jsaac Collomare, Son of Jsack & Thankfull was baptized by the Revd Mr Bourn may 30th 1736.

Joſeph Clap, Son of Joſeph & Hannah was Baptized June 6th 1736.

Adult Richard, a Negro Slave of Mr Anthony Collomare was Baptized June 6th 1736

{ June 9th 1736. Thomas Otis an Infant Child of Dr Jsaac otis's being ſick was baptized in private.

Lydia Turner of Wm & Abigail was baptized June 13th 1736

Bradbury Dwelle of Joſeph & Mary was Baptized June 13. 1736

{ Iune 18th ——— Hatch an Jnfant Child of a bout four years son of David Hatch, being ſick of a dangerous Diſeaſe was baptized in private.

Joſeph Turner Son of Benjm & Mercy, was baptized. June 20. 1736

John Roſe ſon of Joſhua and Elizabeth of Marſhfield was baptized June 27th 1736.

Elizabeth Perry Daughter of Saml & Eliz:th was baptized July 4th 1736.

George Cuſhing ſon of Joſeph & Lydia was baptized July 11th 1736

Samuel Hatch Son of Jsaac & Penelopy was baptized Augt 1st 1736.

Elizabeth Copeland daughter of Joſeph and Eliz: was baptized Augt 1. 1736

Joſhua Dwelle Son of Jedidiah & Eliz: was baptized Augt 1st 1736.

Joſeph Clyft, of William & Judith of Marſhfield was Baptized Augt 8th

Rebecca King of Joſeph & Thankfull was baptized Augt 8th 1736.

Luther Marble Son of David & Abigail was baptized Augt 15th 1736

Sarah Woodart daughter of James & Sarah was baptized Augt 15th 1736.

Abigail Clap, daughter of Benjamin and Grace, of the North Precinct was baptized Augt 29th 1736.

Jsaac Perry Son of Amos & Ruth was baptized Sept 5th 1736.

Edward Cuſhing of John and mary was baptized Sept 12 1736

Ruth Torrey, of Caleb & Mary was baptized Sept 12th 1736.

George Bryant of Benjamin & Abigail was bapt^{d} Sep^{t} 12 1736.
Sage Randal of Caleb and Hannah was baptifed Sep^{t} 12. 1736.
Paul Randall, Son of Benj^{m} & Sarah was baptized Oct: 3^{d} 1736.
Rachel Lincoln of Jofhua & Mercy was baptized oct: 17th 1736.
Elizabeth Wade of Jofeph & Rachel was baptized Oct: 24th 1736.

1737

{ Hannah North Eells daughter of Saml & Hannah Eells of Hanover being fick & in a dangerous Condition was Baptized Jn Private Jan: 18. 1736/7

Relief Jacob Daughter of Jofeph & Mary, was baptized Feb: 6th 1736/7

{ Thomas King an Jnfant Child of John Kings of Marfhfield being dangeroufly fick was Baptized in Private Feb: 22^{d} 1736/7

Lydia Beftow daughter of Saml & Margret Beftow of Hanover was baptifed by me at Hanover March 20 1736/7

Adult Michael Hatch, & Prifcilla his wife were baptized April 3^{d} 1737.

Samuel Collamare son of Anthony was baptized April 3^{d} 1737
Elifha Curtice Son of Elifha & Martha was baptized April 3^{d} 1737

April: 24 1737 J preached at Marfhfield, & Baptized Stephen Lappam Son of David & Rebecca.

Hatherly Fofter Son of Jofeph & Abigail was baptized by the Revd Mr Bourn April 24th 1737.

{ William Barker Son of Barnabas & Mary Barker was Baptized In Private being fick & not Likle to Live. May 1st 1737.

Jsaac Clap Son of John & Mercy was baptized May 8th 1737
Deborah Stetfon of Abijah & Deb: was baptized May 8th 1737
Patience Hatch of Hzekiah & Patience was Baptized May 8th 1737.
Thomas Turner Son of Thom^{s} & Mary was Baptized May 15th 1737
Gidion Stetfon Son of Gidion & Lydia, was baptized May 29 1737

Abigail Proutte daughter of Edward & Rebeccah was baptized June 12th 1737.

Adult { Cefar Anegro Slave of Capt Caleb Torry, was baptized June 12th 1737.

Ruth Bowker of James & Hañah was baptized June 26th 1737
Jofhua Jacob son of Jofhua & Mary was baptized July 3^{d} 1737

{ Jofeph Copeland, an Jnfant Child of Jofeph & Elizabeth, was baptized in private, being fick, on Satturday Eve, Auguft 6th 1737.

{ Jofeph Lambert An Jnfant Child of John Lambert was Baptized in private Augt 26 1737.

Hannah Magoon daughter of John & Abigail was baptized Sep^{t} 11th 1737.

Mercy James daughter of Benj^{m} & Mercy was baptized Sep^{t} 18. 1737
Jofeph Dwelly Son of Jofeph & Mary was baptized Oct: 16. 1737

Hannah Faunce of Plymouth dauter of Thomas & Hanah was Bap: Oct: 16. 1737

Elizabeth Turner daughter of Hawkins & Lufanna was bapt^{d} oct 23 1737.

Adult. Mary Braimen was baptized Nov 20th 1737

Iofeph Collomare Son of Jsaac was baptized Dec: 4th 1737

{ Mary Hayden daughter of Hayden & his wife was baptized in Private being fick Dec: 9th 1737

RECORDS OF THE SECOND CHURCH OF SCITUATE, NOW THE FIRST UNITARIAN CHURCH OF NORWELL, MASS.

Communicated by WILFORD JACOB LITCHFIELD, M.S., of Southbridge, Mass.

1738

Stephen Brooks Son of Nat[ll] and Mary was baptized January 1st 1737/8

Bethia Spooner daughter of John Spooner of Marſhfield was baptized Jan: 15th 1737/8.

Hannah North Eells daughter of Samuel & Hannah Eells of Hanover was Baptized Feb: 5th 1737/8.

Simeon Rogers Son of Sam[ll] Rogers jun[r] of marſhfield was baptized Feb: 12 1737/8

Mary Truant daughter of John [?] Truant of Marſhfield was baptized Feb 12th 1737/8

{ Benj[m] Palmer an Jnfant of Bezelial Palmer was baptized in private being Sick, on Feb: 25th 1737/8

Robinſon Turner Son of Abiell & Eliz: was baptized Feb: 26. 1737/8

Sarah Hammon of Benj[m] & Sarah was baptized Feb: 26 : 1737/8

John Eells son of John & Abiah Eells was baptized March 5th 1737/8

Mary Curtice, Daugh of Benj[m] & Rebecca was Baptiſed March 19th 1737/8

Bethiah Woodart daughter of James Woodart & —— his wife was baptized march 19th 1737/8.

Adult. Lydia Clift the wife of Saml Clift of Marſhfield was baptized at the North Meting houſe in Marſhfield march 26th 1738

Benjamin Dammon Son of Ebenezar Damon of Marſhfield was baptized march 26th 1738

Hannah Holmes daughter of Joſiah Holms of Marſhfield was bapt^{d}: March 26. 1738

Mercy Lincoln daughter of Joſhua & mercy, was baptized April 23^{d} 1738

Micael Hatch Son of Micael and Priſcilla was bap^{d}: April 23. 1738.

Jedidiah Dwelle son of Jedidiah and Elizabeth was baptized April 30th 1738

Colebourn Barrel Son of Wm Barrell was baptized May 7th 1738

Mercy Barker daughter of Barnabas, was baptized May 7. 1738

Gidion Randal Son of Caleb and Hannah was baptized May 14th 1738

May 21st 1738 J preached at Hingham for the Revd Mr Gay, and baptized Lydia Whitten daughter of Jsaac & Lydia.

May 26th 1738 George Turner ſon of Charls & Eunice, being ſick was baptiſed in private.

Adult. Benjamin Bowker was baptiſed June 4th 1738.

The same day was baptized his Jnfant Child whoſe name is Benjamin.

Adult. Rebecca Bowker was baptiſed June 4th 1738.

Eliſha Silveſter Son of Eliſha & Eunice, was bapt: June 4th 1738.

George Neal Son of John Neal, Late of Jreland was baptized June 4th 1738

Ruth Clap. of Joſeph & Hannah was baptized July 2^{d} 1738.

Lydiah King, of John & Mary of Marſhfield was baptized July 2^{d} 1738

Thomas Collomare, of Thomas & Hannah was Baptized July 2^{d} 1738.

Caleb Torry Son of Caleb & Mary was baptized July 9th 1738

Mary Fiſh daughter of Ebenezar [&] Deborah of Duxborough was baptized July 9th 1738.

Lillis Bryant daughter of Benj^{m} and Abigail, was baptiſed July 23. 1738

Martha Hatch daughter of Nehemiah & Martha was baptized July 23. 1738

{ Thomas Otis an Jnfant Child, ſon of Jsaac & Deborah being dangerouſly sick was baptized in private. July 25th

Adult Jeremiah Hatch (aged about —— years) was baptized Augt 6th 1738

Joſeph Lambert ſon of James, was baptized Augt 6th 1738.

Luſanna Randall daughter of Capt Nehemiah Randal, bap: Augt 13th 1738

Sarah Gray daughter of Thomas Gray & Sarah his wife, Baptized Augt 13. 1738

John Vinal, Son of John & Mary was baptized Augt 13th 1738.

Chriſtian Farrow, a Child of Benj^{m} Farrow, was baptized Augt 20. 1738

Ephraim Marble Son of David & Abigail was bap^{t} Augt 20th 1738

Deſire Silveſter a Child of Nehemiah Silveſter, bap^{td}: Augt 20th 1738

Mercy Turner daughter of Benj^{m} & Mercy, was bap^{td} Augt 27th 1738

Sep^{t} 10th 1738 J preached at Wetherſfield in Connecticut: & baptized a child for Gideon Dem̄ing named *Mercy.*

Deborah Woodart, daughter of Benjamin & Deborah, of Leiſter, was baptized Sep[t] 17.th 1738.

William Stetſon & Stephen Stetſon } Children of W[m] Stetſon & Hannah were baptized in private Sept: 28th 1738.

Stanton James Son of John & Prudence, was baptiſed oct: 15th 1738

Patience Brook daughter of W[m] & Mary, was baptized oct: 15th 1738.

Samuel Lappam Son of Joſhuah & Mary was baptized Oct: 22[d] 1738.

Elijah Stoddard son of Benj[m] & Ruth was baptized oct: 22. 1738

Abſolom, Son of Ceſar a negro Serv[t] to Cap[t] Torry was baptized oct: 22. 1738.

1739

Hannah King daughter of Joſeph of Marſhfield was baptized Jan. 21st 1738/9

Abigail Foſter daughter of Joſeph & Abigail was baptized Feb: 18th 1738/9.

Benjamin Bowker Son of Benj[m] & Hannah was baptized Feb: 18th 1738/9

Ann Neal of Joſeph & Allice was baptized Feb: 25th 1738/9

Thankfull Collomare of Jsaac & Thankfull was baptized March 4th 1738/9

March 22[d] 1738/9 John Groſs an Jnfant Child of Edmund & Olive Groſs being dangerouſly Sick was baptized.

March 23[d] 1738/9 Ann Bryant an Jnfant Child of David Bryant being dangerouſy ſick was baptized.

Elizabeth Randall of Benj[m] & Sarah was baptized April 1[st] 1739.

April 22[d] 1739 J preach[ed] at Marſhfield north meeting houſe and Baptized
Sarah Clift daughter of william.
Benjamin Lappam son of David.
Eliſabeth Silveſter daughter of John.
Rhoda Roſe, daughter of Joſhua

April 29[th] 1739 J preach[e]d at Duxboroug[h], and Baptized
Nathanael & Lemuel Turner Children of Amaſa & Rebecca
Philip Chandler ſon of Philip and Rebecca.
Silvanus Curtice, Son of Silvanus and Dorothy.
Warren Weſton Son of Eliphaz and Priſcilla.
Williams Fiſh son of Nathan[ll] and Mary.

Mercy Cuſhing daughter of Joſeph & Lydia, was baptized May 6th 1739

Charls Silveſter Son of William & Mary was baptized May 6th 1739.

Ruth Copeland daughter of Joſeph & Elizabeth was baptized May 6th 1739

Hannah Jacob daughter of Joſeph and Mary was baptized May 13. 1739.

Lemuel Church son of Nathan[ll] Church jun[r] was baptized in private being sick & not Likely to Live May 25th 1739

Priſcilla Hatch daughter of Micael & Priſcilla was Baptized May 27 1739

Jonathan Hatch Son of Hezekiah & Hannah was baptized June 17. 1739

Conſider, & Seth Jones twin Children of Ebenezar & Jane Jones of Marſhfield were baptized June 24 1739.

Nehemiah Prouty, Son of Margret Prouty, was baptized June 24. 1739

Experience Palmer & Jsaac Palmer Children of Jofeph Palmer & Mary his wife were baptized July 1st 1739

Daniel Faunce son of Thomas and Hannah his wife of Plymouth was baptized July 1st 1739.

Ruth Randall & Elifha Randal } children of Mary Randal were baptized July 8th 1739.

Betty Jones of Elifha & Sarah of Marfhfield was baptized July 22. 1739.

James Stockbridge Son of Sam^{ll} & Sarah, was baptized July 29. 1739

Deborah Silvefter, of Jofeph & Lydia was baptized Auguft 5th 1739

Amos Clift, & Mary Clift, Children of Sam^{ll} & Lydia of marfhfield, were baptized Augt 12. 1739.

{ Nabby Otis an Jnfant of Dr Jsaac Otis [&] Deborah, his wife being fick, was baptized in private Augt 22 [?] 1739*

Betty Turner daughter of Hawkins & Lufanna, was baptized Sep^{t} 2 1739.

Adult. Patience Pamalich an Jndian woman was Baptized Sep^{t} 2^{d} 1739.

Bennony Pamalich Son of the above S^{d} Patience was baptized Sep^{t} 2^{d} 1739

{ Edward Turner Son of Charls & Eunice being fick was baptized in private, Sep^{t} 3^{d} 1739

Solomon Lincoln Son of Jsaac & Abigail was baptized Oct: 28 1739.

John Stockbridge Son of Micael & Mary was baptized oct 28th 1739.

Hannah Clap, of Nathan^{ll} Clap & his wife, was baptized nov: 18 1739 by the Revd Mr Gay of Hingham

Elizabeth Turner of Abiel & Eliz: his wife was baptized nov: 18 1739, by the Revd Mr Gay of Hingham

Ezra Tolman of Elkana Tolman & ——— his wife was Baptized Nov: 25. 1739

Zechariah Curtice of Elifha Curtice and ——— His wife, was baptized Nov. 25. 1739

Adult. Cefar Burges a negro man was Baptized Dec: 9th 1739.

1740

Sufanna Collomare of Anthony & his wife was baptized Jan: 27th 1739/40.

Nathanael Turner, of W^{m} & Abigail was baptized Feb: 10. 1739/40

Ruben Turner of Jonathan & Abigail was baptized Feb: 24th 1739/40.

Mary Vinal, daughter of John & Mary was baptized April: 13. 1740

Betty Bryant daughter of Benj^{m} & Abigail was baptized. April 13th 1740

John Fofter Son of Elifha & Temperance was baptized April: 13. 1740.

Adult. Rachel Tailer, a widow was baptized April 20th 1740 &

Lettice Tailer her daughter was baptized at the fame time.

Betty Collomare daughter of John Collomare was baptized April 20th

Hannah Collomare daughter of Thomas Collomare was baptized April 20. 1740.

Sam^{ll} Clap Son of Sam^{ll}. & Sarah was Baptized April. 27. 1740

Afahel Rofe Son of Gidion & Lydia was baptized April. 27. 1740

Deborah Lincoln daughter of Jofhua and Mercy, was baptized April. 27. 1740.

Sarah Woodart daughter of James and Sarah was baptized April. 27. 1740.

* This date is blotted.

Mehitabel Marvel daughter of David marvel was baptized by mr Bourn May 18th 1740

Robert Stetſon Son of Robert Stetſon was baptized by mr Bourn May. 18th.

Joſeph Bowker ſon of James, was baptized by mr Bourn May 18th 1740

Seth Silveſter ſon of Nehemiah was baptized by mr Bourn May 18th 1740

Jſaac Torry Son of Caleb, was Baptized June 1st 1740

June 8th 1740. J preach'd at Hingham the second Sab: after Mr Hobarts death; and Baptized two children, viz:
Jonathan Marvel, Son of Nathanll & Hannah Orcot daughter of Emerſon orcot.

Ionathan Perry Son of Amos & Ruth was baptized in Private July 17th 1740

Rachel Brooks daughter of Gilbert was baptized July 20. 1740

John Brooks ſon of Gilbert Brooks junr & Deborah his wife was baptized Augt 17. 1740

memorandum Augt 10 1740 J preach[e]d for mr Bourn & baptiſed a child of John Bates's whoſe name J have forgott.

Eunice Jacob daughter of Joſhua & Mary was baptized Sept 14th 1740.

Mercy Clap daughter of John Clap and mercy his wife, was baptized Sept 28th 1740.

Hannah Tolman daughter of Joſeph and Hannah [h]is wife, was baptized Sept 29.

William Perry An Jnfant Child of Benjm Pery & Ruth his wife was baptized in private, being ſick. Oct: 2d 1740

Elizabeth Prouty, William Prouty, & Richard Prouty Children of Wm & Elizabeth were baptized Oct: 12th 1740.

Luſannah Prouty, Deborah Prouty & Jonathan Prouty Children of William & Jemimah Prouty were baptized Oct: 12th 1740.

Edward Prouty Son of Edward & Rebecca Prouty was baptized oct: 26. 1740:

John Hunt ſon of John Hunt & his wife was bap: nov. 2. 1740

Mary Copeland, of Joſeph & Elizabeth was baptized Nov: 9.th 1740

Joſhua Barker ſon of Barnabas & Mary was baptized Nov: 16th 1740.

James Silveſter ſon of Eliſha & Eunice was baptized nov: 23d 1740.

Joſhua Collomar ſon of Jsaac Collomare was baptized Nov: 23. 1740.

1741

Hannah Bowker daughter of Benjm & Hannah was baptized Jan: 18 1740/1

mehitabel Brooks daughter of * & Meriam Brooks was Baptized Feb: 22 1740/1

mercy Toby daughter of Eliſha Toby & ——— his wife was baptized march 1st 1740/1

Abigail Lincoln Daughter of Jsaac & Abigail was baptized March 8th 1740/1

Lot, Son of widow Eliſabeth Dwelle was baptized in private it being sick & not Likely to recover march 16. 1740/1

Prudence James daughter of John & Prudence was baptized march 22d 1740/1

Hannah Brooks daughter of Wm & mary Brooks was baptized March 29th 1741

* This name is badly blotted, but is probably *Tailor*.

Simeon Rofe Son of Gideon & Lydia was Baptized April 26. 1741

Seth Stoddard fon of Benj^{m} Stoddard jun^{r} and his wife ——— was baptized April 26th 1741

——— Turner an Jnfant Child of Charls and Eunice Turner was Baptized in private Jt being fick & not Like to Live May 6th 1741

Robert Corthel Son of Robert & mary was baptized May 17th 1741.

Abiel Turner Son of Abiel and Eliz.th was bap^{t} May 10 1741.

Peleg Turner Son of Benj^{m} & Mercy was baptized may 24 1741

Betty Fofter, daughter of Jofeph & Abigail, was baptized May 24 1741

Defire Clap Daughter of Nathan^{ll} & Defire was baptized May 24th 1741.

Rachel Gilkey daughter of James and Grace was baptifed may 24. 1741.

Defire Bowker daughter of James & Hannah was bapt^{d} June 7th 1741

Sarah Jacob daughter of Deacon Jofeph Jacob & Mary his wife was baptized June 14 1741

July 26, 1741. J preach^{d} at Taunton and baptifed: William Codden Son of George & Eliz: Codden: & Prudence Hofkins daughter of Jofhua & Lydia Hofkins.

Mary Silvefter daughter of W^{m} & Mary, was baptized Aug 2^{d} 1741.

{ John Hatch an Jnfant Child of Micael & Prifcilla was baptized Jn private On Sabbath Evening Augt 2^{d} 1741

Edmund Grofs son of Edmund & Oliffe, was baptized Sep^{t} 6th 1741

Allice or Elfe Neal daughter of Jofeph and Allice Neal was baptized in private Sep^{t} 16. or 17. 1741

Nathan Cufhing Son of Jofeph and Lydia was baptized Sep^{t} 27 1741.

Lemuel Dwelly Son of Jofeph & Mary was baptized Oct: 4th 1741

Adult. James Northy was Baptized Oct: 18th 1741

Adult. Mary Northy, &

Adult: Mehitabell Northy Children of James North[y] were baptized after y^{y} had own'd the Cov^{t} Oct: 18.

Ebenezar Northy, Anna Northy, Sarah Northy, Deborah Northy & Jeffe Northy Children of James & mary Northy were baptized oct: 18 1741.

Elizabeth Gray daughter of Thos. Gray from Jreland was baptized oct 18th 1741.

Calvin Powers Son of Walter Powers was baptized Oct: 18th 1741.

Hawkins Turner Son of Hawkins and Lufanna his wife was baptized Nov 1st 1741.

Sarah Hart daughter of William and Mary Mallus [or Mellus] was bap: Nov: 15. 1741

{ Mercy Turner an Jnfant of Jeffe & Lydia Turner, being fick was baptized Jn private Dec: 11th 1741.

Nehemiah Randal Son of Elifha & Zeporah was baptized Dec: 13th 1741

{ Dec: 27. P: M: J preach'd at Taunton and Baptized my GrandChild, Enos Williams, Son of Seth & Mary Williams

1742

Adult. Iames Northy Son of Iames & Mary his wife being some what delirious, was baptifed at the requeft of his Parents, he defiring of it alfo. Jan: 10th 1741/2

Caleb Randal fon of Caleb & Hannah Randal of Hanover was baptized Jan: 10th 1741/2.

Keziah Stockbridge daughter of Mical & Mary Stochbridge, was baptized Jan: 10th 1741/2

Amos Stetfon son of Gidion Stetfon was baptized Jan: 24 1741/2

{ Feb 4th 1741/2 Abigail Hatch an Jnfant Child of Hezekiah Hatches being ſick was baptized in private }

William Randal Son of Benjamin & Sarah was baptized March. 28th 1742

Joſeph Silveſter Son of Joſeph & Lydia was baptized May 16th 1742

Edward Prouty ſon of Edward & Rebecca, baptd may 16. 1742

Mary Palmer of Joſeph & Jane was baptized may 16 1742

Nehemiah Silveſter Son of Nehemiah & Mehitabel bap: may 16 1742

Isaac Lincoln ſon of Jaac [Isaac] Lincoln & ——— His wife bapd May 16th 1742

P[h]ilip Turner Son of Jsrael & Deborah was baptized may 16. 1742

Luſanna Collomare daughter of Anthony & Suſaña bapd May 23 1742

Luce Lambert of James & Sarah was baptized May 30th 1742

Benjamin Palmer of Bezalael & Anna, was baptized may 30. 1742

Caleb Nicols of Jsrael & Elizabeth was baptized June 6th 1742.

Rhode Marvel Daughter of David & his wife ——— was baptized by Mr Wales June 13. 1742

Martha Stetſon daughter of Anthony & Ann his wife, was baptized by Mr Wales June 13. 1742

William Wilſon Son of Wm & Hannah was baptized June 13th 1742

Adult. John Wheelwright was baptized June 20th 1742.

Levi Corthel Son of Robert & mary was baptized June 20th 1742.

Mary Woodart daughter of James & Sarah was baptized June 27th 1742

{ Thankfull Hatch an Jnfant child of Micael Hatch & Priſcilla his wife being Sick, was baptized Jn private June 28th 1742 }

Adult. Judith Dammon wife of Daniel Damon was baptized July 4th 1742.

Aſa Roſe Son of Gidion & Lydia was baptized July 4th 1742

Simeon Naſh Son of Symion & Lydiah was baptized July 4th 1742

Hannah Barker of Samll Barker junr was baptized. July 7th 1742

Abigail Barrel of William & Abigail was baptized July 18th 1742

John Collomare Son of John & Margret was baptized July 18th 1742

Lydia Collomare of Thomas & Hannah was baptized July 18th 174. [1742]

Ruben Buck Son of Jsaac Buck junr & Mary, was baptized July 18. 1742.

Rebecca Collomare daughter of Jsaac & Thankfull was baptized Augt 1st 1742.

Daniel Dammon Son of Daniel & Judith was baptized Augt 22. 1742.

Grace Stetſon, daughter of Matthew and Hannah was baptized oct. 10. 1742

Nathan Cuſhing Son of Joſeph & Lydia was baptized Oct: 10th. 1742

Ezekiel Vinal ſon of John & Mary was baptized oct: 10th 1742

Rhode James daughter of John & Prudence James was baptized oct: 10th 1742

Miriam Tolman daughter of Eliſha & Miriam his wife was baptized oct: 17. 1742.

Adult. Samuel Holman was Baptized in Private, Oct: 31. 1742.

Adult. Grace Siſco a negro Servt formerly to Joſeph Clap of this town, now to John Hall of hingham, after her Confeſſion * * * was read to the Chh. and accepted, was baptized Nov. 14 1742

Sarah Brooks daughter of William & Mary, was baptized Nov. 21. 1742

Lufanna Eells daughter of John & Abiah, was baptized Dec: 19th 1742

Sarah Curtice daughter of Elifha & Sarah was baptized Dec: 19th 1742

Dec: 26 1742 J preach'd at Pembrok vilage for mr Lemuel Bryant and baptized three Children *viz.*

Seth Pierce Son of Jofhua Pierce, Pierce [*sic*] and his wife.

Patience & Prince, Children of Richard, a Negro Servt of mr Jofiah Cufhings.

RECORDS OF THE SECOND CHURCH OF SCITUATE, NOW THE FIRST UNITARIAN CHURCH OF NORWELL, MASS.

Communicated by Wilford Jacob Litchfield, M.S., of Southbridge, Mass.

1743

Jonathan Turner, Son of Jeffe and Lydia, was Baptized Jan: 9th 1742/3

Silvanus Clap, Son of Natll & Defire Clap was was [*sic*] baptized. Jan: 23d 1742/3

Jofhua Lincoln Son of Jofhua & Mercy was Baptized Jan: 23/ 1742/3

Sufanna Sterer daughter of Benjm & Ruth, was baptized Jan 23. 1742/3

Barfheba Fofter daughter of Elifha & Temperance was baptized by mr wales of Marfhfield Jan: 16. 1742/3

Iofeph Fofter fon of Jofeph & Abigail was baptized March 6th 1742/3

Hannah Copeland daughter of Jofeph & Eliz: was baptized march 6th 1742/3.

Olive Grofs daughter of Edmund & Olive was Baptized march 6th 1742/3

Samuel Brooks, Son of Gilbert & Deborah was baptifed March 6th 1742/3

Sylla [?] Soul, & Abigail Soul, Children of Jchabod Soul deceafed, & his widow was baptized march 6th 1742/3

Iames Jacob, fon of Jofhua & Mary was baptized march 20th 1742/3

Mary Torry daughter of Caleb and Mary was baptifed April 3d.

John Cufhing, fon of John Cufhing junr & Deborah was baptized April 3d 1743

Sarah Hatch dater of Mical & Prifcilla, was baptized May 1. 1743.

Conftant Church & Lemuel Church children of Nathanael and Jerufha, were baptized May 8th 1743

Sarah Eells daughter of John & Abiah was baptifed May 8th 1743

Lydia Jacob daughter of Deacon Jofeph Jacob and ——— his wife, baptd June 5th 1743

Conftant Clap fon of Capt John Clap & Mercy his wife, was baptized June 5th 1743

Simeon Silvefter fon of Elifha & Eunice was baptized June 5th 1743.

Defire Eells daughter of North Eells & Ruth his wife an Jnfant of nine days old, being fick and not Likely to Live was baptized in private June 17th 1743.

Luce Barker of Barnabas & Mary was Baptifed June 26. 1743

Malachi Stetfon of Job & mary was Baptized June 26. 1743.

David Tower Son of Benjm Tower junr was baptized July 10th 1743

Simeon Curtice fon of Simeon Curtice was baptized July 10th 1743

James Gilkey Son of James & Grace, was baptized July 24th 1743.

Elizabeth Church daughter of Jofeph & Grace, was baptized July 31. 1743.

Miriam Brooks daughter of Tailor Brooks & Miriam his wife was baptized July 31. 1743

Ruben Rofe Son of Gidion & Eliz: was baptifed oct: 30. 1743

Richard Silvefter fon of nehemiah was baptized oct: 30. 1743

David Collomare Son of Jsaac was baptifed Nov: 6th 1743

Iofeph Dammon Son of Jofeph was Baptized Nov: 6th 1743

James, & Benjamin Cufhing Children of James Cufhing junr were baptized Nov: 6th 1743

Deborah Nafh daughter of Simeon was bap: Nov: 6. 1743

Elizabeth Brooks daughter of Natll & Eliz: was baptifed Nov: 6th 1743

Abigail Turner Daughter of Abiel & Elizth. was Bapd Dec: 4th 1743

Lufanna Negro daughter of Cefar negro, Slave to Capt Caleb Torry, was baptized Dec: 11th 1743

1744

Ruth Dwelle daughter of Jofeph & Mary was baptized Jan: 15th 1743/4

Adult: Mary Bowker daughter of Richard was Bapd Jan: 22.

Sarah Prouty daughter of Edward & Rebecca Prouty was baptized Jan: 29 1743/4

Samuel Tolman fon of Jofeph & Mary was baptized Jan: 29 1743/4.

Pickles Cufhing Son of Deaccon Jofeph Cufhing & Lydia his wife, was baptized Feb: 19th 1743/4.

Ruth Hatch daughter of Hezekiah was baptized March 11th 1743/4

Zenos Stetfon Son of Gidion was baptized march 11. 1743/4

Lazarus Bowker fon of Lazarus was baptized Mr [March] 11. 1743/4

Jabez Standly Son of Jabez & Deborah was baptized March 18 1743/4

Ephraim Palmer Son of Jofeph & Jane was Baptifed April 22ᵈ 1744.
Afa Turner Son of Jonathan & Abigail was baptized April 22ᵈ 1744.
Mary Lincoln daughter of Josfhua and Mercy was baptized May 13ᵗʰ 1744
Lydia Cufhing daughter of James Cufhing junʳ was baptized May 13. 1744
Mary Corthel daughter of Robert Corthel, was baptized May 13. 1744
Elifabeth Cufhing daughter of John Cufhing junʳ was baptized May 27. 1744 by Mʳ Bourn
Thankfull Hatch daughter of Micael Hatch was baptized May 27. 1744 by Mʳ Bourn.
Jonatha[n] Star Turner Son of Hawkins Turner was baptized June 10ᵗʰ 1744
Rhode Bowker daughter of James & Mary Bowker was baptifed June 17ᵗʰ 1744.
John Dammon son of Daniel & Judith was baptized July 1ˢᵗ 1744
Hannah Nichols daughter of Jsrael and ——— his wife was baptized July 15ᵗʰ 1744.
Rebecca Neal daughter of Jofeph Neal & ——— his wife was baptized July 15ᵗʰ 1744.
Mary Ewell daughter of Peleg Bryant & ——— his wife was Baptized July 15ᵗʰ 1744
Jofeph Church Son of Jofeph & Grace, was baptized July 22ᵈ 1744
Roland Cufhing Son of the Honourable John Cufhing & Mary his wife, was baptized July 29ᵗʰ 1744. by the Revᵈ Mʳ Bourn
Ruth Bryant daughter of Benjᵐ & Abigail, was baptized Aug: 5ᵗʰ 1744.
{ Jofeph Lambert Son of Jofeph Lambert & ——— his wife was baptized in Private he being Sick, in the Evening after the Sabbath Augᵗ 5ᵗʰ 1744. an Jnfant Child.
Calvin Wade fon of Jofeph & Rachel was baptized Augᵗ 19. 1744.
Sarah Lincoln daughter of Jsaac & Abigail was baptized Augᵗ 19. 1744.
Elifha Tolman fon of Elifhah & Miriam Tolman was Baptized Augᵗ 19ᵗʰ 1744.
Luce Silvefter daughter of Jsrael Silvefter & ——— his wife, was baptized Aug: 19. 1744.
Elifha James Son of John James junʳ & Prudence his wife was baptized Augᵗ 26. 1744
Charls Curtice Son of Benjᵐ & Rebecca was baptized Sepᵗ 2ᵈ 1744.
Martha Collamer daughter of Thom.ˢ & Hannah was baptized Sepᵗ 2ᵈ 1744.
Stephen Dammon Son of Jsaac & Lydia was baptized Sepᵗ 9ᵗʰ 1744.
Zepparah Randal daughter of Elifha & Zeporah was baptized Sepᵗ 16. 1744
Mary Buck daughter of Jsaac Buck junʳ and Mary his wife was baptᵈ Sepᵗ 16. 1744
Tamar daughter of Cefar Negro, & Sarah his wife was Baptized Sepᵗ 23. 1744
William Church Son of Nathanˡˡ & Jerufha was baptized Sepᵗ 30. 1744.
Luce Barker, daughter of Barnabas & Mary, was baptized Oct: 7ᵗʰ 1744.
Defire Eells daughter of North & Ruth Eells was Baptized Oct: 14ᵗʰ 1744.
Simeon Perry Son of Abner & Sarah was baptifed oct: 14ᵗʰ 1744.

Lufanna Turner daughter of Benj^m & mercy was baptized Oct: 28. 1744.

Elifabeth Vinal daughter of John & Mary was baptifed Oct: 28. 1744.

Abigail Turner daughter of Jeffe & Lydia was baptized Oct: 28. 1744.

Jofeph Woodart Son of James & Mary was baptized Oct: 28. 1744.

Noah Brooks Son of Tailor & Miriam was baptized Nov: 4. 1744.

Sarah Stockbridge daughter of Samuel Stockbridge jun^r & Sarah his wife was baptized Dec: 9th 1744.

Eunice Bowker daughter of Benj^m & Hannah was baptifed Dec: 9th 1744.

Jofeph Benfon Son of Jofeph & Abiel was baptized Dec: 16. 1744.

John Neal Son of Job & Sarah was baptized Dec: 23. 1744. *Baptifms this year 50*

1745.

Jofeph Stetfon an Jnfant child of Jof: Stetfon & ——— his wife was baptifed in Private, not being Likely to Live, on Saturday Jan: 19th 1744/5.

Seth Brooks Son of william an infant was baptized Jn private not being Likely to Live: Jan: 28th 1744/5.

Rhoda Stetfon daughter of Job & mary was baptized Feb: 10. 1744/5.

Hawkes Cufhing Son of Joseph & Lydia was baptized Feb. 17th 1744/5

Temperance Clap Daught^r of Nat^ll & Defire was baptized Feb. 17th 1744/5

Abigail Clap an Jnfant of Jofeph Clap being Sick was baptized in private. Feb: 27. 1744/5

Timothy Fofter Son of Jofeph & Abigail was baptifed March 24. 1744/5

John Skiffe Son of Samuel and Elifabeth was baptized April 7th 1745

Hannah Willfon daughter of W^m & Hannah was Baptifed April 14th 1745

Simeon Perry fon of Jofeph & rachel was baptized April 14th 1745.

Iofeph Jacob, fon of Deacon Jofeph Jacob & mary his wife, was baptized April 28th 1745

Rhode Copeland daughter of Jofeph & Eliz^th Baptifed April 28: 1745

Melzar Curtice Son of Simeon & ——— his wife, baptifed April 28th 1745

{ Elizabeth Randal an Jnfant Child of Gerfhom & Elizabeth Randal was baptifed in Private May 3^d 1745 Jt being dangeroufly fick

Elifha Fofter Son of Elifha & Temperance was baptized May 5th 1745

Richard, & Thomas, negro Children of Cuba, a Negro Slave to m^r Jsaac Turner, were baptifed; may 5th 1745.

Lenthall Eells daughter of John & Abiah Eells was baptized may 19th 1745

Daniel Randal Son of Benj^m and Sarah was baptized May 26. 1745

Katherine, a Negro Child of Cuba a Negro Slave, to Mr Jsaac Turner was baptifed may 26th 1745.

Martha Curtice daughter of Elifha & Sarah Curtice was baptized June 2^d 1745

Iohn Gilkie Son of James & Grace, was baptized June 16. 1745.

Enoch Collamar fon of John & margret was baptized June 30. 1745

Dwelle Clap, fon of David Clap jun^r was baptized July 28th 1745.

Margret Turner daughter of Abiel & Elifabeth was baptized. Augt 11. 1745

Ifrael Turner Son of Jsrael & Deborah was baptized Aug[t] 25. 1745

*Ad.** Leah Fother [?] a Negro woman Living with M[rs] Amy Dwelly was Baptifed Sep[t] 1st 1745.

Ruth Stoddard daughter of Benj[m] & Ruth was baptized fep[t] 22. 1745

Mary Tolman daughter of Jofeph & Mary, was baptized Nov: 3[d] 1745

Ephraim Stetfon fon of Matthew & Hannah was baptized Nov: 17. 1745.

Samuel Cufhing Son of James Cufhing jun[r] & his wife ——— was baptized Nov 24

Mary Gray daughter of James Gray & his wife ——— was baptifed Nov: 24. 1745

Abigail Bowker an Jnfant of Lazarus Bowker & Abigail his wife was baptized in private Nov: 30. 1745.

Francis Cufhing fon of John & Deborah was baptifed Dec: 1st 1745.

35 Baptifms 35 this Last year

1746

Ruben Hatch Son of Nehemiah & Mary his wife was baptized Jan 19 1745/6.

Lydia Stetfon daughter of Gidion Stetfon and ——— his wife was baptifed march 23. 1745.6

Samuel Curtice Son of Amos & Mary his wife was baptifed April. 6[th] 1746

Benjamin Perry fon of Benjamin & ——— his wife was baptized April 20[th] 1746

Elijah Silvefter Son of William & Mary was baptized April. 20 1746.

Abigail Tower daughter of Benj[a]min Tower jun & his wife, was Baptifed May 4[th] 1746

Jemima Farrow daughter of Thomas & Jemimah was baptifed May 4. 1746

Elifabeth Rofe Daughter of Gidion & Lydia, bapt[d], may 11[th]

Rebecca Neal, daugter of Jofeph & Allice, bap[d] May 11 1746

Mary Brooks daughter of W[m] & Mary bapt[d] May 11 1746.

Jofeph Dammon fon of Jofeph & IoAnna was baptized May 18th 1746

Nehemiah Silvefter, Son of Nehemiah & Mehitabel, was bap[d] May 25. 1746.

Abigail Collamar daughter of Anthony Collomar deceafed was Baptized June 1. 1746

Lurana Lambert daughter of John Lambert and his wife ——— was baptifed June 1. 1746.

Jsaac Silvefter fon of W[m] & Mary was paptized July 5th 1746.

William James fon of John & Prudence was baptized July 13th 1746.

Jofhua Hatch fon of Micael & Prifcilla was Bapt[d] July 20, 1746.

Prince Bryant fon of Benj[m] and Abigail was baptized July 27. 1746.

Lufanna Stetfon daughter of Jofeph & Mary was baptized July 27. 1746.

Sufannah Prouty of Edward & Rebecca Prouty, was baptized Aug[t] 24 1746

Lufanna Buck of Jsaac Buck jun[r] & Mary his wife was baptized Aug[t] 24 1746.

Oliver Nafh: & Church Nafh Children of Simeon and Lydiah Nafh were baptifed by my Son Edward Aug[t] 10. 1746.

* Adult.

Abner Perry Son of Abner Perry deceafe[d] and Sarah his widow was baptized Sep^{t} 7th 1746.

Enofs Briggs Son of Seth & Abigail was baptized Sep^{t} 7. 1746.

Cornelius Bowker Son of James Bowker jun^{r} & his Wife was baptized Sep^{t} 28. 1746

Jffachar, Son of Cefar Negro and his wife Sarah; Indn* was baptifed Sep^{t} 28. 1746.

Sarah Dwelle daughter of Jofeph was Baptized Oct: 5th 1746

Jofeph Church Son of Jofeph & Grace was Baptized oct: 5th 1746

Lydia Turner daughter of Jonathan and Abigail was baptifed Oct 26 1746

Peleg Bryant Son of Peleg & his wife was baptized Oct: 19th 1746.

Lemuel Cufhing fon of Jofeph Cufhing jun^{r} & Lydia his wife was baptized nov. 23. 1746

Abner Wade fon of Iofeph Wade and Rachel his wife was baptifed Nov 23. 1746.

Iofhua Barrel Son of William & Lydia was Baptifed Nov: 30 1746.

Job Neal Son of Job & Sarah was baptifed Nov: 30. 1746.

Seth Turner Son of Jeffe & Lydia was baptized Dec: 21. 1746

The whole Number of those baptifed Anno 1746 is 36

RECORDS OF THE SECOND CHURCH OF SCITUATE, NOW THE FIRST UNITARIAN CHURCH OF NORWELL, MASS.

Communicated by WILFORD JACOB LITCHFIELD, M.S., of Southbridge, Mass.

1747

Nathanæl Eells fon of North Eells and Ruth his wife was born Jan: 1st 1746/7———And Baptifed Jan: 18.——

William Turner Son of Charls & Unice, was baptifed Jan: 25th 1746/7.

Mary Clap daughter of Nat^{ll} & Defire was baptifed Jan: 25th 1746/7

Elifabeth Curtice of Sam^{ll} & Rachel was baptifed Feb: 15. 1746/7

Sarah Riply daughter of Jofhua Riply and ——— his wife was Baptifed Feb: 22 1746/7

Temperance Fofter daughter of Elifhah & Temperance his wife was baptifed march 29. 1747.

Hannah Brigs daughter of James Briggs & Hannah his wife was Baptifed march 29. 1747

Content Barker daughter of Barnabas Barker & his wife ——— was baptized April 5th 1747.

Lufanna [or Lufanda] Perry daughter of Jofeph Perry & his wife was bap^{t} April 26 1747.

* Indian ?

Elifabeth Turner of Benj^{m} & Mercy was baptifed May 17th 1747.

Sarah Bryant of Thom^{s} & Sarah was baptifed may [? 17] 1747.

Deborah Jacob daughter of Deacon Jofeph Jacob & Mary his wife was Baptized May 24. 1747

Deborah Torry of Capt Caleb Torry & mary his wife was baptifed may 31. 1747.

Ruth Vinal daughter of John & Mary, was baptifed June 7th 1747

Jofeph Eells Son of John & Abiah Eells was baptifed June 21st 1747.

Abigail Wilfon daughter of W^{m} & Mary wilfon was baptifed June 21st 1747

John Right Son of Mercy Right was baptifed June 21st 1747.

Luce Cufhing daughter of the Honourable John Cufhing Esqr And Mary his wife was Baptifed June 28th 1747.

John Woodart fon of James & Sarah was baptifed June 28th 1747.

{ Luke Palmer an Jnfant Child of Jofeph and Jane Palmer being fick with the throat trouble was baptifed Jn private June 30th 1747.

Roland Turner & Anna Turner Twinn children of Abial and Elifabeth Turner were baptifed July 5th 1747

Robert Cufhing Son of John Cusfhing jun^{r} and deborah his wife was baptifed July 5th 1747.

{ Iuly 7th 1747. J baptifed two Children of Jofhua & Lydia Palmer. they being dangeroufly Sick. the name of the one was Lydya the name of the Other was ———

Anna Hatch daughter of Nehemiah Hatch and Mary, was baptized July 19th 1747

Lydia Copeland daughter of Jofeph & Elifabeth was baptifed July 26th 1747.

Mercy Tolman daughter of Elifha & Miriam, was baptifed Augt 2^{d} 1747.

Charls Samfon had a child baptifed by the Revd Mr Bryant of Braintree, on the 9th of Auguft 1747.

William Lincoln Son of Jsaack & Abigail was baptifed Augt 30th 1747.

Nehemiah Randal Son of Gerfhom & Elifabeth was baptifed Sep^{t} 6. 1747.

Iacob Stetfon Son of Matthew & Hannah was baptifed Sep^{t} 27th 1747.

Calvin Curtis, Son of Elifha & Sarah was baptifed Sep^{t} 27. 1747.

Sufannah Randal daughter of Perez and Sarah was baptifed Sep^{t} 27. 1747.

Gerfhom Bowker Son of Lazarus & Abigail was baptifed Oct: 4th 1747.

Deborah Bowker daughter of John & Ann was baptifed Oct: 4th 1747.

Lydia Randal daughter of Elifha & Zeporah was baptifed oct: 11. 1747.

Luce Turner daughter of Hawkins & ——— was baptifed Oct 11. 1747.

Jofhua Turner Son of Jsrael & Deborah was baptized Oct: 25. 1747

Eunice Stetfon daugher of George & Eunice was baptifed oct: 25 1747

Elizabeth Tolman daughter of Jofeph & Mary was baptifed Nov: 8. 1747.

Mary Church daughter of Thomas and Mary; was baptifed Nov: 29 1747.

The whole number of the baptifed this year is 42

1748

Sarah Wheelwright daughter of John & Sarah, was baptifed Ian: 10. 1747/8.

Lucresia Gilkie, daughter of James and Grace was baptised Jan: 24. 1747/8.

Lydia Collomar daughter of Thomas Collomar & Hannah his wife was baptised Feb: 14. 1747/8

Amos Curtice Son of Amos & Mary was baptised Feb. 14. 1747/8

Martha Farrow daughter of Thomas & Jemimah, was baptised Feb: 14. 1747/8

Iacob Lincoln Son of Jsaac & Abigail was baptised March 6th 1747/8.

Margret Briggs daughter of John And Abigail Brigs was baptized March 27. 1748

Eunice James daughter of John and Prudence was baptized April 3, 1748.

Ann Bryant of Peleg & Mary was Baptised April 3d 1748.

Samuel Stockbridge Son of Samll & Sarah was baptized April. 17. 1748.

Lydiah Tower of Jonathan & Lydia was baptised April 17th 1748.

Bathsheba Damon daughter of Danniel & Judith, was baptized May 1st 1748.

Stephen Silvester son of Nehemiah & ——— his wife was baptized may 8th 1748.

Jsrael Silvester Son of Jsrael and his wife was baptised May 8. 1748.

Abigail Bryant daughter of Samll Bryant and mary his wife was baptised May 8. 1748.

Deborah Man an Jnfant of Josiah & Mary Man was baptised in private, being sick. may 13.

Mary Palmer of Josehp [*sic*] & Jane his wife was Baptised may 15th 1748.

Joshua Bowker Son of Bemjm [*sic*] and Hannah was Baptised May 22. 1748.

Iune 4th 1748. J baptised an Jnfant child of Jonathan & Elisabeth Elems which child died Jun 6th

{ June 7th J baptized, Abigail Bryant an Jnfant Child of Benjmin Bryant and his Wife ——— }

Thomas Cushing Son of Joseph and Lydia, was baptized June 26. 1748

Lusannah Prouty daughter of William and his wife was baptised June 26. 1748

Abigail Cushing daughter of the honourable John Cushing, Esqr, & Mary his wife, was baptised July 3d 1748.

Lurania Silvester daughter of Elisha Silvester an[d] ——— his wife was baptised July 3d 1748.

Job Curtice Son of Samuel & Rachel was baptised July 10th 1748.

Adult. Sarah Hooper a young woman Living with Mr Samll Stockbridge was baptized July 10. 1748

Hannah Stetson, daughter of Gidion Stetson & ——— his wife baptized July 24

Jsaac Dammon Son of Jsaack & Lydya was Baptised July 24, 1748.

Elisabeth, daughter of Cesar a negro Servant or Slave, to Capt Torry, and Sarah his wife, a free Jndian woman was baptized Augt 28. 1748.

Desire Stoddard daughter of Benjm Stoddard & his wife, ——— was-baptised Augt 28. 1748.

Abigail Standly daughter of Jabez & Abigail Standly was baptised Sept 11. 1748.

{ Bartlet Bowker an Jnfant Son of Lazarus Bowker was baptised in Private, Sept 12, 1748. }

Sarah Cole daughter of James Cole & Sarah his wife was baptifed Sep[t] 25. 1748.

Jsaack Buck, son of Jsaac & mary was baptifed Sep[t] 25. 1748

Molly Stetfon daughter of Jofeph Stetfon & ——— his wife was baptifed Sep[t] 25 1748

{ Samuel Eells Son of North & Ruth Eells was baptifed Sept 26 1748 in private, being fick & not Likely to Live

Nathanael Jacob Son of Deacon Jofeph Jacob & ——— his wife was bap[d] Oct 9th

Jofeph Neal son of Job & his wife was baptifed Oct: 9th 1748.

Macael Hatch Son of Michael & his wife Oct: 23. 1748

Sufanna Clap of Nath[ll] & defire his wife was baptifed Oct: 30th 1748

{ Defire Elmes daughter of Jonathan Elmes & ——— his wife an Jnfant was baptifed in Private oct: 31. 1748

Luce Jacob daughter of Jofhua & Mary was baptifed Nov: 13. 1748.

Hannah Silvefter daughter of W[m] and Mary was baptifed nov: 20. 1748

Luce Cufhing daughter of James Cufhing jun[r] & his wife baptifed Nov: 27. 1748.

Huldah Lambert of John Lambert & his wife, baptifed Nov: 27. 1748.

Sarah Briggs, of James & Hannah was baptifed Dec: 11. 1748.

{ Lydia Barrel, daughter of William Barrel, & Lydia his wife deceafed was baptized in private Dec: 16. 1748

Seth Turner fon of Jeffe & Lydia was baptifed Dec: 18. 1748.

Bartlet Bowker of John Bowker and his wife was baptifed Dec. 25 1748.

The whole number of the baptifed this year amounts to 50.

1749

Sufanna Brooks daughter of W[m] Willian [*sic*] Brook[s] & his wife ——— was Baptized Jan 22 1748/9.

Deborah Cufhing daughter of John Cufhing & Deborah was baptifed Jan: 29 1748/9.

Samuel Bryant Son of Sam[ll] Bryant Jun[r] & Mary his wife was baptifed march 5.

Adult. Sarah houfe Daughter of David Houfe deceafed was baptifed March 5. 1748/9

Molly northy Hatch daughter of nehemiah Hatch was baptifed by m[r] Bourn march 19.

Sarah Fofter daughter of Elifha Fofter & his wife ——— was baptifed April 2[d] 1749

Luther Curtice Son of Elifha Curtice & his wife was baptized April 9th 1749.

John Dwelly Son of Jofeph Dwelly deceafed and Mary his widow was baptized April 9th 1749

Rachel wade, daughter of Jofeph & Rachel was baptized April 9th 1749

Robert Randal Son of Perez & Sarah Randal was baptized April 9th 1749.

Hannah Clap daughter of Jofeph Clap and ——— his wife, was baptifed April. 23. 1749

Mary Man daughter of Jofiah man and Mary his wife was baptifed April 23. 1749

Margret Briggs daughter of John & Abigail was baptifed may 14th 1749

Thomas Cufhing Son of Deacon Jofeph Cufhing jun[r] & Lydia his wife was baptifed June 4th 1749

Margret Bowker daughter of Benj^{m} and Hannah was baptifed June 4th 1749.

Calvin Turner Son of Jonathan and Abigail was baptifed July 2nd 1749

Barne Wade & Zebulon Wade Children of Zebulon wade and his wife were baptized in private July 19th [?] 1749.

Adult Mary Turner wife of Nat^{ll} Turner was baptized July 23 1749.

Elijah Turner fon of Nathan^{ll} & Mary was baptized July 23. 1749

Betty Woodart daughter of James woodart his wife deceafed was baptized July 23 1749.

Efter [Esther] Tower daughter of Benj^{m} & his wife ——— of Abbinton was baptized Aug 6th 1743.

Jofeph Copeland, fon of Jofeph & Elizabeth was Baptized Sept 3^{d} 1749

Adult Philifs a Negro Slave to Dr Otis was baptifed Sept 3^{d} 1749

Olive & Betty, & Ruben three Children of the above named Philis were Baptised Sept 3^{d} 1749

Thankfull Eells, daughter of North Eells, & Ruth, his wife, was Baptifed In private about five of the Clock in the morning, and died between Twelve and one of the Clock Oct: 8 1749.

Zechariah Dam̄on Son of Zechariah Dammon, and Anna Lenthall his wife, was baptized Oct: 15th 1749

Rhoda Bryant daughter of Peleg & Mary was baptifed December 3^{d} 1749

Lydia James daughter of John James & Prudence his wife was baptifed Dec: 31. 1749

The whole number of the baptifed this year amounts to 31

1750.

Iacob Turner Son of Jsrael & Deborah was baptized March 25. 1750.

Lydia Stockbridge of Sam^{ll} & Sarah was baptifed April 1st 1750.

Demmick Bowker of Lazarus & Abigail was baptifed April 1st 1750.

BathSheba Barker of Barnabas & Mary was Baptifed April 15th 1750

Samuel Dammon of Daniel & Sarah was Baptifed April 15th 1750.

Luscenda Stetfon of Jofhua & Lillis was baptized April 29. 1750

Nathanael Jacob, Son of Deacon Jofeph Jacob & mary his wife was baptifed May 6th 1750

Luther Stetfon fon of Job & Mary was baptifed may 6th 1750.

Silva Church daughter of Jofeph, & Grace his Widow was baptized May 6th 1750.

Adult Philis a Negro Servant to Deacon Jofeph Cufhing was baptized June 3^{d} 1750.

Caleb Cufhing fon of Jofeph & Lydia was baptifed July 1st 1750.

Sufanna Man daughter of Jofiah man & ——— his wife was baptifed July 8th 1750.

Sufannah Randal daughter of Benja^{m} Randal jun^{r} & Hannah his wife was baptized July 15th 1750.

Nathanael Silvefter Son of Nehemiah & Mehitable was Baptifed July 29. 1750

Anna Wade daughter of Zebulon Wade and ——— his wife was Baptifed Augt 5th 1750.

Samuel Curtice Son of Sam^{ll}: & Rachel was baptifed Augt 12th 1750.

At a Meeting of the 2^{d}. Church of Christ in Scituate on ye 11th. Day of Oct^{o} 1750 being the first Chh. Meeting after the Death of the Revd Mr Eells. S^{d} Church chose ye Revd Mr Shearj^{a}. Bourn Moderator of the S^{d}

Meeting and after Prayer to God for his presence & Direction S[d] Church chose Joseph Cushing Jun[r] Clerk of S[d] Church during the prefent Vacancy.

Sarah Buck Daughter of Isaac Buck Iun[r] and Mary his wife was Baptised September y[e] 2[d] 1750 by M[r] Lewis.

Charles Tolman Son of Elisha and Miriam Tolman and James Gilkey Son of James and Grace Gilkey were Baptised September y[e] 9th 1750 by M[r] Niles.

Barker Cushing Son of M[r] John Cushing Iun[r] and Deborah his Wife and Bailey Randall Son of Perez and Sarah Randall and William Son of Sambo a free Negro and Martha his Wife an Jndian were all Baptised October y[e] 14th 1750 by M[r] Anger [Angier].

Joseph Tolman Son of Joseph and Mary Tolman was Baptised Oct[o] y[e] 28th 1750 by M[r] Nath[ll] Eells of Stonington

Abigail Eells Daughter of John and Abiah Eells was Baptised November y[e] 4th 1750 by M[r] Edward Eells.

Jra Bryant Son of Samuel Bryant Iun[r] and Mary his Wife was Baptised November y[e] 4th 1750 by M[r] Edw[d] Eells

Sarah Cushing Daughter of James Cushing Jun[r] & Mary his Wife was Baptised Novemb: y[e] 4th 1750 by M[r] Edw[d] Eells

Ruth Dammon, Joanna Dammon, and Leafa Dammon Daughters of Joseph and Joanna Dammon were Baptised November y[e] 4th 1750 by M[r] Edw[d] Eells of Middletown

Steel Foster Son of Cap[t] Joseph Foster and Abigail his Wife was Baptised Ianuary y[e] 6th 1750 by M[r] Gay

Thankful Eells Daughter of North Eells and Ruth his Wife was Baptised January y[e] 20th 1750 by M[r] Wales of marshfield.

Abigail Clap Daughter of Nathan[ll] Clap Esq[r] and Desire his Wife, was Baptized February y[e] 10th 1750/1 by M[r] Bourn.

Nathaniel Dammon Son of Zachariah Dammon Jun[r] and Anna Lenthal his Wife Was Baptized February y[e] 24th 1750/1 by M[r] Bafs.

Bethiah Turner Daughter of Abiel Turner and Elizabeth his Wife and George Stetson Son of George and Unice Stetson his wife and Lucy Brigs Daughter of James Briggs Jun[r] and Hannah his Wife and Mary Stetson Daughter of Gideon Stetson were all Baptized June y[e] 2[d] 1751 by M[r] Edward Eells of Middletown.

Iane Palmer Daughter of Joseph Palmer and Jane his Wife and James Cole Son of James Cole and Lucy Stodder Daughter of Benjamin Stodder Iun[r] were all Baptised June ye 2[d] 1751 by the Rev[d] M[r] Edward Eells of Middletown.

Nathaniel Cushing Son of Joseph Cushing Iun[r] and Lydia his Wife ——— and Seth Turner Son of Jonathan Turner & Abigail his Wife, and John Briggs Son of John Briggs and Abigail his wife and Lucy Bowker Daughter of John Bowker and Ann his Wife were all Baptised June y[e] 23[d] 1751 by the Rev[d] M[r] Gay.

James Briant Son of Peleg Briant and Mary his Wife and James Barrel Son of James Barrel and Deborah his Wife were both Baptised June y[e] 30th 1751 by M[r] Bourn.

[This concludes the baptisms of the "Rev. Nathaniel Eells book," so-called. The entries from the death of Rev. Mr. Eells were made, undoubtedly, by Joseph Cushing.]

RECORDS OF THE SECOND CHURCH OF SCITUATE, NOW THE FIRST UNITARIAN CHURCH OF NORWELL, MASS.

Communicated by WILFORD JACOB LITCHFIELD, M.S., of Southbridge, Mass.

A Catalogue of the Members of the second Church of Christ in Scituate, Nov^{r}: 13. 1751.*

Ioseph Cufhing: ye Deacon. Senr:
Elifabeth Curtice, ye Widow
Stephen Clap.
Temperance his Wife.
Abagail Collamore, ye Widow
Elifabeth Prouty, ye Widow
Elifabeth Turner, Widow
Sarah Pinchion,—Widow
Ann Stetfon, Wife to Mr Gerfhom S^{n}.
Miriam Curtice.
Mary Cufhing, Wife to Mr Iames Cufhing.
Elifabeth Tolman, Wife to Mr Benjamin Tolman.
George King, &
Deborah, his Wife.
Elifabeth Brooks.
Zachariah Damon, &
Mehetabel, his Wife.
Iames Briggs, &
Anna, his Wife.
Mary Brooks, Wife to Mr Nathl B.
Iohn James, Senr &
Samuel Stockbridge, Senr: &
Lidia his Wife.
Ierufha Church, wife to M^{r}: Nath. Iun^{r}
Eunice Sylvefter, wife to M^{r}: Elisha S.
Rachel Spooner, Widow.
Mary Barker, wife to M^{r}: Iames B.
Mary Cufhing, wife to Hon^{l}. Iohn C., Esq:
Margarett Collamore, wife to M^{r}: John.
North Eells, &
Ruth, his Wife.
Mary Sylvefter, wife to M^{r}: Zebulon S.
Temperance Fofter Wife to M^{r}: Elifha.
Ruth Perry.
Anna Lenthal Damon Wife to M^{r}: Zach.
Iofeph Copeland &
Elifabeth, his Wife.

* The following entries are from the third book of records called "The Church Book —Jonathan Darbys—1752." He was pastor until 1754, and was succeeded by Rev. David Barns, D.D.

Lidia, his Wife.
Timothy Symmes, &
Elifabeth, his Wife.
Benjamin Perry.
Rachel Turner.
Abigail Hobart.
Ifaac Otis &
Deborah, his Wife.
Defire Sylvefter.
Ifaac Buck
Ionna Ruggles, Wife to M[r]
Iohn Ruggles.
Elfe Benfon, Wife to M[r]
Jofeph Benfon.
Sarah Lambert, Wife to M[r]
Iames Lambert.
Iofeph Jacob, y[e] Deacon.
Mercy Turner, Widow.
Benjamin Curtice &
Rebecca, his Wife.
Abigail Turner, Wife to M[r]: W[m]: T.
Iemima Damon, Widow.
Lidia Simmons.
Ionah Stetfon &
Mercy, his Wife.
Ruth Perry.
Rebecca Prouty, Widow.
William Barrel &
Abigail, his Wife.
Iofeph Cufhing, Jun[r]: y[e]: Deacon
Margarett Turner.
Rachel Stetfon, Wife to M[r]: Sam[l]: S.
Nathan Pickles.
Richard Turner.
Benjamin Randal &
Sarah, his Wife.
Abigail Fofter, Wife of M[r]: Jof[h]: F.
Lufanna Turner, wife to M[r]: Hawkins T.
Iudah Dwelly, Widow.
Iofeph Dunham &
Iane, his Wife.
Iohn Iames, Iun[r] &
Prudence, his Wife.
Lidia Sylvefter, Wife to M[r]: Ioseph S.
Mary Barker, wife to M[r]: Barnabas, Sr:
Hannah Merit, wife to M[r]: David M.
Hannah Bowker, wife to M[r]: Iames B.
Iofeph Clap, &
Sarah, his wife.
Iofeph Damon &
Ioanna his Wife.
Iofeph Palmer &
Iane, his Wife.
Iemima Farrow, Wife to M[r]: Tho[s]: F.
Sarah Barker, Wife to M[r]: Barnabas, Jun[r]:
Sarah Stockbridge, Wife to M[r]: Samuel, Jun[r]:
Mary Neal, Wife to M[r]: John N.
William Sylvefter &
Mary his Wife.
Mary Buck, Wife to Isaac B., Jun[r]:
Prifcilla Hatch Wife to M[r]: Michael H.
Deborah Turner, Wife to M[r]: Ifrael T.
Edmond Grofs &
Olive, his Wife.
Mary Brooks, Wife to M[r]: Wm:
Hannah Stetfon, Wife to M[r]: Mathew S.
Mary Torry, Wife to M[r]: Caleb T.
Hannah Collamore, Wife to M[r]: Tho[s]:
Abigail Turner, Wife to M[r]: Jon[a]: T.
Iemima Prouty, Wife to M[r]: W[m]: P.
Ruth Randal, Widow.
Abigail Bowker, Wife to M[r]: Lazarus B.
Ifaac Damon &
Lidia, his Wife.
Benjamin Stoddard &
Mary his Wife.
Patience Iordan, Widow.
Cuba, a Servant to M[r]: Ifaac Turner.
Deborah Oakman, Wife to M[r]: Sam[l]: O.
Abiel Bryant, Wife to M[r]: Iohn B.
Mary Bryant, Wife to M[r]: Sam[l]: B.
Iael Whitton.
Hannah Turner, Wife to M[r]: Lemuel T.
Mary Northy, Wife to M[r]: Iames N.
Sarah Ruggles.
Abigail Bryant, Wife to M[r]: Benjamin B.
Mary Sampfon, Wife to M[r]: Charles S.

The Names of those Admitted into full-Communion

1752

April. 5. Mary, ye: Wife of Robert Damon.
May. 3. Iofhua Lincoln & Huldah his Wife.
June. 7. Gilbert Brooks.
Nov: 5. Iofeph Tolman & Mary his Wife.
Thomas Pinchion & Agatha his Wife.

1753.

June. 10. Oliver Winflows, difsmifion from ye: 1t. Chh: of Marfhfield, was read & he recieved.
Octo: 7. Hannah, ye. Wife of Mr: Wm: Stetfon.
15. The Honl: Iohn Cufhing Efqr: being in full Communion with ye: eftablifhed Chh: & defiring ye: ordinances of Chrifti-anity with us & ye: Privilidges of this Chh: his Request Was granted by a Unanimous Vote.
Novr: 4. Mrs: Mary Cufhing & Mr: Wm: Cufhing—the Children of Iudge Cufhing.
December ye 4th. 1754 Mr. David Barns's Dismifsion from the Chh in Littleton was Read & He Received into the 2d. Chh in Scituate.
Attest Joseph Cushing Junr. Clerk of Sd. Church During the Vacancy.
Octbr 5. 1755 John Ruggles, Jun.
Dcembr: 3: Elifabeth Wife to Mr Jofeph Toleman
Iannary 1756: Nehemiah Porter and his Wife. Prince Rofe
March: 7. John Cufhing Jun & Deborah his Wife
April: 4: Abiel Turner and Elifabeth his Wife
Grace ye Wife of Elifha Sylvefter
May 2: the wife of Deacon Cufhing & his Son Jofeph
Samll Clap Jun and his wife Lucy
Ruth Torry D. to Capt Torry
June 6. 1756 Nehemiah Hatch & Wife
The Widdow Hannah Bowker Lucy Bryant & Hannah Sparhawke
July 4. Elifha Tolman and his wife
Gilbert Brooks and Prifcilla Perry.
Novbr. 4 Elifabeth Curtice

The Names of those who are baptized.

1751

Nov: 17. Lucy, daughter to Cap: Iohn Iames jr:
Melzar & Mary, Children of Charles Sampfon.—By Revd: Mr: Bourn.
Decm:. 1. Deborah, daughter to Mr: Gerfhom Randal. Prudence, D. to Mr: Jofeph Stetfon. Iohn Son to Mr: Iohn Bryant. (This Child Was baptized ye: Sabbath before Viz. Novr: 24. ye: 1st: I baptized).
8. Mary, daughter to Mr: Elifha Fofter. by Revd: Mr: Bourn.

Friday. 20. all y[e]: Children of M[r]: Richard Turner in his houfe, he being Sick. Viz. Iemima, upon her defire. Iohn, Vine, Iofeph, Confider, & Ruth. (6)

1752

Jan[y]: 26. Sarah, daughter to Iob Neal.
Feb. 23. Iohn, Son to Barnabas Barker Iun[r]:
25. being Tuefday, Confider, son to Ion[a]: Elms, in his house it being Sick.
March. 8. Benjamin, Son to Benj[a]: Randal jun[r]:
29. Elijah, son to Sam[l]: Briant, &
Nathaniel, son to Nath[l]: Turner.
April. 5. William, son to Iofeph Copeland,
Thomas, son to Tho[s]: Farrar, &
Caleb, son to amos Damon.
12. Caleb, son to Iofeph Wade–William son to Will[m]: Brooks, & William son to M[r]: Will[m]: Merchant of Bofton.
26. Lebeus, son to Sambo, a free Negro.
May. 3. Ruth, daughter to Ifaac Stetfon.
May. 10. Mary, D. to Deacon Iofeph Iacob, &
Mary, D. to Robert Damon.
June. 7. Hannah, D. to Cap. Caleb Torey, &
Ionathan, Son to Lazarus Buker, [Bowker] &
Mary, D. to Ifaac Buck.
21. Elifha, son to Benj[a]: Buker. Iacob son to Iames Gilkey. Mary, D. to [omitted] Burrel. Deborah, D. to y[e]: Widow Ruth Turner.
Iuly. 5. Deborah, D. to Dea[n]: Iof[h]: Cufhing Iun[r]:
12. Iofeph, Abigail, & Peleg, Children of m[r]: Ifrael Smith. North, son to M[r]: North Eells.
Aug. 30. Abiel D to M[r]: Sam[l]: Stockbridge Iun[r]:
N. Stile begins — Simeon Son to M[r]: Dan[l]: Damon.
Sept. 24. David, S. to Widow Mary Clap, & David Clap Iun[r]: dec[d]:
Stephen, S. to Sam[l]: Clap & Lucy his Wife.
Oct[o]: 10. Tuefday. Simeon, S. to Tho[s]: & Agatha Pinchion at her Defire.
22. Zipporah, D. to M[r]: Barnabas Barker Sen[r]:
Celia, D. to Ifrael Sylvefter, by M[r]: Bourn.
Oct[o]: 29. Tho[s]: Pinchion Sen[r]: Tho[s]: Pinchion jun[r]:
Mary & Iudeth, Children of Tho[s]: Pinchion Sen[r]:
Enoch, Son to Sam[l]: Curtice.
Nov[r]: 5. Anna, D. to M[r]: Iohn Bowker.
Nov[r]: 12. Perfis, D. to M[r]: Ion[a]: Turner.
19. Elizabeth Hooper, AEt [omitted]:
Dec[r]: 3. Edward, Son to Iohn Cufhing Iun[r].

1753

Jan[y]: 14. Bethiah, D. to M[r]: Abiel Turner.
Feb. 18. Lydia, D. to M[r]: Iefse Turner.
Abigail, D. to M[r]: Iohn Briggs.
Elifha, Son to M[r]: Elifha Silvefter.
Feb. 25. Stephen, Son to M[r]: Zach[h]: Damon Jun[r]:

March 22. Huldah, D. to M^{r}. Iofhua Lincoln, apprehended near its end, Was baptized in their house.

April. 1. David, Son to M^{r}: William Prouty, & Iames, Son to M^{r}: Iames Briggs Iun^{r}:

15. Eunice, D. to Nathl: Clap, Esqr:

May. 13. Abigail (Smith) D. to y^{e}: Widow Rachel Spooner, & Elifabeth, D. to M^{r}: Ionah Stetfon Iun^{r}:

27. Marlborough, Son to M^{r}: W^{m}: Silvefter.

Iune. 3. Luke, Son to M^{r}: Luke Silvefter.

10. Edward, Son to Capt: Peleg Bryant.

July. 15. Thomas, Son to Capt Iohn Iames Iun^{r}:

Sarah, D. to Bazaleel Palmer, by M^{r}: Bourn.

16. Mark, son to Philis, Negro Servant of Deacon Iofeph Cufhing Iun^{r}:

29. Freeborn, Son to Sam^{ll}: Bow, a Negro Man, free.

Aug^{t}: 5. Mary, D. to Sam^{ll}: Randal & Sarah his Wife, Who own'd y^{e}: Covenant.

Deborah, D. to Iacob Silvefter, Who own^{d}: Covenant.

26. Ionathan, Son to Ion^{a}: & Lydia Tower.

Sept: 2. Damaris, D. to Nehemiah & Lettice Prouty.

23. Submit, D. to Thos: & Han^{h}: Collamore.

Molly, D. to M^{r}: Saml: & Mary Bryant.

30. David, Son to M^{r}: Robert & M^{rs}: Mary Damon.

Oct^{o}: 14. David, Son to M^{r}: Ifrael & M^{rs}: Deb: Turner.

William, Son to M^{r}: Iames & M^{rs}: Deb: Barrel.

21. Anna, D. to M^{r}: Luke & Ionna Bowker—y^{y}: own^{d}: Covenant.

28. Iofeph, Son to M^{r}: Oliver Winflow. By M^{r}: Bourn.

Simeon, Son to M^{r}: Thos: & M^{rs}: Agatha Pincheon.

Ebenezer, Son to M^{r}: Iof: & M^{rs}: Elif: Copeland.

Nov^{r}: 4. Iob, Son to M^{r}: Iob Neal.

18. Martha D. to M^{r}: Iof: & M^{rs}: Iane Palmer.

Dec^{r}: 2. Hannah, D. to M^{r}: Benj^{a}: & M^{rs}: Han^{h}: Randal.

9. Sarah, D. to M^{r}: Elifha & M^{rs}: Mer^{m}: Toleman. By M^{r}: Bourn.

1754.

Ian^{y}: 10. Molly, D. to Nathl: & Mary Mayo being sick, Was baptized at her defire & upon her account.

13. Ruth, D^{r}: to M^{r}: Elifha & Temperance Fofter.

20. Lidia D. to M^{r}: Nathl: Mayo, & Mary his wife upon her account.

Feb. 24. William, Son to M^{r}: W^{m}: Iones of Marfhfield, Who own'd y^{e}: Covenant.

March. 30. Ionathan, Son to M^{r}: Lazarus Bowker & Abigail his Wife, being dangeroufly ill.

April. 2. M^{r}: Ifaac Prouty AEt: 65, on his Death Bed.

7. Mary, D. to M^{r}: Barnbas Barker Iun^{r}:

The Rev^{d}. M^{r}. Dorby Departed this Life April ye 22^{d}. 1754 In the 28th. Year of His Age and in ye 3^{d}. Year of His Ministry.

At a Church Meeting of ye 2^{d}. Church of Christ in Scituate on ye 7th. Day of May A.D. 1754 being the first Chh. Meeting after the Death of the Rev^d^. M^r^. Dorby S^d^. Church Chose ye Rev^d^. Mr Bourn Moderator of S^d^. Meeting.

Also S^d^. Church Chose Joseph Cushing Iun^r^. Clerk of S^d^. Chh. during the present Vacancy

Baptized. 1754

April. 28th. Rebecca Curtis Daughter to Elisha and Sarah Curtis By ye Revd Mr Gay

May. 5th. Elisabeth Stetson Daughter to Isaac Stetson, By ye Rev^d^. M^r^. Perkins.

May. 19th. Betty Stodder Daughter to Benj^a^ Stodder Iun^r^. Martha Daughter to Thomas Farrow and Amos Dammon Son to Amos Dammon all by the Rev^d^. M^r^. Bourn.

May 26 Abigail Iacob Daughter to Dea^n^. Ioseph Iacob by the Rev^d^. M^r^. Smith

June y^e^. 2^d^. Desire Silvester Daughter to Nehemiah Silvester, Lucy Smith Daughter to Jsrael Smith. Lucinda Clap Daughter to Samuel Clap Iu^r^ Jsrael & Ruth Lappum Children of Thomas Lappum and Asher Son to Philis Slave to Doc^tr^ Otis all by the Rev^d^. M^r^. Wales

September ye 29th. 1754 Mehitabel Cole Daughter to James Cole and Ezekiel Sprague Son to Ezekiel & Priscilla Sprague. all by the Rev^d^ M^r^. Smith of Wey^o^. [Weymouth]

October ye 20th. 1754 Caleb Cushing Son to Dea^n^. Ioseph Cushing Iu^r^. Samuel Stetson Son to George Stetson and Samuel Randall Son to Samuel Randall all by the Rev^d^ M^r^. Nat^h^ Eells of Stonington.

October ye 27th. 1754. Ann Briggs Daughter to Iohn Briggs and Iohn Bowker Son to Iohn Bowker by the Rev^d^. M^r^. Edward Eells of Middletown.

David Barns [his autograph]

The names of those y^t^. were Baptized Since I was Ordained. Decem^br^. 4: 1754

Decr 15: David, Son of M^r^. Iesse Turner Chriſtopher, Son to Mr Sam^ll^. Curtice

1755

Feb. 8 Thomas Son to M^r^ E: Sylveſter

Feb: 16: Robert, Son to M^r^ I: Cuſhing
Lemuel Son to Mr Laz: Bowker

Feb 23 Martha Daughter to M^r^ A: Turner

March. 2 Rachel Daugh^tr^. to Nath: Clap Esq

March. 23 Elisabeth Daugh^r^ to Gerſh: Randal

April 6: James: Son to Caleb Tory

1755

Apr: 24 Ruth: D: to North Eells

May 18 Ceſar in Private by Reaſon of Sickneſs Sev^t^ [Servant to] John Elms

May 18 Rhoda D: to M^r^. Peleg Briant
Edward Son to Zec^h^. Damon
Joſeph Son to Ezra Randal.

May	25	Gilbert Son to W^{m}. Brooks
		Bathſhebah D to Luke Bowker
June	1	Eliſabeth : D : to Amos Damon
		Hannah : D : to W^{m}. Damon
June	8	Zine : D : to Sam^{ll}. Briant
Aug :	3 :	Benjamin Son to Joſh Lincoln
		Celia : D : to Jsrael Sylveſter
		Job Son to Nathl : turner.
		Lucy D : to James Cuſhing
Aug :	23 :	Abiah D : to John Briant
N : B :		Sarah D to Waterman Eells. this Day w : Eells & wife y^{r} confeſsion . . . . . . owned y^{e} cov^{t} and had y^{r} Child Babtized Sarah D : Nath Church
$Octb^{r}$:	5 : 1755/	
		Rebeckah D : to Joſeph Copeland
		$Nath^{l}$. Son to Na^{th} Broks [Brooks]
		Huldah D : to Bezelael Palmer
		Rachel : D : w^{m}. Brigs
$Octb^{r}$	26/	Lydia D : to Jonah Stetſon
		Anna D : to Job Neal
Nov^{br}	16/	Jonathan Son to $Nehe^{m}$ Prouty
Nov :	23/	Sarah : D ; Benja : Randal Ju
Dec^{br}	7/	Eliſabeth Wife to Joſeph toleman
		Charles Son to Israel Smith
Feb 1 :	1756	Ruth D : to $Jona^{th}$. turner
		Abigail D : to Ezek : Sprague
Feb/	8/	Joſeph Son to John Brigs
Feb	29/	Lydia D : to Deacon Cuſh [Cushing] :
		Sarah D : to Sam^{ll} Randal
May	16/	W^{m}. Haden & wife made confeſsion and owned y^{e} Cov^{t}. and with his Children 5 in Number w^{r} Baptized
May	16 :	Damſon D : to John Bowker
		Hannah D : to Jom [? John or James] Nicolſon
May	23 :	Mercy D : to a negro of Dr Otis
May	30/	John Son to Michael Hatch
		Marcy D : to Eliph : Nothe [Northy]
June	20 :	Nath : ſon to Nath Clap
		Johanna D : $thom^{s}$ Farrar
		Jemimah D : to Amos Damon
		Sarah Da : Benja. Collomore
		Mary *Ditto*
		Hannah *Ditto*
		Benja Son to S^{d} Collomore.
June	30/	Thomas Son to J^{n} Nicols
Sept :	19/	Betty Jones : D : to John Jones
		Barnabas Son to $B.^{ar}$ Barker

1757

Jan	16	Deborah D to Jsrael Turner
		Abigail D to Ezra Randal
March 20 :	1757	Nehemiah Son to Mr Nehemiah Porter
	26 :	Nabby : D : to Lazarus Bowker Baptized in private by Reaſon of Sickneſs

April : 3 : [blank] to Jonah Stetſon Jun
10 Barker Son to J^{n}: Cuſhing Jun
17 Sarah D to Widdow [blank] Palmer
24 Sam^{ll}: Son to Eliſha Tolman
Ezekiel son to Peter Collmore
24 John Son to Sam^{ll} Bryant :
24 : Orphan D. to ye Widdo Peterſon owned ye covenant & was Baptized
May 8 1757 Ezekiel Son of Isai. Stoddard
15 Eliſha Son to Lemuel Sylveſter
Lucy : D : to Isaac Damon
22 Sarah D : to John Homes
29 : Elijah Son to Joſeph Clap S^{r} [?]
Lydia D : to John Curtice
Abigail D : to M^{r} : Stephen Lapham
Priſce [Priscilla] : D to Jsaac Prouty.
Before Baptiſm ye same Day ye S^{d} Prouty and wife owned ye Covenant
June 19 1757 Allice : D : to Deacon Cuſhing Jun
July 3 Lydia D to Nath Brooks Jun
10 Barſtow Son to Capt. W^{m}. Sylveſter
Rhoda D : to Michael Hatch
17 : Rachel : D : to R^{d} David Barns and Rachel his wife
23 : Thomas, Sam^{ll}. Abel, Sons, to Simeon Naſh and Lydia his Daughter
31 Cynthia D : to Elijah Curtice
Aug 14 : Thomas Barker Son to M^{r}. James Brigs
21. Joſeph Son D^{cn}. Joſeph Jacob
28 : Unice : D : to Isaac Stetſon
Sept : 1757 Oliver Son of Oliver winſlow
Ceberry [Sebre] D : to John Brigs
Allice : D : to Israel Smith
Eliphalet Son to Eliph Nothe [Northy]
Octbr 2 1757 Martha D : to Peleg Bryant
9 Damaris D : to : Nehe^{m} : Prouty
Ruth : D : to Cornelius Brigs
16 Molly : D to Benj^{a} : Randall.
nov : 6 : Mary : D : to Math : Stetſon
Abigail D to [blank] Tore [Torrey]
Mercy : D : to Antony Eames
Hannah his wife His wife owned ye Cov : Bapt : on His account
Gidion Son to Gidion Roſe Jun brot out by her alone and Baptized on Her account
20 Gerſhom Son to Mr Nehemiah Sylveſter
Betty : D : to Benj^{a} Collmore Baptized on Her Account
Decb^{r} 4 : Ebenezer & Grace Totman owned ye Covenant and y^{r} children w^{h} [were] Baptized Thomas and Stephen
Charles Son to John Bowker
Jenny D : to Nath Mayhew Baptized on Her Account

RECORDS OF THE SECOND CHURCH OF SCITUATE, NOW THE FIRST UNITARIAN CHURCH OF NORWELL, MASS.

Communicated by WILFORD JACOB LITCHFIELD, M.S., of Southbridge, Mass.

May 15. 1791*		Clarriſsa & Lucinda twins Daughters to Sam^{ll}: Damon and Wife.
May	22	Lydia Daughter to Simeon Daman & wife
June	5	Clarriſsa D. to abiel Turner Junr. & wife
		Galen Clapp Son to Capt John James & wife
		Rebeckah in Private D. to Thos. Lapham Junr & wife
July	3	George & Ruth, Son and D. to Thos. Lapham Jun and wife
		Deſire Eells D. to Calvin Daman and Wife
		Elias Son to James Barrell Junr. And Wife
Augst	7:	Quintus Carolus. Son of Charles Turner Eſq^{r}. & Wife
		Lucinda D: to Elijah Turner and wife
Augst	14	Tryphine D to Thos. Sylveſter Junr. & Wife
Augst.	21	Sylveſter Son to Charles Tolman & wife
Augst	27	Joseph Son To Roland Turner and wife
Sept	7:	Thomas Son to Thos. Waterman and Wife
Jany 9 1792		Luſstanos. Son to Bryant Stephenſon & wife
Feb	14	Mary Collier[?] D to Galen Daman & Wife in private
Feb^{y}	20	Zacheriah adult in ye other Pariſh very Sick. His other name Naſh.
May	27	Charles, Son to Noah Meritt in private
June	3	Eliſha Son to Eliſha Young & wife
		Benj^{a} Turner Son to Benj^{a} Lane & wife
May	13	Horace Son to Capt Enoch Collmomore [*sic*] and wife
June	10	Experence D to Sam^{ll}. Randall and Wife
June	17	Hannah D to Capt John James and wife
June	24	Hannah D to Nath^{ll} Waterman and wife
July	1	Thirzby D to Joſhua Bryant Junr. & wife
		Betſy D. to Mathew Tore [Torrey] & Wife
		Chloe D to Benj^{a} Bowker Junr. and wife
July	15	Thomas Son to tho^{s}. Ruggles & wife
July	22	Sam^{ll}. Son to Charls Turner Eſq^{r}. & Wife.
July	29	Mary D to Sam^{ll}. Curtis & wife
		Leafe D to Joſeph Cuſhing & wife
		Harris Son to Gerſhom Bowker in Private
Sept	9	Lucy & Ruth Daughters to Willm Barrell and wife
Augst.	19	Samuel Son to Charles Turner Eſq^{r}. and wife
Sept.	16	Lydia, Betſy, Hannah, D^{s}: William Joſiah Levitt Sons to William James & wife.
		Polly D: to s^{d}. James & wife Baptized in private

* This entry begins what is left of the church baptisms of Rev. David Barnes—contained in loosely-sewed sheets, without covers, preserved at the Norwell Bank. There appears to be a hiatus in these records from 1757 to this entry. Rev. Dr. Barnes retired from the ministry in 1809, and was succeeded by Rev. Samuel Deane. Besides the baptisms, there are marriages, church admissions, dismissals, etc.

Sept 16 Elijah Stowers Son to Elijah Curtice Junr & wife
Lucy Cuſhing D. To Stephen Bowker & wife
Sept 23 Elijah Son to John Hatch and wife.
Sept 31 [*sic*] Calvin Son to Calvin Daman & wife
Artimiſsa: D to Jonathan Hatch Junr. and wife
Octob^{r}: 7 James Son to Jeſse Wright & wife
Juda Litchfield D. To Joſhua Daman & wife
Polly D: to Thos. Lapham Junr. and wife
Octo^{b}. 14 Eleanor Wife of Robert Northy.
Eleanor D: & James Son to Robert Northy and Wife
Nov^{b} 3 Joſeph Son to Sam^{ll}. Simmons & Wife
Nov^{b} 4 Mary Turner D. to Joſeph Tolman Junr & Wife
Decb^{r} Thankfull Wife to Sam^{ll}. Simons Adult
Peleg & Sam^{ll}. Sons to Sam^{ll}. Simons and wife
Jany 13 1793 Luther son to Luther Barrell and Wife
Feb 24 Benj^{a}. Hearſsy son to Braddock Jacobs and wife
May 5 Marcus Son to Sam^{ll}. Tolman & wife
John Son to Elijah Bowker and wife
June 2 Elijah Son to William Brooks Junr & wife
Augt 4. Clarriſsa D: to Joſeph Jacobs and Wife
Aug^{t}: 18. Lucy D. to Benj^{a} Lane and Wife
Sept 8. Anna D. to Eliſha Briggs and wife
Sept 22 Bettſy D: to Israel Turner & wife
Octo^{br} 6 Gorham Son to Joſeph Benſon & wife
Octob^{r}. 13 Betſey D. to Nath^{ll}. Cuſhing & wife
Novb^{r}. 24 Lucy D. to Joſeph Cuſhing and wife
Decm^{r}. 7 Abigail D to Gerſhom Bowker and wife in private
Feby 3 1794 Eliſha Son to David Clapp & wife in private
april 13. Lucy D. to Nath^{ll} Chittenden & Wife
Nancy D to Lemuel Jacobs & wife
May 22 Horrace Son to John James and wife
June 8 Hannah Tolmon D. to Charles Turner Eſq^{r}. & Wife
Eſther D to Charles Cole & wife
June 29 Alpheus Son to Micah Stetſon & wife
Augst. 24 Eſther D to Charles Cole and wife
Augſt. 31 Eldward [or Edward] son to Nath^{ll}. Cuſhing Junr. and wife
Sept 14. Benjamin son to Roland Turner and wife
Johannah D. to Eliſha Young and wife
Turner son to Jonat^{h}. Hatch Junr: and wife
Sept 28 Sam^{ll}. Stanly Son to Sam^{ll}. Bowker Negro and wife
Harriot, Stanly D^{r} to Prince Freeman Negro & wife
Octo^{br} 5 Nabby D: to Stephen Bowker and wife
Sam^{ll}. Litchfield Son to Simion Daman & wife
Betſey. D to Thos. Ruggles and wife
Nov^{br} 2. Fanny D to David Clapp and wife
Elijah Son to David Clapp and wife
Tryphoſy D to Thos. Sylveſter & wife
Decm^{br}. 7 Eliza. Bailey. Son to Elijah Turner Eſq^{r}. and wife
May 10 1795 Ruth Tillden D: to Calvin Daman & Wife
June 7 Son to Pickles Cuſhing Junr. and wife
Joſeph Copeland son to Sam^{ll}. Tolman & wife
June 14 Sarah Jacobs Daughter to Eliſha Briggs & wife
July 26 Loring Cuſhing son to Micah Lapham & wife

Augst	9:	Nabby Leavet D. to Luther Barrell & wife
Augst.	23	Affee[?] D: to Co^{ll}. Willm. Turner & wife
		Fanny D. to Benj^{a} Lane and wife
Sept	27	Theadore son to Charles Turner Efq^{r}. and wife
Octob^{r}.	4	John son to John Foſter Junr. & Wife
		Lydea D. to Braddock Jacobs and wife
Octo^{br}	18	Betſy. D to Gerſhom Ewell and wife
Octo^{br}.	25.	Charles. son to David Clapp and wife
Nov^{br}	1	Seth Stoddard Junr. and wife Owned the Covenant He was Baptized with two of y^{r}. Children Named Benjamin and Temperance
Nov^{br}.	8	Lucinda an adult D to Sylvanus Daman.
April 4 1796		Demick Bowker son to Galen Daman & wife in private
May	1	Joſiah son to Charles Briggs and wife
May	8	Joſhua Dauis son of Harris Turner and wife
May	20	Charles son to Stephen Totman & wife
May	29	Thomas son to Sam^{ll}: Simmons and wife
July	5.	Nabby an adult Wife to Ezra Dingley of Duxbury
Augst.	14	Lydia D. to Elijah Curtice & wife.
Augst.	14	Cloe Stowers D. to John Turner & wife
Augst.	21	Anna D. to Simeon Daman & wife
Augst.	28	Abiah Joice D to Thos Lapham Junr and wife
		Harriot D to Nath^{ll}. Chittenden & wife
Sept	4	Hannah an adult wife to Elijah Briggs
		James Buffinton son to Elijah Briggs & wife
		Eliſabeth Daughter to Elijah Briggs & wife
Sept	6.	Baptized the Children of Confider Merritt & wife in private they being Sick of ye Canker Raſh—Polly: D. Joce[?] D: Benjamin Son. Roxa[?] D: Confider son Joſeph son Priſsa D
Octo^{br}.	23.	Delight D to Elijah Bowker and wife
Nov^{br}.	13	Lydia Ford. D: to Micah Stetſon & wife
	20	Molly Dau^{tr}. to William James & wife
May 21 1797		Mary Rand. D: to Charles Turner Efq^{r}. & wife
July.	9.	Hannah Chandler Daug^{h} to Cha[n]dler Cole and Wife
		Anſon son to Jonth Hatch Junr. & wife
Octo^{br}:	8:	Ruth Turner D to Thos. Cuſhing & wife
		Ruth Thomas D to Picles Cuſhing & wife
Octo^{br}.	29	Lazerus Bowker, Son to Galen Daman & wife
		Bethyah Woodard: D to Willm Gallon[?] Junr & wife
		Stephen. Son to Joſeph Cuſhing & wife.
Nov^{br}.	2	Debbe Cuſhing D. to John Naſh & Wife in private
Nov^{br}.	5.	Samuel Oakman son to Thos. Ruggles & wife
Nov^{br}.	12.	William son to Charles Lapham & Wife
		Lucy D: to Nath^{ll} Winſlow Junr. & wife
Nov^{br}.	19	Sarah Turner D. to Benj^{a} Turner Lane & wife
Jany 11 1798.		Nathan Son to William Brooks and wife in private
April.	28.	Turner. Son to Sam^{ll}. Tolman and wife in private
May	19:	Sarah D to Eben^{r}: Copeland & wife
July	1.	Noah Son to Joſhua Bryant and wife
		Deborah Richmond: D to Perez Jacobs and wife
July	8	Sam^{ll}. Weſt son to Nath^{ll}. Cuſhing and wife
		Gracy D to James Torry & wife

July	22	Lucy Daughter to John James and wife
Aug[st]	5	James Newton Son to James Sparrell and wife
Aug[st].	5.	Hannah Waterman. D to Jofhua Jacobs Jun[r]. and wife
Sep[t]	30	Fanny D to Luther Barrel and wife
Octo[br].	7	Juda Hatch D to Harris Turner & wife
June 16	1799	Lucy Sylvefter D to John Ewell and wife
		Mary D to Elijah Curtice & wife
June	30	James Son to Thomas Southward & wife
July	7	Elifha son to Micah Stetson and wife
Sep[t]	1	Joanna & Hannah Daughters to Braddock Jacobs & wife
		Sarah Stockbridge D to Perez Turner & wife
Sept	29	Joanna Turner. D to Capt Benj[a] Lane and wife
Octo[br].	6:	Francis Son Col[l]. Charles Turner and wife
		Charles son to Charles Cole and wife
		Abiel son to Roland Turner and wife
		Mary D to Nath[ll] Winflow Jun[r]. & wife
		Charlotte D to Charles Lapham & wife.
Octo[br].	13	James So[n] to John Fofter Jun[r] & wife
Octo[br]	20	John son to John Nafh and wife
		Hannah Stowel D to Elifha Briggs and wife
		Sally D to Robert Northy and wife
Nov[br].	3	Howard son to Galen Daman and wife

RECORDS OF THE SECOND CHURCH OF SCITUATE, NOW THE FIRST UNITARIAN CHURCH OF NORWELL, MASS.

Communicated by WILFORD JACOB LITCHFIELD, M.S., of Southbridge, Mass.

[The following records, on four loose sheets badly worn and broken, were found in Norwell since the appearance of the instalment on pages 271–274, *ante*, and belong to the pastorate of Rev. David Barnes.] *

(Sheet No. 1, one side)

A Liſt of thoſe who Joined to the C^{hh} in 1786

July 21	1786	Elijah Whitman was received to Communion with the Church
July 6	1788	Charles Turner Junr.
Augst 3	1788	Eunice The Wife of Nath^{ll} Jordan
Octo^{br} 5	1788	Hannah Otis Daughter of Dr Otis
Octob^{r} 4	1789	Joſhua Clapp was admitted
May 2	1790	Nath^{ll} Winſlow and wife were admitted
Augst 7	1791	Hannah Turner wife to Charles Turner Eſq^{r}
Sep^{t} 4	1791	Thos Jenkins and wife were admitted to Communion
Nov^{br} 6	1791	Abiel Turner Junr
July 1	1792	Betſy Otis was admitted
Sept 2	1792	Foſter Waterman W^{r} And the widdow Sarah Neal
Sept 1	1793	The Wife of Luther Barrell belonging to The firſt Chh in Hingham beng diſmiſsed from y^{t} C^{hh} and recommended was received into this C^{hh}
		Elijah Whitman was diſmiſsed and recommended to ye firſt C^{hh} in Pembroke
June 1	1794	Polly Turner Daughter to Hon^{bl} Charles Turner was admitted to full communion
Sep^{t} 28		Mrs Hannah Stone wife to the Revd Mr Stone of Yarmouth
June 7	1795	Bethiah Winſlow of Scituate was admitted
July 5		Hannah Tolman
Auguſt: 2		John Briggs
Octob^{r} 4		The Wife of John Foſter Junr
Nov^{br} 5;	1797	Nath^{ll} Winſlow Junr and Wife
May 6	1798	Eben^{r} Copeland & Wife
		Hannah Copeland

*pp. 404-407, this volume.

June 3 — Sally Southworth wife to Thos Southworth
Cloe Sylveſter

July 1: — Joſhua Bryant and wife
Nabby Cuſhing Daughter to Nathaniel Cuſhing
Ruth Cuſhing wife to Pickles Cuſhing
Sally Turner
Lucy Sylveſter

(Sheet No. 1, other side.)

Augt 5 1798 — Joſhua Jacobs Junr And Wife
James Sparrel and wife
Deborah Waterman Junr was baptized and rec^{d} into ye C^{hh}
Bathſheba Houſe was alſo admitted

Nov^{br} 4 — Deborah Waterman

July 1799 — Polly Simons was admitted to communion

Octo^{br} 5 1800 — Samuel Waterman was admitted to communion

May 3 1801 — John Foſter admitted to communion

Sept. 6 — Thos Cuſhing & Wife

Octob^{r} 4 — William Barrel

Sept 4 1803 — John Hatch and his wife

Nov^{br} 11 — The Wife of Deacon John Ruggles

May 12 1805 — Ruth, the wife of Deacon Eliſh James
Mary The Wife John Foſter Senr
Ruſha Tower, D to Mathew Tower
Bathſheba Jones

June 2 — Baſhua Tower wife to Mathew Tower

May 4 1806 — John Jones was received into Communion

July 6 1806 — James Curtiſs Junr & Wife
The Widdow Prudence Turner
Emelia Sprague, Cynthia Nicols

July 27 — At a meeting of the Church regularly Notified The C^{hh} made choice of Thos Cuſhing for a Deacon. He accepted ye Office

May 10 1807 — Nabby Foſter wife to Capt Seth Foſter
Eunice Torry Daug^{ter} to James Torry

June 7 — James Barril

Sept 6 — Hitte Curtice wife To Sam^{ll} Curtice was received into the C^{hh} tho' not preſent She being confined by ſickneſs
The same day Hitte Curtice Junr and Sophia Curtice Daughters of Sam^{ll} Curtice w^{r} Admitted to communion

(Sheet No. 2, one side.)

Deaths for the Year 1786.

Jany 1786 — Abraham a Negro Aged about 70 of Old age The Palſy and the relicks of the Omerial Diſeaſe

Jany 29 1786 — The Widdow Anna Soper aged about 60, of a Motification

March 28 1786 — Paul Curtice, Etat: 19: Suddenly by the overſetting of a loaded Carte

May 2 — —— Elms aged 9, of a Nervous Fever in the begin[n]ing which ended in a Conſumption

May 10 — Jemima Hatch aged 70 of a Dropſie

May 30 — An infant belonging to Elijah Turner & wife w^h lived a few momints
June 8 — Capt Benj^a Randall aged 62 of a Mortification as was fupposed in his Bowells
June 27 — An infant belonging to Elifha Young and wife Aged about 3 Months of Convulfion fits
July 17 — The wife of Jofhua Clapp Aged [*blank*] of a Confumption
[*torn*]ug^st 9 — The Widdow Stockbridge Aged 78 of a Complication of diforders
[*torn*]tob^r — The Widdow Perry aged 61 of a complication of diforders
[*torn*]cem^br 15 — Elifha Fofter's Daughter aged 4^rs of a Difsentery
[*torn*]n^y 2 — Dr Ephraim Otis's Son aged 3 ^yrs of a Quinfy
[*worn*]an^y 13 — John Stetson aged 92 of old age
Feby 19 — Mercy Turner Widdow aged 83 of old age
March — A Child of Nath^ll Brooks Junr aged 18 month of a Confumption
March — Mercy Clapp Aged [*blank*] of a billious Cholick
April — The widdow Hannah Hatch aged 78 of old age
Aug^st 31 — Hannah Collmore wife to Benj^a Collmore aged 64, of a billious Diforder
Octo^br 17 — A Child of Calvin Daman and Wife aged 7 months of the Canker
Octo^br 18 — Lazarus Bowkers Junr wife aged 41 of a Canker Fever
Octo^br 23 — An Infant of Nath Jordan and Wife 14 Day old Diforder Unknown
Decmb^r 16 — Hannah Vinal aged 84 of old age
[*worn*]an^y 7 1788 —— Cole Wife to James Cole aged 68 of a billious diforder
[*worn*]eb^y/5 — A Daughter of Dea^n James aged 6^yrs of a billious diforder & [*worn*]
[*torn*]^y 6 — —— Stoddard wife to Benj^a Stoddard aged 72 of a [*worn*]
[*torn*] — a child of Thos Church Junr aged half an hour [*worn*]
[*torn*] — Jacob Vinal aged 88 of old age [*worn*]
[*torn*] — [B]arrell Daughter to James Barrell aged 26 of a [*worn*] of [*worn*]

(Sheet No. 2, other side.)

Feby 7 1794 — Revd Nathan Stone of Yarmouth & Mifs Hannah Clapp, Scituate
March 6 — Jofhua Herfy Junr of Hingham & Lucy Jacobs, Scituate
Nathan Hunt of Quincy & Polly Turner of Scituate
May 18 — Lazarus Bowker and Sarah Turner both of Scituate
July 6 — Bartlett Barrell & Relief Nafh both of Scituate
July 9 — Thomas Ford of Duxborough & Hannah Church of Scituate
Sep^t 1 — Sam^ll Lewis of Falmouth and Nabby Turner Tolman, Scituate
Nov^br 26 — Edmond Whitemore & Jane Cortherill both of Scituate
Jany 1 1795 — John Turner and Cloa Clapp both of Scituate
March 22 — Abijah Otis & Mary Turner both of Scituate
May 28 — Fruitfull Sylvefter & Patty Clapp Negroes both of Scituate
June 7 — David Whitcomb [in pencil] of Cohafset and Prudence Dorithy of Scituate

June 18 Charles Lapham & Temperance Clapp both of Scituate
Aug[st] 4 David Prouty and Lydia Stoddard both of Scituate [*worn*]
Sept 30 1795 Paul Otis and Lucy Bailey both of Scituate
Octob[r] 4 1795 John Cudworth Jun[r] & Patty Litchfield both of Scit[*worn*]
Nov[br] 29 Thomas Cufhing and Ruth Turner both of Scituate
Charles Whiting Cufhing of Hingham & Deborah Jacobs of Scituate
December 2 1795 Elijah Randal and Ruth Woodward both of Scituate
January 1 1796 Nath[ll] Stevens of Marfhfield and Lydia Church of Scituate
March 27 Confider Howland of Marfhfield and Ruth Church of Scituate
Octo:[br] 26 Cato Negro man of scituate & Joanna Negro woman refident in Scituate
[*worn*][br] 13 Willam Cufhing of Pembroke & Ruth Briggs of Scituate
[*worn*] Nath[ll] Tnrner and Rachell Turner both of Scitua[*worn*]
[*worn*] Ebenezer Copeland & Sarah Waterman both of Scituate
[*worn*]is Whiting of Hingham & Abigail Bowker of Scituate
[*worn*] Nafh and Debby Cufhing both of Scituate
[*worn*] Keen of Marfhfield & Sufannah Church of Scit[*worn*]

(Sheet No. 3, one side.)

Decem[ber] 20 1787 M[r] Jonathan Cufhing of Hingham & Mifs Sarah Simmons [*worn*] Scituate.
March [*worn*] (20?) 1788 Perez Jacobs of Hanover & Relief Bowker Scituate
March 25 Elijah Bowker & Anna Sylvefter both of Scituate
April 17 Bela Mann of Hanover & Anne Bryant of Scituate
May 24 Wil[m] Jackfon of Plymouth & Nancy Barnes of Scituate
June 8 John James and Patience Clapp both of Scituate
Dcemb[b] 25 Samuel Sprague and Lydia Mayhew, ditto
April 9 1789. Cap[t] James Shaw of Abington and the Widdow Mary Turner of Scituate
April 9 Sam[ll] McChane of briftol in the County of Lincoln & Phebe Cudworth in y[e] County of plymouth
April 30 Stephen Bowker and Lucy Cufhing both of Scituate [*torn*]
June 12 Benj[a] Hayden of Scituate & Ruth Lincoln of Cohafset
Sept 21 Charles Turner Ju[r] Efquire & Hannah Jacobs both of Sci[*worn*]
Octob[r] 14. Elifh Grofs and Deborah Sylvefter both of Scitu[*worn*]
Nov[br] 19 M[r] Jofiah Cotton of Plymouth Clerk of the Court, To Rachell Barnes of Scituate
Nov[br] 26. Tho[s] Waterman and Sally Winflow b[*worn*] of Scituate
Decem[br] 17. Calvin Damon and Mercy Eelles both of Scituate
March 11 1790 Mical Clapp and Eunice Sylvefter bot[*worn*] of Scituate
[Dates of the following are worn off]
Sam[ll] Griffin of Fitswilliam and Hannah Bowker of Scitua[*worn*]
Jofeph Cufhing and Defire Bowker of Scitu[*worn*]
Elijah Lewis of Hingham & Sarah Stockbridge of Scit[*worn*]
[*worn*][ll] Tylden of Marfhfield and Peggy Fofter of Scit[*worn*]
[*worn*] Turner Lane and Lucy Stetson both of Scituate
[*worn*] Daman of Scituate to Hannah Dam[*worn*]

(Sheet No. 3, other side.)

[*worn*]an^{y} 27 1791	Benjamin Brooker [or Brookes] of Roxbury and Harriot Grandifon of Scituate
April 27	James Ewell of Marfhfield & Elifabeth Crague of Scituate
May 22	Gad Levet of Pembroke and Huldah Perry of Scituate
June 2 (?) 1791	Bille Corlew And Sarah Bourn both of Scituate
June 30 1791	Benjamin Bowker Junr and Cloa Stetson both of Scituate
Octob^{r} 2 (?)	Elifha Briggs and Abigail Fofter both of Scituate
Octob^{r} 13	Elijah Sylvefter of Hanover & Elifabeth Briggs of Scituate
Nov^{br} 17	Paul Otis & Penelopie Nichols both of Scituate
	John Cafwell & Chriftiana Perry of Hanover.
Nov^{vr} 24	Jefse Curtis of Hanover & the widdow Lucy Morton of Scituate
Nov^{br} 21	Abner Crooker of Marfhfield & Deborah Stutson, Scituate
[*torn*] Decem^{br} 22	Thatcher Tilden of Marf[h]field & Lucy Turner of Scituate
Decem^{br} 25	Amos Litchfield and Afenath Stockbridge both of Scituate
[*torn*]an^{y} 1 1792.	Jofeph Gannett & Ruth Gannett both of Scituate
Jany 19 1792	Pickles Cufhing & Ruth Cufhing both of Scituate
Feby 5 1792	Jofeph Battles and Sarah Turner both of Scituate
March 9 1792	Nath^{ll} Eelles & Elifabeth Randall both of Scituate

Carried to the Town Clerk.

April 3. 1792	Sam^{ll} Fofter of Kingfton and Mary Otis, Scituate
June 10	Caleb Torry & Sufannah Litchfield both of Scituate
June 17 : 1792	Capt: Willm Church and the Widdow Jael Henderfon both of Scituate
[*torn*]gst 12	Ward Jackfon & Lucy Nafh both of Scituate
Octo^{br} 22	Pollicarpus Jacobs & Lydia Clapp both of Bofton
Octo^{br} 25	Thos Carlow of Springfield & Abigail Carlow of Scituate
Octo^{br} 28	Elifha Turner & Lydia Briggs both of Scituate
Nov^{br} 4	Hawke Cufhing and Abigail Clapp both of [*torn*]
[*worn*]^{br} 8	Seth Stoddard and Martha Stockbridge both of [*worn*]
[*worn*]^{br} 24	James Wright and Lucy Brown both of Scituate
[*worn*] 1793	Isaac Thomas of Marfhfield, & Temperance Turn[*worn*]
	Simion Litchfield and Lucy Hatch Both of Sci[*worn*]
[*worn*] 13	Henry Joflyn of Pembroke and Lou[*worn*]
[*worn*]	Micah Lapham and Sarah Cufhin[*worn*]
[*worn*]	Zacheus Lambart & Zipporah Cu[*worn*]
[*worn*]	Samuel Donnely (?) [*the rest indistinct*]

(Sheet No. 4, written only on one side.)

[No year date appears]

[*worn*]arch 10	Sarah Fofter wife of John Fofter aged 46 of a Confumption
	Afhur Spragues wife Aged 43 Diforder unknown
June 1	Nath^{ll} Eells wife aged 39 of a putrid fever
	A Child of Willm Studly and Wife aged one Yea[r] of a Confumption
July	The widow Damon aged 52 of a Languifhment
July	The wife of Hawke Cufhing aged 41 of a Confumption

Octob 1 — The Widdow Standley Aged 83 of old age
Octob^{r} 30 — The Wife of James Colman aged 49 of a Dropſy

[The following records are a continuation of those appearing on pages 271–274, *ante.*]

Jany 5 1800 — Elizabeth D to Sam^{ll} Tolman and wife in private
July 13 — Mary D to Joſhua Jacobs Ju^{r} & wife
Sept 14 — Eliza D to John Ewell and wife
14 — Sarah Cuſhing D to Sam^{ll} Waterman and Wife
21 — Margaret D to Willm Gallow and Wife in private
Octob^{r} 26 — Caroline D to Thomas Cuſhing & wife
Lydia D to Micah Lapham and Wife
Hannah Cuſhing D to Perez Turner & Wife
Nov^{br} 2 — Charlotte Appleton D to Sam^{ll} Kent and Wife
Hannah wife to Sam^{ll} Kent at ye same time
John Son to Nath^{ll} Cuſhing and Wife
Decm^{r} — Mary D to Pickles Cuſhing Junr & wife in private

---

RECORDS OF THE SECOND CHURCH OF SCITUATE, NOW THE FIRST UNITARIAN CHURCH OF NORWELL, MASS.

Communicated by Wilford Jacob Litchfield, M.S., of Southbridge, Mass.

April 26 1801 — Matilda D to Charles Turner Eſq^{r} and wife
May 3 — Amaſa son to Harris Turner and wife
May 10 — Maryann D to Walter Jacobs & wife
May 31 — Paul son to Elijah Curtice & Wife
Auguſt 9 — John son to John Ewell and wife
October 18 — Sarah Smith D to Eliſha Briggs & wife
Charlott D to Elijah Bowker & wife
Caroline D to Warren Bowker & wife
Octo^{br} 25 — { Enoch son to James Cole and wife / Mary Clapp D to James Cole and wife } twins
Nov^{br} 1 — Caroline D to Seth Foſter and Wife their first child.
Charlotte Curtiſs D to Nath^{ll} Winſlow & wife
Decemb^{r} 13 — Deborah Clapp D to Thos Briggs and wife ——
April 5, 1802 — Mary Perry Church adult in private Sick
May 2 — Joſhua Son to Capt Joſhua Jacobs Junr & wife
Damſon D. to —— Simonds & wife
June 27 — John King son to John Nash and wife
Hannah williams Da to Sam^{ll} Kent & wife

June 30	Abigail Daughter Thomas Lapham Jun[r]
Aug[st] 1	Maria D. To Capt Benj[a] Lane and wife
	Elifabeth wife to Ebenezer Osborn
	Ebenezer son to Ebenezer Osborn & wife
Augft 8	Hannah Schiverick D. To Nath[ll] Eelles Jun[r] & wife
Aug[st] 29.	Betfy Turner D. to Walter Jacobs & wife
Sept 5	Afa Delano son to Afa Waterman & wife
October 3,	Peter Thatcher son, Lucy Turner, Daughter Atherton Wales, son, Henry, son, Children of Thatcher Tilden and wife
May 30 1803	Lucy Sylvefter in private near her end
June 5.	Michal D. and John son—twins of John Collamore & wife
July 10	John Turner son to Sam[ll] [" James " careted in another hand] Sparrell and wife
Aug[st] 7	Alfred Brunfon son to Capt Seth Fofter and wife
	Matilda D. to Jofeph Cufhing and wife
October. 9	Betfy. D. to Thatcher Tilden and wife
Octob[r] 16	R D. to Elijah Bowker and wife
	Mary D to Pickles Cufhing Jun[r] and wife
Octo[br] 23	Thomas son to John Jones and wife
	Julia D. to Col Charles Turner & wife.
Octo[br] 30	[blank] Turner D. to Jonathan Hatch Jun[r] & wife
	Unice Whiting D to Harris Turner ——
October 25	in private Hannah Totman. D. to Stephen Totman adult being very Sick
April 22 1804	Edmond son to Warren Bowker & wife
May 20	Sarah [over " Mary," crossed out] south worth D. to John Fofter Jun[r] and wife
	Mary Elifabeth D to Will[am] Delano & wife
	Mary Stockbridge D. to Elnanathan [*sic*] Cufhing & wife
June 3	Thophilus son to Capt Jofhua Jacobs Jun[r] & wife
	Mary D. to Sam[ll] Simons and wife
June 24	Charles Henry son to Charles Lapham & wife
July 1	George son to Benj[a] Lane and wife
	Nath[ll] Cufhing son to John Nafh and wife
July 15	Calvin son & Sufannah D to Galen Daman & wife
Aug[st] 5	Nancy D to Charles Cole & wife
Sept 2	Eliza D to Eben[r] Ofborn & wife
Sept 23	Luther Albert Son to Luther Tilden & wife
	Mary Turner D to James Torry Jun[r] & wife
Sept 30.	Huldah D. Ebenezer Copland and Wife
	Joseph and Charles Sons to Major John James and wife
	Jane, Daugter William Corlew in private
Octo[br]	William Hart Son to William Delano and wife
	Dolly [over " Mary," crossed out] D. to Joseph Stockbridge & wife.
Nov[br] 4	Rufus Litchfield adult Rufus son to Rufus Litchfield and wife
March 20 1805	Jerufha Gay D to Elnathan Cufhing & wife
May 12	Charlotte Cushing D. to Sam[ll] Waterman & wife
	Almira D to Major John James & wife

William, son Coll Charles Turner & wife
David Jacob son to Nath^{ll} Cuſhing & wife
Temperance Freeman D. to Timothy Foſter & wife
James Otis Son, James Curtis and wife
June 2 Amelia adult, Daughter to Aſhur Sprague
June 30. Henry Turner son to Thos Ruggles and wife
Augst 4 Luther Turner and his child named Lucy
Elvira D to Demick Bowker & wife
Octo^{br} 13 1805 John Son to Joſeph Cuſhing & wife
Nov^{br} 3 Edward Son to Foſter Jacobs & wife
Lucy Clapp, Daughter to the same
Mary D. to Wm Whiting of Hanover
Decemb^{r} 8 Harriot D to Pickles Cuſhing & wife
John Son to Jonath Hatch & wife
June 15 1806 Eliſha Heyden adult at ye same time
Eliſha son to Eliſha Heyden & wife
June 29 Ame Cuſhing D to Capt. Joſhua Jacobs Junr & wife
July 6 Hannah Wife to Warren Sylveſter & their child Almira
Phebe Cuſhing D to James Curtiſs & wife
In private Catherine Sylveſter a black woman
Augst 3: Eliſha son to Eliſha Foſter Junr & wife
Prudence Clark D. to Willm Delano & wife
Augst 14 Temperance Cuſhing D. of Sylvanus Daman an adult.
October 5 Melzar Stoddard son to Luther Turner formerly of Pembroke
Nov^{br} 9 Nathan son To Capt^{t} Thos Southard & wife
Nov^{br} 26 Mary Daughter To Rufus Litchfield and wife
May 10 1807. William, Son to Harris Turner & wife, lately moved to Townſend
Julia D to Luther Tilden & wife
May 24 William son to Timothy Foſter & wife
July 5 Joſiah son to Thomas Cuſhing & wife
Octob^{r} 11 Deborah D to Eliſha Heyden & wife
Zilpah Turner to Nath^{ll} Eells & wife
Prudence Clark D to Willm Delano & wife
Charles Warren son to Warren Sylvester & wife
Nov^{br} 1 Edward Bartlett son to Thacher Tilden and wife
David William son to Amiel Studly & wife
Rachel Wife to Bayley Jenkens
Thomas Bailey & William Woodward sons to Bailey Jenkens & wife
George Anſon Son to Anſon Robbins & wife
Temperance D to Micah Lapham & wife
Nov^{br} 8 Francis. D. To Sam^{ll} Waterman & wife
Nov^{br} 15 Julia D: to Pickles Cuſhing & wife
Decm^{br} 23 Mary Stetson & Eliza Stutson both adults in private on account o Sickneſs.
Jany 24 1808 Harriette D to Seth Foſter and wife
April 24 Grace Turner ["Barstow," written above "Turner"] D to Eliſh Foſter & wife
Thomas son to Thos Southward & wife
May 1 Eliza Daughter Major John James & wife

June 5 Rachel Wife to Perkins Clapp
Rachel D to perkins Clapp and wife
Sam^{ll} son to perkins Clapp & wife
June 4 a Child belonging Prince & wife in private on account of Sicknefs
July 3 Hannah D To Jofiah Stoddard and wife
Augst 8 Bela Tower son to Jofhua Jacobs Ju^{r}
Augst 2 Frederick son to James Curtice & wife
Augst 14 Jofeph Warren son to Elifha Brigs & wife
Sept 2 [?] Lucy D to Allen Clapp & wife
Octo^{br} Anna Eliza D to [blank] Turner & wife.
Eunic D to David Bowker & wife
Nov^{br} 13 Betfey D to James Sparrel & wife
March 5 1809 Harriot D to Allen Clap & wife
June 4 Nath^{ll} son to Nathaneel Eells & wife
Jane Daughter to Nath^{ll} Cufhing Junr & wife
July 2 Benj^{a} Hatch Tower to Sam^{ll} Eells and wife
Lufannah Ruggles D to George Hatch & wife
July 9 Eliza D to John Nafh and wife
Harrifon son to Dea^{n} Thomas Cufhing & wife
July 16 Polly Da to Elifha Tolman and wife
Sarah D to Capt Southward & wife in private
Sarah D to Luther Tilden and wife
Augst 6 Walter son to Anson Rollins [? Robbins] & wife
Aug 13 Francis son to Timo^{t} Fofter & wife
Sept 19 Anna D to Jofeph Cufhing & wife
Sept 5 Charles son James Curtice & wife
Mary D to Luther Tilden & wife
Septr Francis son of John Ewell & Wife
Novr 5 Elisha Son of Foster Jacobs & Wife
William Son of William Studley & Wife
William Son of Elisha Hayden & Wife
Nov^{br} 1 1807 Widdow Rhoda Ford Lucy Ford & Rhoda Ford Junr Nabby Barker James Curtifs were addmitted members of the chh
July 3 1808 The wife of George Torry admitted
Nov^{br} 13 Jofeph Turner & Franie Cufuhing [*sic*] admitted
April 2 John Nafh and wife were admitted

Deaths for the Year 1799

February 7 1799 The Widdow Elms Ætat. 68 of a complication of diforders
May Lucy Sylvefter of a confumption
A child of David Prouty
another of Benj^{a} Bailey
John Hatches wife of a confumption
October 7 1803 The C^{hh} difmifsed the Revd Charles Turner and recommended him to the c^{hh} of Chrift in Turner [Maine, probably].
Octob^{r} 16 1803 The c^{hh} difmifsed the wife of Luther Barrell and recommended her to the c^{hh} of Chrift in Afhburnham

[This completes the book of Rev. David Barnes.]

RECORDS OF THE SECOND CHURCH OF SCITUATE, NOW THE FIRST UNITARIAN CHURCH OF NORWELL, MASS.

Communicated by WILFORD JACOB LITCHFIELD, M.S., of Southbridge, Mass.

CHURCH MEMBERS AND ADMISSIONS.*
1810–1850.

WHEN I came into the ministry in Scituate, there appeared to be a loss of a part of the Church records, during the ministry of my venerable predecessor Dr. Barnes. I was, therefore, unable to ascertain the names of the Church members then living, except by enquiry. In this manner the following list was collected, of the names of the members of the 2d Cong. Chh. in Scituate liveing in Feb. 1810. SAMUEL DEANE.

* From the Church Book of Rev. Samuel Deane, pages 70–77 inclusive. The Baptisms in the first part of this book will appear later in the REGISTER.

This is undoubtedly imperfect and does not pretend to chronological arrangement.
REV. DAVID BARNES, D.D., Sen. Pastor.

Hon. William Cushing
M[rs] Hannah his wife
Hon. Nathan Cushing
M[rs] Abigail his wife
Dea. Elisha James
Ruth, his wife
Dea. Thomas Cushing
Ruth his wife
Hon. Charles Turner J[r].
Hannah his wife
John Foster Sen.
Mary his wife
Dea. John Ruggles
William Briggs
M[rs] Eliz[th] his wife
Wid Rhoda Ford
Rhoda Ford J[r]
Samuel Waterman
Sally his wife
M[rs] Bathsua Town (of Matther)
Charles Tolman Sen.
Mrs Mary his wife
Wid Experience Stetson
Naby Foster (wife of Cap. Seth)
Thomas Ruggles
Nabby Barker. dis.
William James Sen.
Mary his wife
Sally Young
Wid. Marcy Turner (Israel)
Wid. Ruth Jenkins
Caleb Torrey Sen.
Rev. W[m] Torrey
Mary Cushing (wid. of John)
John Jones Sen.
Hannah Brooks (wife Simeon)
Bathsheba Daman (wife Melzar)
Joseph Jacob.
Hannah, his wife
Huldah Church (wife of Thomas)
Sarah Bowker (wife Lazarus)
Eunice Torrey (wife of James)
Nathaniel Winslow
M[rs] Sarah his wife
M[rs] Sarah Winslow (wid. of Maj.)
Cap. Joshua Jacob.
Hannah his wife.
Bathsheba House.
Jerusha Eells (wife Sam[l])
Miss Emily Sprague.
Miss Cynthia Nichols.
Miss Eunice Torrey
Thankful Torrey (wife Geo)
Col. John Jacob.
Lucy Copeland (wife of W[m] Jr)
Nabby wife of J[n] Foster J[r]
Abigail Otis (wife of D[r]. C. O.)
Miss Frances Cushing.
Miss Betsey James
Thomas Lapham Sen.
Abiah his wife
Hette Curtis (wife of Sam[l])
Miss Sophia Curtis
Miss Hette Curtis
James Barrell Sen.
M[rs] Mary his wife
Wid. Zeporah Randall
James Turner
Wid. Lucy Briggs
Miss Betsey Otis
John Nash
Deborah his wife
Wid. Deb[r] Waterman
Wid. Hannah James
Patience Oldham (of Jon[a])
Wid Eliz[th] Stetson
Wid Ruth Craig
Joshua Bryant.
M[rs] Abiel his wife
Wid. Marcy Brooks
John Hatch
Lucy his wife
Cap. Tho[s] Southworth
Sally his wife
Elizabeth Clap (wife of Sylvanus)
Eunice Jordan (wife of Nath[l])
Lydia Woodward
Benj[n] Stetson
Mary Delano (wife of Benj[a])
Cap James Curtis
Phebe his wife
M[rs] Hannah Stone
Nathaniel Jacob.
Edmund Bowker.
Lydia his wife
Cap James Sparrell
Betsey his wife
Eben[r] Copeland
Sally his wife
Hannah Copeland
Lydia Copeland.

Names of Church Members in Scit. South Parish. admitted since Jan. 1810. S. Deane.

1810	June	3^{d}	Miss Eunice Brooks.
	Aug.	5	Cap. Willm Brooks
			Mrs Lucy Brooks, (his wife)
			Miss Betsey Brooks.
			Mr Samuel Foster.
			Mrs Sarah Foster. (wife)
			Mr Nathl Cushing.
			Mrs Jane Cushing. (wife)
	Oct.	7	Miss Thirza Bryant
			Miss Betsey Torrey.
1811.	June	2	Mr Gershom Ewell.
			Mrs Hannah Ewell (his wife)
			Mrs Sarah Stetson.
			Miss Elizabeth Studley.
	Sept.	1st	Miss Lucy Cushing.
	Oct.	6th	Miss Elizabeth Stetson.
			[None in 1812]
1813	May	2^{d}	Mrs Patience James.
			Maj. Jno. Jas. wife.
	Sept.	5	Mr Silas Stetson.
1814	May	1st	William Studley Sen
			Mrs Asenath Litchfield
			Miss Lucy Stockbridge
	June	5th	Mrs Esther Cole
			Mrs Mary Studley.
1815	Sep	3^{d}	Hannah Lincoln Elms
	Oct.	1st	Mr Thomas Lapham
			Mrs Sally Lapham (his wife)
	Nov	12th	Mrs Polly Harris methodist [in pencil]
1816	June	2^{d}	Elizabeth Lincoln
	July	7	Dr Cushing Otis.
	Aug.	4	Mr Samuel A. Turner
			Mrs Nancy Magoun
	Sept	1st	Wid Elizabeth Elms
1817	Aug	3	Mr Noah Nichols
	Sep.	7	Mrs Lydia Parsons.
			Mrs Betsey Penniman.
			Pickles Cushing J^{r}
			Mrs Rachel Cushing (his wife)
			Miss Deborah Hatch
1818	July	5th	Christopher Cushing Esqr
			Mrs Lucy Cushing (his wife)
			Mrs Stella Deane
			[None in 1819]
1820	July	2^{d}	Wid. Alice Cushing
			Cap. Perez Turner
			Mrs Hannah Turner his wife
	Aug.	6th	Timothy Foster
			Jacob Read

	Sep.	3d	Joshua James
			Sally James his wife
1821	July	1st	Hannah James
			Caroline Foster
	Sep.	2d	Cap. Luther Tilden
			Mrs Philenda Tilden his wife
1822	Oct.	6th	Wid. Sarah Delano
1823	June	1st	David Bowker
			Mrs Eunice Bowker his wife
	July	6th	Lemuel Jacobs Sen.
			Mrs Sarah Jacobs his wife
	Sep.	7th	Wid. Lydia Turner (of Elisha Turner)
1824	June	6.	Wm Hammatt Esq.
			Mrs Huldah Jacob.
			Mrs Sarah S. Benson
	July	4th	Wid. Deborah Turner.
	Sep.	5th	Mrs Nabby Eells (wife of Nathl Ells)
	Sep.	5.	Charles Foster
			Mrs Eunice Foster
1825	May	1st	Miss Betsey Cushing
			Miss Deborah C. Briggs.
	June	12th	John Foster
			Miss Nabby Nichols.
			Mrs Betsey Jones.
			Mrs Lydia Turner.
			Mrs Sally Meritt
			Miss Ruth Cushing
			Miss Caroline Cushing.
	Sep	4th	Samuel Curtis Sen.
			Mrs Welthea James
1826			[no entries]
1827	Sep.	2d	Miss Lydia Cushing
			Miss Temperance Foster.
1828	July	6th	Wid. Betsey Jacob of Walter [written above Betsey]
	Sep.	7th	Mrs Thirza Bowker (wife of Dimmock Bowker.)
			Miss Nebby Nash
	Oct.	5th	Mr Lot Litchfield
			Mrs Dolly Litchfield his wife
			Mr Benjamin Turner
			Mrs Hannah C. Turner his wife.
1828	Oct.	5	Miss Hannah Jacob.
	Nov.	2d	James N. Sparrell
			Mrs Desire Sparrell his wife
1829	July	12.	Nathl Clap.
			Mrs Anna Clap. his wife
	Dec.	6.	Elijah Daman.
			Mrs Lucy Daman his wife
			[None in 1830.]
1831	May	3.	Charles Cole sen
			Mrs Martha Clap wife Elijah sen
	June	5.	Mrs Rachel Jenkins wife of Bailey J. . . .
			Mrs Rachel Litchfield wife of Rufus L

	July	3	Wid. Rachel Clap (of Perkins)
			Wid. Rachel Gardner (of Seth)
	Sep.	4.	Miss Julia Tilden
1832	July	1.	Wid. Bethia Tolman
			M[rs] Lusanna Turner wife of Lem[l] T.
			John K. Nash Esq.
			Eliza Nash
			Lucy Southworth
			Martha P. Deane
1832	July	1	Sarah Otis Curtis
			Abigail Tilden Otis
			M[rs] Sally Foster (wife of Elisha)
			Grace B. Foster
			Sarah D. Foster
			Sally Lapham
			William Hart Delano
			M[rs] Sarah Delano (his wife)
	Aug.	5.	M[r] Ebenezer Stetson
			M[r] James Southworth
			Wid Charlotte Clapp
	Sep.	2[d].	Cap. Job Cowen
			M[r]. Alfred Litchfield
			M[rs] Mary Litchfield his wife
			Lucy Nichols Curtis.
	Oct.	7th	M[rs] Briggs (wife of Cap. Benj.)
			Miss Sarah
			Miss Harriet her daughter
1833	Aug.	3.	M[r] Nath[l] Brooks
			M[rs] Charlotte his wife
1834	June	6	Henry Briggs
			Caroline Otis Briggs (his dau)
			[None in 1835, 1836, 1837.]

Persons admitted to this church* since 1836.

1838	April	1.	Mary R. James.
	July	1.	Mrs. Mary Otis Robbins
1839	May	5.	Emily Cushing.
	"	"	Clarifsa Cushing.
	June	2	Elijah Brooks & his wife
			Maria Brooks.
	"	"	Mrs. Jane Delano.
			Abiel Turner & his wife
			[blank] Turner [blank]
1841	Oct.	10	Mrs Sophia Tilden
1842	April	24	Mr Elnathan Cushing
			Louisa Cushing, his wife.
	May	1	Caroline Tilden.
	July	3	Mr. David Torrey
			Mrs. Vesta Torrey.

* Rev. Samuel Deane died Aug. 9, 1834, and Rev. Samuel J. May was installed Oct. 26, 1836. He was succeeded by Rev. William O. Mosley, ordained Feb. 15, 1843, and he was followed, in 1848, by Rev. Caleb Stetson, who was pastor for eleven years.

Persons admitted to the Church.

Sepr 4, 1842	Mary E. Delano
	Prudence Delano
	Lucy Delano.
October 2d 1842	Rachel Turner
	Deborah Anne Clapp.
	Antoinette Clapp
Sep 3, 1843	Dr Amory Gale and Patty Gale his wife.
	Mrs Dama Stockbridge
	Susanna Stowell Stockbridge
	Elisabeth Richmond Stockbridge
	Mrs Lydia K. Litchfield.
November 5	Charlotte A. Clapp.
	Susanna Damon
October 6, 1844	Joseph Clapp,—and Lucy Clapp his wife.
July 6, 1845	William James
	Mrs Maria Hatch.
1846 Nov. 1.	Lucretia Clapp.
1847 September 5.	Mary Clapp.
October 3.	Mrs. Lucinda Turner.

Ministry of Rev. C. Stetson

1849 Jany Mrs Julia Ann Stetson wife of the Pastor, from the 1st Church Medford

[The list of admissions will end here.]

RECORDS OF THE SECOND CHURCH OF SCITUATE, NOW THE FIRST UNITARIAN CHURCH OF NORWELL, MASS.

Communicated by WILFORD JACOB LITCHFIELD, M.S., of Southbridge, Mass.

Baptisms in Scit. South Parish, from 1st. January, eighteen hundred ten.—S. Deane.

1810		*Children Bap.*	*Parents of the Children.*
May	6.	Joshua Turner	Cap. Elisha Foster
June	3^{d}.	Turner Hatch	Bailey Jenkins
June	17	Alvan	Melzar Damon
July	19	Martin (in private)	Jos. Cushing
Aug.	5.	Nathaniel	Nathl Cushing 2^{d}
Sep^{t}.	2	Elnathan	Elnathan Cushing
Sep.	2	Ann. Jane	Elnathan Cushing
Sep	2	Sarah Delano	Saml. Foster
Oct.	7	Betsey (adult)	George Torrey
Oct.	14	Jane	Seth Foster
Oct	28	Hervey Turner [by Mr	Warren Sylvester
Oct.	28	Mary Thomas]	Maj Jno. James
Dec.	2^{d}.	James [by Mr Allen]	Elisha Briggs
1811.			1811.
March	3^{d}	Wm Cushing	Cap Josh^{a} Jacobs
Ap	21	Albert	Pickles Cush^{g} [Cushing] J^{r}.
Ap.	26	Israel (in private)	John Nash
May.	19	Temperance James	Cap. Thos Southworth
June	2	Samuel	Saml Waterman
June	16	Dorcasina & Ruth }	Elijah Bowker
July	7th	Abigail Tilden	D^{r}. Cushing Otis
		Matilda	Anson Robins
		Sarah Otis	James Curtis.
		Frances	Elnathan Cushing
		Theodore Parsons	David Bowker
		Gracy	Rufus Litchfield

	Wm Phillips	Cap Luther Tilden
	Henry	Dimick Bowker
Sep 29	Sarah Hatch	Elisha Tolman
Oct. 13	Martha Turner	Nath[l]. Eells.
Nov. 24	Mary Ann.	Elisha Heyden.
Dec. 1st.	Emily	Dea. Thos. Cushing.
1812		1812
May 10	Ebenezer (adult in priv.)	Stephen Totman.
" "	James	Ebenez[r] Totman.
" "	Joseph	Eben[r]. Totman.
June 7.	Mary Jacobs	Tim[o] Foster
Aug. 2.	Martha Phillips [?]	Rev. Sam[l]. Deane
" "	George	Cap Elisha Foster
Aug. 28	Mary (adult)	Nath[l]. Turner.
Sep 27	Hayward Pierce	Nath[l]. Cush[g]. 2[d].
Oct. 1st	Sam[l]. Stetson	Cap. Storer of Portl[d] [Portland]
Oct. 11th	Rachel Woodw[d]	Bailey Jenkins.
Oct. 25	William	Allen Clapp
" "	Julia	Rufus Litchfield.
Nov. 22d	Allyne	Joseph Cushing.
1813		1813
June 23.	James Otis	Cap. Seth Foster.
June 4	Joanna	Melzar Daman
July 4	Williams	Elnathan Cushing
July 11	Geo. Partridge	Cap Jas. Sparrell
Aug. 15	Jno. Hillard	David Bowker
Aug 22	Desire Otis	James Curtis
Sep 5th	Chas. Freder[k]	Rev. Sam[l]. Deane
Sep 19	Eliza	Pickles Cushing Jr
Oct 31	Piam	Cap Josh[a]. Jacobs
Oct 31	Thirza	Dimick Bowker
1814		1814
June 19	Sarah	Nath[l]. Eells
July 17	Rufus	Rufus Litchf[d].
Oct. 2d	Nathan	Nath[l]. Cushing 2[d].
Sep. 27	Enoch	Abr[m]. Harris.
Dec. 22d	Levi (adult. private)	Dwelly Clap
1815		1815
Ap. 3d	John (in private)	Cap.Thos.South[th].[Southworth]
June 4	Joseph	Timo[y]. Foster
June 11	Annah Brooks	Allen Clap
July 16	Rhoda	Josi[h]. Stodart.
July 17	George (private)	Cap: Thos. Southw[th].
July 30	Clarissa	Dea. Thos. Cushing
Aug 5	Lem[l]. Cushing	Sam[l]. Waterman
Sep 3d	Hann[h] Lincoln (adult)	Sam[l] Elms
Sep. 10	Lucy Nichols	James Curtis
Oct. 1st	Benjamin, Sally, Israel, Rachel Clap }	Thom[s]. Lapham
Oct. 1st	M[rs] Sally.	Tho[s]. Lapham & wife

Nov.	5th	Eunice	David Bowker
Nov.	12th	Stephen }	Abrahm. Harris
"	"	Samuel }	
1816			1816
June	2d	Elizabeth (adult)	Solomn Lincoln
June	9th	Martha	Elisha Hayden
July	7	Rachel	Cap Jas. Sparrell
July	7	Lydia	Melzar Daman
July	14	Sally	Cap Elisha Foster
Sep	1st	Sally.	Cap Wm Brooks Jr.
Nov	3	Geo. Ward	Cap. Josha. Jacob.
Dec.	1st	Lydia King	Pickles Cushing Jr.
Dec.	8	Lydia King	Thomas Lapham
1817.			1817.
Oct.	5th	Polly Bowker	Allen Clap.
Oct.	19	David Richmd.	Joshua Jacob
Nov.	9th.	John Milton	Rev. Samuel Deane
1818.			1818.
June	7.	Hannah Clap	Timothy Foster.
Aug	16	Benjamin	Nathaniel Eells.
1819.			1819
June	6th	Chas. Cushing	Henry Sheafe Esqr
July	4th	William	Elisha Hayden
Aug	1st	Lucy Brooks	Cap. Luther Tilden.
Nov.	7th	Philip	Cap. Elisha Foster.
1820			1820
July	2d	Abigail	Samuel Adams Turner.
Aug	6th	Catharine Whiton	David Bowker.
Aug.	6	James Clapp	David Bowker.
Aug.	6	Joshua Bryant	Jacob Read.
Sep.	3d	Emily.	Joshua James.
Oct	20th	James.	Samuel Turner.
Nov.	2d	Harriet	James Curtis Jr
Nov.	2d	Saml. Deane	James Curtis Jr
1821			1821
July	1st	Lucretia }	Allen Clapp
		Helena }	
Sep.	2d.	Caroline.	Cap. Luther Tilden.
Oct.	7th	Jos. James. Lloyd [three sons]	Cap. Isaac Whittemore (deceased)
do.	do.	Geo. Parsons	Mr. Ebr. Thayer Fogg.
do.	do.	Hervey Hatch	Bailey Jenkins.
1822			1822
June	8.	Thompson Philips.	Maj. Wm Hamatt
Sep	1st.	Helen Maria	Rev. Saml. Deane
Oct.	6th	{ Benja Franklin	{ Wid. Sarah Delano. (wid. of Wm)
		Edwd. Hart.	
		Sarah.	
		Lucy Snow }	
Oct	6th	Helena Clap.	David Bowker.
1823			1823
June	17th	Mary Loisa *in private*	Samuel Foster.

Date	Name	Parent
Aug 3d.	Eunice John Thaxter	Cap. Wm Brooks
Sep. 28th	Julia	Allen Clap.
Oct. 5th.	Chas. Walter	Elisha Hayden.
1824		1824
June. 6	Mrs. Huldah Jacob (adult)	dau. of Lazarus Bowker
do do	Freeman Dexter	childn. of Mrs. Huldah Jacob.
do do	Mary Henry	Cap. Elisha Foster.
July 4th	Helen	Joshua James.
do do	Deborah Hannah Jacob	Wid. Debr. Turner.
Aug 1.	Edwin	David Bowker.
Sep 5.	Chs. Thomas Walter	Charles Foster
Nov 7	Cushing Otis	Cap. James Curtis
1825		1825
June 12	Noah Nichols William Cushing	Charles Jones
Aug 15th	John Howland (in private)	Wm. Hammatt Esq.
Sep. 10	Allen ——	Allen Clap.
Oct 2d	Mary Randall Anne Appleton William Henry	Wm. James Jr.
1826	[none]	
1827		1827
Feb. 4th	Stephen.	Stephen Benson.
July 22d.	Albert	William James Jr.
Aug. 5.	Horace Tower Chas. Edward Ebenezer Thayer	Ebenr. T. Fogg, Esq.
Aug 31st	Mrs Lydia Bowker Bishop	wife of Chas. D. Bishop.
Oct. 14	Charles ——	Sam. A. Turner
1828		1828
Oct. 5.	Roland Elizth. Robinson Peres Martha David Shiverick	Benja. Turner
	Mr. Lot Litchfield adult	son of Amos Litchfield
Nov. 2.	Mrs. Desire Sparrell (adult)	daughter of Mr James Barrell and wife of James N. Sparrell
Nov. 16	Martha James James Newton Mary Turner	children of James N. Sparrell
do.	Sarah Ann	Stephen Benson.

Date	Name	Parent
1829		1829
Oct. 22d.	George / Laurinda in private	David Bowker.
Dec. 6.	Mrs Lucy wife of	Elijah Daman
do.	Debby Cushing Nash	d[au.] of James N. Sparrell.
1830		1830
Nov. 2	John	Saml A. Turner Esq.
do	Welthea Alden	William James Jr.
1831		1831
Ap 24.	William Harper aged 7 / Rebecca Cushing " 5 / Lucy Ann " 3	Wid Lucy Bean.
Sep 4	George Henry	James N. Sparrell.
1832		1832
Ap. 5.	Relief (dautof Bartlett Barrell)	Wife of John Gregory.
July 1.	Sarah (d. of Simn. Brooks)	wife of Willm. H. Delano.
July 1.	Sarah Ann / Mary Frances	childn of Wm. H. Delano.
Sep. 2d	Mr Alfred Litchfield (adult)	son of Dea. Israel Litchfield.
do.	Esther Cole	Mr Alfred Litchfield.
1833		1833
	Nathl. Milton 10 / Charlotte Elizabeth 4	children of Nath & Charlotte Brooks.
same time	Mr Nathl. Brooks	Father of children above.
1834 (June 6*)		
Caroline Otis / Geo. Henry / Mary / Elizabeth Ruggles		children of Mr. Henry Briggs & his late wife, Betsey, Daughter of Thomas Ruggles.
Thomas Wales / John Ruggles / Lucy Turner		[names of parents not given.]
Aug 3*		
Ellen		Daughter of Timothy Foster.

Miscellaneous Records.

1810, July 1st *Voted*—To dismiss Mrs Hannah Stone, and to recommend her to the fellowship and commn of the church of Christ in Dennis.

1813. Jan. 31st *Voted* to dismiss Mr William Torrey, and to recommend him to the fellowship and communion of the church of Christ in Canandagua N. York.

1818 May 3d The church *Voted* to dismiss Nathaniel Jacob and to give him a recommendation to the Church of Christ in Hanover, under the Pastoral care of the Rev. Calvin Chadwick.

1820. Sep. 3d Nabby Barker dismissed at her own request to the church in Hanover.

1826. May 14th. Cap Joshua Jacob, Mr Joshua James, and Mr. Charles Foster chosen Deacons.

[This completes the abstracts from Samuel Deane's book, and the church records to 1850, except some omissions and corrections to appear next.]

*These two entries were "copied from an imperfect leaf, taken out" of the book, by Rev. W. H. Fish, successor of S. Deane.

RECORDS OF THE SECOND CHURCH OF SCITUATE, NOW THE FIRST UNITARIAN CHURCH OF NORWELL, MASS.

Communicated by WILFORD JACOB LITCHFIELD, M.S., of Southbridge, Mass.

OMISSIONS.

Ante, Vol. 58.

Page 86, *after* line 6, *insert:* (p. 316, this volume.)

Joseph Dwelly son of John Dwelly, May 6 [baptized]

Page 261, *after* line 32, *insert:* (p. 354, this volume.)

Jsaac Stetſon Son of Antnony and Anna Stetſon, Baptized Oct: 12 1719

Mary Bowker daughter of James Bowker jun[r] & Hannah his wife was baptized Nov: 1st 1719

Joſeph Ramſdel ſon of Joſeph & mary Ramſdel of Pembroke was Baptized Nov: 1st 1719

John Woodward ſon of John Woodward & Mary his wife was Baptized november 29th 1719.

John Hatch, the Son of John Hatch jun[r] & Grace his wife, An Jnfant being Sick, & as was Suppoſed nigh unto death, was Baptized in private Feb: 25th 1719/20

Page 391, *after* line 5, *insert:* (p. 365, this volume.)

1726

Sarah Dwelle daugnter of Abner & Sarah Dwelle was baptized Dec: 1st 1726 in private. She being ſick and not Likely to recover.

Charls Stetſon Son of Anthony & Anna Stetſon, was baptized Dec: 25th 1726.

1727

Adult. Benjamin Randal was baptized Feb: 5th 1726/7

Adult. Joſhua Turner was baptiſed Feb: 12th 1726/7

Rebecca Stetſon, Lydia Stetfon & Samuel Stetfon Children of Samuel & Rebecca Stetſon were Baptized Feb: 19th 1726/7

James Rogers, & Jeremiah Rogers, Children of John Rogers & Deborah his wife, were baptized Feb: 19. 1726/7.

Margret Curtice daughter of W[m] Curtice & Margret his wife was baptized Feb: 26. 1726/7

Rachel Briggs daughter of James & Hannah Brigs was baptized Feb: 26. 1726/7

Elizabeth Turner; Jael Turner Princes Turner & Lurana Turner Children of Joſhua & Elizabeth Turner, were baptized Feb: 26th 1726/7

Micael Clap Son of Sam[ll] and Sarah Clap was baptized March 26.th 1727

Adult. Lydia James wife of John James was Baptized April 2[d] 1727

Abel woodwart Son of Benjamin & Mary woodwart was baptized April 2[d] 1727.

Ann Woodworth daughter of Ebenezar & Joanna woodworth, was baptized April 2[d] 1727.

Sarah, daughter of Zecheriah, & Mehittable Dammon, was Baptifed May 14. 1727

Robert Son of Daniel & Jemimah Dammon was baptized, May 14 1727

Thomas Buck Son of Jsaac Buck & Mary his wife was Baptized June 4th 1727.

Noah Torry Son of Jofeph & deborah Torry was baptized June 4th 1727

Luce Turner daughter of Benjm & Mercy Turner was baptized June 4th 1727

Mary Ruffel Servt child to John Ruggles was baptifed June 4th 1727

Adult: Rebecca Sprague was Baptized June 4th 1727.

Rebecca Berftow daughter of Benjmin Beftow & his wife was baptized June 11th 1727.

Ezekiel Lamb and James Lamb, Children of James Lamb (Indns) and Patience, (a Melatto) his wife were baptized June 18th 1727.

Luke Toby, Son of Thomas Toby & Mary his wife was Baptized July 2d 1727.

Hannah Bowker daughter of James & Hannah Bowker was Baptized. July 2d 1727.

Elizabeth Beftow daughter of Saml & Lydia Beftow was Baptized July 23. 1727

Jofiah Cornifh Son of Jofeph & Patience Cornifh of Hanover was baptized Auguft 6th 1727

John Ruggles Son of John & Joanna Rugles was baptized Sept 10th 1727

Sept. 24th 1727 J preached at the north Precinct for Mr Bourn, & Baptized: Nathanael Brigg son of Jofeph and Deborah Briggs.

Oct 8th 1727 J preached at Hanover and after Sermon J Baptized.

Adult william Cocks. Jsaac & Mary Hatch Children of Jsaac Hatch.

Benjamin Man, Son of Benjm man.

Adult Judith Rogers, wife of Jofeph Rogers of marfhfield was Baptized oct: 15th 1727

Jofeph Silvefter son of Jofeph & Mary Silvefter of Marfhfield was Baptized Oct: 15. 1727.

Adult Abigail Studly was Baptized Oct. 22. 1727

Adult. Deborah Stetfon daugter of Sergt Saml ftetfon was baptized oct: 22. 1727

Prince Rofe Son of Gidion & Lydia Rofe was baptifed oct: 29 1727.

William Turner Son of wm & Abigail Turner was baptized nov: 26 1727

Samuel Oakman Son of Saml & Elizabeth oakman of marfhfield was Baptifed nov: 26. 1727

Adult. Penelipah Hatch wife of Jsaac Hatch was baptized Dec: 24 1727

Seth Hatch Son of Jsaac and Penelipah Hatch was baptized Dec: 24th 1727.

Mary Brooks daughter of Nathanl & mary Brooks was baptifed in Private Dec: 1727

1728

Elizabeth Brooks daughter of Gilbert Brooks & Abigail his wife was baptized Jan: 1st 1727/8

Jofeph Turner Son of Jofeph & Elizabeth Turner was baptized Jan: 28th 1727/8.

January 30th 1727/8 Sarah Jacob an Infant Child of Jofhua & Mary Jacob was Baptized in Private, it being Sick & not Likely to recover.

Corrections.

Ante, Vol. 57. (see p. 431 for page nos.)

Page 82, line 19, *for* Guilulmo, *read* Guilielmo; 84, line 35, *for* Burrouges, *read* Burroughs, line 39, *for* May 11, *read* May 14; 178, line 16, *for* Hicks, *read* Hicke; 179, line 31, *for* Mar. 21, *read* Mar. 24; 180, line 13, *for* Gener (?), *read* Grace ye, line 18, *for* July 3, *read* July 31, line 26, *for* Loy, *read* Loys, line 28, *for* L. [?], *read* Rogers, line 45, *for* Cushion, *read* Cushen; 181, line 1, *for* Blackmore, *read* Blackmoor, line 9, *for* Cushion, *read* Cushen, line 32, *for* Bryant, jun^{r}., *read* Briant sen^{r}, line 38, *for* Barsto, *read* Bersto, line 45, *for* Curlien (?), *read* Curtice, line 47, *for* Andrew, *read* Anthonie, line 50, *for* Sept. 20, *read* Sept. 23, last line, *for* Oct. 2, *read* Oct. 2 [worn]; 182, line 3, *for* Bumpas, Apr. 4, *read* Bumpus, Apr. 7, line 4, *for* Witherell, *read* Wetherel, line 9, *for* Marcy Whiston, *read* Mercy Whetston, line 15, *for* Barsto, *read* Bersto, line 17, *for* Studson, *read* Sturtson, line 31, *for* Mary Curtis, *read* Marcy [or Mercy] Curtice, line 35, *for* Mary, *read* Mercy, lines 39 and 41, *for* Studson, *read* Sturtson, line 42, *for* Nickells, *read* Nickolls, line 52, *for* Barrel, *read* Barret; 183, line 1, *for* August 4, *read* August [worn], line 5, *for* junior, *read* senior, line 8, *for* Studson, *read* Sturtson, line 10, *for* Witherel, *read* Wetherel, line 12, *for* Studson, *read* Sturtson, line 16, *for* Witherell, *read* Wetherell, line 18, *for* Brooks, *read* Brooke, line 19, *for* junior, *read* senior, line 20, *for* Barsto, *read* Bersto, line 22, *for* Jenkins, *read* Jenken, line 23, *for* Whiston, *read* Whetestone, line 28, *for* Bumpas, *read* Bumpus, line 31, *for* Badcock, *read* Badcoke, line 37, *for* Barsto, *read* Bersto, line 37, *for* November [?], *read* November 7, line 39, *for* Zoar, *read* Isaac, line 41, *for* ———, *read* Alce, line 41, *for* Zoar [?], *read* Isaac Prince, line 46, *for* Witherell, *read* Wetherell, line 47, *for* Studson, *read* Sturtson, line 52, *for* Sprout, *read* Sprut, last line, *for* Whiston, *read* Wheteston; 184, line 4, *for* Witherell, *read* Wetherell; 318, line 22, *for* Jinkins, *read* Ginkins, line 24, *for* Clarke, *read* Clape, line 39, *for* Joslin, *read* Joycelin, line 44, *for* Curtise, *read* Curtice; 319, line 10, *for* Briant, *read* Orcut, lines 42 and 43, *for* Witherell, *read* Wetherell; 320, line 15, *for* Curtise, *read* Curtice, line 32, *for* Marry, *read* Mercy; 321, line 33, *for* Marry, *read* Marcy; 322, line 20, *for* Mighell, *read* Mighil, line 27, *for* Abuah, *read* Abnah, line 40, *for* Curtiss, *read* Curtise; 323, line 1, *for* M^{r}. [Hobart?], *read* M^{r}. Jer. Hobart, line 8, *for* bosby *read* besby, line 13, *for* Bastow, *read* Bestow, line 31, *for* Jerimiah, *read* Jemimah; 324, line 42, *after* Clap, *insert* &, line 10, *for* 30, *read* 10, lines 39 and 40, *for* Collomer, *read* Collomar; 398, line 37, *for* 7th, *read* 6th; 401, line 11, *for* 17, *read* 12; 403, line 5, *for* 30th, *read* 10th, last line, *for* Judix [?], *read* Indians.

Vol. 58. (see p. 431 for page nos.)

Page 84, line 1, *for* Micah, *read* Micael, line 30, *for* Gorden, *read* Jorden, line 34, *for* Foster, *read* Fother, line 42, *insert* Apr. 3^{d}; 85, line 1, *insert* Aug. 6, 1749; 86, line 23, *for* 22, *read* 12; 87, line 22, *for* 3, *read* 1, line 38, *for* 15th, *read* 11th, line 49, *for* Collamare, *read* Collomare; 88, line 37, *for* Staples, *read* Steples; 169, line 3, *for* Susannah, *read* Lusannah; 170, line 47, *for* Zebulem, *read* Zebulun; 171, line 15, *for* ftutfon, *read* Hutson; 172, line 27, *after* of, *insert* John Palmer and; 173, line 25, *for* Tounsand, *read* Townsand; 174, line 17, *for* 24, *read* 23; 175, line 9, *for* Stutfon, *read* Hutfon; 176, line 28, *for* Bathfhebah, *read* Barfhebah; 264, line 20, *for* Gael, *read* Jael; 390, line 43, *for* Symons, *read* Symmons.

Vol. 59.[1]

Page 75, line 43, *for* Jerifha, *read* Jerufha; 76, line 1, *for* Lambert, *read* Lumbert: 135, line 11, *for* 1734, *read* 1732.

Vol. 60.[2]

Page 180, line 45, *for* 18, *read* 12; 182, line 40, *after* Eames, *insert* [and]; 271, line 41, *after* wife, *insert* (baptized twice); 272, line 48, *for* Eliza, *read* Elija; 273, line 40, *for* Gallon [?], *read* Gallow; 339, line 11, *after* Perry, *insert* both, line 34, *after* [worn], *insert* 7.

Vol. 61.[3]

Page 57, line 19, *for* R——, *read* R[e]bekah, line 28, *for* south worth, *read* southworth; 173, line 22, *for* Matther, *read* Matthew; 175, line 36, *for* Nebby, *read* Debby.

Vol. 57.
p. 82 is p. 312, this volume.
p. 84 is p. 314, this volume.
p. 178 is p. 317, this volume.
p. 179 is p. 318, this volume.
p. 180 is p. 319, this volume.
p. 181 is p. 320, this volume.
p. 182 is p. 321, this volume.
p. 183 is p. 322, this volume.
p. 184 is p. 323, this volume.
p. 318 is p. 323, this volume.
p. 319 is p. 324, this volume.
p. 320 is p. 325, this volume.
p. 321 is p. 326, this volume.
p. 322 is p. 327, this volume.
p. 323 is p. 328, this volume.
p. 324 is p. 329, this volume.
p. 398 is p. 330, this volume.
p. 403 is p. 335, this volume.

Vol. 58.
p. 84 is p. 338, this volume.
p. 85 is p. 339, this volume.
p. 86 is p. 340, this volume.
p. 87 is p. 341, this volume.
p. 88 is p. 342, this volume.
p. 169 is p. 345, this volume.
p. 170 is p. 346, this volume.
p. 171 is p. 347, this volume.
p. 172 is p. 348, this volume.
p. 173 is p. 349, this volume.
p. 174 is p. 350, this volume.
p. 175 is p. 351, this volume.
p. 176 is p. 352, this volume.
p. 264 is p. 357, this volume.
p. 390 is p. 364, this volume.

[1] p. 75 is p. 367, this volume.
p. 76 is p. 368, this volume.
p. 135 is p. 372, this volume.

[2] p. 180 is p. 401, this volume.
p. 182 is p. 403, this volume.
p. 271 is p. 404, this volume.
p. 272 is p. 405, this volume.
p. 273 is p. 406, this volume.
p. 339 is p. 412, this volume.

[3] p. 57 is p. 414, this volume.
p. 173 is p. 418, this volume.
p. 175 is p. 420, this volume.

EPITAPHS IN THE OLD BURYING-GROUND IN NORTH DENNIS, MASS.

[Copied by **Mercie Sears Crowell**.]

Here lies the body
of the
Rev[d] Josiah Dennis
Pastor of East Church
in Yarmouth,
who died Aug 31st 1763
in the 69th year of his age
and 37th of his ministry.

Here Lyes Buried y[e] Body
Of M[rs] Bathsheba
Dennis Wife to y[e]
Rev[d] M[r] Josiah Dennis
Who Departed This Life
Nov y[e] 20th 1745 in y[e]
45th Year Of Her Age.

Here lies the body of
Mrs Phebe Dennis
Wife to the Rev[d]
Mr Josiah Dennis,
Who departed this life,
Oct the 2nd 1775
in the 63rd year
of her age.

Rev Nathan Stone Pastor of the east church in Yarmouth, now Dennis departed this life April 26, 1804 in the 67th year of his age, and 40th of his ministry, Endeared to his family and friends in life and lamented by all at his death.

Of temper humble, mild and kind,
To hospitality inclined
This world's vain wealth he ne'er could prize,
But laid up treasure in the skies.

Mrs Mary Stone consort of the Rev Nathan Stone departed this life the 28th of April 1790, in the 49th year of her age, endeared to her family and friends in life and lamented by all at her death.

We Abner, Elisha and Zenas Howes with filial affection place this stone over the mortal remains of Elisha Howes our parent, who was born April 2, 1754 and died May 3, 1831. For the information of his descendants we add, he was the son of Stephen Howes, a son of Amos, the son of Joseph, the son of Thomas Howes, our English Ancestor, who came to this country A. D. 1637.

Howes Cemetery, North Dennis, Mass., Inscriptions:—It should be stated that at the time of copying these grave records the stones of Thomas[1] Howes and his two older sons, Joseph[2] and Thomas,[2] were not found; nor was that of his Widow Mary, who married (second) Governor Thomas Prence, and who undoubtedly was buried there, as stated by Mr. J. C. Howes in his Genealogy of the Howes Family.

Thomas Howes died Nov. 22, 1737, in his 74th year.
Mrs. Sarah Howes, wife of Thomas, died in March, 1776, in her 100th year.
Thomas Howes died Sept. 11, 1771, in his 66th year.
Hannah Howes, wife of Thomas, died Nov. 7, 1739, aged about 25 years.
Thomas Howes, son of Thomas and Hannah, died Dec. 17, 1739, aged about 3 years.
Prince Howes died Oct. 2, 1753, in his 84th year.
Dorcas Howes, wife of Prince, died Nov. 14, 1757, in her 86th year.
Sarah Howes, daughter of Prince and Dorcas, died Oct. 11, 1734, in 23d year.
Samuel Howes died Dec. 27, 1882, aged 65 y. and 2 d.

Jerusha Howes, widow of Samuel, died Oct. 29, 1801, in 86th year.
Capt. Thomas Howes died Nov. 19, 1764, in 65th year.
Deborah, wife of Capt. Thomas Howes, died Sept. 11, 1781, in 77th y.
Lydia Howes, wife of Capt. Ebenezer, died Nov. 4, 1755, in 71st y.
Capt. Ebenezer Howes died Jan. 8, 1726, aged about 53.
Sarah Howes, wife of Ebenezer, died Sept. 9, 1705, aged about 27.
Mrs. Mary Howes died Nov. 16, 1725, in 28th y.
Jeremiah Howes, aged about 71, died Sept. 9, 1708.
Sarah, wife of Jeremiah Howes, died Mch. 3, 1706, in 60th year.
Mrs. Annar Howes died Sept. 22, 1758, in 43d y.
Betsey, wife of John Howes, died Mch 3, 1777, in 25th y.
John Howes died Sep. 11, 1832, aged 86.
Miss Sarah Howes died Sept. 30, 1816, aged 41.
Mary, wife of Joseph Howes, died May 17, 1790, in 89th y.
Priscilla, wife of Jeremiah Howes, died July 6, 1783 in 39th y.
Isaac Howes d. Sept. 20, 1728, aged 29.
Ebenezer Howes, drowned in Norfolk River and buried on Sewels Point, Aug. 17, 1808, aged 20, and [on same stone].
Ezriah Howes, died Sept. 1790, aged 8 weeks, sons of Jonathan and Susan.
Lot Howes, Jr. died May 6, 1792, aged 45
Lot Howes died July 1, 1791, aged 83.
Thankful, wife of Lot Howes, died July 21, 1790, in 77th y.
Prince Howes died Jan. 9, 1799, in 81st y.
Hannah, wife of Joseph Howes, died Mch. 29, 1723, in 59th y.
Mary, wife of Joseph Howes, died Mch. 14, 1712, in 49th y.
Joseph Howes d. Dec. 24, 1743, in 84th y.
Levi Howes died Mch. 9, 1825, aged 75.
Deborah, wife of Levi Howes, died Dec. 31, 1842, aged 90.
Temperance, wife of Isaac Howes, and daughter of Christopher Crowell, died Mch. 17, 1763, in 30th y.
John Howes, son of Josiah and Lydia, died Jan. 28, 1792, in 23d y.
Susannah Howes, daughter of Josiah and Lydia, died July 25, 1803, in 18th y.
Lydia Howes, daughter of Josiah and Lydia, died Feb. 7, 1792, in 18th y.
Josiah Howes died June 12, 1810, aged 72.
Lydia, widow of Josiah Howes, died May 23, 1823, aged 81.
David Howes died Nov. 16, 1838, aged 71.
Mary, widow of David Howes, died Apr. 11, 1856, in 87th y.
Temperence Howes, wife of Perez, d. Oct. 13, 1801, in 28th y.
Samuel Howes, Jr. d. Aug. 25, 1798, in 23d y.
Mary Howes, daughter of Isaac and Hannah, d. Feb. 21, 1784, in 10th y.
Anna Howes, wife of Dea. Joseph, d. Oct. 18, 1797, aged 79.
Abigail, wife of Samuel Howes, d. Nov. 19, 1807, in 65th y.
Deacon Joseph Howes, d. Aug. 24, 1787, aged 69.
Mrs. Lydia Howes died Jan. 5, 1787, in 78th y.
Joseph Howes d. Dec. 6, 1750, in 61st y.
Elizabeth Howes, wife of Joseph, died Jan. 11, 1759, in 67th y.
Mrs. Experience Howes died Apr. 2, 1757, in 65th y.
Betty, wife of Nathaniel Howes, died Oct. 2, 1806, in 34th y.
Miss Ruhamah Howes died May 29, 1812, in 30th y.
Miss Polly Howes d. June 8, 1851, aged 75 years, 4 mo.
Miss Ruth Howes d. Mch. 8, 1851, aged 71 y. 7 m.
Miss Mercy Howes, b. Aug. 1, 1770, d. Aug. 21, 1830, ae. 60 y. and 20 d.
Mrs. Ruth, wife of Edward Howes, b. Sept. 15, 1744, died Aug. 29, 1830, aged 85 y. 11 m. 12d. "Fifth Descendant from English Ancestors" . . . [the line being given: Philip,[4] Joseph,[3] Joseph,[1] Thomas[1]].
Edward Howes, born Mch. 21, 1739, died June 1, 1811, aged 72 y. 72 d. [His line is given: Samuel,[4] Ebenezer,[3] Jeremiah,[2] Thomas[1]].
Jonathan Howes, son of Thomas and Jerusha, died Dec. 8, 1806, in his 10th y.
Marcy, daughter of Thomas and Jerusha Howes, d. Nov. 15, 1805, in 21st y.
Joseph Howes, son of Joshua and Levina, d. July 9, 1801, aged 10 mo.
Thomas Howes d. June 10, 1796, in 32d y.

Joshua Howes d. June 5, 1765, aged 27.
Mercy, widow of Joshua Howes, d. May 26, 1822, aged 82.
Thankful Howes, daughter of Thomas and Marcy, d. Mch. 31, 1741.
Henry Howes d. Feb. 24, 1779, in 23d y.
David Howes d. Sept. 28, 1759, in the 24th y.
Mary, wife of Joshua Howes, d. Dec. 1, 1774, in 25th y.
Nathaniel Howes d. Mch. 5, 1759, in 48th y.
Miss Thankful Howes d. Sep. 17, 1810, in 44th y.
Thomas Newcomb d. Mch. 18, 1795, in 61st. y.
Nathaniel Howes, son of David and Hannah, d. Aug. 30, 1751, in 14th y.
Anthony Howes, son of David and Hannah, d. Jan. 19, 1740, aged 7 y.
Marcy Howes, wife of Thomas, d. Feb. 5, 1792, in 78th y.
Mrs. Bety Howes d. Aug. 6, 1756, in 63d y.
John Howes d. July 17, 1750, in 50th y.
James Howes d. Aug. 1, 1745, in 37th y.
Nathaniel Howes d. July 26, 1745, in 74th y.
John Howes d. Apr. 30, 1736, in 72d y.
Mary, wife of John Howes, d. Apr. 8, 1746, in 77th y.
Elizabeth, wife of Joseph Howes, d. Jan. 11, 1759, in 67th y.
Joseph Howes, d. Dec. 6, 1750, in 61st y.
Deborah, widow of Levi Howes, d. Dec. 31, 1842, aged 90 y.
Levi Howes, d. Mch. 9, 1825, ae. 75.
Isaac Howes d. Sept. 20, 1728, aged 29 y.
Joseph Howes d. Dec. 24, 1743, in 84th y.
Mary, wife of Joseph Howes, d. Mch. 14, 1712, in 49th y.
Hannah, wife of Joseph Howes, d. Mch. 29, 1723, in 59th y.
Rebecca, wife of Jonathan Howes, Esq., born 1729, died July, 1807, aged 79.
Jonathan Howes, Esq. born 1729, died Oct. 15, 1801, aged 72 y.
David Howes, d. Feb. 3, 1781, in 83d y.
Hannah, wife of David Howes, d. July 11, 1790, in 82d y.
Martha, wife of Anthony Howes, d. July 7, 1789, in 36th y.
Joshua, son of Philip Howes, d. Oct. 12, 1792, aged 2 m. 9 d.
Philip Howes d. Oct. 11, 1805, in 43d y.
Mrs. Keziah Howes d. Apr. 23, 1843, aged 78.
Elizabeth Howes, wife of Thomas, d. Oct. 31, 1848, aged 63.
Thomas Howes d. Oct. 1, 1851, aged 72.
Jonathan, son of Thomas and Priscilla Howes, died in Liverpool, Eng., Aug. 22, 1831, aged 23.
Thomas Howes, born July 2, 1812, died Apr. 26, 1882.
Mary Jane Howes d. Apr. 4, 1891, aged 83.
Eben Foster Howes d. June 22, 1864, aged 32. Buried in Lone Mountain Cemetery, San Francisco, Cal.
Judah Howes d. Aug. 5, 1842, aged 36 y.
Barnabas C. Howes born July 28, 1839, died Mch. 7, 1892.
William C. Howes, son of Thomas and Deborah, d. Sept. 8, 1848, ae. 2 y. 5 m.
Thomas B. Howes, son of Thomas P. and Deborah, d. Sept. 12, 1848, ae. 4 y. 9 m.
Richard Evans Howes, son of Thomas Prince and Deborah Howes, d. Aug. 5, 1861, aged 13 m.
Thomas Prince Howes d. June 26, 1894, aged 76.
Deborah, wife of Thomas Prince Howes and daughter of Thomas Basset of Plainfield, Mass., d. July 7, 1860, aged 44.
Oren Howes d. Apr. 10, 1877, aged 72 y. 7 m.
Sukey N., wife of Oren Howes, d. Aug. 13, 1885, aged 76 y. 8 m.
Fannie, wife of Jonathan Howes, died Feb. 13, 1878, aged 64 y. 2 m.
Jonathan Howes d. July 21, 1880, aged 73 y. 9 m.
Cyrus, son of Alexander and Persis Howes, d. Feb. 23, 1808, aged 10 weeks.
Alexander Howes, son of Alexander and Persis, d. Aug. 2, 1814, ae. 3 y. 5 m.
Alexander[6] Howes [Jonathan,[5] Lot,[4] Prince,[3] Jeremiah,[2] Thomas[1]], d. Nov. 30, 1849, aged 65 y.
Persis, wife of Alexander Howes, d. Sept. 19, 1848, aged 62.
Olive, daughter of Alexander and Persis Howes, d. Jan. 4, 1833, aged 16 y. 4 m.

Sarah Adeline, widow of Capt. Nathan Crowell, d. Jan. 19, 1846, in 33d y.
Capt. Nathan Crowell d. July 9, 1838, at sea, on his passage from Liverpool, Eng., to Boston, in his 39th y.
Susannah, wife of Jonathan Howes, d. Feb. 2, 1828, aged 75.
Jonathan Howes d. May 19, 1834, aged 82 y.
Seth Howes, born Feb. 3, 1737, d. Feb. 19, 1819, aged 82 y. 16 d.
Miss Susannah Howes d. Feb. 13, 1820, aged 17.
Solomon Howes d. July 22, 1831, aged 42.
Leonard Howes d. Aug. 1831, aged 14.
Nancy, widow of Solomon Howes, d. Dec. 1, 1865, aged 74 y. 3 m. 15 d.
Huldah, wife of Abraham Howes, d. Aug. 3, 1877, aged 63.
Abraham Howes d. May 28, 1867, aged 57.
Hepsy, wife of Micah Howes, d. Sep. 8, 1844, aged 65.
Micah Howes d. May 27, 1842, aged 67.
Also three sons: Solomon, d. Sep. 12, 1832, aged 27.
Judah, d. Apr. 24, 1835, aged 22.
Samuel, d. Oct. 3, 1841, aged 18, "lost at sea".
Thankful Howes, widow of Judah, d. Nov. 3, 1816, aged 39.
Judah Howes d. Aug. 23, 1807, in 30th y.
Olive Howes, daughter of Judah and Thankful, d. Nov. 17, 1805, in 6th y.
Eben Howes, son of Judah and Thankful, d. July 6, 1818, aged 11.
Mrs. Lydia Howes d. June 20, 1835, aged 77.
Isaiah Howes d. May 18, 1885, aged 75.
Thomas Howes, b. July 2, 1812, d. Apr. 26, 1882.
William Howes, d. Nov. 17, 1809, aged 78.
Mary, wife of William Howes, d. May 30, 1806, in 77th y.
Mary, wife of Philip Howes, d. Oct. 28, 1790, in 78th y.
Philip Howes, born May 25, 1705, died Feb. 28, 1787, aged 81 y. 9 m.
Judah Howes d. Jan. 5, 1786, aged 85.
Susannah Howes, wife of Judah, d. Feb. 14, 1788, in 77th y.
Huldah, wife of Noah Howes, d. July 14, 1798, aged 85
Seth Howes, born Feb. 3, 1737, d. Feb. 19, 1819, aged 82 y. 16 d.
Jonathan Howes d. May 19, 1834, aged 82.
Rebecca, Wife of Noah Howes, d. July 24, 1803, aged 81.
Noah Howes d. June 24, 1838, in 78th y.
Keziah Howes d. Mch. 14, 1819, in 25th y.
Abraham Howes d. Jan. 19, 1817, in 77th y.
Lydia, wife of Abraham Howes, d. Nov. 24, 1805, in 66th y.
Miss Susannah Howes d. Feb. 13, 1820, aged 77 [?].
Elvira, widow of Isaac White, Jr., d. Feb. 6, 1841, aged 32 y. 6 m.
Serviah, wife of Josiah Howes, d. Aug 11, 1840, aged 58 y. 7 m.
Thankful, their daughter, d. Apr. 3, 1849, aged 29 y. 3 m.
Josiah Howes d. Feb. 2, 1836, aged 57.
Thankful, daughter of Josiah and Serviah Howes, b. Jan. 17, 1815; died Jan. 13, 1818.

Jamaica Plain, Mass. Miss Ella F. Elliot

INSCRIPTIONS UPON GRAVESTONES IN THE OLD CEMETERY AT ORLEANS, MASS.

[Communicated by JOSIAH PAINE, Harwich, Mass.]

HERE LYES THE BODY | OF MR. THOMAS MAYO | OF EASTHAM, DEC'D APRIL 22, 1729 | IN YE 79 YEAR | OF HIS AGE.

[Thomas Mayo was born in Eastham, Dec. 7, 1650. His father was Nathaniel, who married Hannah Prence, Feb. 13, 1650, and who died in 1661. His grandfather was Rev. John Mayo. He married Barbara Knowles, of E., June, 1677, and had Thomas, who was born in 1678; Theophilus, born in 1680; Mary, born in 1683; Maria, born in 1685; Ruth, born in 1688; Judah, born in 1691; Lydia, born in 1694; Richard, born in 1696, and Israel, in 1700. He was a prominent citizen of Eastham, and was twelve years Selectman.—J. P.]

HERE LYES THE BODY | OF MR. JONATHAN SPARROW | DIED MARCH 9TH, 1739-40, IN YE 75TH YEAR | OF HIS AGE.

[Jonathan Sparrow was born in Eastham, July 9, 1665. He was the sixth child of Capt. Jonathan Sparrow, by his second wife Hannah, the widow of Nathaniel Mayo, and daughter of Gov. Thomas Prence. His father, Capt. Jonathan, was the most prominent citizen of that place, where he died aged 73, March 21, 1706.—J. P.]

HERE LYES YE | BODY OF MR. | RICHARD SPARROW | AGED 53 YEARS | DEC'D | APRIL YE | 13, 1728.

[Richard Sparrow was the younger brother of Jonathan. He married Mercy Cobb, of Barnstable, it is supposed.—J. P.]

HERE LYES YE BODY | OF MR. JOHN SPARROW | AGED 78 YEARS 3 MONTHS AND 20 DAYS | DEC'D FEB. YE 23, 1734–5.

[John Sparrow was the eldest son of Capt. Jona. Sparrow. His mother was Rebecca, d. of Edward Bangs.—J. P.]

HERE LYE THE BODY | OF MRS. MARY HOPKINS | DIED MARCH | YE 1 DAY 1734.

[Mary Hopkins was the wife of Joshua Hopkins, whom she married May 26, 1681, and daughter of Daniel and Ruth Cole, of Eastham. She was the sixth child, and was born March 10, 1658. She bore her husband eight children. Her youngest daughter, Phebe, married Bixby, who settled in the State of New York. Her son Elisha, born in 1688, married and settled at Chatham, where he became one of the wealthiest men of the place. Joshua Hopkins, her husband, was the grandson of Stephen Hopkins, the pilgrim. His death occurred in or about 1738. He was one of the most opulent men of his time in Eastham.—J. P.]

HERE LYES THE BODY OF MR. SAMUEL KNOWLES | FORMERLY REPRESENTATIVE FOR THE TOWN OF EASTHAM | WHO DIED JUNE YE 19 | 1737, IN THE 86TH YEAR OF HIS AGE.

[Samuel Knowles was one of the most eminent men of Eastham. He was many years a Representative and Selectman. His father was Richard Knowles, who married Ruth Bower, of Plymouth, Aug. 15, 1639. He was born at Plymouth, Sept. 17, 1651. He married Mercy, daughter of Major John Freeman, of E., in Dec., 1679. She died in 1744. The inscription upon her gravestone has become illegible.—J. P.]

HERE LYES BURIED | THE BODY OF MR. JOHN PAINE | AGED 70 YEARS | 7 MONTHS AND 12 DAYS | DEC'D OCT. YE 26 | 1731.

[John Paine was born in Eastham, March 14, 1661–2. His father was Thomas Paine, who came over from Kent, England, "in 1622" "when a lad" about "ten or twelve" years of age, with his father of the same name, and who married Mary, daughter of Nicholas and Constance Snow, and granddaughter of Stephen Hopkins the Pilgrim, not far from 1650, and who died very aged, August, 1706. John Paine was twice married. For his first wife, he married Bennit Freeman, March 14, 1689; she dying May 30, 1716, for his second wife he married Alice Mayo, March 3, 1719–20. By these two wives he had seventeen children. His son Thomas was a leading man in Eastham during the Revolutionary struggle, and died at Portland in 1802, whither he had removed. During his time John Paine was the leading man in Eastham. A Diary kept by him between the years 1695 and 1718 is yet in existence in the hands of a lineal descendant now resident of Salem, Mass.—J. P.]

HERE LYES YE BODY OF | MRS. ALICE PAINE | WHO DIED YE OCT. 12, 1748 | IN THE 63 YEAR | OF HER AGE.

[Alice Paine was wife of John Paine. Her father was Nathaniel Mayo, grandson of Rev. John Mayo.—J. P.]

HERE LIES BURIED THE BODY OF | JOSEPH DOANE, ESQ. OF EASTHAM | WHO DIED THE 27TH OF JUNE, ANNO DOM. | 1757, IN THE 89 YEAR OF HIS AGE. | HE WAS DEACON OF THE FIRST CHH | IN EASTHAM ABOUT FORTY YEARS | AND IN COMMISSION FOR THE PEACE IN | THE COUNTY OF BARNSTA-

BLE FOR ABOUT FIFTY YEARS | WHICH OFFICE (WITH OTHERS HE SUSTAINED) HE DISCHARGED WITH FIDELITY AND HONOR.

[Joseph Doane was born in Eastham in 1669. His father was Daniel Doane, and grandfather was Dea. John Doane, one of the seven first settlers of Eastham. For his first wife, Joseph Doane married Mary Godfrey, January 8, 1690; she dying Jan. 22, 1725, he again married Mrs. Desire Berry, Feb. 29, 1726–7. By these two wives he had twelve children. Daniel and Elisha his sons settled in Harwich; Joshua, the youngest son, settled in Connecticut. Esqr. Doane held many offices within the gift of his townsmen.—J. P.]

HERE LIES BURIED | THE BODY OF DOCT. JONATHAN KENWRICK | DIED JULY YE 20TH, 1753 | IN THE 38TH YEAR OF HIS AGE.

[Edward Kenrick, the ancestor of the Cape family, and father of Dr. Jonathan, came, according to tradition, from the "West of England." He settled in that part of Harwich now So. Orleans, after 1706. The name is written in various ways upon the records. Sometimes, it appears as "Cenrick," "Kendrick," and "KENRICK." The name is now written by the descendants of Dr. Jonathan—"Kenrick," and by the descendants of Thomas, his brother—"KENDRICK." The former mode of writing it, KENRICK, is perhaps the true one. Edward, the ancestor, married twice. For his first wife he married Elizabeth Snow, Dec. 3, 1706, by whom he had Thomas and Solomon; she dying, he again married Deborah Tucker, April 30, 1713, by whom he had Susannah, who was born Jan. 24, 1713–14; and Dr. Jonathan, born Nov. 14, 1715. He died about 1741. Dr. Jonathan married Tabithy Eldridge, of Chatham, and had three children, viz.: Samuel, who married Esther Mayo, Feb. 26, 1761, and became a skilful physician; Anson, born about 1743, who married Azubah Sears, Oct. 29, 1765, and removed to Nova Scotia; Jonathan, born Feb. 19, 1745, whose wife was Hannah. Dr. Jonathan, though young when death took him away, had attained to eminence as a skilful physician. His widow survived, and married Theophilus Hopkins, July 24, 1754. By him she had several children, one of whom, called Theophilus, became a physician. Capt. John Kendrick, his nephew, who was born in Harwich, where he spent his boyhood, and whose father Solomon emigrated to Nova Scotia before the Revolution, was the first shipmaster who went on a voyage of trade to the North West Coast, from the United States.—J. P.]

HERE LYES THE BODY OF | MRS. SARAH PAINE | THE WIFE OF WILLIAM | PAINE, ESQ., DIED JANUARY THE 16TH | 1734, AGED 36 YEARS.

[William Paine, Esq., was son of Dea. John Paine, and for many years a Representative from Eastham. He died at Louisburg in Aug., 1746. His wife Sarah was daughter of ——— Bacon, of Barnstable, whom he married in 1727.—J. P.]

HERE LIES THE BODY OF | NATHANIEL FREEMAN, ESQR. | WHO DEPARTED THIS LIFE | JANUARY YE 4TH, 1760 | IN THE 91ST YEAR | OF HIS AGE.

[Nathaniel Freeman, Esq., was son of Major John Freeman, of Eastham; an account of his family is given in volume xx. of the Historical and Genealogical Register.—J. P.

IN MEMORY OF | JOHN FREEMAN, ESQR. | DEACON OF THE CHURCH | IN THIS PLACE DIED | THE 9 OF JUNE, 1772 | IN THE 76 YEAR | OF HIS AGE.

[John Freeman, Esq., was son of Nathaniel. An account of him is given in volume xx. of the Register.—J. P.]

HERE LIES BURIED THE BODY | OF MR. SAMUEL BATY | WHO DIED AUGT. YE 30TH | 1768 IN THE 57TH YEAR | OF HIS AGE.

IN MEMORY OF | MAJOR GIDEON | FREEMAN WHO | DIED NOV. 4TH | 1807, IN HIS | 82D YEAR.

[Major Gideon Freeman was son of John Freeman, Esq. He was a wealthy and influential citizen of Orleans. He married Hannah, daughter of Samuel Freeman, of Eastham, and had seven daughters. Rebecca married Simeon Kingman, Esq.; Betsey married Rev. Jonathan Bascom, Feb. 10, 1785; and Hannah married Allen Bourne, Esq., of Sandwich.—J. P.]

IN MEMORY OF | MRS. HANNAH FREEMAN | WIFE OF MAJ. GIDEON FREEMAN | WHO DIED AUG. 15, 1795 | IN THE 69TH YEAR | OF HER AGE.

TO THE MEMORY OF MRS. ELIZABETH ROGERS | WIFE OF MR. JUDAH ROGERS | WHO DIED MAY 28, 1794 | IN THE 83 YEAR | OF HER AGE.

ERECTED IN MEMORY OF DOCT. SAMUEL KENWRICK, ELDEST SON OF DOCT. JONATHAN KENWRICK, WHO LIVED BELOVED AND DIED LAMENTED, FEB. 10, 1791, ÆT. 49.

How lov'd, how valued once, avails thee not,
To whom related or by whom begot;
No longer thy all healing art avails,
But every remedy its master fails.

[Dr. Samuel Kenrick was a very skilful physician. His practice was extensive. He left several sons, one of whom became a physician, and settled in Wellfleet.—J. P.]

EARLY ORLEANS, MASS., ALMANACS

Kept by Clara Snow Crosby, 1838–1899

Contributed by Mrs. Muriel L. MacFarland of Kansas City, Missouri

The following are excerpts from recordings kept on almanacs by Clara Snow Crosby, 1838–1899, of events that came to her attention while living in Orleans, Mass., the originals now being in the possession of Mrs. Warren M. Crosby of Topeka, Kansas, and contributed to The Register by Mrs. Muriel L. MacFarland of Kansas City, Mo. The complete detailed records have been deposited with the New England Historic Genealogical Society.

1862

Jan. 1. Albert Freeman presented with a son.
7. Lucia Snow died.
11. Almond G. Crosby's 24th birthday.
20. Child of James R. Rogers buried.
22. Samuel S. Freeman married Betsey Jane Snow of Harwich.
28. Amariah Mayo married Hannah Ford.
Feb. 5. Mary, wife of Jonathan Higgins, died.
March 13. Theophilus Hurd married Melissa B. Mayo.
15. Jesse Sparrow died.
18. Solomon Taylor and Zeviah T. Snow married.
April 11. Tommy, son of Mrs. Harriet Freeman, died.
13. Lydia B. Snow married in the Orthodox Church to Levi C. Long of Harwich.
June 8. Josiah Gould and Lydia S. P. Sparrow married.
20. Thomas Gould buried.
23. Seth Sparrow died.
30. Clara Cole, daughter of Ephraim Cole, died.
July 19. Caleb S. Hayden and Emmeline Rogers of Harwich married.
28. Loui, wife of William F. Mayo, died.
Aug. 8. Edwin E., son of Solomon Crosby, died.
13. Charles A. Berry and Lucinda Higgins married.
Sept. 3. Sophia Thomas has got a boy.
7. Joshua Sparrow and Charlotte E. Linnell married.
10. Louisa, wife of John Young, died.
14. Josiah Young buried. Son of Zebediah Young.
19. Child of Martha Higgins died.
28. Joseph Cummings and Helen E. Linnell married.
Oct. 6. Rueben S. Snow buried in Truro.
9. Hannah C. Freeman and Heman Cook of Provincetown married.
21. Uncle Luther Snow died.
28. Hear of Gilbert Doane's death by shipwreck August 17th.
28. Lucia Smith, a girl.
30. Joseph Higgins wife, a boy.
31. The Schooner A. F. Linnell lost on Anegada reef.
Nov. 1. A baby boy for myself, Walter Elmond.
21. Samuel S. Freeman's wife, a boy.
Dec. 6. Amariah Mayo's wife, a baby.
11. Betsey, wife of Jesse Sparrow, died.
30. Bradford and Melissa married.

1863

June 28. Almond S. Crosby died.
July 17. Daniel Hopkins died in Eastham.
Nov. 1. Amanda W. Freeman married November 1863.

1864

Dec. 19. Amanda W. Freeman died, aged 24 years, 2 months.

1865

April 11. Julia W., daughter of Abner F. Linnell, died.
June 19. Harriet Newell, wife of Vickery N. Crosby, died.
Dec. 6. Rail cars first come to Orleans.
March 28. Dorra F. Arey married, died March 12, 1866.
April 3. Rev. Jacob White, 20 years preacher in Orleans died in South Linnboro, N. H. [Lyndeborough]. Brought to Orleans and buried April 9.
April 4. Grandma Crosby died, aged 84 years.

1866

Jan. 7. Joshua Calvin, son of Franklin and Lucy Freeman, died.
Feb. 12. Ship Hamlet ashore.
18. Schooner Ida ashore on Nauset Beach.
April 4. Sally Freeman, wife of Joshua Crosby, died, 84 years.

1867

Jan. 29. Olive Adelia, wife of Elisha P. Freeman, died.
Feb. 21. Silvanus Snow, Jr., married.
Dec. 16. Julia F. Snow died.

1868

Sept. 1. Benoni Baker died.
5. Mr. John Higgins died.
8. Mrs. Sherman died.
10. Deborah, wife of Elisha Cole, died.
Nov. 15. Porter and Ella married.
19. Moses Wiles married.

1869

June 20. Mother Crosby died.
Oct. 14. Father Crosby married.

1870

May 8. John F. Crosby and S. Ada Young married.
June 19. Henry T. and Eliza Snow married.
Aug. 7. Olive Snow married.
Sept. 2. David Snow's wife died.
10. Uncle Willis gets run over.
Nov. 16. Aunt Olive Snow died.
Dec. 30. Brig. Alvarado ashore with coal, 1 man lost.

1871

April 22. Barque Wavelot ashore this morning with shooks.
June 7. Abigail Gould died.
20. Hear of Aunt Mary L. Arey's death, died April 10, 1871—also little Dorras.
July 23. Uncle Henry Snow married.
Oct. 1. Morey Gould married.
Nov. 28. Leander and Dorcus married.
Dec. 21. Uncle Dean married.
19. Sparrow Higgins and Jamie Linnell married.

1872

Jan. 28. Thacher Snow died.
Feb. 13. Mary Ann, wife of Nathan G. Taylor, died.
March 1. Leander Crosby died.
8. Joshua L. Crosby died.
12. Schooner Alexander ashore.
July 28. Aunt Lydia Cummings buried.
Sept. 25. Calvin Cummings died.
Nov. 12. Absalom Linnell died.

1873

March 31. Loui, wife of Asa Rogers, died.
June 22. Benjamin Gould drowned.
July 7. May S. Hayden died.
July 22. Cars go through to Provincetown.
Aug. 6. Dean Nickerson died.
18. Reuben Smith died.
Sept. 3. Hopey, wife of Albert Freeman, died.

1874

Aug. 6. Esther M. Doane died.
10. Hattie Young died.
Nov. 8. James (?) M. Snow married Matilda Cole.
Dec. 16. Mr. and Mrs. J. L. Sparrow's golden wedding.

1875

Jan. 31. Walter C. Mahan died.
March 12. Wallace Mayo drowned.
April 14. Elliott E. Crosby married.
June 1. Aunt Phebe Freeman died.
Oct. 1. Clarence S. Hopkins died.
Dec. 20. Brig Anna Lydia ashore.
Dec. 26. Mr. Pope preaches and resigns.

1876

Feb. 10. Daniel Higgins died.
10. Marion Snow died.
March 29. Henry B. Nickerson died, aged 28 years.
June 14. Mr. Stiles ordained as a Universalist preacher.
Aug. 28. Henry Judson Hopkins died in Grand Rapids, Mich.
Oct. 15. Rev. Mr. Stiles married in Universalist church.
Dec. 7. Lizzie Crosby married.
28. Charlie Mayo and Martha A. Hopkins married.
29. S. Walter Hopkins died.
31. Silvanus Snow, Jr.; married.

1877

Oct. 12. Lewis Higgins' wife died.
20. Martha, wife of Charlie Mayo, died.
22. Marcha, wife of Samuel Sherman, died.
Nov. 24. Ella, wife of E. P. Freeman, died.
29. S. Emerson Sparrow married.

1878

March 16. Mrs. Jabey Higgins died, aged 80.
21. Aunt Sally Sparrows' 80th birthday.
April 10. Aunt Abigail Snow died, aged 77.
April 27. Aunt Olive Freeman died.
May 26. W. C. Stiles' farewell sermon.
July 2. Abba Wheldon, wife of Joseph L. Snow, died.
4. Sukey F., wife of George W. Cummings, died.
31. Mrs. Hanson R. Higgins died.

Oct. 10. Captain David Snow married in N. Y.
Nov. 14. Samuel S. Hopkins died.
18. Millie Sparrow died.
Dec. 2. Johnnie Mayo & Sparrow S. Hayden drowned.
15. Sister Emma married to E. Porter Freeman.

1879

Jan. 6. Mr. Edmund Snow died.
21. Mrs. Elisha Snow died.
March 6. Dea. Asa Hopkins died.
7. Mrs. Sully Freeman died.
24. Laura A., wife of Asa Nickerson, died.
April 14. "Little Abba", child of James M. and Matilda C. Snow, died.
29. Matilda Cole, wife of James M. Snow, died.
June 5. Dr. S. T. Davis commenced practice in Orleans.
July 15. George W. Cummings & Delilah Mayo married.
Aug. 5. Victoria, wife of Josiah C. Hopkins, died.
Sept. 26. Bertie Hopkins died.
Oct. 9. Mr. Silvanus Snow died, aged 79.
15. Ina May P., aged 2 weeks short of 14 years.
16. Capt. Hiram Bangs died, aged 55.
24. Brother Leander's little Mamie died.
Nov. 5. Sister Emma, a boy.
16. Ocean cable from France lands on Eastham beach.
Dec. 10. Marin Judson, wife of J. F. Smith, died.
24. James Alvers Gould married Desiah B. Eldredge.
27. Mrs. White died.
29. Great fire in Boston.

1880

Jan. 2. Mr. Franklin Freeman died.
6. Gracie Snow brought to Orleans for interment.
Feb. 3. Elenor, wife of Joseph L. Snow, died.
5. Willie Hodgen died.
March 14. Deacon Franklin Snow of Boston died.
16. Aunt Ruth Gould died.
April 3. Mr. Vose died.
8. Joseph L. Snow and Mrs. Mary Eldredge married.
Sept. 10. Uncle Russell Snow died.
Dec. 13. Joshua Snow died in Provincetown.
23. James H. Sparrow died.
24. Herman Swaine died.

1881

Jan. 7. Mrs. Olive Snow Burrill died.
12. Mr. James Freeman died.
Feb. 23. Silumeth Linnell died.
April 24. Grandma Freeman died, aged 95 yrs. 3 months, 9 days.
May 4. Miss Polly Higgins died.
July 3. President Garfield shot.
Sept. 19. President Garfield died.
26. Funeral services in town hall in memory of Garfield.
Oct. 20. Mrs. Mehittable L. Knowles died.
Nov. 8. Jabey Higgins died.
26. Davis Hurd died.
28. Sarah, wife of Caleb Hopkins, died.
Dec. 22. Mary L. Hursey & Joseph Cobb, married.

1882

Jan. 6. Delia Porter Freeman died, aged 15 yrs., 4 months.
31. Capt. Winsor Snow died in Somerville.
March 21. Alfred Rogers died.
April 12. Allie Austin Freeman married.
June 22. Frank M. Hayden died.

Aug. 4. Mrs. Almira Higgins died.
15. Ezro Kelly & Child buried.
27. Charles Chase & Mary Steele married.
Sept. 15. Mrs. Thankful L. Hopkins Smith died.
Oct. 2. Mrs. Phebe Smith died.
7. Mrs. Ann S. Young of Barnstable died.
18. Elbredge Walker and Fanny Walker married—Chicago.
Nov. 23. Mrs. Freeman H. Hayden died.
Dec. 8. Ensign B. Rogers died.

1883

Jan. 4. Warren married.
11. Mattie, child of Sparrow S. Higgins, died.
24. Etta Nickerson married.
Feb. 7. Jesse Snow attempts to take his life.
July 13. Edith G. Snow died.
16. Mrs. Insie White buried—Spiritualist.
Aug. 26. Anna Charles married.
Oct. 14. Augustus Percival died at sea.
20. 8 men lost in Barnsatable Bay from Sch. Helen M. Crosby.
25. Mr. Solomon Mayo died in Town Hall.
Nov. 4. Abel H. and Lizzie Knowles married.

1884

Jan. 1. Willie Snow married.
7. George Snow married.
Feb. 13. Mrs. Couden died.
July 23. Mrs. George P. Power (pomer?) died.
Aug. 24. Dr. B. F. Seabury's wife died.
Oct. 22. Sylvester D. Hopkins died.
Nov. 8. Aunt Polly Snow died.
18. Philander A. Crosby married.
28. Capt. Jesse C. Snow died.
30. Nellie Higgins died.

1885

Feb. 13. Mr. Albert Hopkins died.
20. Sabina Nickerson died.
March 14. Thomas C. Snow died.
29. Uncle Jonathan Linnell died—aged 98 yrs., 4 months.
April 7. Mr. Solomon Linnell died, aged—
28. Aunt Sukey Sparrow died & Mrs. Elisha Hopkins.
30. Mr. William Freeman died.
May 21. Ebbie S. Freeman married.
July 22. Gen. Grant died.
Sept. 30. Mrs. Susan Benson died.
Dec. 17. Gracie B. Young died.

1886

Feb. 15. Eliza, wife of Frank M. Cummings, died.
25. Daniel B. Gould & Celena M. Wiles married.
March 5. Eldo, wife of D. I. Cummings, died.
14. Thankful Crosby, wife of John Hendrick, died, 67 yrs., 7 months.
April 3. Miss Amanda Snow buried in Orleans.
7. Mr. Abel Chattuck died.
23. Lillian F., wife of J. C. Hopkins, died.
July 13. Miss Alice G. Egerton died—27th funeral Boston.
Aug. 24. Aunt Sally Gould died.
31. Hannah R. Gould & Capt. Wm. Freeman married.
Sept. 9. Frank Higgins & Eliza F. Hayden married.
16. Thomas Spencer Snow died.
21. Mrs. Tracy Kenney died.
24. Aunt Sally Sparrow died.

Oct. 10. Everett MacCarter & Alice R. Snow married.
30. Mrs. Nabbie, widow of Mr. William Freeman, died.
Dec. 22. Marcus R. Taylor & Carrie G. Crosby married.
30. Mary Harney, wife of Isaac Cobb, died.

1887

Jan. 3. Capt. James Smith died.
3. Mr. Freeman Doane died.
18. Capt. Dean S. Linnell & Emogene Eldredge married.
18. Jane, wife of S. Emery Mayo, died.
March 8. Henry Ward Beecher died.
17. Lennette M. Rogers & B. F. Bee married.
June 11. A little girl to Dan and Lena.
Sept. 5. Mr. Davis Hopkins died.
7. Mr. Edmund Linnell died.
18. John Snow and Mrs. Abba Hopkins married.
Oct. 2. Mrs. Susan Rogers died in Dedham.
10. Herbert R. Sparrow died.
Nov. 12. Sylvia, widow of Joshua Snow, died.
23. Alice Kendrick buried.

1888

Feb. 8. Ruth C. Eldedge died.
13. Susan, wife of Capt. A. F. Linnell, died.
21. Capt. S. Newell Smith died.
23. Mrs. Aruzina Sparrow died.
March ? Haskel Crosby & E. May Freeman married.
? S. E. Mayo & Olive C. Doane married.
April 30. Henry Cummings & Theresa Paine married.
June 3. Bert Higgins & Ada Hopkins married.
13. Mrs. Abel Chattuck died.
24. Imogene, wife of Dean S. Linnell, died.
30. Miss Rosilie Hopkins died—born July 1813.
Oct. 28. Abba Lillian Nickerson married.
Nov. 14. Willie Jameson & Mary O. Sparrow married.
? Father Crosby died, born November 22nd, 1809.
Dec. 19. Mrs. Tamzen Snow died.
28. Mrs. Frederick Kendrick died.

1889

Jan. 7. Rev. Donald Frazer's babe died.
7. Ada, wife of Morris A. Hayden, died.
13. Elisha Cole died.
19. Luella, wife of Henry M. Percival, died.
Feb. 20. Lizzie Taylor & (?) married.
March 3. Wallace Baker & Alice E. Cole married.
March 6. Frank Crosby of Brewsters & "Sis" Oliver married.
17. Mrs. Bangs Taylor died.
Aug. 12. First Universalist S.S. in Eastham organized with 6 teachers and 33 scholars.
19. Bertie, son of Allie A. Freeman, died.
30. Capt. Jonathan Snow died in Provincetown.
Sept. 16. Ada Hopkins baby died.
28. Emma's baby born—Bennie.
Nov. 25. Sara Louisa Keeler died.

1890

Jan. 11. Daniel Smith died.
25. Mr. William Mayo died.
27. Mr. Nickerson died (Reuben).
29. New Universalist church in Eastham dedicated.

Feb.	24.	Benjamin F. Freeman died.
	26.	Dr. Benjamin F. Seabury died.
	27.	Uncle Willis Snow gets hurt at the wreck & died March 1st.
March	13.	Washie Taylor gets hurt, died 20th.
	27.	Aunt Mary Crosby died, Father Crosby's second wife.
	18.	Caleb Hopkins died.
	20.	Mr. ——— Chandler died.
May	1.	Mrs. Zehiva Nickerson died.
	18.	Mrs. Eliza I. Mahan died.
June	7.	Mrs. Emily D. Wilson died.
Aug.	27.	Mrs. Joseph Gould died.
Dec.	17.	Olive S., widow of Solomon Higgins, died.
	22.	Mrs. Freeman Mayo died.
	24.	Sister Emma, a boy.
	30.	Mrs. Jacob W. Mayo, a boy.

1891

Feb.	14.	Julia D., wife of Frank W. Hopkins, died.
March	22.	Mrs. Samuel Rogers died.
	27.	Mrs. Nettie M. Rogers Bee died.
April	12.	Clifton Hayden married to Lizzie Sawyer of Providence, R. I.
	28.	A boy to Mr. and Mrs. Dannie B. Gould.
May	18.	Uncle James L. Sparrow died, aged 2 weeks short of 90 years.
	20.	Miss Nettie Newton died.
June	4.	Moses Eames of Upton died.
June	25.	Mrs. Elisha L. Freeman died (Mary Foster Hopkins).
July	5.	Orville W. Crosby and Celia H. Walker married.
	15.	Mr. Jonathan Young died.
Aug.	10.	Dean G. Linnell died.
Oct.	5.	Charlotte J. Sparrow & Homer White of N. H. married.
	27.	Allan Smith & Eva G. Higgins married.
Nov.	15.	Harry Ditson died.
	17.	John Kendrick Esq., married to Miss Kate Crosby of Brewster.
	26.	Mr. Joseph W. Rogers died, near 69 years.

1892

Jan.	4.	Mrs. Stephen Snow of Brockton died.
	6.	Mr. Edwin Smith died.
	7.	Uncle Abijah Baker died, aged 75.
	13.	Capt. John Linnell's wife died.
	24.	Willie F. Gould and Bertha Norris married.
	25.	Mr. Abner Freeman died.
Feb.	5.	Mr. Joshua Sparrow died.
	28.	Mr. Frederick Kendrick died.
	28.	Rev. Mr. Pierce comes to preach in Universalist church. (No date)
March	1.	Mrs. Abijah Baker died, aged 74.
April	5.	Mrs. Alvin Smith died.
	24.	Miss Susan Mayo died aged 42.
May	4.	Mr. Franklin Gould died.
	4.	Mr. Oliver Linnell died.
	10.	Aaron Snow died.
June	1.	Mrs. Mary Jane Tutty, wife of Aaron Snow, died.
July	3.	Mrs. Thomas Newcomb died.
Sept.	9.	Henry Harding died.
	15.	Mrs. Joshua Sparrow died.
	30.	Calvin Snow died.
Nov.	4.	Mrs. Caleb Hayden died.
	7.	Emma, a little girl.
	10.	John Harris Snow died.
	29.	Aunt Darcus Myrick died.

Dec. 4. Mrs. Ephraim Cole died.
13. Aunt Lucy E. Freeman—died Widow Franklin Freeman.
20. Diana Snow, wife of Levi Long, died.
23. Edward Hurd died.

1893

Jan. 2. Eva married.
4. Florence A. Taylor & Edward Roberts married, both mutes.
Feb. 1. Lucinda S. Snow, wife of Willie Smith, died.
28. Joseph Mayo of South Orleans died.
March 3. Elisha L. Freeman died.
4. Freeman Mayo died.
8. A boy to Mr. & Mrs. Dan B. Gould, Alvus Benson.
28. Ralph W. Sanborn & Rena Barrett married.
May 14. Mr. George Drummond dies.
June 6. Uncle Harvey Sparrow died, born 11/14/1795.
16. Albert Austin Freeman died—aged 38 yr. 11 mo.
30. Mrs. Joshua Lewis Crosby buried.
July 21. Mr. Thomas Linnell died.
30. Susan, wife of Thomas Higgins, died.
Oct. 9. Augustus E. Higgins & Marion E. Campbell married.
25. Mr. Thomas Higgins died.
Nov. 17. Mrs. Mary, widow of Isaiah Crosby, Jr., died.
22. Samuel Sparrow died.
Dec. 20. W. S. Rogers died.

1894

Jan. 12. Freeman G. Crosby died.
22. Marcus Pierce's father died.
25. Mark T. Worcester, a peddler, died suddenly in town. (Carried to Nantucket).
26. Wilcox had his leg taken off and died.
30. Henry C. Nickerson & Dora Malana Mayo married.
Feb. 4. Rev. Edwin W. Pierce preaches his last sermon, lived in town 2 years.
11. A. Lizzie Snow died, aged 33 years, 4 months.
March 16. Mrs. William Crosby died.
16. Mrs. William Steele died.
April 1. Frederick Percival died.
8. Rev. F. W. Evans preaches his first sermon here and married April 25th.
May 12. Capt. David Snow died, aged 72.
14. Alville B. Nickerson died, aged 25 years.
17. John Chandler died.
18. Abba Hopkins, wife of John S. Snow, died.
June 27. Zelotus Rogers found dead.
Aug. 14. John Martin died.
22. Mrs. May, widow of Seth Doane, died and
29. Miss Martha Doane, her sister, died.
Sept. 2. Norris A. Hayden married to his 3rd wife.
3. Mamie Newcomb elopes.
4. Alice Mayo married.
Oct. 14. (Adaline Linwood), a girl to Mr. and Mrs. Augustus E. Higgins of No. Cambridge, Mass.
24. Susan, widow of Jonathan Snow, died in Provincetown.
Nov. 8. John Kanler died.
21. Mr. John Keeler died.
Dec. 12. Mrs. Roxanna, widow of Jonathan Mayo, died.
31. Jonathan S. Freeman died (soldier).

1895

Jan. 2. Hattie Knowles married.
24. Freeman E. Snow & Ada C. Baker married.
Feb. 5. Mrs. Josiah (Aunt Tannie) Hopkins died.
24. Mrs. Rosanna Higgins died.

March 11. Twin boys to Mr. and Mrs. Weston Taylor.
16. Mrs. Eben H. Linnell died, aged 81 years.
18. Mrs. Tamzen Doane, widow of Clarenton Mayo, died, 69 years.
22. A girl, to Mr. and Mrs. Evans (Rev.)
23. Mrs. Julia A. Doane, widow of Leander Crosby, died—sister of Mrs. Tamzon Doane.
May 12. Mr. Solomon Crosby died.
28. Mr. Hiram Myers takes the census (no date).
June 6. Lawrence Monroe Rogers & Mary B Crowell married, of East Harwich.
11. Mrs. Elikeem Higgins died.
13. Orrin Higgins' youngest daughter married.
20. Mr. Gould Linnell died.
23. Mrs. Sarah Carpenter 2nd., wife of John Snow, died, aged 81.
Oct. 1. A girl to Mr. and Mrs. Daniel B. Gould.
17. Thomas S. Snow and Fanny Lewis married.
23. Chester L. Freeman and Louisa Rogers Mayo married.
27. Rev. Mr. Leah preaches his first sermon.
28. Elwood B. Freeman died—son of Silvanus F., aged 34 years.
Nov. 1. John(?) Young died.
27. Mrs. Evans (Rev. Mr. Evans' mother) died in Chelsea.
28. News of Effie Holmes Wood death in India.
Dec. 8. James Rogers of Eastham died.
25. Willie Higgins & Lottie Crosby married.
31. Ben H. Nickerson & Nellie Cummings married.

1896

Jan. 17. Capt. Alfred Kendrick died—born May 30, 1800.
28. Mrs. Mercy Freeman Doane died in California.
29. Helen, daughter of Fred and Lizzie R. Snow of Chelsea, died.
Feb. 16. Mercy Gould, wife of James Taylor, died.
March 5. Governor F. T. Greenhalge died.
April 4. Marion's father brought to Orleans and buried.
12. Mrs. Jesse C. Snow (Elvir) buried 12th, age 90.
16. Capt. Lot Higgins died, born Sept. 10, 1800.
29. Mrs. Margaret, widow of Winsor Snow, buried, aged 75 years.
May 17. Miss Hanard of Brewster shot by a Mr. Alexander who then took his own life.
28. A son to Mr. and Mrs. Freeman E. Snow.
June 9. Mrs. Gould Linnell died.
16. Patty Young Smith died.
20. Mrs. Susan Snow Link died.
27. James M. Snow died in Boston hospital and buried in Duxbury.
July 2. Samuel Sherman died.
6. Mrs. Emmeline Gould died.
16. Gov. William E. Russell died.
Aug. 2. Eddie and Paul Bramhall died and buried in Orleans.
Sept. 6. Frank W. Snow and Emmie Modena Hayden married in Boston.
27. Angela Adalaide Keeler died.
Oct. 2. Died in Orleans, John Tutty, a native of Chelsea, aged 99 years, 8 months.
11. Hanson R. Higgins died.
16. John G. Snow died, 85 years.
Nov. 10. Miss Mercy T. Snow brought to Orleans and buried.
14. Mr. Bangs Hurd died.

1897

Jan. 6. Winsor Nickerson died and carried to Whitman & buried.
Feb. 12. Mrs. Mehitable, widow of Dean G. Linnell, died.
18. Winfred W. Rogers died in Chatham, aged 24 years.
26. Freeman H. Snow died.

March 22. Pamelia Ann Snow (Mrs. Linnell) brought to Orleans and buried.
22. Died in Orleans, Rev. Charles E. Harwood, Orthodox preacher. Carried to Endfield & buried, aged 54 years, 9 months.
April 2. Abigail Smith, wife of Solomon Linnell, died, aged 71 years.
May 28. Died in Taunton, April 28th, Francis G. Freeman of Wellfleet, aged 61 years, 5 months.
June 1. A daughter to Mr. and Mrs. Wilfred H. Crosby.
1. French steamer arrived with cable, landed cable and leaves.
17. Ella F. Freeman & Overy P. Mayo married.
18. Deacon Jonathan Higgins died.
Aug. 30. Abigail Snow, widow of Sylvester Hopkins, died.
Sept. 3. A girl Lillian Madaline, to Mr. and Mrs. Dan B. Gould.
24. Joseph L. Higgins died, aged 79 years, 9 months.
? Capt. Dean S. Linnell married his second wife.
Oct. 1. Mrs. D. I. Cummings died.
7. Finished laying French cable to shore at East Orleans.
18. Died in Dennis, Mrs. Luther Hall.
25. Thomas Doane buried in Orleans.
28. Isaiah T. Hatch and Miss Datie B. Rogers married.
29. Bennie Nickerson died.
Dec. 6. Mrs. Rebecca (Kendrick) Anderson died.

1898

Jan. 5. Mrs. Darcus Eldredge of East Harwich died, aged 71.
Feb. 20. Ship Asia ashore on a ledge in Vineyard Sound and 16, including Capt. ———, wife and daughter lost—3 saved.
28. Mrs. Rebecca Rogers Young died, aged near 81 years.
March 13. Philander Artemus Crosby died in South Braintree & brought back to Orleans, age 40 years, 11 months.
March 31. Died in Washington, D. C. & brought back to Yarmough, March 31st, Hon. John Simppins, first Congressman from Cape Cod.
April 19. Spend the day in East Boston & see the Barkentine Herbert Truller on board of which 3 persons were murdered by Thomas M. Bram, July 13th, 1896.
21. Isaac L. Gould died.
24. Mrs. Sarah Hopkins died, aged 78.
27. Mertie Snow of Craig, Nebraska, a baby girl.
May 2. Capt. John Linnell died.
17. Mrs. Edwards (Marrietta Linnell), daughter of Capt. John Linnell, died.
June 8. Fred, son of Mr. and Mrs. Luther Hurd, died, aged 22.
Sept. 4. A daughter (Alice Roberts) to Mr. and Mrs. Daniel B. Gould.
11. Myra Lewis married.
23. Will Potter & Ruthie Walker married.
Oct. 12. Rollin W., son of Orville W. and Celia H. Crosby, died, aged 5 years 10 months.
17. Doctor W. H. Stone of Wellfleet died.
Dec. 8. Miss Laura Young died.
22. D. Johnson Cummings & Mary Eliza Hopkins married.
26. Walter Mayo and Bertha Newcomb married.
26. Uncle John Kendrick died.
28. A boy to Ovey P. and Ella F. (Freeman) Mayo.
28. A boy to Frank W. and E. Modena (Hayden) Snow.
29. Marcia B. (Mayo), wife of E. Kendrick, died.

1899

Jan. 7. Mrs. Lydia Bangs (Snow) Long died.
18. A son to Mr. and Mrs. Norton Steele (Myra Lewis).
18. Lottie I. Snow and Andrews married.
Feb. 5. Clarence, son of John C. Rogers, died, aged 19.
March 21. Almond has the doctor—22nd—23rd.

"Almond" was Almond Otis Crosby, born 8/20/1860. Died March 26, 1899—son of Clara Snow Crosby who kept the almanacs she died March 31, 1899.

MARRIAGES SOLEMNIZED IN PEMBROKE, MASS., BY THE REV. THOMAS SMITH, 1755–1787.

Communicated by H. H. EDES, Esq., of Boston, Mass.

THE following list is thought to contain a complete record of all the marriages solemnized by the Rev. Thomas Smith during his ministry in Pembroke. It was copied by me from what appeared to have been Mr. Smith's original minutes, kept in a book of accounts, still in the possession of his descendants, where I discovered them by accident during a visit to the present owner of the volume. From these minutes returns were made in due form to the town clerk, at proper intervals, as indicated in the following pages, which are as near a *fac-simile* of the original record as modern type can make them. The manuscript was in some places nearly illegible by reason of the fading of the ink, and of the careless manner in which these minutes were jotted down. Several entries about which a doubt existed as to my own rendering, were drawn off and sent to Mr. George H. Ryder, the present town clerk of Pembroke, with a request that he would verify or correct my transcript by the town books. To this request a most courteous reply was returned, which enables me to present in print an accurate copy of the entire manuscript by which the proof has been corrected.

The Rev. Thomas Smith, whom the biographical dictionaries dismiss with a few lines when mentioning him at all, was a man of note in his day and generation, and sprang from an honored ancestry; while the family into which he married was of even more distinguished extraction. His emigrant ancestor was the Rev. JOHN SMITH,[1] who was early located in Barnstable, where in 1643 he married Susannah Hinckley, a sister of Gov. Thomas Hinckley, joined the church Oct. 13, 1644, and still later was settled over the parish as its pastor; but "being disliked" by his gubernatorial brother-in-law,—so the record reads,—he withdrew to Long Island, thence to New Jersey, and finally returned to the Old Colony, succeeding, in 1658, the Rev. William Leverich in the Sandwich pulpit. His ministry was harassed by dissensions and party strife, and he laid down his charge in 1688, at the age of seventy-four, after a service of thirty years.[2]

[1] By a deposition of his, taken in the settlement of some probate matters, quoted in Freeman's History of Cape Cod (ii. 80), it appears that he was son of Thomas Smith, of Brinspittae (a place I fail to locate upon any map at my command),* said to be about five miles from Dorchester, in Dorsetshire; was now, "February 8, 1651, in Barnstable * * * only son and heir, supposeth his age about 37 it being, next May, 21 years since he came out of England," and that he had sisters Hannah and Tumson then living in England. It would seem, therefore, that he was born in or about 1614, and came to New England in 1630.

[2] Vide Freeman's History of Cape Cod, i. 80.

* Adams's "Index Villaris" (ed. 1680) gives Brinspudel in Dorsetshire, Lat. 50° 49', Long. 2° 20' W., probably the place now called Bryant's Piddle, a tything in the parish of Aff Piddle.—ED.

Mr. Smith was the father of thirteen children, the last of whom was JOSEPH SMITH, who was born December 6, 1667. He lived at Barnstable, where, April 29, 1689, he married Anna Fuller, who died July 2, 1722. By her he had fourteen children[1]—among whom was Thomas, the minister at Pembroke—and died March 4, 1746.

The Rev. THOMAS SMITH was born in Barnstable, Feb. 6, 1705–6, and graduated at Harvard College in 1725. In 1729 he succeeded the Rev. Daniel Greenleaf as pastor of the church in Yarmouth, where he labored for twenty-five years. In 1754 he requested a dismission, "leaving for lack of competent support," and accepted a call to Pembroke, where he was installed as the successor of the Rev. Daniel Lewis,[2] Dec. 4, 1754. His ministry continued thirty-four years, during which time the meeting-house was enlarged. He preached until his sight failed, and died July 7, 1788, in the eighty-third year of his age. The Rev. Morrill Allen, lately deceased, one of his successors in the Pembroke pulpit, speaks of him as a fine scholar, and the most distinguished man who had ever been settled in the town.

Mr. Smith was married Aug. 28, 1734, to Judith Miller, who was born Aug. 23, 1716. She brought him these twelve children, and died July 31, 1785.

i.	Mary,	born	May	18, 1735,	in Yarmouth.	
ii.	Josiah,	"	Feb.	26, 1738,	"	
iii.	Joseph,	"	Nov.	22, 1740,	"	
iv.	Thomas,	"	July	24, 1742,	"	
v.	Joshua,	"	July	27, 1744,	"	
vi.	Nathaniel,	"	May	29, 1746,	"	d. Dec. 26, 1746.
vii.	Judith,	"	Nov.	4, 1747,	"	
viii.	Thankful,	"	Feb.	26, 1749,	"	
ix.	Nathaniel,	"	Feb.	16, 1752,	"	
x.	Edward,	"	May	16, 1754,	"	
xi.	Catharine,	"	March	21, 1756,	in Pembroke.	
xii.	Christopher,	"	Dec.	22, 1757,	"	

The Rev. JOHN MILLER, who was early of Roxbury, and by some writers is thought to have been of Dorchester likewise, came to New England in 1634, bringing his wife Lydia and son John. He was bred at Gonville and Caius College, Cambridge, where he took his A.B. in 1627, and in the Magnalia is included by Mather in his "*first* classis." While in Roxbury he was an elder of Eliot's church. From 1639 to 1641, he was an "assistant" to the Rev. Ezekiel Rogers, at Rowley, where he also filled the office of town clerk. In the latter year he received and declined a call to the Woburn church, and in 1642, on account of his health, declined a mission to Virginia,

1 *Vide ante*, vol. iii. 275.

2 We hope to present to our readers, in the April number, a transcript of Mr. Lewis's original record of admissions to the Pembroke church from its foundation in 1712, to the close of his ministry in 1753, together with other interesting items relating to the church.—ED.

on which it was proposed to associate with him the Rev. George Phillips, of Watertown, and the Rev. William Thompson, of Braintree. The same year he was a grantee of Newbury. Johnson, in his Wonder-Working Providence, says that he remained in Rowley till called to Yarmouth, whither he went about 1646, as the successor of the famous Marmaduke Matthews. After the death of his wife, which occurred in Boston, Aug. 7, 1658,[1] he seems to have preached "where any temporary want existed," until about the time of the settlement of Groton, whither he appears to have gone with the first settlers of the town, or to have followed them immediately, for a vote of the inhabitants, passed March 18, 1662–3, requested the Rev. John Miller "to continue with them," if he was "moved" to do so; while by another vote of the same date, lands were assigned to him. His ministry in Groton was short, as he died June 12, 1663, and was succeeded by the Rev. Samuel Willard, who was ordained July 13, 1664. He is said to have been a man of high literary attainments.

Mr. Miller had several children born at different places; but it is his son JOHN MILLER, born in England, in March, 1631–2, in whom we are most interested. On the 24th of December, 1659, he was married to Margaret Winslow, daughter of the first Josiah Winslow, and niece of Gov. Edward Winslow, who was born July 16, 1640. He settled in Yarmouth, where he filled various offices of trust, and was frequently its representative in the General Court. He was the father of eleven children, and died in the home of his adoption in June, 1711, at the age of 79.

JOSIAH MILLER, son of John and Margaret (Winslow) Miller, was born in Yarmouth, Oct. 27, 1679, and was very prominent in the public affairs of the town. Aug. 13, 1708, he married Mary Crosby, who was born April 14, 1678, and died in Pembroke, Feb. 15, 1772, at the advanced age of nearly 94 years. Her husband had died more than forty years before in Yarmouth, April 15, 1729. Judith Miller, before mentioned as the wife of the Rev. Thomas Smith, was their daughter.

MARRIAGES.

—— Newel to Rebecca M^c^Farland........................*Folio* 132 A
Dec^br^ 1755. James Bonny to Keturah Bishop.
1756. July 22^d^. Hudson Bishop to Abigail Stetson.
John Ford J^nr^ to Mary Baker.
Ebenezer Cain to Mary Tubbs.
1757. Thomas Tyrrel to Lucy Taylor, Feb. 14.
1757. Nov^br^ 17th. Jethro Hector to Sylva Molatto.
1757. Ichabod Richmond to Abigail Ford.
1757. Dec. 29. Nehemiah Ramsden to Rebecca Chamberlain.
—— Packard to Ruth Bonny.

[1] Lydia, wife of Mr. John Miller, minister of Yarmouth, died, at the house of Thomas Bumstead, of Boston, the 7th of August, 1658.—(Boston Records.)

March 7th. 1758. Prince Keen to Elizabeth Ford.
July 20. 1758. Job Clap to Penelope Hatch.
Novembr 6th. David Philips to Lydia Hatch.
1759. Jan. 4th. Benj. Samson to Deborah Cushing.
1759. May 20th. Robert Barker to Betty Turner.

1759. October 1st. Isaac Lane to Sarah Hatch.
July 30th. Edward King to Alice Perry.
Novbr 12. John Chubbuck to Lydia Crooker.
Thomas Church to Huldah Soul, Febr. 24, 1760.
1760. June 15th. Josiah Smith to Mary Barker.
1760. July 10th. Charles Josselyn to Rebec Keen, ye 3d.
1760. Sept. 14th. Ichabod Bonny to Mary Turner.
1760. October 15. Wm Hearsey to Patience Bisbe.
1760. October 27. Isaack Little to Lydia Hatch.
1760. Asa Bearse to Mary Randal 3d, Novbr 27.
1761. Freedom Chamberlain to Deb. Turner, Jan. 8th.
1761. Ichabod Thomas to Ruth Turner, Jan. 22d.
1761. Mathew Stetson to Mary Randal, Feb. 5.

1761. Ebenezer Barker to Priscilla Loring, April 2d.
1761. Abishar Stetson to —— Crooker, April 16th.
1761. Joseph Taylor to Thankful Clark, May 3d.
1761. Pool Spear to Christina Turner, May 10th.
1761. Joshua Turner Jnr to Betty Benker, June 22d.
1761. Thomas Randal to Deborah Barker Jnr Sept. 10.
1761. Nathaniel Cushing to Lucy Turner, Sept. 24.
1761. { Isaac Ford to Lucy Josselyn.
{ Perez Sampson to Mary Taylor, Octbr 1st.
1761. { Lemuel Bonny to Lucy Bonny.
1761. { Nathaniel Stetson to Sarah Bishop, December 3.
1762. Janry 7th. Joseph Dwelle to Mary Mcgoon.
1762. Feb. 18. Asa Keen to Zilpah Hatch.
1762. Wm Hayford to Betty Bonny, March 11.

1762. Caleb Howland to Deb. Oldham, May 2d.
1762. Jesse Lapham to Mercy Randal, Novbr 25.
1763. Febr 24th. Jedediah Dwelle to Lydia Soule.
1763. April 28. Diman Perry to Nabbe Cushing.
Carried to Town Clck.

1763. June 2d. Jno Mitchel to Rispha Richards.
1763. Octbr 13th. Robert Mclathlin to Mary Keen.
Octbr 18th. Adam Turner to Chloe Bonny.
1763. Novbr 28th. Isaac Hatch to Sarah Cushing.
1764. Febr 22d. Jonathan Turner to Hannah Ford Jnr.
1763. Decem. 6th. Danil Tubbs to Hannah White.
1763. Will Standish to Abigail Stetson, Decembr 8.
1764. March 8. Seth Fuller to Deborah Ford.
1764. March 22d. Sylvanus Cook [of Kingston] to Sarah Barstow.

1764. Thomas Curlew to Mary Russel, July 18th.
1765. Abel Russel to Lydia Garnet, May 7th, 1765.
1765. Abner Megoon to Ruth Briggs, Oct. 14.
1765. Ezra Lawrence to Mol Geofry, Sept. 26.
1765. Nath Winslow to Sarah Hatch Jnr, Nov. 21st.... ....*Folio*
1766. Thos Lincoln to Lydia Randal, Febr 13th. 132 B

John Jordan to Chloe Tubbs, Feb. 23.
Daniel Bonny to Elizabeth Burton, May 15.
Robert Page to Susannah Bennet, May 26.
1766. Elisha Hatch to Bettsy Howland, August 7th.

1766. Nov. 13. Revd Isaiah Dunster to Mary Smith.
December 8. Amariah Goodwin to Thankful Russel.
1767. Jan. 8th. Thomas Barker to Olive Ford.
29 Jan. Ichabod Bearse to Eunice Witherel.
7 April. Stephen Richardson to Mercy Darling.

1767.

October 29. Zelek Basset to Huldah Garnet.
Dec. 10. Lemuel Church to Susannah Baker.
Dec. 24. Sam'l Jennings to Keziah Bearse.[1]
Amos Withrel to Ruth Stetson.
Mrch 1. Apollos Cushman to Eleanor Keen.
Mrch 10. Japhet Crooker to Lydia Turner.
Mrch 18. Joseph Turner to Elizabeth Crooker.

May. Windsor to
June 14. Nathaniel Turner to Sarah Rogers.
July 7th. James Glover to Rachel Bonny.
Nov. 24. Stockbridge Josseyln to Olive Standish.
1769. May 23d. Joseph Peirce to Oliff Fish.
June 15th. Daniel Oldham to Withrell.
Novbr 16. Ebenezer Beerse to Lydia Jennings.
Sept. 28. Hezekiah Bryant to Debrah Crooker.
Decbr 25. Joshua Withrel to Mary Standish.

1770.

Jan. 18. Simeon Nash to Hulda Bates.
Feb. 1. { Joseph Ramsden to Elizabeth Barker. and Thomas Crooker to Nabby Randal.
15. James Cox to Ruth Mcgoon.
Mrch 26. Thomas Cooke to Hannah Lincoln.
June 10. John Thomas to Sarah Loring.
Sept. 16. Zadock Reed to Lucee Garnet.
Octo. 22. Shubael Butler to Hannah Garnet.
Nov. 22. Caleb Barstow to Sylvina Mcgoon.

1771.

April 25. Melzer Curtis to Keziah Hall.
May 30. Caleb Tilden to Joanna Barker.
Sept. 1st. Nathl Loring Jnr to Sarah Baker ye 3d.
Octo. 31. David Crooker Jnr to Ursula Turner.
Nov. 20. Benj. Barns to Luciana Ramsden.
Nov. 21. Isaack Brewster to Leonice Soul.
Philip Turner to Judith Hatch.
Decbr 1st. Ephraim Lindsay to Ann Bonny.

1772.

Janry 16th. Wm Reading to Elizabeth Bates.
Mrch 19. Benj. Cox to Deborah Russel.
April 30. Isaiah Cushing to Lydia Fish Jnr.

[1] This entry and that following are opposite "Dec. 24."

May 17. Moses House [of Marshfield] to Lydia Russel.
Octo. 1st. Ebenezer Man to Ursula Randal Jnr.

1773.

August 5. Lemuel Crooker to Rachel Foster.
August 19. Constant Little to Sarah Barker Jnr.
Sept. 5. Zebulun Buker to Debrah Randal.
Ditto. Maurice Tubbs to Betty Randal.
Octo. 16th. Isaac Tubbs to Hannah Crooker.
Decembr 30. Diman Perry to Susannah Lincoln.
John Randal to Sarah Eames, June 9, 1774.......*Folio* 133 A
1774. Saml Rider to Peggy Keen, June 19, 1774.
all in ye Back page have been returned to ye Clerk — Saml Chandler to Rebecca Darling, Octo. 27th, 1774.
Abel Nash to Susannah Tracy, Decem. 15th.

1775.

Eben Crooker to Cloe Gardner, Nov. 25, 1773, omitted in former list.

Jan. 11th Eleventh. Asher Keen to Desire Witherel.
Feb. 21st. Ebenezer Withrel to Rebecca Macfarland.
Joseph Mcgoon to Sarah Mcgoon.
23d Novmbr. Andrew Bradford to Mary Turner 3d.

1776.

Feb. 1st. Isaack Mcgoon to Lydia McFarland.
March 14. Isaiah Stetson to Susa Bonney.
Ditto 28. Nathaniel Randal to Deborah Stetson Jnr.
May 5. Job Turner to Sarah James.
May 16. Eliphalet Bishop to Elizabeth Tubbs.
Nov. 7th. James Sprague Jnr to Lydia Barker.

1777.

Janry 13. Elijah Baker to Mary Wittemore.
Janry 23. William Cushing to Abigail Turner Jnr.
March 13. Caleb Lapham to Sarah Fish.
Sept. 14. Philip Turner to Mercy Turner.
Novbr 20. Elisha Briggs to Laurentia Hall.
Dec. 25. Saml Loring to Prudence Chapman.

1778.

Mrch 15. Nathaniel Fish to Mary Leavit.
June 25. Abiel Sherman to Lydia Walker.
Octo. 1st. Benjamin Highland to Content Lincoln.
Decembr 3d. Edward Stevens Jnr to Mehetabel Newberry.
Decembr 24. David Man to Elizabeth Bates.

1779.

Janry 7th. Jacob Tubbs Jnr to Desire Crooker Jnr.
Mrch 18. Lemuel Little to Mary Lapham.
May 20. Jesse Torrey to Mary Chamberlain.
June 6. Nathaniel Bishop to Abigail Bearse Jnr.
July 8. Joseph Byron to Alice Garnet.
July 25. Perry Harden to Moll-Swan-Keen.
August 18. Daniel Russel to Susanna McFarland.
Nov. 2. Ebenezer Whitman 3d to Ruth Delano.
Nov. 23. John Lowden to Hannah Gould.
Novbr 25. Zacheus Fish to Rachel Stetson.
Dec. 8. Ezra Warren to Saba Tirrel.
Decem. 23. Alexander Garnet to Ruth Tubbs.

1780.

Feb. 24. John Briggs Jnr to Hannah Bearse Jnr.
May 3d. Jesse Turner to Bathsheba Lapham.
June 26. Wait Ford to Hannah Loring.
July 3d. Joseph Henney to Sylvina Richards.
July 6. Saml Peterson to Lydia Cowin.
July 13. Joshua Keen Jnr to Lydia Crooker.
July 26. Joseph Sherman to Sylvester Josselyn.
Augt 17. Isaac Foster Jnr to Urania Taylor.
Sept. 3. Comfort Bates Jnr to Nabby Mcgoon.
Octo. 1. Amos Hatch to Hannah Philips.
Nov. 23. Charles Ford to Polly Bisbe.
Nov. 30. Hadly Standish to Nabby Garnet.
Decem. 7th. Thomas Nash to Betty man.

All ye above returned to the Town Clerk.

1781.

Sept. 7th. Bille Ford to Lucene Howland.
Octobr. 7. Noah Bonney to Nancy Tory—Octo. 7.
Octobr 25. Joshua Mcgown to Sylvina Stetson.
Nov. 15. Gideon Thomas White to Sarah Crooker.
Nov. 25. Tilden Crooker to Priscilla Barker Jnr.
Decembr 9th. Isaac Thomas to Catharine Smith.
Decembr 13. James Barstow to Sarah Leavit.
26. Elisha Turner to Sarah Keen.

1782........................Folio

Janry 1. Joseph Smith to Bathsheba Torrey. 133 B
Janry 6. Daniel Baker to Priscilla Loring Jnr.
Janry 31. Thomas Fish to Ursula Crooker Jnr.
July 2d. Seth Perry to Hannah Josselyn Jnr.
July 4th. Nathan Stetson to Bethia Crooker.
August 1st. Joseph Bobbins to Lucy Cushing Both of Hanover.
Sept. 12. Saml Webb to Betty Baker.
Nov. 27. Richard Withrel to Sally Randal.
Decem 1st. Abel Stetson to Sally Oldham.
Decem. 12. James Brand to Hannah Ned.

1783.

Febr 20. Isaack Tubbs to Betty Tubbs.
Febr 27. John Young to Leah Bonny.
July 17. Saml Elles to Lydia Josselyn.
Sept. 18. Luther Samson to Abigail Foord.
Octobr 2. Isaac Walker to Lydia Dowse.
Decembr 11. Harris Hatch to Deborah Chamberlain Jnr.

1784.

Janry 22d. John Chubbuck to Mary Forster.
Do Lemuel Keen to Mary Josselyn.
April 8. John Tolman to Dorothy Hall.
April 22d. Arannah Fullington to Lyllis Stetson.
May 9th. Jesse Delano to Margaret Leavit.
July 15. Christopher Thomas to Huldah Dwelle.
Novmbr 14. Ichabod Thomas Jnr to Polly Thomas.
Novmbr 25. John Josselyn to Lucy Lowden.
Decembr 16. Isaiah Bonny to Aphia Pompele.

Decembr 30. Isaack Fish to Deborah Fish.

All ye above Returned to ye Town Clerk.

1785.

March 2^{d}. Jacob Peterson to Betse Turner J^{nr}.
March 31st. Winslow Turner to Molly Standish.
April 24. Christopher Pierce to Lydia M^{c}goon.
June 30. Fredom Chamberlain J^{nr} to Priscilla Josselyn.
Novembr 27. Alanson Carver to Huldah Barstow.

1786.

Febry 23. John Lowden to Ruth Josselin.
March 9th. Seth Sampson to Appie Pompelie.
April 23. Thos M^{c}gown to Priscilla Barker.

1787.

March 15. Lot Foord to Naomi Lapham.
July 26. Benjaman Tolman to Rebecka Lincoln.

1786 December.................... *Folio* 134

Richard Hite to Suke Osgood.

August. 1787. Uriah Iues to Sarah Samson.
October 28. 1787. Jonathan Bonney to Peggy Torrey.
Novem 29th. 1787. William Briggs to Nabby Briggs.

BAPTISMS IN THE SECOND CHURCH OF CHRIST IN PEMBROKE, MASS., FROM 1748 TO 1803.

Communicated by MRS. ELROY M. AVERY of Cleveland, Ohio.

THE Rev. Gad Hitchcock was ordained pastor of the Second Church of Christ in Pembroke (now Hanson), Plymouth County, Mass., in October, 1748. He died in 1803. The following records are transcribed by me from a book in his own handwriting and bearing his signature. The book was the property of the late Calvin T. Phillips, one of his descendants.

1748.

October 9, 1748. Abigail, Daughter of Samuel Howland.
" 9, Content, Daughter of Abraham Howland.
" 16, Sarah, Daughter of James Hanks.
" 23, Obadiah, Son of James Bearse.
November 20, Isaac, Son of Isaac Hamlin, per Mr. Brown.

1749.

January	29, 1749.	Dorothy, Daughter of Abraham Josslyn.
March	5,	Noah, Son of Ezekial Bonny.
"	5,	Matthew, Son of Matthew Whiting.
April	14,	Abraham, Son of Benjamin Howland, it being Sick Baptism was administered in private house.
May	9,	Isaac, Son of William Cox.
"	9,	Thomas, Son of John records, baptised on account of William Cox.
July	2,	Job, Son of Jacob Bearse.
August	13,	Isaac, Son of Captain Josiah Cushing.
Sept.	3,	Richard, son of Richard and Pegg, negro servants of Captain Josiah Cushing.
October	3,	Gamaliel, Son of Jonah Bisbee.
November	5,	Gad, Son of Rev. Gad Hitchcock.

1750.

April	5, 1750.	Abel, Son of Jabez Cole, on account of his wife.
"	6,	Rebecca, Daughter of Abraham Howland, in a private house being sick.
"	8,	Isaac, Son of Abraham Howland.
"	22,	Job, Son of Job Bonney.
"	29,	John, Son of Deacon John Bisbee.
June	17,	Elizabeth, Daughter of Elisha Faxon.
"	24,	Alexander, Son of Alexander Soper, Baptised on account of his mother.
July	5,	Nathan, Son of Daniel Crocker.
August	19,	Priscilla, Daughter of Thomas Faxon.
November	11,	Nathaniel, Son of Edward Thomas.
December	16,	Abner, Son of Isaac Hamlin.

1751.

January	20, 1751.	Benjamin, Son of Benjamin Howland.
February	24,	Lemuel, Son of Ebenezer Bowen.
March	3,	Isaac, Son of Abraham Josslyn.
April	27,	Studley, Son of Aaron Bisbee of Duxburough.
"	27,	Elizabeth, Daughter of David Hersey, Jun, of Plympton.
May	19,	Ephraim, Son of John Allen and
"	19,	Jotham, Son of Gideon Bisbee, both per Mr. Shull.
June	16,	Matthew, Son of Matthew Whiton, per Mr. Angier.
"	24,	William, Son of Ezekial Bonney.
"	24,	Ruth, Daughter of Samuel Howland.
"	24,	Sarah, Daughter of Elisha Faxon.
October	27,	Mary, wife of Thomas Moore, an Adult.
November	3,	Mary and John, children of Thomas Moore, Baptised on account of his wife, Mary Moore.

1752.

March	15, 1752.	Daniel, Son of Daniel Hayford Junr Baptised on account of his wife.
"	27,	Sarah, Daughter of Samuel Bisbee.

April 26,	Adam, Son of Samuel Perry.
" 26,	Hannah, Daughter of Jacob Bearse.
May 10,	Rebecca, Nathaniel, Hannah, James, John and Benjamin, Children of Edward Cox.
" 24,	David, Son of Isaac Hamlin.
" 24,	Matthew, Son of Richard and Pegg, Negro Servants belonging to Captain Josiah Cushing.
June 7,	Mary, Daughter of Alexander Soper, Baptised on account of his wife.
" 21,	Charles and Luke, twin Sons of Job Bonney.
" 29,	Simeon, Son of Joseph Ramsdell.
October 8,	Elizabeth, Daughter of Elnathan Watson of Duxburough.
" 15,	Mary, Daughter of Daniel Crocker.
" 15,	Richard, Son of Richard Phillips.
" 15,	Lydia, Daughter of Mr. Castle, Baptised on account of his wife.
November 19, N. S.	Ruth, Daughter of Thomas Faxon.

1753.

March 25, 1753.	Stetson, Son of William Holmes, Baptised on account of his wife.
April 8,	Joseph, Son of Edward Thomas.
" 8,	Elisha, Son of John Records, Baptised on account of his wife.
May 13,	Rebecca, Daughter of Gideon Bisbee.
" 13,	Allathea, Daughter of Benjamin Howland.
" 27,	Isaac, Son of Thomas Moore, Baptised on account of his wife.
September 9,	Nelson, Son of Richard Beuker, Baptised on account of his wife.
" 9,	Abigail, Daughter of Abraham Jossylin.
October 28,	Jonathan, Son of Ezekiel Bonny.
" 28,	Ford, Son of Jacob Bearse.
" 28,	Edward, Son of Daniel Hayford Junr.
November 4,	Deborah, Daughter of Mr. Castle, Baptised on account of his wife.
December 2,	Elisha, Son of Elisha Faxon.
" 8,	Susanna, Daughter of David Gardner, Pembroke, old precinct.
" 22,	Marlborough, Son of Matthew Whiten, it being Sick baptism was administered in private.

1754.

January 13, 1754.	Ichabod, Son of Widow Sarah Howland.
" 13,	Sarah, daughter of Ephraim Paddock.
February 10,	Calvin, son of Reuben Carver.
" 24,	William, son of Richard and Pegg, negro servants belonging to Captain Joseph Cushing.
March 17,	Abagail, daughter of Joseph Cole, baptised on account of his wife.

April	25,	Margaret, daughter of Henry Monroe.
"	25,	Olive, daughter of Joseph Ramsdell, jr.
"	28,	Molly, daughter of Ebenezer Bourn.
May	19,	Margaret, daughter of Lemuel Crocker.
July	28,	Tabitha, daughter of Mrs. Keen.
August	11,	Sarah, daughter of Benjamin Paris.
September	21,	Isaac, son of Richard Phillips.
"	21,	Spencer, son of Comfort Bates, Jun, lower parish, being sick baptism administered in private house.
October	13,	Jacob, son of Abraham Howland.
"	20,	Barnabas, son of Elijah Faxon.
"	20,	Edmund, son of Benjamin Ramsdell.
"	20,	Mary, daughter of Job Bonny.
"	20,	Eleazer, son of Jonah Bisbee.
"	20,	Samuel, son of Levi Keen.
November	24,	Deliverance, daughter of Samuel Hayford.

1755.

January	15, 1755.	Marlborough, son of Matthew Whitton.
February	2,	Sarah, daughter of Edward Cox.
"	8,	Sarah, daughter of Edward Thomas.
"	8,	Betty, daughter of Alexander Soper, on account of his wife.
April	13,	Tilden, son of Daniel Crocker.
May	25,	Content, daughter of Samuel Ramsdell.
August	17,	Laurina, daughter of Job Castel, on account of his wife.
"	31,	Gideon, son of Gideon Bisbee.
September	7,	Sylvester (?) daughter of Ezekiel Bonney.
"	14,	Abigail, daughter of Increase Robinson.
"	14,	Nathaniel, son of Daniel Hayford, Jun.
October	12,	Samuel, son of Benjamin Paris.
"	26,	Abigail, daughter of Abraham Josselyn.
November	9,	Mary, daughter of Reuben Carver.
"	30,	Jonathan Finney, son of William Holmes, baptised on account of his wife.

1756.

January	18, 1756.	Abigail, daughter of Samuel Hayford.
"	25,	Richard Hill, son of Widow Phebe Beuker.
February	15,	Thomas, son of Thomas Moore.
April	14,	Betty, daughter of Isaac Soul.
May	2,	Lucinda, daughter of Hezekiah Holmes.
"	30,	Bennet, son of Henry Monroe.
June	6,	Molly, daughter of Elisha Foxson.
"	20,	Ephraim, son of Ephraim Paddock.
August	1,	Rachel, daughter of Nehemiah Pierce.
"	8,	Margaret, negro woman belonging to Josiah Cushing, an adult.
"	15,	Asaph, son of Elijah Faxon.
October	3,	———, daughter of Richard and Pegg, negro servants of Josiah Cushing.

November	21,	Rebecca, daughter of Edward Cox.
"	28,	Elijah, son of Elijah Cushing, Jun.
December	12,	Benjamin, son of Lemuel Crooker.

1757.

January	7, 1757.	Josiah, son of Josiah Foster, by Mr. Dodge.
"	23,	Gaius, son of Richard Phillips.
"	23,	Abigail, daughter of Samuel Ramsdell, Jun.
June	13,	Rebekah and Richard, children of Richard Beuker, baptised on account of his wife.
July	3,	Jemima, daughter of Widow Hill.
"	24,	Isaih, son of Joseph Cole, baptised on account of his wife.
August	21,	Mary, daughter of Matthew Whitton.
September	1,	Ebenezer, son of James Bourn.
"	11,	John Blainey, son of Reuben Carver per Mr. Shull.
October	9,	Bethiah, daughter of Daniel Crooker.
"	16,	Orsamus, son of Hezekiah Holmes.
"	16,	Asia, Betty, Alie, children of Mrs. Hamblin, wife of E. Hamblin, baptised on her account.
November		Crispa, daughter of Sylvester Prince.
"	20,	Jonathan, son of Gideon Bisbee.

1758.

February	26, 1758.	Africa, son of Eleazer Hamblin, baptised on account of his wife.
April	23,	Lucy, Sarah and Deborah, children of —— Dunbar.
"	23,	Lydia, daughter of Abraham Josselyn.
"	23,	Parmelia, daughter of John Records, baptised on account of Sarah, his wife.
May	14,	Nathaniel, son of Alexander Soper, baptised on account of his wife.
"	21,	Oliver, son of Ezekial Bonney.
"	28,	Job Caswell, an adult.
November	5,	Samuel, son of Thomas Moore.
"	5,	John, son of Simeon Ramsdell.
"	5,	Samuel, son of Elisha Faxon.
"	5,	Christopher, son of George Stetson.
"	5,	Cinthia, daughter of Richard Phillips.
"	19,	George William, son of Henry Monroe.
"	19,	Alice, daughter of Job Caswell.
December	31,	Tamson, daughter of Lieut. Elijah Cushing.

1759.

January	21, 1759.	John, son of Samuel Ramsdell, jun.
March	11,	Thomas, son of Jacob Bearse.
April		Lucy, unknown child, on account of Isaac Soul.
"	29,	Crispe, daughter of Sylvester Prince.
May	6,	Zebulon, son of Zebulon Howland.
August		Elizabeth, daughter of Edward Cox. Being sick baptized in private.
"		Deborah, daughter of James Bourn.

August	26,	Mary White and Anne, daughters of Theophelus Cushing.
September	1,	Rebecca, daughter of Joseph Newell.
"	1,	Deborah, daughter of Daniel Crooker.

1760.

January	6, 1760.	Anna, daughter of Captain Cushing.
February	10,	Lydia, daughter of Mathew Whitten.
March	29,	Isaac, son of Howland Beals.
April	6,	Ruth, daughter of John Delano, on account of his wife.
"	20,	Europe, son of Eleazer Hamblin, on account of his wife.
June	29,	Cynthia, daughter of Hezekiah Holmes.
July	4,	Mercy Monroe, daughter of Simeon Ramsdell.
"	11,	Joseph Ramsdell, an adult.
"	13,	Ann, daughter of Samuel Hayford.
August	24,	Cela, child of Abraham Josselyn.
November	2,	Betty, child of Thomas Moore.
"	16,	Jairus, son of Richard Phillips.
"	16,	Mary, daughter of Webster Hayford.
"	16,	Walter, son of Hatch.
"	23,	Hannah, daughter of William Phillips, jun.

1761.

February	27, 1761.	Barker, son of Zebulon Howland.
March	15,	Malsey, son of Ephraim Lynsey.
April	19,	Mary, daughter of John Hatch.
May	3,	John, son of John Allen.
"	31,	Sybyll, daughter of Jonathan Dunbar.
"	31,	John, son of Howland Beals.
June	7,	Hannah and Anna, daughters of Jonah Newell.
"	7,	Betty, daughter of Elijah Faxon.
October	4,	Mercy, daughter of Benjamin Bonney.
"	25,	Nehamiah, son of Nehamiah Ramsdell.
November	1,	Allen, son of Elisha Faxson.
"	22,	Job, son of Job Caswell.
"	22,	America, son of Eleazer Hamblin.
December	9,	Nehemiah, son of Theophilus Cushing.

1762.

February	6, 1762.	Eleazer Hamblin, an adult.
April	18,	George Williams, son of Moses Soul.
"	18,	Joseph, son of Increase Robinson, jun.
"	18,	Lydia, daughter of James Bourn.
"	25,	Ruth, daughter of Jabez Cole, baptised on account of his wife.
"	25,	Samuel Baker, son of Henry Perrey.
"	25,	Hannah Barker and Lydia Cushing, daughters of Zebulon Howland.
May	9,	Mary, daughter of Thomas Hill.
"	30,	Anna, daughter of ——— Dammon.
"	30,	Esther, daughter of Noah Cole, baptised on account of his wife Jane.

July	4,	Anna Stockbridge.
"	11,	Nathaniel, son of Nathaniel Cushing.
August	15,	Elisha, son of William Phillips.
October	24,	Molly, daughter of John Read, baptised on account of his wife.
"	31,	Eleaxor, son of Abraham Josselyn.
"	31.	Laurana, daughter of Hezekiah Holmes.
November	14,	Thomas, son of Thomas Josselyn.
"	14,	James, son of Ephraim Linsey.
"	28,	Elisha, son of Elisha House.
December	5,	Chloe, daughter of Richard Phillips.
"	5,	Ruby, daughter of Matthew Whiten.
"	19,	Mercy Freeman, daughter of Samuel Hayford.
"	26,	Deborah, daughter of Simeon Jones.

1763.

March	1763.	Abraham, son of Benjamin Howland, on account of his wife.
April	3,	Sarah, daughter of John Delano on account of his wife.
"	3,	Ezekial, son of Thomas Moore.
"	3,	Theofolous, son of Thomas Moore.
May	1,	Nathaniel, son of Nehemiah Ramsdell.
June		Deborah, daughter of ——— Ershine.
"		Mary, daughter of William Cox, jun.
July		John Bisbee, son of John Thompson.
"		Laben, son of Japhet Allen.
August		Webster, son of Webster Hayford.
"		William, son of William Hayford.
"	28,	Isaah, son of Howland Beals.
September	25,	Issachar, son of Caleb Howland.
		Daniel, son of Theophalus Cushing.
November		Allen, son of John Hatch.
"		Lydia, daughter of Eleazer Hamlin.
December	25,	Hannah, daughter of Lemuel Bonney.
		Priscilla, daughter of Increase Robinson, jun.

BAPTISMS IN THE SECOND CHURCH OF CHRIST IN PEMBROKE, MASS., FROM 1748 TO 1803.

Communicated by MRS. ELROY M. AVERY of Cleveland, Ohio.

1764.

	1764.	Sarah, daughter of Noah Cole.
		Eleoner, daughter of Moses Soul.
April	29,	Henry, son of Henry Perrey.
May		Benjamin, son of Elisha Faxon.
July		Job, son of Job Caswell, on account of his wife.
"		Peter, son of John Thompson, Bridgewater.
"		Betty, daughter of William Phillips.
		Lucy, daughter of Nathaniel Cushing.
August	5,	James, son of James Bourn.
September	1,	Seth, son of Reuben Carver.

	Rebecca, daughter of William Hayford.
September	Jonathan Bonney, son of Webster Hayford.
October 8,	Mary Brackley, daughter of Ephraim Lindsey.
November 4,	Daniel, son of Theophilus Cushing.

1765.

January 20, 1765.	Simeon, son of Simeon Jones.
March 20,	Abiah, daughter of Hezekiah Holmes.
" 31,	Betty, daughter of William Hayford.
April 14,	John, son of John Delano, on account of his wife, per Mr. Badwin.
" 28,	Lydia, daughter of Joseph Bonney.
May 5,	Patience Howland, daughter of Thomas Josselyn.
" 26,	Nabby, daughter of Daniel Crooker.
" 9,	Tamar, daughter of Abraham Josselyn.
" 9,	Ichobod, son of Richard Phillips.
" 9,	Abner Turner, son of Simeon Ramsdale.
September 8,	William, son of Jahesh Cole, baptised on account of his wife.
" 8,	Asa, son of Increase Robinson, Jun'r.
" 15,	Levi, son of John Reed.
" 22,	Isaac, son of William Cocks, Jun'r.
" 29,	Eleazer, son of Eleazer Hamlin.
" 29,	Sarah Lindsey, daughter of Thomas Hill.
	Lucy, daughter of Lemuel Bonney.
October 6,	Isaac, son of Alexander Soper.

1766.

February 2, 1766.	Oliver, son of Matthew Whitten.
" 26,	———, child of William Phillips, Jun'r.
"	Deliverence, daughter of Webster Hayford.
April 6,	Deborah, daughter of John Hatch.
" 13,	Buzi, son of John Hunt.
"	Tamar, daughter of Lieut. Elijah Cushing.
May 11,	Lydia, daughter of Jeremiah Cushing.
" 17,	George, son of Noah Cole.
" 25,	Ezra, son of Howland Beals.
June 19,	Betty, daughter of Daniel Crooker.
" 13,	Seth, son of Nehemiah Ramsdell.
" 27,	Artemisia, daughter of William Hayford.
	James, son of John Thompson, Bridgewater.
August 24,	Seth, son of Seth Cocks.
September 28,	Bildad, son of Moses Soul.
October 12,	Huldah, daughter of John Hobert.
" 19,	Ruth, daughter of Ephraim Lindsey.

1767.

March 1, 1767.	Nathaniel, son of Simeon Jones.
April 26,	Ruth, daughter of Richard Phillips.
" 26,	Bethiah Thacher, daughter of Thomas Josselyn.
" 26,	Richard, son of Richard Lowden.

May 31,	Bethiah, daughter of James Bourn.
June 7,	John, son of Mercy Hayford, baptised on account of Captain Josiah Cushing and wife who have engaged for the religious education of it.
" 14,	Juba, a black boy belonging to Gad Hitchcock.
" 14,	Lilly, a black girl belonging to Blany Phillips, both on account of their respective masters.
July 9,	Abner, son of Hezekiah Holmes.
" 19,	Betty, daughter of Thomas Moore.
" 19,	Elizabeth Ramsdell, daughter of Elijah Croker.
"	Lemuel, son of Lemuel Bonney.
August 23,	Mary White, daughter of Theophalus Cushing, baptised on account of his wife.
September 6,	Hannah, daughter of Joseph Bonney.
" 13,	Molly, daughter of Eleazer Hamlin.
" 20,	Israel, son of John Delano, baptised on account of his wife.
November 14,	William, son of William Cocks, Jun'r.
" 15,	Matilda, daughter of William Hayford.
	Elizabeth, daughter of Increase Robinson.
December 13,	Cephas, son of Joseph Cole.

1768.

January 1768.	Isaac, son of Nathaniel Cushing.
" 17,	Mercy, daughter of John Hunt.
February 26,	Phebe, daughter of James Hatch, baptised on account of his wife.
March	Edward, son of Lieut. Elijah Cushing.
April	John, son of William Phillips, Jun'r.
"	Bartlett, son of Nehemiah Ramsdell.
"	Martha, daughter of Noah Cole.
May 3,	John, son of Samuel Darling.
"	James and John, twin sons of Henry Perry.
" 29,	James Hatch, an adult.
" 29,	Mary and Charlotte, daughters of James Hatch.
June	William, son of John Thompson, Bridgewater.
July	Lilly, a negro woman belonging to Lieut. E. Cushing.
August	Mary Rose, daughter of Jeremiah Stetson.
"	Elizabeth, daughter of James Hatch.
September	Joseph and Ruth, son and daughter of ——— Briggs.
October 2,	Isaac, son of Abraham Josselyn.
"	Samuel, son of Samuel Hill.
" 2,	Oliver, son of John Reed.
" 16,	Ephraim, son of Ephraim Lindsey.
" 30,	Elijah Cushing and Briggs, sons of Zebulon Howland.
November 5,	Lydia, daughter of William Cocks, Jun'r.
"	Charles, son of Simeon Jones.

1769.

January 1769.	Sarah, daughter of Hezekiah Holmes.
February	Abiah, son of Nathaniel Chamberlen.
March 19,	Luther, son of Lemuel Bonney.

April 9,	Lydia, daughter of William Phillips, Jun'r.
" 30,	Lydia, daughter of Daniel Crooker.
June 11,	Moses, son of Moses Soul.
July 9,	Joseph Barker, son of Thomas Josselyn.
" 23,	Dinah, a black girl belonging to Gad Hitchcock.
August	Cyrus and Hannibal, twin sons of Eleazer Hamlin.
" 20,	Lydia Bonney, daughter of Richard Phillips.
	Molly Watterman, daughter of Samuel Hayford.
September 17,	Ephraim, son of Seth Cocks.
November	Sarah, daughter of Thomas Moore.

1770.

March 1770.	Elizabeth, daughter of Joseph Bonney.
April	Priscilla, daughter of James Bourn.
" 22,	Mercy, daughter of Samuel Darling.
May	Ephraim, son of Ephraim Briggs.
June 16,	Cynthia, daughter of John Thompson, Halifax.
July	Esther, daughter of John Hunt.
"	Eunice, daughter of Abraham Josselyn, Jun'r.
" 8,	Elvin, son of Increase Robinson.
" 8,	Elijah, son of Elijah Crooker.
" 15,	Deborah, daughter of Alexander Soper, baptised on account of his wife.
" 15,	Chloe, daughter of Nathaniel Chamberlin.
August	Charles, son of Ensign Nathaniel Cushing.
"	Abel, son of John Delano, baptised on account of ye mother.
October	Seth, son of Howland Beals.
November 18,	Arvada, son of William Hayford.
December 2,	Thomas, son of Lieut. Elijah Cushing.
"	Anne, daughter of James Hatch.
" 20,	Rebecca, Howland, an adult.

All above this date, December 30, 1770, are 386.

1771.

April 1771.	Rebecca, daughter of Nathaniel Ramsdell.
"	Deborah, daughter of John Thomas.
" 28,	Hannah, daughter of Simeon Jones.
May	———, daughter of John Hatch.
"	Mercy, daughter of William Phillips, Jun'r.
June	Rebecca, daughter of Sylvester Mo(?).
"	Hannah, daughter of Hannah Stetson.
August 11,	Ensign, son of Daniel Crooker, Jun'r.
September 22,	Bethany, child of Elijah Crooker.
" 29,	Enos, son of Seth Cocks.
November 15,	Lucy, daughter of Samuel Howland.

1772.

January 12, 1772.	Nathaniel, son of Joseph Symmons.
March 1,	Martilla, daughter of Increase Robinson.
May	Nathaniel, son of Nathaniel Chamberlain.
June	Samuel-William, son of Thomas Josselyn, Jun'r.

June 28,	Bennet, Elizabeth, Apphia, John, Reuel, Barnard, the children of John Pumpely, baptised on account of Apphia, his wife.
" 28,	Barzillai, son of John Thompson, Halifax.
July	Simeon, son of Ruben Clark.
"	Amy, daughter of Joseph Bonney.
August 16,	Ezekial, son of Nehemiah Ramsdell.
"	Elizabeth, Cushing, daughter of Zebulen Howland, resident at Fox Island.
September	Sylvia, daughter of Joseph Howland, baptised on account of his wife.
"	Sarah, daughter of Ephraim Briggs.
October	Elizabeth, daughter of Jeremy Stetson.
"	William, son of Noah Cole, baptised on account of his wife.
"	Ancell, child of Mercy Farr.
"	Benjamin, son of Nathaniel Cushing.
"	Lucy, daughter of Lemuel Bonney.
November	James, son of James Hatch.
December	Bennett, son of Henry Monroe.

1773.

January 1773.	Gustavus, son of William Hayford.
March	John, son of John Stetson, baptised on account of his wife.
May	Lydia, daughter of Content Ramsdell.
" 23,	Joshua, son of Joseph Nichols.
"	Sarah, daughter of John Thomas.
"	Mary Gary, an adult.
June	Anne, daughter of Captain Elijah Cushing.
"	Mary, daughter of Howland Beals.
"	William, son of William Phillips, Jun'r.
August 2,	Ebenezer, son of Betty Robinson Corbet.
" 22,	Noah, son of Noah Perry.
September 19,	Ethelbert, son of Ephraim Lindsey.
October	Benjamin, son of Richard Phillips.
" 31,	Susannah, daughter of Increase Robinson.
November 14,	Seth, son of Gideon Ramsdell, Jun'r.
"	Avice, daughter of Ephraim Briggs.
" 28,	Phebe, daughter of Samuel Hill.

BAPTISMS IN THE SECOND CHURCH OF CHRIST IN PEMBROKE, MASS., FROM 1748 TO 1803.

Communicated by Mrs. Elroy M. Avery of Cleveland, Ohio.

1774.

January 1774.	Zeheniah, son of Nathaniel Chamberlain.
March	Sarah, daughter of Samuel Howland.
"	Hannah, daughter of Hannah Cole.
"	Jacob, son of Jacob Bearse.
April	Christina, daughter of William Hayford.
" 24,	Hannah, daughter of Simeon Jones.
May 22,	Asia, son of Eleazer Hamlin.
" 22,	Calvin, son of John Thompson.
June 5,	Lurenna, daughter of John Hatch.
"	Eunice, daughter of Blaney Phillips, Jun'r.
"	John Allen, son of James Bourn.
July 3,	Chloe, daughter of Joseph Bonney.
August 14,	Elizabeth Josselyn, daughter of Seth Cocks.
" 20,	Abraham, son of Abraham Josselyn.
September	Elizabeth, daughter of Job House.
October 9,	William, son of William Cocks, Jun'r.
"	Joseph, son of Daniel Gardner, administered on account of his wife.
" 23,	Joshua, son of Joshua Barker.
" 23,	Mary, daughter of Joseph Nichols.
November	Samuel, son of John Pumpilly, baptised on account of his wife.
" 26,	Sarah Barstow, Lazarus, Alderson, children of Benjamin Ramsdell, Jun'r.

1775.

January 29, 1775.	Oliver Reed, son of Richard Smith, baptised on account of his wife Rhoda.
February 5,	Sarah, daughter of David Tilden.
" 19,	Betty, daughter of Nehemiah Ramsdell.
March 5,	Joseph, son of John Stetson, baptised on account of his wife.
" 25,	Luther, son of Ephraim Briggs.
" 26,	Hannah and Mary, twin daughters of Henry Monroe, Jun'r.
April 2,	John, son of Thomas Record.
" 9,	Levi, son of Nathaniel Chamberlain.
" 15,	Mary, daughter of Noah Perry.
May 7,	Betty, daughter of Captain Elijah Cushing.
" 7,	Job, son of Gideon Ramsdell.
" 14,	Benjamin, son of William Delano.

May 14, 1775.	Betsey, daughter of James Hatch.
" 14,	Seth, son of Howland Beals.
" 14,	Nathaniel, son of West Cole.
June 4,	Peggy, daughter of Joseph Howland, baptised on account of his wife.
July 31,	Increase, son of Deacon Increase Robinson.
August 13,	Anne Howland, daughter of Ephraim Lindsey.
" 13,	Rachel, daughter of Joseph Hanks, baptism administered on account of his wife.
" 27,	Ruth, daughter of John Thomas.
September 10,	Elizabeth, daughter of John Thompson.
November 19,	Warren, child of Samuel Howland.
December 10,	Joseph, son of (Jacob?) Gannett.

1776.

January 26, 1776.	Sarah, daughter of Eleazer Hamlin.
February 25,	Mary, daughter of Widow Hannah Phillips baptised on the Sabbath after the death of her husband.
" 25,	Gershom, son of Gershom Ramsdell.
March 24,	Ruben, son of Ruben Clark.
April 21,	Sophia, daughter of Gammelial Bisbee.
May 5,	Betty, daughter of Thomas Record.
" 26,	Gad, son of Lindes Tower, offered for baptism by Gersham Ramsdell and wife who have the care of the child.
June 2,	Mary, daughter of Matthew Whitten, Jun'r.
" 9,	Isaac and Harlow, sons of Samuel Harding, baptism administered on account of his wife.
" 16,	Sally, daughter of Richard Smith, baptism administered on account of his wife.
July 21,	Abner, son of Abraham Josselyn.
August 18,	Thirsa, Daughter of John Hatch.
" 25,	James, son of James White Cushing.
" 25,	Will, an Indian child baptised on account of Jackson's wife.
September 1,	Nathaniel, son of Nathaniel Thomas.
" 22,	Nathaniel, son of Joseph Bonney.
October 20,	Perez, son of Joseph Howland, on account of his wife.
" 27,	Anna Stockbridge, daughter of Thomas Josselyn, Jun'r.
" 27,	Polly, a child offered by William Cocks and wife as the care of it is committed to them.
November 3,	Samuel, son of Job House.
" 3,	Nathaniel, son of Major David Tilden.

1777.

January 25, 1777.	Ruth, daughter of Elisha Records.
April 6,	Joseph, son of Joshua Barker.
" 6,	Rachel, daughter of Zadoc Reed.
" 20,	Sarah, daughter of Gideon Ramsdell.
May 18,	Cloe, daughter of Nathaniel Chamberlain.

May	18, 1777.	Levi, son of William Hayford.
"	18,	Benjamin, son of Benjamin Monroe.
"	25,	Elijah Turner, son of Nathaniel Cushing.
June	2,	Rachel, daughter of Capt. Elijah Cushing.
"	2,	Gershum, son of Gershum Ramsdell.
"	8,	Nathaniel, son of William Delano.
"	14,	Christopher, son of Christopher Phillips.
"	22,	Sarah, daughter of John Thompson.
July	12,	Orphy, daughter of Lemuel Bonney.
"	27,	Lucy, daughter of Ephraim Briggs.
"	27,	Louise, daughter of Gamaliel Bisbee.
August	24,	John, son of Ephraim Lindsey.
"	24,	Anne, daughter of Howland Beals.
"	31,	Priscilla, daughter of Edward Hayford of Bridgewater.
September	14,	Enoch, son of Jacob Gannet.
"	28,	Cynthia, daughter of Thomas Record.
October	26,	Abigail, daughter of Benjamin Barnes.
November	9,	Nathaniel, son of Capt. James Hatch.
December	26,	Samuel, son of Samuel Ramsdell.

1778.

February	1, 1778.	Daniel, child of Doct. Daniel Childs.
March	29,	Eli, son of Alexander Soper, Jun'r.
April	26,	Rebecca, daughter of Noah Cole, baptised on account of his wife.
May	24,	Jonathan Bisbee, son of Joseph Nichols.
June	24,	Margaret, daughter of Matthew Whitten, Jun'r.
"	28,	Sylvina, daughter of Samuel Harding, administered on account of his wife.
July	5,	Jonathan, son of Samuel Howland.
"	26,	Nathaniel Twynge, son of Major David Tilden.
		Harvey, son of Lot Stetson.
August	26,	Mary, daughter of Job House.
September	27,	Henry, son of Henry Monroe, Jun'r.
October	18,	Elizabeth, daughter of Adam Perry.
"	30,	Barnabus, son of Barnabas Jackson.
November	8,	Betsey, daughter of Ruben Clarke.
"	29,	Betsey, daughter of Gersham Ramsdell.
December	20,	Betsey, daughter of Nathaniel Thomas.

1779.

February	7, 1779.	Edward, son of John Thomas.
"	21,	Dorothy, daughter of Doct. Gad Hitchcock.
"	21,	Joseph, son of Henry Monroe, Jun'r.
March	14,	Simeon, son of Zadoc Reed.
April	14,	Nancy, daughter of William Cocks, Jun'r.
"	11,	Sylvester, daughter of Joseph Bonney.
"	11,	Sarah, daughter of Nathaniel Chamberlain.
"	11,	Thomas, son of Elisha Records.
"	11,	John, son of Richard Smith, adminstered on his wife's account.

May	2, 1779.	Ruth, daughter of Doct. Daniel Childs.
"	2,	William, son of William White, baptism administered on account of his wife.
"	15,	Lydia, daughter of Ephraim Briggs.
"	15,	Ethelbert, daughter of Widow Anne Lindsey, born a few months after her husband's death.
"	23,	Elizabeth, daughter of Joshua Barker.
June	7,	Peddy, daughter of Joseph Howland, baptism administered on account of his wife.
"	13,	Rizpey, daughter of Gamaliel Bisbee.
"	13,	Ruth, daughter of Jos. Waterman.
"	20,	Olive, daughter of Adam Perey.
September	21,	Silvanus, son of Captain Joseph Smith.
October	31,	Richard, son of Samuel Hill.
December	5,	Tracey(?), son of Benjamin Barnes.

1780.

March	26, 1780.	Fanny, daughter of Doct. Gad Hitchcock.
April	16,	Ezra, son of Lot Phillips, baptism administered on his account only.
"	20,	Levi, son of Samuel Ramsdell, Jun'r.
May	7,	Isaac, son of Captain Elijah Cushing.
"	28,	Cyrus, son of Benjamin Monroe.
June	4,	Isaac, son of Richard Lowden.
July	2,	Cloe, daughter of Mathew Whitten.
"	2,	Nathan, son of Nathan Stephens.

[Leaves seem to be missing from the book and the next baptism recorded is Nov. 9, 1783.—Mrs. E. M. A.]

1783.

November	9, 1783.	Mary, daughter of John Barstow.
"	23,	Daniel, son of Noah Perrey.

1784.

May	30, 1784.	Lucy, daughter of Richard Smith, administered on account of his wife.
June	6,	Edward, son of Nathan Stevens, administered on account of his wife.
"	27,	Oliver, son of Nathaniel Chamberlain.
July	4,	Sylvia, daughter of Mathew Whitten, Jun'r.
August	1,	Clarissa, daughter of Joseph Bonney.
"	8,	Susannah, daughter of Abel Bourn.
"	8,	Lydia, daughter of Isaac Keen, die eod ' et anno.
September	5,	Lucy, daughter of Alexander Soper, Jun'r.
"	12,	Lowis, daughter of Leonard Hill.
"	26,	Anne, daughter of Capt. Elisha Cushing.
October	10,	Crowell, son of Noah Bonney.
"	24,	James, son of Job House.
November	7,	Lucy, daughter of Nathaniel Clark.
December	5,	Mary, daughter of Benjamin Barnes.

1785.

April 8, 1785.	Samuel, son of Samuel Howland.
" 24,	Susey, daughter of Capt. Isaah Stetson, on account of his wife.
May 1,	Lewis, son of Christopher Phillips.
" 15,	Lupira, daughter of Gamaliel Bisbee.
" 22,	Lettice, daughter of Joshua Barker.
June 5,	Francis, son of Francis Josselyn.
July 3,	James, son of Henry Monroe, Jun'r.
" 10,	Lucia, daughter of Capt. Joseph Smith.
	——(?) Hatch, daughter of Deborah Hatch.
August 14,	Joshua Pratt, Jun'r, an adult.
" 21,	Samuel, Matilda, Alpheus, John, Levi, Mercy, Joshua, children of Joshua Pratt, Jun'r.
" 21,	Abigail, daughter of Benjamin Mouroe.
" 21,	Lucinda, and Benjamin, children of —— Stetson, baptised on account of Hannah Stetson, his wife.
September 11,	Anna, daughter of Zadoc Reed.
" 18,	Anna, daughter of Joseph Barstow.
October 2,	Mehitabel, daughter of Mathew Whiten, Jun'r.
"	Mary, daughter of Richard Smith, baptism administered on account of his wife.
November 27,	Lydia, danghter of Jeremiah Stetson, Jun'r.

1786.

March 26, 1786.	Mary, daughter of Nathaniel Thomas.
April 29,	Hannah, Charles, John, children of Calley and Margaret his wife, baptised on account of Margaret.
May 9,	Lydia, daughter of Lot Phillips, baptised on account of the father.
" 14,	Lydia, daughter of Eleazer Josselyn.
" 14,	Rebecca, daughter of Reuben Hardin, baptised on account of his wife.
June 4,	Betty, daughter of Doct. Gad Hitchcock.
" 11,	Priscilla, daughter of James Bourn, Jun'r.
July 2,	Nathan Turner, son of Nathan Sprague.
" 9,	Joseph, son of Joseph Thomas.
" 30,	Benjamin, son of Benjamin Pratt, Jun'r.
November 5,	Anne Cushing, daughter of Isaac Thomas.
" 26,	Hervey, child of Noah Bonney.
	Hannah, child of Nathan Hill.

1787.

April 16, 1787.	Mary, daughter of Zadoc Thomas.
May 27,	Nathaniel, son of Alexander Soper, Jun'r.
June 3,	Lucy, daughter of Samuel Briggs, baptised on account of his wife.
" 10,	Bathsheba, daughter of Capt. Joseph Smith.
" 10,	Eunice, daughter of Reuben Clarke.
July 1,	Oliver, son of Abel Bourn.

July	1, 1787.	Ruth Sprague, daughter of Isiah Keen, baptised on account of his wife.
"	8,	Chloe, daughter of Isiah Stetson, administered on account of his wife.
"	8,	Peter, son of Francis Josselyn.
August	25,	Salome Barstow, son of Samuel Harding, administered on account of his wife.
"	25,	John Hatch, son of Ichabod Howland.
September	9,	Nathaniel, son of William Collamore.
"	9,	Benjamin, son of Thomas Stetson.
"	16,	Phebe, daughter of Gamaliel Bisbee.
"	30,	Margaret, daughter of Henry Munroe.
October	7,	Beckey, daughter of Benjamin Beuker, administered on account of his wife.
"	14,	Sarah, daughter of George William Munroe.

1788.

March	8, 1788.	Abner, son of Benjamin Studley.
"	8,	Sylvester, daughter of Benjamin Studley.
May	2,	Gad, son of Doct. Gad Hitchcock.
"	18,	Benjamin, son of John Thomas.
"	18,	Eleazer, son of Eleazer Josselyn.
June	1,	Wealthy, daughter of Nathaniel Thomas.
"	1,	Samuel, son of Joseph Barstow.
"	15,	Jeremiah, son of Jeremiah Stetson, Jun'r.
"	15,	Seth, son of Seth Harding, administered on account of his wife.
"	22,	Betty, daughter of Capt. Elijah Cushing.
"	22,	Lucinda, daughter of Capt. William White, baptised on account of his wife.
		Joseph, son of Joseph Howland, administered on account of his wife.
		Isaac, son of James Bourn, Jun'r.
July	6,	Deborah, daughter of Isaah Keen, administered on account of his wife.
"	13,	Celia, daughter of Nathan Sprague.
August	23,	Sally, daughter of Lot Phillips.
"	23,	Patty, daughter of Richard Lowden, Jun'r.
		Harriott, daughter of Nathaniel Clarke.
"	31,	Martin, son of Leonard Hill.
"	31,	——— (?) Cushing, daughter of Christopher Phillips.
September	28,	Lydia Cushing, daughter of Isaac Thomas.
October	12,	Nathan, son of Isaac Beals.
November	9,	Melinda, daughter of Ezekial Bonney.

1789.

April	5, 1789.	Anne Thomas, daughter of Samuel Briggs, administered on account of his wife.
"	12,	Nancy, daughter of Barnabas Holmes, administered on account of his wife.
"	19,	Nancy, daughter of Noah Bonney.
May	24,	Nathaniel, son of Nathaniel Hill.

May	24, 1789.	Thomas Hill, son of Francis Josselyn.
"	24,	Benjamin, son of Benjamin Bowker, administered on account of his wife.
June	14,	Salome, child of Charles Ramsdell.
"	21,	Jubetta, daughter of Alexander Soper.
July	5,	Abigail, daughter of Isaac Josselyn.
"	26,	Judith Miller, daughter of Capt. Joseph Smith.
August	9,	Sarah, daughter of Abel Bourn.
"	30,	Deborah, wife of George Osborn.
"	30,	Elizabeth, Levi, Ebenezer, Deborah, Baruch, the children of George Osborn.
September	20,	Bartlett, son of John Ramsdell.
November	15,	Judith, daughter of Joshua Pratt.

1790.

January	3, 1790.	Ezekial, Dodge, son of Nathaniel Cushing, Jun'r.
March	28,	Daniel, son of Doct. Gad Hitchcock.
May	2,	Deliverence Crooker, an adult.
"	20,	Calvin, son of Nathaniel Thomas.
June	6,	Sarah Osbourn, an adult.
"	27,	Luther, son of Zadoc Reed.
July	4,	Ephraim Allen, son of Eleazer Josselyn.
"	4,	Nathaniel, son of Samuel Briggs, baptism administered on account of his wife.
"	11,	Lucy, daughter of Nathaniel Clarke.
"	14,	Lydia, daughter of Isaac Beals.
September	5,	Hetty, daughter of Seth Cocks, Jun'r.
"	5,	Betty, daughter of Isaac Keen, baptism administered on account of his wife.
October		Elizabeth, daughter of Henry Monroe, Jun'r.
"	17,	Tamer, daughter of James Bourn, Jun'r.
"	17,	Rudolphus, son of Nathan Sprague.
"	31,	Lydia, daughter of Samuel Hill, Jun'r.
November	7,	Avetus, son of Gameliel Bisbee.
"	7,	Judith, daughter of Barnabas Holmes of Plymouth, administered on account of his wife.

BAPTISMS IN THE SECOND CHURCH OF CHRIST IN PEMBROKE, MASS., FROM 1748 TO 1803.

Communicated by MRS. ELROY M. AVERY of Cleveland, Ohio.

1791.

February	27, 1791.	Nathaniel, son of Henry Perry, Jun'r.
March	5,	Clarissa, daughter of John Ramsdell.
"	31,	Josiah Cushing, son of Isaac Thomas.
April	17,	Debby Allen, daughter of Richard Lowden, Jun'r.
May	7,	Benjamin, son of Thomas Stetson.
"	23,	William, son of Gersham Ramsdell.
"	22,	Chloe, daughter of Reuben Harding, administered on account of his wife.
"	29,	Gideon Thomas, son of Elijah Damon, Jun'r.
June	5,	Sarah, daughter of Snow Baker.
"	5,	Fanny, daughter of Reuben Clark.
"	5,	Rachel, daughter of Ebenezer Bonney.
"	5,	Dianna, daughter of Lot Phillips.
July	10,	Joseph, son of Capt. Joseph Smith.
"	15,	Sarah Lindsey, daughter of Nathaniel Hill.
"	15,	Christiana, daughter of Isaac Josselyn.
"	17,	Richard, son of Benjamin Beuker, administered on account of his wife.
August	14,	Ezra, son of Noah Bonney.
September	5,	Warren, son of Abel Bourn.
"	5,	Gad, son of Alexander Soper, Jun'r.
October	2,	Calvin, son of Nathaniel Thomas.
"	30,	Ebenezer Standish, son of Isaac Thomas, Jun'r.
"	30,	Roland, son of Ezekial Bonney.

1792.

March	11, 1792.	Mehetabel, daughter of Nathaniel Cushing.
"	25,	Sagey, daughter of Doct. Gad Hitchcock.

May 13, 1792.	Lurania, daughter of Ichabod Howland.
June 3,	Jemima Lindsey, daughter of Francis Josselyn.
" 10,	Priscilla, daughter of Isaac Josselyn.
" 17,	Sally, daughter of Isaah Keen, administered on account of his wife.
" 17,	Charles William, son of Charles William Soul.
July 1,	Betty, daughter of Charles Ramsdell.
" 15,	Elijah, son of Samuel Ramsdell, Jun'r.
" 15,	Isaac, son of Isaac Beals.
" 29,	Lyman, son of Eleazer Josselyn.
August 5,	Jotham, son of Joshua Pratt, Jun'r.
" 26,	Earl, son of Joseph Josselyn, Jun'r.
" 26,	Betty, daughter of John Beals.
" 26,	Nabby, daughter of Nathan Sprague.
October 2,	Nancey, daughter of Snow Baker.
September 8,	Nabby, daughter of Samuel Holmes, administered on account of his wife.

1793.

March 7, 1793.	Bethiah Barker, daughter of Barnabas Perry.
May 4,	Zavan, infant Christopher Phillips.
" 26,	Lettuce, daughter of Samuel Hill, Jun'r.
June 9,	William Peaks, son of Elijah Damon, Jun'r.
July 7,	Elizabeth Paris, daughter of Ebenezer Bonney.
" 7,	Joe, daughter of Reuben Harding.
"	Lucy, daughter of Zadoc Reed.
" 25,	Roxanna, daughter of Ezekial Bonney.
"	Isaac, son of Seth Cocks.
August 11,	Bethiah, daughter of James Bourn, Jun'r.
" 18,	Orphey, daughter of Gamaliel Bisbee.
September 15,	Elizabeth, daughter of Bowen Baker.
" 22,	Martin, son of John Ramsdell.
" 29,	Joshua, son of Capt. Joseph Smith.
October 27,	Isaac Smith, son of Isaac Thomas, Jun'r.
November 24,	Chrissey Wadsworth, daughter of Lot Phillips.

1794.

March 23, 1794.	Nathaniel, son of Nathaniel Cushing.
" 23,	Judith, daughter of Jeremiah Stetson, Jun'r.
" 23,	Harriott, daughter of George William Munroe.
" 30,	Luther, son of Nathaniel Thomas.
April 20,	Lydia West, daughter of Barnabas Holmes, administered on account of his wife.
May 4,	Sophia, daughter of Isaac Josselyn.
June 1,	Turner, son of Nathaniel Clarke and Sally, daughter of Nathaniel Clark.
" 1,	Mary, daughter of Francis Josselyn.
" 8,	Judah, son of Noah Bonney,
" 15,	Alexander, son of Alexander Soper, Jun'r.
" 15,	Avice, daughter of Abel Bourn.
" 22,	Lydia, wife of Gersham Ramsdell.

June 22, 1794.	Edna, daughter of Isaih Keen, administered on account of his wife.
" 29,	Mary, daughter of Gersham Ramsdell.
July 5,	Katey, daughter of Henry Perry, Jun'r.
September 14,	Charles, son of Doct. Gad Hitchcock.
October 12,	Cushing, son of Snow Baker.
" 12,	Nathan, son of Eleazer Josselyn.
November 16,	Nahum, son of Richard Lowden, Jun'r.
" 30,	Polly Turner, daughter of Bowen Barker.
December 28,	Betsey, daughter of Nathan Dwelling (Dwelley?).

1795.

March 29, 1795.	Debby Hatch, daughter of Joseph Josselyn.
May 10,	Luther, son of Isaac Beals.
" 17,	Seneca, son of Samuel Briggs, administered on account of his wife.
June 14,	Betty, daughter of Elijah Damon, Jun'r.
" 14,	Zavon, son of Christopher Phillips.
" 28,	Mercy, daughter of Henry Munroe.
" 28,	Ebenezer, son of Ebenezer Bonney.
"	Richard, son of Nathaniel Hill.
July 5,	Sally, daughter of Isaac Soper.
August 30,	Charles, son of Nathan Sprague.
September 6,	Briggs, son of Leonard Hill.
October 4,	Avenic Standish, daughter of Isaac Thomas, Jr.
" 25,	David, son of Samuel Ramsdell, Jun'r.
" 25,	Joshua, son of Gersham Ramsdell.
November 15,	Thomas, son of Capt. Joseph Smith.
December 6,	Rhoda, daughter of John Perry.

1796.

January 17, 1796.	Roland, son of Ezekial Bonney.
March 27,	Lucy, daughter of Nathaniel Cushing.
April 17,	Polly, daughter of Zadoc Reed.
May 22,	Isaac Bourn, son of Isaac Josselyn.
June 19,	Sibyll Angier, daughter of Dr. Gad Hitchcock.
July 3,	Betty, daughter of Alexander Soper, Jr.
" 3,	Reuben, son of Reuben Harding, administered on account of his wife.
August 7,	Isaac, son of Isaac Soper.
" 14,	Bethiah, daughter of Eleazer Josselyn.
" 28,	Nabby Colemore, an adult.
September 11,	Thirsa, daughter of Isaiah Keen, on account of his [wife.
" 18,	Hannah Josselyn, daughter of George William Monroe.
October 16,	Polly, daughter of Nathan Sprague.
" 30,	Ruth, daughter of Isaac Bowen Barker.
" 30,	Lucy, daughter of Oliver Whitten.
November 6,	Sarah, daughter of Gersham Ramsdell.
" 13,	Deborah, daughter of Abel Bourn.
" 13,	Roland, son of Nathaniel Hill.
December 15,	Eli, son of Thomas Stetson.

1797.

February	12, 1797.	Benjamin, son of Isaac Beals.
"	19,	Polly, daughter of John Beals.
April	23,	Lurania, daughter of Nathaniel Jones.
May	7,	Nabby Barker, daughter of Henry Perry, Jun'r.
"	7,	John, son of Jeremiah Stetson, Jun'r.
"	7,	Nathan, son of Nathan Dwelley.
June	4,	Thomas, son of Samuel Hill, Jun'r.
"		Blaney, son of Lot Phillips.
"	18,	Lucy, daughter of Bennet Munroe.
"	25,	Lucia, daughter of Noah Bonney.
July	23,	Betsey, daughter of Simeon Jones.
August	27,	John, son of John Perrey.
September	3,	Elizabeth Paris, daughter of Ebenezer Bonney.
"	3,	Elijah, son of Elijah Damon.
"	5,	The Widow Honor Prat, an aged person.
"	17,	Stetson, son of Gamaliel Bisbee.
November	12,	Charles, son of Charles Cushing.

1798.

January	21, 1798.	Deborah Thomas, daughter of John Briggs, now resident at Salem.
March	18,	Priscilla, daughter of Eleazer Josselyn.
April	1,	Ezekial, son of Ezekial Bonney.
"	5,	Thankful, daughter of Captain Joseph Smith.
"	12,	Emala, daughter of Elisha Josselyn.
May	20,	Branch, son of Joseph Josselyn.
June	10,	Osen, son of Charles Josselyn, Jun'r.
"	10,	Sarah Hill, daughter of Frank Josselyn.
"	23,	Isaac, son of Samuel Briggs, baptised on account of his wife.
September	9,	Luther, son of Gersham Ramsdell.
"	16,	Maria, daughter of Isaac Bowen Barker.
"	23,	Nathaniel, son of Nathaniel Cushing.
October	28,	Deborah, daughter of Nathaniel Thomas.
"	28,	Priscilla Bourn, daughter of Isaiah Keen, administered on account of his wife.
"	28,	Charles, son of Isaac Thomas 2d.
November	11,	Heman, son of Isaac Soper.
"	25,	Lucy, daughter of Lemuel Bonney, Jun'r.

1799.

May	17, 1799.	Lydia, daughter of Snow Baker.
"	17,	Eunice Buck, daughter of Nathan Sprague.
"	17,	Eleanor, daughter of Isaac Josselyn.
June	9,	Luther, son of Zadoc Reed.
July	23,	Abel, son of Abel Bourn.
"	23,	Perez, son of Isaac Beal.
October	6,	Mary Sheldon, daughter of Dr. Gad Hitchcock.
"	6,	Lewis, son of John Perry.
"	6,	George, son of Nathaniel Cushing.

October	6, 1799.	Dolly, daughter of Nathaniel Jones.
"	6,	Nathaniel, son of Elijah Damon, Jun'r.
"	6,	Hannah, daughter of Samuel Hill.
"	6,	Lucy, daughter of Alverson Ramsdell.
November	17,	Lydia, daughter of Enos Cocks.
"		Samuel Williams, son of Samuel Josselyn.

1800.

April	13, 1800.	Bennet, son of Bennet Monroe.
June	8,	Bowen, son of Isaac Bowen Barker.
"	8,	Rufus, son of Gersham Ramsdell.
"	8,	Joseph, son of Joseph Monroe.
"	8,	Mary, daughter of Jacob Bearse, Jun'r.
"	8,	Charles Josselyn, son of William Monroe.
"	8,	Thirza Hatch, daughter of Seth Beal.
"	8,	Samuel, son of Samuel Briggs.

Here the record stops abruptly, but his son Dr. Gad Hitchcock records: "My honored father died Aug. 8, 1803, after an indisposition and confinement of four years."

Pembroke (Mass.) Records. — In an interleaved copy of "An Astronomical DIARY, OR, AN ALMANACK For the Year of our Lord CHRIST, 1742. . . . . . By Nathanael Ames. . . . . . . *BOSTON* in *NEW-ENGLAND:* Printed by *John Draper*, for the Booksellers, 1742," a little book (unbound) measuring about 6½ inches in height by 4¼ inches in width, are many brief entries written by a minister, probably Rev. Daniel Lewis, who was pastor of the First Church of Pembroke, Mass., from 1712 until his death on 29 June 1753, in his 68th year. The state of the weather and the various texts from which the writer preached his sermons are the chief subjects of record in this diary; but there are also some records of marriages and deaths, and these, together with a few other interesting entries, are given below. Several of these vital records do not appear in the printed Vital Records of Pembroke.

January 1742.

9. . . . . Baptized *Jno Lincoln* Jur's Child being Sick.
11. . . . . . *Jno Lincoln's* Child dyed.
12. . . . . *Jno Lincoln's* Child Buried.
17. . . . . *Barnabas Ford's* Chd dyed
18. . . . . *Joseph Josselyn's* Child *Buried.*
19 . . . . At the *funal* of *Barnabas Ford's* Child.
20. . . . . at the funal of Josiah *Foster's* Wife

February 1742

18 . . . . Ruth Star dyed
20. . . . . *Ruth Star* buried. aged 57.
22 . . . . Between 3 and 4 a Clock this morning looking out of my Window towards the East just before I was going to bed, I saw a *blazing Star*, which seemed to be almost directly in the East, somewhat more than two hours high, as it then appeared to Me.
25 . . . . In ye night about 5 [?] o'C[l]ock saw the blazing Star.

May 1742.

31. . . . . *Wm. Page* Married

June 1742.

3 . . . . Joshua Briggs Married.

July 1742

22 . . . . [At Hingham.] Went to see Aunt Lasell, who is Sick.

Mr Daniel Lewis died February 18th 1829 Marshfield [*This entry written in pencil in later handwriting.*]

Dec. ye 31st [1742] This day, when concluding the Publick Worship of the *Last day* of the Year, I was taken, with an *Apoplectik* fit, which Laid the Foundation of a *Sickness*, that Lasted so long, that I preached no more, till the 25th of *March* following.

Death's This Year 1742.

1. *Thomas Lincoln*, son of Jno Lincoln Jur Dyed about noon Jan. 11th Aged about 2 or 3 Weeks.

2. A Child of *Barnabas Fords*, dyed just after it was born, a son, *Jan.* 17th
3. *Tryphena Foster*, Wife of Josiah Foster, dyed between 12 & 1 a Clock at noon, about 77. Years old.
4. *Ruth Star*, Widdow, Dyed at *Pembroke*, *Feb.* 18th Aged 57 Years this month. She was born at *Hingham*, Married and lived at Boston, where she lived till about 2 years ago. When she came to *Pem.* she was under decays as to her understanding and reason, which prevailed at last to such a degree, that for above a year before she dyed she kept her bed, and took no more notice of things, and seemed to be as help less, as a little Infant.
5. *Jenny*, A Negro woman belonging to Capt. *Nah. Cushing* dyed of a Consumption. about 3 o'Clock on a Sabbath day Morning April 11th
6. *Sylva Clark*, Daughter of Jno Clark, dyed suddenly, of a Cold accompanied with the *Phthisich*, *May* 26. Aged 5 Years 11 Month, and 18 days.
7. *John Chamberlain*, Son of Freedom Chamberlain, dyed Sept. 3d 1742. The Means of his Death was a *Scold* he met with some time before; he was aged about 3 Years And 3 quarters.
8. *Beersheba Garnett*, Wife of samuel Garnet, dyed after a short ill ness of about 3 or 4 days, *Dec.* 18. Day. Aged

Capt. Jno Magoun dyed of a *Consumption*, Aug. 19th 1743. Aged 40 Years, and One week.

5 Park Street, Boston, Mass. CHARLES ELIOT GOODSPEED.

THE ORIGINAL CHURCH RECORDS OF GAD HITCHCOCK, D.D., 1748 TO 1803: DEATHS

Barbara L. Merrick

Reverend Gad Hitchcock was the first minister of the Second Church of Christ in the West Parish of Pembroke, now Hanson, Massachusetts. He was born at Springfield, Massachusetts, 12 February 1719 and died 8 August 1803, son of Captain Ebenezer[3] Hitchcock and Mary Sheldon. He graduated from Harvard College and was ordained October 1748.

A strong spiritual and political leader in Pembroke at the time of the Revolution, Hitchcock is best remembered for his great Election Sermon. Delivered in the presence of Governor Thomas Gage, the text was extracted from Proverbs 29:2: "When the righteous are in authority, the people rejoice; when the wicked beareth rule, the people mourn." The legislative body proceeded to heed Reverend Hitchcock's sage advice, invoking Governor Gage's wrath and contributing to a colorful period of American history.

Hitchcock earned respect as a chaplain in the Revolution and served with distinction in the Constitutional Convention of the Commonwealth. He was awarded the D.D. from Harvard College in 1787.

During his ministry at Pembroke's West Parish, Hitchcock recorded in a diary in his own handwriting the christian events at which he officiated. The diary is directly quoted several times in Mrs. Edward Hitchcock, Sr., and Reverend Dwight W. Marsh's book *The Genealogy of the Hitchcock Family* (Amherst, Mass., 1894), and the baptisms were printed in the *Register* (49[1895]:286-292, 426-430; 50[1896]:177-183, 317-321). This* book also contains admissions and dismissals from the church plus church votes taken during the years. The marriages are documented by the *Vital Records of Pembroke, Massachusetts to the Year 1850* (Boston, 1911). The burial and death records are of great significance, for they have never before been published.

At the time the baptism records were extracted for the *Register* by Mrs. Elroy M. Avery of Cleveland, Ohio, the book was the property of the late Calvin T. Phillips, a descendant of Gad Hitchcock. For many years the whereabouts of the diary was unknown, until it was found in a Pennsylvania bookstore. Now it is the property of the Pembroke Historical Society and is maintained with the town records at the office of the town clerk, Pembroke.

The Hitchcock diary was without covers and consisted of 120 pages of manila paper, measuring 4 by 6½ inches, which were sewn together by hand with white linen thread. The pages were brittle and the edges frayed. The ink had turned brown and was heavily applied in some places, yet faded so that it was hard to read in others. Many times the ink had blotted through the page to the other side of the paper, so that it was extremely difficult to read the reverse side of the page.

*See p. 457, this volume.

Death records appearing in the Hitchcock diary are arranged below by year, with month and day appearing to the left of each entry. Original spelling and punctuation are retained, except in bracketed editorial insertions, where the spelling of names is standardized.

1748/1749

Alimelich, Son of Jonah Bisbee
Tabitha, Wife of Solomon Leavitt [daughter of Ebenezer Crane & Mary Tolman]
Mary, Daughter of William Gould
Thomas, Son of William Gould
Grace, Daughter of William Gould
Jonathan, Son of Ebenezer Records

1749

April 15,	Abraham, Son of Benjamin Howland
June 13,	Child of Josiah Bourn Junior
October 22,	Samuel Sikes, a lad belonging to Thomas More
" "	Child of Mercy Sole

1750

January 3,	Child of Gideon Bisbee
March 10,	Young son of Samuel Wade
April 9,	Martha, Wife of Samuel Ramsdell [daughter of James Bowker]
April 15,	Rebecca, Daughter of Abraham Howland
May 13,	Solomon Beals
May 19,	Child of Solomon Leavitt
June 3,	Isaac, Young son of William Cox
July,	Child of John Gould
July 13,	Colson, Son of Benjamin Howland
July 30,	Matthew, Son of Matthew Whiten
November 10,	Sarah, wife of Richard Buker [daughter of Elnathan Palmer & Mercy Clarke]

1751

January 16,	Child of Thomas Moore
September 3,	Sarah, Wife of Theophilus Witherly [Sarah Records]

1752

February 10,	Child of Thomas Moore
March 19,	Thomas Paris
" "	Child of Solomon Leavitt
August 7,	Child of Nehemiah Peirce
September 14,	Mrs. Dorothy Angier [widow of Samuel, daughter of Dr. Jonathan Avery & Sybil Sparhawk] NOTE: if to me had not been reduced to New Stile, it would have been September 3, 1752
December 1,	N.S. Child of Lydia Allen
December 5,	Joshua, Son of John Allen
December 6,	Bethiah, Daughter of John Allen
December 8,	Ephraim, Son of John Allen

1753

February 9,	Mary, Daughter of Solomon Leavitt
April 5,	Samuel Howland
April 23,	Mrs. Paris [widow of Thomas, widow of John Records, Grace ———]

April 25,	Child of Solomon Leavitt
	Thomas Hayford
	Son of George Russell
	Child of Samuel Wade
July 2,	Joseph, Son of Edward Thomas
September 23,	Abigail, Wife of Aaron Bisbee
November 23,	Aaron Bisbee

1754

January 4,	Marlborough, Son of Matthew Whitten
January 13,	Wife of Joseph Newell's
May 15,	Dido, Indian woman belonging to Henry Munroe
December 14,	Child of William Gould, Junior

1755

July 16,	Child of Abraham Josselyn

1756

January 1,	James, Son of James Hall
January 4,	Ebenezer Jones
January 9,	Elizabeth, Wife of Eliashib Faxon [daughter of Ebenezer Crane & Mary Tolman]
January 19,	Richard Beuker Junior
April 7,	Wife of Solomon Leavitt [Susanna Harden]
May 11,	Bethiah, Wife of John Allen [nee Crooker]
May 30,	Ebenezer Bourn
June 6,	Mary Gardner
June 11,	Child of James Bourn
June 19,	Grace, Negro servant of Capt. Joseph Cushing
July 4,	Rebecca, Daughter of Edward Cox
October 9,	Elizabeth, Daughter of Elisha Faxon
October 10,	Oliver, Son of Josiah Bourn Junior
October 16,	Child of Widow Abigail Bourn
	Seth Harden, in ye Army
	James Hall, in Army
December 4,	Child of Widow Foster
December 25,	Mary, Daughter of John Bonney
	Jonathan, Son of Job Bonney, in army
	James Hanks, in army
December 31,	Anne, Daughter of Capt. Josiah Cushing

1757

February 8,	Margaret, Daughter of Henry Munroe
February	Child of Widow Beuker [Richard Hill Bowker]
February 22,	Child of Job Bonney
February 23,	Abijah Leavitt
March 22,	Son of Richard Hill [Joseph]
April 5,	Richard Hill Junior
October	Patience, Daughter of George Russell
November 19,	Crissa, Daughter of Sylvester Prince

1758

January 16,	Ezra, Son of Solomon Beals
March 14,	Deliverance, Daughter of Samuel Hayford
	Widow Christophers
	Widow Jane Jones
	Grand child of Josiah Bourn
	Abram Harding killed

	David Bonney Dyed
	Ezekiel Bonney Junior Dyed
	Richard Osgood, Indian, in army
December 15,	Child of Joseph Josselyn
	George Russell Junior, in army

1759

January 3,	Wife of Increase Robinson
January 14,	Wife of Benjamin Taylor [daughter of John Russell Jr. & Mercy Crooker]
February 1,	An Indian woman, a transient person
March	Child of William Gould Junior
April 4,	Gaius, Son of Richard Phillips
	Lucey, unknown child at house of Isaac Soul
June 8,	Mercy, Wife of Sylvester Prince
June 11,	Elizabeth, Daughter of Edward Cox
July	Deliverance, Daughter of Samuel Hayford
November	Samuel Ramsdell Senior
December 16,	Mercy, Daughter of Henry Munroe, Sm Pox
December 20,	Hannah, Wife of Henry Munroe [daughter of Henry Josselyn & Hannah Oldham] of the Small Pox
December 29,	Bennet, Son of Henry Munroe, Small Pox

1760

March 16,	Boston, Negro man belonging to Col. Elijah Cushing
September 6,	Deacon John Bisbee
	Gideon Bisbee, of Small Pox in army
December 21,	Ebenezer Jones of small pox
December 28,	Mrs. Mary Bryant
December 29,	Child of Ruben Carver

1761

January	Susanna Hayford
	Benjamin, Son of Nehemiah Peirce, army
	John, Son of John Allen, in army (1760)
	Son of Samuel Wade, in army (1760)
January 31,	Joseph Ramsdell
January	Resus Records
February 27,	Barker, Child of Zebulon Howland
March 2,	Mary Newell
March 4,	Child of Ephraim Lindsey
March 29,	Tamar, Wife of Lieut. Elijah Cushing, of Small Pox [daughter of Theophilus Cushing & Hannah Waterman]
April 17,	Rebekah, Wife of Edward Cox
May 9,	Eliashib Faxon
May 26,	Cynthia, Daughter of Hezekiah Holmes
May 28,	Solomon, Kinsman of George Russell
August	Hearsy
December 9,	Polley, Daughter of Theophilus Cushing

1762

January 9,	Child of Sylvester Prince
	Son of Increase Robinson, in army
April 29,	Hannah, Wife of Jabez Bolton [daughter of Jonah Bisbee & Ruth Briant]
June 26,	Col. Elijah Cushing Esq. Suddenly at Boston
July 9,	Job, Child of Job Caswell
	——— Bolton, Son of Elisha, in army
December 30,	Ebenezer Bonney

1763

February 13,	Child of Ruth Records
May 20,	Wife of Deacon William Phillips [Hannah, daughter of John Prior & Bethiah Allen]
June	Daughter of Jacob Bearse
July 9,	Jacob Bearse
July 24,	Elijah Faxon
November	Daniel, Son of Theophilus Cushing

1764

January 31,	Betty, Daughter of Thomas Moore
April 9,	Mr. Jesse Thomas
December 11,	Deacon Daniel Hayford
December 29,	Child of Nehemiah Ramsdell

1765

April 4,	Son of Jeremy Stetson drowned
April 22,	Widow Dawes

1766

[no date]	Asa, Son of Increase Robinson
January 29,	Child of William Gould Junior
March 3,	Lucy, Daughter of Lemuel Bonney
March 22,	Hannah, Daughter of Lemuel Bonney
August 17,	Isaac, Son of Abraham Josselyn

1767

March 24,	Elizabeth, Wife of Elijah Crooker [daughter Samuel Ramsdell Jr. & Dorothy Bishop]
May 4,	Mary, Daughter of Thomas Rickard
November 14,	William, Son of William Cocks
December 1,	Increase Robinson

1768

April 13,	John, Son of William Phillips Junior
	Child of Jabesh Bolton
September 7,	Wife of Christopher Ripley
September 12,	Another child of Jabesh Bolton
December 23,	Hannah, Daughter of Isaiah Keen

1769

January 11,	Sarah, Daughter of Hezekiah Holmes
April 6,	Child of Jabesh Bolton
August 12,	Lydia, Wife of Eleazer Hamlin [daughter Ichabod Bonney & Elizabeth Howland]
September 27,	Abigail, Daughter of Elisha Bolton
December 13,	Buzi, Son of John Hunt

1770

March 30,	Josiah Bourn
August	Child of Amos Gardner
October 12,	Mary, Wife of Thomas Records [Mary Dawes]
November 7,	Anne, Wife of Ephraim Lindsey
November 12,	Elisha Hearsey
December 24,	Child of Lemuel Bonney

1771

January 7,	Thomas Records
January 9,	Mrs. Witherly, Widow
March 12,	Nathaniel Harding
June	Benjamin Phillips, died at sea
July	John Delano, died at sea

1772

March 8,	Hannah Curtis
March	Jonathan, Son of Widow Rebecca Bisbee
June 2,	Wife of Nathaniel Harding
June 3,	Grace, Wife of Jabesh Cole [daughter of Samuel Keen & Ruth Sprague]
August 8,	Ezekiel Bonney
August 17,	Hannah, Child of Simeon Jones

1773

February	Child of Abraham Josselyn Junior
February	Oliver, Son of John Reed
March 6,	Chloe, Daughter of Nathaniel Chamberlain
April	Child of William Gould Junior
April 10,	Deborah, Wife of Josiah Cushing [daughter John Cushing & Deborah Barker]
May	Joshua Pratt
May 31,	Seth, Son of Howland Beals
	Asia, Son of Eleazer Hamlin at N. York in January
July 24,	Mary, Wife of Robert White [daughter Daniel Crooker & Mary Ramsdell]
July 27,	John Allen
August 2,	John Bisbee
August 2,	Widow Almsburg
November 6,	Deacon Daniel Crooker

1774

February	Shubial Bearce
April 8,	William Gould
April 15,	Rouse Howland
June 15,	Mary Ramsdell
November 11,	Experience Daws
December 9,	Child of William Chapman

1775

January 20,	Isaac, Son of Josiah Cushing Esq.
March 2,	Grace Gould [Widow of William]
May 15,	Zeruah Finney, a School Mistress
August	Widow Mary Bisbee
September	Joseph Hanks, in Roxbury Camp
September 11,	Hannah, Wife of Benjamin Ramsdell Junior [Hannah Ladd]
September 22,	Egartha, Wife of Isaac Soul [daughter of Henry & Mary Parry]
September 22,	Betty, Daughter of John Pumpely
September	Child of Samuel Harding
September 25,	Abigail, Wife of Daniel Crooker
September 26,	Hannah, Wife of Jonathan Dunbar
September 27,	Child of Samuel Harding
October 5,	A third child of Samuel Harding
October 11,	Dorothy Soul
October 15,	John Whitten
October 22,	Isaac Soul

October 27,	Mary Whitten Junior
October 30,	Nathaniel, Son of Nathaniel Thomas
December 22,	Consider Cole, in army, Roxbury

1776

January 8,	Widow Betty Bearse [Betty Records, widow Shubael Bearce]
January 19,	Widow Mary Crooker [widow Daniel, daughter Samuel Ramsdell & Martha Bowker]
February 12,	Rebecca, Wife of Lindes Tower [daughter Richard Beuker & Mary Pratt]
February	William Phillips Junior
February 27,	Child of Joseph Howland
March 12,	Gershom, Son of Gershom Ramsdell
April 6,	John Allen, Son of James Bourn
April 7,	Child of Christopher Phillips
June 20,	Ruth, Wife of Dr. Daniel Child [Ruth Record]
July	Wife of Jonathan Gannett [Hannah, daughter Christopher Dyer & Hannah Nash]
July 31,	Deacon William Phillips
	[Joseph] Hollis, died in army at New York
August 7,	Elijah Crooker, died in army at New York
September	Matthew, a Negro man belonging to Josiah Cushing Esqr, in army at New York
October 12,	Widow Susanna Harding [widow Nathaniel, daughter James Lathan & Deliverance Alger]
November 7,	Seth Bearse
November 15,	Elijah, Son of Elijah Cushing
" "	Nehemiah, Son of Elijah Cushing
	Nehemiah, Son Theophilus Cushing, in army at New York
December 17,	James Loring, by an accident

1777

January	Tilson Gould, by a wound
February 2,	West Cole
	Thomas Bearse, at Connecticut
April 23,	Ruth, Wife of Jonah Bisbee [daughter Stephen Bryant & Bathsheba Briggs]
May 18,	Isaiah Keen
September	Abijah Leavitt, in the army
September 27,	Nathaniel, Son of Major David Tilden
November 2,	Captain Chapman, a Stranger belonging to Whitby, Yorkshire, England at 11 o'clock at night

1778

January 4,	Ethelbert, Son of Ephraim Lindsey
February 4,	Thomas Records
February 17,	The widow Ruth Faxon in 99th year of her age
March 13,	Polly, a child committed to the care of William Cocks & his wife
March	Ephraim Gould, of the Small Pox
March 30,	Sarah, Wife of George Osborne
April 20,	Ford Bearse of small pox
May 7,	Lieut. Edward Thomas, of the Small Pox
	Simeon Reed, in the army
May 27,	Abraham Josselyn, of the Small Pox
June 24,	Child of Noah Perrey
October 12,	Edward Cox
August 26,	Ephraim Lindsey, in the army
October 19,	Sarah, Child of Ebenezer Barker

1779

January 9,	Richard Hill
February 7,	Child of Levi Wade
March 22,	Hannah Hammot, a Negro woman belonging to Lemuel Jackson
May 11,	Anne, Daughter of Capt. James Hatch
June 6,	Mary, Wife of Capt. James Hatch [Mary More]
October 4,	Anne, Daughter of Capt. Elijah Cushing
November 27,	Jonathan Dunbar
December 7,	An Infant of Alexander Soper Junior

1780

January 12,	Lot Dwelly, in army
March 18,	Lucy, Wife of Capt. Joseph Smith [daughter of Peleg Wadsworth & Lusanna Sampson]
April 12,	Tracey, Son of Benjamin Barnes
May 27,	Pomp, a Negro
August 27,	Lydia, Child of Samuel Howland
October 3,	Hannah, Wife of John Bonney [Hannah Gould]
October 25,	Nathaniel, Son of Capt. James Hatch
November 7,	Betty, Daughter of Capt. Elijah Cushing
November 11,	Betsey, Daughter of Capt. James Hatch

1781

February 14,	Samuel Perry
April 15,	Deborah, Wife of Jedudiah Beals [daughter Samuel Boles & Lydia Balch]
April 20,	House, Son of Samuel Barstow
May 4,	Betty, Wife Ruben Harding [Betty Pynchon]
June 22,	Two twin Infants of Alic Gardner, one of them indeed was stillborn
June 27,	Sarah, Wife of Samuel Wade [Sarah Cortis]
July 31,	Eliseus Taylor

1782

February 23,	Child of Adam Perrey
April	Rachel Reed
May 23,	John, Son of Walter Hatch
	Sprague Keen in Prison Ship N. York 1781
June 4,	Cyrus, Son of Benjamin Munro
June 14,	Benjamin, Son of Benjamin Munro
	Peleg Osborn and his Brother
October 3,	Gammy Lindsey
November 8,	Mrs. Elizabeth Cushing

1783

March 28,	Pamela, Wife of Joseph Hearsey [nee Recods]
May 29,	John Reed
June	The Widow Keen [Ruth]
August 9,	Olive, Daughter of Adam Perrey
August 30,	Thomas Hill, Child of Francis Josselyn

1784

January 15,	Alexander, Son of Alexander Soper Junior
	Infant of Betty Humphry
August 10,	William Cocks, suddenly
September 3,	Stillborn Infant of William Richman
December 22,	Ben Still

1785

January 22, Lemuel Jackson
March 26, Katherine, Wife of Isaac Thomas [nee Smith]
April 13, Samuel, Son of Samuel Howland
May 15, Andrew Lindsey
June 18, Child of Calley, a Negro
July 11, Widow Hannah Bonney [widow Ezekiel, daughter Stephen Briant & Bathsheba Briggs]
August 13, Reuben, Son of Reuben Clark
September 11, Widow Hannah Bearse
October Widow Bourn
December 21, Sarah Durfey
December 23, Elijah Turner, Son Nathaniel Cushing

1786

June 13, Charles, Son of Calley, a Negro
July 1, Wife of Benjamin Taylor [Abiah Phillips, daughter Thomas Phillips & Mary Eames]
August 5, Phebe Beauker [probably daughter of Richard Hill and Jemima Ramsdell]

1787

January 19, Blaney, Son of David Bouls
January 25, Mary, Daughter of Joshua Barker
January 29, Child of Samuel Howland
February 3, Wife of Deacon William Delano [Eleanor Stevens]
February 12, Mary, Wife of Alexander Soper [daughter William Cox & Mary Ramsdell]
April 29, Infant Child of John McDaniel
May 12, Child of Dick Joel, a black
October 26, Child of Charles Ramsdell
October 31, Child Alice Gardner
Wife of Lemuel Little [Mary Lapham]
December 12, Richard Bowker

1788

March 8, Sylvester, Daughter of Benjamin Studley Jr.
April 10, Mary, Wife Gershom Ramsdell [Mary Garey]
May 15, Child of Richard Joel
June 8, Theophilus Cushing
July Child of Thomas Josselyn Junior
August 25, Lucia, Daughter of Abner Magoun
November 7, Cynthia Briggs, Daughter of Abner Magoun
November 14, Mary, Wife of Othniel Ford
November 25, Widow Elizabeth Bonney

1789

February 20, Sarah, Wife of Capt. James Hatch [nee Cushing]
February 20, Lydia, Wife of Capt. Josiah Cushing
May 14, Widow Betty Jackson [Betty Wade, Widow of John]
June 13, Peniah, Daughter Daniel Crooker, drowned
September 10, Lucey, Daughter Nathaniel Clark
October 10, Nathaniel Harding
October 11, Pegg, a Negro woman
18, Benjamin, Son of Thomas Stetson
December 31, Widow Eunice Hicks [widow Benjamin, nee Briggs]

1790

May 22, Calvin, Child of Nathaniel Thomas

June 21, Richard Everson
September 25, Huldah, Wife Samuel Barstow [daughter of Samuel House & Deborah Barstow]
November 29, Widow Deliverance Crooker [widow Elijah, daughter Rouse Howland & Anne Bonney]
December 3, Mr. Nathaniel Cushing
December Lilly, a Black

1791

January 13, Salome, Daughter of Daniel Crooker
January 22, Widow Betty Brown, a black
March 22, Josiah Bourn, Suddenly in the woods
April 18, William Niles
September Hannah Rider, an Indian woman
November 25, Widow Elizabeth Barker [widow Elisha, daughter Isaac Bowen & Elizabeth Tucker]

1792

January 1, Thomas Hill, Son of Francis Josselyn
February 14, Ebenezer Record
April 22 Chriss, a black
May 6, William Bonney
May 8, Sarah, Second wife of Gershom Ramsdell, [daughter John Delano & Ruth Cox]
November 25, Silvia, Daughter Joseph Howland
December 11, Joshua Pratt

1793

March 3, Drusilla, Daughter of Thomas Hobart
Joshua, Son of Capt. Joseph Smith, at Sea
March 28, Child of Abel Bourn
May 4, Zavan, Infant Christopher Phillips
June 5, Danah, a Black, Wife of Joseph Warrick
July 15, Roland, Child Ezekiel Bonney drowned
August 4, Infant child of Oliver Whitten
December 11, Josiah Cushing Esqr

1794

January 30, Thomas Hobart
April 14, Henry Munroe
April 18, James Clark
July 1, Isaac Taylor
December 8, Rachel, Wife Capt. Edward Thomas [daughter Nehemiah Cushing & Sarah Nichols]
December 19, Widow Anne Ramsdell

1795

February 21, Widow Eunice Perry [widow Samuel, daughter Samuel Witherell]
March 12, Widow Margaret Clark
March 28, Ruth Clark
May 18, Eunice, Wife of Joseph Dawes Ramsdell [daughter of Thomas Nash]
June 19, Noah Perrey Junior, drowned
August 9, Mary Tubbs
August 21, Child of Zadoc Reed
November 3, Mr. Thomas Collemore

1796

February 6,	Richard Lowden Junior
March 10,	Priscilla, Wife of Isaac Josselyn [nee Bourn]
March 12,	Sambo, a black
April 10,	Child Lydia Sambo
April 21,	Nabby, Daughter Benjamin Barnes
September 2,	Elizabeth Paris, Daughter Ebenezer Bonney
September 13,	Nathaniel, Son of Nathaniel Cushing
December 26,	Nahum, Child Widow Lowden

1797

May 3,	A mullatto Infant
July 24,	William Whitman, an unfortunate fall from a Load of Hay
September 25,	Lydia, Wife of Samuel Howland [nee Robinson]
October 14,	The widow Jane Hobart who died at Boston and was brot here to be buried
November 26,	The widow Honor Pratt

1798

February 18,	Samuel Howland
February 24,	Isaac, Son of Seth Cocks junior, in consequence of the bite of a mad dog
March 14,	The Widow Mary Cocks [Widow of William, daughter Thomas Ramsdell & Sarah Alverson]
April 10,	The Widow Mary Beuker [Mary Pratt, Wid. Richard]
April 22,	Nathaniel Lincoln, late of Oakman, found dead in the woods, supposed to have perished the 18th.
May 11,	An Infant of Jacob Bearse Junior
June 2,	Benjamin Beauker
August 31,	Mrs. Sherman of a Cancer
October 6,	Mrs. Christian, Wife of Mr. Blaney Phillips [daughter of Christopher Wadsworth & Mehitable Wormall]
October 16,	Nathaniel, Infant Son of Nathaniel Cushing
October 23,	Widow Ruth Lincoln [widow Nathaniel Lincoln and John Delano, d. William Cox & Mary Ramsdell]
December 14,	Abigail Soul

1799

January 19,	Child of Reuben Harding
February 2,	Abithiah, Wife of Matthew Whitten Junior, of fatigue and cold, as she was returning home.
March 30,	Benjamin Ramsdell
May 10,	Widow Content Whitman [widow of William, Content Cole]
May 13,	Isaac Buck
December	Mary, Wife of Jacob Bearse [Mary Munro]
	Jonah Bisbee February 1799

1800

April 5	Levi Everson

The final page of the diary contains personal items from the life of Gad Hitchcock, D.D.

Gad Hitchcock, born upon Thursday November 2, 1749 Old Style, Pembroke

My Hon'd Mother, Mary Hitchcock, died at Springfield, January ye 8th, 1760

Juba Violet a Child born February 16, 1761

Sister Dinah, Wife of Mr. James Sheffield died Sept. 29, 1761
Mrs. Gay, Wife of Revd Ebenezer Gay, Suffield, died Apr. 20, 1762
Dinah Violet daugh: Born April 11, 1769
Joanna Dinahs daugh: Born July 10, 1788
My Hon^{d} Father Dyed January 18, 1776
My Brother Col^{o} Daniel Hitchcock died the army at Morristown Jersey January 13, 1777

Barbara L. Merrick, Historian of the Massachusetts Society of Mayflower Descendants and of the Elder William Brewster Society, is a resident of Pembroke, Massachusetts.

THE PASSENGERS OF THE MAY FLOWER IN 1620.

BY NATHANIEL BRADSTREET SHURTLEFF, M. D.

As early as the year 1602, several religious people residing near the joining borders of Nottinghamshire, Lincolnshire, and Yorkshire, together with their pious ministers, being grievously oppressed by courts and canons, resolved to shake off the yoke of antichristian bondage, and, as the Lord's free people, to form themselves by covenant into a church-state, to walk in all his ways according to their best knowledge and endeavors, cost them whatever it might.

In the year 1606, by reason of the distance of their habitations, these people were obliged to assemble in two places and become two distinct churches; over one of which Mr. John Smith was established pastor, and among the others were Mr. Richard Clifton and Mr. John Robinson, two very excellent and worthy preachers.

In the fall of 1607, Mr. Clifton and many of his church, being extremely harassed, removed themselves and families to Holland, where, in the spring of 1608, they were followed by Mr. Robinson and the rest. They settled first at Amsterdam, where they remained a year; but finding that Mr. Smith's church, which was there before them, had fallen into contention with others, they, valuing peace and spiritual comfort above other riches, removed with Mr. Robinson, their pastor, to Leyden, Mr. Clifton remaining in Amsterdam, where he soon died.

Soon after their arrival in Leyden, they chose Mr. William Brewster to assist the pastor, as Elder of the Church. In their new place of abode they lived in love and harmony with each other, and on friendly terms of intercourse with their neighbors, till they removed to America.

By the year 1610, many had come over to them from various parts of England, and they had increased and become a great congregation.

In 1617, Mr. Robinson and his church began to think of emigrating to America; and, as a preparatory step, sent Mr. Robert Cushman and Mr. John Carver from Leyden over to England, to treat with the Virginia Company, and also to see if the King would grant them the liberty of conscience there, which was refused them in the land of their birth. Although the agents were not able to obtain from the King their suit for liberty in religion under the broad seal, as was desired, nevertheless, they prevailed so far as to gain the connivance of the King that he would not molest them, provided they carried themselves peaceably. In 1618, the agents returned to Leyden, to the great discouragement of the people who sent them; who, notwithstanding, resolved, in 1619, to send again two agents to agree with the Virginia Company; and at this time they sent Mr. Cushman a second time, and with him Mr. William Bradford, who, after long attendance, obtained the patent granted by the Company to Mr. John Wincob, which was never used.

Notwithstanding all these troubles, so strong was their resolution to quit Leyden and settle in America, that they entered into an arrangement with Mr. Thomas Weston, a merchant of London, for their transportation, and sent Mr. Carver and Mr. Cushman to England, to receive the money of Mr. Weston, to assist in their transportation, and to provide for the voyage. By direction, Mr. Cushman went to London and Mr. Carver to Southampton, where they finally joined with Mr. William Martin, who had been chosen to assist them.

A vessel of sixty tons, called the Speedwell, was bought and fitted in Holland, to be used in their transportation, and was designed to be kept for use in their new country. Mr. Cushman, in June, 1620, also hired at London the renowned May Flower, a vessel of ninescore tons, and also Mr. Clarke, the pilot.

Mr. Cushman, having procured the May Flower at London, and fitted it for the voyage, proceeded in it to Southampton, where he and Captain Jones, together with the other agents, remained seven days, until the arrival of the Pilgrims who left Leyden in July, embarking from Delft Haven.

On the 5th of August, both vessels, the May Flower, Capt. Jones, and the Speedwell, Capt. Reinolds, set sail from Southampton. The small vessel proving leaky, they both put in to Dartmouth about the 13th of August, where they remained till the 21st, when they set sail again. Both vessels were obliged to return a second time on account of the leakage of the Speedwell; and this time they put back to Plymouth, where they gave up the small vessel and dismissed those who were willing to return to London, Mr. Cushman and his family returning with them.

On the 6th of September, their number then consisting of one hundred persons, they made their final start, and arrived at Cape Cod on the eleventh day of November, when they signed the famous compact, and landed at Plymouth, in America, on the eleventh day of December, Old Style, or on the *twenty-first* of December, *New Style*, in the year 1620.

During their passage, one only died, William Butten, a young man, servant to Mr. Samuel Fuller, the physician of the new colony, who was included in Mr. Fuller's family, according to Governor Bradford, although dead at the time of the signing of the compact.

One person was born during the passage, Oceanus Hopkins, a son of Mr. Stephen Hopkins, who did not survive long after the landing.

At the commencement of the voyage, the number of passengers of the May Flower was one hundred, and at the time of the arrival at Cape Cod Harbor it was the same; one having died, and one having been born, thus preserving the integrity of the number. Both of these persons, however, are numbered among the passengers, and hence the number is generally stated as one hundred and one.

Peregrine White, son of Mr. William White, was born in Cape Cod Harbor, in November, after the signing of the compact and before the landing, and is not included with the voyagers. He enjoyed the distinction of being the first born white child in New England, of the Leyden Pilgrims.

The first child born after the landing on the twenty-second day of December, 1620, was a son of Mr. Isaac Allerton, but it did not survive its birth.

The May Flower has already been stated to have been a vessel of about ninescore tons, and was procured at London by Mr. Robert Cushman, who was debarred the privilege of coming over with the infant colonists, as it was necessary that he should remain in England, to keep together those who were left behind, and to provide for their future emigration, as he had done for that of those of the first passage. This he did by procuring the Fortune, and sailing from London in July, 1621, and arriving in New England on the 9th of November of the same year. It is also highly probable that he obtained the other early vessels, as he continued to be the agent of the Pilgrims till his death, which occurred in England, just as he was ready to come to spend the rest of his days in New England. In 1624, when the first division of land for continuance took place, Mr. Cushman, although in England, was placed at the head of the list of those who came in the May Flower; an act of justice alike creditable to our forefathers and honorable to him.

The May Flower not only brought over the first of the Leyden Pilgrims, but also, in the year 1629, with four other vessels, transported Mr. Higginson and his company to Salem; and in 1630, was one of the fleet which conveyed to New England Mr. Winthrop and the early settlers of the Massachusetts Colony.

A vessel bearing this name was owned in England about fifteen years or more before the voyage of our forefathers; but it would be impossible to prove or disprove its identity with the renowned May Flower, however great such a probability might be. It is known, nevertheless, that this identical famous vessel afterwards hailed from various English ports, such as London, Yarmouth, and Southampton, and that it was much used in transporting emigrants to this country. What eventually became of it, and what was the end of its career, are equally unknown to history.

The following list of passengers is made up from various sources. By referring to the list of those who signed the compact at Cape Cod, taken from Governor Bradford's folio manuscript, we know who signed the compact, and the number of persons in the family of each; who of the signers brought wives, and who died the first winter. By the pocket-book of Governor Bradford we know the names and dates of the deaths of sixteen who died the first season, and how many died before the arrival of the Fortune, on the 9th of November, 1621. By an examination of the Old Colony Records, we know to whom land was assigned in 1624, and what families were extinct at that time; and, as the families were arranged according to the vessel in which they came, and an acre was granted to each individual, we know how many were at that time in each family. Smith has also told us that none of the first planters died during the three years preceding the close of the year 1624. By the division of cattle, in the year 1627, a record of which was made at Plymouth, we know every individual who was living at that date, and the relative age of each person in every family. By wills, records, and gravestones, we know the ages of many of the Pilgrims and their children.

From such materials, and with such authorities, the following table has been constructed; and it is believed, that, although there is a possibility of the existence of small errors which can never be proved, the list is entirely or very nearly correct.

In order to save space and unnecessary printing, and to exhibit more readily for reference some of the most important facts, the following distinctive marks are made use of.

Those who signed the compact at Cape Cod, on the 11th of November, 1620, are in capitals.

The number in each family is indicated by the Arabic numeral.

Those who brought their wives have this mark, †.

Those who left them for a time in Holland or England are thus distinguished, ‡.

Those who died before the arrival of the Fortune on the 9th of November, 1621, have an asterisk, *.

Those who died before the division of cattle in 1627, are in italics.

The dates of those who died the first season are given as taken from Bradford's pocket-book.

JOHN CARVER, died in April, 1621. †*
Mrs. Carver, (his wife,) died in May, 1621. *
Elizabeth Carver, daughter of Mr. Carver and also wife of John Howland.
Jasper, (the boy of Mr. Carver,) died Dec. 6, 1620. *
John Howland.
Three others of this family died before 1627. * 8

WILLIAM BRADFORD. †
Mrs. Dorothy Bradford, (his wife,) drowned Dec. 7, 1620. * 2

EDWARD WINSLOW. †
Mrs. Elizabeth Winslow, (his wife,) died March 24, 1620–1. *
Edward Winslow, Jr., son of Edward.
John Winslow, son of Edward. 5

GEORGE SOULE. 1

WILLIAM BREWSTER. †
Mrs. Brewster, (his wife.)
Love Brewster, son of William.
Wrestling Brewster, son of William.
Mrs. Lucretia Brewster, wife of Jonathan, the oldest son of Elder Brewster.
William Brewster, son of Jonathan. 6

ISAAC ALLERTON. †
Mrs. Mary Allerton, (his wife,) died Feb. 25, 1620-1. *
Bartholomew Allerton, son of Isaac.
Remember Allerton, daughter of Isaac.
Mary Allerton, daughter of Isaac, and also wife of Elder Thomas Cushman.
Sarah Allerton, daughter of Isaac, and also wife of Moses Maverick. 6

MILES STANDISH. †
Mrs. Rose Standish, (his wife,) died Jan. 29, 1620-1. * 2

JOHN ALDEN. 1

SAMUEL FULLER. ‡
William Butten, (his servant,) died Nov. 6, 1620. * 2

CHRISTOPHER MARTIN, died Jan. 8, 1620-1. †*
Mrs. Martin, (his wife,) died the first winter. *
Solomon Martin, son of Christopher, died Dec. 24, 1620. *
One other of this family died the first winter. * 4

WILLIAM MULLINS, died Feb. 21, 1620-1. †*
Mrs. Mullins, (his wife,) died the first winter. *
Priscilla Mullins, daughter of William, and also wife of John Alden.
Two others of this family died the first winter. * 5

WILLIAM WHITE, died Feb. 21, 1620-1. †*
Mrs. Susanna White, (his wife,) afterwards wife of Governor Winslow.
Resolved White, son of William.
William White, Jr., son of William.
Edward Thompson, died Dec. 4, 1620. * 5

RICHARD WARREN. ‡ 1

STEPHEN HOPKINS. †
Mrs. Elizabeth Hopkins, (his wife.)
Constance Hopkins, daughter of Stephen and also wife of Nicholas Snow.
Giles Hopkins, son of Stephen.
Caleb Hopkins, son of Stephen.
Oceanus Hopkins, son of Stephen, born at sea. *

EDWARD DOTEY.

EDWARD LEISTER. 8

EDWARD TILLEY, died the first winter. †*
Mrs. Tilley, (his wife,) died the first winter. *
Two others of this family died the first winter. * 4

JOHN TILLEY, died the first winter. †*
Mrs. Tilley, (his wife,) died the first winter. *
One other of this family died the first winter. * 3

FRANCIS COOKE. ‡
John Cooke, (called the younger,) son of Francis. 2

THOMAS ROGERS, died the first winter. *
Joseph Rogers, son of Thomas. 2

THOMAS TINKER, died the first winter. †*
Mrs. Tinker, (his wife,) died the first winter. *
One more of this family died the first winter. * 3

JOHN RIDGDALE, died the first winter. †*
Mrs. Ridgdale, (his wife,) died the first winter. * 2

EDWARD FULLER, died the first winter. †*
Mrs. Fuller, (his wife,) died the first winter. *
Samuel Fuller, (called the younger,) son of Edward. 3

JOHN TURNER, died the first winter. *
Two others of this family died the first winter. * 3

FRANCIS EATON. †
Mrs. Eaton, (his wife,) died before 1627.
Samuel Eaton, son of Francis. 3

JAMES CHILTON, died Dec. 8, 1620. †*
Mrs. Chilton, (his wife,) died the first winter. *
Mary Chilton, daughter of James and also wife of John Winslow, the brother of Edward. 3

JOHN CRACKSTON, died the first winter. *
John Crackston, Jr., son of John. 2

JOHN BILLINGTON. †
Mrs. Helen Billington, (his wife.)
Francis Billington, son of John.
John Billington, Jr., son of John. 4

MOSES FLETCHER, died the first winter.	*	1
JOHN GOODMAN.		1
DEGORY PRIEST, died Jan. 1, 1620-1.	*	1
THOMAS WILLIAMS, died the first winter.	*	1
GILBERT WINSLOW, brother of Edward.		1
EDWARD MARGESON, died the first winter.	*	1
PETER BROWN.		1
RICHARD BRITTERIGE, died Dec. 21, 1620.	*	1
RICHARD CLARKE, died the first winter.	*	1
RICHARD GARDINER.		1
JOHN ALLERTON, (seaman,) died the first winter.	*	1
THOMAS ENGLISH, (seaman,) died the first winter.	*	1
Total,		101

The number of deaths of the first planters that occurred from the time the May Flower left England, to the year 1625, may be thus enumerated: —

In November, 1620,	1
In December, "	6
In January, 1620-1,	8
In February, "	17
In March, "	13
In April, 1621,	1
In May, "	1
From April 6 to November 9, 1621,	4
From November 9, 1621, to 1625,	0
Total,	51

Of these were, —		
Signers to the compact,		21
Wives of the signers,		13
Known members of families, viz: William Butten, Edward Thompson, Jasper, the boy, Solomon Martin, and Oceanus Hopkins,		5
Unknown members of the following families, viz:		
Of Carver's,	3	
Of Martin's,	1	
Of Mullins's,	2	
Of Edward Tilley's,	2	
Of John Tilley's,	1	
Of Tinker's,	1	
Of Turner's,	2	12
Total,		51

In the division of land in 1624, Henry Samson and Humilitie Cooper had land assigned them among those who came in the May Flower, and for this reason they have been generally believed to have been among the passengers of that vessel. If such is the case they can be placed in the family of Mr. Carver better than that of any other. But, as Mr. Cushman is also placed on that list, it may be reasonably inferred that others were put there for some other reasons, as perhaps Samson and Cooper, who are therefore excluded in this account.

John Goodman is marked in Bradford's manuscript as among those who died the first season. But as his name occurs among those who had garden lots in 1620, and also in the division of land in 1623, it must be inferred that he was marked by mistake, or else Mr. Prince committed an error in taking his copy for the Annals.

Three of the wives of the signers were left in Europe; namely, Bridgett, the wife of Dr. Samuel Fuller, Hester, the wife of Francis Cooke, and Elizabeth, the wife of Richard Warren. These afterwards came over in the Ann, in 1623.

Five lost their wives and married again; namely, William Bradford, who married widow Alice Southworth; Edward Winslow, who married widow Susanna White; Isaac Allerton, who married Fear Brewster, and afterwards, Joanna ———; Miles Standish, who married Barbara ———; and Francis Eaton, who married Christian Penn.

Others were married for the first time; namely, John Howland and Elizabeth Carver; George Soule and Mary; Love Brewster and Sarah Collier; John Alden and Priscilla Mullins; Resolved White and Judith Vassal; Giles Hopkins and Catherine Wheldon; Edward Dotey and Faith Clarke; John Cooke and Sarah Warren; Samuel Eaton and Martha Billington.

Several of the Pilgrims had children born in New England, an account of whom may form another article at some future time.

NOTE.

The following mistakes, not attributable to the author, should be thus corrected:

On page 50, line 15, "John Howland" should be in Roman Capitals. [1]

On page 50, lines 12, 34, 36, and 49, the word "also" should be "afterwards." [1]

On page 50, line 23, "George Soule" should be included in the family of Edward Winslow, and the numeral 1 against his name erased. [1]

On page 51, lines 9 and 41, the word "also" should be "afterwards." [2]

On page 48, line 51, the word "the", before infant, should be "its." [3]

[1] p. 50 is p. 497, this volume.
[2] p. 51 is p. 498, this volume.
[3] p. 48 is p. 495, this volume.

LIST OF THOSE ABLE TO BEAR ARMS IN THE COLONY OF NEW PLYMOUTH IN 1643.

[Communicated by NATHANIEL B. SHURTLEFF, M. D.]

The fact that this list of names is one to which constant reference is had, in all genealogical inquiries of the old families of the Old Colony, is a sufficient reason for its insertion in this work. As this copy is made from the one taken in 1819, by the Commissioners appointed by the General Court, the present copyist cannot be responsible for its perfect accuracy. It has, however, been carefully collated with the original, by William S. Russell. Esq., of Plymouth, the obliging Register of Deeds, who has the custody of the Old Colony Records. The names distinguished by an asterisk are crossed out in the original.

"August 1643. The names of all the males that are able to beare armes from XVI yeares old to 60 yeares wthin the seuerall Touneshipps.

Plymouth.

Mr Wm Hanbury
Raph Joanes
*John Jenkine
Charles Thurstone
Robte Eldred
Robte Wickson
George Crips
John Howland Sen
John Howland Jun
Jacob Cooke
*Francis Cooke
John Cook his boy
Samuell Eaton
Willm Spooner
Phineas Pratt
*George Clarke
Francis Billington
Benjamin Eaton
*Abraham Pearse
The blackamore
Mathew Fuller
John Bundy
Thomas Southwood
Mr John Done
James Cole Seni
James Cole Jun
Heugh Cole
John Grome
Thomas Lettis
*John Cooke Sen
Samuell Hicks
Thomas Willet
Thurston Clarke Junr
*Gregory Armstrong
Robte Lee
Nicholas Hodges
Thomas Gray
*John Shawe Sen
James Shawe
John Shawe Jur
*Stephen Bryan
John Harman
John Winslow
Samuell Kinge
Edward Dotey
Willm Snowe
John Holmes
Willm Hoskine
*James Hurst
George Lewes
*Mr John Atwood
Willm Crowe
Ephraim Hicks
Richard Knowles
James Renell
*James Adams
John Yeonge
Edward Holman
*Caleb Hopkins
John Heyward
Willm Baker
Richard Bushop
John Gorame
Mr Wm Paddy
Henry Atkins
Mr Bradford
John Bradford
Samuell Stertevant
Samuell Cutbert
Mr Thomas Prence
Thom. Roberts
Willm Nelson
John Smyth
Nathl Sowther
Mr John Reynor
Samuell Fuller
Samuell Eddy
Richard Sparrow
John Kerby
*John Jenney Sen
*Samuell Jenney
John Jenney Jur
Richard Smyth
Josias Cooke
John Wood
Henry Wood
Steephen Wood
Robte Paddock
Josuah Pratt
Richard Wright
Andrew Ringe
Gabriell Fallowell
Thomas Cushman
Thom. Sauory
John Finney
*Webb Addey
Thomas Pope
Giles Rickett Sen
John Rickett
Giles Rickett Jun
George Watson
John Barnes

*Edward Edwards
John Jordaine
John Dunhame
Thom. Dunhame
Samuell Dunhame
Edmond Tilson
John Smaley
*Francis Goulder
Thomas Whitney
Ezra Couell
Anthony Snow
Richard Higgens
John Jenkine
Nathaniell Morton
Manasseth Kempton
John Morton

Ephraim Morton
James Glasse
Edward Banges
Joseph Ramsden
Jeremiah Whitney
Nicholas Snow
Marke Snowe
*Willm Fallowell
Rob^{te} Finney
John Smith Senr
Thom Clarke
George Bonum
*Willm Shercliffe
John Churchell
Joseph Greene

Thomas Morton
Thomas Williams
John Faunce
Richard Church
*Gabriell Royle
Nathaniell Warren
Joseph Warren
Rob^{te} Bartlett
Thom. Shreeue
Thom. Little
John Tompson
Ephraim Tinkham
* Willm Browne
Thomas Tiley
*Wm Hartopp

Duxborrow. 1643.

Moyses Symons
Samuell Tompkins
James Lyndall
Thom Ouldame
Edmond Weston
Willm Foard
Francis West
Francis Godfry
Solomon Lenner
John Irish
Phillip Delanoy
Mr John Alden Sen
John Alden Jun
[Jo Alden]
Morris Truant
John Vobes
Willm Sherman
Samuell Nash
Abraham Sampson
George Soule
Zachary Soule
Wm Maycumber
Wm Tubbs
Wm Paybody
Wm Hillier
Experience Michell
Henry Howland

Henry Sampson
John Browne
Edmond Hunt
Willm Brett
John Phillips
Thomas Gannett
Wm Mullens
John Tisdale
Nathanell Chaundor
John Harding
John Aymes
Francis Goole
John Wasborne Sen
John Washborne Jun
Phillip Washborne
Wm Bassett Sen
Wm Bassett Jun
Francis Sprague
Willm Laurance
John Willis
Jonathan Brewster
Willm Brewster
Loue Brewster
Constant Southworth
Capt. Standish
Alexander Standish

John Heyward
John Farneseed
Thom. Bonney
Rob^{te} Hussey
Richard Wilson
Thom. Heyward Sen
Thom. Heyward Jun
Tho. Robins
Arthur Harris
Edward Hall
Christopher Waddesworth
Willm Clarke
Mr Comfort Starr
John Starr
Daniell Turner
George Patrick
John Maynard
Steephen Bryan
John Roger
Joseph Rogers
Joseph Pryor
Benjamin Reade
Abraham Pearse
Wm Merick
Will Hartub

Yong: Jo: Brewster; † Haden; Sam Chanler,

Scittuate. 1643.

Mr Charles Chauncey
Thomas Hanford
Robert Haward
Raph Elemes

Nathaniell Mote
Henry Advard
Willm Parker
John Hollett

Gowen White
Willm Perrie
Willm Holmes
Thomas Ensigne

† Probably Brewster, Haden, and Chanler were added subsequently.

George Willerd
Richard ———
Walter Briggs
John Hore
John Wadfeild
Thomas Allen
John Hewes
James Cudworth
John Whistons
Nicholas Wade
John Tilten
Thomas Symons
*Edward Foster
Thomas Rawlins Sen[r]
Thomas Rawlins Jun
Rob[te] Brelles
John Witherden
John Beamont
Richard Toute
Georg
Thomas Tarte
John Dammon
John Hammon
Christopher Winter
Henry Merrite
John Merrite
Isaac Chittenden
Joseph Collman
John Whitcombe
Thomas Lapham
Thomas Pynson

Richard Gannett
Will[m] Randle
Will[m] Hatch
John Lewes
Thomas Wyborne
John Winter
Humfrey Turner
John Turner
John Turner†
John Hewes
John Williams Sen
John Williams Jun
Edward Williams
James Cushman
Jeremie
Peter Collemore
Will[m] Wills
Samuell Fuller
Isaac Buck
Will[m] Hatch
Walter Hatch
Harke Luse
Edmond Eddenden
Thomas Hyland
John Rogers
Thomas Chambers
Richard Curtis
Will[m] Curtis
Joseph Tilden
Thom. Tilden
Edward Tarte

Georg Sutton
Symon Sutton
Thomas Clay
Goodman Read
Thomas Robinson
Edward
*Ephraim Kempton Sen
Ephraim Kempton Jun
Isaack Stedman
Walter Woodworth
George Russell
George Moore
Mr William Vassell
John Vassell
Resolued White
Will[m] Pakes
Jacob
Thomas King
Mr Weatherell
Thomas Byrd
Edward Jenkins
George Kennerick
Mr Garrat
Henry Mason
Elisha Besbeach
John Bryant
John Hatch
John Stockbridge
*James Till
Robert Stutson
——— Glasse

Sandwitch. 1643.

Henry Feake
Daniell Wing
Peter Gaunt
Thomas Johnson
Miles Black
Nicholas Wright
Edward Dillingham
John Fish
Richard Kerby
Thomas Launder
Henry Saunderson
John Winge
Will[m] Wood
John Ellis
Thomas Nichols
Anthony Bessy
Joseph Winsor
Nathaniell Willis

Anthony Wright
*Richard Chadwell
Jonathan Fish
Samuell Arnold
George Allen
Richard Burges
Henry Cole
Joseph Holly
Thomas Burges Sen[r]
Thomas Burges Jun[r]
Thomas Tuper
Henry Dillingham
Henry Sephen
Thomas Butler
James Skiffe
Lawrance Willis
John Presbury
John Freeman

Edmond Clarke
Will[m] Swyft
Michaell Turner
Peter Wright
Stephen Winge
Thomas Bordman
Raph Allen
Francis Allen
Thomas Gibbs
Edmond Freeman Ju[r]
Nathaniell Fish
Rob[te] Botefish
Thomas Greenfeild
Mathew Allen
John Johnson
John Bell
Peter Hanbury
John Greene

† Is this a repetition, or does it mean the other John Turner, called 2d, who was own brother to John Turner, both being sons of Humphrey Turner?

Richard Burne
Thomas Shillingsworth
John Dingley
John Vincent
John Joyce
Willm Newland
Edmond Berry
George Buitt
John Newland
Benjamin Noy
George Knott
John Blakemore
Mr Willm Leuerich
Mr Edmd Freeman Sen

Barnstable. 1643.

Mr John Lathrope
Mr John Mayo
Thomas Dimmock
Richard Foxwell
Nathaniell Bacon
Samuell Mayo
John Scudder
Roger Goodspeed
Henry Cobb
Barnard Lumbard
Thomas Huckings
Edward Fitzrandle
George Lewes
Isaack Wells
Henry Rowley
Thomas Lothrope
John Hall
Thomas Lumbard
Robte Linnett
Willm Casley
John Bursley
Thomas Allen
Samuell Jackson
Willm Tilly
Samuel Hinckley
Thomas Hinckley
John Smyth
James Cudworth
Mr Nicholas Symkins
James Hamblin
Henry Coggen
Henry Borne
Willm Crocker
Austine Bearse
Thomas Shawe
John Cooper
Thomas Hatch
Robert Shelly
Willm Beetes
John Crocker
Abraham Blush
Henry Ewell
Dolor Davis & his sonns
Laurance Lichfeild
Thomas Boreman
Anthony Annable
John Casley
John Russell
John Foxwell
Thomas Blossome
Samuel Lothrope
Joseph Lothrope
David Linnett
Nathaniel Mayo
*Willm Pearse
Richard Berry
John Blower
Francis Crocker
Benjamin Lothrope
John Davis
Nicholas Davis

Yarmouth. 1643.

Robert Dennis
Thomas Flaune
*Nicholas Sympkins
Willm Chase Senr.
Willm Chase Junr
Anthony Thacher
Andrew Hellot Jun
Samuell Williams
John Derby
Thomas Payne
Willm Ttwineing
James Mathews
Yelverton Crowe
John Crowe
Tristrame Hull
Edward Sturges
Anthony Berry
Thomas Howe
Thomas Falland
Nicholas Wadiloue
Samuel Hellott
Willm Palmer
Richard Taylor
Willm Lumpkine
Willm Grause
Henry Wheildon
Samuell Rider
Richard Prichett
Richard Temple
Thomas Starr
Benjamin Hamond
James Bursell
Willm Edge
Robert Davis
Richard Seeres
Heugh Norman
Peter Worden
Willm Nicholsone
John Burstall
Emanuell White
Willm Northcutt
Mr Marmaduke Mathews
Richard Hore
Roger Else
John Gray
Andrew Hellott Sen
Job Cole
Daniell Cole
Heugh Tilly als Hillier
John Joyce
Wm Pearse
Boreman

Taunton. 1643.

Mr John Broune
Mr Willm Poole
John Browne
James Browne
James Walker
Oliver Purchase
Thomas Gilbert
Richard Stacye
Willm Hollway
Tymothy Hollway
Willm Parker
Peter Pitts
John Parker
Willm Hailstone
Wm Hodges

EARLIEST INSCRIPTIONS FROM PLYMOUTH BURYING HILL.

Here lies the body of Edward Gray, Gent, aged about 52 years, and departed this life the last of June, 1681.

Here lies buried the body of M[r]. Wm. Crow, aged about 55 years, who decd January 1683–4.

Here lyeth buried ye body of that precious servant of God, Mr Thomas Cushman, who, after he had served his generation according to the will of God, and particularly the church of Plymouth, for many years in the office of Ruling Elder, fell asleep in Jesus, December ye 10th, 1691, and in the 84th year of his age.

Here lyes ye body of Mr. Thomas Clark, aged 98 years. Departed this life March 24th, 1697.

ABSTRACT OF THE FIRST WILLS IN THE PROBATE OFFICE, PLYMOUTH.

[These Extracts were made by Mr. Justin Winsor, now of Harvard College, Cambridge, the author of the Hist. of Duxbury. Will some of our Plymouth friends furnish us with a continuation?]

I *Samuell Fuller* the Elder being sick & weake, but by the mercie of God in pfect memory ordaine this my last will and testm^t^. I doe bequeath the Educacon of my cheldren to my Brother *Will Wright* & his wife, onely that my daughter *Mercy* be & remaine to goodwife *Wallen* so long as she will keepe her at a reasonable charge. But if it shall please God to recover my wife out of her weake state of sickness then my children to be wth her or disposed by her. I desire my Brother *Wright* may have the bringing up of a childe comitted to my charge, called *Sarah Converse;* but if he refuse then I comend her to my loving neighbor and brother in Christ, *Thomas Prence.* Item, whereas *Eliz. Cowles* was submitted to my educacon by her father and mother still living at Charlestowne, my will is that she conveniently appelled & returne to her ffather or mother. And for *George ffoster* being placed wth me by his parents still living at Sagos, my will is that he be restored to his mother. Item, I give to my son *Samuel,* my house and land at the Smelt river. I order certain portions of my Estate [naming them] to be sold to Educate my two children, *Samuell* & *Mercy.* I give land adjoining Mr. Isaac Allerton's to my son *Samuel,* and also land at Strawberry hill given me by *Edward Bircher,* if Mr. *Roger Williams* refuse to accept it as he has formerly done. Item. My will is that my cozen *Samuel* goe freely away with his stock of cattle and swine, without any further recconing. Item. My estates, and cattle with my two servants *Thomas Symons & Robt. Cowles* be employed for the good of my Children, by my Brother *Wright* and *Priscilla* his wife. I give to the Church of God at Plymunt^h^ the first Cow calfe that my browne cow shall have. I give to my sister *Alice Bradford* twelve shillings to buy her a pair of gloves. Whatever is due to me from *Capt. Standish,* I give unto his children. Item. That a paire of gloves of 5 sh. be bestowed on Mr. *Joh. Winthrop,* Govr. of the Massachusets. It. Whereas *Capt. John Endecott* oweth me two pounds of Beaver, I give it to his sonne. It. My will is that my children be ruled by my overseers in marriage. It. I give unto *John Jenny & Joh. Winslow* each of them a paire of gloves of five shillings. It. I give unto *Mr Heeke,* the full sum of twenty shillings. I give unto *Mr. William Brewster,* my best hat and band, wch I never wore. I give to *Rebecca Prence* 2sh. 6^d^ to buy her a paire of gloves. My will is that in case my son *Samuel* die before he come into inheritance of my Estates, then they are to go to my kinsman *Samuel Fuller,* now in the house with me. I appoint my son *Samuel* my Executor, and *Mr. Edward Winslow, Mr. William Bradford & Mr. Thomas Prence,* my overseers To my Daughter *Mercy* one Bible with a black cover. It. Whatsoever *Mr. Roger Williams* is indebted to me upon my booke for phisick I freely give him.

SAMUELL FFULLER.

July 30, 1633.

Memorand. Whereas the widow *Ring* submitted to me the oversight of her sonne *Andrew*, my will is that *Mr. Prence* take charge of him.

Witnesses hereunto,

Robt. Heeks
John Winslow

[In Gov. Winslow's hand-writing.]

Widow Mary Ring.

Oct. 28, 1633. I *Mary Ring*, being sicke in body; but of pfect memory, thanks be to God, doe make this my last will. To *Andrew*, my sonne; to daughter *Susan*; to *Stephen Deane* ['s] *Childe* (a daughter); to my daughter *Eliz. Deane;* to *Mrs. Warren* as a token of love, a wodden cupp; son [in law] *Stephen Dean*. I appoint *Samuel Fuller* and *Thomas Blossom* my overseers.

Witnesses

Samuel ffuller
Thomas Blossom

Mary Ring.

Following is an inventory of her Estate.

Peter Browne of New Plymouth.

Inventory of his Estate. Oct. 10, 1633. Taken by *Capt. Standish* and *Elder Brewster*.

He died intestate, and his Estate was settled by a Court held Nov. 11, 1633.

Martha Harding.

Inventory given to the Court, 8 Oct. 1633. Taken by *James Hurst*. *Francis Cook* and *John Done*. Amount £20, 18, 6. She died leaving one son in the custody of *Mr. Done*.

Richard Hanckford.

He died, Sep. 14, 1633. Inventory taken by *Joshua Pratt* and *Edward Foster*. *Edw. Winslow*, Administrator.

Godbert Godbertson, & Zarah, his wife.

Inventory by *John Done & Stephen Hopkins*, Oct. 23, 1633.

John Adams late of Plymouth.

Inventory by by *John Winslow* and *John Jenny*, Oct. 24, 1633. Amount, £71 – 14.

Joh Thorp, Carpenter, of Plymouth.

Inventory by *Capt. Standish* and *Elder Brewster*, Nov. 15, 1633

Francis Eaton, Carpenter, of Plymoth.

Inventory by *James Hurst, Francis Cook*, and *Phineas Pratt*, Nov. 8, 1633.

William Wright.

His Will. — To *Priscilla*, his wife, his house at Plymouth, and all his property, excepting a Ewe lamb, which was given to Plymouth Church, and some clothes, given to him by his brother *Fuller*, which were given to *Elder Brewster*. He appointed his beloved friend and brother *William Bradford*, to have an oversight of this will.

Sep. 16, 1633.

Wittnessed by — Will. Wright.

Will. Bradford,
Christopher Wadsworth.

Inventory by *Manassah Kempton*, and *John Hanks*. Amount, £99 – 12.

Samuel Fuller, the Elder.

Inventory by *Stephen Hopkins* and *John Jenny*. Library, 27 volumes.

1634. A Deposition concerning the affair at Kennebec, wherein *Hocking* was killed.

Stephen Deane.

Inventory Oct. 2, 1634, by *Stephen Hopkins* and *Robt. Hicks*. Amount, £87. 19. 6.

Thomas Evans.

He died, 27 Jan. 1634; inventory by *Mr. John Howland* and *Jona. Brewster*, Feb. 18, 1634.

William Palmers.

His will. I *William Palmer*, of Duxborrow, Nayler, appoint my loving friends, *Mr. Bradford*, *Mr. Winslow*, and *Mr. Prence*, my executors. Whereas I have married a young woman who is dear unto me, I desire she may have not less than one third of my estate. to *Rebecca* my grandchild, and *Moyses Rowly*, whom I love, but not so as to put it into their father's or mother's hands. I desire my executors to give something to *Stephen Tracy*, something to the Plymouth Church, and also wish that young *Rowly* may be put with *Mr. Partridge* [minister of Duxbury] that he may be brought up in the fear of God, and to that end if his father suffer it, I give *Mr. Partridge* five pounds. To my son *Henry*, and daughter *Bridget*, 40 shillings.

The mark of
Wm. X Palmer.

Witnessed
Thomas Barnes
William Basset.

Dec. 4, 1637.

Inventory, Nov. by *Jona. Brewster*, *Edmund Chandler*, *Wm. Basset*, and *John Willis*. Amount, £111. 12. 4.

John Cole.

His will. To my brother *Job Cole;* sister *Rebecca;* to *Eliza Collyer;* to each of Master *Collier's* men, viz, *Edward*, *Joseph*, *Arthur*, *Ralph* and *John;* to my brother *Daniel*. John Cole.

Witnesses
John Maynard,
Edward Paul.

John Bryant.

His will. June 17, 1638. *Richard Paul*, and *William Cradding* testify, that *J. B.* deceasing at Cohannack, April, 28, 1638, did two days before did declare this will. All his good and chattels to *John*, his son ; except a platter and a bottle which he gave to *R. Paul;* and he desired Mr *John Gilbert*, to take charge of the property for his son.

Inventory by Mrs. *Eliz. Poole*, Mrs *Jane Poole*, *William Cradding*, and *Richard Paul*. Amount £43.

Thomas Hampton. (Sandwich.)

His Will. March, 1637.

To Mr, *Leverich* of Sandwich, and his wife. To *Thomas Chillingworth*. To *Thomas Tupper*, *Peter Gaunt*, *Richard Kirby*. To *Wm. Harlow*. Witnessed by *Leverich*, *Gaunt* and *Harlow*.

Peter Worden, the Elder. (Yarmouth.)

Feb. 9, 1638. To my only Son *Peter Warden*, my whole property, and he to give *John Lewis* a goat.

Witnessed by *Nicholas Simpkins*, Mr. *Tilley*, and *Giles Hopkins*.

Thomas Pryor. (Scituate.)

June 1639. To my two sons in Old England, *Samuel* and *Thomas ;* to two daughters in Old England, *Elizabeth* and *Mary*. To son *Joseph*. To the pastor of Scituate. To my sons *John* and *Daniel*. Mr. *Timothy Hatherley* to have oversight of this. Witnessed by *John Winter*, *Joseph Tilden*, *Wm. Crocker*, *George Kennerich*.

Inventory, Sep 28, 1639. Amount £22. 7. 6.

Daniel Standlake. (Sciatuate.)

His noncupative will. He died May, 1638 ; Made by *Thomas Richard*, and *Wm. Crocker*. His property to his wife, except two kine goats, which he gives to his two children.

William Gilson. (Scituate.)

His will Jan. 27, 1639. To his wife *Francis Gilson ;* his cozen *John Dammon*, his cozen *Hannah Dammon ;* his cozen *Daniel Romeball ;* Mr. *John Lathrop*. He died at Scituate, Feb. 1, 1639.

Inventory by *Anthony Annable*, *Henry Cobb*, and *Edw. Foster*. Amount. £229, 3, 2.

Added thereunto is a *Codicill*.

John Dammon was his kinsman and servant, and he requested his Aunt (i. e. *Gilson's* wife, cozen being synonymous with nephew) to employ him in the wind mill, and this is the substance of the *Codicill*.

ABSTRACT OF THE EARLIEST WILLS IN THE PROBATE OFFICE, PLYMOUTH.

[Communicated by MR. JUSTIN WINSOR, of Boston.]

NATHL TILDEN (Scituate)
His Will. May 25, 1641.

To *Lydia*, my wife, most of my property, including the house, wherein one *Richard Lambert* dwelleth being in Centerden in Kent, Old England; and to my two Youngest Children, *Lydia* and *Stephen* their maintenance of their mother. To my son *Joseph*. To son *Thomas;* To my daughter *Judith;* To my daughter *Mary*, the wife of *Tho. Lapham*, and to *Sarah*, my daughter, wife of *Geo. Sutton*. My Servants *Edward Ginkins*, and *Edward Tarte*, to serve son *Joseph*.

Witnesses
Symon Sutton his mark
Thomas Hatch

Inventory. 31 July 1641. by *Wm. Vassall*, *Tho. Chambers*, *Wm. Patch*.

KATHERNE BRIGG'S Administration of the estate of her husband *John Brigg's* deceased, late of Sandwich. Administration granted June 1, 1641. His Estate amounted to £55, 2. Inventory taken by *Edw. Dillingham* and *Tho. Tupper*. He had children, *Samuel*, and *Sarah*.

MR WILLIAM KEMP. (Duxbury)

Inventory 23 Sep 1641. by *Wm Collier*, *Jona. Brewster*, *Christopher Wadsworth*, and *Comfort Starr*. Amount £172. 9. 5. His wife *Elizabeth* administratrix.

WILLIAM SWYFT. (Sandwich.)

1643. Administration by *Joane* his wife. Jan. 1643. the Inventory was showed at Court. Am't £72. 11. 1. He had a house at Sudbury mortgaged to one Mr. *Burton*.

MR. JOHN ATWOOD. (Plymouth)

I, *J. A.* gentleman, this 20th of Oct. 1643, make this my last will and testament. " For my Brethren God hath blessed them that they may be as well to give to me as I to them, and for their children they may be many, I do here give & bequeath them greate and smale young and old male and female which were borne before the date of these ꝑsents twelve pence apiece if demanded, and for my litttle kinsman Wm. Crowe & my Brother and sister Lee and their two children Ann & Mary I leave them to the will of my wyfe to deale with them as shall seem good to her and I do therefore ordain my loving wife Anne Atwood to be my sole Executrix to whom I will and bequeath all the rest of my estate my debts being first payd and she paying my debts and legacies before mentioned " &c.

Witnesses *JOHN ATWOOD.

Wm Bradford.

Rob[t] Hicks.

Inventory taken Feb. 27, 1643–4 by R. Hicks, Wm Paddy, Thomas Southworth, and Nath[l] Souther. Am't £186. 14.

JOHN JENNY. (Plymouth.)

To my Eldest Son *Samuel Jenny*, a double portion. To my wife *Sarah* whom I ordain my Executrix, my dwelling and mill adjacent. Where as *Abigail* my eldest daughter had somewhat given her by her grandmother and *Henry Wood*, of Plymouth aforesaid, is a *suter* to her in way of marriage, my will is that if she shall dwell one full year with Mr *Chas. Chauncy* of Scituate before her marriage (provided he be willing to Entertain her) that then she have two cows and my full consent to marry. My estate after my wife's death to be distributed among my Children *Samuel, John, Abigail, Sarah*, and *Susan*. I appoint Mr *W[m] Bradford*, and Mr *Tho. Prence* overseers of this will, and give them each a pair of gloves of 5 shillings cost.

Dec 28, 1643. JOHN JENNY.

Witnesses

Edw Winslow

Tho. Willet

Wm Paddy.

Inventory May 25 1644, by Mr *Paddy* and *Nath Souther*. Am't £108. 3. 3

ELDER BREWSTER. (Duxbury.)

Letters of administration on the estate were granted to his sons, *Jona.* and *Love*, June 5, 1644.

Wearing apparell, household utensils &c. appraised by Capt *Standish* and *John Done*. May 10, 1644.		28.	8.	10.
Articles at his house in Duxbury, by *Standish* & *Prence*, May 18.		107.	0.	8.
His Latin books by Mr. *Bradford*, Mr. *Prence* and Mr. *Reyner*, May, 18, sixty three volumes		15.	19.	4.
His English books by Mr. *Bradford* and Mr. *Prence*. Between three and four hundred volumes		27.	0.	7.
Latin and Eng. books	42 19 11			
Total sum of goods.		150.	0	7

---

* This is Mr. John Atwood, the assistant, generally styled gentleman, formerly of London. He left no issue, and is often confounded, by genealogists, with John Wood, alias Attwood, who was also of Plymouth. S.

ABSTRACT OF THE EARLIEST WILLS IN THE PROBATE OFFICE, PLYMOUTH.

[Communicated by MR. JUSTIN WINSOR, of Boston.]

THE first volume of Wills is labelled, "Plymouth Colony Records. Wills, &c, Vol. I. 1633–1654," and is entitled thus: —

"New Plymouth.

A Register of the wills and Testaments of the deceased wth a true coppy of the Inventories of their goods and chattels, as they were presented in publick Court uppon oath.

Anno Dom. 1633.

As also the Inventories of the goods of such as died without wills."

Subjoined to this inscription, in a later hand, is written: —

"Likewise the depositions of witnesses"

EDWARD FOSTER. (Scituate.)

His will, dated Nov. 24, 1643, makes his wife, *Lettice*, his Executrix, and bequeaths to her his lands at North River and Stoney Brook. He names also his son *Timothy*, then a minor, and an *infant* yet unborn. He appoints, as his overseers of his will, *Timothy Hatherly*, father *Richard Sillis*, *Edmond Eddenden*. It was witnessed by the same, and *Thomas Hanford*. The Inventory was taken, Feb. 1643, by *Hatherly*, *Sillis*, and *Eddenden*. Amount, £42. 3.

STEPHEN HOPKINS. (Plymouth.)

His will, was exhibited at Court, Aug. 1644, and dated June 6, preceding. He desires to be buried near his deceased wife. He names his son *Caleb*, as "heir apparent," and executor of the will, and, together with *Capt. Standish*, supervisor; also another son, *Gyles* (and his son Stephen;) daughters, *Constance* (wife of *Nicolas Snow*); *Deborah; Damaris; Ruth;* and *Elizabeth*. Witnessed by *Myles Standish* and *William Bradford*. [Though attached to the instrument in the *Record*-book, the names of the witnesses appear to be autograph signatures.] An Inventory of his estate was taken, July, 1644, by *Capt Standish, Tho. Willet*, and *John Done*. 'Amount £25. 14. 5.

EPHRAIM KEMPTON, SEN. (Scituate.)

A tailor, "being lately deceased May the fift, Anno Dom. 1645." His Inventory. Amount £47. 16. 10.

DIVISION OF THE ESTATE OF STEPHEN HOPKINS.

"The seu'all porcons of the children of Mr STEVEN HOPKINS, deceased, as they were divided equally by Capt. *Myles Standish, Caleb Hopkins*, their brother." Then follows an enumeration of the allotted "porcons" of *Deborah, Damaris*, and *Ruth*, each amounting to £9. 6. 8. In relation to the other daughter, Elizabeth, there is a paper containing six articles, signed by *Standish, Caleb Hopkins*, and *Richard Sparrow*, being an agreement by which she was "put out" to Sparrow, until she should become of the age of 19. or until her marriage, and "in consideracon of the weaknes of the child and her inabillytie to p[r]forme such service as they acquite their charges in bringing of her up," Sparrow was to receive into his hands her "porcon" of the estate, provided if "goodwife Sparrow" should die, Standish and her brother might dispose of Elizabeth as they thought best. Witnessed by *Wm Paddy*, and *Thomas Willet*. Next follows a paper by *Sparrow*, promising payment in consideration of the above, and witnessed by *Paddy*, and a receipt by *Standish*, dated May 19, 1647.

"The coppie of JOB LANE's refusall to accept of the executorship of *Thomas Howell's* last will and testa[mt], directed to the Gou[r]nor". By this it appears Lane was a carpenter of Dorchester, and a nephew of Howell, and was in Old England at the time of his decease. Dated 19 Oct. 1647. Witnessed by *Edmond Weston.*

THOMAS BLISE. (Rehoboth.)

Will, dated 4, 8°, 1649. Exhibited at Court June 8, 1649. He bequeaths his house to his son *Jonathan*. Names his eldest daughter, wife of Thomas *Williams;* his da. Mary, wife of Nathaniel *Harmon;* his son-in-law, Nicolas *Ide*, and his son Nathaniel. Appoints his well-beloved friends, *Richard Wright*, and *Stephen Paine*, overseers. Witnessed by *Paine*, and *Edward Smith.*

Inventory was taken by *Paine*, and *Richard Bowin*, 21 6mo. 1647. Am't, £117. 16. 4.

ROBERT HICKS. (Plymouth.)

"Deceased the 24th Mar., 1647." Inventory, July 5, by *Wm. Paddy and Thomas Cushman*. Amount £39. 13. Was formerly of Duxbury. His will, dated May 28, 1645. To his son *Ephraim*, his house at Plymouth, and land lately purchased of *John Alden*, and also land at Island Creek, on Duxbury side; his oldest son, *Samuel;* his wife, *Margaret*, to have the use of three rooms in his house during her lifetime, and to be Executrix of the will: To his grandson *John Bangs;* To Rev. *John Reyner's* son John; To *John Watson;* "To the younger of *M[r]. Charles Chauncey's* sonns, which his wife had at one birth, when hee dwelt at Plymouth;" To Plymouth town, a "cow calfe:" To *Wm Pontus, Phineas Pratt, John Faunce, Nathl. Morton, Thomas Cushman*, 20. each; To *Joshua Prat* and *Samuel Eddy*, a suit of clothes. *John Howland, Manasseh Kempton*, and *Thomas Cushman*, Overseers. Witness, *Nathl. Souther.*

JOSEPH HOLIWAY. (Sandwich.)

Inventory by *Edw. Dillingham* and *Wm. Newland*, Dec. 4, 1647. Amount £205. 6. His wife "*Rosse*" certified before *Tho. Prence* 30. 10mo. 1647.

THOMAS HOWELL. (Marshfield.)

A "full manifestation of *Thomas Howell's* desire on his death bed," June 6, 1647. His property to be divided equally between his wife and children. Appointed *Job Lane*, his kinsman, now in England, his executor, and requested *Edmond Weston* to be agent in trust until he returned.

Inventory, May 31, 1648, by *Thomas Bourn*, *Kenelm Winslow*, and *Joseph Biddle*. Amount. £38. 2.

ALEXANDER WINCHESTER. (Rehoboth.)

Will, dated 4. 4mo 1647, and exhibited at Court June 8, 1648. He gave one half of his property to his wife, whom he made his executrix, and the rest to his children, when they became fifteen years of age. *John Hazell, Walter Palmer*, and *Wm. Cheesborough*, supervisors. Witness, *Cheesborough*.

"*Richard Bullock*, aged 25 yrs., testifies that after the death of Winchester, he enquired of his widow, how she would dispose of the children, and she answered her husband has taken course for them, and left them to the overseers of his will. Hee being then sick and dyed the 16th July, 1647.

JOHN BROWN.
RICHARD BULLOCK."

Inventory, 30th 1mo 1647, by *Steven Paine, Richard Bowin*, and *Joseph Pecke*.

JAMES CUSHMAN, ALS. COACHMAN. ("Seteat.")

Will, April 25, 1648; proved May 24, 1648. To "cozin" *John Twisden*, of Gordiana, in the county of Devon, province of Mayne: To *Wm. Witherell*, of Seteat; To "cozin" Mr. *John Ferniside*, of Duxbury: Appoints *Thos. Lapham* his executor. Witnessed by *Wm. Witherell* and *Joseph Tilden*.

Inventory, May 29, 1648, by *Wm. Vassall* and *Joseph Tilden*. Amount £29. 19. 10.

WILLIAM LAUNDERS. (Marshfield.)

Inventory, Jan. 1, 1648, by *Josiah Winslow* and *Anthony Snow*. Amount £18. 1. 8.

"Being requested by *William Launders* of Marshfield now lying sick and weak at the dwelling house of *Francis Sprage* of Duxbery, to make his will & testament," the following certified as to the disposition of his estate then made by him.

JONATHAN BREWSTER,
THOMAS BURNE,
ROBERT WATERMAN.

GRACE GRANGER.

Widow. Her will dated Nov. 24, 1648. Gives to her son *John*, her house, when he shall become of age. Names her dau. *Elizabeth*. Witnessed by *Timothy Hatherly*, *John* —— (his mark), and *Richard Beare*, (his mark.)

Note.—*Thomas Graunger*, servant of *Love Brewster*, was hung for a capital crime, 1642; and a *John*, died at Marshfield, Oct. 4, 1655, and was buried at Scituate, W.

THOMAS RICKARD. (Scituate.)

His will, dated Nov. 14, 1648, and witnessed by *Richard Garret* and *Jo-*

seph Tilden. He bequeaths to *Thomas Pincheon*, the elder, and his wife *Joan*, and their children, *Thomas and Hannah.* To *Laurrance, Letchfield, Henery Atwood, Thomas Ingham, Joan* and *Richard Stanlake*, "Cozin" *Henry Borne, John Bisbee*, (son of Elisha,) *Wm. Parker, Isaac Birch*, and *Richard Garrett.*

Inventory, Dec. 2, 1648, by *Humphrey Turner* and *Joseph Tilden.* Amount £25. 12. 3.

GEORGE KNOT. (Sandwich.)

Nuncupative will, dated May 1, 1648. To wife *Martha*, executrix of the will; To son *Samuel;* To dau. *Martha*, "if she maries and lives in Sandwich," and to *Thomas Dunham*, "in case he maries my daughter." Overseers, *Wm. Leveridge* and *Wm. Newland.* Taken by *Leveridge* and *Thomas Nichols.*

Inventory, June 1, 1648, by *Edward Dillingham* and *Wm. Newland.* Amount, £69½.

GEORGE ALLEN, THE ELDER. (Sandwich.)

Will. Names his sons *Matthew, Henry, Samuel, William*, and his "five least children." His wife *Catherine*, executrix. *Ralph Allen* and *Richard Bourn*, overseers. Witnesses, *Wm. Leveredge, John Vincent*, and *Richard Bourn.*

Inventory, Sept. 22, 1648, by *Edward Dillingham and Richard Bourn.*

HENRY COGGEN. (Barnstable.)

He "deceased in England, about the 16th of June last." Inventory, Oct. 3, 1649, by *Henry Cobb, Barnard Lumbert*, and *Thomas Hinckley.* Amount, £28. 14. 8., certified to by *Mrs. Abigail Coggen.*

EPHRAIM HICKS. (Plymouth.)

Inventory taken on the oath of *Mrs. Margaret Hicks* by *Capt. Standish, Thomas Willet, Wm. Paddy, Mannaseh Kempton, and Thomas Southworth.*

THOMAS BLOSSOM. (Barnstable.)

Inventory taken on oath of *Sara Blossom*, widow, by *Henry Cobb* and *Thomas Huckins.* Amount, £37. 10s. 9d.

LOVE BREWSTER. (Duxbury.)

Will dated Oct 1, 1650, and exhibited at Court, March 4, 1650. To children, *Nathaniel*, the heir apparent, the estate in Duxbury; *William, Wrestling*, and *Sarah.* And to his three sons jointly "all such land as is of right due to mee by purchase and first coming into the land, which was in the yeare, 1620." His wife Sarah, executrix. Witnessed by *Myles Standish.*

Inventory (including books to the number of 30 volumes) taken Jan, 31, 1650, by *Wm. Collier* and *Capt. Standish.* Amount, £97. 7. 1.

ABSTRACT OF THE EARLIEST WILLS IN THE PROBATE OFFICE, PLYMOUTH.

[Communicated by Mr. Justin Winsor, of Boston.]

Nicholas Robbins. (Duxbury.)

His will, dated 9, 12mo, 1650, gives his house to his wife *Ann;* names his children, *John*, *Rebecca*, *Mary*, *Hannah*. Witnessed by *Ralph Partridge* and *John Willis*.

Inventory, 1650, by *John Willis*. Amount, £38. 13. 9.

Henry Smith. (Rehoboth.)

Will, dated Nov. 3, 1647; gives his wife his house, and makes her the executrix of his will. Names brother *Thomas Cooper*, and sons, *Henry and Daniel*, and da., *Judith*. Witnessed by *Stephen Paine*, *Thomas Cooper*, and *Joseph Peck*.

Inventory taken, 21, 10mo, 1649, by *Cooper* and *Peck*. Amount, £149. 16.

William Thomas. (Marshfield.)

His will, dated July 9, 1651. He leaves to his son *Nathaniel* the farm, whose wife is also mentioned, and likewise his children, *Nathaniel*, (who received a house and land at Eagle Nest,) *Mary*, *Elizabeth*, and *Dorothy*. To Marshfield Church, "a draper table-cloth of nine foot longe." To *Wm. Collier* and *Edw. Bulkley*, (a "siluer beer bowl,) who were made overseers of the will. To *Edward Bumpas*. Witnessed by *John Russell* and *Henry Draiton*, (his mark.)

Inventory taken Sept. 26, 1651, by *George Soule* and *Josiah Winslow*. Amount, £375. 7.

Thomas Lapham. (Scituate.)

Will dated June 15, 1644, signed by his mark; makes his wife, *Mary*, executrix, and names his children, *Elizabeth*, *Mary*, *Thomas*, and *Lydia*. Witnessed by *William Wetherell* and *Joseph Tilden*.

Inventory, Jan. 23, 1648, by *Wm. Hatch* and *J. Tilden*. Amount £68. 0. 4.

John Hazell. ("Secunke," alias Rehoboth.)

Will, 19, 9mo, 1651. "To every one who can make it appear they are my kindred, 12^{d}." To *William Devell*. Appoints *John Clark*, of R. I., and *Nathl. Biscoe*, of Watertown, executors. Witnessed by *John Warren* and *Thomas Arnoll*, of Watertown.

Next follows a letter of attorney from *Clark* and *Biscoe* to *Thomas Broughton*, of Boston, for the settlement of Hazell's estate. Witnessed by *Richd. Croade* and *Nathl. Biscoe, Jr.*

Inventory taken by *Edward Smith* and *Joseph Torrey*, 11, 8mo, 1651. Amount, £165. 19.

Henry Drayton.

Inventory, Dec. 12, 1651, by *Kenelm Winslow*, *Josiah Winslow*, and *John Burn*. Amount, £21. 14. 3.

WEBB AUDEY.

Nuncupative will by *John Bowen*, *Susanna Jeney*, and *Martha Sherive*. To *Rev. Mr. Reyner*, 30^{s}. One house he had sold to *Thomas Sherive*, and in relation to another he said "there were poor enough in the town." To goodmen *Pratt*, *Savory*, and *Sherive*.

Inventory taken March 19, 1651.

John Bowen, as overseer, in lieu of the 30^{s} bequeathed to *Mr. Reyner*, made over to him the small house, that being valued at that sum.

WILLIAM HATCH, SEN. (Scituate.)

His will, dated Nov. 5, 1651. Styles himself a planter. Gives to his wife *Jane* one half of his house. Names his da. *Jane Lovell*, and grandson *John Lovell;* his da. *Ann Torrey*, and grandchildren *James*, *William*, *Joseph*, and *Damaris Torrey;* and sons *Walter* and *William*, whom he made executors of his will. Witnessed by "*Guilielmo Wetherell*, *James Torrey*, *Willam Hatch*, the son of *Thomas Hatch*."

Inventory taken by *Thomas Chambers*, *Ephraim Kempton*, and *James Torrey*. Amount, £95. 3. 4.

JAMES ADAMS.

"Who died att sea in the good shipp called the James of London the 19th of January, 1651, to which Captaine *John Allin* was master, and cheife commander of the said vessell."

Inventory by *James Nash* and *Anthony Snow*. Amount, £34. 15. *Kenelm Winslow* appointed administrator of his estate.

JOHN EWER. (Barnstable.)

Inventory by *Wm. Crooker* and *John Smith*, of Barnstable, May 31, 1652. Amount, £19. 7. 5., exhibited at court, June 29, 1652, on oath of *Mary Ewer*, widow.

JUDITH SMITH. (Rehoboth.)

Widow. Her will, dated Oct. 24, 1650. Names her son *Henry*, da. *Judith*, son and da. *Hunt*, son *John's* three children, son *Daniel*, and the three children of her son *Hunt*. Witnessed by *John Pecke* and *Magdalen Smith*, her mark.

Inventory, 14, 10[mo], 1650, by *Joseph Pecke* and *Thomas Cooper*. Amount £120. 6.

JAMES LINDALE. (Duxbury.)

Will dated Aug. 10, 1652, and exhibited at court Mar. 4, 1652. To his wife, *Mary*, the executrix of the will, he gives his house and land at Duxbury and at Marshfield, provided she "continue in her widowhood." Names his son *Timothy* and daughter *Abigail*. To the Duxbury church "one cow-calfe." Appoints his "highly and well beloved friend and neighbour, *Constant Southworth*, supervisor." Witnessed by *Standish* and *Alden*.

Inventory, Oct. 29, 1652, by *Collier*, *Alden*, and *Standish*. Amount, £130. Next follows "A review of the inventory of the estate of *James Lindale*, taken after the decease of *Mary Lindale*, his wife," Feb. 8, 1652, by the same.

ABSTRACTS OF THE EARLIEST WILLS IN THE PROBATE OFFICE, PLYMOUTH.

[Communicated by Mr. Justin Winsor, of Boston.]

WILLIAM PONTUS, (Plymouth.)

Will dated Sep. 9, 1650 signed by his mark. Gives his house to his eldest daughter *Mary*. Names another da. *Hannah*, and appoints his son-in-law *James Glass*, executor. Witnessed by *Joshua Pratt*, *James Hurst*, and *John Donham*, his mark.

Memorandum *John Dunham* testifies that he heard Pontus say that he had given his son-in-law, *John Churchill*, and *Hannah* his wife one half of the meadow at the watering place, Plymouth; and also that the other daughter, the widow *Mary Glass* consented.

Inventory taken Feb. 20, 1652, by *Nathaniel Morton* and *Ephraim Morton*. Am't £12. 17 s.

JAMES GLASS, (Duxbury.)

Inventory taken on oath of his widow, *Mary*, by *John Donham* and *Ephraim Morton*. Am't £32. 6s. 5d. He d. Sept. 3, 1652.

MR. HENRY ANDREWS, SEN., (Taunton.)

Styled "yeoman," will dated Mar. 13, 1652. To daughter *Mary Hedges* wife of *Wm. Hedges* a dwelling house near his own in Taunton, and after her to his grandson *John Hedges*. To daughters *Sarah* and *Abigail*, £130 in the hands of *John Parker*, shoemaker, of Boston. To son, *Henry* his house. Names his wife *Mary*. Makes a bequest to the Minister of the town, and to *Elisabeth Harry*, widow, one of the poor of the church. Appoints *James Wyate* and *Walter Dean*, overseers. Witnessed by *Wm. Parker*, *James Wyate*, and *John Jollop*.

Inventory taken Feb. 10, 1652, by *Walter Dean*, *James Wyate*, *Wm. Parker*, and *Ric'd Williams*. Am't £330. 16 s.

ROBERT WATERMAN, (Marshfield.)

Inventory taken Jan. 13, 1652, on the oath of *Elizabeth Waterman* by *Anthony Eames*, *Edmond Hincksman*, *Mark Eames* and *Anthony Snow*. Am't £78.

JOHN BARKER, (Marshfield.)

Inventory taken Dec. 17, 1652, on the oath of his widow *Anna*, by *Kenelm Winslow*, *Edmond Hincksman*, *Joseph Beadle*, *John Bourn*. Am't £131. 11 s.

THOMAS CHILLINGWORTH, (Marshfield.)

Inventory exhibited at court, June 7, 1653, taken by *John Dingley*, *Arthur Howland*, *John Russell*. Am't £180.

WILLIAM HALOWAY, (Marshfield.)

Inventory taken (no date) by *John Dingley*, *Robert Carver*, and *John Russell*. Am't £65. 15 s.

JOHN FAUNCE, (Plymouth.)

Inventory 15 Dec. 1653, by *Lt. Tho. Southworth* and *Nathl. Morton*. Am't £27. 10s. 6d.

THOMAS HICKE, (Scituate.)

His will signed by his mark, Jan. 10, 1652. His wife *Margaret*, Executrix. To his sons, *Zachariah*, *Daniel*, and *Samuel*.

Inventory by *Walter Woodward*, and *Wm. Brooks*. Am't £18. 2s. His widow *Margaret* took oath to it, Oct. 3, 1653.

MR. JOHN LOTHROP, (Barnstable.)

Pastor of the church. His will dated Aug. 10. 1653. To his wife, the house he then lived in. To his eldest son *Thomas*, the house formerly occupied by him in Barnstable. To son *Benjamin*. To son *John*, who is in Eng^d^. To daughters *Jane* and *Barbara*. He requests his children to take in order of their ages such of his books as they may wish, and the rest he orders to "bee sold to any honest man whoe can tell how to make use of them."

Inventory, Dec. 8. 1653. By *Thomas Dimmack*, *Henry Cobb*, *John Cooper*, and *Thomas Hinckley*. Am't £72. 16s. 6d.

HENRY MERRITT, (Scituate.)

Inventory, Jan. 24, 1653, by *James Cudworth* and *John Williams*. Am't £121. 16s. 3d.

Inventory of things jointly purchased by *Henry Merritt*, dec^d^., and his brother *John Merritt*, which remained undivided.

MRS. ANN ATWOOD, (Plymouth.)

Her will dated April 27, 1650. "Widow sometime wife of *Mr. John Atwood*, Gent. being in p^r^fect health and strength and in p^r^fect memory, yett considering our frayle estate, that our waies are like unto to the grasse that soone withereth," ordaineth as follow: To my brother and sister, *Robert* and *Mary Lee*, "unto whome both myselfe and my deceased husband have formerly shewed what healp and kindness wee could." To loving nephew, *Wm. Crow*, the rest of my property, and if he die, then the estate to be devided among his brothers and sisters, that bee by his own father and mother. Appoints him the executor of the will. Witnesses,

Wm. Bradford,
Nathl. Morton.

ANN her × mark ATWOOD.

Inventory taken, June 1, 1654, by appraisers appointed by *Governor Bradford*.

[Here ends the first Volume of Plymouth Wills, containing forty-two Wills with Inventories attached, (five of which are nuncupative) and thirty Inventories of intestates, and a few miscellaneous papers. It was commenced in 1633 and ended in 1654.]

BEGINNING WITH "VOLUME II. 1654–1669."

WILLIAM PHILLIPS, (Taunton.)

His will dated April 16, 1654. He says therein he is "aged three score years and ten att the least." He bequeathes his house to his wife *Elizabeth*, and to his son *James*, whom he made Executor of his will, and provided that if he should die without issue, it might descend to the children of his son-in-law, *James Walker*. He mentions also his daughter [in-law?] *Elizabeth Walker*, and her little daughter *Hester Walker*.

Inventory Mar. 1, 1644, by *William Hailston* and *William Otway*. Am't £78. 8.

THOMAS COGGEN, (Taunton.)

Deceased March 4, 1653. Inventory by *George Hall* and *Richd Williams.* Am't £23. 8s.

MARY HEDGE, (Taunton.)

Her will disposes of the estate left her by her husband to her sons *John* and *Henry.* It mentions *Henry Cobb* and brother *Henry Andrews.* I request *Peter Pitts* "to perform these conditions in case I make him my husband."

WILLIAM HEDGE, (Taunton.)

Deceased Ap. 2, 1654. Inventory taken by *James Wyate, Wm. Barker, Oliver Purchas.* Am't 157. 9s.

MARY ANDREWS, (Taunton.)

States in her Will, she is aged 43 years. Disposes of her estate left her by her deceased husband, *Mr. Henry Andrews,* to son *Henry* (whom she appoints her executor ;) to daughter *Abigail:* to little daughter *Sarah* ; to son-in-law, *Wm. Hedge,* and daughter *Mary Hedge.* Appoints her kind and beloved friends, *Oliver Purchis, James Wyate, Walter Deane,* overseers. Signed Feb. 14, 1653 : by her mark.

ANTHONY GILPIN, (Barnstable.)

His Will was exhibited at Court, June 5, 1655. To his kinsman in England, *Wm Hodges* of Darnton, Yorkshire, together with his five *sisters,* all of whom were made his heirs. He gave, to *Nathaniel Bacon* of Barnstable, all his property in trust for his heirs. Accompanying this are several papers signed by *Bacon,* relating to the estate.

Inventory, Apr. 2, 1655. Amt £57. 9^{s}.

JAMES PILBEAME, (Rehoboth.)

Inventory taken 6 3 mo. 1653, by *Stephen Paine,* and *Robert Martin,* Amt. £48. 6^{d} 10^{s}.

Lenard Ryce, being son-in-law of Pilbeame, is allowed to be administrator.

THOMAS GANNATT, (Bridgewater,)

"Sometime of Duxbury, now of Bridgewater." Will dated June 19, 1655. To his wife. To his brother *Matthew Gannatt.*

Witnesses, *Wm. Brett, Wm. Bassett, Thomas Haward.*

Inventory, July 10, 1655. Am't £41. 19 s.

EDWARD DOTEN, SEN., (Plymouth.)

Will dated May 20, 1655. To his wife, his house. To son *Edward.* Signed by his mark. Witnessed by *John Hawland, James Hurst, John Cook, William Hoskins.*

Inventory, Nov. 21, 1655, by *Hoskins* and *Ephraim Tinckham* (his mark.) Am't £137. 19^{d} 6^{s}.

Mrs. Sarah Jeney, (Plymouth.)

Widow. Her Will dated April 4, 1654, witnessed by *Thomas Southworth.* To daughters *Sarah Pope* and *Abigail Wood.* To grand-dau. *Sarah Wood.* To son *Samuel.* To son [in-law] *Bein Bartlett.* To Rev. Mr. *Reyner.* To *Elder Cushman*, the Bible which was my daughter *Susannah's.* To *Tho. Southworth.*

An addition to her Will, dated Aug. 18, 1655, mention is made of son *Samuel's* children; of her grand-children *Sarah Wood, Susannah Pope,* and *Sarah Jeney.* This last witnessed by *Wm. Bradford* and *Allice Bradford*, (her mark.) Her Inventory taken 18 Feb. 1655, by *Tho Willet* and *Tho. Southworth.* Am't £248. 5s. 8d.

John Graunger, (Marshfield.)

Inventory of J. G. deceased, 24th 7th mo., November, (?), 1656, taken by *Anthony Eames, Francis Crooker,* and *Morris Truant.*

Richard Mann, (Scituate.)

Inventory, taken Apr. 14, 1656, by *James Cudworth* and *Walter Briggs.* Am't £92, 2s.

Mrs. Elizabeth Poole, (Taunton.)

Her Will is dated 17 3 mo., 1654, Aged 65 yrs. "Being sicke and weake under the vistation of the Lord, yett being of p'fect memory, & understanding, and willing to set my house in order according to the direction and message of the Lord unto Hezekiah, when he was sicke, that I might leave mine affairs soe as might bee peaceable and comfortable to my friends remaining behind me, I therefore committ my body to the grave according to the appointment of god, whoe tooke me from the dust, and saith wee shall return unto the dust, there to remaine untill the resurection, and my soul into the hand of god, my heavenly father, through Jesus Christ, whoe is to me all in all, and hath as I believe and ame persuaded through the mercy of God reconciled mee unto god, and taken away the guiltiness of sin and fear of death, which would otherwise have been heavy to bear, and makes me willing to leave the world, and desire to be with Christ, which is best of all. And as to that portion of wordly goods which the Lord of his mercy hath yet continued unto me, I give and bequeath as followeth:"

To my brother *Capt. William Poole* of Taunton, my house now occupied by him, which I built, and have lived in until of late. To my "cousen" *John Pole*, "my brothers eldest sonne," I give him, if he marries before his father dies, the house I now live in, which I bought of *Robert Thornton.* To my "cousens" *Timothy* and *Mary.* To the church of Taunton. To my "*cousen John Pole*, my pts in the Iron works to be for the furtherance of him in learning, which I desire him to attend unto." The same provisions were made for *Nathaniel Pole.* To my "kind old frind, sister *Margery Paule*, widdow." I appoint *John Pole* my executor, and my "frinds *Richard Williams* and *Walter Deane*, deacon of the Church of Taunton, and *Oliver Purchis*," my overseers.

Witnessed by *James Wyate, Oliver Purchis, Richard Williams.*

She died May 21, 1654. Her Inventory taken by *Wm. Hailstone.* £188. 11s. 7d.

ABSTRACTS OF THE EARLIEST WILLS IN THE PROBATE OFFICE, PLYMOUTH.

Communicated by Mr. JUSTIN WINSOR, of Boston.

JOHN DARBY, (Yarmouth.)

Inventory taken Feb. 22d, 1655, by *Edmund Hawes* and *Robert Dennis.*

RICHARD SILLIS, (Scituate.)

Inventory taken March 26, 1656, by *Jas. Cudworth* and *John Hallet.* Am't £67. 1s. 4d.

The will of Richard "*Sealis*," dated 17, 7 mo. 1653, styles himself "planter," names his wife *Cyline*, his da. *Hannah Winchester*, and *John Winchester*, and another daughter *Hester*, wife of *Samuel Jackson.* Witnessed by *Charles*, *Isaac*, and *Ichabod Chauncye.*

EPHRAIM KEMPTON, (Scituate.)

Inventory taken 22 July, 1655, by *James Torrey* and *Thomas King.* Am't. £64. 13s. 4d.

WILLIAM DENNIS, (Scituate.)

Will dated Feb. 16, 1649. To his wife *Judith*, whom he made executor. To his son-in-law, *Wm. Parker.* To *Remember*, *Dependence*, and *Experience Leichfeild.* Witnessed by *Hatherly* and *Cudworth.*

Capt. MYLES STANDISH, (Duxbury.)

Next follows a part of Standish's will, crossed diagonally by several strokes of the pen, but on the opposite page it stands recorded entire, as follows:

"The Last will and Testament of captaine Myles Standish, Exhibited before the Court held att Plymouth the 4th of May, 1657, on the oath of captaine James Cudworth, and ordered to be recorded as followeth:

Given under my hand this March
the 7th 1655.

Witnesseth these presents that I Myles Standish, Seni'r, of Duxburrow being in p'rfect memory, yett deseased in my body and knowing the fraile estate of man in his best estate, I doe make this to bee my last will and testament in manor and forme following:

1. my will is that out of my whole estate my funerall charges be taken out and my body to bee buried in decent manor, and if I die att Duxburrow, my body to bee layed as neare as conveniently may bee to my two dear daughters, Lora Standish my daughter and Mary Standish my daughter-in-law.
2. My will is that out of the remaining pte of my whole Estate that all my just and lawful debts, which I now owe or att the day of my death may owe be paied.
3. Out of what remaines according to the order of this Goverment my will is that my dear and loveing wife Barbara Standish shall have the third pte.
4. I have given to my son Josias Standish upon his marriage one young horse, five sheep and two heiffers, which I must upon that contract of

marriage make forty pounds, yett not knowing whether the estate will bear it att p^r^sent; my will is that the resedue remaine in the whole stocke and that every one of my four sons, viz, Allexander Standish, Myles Standish, Josias Standish, and Charles Standish may have forty pounds apeec; if not that they may have proportionable to ye remaining pte bee it more or lesse.

5. My will that my eldest son Allexander shall have a doubble share in land.
6. My will is that soe long as they live single that the whole bee in ptenership betwix them.
7. I doe ordaine and make my dearly beloved wife Barbara Standish, Allexander Standish, Myles Standish and Josias Standish joynt exequitors of this my last will and testament.
8. I doe by this my will make and appoint my loving frinds Mr Timothy Hatherly and Capt James Cudworth supervissors of this my last will, and that they wilbee pleased to doe the office of Christian Love to bee healpfull to my poor wife and children by theire Christian counsell and advisse, and if any difference should arise which I hope will not, my will is that my said supervissors shall determine the same, and that they see that my poor wife shall have as comfortable maintainance as my poor estate will beare the whole time of her life, which if you my loveing friends pleasse to doe though neither they nor I shalbe able to recompenc, I doe not doubt but the Lord will.

By me MYLES STANDISH.

further my will is that Marrye Robenson, whome I tenderly love for her grandfather's sacke shall have three pounds in som thing to goe forward for her two yeares after my decease, which my will is my overseers shall see pformed.

ffurther my will is that my servant John Irish Juni^r^ have forty shillings more than his covenant which will apeer upon the towne booke alwaies.

prouided that he continew till the time hee covenanted bee expired in the service of my exequitors or of them with theire joynt consent.

March 7th 1655 By me MYLES STANDISH

9. I give unto my son and heir aparent Allexander Standish all my lands as heire apparrent by lawful decent in Ormistick Bousconge Wrightington Maudsley Newburrow Cranston and in the Isle of man, and given to mee as right heire by lawful decent, but surreptitiously detained from me my great grandfather being a 2^ond^ or younger brother from the house of Standish of Standish. by mee

March the 7th 1655. MYLES STANDISH

Witnessed by mee James Cudworth."

NOTE. The word "surreptitiously" in the last clause was inserted, (in a blank left between the preceding and following word,) apparently at a subsequent time, yet appears to be in the hand of Sec. Morton.

"An inventory of the goods and chattles that Captaine Miles Standish, gent, was possessed of att his decease as they were shewed to us whose names are underwritten this 2^ond^ of desember, 1657, and exhibited to the Court held att Plymouth the 4 May 1657, on the oath of Mi^s^ Barbara Standish.

	£	s.	d.
It. one dwelling house and outhouses with the land thereunto belonging	140	00	00
It. 4 oxen	24	00	00
It. 2 mares, two coults, one young horse	48	00	00
It. 6 cowes, 3 heifers and one calf	29	00	00

	£	s.	d.
It. 8 ewe sheep, two rames and one wether	15	00	00
It. 14 swine great and small	03	15	00
It. one fowling peece 3 musketts, 4 carbines 2 small guns, one old barrell	08	01	00
It. one sword one cutles 3 belts	02	07	00
It. the history of the world and the Turkish history	01	10	00
It. a cronicle of England and the countrey ffarmer	00	08	00
It. y[e] history of Queen Elisabeth, the state of Europe	01	10	00
It. Doctor Hales workes, Calvin's institutions,	01	04	00
It. Wilcock's workes and mayor's	01	00	00
It. Rogers' seaven treatises and the ffrench akadamey	00	12	00
It. 3 old bibles	00	14	00
It. Ceser's comentaryes, Bariff's artillery	00	20	00
It. Preston's Sermons, Burroughes Christ in contentment, gosspel conversation, passions of the mind, the phisisions practice, Burroughes, Earthly mindedness, Burroughes discovery	01	04	00
It. Ball on faith, Brinsley's watch, dod on the Lord's Supper, Sparke against herisye, davenporte apollogye.	00	15	00
It. A reply to Doctor Cotten on baptisme, The Garmon History, the Sweden Intelligencer, reasons discused.	00	10	00
It. 1 testament, one psalme booke, Nature and grace in conflict, a law booke, The mean in mourning allegation against B. P. of Durham, Johnson against hearing.	00	06	00
It. a pcell of old bookes of divers subjects in quarto	00	14	00
It. Wilson's dixonary, homer's Illiad, a comentary on James Ball catterkesmer	00	12	00
It. an other pcell in octavo	00	04	00
It. halfe a young heifer	-1	00	00
It. one feather bed, bolster, and 2 pillowes	04	00	00
It. 1 blankett, a coverlid and a rugg	01	05	00
It. 1 feather bed, blanket and great pillow	02	15	00
It. 1 old feather bed	02	05	00
It. I feather bed and bolster	04	00	00
It. 1 blankett and 2 ruggs	01	15	00
It. 1 feather bolster and old rugg	00	14	00
It. 4 paire sheets	03	00	00
It. 1 paire fine sheets	01	04	00
It. 1 table cloth, 4 napkins	00	10	00
It. his wearing clothes	10	00	00
It. 16 peeces of pewter	01	08	00
It. Earthern Ware	00	05	00
It. 3 brasse Kettles, one skillett	02	00	00
It. 4 iron potts	01	08	00
It. a warming pan, a frying pan and a cullender	00	09	00
It. one paire stillyards	00	10	00
It. 2 bedsteads, one table, 1 forme chaires, 1 chest and 2 boxes.	02	13	00
It. 1 bedstead, one settle bed, one box, 3 casks	01	07	00
It. 1 bedsted, 3 chists, 3 vasses with sence bottles, 1 box, 4 casks	02	06	06
It. 1 still	00	12	00
It. 1 old setter, 1 chaise, one kneeding trough, 2 pailes, 2 traies	00	16	00

	£	s.	d.
It 2 beer casks, 1 chern, 2 spining wheels, one powdering tubb, 2 old casks, one old flaskett	00	15	00
It. 1 mault mill	02	00	00
It. 2 sawes with divers carpenter's tooles	01	19	00
It. a timber chaire with plow chaires	01	06	00
It. 2 saddles, a pillion, one bridle	01	00	00
It. old iron	00	11	00
It. 1 chist and a husking tabl	00	08	00
It. 1 hachett, 2 tramells, 2 iron doggs, 1 spitt, one fier-forke, 1 lamp, 2 gars (?), one lanthorn, with other old lumber	02	01	00
It. in woole	00	15	00
It. in hemp and flax	00	06	00
It. eleven bushells of Wheat	02	05	00
It. 14 bushells of rye	02	02	00
It. 30 bushells of pease	05	05	00
It. 25 bushells of indian corn	03	15	00
It. cast, and peakes, and plow irons, and 1 brake	02	05	00
It. axes, sickles, hookes, and other tooles	01	00	00
It. eight iron hookes, 1 spining wheel, with other lumber	00	14	00
	22	03	00
	55	18	00
	280	06	00
John Alden James Cudworth	358	07	00

JOSHUA PRATT, (Plymouth.)

Inventory taken on oath of *Bathsheba Pratt* by *Thomas Cushman* and *Nathl Morton*, and exhibited at Court, Oct. 6, 1656. Am't, £18. 11s. 3d.

WIDOW KEMPTON, (Scituate.)

Inventory, 10 Apr. 1657, by *James Torrey, John Bryant, and Wm. Brooks*. £38. 11s. 6d.

WILLIAM HATCH, JR. (Scituate.)

"Late deceased in Verginia, being upon a journey to Verginia." His will dated Sep. 13, 1653. To daughter *Phebe*, to be paid in 1668. Appoints his wife *Abigail*, executrix. Witnesses, *Geo. Sutton, James Torrey*, aged 44 years. His inventory, Apr. 7, 1657, £56. 3. 6d. by *Edw. Jenkins, Thomas Turner.*

MR. JOHN GILBERT, SEN^R. (Taunton.)

of Pondsbrooke, Taunton. Will, 10 May, 1654. To son *Gyles* his farm of 100 acres—sons *Joseph, Thomas, John*,—daughter *Mary Norcrosse*, and her daughter Mary. To his wife's grand child *Elizabeth Peter*. To his wife *Winnifred.*

Nicolas Steel, Wm. Pole } Witnesses — Nicolas Steel, Richd Williams } overseers of the will.

Inventory exhibited at Court, June 3, 1657.

ABSTRACTS OF THE EARLIEST WILLS IN THE PROBATE OFFICE, PLYMOUTH.

Communicated by Mr. JUSTIN WINSOR, of Boston.

SAML. WILBOR, (Taunton.)

His original will is in the Massachusetts Colony, but this copy was ordered to be made here. Apr. 30. 1656.

To his wife *Elizabeth.* He names his house in Boston, where he then lived.

To his eldest son *Samuel,* land in Rhode Island.

To his son *Joseph,* his house at Taunton.

To his youngest son *Shadrach.*

To *Robert Blott* of Boston, *Goodman Blacke,* Servant *John Markelett,* a Scotchman.

Witnesses
Robert Howard
Wm. Colbron.

Inventory, 23d Oct. 1656.
£282, 19, 6d,

ANTHONY BESSEY, (Sandwich.)

His will. Feb, 10. 1656. To his wife *Jane* (the Executrix), his daughters, *Ann, Mary, Elizabeth,* sons *Nehemiah* and *David.*

James Skiffe and *Richd. Bourn,* overseers and witnesses to the will.

Inventory, 21 May, 1657.

GOV. WILLIAM BRADFORD, (Plymouth.)

"The last will and testament nunckupative of Mr William Bradford, seni^{r} deceased May the 9th, 1657, and exhibited to the Court held att Plymoth, June 3^{d} 1657.

Mr. William Bradford Senr being weake in body, but in ppct memory having deferred the forming of his will in hopes of having the healp of Mr. Thomas Prence therein, feeling himself very weake and drawing on to the conclusion of his mortall life, spake as followeth. I could have desired abler then myselfe in the desposing of that I have, how my estate none knowes better then yourselfe, said he to Leiftenant Southworth, I have desposed to John and William alreddy theire proportions of land, which they are possessed of.

My will is that what I stand engaged to p^{r}forme to my children and others may bee made good out of my estate, that my name suffer not.

Ffurther my will is that my son Joseph bee made in some sort equall to his brethren out of my estate.

My further will is that my dear and loveing wife Allice Bradford shall bee the sole Exequitrix of my estate, and for her future maintainance my will is that my Stocke in the Kennebecke trad bee reserved for her comfortable subsistence as farr as it will extend, and soe further in any such way as may be judged best for her.

I further request and appoint my wel beloved Christian ffrinds, Mr. Thomas Prence, Captain Thomas Willet and Leiftenant Thomas Southworth to be the suppervissors of the desposing of my estate according to the p^{r}mises confiding much in theire faithfulness

I comend to youer wisdome some small bookes written by my owne hand to bee improved as you shall see meet. In speciall I comend to you a little booke with a blacke cover, wherein there is a word to Plymouth, a word to Boston, and a word to New England, with sundry useful verses.

These pticulars were expressed by the said William Bradford, Govr, the 9th of May, 1657, in the p^rsence of us, Thomas Chushman
Thomas Southworth
Nathaniel Morton"

The inventory of his estate was taken by Tho. Cushman and John Dunham. There is an account contained in it of articles "in ye old parlor, in the great room, in the kitchen, in the new chamber, in the studdie"

Major William Holmes.

Who died at Boston Nov. 12, 1649. His will. Names kinswomen *Margaret* and *Mary Holmes*, residing in the island of Antego, and daughters of his deceased brother, *Thomas Holmes*. Also mentions his estate in that island, and his sister-in-law *Margaret Webb*, alias *Holmes*, late wife of his brother *Thomas Holmes*, and her daughters, *Rachell* and *Bathsheba*, all now living in London. He gave them his farm in Scituate "if they come to New England". He also speaks of "arrears due to him for being a soldier and commander in the army and service of the king and parliament." He calls *Job Hawkins* of Boston, "his loving and kind kinsman."

Witnesses
John David
Nicholas Simpkins
John Butworth
John Richbell

Executors,
James Penn
Robt Scott.

Deposition by *James Penn*, that he had written to St. Antego, but had received no answer, and had also sent to the kindred in England, that they were poor, and could not come over, and that thus none appear to have rightful claim to the property but *Job Hawkins.*

Deposition by *Isabel Simpkins*, aged 44 years, that when Major Holmes came last into this country, he told her that he was very poor and that he was supported by Job Hawkins, who furnished him clothes, &c., and "put him in credit in the taverns" June. 1654.

Deposition of *Capt. Nicholas Simpkins*, aged 54 years, that when Maj. Holmes came last into this country, about 1649, he was "very mean in apparel", and that Hawkins paid his "scores att the tavernes, tho he kept companie much with divers gentlemen". June 1654.

Deposition of *Lenard Buttels*, aged 41 yrs, that he paid Maj. Holmes £4, on Hawkins' account.

Some other papers.

Edward Hunt, (Duxbury.)

May 20, 1656. Inventory by Christopher Wadsworth and Constant Southworth. Am't. £51. 11s. 9d.

James Hurst, (Plymouth.)

Will dated Dec. 10. 1657. To his wife *Gartend* (Executrix) he gave his house at P. To his grand children, *John*, *Gershom*, *James*, *Eleazer*, *Hannah*, and *Patience Cobb*, and *Mary Dunham*. Supervisors, *Mr Cushman* and *Gyles Richards sen*. Witnesses, *Tho: Southworth* and *Wm Bradford.*

Inventory by *T. Southworth* and *Wm. Hoskins*, 24 Dec. 1657. £97 6s.

Note.—Mary Cobb m. Jona. Dunham 16, Oct. 1657. Dunham's first wife Mary Delano, daughter of Philip, he m. Nov. 29, 1655.—W.

REV. RALPH PARTRIDGE, (Duxbury.)

His will was exhibited at Court on the oath of *Wm. Collier*, May 4, 1658.

To his da. *Elizabeth Thacher* all his landed estate in N. E, and after her to her second son *Ralph Thacher*, Excepting one parcel of land "at Hicks his necke", which I bought of *Mr Hicks* of Plymouth, and another lot of 10 acres which I give to her eldest da. *Patience Kemp*, and to her youngest son *Peter Thacher*, my part of lands which were purchased of Ussamequen, called the New Plantation. He names also her eldest son *Thomas Thacher*. To this da. he also gave his house in Old. England.

To his eldest da. *Mary*, wife of *John Marshall*, and hir sons *Robert* and *John*.

Names his wife *Patience* who had previously deceased, and his "late deceased attorney Mr *Thomas Cullen*, the elder",

Bequeaths also to *Wm. Brett*, to *Joseph Prior*, his man serv't, and *Anna Reiner*, his maid serv't. Names his sister *Elizabeth Tidge*.

Witnessed by Signed Sep 29. 1655,
Wm. Collier
Robert Husey

His inventory taken 25 2mo 1658 by *Wm Collier*, *John Alden*, *Constant Southworth* and *Christopher Wadsworth*. It names articles in "the Studdy (his library, 400 volumes), the little room next the studdy, the parlor, the parlor chamber, kitchen chamber, Leanto chamber, garrett, kitchen, sellar". An account of his lands is also given, naming 40 acres, which he bought of *C. Wadsworth*, 3 of "medow", 10 at Morton's hole, 10 in the common field with a house, 25 which he bought of *Arthur Harris*, 59 bought of *Mr Reyner*, 3 at Blue fish river, 40 purchased of *John Willis*, and his own house, with lands adjoining, orchard &c, and a full purchase at Bridgewater.

THOMAS DIMACK, (Barnstable.)

Nuncupative will by *Anthony Annable* and *John Smith*, that "when he was sick last summer, he said what little he had he would give to his wife, for the children were hers as well as his"

DANIEL WING. (Sandwich?)

May 3. 1659. Inventory, by *John* and *Stephen Wing*, of a small estate confirmed to the children of Danl. Wing.

WILLIAM CARPENTER, SEN. (Rehoboth.)

Will, dated 10 10mo 1659. Names his wife; his sons *John* (and his son) *William* (and his son John) *Joseph* (and his son Joseph) *Abijah*, and *Samuel*. His daughters *Hannah* and *Abigail*.

To John Titus' son. Witnessed by *John Peck* and *Richd. Bullock*. Executors, *Richd Bowin* and *John Allin*.

His inventory, an extensive one, follows.

ELIZABETH HOPKINS, (Plymouth.)

Inventory of her property in the hands of *Jacob Cook* and *Andrew Ring*, Oct. 6. 1659. Am't. £26. 14s. by *Tho. Southworth John Morton*.*

A writing by *John Freeman* and *Edwd. Bangs*, 29. 7mo 1659, about the cattle of *Gyles* and *Elizabeth Hopkins*, accompanied by orders of Court.

* In connection with this estate at this date is mentioned the name of Mrs. Standish, which shows that she was alive in 1659. The Captain died in 1656, and it is known his wife survived him, but how long is doubtful.—J. W.

[Here ends Part I, of the 2nd volume. In Part II, from page 1 to page 59, are contained the years 1663 – 1669; and from p. 59 to p. 84, the years 1660 – 1663. For the sake of preserving the chronological order, the following abstracts commence with page 59, and having continued through the volume, will recommence with the first page and complete the book.]

JOHN GREEN, (Sandwich.)

Will dated last of Feby 1659, conveys power of attorney to *James Skiffe*, names his *sister* and her child. Witnessed by *Stephen Wing* and *Benj. Nye*. Inventory, £79. 9s. 9d, taken May 21, 1660.

JOHN DEANE, (Taunton.)

Will dated, 25 2mo 1660. Calls himself 60 yrs. old. Appoints his wife *Alice*, executrix. Gives to his son *John*, his house; to his 2^d son *Thomas*, 3^d son *Israel*, his two youngest sons *Isaac* and *Nathaniel* His da. *Elizabeth*. His brother *Walter Deane*.

Witnesses
Hezekiah Hoare
Anthony Slocum
James Wyate

Inventory,
June 7. 1660
£150

MR. JOHN BURSLEY, (Barnstable.)

Inventory, 21 Aug. 1660 by *John Smith* and *John Chipman*. Am't. £115. 5s.

WILLIAM CHASE, (Yarmouth.)

His will. "Being aged" he bequeaths to his sons *Benjamin* and *William*. His wife *Mary*. Appoints neighbor *Robt. Dennis* and *Richd. Taylor* overseers. Witnessed by *Richd. Hoare*, and *Mary Dennis*. Dated May 4, 1659.

Inventory by *Dennis*, *Taylor*, and *Edmund Hawes*, 14th Sep. 1659.

EDWARD TILSON, (Scituate.)

Inventory by Nathl. Morton, Samuel Dunham, Walter Hatch and Thomas Bird. Am't £73 13s. 6d, May 5. 1660.

THOMAS HATCH, (Barnstable)

Inventory, May 27. 1661. taken by Isaac Robinson, Tho. Ewer. Sworn to by his widow Grace. Amt £14. 18s.

RICHARD SPARROW, (Eastham.)

Will. Desires to be buried at Eastham. To his wife *Pandora* his house, whom together with his son *Jonathan*, he makes his executors. Names his grand children, *John*, *Priscilla*, and *Rebecca Sparrow*. Dated 19 9mo 1660. Appoints *Tho Prence*, *Tho Willes*, and *Lt. Tho Southworth*, his overseers.

Witnesses
Josiah Cook
Saml. Freeman

Inventory (£85) by
Josiah Cook
Nicolas Snow

ABSTRACTS OF THE EARLIEST WILLS IN THE PROBATE OFFICE, PLYMOUTH.

[Communicated by Mr. JUSTIN WINSOR, of Boston.

ROBERT MARTIN. (Rehoboth.)

Will dated 6 3mo 1660. Names his wife *Joan*, and his brother *Richd Martin* in Old England, and his children. Gives also to his Elder brother *Abraham* "if his need calleth for it." Appoints *Tho Cooper* sen, *Wm Sabin* of Rehoboth, and "cozen" *Robt Clapp* of Dorchester, overseers; and *Rev Saml Newman* and *Nathl Paine*, Executors. Witnessed by *Stephen Paine Senr* and *George Robinson.*

Inventory, "19 5mo, June, 1660." Am't. £193. 1^s.^ 6^d.^

JOHN ROGERS, SEN. (Marshfield.)

Will, dated Feb. 1, 1660. Names wife *Frances*, (executrix), Sons *John*, *Joseph*, *Timothy*, and daughters, *Ann Hudson*, *Mary*, *Abigail*, and grand children, *George* and *John Russell*. *John Hudson* lived on his land at Namasakeeset. Witnessed by *Anthony Eames*, *Wm Maycomber*, *Mark Eames*, *Richd Beare.* Inventory by *A. Eames*, *Tho. King*, and *John Rogers*. Am't. £125. 17^s.^

THURSTON CLARK. (Duxbury.)

Inventory Dec. 10, 1661. Taken on oath of his widow *Faith*, by *Christopher Wadsworth*, *Joseph Andrews*, *John Rogers*, and *John Tracy* Am't. £97. 12^s^ 6^d.^

NATHANIEL MAYO. (Eastham.)

His will dated 19 10mo 1661, names his sons *Thomas* (eldest), *Nathaniel*, *Samuel*, *Theophilus;* his daughter *Hannah;* his wife *Hannah*, the executrix of the will; appoints his father (in-law) *Thomas Prence*, and brother (in-law) *John Freeman* and *Nathaniel Bacon*, overseers of the will, which was witnessed by *Edwd Bangs* and *Josiah Cook*.

Inventory taken by *John Done* and *Wm Merrick*, and Exhibited at court 4 Mar. 1661. Am't. £202. 4^s.^ 8^1.^

WILLIAM PARKER. (Taunton.)

Will dated Mar 15. 1659, then being aged 60 years. Gives to *James Phillips*, and to *Elizabeth* wife of *James Walker*, and makes his wife *Alice*, residuary legatee, and executrix of the will.

Overseers of the will.	Witnesses
Richard Williams	*Richd Williams*
James Walker	*Peter Pitts*

Inventory taken 10 of last mo. 1661, by *Williams* and *James Wyate*.

THOMAS BILLINGTON. (Taunton.)

Isaac Hall aged 24 yrs, deposes that he heard T. B. on his death bed, three or four days before death, say that he gave all his property to *James Leonard, Sen.* May, 1662.

John Wood, aged 42 yrs, the same.

Inventory, May 1, 1662, by *Richd Williams* and *George Hall.*

JOSEPH WORMALL. (Scituate.)

His will exhibited at court, June 24, 1662. To his wife *Merriam*, son *Josias*, daughters *Sarah* and *Hester*. Overseers, *Abraham Sutlieff*, *Matthias Briggs*, *James Torrey*. Dated Feb. 4, 1661. Witnessed by *Josiah Turner*, *Elijor Clapp* and *James Torrey*.

Inventory by *John Cushing* and *James Doughtey*.

EDMOND CHAUNDELER. (Duxbury.)

Will dated May 3, 1662. "being old." To his sons *Samuel*, *Benjamin*, and *Joseph* (executor); daughters *Sarah*, *Anna*, *Mary* (to these three property at Barbadoes, sugar) and *Ruth*.

Witnesses, *John Alden* and *Constant Southworth*;

Inventory by *Alden* and *Philip Delano*, 24mo 1662.

JOHN ALLIN. (Scituate.)

Nuncupative will. *Nicolas Baker* aged 53 years, deposes that *Timothy Hatherly* and himself, heard the said Allin, two days before he died make the following distribution of his estate,—to *Josias Leichfield*, the house he lived in,—to his *wife* the other house, where *Jonas Littles* lives. June 2, 1663.

Inventory, 25 Sep 1662, by *Hatherly*, *Baker*, *Walter Briggs*, *John Woodfield*, and *James Cudworth*. Am't. £168. 14s. 6d.

JOHN BROWN, JR. (Rehoboth.)

His will styles him of Wannamoiset. To his wife the three-score pounds, my father-in-law, *Wm Buckland*, was to pay as a marriage portion in 1660. To eldest son *John*. To his brother *James*. Gives to the care of his father, Mr *John Brown* (the executor of the will) five of his children for him to bring up. March the last, 1662. Witnesses, *John Allin and Thomas Willet*

Inventory (£350) by *Stephen Paine*, *Thomas Cooper and Peter Hunt*.

MR JOHN BROWN, SEN'R. (Rehoboth)

Will dated April 7. 1662. To da. *Mary*, wife of *Thomas Willet*—To grand child *Martha*, wife of *John Saffin*—To grand child *John Brown*, the house his father died in, 700 acres in the Narraganset country, 350 of which is on Great Neck—To grand children *Joseph* and *Nathaniel Brown*, 500 acres in the same place—To grand Children *Lydia* & *Hannah Brown*, the same quantity, their uncle *James* to dispose of it.

His son *James* and wife *Dorothy*, executors.

Witnesses	Inventory (£655, 1s. 2d)
John Allin	by *Stephen Paine*
Richd Bullock	*Thomas Cooper*
Sampson Mason	*Peter Hunt*

This copy of the will endorsed by an order of Court.

JOHN CHURCHILL, SEN'R. (Plymouth)

Nuncupative will exhibited at court May 3. 1662. *Abigail Clark* aged 20 yrs, deposes that on Tuesday, 24th Dec last, her kinsman, J. C. Senr being ill, did express himself in manner &c, as followeth, that he gave to his son *Joseph* & *Eleazer* lands at Plymouth, and to sons *John* and *William* other property, all of which was confirmed by *Joseph*.

Inventory (£74. 14s. 6d.) by *Nathl* & *Ephraim Morton*.

THOMAS BURMAN. (Barnstable.)

Will, May 9. 1663. To his wife *Hannah* (the executrix of the will.) To his sons *Thomas*, *Trustrum* and *Samuel*, and daughters *Hannah*, *Desire*, *Mary* and *Mehetabel*. Signed by his mark. Witnessed by *John Smith* and *John Chipman*.

Inventory by *Wm Crocker*, *John Howland*, and *Moses Rowley*.

A paper signed by *James Phillips* husbandman, stating that he had received the bequest of his uncle *Wm Parker* and his aunt *Allis Paine*, and binds himself &c, never again to molest their estates.

Here closes the volume, with the exception of four papers, recorded by order of Court, letters from the quaker, Humphrey Norton, &c. To continue chronologically, these extracts, now begin with p. 1 of part ii. of this 2d volume, and finishing p. 57, a complete abstract of the volume is thus given.

FRANCIS COOKE. (Plymouth.)

His will dated 7 10mo 1659. Makes his wife *Hester* and son *John*, executors. Witnessed by *Howland* and *Alden*.

Inventory, May 1, 1663, taken by *Eph. Tuckham* and *Wm Crowe*. Amt. £86. $11^{s.}$ $1^{d.}$

SAMUEL HINCKLEY, Sen. (Barnstable.)

Will. To wife *Bridget*, sons *Samuel*, *John* and *Thomas*, daughters *Susannah*, *Sarah*, *Mary*, *Elizabeth* and *Bathshoa*, (da. of Thomas,) To his son [in law] *Henry Cobb's* sons *Samuel* and *Jonathan*.

Inventory (£162. $16^{s.}$) by *Henry Cobb* and *Wm. Crocker*.

SAMUEL HOUSE. (Scituate.)

Inventory at the request of his children *Samuel and Elizabeth House*, taken 12 Sep 1661, by *Timothy Hatherly*, *Nicolas Baker*, *Joseph Tilden* and *Isaac Chittenden*. £249. $17^{s.}$

JOHN FOBES. (Bridgewater.)

Wm Brett and *Arthur Harris* depose that being with *goodman ffobes* of Bridgewater, lying sick and expecting his change, he disposed a part of his Estate to his two eldest sons *John* and *Edward*, and to his daughter *Mary*, and left the remainder to be divided by his *wife*.

Inventory, July 31, 1662.

MITCHELL. (Duxbury.)

"Loveing frind Experience Michell, my love and my wife's remembered unto thee and thy wife. I thought it fitt to acquaint you with the death of my [thy ?] Sister's Son John, whoe died att my house on the sixt day of the week, being as I judged, about the 10th day of July, 1661; hee was sensable untill about two houres before hee died and did say, Oh Lord, when shall my change come; hee was not affraid of death; hee was with Mistress Swift to bee cured of his desease. The land his father gave him, John gave to his brother Willam, onely Edward is to have his choise, when they do devid the two Shares, his love he remembered to his Mother and to his brothers and Sisters; hee was buryed on the last day of the week. I have sent his clothes by John Smith, of Plymouth, they will be left at John Smithes house of Plymouth, that if there bee an opportunitie to convey them to his mother, you may know where they are,

Soe I rest
Youer frind,
George Allin of
Sandwich.

" Postscript—"
You may send this writing
to his mother, as you have
oppertunitie.

And Subscribed thus—
To his Frind Experience
Michell of Duxburrow,
give this.

RICHARD SYLVESTER, Sen. (Marshfield.)

His will appoints his wife *Naomy*, Executrix.
To Sons *John*, *Joseph*, *Israel*, *Richard* and *Benjamin*, and daughter *Lydia*, *Dinah*, *Elizabeth*, *Naomy* and *Hester*,
Witnesses.
John Hanmore,
James Torrey, *Sen*,

Inventory,
Sep. 24, 1663,
£244, 5[s] 11[d].

NATHANIEL RAWLINS. (Scituate.)

Inventory, 29 Dec. 1662, taken on oath of his widow *Lydia* by *Thomas King* and *Humphrey Johnson.*

REV. SAMUEL NEWMAN, (Rehoboth.)

Will dated Nov. 18, 1661. Names his wife *Sybil*, his Son, *Samuel*, *Antipas*, *Noah* (to whom he gave his library), and da. *Hopestill*. Mention is also made of 3 daughters. Gives bequests to his old servants *Mary Humphreyes* of Dorchester, *Elizabeth Cubby*, of Weymouth, *Elizabeth Palmer*, of Rehoboth, and *Lydia Winchester*, my present one.

He died July 5, 1663. His will witnessed by *John Hinckley*, *Sam[l]. Newman*, Jr. He appointed *Stephen Paine*, *Sen. Dea Thomas Cooper*, and *Lt. Hunt*, overseers of his will.

Inventory taken by overseers, July 31, 1663.

ROBERT ABELL. (Rehoboth.)

Inventory, 9 Aug 1663. (£354. 17[s]. 9[d].) by *S. Paine*, *T. Cooper* and *Peter Hunt.*

In connection are named his " eldest son, his widow, his daughter *Mary*, and his 5 children."

JOAN SWIFT. (Sandwich.)

Will dated 12 8[mo] 1662. To *Daniel Wing's* two sons *Samuel* and *John*—to grand children *Hannah Swift* and *Experience Allin*—to *Mary Darby*—to *Hannah Wing*, the elder and her daughters—to *Zebediah Allin*—to son *William* (executor) and his children. Appoints as overseers the witnesses *John Vincent* and *Benj. Hammond.* Inventory taken 25 10[mo] 1663 by *Rich[d] Brown* and *James Skiff*.

ABSTRACTS OF THE EARLIEST WILLS IN THE PROBATE OFFICE, PLYMOUTH.

[Communicated by Mr. JUSTIN WINSOR, of Boston.

JOHN FISH. (Sandwich.)

Inventory on oath of *Mrs. Cecelia Fish*, by *Richard Bourn* and *Nath*[l] *Fish*, Nov. 18, 1663.

ZACARYA SOULE. (Duxbury.)

Inventory taken on oath of his widow *Margaret*, Dec. 11, 1663, by *John Alden* and *Constant Southworth.*

THOMAS ENSIGN. (Scituate.)

Inventory, 17 Feb. 1663, (£71. 9*s*.) by *Nic. Baker*, *Edw. Jenkins*, and *Isaac Buck*.

GEORGE LEWIS, SEN. (Barnstable.)

Will exhibited at court 3 Mar. 1663. To his wife *Mary;* to sons *Ephraim*, *George*, *Thomas*, *James*, *Edward* and *John ;* to daughter *Sarah*. Witnessed by *Thomas Allin* and *Wm. Casley.*

THOMAS ENSIGN. (Scituate.)

Will dated July 16, 1663. To wife *Elizabeth*, his house. To son *John*. To daughters *Hannah* and *Sarah*. To *Sarah Underwood*, his wife's sister's daughter, when she becomes 15 yrs of age. Witnessed by *Timothy Hatherly* and *Nic. Baker*.

THOMAS BOURN. (Marshfield.)

Will dated May 2, 1664. To daughters *Martha Bradford*, *Anne Smith*, and *Margaret Winslow*. To son *Nath*[l] *Tilden*. To daughter *Lydia Tilden's* daughter *Lydia*. To *John*, *Thomas*, *Joseph*, and *Robert Waterman*. To *Mr. Arnold*. Makes his son *John* his right heir, and Executor of the will. Witnessed by *Sam*[l] *Arnold*, and *Anthony Snow*.

Inventory (£138. 14*s*. 2*d*.) by Sergt. *Joseph Riddle*. *A. Snow*, and *Thomas Doged*.

JAMES PITNEY. (Marshfield.)

Nuncupative will by *John Bradford* (who was made overseer) and *John Bourn*, March 14, 1663. The testator aged 80 years. Leaves his property to his sons *John Thomas, Sen.*, and *James Pitney*, and daughters *Abigail* and *Sarah Thomas*, (and her children) who was made executrix of the will.

Inventory taken March 21, 1663. Am't £31. 9*s*.

LT. JAMES WYATT. (Taunton.)

Inventory by *Rich*[d] *Williams*, and *Walter Deane*, July 27, 1664. Am't. £232. 7*s*. 3*d*. Debts £65.

THOMAS BIRD. (Scituate.)

Will, To *Gershom*, son of *Anthony Dodson*, of S, his two dwelling houses, and land betw. *Tho. Oldham's* and *John Bisbee's*, he paying to the church of Marshfield 20 shillings a year—To *Jonathan Dodson*, brother of G,—To the 3 daughters of *A. Dodson*—To *Mr. Wm. Witherell*, minister of S—To kinsman *Rob*[t] *Marshall*—To *Wm. Brooks*, of S—To *John* son of *Elisha Bisbee*—To *James Torrey, Sen*[r]—To *Deborah Bunden* (?)—Makes his wife *Ann* residuary legatee.

Feb. 4th, 1663.

Overseers.	Witnesses.
Wm. Witherell,	*Thomas Oldham,*
Jas. Torrey.	*John Hammer* (mark)

Inventory taken July 8, 1664. (£211. 1*s*. 0*d*.) by *Thomas Kinge, John Ottis, John Hollett*, his mark.

THO. LUMBERT. (Barnstable.)

Mar. 23[d], 1662-3, his will. To his wife—Son *Caleb*, his house—To sons *Jedediah* and *Benjamin*—It mentions that he formerly gave property to his sons *Barnard, Joshua, Joseph*, and his son in law *Edw. Coleman*. It mentions his daughter *Margaret Coleman*.—His grandchild *Abigail*.

Witnesses, *John Gorum* and *Barnard Lumbert*.

June 10, 1663, Will again acknowledged by testator before *Anthony Thacher* and *Tho. Thornton*.

Inventory at Court Mar. 7, 1664, on oath of *Joyce Lumbert*, widow.—Taken Feb. 8, 1664. £210. 8*s*. 6*d*.

By *Henry Cobb, John Gorum, Nath*[l]. *Bacon*.

GOWIN WHITE.

Inventory, 8 Dec. 1664.—Exhibited on oath of *Timothy* and *Joseph White*. £59. 15*s*. 0*d*.

Taken by *Isaac Barker* and *James Cudworth*.

ANNA VINALL. (Scituate.)

Inventory. She d. 6 Oct. 1664. On oaths of *Stephen* and *John Vinall*. £87. 10*s*. 10*d*. (excepting lands). By *Nic.* and *Nat. Baker*.

WILLIAM SHEPHEARD. (TAUNTON.)

Inventory of goods left at house of *Tho. Jones*, of T. Feb. 27, 1664. By *Walter Deane, Geo. Hall* and *Nic. White*.

CORNELIUS. (Barnstable.)

Inventory of a certain Irishman, named *Cornelius*, who d. at B. 15 Dec. 1664. £1. 18*s*. 6*d*. Debts, £1. 12. 0. By *Barnard Lumbert*.

RICHARD ORMSBY. (Rehoboth.)

Inventory, 3d, 5 mo, 1664. £45. 14[s] 6[d].

THOMAS BOWEN. (Rehoboth.)

Will, 11 April, 1663, late of New London, in Connecticut. To son *Richard*—To wife *Elizabeth*—His wife executrix—To his brother *Obadiah Bowen*.

Witness, *Daniel Smith*.

JOHN WALKER. (Marshfield.)

Inventory Dec. 28, 1663, £57. 9*s*. 9*d*. By *Wm. Foard* and *John Bourn*. *Lydia*, his widow, took oath. His daughters *Lydia*, *Martha* and *Mary*, mentioned, not of age.

FRANCIS STREET. (Taunton.)

Inventory, June 3d, 1665. £42. 19s. By *Wm. Harvey*, *Edw. Babbitt*, *Jona. Briggs*. His widow *Elizabeth*, took oath.

JONAS PICKLES. (Scituate.)

Will, nuncupative. By *Lydia Springe* and *Hanah Ganett*, wife of *Matthew Ganett*. To his *wife* and *children*. Dec. 15, 1664.

Inventory, Dec. 15, 1665. £79. 2. 0. By *Edw. Jenkins* and *Isaac Chetenden*.

LT. JAMES TORREY.

Inventory 15th Sept., 1665, on oath of his widow *Ann*. £102. 1*s*. 0*d*. By *James Cudworth*, *Thos. King*, *John Cushen*, and *Joseph Tilden*.

NICHOLAS MILLER *alias* HODGIS.

Will, Oct. 24, 1665. To *Peter Reife*—To *John Hoskins* and *Wm. Hoskins, Jr.*—To *Mary Cobb* and *Daniel Ramsden*, and *Hannah Reife*.

Inventory, Oct. 31, 1665. By *Jas. Cole, Jr.* and *Jona. Shaw*.

THOMAS HOWES. (Yarmouth.)

Will, 26th Sept., 1665. To sons *Joseph*, *Thomas* and *Jeremy*—To wife *Mary*.

Witnesses, *Tho. Thornton*, *Anthony Thacher*.

Inventory, 18th Oct., 1665. £242. 14. 0. *Mistress Mary Howes*, widow, took oath.

MARGARET HICKES. (Plymouth.)

Will, July 8, 1665; widow. To son *Samuel;* daughter-in-law, *Lydia;* son Samuel's *chd;* son *Ephraim*, now deceased. To grand child *John Banges*. To the son of her son-in-law, *George Watson*, husband of her da *Phebe*, dec.

Geo. Watson, } Overseers.
Capt. Southworth, }

Inventory 5th March, 1665. By *Capt. S.* and *John Morton*. £53. 12*s*. 6*d*.

TIMOTHY HATHERLY. (Scituate.)

Will. To wife *Lydia*—To *Edw. Jenkins*, his *wife* and *chd*—To *Nic Wade*, his *wife* and *chd*—To *Susanna*, wife of *Wm. Brooks*, and her *children*—To *Timothy* and *Elizabeth Foster*—To *Mr. Tho. Hanford*—To *Fear Robinson*, "now the wife of *Samuel Baker*," and to the other three chd of *Isaac Robinson*, *John*, *Isaac* and *Mercy*. To *Lydia Ganett*, his wife's daughter, and her *four* chd. To *George Sutton*, his *wife* and *chd*.—To the wife of *Wm. Basset*, his wife's daughter—To widow *Preble*, his wife's daughter—To *Lydia* and *Thomas Lapham*—To *Stephen Tilden*, and *Nic Baker*—To his man, *Tho.*

Savory—To *Lydia*, daughter of *Wm. Hatch*—Makes *Joseph Tilden*, residuary legatee. Sept. 20, 1664. Witnessed by *Nic Baker* and *Isaac Chettenden*.

MR. JOHN JOYCE. (Yarmouth.)

Will, 20 Nov., 1666. To *Dorothy*, his wife. To *Hosea Joyce* his only son. To his two daughters *Mary* and *Dorias* (?)—To *Rev. Tho. Thornton* and *Richd Taylor*.

Witnesses, *Tho. Thornton* and *Anthony Thacher*.

Postscript names *Thacher*, *Edmund Hawes* and *Andrew Hallett*, as overseers.

Inventory 18th, 12th mo. 1666. £232. 1. 0.

EDWARD DILLINGHAM.

Will. To sons *Henry* and *John Dillingham*. May 1st., 1666.

Witnesses, *Stephen Wing*, *Wm. Griffith* (?) and *John Newland*.

Inventory by *Stephen Wing* and *Stephen Skiffe*.

WM. BASSETT, SEN. (Bridgewater.)

Will, 3d, 2 mo., 1667. To his *wife* his moveables. To his son *William's* son—To son *Joseph*.

Witnesses, *Wm. Brett* and *John Carey*.

Inventory, May 12, 1667. His relict *Mary* took oath.

TIMOTHY HATHERLY. (Scituate.)

Inventory Nov. 9, 1666. £224. 12. 8. By *John Hollett*, *Rodolphus Elmes* and *Jas. Cudworth, Senr*.

Letters of administration granted to *Joseph Tilden*.

WILLIAM HACK.

Inventory on oath of *Mary Hack*, his wife, June 1, 1667. £35. 3*s*. 0*d*.

Thomas Linton of Taunton, testifies, that said H., when he left for England, promised to return to his wife in the summer following. *Henry Andrews* the same. *Robt. Thornton*, being in Boston, two years ago, was told by a seaman from London, who knew said H. there, that he, said H., was married. Signed May 31, 1667.

JOHN PAYBODY. (Duxbury.)

Will, 16 July, 1649. To eldest son *Thomas*, second son *Francis* and youngest son *William*. To his da *Annis Rouse*—To *John*, son of *John Rouse*, his land at Causwell, after his wife's death. To *John*, son of *William*—To his wife *Isabel*.

Witness, *John Fernessyde*.

Boston, April 27, 1667. Said *F*. took oath to the will.

TRISTRUM HULL. (Barnstable.)

Will, Dec. 20, 1666. To son *Joseph*—To his wife *Blanch*—To chd, *John*, *Mary*, *Sarah*, *Hannah*. To *Robert Davis*.

Witnesses, *Mark Ridley* and *Matthew Fuller*.

His Inventory by *Barnabas Lathrop* and *John Crocker*.

THOMAS EWER. (Sandwich.)

Inventory, May 31, 1667. His widow *Hannah* took oath. £30. 3*s*. 6*d*.

ABSTRACTS OF THE EARLIEST WILLS IN THE PROBATE OFFICE, PLYMOUTH.

[Communicated by Mr. JUSTIN WINSOR.]

JOHN TURNER.

Inventory 31 May, 1667, by *John Chipman* and *John Ottis.*

MR. ANTHONY THACKER (Yarmouth.)

Inventory, he d. Aug. 22, 1667. Taken 13 Sep. by *Edmund Hawes*, *Robt Dennis*, and *John Gorum*. £266, 9s. 9d.

ROBT HUSEY (Duxbury.)

Inventory exhibited at Court, 30 Oct., 1667, £21, 18s. 6d. by *John Haward.*

NATHANIEL WARREN, Senr. (Plymouth.)

Will. To wife *Sarah*, and his *chd;* names his lame and impotent *daughter*, and his eldest *son*. Appoints *Thomas Southworth*, his brother *Joseph Warren*, and *Lt. Eph. Morton*, Intervisers. June 29, 1667. Witnesses, *Hugh Cole*, *Nathl Morton*. A supplement names his mother, *Mistress Elizabeth Warren*, and his sisters *Mary Bartlett*, Sen., *Ann Little*, *Sarah Cooke*, *Elizabeth Church*, & *Abigail Snow*. July 15, 1667. Inventory, Oct. 21, 1667. £475. Taken by *Joseph Warren*, *Eph. Morton*, *Thomas Southworth.*

GABRIEL FALLOWELL (Plymouth.)

Will. To *Sarah*, da. of *John Wood;* to my grandchild *Jona. Fallowell*, to *Catherine*, his loving wife. His brother *Robt Finney*. Oct. 14, 1667. Inventory, Feb. 1667. £45, 15, 6.

JOHN PARKER (Taunton.)

Will, 6 Nov., 1665. To his wife *Sarah*. Speaks of his house at Boston. To his wife's sister's son, *Nathl Smith*, to his brother *Mr. John Summers*, minister, and his chd, *Samuel*, *Elizabeth*, *Mary*, *Abigail*, and to chd of his sister *Smith*,—to sister *Faben's* (?) chd, *John*, *Joseph*, *Daniel* and *Annis*, to *Mary Parker*, and sister *Elizabeth Phillips* of Taunton, to *James Phillips* of Taunton and his two *sons*, to cousin *James Walker's* children of Taunton, to the church of Taunton. He d. Feb. 26, 1667. Inventory, £406, 0, 9.

RICHD BULLOCK (Rehoboth.)

Inventory, Nov. 22, 1667. £81, 12, 3.

RICHD FOXWELL (Barnstable.)

Will names sons *Samuel Bacon*, *Hugh Cole*, and son and da. *Nelson*. To church of Barnstable, for the poor. Names *Mr. Adams*, "woolen draper which did dwell in London." 1668, April 7th. In a supplement names his son *Nelson*, with "my daughter *Ruth*." Inventory 30 May 1668, by *Henry Cobb* and *Thomas Huckens*. £26, 18s. 6d.

JOHN WILLIAMS, Sen. (Scituate.)

Will. To da. *Mary Dodson;* his son *John;* to *Ann*, wife of *John Pratt*, and *Deborah*, wife of *Wm. Burden*. To *Mary Barker*, and to his two grandchd *John* and *Abraham Barker*. To *Nic. Baker* of Scituate. Dec. 19, 1667.

WILLIAM CLARK (Yarmouth.)

Barnard Lumbert, aged 60, testifies that Wm Clark of Yarmouth gave, by nuncupative will, his property to *Joseph Benjamin*, 28th 12 mo 1668. *Clark* d. Dec. 7, 1668. Inventory, £8, 3s. 0d.

Widow SILVESTER (Scituate.)

Inventory 26 Nov 1668 on oath of *John Silvester*. £87. Taken by *John Cushen* and *Robert Stetson*.

WM BURDEN

Heretofore of Concord, Mass., now resident in Duxbury, testifies, that he rec[d] in right of his wife, *Deborah*, da. of *John Barker*, late dec[d], money from *Abraham Blush*. March 1, 1660. *John Pratt* is called father in law of *Abraham Blush*.

JOANNA MARTIN (Rehoboth.)

Inventory, Feb. 26, 1666. £193. 12. Taken by *Tho. Cooper sen*, *Peter Hunt*, *Henry Smith*, *Wm Sabine*. Her will, April 6, 1668. To loving kinsman *John Ormsley;* to sister *Smith;* to cousins *Grace Ormsley*, *Thomas Ormsley*, and *Jacob Ormsley*. To cousin *Clapp*, and kinswoman *Jane Clapp;* to brother *Upham* his *chd* at Mauldin. *Stephen Paine Jun. Richd Bowin Jun.* overseers.

JEREMIAH BURROWES (Marshfield.)

Inventory, 22 Nov. 1660. £47, 13, 8. Taken by *Josias Winslow* & *Wm Sherman*.

JOHN DUNHAM Sen (Plymouth.)

Will, Jan 25, 1668. To sons *John* (eldest), *Benajah*, *Daniel*, and son in law *Stephen Wood;* and wife *Abigail*. Witnesses *Tho Southworth John Cotton Tho Cushman*. Inventory, 16 Mar. 1668. by *Tho. Southworth* & *Thomas Cushman*.

THOMAS CHETTENDEN (Scituate.)

Will; calls himself weaver, 7 Oct. 1668. To my sons *Isaac* & *Henry*. Inventory, 9 Nov 1668, £63. 02s, 01. By *Jas. Cudworth* and *Stephen Vinall*.

WILLIAM BERSTOW.

Inventory sworn to by his *widow* Apr. 5, 1669. By *Robt Stetson* & *Joseph Silvester*.

JOHN CROCKER (Barnstable.)

Will 10 Feb. 1668. To his loving wife *Jone;* to brother *Wm Crocker's* sons, viz, *John*, *Job*, *Samuel*, *Josias*, *Elisha* and *Joseph*. His kinsman *Job Crocker*, Executrix. Inventory, £57. 02. 02, by *Wm Crocker*, *Tho. Haskins* & *John Tompson*.

FRANCIS STEVENS Sen. (Rehoboth.)

Inventory by *Wm Carpenter* and *John Ormsley*, Apr. 1. 1669.

FRANCIS GODFREY (Bridgewater.)

Will, calls himself "aged inhabitant of the town of B." 1666. To wife *Elizabeth*. To his gd. child *John Carye*. To his da. *Elizabeth Carye*, and her child *Elizabeth*. To his servant *John Pitcher*. To son in law *John Carye*. Witnesses *Wm Brett*, *Jas Keith*, *Nathl Willis*, *John Hill*. Inventory, 30 July, 1669. £117. 17s. 5d.

JOHN WOODFIELD (Scituate.)

Will. To wife *Hester*, who is made Executrix. June 4, 1669. Witnesses, *Nic Baker*, *Micaell Peirse*. Inventory, 18 June 1669, by *John Hallet* and *Isaac Chettenden*. £64. 4. 0.

Here ends the volume marked "PLYMOUTH COLONY RECORDS, *Wills, &c.*, VOL. II, 1654–1669."

Beginning with "Wills, &c., Vol. III, 1669–1678."

On the first page some scattering memoranda, and numerical accounts.

Capt. THOMAS SOUTHWORTH.

Will, 18th Nov. 1669. To da. *Elizabeth Howland*, housing and lands in Plymouth; to her husband *Joseph Howland*, his rapier and belt. To *Thomas Faunce*, *Deborah Morton*, and *Wm Churchill*. To his *brother Constant Southworth*, whom he charges "for the support of my wife in her poor condition." Witnesses, *John Morton*, *George Bonum*. Inventory by *Geo. Watson*, *John Morton*, and *Eph. Morton*. Exhibited at court, Mar. 1, 1669, on oath of *Joseph Howland*.

Mistress ALICE BRADFORD (Plymouth.)

Will. "Wishes to be interred as near to her decd husband, *Mr. Wm Bradford*, as conveniently may be." To sister *Mary Carpenter;* to sons *Constant Southworth*, *Joseph Bradford;* to grandchild *Elizabeth Howland*, da. of my decd son, *Capt. Tho. Southworth;* to servant maid *Mary Smith*. Her mark. Inventory, March 31, 1670, on oath of Mistress *Carpenter*, £162, 17s. By *Geo. Watson*, *Eph. Morton*, *Wm Harlow*.

Joseph Tilden (Scituate.)

Will, May 12, 1670. "Yeoman," to wife *Elizth Tilden;* sons *Nathl, John, Stephen, Samuel* and *Benjamin*, none of them 21 years old at this date; daughters, *Rebecca, Elizabeth* and *Lydia.* To sister Elizabeth Garrett; brother Stephen Tilden. Inventory, May 31, 1670. £1367. 5s.

Wm Macomber (Marshfield.)

Inventory, 27 May, 1670. £102. 1s. On oath of *Priscilla* Macomber, *Thomas* Maycomber, *Matthew* Maycomber.

Samuel Sturtevant (Plymouth.)

Will, Aug. 1st, 1669. Son-in-law *John Waterman;* sons *Samuel, James, John* and *Joseph*, and a child, "his wife goeth with." To his wife. Witnesses, *Wm Crow, John Smith.* Inventory, 22 Oct. 1669. £23, 18s.

Joseph Burye,

Aged 30 years, testifies that he heard *Robert Rollock* say that he intended to marry his landlady this fall, about a month or six weeks before he died. Oct. 28, 1669.

Robert Rollock (Sandwich.)

Inventory, 15 Sept., 1669. By *Rich. Bourne, Nathl. Fish, Tho. Lobey, John Ellis.*

John Richmond, Senr. (Taunton.)

Will, 14 Dec. 1663. To eldest son *John Richmond;* son in law *William Paule,* and *Mary* his wife, and to their children. To younger son *Edward* and his son *Edward;* to son in law *Edward Rew*, and *Sarah*, his wife; son *John's* son *Thomas.* Witnesses, *Joseph Wilbore, Shadrach Wilbore.* He decd 20 March, 1663–4, aged 70 years. Inventory, £10. 11s. 09d. *Edward Richmond* lived at Newport, R. I.

George Hall (Taunton.)

Oct. 1669. Will. To wife *Mary;* sons *John, Samuel, Joseph;* da. *Charity, Sarah;* grandchildren; to the church in Taunton 40 shillings to buy cups, to *Wm Evens.* Witnesses, *Richd. Williams, Walter Deane.* He died Oct. 30, 1669. Inventory, £170. 15s.

Catherine Hurst.

Widow, inventory, 30 May, 1670. £39. 3. 0.

Nathl Goodspeed (Barnstable.)

Inventory 23d May, 1670. £72. 0. 0. His relict was *Elizabeth*, and father was *Roger*, both alive at this date.

ABSTRACTS OF THE EARLIEST WILLS IN THE PROBATE OFFICE, PLYMOUTH.

[Communicated by Mr. JUSTIN WINSOR.]

CAPT WM HEDGE, (Yarmouth.)

Will. To sons *Abraham*, *Elisha*, *William*, *John*, *Elemuel;* to daughters *Sarah Matthews*, *Elizabeth Barnes*, *Mary Sturgis*, and *Mercy Hedge;* to sister and brother *Brooks*. His wife *Blanch* "had dealt falsely with him in the covenant of marriage, and departed from him." He gave her 12d. 30 June 1670. *Matthew Fuller*, *John Gray*, *John Davis*. Inventory £487. 16. 0.

WM BASSET (Sandwich.)

Inventory, 9 Aug. 1670, on oath of *Mis. Mary Basset*. £184. 10s.

NONQUID NUMMACK.

Will, March 1, 1669. Desires *Edw Freeman Senr* and *Richd Bourne* to watch over his children, whom he desires to be brought up in the Christian faith. To sons *Tequatohaohom* (?) and *William Numack* and *Jonas Numack;* to da. Margery and her son Samuel. His mark.

GEORGE PETCOCK (Scituate.)

Being weak and impotent, and not able to dispose of his affairs, resigns his body and property to the town of Scituate. 27 Nov. 1670. *Cunel Studson* and *Mark Chettenden* were appointed to take charge.

ABRAHAM MARTIN (Rehoboth.)

Will. To the chd of brother *Richd* and the children of *John Ormsbey;* to Mr *Hubbert*, pastor at Hingham; to *Hannah Hill*, of a place near Medfield; to *Moses Mavorick* at Marblehead; to *Samuel* son of *Stephen Paine;* £1 to improve the burial place, and £1 for a bell on the church; and 10s for a "bear." Sep. 9. 1669. Inventory £66. 1. 8.

HENERY HOWLAND (Duxbury.)

Will. To sons *Joseph*, *Zoeth*, *John*, *Samuel*. To das. *Sarah*, *Elizabeth*, *Mary*, *Abigail*. To his wife *Mary*. 28 Nov. 1670. *Samuel Nash*, *John Sprague*. Inventory £141. 4s. 0d. 14. 11 mo. 1670.

HENERY WOOD (Middlebury.)

Inventory on oath of *Abigail*, widow. By *John Morton*, *Jonathan Dunham*, *Francis Combe*, *George Vaughan*. £63. 03. 03.

JOSEPH LUMBERT,

Aged 29 yrs. in Boston in 1667 met *Simon Bringley* in the street, who told him that *John Turner*, before he went his voyage gave to *Matthew*

Darbey of Barnstable, all his property in Barnstable, if he should not return from sea. July 1671.

Mr William Lumpkin (Yarmouth.)

Will. To wife *Tamasin Lumpkin ;* to da. *Tamasin*, the wife of *John Sunderling ;* to gd. chds. *Wm. Gray*, *Elisha Eldred* and *Bethiah Eldred.* 23d July 1668. Inventory £93. 3s. 6d. By *John Crowell* and *John Hall.*

Mr John Barnes (Plymouth.)

Will, 6 Mar. 1667–8. To wife *Jone ;* son *Jonathan ;* to grd-son *John Marshall ;* to his *cousin* the *wife* of *Henry Sampson ;* to kinswoman *Ester Richard.* Witnesses, *Geo Soule Sen*, *Samuel Seabury*, *Saml Hunt.*

Edward Hall, (Rehoboth.)

Will 23d Nov. 1670. To wife *Ester*, son *John.* Inventory 6 Mar 1670. £84.

Ester Woodfield (Scituate.)

Will. To *Nic Baker* Sen ; to *Isaac Buck* and his wife *Frances ; Experience Litchfield* of Scituate ; to *Judith*, wife to *Wm Peakes*, *Senr. ;* to *Israel and Wm Peakes ;* to *Ryah Peirce*, and *Pensis Peirce*, and to *Philip*, the servant of *Michael Peirce ;* to *Elizabeth*, wife of *Francis James* of Hingham ; to *Robt Whetcome* Senr of Scituate ; to servant *Hannah Ewell ;* to *Elizabeth* wife *Nic Coade ;* to *Saml Jackson*, and to the wife of *Thomas Hiland.* 1672. 27 May.

Wm Joanes (Scituate.)

He d. 29 Jany. 1671. Inventory on oath of *Dorothy Tubbs.* £16. 19. By *Thomas Clap* and *Walter Woodworth.*

Ralph Chapman (Marshfield.)

Will. To da. *Sarah* and her husband *Wm Norcut ;* to younger son *Ralph ;* to children *Isaach*, *John* and *Mary.* 28 Nov 1671. Witnessed by *Peregrine White* and *Eph Little.* Wm Ford Sen, aged 67 ; Thomas Tilden aged 50, Anna Little aged 60 yrs ; and Eph Little aged 22 yrs, testify that at the making of his will, R. Chapman's hands were so swelled, that he could not sign it. Inventory £46. 5s. 9d.

Thomas Shaw (Barnstable.)

Will 1672, June 25. To kinsman *Robt Parker ;* to *John Crocker ; Joshua Lumbert ; Elder John Chipman ; Jas Hamblin* Jr ; *Ann,* wife of *Anthony Annable ; David Linnet.* Inventory £50.

Joseph Biddle (Marshfield.)

Will April 17, 1671. To *Mr Samuel Arnold ;* to the town's poor ; to *Edward Bumpas Senr ;* to *Jacob Bumpas*, his late servant ; to wife *Rachel*, and her da. *Martha Deane.* Inventory 26 Sep. 1672. £221. 7s. 10d.

PLYMOUTH COLONY RECORDS.

[Copied from the originals by the HON. ELIJAH HAYWARD, and by him communicated for the Register.]

MARRIAGES.

Yarmouth, Benjamin Vermages, to Mrs. Mercy Bradford, June 15, 1648.
Sandwich, Thomas Burgess, to Elizabeth Bassett, Nov. 8, 1648.
Plymouth, William Brown, to Mary Murcock, [Murdock ?] July 16, 1649.
" William Harlow, to Rebekah Bartlett, Dec. 20, 1649.
Sandwich, John Freeman, to Mary Prence, Feb. 14, 1649–50.
Plymouth, Edward Gray, to Mary Winslow, Jan. 16, 1650–1.
" John Dickarson, to Elizabeth Hicks, July 10, 1651.
" John Howland, to Mary Lee, Oct. 26, 1651.
" Giles Rickard, Jr., to Hannah Dunham, Oct. 31, 1651.
" Arthur Hathaway, to Sarah Cook, Nov. 20, 1652.
" James Shaw, to Mary Mitchell, Dec. 24, 1652.
Eastham, Mark Snow, to Ann Cooke, Jan. 18, 1654–5.
Plymouth, William Shirtley, to Elizabeth Lettice, Oct. 18, 1655.
" Benajah Pratt, to Pesis [Persis ?] Dunham, Nov. 29, 1655.
" Jonathan Dunham, to Mary Cobb, Oct. 15, 1657.
Abraham Jackson, to Remember Morton, Nov. 18, 1657.
Scituate, John Bryant, to Mary, d. of George Lewis, of Barnstable, Nov. 14, 1643.
" Ephraim Kempton, to Joanna, d. of Thomas Rawlins, Jan. 28, 1645–6.
" Resolved White, to Judith, d. of William Vassall, April 8, 1640.
" William Parker, to Mary, d. of Humphrey Turner, Nov. 13, 1651. She died Aug. 1651.[?]
" James Adams, to Frances, d. of William Vassall, July 16, 1646.
" Joseph Tilden, to Ellice [Alice ?] Twisden, Nov. 20, 1649.
Plymouth, Samuel Hooker, to Mary Willet, Sept. 22, 1658.
" Robert Marshall, to Mary Barnes, between Dec. 2, 1658, and Oct. 25, 1660.
" Benajah Dunham, to Elizabeth Tilson, Oct. 25, 1660.
" Samuel Eaton, to Martha Billington, Jan 10, 1660–1.
" Mr. John Holmes, to Mary Atwood, Dec. 11, 1661.
" Anthony Sprague to Elizabeth Bartlett, Dec. 26, 1661.
" Thomas Leonard, to Mary Watson, Aug. 21, 1662.
" Zachariah Eddy, to Alice Paddock, May 7, 1663.
" William Crow, to Hannah Winslow, April 1, 1664; she m 2d, John Sturtevant, and was great-grandmother to Rossete Cotton.
" Jonathan Pratt, to Abigail Wood, Nov. 2, 1664.
" Joseph Howland, to Elizabeth Southworth, Dec. 7, 1664.
" William Harlow, to Mary Shelley, Jan. 25, 1665–6.
" John Smith, Jr., to Deborah Howland, Jan. 4, 1648–9.
" Samuel Dunham, to Martha Holloway, June 29, 1649.
" Ephraim Hicks, to Elizabeth Howland, Sept. 13, 1649.
Sandwich, William Allen, to Priscilla Browne, March 21, 1649–50
Plymouth, Ralph James, to Mary Fuller, April 17, 1650.
" Thomas Roberts, to Mary Padduck, March 24, 1650–1.

Plymouth, Richard Foster, to Mary Bartlett, Sept. 10, 1651.
" John Rickard, to Hester Barnes, Oct. 31, 1651.
" William Spooner, to Hannah Pratt, March 18, 1651-2.
" James Cole, Jr., to Mary Tilson, Dec. 23, 1652.
Eastham, Jonathan Sparrow, to Rebeckah Bangs, Oct. 26, 1654.
" William Walker, to Sarah Snow, Feb. 25, 1654-5.
Plymouth, Jonathan Dunham, to Mary Delanoy [Delano ?], Nov. 29, 1655.
" Samuel Rider, to Sarah Bartlett, Dec. 23, 1656.
" Jonathan Shaw, to Phebe Watson, Jan. 22, 1656-7.
" Joseph Dunham, to Marcye [Mercy ?] Morton, Nov. 18, 1657.
" William Harlow, to Mary Faunce, July 15, 1658.
" John Saffin, to Martha Willet, Dec. 2, 1658.
" Benjamin Edson [Eaton ?], to Sarah Hoskins, Dec. 4, 1660.
" John Holmes, to Mary Faunce, Nov. 20, 1661.
" Daniel Wilcockes, to Elizabeth Cook, Nov. 28, 1661.
" Giles Rickard, Sr., to Jone [Jane ?] Tilson, May 20, 1662.
" Edward Doty, to Sarah Faunce, Feb. 26, 1662-3.
" Jonathan Morrey, to widow Mary Foster, July 8, 1659.
" Thomas Cushman, to Ruth Howland, Nov. 17, 1664.
" George Morton, to Joanna Kempton, Dec. 22, 1664.
Eastham, John Freeman, to Mercy Prince, Feb. 13, 1649-50, and had John, b. Feb. 2, 1650-1, d. an infant; John, Dec. 1651; Thomas, Sept. 1653; Edmund, June, 1657; Mercy, July, 1659.
" Nathaniel Mayo, to Hannah Prence, Feb. 13, 1649-50.
" Joseph Rogers, to Susanna Deane, April 4, 1660.
" John Bangs, to Hannah Smalley, Jan. 23, 1660-1.
Scituate, Stephen Tilden, to Hannah Little, Jan 15, 1661-2.
" Thos. Pinson [Pincin ?], Jr., to Elizabeth White, Sept. 18, 1662.
Taunton, Thomas Auger [Alger ?], to Elizabeth Packer [Packard ?], of Br., Nov. 14, 1665.
Plymouth, John Waterman, to Ann Sturtevant, Dec. 7, 1665.
" Isaac Barker, to Mrs. Judith Prence, Dec. 28, 1665.
" Ephraim Tilson, to Elizabeth Hoskins, July 7, 1666.
" Benjamin Bosworth, to Hannah Morton, Nov. 27, 1666.
" John Phillips, to Ruth Dotey, March 14, 1666-7.
" John Doged, of Martin's Vineyard, to widow Bathshebath Pratt, Aug. 29, 1667.
" Nathaniel Holmes, to Marcye [Mercy ?] Faunce, Dec. 29, 1667.
" John Ivey, of Boston, to Marcye [Mercy ?] Bartlett, Dec. 25, 1668.
" Joseph Dunham, to Hester Wormall, Aug. 20, 1669.
" Nathaniel Bosworth, of Hull, to Elizabeth Morton, Dec. 7, 1670.
" Joseph Prince, of Hull, to Joanna Morton, Dec. 7, 1670.
" John Laythrope [Lathrop ?], to Mary Cole, Jr., Jan. 3, 1671-2.
" Joseph Churchill, to Sarah Hicks, June 3, 1672.
" Nathaniel Morton, to Anne Templar, of Charlestown, April 29, 1674.
Taunton, William Briggs, to Sarah Macumber, of Marshfield, Nov. 6, 1666.
" John Eddy, to Susanna Paddock, of Dartmouth, Nov. 30, 1665.

Taunton, Richard Briggs, to Rebeckah Hoskins, of Lakenham, Aug. 15, 1662.
Taunton, John Deane, to Sarah Edson, of Br., Nov. 7, 1663.
Barnstable, Anthony Annible, to Anne Alcocke, March 1, 1645–6. She d. buried May 16, 1651; and he afterwards m. Hannah Barker.
" Thomas Burnam, to Hannah Annible, March 1, 1645–6.
Scituate, Thomas Oldam, to Mary Witherell, Nov. 20, 1656.
Swansey, Thomas Manning, to Rachel Bliss, Oct. 28, 1674.
Rehoboth, John Fuller to Abigail Titus, April 25, 1673.
John Kinsley, to Mary Maury, March 16, 1673–4.
Eastham, Jonathan Bangs, to Mary Mayo, July 16, 1664.
" Ephraim Done [Doan?], to Mercye [Mercy?] Knowles, Feb 5, 1667–8.
" Stephen Merricke, to Mercy Bangs, Dec. 28, 1670.
" Joshua Bangs, to Hannah Scudder, Dec. 1, 1669.
Taunton, John Smith, Sr., to Jaell Packer [Packard?], of Br., Nov. 15, 1672.
Rehoboth, Thomas Read, to Anna Perrin, June 16, 1675.
Taunton, James Leonard, Jr., to Lydia Caliphar, of Milton, Oct. 29, 1675.
Eastham, Joseph Harding, to Bethah Cook, April 4, 1660.
" Mark Snow, to Jane Prence, Jan. 9, 1660–1.
" Jonathan Higgens, to Elizabeth Rogers, Jan. 9, 1660–1.
Scituate, George Young, to Hannah Pinson [Pincin?], Jan. 15, 1661–2.
" Edward Wright, to widow Lydia Rowlins, May 25, 1664.
Plymouth, John Bryant, to Abigail Bryant, Nov. 23, 1665.
" Edward Gray, to Dorothy Lettice, Dec. 12, 1665.
" Jonathan Barnes, to Elizabeth Hedge, Jan. 4, 1665–6.
" Jacob Mitchell, to Susanna Pope, Nov. 7, 1666.
" Robert Barrow, to Ruth Bonum, Nov. 28, 1666.
" John Cole, to Elizabeth Rider, Nov. 21, 1667.
" John Followell, to Sarah, d. of John Wood, Feb. 13, 1667–8.
" Giles Rickard, Jr., to Hannah Churchill, June 25, 1669.
" Jacob Cook, to Elizabeth Shirtliff, Nov. 18, 1669.
" Richard Willis, to Patience Bonum, Dec. 28, 1670.
" Francis Curtice [Curtis?], to Hannah Smith, Dec. 28, 1670.
" Nathaniel Southworth, to Desire Gray, Jan. 10, 1671–2.
" Thomas Faunce, (the elder), to Jane Nelson, Dec. 13, 1672.
Taunton, Joseph Gray, to Rebeckah Hill, Feb. 25, 1667–8.
Swansey, John Paddock, to Anna Jones, Dec. 21, 1673.
Scituate, John Bryant, to Elizabeth Witherell, Dec. 22, 1657.
Rehoboth, James Willett, to Elizabeth Hunt, April 17, 1673.
" Samuel Fuller, to Mary Iyde [Ide?], Dec. 12, 1673.
Taunton, John Pollard, to Mary Leonard, of Br., Dec. 24, 1673.
Eastham, John Cole, to Ruth Snow, Dec. 10, 1666.
" John Knowles, to Apphiah Bangs, Dec. 28, 1670.
" Stephen Hopkins, to Mary Merricke, May 23, 1667.
Taunton, Thomas Deane, to Katharine Stevens, Jan. 5, 1669–70.
Swansey, Hezekiah Willet, to Andia Browne, Jan. 7, 1675–6.
Sandwich, John Redding, to Mary Bassett, Oct. 22, 1676.
Taunton, Daniel Reed, to Hannah Pecke, March 20, 1676–7.
" Moses Read, to Rebeckah Fitch, Dec. 6, 1677.
" Noah Mason, to Sarah Fitch, Dec. 6, 1677.

Taunton, William Hoskins, to Sarah Casewell, July 3, 1677.

" Thomas Gilbert, at Boston, to Anna Blake, of Milton, Dec. 18, 1676.

Rehoboth, Thomas Wilmoth, Sen., to Rachel Read, June 27, 1678.

" John Thompson, to Sarah Smith, Sept. 19, 1682.

Taunton, Benjamin Deane, to Sarah Williams, Jan. 6, 1680–1.

" John Eddy, to Deliverance Owin, of Braintree, May 1, 1672.

" Benjamin Leonard, to Sarah Thrasher, Jan. 15, 1678–9.

" Ezra Deane, to Bethiah Edson, of Br., Dec. 17, 1678.

" James Reed, to Susanna Richmond, April 18, 1683.

Benjamin Dunham, to Mary Tilson, Oct. 25, 1660.

William Merricke, of Eastham, to Abigail Hopkins, May 23, 1667.

John Martin, of Rehoboth, to Mary Billington, June 27, 1681.

Mark Snow, to Ann Cook, Jan 18, 1654–5. She died July 24, 1656.

Taunton, Isaac Williams, to Judith Cooper, Nov. 13, 1677.

Plymouth, Joseph Faunce, to Judith Rickard, Jan. 3, 1677–8.

Taunton, Isaac Deane, to Hannah Leonard, Jan. 24, 1677–8.

Plymouth, Joseph Browne, at Rehoboth, to Hannah Fitch, Nov. 10, 1680.

Taunton, Samuel Rider, to Lydia Tilden, of Plymouth, June 14, 1680.

" John Eddy, to Susanna Paddock, of Dartmouth, Nov. 12, 1665.

" Isaac Negus, to Hannah Andrews, April 7, 1679.

" Richard Godfrey, to Mary Richmond, Jan 1, 1679–80.

" Hugh Briggs, of Taunton, to Martha Everson, of Plymouth, March 1, 1683–4.

Rehoboth, Thomas Cushman, to Abigail Fuller, Oct. 16, 1679.

Joseph Gannett, of Scituate, to Ruth Buck, Jan. 17, 1676–7.

DEATHS.

Plymouth, Glass, Hannah, d. of Jame, June 15, 1648.

Sandwich, Wright, William, buried, May 2, 1648.

Plymouth, Hicks, Ephraim, Dec. 12, 1649.

" Morton, Eliezer, son of Nathaniel, Jan. 16, 1649–50.

" Paddy, Joseph, son of William, Feb. 18, 1649–50.

" Wright, Mordeci, buried March 20, 1649–50.

" Paddock, Robert, July 25, 1650.

" Dunham, Jonathan, son of John, Aug. 26, 1650.

" Sturtevant, John, son of Samuel, Oct. 30, 1650.

" Morton, still born d. of Nathaniel, Nov. 23, 1650.

" Paddy, Alice, wife of William, April 24, 1651.

" Dunham, two sons, twins of Samuel, d. within 6 day, b. Dec. 29, 1651.

" Pontus, William, Feb. 9, 1652–3.

" Jennings, Susanna, March 23, 1653–4.

" Shaw, Alice, wife of John, March 6, 1654–5.

" Rickard, Judith, wife of Giles, Feb. 6, 1661–2.

" Kempton, Manasses, Jan. 14, 1662–3: "He did much good in his place the time God lent him."

" Cook, Francis, April 7, 1663, the ancestor.

" Harlow, Mary, wife of William, Oct. 4, 1664.

Eastham, Rogers, Joseph, Jr., Jan 27, 1660–1.

Eastham, Snow, Anna, wife of Mark, and d. of Josias Cook, July 24, 1656.
Plymouth, Thomson, John, son of John, Feb. 11, 1648–9.
Sandwich, George Allen, Sr., buried May 2, 1648.
Plymouth, Morton, John, son of John, Dec. 20, 1649.
" Bonum, Sarah, 1649–50, before Feb. 18.
" Faunce, Elizabeth, d. of John, March 3, 1649–50.
" Finney, mother, April 22, 1650, ae. upwards of 80.
" Holmes, Mis Sarah, Aug. 18, 1650.
" Harlow, William, son of William, Oct. 26, 1650.
" Lettice, Thomas, son of Thomas, Nov. 3, 1650.
" Barnes, Mary, wife of John, June 2, 1651.
" Willet, Hezekiah, son of Capt. Thomas, July 26, 1651.
" Willet, Rebeckah, April 2, 1652.
" Gray, Thomas, Nov. 29, 1652.
" Atwood, Mis Ann, June 1, 1657.
" Dotey, Edward, Aug. 23, 1655.
" Churchill, John, Jan. 1, 1662–3.
" Morton, Phebe, wife of George, May 22, 1663.
" Kempton, widow of Manasses, Feb. 19, 1664–5, ae. 81.
Rawlins, Nathaniel, Dec. 23, 1662.
" Morton, Nathaniel, son of Nathaniel, Feb. 17, 1666–7.
" Followell, Gabriel, Dec. 28, 1667, ae. 80, "much respected and greatly lamented."
" Dunham, John, Sr., March 2, 1668–9, ae. about 80. He was deacon of the church, &c.
" Southworth, Capt. Thomas, Dec. 8, 1669, ae. about 53. A great and good man, &c.
" Bradford, Mrs. Alice, widow of Gov. William, March 26, 1670 or '71. A most excellent woman; ae. about 80.
" Bradford, Alice, Jr., Dec. 12, 1671, ae. about 44.
" Prence, Gov. Thomas, March 29, 1673, in his 73d year.
" Morton, Lydia, wife of Nathaniel, Sept. 23, 1673.
" Morton, John of Mido., Oct. 3, 1673. "A Godly man," &c.
Barnstable, Annible, Jane, wife of Anthony, buried about Dec. 1643.
" Annible, Hannah, 3d wife of Anthony, buried about March 16, 1657–8.
Scituate, Bryant, Mary, wife of John, July 2, 1655.
" Kempton, Hannah, wife of Ephraim, March 31, 1656.
Rehoboth, Reed, Sarah, d. of John, Jr., July 19, 1673.
" Holmes, Samuel, son of Samuel, buried Sept. 13, 1674.
Taunton, Leonard, Hannah, d. of James, Feb. 25, 1674–5.
Rehoboth, Read, John, Jr., buried April, 1676.
" Willet, Ellice [Alice?], wife of James, buried, July, 1676.
" Fuller, Sarah, wife of Robert, buried Oct. 14, 1676.
" Fitch, Jeremiah, buried Oct. 15, 1676.
Taunton, Leonard, James, son of James, Dec. 30, 1674.
Plymouth, Rickard, Mercy, d. of John, son of Giles, Feb. 12, 1682–3.
Taunton, Briggs, Sarah, wife of William, March 20, 1680–1.
Howland, John, Feb. 23, 1662–3.
Plymouth, Dunham, Mercy, wife of Joseph, Feb. 19, 1666–7.
" Howland, John, Sr., Feb. 23, 1672–3.
" Bosworth, Elizabeth, wife of Nathaniel, April 6, 1673.

Plymouth, Warren, Elizabeth, widow, Oct. 2, 1673, ae. about 90.
Taunton, Deane, John, son of John, Aug. 6, 1670.
Barnstable, Annible, Anne, 2d wife of Anthony, buried May 16, 1651.
Swansey, Browne, wife of John, Sr., Jan. 27, 1673–4, in her 90th year.
Scituate, Kempton, Ephraim, 24th, 1655.
Swansey, Willet, Capt. Thomas, Aug. 3, 1674.
Rehoboth, Blackston, Sarah, wife of William, middle of June, 1673.
" Reed, Elizabeth, wife of Thomas, buried Feb. 23, 1674–5.
" Read, Sarah, d. of John, b. or d. Jan. 1675–6.
" Read, John, son of Thomas, buried Dec. 4, 1676.
" Fuller, Samuel, buried Aug. 15, 1676.
" Fuller, John, buried Aug. 23, 1676.
" Leonard, Sarah, d. of Krie, [Rice?] buried March 16, 1676–7.
" Read, Zachariah, son of Moses, buried, Jan. 1678–9.
Taunton, Eddy, Susanna, wife of John, March 14, 1670–1.

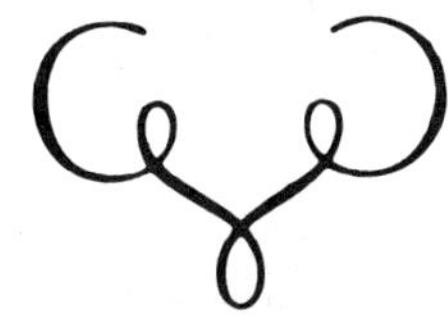

BIRTHS, MARRIAGES, AND DEATHS OF PROVINCETOWN, MASS.

[Copied from the First Book of Records, by DAVID HAMBLEN of Boston.]

Stephen Atwood and wife Sarah had ch.: Jonathan, b. Aug. 2, 1731; Stephen, b. Dec. 25, 1733; Martha, b. Jan. 24, 1735–6; Rebeckah, b. May 1, 1738; Sarah, b. Aug. 10, 1740; Susannah, b. July 16, 1743.

Henry Atwood and wife Thankful had ch.: Thankful, b. Aug. 17, 1729; Kezaiah, b. Feb. 22, 1732–3; Henry, b. Oct. 11, 1735; Elisabeth, b. Sept. 27, 1737.

Joseph Atwood and wife Lydia had ch.: Lydia, b. Sept. 8, 1733.

Joshua Atwood and wife Sarah had ch.: Samuel, b. Aug. 24, 1735; Mary, b. Feb. 13, 1745; John, b. March 24, 1756.

Samuel Atwood and wife Barsheba had ch.: Joshua, b. July 3, 1767; Henry, b. Sept. 9, 1768; Sarah, b. Dec. 26, 1769; Mary, b. Aug. 16, 1773; Samuel, b. June 11, 1776; Elisabeth, b. Feb. 17, 1779; Bethsheba, b. July 18, 1781; John, b. Sept. 11, 1784.

John Atwood and wife Mary had ch.: Marcy, b. Oct. 13, 1781; Martha, b. Oct. 30, 1783; Asa, b. Aug. 20, 1789, d. same date.

Jonathan Atwood and wife Nabby had ch.: Rebecca, b. July 11, 1757; Nathan, b. Aug. 11, 1759; Hannah, b. July 2, 1763; Henry, b. March 8, 1766; Nabby, b. Aug 11, 1769; Jonathan, b. Nov. 20, 1772; James, b. June 2, 1776.

Joshua Atwood and wife Betsey had ch.: Mary, b. Feb. 25, 1787; Nathaniel, b. June 20, 1789.

Silas Atkins and wife Bethiah had ch.: Isaiah, b. Oct. 16, 1786; Bethia, b. Feb. 20, 1789; Martha, b. June 5, 1793; Joshua, b. March 16, 1795.

Joseph Atkins and wife Ruth had ch.: Joseph, b. June 28, 1789; Freeman, b. Oct. 8, 1790; Ruth, b. Feb. 25, 1793.

David Brown and wife Eunice had ch.: Ebenezer, b. July 14, 1791.

Timothy Barnab[y?] and wife Martha had ch.: Stephen, b. Oct. 13, 1728; Ruth, b. Nov. 11, 1735.

Joseph Barneby and wife Lidia had ch.: Joseph, b. July 14, 1736.

Barnabas Briggs and wife Abigail had ch.: Seth, b. Sept. 24, 1778; Mercy, b. Aug. 3, 1780; Sally, b. July 29, 1784; Cate, b. June 19, 1786; Barnabas, b. Aug. 23, 1788; Mahala, b. Sept. 24, 1791.

Rev. Jeremiah Cushing and wife Hannah had ch.: Ezekiel, b. April 28, 1698.

Ezekiel Cushing m. Hannah, she b. Dec. 1, 1703, had ch.: Loring, b. Aug. 10, 1721; Ezekiel, b. June 3, 1724; Jeremiah, b. Oct. 7, 1729; Hannah, b. Feb. 9, 1731–2; Lucia, b. July 13, 1734; Lucia, b. Dec. 27, 1735; Phebe, b. April 15, 1738.

Jeremiah Cushing m. Mary, had ch.: Jonathan, b. Aug. 25, 1732; Mary, b. March 15, 1733; Luranah, b. Dec. 20, 1735; Sarah, b. Oct. 13, 1737; Hannah, b. Oct. 28, 1740.

Joshua Cook m. Zerviah, had ch.: Joshua, b. June 10, 1725; Elnathan, b. April 15, 1727; Elisabeth, b. Feb. 20, 1729; Martha, b. June 1, 1731.

Jacob Cook m. Mary, had ch.: Ebenezer, b. Dec. 2, 1731.

John Cook m. Desire, had ch.: Mary, b. April 27, 1728; John, b. Aug. 23, 1730; Jabez, b. June 17, 1732.

Solomon Cook and wife Rebecka had ch.: Mary, b. Oct. 3, 1733;

Solomon, b. Sept. 12, 1737; Rebecka, b. June 26, 1740; Edward, b. April 29, 1746.

Solomon Cook and wife Rebecka had ch.: John Covel, b. Jan. 4, 1760; Rebeckah, b. Aug. 1, 1762.

Solomon Cook and wife Baty had ch.: Solomon, b. Aug. 12, 1764.

Edward Cook and wife Experience had ch.: Hannah, b. Oct. 24, 1767.

Solomon Cook and wife Elizabeth had ch.: Rebecca, b. Aug 1, 1762.

Ebenezer Cook and wife Jane had ch.: Ebenezer, b. Oct. 21, 1788.

Samuel Cook and wife Jane had ch.: Jesse, b. June 13, 1783; Stephen, b. Oct. 29, 1786.

John Cook and wife Mary had ch.: James, b. Sept. 15, 1771; Isaac, b. Dec. 24, 1775.

Elisha Cook and wife Susannah had ch.: Lemuel, b. Aug. 5, 1766; Sarah, b. Aug. 16, 1768; Elisha, b. Oct. 11, 1770; David, b. Dec. 20, 1774.

Jonathan Cook m. Mercy Tilton, April 16, 1773.

Elisha Cobb and wife Mary had ch.: Mary, b. June 1, 1726, d. Jan. 30, 1729.

John Connit and wife Kezia had ch.: Elizabeth, b. Sept. 30, 1726; John, b. Aug. 17, 1730; Sarah, b. Sept. 30, 1732.

John Conant and wife Abigail had ch.: John, b. Dec. 19, 1763; Samuel, b. Aug. 22, 1765; Bettey, b. Sept. 20, 1768; Abigail, b. Aug. 6, 1770, d Dec. 27, 1772; Sarah, b. Oct. 6, 1772.

John Cash and wife Mary had ch.: Stephen, b. Sept. 5, 1769.

Samuel Cash and wife Eals had ch.: Samuel, b. Oct. 12, 1744; Daniel, b. Oct. 20, 1746.

Stephen Cash and wife Mary had ch.: Stephen, b. Aug. 22, 1797.

Edmon Chase and wife Abigail had ch.: Abigail, b. Nov. 17, 1769.

James, son of Thankful Colliner, b. Sept. 15, 1757.

Solomon Crowell and wife Sarah had ch.: Solomon, b. July 17, 1771; Sarah, b. July 17, 1771.

Solomon Crowell and wife Thankful had ch.: Josiah Clark, b. July 19, 1790.

James Hatch Creed and wife Moller had ch.: John, b. Aug. 8, 1794.

Ephraim Deane and wife Ann had ch.: Eunice, b. Nov. 10, 1725; Thankful, b. Feb. 8, 1727–8; Ann, b. March 4, 1730–1.

Thomas Delano and wife Sarah had ch.: Thankful, b. Aug. 9, 1727; Sarah, b. June 17, 1729, d. July 18, 1730; Sarah, b. May 24, 1731; Hannah, b. Aug. 4, 1733; Sarah, b. April 19, 1735.

Ephraim Doane and wife Mary had ch.: Ephraim, b. May 22, 1717; Nemiah, b. Oct. 13, 1720; Betsy, b. Sept. 1, 1724; Joshua, b. June 1, 1727; Mary, b. July 24, 1729; Elisha, b. March 22, 1731–2.

James Doane and wife Mary had ch.: Lidia, b. July 29, 1735; Jeremiah, b. Aug. 27, 1737.

Hezekiah Doane and wife Hannah had ch.: Ephraim, b. April 1, 1696.

Adam Milston Dyer and wife Sarah had ch.: Adam, b. April 6, 1789; William, b. Sept. 7, 1791.

Jesse Dyer and wife Roda had ch.: Jesse, b. Aug. 18, 1789; David, b. Oct. 21, 1791.

Micah Gross and wife Elisabeth had ch.: Micah, b. Jan. 28, 1782.

Alexander Gross and wife Elisabeth had ch.: Janne, b. Nov. 28, 1793.

Joshua Freeman Grozier and wife Martha had ch.: William, b. April 17, 1794.

Beriah Higgins and wife Desire had ch.: Debrow, b. Oct. 26, 1725; Beriah, b. April 1, 1727; Phebe, b. May 17, 1736.

Thomas Hoage and wife Mary had ch.: John, b. Oct. 4, 1717.

Ezra Hudson and wife ——— had ch.: Betsey, b. Dec. 10, 1793; Sally, b. Aug. 6, 1795.

John Hill and wife Susannah had ch.: Josiah, b. Nov. 25, 1797.

John Hill and wife Salone had ch.: John, b. April 3, 1802.

Hannah, dau. of Ebenezer and Abigail Haywood, b. July 17, 1736.

Thomas Kilborn m. Mehitable Rider, April 7, 1748, had ch.: Thomas, b. June 26, 1750; Mehitable, b. Aug. 1, 1752; Ruth, b. Jan. 2, 1755; Andrew, b. May 12, 1757; William, b. Aug. 11, 1759; David, b. Nov. 14, 1761.

Thomas Kilborn and wife Batey had ch.: Batey, b. Aug. 10, 1746.

William Kilborn and wife Mary had ch.: William, b. Sept. 11, 1785.

Benjamin Kinyer and wife Susannah had ch.: Benjamin, b. Sept. 1, 1783.

Silas Knowles and wife Phebe had ch.: Mary Freeman, b. Nov. 22, 1791; Silas, b. Nov. 20, 1794.

Garvitt Linch and wife Lydia had ch.: Rose, b. Aug. 22, 1735.

John Larry and wife Betty had ch.: John, b. Jan. 13, 1764; Martha, b. Aug. 10, 1767.

John Larry and wife Abigail had ch.: John, b. Oct. 10, 1785; Nabby, b. June 29, 1790; William, b. Dec. 24, 1791.

Robert Mayo and wife Deborah had ch.: Mary, b. Nov. 12, 1724; Thankful, b. July 12, 1727; Gamalel, b. Dec. 8, 1729; Surviah, b. April 10, 1732; Robert, b. Dec. 28, 1736.

James Mayo and wife Lettis had ch.: Bety, b. May 10, 1727; Henry, b. July 28, 1729, d. June 29, 1730; Lettis, b., no date, d. June 7, 1732.

James Mayo and wife Susannah had ch.: James, b. Nov. 3, 1733; Lettice, b. April 11, 1736; Whitford, b. June 30, 1739.

Joshua Atkins Mayo and wife Martha had ch.: Bethiah, b. Sept. 1, 1782; Joshua Atkins, b. Sept. 30, 1786; Thomas, b. Feb. 21, 1789; Joseph, b. Sept. 3, 1791; Martha, b. Sept. 23, 1794.

Elisha Mayo and wife Martha had ch.: Samuel, b. Sept. 11, 1729; Jerusha, b. Oct. 21, 1733; Sarah, b. July 11, 1736; Elisha, b. July 3, 1738; Martha, b. July 31, 1743.

Jeremiah Miller and wife Sarah had ch.: William, b. Dec. 30, 1760.

William Miller and wife Rebecca had ch.: Sally, b. Sept. 22, 1785.

Phineas Nickerson and wife Susannah had ch.: Jane, b. Dec. 12, 1757.

Phinehas Nickerson and wife Phebe had ch.: Phebe, b. Oct. 5, 1792; Mary, b. Dec. 9, 1790.

Stephen Nickerson and wife Hannah had ch.: Mary, b. June 22, 1783.

Seth Nickerson and wife Martha had ch.: Jonathan, b. July 5, 1754; Stephen, b. Sept. 6, 1756; Martha, b. May 7, 1759; Joshua, b. Dec. 7, 1761; Seth, b. April 17, 1764.

Seth Nickerson and wife Phebe had ch.: Lydia, b. Aug. 26, 1789; Seth, b. Feb. 23, 1791; Nancy, b. June 6, 1793; Sally, b. June 15, 1795.

Seth Nickerson and wife Mary had ch.: Hannah, b. Feb. 6, 1762; Nathan, b. Dec. 11, 1763; Elisabeth, b. June 19, 1766; Ebenezer, b. Aug. 17, 1768; Eneas, b. Sept. 19, 1770.

Seth Nickerson and wife Mary had ch.: Mary, b. June 13, 1778; Hannah, b. June 13, 1778.

Seth Nickerson and wife Isabel had ch.: Mina, b. Oct. 2, 1781; Jane,

b. Sept. 9, 1785; Thankful, b. March 26, 1787; Sally, b. March 18, 1789; Seth, b. Jan. 1, 1791; Jesse, b. Sept. 18, 1792.

Jonathan Nickerson and wife Sarah had ch.: Seth, b. May 28, 1734.

Seth Nickerson and wife Martha had ch.: Rebecca, b. Aug. 25, 1766; Bethiah, b. April 4, 1768; Ruth, b. June 4, 1771; Sarah, b. June 29, 1773; Nathaniel, b. Dec. 24, 1775; Reuben, b. Nov. 21, 1777.

Jonathan Nickerson and wife Bethiah had ch.: Abigail, b. Aug. 26, 1777; Isaiah, b. March 18, 1779; Jonathan, b. Aug. 19, 1781; Elisha, b. July 15, 1783; Levi, b. Nov. 2, 1785.

Joshua Nickerson and wife Rebecca had ch.: Isaac, b. Aug. 28, 1784; Joshua, b. Sept. 10, 1786; Rebecca, b. Nov. 9, 1788; Abraham, b. July 25, 1791.

Ebenezer Nickerson and wife Solone had ch.: Eunice, b. Aug. 30, 1794.

Nathan Nickerson and wife Sarah had ch.: John, b. Dec. 11, 1786; Nathan, b. Nov. 5, 1790.

Enos Nickerson and wife Deborah had ch.: Nehemiah K., b. Feb. 11, 1783.

Elijah Nickerson and wife Jemima had ch.: Josiah, b. Nov. 7, 1770; Elijah, b. Aug. 7, 1772; Elijah, b. Aug. 29, 1774; Joseph, b. Sept. 27, 1776; Hannah, b. Sept. 4, 1782; David, b. Sept. 11, 1785.

Alen Nickerson and wife Polly had ch.: James C., b. Nov. 13, 1784; Rebecca, b. Nov. 3, 1786; Alen, b. Feb. 2, 1789.

Thomas Newcomb and wife Hepzebah had ch.: Sarah, b. Jan. 20, 1723; Silas, b. April 19, 1725.

Thomas Newcomb and wife Marce had ch.: Hepzebah, b. June 3, 1734; Peggy, b. Feb. 16, 1736; Bety, b. May 10, 1738; Thomas, b. Sept. 30, 1740; Mary, b. Jan. 31, 1743; Jenah, b. Feb. 4, 1745.

Silas Newcomb and wife Susannah Kilborn, m. Aug. 4, 1748, had ch.: Susannah, b. Sept. 6, 1750; Jeremiah, b. Nov. 8, 1753; Sarah, b. Sept. 8, 1755; Mary, b. Dec. 9, 1758; Silas, b. Dec. 16, 1761.

Silas Newcomb and wife Azubah had ch.: Levi, b. Jan. 1, 1791.

Jeremiah Newcomb and wife Rachel had ch.: Andrew, b. June 11, 1778; Ebenezer, b. Dec. 24, 1781; Reuben, b. Aug. 6, 1783; Cate, b. July 7, 1785; Rachel, b. Aug. 1, 1788; Jeremiah, b. July 19, 1794.

Richard Parry and wife Rebeckah had ch.: Eleanor, b. Oct. 9, 1768; Jemimah, b. Oct. 13, 1770; Richard, b. May 6, 1774.

Henry Paine and wife Mary had ch.: Henry, b. Aug. 3, 1791; Ephraim, b. Nov. 12, 1792.

Joshua Parce and wife Hepzebah had ch.: Marcy, Sept. 9, 1754; Joshua, b. Oct. 3, 1756; Margaret, April 1, 1759; Eunice, b. June 9, 1761; Bety, b. May 11, 1764; Thomas, b. June 24, 1766; William, b. Oct. 15, 1768; Jane, b. Sept. 15, 1771; Phebe, b. Oct. 1, 1774.

Zephaniah Parce and wife Margaret had ch.: Nancy, b. July 12, 1790.

William Prince and wife Sally had ch.: John, b. July 20, 1791.

Rev. Samuel Parker m. Mrs. Mary Smith, Jan. 14, 1785.

Benjamin Rider and wife Mehetable had ch.: Benjamin, b. Aug. 28, 1725; Mehetable, b. Sept. 7, 1729; Mary, b. Feb. 25, 1732; Ann, b. Feb. 25, 1732, twins.

Benjamin Rider and wife Experience had ch.: Daniel, b. July 26, 1758; Benjamin, b. Sept. 3, 1761; Isaiah, b. Aug. 14, 1773.

Samuel Rider and wife Experience had ch.: Samuel, b. May 22, 1725; Joseph, b. March 29, 1727; Desire, b. Oct. 4, 1728; Joseph, b. Oct. 11,

1730; Lydia, b. Oct. 8, 1732; Experience, b. Sept. 20, 1737; Sarah, b. Oct. 31, 1739; Joshua, b. April 26, 1742.

Samuel Rider and wife Lydia had ch.: Nathaniel Godfrey, b. Aug. 7, 1782; Samuel, b. Aug. 1784; Bethia, b. July 21, 1787; Lydia, b. March 21, 1789; Benjamin, b. June 6, 1791; Atkins, b. May 18, 1795.

Gershom Rider and wife Barsheba had ch.: Gershom, b. Oct. 1, 1732; Marce, b. March 9, 1735; Thomas, b. July 25, 1737; Elisabeth, b. Jan 23, 1740; Barsheba, b. Feb. 25, 1742; John, b. May 16, 1744; Lot, b. Feb. 10, 1746.

Gershom Rider and wife Elisabeth had ch.: Gershom, b. May 5, 1762.

Ebenezer Rider and wife Hannah had ch.: Samuel, b. Dec. 13, 1757.

Joshua Rider and wife Hannah had ch.: Elisabeth Nelson, b. Sept. 29, 1791; Rebecca, b. July 1, 1794.

David Rider and wife Anna had ch.: David, b. Oct. 2, 1790; Jesse, b. June 30, 1792; Elisha, b. Nov. 24, 1794.

Thomas Rider and wife Rebecca had ch.: Nathaniel, b. May 12, 1775.

Ebenezer Rider and wife Ruth had ch.: Samuel Hinks, b. Oct. 27, 1795.

Lot Rider and wife Mary had ch.: Joseph, b. June 18, 1775; Mary, b. Dec. 27, 1777; Lot, b. June 16, 1780; Desire, b. March 2, 1783; John, b. Aug. 3, 1785; Thomas, b. May 19, 1788.

Benjamin Rotch and wife Martha had ch.: William, b. Oct. 23, 1729; Prince, b. Nov. 1731; Joseph, b. Nov. 13, 1733; Benjamin, b. Nov. 4, 1735.

William Robbinson and wife Polly had ch.: Thomas, b. Nov. 24, 1792; Marcey, b. Nov. 3, 1794.

Anthony Strout and wife Abigail had ch.: Debrow, b. March 22, 1725; Rebecka, b. May 21, 1727; Rebecka, b. May 3, 1729; Job, b. Sept. 14, 1730; Rebecka, b. Feb. 21, 1730–31; Job, b. March 26, 1729; Daniel, b. Feb. 20, 1732–3; Abigail, b. July 7, 1735.

[There is evidently a mistake in the Records of this Family. I have given them just as they read.—D. H.]

John Strout and wife Ruth had ch.: Ruth, b. Feb. 19, 1735–6; Eleazer, b. Oct. 29, 1737.

Christopher Strout and wife Mary had ch.: Mary, b. Jan. 25, 1718; Christopher, b. June 26, 1720; Ruth, b. March 11, 1722–3; Dorcas, b. July 14, 1724; William, b. Sept. 13, 1726; Betty, b. March 17, 1728–9; Bersiler, b. March 23, 1731–2.

Joseph Strout and wife Rachel had ch.: Barnabas, b. June 24, 1729; Sarah, b. Aug. 2, 1731; Hezekiah, b. Jan. 19, 1735.

George Strout and wife Keziah had ch.: George, b. Sept. 1, 1730, d. July 13, 1731; Isaiah, b. July 28, 1732; Keziah, b. Sept. 16, 1734; Levi, b. Oct. 21, 1737. Keziah d. Aug. 6, 1732. Think it should be Isaiah instead of Keziah.

Elisha Strout and wife Ela had ch.: Ela, b. Oct. 18, 1737.

Samuel Smith and wife Abigail had ch.: James, b. Aug. 20, 1730, d. April 26, 1758; Samuel, b. Oct. 4, 1733; Simeon, b. Oct. 9, 1735; Susannah, b. Sept. 4, 1738; Abigail, b. June 15, 1740; Rebeckah, b. Oct. 25, 1743; Sarah, b. May 25, 1745.

Samuel Smith and wife Ruth had ch.: Ephraim, b. Jan. 31, 1757; Hannah, b. March 22, 1759; John, b. Aug. 29, 1761; Jesse, b. July 17, 1765; Chloe, b. Oct. 10, 1767; Ruth, b. Jan. 3, 1770.

Samuel Smith and wife Abigail had ch.: Samuel, b. Sept. 17, 1798.

Beriah Smith and wife Elisabeth had ch.: Ebenezer, b. Aug. 11, 1735.

Simeon Smith and wife Susannah had ch.: Margaret, b. May 3, 1759; James, b. Aug. 9, 1763; Susannah, b. July 1, 1765; Abigail, b. Dec. 17, 1767; Samuel, b. Nov. 26, 1772.

James Smith and wife Elisabeth had ch.: Mary, b. Dec. 16, 1753; Enock, b. Oct. 16, 1755; James, b. Jan. 13, 1758.

Enock Smith and wife Mary had ch.: Sarah, b. May 26, 1784; Enock, b. Aug. 23, 1786; David, b. Sept. 23, 1791; Jesse, b. Oct. 9, 1793; Joseph H., b. Oct. 14, 1797; Zubah, b. Dec. 25, 1795.

Daniel Smith and wife Martha had ch.: Lewis L., b. Oct. 8, 1789; Daniel, b. Sept. 10, 1791.

Seth Smith and wife Eliza had ch.: Elbridge, b. Aug. 27, 1784; David, b. April 15, 1781.

John Small and wife Hannah had ch.: Lydia, b. Oct. 26, 1729; John, b. Oct. 8, 1731; Hannah, b. March 26, 1734; David, b. May 19, 1736.

Edward Small and wife Abigail had ch.: Abigail, b. Sept. 30, 1731; Micho, b. April 6, 1733; Job, b. Sept. 9, 1734; Edward, b. April 1, 1736.

Elisha Small and wife Bethiah had ch.: Nathaniel, b. Aug. 10, 1736.

John Savage and wife Deliverance had ch.: Abigail, b. July 6, 1793.

Richard Stevens and wife Mercy had ch.: Richard, b. July 21, 1771.

Robert Soaper and wife Isabel had ch.: Samuel, b. July 21, 1791; Elisabeth, b. Oct. 10, 1793.

Tailer Smalley and wife Mary had ch.: Tailer, b. June 6, 1792; John, b. Oct. 1, 1794; Mary, b. Oct. 28, 1796; Benjamin, b. Dec. 20, 1802.

Philip Tilton and wife Desire had ch.: Experience, b. Nov. 26, 1747; Marcy, b. Oct. 12, 1750; James, b. April 19, 1753; Desire, b. Aug. 29, 1755; William, b. July 28, 1759; Rodah, b. Aug. 28, 1762.

William Tilton and wife Marca had ch.: William, b. Sept. 16, 1723; Philip, b. Sept. 16, 1723, twins; Rhoda, b. Nov. 25, 1726; James, b. May 10, 1731.

Nathan Tubbs and wife Dorcas had ch.: Peggy, b. May 6, 1788.

George Whitford and wife Susannah had ch.: Rebeckah, b. Dec. 21, 1730.

Christopher Webber and wife Mary had ch.: Sarah, b. Jan. 19, 1731; John, b. Sept. 13, 1732.

Thomas Watkins and wife Sarah had ch: Joanna, b. Aug 18, 1780.

Jabez Walker and wife Sarah Atwood m. July 17, 1748, had ch.: Jabez, b. Dec. 7, 1749; James, b. Dec. 5, 1752.

George Whorff and wife Mehitable had ch.: Susannah, b. Nov. 19, 1787.

John Whorff and wife Rebecca had ch.: Mary, b. June 19, 1783; John, b. Aug. 17, 1785; Thomas Rider, b. Jan. 10, 1788; Rebecca, b. July 20, 1790; Sally, b. Jan. 22, 1793; Betsey, b. Nov. 7, 1794.

John Whorff and wife Sarah had ch.: George, b. May 15, 1763; Isaac, b. Oct. 29, 1765; Joseph, b. Aug. 12, 1768; Samuel, b. April 29, 1772; Sarah, b. Sept. 16, 1758.

William Wareham and wife Jane had ch.: Martin, b. Oct. 2, 1792; Martin, b. Dec. 2, 1793.

Robert Wickson and wife Zuby had ch.: Crowel, b. Jan. 13, 1780; Isaiah, b. Feb. 1, 1783; Robert, b. Aug. 20, 1788.

David Young and wife Joanna had ch.: Joanna Walker, b. July 18, 1783.

Samuel Young and wife Marcy had ch.: Mary, b. Oct. 7, 1783.

Mary, wife of Samuel Young, d. May 7, 1783.

FIRST BOOK OF RAYNHAM RECORDS.

From a copy in the possession of the SOCIETY.

[Page 1.]

1735–6	Feb.	23	m.	Edward Austin & Zipporah Haskins of Raynham by Mr. Wales.
1742	Oct.	21	"	Edmund Andrews of Taunton & Keziah Dean of R. by Do.

Deaths of children of John King & Alice his wife.

1700	Dec.	22	d.	Judith their dau.
1716	Apl.	2	"	Ruth.
1717	Aug.	13	"	Mercy.
1720	May	11	"	Ebenezer.
1727	Aug.	21	"	Isaac.
1729	Oct.	29	"	Josiah.
1741	"	5	"	John King the father of three children.
1746	May	22	"	Alice King his wife.
1753	July	6	"	David their son.
1754	Mar.		"	Jonathan.
1760	Nov.	18	"	John.

Recorded by Mason Shaw, August 5, 1779.

[Page 2.]

John King & Alice Dean m. feb. 1, 1699–1700.

1700	Dec.	8	b.	Judith.
1702	Aug.	5	"	Philip.
1703	Oct.	13	"	John.
1704–5	Feb.	28	"	Hannah.
1706	Oct.	30	"	Isaac.
1710	July	7	"	Abigail.
1712	Oct.	17	"	Jonathan } twins.
			"	David } twins.

1714	Sept. 10	b.	Josiah.
1715–16	Mar. 18	"	Ruth.
1717	May 23	"	Marcy.
1718	Oct. 21	"	Benjamin.
1719–20	Mar. 24	"	Ebenezer.

Recorded by Mason Shaw, Town Clerk, Oct. 5, 1779.

Children of John King & Catharine his wife.

1756	Mar. 5	b.	John.
1758	May 28	"	Nathan.
1760	June 7	"	Isaac.
1763	June 22	"	Nabby.
1765	Nov. 3	"	Silas.
1768	July 31	"	Zenas & d. Aug. 31, 1775.
1770	Dec. 7	"	Catharine.
1773	Oct. 12	"	Bathsheba.

Recorded by Josiah Dean Jr. Town Clerk, March 21, 1805.

[Page 3.]

1713	Dec. 10	b.	Samuel Baker the son of Thomas Baker & Abigail his wife.			
1716	Mar. 19	"	Abigail Baker	dau.	do.	do.
1721–2	Jan. 25	"	Elijah Baker	son	do.	do.
1727	Juue 1	"	Mary Baker	dau.	do.	do.
1729–30	Feb. 28	"	Thomas Baker	son	do.	do.
1735	Nov. 24	"	Simeon Baker	"	do.	do.
1735	May 20	m.	Ebenezer Brittun & Tabitha Leonard both of R. by Mr. Wales.			
1737	Sept. 15	"	Seth Basset & Mary Hayward by Mr. Wales.			
1740	Apl. 18	"	Levi Blossome the son of Sylvanus Blossome & Charity his wife.			
1742	July 6	"	Elijah Blossome the son of Sylvanus Blossome & Charity his wife.			
1749	Oct. 23		The Rev[d] Mr. Eliab Byram of Mendum in the county of Morris in the Province of New Jersey Resident now in Raynham and Mrs. Sarah Leonard of Raynham were married by Samuel Leonard Justice Peace.			

[Page 4.]

1749 Feb. 22 Providence ss. These may certify that Ebenezer Brettun & Sarah Bullock were Lawfully joined in marriage by me John Andrews J. Peace.

Rec[d] pr Josiah Dean Town Clerk.

Here follows the children of Abiel Brettum & Mary his wife.

1729	July 7	b.	Abiel.
1734	June 5	"	Charles.
1738	" 22	"	Benjamin.
1739	Apl. 6	"	James ——d. July 28, 1756.
1743	Sept. 22	"	Mary.
1745	Apl. 1	"	Hepsibah.
1748	May 11	"	Patience.

1750	Nov.	12	b.	Susannah.
——	——		"	Prudence.

[Page 5.]

1733	Apl.	5	m.	Phineas Crossman & Lydia Shelly both R. by Mr. Wales.
				Y^e last that was sent to the Clerk of the Sessions April 1733.
1733	Oct.	12	m.	Theophilus Crossman & Elizabeth Maturin both of R. by Do.
1733–4	feb.	28	m.	Gabriel Crossman & Phebe Briggs by Mr. Wales.
				This the last sent April 1734 to ye Clerk.
1733	Nov.	9	b.	Rachel Crossman dau. Phineas Crossman & Lydia his wife.

Here follows the names & the births of the children of Thomas Crossman of Raynham and Joannah his wife.

1723–4	Jany	8	b.	Zibiah	dau.
1726	Aug.	28	b.	Abiah	dau.
1728	Dec.	22	b.	two daughters at a birth & died Dec. 27, 1728.	
1729	Dec.	24	b.	Keziah	dau.
1732–3	Jany	28	b.	Leonard	son & d. 25 feb. following.
1734	Oct^o.	19	b.	Anna	dau.

[Page 6.]

1734–5	Jany	12	b.	Robert Crossman son of Gabriel Crossman & Phebe his wife.
1736	Dec.	16	m.	Joshua Campbell & Abigail Brettun both of R. by Wales.
1737	Apl.	24	m.	Judah Chase of Taunton & Judith Leonard of R. by Wales.
1737	Sept.	13	b.	Abigail Campbell dau. Joshua Campbell & Abigail his wife on Tuesday.
1737	Nov.	9	b.	Phebe Crossman dau. Gabriel Crossman & Phebe his wife.
1738–9	Feb.	13	b.	Joanna Crossman dau. Thomas Crossman & Joanna his wife Tuesday.
1739	Oct.	13	b.	Mary Crossman dau. Gabriel Crossman & Phebe his wife Saturday.
1739	Nov.	22	d.	Keziah Crossman dau. Thomas Crossman & Joannah his wife.
1740	June	26	b.	Rebeckah Campbell dau. Nehemiah Campbell & Jemima his wife.
1741	Apl.	21	b.	*Welthy* Crossman dau. Gabriel Crossman & Phebe his wife.

[Page 7.]

Nehemiah Dean & Mehitable Hall both of Raynham m. Dec 16, 1731 by Wales.

Elijah & Susannah Dean's children.

1730	Dec.	4	b.	Hannah.
1733	Apl.	8	"	Abigail & d. 8 May 1734.

Susannah wife of Elijah d. 25 Apl 1734.

Children of Josiah Dean & Jane his wife.

1738	Dec.	30	b.	Nehemiah—Sater Day.
1740	Sept.	21	"	Abigail —Sabeth Day.

Jerusha Dean wife of Ensign Elijah Dean dye^{d} in Raynham January 29, 1741–2 —very suddenly.

Ensign Elijah Dean & Sophia Leonard were married by the Rev^{d} Mr. John Wales June the 2. 1742.

Children.

1743	Sept.	26	b.	Susannah.
1745	June	18	b.	Jerusha.
1747	Apl.	17	b.	Elijah.
1749	Mar.	18	b.	Samuel.

[Page 8.]

Thomas Dean ye 3^{d} Deceas^{d} febru^{r} ye 3. 1719–20 in ye 23^{d} y. of his age.

Josiah Dean & Jean Washburn m. Aug. 18, 1737 by Revd Daniel Perkins.

Thomas Dean ye 2^{d} deceased September ye 10, 1747 aged about 74.

Mary Dean widow of Thomas Dean 2^{d} Dec^{d} february ye 1st 1749 aged about 74 years.

Children of Josiah & Jane Dean.

1749	feb.	13	died	Nehemiah aged about 11 years [*See* page 7. W. R. D.]
1743	Aug.	20	born	Mary —Saterday.
1748	Mar.	6	"	Josiah—Sunday.
1751	Nov.	15	"	Job —Fryday in ye 11th hour at night.

Ensign Elijah Dean Dec^{d} Apl. ye 29, 1750 aged 49 years.

Marriages by Zephaniah Leonard.

1748–9	Feb.	9	m.	Shubal Campbell of Norton with Mary Jones of R.
Same date.			"	Edmund Leonard with Mary Jones both of R.
1749	Oct.	26	"	David White of Raynham & Bethiah Daggett of Attleboro.
1749	Nov.	15	"	Ebenezer Jones of R. & Mary Finney of Norton.

[Page 9 — marriages by Z. L. continued.]

1750	Oct.	30	m.	Henry Hicks of Middleboro & Hannah Smith of Taunton.
1751	June	27	m.	Thomas Baker of R. & Hannah Crossman of Middleboro.
1752	Dec.	8	m.	Benjamin Walker of Taunton & Silva Keith of Bridgewater.
1757	Aug.	16	m.	Lemuel Wilbore & Sarah Holden both of R.

Rec^{d} by Josiah Dean, Town Clerk.

Josiah Dean died March 23, 1778 in y^{e} 76 year of his age.

Jane widow of Josiah Dean died May 26, 1790 in y^{e} 75th year of her age.

FIRST BOOK OF RAYNHAM RECORDS.

From a copy in the possession of the SOCIETY.

[Page 10 is blank, there being nothing on it. W. R. DEANE.]

[Page 11.]

1762	Mar.	31	b.	Sarah Fuller da. Nathaniel Fuller & Mary his wife.
1788	July	18	m.	Wm French Jr. & Mary Hewitt by Josiah Dean Esq.
1792	Sept.	6	m.	Charles Frazier & Tabitha Leonard by Do.
1801	Aug.	17	b.	Archelaus Bolton son of Gamaliel Bolton & Sally his wife.
1803	Nov.	22	b.	Nelson Bolton son of Do & Do
				Rec[d] Jany 18, 1805 [means Bolton W. R. D.]

[Page 12.]

1802	June	13	b.	Samuel Holmes son of John Holmes & Almy his wife.

[Page 13.]

1756	Apl	28	b.	Lemuel son of Andrew Gilmor & Abigail his wife.			
1756	Oct.	19	d.	Hannah dau. of	Do	&	Do
1756	"	22	d.	Andrew son of	Do	&	Do
1758	Mch	16	b.	Daniel son of	Do	&	Do
1759	July	11	b.	Mercy dau. of	Do	&	Do
1760	Dec.	29	b.	Elisha son of	Do	&	Do
1762	June	9	b.	James son of	Do	&	Do
1764	July	23	b.	Andrew son of	Do	&	Do
1766	July	9	b.	Peres son of	Do	&	Do

[Page 14.]

Samuel Gilmor & his wife Chloe were married Aug. 20, 1778, by the Rev. Mr. Fobes.

Children.

1779	June	7	b.	Ornan
1781	"	20	b.	Nabby
1783	Mch	22	b.	Chloe
1785	Aug.	26	b.	Buara *dau.*
1787	June	30	b.	Arba *son*

Abigail Hall of Raynham widdow of Samuel Hall of Taunton deceased dyed July 6, at night, 1734.

Here follow the births of the children of James Hall & Sarah his wife togather with their names. Entered May y[e] 15, 1736, from his own Record.

1713	Apl	23	b.	James.
1714	Nov.	21	b.	2[d] son [no name, W. R. D.] & d. 25 day novemb. 1714.
1715	Nov.	16	b.	Nathan
1718	Apl	12	b.	Macy *son*
1720	May	7	b.	Mary
1722/3	Feb.	9	b.	Edmund
1725	May	14	b.	David
1729/30	Feb.	24	b.	Sarah

James Hall father of the above named children d. Dec. 4, 1735, being within 4 days of sixty years old.

Children of John Hall & Hannah his wife.

1728	July	29	b.	John—Monday
1730	Nov.	11	b.	Hannah—thursday
1732	Dec.	6	b.	Elkanah—wednesday
1735	Sept.	10	b.	Elisha— do.
1737	Mch	18	b.	Joseph—Saturday

These all entered May y[e] 9th 1738.

FIRST BOOK OF RAYNHAM RECORDS.

From a copy in the possession of the SOCIETY.

[Page 16.]

1738	Dec	28	m.	Jonathan Hall & Lidia Leonard by Mr. Wales

Children.

1739	Sept	26	b.	Jonathan — died Nov 22, 1739

1740	Oct	4	b.	Seth — Saturday Rec[d] Mar. 25, 1741

The names & births of the children of Jonathan Hall the first and Sarah his first wife are as followeth:—

1716	May	3	b.	Jonathan — Thurs.
1718	July	16	b.	Sarah & d. feb 11, 1725/6
1720	Apl	5	b.	Amos — Tues.
1722	May	21	b.	Rebeckah & d. May 15, 1723
1724	May	15	b.	John — Frid.
1725/6	Jany	28	b.	Mason — Frid.

Sarah the first wife of the above Jonathan Hall died Mar. 28, 1726

Here follows the names & the births of the children of the said Jonathan Hall & Sarah his second wife

1728	May	2	b.	Elizabeth — Thursday
1734	Mch	25	b.	Hannah — Monday

[Page 17.]

1732	Nov	16	m.	Hatherly Jones & Abigail Rogers by Rev. John Wales of Raynham
1734/5	Mch	18	d.	Abraham Jones of Raynham in the 76th year of his age
1727	Nov	30	b.	Timothy Jones son of Timothy Jones & Sarah his wife of Raynham
1730	"	2	b.	Abraham Jones son Do & Do do
1733	"	19	b.	Hannah Jones dau. Do & Do do
1734	Oct	6	b.	John Jones son of Hatherly Jones & Abigail his wife — Sabbeth
1738	May	7	b.	Ephraim Jones son Do & Do Sabeth
1738	Nov	15	b.	Samuel Jones son of Timothy Jones & Sarah his wife
1743	Apl	5	b.	Bathsheba Jones dau. of Nathan Jones & Bathsheba his wife
1749*	Nov	20	m.	Elnathan Jones & Silence Hewit by Sam[l] Leonard Esq. Jus. Peace
1789	Aug	27	m.	Solomon Jones & Tabitha Knapp by Josiah Dean Esq

---

[Page 18.]

Here follows the names of the children of Joseph Jones y[e] 2[d] of Raynham (d. Apl 25, 1744) & Elizabeth his wife (d. Nov. 23, 1750)

1724	Dec	5	b.	Elizabeth
1726	Oct	1	b.	Ebenezer
1728	Nov	29	b.	Lydia
1730	Dec	15	b.	Mary
1733	Feb	28	b.	Joseph
1735	Oct	18	b.	Nehemiah
1738	May	18	b.	Bethiah
1740	"	26	b.	Ephraim — d. June 16, 1742

* The 9 is blotted, may be 7. W. R. D.

1741	Nov	9	b.	Seth Jones son of Hatherly Jones & Abigail his wife — Monday
1745	July	26	b.	Abigail Jones dau. Do & Do — Fryday

FIRST BOOK OF RAYNHAM RECORDS.

From a copy in the possession of this SOCIETY.

[Page 18.]

1768	July	24	m.	Job Godfrey of Taunton to Abigail Jones of R. by Zeth Leonard Jus. P.
				Son of above below
1769	July	9	b.	Job. Sunday

[Page 19.]

1734	Oct	17	m.	Ichabod Keith of Bridgewater & Lydia Williams of R. by Wales
1735	June	5	m.	Amos Keith of Do & Sarah Robinson of R. by do.
1736/7	Feb	17	m.	David King & Rebecca Dean both of R. by do.
1737	June	22	m.	Jonathan King & Phebe Leonard by do
1743	Nov	22	m.	Benjamin King & Abiah Leonard by do
				Child of Benj.' & Abiah viz.
1744	Nov	27	b.	George — Tuesday about 3 o'clock in the afternoon [See below W. R. D.]
1742	Aug	12	m.	Samuel Kinsley of Easton & Sophia White of R. by Wales
1745	Apl	11	m.	George Knapp & Sarah Atherton both of R by do.
1743/4	Feb	28	m.	Robert King of Rehoboth and Mercy Dean of R by do
1746	Nov	15	b.	Anna King, dau. of Benjamin King & Abiah his wife — 10 oclk at night. Sat.

[Page 20.]

Children of Benj. King continued.

1748 Jany 30 b. William King son of Benjamin King & Abiah his wife — Monday morning about one of the clock
1750/51 Feb 24 b. Asa King son Do & Do Sunday morning 10 o'clock.
1753 Aug. 1 b. Hazadiah King dau Do & Do. Wednesday, 10 o'clock at night.
1756 Mch. 9 b. Gaius King son Do & Do. Tuesday
1758 July 3 b. Stephen King son of Benjamin King & Deliverance his wife
1759 Nov 17 b. Eli King son Do & Do.
1761 Feb 6 b. Abigail King dau. Do & Do.
1762 June 29 b. Abia King dau Do & Do.
1764 Apl 30 b. Sarah King dau Do & Do
1766 Aug. 30 b. Barzelia son Do & Do

[Page 21.]

1726/7 Feb 16 m. Samuel Leonard Jr. & Abigail Shaw then both of Taunton by Seth Williams Esq.

Children.

1727 Dec. 20 b. Nathan son of Sam[l] Leonard Jr & Abigail his wife
1730 Apl 19 b. Samuel son Do & Do.
1733 May 6 b. Abigail dau Do. & Do. & d 26 May 1733
1734 Aug 7 b. Katherine dau Do & Do.
1737 Aug 16 b. Jonathan son Do & Do.
1739 Apl 20 b. Bethiah dau Do & Do
1743/4 Feb. 14 b. Nathaniel son Do. & Do.

1724 Apl 24 m. Zephaniah Leonard & Hannah King, then of Taunton now of R.

Their children viz.

1724/5 Jan 5 b. Joshua — Tues.
1726 Sept 22 b. Mary — Thurs.
1729 Mar. 23 b. Prudence — Sabbath Day — & dec[d] Jany 1. 1730/1
1731 Apl 27 b. Silence — Tues.

[Page 22.]

1732/3 Mch 1 b. Anna — Thurs.
1734/5 Jan. 31 b. Abigail* — Frid.

All the foregoing record concerning Zephaniah Leonard & his children was recorded by me May 31. 1735 SAMUEL LEONARD JR. Town clerk.

1736/7 Jany 18 b. Zephaniah Tues. son of Zeph & Hannah L. [Same family as above W. R. D.]
1738 Nov 10 b. Phebe* *dau.* Do. & Do.

[Here follows the births of three of the children of Major Zephaniah Leonard and Hannah his wife viz

1744 Aug 3 b. Appollos — Frid.

* Both buried in the same grave.

1746	July	16	b.	Phebe — Wed. & d. June 17. 1752 Wed.
1748	April	8	b.	Silas — Frid & d. May 15. 1752 Frid
1750	Dec.	6	b.	Samuel Thurs.]

Madam Rebeckah Leonard Relict of James Leonard late of Taunton deceased. Dyed in Taunton April ye 3. 1738 in ye 77 year of her age

1726	June	23	m.	Thomas Leonard Jr. & Sarah Sulker by Rev Mr. Danforth

Their children as follows

1727	Oct	5	b.	Mary — Thurs.
1729	June	26	b.	Sarah — Thurs
1731	July	18	b.	Hannah — Sabbath Day
1733	Apl	30	b.	Gamaliel — Monday

[Page 23.]

Children of Ebenezer Mohurin of Raynham & Bathshua his wife.

1720	Nov	9	b.	Stephen
1727	Mch	27	b.	Mary
1729	Nov	11	b.	Seth
1731/2	Mch	24	b.	Betty

1733	July	12	m.	John Macomber of Taunton & Lydia Williams of R.	by Wales
1742/3	Jany	18	m.	Ebenezer Mayo, Resident of Raynham & Abigail Baker	by Do.
1744	May	7	m.	John Murphy & Mary Griffin both of R.	by Do.
1750	Dec.	6	b.	Samuel son of Zephaniah & Hannah Leonard — Thursday	

[Page 24.]

Children of Nehemiah Washburn & Polly his wife

1784	Feb	16	b.	Cromwell
1785	Sept	8	b.	Thirza
1787	Jany	10	b.	Mahala
1788	Dec	12	b.	Fanny
1791	Jany	1	b.	Nehemiah
1792	Aug	12	b.	Davis
1794	July	28	b.	Calvin
1796	Mar	12	b.	Lysander
1797	Oct	1	b.	Isaac
1799	Nov	29	b.	Nancy
1801	July	23	b.	John Marshall

Rec^d Sept. 10, 1802

[Page 25.]

1727/8	Mar.	19	m.	Philip King and Abigail Williams

Children follow, viz.

1728/9	Mar	17	b.	Abigail — (Monday)
1730	Aug	26	b.	John — (Wed.)
1732	Dec	17	b.	Prudence — (Sunday)
1734	Nov	28	b.	Hannah — (Thurs.)
1736	Sept.	17	b.	Alles [Alice. W. R. D.] — (Frid.)
1738	Oct	23	b.	Philip — (Mond.)
1740	Aug	23	b.	Bethsheba — (Sat.) & d. Aug. 8. 1741 — (Sat.)

1742 May 26 b. Mary — (Wed.)
1743/4 Mar. 20 b. Bathsheba — (Tuesd.) 2^d of the name
1746 Dec 24 b. Rhoda — (Wed.) & d. Dec. 21. 1758 — (Thurs.)

[Page 26.]

Philip & Abigail King's children, continued.

1748 Mar 10 b. Samuel — (Frid.) & d. July 26. 1770 — (Thurs)
1751 Oct 25 b. Nathan — (do) & d. Nov 10. 1756 — (Wed.)
1756 Oct 6 *d.* Abigail King the wife of Capt. Philip King

1768 May 22 b. Joseph Presho
1768 Apl 2 b. Sarah Presho

Children of above, viz

1790 Sept 25 b. Sally
1792 Nov 27 b. Joseph. Jr
1794 Dec 9 b. Phebe
1797 Mar. 20 b. Peter
1799 June 24 b. Damaris
1801 Dec 18 b. Elijah Williams

Rec^d Sept. 13. 1802

Same family continued

1805 Aug 2 b. Clarissa
1807 Dec 18 b. Hosea
1810 Apl 2 b. Varánes
1812 Sep. 30 b. Phebe

[Page 27.]

1733/4 Feb 14 m. Nicholas Power & Lydia Brettun, by Wales
1745 Nov 21 " Joseph Presbrey of Taunton & Mary Baker of R. by Do.
1760 Oct 3 b. Elizabeth Presho dau. Peter Presho & Elizabeth his wife
1761 Nov 19 b Peter " son Do & Do.

1786 Mar 31 b. Laban son of Samson Presho & Abi his wife
1790 June 11 b. { Anna dau / Samson son } of Do. & Do — (*twins*)
1794 May 20 b. Hannah dau Do & Do.
1796 Feb 7 b. Polly " Do & Do.
1798 June 8 b. Luin* son Do & Do
1800 Aug 21 b. Vison* son " "
1788 Feb 16 b. Malinda* dau " " born in Middleboro
1792 Apl 28 b. Hannah* " " "
1804 Dec 9 b Drusilla* " " "
1805 Nov 30 b. Billings Whitfield* son " "

[Page 28.]

1737 Feb 17 m. David King (died July 6. 1753) & Rebecka Dean

Children

1738 Aug 11 b. David — & d. Dec 16. 1754
1740 Dec 29 b. Isaac & d July 30. 1759

[* These are undoubtedly of the same family. *W. R. D.*]

1743	June	12	b.	Job
1745	Dec	26	b.	Mary
1750	Oct	16	b.	Zebulon

1775	June	6	b.	Zibeon Wilbur }
1781	Apl.	11	b.	Lydia Wilbur }
				Their children below
1798	Sept	17	b.	Lydia
1801	Feb	22	b	Dinah
				Rec[d] Sept 13. 1802
1773	June	17	b.	James Wilbur
1781	Oct	6	b.	Hannah Wilbur
1799	Feb	11	b.	Sally Wilbur
1800	May	17	b.	James Wilbur Jr
				Rec[d] Sept 13. 1802
1803	May	28	b.	Roxana
1807	Jany	17	b.	Elcana

[Page 29.]

1736	Aug.	19	m.	John Rowland & Mary Robinson — in Raynham	by Wales
1742/3	Mar	9	"	John Robinson & Lydia Bryant — both of R	by Do
1740	June	11	"	Josiah Robinson & Bethiah Robinson both of R,	by Do

1745	Oct	15	b.	Luther Robinson
1748	June	22	b	Hannah Gushee
1771	Apl	24	b	Parna Robinson
1772	Sept	21	b	Selina Robinson
1777	May	7	b.	Hannah Robinson
1785	Apl	13	b.	Lydia Robinson
1755	May	12	b	Philip Knapp son of George Knapp & Sarah his wife

---

[Page 30.]

Children of John Robinson Jun[r] & Welthy his wife

1769	May	2	b.	Perez — Thursday morning
1770	Nov	1	b.	Welthy — Thursday 12 noon
1773	June	23	b.	Eliab — Sunday, 9 o'clk
1777	Aug	27	b.	Sylvester — Thursday, 2 o'clk
1779	June	23	b.	Alvan
1781	Aug	7	b.	Abigail
1783	Sept	22	b.	Josiah
1786	Mar	23	b	Polly

[Page 31.]

1732	July	26	m.	Ebenezer Shaw of R. & Hannah Fobes of Bridgewater, in R. by Wales
1731/2	Feb	24	b.	Jonathan Shaw son of Jonathan Shaw & Mercy his wife

1720	Sept	27	b.	Benjamin Shelly son of Benj[n] S. & Allice his wife. *Note* He was born in Taunton before Raynham was constituted a town.
1721	Mch	11	b.	Mehitable Shelly dau Do & Do.
1734	June	12	*m.*	Isaac Sampson of Plympton & Elizabeth Shaw of R. by Wales
1736/7	Jany	15	b.	Mason son of Jonathan Shaw of R. & Mercy his wife
1734	July	19	b	John son Do & Do (this should be first)
1738	Apl	4	b.	Jonathan Shelly son of Joseph S. & Thankful his wife — Tuesday
1739	June	7	b	Rebeckah dau Jonathan Shaw & Mercy his wife & d. June 27 æt 20 *d.*

[Page 32.]

1740	Sept	14	b	Susannah dau Jonathan Shaw & Mercy his wife — Sabbath day night
1745	Sept	7	b	Gideon Shaw son of Jonathan Shaw & Mercy his wife
1747	Nov	23	b	Silas " " Do & Do & d. feby 7, 1747
1749	Jany	8	*d.*	Mercy Shaw wife of Dea. Jonathan Shaw in the 44th year of her age
1768	Oct	1	*d.*	Dea. Jonathan Shaw in the –7 of his age
1745	June	11	m.	Samuel Shaw & Phebe Hall both of R. by Wales
1745	Dec	10	m.	Nath[l] Shaw & Elisabeth Hall both of R. by Wales
1750	Apl	1	b.	Joseph son of Joseph Shaw & Mary his wife & d. next day
1751	Nov.	6	b	Joseph 2[d] son Do & Do
1753	June	7	m.	Ebenezer Stutson of Taunton & Hannah Hall of R. by James Williams Just. P. Taunton

FIRST BOOK OF RAYNHAM RECORDS.

From a copy in the possession of this Society.

[Page 33.]

1739	Dec	12	b.	Abigail dau. of John Tuell & Abigail his wife

[Page 34.]

1740	May	19	b	Wealthy dau. Israel Washburn & Leah his wife & d. Aug 23, 1747
1741/2	Mar	19	b.	Mary dau. Do. & Do. — & d. Aug 16. 1747
1744	June	8	b.	Israel son Do. & Do. — & d Aug 24, 1747
1749	Nov	20	b.	Leah dau Do & Do
1752	Aug	8	b.	Olive dau Do & Do
1755	Jany	30	b.	Israel son Do & Do
1759	June	16	b.	Nehemiah, " Do & "
1761	Sept	29	b	Seth " " "
1764	May	14	b	Oliver " " "
1785	Mch	27	b.	John G. Dean son of Joseph Dean & Polly his wife
1790	Sept	25	b	Polly Dean dau Do. & Do. m. Abiezer Dean
1802	June	25	b.	Joseph Augustus Dean son Do & Do

[Page 35.]

1786*	Mar	4	b	Hannah dau. Ephraim Wilbore & Hannah his wife
1786*	Oct	1	b.	Patience dau Do. & Do.
1788	July	17	b.	Reuben son Do. & Do
1790	June	24	b.	Versina dau Do & Do
1784	Nov	4	b.	Elijah son of Ebenezer Wilbur & Elizabeth his wife & d. Sept 13, 1785
1786	July	3	b.	Elizabeth dau. Do & Do.
1788	May	12	b	Ebenezer son Do & Do.
1790	Apl	21	b.	Reuel son Do & Do.
1792	Aug	31	b.	Ziba son Do & Do.
1795	Feb	22	b.	Susannah dau Do & Do.
1799	Mch	24	b.	Bathsheba

[Page 36.]

1731	June	27	b.	David White son of John White & Elizabeth his wife

"The Rev[d] Mr. John Wales & Mrs. Hazadiah Leonard were married November the 8th 1733 by the Rev[d] Mr. Clap."

1732	Nov.	10	b.	Lydia dau. Samuel White & Susannah his wife
1734	Aug.	16	b.	John son Rev[d] Mr. John Wales & Hazadiah his wife
1734	June	20	m.	Stephen Wood & Remember Hodges by Wales
1736	Sept.	12	b.	Prudence dau. Rev[d] Mr. John Wales & Hazadiah his wife Sunday

[* Query? *W. R. D.*]

1735	May	8	m.	Thomas White of Taunton & Sarah Brettun of R. by Wales
1736/7	Jany	18	m.	Timothy Williams of Taunton & Elizabeth Brettun of R. by Do.

[Page 37.]

1724	Aug.	16	b.	Mary dau Shadrach Wilbore Junr & Anna his wife
1732	May	6	b.	Shadrach } Anna } twins, son & dau. Do & Do
1737	July	7	d.	Anna Wilbore wife of the above Shadrach Wilbore Jr.
1738	Dec	7	b.	Mary Wales dau. Rev^{d}. Mr. John Wales & Hazadiah his wife
1740/1	Jany	17	b.	Nathl. Wales son Do. & Do.
1738	Sept	12	b.	Mary dau. Nathl. Williams & Mary his wife
1739	June	27	b.	Edmund son of Edmund Williams & Lydia his wife Wed $8\frac{1}{2}$ o'clk A.M.
"	Oct.	13	d.	John White son John & Elizabeth W. in 14th year of age

[Page 38.]

1737	Nov	6	m.	Edmund Williams & Lydia Crane by Wales
1741	May	8	b.	Lydia dau Edmund & Lydia Williams $\frac{1}{4}$ before 3 Friday morning
1742	Feb	13	b.	Jason son Do & Do. — Sunday
1743	July	1	b.	Elkanah son Rev^{d} Mr. John Wales & Hazadiah his wife
1744	Feb	6	b	Anne dau Edmund & Lydia Williams 40 min. past 9 o'clk A.M. [& *(p. 53)* d. 4 Sept 1763 Sunday $\frac{1}{2}$ past 2 P.M. aged 18 yrs 16 m. 26 d.]
1739	Nov	8	m.	Shadrach Wilbore Jr. & Mehitable White both of R. by Wales
1742	Aug	26	m.	Simeon Williams of Easton & Zipporah Crane of R. by Wales
1742/3	Feb	18	m.	Seth White of Norton & Naomi White of R. by Wales
1744	May	30	m.	Abijah Wilbore & Phebe White both of R. by Wales

[Page 39.]

1796	Dec	17	b.	Polly White dau. Elijah White Junr. & Mary his wife
1799	June	22	b	Rhoda White 2^{d} dau Do. & Do.
1800	Mch	13	b.	Eliza White 3^{d} dau Do & Do
1802	Mch	8	b.	Elijah White son — Do & Do
1804	June	11	b	Adeline White dau — Do & Do.
1808	Sept	20	b.	Elijah White son — Do & Do
1793	July	1	b.	Asa son of Zadock Presho & Orphah his wife.
1794	July	24	b.	Laura dau Do. & Do.
1795	Sept	4	b.	James son Do. & Do.
1797	Jany	19	b.	Sullivan son Do. & Do.
1798	Nov	14	b.	Ebenezer son Do. & Do.

1800 Mch 19 b. Ezra — son Do. & Do.
1801 June 29 b. Daniel son Do & Do.
1803 Dec 30 b. Ruth Forbes dau Do & Do.
1804 Apl 5 b. Almira dau Do & Do.
1807 July 10 b Isaac — son Do & Do
1809 Apl 21 b. William Henry son Do & Do
1805 May 26 b. Zadock — son Do & Do

[Page 40.]

1738 Nov 10 b. Phebe* dau Zephaniah & Hannah Leonard Frid. & d Nov 9. 1739
1739 Nov 8 *d.* Abigail* dau Do. & Do.
1740 Aug 4 b. Prudence dau Do. & Do. Monday abt. 11 o'clk at night *N.B.* She was his 2^{d} child of that name. She d. June 12. 1752 Monday
1735 Nov 17 b. Paul son of Thos. & Sarah Leonard Monday
1738 July 3 b. Caroline dau Do & Do do.
1737 Nov 17 m. David Simeon & Thankful Shelly by Wales
1737 Aug 16 b. Jonathan son of Samuel Leonard Jr. & Abigail his wife Tues. & d Oct. 18, 1737, Tues.

[Page 41.]

1740 July 22 b. Phebe dau. Thomas & Sarah Leonard Tuesday 8 A.M.
1742 May 19 b. Abigail dau. Capt Zephaniah Leonard & Hannah his wife — The 2^{d} dau of that name
1745 Apl 13 *d.* Samuel Leonard Esq. of Raynham on Satterday a little after Sunset aged 71 years 2 mo & 12 days.
1739 Sept 27 m. James Leonard of Taunton & Mary Dean of R. by Wales
1739 Apl 20 b Bethiah dau. Samuel Leonard Jr. & Abigail wife — Frid.
1743/4 Feb 14 b. Nathaniel son Do. & Do. — Tuesday 8 o'clk M.

[Page 42.]

Children of Zephaniah Leonard & Hannah his wife viz.
1744 Aug 3 b. Appollos — Friday
1746 July 16 b. Phebe — Wed. & d. June 17. 1752 Wed.
1748 Apl 8 b. Silas — Frid. & d. May 15. 1752 Frid.

1750 July 7 b Ezra son of Josiah Leonard & Hannah his wife
1741 May 4 *m.* Philip Leonard & Lydia Chase both of R. by Wales
1743 Nov 1 m. Nicholas Leonard of R. & Hannah Stimpson of Taunton by Do.
1746/7 Mch 4 m. Josiah Leonard & Hannah Campbell both of R. by Do.
1747 Nov 23 b. Josiah son of Josiah Leonard & Hannah his wife
Josiah Leonard Jr. dyed Nov 13. 1777
1748 Sept 19 *d.* at Boston about 5 o'clk A.M. Mary Leonard the daughter of Maj. Zephaniah Leonard & Hannah his wife aged 22 years wanting 3 days & was brot. to Raynham and Interred there Sept. 21, 1748

* Both buried in the same grave.

[Page 43.]

Samuel Leonard y^{e}. 2^{d}. Esq. Deceased December 21. 1749 & Nathan his son deceased Feb 16th 1749/50 & Samuel Leonard the 3^{d} his son deceased July 14, 1750

1750	Dec.	6	b.	Samuel son Zephaniah Leonard & Hannah his wife — Thurs.
1749	Feb	15	b.	Ephraim son of Edmund Leonard & Mary his wife
1751	Mch	31	b.	Dorcas dau. Do & Do. & d. Nov 14, 1752 N. S. aged 12 yrs 7 m. 3 d.
1752	May	5	b.	Seth son — Do & Do.
1754	Apl	3	b.	Simeon son — Do & Do
1759	May	30	b.	Solomon son — Do & Do.

Children of Philip Leonard & Lydia his wife

1742	Feb	14	b.	Judith
1743	Aug.	14	b.	Philip
1744	Jany	12	b.	Lydia
1743	July	10	b.	David [*Qu.* 1745? *J. D.*]
1747	July	28	b.	Rebeckah
1749	June	21	b.	Reuben

[Page 44.]

1753	Jany	15	d	Sarah wife of Thomas Leonard 3^{d}.
1763	Feb	24	m.	Ebenezer Stetson of Dighton & Anna Leonard of R. by Wales
1774	July	1	d.	Mr. Thomas Leonard
1778	Sept	20	b.	Rhoda dau. of Libeus Shelly & Bethany his wife
1782	Jany	30	b.	Lot son Do & Phebe his wife
1784	Aug	13	b.	Green " Do & Do.
1786	Nov	7	b.	Phebe dau Do. & Do.
1788	June	23	b.	Polly " Do. & Do.
1790	Mch	11	b.	Libeus son Do. & Do.

[Page 45.]

1740	Apl	3	m.	Philip Hall & Huldah Leonard by Wales Child
1740/41	Jany	18	b.	Huldah dau Philip Hall & Huldah his wife
1741	Dec.	26	b.	Noah son John Hall & Hannah his wife — Saturday

John Hall the son of Jonathan Hall & Sarah his first wife (whose maiden name was Sarah Ockington) Dyed in the battle of the seige at Cape Breton on May 26. 1745 in attacking the Island Battery

1744	Dec	20	m.	Amos Hall & Abigail Blake both of R. by Wales
1742/3	Feby	4	b	Silas son of Jonathan Hall Jr. & Lydia his wife—Friday
1744/5	Mar	20	b.	Prudence dau Do. & Do. — Wednesday [see death p. 46 W. R. D.]
1747	Oct	21	b.	Lydia " Do & Do. ——
1750	Aug	14	b	Jemima " Do & Do ——

[Page 46.]

Jonathan Hall the 1st. of Raynham Deceased April 19. 1750
Said Hall's 2d wife died July 1754

1727	July	9	b.	Brian son of John Hall 3d of Taunton & Mary his wife
1752	June	21	*d.*	Prudence dau Dea. Jona. Hall & Lydia his wife
1753	June	10	b.	Jonathan son of Jonathan Hall & Lydia his wife Sunday
1755	Nov	12	b.	Hezekiah son of Dea. Jona Hall & Do Wed
1757	Dec	23	b.	Obed son Do & Do ——
1757	Nov	27	b	Mary dau. Abel Hayward & Mary his wife
1765	Feb	14	b.	Charlotte, 2nd. dau Do & Do

[Page 47.]

1775	Oct	29	d.	Nehemiah Hall, 70 years 9 mos & 3 days old
				Children of Dea. Jonathan Hall & Lydia his wife, viz.
1759	Dec	25	b.	Ebenezer
1762	June	6	b.	Abigail & d. Apl 3. 1765
1764	Apl	26	*m.*	Dea Jonathan Hall & Hannah Hall
1765	May	17	b.	Linus their son
1777	Mch	4	b.	Lois dau. Hezekiah Hall & Sarah his wife
1779	Jany	24	b.	Bezer son Do. & Do. & d. Aug 5. 1780
1781	June	26	b.	Eliphalet son Do. & Do — born in Bridgewater
1783	July	30	b	Adrastus son Do. & Do.
1786	Apl	3	b.	Bezer son Do & Do

[Page 48.]

1743	Aug	5	b.	Annie dau. Gabriel & Phebe Crofsman
1744/5	Jany	18	m.	Onesimus Campbell of Raynham & Allice Richmond of Taunton by Sam1. Leonard Jr. J: P.
1739	Nov	8	m.	Nehemiah Campbell & Jemima Leonard both of R. by Wales
1738	Feb	13	b.	Joanna dau. Thomas Crossman & Joanna his wife
1741	Aug	28	b.	Allice dau. Do. & Do
1744	May	12	b.	Thomas son Do. & Do
1748	Feb	6	b	Elizabeth dau. Do. & Do.
1745	Oct	1	b	Seth son Gabriel Crossman & Phebe his wife
1748	Jany	7	b	Hannah dau. Do. & Do.
1750	June	25	b.	Gabriel son Do. & Do.

[Page 49.]

1736	Dec	28	b.	Hannah dau. Stephen Dean & Hannah his wife & d. Jany 8 1736
1747	Apl	30	b	Stephen son. Do. & Do.
1749	Oct	19	d.	Stephen Dean ye. father of the above named children, aged 41 *yrs* 20*d*.
1762	July	3	d.	Sophia Dean widow of Elijah Dean
				Children of Stephen Dean & Hannah his wife
1768	Feb	22	b.	Zoheth — Monday — 1st son

1770	May	21	b.	Cassandra — Do — 1st dau.
1773	Oct	19	b.	Stephen — Tuesday — 2^d^. son
1776	June	6	b.	Arnold — Thursday — 3^d^. son

[Page 50.]

Children of Samuel Leonard & Anna his wife

1768	Mch	4	b.	Samuel
1770	Aug	26	b.	Job
1773	Feb	22	b.	Jane
1777	Aug.	14	b.	Anna
1781	July	31	b.	Hannah
1786	Oct	4	b.	Wetherell
1791	Nov	26	b.	David
1795	Feb.	17	b.	Elijah

Rec^d^ Oct 13. 1801

Children of Simeon Leonard & Keziah his wife

1787	Dec	16	b.	Demas [guess a daughter. W. R. D.]
1789	Sept	14	b.	Marshall — son
1792	Nov	7	b.	Arnold — do.
1794	July	20	b.	Sebury
1796	July	4	b.	Levi
1799	Mch	1	b.	Melansa

[Page 51.]

Children of Capt. Joshua Leonard & Hannah his wife

1769	June	25	b.	Joshua — 1st son
1770	Sept	8	b.	Hannah — 1st dau
1772	Mch	11	b.	Silas — 2^d^. son
1773	Aug	29	b	Mary — 2^d^. dau
1775	Feb	12	b.	Peyton Randolph — 3^d^. son
1776	Aug	29	b	Isaac 4th son

FIRST BOOK OF RAYNHAM RECORDS.

From a copy in the possession of this Society.

Children of Captain Joshua Leonard and Hannah his wife
(Continued.)

1778	Feb	21	b	Anna Sarah – 3d dau
1780	May	24	b.	Olive
1782	Jany	9	b.	Sorannus
1783	July	25	b.	Artemas
1788	July	22	b.	Olive
1790	Aug.	14	b.	Isaac

Recd Apl 9. 1804

1778	July	21	b.	Ameida dau. of Jonah Wilbore & Lydia his wife
1802	Feb	14	b.	Ithiel son of Joseph Wilbore & Hannah his wife
1760	Apl	28	b.	Elijah son of Elijah Leonard & Hannah his wife
1800	Feb	27	b.	Abisha son of Ambrose Lincoln & Lois his wife

[Page 52.]

1745	Oct	13	b.	Bathsheba dau. Rev Mr. John Wales & Hazadiah his wife

1746 Mch 3 b. Sarah dau. Edmund Williams & Lydia his wife ½ past 9 A.M.
1748 Jany 2 b. Nathan Do & Do
1750 Sept 28 b Huldah dau. Do & Do — Friday 3 A.M.
1752 Nov 10 N.S. b Stephen son Do & Do.
1754 Aug 11 b. David son Do & Do

1743 Apl 27 b. Hannah dau Joseph Wilbore & Susannah his wife
1745 Sept 27 b. Jacob son Do. & Do.
1748 Sept 22 b. Rebeckah dau Do. & Do.
1750/1 Mch 8 b. Abia dau Do. &, Do. Friday

[Page 53.]

1756 Aug 5 b. Noah son of Edmund Williams & Lydia his wife
1758 Aug 28 b. Silas son of Do. & Do. & d. Feb 22, 1762 aged 3 yrs 5 mos. 23 ds.
1763 Sept 4 *d* Anne dau of Do. & Do. Sunday ½ past 2 P.M. aged 18 yrs 6 mos. 26 d.
1754 Oct 23 b. Nathaniel son of Joseph Wilbore & Susannah his wife
1758 Aug 10 b Mehitable dau. of Meshack Wilbore Jr. & Mehitable his wife
1760 Aug 1 b Abigail dau of Meshack Wilbore Jr. & Do
1761 May 26 b Meshack son of Do & Do
1731 Dec 6 b. Meshack Wilbore Junr. the Father of the above named children & son of Meshack Wilbore & Elizabeth his wife
1762 May 18 m. James Williams Jr. of Taunton & Susannah Shaw of R. by Jas. Williams J.P.

[Page 54.]

1754 July 26 m. Silas son of Joseph Shaw & Mary his wife

Children of Nathaniel Shaw & Elizabeth his wife are as follows

1746 Aug 6 b. Nathaniel Jr.
1748 Feb 25 b. John
1753 Sept 28 b. Betsey
1751 Nov 25 b Asal
1755 Sept 28 b. Jairus
1758 Nov 21 b. Sarah

1763 Jany 12 b. Phebe Williams dau Edmund Williams & Lydia his wife

"Lydia wife of Edmund Williams died May 14, 1781 aged 61 years ye 4 of August last Old Stile."

[Page 55.]

1765 Oct 30 m. Zephaniah Leonard of Raynham & Abigail Alden of Middleborough by Rev^d Mr Solomon Reed— Rec^d by Zeph. Leonard T.C.

Children of above, viz

1766 Mch 19 b Zephaniah & d. Mch 7. 1769
1767 Dec 28 b. Wm Augustus & was drowned Nov. 9. 1774

1769 July 10 b. Nabby — Monday
1771 Nov 8 b. Clarissa — Friday
1773 Apl 18 b. Zephaniah — Sunday
1775 Sept 27 b. Wm Augustus, their 4th son
[Continued next page]

[Page 56
Children of Z & A. Leonard, continued]

1780 Dec 28 b Horatio
1785 Apl 19 b. Fanny

1763 June 16 m. Mason Shaw & Mary King both of R. by Wales. — Recd by Mason Shaw T.C.
Children
1764 July 11 b Hannah — Wednesday
1767 Jany 23 b. Mason — Friday — & d Dec 25. 1770 Tuesday
1769 June 8 b. Jahaziah — Thursday
1773 May 24 b. Mason — Monday
1777 Mch. 3 b. Lloyd — Monday

[Page 57.]

1765 Oct 10 m. Philip King & Mary Wales both of R.
Children
1766 Sept 12 b. Polly
1768 Jany 14 b Prudence- 2d dau

1776 Sept 15 b. Abiah Andrews dau. of Rufus Andrews & Alathea his wife
1779 Aug 30 b Alfred Andrews
1781 June 24 b. Walter Andrews
1784 Oct 14 b. Dianna Andrews
1787 May 12 b. Phylena Andrews
1792 Mch 12 b. Asaph Andrews
1797 Oct 27 b. Belara Andrews

[Page 58.]

Children of Saml Baker of Raynham & Mehitable his wife
Mehitable Baker was born

1785 Dec 26 b. James, son of Charles Frazer & Phebe his wife
1788 Feb 6 b. Matilda — their dau
1790 June 7 b. Samuel W — their son
1793 Nov 15 b. Reuben L. son of Charles Frazer & Tabitha his 2d wife
1795 June 14 b. Charles, their son
1797 Mch 9 b. Oliver — their son
1799 June 26 b George Washington Frazer
1801 Sept 21 b. Philip Leonard Frazer
1807 Mch 25 b. Rebeckah Leonard Frazer

[Page 59.]

1759 Sept 25 b. Hannah dau. of Abiel Williams & Zeruiah his wife
1762 Feby 2 b. Mary their 2d dau

1764 June 8 b. Jonathan their son
1766 Aug 8 b. Anna their 3d dau
1769 May 6 b. Macy their 2d son
1772 Feb 2 b. Zeruiah their dau — Sabbath day

1773 Mch 5 b. Hannah dau. of Ephraim Wilbore & Hannah his wife
1791 Feb. 11 b. Leonard 5th son of Gabriel Crossman & Phebe his wife

---

[Page 60.]

Children of Shubael Campbell & Mary his wife

1749 Dec 3 b. Coomes Campbell
1751 July 31 b. Shubael "
1752 July 17 b. Hannah "
1751 Oct 10 d. said Shubael Campbell — all in old stile

1761 Jan. 17 — "marriage is intended betwixt Shobel Campbell of Raynham & Mary Pratt of Norton both in Bristol County, & publication of such intention has been made in Raynham according to Law February ye 9th 1761."

1764 Apl. 23 b. Hannah dau of Sherebiah Cobb & Hannah his wife
1772 Dec 13 b. Elkanan son of Gabriel Crossman & Phebe his wife
1775 Mch 23 b. Barzillai their 2d son
1785 Apl. 13 b. Bradford their 3d son
1789 Jan 13 b. Alvin their 4th son

[See above p. 59 for their 5th son. J. D.]

[Page 61.]

1757 Nov 17 m. Jonathan Shaw Jr. & Bethiah Hall (d. Apl 17. 1781) by Wales

Children

1758 Sept. 6 b Jonathan — Wednesday
1759 Nov 13 b. Bethiah — Tuesday

1766 Apl 11 b. Squier 1st son of Gustus Stevens & Bathsheba his wife
1767 Mch 15 b. Ebenezer 2d son of do. & do.
1771 Mch 29 b. Joseph 3d son of do. & do.

1769 Sept 2 b. Nabby dau. of Gideon Shaw & Abigail his wife
1772 May 17 b. Philena dau. of do. & do.
1775 Mch 3 b Melaneia dau. of do. & do

1768 June 5 b. Daniel son of Nathaniel Shaw & Lydia his wife
1799 June 3 b. Leonard Stephen son of David Dean & Polly his wife

[Page 62.]

Children of Jona^{n} Shaw Jr & Lydia his wife

1779	Oct	7	b.	Permenis Calisthenes
1782	Dec	10	"	Cassini
1785	Sept	5	"	Amyntas
1788	May	10	"	Lydia
1790	Sept	10	"	Cassini
1793	Jany	8	"	Henrietta Maria Antoinette
1795	Aug.	5	"	Lydia

[Page 63.]

1756	Jany	18	b.	Elijah son of Thomas Baker & Experience his wife—1st dau. [? J. D.]
1758	Jany	5	"	Zilpha dau of do & do — 2nd dau
1759	Jany	3	"	Leby dau of do & do — 3rd dau
1765	May	11	"	Ebenezer son of do & do — son

1781			m	Cyrus Crossman to Charity Gardner

Children of Jabez Carver & Phebe Carver

1775	July	9	b.	Phebe
1777	Nov	30	"	Jabez
1780	Nov	14	"	Sarah
1783	Feby	8	"	Rhoda
1785	Jany	6	"	Olive

1775	Sept	4	b.	Hannah Dean Carver dau. of John Carver & Bathsheba his wife
1780	Sept	27	"	Clifford Carver son of do. & do.

[Page 64.]

1747	Sept	10	d.	Thomas Dean ye 2^{d} in ye 74 year of his age
1749	Feb	1	"	Mary Dean widow of s^{d} Thomas Dean in ye 74 year of her age

---

1737	Aug.	18	m.	Josiah Dean & Jane Washburn by Rev^{d} Mr. Daniel Perkins.
				Children
1738	Dec	30	b.	Nehemiah (Saturday) & d. Feby 13. 1749 aged about 11 years
1740	Sept	21	"	Abigail (Lords day)
1743	Aug	20	"	Mary (Saturday)
1748	Mar	6	"	Josiah (Sunday)
1751	Nov	15	"	Job (Friday)

1793	Sept.	2	b.	Cassandra dau of Zoheth Dean & Asenath his wife
1795	Mar.	26	"	Fanny dau. of Do. & Do.

[Page 63 second.]

Children of William Woodward & Rachel his wife

1767	Jany	5	b.	Irana their dau. Fryday
1768	Aug	3	"	Ozias " son, Wed.
1770	Nov.	17	"	Apollos " ", Sat.

1772	Jan	7	b.	Rachel Woodward, their 4th child

1778	Mar	5	b.	Hannah dau. of Ephraim Wilbore & Hannah his wife

1770	Aug.	26	b.	Betsy dau. of Joseph Cole & Zerushah his wife
1772	Oct	3	"	Sophiah their 2^{d} dau

1774	Oct	15	b.	Abiah dau. of Ephraim Wilbour & Hannah his wife & d Apl 17. 1778
1776	Oct	15	"	Ephraim their son & d. Dec 29. 1777
1778	Apl	12	"	Hannah their dau.
1779	June	12	"	Patience their dau.
1781	Aug.	s^{d}	"	Elizabeth their 4th dau
1783	Oct	25	"	field, their 2^{d} son

[Page 64 second.]

1772	Apl	16	b.	Zipporah dau. of Job King & Zipporah his wife
1774	Apl	2	"	David son of Do. & do.
1776	Apl	5	"	Rebeckah dau. of Do & Do
1778	Nov.	8	"	Job son of Do. & Do

1774	May	17	b.	Molly dau. of Job Dean & Judith his wife & d. feb 18. 1783
1776	Mar	7	"	Phebe dau of Do. & Do
1778	Jany	29	"	Judith dau. of Do. & Do.
1780	Mch	9	"	Belinda dau of Do & Do & d. Dec. 24. 1783
1782	May	13	"	Williams son of Do. & Do.
1784	Sept	5	"	Polly dau. of Do. & Do.
1786	Aug.	22	"	Zephaniah son of Do. & Do.
1789	Feby	15	"	{ Martin, Marcus } sons of Do & Do
1791	June	6	"	Nabby dau. of Do. & Do.
1793	June	9	"	Job Williams son of Do. & Do.
1795	Aug	23	"	Parmenus " of Do & Do
1799	Apl	28	"	Jeziah dau of Do. & Do
				Phebe Bassitt their grand daughter was born at New Gloucester Dec 8. 1798

[Page 65.]

1768	Apl	28	m.	Edmond Williams Jr. to Susannah Williams by James Williams Esq.
1769	Nov	15	b.	Susannah, their daughter
1771	Aug	2	"	Silas, their son
1773	Mch	24	"	Nancy, their dau.
1774	Nov	20	"	Edmund, their son & d. Oct 5. 1780
1775	Sept	3	d.	Edmond Williams Jr. above named
1775	July	23	d.	David son of Edmond Williams & Lydia his wife
1776	Dec	3	d.	Jason son of Do. & Do. — d. at Albany Hospital

[Page 66.]

1793	Aug.	28	b.	Jane Chamberlain dau. of James Chamberlain & Jane his wife
1797	Oct.	8	"	Melinda Chamberlain
1799	Aug.	30	"	Susanna Pratt Chamberlain

1801	Oct	15	b.	Joseph Feeto, son of Gabriel Feeto & Hannah his wife & d Nov. 15 1809 aged 8
1803	Dec	3	"	Philander Feeto

[Page 67.]

1755	May	8	b.	Bethiah dau. of Gamaliel Leonard & Bethiah his wife. Thurs. 5 P.M.
1757	"	31	"	Gamaliel son of Do. & Do. — Tues. 1 A.M.
1759	Aug	19	"	Phebe dau of Do. & Do. — Sunday ½ past 10 P.M.
1762	Mch	1	"	Molly dau. of Do. & Do. — Monday ½ " 7 P.M.
1764	Apl	24	"	Thomas son of Do. & Do. — Tues. 11 A.M.
1766	May	11	"	Keziah dau. of Do. & Do. — Sunday 8 P.M.
1768	Sept	30	"	Katharine dau of Do. & Do. — Friday 10 A.M.
1771	Mch	15	"	Simeon son of Do. & Do. — Friday 5 A.M.
1773	July	17	"	Eliakim son of Do. & Do. — Saturday 7 P.M.
1776	June	26	"	Cynthia dau of Do. & Do. — Wed. 4 P.M.

[Page 68.]

1796	May	20	b.	Sally dau. of Apollos & Sally White
1798	Aug	1	"	Wm Shepherd son of Do & Do.
1801	Jany	23	"	Minus son of Do & Do.
1805	Dec.	23	"	Harriet dau. of Do & Do
1808	Nov	1	"	Harrison Gray Otis son of Do. & Do.
1812	Mch	10	"	Martin son of Do. & Do.

1783	Nov.	15	b.	Daniel White son of Daniel White & Anna his wife
1785	July	21	"	Nancy White dau of Do. & Do

MARRIAGES AND BAPTISMS IN RAYNHAM, MASS.

Copied by FRANCIS E. BLAKE, Esq., from manuscripts found among papers of Rev. Perez Fobes, D.D., of Raynham.*

MARRIAGES.

December 16, 1782 Elijah Gashee and Sarah king where Married, both of Raynham.

January 9, 1783 Joseph Dean and Mary gilmore were Maried both of Raynham.

Feb. 20, 1783 Mr. Nehemiah washburn and Mrs. Polly Presho where Married both of Raynham.

Mr. philip elis (?) and Mrs. Sarah hall where Married March 16, 1783 both of Raynham.

April the 3, 1783 Mr. Daniel white and Mis anna hall where Maried Both of Raynham.

May the 25, 1783 where Married Philena Hall of Raynham and Samuel hood of taunton.

June ye 12th 1783 Were Married Capt. Israel Washburn & Mrs. Abiah King both of Raynham.

November 30, 1783 where Married Seth Silvester of Bridgewater and hannah hall of Raynham.

December 16, 1783 were married Cæser Crane of Bridgewater & Bridget Lincoln of Raynham. Blacks.

September 16, 1784 were married Dec[n] Nathaniel Shaw and Rebachah Jones both of Raynham.

September 16, 1784 were married David haard of taunton and Noami knap of Raynham.

October 14, 1784 Were Married Mr. Jonathan Wiliams of this Town and Miss Polly Dean of this Town.

November 17, 1784 Were Married Mr. Nathan Bakas of Middleborough and Miss Bethiah Leanard of this Town. (Another record has Nov. 19.)

January 1, 1784 Were Married Mr. James Williams Juner of Taunton and Miss Polly Hall of Raynham.

January 11, 1784 were Married Ebenezer Wilbore & Elizabeth Presho both of this Town.

February 26, 1784 Were Married Mr. Samuel Gashee and Miss Hannah Gillmor, both of Raynham.

May 6, 1784 Were Married Obed Hall and Abigail Dean both of Raynham.

* Rev. Perez Fobes, D.D., was pastor of the church in Raynham, Nov. 19, 1766, till his death, Feb. 23, 1812. Most of the entries are in his handwriting. He married a daughter of his predecessor, Rev. John Wales.

July 8th, 1784 were Married Mr. Elezar Clap of Norton & Widow Silvia Gusshee.

Sept. 9, 1784 Nathaniel Richmon & Susanna Lambart both of this Town.

Septem[r] 9, 1784 Simeon Leonard & Kezia Andrews.

March 23, 1786 were maried Linus & Selah.

may the 11, 1786 were married Thomas Leonard both of Raynham. [*sic.*]

october 1786 Were Married Meshack Wilber and Kesiah Leonard both of Raynham.

December 28, 1786 Were Married Samuel Tubbs of Berkely & Ascenath Shelly of Raynham.

January 11, 1787 were Maried William Shaw and olive Dean both of Rainham.

May the 3, 1787 were Maried Isaak hall & Polly Leonard both of Raynham.

August 23, 1787 were Maried Andrew Gillmor and Hannah Makepiace both this town.

october 11, 1787 were Maried Siles King & Sally Hall both of Raynham.

October 25, 1787 were Maried James Gillmor and Anny Wilbur both of Raynham.

November 29, 1787 Joseph Tucker Junr and Betesey Aldrich were Maried both of Raynham.

January 17, 1788 were Maried Oliver Wasbern & Sarah Leiscomb both of Rainham.

April 17, 1788 were married Samuel Read of Dighton & Mercy Gillmor of Raynham.

May 11, 1788 were Married Amariah Hall & Sybble Whilee both of Raynham.

May 14, 1788 were Married Seth Read of Dighton and Casandnaia Dean of Raynham.

October 21, 1788 Were Married Isaack Marlow and Susannah Shaw of Raynham.

October 30, 1788 Were Married Ephrem Raymontd and Polly Dean of Raynham.

Novembr 20, 1788 were maried Robbert Jun Britton [*sic.*] & Sally Fales.

December 17, 1788 were Maried Peres Elice and Polly Hathaway.

December 25, 1788 Were Maried Standly Carter and Bethiah Leonard.

February 19, 1789 Were Maried William Hoard of Taunton and Polly English of Raynham.

February 26, 1789 Were Maried Israel Gillmor of Franklin and Lucinda Ellis of Raynham.

october , 1789 Were Maried Stephen King & Miss Hannah Shaw Both of Raynham.

November the 26, 1789 Were Maried Frances Jones and Isabel Gillmor both of Raynham.

December 15, 1789 Were Maried Asael Jones and Katy Leonard Both of Raynham.

January 26, 1790 Were Married Parna Robinson of Raynham and John thatcher of Wareham.

April 30, 1790 Were Married Alexander Kingman of Bridgewater and the Widow Abiah Knap of this Town.

June 14, 1790 Were Married Esq. Israel Washburn and Mrs. Hannah hall both of Raynham.

June 20, 1790 Were Married Elkanah Barny of Taunton and Catharine King of Raynham.

July 22, 1790 were Married Joseph Cole and Chloe Jones of Middlebury.

August 5, 1790 were Married Eliacam Howard and Anny Williams.

August 26, 1790 were Married Oliver Campbell and Sally Andrews both of Raynham.

November 25, 1790 were Married Mr. William Breaton of Easton and Mrs. Mary Briton of this Town.

December 2, 1790 Were Married Meshack Wilbere tirshus and Nancy Williams both of this Town.

February 3, 1791 Were Married Mr. Mart Lincon of Taunton and Miss Susana Hall of this Town.

February 17, 1791 Were Married Asael Macket [Hacket?] and Lydia French of this Town.

October 2, 1791 Were Married Nehemiah Jones and Polly Alden both of Raynham.

November 17, 1791 Were Married Elijah White and Annah Whiles both of this Town.

January 26, 1792 were Married Mr. Hezikiah Hayward of Bridgewater and Hassadiah King of this Town.

May 13, 1792 Were Married Rev[d] Elijah Leonard of Marshfield and Miss Molly Wales Fobes of this town.

May 27, 1792 Mr. Isaac White of this town & Miss Olive Fobes of Bridgewater.

[ ] Mr. Berzella King and Mrs. Lesenda Gillmor both of this town.

July 26th, 1792 were Married Mr. Isaiah Keth and Miss Polly Basset both of this Town.

Sept. 27, 1792 were Married Mr. Zadock Presho and Miss Orpha Alden both of this Town.

[ ] Mr. Thomas Green of Coventry in the State of Rhode Island and Miss Jane Dean of this town.

October 18, 1792 were Married David Dean and Hannah hall both of this Town.

This Certifies, That the Intentions of Marriage between Capt. John Williams of Taunton, and Miss Silence Dean of Raynham, both in the County of Bristol, have been enterd in the Town-Clerk's Office and published in the Town of Raynham according to Law.

Certified at Raynham aforesaid, the Eleventh day of June in the year of our Lord one thousand eight hundred and four.

Seth Washburn, Town-Clerk.

Raynham April 22, 1799.

This certifies that Mr. Lemuel Brient & Miss Polly Keith both of this Town have had their intentions of Marriage published according to Law. Seth Washburn, Town-Clerk.

This Certifies, That the intentions of Marriage between Mr. William Henry Williams of Taunton & Miss Elizabeth Williams Shaw of Raynham have been entered in the Town Clerk's Office, and published in the town of Raynham according to Law.

Certified at Raynham aforesaid, the eighth day of November in the year of our Lord one thousand eight hundred and thirty three.

Wm. Snow, Town Clerk.

MARRIAGES AND BAPTISMS IN RAYNHAM, MASS.

Copied by FRANCIS E. BLAKE, Esq., from manuscripts found among papers of Rev. Peres Fobes, D.D., of Raynham.

MARRIAGES (Continued).

THIS CERTIFIES, That the intentions of Marriage between Mr. Enoch Robinson & Miss Sophia V. Saunders both of Raynham have been entered in the Town Clerk's Office, and published in the Town of Raynham, according to law.

Certified at Raynham aforesaid, this fifteenth day of June in the year of our Lord, one thousand eight hundred and thirty three.

Attest, WM. SNOW, Town Clerk.*

I hereby certify that the Intention of Marriage between Philip S. Dean of Taunton and Mary D. Bates of Raynham have been entered in the town Clerks office in said Taunton fourteen days and published in said Taunton according to Law Dated at Taunton this tenth day of April the year of our Lord one thousand eight hundred and thirty two.

Attest ALFRED WILLIAMS, Town Clerk.

This may certify that the Intention of Marriage between William H. Williams of Taunton and Elizabeth W. Shaw of Raynham have been entered in the Town Clerks office in Taunton and published in said Town according to Law.

Taunton Nov. 10, 1833.

Attest ALFRED WILLIAMS, T. Clerk.

BAPTISMS.

April 6, 1783 Bethiah was Baptized the Daughter of Seth & Hannah Robinson.

April 20th, 1783 Gustavus the Son of Zephaniah and Abigail Leonard.

April 27th, 1783 Silas the Son of Nathaniel Dean and Elizebeth.

August 10th, 1784 Anna the Daughter of Jonathan Shaw and Lydia.

Sept. [7] 1783 Artemas the Son of Capt. Joshua and Hannah Leonard.

October 27th, 1783 Josiah the Son of John and Welthy Robinson.

October 29 1783 William the Son of Jonathan and Phebe Robinson.

Feb [19] 1784 Jonathan the Son of Wiliam and [Lyd]ia French.

*[Note in pencil.] Married June 23rd, 1833 by Rev. Simeon Doggett of Raynham, per memo. in Almanac.

June 8th, 1784 Olive the Daughter of Ezra & Elizabeth Leonard.

August 8th, 1784 Enoch the Son of George Wiliams and Bathsheba.

November 28th, 1784 Baptized Anny the Daughter of Nathaniel & Elizebeth Dean.

March 27th 1785 Josiah the Son of Josiah and Sarah Dean.

May 29th 1785 Lydia the Daughter of Luther Robinson and Hannah.

June 5th, 1785 Fanny the Daughter of Col Zephaniah and Abigail Leonard.

June 26th, 1785 Anny the Daughter of Seth Robinson and Hannah.

November 20th, 1785 Parmenia, Calisthenes, Cassine & Amyntas the Sons of Jonathan Shaw Jun. and Lydia his wife.

Feb. 26th 1786 Samuel King the Son of George Wiliams and Bathsheba.

May 28th, 1786 Polly the Daughter of John Robinson and Whelthy.

June 10th, 1787 Simeon the Son of Seth and Hannah Robinson.

May 25th 1788 Asa the Son of Nathaniel and Elizabeth Dean.

June 8th, 1788 Lydia the Daughter of Jonathan Shaw Jun. & Lydia.

July 27, 1788 was baptized Elial Byram Son of Esq Dean his wife Sarah.

Sept 14, 1788 was baptized Olive the Daughter of Capt Joshua Leonard his wife Hannah.

February 19, 1789 Was Baptized Polly the Daughter of Silas Shaw His Wives Name Elizabeth.

June 8, 1789 Was Baptized Sally Daughter John Robinson & his Wife Whelthy.

September 13, 1789 baptized Beazer [*sic*] the Son of Seth Robenson and Hannah.

November the 29, 1789 was Baptized Basheba King.

December 6, 1789 was Baptized Catharine King.

Jannary 31, 1790 Was baptized Silis Shaw the Son of Silis Shaw and Elizabeth his wife.

August 22, 1790 was baptized Polly the [daughter] Stephen King and Hannah his wife.

September 19, 1790 was baptized Susanna the Daughter of Thomas Dean and Susanna.

BAPTISMS, FROM REHOBOTH CHURCH RECORDS.

[Transcribed by ELISHA L. TURNER of Dedham.]

Hannah Greenwood; Rebeckah, ye daughter of John Pain, bap. Feb. 17, 1694.

Judith ye daughter of Sam[ll] Pain, bap. March 7, 1695.

Judith ye daughter of John Hunt, bap. April 14, 1695.

Abigail ye daughter of George Robinson, and Elizabeth daughter of Israel Read, bap. May 12, 1695.

Abigail ye daughter of John Titus, bap. May 26, 1695.

Jonathan son of James Thirber and Bathsheba daugh[r] of Saml Newman, bap. July 28, 1695.

John son of John Read, bap. November 17th, 1695.

Sarah daugh[r] of Phill. Walker, bap. Jan. 12, 1695–6.

Rebeckah daugh[r] of Enoch Hunt, Elizabeth daugh[r] of Sam[ll] Pamer, Feb. 16, Hezekiah son of Hez. Peck, Elizabeth daugh[r] of Josiah Peck, Jun., Hannah daugh[r] of Joseph Dagget, bap. 5 April, 1696.

John son of John Lane, bap 19 April, 1696, also wife of Sam[l] Sabin, sen[r].

An daugh[r] of Israel Read, bap. May 3, 1696.

James son of James Sabin, & Noah ye son of Joseph Titus, bap. May 24, 1696.

Adin: Josiah son of Josiah Carpenter, & Rachel & Experience, daugh[rs] of Tim: Ide, bap. July, 1696.

Obediah son of Israel Ingraham, & Thom. son of John Friend, bap. Oct. 5, 1696.

Daniel, Ichabod, Solomon, Jethniel, Esther, children of Jethniel Peck, bap. Ap: 11, 1696.

Noah son of Sam[l] Pain, bap. April 25, 1697.

Jabish son of Doct[r] Brown, bap. May 9, 1697.

Henry, Joshua, Rebeckah, Elizabeth, children of Joshua Smith, & Nathaniel, Deliver, children of John Smith, all bap. 9 May, 1697.

John Greenwood & ye Wife of John Sheperdson, bap. May 30, 1697.

Ebenezer son of Jethniel Peck, bap. June 14, 1697.

James, Phillip, Esther, children of Phillip Walker, bap. July 4, 1697.

Solomon son of John Pain, & Hannah, daugh of John Hunt, bap. July 18, 1697.

Daniel son of Mary Newman, bap. Aug. 1, 1697.

Nathaniel, Josiah, Susannah, children of Thom. Cooper, Jun[r], bap. Aug. 15, 1697.

Abia Carpenter, bap. in a private house, Sept. 1, 1697.

Eben son of Sam[l] Robin, bap. Sept. 5, 1697.

Abia, Thomas, Mehitabel, Sarah, children of Abiah Carpenter, and Elizabeth, daugh[r] of Capt. Mason & a member of the Church at Norwich, bap. Sept. 12, 1697.

Tabitha & Sibill children of Benj. Hunt, Sept. 19, 1697.

Sarah Fuller & Elizabeth Allen, bap. (in a private house) Oct. 27, 1697.

Nat. Chaffe, Jan. 2, 1697–8.

Huldah Hunt, March 20, 1698.

Hannah daughter of George Robinson, Ruth, daugh[r] of Is. Read, Mar. 27, 1698.

Leah daugh: of Nat. Carpenter, Joseph, Deborah, Martha, children of Jos. Buckland, Jun. bap. on ye 17 April, 1698.

Israel son of Josiyah Peck, Noah, son of Tho. Cooper, Junr, Nat., Phillip, Elizabeth, Rachel, Experience, children of Nat Whittaker, Susannah, daughr of Jos Kent, sen. bap. April 24, 1698.
Moses son of John Read, May 26, 1698.
Bathshebah daughr of John Smith, Rachell daughr of Hezekh Peck, June 19, 1698.
Ezekiel son of Benj. Fuller, bap. Nov. 13, 1698.
Rebeck: daughr of David Carpenter, Nov. 27, 1698.
Josiah son of Tim. Ide, bap. Dec. 21, 1698, Joseph Polley ye same time, Israel Peck being sponsor.
Rachell daughr of Saml Cooper, Jan. 8, 1698–9.
Martha daughr Joseph Titus, Jan. 15, 1699.
David son of James Sabin, bap. Feb. 12, 1698–9.
Benjamin son of John Lane, Ephraim son of John French, bap. Feb. 20, 1698–9.
Benjamin son of Joseph Buckland, bap. Mar. 5, 1699.
Sarah daughr of John Peck, & Sarah daughr of John Sheperdson, bap. Apr. 16, 1699.
Noah Greenwood, Joseph son of Joseph Dagget, bap. April 25, 1699.
Ezra son of Nat Carpenter, & Rebeckah, daughr of Nat. Whittaker, bap. April 30, 1699.
Hannah Graunt (personally owning ye covenant) was bap. June 4, 1699, also Sarah daughr of Charles Williams ye same time.
Elizabeth wife of Saml Titus & her children Elizabeth & Abigail, bap. June 11, 1699.
Ebenezer son of John Butterworth, Rachell daughr of Abia Carpenter, bap. June 18, 1699.
Stephen son of Saml Pain, bap. Aug. 6, 1699.
Sarah daughtr of Abraham Follet, bap. Aug. ye 13, 1699.
Joshua son of Israel Read, bap. Oct. 8, 1699.
Sarah daughr of Elisha Maye, and Abigail daughr of Stephen Read, bap. Oct. 21, 1699.
Elizabh wife of Benj. Wilson, Benj. son of John Pain, Ebenezer son of Danl Pamer, Mercy daughr of Leonard Newsom, bap. Novemr 19, 1699.
John, Amos sons of Benjamin Fuller, bap. Decemr 10, 1699.
Benjam: Mary children of Benj: Fuller bapt: Decemr 21, 1699.
Obediah son of Robert Fuller, bap. Mar. 3, 1700.
Benjamin, Nicholas sons of Nicolas Ide, Timothy son of John Reed, also Elizabeth daughr of Josiah Carpenter, bap. March 24, 1700.
Mary daughr of Phillip Walker, bap. March 31, 1700.
Oliver, Hezekiah sons of Jabesh Brown, Bap. May 5, 1700.
Hector, (Negro man servant of Benj. Allen,) bap. May 26, 1700.
James son of Jonathan Viall, bap. July 14, 1700.
An daughr of Mr. Lowe, bap. Sept. 1, 1700.
James son of Thos. Cooper, John son of Hezekiah Peck, bap. Oct. 13, 1700.
Sarah daughr of Samll Newman, & Mercy daughr of Saml Pamer, bap. Feb. 2, 1700–1.
Elijah son of Nat. Carpenter, bap. Mar. 30, 1701.
Rebeckah daughr of Benj. Wilson, bap. Aprll 6, 1701.
Rebeckah daughter of Jabesh Brown, bap. April 20, 1701.
Hannah daughr of Nat. Whittaker, also Noah & Saml sons of David Newman, bap. April 27, 1701.
Ephraim son of Joseph Ingraham, bap. May 11, 1701.

Rebeckah daugh[r] of Jethniel Peck, Peter son of Abia Carpenter, Freelove & Abigail daugh[s] of Daniel Smith, also Peter & Judah, children of Nat. Cooper, bap. May 25, 1701.
David son of David Carpenter, Sam[l] son of Sam[l] Loe, John son of Joseph Bucklen, John son of John Smith, bap. June 8th, 1701.
Joshua son of Benj. Fuller, bap. June *ult*, Sabbath.
Daniel son of Tim. Ide, bap. July 14, 1701.
Isaac & Rebeckah children of Abraham Follet, bap. July 21, 1701.
Jonathan son of Mr. Jonathan Viall, bap. Aug. 17, 1701.
Esther Greenwood, Nathan son of John Pain, also Sarah daugh[r] of John Lane, bap. August 24, 1701.
Hannah daughter of David Newman, & Abigail daugh[r] of John Follet, bap. August 31, 1701.
Mercy daugh[r] of Joseph Titus, bap. Sept. 28, 1701.
Hephzibah and Martha daugh[s] of Joseph Dagget, bap. Dec. —, 1701.
Judah daugh[r] of Is: Reed, bap. Dec. 10, 1701.
Nat. son of Nat. Cooper, bap. Jan. 25, 1701–2.
David son of Daniel Smith, Jain daugh[r] of Phillip Walker, bap. March 29, 1702.
Daniel son of Sam[l] (——), Martha daugh[r] of James Sabin, bap. April 12, 1702.
Mary daugh[r] of Sam[l] Cooper, bap. June 7, 1702.
Stephen son of Joseph Peck, and Joseph son of Jethniel Peck, bap. 14 June, 1702.
Eliezar son of Sam[l] Palmer, bap. July 12, 1702.
Mary daugh[r] of Leonard Newsom, bap. 2 August, 1702.
Elizabeth daugh: of Cornet Walker, bapt: Aug. 16, 1702.
Jerusha dau: of Jabesh Brown, bapt: Sept. 27, 1702.
Rachell daughter of Sam[ll] Lowe, bapt: Novemb: 1, 1702.
Benj., Jonathan and Hannah, children of Benj. Wilson, bap. Nov. 14, 1702.
Sarah daugh[r] of John Reed, April 11, 1703.
Mary daugh[r] of Joseph Ingraham, Experience daugh[r] of Goodman Wedge, bap. May 9th, 1703.
Sarah daugh[r] of Baruck Buckland, bap. June 22, 1703.
Jonathan son of John Smith, bap. July 1, Sab: 1703.
Dan. son of Nat. Carpenter & Margaret daugh[r] of Nat. Whittaker, bap. 18, 1703.
Joseph son of John Follet, bap. March 25, 1703.
Benjamin son of Cornet Walker, Melatiah son of John Lane and John son of Sam[l] Titus, bap. —— 15, 1703.
Martha d. of John Hunt, bap. Aug. 29, 1703.
Hannah daugh[r] of Sam[l] Peck, bap. Sept. 12, 1703.
Lidia daugh[r] of Joseph Titus, bap. Sept. 19, 1703.
Ebenezer, Nath[l], Thomas sons of Nath[l] Peck, bap. Sept. 26, 1703.
Gideon son of John Pain, Christopher, Ichabod, Dan, Peter, Mary, children of Rich[d] Bowen, bap. Oct. 10, 1703.
Henry, Paul, Sam[l], Thom., Will[m], Phebe, children of Paul Healy, bap. Jan. 2, 1703–4.
Rachel daugh[r] of Jos. Buckland, bap. Jan. 30, 1703–4.
Nat. son of Phillip Walker, bap. Feb. 6, 1703–4.
Ruth daugh[r] of Elisha Maye, bap. March 12, 1704.
John son of Benj. Viall, bap. Mar. 19, 1704.
My own daugh[r] Elizabeth, bap. April 4, 1704.

Israel son of Joseph Dagget, bap. April 30, 1704.
Ruth, daugh^r of Saml Cooper, bap. May 7, 1704.
Jonathan & Hannah children of Jonathan Carpenter, bap. May 21, 1704.
An, daugh^r of Jethniel Peck, bap. May 28, 1704.
Abigail daugh^r of James Sabin, bap. June 25, 1704.
Margaret daugh^r of David Newman, bap. 23 July, 1704.
Persis daughter of John Follet, bap. August 6, 1704.
Isaac, Samuel, Grace, Experience children of Saml Sabin, and Noah and Miriam children of Noah Carpenter, bap. Aug. 13, 1704.
Eben. son of Eben. Smith, bap. August 27, 1704.
Elizabeth daugh^r of Paul Healy, Sept. 2, 1704.
Sarah daugh^r of Ichabod Bozzard, bap. Sept. 14, 1704.
Elizabeth daugh^r of Solomon Miller, bap. Oct. —, 1704.
Francis son of Benj. Wilson, bap. 8 Oct. 1704.
Amos son of John Shepherdson, and Rebeckah daugh^r of Noah Peck, bap. Novem. 19, 1704.
Abiel son of Benj. Fuller, and Sarah daugh^r of Noah Carpenter, bap. Dec. 1704.
Solomon son of Danl Smith, bap. Feb. 18, 1704.
John son of Joseph Tree, bap. March, ult. sabbath, 1705.
Rachel daugh^r of Saml Peck, bap. April 22, 1705.
Mary daugh^r of Abia Carpenter, bap. April 29, 1705.
Joseph son of Joseph Ingraham, bapt: May 27, 1705.
Lydia daught: of Jos. Peck, bapt. June 17, 1705.
James son of Geo. Bastoe, bap. May 6, 1705.
Rachel daugh^r of Nat. Carpenter, bap. May 20, 1705.
Jonathan, Jacob, Elisha, Ephraim, Daniel sons of Timothy Bliss, Abraham son of Joseph Follet, bap. May 24, 1705.
Noah son of Noah Peck, & Rich^d son of Rich. Bowen, bap. July 8, 1705.
Edward son of Saml Daye, bap. July 15, 1705.
Elizabeth daughter of John Lane, bap. July 29, 1705.
Anne daughter of David Newman, bap. August 26, 1705.
Abigail daugh^r of John Wedge, bap. Sept. 30, 1705.
Miriam daugh^r of Jonathan Bliss, bap. Oct. 14, 1705.
Nat^l son of Benj. Viall, bap. Nov. 11, 1705.
Jonathan son of Jonathan Amsbury, bap. Dec. 9, 1705.
Obadiah son of John Reed, bap. Jan. 13, 1705–6.
Martha daugh^r of Jonathan Carpenter, bap. Feb. 17, 1705–6.
Eben. son of Eben. Smith, bap. Mar. 17, 1706.
Nathl son of Paul Healy, bap. Mar. 24, 1706.
Mehitabel daugh. of Saml Cooper, bap. Mar. ult. 1706.
Elizabeth daugh^r of John Streeter, bap. May 19, 1706.
Benj. son of Jethniel Peck, bap. 26, 1706.
Martha wife of Elisha Peck, and Nehemiah son of Joseph Buckland, bap. July 14, 1706.
Richard, Sarah children of Henry Joslen, bap. July 28, 1706.
Elizabeth d. of Benjamin Willson, bap. Aug. 4, 1706.
Asa son of Jabesh Brown, bap. Aug. 25, 1706.
Mercy daugh^r of Saml Sabin, bap. Sept. 15, 1706.
Benj., Jonathan sons of Banfield Capron, Stephen son of Noah Carpenter, Mary daugh^r of Ichabod Bozzard, bap. Sept. 29, 1706.
David Walker son of Phillip Walker, Saml son of John Follet, & Margret daugh^r of Joseph Peck, bap. Oct. 13, 1706.

Mary daughter of Abraham Follet, bap. Oct. 20, 1706.
Ranur daugh^r of John Pain, bap. Nov. 17, 1706.
Abijah daugh^r of Joseph Titus, bap. Dec. 8, 1706.
Hannah, daugh^r of Ephraim Maye, bap. Feb. 23, 1706–7.
Bridget daugh^r of Henry Joslen, bap. Mar. 16, 1707.
Daniel son of Nat. Peck, & Saml son of Samuel Peck, bap. April 13, 1707.
James son of John Streeter, bap. May 4, 1707.
John son of John Fuller, bapt. May 18, 1707.
Bennet son of Joseph Ingraham, bap. June 29, 1707.

Priscilla wife of Eben. Smith, Constant son of Jonathan Viall, Ebenezer son of John Lane, & Jael daugh^r of Elisha Peck, bap. July 13, 1707.

Esther wife of Thom. Tingley, Sarah daugh^r of Jonathan Amesbury, William son of Will Bishop, Zeruiah daugh^r of Richd Bowen, Cornelius son of Abia Carpenter, James son of James Jordan, Patranelle, daugh^r of Hezekiah Peck, Elizabeth daugh^r of Jethniel Peck, Abigail daugh^r of Eben. Smith, Abishai son of Jonathan Carpenter, Jonathan, Nat., Hannah children of Jonathan Chaffey, Sam^{ll} son of Benj: Willson, Edward, Obad: sons of Obad: Carpenter, Nat. son of Danl Smith, David son of Nathl Peck, Henry son of Henry Joslen, Asa son of Noah Carpenter, Martha daugh^r of Samuel Cooper, Abigail daugh^r of Danl Perrem, John son of John Shepherdson, Stephen son of Stephen Pain, David son of Joseph Buckland, Joseph Buckland, Jun., Zach. Carpenter, his wife Martha, his child^n Zack. and Keziah, together with Caleb son of Goodman Lyon, all bap. April 17, 1709.

Mary Rowland and Smith her son, Ephraim son of Ephraim Carpenter, Ebenezer son of James Jourdan, and Patience daugh^r of Deacon Perry, all bap. May 1, 1709.

Daniel Allen and Christian his daugh^r, Mercy wife of John Marten, Comfort son of Josiah Carpenter, and Phebe daugh^r of Joseph Titus, Elizabeth wife of Paul Healy, Lydia daugh: of Jabesh Brown, Esther Greenwood, Joseph son of Jonathan Vial, Elizabeth daug^r of John Follet, Ichabod, Beriah children of Danl Reed, John son of John French, Susannah daugh^r of Danl Perrem, Ephraim son of Ephraim Maye, Daniel son of Nat. Wilmeth, Thomas son of Danl Allen, Sarah daugh^r of Saml Cooper, Mary wife of James Read, James, Elizabeth, Mercy, Susannah children of James Read, Dorothy daugh^r of Nat^h Chaffey, Edward son of Stephen Pain, Mary daugh^r of Noah Carpenter, Ebenezer son of Paul Healy, Aaron son of James Read, Ruth daugh^r of Benj. Willson, Thom. son of Benj. Vial, Mercy daugh^r of Solomon Miller, Solomon servant of Is. Peck, Martha daugh^r of Zach Carpenter, Andrew negro man servant of Ensign Ide, Uriel son of Richd Bowen, Abraham, Abiel children of Abia Carpenter, Jonas son of Hen. Dyer, Jonah son of John Titus. Urania daugh^r of Doct. Bowen, Jerusha daugh^r of Elisha Peck, Saml, Eben., Dorothy & Ruth children of Saml Fuller, Elizabeth daugh of Leiv: Hunt, Johanna daugh^r of John Smith, Timothy, Ephraim, Thomas, Elisab: children of Tho. Tingley, Elizabeth, Mary children of Nat^l Shepherdson, Jonathan son of John Fuller, Caleb, Johannah, Dorothy children of Eben. Walker, Hannah daugh^r of Noah Peck, Henry son of Ich. Boz., Esther daugh^r of Jos. Buck, James son of James Buck, John son of Jabesh Brown, Abigail, Mary, Esther, Rebeckah daugh^{rs} of Ensign Dean, Jacob Ide & Sarah his wife, Saml Tingley, John Ide, Patience Ide, Jacob son of Jonathan Amesbury, Danl son of Jonathan Chaffey, Unice daugh^r of Elisha Peck, Abigail daugh[r] of Daniel Read, Sarah daugh[r] of Jacob Ide, Timothy son of Sam[l] Fuller, Edward son of Sam[l] Bishop, Jonathan Carpenter, Sarah wife of Nat. Perry, Saml son of N. Read, Ichabod son of Sam[l] Brown, Josiah, Robert, Sarah, Elizabeth children of Robert Fuller, Mary daugh[r] of Silas Titus, Mehitabel d. of Nat[l] Willmarth, Elizabeth daugh[r] of John Streeter, Benj. son of Jonathan Viall, Mehitabel daugh[r] Nath[l] Peck, Elizabeth daugh[r] of Dan[l] Allen, Tho. Amesbury son of Daniel, Daniel Perrem, Priscilla daugh[r] of Sam[l] Daye, Elizabeth daugh[r] of Eben. Walker, Eliza. Susan daugh[r] of George Hill, Jonathan son of John Follet, Mary daugh[r] of Mich. Pullen, Ruth daugh[r] of Solomon Miller, Caleb, Tho., Experience children of Tho. Amesbury, Esther daugh[r] of Dan[l] Smith, Esther dau. of Dan. Reed, Bethya daugh[r] of Benj. Willson, Elizabeth daugh[r] of Edward Glover; John son of Sam[l] Bliss, Hannah daugh[r] of John French, Ruth daugh[r] of Sam[l] Walker, Miriam daugh[r] of Jonathan Chaffey, Nat[l] son of Nat[l] Reed, Mary daugh[r] of Joshua Amesbury, Susanna daugh[r] of Mr. Sam[l] Vial, Tim. son of James Buckland, Mary daugh[r] Jonathan Bliss, Sarah, Elizabeth d[rs] of Israel Sabin, Sam[l] son of Sam[l] Cooper, Thom. son of Thom. Reed, (Inspersion?) daugh[r] of Elisha Peck, Elizabeth daugh[r] of Jabesh Brown, Nat[l] son of Jacob Ide, Solomon son of Nat[l] Peck, Hannah daugh[r] of Ensign Viall, Daniel, Elisha, Jabesh, Eliezar, Bethia child[n] of Dan[l] Carpenter, Hannah daugh[r] of John Lion, Dan[l] son of Dan[l] Read, Mary daugh[r] of Sam[l] Fuller, Sarah wife of Dan. Brown, Sarah daugh[r] of Dan[l] Brown, Abigail daugh[r] of Benj: Wilson, Mercy daugh[r] of Jonathan Amesbury, Jonathan son of Joseph Buckland, Hannah daugh[r] of Sam[l] Woodword, Will. Blanding, Will., Elizabeth children of Will. Blanding, Will[m], John, sons of Mich. Pullen, Mary daugh[r] of John Robinson, Susan, George, Nat. son of Nat[l] Willmath, Jane wife of Joseph Titus, John son of Sam[l] Thurston, Michael, Stephen children of Joseph Titus, Daniel son of Noah Whittaker, Martha daugh[r] of Eben. Walker, Mary daugh[r] of J. Jordan, Benj. son of Elisha Maye, Eben. son of John Titus, John son of John Perren.

DISMISSIONS FROM THE FIRST CHURCH OF SANDWICH, MASS., 1749-1818

Copied by FLORENCE CONANT HOWES

1749. 29 Jan. voted to dismiss Mercy Hall, (once Fish) from this Chh. & recommend her to notice of the Chhs in Hebron.

1749 10. Dec: Martha Hatch (once Garret) by Consent of ye Chh dismissed & recommended to the Chh in Falmouth.

1749/50 11 March. Voted to dismiss Patience Ellis (once Blackwell) ye wife of ye Revd. mr. Jon^th^ Ellis & recommend to ye Chh. of Christ in Littlecompton. (or Second)

1750. 24. May. Seth Pope a member of this Chh. by Consent of ye Chh. (at his Request) dismissed & recommended to ye Chh in Lebanon under ye pastoral Care of ye Rev^d^ mr. Sol. Williams.

1751. Mary Bates (now Bumpus) a member of this Chh. at her Request dismissed y^th^ Consent of ye Chh & recomended to ye Chh in Wareham.

—— 18 Augt. Israel Tupper jun^r^ & Wife members of this Chh at their Request dismissed & recommended to ye Chh in Dartmouth. wth Consent of Chh

1752. 7 Jun. Phebe Ellis this Chh consented to dismiss & recomend to the Chh in Plimpton under the pastoral Care of Mr Parker.

1752. 9 Aug. Zaccheus Handy a member of this Chh. by Consent of ye Chh dismissed to ye first Chh in Rochester under ye Pastoral Care of mr. T. Ruggles.

1752. 9 Aug. Thos. West & his Wife members of this Chh. by Consent of ye Chh dismissed to ye Chh in Dartm^o^- under ye Pastoral Care of mr Jn. Cheever.

1756 Oct 31. Bethiah Freeman a member of ye Chh dismis^d^ by Consent of Chh. to ye Chh. in Middleborough under ye Care of Rev mr Conant

1762 Jun 27. Joanna Paige (once Freeman) a member of ye Chh dismis^d^ by Vote of Chh to ye Chh. in Hardwick. Mr White Pastor.

1762 Aug. 29. Mary Nye (now Barlow) of ye Chh dismis^d^ & recommended by Vote to 2 Chh - Rochester mr Hovey Pastor

1764 Apr. 15. John Peckum a member of this Chh dismissed & recomended, by Vote to ye Chh of X in Bristol & Oct 20th 1765. S^d^ John Peckum returning from Bristol & being dismissed from y^t^ Chh was rec^d^ here again

1766 18. May. Eliz^a^ Pike (now Lombard) dismissed by Vote & recommended to the Chh in Truro—

1766. 12. Oct. Rebecca Swift (wife of Lem^l^) dismissed & recommended by Vote to ye Chh in New-Braintree under the Pastoral Care of ye Rev^d^ mr Benj^a^ Ruggles

1768 2 Oct. Martha Robinson (W. of Dunson) dismiss'd & recomended by Vote to ye Chh in New Rutland

1769. 6 Aug. Wm. Basset & Lydia Basset his wife dismissed & recommended by Vote to ye 1st. Chh in Rochester

1770. 28 Oct. Sol^o^ Foster & Rebecca Foster his Wife dismiss'd & recommended by Vote to 2^d^. Chh. in Brookfield

1772. 30 Aug. Hannah Smith (once Barlow) (now wife of James Smith) dismiss'd & recommended by Vote to W. Chh. in Barnstable

1775. 15. Oct. Tho[s]. Smith Esq[r]. of Falm[o] dismissed & recommended by Vote to the Chh in Falmouth

1780. 1 Oct. Jn[o] Peckam & Mercy Peckham his Wife dismissed & recommended to the Chh in Petersham by Vote-

1784 21 Mar. Hannah Bourn[?] (wife of Stephen) dismissed & recommended to y[e] Chh in Wareham by Vote

1785 Silas Tupper & Hannah Tupper dismissed & recommended to ye Chh in Barnard July 3d.

1789 Jan[y]. 25 Voted to dismiss Hannah Jones (wife of John) & to recommend her to the church in Barnard.

1790. Anna Williams, now Smith, wife of Rev[d] Jonathan Smith of Chilmark, dismissed, & recommended to y[e] chh in that place, Jany 17.

1791. June 12. Abigail Smith, now Tobey, wife Thomas Tobey of Rochester dismissed & recommended to the2[d] church in that place.

1791. August 30. Elizabeth Fish, wife of Ellis, dismissed & recommended to the church in Randolph, State of Vermont.

1799 Jan[y] 27. Elizabeth Fish wife of Alven, dismissed & recommended to the church in North-Granville, State of N. York- afterwards recommended to the chh in Randolph, Vermont.

1799 July 21. Bathsheba Crocker, now Haskell, dismissed & recommended to the Church in Rochester.

1800. July 6. Mary Yost, now Nye, dismissed & recommended to the church in Falmouth.

1801. April 12. Esther Tupper, now May, dismissed & recommended to the church in Winthrop. October 4. Hannah Fish, wife of Stephen, dismissed & recommended to the Church in Randolph, State of Vermont.

1808 March 20. Elizabeth Atkins, now Jenkins, dismissed & recommended to the West church in Barnstable.

1815 Sept. 24. Alden Gifford & Mercy his wife, dismissed & recommended to the chh in Locke, State of N. York.

Nov. 22 Ruth Fish now Howland, dismissed & recommended to y[e] chh in Lee.

Aprl 2. 1818. Jane, wife of Rev. P. Crocker, dismissed & recommended to the Chh. in Dartmouth——

SCITUATE AND BARNSTABLE CHURCH RECORDS.

[Copied for the Register by Amos Otis, Esq., of Yarmouth Port, Ms. Mr. Otis says, "The dashes and asterisks occur in Dr. Stiles' MS., and I presume indicate imperfections in the original record." The Rev. Mr. Carleton of West Barnstable made a copy, from that made from the original by President Stiles, and preserved in the Library of Yale College. Mr. Carleton's copy was used by Mr. Otis, who, with Mr. C., collated his own with another copy of the original, made by the Rev. Mr. Russell. "In the list of baptisms at Barnstable," Mr. Otis says, "I have supplied the omissions from the copy made by Rev. Mr. Walley, and they are distinguished by being placed in brackets. In the Barnstable Church Records I find several matters of historical interest, which I will hereafter transcribe for the Register. I observe that at the settlement of Rev. Jona. Russell, senior, [in 1683], Anna Lothrop, widow of Rev. John, and Sarah Walley, widow of Rev. Thomas, were living in Barnstable; that Isaac Robinson, (son of Rev. John) was then a resident at 'Martin's Vineyard.'"

Explanatory Letter of Dr. Stiles.

Newport, Rhode Island, Aug. 24, 1769.

Records of the Beginning of the Churches of Scituate and Barnstable, which I copied from an original manuscript in the autographical hand-writing of Rev. John Lothrop their first Pastor. This MS. I found A. D. 1769, in the hands of the Revd. Elijah Lothrop of Gilead in Connecticut. I account it the more valuable as these chhs. of Scituate and Barnstable have no records till many years after their gathering, particularly tho' the chh. of Scituate was gathered January 8, 1634, yet there are no chh. records to be found there, (as the Rev. Mr. Grosvenor, the present Pastor, told me 1768), for more than seventy years till Mr Pitcher's day, who begun their present chh Records at his ordination, Sept. 24, 1707, from which time they have been kept regularly. EZRA STILES.]

Toutching the Congregation . . . .* of Christ collected att Situate.

The 28 of September 1634, being the Lord's day, I came to Situate the night before and on the Lord's day spent my first Labours, Fornoone and afternoon.

Upon the 23 of Novemb. 1634 or Breathren of Situate that were members at Plimoth were dismissed from their membershipp, in case they joyned in a body att Situate.

Uppon January 8, 1634, Wee had a day of humiliation and then att night joyned in covenaunt togeather, so many of us as had beene in Covenaunt before. To witt,

2. Mr. Gilsonn and his wife
4. Goodman Anniball and his wife
6. Goodman Rowly and his wife
8. Goodman Cob and his wife
9. Goodman Turner
10. Edward Foster
11. Myselfe
12. Goodman Foxwell
13. Samuell House
15. Mr. Hetherly and his wife joyned Janu. 11, 1634.
17. Mr. Cudworth and his wife joyned Janu. 18, 1634.
18. Hennery Borne joyned Janu. 25, 1634.

1635.

22. Symeon Hayte and Bernard Lumbard and their wives joyned Aprill 19, 1635.
23. Thomas Boiden, Brother Gilsons Servaunt joyned May 17, 1635.
25. My Wife and Brother Foxwell's wife joyned having their dismission from elsewhere June 14, 1635.
26. Jane Harrice joined, June 21, 1635.

* The blank should probably be filled with—*and church.* Ed.

27. Goody Hinckley joyned, Aug. 30, 1635.
28. Goodman Lewis Senior joyned, Septemb. 20, 1635.
29. William Betts joyned, Octob. 25. 1635.
30. Egglin Hanford, Mr. Hatherleys Syster joyned Novemb. 21, 1635.
31. Goody Turner joyned Janu. 10, ——
32. Hennery Ewell joyned April 3, 1636.
33. Elizabeth Hammon my Sister having a dismission from the church at Watertowne was joyned, Aprill 14, 1636.
34. Thomas Lappham joyned Ap. 24. 1636.
35. Goodman Steadman joyned July 17, 1636.
36. Isaac Robinson and my Sonn Fuller joyned haveing their Letters dissmissive from the church att Plimoth unto us Novemb. 7, 1636.
38. Mr. Vassel joyned Novemb. 28, 1636.
hee the first joyned in our new meeting house.
39. Goodman Crocker and
40. Goody Foster joyned } Decemb. 25, 1636.
42. Goodman Chittenden and his wife joyned Febru. 12, 1636.

1637.

43. Goodman Cointer and Goodman
45. Kinricke and his wife joyned } Aprill 9, 1637.
46. Goody Merrett and
47. Goodwife Stedman joyned } April 16, 1637.
48. Goodman Besbitch joyned April 30, 1637.
49. Goodman Shelly
50. Edward Fitts Surrandolfe
51. My Sonn Thomas Lothropp
52. Sarah Tinker } joyned May 14, 1637.
53. Goodwife Robbinsonn
54. Goodwife Stockbridge
55. Judeth Vassell } joyned July 16, 1637.
56. Richard Syllice
57. Christopher Cointer } joyned Decmb. 24, 1637.
58. Goodman Jackson
59. Thomas King } joyned Febru. 25, 1637.
60. My Brother Robert Linnell and his wife having a letter of dismission
61. from the church in London joyned to us Septemb. 16, 1638.
62. Syster Bourne dismissed from the church att Hingham joyned November 11, 1638.

Austin Berce joyned Aprill 29, 1643.
Isaac Wells joyned May 27, 1643.
Mestresse Bursly joyned July 22, 1643.
Our Brother Fittsrendolfe wife joyned August 27, 1643.
Alice Goodspeed joyned Decemb. 31, 1643.
Roger Goodspeed joyned July 28, 1644.
Judith Shelley joyned by dissmission from ye church att Boston, August 25, 1644.
Mestres Chamberlin joyned Octob. 6, 1644.
John Smith joyned Octob. 13, 1644.
Nathaniell Bacon joyned May 3, 1646.
Joshua Lumbard joyned March 14, 1646, expressing in his confession many sadd temptations God carryed him through for the space of Some 8 yeares, repeating of many Sweete Scriptures.

Dolor Davis and his wife being dismissed from the church att Duxbury, was joyned to ours, Aug. 27, 1648.
Hannah wife of Nathaniell Bacon joyned March 18, 1648.
Sarah the wife of Henry Cobb, and the wife of Samuell Mao joyned to the Congregation in my house, Janu. 20, 1649.
Brother Beirce his wife and Goody Chippman joyned to the Congregation ye day yt Brother Dimmick was invested Elder Aug. 7, 1650.
Susannah wife of John Smith joyned Jun 13, 1652.
John Finney joyned August 29, 1652.
John Chippman joyned Janu. 30, 1652.

Situate Baptized.—Mary, Daughter of Humfery Turner baptized att my first House Janu. 25, 1634,
uppon which day alsoe wee first enjoyed in ye same place the blessed privilidge of the Sacrament of the Lord's Supper.
James the sonn of Mr. Cuddworth bapd. in his house May 3d, 1635.
Mary ye daughter of Brother Foxwell bapd Aug. 30, 1635.
Elizabeth daughter of or Syster Hinckley bapd. Sep. 6, 1635.
Timothy Sonn of Edward Foster baptd. March 7, 1635.
Bernabas Sonn of John Lothropp bapd. June 6, 1636.
Elizabeth Daughter of Samuell House bapd Octob. 23, 1636.
Joseph Sonn of Humfery Turner baptizd. ye first in or new meeting house Janu. 1, 1636.
Mary Daughter of or Brother Cobb March 26, 1637.
Deborah Daughter of or Brother Anniball May 7, 1637.
John Sonn of Brother Crocker Jun. 11, 1637.
Hannah Daughter of Robert Shelley July 2, 1637.
Mary Daughter of James Cudworth July 23, 1637.
Hannah Daughter of or Syster Stockbridge, baptized Septem. 24, 1637.
Mary Daughter of Bernard Lumbard Octob. 8. 1637.
Elizabeth, Daughter of Goodman Steadman Novemb. 24, 1637.
Susannah Daughter of Isaac Robinsonn Janu. 21, 1637.
Samuel Sonn of Samuell Hinkley Febru. 4, 1637.
Samuel Sonn of my Sonn Samuel Fuller Febru. 11, 1637.
John Sonn of George Lewice March 11, 1637.
1638.—Anna Daughter of Samuell Jacksonn March 25, 1638,
who was borne tow or three yeares before.
John Sonn of John Winter April 1, 1638.
Timothy Sonn of Edward Foster }
Martha daughter of Brother Foxwell } Aprill 22, 1638.
Elizabeth daughter of Thomas Lappham and }
Thomas Sonn of Goodman Rogers of Duxberry } May 6, 1638.
Jonathan Sonn of James Cudworth Septem. 16, 1638.
Deborah Daughter of George Kinerick Novem. 25, 1638.
Samuell Sonn of Samuel Hinckley Febru. 10, 1638.
Nathaniel Sonn of Umphrey Turner March 10, 1638.
1639.—Hannah Daughter of Brother Cobb Octob. 5, 1639.

Since our Comeing to Barnstable, Octob. 11, 1639.

Abigaill daughter of John Lothropp ye 1st. }
Martha daughter of Bernard Lumberd ye 2d. }
and Mary daughter of Robert Shelley ye 3d. } Novem. 2 1639.
att Mr Hull's house.* }

* Doct. Stiles' copy, "att my house;" Barnstable Ch. Rec., "att Mr. Hull's House."

Elizabeth daughter of Brothr Crocker Decb. 22, 1639.
Timothye Sonn of Mr. Dimmock Janu. 12, 1639.
Hannah daughtr of William Betts Janu. 26, 1639.
Thomas Sonn of Hennery Cogaine March 2, 1639.
John Sonn of Hennery Ewell March 9, 1639.
Naomi daughter of Mr. Hull March 23, 1639.
1640.—John Sonn of Isaac Robinsonn, April 5, 1640.
Nathaniell Sonn of Edward Fitts randolfe August 9, 16[40.]
Mary Daughter of Thomas Lothropp Octob. 4, 1640.
John Sonn of Phillipp Tabor dwelling att Yarmouth a member of the church att Watertowne, Novem. 8, [1640.]
Manasseh Sonn of Mr. Mathews of Yarmouth Janu. 24, [1640.]
Bethiah daughter of Robert Linnell Febru. 7, 1640.
Bethiah daughter of Samuell Jackson March 14, 1640.
1641.—Ruth daughter of Richard Foxwell April 4, 1641.
Israell Sonn of James Cudworth April 18, 1641.
Ruth daughter of Joseph Hull May 9, 1641.
Thomas Sonn of Thomas Holland May 9, 1641.

Both these from Yarmouth, ye parents of the first beeing yett members with us—ye Father of the 2d beeing a member of a Separated Church in Old England

Jabez Sonn of Bernard Lumberd July 4, 1641.
Ephraim Sonn of George Lewice July 25, 1641.
Sarah daughter of Samuell House }
Sarah daughter of Samuell Fuller } August 1, 1641.

both which were borne at Situate.

Jedidiah Sonn of Thomas Lumbard Septem. 19, 1641.
Sarah daughter of Abraham Blush Decemb. 5, 1641.
Bathsua daughter of John Lothrop Febru. 27, 1641.
Patience daughter of Brother Cobb March 13, 1641.
1642.—Mehetabel daught. of Maister Dimmock, Aprill [18, 1642]
Bartlemew Sonn of James Hamling April 24, [1642.]
Nathaniel Sonn of Edward Fitts Randolfe May 15, [1642.]
Samuell Sonn of Brother Willi. Crocker July 3, 1642.
Joseph Sonn of John Hall July 3, 1642.
Samuel Sonn of Samuell Hinckley July 24, 1642.
John Sonn of Robert Shelley July 31, 1642.
Isaac Sonn of Isaac Robinson Aug. 7, 1642.
Hannah Daughter of Thomas Lothropp Octo. 18, 1642.]
Hester daughter of Samuell Jackson Febru. 5, 1642.
Eben-ezer Sonn of Hennery Ewell }
Samuell Sonn of William Betts, } Febru. 12, 1642.
John Sonn of Hennery Cogain }
1643.—Joannah daughter of James Cudworth March 25, 1643.
Mary and Martha, daughters of Austen Berce baptized May 6, 1643.
Mary daughter of Mrs. Bursley July 29, [1643.]
Beniamin Sonn of Brother Lumbar, Senior baptized August 5, 1643.
Nathaniell Sonn of Roger Goodspeed Janu. 14, 1643.
Sarah, daughter of George Lewice Febru. 11, 1643.
Samuell Sonn of Thomas Allen Febru. 18, 1643.
Priscilla daughter of Austin Berce baptized Mar. 11, 1643.
1644.—Ruth daughter of Dollar Dauice March 24, 1644.
John Sonn of Samuell Hinckley May 26, 1644,

our meeting beeing yt day att ye end of Mr. Bursley's house.

Mary daughter of Samuell Fuller — Jun. 16, 1644.
John Sonn of James Hamling — Jun. 30, 1644.
Thomas Son of Thomas Lothropp — July 7, 1644.
Lyddia Daughter of Thomas Huggins — July 7, 1644.
Beniamin Sonn of John Hall — July 14, 1644.
Mary daughter of Thomas Hinckley — Aug. 4, 1644.
Shubeall Sonn of Mr Dimmick — Septemb. 15, 16[44.]
John Sonn of Mr Bursley — Septemb. 22, 1644.
Mary daughter of Edward Fittsrandolfe — Octob. 6, 1644.
Samuell Sonn of John Smith — Octob. 20, 1644.
Hannah daughter of Nathaniell Bacon — Decemb. 8, 1644.
Gershom Sonn of Brother Cobb, baptizd — Janu. 12, 1644.
Feare, daughter of Isaac Robinsonn — Janu. 26, 1644.
John Sonn of John Lathropp baptizd. — Febru. 9, 1644.
Job Sonn of William Crocker, baptized — March 9, 1644.
Hope Sonn of William Betts, baptizd. — March 16, 1644.
1645.—Mary daughter of Hennery Cogaine baptizd — Aprill 20, 1645.
Sarah daughter of John Smith baptizd — May 11, 1645.
John Sonn of Samuel House baptizd — May 18, 1645.
John Sonn of Roger Goodspeed baptizd — June 15, 1645.
Sarah daughter of Hennery Ewell, — Sept. 14, 1645.
Samuel Sonn of Anthony Anniball and
Nathaniel Sonn of John Hall } — Febr. 8, 164[5.]
Nathaniell Sonn of Nathaniell Bacon — Febru. 15, 16[45.]
Johannah daughter of Maistr Bursley — March 1, 1645.
1646.—Sarah Daughter of Austen Beirce &
Mary daughter of Thomas Huggins } — March 29, 16[4]6.
Elizabeth Scudder and Sarah Scudder
Daughters of John Scudder. } — May 10, 1646.

William sonn of William Nichollson and
Mary daughter of Edward Sturgess and
Dorcas daughter of Andrew Hallet and
Abigail daughter of John Joyce
} of the church of Yarmouth, bee-ing ye 2d Sab-baoth of or meet-ing in our new meeting-house. — Baptised June 1, 1646. being Children

John Sonn of Thomas Allen — Septemb. 27, 1646.
Henry Sonn of Henry Cogaine — Octob. 11, 1646.
Eben-ezer, Sonn of John Smith and
Melatiah Sonn of Thomas Lothrop } — baptised Novem. 22, 1646.
Sarah daughter of Thomas Hinckley, bapizd — Decemb. 6, 1646.
Samuell Sonn of Samuel Jackson, bapt — Februa. 7, 1646.
1647.—Mercye daughter of Isaac Robinsonn baptized — July 4, 1647.
Marye daughter of Roger Goodspeed — Septemb. 12, [1647.]
Josiah Sonn of William Crocker bapd — Septemb. 19, 1647.
Sarah daughter of James Hamling bapd — Novemb. 7, 1647.
Mary, Daughter of John Smith bapd — Novemb. 21, 1647.
Abigaile daughter of Austen Beirce bapd — Decemb. 19, 1647.
Isaac and Marye Twinnes, children of
John Smallee of Nosett and
Elizabeth daughter of Thomas Huggins } — baptized February 27, 1647.
Gershom, Sonn of John Hall bapd — March 5, 1647.
1648.—Eleazar, Sonn of Henry Cobb baptizd — Aprill 2, 1648.
Joseph Sonn of Abraham Blush, bapd — Aprill 9, 1648.

Hannah daughter of Edward Fittsrandolfe, and
Jonathan Sonn of Andrew Hallet of Yarmouth } baptized Aprill 23, 1648.
Mary, daughter of Nathaniell Bacon bapd August 20, 1648.
Mehetabell, daughter of Thomas Allen
Melatiah daughter of Thomas Hinckley } bapd Novemb. 26, 1648.
1649.—Elizabeth daughter of Mr Bursley baptized by my Brother Mao March 25, 1649.
John, Sonn of Roger Else of Yarmouth baptized here Aprill 15, 1649.
Esek Sonn of Anthonye Anniball baptized Aprill 29, 1649.
Bethiah, daughter of Thomas Lothropp bapd July 23, 1649.
John sonn of Thomas Huggins baptizd Aug. 5, 1649.
Hannah, daughter of Austen Beirce baptizd, Novemb. 18, 1649.
Mary the daughter of Samuell Mao and Samuell the sonn of Samuell Mao were baptized Febru. 3, 1649.
Eleazer Sonn of James Hamling baptizd March 17, 1649.
1650.—Benjamin, Sonn of Roger Goodspeed baptizd May 19, 1650.
Marye, daughter of Edward Fittsrandolfe baptized June 2, 1650.
Eleazar, sonn of William Crocker baptizd July 21, 1650.
Alice, daughter of Abraham Peirce of Plimoth, beeing brought hither by Goody Scudder, his wives Syster and here baptized July 21, 1650.
Dorcas, daughter of John Smith and
Elizabeth daughter of John Chipman } baptizd Aug. 18, 1650.
Hannah daughter of Samuell Mao bapd Octob. 20, 1650.
Samuell, Sonn of Nathaniell Bacon, baptized March 9, 1650.
1651.—Hannah, daughter of Thomas Hinckley and
Thomas, Sonn of Thomas Huggins baptized, } Aprill 27, 1651.
Thomas Sonn of Samuel Fuller baptized, May 18, 1651.
William, Sonn of John Hall baptized June 8, 1651.
Mehetabell, daughter of Hennry Cobb baptizd Septemb. 7, 1651.
Israel, Sonn of Isaac Robinson and
Hannah daughter of John Scudder } baptized Octob. 5, 1651.
Joseph, Sonn of Austen Beirce baptised Janu. 25, 1651.
John, Sonn of John Smith baptised Febru. 22, 1651.
1652—Abigaile, daughter of Joshuah Lumber baptizd Aprill 11, 1652.
John Sonn of John Bursley baptizd Aprill 11, 1652.
Israell Sonn of James Hamling baptizd June 25, 1652.
Hope, daughter of John Chipman baptizd Septemb. 5, 1652.
John Sonn of Edward Fittsrandolfe baptizd Janu. 2, 1652.
Samuel, Sonn of Thomas Hinckley baptizd Febru. 20, 1652.
Shubaell, Sonn of John Smith baptizd March 13, 1652.
1653.—Jacob, Sonn of Isaac Robinsonn and
Ruth, daughter of Roger Goodspeed } baptizd May 15, 1653.
Elizabeth daughter of Samuel Mao baptizd May 22, 1653.
Beniamin Sonn of John Hall baptizd May 29, 1653.
John, Sonn of John Finny baptizd being of ye age of 14 yeeres July 31, 1653.
Hester, daughter of Austen Beirce baptizd Octob. 2, 1653.
Desyre daughter of Anthonye Anniball and
Hannah daughter of Thomas Huggins baptizd } Octob. 16, 1653.

Buryed Situate.

Brother Anniball buryed a Maide child beeing borne somewhat before the tyme, Aprill 8, 1635.
A Servaunt of Goodman Lewice Junior buryd March 6, 1635.

Jervice Large, Goody Hinckleys Servaunt buryed Aug. 9, 1636.
George —— dwelling wt Goodman Hinckley buryed March 25, 1637.
Timothy, the child of Brother Foster buryed Decemb. 5, 1637.
One Linkes Slaine by a bow of a tree in ye cutting downe of the tree, March 6, and buryed in the way by John Emmersonn's House neere Goodman Stockbridge March 10, 1637.
Goodman Standley buryed May 7, 1638.
My child a daughter buryed unbaptized July 30, 1638.
A maide child of Goodmā Twisdens borne before its time buryed Aug 9, 1638.
Jonathan Sonn of James Cudworth, Sept. 24, 1638.
Deborah daughter of George Kenrick Febru. 21, 1638.
Brother Jacksonn's wife of a consumption March 4 or 5, 1638.
Goody Standley's youngest child, a little girle Aprill 19, 1639.
Goodman Pryer June 22, 1639.
Buryed at Barnstable 1640.—Imprimis, Timothy Sonn of Mr Dimmick in the lower Syde of the Calves pasture, June 17, 1640.
Goodman Hinckley's child, a daughter uppon their comeing hither buryed unbapized, July 8, 1640.
Nathaniell sonn of Edward Fittsrandolfe Decemb. 10, 1640.
Mr. Bursley's child dyed Suddenly in the night and buryd Janu. 25, 1640.
Goodman Hinckley's child a twinn buryed upbaptized Febru. 6, 1640.
Mr. Dimmick his 2 childrē twinnes a sonn and a daughter unbaptized, buried March 18, 1640.
Goodman Hinckley's other twinn buryed March 19, 1640.
Samuell Sonn of Goodmā Hinckley buryed March 22, 1640.
Elizabeth Ewer daughter of my daughter Lothropp Aprill 9, 1641.
Mrs. Carseley miscarried May 7, 1641.
John Oates buryed a little from Mr Carsleys house May 8, 1641.
1642 *Buryed at Barnestable.*—The Stillborne mā child of Hen. Borne May 28, 1642.
1643.—Syster Anniball buryed ye 13th day of ye tenth month 1643 in in the Calves pasture.
1644.—A man child of James Cudworth, unbaptized June 24, 1644.
Benjamin Sonn of John Hall July 23, 1644.
Liddia, daughter of Thomas Huggins, buryed July 28, 1644.
John Sonn of Mr Bursley buryed Septeb. 27, 164–.
1645.—Mary, daughter of Hennery Cogaine buryd May 3, 1645.
**Samuell Sonn Anthony Anniball* *March* 8, 1645.
1646 Buryed.—John Foxwell Son of Brother Foxwell Sept. 21, 1646.
The Stillborne child of James Hamling buryed, Decemb. 2, 1646.
Eben—ezer Sonn of John Smith buryd Decemb. 17, 1646.
**Samuel Son of Samuel Jackson.*
1648.—Patience wife of Henrye Cobb buryed May 4, 1648, the first that was buryed in our new burying place by our meeting house.
Mary, wife of Thomas Huggins buryed 28 of July, 1648.
Elizabeth daughter of Thomas Huggins buryed Decemb. 8, 1648.
1649.—The Stillborne man child of John Carseley buryd Apr. 11, 1649.
The wife of Isaac Robinsonn buryed June 13, 1649.

And a maide childe borne of her before the ordinary tyme buryed the week before.

---

* Erased in Dr. Stiles' MS.—E. C. H.

The maide childe of William Carseley buryd Septemb. 6, 1649.
Mary daughter of John Scudder buryed Decemb. 3, 1649.
A man childe of John Lothropp dyeing immediately after it was borne buryed Janu. 25, 1649.
1650.—Thomas Blossome and Samuell Hollet drowned att the Harbour of Nocett att their first Setting out from thence aboute a fishing voyage Aprill 22, 1650.
The Stilleborne maide childe of John Chipman buryed Sept. 9, 1650.
The Still borne maide childe of Joseph Lothropp buried the 20th day of Novemb. 1651.
John Sonn of John Smith buryed Febru. 24, 1651.
1652.—Mehetabell Daughter of Henry Cobb buryed March 8, 1652.
Mary daughter of Goodman Chase ye elder buryed Octob. 28, 1652.
1653.—Syster Finney buryed May 7, 1653.
Syster Blush buryed May 26, 1653.
Marryed.—My Sonn Fuller and my Daughter Jane, and Edward Foster and Lettice Handford marrd att Mr. Cudworths by Captaine Standige Aprill 8 ye 4th day of the weeke, 1635.
Isaac Robinsonn and Margaret Handford contracted at Mr. Hetherlyes June 27, 1636, and by him Robert Shelly and his wife from Boston marryed here Sepemb. 26, 1636.
Mr Tilldens two daughters mard March 13, 1636.
Edward Fittsrandolfe and Elizabeth Blossome, May 10, 1637.
Richard Syllice and Egglin Handford ye 6th day of ye weeke beeing the 15 day of Decemb. 1637.
My sonn Emmersonn and my daughter Barbarah marryed att Duxberry by Captaine Standige, July 19, 1638.
William Wills and Luce his wife marryed att Plimoth att ye tyme of ye Court either upon the 4 or 5 day of Septemb. 1638.
Goeing White and Elizabeth, Servaunt to Mr. Hatherlye and John Winchester and Hannah Syllice, marryed here att Situate by Maister Gin-ings Octob. 15 1638.
Henery Ewell and Sarah Anniball at Greens-harbour by Mr. Winsloe Noveb. 23, 1638.
William Betts and Alice—Goodmā Ensygnes maid in the Bey Febru. 27 or 28, 1638.
Marryed Since my Comeing to Barnestable beeing Octob. 11, 1639.—William Carseley and Mrs. Mathews Systr of Yarmouth and Mr Bursley and Mr Hulls daughter aboute the 28 of Novemb. 1639, att Sandwidge.
My Sonn Tho. and Brother Larnetts daughter, widdow Ewer, in the Bey Decemb. 11, 1639.
My sonn Samuell, and Elizabeth Scudder marryed att my house by Mr. Freeman, Novemb. 28, 1644.
Thomas Blossome and Sarah Ewer marryed att my sonn Thomas his house by Mr Freeman June 18, 1645.
Edward Coleman of Boston and Margarett Lumbard marryed att Nocett by Mr. Prince Octob. 27, 1648.
Thomas Huggins and Widdow Tillye marryed at Norett by Mr. Prince Novemb. 3, 1648.
John Davis and Hannah Linnett marryed att Nocett by Mr Prince March 15, 1648.
Richard Childe and Mary Linnett marryed the 15th day of October 1649 by Mr. Collier at my Brother Linnett's house.

Henry Cobb and Sarah Hinckley marryed by Mr. Prince Dec. 12, 1649.
John Fennye and Syster Coggin marryed by Brother Thomas Hinckley; they the first marryed by him July 9, 1650.
John Allen and Elizabeth Bacon marryed alsoe by him Octob. 10, 1650 both Anabaptists.
Joseph Lothropp and Mary Ansell marryed alsoe by him Dec. 11, 1650.
Henry Tayler and Liddiah Hatch marryed alsoe by him Dec. 19, 1650.
Joshuah Lumber and Abigaill Linnett marrd by him May 27, 1651.
David Lynnett and Hannah Shelley marryed by him March 9, 1652.
Thomas Lewice and Mary Davice marryed by him June 15, 1653.

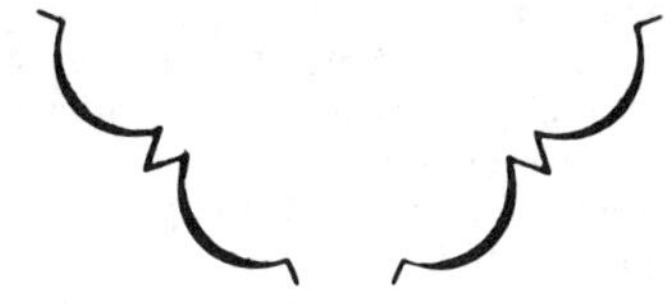

Situate. Some Acts of y^e People & Church.

Dayes of Humiliation.

1. Novemb 6 1634 att Mr. Cudworths
2. Decemb. 25 1634.
3. Janu: 8 1634 which day wee joyned into covenant
4. Janu: 19, 1634 att my house, uppon wch day I was chosen Pastour & invested into office
5. August, 13, 1635 y^t God might direct us for further officers particularly for Deacons.
6. Decemb. 15, 1635 our Brother Cobb was invested into the Office of a Deacon.
7. Aprill. 7, 1636, in respect of p^rsent outward Scarcity & in respect of helpes in ministery, as also for the p^evention of Enemies.
8. Novemb. 11 1636 Ffor a blessing uppon their consultation aboute the Lawes for Settling the State of this Patten. Some differences arising aboute some p ticulars in iudgement, wee were by the mercye of God reconciled joyntly. Aprill ye 27, 1637 Ffor this purpose I had taught out of Gen. 13, 8.
9. June 22, 1637. Ffor Successe in warring against the Pequeuts, as alsoe for composing differences amongst o^r Breathren in ye Bey, & for helpe in ye Ministerye in respect of our selves.
10. Ffebru. 22, 1637, partly for the tow Deacons more, but especially for our removeall, as alsoe for the remoueall of these Spreading opinions in the churches att ye Bey, as alsoe for the preventing of any intended evill against the churches here, uppon wch day Broth Ffoster, and Brother Besbetch were invested into the office of Deacons
10. Novemb. 29, 1638 especially for the grevious affliction uppon Gods people in Jermany & elsewhere, as alsoe for our further Successe in our Remoueall.
11. Janu. 23 1638 Wee that were for Sippicann devided into 3 companies in this service for preventing of exceptions. Wherein wee petitioned for Direction in Electing of Committyes for the Setting downe of our towne, for good orders in beginning and proceeding, for more Spirituall helpe for us, as alsoe for our Breathren here.
12. June. 13, 1639, First occasioned by reason of much drought, as alsoe in regard of great dissentions in generall, as alsoe for Gods directing & provideing for us in the point of remoueall.

June 26, 1639. Ffor the presence of God in mercy to goe with us to Mattakeese.

Dayes of Humiliation at Barnestable.

Octob. 31, 1639. Ffor the grace of our God to Settle us here in Church Estate, and to unite us togeather in holy Walkeing, and to make us Faithfull in keeping Covenaunt wth God, & one to another.

2. Aprill. 15, 1640, att the investing of my Brother Mao into the office of a Teaching Ellder, uppō whome, my Selfe Brother Hull, Brother Cobb Lay on hands, and for the Lord to finde out a place for meeting, & that wee might agree in it, as also y^t wee might agree aboute ye division of Lands.
3. August 5 1640, in the behalfe of England, the Sadd differences be-

twixt it & Scotland as alsoe for direction and Successe in our private com̄union and for the continuance of peace & good agreement amongst us.

Dayes of Humiliation.

March 24, 1640. In regard of England & for others, & our owne particular, our Brother Cooper then invested into ye office of a Deacon, I Brother Mao, & brother Cobb laying on handes.

June, 10. 1641 In regard of ye wett & very cold Spring, as also for the quelling of Strange & heretical tenets raised principally by the Ffamilists, as alsoe for ye healing of a bloodye Coffe amonge children especially at Plimouth.

Septemb. 23, 1642 Ffor old England & Ireland, & for the prvention of ye Jndians here, & our owne Sinnes

March. 21, 1642. Ffor old England—and Ireland—& for or owne P ticulars

May ye 10th 1643 Ffor old England—& for our Selves.

October, 3, 1643. Ffor old England & for ourselves.

Dayes of Humiliation.

November ye 30, 1643. Ffor old England & for ourselves

August ye 1, 1644. Ffor old England & for ourselves

August, ye 14, 1645, Ffor old England & for ourselves

July ye 22, 1646 Ffor the reforming of things amongst ourselves, especially ye Deadnes & drousynes in publique dutyes.

Aprill the 22, 1647, partly for old England, partly for the State of this countrey, to prevent any evill that might come by their Synod, or by discontented persons. & partly for ourselves Ministery with us beeing uppon the pointe to be laid downe, & spirituall deadnes yett much continuing, & for reforming other thinges.

July the 22, 1647, partly for old England, partly for this countrey As alsoe in Speciall for ourselves for the redressing of our Spirituall evills, & for a Sanctifyed use of Gods generall correction of Sickness uppon every ffamily—in a manner of every one in every ffamilye.

Dayes of Humiliation.

March 16 1647 principally for old England requested by Sr Thomas Fairfax and the parliment, in regard of many feares of the presbyterians, with many others to raise upp new warres in the Land, and notwithstanding all their troubles much pride & excesse abounding, with an unframed Spiritt to humble themselves by praying and Seeking unto God.

November 15, 1649—principally for old England & alsoe for our owne particulars, God's hand beeing uppon us by Sicknesses & disease many Children in the Bey dyeing bye the Chin cough & the pockes & wee beeing alsoe many visitted to Sicknesses or diseases.

December 19, 1649. In regard of our owne particulars, very many amongst us beeing visitted with colds and coughes in a strange manner especially children theire coughing constraineing casting & bleeding att ye nose & mouth, & principally in regard of my selfe beeing brought very low by the cough & Stitch in my left side, by reason whereof I was detained from Ministery seven weekes, but our God was intreated to shew mercye

Dayes of Humiliation.

August, ye. 7, 1650. Ffor the investing of my Brother Dimmicke into the office of an Ellder

Aprill y[e] 9, 1651. Ffor getting & obtaining an able & godly minister or Teacher from God. As alsoe in speciall & particular in the behalfe of my selfe toutching the Recovery of my weakeness, and the raising upp of my Spirit with Cheerfullnes in performance of my Ministerye Upon which day I was att home beeing weake.

March, 30, 1653. Ffor the preservation of Gods people in this Land from the purposed invasion of the Indians, especially the Narragansetts, being instigated thereunto by the Dutch even to cutt of all y[e] Inglish, uppō which day I was absent frō the people, haveing a great cold & cough, & alsoe for our owne countrey beeing att warr with the Dutch.

May 11, 1653. Beeing requested by our Governours, Maiestraites & Commissioners being att Boston in Consultation togeather aboute their present conceived dangerous Estate of the Inglish, and haveing sent Messengers unto the Dutch here in this Land.

Contraction.

John Smith & Susannah Hinckley contracted at o[r] Syster Hinckleyes house—P me I: Lo:

May 22, 1643, exercised uppon this Scripture Lett yo:[r] conversation be as becomes y[e] Gospel Phil: 1. 27.

Our Syster Hull renewed her Covenaunt with us, renounceing her joyneing wth thē . . . . . at Jarmouth confessing her evill in soe doeing w[t] Sorrow . . March. 11, 1642.

Henry Actkins: & Elizabeth Wells contracted by my Brother Cobb, att Brother Wells his house July y[e] 9, 1647.

Dayes of Thanksgiveing.

1. Decemb: 22, 1636, in y[e] Meetinghouse, beginning some halfe an houre before nine & continued untill after twelve a clocke, y[e] day beeing very cold, beginning w[t] a short prayer, then a psalme sang, then more large in prayer, after that an other Psalme, & then the Word taught, after that prayer—& thē a psalme,—Then makeing merry to the creatures, the poorer sort beeing invited of the richer.

October. 12, 1637, performed much in the same manner aforesaid, mainely for these tow particulars. 1. Ffor the victory over the pequouts, y[e] 2. Ffor Reconciliation betwixt Mr. Cotton, and the other ministers.

Dayes of Thanksgiveing since we came to Barnestable.

Decemb. 11, 1639, att M[r]. Hulls house, for Gods exceeding mercye in bringing us hither Safely keeping us healthy & well in o[r] weake beginnings & in our church Estate. The day beeing very cold o[r] praises to God in publique being ended, wee devided into 3 companies to feast togeather, some att Mr Hulls, some att M[r] Maos, some att Brother Lumbeids senior.

Dayes of Thanksgiveings

September 2, 1641, Especially for good Tydeings frō old England, of amost happie beginning of a gracious Reformation both of Religion and State, the Lord in the tyme of Reformation, discovering & also preventing sudry Treasons, one amongst others was this a diabolicall intendment to sett y[e] cittye of London on fire att six sundry places haveing an armie prepaired uppon it to massacre whome they thought good, but that snare is broken, & Gods people in England are yett preserved blessed be God. as alsoe for Gods good hand of providence over us & his churches here.

Octob. 14, 1647. Both in regard of our native countrey, God in his infinite Love, goeing on with his Servaunts raised upp by him to doe his worke there, giveing them admirable successe, and in particular by the hand of Sr Thomas Ffarefax and his armie, as alsoe for many singular mercyes bestowed uppon us here, and in and among the rest, ffor recovering us, & all the people in this countrey from a generall visitation of sickenes, none or very few dyeing of it, and likewise for continueing our outward peace and Liberty, with the blessed privilidges of Gods House.

Dayes of Thanksgiveing.

March 13, 1649. Ffor God his gracious restoreing & recovering manye of our Little children who hadd beene very nigh death with very violent coughings, & my selfe alsoe in my left syde God beeing by the congregation sought unto herein, and beeing intreated, shewing mercy, wee as duely required, rendered praise.

January, y[e] 8, 1650, Ffor gods exceeding mercyes towards old England in the prosperous good successe of the armie there under the conduct of Coronall Crumwell, & particularly for their prevaileing against the Rebells in Ireland, as alsoe their admirable victory against the Scotts, The Inglish beeing but a Leaven thousand att the most, But they at Least one & twenty thousand.

March 24, 1652. Ffor the Lords admirable powerfull workeing for old England by Coronall Crumwell & his Armye against the Scotts

June 14, 1652, w[ch] should have beene a day of humiliation for want of Raine, but the Lord giveing us in mercy on the day before raine, itt was turned into a day of Thankesgiveing

Children of the Church—

Martha Ffoxwell dwelling w[t] Goody Hull summoned before y[e] congregation in publique, & delt w[t] & reproved for ioyneing w[t] her Dame in beateing the maide Servaunt of Samuell Mao. delt w[t] for itt, Ffebru. 22, 1651.

David Linnell & Hannah Shelley beeing questioned by the church uppon a publique ffame toutching carnall & uncleane carriages betwixt them tow, beeing in y[e] congregation confessed by them, they were both by the sentence & joynt consent of the church, pronounced to bee cutt off from that relation w[ch] they hadd formerlye to the church, by virtue of their parents covenaunt, acted & done by y[e] church, May 30, 1652. —They both were for their ffaults punished with Scourges here in Bernestable by the Sentence of Magestracye Jun. 8, 1652

Excommunicated out of the Church of Christ att Situate

Christopher Winter, partlye for marrying of one M[rs] Cooper a woman of scandalous carriage, beeing vaine, light, proud, much given to scoffing: and partlye for his unchristian passages in his proceeding, as,

1. making a soelaim covenaunt to her not acquainteing any of the Brethren therewith.
2. pretending sometymes to us hee had made noe absolute covenaunt with her
3. Breakeing frequentlye his word & promise, in promising to us hee would not proceed therein without the church consent.

Lastly in his finall Summons before the church he seemed to cast asper. tions uppon the church, & raither to justifye than to humble himselfe-Exco m̄unicated, Aug. 26, 1658.

Hereunto M[r] Vassell didd not consent, no[r] Goodman Raylings, who purposely went out of the congregation before w . . . . delt with him.

Nor Mr. Hetherly who . . . . discontent to ye Greife of . . . . went out, while wee w . . . . dealeing wth him.

att Barnestable

William Carsley excommunicated & cast out of the church att Bernestable for carnall carriages [&c., ... 9 lines omitted . . . . . .] Hee was alsoe much given to Idleness, & too much to Jearing and had of late tymes slacked in the duty of prayer, observed alsoe by some to bee somewhat proud.—The sentence of Excommunication was pronounced by Brother Mao. William Carsley tooke it patiently. Excom̄unicated, Septemb. 5, 1641

Mr. Hull excommunicated for his willfull breakeing of communion w^t us, & joyneing himselfe a member w^t a companie at Yarmouth to be their Pastour: contrary to ye advise and Counsell of o^r Church, May, 1, 641

Mr. Hull in the acknowledgeing of his sinn, & renueing his covenaunt was received againe into fellowshipp with us, August, 10, 1643.

Samuell Jacksonn excom̄unicated, & cast out of ye church for Lyeing & sundry suspitions of stealeing, as pinnes wch were John Russells & divers other thinges from others, Ffebru: 23, 1644.

Samuell Jacksonn in the acknowledging of his Evills, & renueing his covenaunt, was received againe into fellowshipp with us January 31, 1646, & went from us to live at Situate, beeing necessitated thereunto. Ffebru: 10, att night 1646.

Goodye Shelley excommunicated & cast out of ye church though absent, for shee would not come, setting att nought ye messengers of the church sent to her, principally for slaundering of 2 systers, Syster Wells & Syster Dimmick saying syster Dimmick was proud, & went about telling Lyes but could never prove any thinge by any Testimonye. And alsoe afirming that myselfe & Brother Cobb, to my syster Wells att her house didd talke of her, uppon a day I went to see . . . . Hukkins beeing sicke there, wee denying . . . . noe speach of her . . . . ontinued from tyme to tyme to affirme it as confidently as if shee hadd hadd a spirit of Revelation, Saying also that I had confessed it, and after didd denye it: and that all the church knew it was soe, but durst not or would not speake, And that I deserved raither to bee cast out then shee, for shee was innocent but I was guilty. Shee would never be convinced of any of her conceived Jealousyes, was wondrous perremptorye in all her carriages, many tymes condemning the Breathren that they delt not with her in a way of God. wee had long patience towards her & used all courteous intreatyes & persuasions, but the longer wee waited the worse shee was. The Beginning of all this was, because uppon some occasion shee was not called to a christian meeting which some of the Systers hadd appointed among themselves. many untrueths shee haith uttered from the beginning unto the end of this busynes. Excommunicated, June, 4, 1649.

Barnestable.

Brother Henricke dealt w^tall for Lyeing & other evills—& some satisfaction given by him, Aboute latter end of Octob. 1640.

We had a meeting uppō ye 7th of Decemb. 1640 to expresse our greivances w^tout takeing exceptions, but noe great satisfaction was in ye thinge, yet wee concluded peaceably & promised not to speake of each others infirmityes to any, but to deale in a way of God, onely we thought it expedient by way of advise to propound a case in generall not nameing any person. Mr Tillden & some of o . . . . concluded peace with Love be . . . . . . them, Decemb. 28, 1636, att our Brother Gillsonns. Divers of the people haveing some dista . . . . to Mr Vassell, & hee wt them, were recon . . . . . . & they & all of us in generall renued our covena . . . . wt God & one another to walke in Love & peace, Novemb. 20, 1637, att our Brother Gillsonnes, & there & att that tyme, Wm Tillden & Hennery Lazell were agreed, or Brother Hennery confessing his faileings in some termes towards him.

Christopher Winter beeing exhorted by my selfe, & other of ye Breathren, Goodmā Anniball, Goodmā Cobb, Goodmā Bessbetch Mr Cudworth, Goodmā Turner, Isaac Robbinson, Goodmā Rowly, either to desist in his suite toutching Mrs Cooper, or at least not to proceed in it, unlesse it might bee apparent that the Lord went on along with him in the same, wch exhortation after many Wordes hee accepted of & promised soe to doe, March 21, 1637, att my house.

The Houses in ye planta . . . . . .
Situate
Att my Comeing hither, onely these
wch was aboute end of Sept. 1634

1. Mr Hatherlyes
2. Mr Cudworthes . . . . now Goodmā Ensiynes
3. Mr Gillsonns
4. Goodman Anniballs — all wch small plaine pallizadoe Houses
5. Goodman Rowlyes
6. Goodman Turners . . now Goodmā Jacksons
7. Goodman Cobbes . . . now Goodmā Rowlyes / now Goodmā Viñalls
8. Goodman Hewes . . . now Goodmā Coopers
9. Edward Ffosters

Since my Comeing to Octo. 1636

10. My House
11. Goodman Ffoxwells . . Hennery Boornes
12. Watts house
13. Goodman Chittendens
14. Goodman Lumbers . . wch is bought by goodmā Winter
15. My sonnes
16. Goodman Haites . . . . wc Mr Bower haith bought
17. Goodman Hatches
18. Goodman Lewice senior . . now Goodmā . . . .
19. Goody Hinkles
20. Mr Tildens

. . . The Smiths. Goodmā Haits brother

22. Goodmā Lewice junior
23. Goodmā Rowleyes new house, on his Lott.

1636.

24. Mr Vassells
25. Goodman Stockbridge ye wheeler
26. Goodmā Stedmans
27. Goodman Lumbers uppon his Lott
28. Meeting House erected & on L . . . Aug. ye 2d & 3d dayes 1636. Exercised in Novemb. 10. & 11. 1636
29. Isaac Robinsons . . . . now Goodmā Twisdens
30. Mr Cudworths house on his Lott

31. Brother Turners, on his Lott
32. Brother Cobbs, on his Lott
33. Goodman Hewes on his Lott
34. Goodman Lewice on his Lott . . now Goodmā Williams
35. Goodmā Lewice Juniour his new house haveing sold his other to Mr Dorkins
36. Goodman Kenricks
. . . Mr Bavers
. . . The young Mās. Edward Ffittsrandolfs
now Goodmā Syllice
39. Robert Shellyes
40. John Hanmers . . . . now Goodmā H . . . .
41. Henney Ewells . . wc Goodmā Merritt haith bough
42. Mr Hatches new House
43. George Suttens
44. Brother Crockers junior
45. John Emmersonns
46. Goodman Hommes
47. John Hammers on the Cliffe
48. Goodmā Birds

1637

49. Isaac Robinsonns new house
50. Goodmā Ffoxwells on his Lott
51. My house on the Lott erected Sept. 26
52. Thomas Lapphams
53. Goodman Edendens
54. Goodmā Hylands
55. Goodmā Rawlings on his Lott
56. William Parkers
57. Goodmā Lewice seniors

[*Note by Dr. Stiles.*]

Transcribed from the Revd John Lothrops originall MS. being all the Entries I find in his own Hand writing

By Ezra Stiles Augt 24, 1769

Children Baptized In * * * ye 17 of Sept 1683, by Pastr. Russell.

Thankful of Barnabas & Susanna Lathrop.
Martha of Jonath: & Martha Russell.
Elizabeth of Saml[l] & Hannah Allyn.
Thomas of Willm. & Mary Troop.
John & Mary of Job & Hannah Crocker.
Benjamin, of John and Mary Phinney.
Mehetabel of Saml. & Mary Stoare.
Job of James & Mary Hamblin Junr.
☞ Thomas of John & Mary Dunham. He being a member at Plymouth.
Mehetable and Benjamin, of Shubael & Joanna Dimock.
Saml. of Nathanl & Sarah Bacon.
Martha of James & Sarah Cob.
Mehetabel of James & Sarah Gorham.
Thankfull of George & Mary Lewis.
Barsheba of Thomas & Elizabeth Lumbart.

Anno. 1683 10th month.

☞ Gershom of John & Bethia Hinckley. She only being A member * * * * this Ch & under Ch censure of admonition wn. this child was baptized, yet ye child being born before she was dealth with * * Ch; they yrfore recd. her child to ye ordinances 10ber 1683.

March 23. 8¾

Jedadiah, Thomas, Experience and & Hannah, of Jedadiah Lumbart ye eldest of ym are * * * 15 years old wn baptised, & yet it was by virtue of his father's covenant, for upon examination of him before the elders of ye Ch, he appeared not of maturity to act for hims: * * Covenants hims: also did desire to bee under his father's tuition and Comand & in his Covenant, yrfore he was Judged on In adult * * * & rcd baptism as one In minority.

March 30. 1684.

James of Barnabas and Susanna Lathrop.

Apr. 6, 84.

Saml. of Jonathan & Hope Cob.
Elisha & Alice of Robert and Patience Parker.
☞ Richard Child senr admitted and baptised May 4. 1684.
Saml. and Thomas, of Richard & Elisabeth Child.
Ebenezer, of John & Mary Dunham.
John, Mary, Martha, Hannah and Elizabeth, of John & Mary Lathrop.
Joanna of Shubael & Joanna Dimock.

8 : 2, 84.

Patience of Thomas & Elizabeth Lumbert.
Jun. Mary of Willm & Mary Troop.
Jan: 28. Jonathan of John & Mary Lathrop.

Feb. 25. Sam[ll]. of Sam[ll] & Mehetable Worden he being A member first Cch at Boston.

March 16 84 Sarah ye wife of Jabez Lumbart, she being y[n] admitted * *

John, Matthew and Bernard, of Jabez & Sarath Lumbard.

Benjamin of James & Mary Hamblin.

Thomas of Increase & Elizabeth Clap.

Sam[ll].
Mercy
Patience
Susanna
Experience } of Bartholomew & Susanna Hamblin.

Mercy of James & Sarah Cob.

June16,85. Abigail of John & Sarah Hamblin.

Samuel of Barnabas & Susanna Lathrop.

July 26. Thomas of James & Hannah Goreham.

30 Jonathan of John & Mary Phinney.

Elisha of Eleazar & Mehetable Hamblin.

1685. John of Jonathan & Martha Russell.

1686. Desire of John & Mary Dunham.

1686. Jonathan of Jonath. & Hope Cob.

Mercy, Stephen, Temperance, of John & Mary Gorham.

—86. Barnabas of John & Mary Lathrop.

Thomas of Sam[ll]. & Esther Stores.

Martha of Thomas & Elisabeth Lumbart.

87. Thankfull of Shuball & Joanna Dimock.

Mercy of James and Hannah Gorham.

Joseph, Mehetabel and Ichabod, of Eleazer and Mehetable Hamblin, y[e] 2 former of these were baptised Sept. 19, 1683.

12. Thomas, of Samuel & Mercy Prince.

Thankful of James & Sarah Cob.

Abigail of Jonathan & Marthy Russell.

10. Timothy of Richard & Elisabeth Child.

Elisha of John & Mary Dunham.

Behia of John & Hannah Fuller. She being A member at Boston.

1688. Dolor of John & Hannah Davis, he being y[n] admitted.

9[r] 30. Mehetable y[e] wife of Little John Fuller.
Elizabeth y[e] wife of Thomas Fuller. } They being admitted.

Octob. 21 Abigail of Elisha Paine.

Timothy, Joseph, Fear, Abigail, Mercy and Mary, of John Robinson, his 2 eld. Sons were adult, y[r]fore not baptised.

Samuel, Thomas, Shubal, of Mehetable Fuller.

Mary and Joseph, of Elizabeth Fuller.

William, Noah and Joanna, of Temperance Crocker.

Decemb 16 Joseph, Benjamin, Ebenezer and John, of Joseph Beare.

Esther of Samuell Storrs.

1 or 23. Joseph, Experience, Nathaniel and Mary, of Allin Nicholls.

febr. 10. Mary of Mercy Prince.

March 3[d] 1689.

John of Mary Gorham,

March 24. Ebenezer of Susanna Hamblin.

April 7. Hannah of John & Mary Phinny.

May 12. Abigail of John Lathrop.
Abigail and James, of Allin Nichols.
May 19. Thankfull of Mehetabell Fuller.
June 2. Hannah ye wife of Jonathan Crocker yn being admitted.
Joseph of James Gorham.

1690.
March 16. Jonathan of Jonathan & Martha Russell.
March 4. Thankful of Hannah Crocker.
Hanna of Dolor & Hannah Davis.
August 3d. Marth of Joseph & Temperance Crocker.
Enoch of Mercy Prince.
7r 21. Joseph of Hope Cob.
Shubal of Elisabeth Ewer.

* March 1691.
Sarah of Job Crocker.
22. John Davis junr was baptized being yn admitted into Ch.

April 19, 1691.
Thankful of John & Mary Gorham.
Josiah of Joseph Bearse.
John, Philip, Timothy, Nathan and Elisabeth, of Joanna Canon.
Apr. 26. Sarah, Anna and Mercy, of Jeremiah Pason.
May 3d Benjamin, John and Nathaniel, of John Davis junr.
May 10 Jabez of John Davis junr
Elizabeth of John & Mary Phinney.
of John Lathrop.
of James Gorham.
July 12. Mehetabell of Hannah y wife of Thô Lumbart—Junr
July 26. Thomas of Thomas Ewer.
Aug. 2. Sarah of Elizabeth Dimmock.
Aug. 23. Benjamin of John Dunham.
Aug. 30. Thomas, Samuel and John, of Samuell Chipman.
Septemb 6. John of John & Elizabeth Scudder.
Nathan and Reuben, of Experience Davis.
Nathaniel of Mercy Otis.
of Jane Claghorn.
8r 8th 1691 Reliance of Hannah Fuller.
Jan 24 Jabez Davis was baptized being newly admitted into Ch.
Abraham of Elisha Pain
* * of * * Phinney.

Anno 1692
March 4. Joseph of Samuel & Sarah Chipman.
March 27. Bathshua of Jabez & Experience Davis.
John Ewer of Thomas & Elizabeth.
James of James & Bethia Pain.
Thankful of Jane Claghorn.
April 3. John of John Hinckley Jnr.
April 17. Eleazer of Jonathan & Martha Russell.
Samuel of Jeremiah Bacon.
Jacob and Mary, of Mary, wife of James Lovell.
May 15. Isaac of Hannah, wife of Jonathan Crocker.
June 5. Shubael and John, of Mary Howland, Anno 1692, Octob. 30th.
Mercy of Samll & Mary Chipmen.
Job of John & Mary Gorham.

Novemb^{r} 13^{t}		
	Mercy	of Jno & Mercy Otis.
2th	Samll.	of Jabez & Experience Davis.
27	Bethia	of Susanna Hamblin.
June 5.	Thomas, Josiah, Ebenezer, Seth, Mercy, Mary, Alice and Malatiah of Malatiah Crocker.	
July ult.	Hannah	of Elizabeth Dimmock.
Sept. 18.	James	of Mary Lovel.
	Anne Howland, being then admitted.	
Jan 29.	Experience	of John Lathrop Senr
febr 5	Elizabeth	of Hannah Lumbart.
Anno 1693, March 5.		
	John	of Mercy Prince.
	Lydia	of Hope Cob.
Anno 1694.		
April 18.	Thomas	of James & Bethia Pain.
April 29.	Job	of Job Crocker.
May 6.	John	of John & Sarah Phinny.
	Patience	of Lydia Goodspeed.
June 17.	Sylvanus	of James Gorham.
	Lawrence	of Abigail Whippo.
	Thomas	of James Claghorn.
July 8.	Samuel	of Thomas & Elizabeth Fuller.
Aug. 12.	Shubal	of John Davis.
Aug. 19.	Ruth.	of Lydia Goodspeed.
	Reliance	of Hannah Crocker.
	Mary	of Elisabeth Dimmock.
Sept. 2.	Moody	of Jonathan & Martha Russell.
Sept. 3.	John	of Hannah Lumbert.
8^{r}. 6. 95.	Shubal	of Eleazer & Mehet Hamb * *
	Jacob	of Sam^{ll} & Sara Chipman.
	John, Mary, Sarah and Mehetable, of Mary Jenkins.	
9^{r} 3^{d}	Reliance	of Susan Hamlin.
9^{r} 18.	James	of Richard Chiles.
9^{r} 25	Barnabas	of Elizabeth Lathrop.
10^{r}. 9.	Nathaniel	of Thomas & Elizabeth Ewer.
Jan^{ry} 13.	James	of John & Elizabeth Scudder.
Feb^{ry} 3.	Anne	of Anne Howland.
17.	Experience	of Daniel & Mary Parker.
24.	Mary	of John & Thankfull Hinckley.
Anno 1695.		
June 23.	Joseph	of Jeremiah & Elizabeth Bacon.
July 7.	Gershom	of Hope Cob.
	Mercy	of Mary Lovel.
	David	of Elizabeth Linel.
Decemb^{r} 22	Mary	of Hannah, wife Andrew Lord.
Anno 1696.		
March 8	Bethia	of James & Bethia Pain.
15th	Daniel	of Daniel & Mary Parker.
April 5th	Mercy	of John & Mary Gorham.
	James	of John Davis.
19th	Thankfull	of Dolor & Hanna Davis.
	John	of Elisabeth wife of Thomas Fuller.

26th	Ebeneser	of James Gorham.
	Ebeneser	of John & Elisabeth Scudder.
May 17th	Jane	of Abigail wife of James Whippo.
24th	Isaac	of Jabez & Experience Davis.
June 9th		of Hanna wife of Andrew Lovell.
14th	Thankfull	of Hanna wife of Thomas Lumbard junr
21st	Thomas	of John & Sarah Phinny.

Samuell, Thomas, John, Mary, Sarah, Abigail and Elizabeth. of Phebe wife of Thomas Bump.

July 5th Jane of Phebe wife of Thomas Bump, ye girl being about fourteen or 15 years old, was examined, & being one of ye family & looked upon in her minority, was Baptised.

July 12th	Desire	of ye wife of Samll Annable
Aug 2	Jonathan	of Thomas & Elisabeth Ewer.
Sept 13.	Mehetable	of Ebenezer Phinney.
Octob 11.	Theophilus	of Elisabeth Dimock.
	Joseph	of Abigail ye wife of Israel Hamlin.
Novembr 1.	Jonathan	of Hannah wife of Jonathan Crocker.
Decmbr 20	Solomon	of John & Mercy Otis.
27th	Barshua	of John Lothrop.
Jan 24	Martha	of Jonathan & Martha Russell.

Jany 31. Joseph, John, Thomas, James, Samuel, Jabish, Hannah, Mary and Hope, of Thomas Huckins.

Anno 1697.

March 28	Abigail	of John & Thankfull Hinckley.
	Lydia	of Lydia Goodspeed wife of Ebenezer.

April 4 Israel, Thankful and Prudence, of Abigail wife of Israel Hamlin.

	Seth	of Samll & Sarah Chipman.
	John	of Ann wife of Isaac Howland.
ay 16	Mercy	of Richard Childs.
	Ebenezer	of John & Mary Davis.
June 27	Martha	of Mary, wife of James Lovell.

October 10 Samuel and Margaret, of Samuell Sheverick.

	Davis	of Job Crocker.
17.	Hezekiah	of Thomas & Elizabeth Ewer.
31.	Anna	of Patience ye wife of Samll Annible.
Novmbr 14	Thankfull	of Thomas & Mary Parker.
	John,	of Experience ye wife of Jabez Lewis.

Thomas and Bethia, of Samll Shiverick.

1698 March 20

	John	of Mary wife of John Clark.
March 27.	Jabesh	of Hanna wife of Thô Lumbart.
April 17	Georg	of Abigail Whippo.
24	Rebecca	of Daniel & Mary Parker.
	Mary	of Ebenezer & Susanna Phinney.
May	John	of Experience wife of Jabez Lewis.
29	Bethia	of James & Bethia Pain.
	Abigail	of Jabez & Experience Davis.

June 19 Moses Hatch who was then also admitted into Ch.

	Ebenezer	of Jeremiah & Elizabeth Bacon.
July 3.	Damaris	of Samuel Shiverick.

Moses and Hephzibeth, of Moses Hatch.

August 11 Jacob — of Susanna Shurtley A member of Plymouth.
Daniel — of Dollor & Hannah Davis.
Septr 11. Timothy — of Elizabeth Dimock.
Octobr 2^d Hannah, Desire, Nathaniel, Patience and John, of John Bacon.
Decemb^r 11 Mehetable — of Thomas & Elizabeth Ewer.
febry 19. Nathaniel — of Sam^ll Sturges.
1699, March 26. — of Joseph Bradford, Lately admitted, 7 Children, viz., Benjamin, Ebenezer, Nathan, Robert, Elizabeth, Rebecca, and Malatiah.
of Desire, wife of John Thatcher, by her husband Dimock—Thomas, Edward, Mehetable, Temperance and Desire.
April 9. Rebecca — of Mary, wife of James Lovel.
May 7. Samuell — of Jonathan and Martha Russell.
July 16. George — of Leift James Lewis, } both then admitted
Elizabeth — wife of Joseph Bodfish, } into Ch.
Noah — of Ann Howland.
Thankfull — of John & Thankfull Hinckley.
July 23. Edward & Thankfull, of John Lewis.
Aug. 6. Joseph of Joseph & Mercy Parker.
Aug 13. James, Ebenezer, Susanna and Sarah, of Ebenezer & Anna Lewis.
William, Timothy, Ebenezer, Mary, Sarah and Mercy, of Mary wife of Caleb Williamson.
Robert — of Jane Claghorn.
Margaret — of Abigail wife of Mr. James Whippo.
Aug 27. Philip — of John & Mary Jenkins.
Hannah — of Thomas Huckins.
Septr 17. Elizabeth — of Jeremiah & Elizabeth Bacon.
Hannah — of Hannah wife of John Whettone } Same
Temperanc — of Hannah wife of Benja. Lumbart } Woman.
Thankfull — of John Linel.
24 Jemima — of Abigail y^e wife of Israel Hamblin.
Octob^r 15 Remember — of Temperance & Joseph Crocker.
James — of Hannah wife of Jonathan Crocker.
Novmb^r 19. Jacob — of Jabez & Experience Davis.
Abigail — of John & Desire Thatcher.
Abigail — of Elizabeth wife of David Lorin.
Decemb^r 3_d 1699.
Mary — of Reliance wife of Nath^ll Stone
31. Samuel — of John Linel.
febry 18 Eleazer — of Isaac & Elizabeth Hamlin.
Jane — of Patience wife of Sam^ll Annable.
March 10 99–1700
Samuel, Sarah, Bathsua and Mary, of Benjamin Lumbart.
17. David — of Thomas & Mary Parker.
Nicholas — of John & Hannah Davis.
24. Ebenezer — of Elizabeth wife of John Dimock.
April 14 Martha — of Mary wife of Caleb Williamson.
21 Hanna and John Lathrop of Bethia Lathrop.
May 12 Thankfull — of Hannah wife of Andrew Lovel.
June 2^d Martha — of Ebenezer & Susanna Phinney.
Edward — of John Lewes.

July 14 Ellis wife of Benj. Hatch of Saconesset yn admitted also.
Benjamin of Ellis wife of Benjamin Hatch.
Solomon, Jethro and Zerviah, of Mary wife of Simon Athearn, of Tisbury, on Marthas Vineyard.
Samuel, John and Mehetable, of John Annable.
Aug. 11 Gershom of Hannah wife of Thô Lumbart.
Aug 18 Mary of James & Bertha Paine.
Aug 25 Job of Dolor & Hannah Davis.
Septr 1. Bethia the wife of Shubal Dimock. She was admitted Aug. 25.
Septr 15 Nathaniel of Jeremiah & Elizabeth Bacon.
Samuel of Samll & Prudence Lewis.
Febry 2 David of Nathll & Ruth Bacon.
Febry Reliance of John & Elizabeth Scudder.
Febry 23. John of John & Thankful Hinckley.
Mary of John Annable.
March 16, 1701.
Elizabeth of Abigail wife of James Whippo.
30 Lazarus of Mary wife of James Lovel.
April 6. Sarah of Joseph & Bodfish.
Ebenezer of Thomas & Mary Parker.
May 4th Solomon of John & Mary Bacon.
Hannah of Ebenezr & Anna Lewis.
June 1. Nathan of Henry Cob.
8 Nathaniel, John, Elizabeth and Edy, of Ellis wife of Benjamin Hatch of Falmouth.
Jedediah of John & Hannah Davis.
July 6. John of Samuel Sturgis.
July 20 1701.
Isaac of Isaac & Elizabeth Hamlin.
Benjamin of Jane wife of Shubael Claghorn.
Phebe of John Lathrop.
27 Elizabeth of John & Temperance Parker.
Aug 3 1701.
Annie ye wife of Joseph Hatch of Falmouth being admitted a Little before.
Joseph, Ichabod, Annie, Ruth and Rebeca, of Annie wife of Joseph Hatch.
7ber 7. Malatiah and Timothy, of Ellis wife of Benjamin Hatch.
Ebenezer and Mercy, of Ebenezer Hamlin.
7ber 14 Joseph of John & Mary Jenkins.
7r 28 Elizabeth of John Lewis.
8r 12th Lydia ye wife of Samuel Hatch of Suconnessit.
Hannah of Ellis wife of Benjamin Hatch.
9r 2. Thankfull of Thomas & Elizabeth Ewer.
9r 9th Keziah and Lydia, of Lydia wife of Samuel Hatch.
Sarah of John & Sarah Phinney.
1702. March 1.
Samuel of Patience wife of Samuel Annible.
April 19. Hannah of Daniel & Mary Parker.
26. Barnabas. of Samuel & Sarah Chipman.
Solomon of Elizabeth wife of David Loring.
June 7. Ebenezer of Annie wife of Joseph Hatch.

SCITUATE GRAVE YARD.

[Communicated by DAVID HAMBLIN.]

Barker, Deborah, wife of Samuel, died Dec. 11, 1738, aged 20 y. 26 d. Barker, Desire, wife of John, died July 24, 1706, aged 53 y. Barker, Sarah, widow of John, died Sept. 7, 1730, aged 70 y. Barker, John, Esq. died Dec. 1, 1729, aged 79 y. Buck, Abbah, dau. of Thomas, died Sept. 1, 1716, aged 2 mos. Barker, Hannah, wife of John, formerly wife of Rev. Jeremiah Cushing, died May 30, 1710, aged 46 y.

Cushing, Jeremiah, pastor of Northport, Scituate, died March 22, 1705–6, aged 52 y. Collin, Anthony, [without date.] Cushing, Jeremiah, died May 30, 1710, 46 y.

Dodson, Abigail, died Nov. 16, '95, aged 44 y.

Gannet, Hannah, died July 10, 1700, aged 78 y. Gannet, Micah, died Oct. 1696, aged 77 y. Gannet, Mary, wife of Matthew Gannet, died June 9, 1713, aged 35 y. Gannet, Joseph, Jr., died March 20, 1723, aged 33 y. Gannet, Joseph, died July 19, 1714, aged 66 y.

Hatch, Elizabeth, wife of David, died March 13, 1764, aged 56 y. Hyland, John, died June 19, 1789, aged 85 y. Hyland, Mrs. Fanna, died Sept. 7, 1803, aged 29 y. Hyland, Capt. Oliver, Jr., died Aug. 21, 1801, aged 29 y.

Jacobs, David, Jr., died Jan. 3, 1714, aged 24 y. Jacobs, Mistress Sarah, died Nov. 29, 1711, aged 17 y. Jacobs, Dea. David, died Feb. 10, 1748, aged 85 y. Jacobs, Sarah, wife of David, died Sept. 24, 1723, aged 52 y.

Little, Mary, wife of Ephraim, died Feb. 10, 1717–18, aged 66 y. Little, Ephraim, late of Marshfield, died Nov. 24, 1717, aged 68 y. Litchfield, Josiah, son of Joseph and Tamson, died Nov. 7, 1752, aged 3 y. 3 m. 3 d. Litchfield, Nicholas, died May 1, 1750, aged 70 y. Litchfield, Josiah, died Dec. 7, 1717, aged 40 y.

Merrett, Nehemiah, died July 13, 1722, aged 17 y. Merrett, John, died June 5, 1740, aged 79 y. 3 m. 16 d. Merrett, Mrs. Elizabeth, wife of John, died April 13, 1746, aged 82 y. 37 d.

Nash, Joseph, died May 23, 1732, aged 58 y. Nichols, Joseph, [broken stone.]

Otis, Josiah, son of Dr. Isaac Otis, died Mar. 23, 1723, aged 17 weeks. Otis, Capt. Stephen, died Aug. 26, 1733, aged 72 y. Otis, Hannah, died May 1, 1729, aged 60 y. Otis, Hannah, dau. of Joshua and Hannah, died Mar. 3, 1744–5, aged 5 y. 11 m. Otis, Luce, daughter of Joshua and Hannah, died Mar. 26, 1744–5, aged 7 y. 7 m. Otis, Joshua, son of Joshua and Hannah, died Mar. 22, 1744–5, aged 1 y. 11 m. 2 d.

Pitcher, Rev. Nathaniel, pastor of North Church, Scituate, died Sept. 27, 1723, aged 38 y.

Stockbridge, James, died June 11, 1725, aged 48 y. Stodder, Seth, son of Samuel and Elizabeth, died Aug. 15, 1712, aged 12 y. 5 m. 20 d. Stodder, Dea. Samuel, died July 25, 1762, aged 92 y. Stodder, Elizabeth, wife of Dea. Samuel Stodder, died Mar. 6, 1749, aged 79 y.

Tilden, Nathaniel, died Dec. 17, 1731, aged 82 y. Tilden, John, died Feb. 9, 1739, aged 87 y. Tilden, Nathaniel, died Sept. 27, 1724, aged 5 y. Tilden, Benjamin, died Oct. 23, 1732, aged 28 y. Thompson, Thomas, son of Robert, died Mar. 3, 1722, aged 2 y. Thompson, Robert, son of Robert, died Feb. 26, 1722, aged 23 y. Turner, Abagail, dau. of Samuel and Abigail, died Jan. 12, 1723-4, aged 3 y. Turner, Liddiah, dau. of James and Mary, died Mar. 26, 1740, aged 4 y. Turner, Abagail, wife of Capt. Samuel, died Dec. 12, 1744, aged 58 y. Turner, Capt. Samuel, died Nov. 3, 1759, aged 89 y. Turner, Nathaniel, son of Capt. Samuel, died May 1734, aged 31 y. 4 m. Turner, David, died May 3, 1698, aged 27 y. 6 m. Turner, James, died May 30, 1776, aged 70 y. Turner, Mary, wife of Capt. James, died Aug. 19, 1775, aged 73 y. Turner, Mary, wife of Col. Amos, died Nov. 3, 1722, aged 62 y. Turner, Left. Seth, died Oct. 10, 1743, aged 38 y. Turner, Col. Amos, Esq., died April 13, 1739, aged 68 y.

Vinal, Ignatious, [broken grave stone.] Vinal, Patience, dau. of Ignatious and Patience, died Sept. 22, 1766, aged 6 m. 7 d. Vinal, Ignatious, Jr., son of Ignatious Vinal and wife Mary, died Sept. 10, 1751, aged 4 y. 9 m. 15 d. Vinal, Mrs. Mary, wife of Ignatious, died July 3, 1751, aged 29 y. 11 m. 27 d. Vinal, Mrs. Patience, wife of Ignatious, died Mar. 27, 1773, aged 37 y. Vinal, Seth, son of Seth and Hannah Vinal, died Oct. 6, 1754, aged 6 y. Vinal, Hannah, wife of Seth Vinal, died April 24, 1757, aged 30 y. 5 m. Vinal, Mrs. Mary, wife of Jacob, died Mar. 1, 1755, aged 77 y. Vinal, Nicholas, son of Jacob, senior, died June 24, 1728. Vinal, Jonathan, son of Jacob, senior, died March 22, 1724, aged 16 y. Vinal, Mrs. Mary, wife of John, died July 18, 1723, aged 53 y. Vinal, Mr. John, died Aug. 21, 1698, aged 62 y. Vinal, Ignatious, died Aug. 1769, aged 79 y.

Williams, Capt. John, died June 22, 1694, aged 70 y.

Young, Thomas, died Dec. 25, 1732, aged 69 y. 1 m. 20 d.

[These Epitaphs I took from the old burying ground in Scituate, Mass, 1852; they are all that remain, and in a very few years will entirely be obliterated. Having a desire to preserve to future generations all facts relating to our early ancestors, I devoted part of a few leisure days while rusticating in that ancient and beautiful town.

A road has been made through this burying ground, which has, undoubtedly, destroyed many of the grave stones. This burying ground was connected with the first church in Scituate.

Scituate began to be settled before 1628, by men from Kent County, England. The town was incorporated Oct. 6, 1636. Mr. Giles Saxton was the first pastor, between 1631-34; as the early parish records are lost, very little is or can be known of their doings.—D. H.]

MARRIAGES AT SCITUATE, MASS., PRIOR TO 1700.

Though these marriages were used by DEANE in his history, the date of the year is only given, and we now give the full date.

W. H. W.

James Terry and Lydia Willes, 1 June, 1666.
Thomas Roose and Alice Hatch, Dec., 1665.
Thomas Woodworth and Debrah Damen, 8 Feb., 1666.
Joseph Woodworth and Sarah Stockbridge, 6 Jan., 1666.
Steven Tillding and Hannah Litell, 15 Jan., 1661.
James Briges and Rebecca Tilden, 8 July, 1673.
Thomas Nicholles and Sarah Whiston, 25 May, 1663.
Jonathan Cudworth and Sarah Jackson, 31 May, 1667.
Samuel House and Rebecca Nicholles, 15 March, 1664.
Thomas King and Elizabeth Clapp, 20 April, 1669.
Thomas Perry and Susanna Whiston, 2 May, 1671.
Josiah Lechfield and Sarah Baker, 22 Feb., 1671.
John Baylis and Sarah White, 25 Jan., 1672.
Theophilus Wetherbee and Lydia Parker, 9 Nov., 1675.
Tristram Davis and Sarah Archer, of Brantry, 19 March, 1694–5.
Joseph Barstow and Susanna Lincoln, of Hingham, 16 May, 1666.
Joseph Randall and Hannah Macomber, of Marshfield, Oct., 1672.
Richard Dwelley and Eame Glass, of Duxbury, 4 April, 1682.
Abraham Pierce and Hannah Glass, of Duxbury, 29 Oct., 1695.
Richard Church and Hannah ———, 2 Feb., 1696–7.
Robert Barker and Hannah ———, 1 April, 1697.
Joseph Stockbridge and Margaret (Turner), 20 Oct., 1697.
Timothy Tileston, of Dorchester, and Hannah ———, 5 Jan., 1697.
William Macomber, of Dorchester, and Elizabeth (Turner), 9 March, 1797–8.
Hatherly Foster and Bathsheba (Turner), 1 Dec., 1698.
Peter Collamer and Abagail Davis, of Roxbury, 8 Nov.,1694.
Elisha Turner and Elizabeth Jacob, 6 June, 1687.
Henry Joslin and Abigail Stockbridge, 4 Nov., 1676.
Nathaniel Tilden and Mary Sharpe, 5 Nov., 1673.
William Ticknor and Lydia Tilden, 2 Nov., 1696.
John Hiland and Elizabeth James, 3 Jan., 1694–5.
Joseph Garrett and Ruth Buck, 17 Jan., 1676.
Thomas Clark and Martha Curtis, 11 or 2 Jan., 1676.
Jacob Bumpas and Elizabeth Blackmer, 24 Jan., 1677.
John Curtis and Miriam Brooks, 4 April, 1678.
Cornelius Briggs and widow Mary Russell, 20 March, 1677.
Thomas Turner and Hannah Jenkins, 9 Feb., 1695.
James Terry and Elizabeth Rollings, 24 Sept., 1679.
Joseph Otis and Dorothy Thomas, 20 Nov., 1688.
William Barrett and Lydia James, 20 April, 1680.

Benjamin Pierce and Martha Adams, 5 Feb., 1678.
Benjamin Audley and Mary Merrill, 7 Oct., 1683.
Steven Otis and Hannah Ensine, 16 June, 1685.
David Jacob and Sarah Cushing, 20 Dec., 1689.
John Booth, jr. and Mary Dodson, 12 Dec., 1687.
Isaac Beck, jr., and Eunice Turner, 24 Oct., 1684.
Nathaniel Tilden and Margaret Dodson, of Hingham, 3 Jan., 1693-4.
John Cushing, jr., and Deborah Loring, 20 May, 1688.
Benjamin Stetson and Grace Turner, 22 Jan., 1690.
Josiah Terry and Isabel Witherlee, 6 Oct., 1684.
Josiah Terry and Sarah Mendall, 12 Jan., 1692.
Samuel House and Sarah Pinson, 25 Feb., 1691-2.
Timothy White and Abigail Rogers, 1 Jan., 1678-9.
Israel Chittenden and Deborah Baker, 25 April, 1678.
Isaac Randall and Susanna Berstow, 19 Nov., 1684.
Isaac Randall and Deborah Buck, 29 Nov., 1692.
John Barstow and Lydia Hatch, 16 Jan., 1678.
Ichabod Ewell and Mehitable Gwinne, 1 May, 1689.
Jonathan Pratt and Margaret Loe, 8 Jan., 1691-2.
Thomas Pinson and Sarah Turner, 26 Dec,, 1693.
Samuel Tilden and Sarah Curtis, 25 July, 1694.
James Whitcomb and Mary Parker, 22 Nov., 1694.
Eliab Turner and Elnathan Hinksman, 22 Nov. 1694.
John Palmer and Mary Rose, 20 Dec., 1694.
Thomas Curtis and Mary Cook, 6 March, 1694-5.
Joseph Thorne and Joanna Pinson, 16 May, 1695.
Elnathan Palmer and Mercy Clark, 25 Dec., 1695.
Amos Turner and Mary Heland, 6 April, 1695.
John Dwelley and Rachel Buck, 4 Jan., 1692-3.
Nathaniel Brooks and Elizabeth Curtis, 25 Dec., 1678.
Thomas Brooks and Hannah Bisher, 6 June, 1687.
Joseph Stetson and Hannah Oldham, 6 Nov., 1688.
Thomas Oldham and Mercy Sproat, 27 June, 1683.
Benjamin Curtis and Mary Silvester, 1689.
William Cliffe and Lydia Wills, 25 Nov., 1691.
Nathan Pickles and Merriam Turner, 3 Aug, 1687.
Thomas Young and Sarah White, Jan., 1688-9.
Benjamin Turner and Elizabeth Hawkins, 14 April, 1692.
Aaron Symonds and Mary Woodworth, 24 Dec., 1677.
William Perry and Elizabeth Lobdell, 31 May, 1681.
John Peirce and Patience Dodson, 12 Dec., 1683.
Zecheriah Damen and Martha Woodworth, June, 1679.
Stephen Chittenden and Mehitable Bucke, 5 Nov., 1679.
Jonathan Merritt and Elizabeth Whiton, 8 Aug., 1710.
Richard Garrett and Persis Peirce, 3 Dec., 1695.
John Jackson, of Plymouth, and Abigail Woodworth, 24 Dec., 1695.
Jacob Vinal and Mary Cudworth, 12 Feb., 1695-6.
Rodolphus Elmes and Bethiah Dodson, 20 Feb., 1695-6.
Thomas Hatch and Hannah Cudworth, 6 March, 1695-6.
John Farrow, of Hingham, and Persis Holebroke, 30 April, 1696.
Zecheriah Colman and Joanna Cudworth, 16 Dec., 1696.

Joseph White, jr., and Oseeth Turner, 16 Sept., 1696.
William Ticknor and Lydia Tilden, 2 Nov., 1696.
Thomas Oliver and Bethiah Coppe (or Clappe), 11 Nov., 1696.
Joseph Nichols and Bathshebee Pinson, 12 Jan., 1696–7.
William Parker and Rachel Clark, 2 March, 1696–7.
Abraham Barden and Mary Booth, 20 Oct., 1697.
John Marshall, of Boston, and Jane Allen, 16 Nov., 1697.
Hezekiah Woodworth and Hannah Clap, 23 Dec., 1697.
Gershom Marble and Waitstill Ingle, 29 Dec., 1697.
Joseph White, Sr. and Elizabeth Vinal, 7 June, 1699.
Thomas King and Deborah Briggs, 15 June, 1699.
Israel Hatch and Elizabeth Hatch, 27 July, 1699.
John Baylie and Abigail Clap, 14 Feb., 1700.
John Baylis and Ruth Clothier, 9 Dec., 1699.
Robert Osgood and Sarah Dodson, 14 Dec., 1699.
Josiah Turner and Hannah Holbrook, 24 Jan., 1700.
Ebenezer Mott and Grace Vinal, 19 Feb., 1700.

NOTE.—The earlier marriages, omitted by mistake, will be printed in the next number.

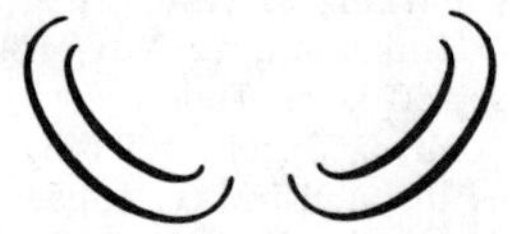

EARLY MARRIAGES AND BIRTHS AT SCITUATE, MASS.

MARRIAGES.

James Torrey m. Ann, dau. of Wm. Hatch, 2 Nov., 1643.
John Bryant m. Mary, dau. of Geo. Lewes, of Barnstable, 14 Nov., 1643.
John Daman m. Katherine, dau. of Henry Merritt, June, 1644.
Ephraim Kempton m. Joanna Rawlings, 23 Jany., 1645.
Rodolphus Elmes m. Catern Whitcomb, 25 Nov., 1644.
Isaac Chittenden m. Martha Vinal, Apr., 1646.
James Adams m. Frances, dau. of Wm. Vassall, 16 June, 1646.
James Doughty m. Lydia, dau. of Humph Turner, 15 Aug., 1649.
John Turner, jr. m. Ann James, 24 Apr., 1649.
Walter Hatch m. Elizabeth, dau. of Thos. Holbrook, 6 May, 1650.
William Peaks m. Judith Lichfield, 2 Oct., 1650.
William Parker m. Mary, dau. of Humphrey Turner, 13 Nov., 1651.

Anthony Dodson m. Mary Williams, 12 Dec., 1651.
Thomas Turner m. Sarah Hiland, 6 Jany., 1652.
Nathaniel Rawlins m. Lydia, dau. of Rich. Sylvester, 4 Sept., 1652.
William Hatch m. Susannah, dau. of Anthony Annable, 13 May, 1652.
Thomas Kinge m. widow Jane Hatch, 3 Mch., 1653.
Thomas Oldham m. Mary Wetherell, 20 Nov., 1656.
John Cowen m. Rebecca Man, 31 Mch., 1656.
John Lowwell m. Elizabeth Silvester, 24 Jany., 1658.
John Bryant m. Elizabeth Wetherell, 22 Dec., 1657.
Jonas Pickles m. Alice Hatch, 23 Sept., 1657.
Samuel Utley m. Hannah Hatch, 6 Dec., 1658.
Daniel Hickes m. Rebecca Hanmoe, 19 Sept., 1659.
John Damen m. Martha Howland, 15 Jany., 1659.
Anthony Collamer m. Sarah Chittenden, 14 June, 1666.
John Sutten m. Elizabeth House, 1 Jany., 1661.
George Young m. Hannah Pierson, 15 Jany., 1661.
Steven Tilden m. Hannah Littell, 15 Jany., 1661.
Thomas Hilland m. Elizabeth Stockbridge, 1 Jany., 1661.
Steven Vinall m. Mary Baker, 26 Feb., 1662.
Thomas Pinson, jr. m. Elizabeth White, 18 Sept., 1662.
Thomas Hatch m. Sarah Elmes, dau. of Rodolphus, 4 Feb., 1662.
John Briant m. Mary Hilland, April, 1664.
Nathaniel Turner m. Mehitable Rigbee, 29 Mch., 1664–5.
John Vinal m. Elizabeth Baker, 2 Feb., 1664.
William Blackmer m. Elizabeth Bankes, 17 July, 1666.
Jeremiah Hatch m. Mary Hawes, 29 Dec., 1657.
Edward Bright m. widow Lydia Rawlins, 25 May, 1664.
Daniel Turner m. Hannah, dau. of Wm. Randall, 20 June, 1665.
Joseph Webb m. Grace Dipple, 16 Apr., 1660.
Samuel Clapp m. Hannah Gill, 14 June, 1666.
Thomas Woodworth m. Deborah Damen, 8 Feb., 1666.
Joseph Woodworth m. Sarah Stockbridge, 6 Jany., 1669.

[The previous article contains later marriages than this.

BIRTHS.

The following births are given from the Scituate Records, with the *full* dates. Deane gives generally only the year.

John Northy had John, b. 8 March, 1675; David, 6 April, 1678; Samuel, 19 July, 1680: Bethiah, 18 Dec., 1682; Sarah, 16 July, 1685; and James, 2 Oct., 1687.

Thomas Perry had Thomas, 26 Jan., 1671; James, 12 March, 1673–4; Susanna, 28 April, 1676; Mary, 18 March, 1677–8; John, 6 June, 1680: Tabitha, 12 April, 1684: David, 16 Nov., 1686.

Nathaniel Turner had Abigail, 10 Feb., 1666; Samuel, 25 Feb., 1671; Mehitable, 29 March, 1673; Lydia, Aug., 1675; Nathaniel, 24 Dec., 1678.

John Turner, Jr. had Japhet, 9 Feb., 1650; Israel, 14 Feb., 1654; Miriam, 8 April, 1658; Ann, 23 Feb., 1662: Sarah, 25 July, 1665; Jacob, 10 March, 1667–8; David, 5 Nov., 1670; Philip, 18 Aug., 1673; —— a son, 9 April, 1676.

Steven Tilden had Hannah, 14 Oct., 1662; Steven, 5 Feb., 1663–4;

Abigail, 11 July, 1666; Mary, 7 April, 1668; Judith, 1 June, 1670; Joseph, 13 May, 1672; Mercy, 1 May, 1674; Ruth, 1 June, 1676; Isaac, 28 Aug., 1678; Ephraim, 20 Nov., 1680; Ebenezer, 16 June, 1682; David, 6 Nov., 1685.

John Cowen had Joseph, 5 Dec., 1657; Mary, 14 May, 1659; John, 10 Jan., 1662; Israel, 10 Dec., 1664; Rebecca, 10 May, 1666.

Steven Vinal had Aaron, 1 Jan., 1664; John, 20 Sept., 1667; Steven, 9 May, 1670; Hannah, 10 July, 1671; Steven, 2 March, 1674–5; Gideon, 17 Aug., 1678; Samuel, 4 July, 1681.

Richard Man had Nathaniel, 25 Sept., 1646; Thomas, 15 Aug., 1650; Richard, 5 Feb., 1652; Josiah, 10 Dec., 1654.

John Magoon had Isaac, Aug., 1676.

Jonas Pickles had Mercy, 8 Dec., 1660; Nathan, 28 Jan., 1661; Lydia, 10 April, 1662; Jonas, 10 March, 1663–4.

Thomas Roose had Thomas, 16 Sept., 1666; Patience, 31 March, 1668; Hannah, 23 May, 1669.

Jonas Dean had Thomas, 29 Oct., 1691; Ephraim, 22 May, 1694.

John Baylie had John, 5 Nov., 1673; Sarah, Oct., 1675; Mary, Dec., 1677; Joseph, Oct., 1679; Benjamin, April, 1682; William, Feb., 1684–5; Hannah, Jan., 1687–8; Samuel, Aug., 1690.

Samuel House had Samuel, 28 March, 1665; Joseph, 10 April, 1667; Rebecca, 12 April, 1670; John, 22 Sept., 1672.

James Doughty had Mary, 23 June, 1650; James, 21 Feb., 1651–2; Elizabeth, 25 Nov., 1654; Lydia, 14 Feb., 1656; Sarah, 2 April, 1662; Samuel, 29 Sept., 1664; Robert, 14 Feb., 1666–7; Susanna, 15 Feb., 1670.

James Woodworth had Benjamin, Aug., 1676; Sarah, Aug., 1678; Elizabeth, Aug., 1680; Eamee, Jan., 1682–3; Abigail, April, 1685; Ruth, May, 1687.

William Blackmore had Phebe, 12 Aug., 1672; William, 25 Feb., 1675.

Israel Silvester had Israel, 23 Sept., 1674.

Edward Wanton had George, 25 Aug., 1666; William, 15 Sept., 1670; Elizabeth, 16 Sept., 1668; John, 24 Dec., 1672; Sarah and Margaret, twins, 22 Sept., 1674. At Boston, Edward, 13 Sept., 1658; Joseph, 1 May, 1664. At Scituate also, Hannah, 25 July, 1677; Michael, 9 April, 1679; Stephen, 5 March, 1682; Philip, 9 May, 1686.

John Sutton had Elizabeth, 20 Oct., 1662; John, 28 Feb., 1663–4; Mary, 22 Jan., 1665; Sarah, 3 Nov. 1667; Hannah, 3 Nov., 1669; Hester, 25 Oct., 1671; Benjamin, 22 March, 1674–5; Nathaniel, 31 July, 1676; Nathan, 6 Aug., 1679.

John Booth had Elizabeth, 5 Oct., 1657; Joseph, 27 March, 1659; John, 1 Jan., 1661; Benjamin, 4 July, 1667; Mary, 6 June, 1669; Abraham, 7 Feb., 1673; Grace, 4 July, 1677; Judith, 13 March, 1680.

Peter Worthelike had Hannah and Alice, 18 Aug., 1676; Sarah, 6 April, 1682.

Thomas Woodworth had Ebenezer, 25 May, 1676; Mary, 8 July, 1678.

Richard Prouty had James, 30 Oct., 1677; Edward, 30 Sept., 1679; Jonathan, 1 Sept., 1681; Isaac, 18 Nov., 1689; Margaret, 2 March, 1691–2; William, 30 Jan., 1694–5. W. H. W.

SCITUATE CHURCH RECORDS.—A book of "Records of the first Universalist Church in Scituate," in the possession of Charles H. Killam of Assinippi, Mass., shows the following as church members, August 30, 1827:

Benjamin Whittemore, Ichabod R. Jacobs, Joshua Damon, Charles Jones, John Grose, Theophilus Corthel, Eleazer Whiting, Michael Jacobs, John Jones, Franklin Jacobs, Loring Jacobs, Mandama B. Whittemore, Sophia Simmons. Lydia Jones, Priscilla Mann, Anne Lenth[ll] Smith, Roxana Gross, and Lucy Clapp.

Sept. 9, 1827, Deborah Corthell was admitted; May 25, 1828, Sally Randall; Sept. 28, 1828, Experience Randall and Amiel Studley; Jan. 2, 1830, Phoeba S. Killam.

On Oct. 27, 1833, reference was made to the death of Franklin Jacobs, and on Nov. 16, 1834, to that of Sophia Simmons.

The church was re-organized in March, 1855.

Boston, Mass. WILFORD J. LITCHFIELD.

VITAL RECORDS OF SCITUATE, MASS. — The following entries have been taken from an old record book formerly belonging to Rev. Thomas Clap of Taunton, Mass., which is in the possession of the Old Colony Historical Society. They appear in a list headed "The following Persons Were Married by me Thomas Clap one of His Majesties Justices of the Peace for the County of Plymouth." They correct the reading of one surname printed in the "Vital Records of Scituate," and supply two dates for marriages of which the intentions only are given in volume 2 of the published records.

Scituate March. 17th 1762 Jacob Lincoln and Sussanna Marvell Both of Scituate were Married together

Scituate June 5. 1766 Thomas Pincin & Elizebeth Nash Both of Scituate were Married Together

Scituate October. 1767. the 15th day of sd Month Joshua Jenkins & Mary Jenkins Both of Scituate were Married together

Boston, Mass. FLORENCE CONANT HOWES.

SEEKONK INSCRIPTIONS.

Providence, Jan. 29*th*, 1856.

Mr. S. G. Drake:

Dear Sir,—Ten years ago I copied from the grave stones in an old burying ground situated at the head of Bullock's Cove, in the town of Seekonk—originally a part of Rehoboth—several inscriptions, some of which you may deem of interest enough to occupy a page of the Register.

The first that I give will be those of Thomas Willett and his wife. The head stones of the Willetts are about six inches thick by fifteen inches wide, and are above the ground about twenty inches; they are rough, without attempt at ornament, except the top being curved, the lettering being legible and tolerably well executed. I copied precisely as the lines, figures, and capital letters are on the stones. J. A. Howland.

[Head Stone.]
1674.
Here lye^h ye body
of ye Wor^l Thomas
Willet esq^r who died
Avgvst ye 4th in ye 64th
year of his age anno.

[Foot Stone.]
Who was the
first Mayor
of New York
& twice did
sustaine y^t place.

[Head Stone.]
1699
Here lyeth ye body of
the vertvovs ^{Mrs} Mary
Willett wife to thomas
Willett esq^r. who died
Janiary ye 8th about ye 65th
year of her age anno.

[Foot Stone.]
Daughter to
the Wor^{ll} John
Brown esq.
Deceased.

In memory of
Lieut James
Brown who
died April 15th
1718 in ye 60th
year of his
Age

In memory of
Mrs Margaret
Brown
Relict of Lieut James
Brown, Who died on
the 5th Day of May
1741 in ye 85th year
of her age

In Memory of Mr
Nathaniel Brown
died Novem^r y^e
13th 1739 In ye 79th
year of his age.

In memory of
Hannah ye Wife
of Nathanael
Brown died
Novem^r 1736
In ye 66th year
of her age.

In memory of
Samuel Brown
Esq. Dec^d June
ye 2^d 1752 in y^e
76 year of
his Age

In memory of
Mrs Sarah Brown y^e
Wife of Mr Samuel
Brown Died ye 9th Day
of June 1740 in y^e
58th year of
her Age

In Memory of Mr
Daniel Brown
Who Departed this Life
December 25 1750

In Memory of
Mrs Kezia
Brown Wife
of Capt. Benjamin
Brown Dec[d] May
17th 1755 in y[e] 52[d]
year of her age

Here lies inter[dd]
y[e] Body of Mr
Nathan Brown
Dec[d] July y[e] 3[d]
1737 in y[e] 46th year
of his age

Here lyeth
the Body of
Josiah Brown
died April y[e] 14th 1724
in y[e] 29th year
of his age

In Memory of
Mrs Anna Brown
Relict of Samuel
Brown Esq[r] Dec[d]
January y[e] 2[d]
1753 in y[e] 63[d]
year of her Age

In memory of
Dorothy Brown
Relect to Nathan
Brown of Rehoboth
She died Janewary
28th 1786 in y[e]
66th year of
her age
Departed this life mid of your tears
Here I shall lie till Christ Appears

In Memory of Mr
Benjamin . Brown
Son of Capt Benjamin Brown
& Mrs Kezia his wife
Departed this Life on the
29th Day of October 1754
in y[e] 28th year of his age.
My Beauty great is all quite gone
My flesh is wasted to the Bone
My house is narrow now and throng
Nothing but truth comes from my tongue
And if you should see me this Day
I do not think but you would say
That I had never been a Man,
So much altered now I am.
For Gods sake pray th' Heavenly King
That he my Soul in Heaven would bring.
All they that pray and make Accord
For me unto my GOD and LORD
GOD place them in his Paradice
Wherein no wretched Caitiff lies

MARRIAGES IN TAUNTON.

The following record of marriages solemnized by Maj. Thomas Leonard, of Taunton, from 1684 to 1713, the year of his death, is from a manuscript volume still extant. The record was printed in the Bristol County Telegram for Nov. 20, 1858, whence we have copied it. For a notice of Maj. Thomas Leonard, see Reg. V. 407.

John Walker and Mary Knoles were married the 22d of July, 1684.
Abraham Hathway and Rebekah Wilbore were mar. August 28, 1684.
Robert Godfree and Hannah Hackit were married Jan. 14, 1684–5.
Samuel Hoskins and Mary Austin married Feb. 5, 1684.
Uriah Leonard and Elizabeth Caswell mar. June 1, 1685.
Joseph Richmond and Mary Andrewes married June 26, 1685.
Abell Burt and Grace Andrewes married June 26, 1685.
James Burt and Mary Thayer married Sept. 2, 1685.
John Knap and Sarah Austin married Oct. 7, 1685.
Joseph Crosman and Sarah Alden married Nov. 24, 1685.
Wm. Makepeace and Abigail Tisdail married Dec. 2, 1685.
James Phillips and Abigaile Hathway married Dec. 9, 1685.
John Macomber, Sen. and Mary Badcock married Jan. 7, 1685–6.
Thomas Braman and Hannah Fisher married Jan. 20, 1685–6.
Walter Merry and Elizabeth Cunnill married Jan. 21, 1685–6.
Mr. George Goodwin and Deborah Walker married Feb. 9, 1685–6.
Henry Andrewes and Mary Dean mar. Feb. 17, 1685–6.
Richard Burt and Eunice Leonard mar. Feb. 18, 1685–6.
William Davis and Mary Makepeace married March 1, 1685–6.
William Wood and Dorothy Irish mar. April 1, 1686.
Samuel Hall and Elizabeth Bourn mar. April 7, 1686.
Samuel Bayley and Mary Thayer married May 17, 1686.
Richard Haskins and Jane Fluster mar. Aug. 2, 1686.
Aaron Knap and Rachel Burt married Dec. 8, 1686.
John Crane and Hannah Leonard mar. Dec. 13, 1686.
Isaac Hathway and Mary Pits married Mar 17, 1686–7.
Jared Talbot and Rebekah Hathway mar. May 4, 1687.
Josiah Smith and Mary Prat, of Dartmouth, married May 25, 1687.
Samuel Knap and Elizabeth Cob married May 26, 1687.
William Briggs and Constant Lincoln married July 13, 1687.
John Packer and Judith Winslow mar. April 12, 1688.
John Burrill and Mercy Alden married June 26, 1688.
Henry Andrewes and Mary Williams mar. July 4, 1688.
Joshua Tisdale and Abigail Andrews mar. July 5, 1688.
Ebenezer Thayer and Ruth Neal married Aug. 2, 1688.
John Hackit and Ealenor Gardner mar. Sept. 10, 1688.
John Whipple and Lydia Hoar married Nov. 16, 1688.
Jonathan Haward and Susana Keith married Jan. 8, 1688–9.
John Knowlman, Jr. and Ealenor Evins married Feb. 5, 1688–9.
James Edmester and Anne Makepeace married April 19, 1689.
Thomas Brigs and Abigail Thayer mar. Oct. 24, 1689.
Thomas Lincolne and Susana Smith mar. Nov. 14, 1689.
John Caswel and Elizabeth Hall married Nov. 26, 1689.
Nath. Bun and Hannah Willims married Nov. 28, 1688.
Edward Cob and Sarah Hackit married Dec. 18, 1689.
Samuel Crosman and Elizabeth Bell mar. Dec. 19, 1689.

Daniel Oen and Hannah Lincoln mar. Dec. 23, 1689.
John Crosman and Johana Thayer mar. Jan. 7, 1689–90.
Jonathan Pratt and Elizabeth Hall married March 3, 1689–90.
Benjamin Williams and Rebekah Macey married Mar. 12, 1689–90.
Samuel Hackit and Mary Crane mar. March 28, 1690.
James Phillips and Elizabeth French married May 7, 1690.
William Thomas and Sarah Prat married July 30, 1691.
Jonathan Hayward and Sarah Dean mar. Oct. 8, 1691.
Joseph Basset and Bathyah Eaton mar. Nov. 5, 1691.
Thomas Caswel and Mary Ransden mar. Dec. 2, 1691.
Stephen Mirack and Anna Wilbore mar. Jan. 25, 1691–2.
Nicholas Stoughton and Sarah Hoar married Feb. 25, 1691–2.
Stephen Burden and Abigale Williamson married March 24, 1692.
Jonah Austin and Tamason Lincolne married April 20, 1692.
Samuel Hoskins and Rebekah Brooks mar. May 12, 1692.
John Paul and Dorothy Walker married May 26, 1692.
Samuel Waterman and Marcy Ransome mar. July 26, 1692.
Samuel Brigs and Mary Hall married July 27, 1692.
John Hall and Ester Bell married Dec. 14, 1692.
Samuel Dean and Sarah Robinson mar. Dec. 15, 1692.
Samuel Staple and Hannah Lillikin married Feb. 9, 1691–2.
Samuel Waldron and Hannah Brigs mar. Apr. 17, 1693.
Edward Paul and Ester Bobbot married Aug. 23, 1693.
William Rypley and Mary Corbison mar. Oct. 11, 1693.
Miles Gorden and Elisa. Smith married Oct. 16, 1693.
William Brigs and Elisabeth Lincolne married Oct. 17, 1693.
Ebenezer Camball and Hannah Prat mar. Mar. 29, 1694.
James Bennet and Ruth Rogers mar. July 12, 1694.
Samuel Richmond and Mahitabell Andrews married Dec 20, 1694.
Christopher Penny and Elisabeth Wallero married Jan. 8, 1695.
Daniel Fisher and Mercy Edy married Feb. 7, 1694–5.
William Cobb and Mary Newland mar. Feb. 11, 1694–5.
Increase Robinson and Mahitabell Williams married Feb. 11, 1694–5.
Benj. Jones and Hannah Walker mar. Apr. 8, 1695.
George Leonard and Anna Tisdale mar. July 4, 1695.
Joseph Tucker and Hannah Wilkinson married Dec. 7, 1695.
Charles Williams and Mary Gladding married Feb. 13, 1695–6.
Joseph Jones and Abigail Caswel married Apr. 6, 1696.
Jacob Staple and Mary Briggs married Sept. 15, 1696.
John Hall and Elisabeth King married Dec. 17, 1696.
Samuel Crosman and Mary Sawyer mar. Dec. 22, 1696.
Eliezer Fisher and Hannah Edy mar. Dec. 24, 1696.
Thomas Randall and Rachell Lincolne married Jan. 20, 1696–7.
Jacob Hathway and Phillip Chase mar. Jan. 28, 1696.
Henry Gaishet and Sarah Haskins mar. Sept. 2, 1697.
Joseph Wood and Abigail Paul married Oct. 18, 1697.
John Simmons and Hannah Hathway married Dec. 14, 1697.
Thomas Makepeace and Mary Burt, married Jan. 10, 1697–8.
Jabiz Prat and Elisabeth Cobb mar. Feb. 23, 1697–8.
Jeremiah Fairbanks and Mary Penfield married April 14, 1698.
Thomas Monrow and Mary Wormwell married Oct. 13, 1698.
William Britten and Lidia Leonard mar. Oct. 26, 1698.
Edward Bobbot and Elisabeth Thayer mar. Dec. 22, 1698.

Israel Woodward and Bennet Edy mar. Dec. 28, 1698.
James Leonard, Junior, and Hannah Stone married Feb. 28, 1698-9.
David Shepard and Rebecca Curtice married Apr. 12, 1699.
John Kennicut and Elizabeth Luther mar. Apr. 14, 1699.
Joseph Benson and Deborah Smith mar. April 17, 1699.
Ephraim Staples and Elisabeth Welsber married Aug. 16, 1699.
Thomas Stephens and Mary Casewell married Sept. 28, 1699.
James Walker and Sarah Richmond mar. Oct. 6, 1699.
Thomas Leonard, Jr. and Johanah Pitcher married Dec. 1, 1699.
Thomas Terry and Abigail Dean mar. Jan. 4, 1699-1700.
John King and Alice Dean married Feb. 1, 1699-1700.
John Smith, son of Nathaniel Smith, and Priscilla Blake were married May 30, 1700.
Samuel Hodges and Experience Leonard were married Dec. 31, 1700.
Eliezer Edy and Elisabeth Randell mar. Mar. 27, 1701.
Samuel Leonard and Katherine Dean mar. Apr. 17, 1701.
Samuel Blake and Sarah Pitts married May 19, 1701.
William Thayer and Sarah Bobbot mar. May 29, 1701.
Israel Packer and Hannah Crosman mar. July 16, 1701.
Remembrance Simmons and Hannah Smith were married Dec. 17, 1701.
John Alger and Johanah King married April 9, 1702.
Sam'l Hoskins, Sr. and Hannah Hall mar. June 4, 1702.
Francis Smith and Ester Holloway mar. July 13, 1702.
Benjamin Newland and Sarah Leonard married July 23, 1702.
Edward Simmons and Ester Reed, both of Swansey, were married Jan. 6, 1702-3.
Joseph Wood and Mary Reed married Jan. 11, 1702-3.
Caleb Edy and Bathyah Smith, both of Swansey, were married Jan. 11, 1702-3.
Peter Pitts and Bathyah Robbinson mar. Mar. 11, 1702-3.
Elkanah Leonard and Charity Hodges m. Mar. 25, 1703.
John Wilbore and Alice Pitts married April 20, 1703.
Nicholas White and Experience King mar. June 2, 1703.
Benjamin Chace and Mercy Simmons married June 23, 1703.
Ephraim Smith and Mary Savage, both of Swansey, mar. Oct. 15, 1703.
Nathaniel Crossman and Sarah Marrick married Oct. 21, 1703.
John Smith and Mary Godfree mar. Nov. 25, 1703.
Moses Choksinah and Elisabeth Joseph married Nov. 26, 1703.
Edward Hammet and Experiance Boles married Jan. 17, 1703-4.
William Corbitt, of Swanzey, and Hannah Negus, of Taunton, married March 23, 1703-4.
Hezekiah Luther, Junior, and Martha Gardner, both of Swanzey, married March 23, 1703-4.
Ebenezer Hall and Jane Bumpus mar. June 22, 1704.
John Smith and Abigail Simmons mar. Oct. 26, 1704.
Robert Woodward and Hannah Briggs married April 2, 1705.
John Terry and Remember Farrah mar. April 3, 1705.
George Townsend and Elisabeth Gilbert married April 27, 1705.
David Gaschit and Alice Godfree mar. June 12, 1705.
John Pain and Rebekah Divis married Oct. 31, 1705.
Amos Briggs and Sarah Pain married Jan. 2, 1705-6.
William Macomber and Sarah Holloway married Jan. 3, 1705-6.
Ebenezer Robbinson and Mary Williams married Feb. 13, 1705-6.

Joseph Dunham and Bathiah Chase mar. June 19, 1706.
James Leonard and Rebeckah Williams married Aug. 29, 1706.
Timothy Cooper and Elisabeth Gurney married Oct. 16, 1706.
Nathaniel French and Abigail Smith mar. Nov. 7, 1706.
Thomas Hix and Abigail Bliffin, both of Swanzey, married Dec. 30, 1706.
Walter Chace and Deliverance Simmons, both of Freetown, married Jan. 29, 1706–7.
Joseph Tisdale, Junior, and Ruth Reed married Mar. 13, 1706–7.
Benjamin Caswel and Mary Briggs married March 17, 1706–7.
Jothathan Williams and Elizabeth Leonard married April 3, 1707.
Joseph Williams and Mary Gilbert mar. Apr. 7, 1707.
Toney we Hanian and Elisabeth Waa married Oct. 10, 1707.
Benjamin Williams and Elisabeth Deane married Dec. 4, 1707.
Abraham Simmons and Anne Lee mar. Dec. 25, 1707.
Samuel Edson and Mary Dean married Jan. 1, 1707–8.
William Brightman and Mercy Spur married Jan. 22, 1707–8.
Joseph Winslow, of Swansey, and Mary Tisdale, of Taunton, married Feb. 11, 1707–8.
John Macomber and Elizabeth Williams married Mar. 17, 1707–8.
Uriah Leonard, Jr. and Abigail Stone married June 12, 1708.
Nathan Walker and Abigail Richmond married July 29, 1708.
William Hodges and Susana Gilbert mar. July 29, 1708.
Joseph Reed, of Freetown, and Sarah Dean, of Taunton, married Dec. 29, 1708.
Joshua Howland, of Freetown, and Elisabeth Holloway, of Taunton, married May 12, 1709.
Richard Godfree, Junior, and Bathsheba Walker married Dec. 15, 1709.
John White, Jr. and Elisabeth Crosman married Dec. 28, 1709.
Israel Dean and Ruth Jones married Jan. 19, 1709–10.
Nicholas Vorce and Mary Bourn mar. March 30, 1710.
Edward White and Rebekah Wetherell married May 3, 1710.
William Corbitt and Mercy Allin mar. July 10, 1710.
John Harvey and Mehetable Leonard married July 23, 1710.
John Briant and Abigail Holloway mar. Sept. 27, 1710.
David Shearmon, of Dartmouth, and Abigail Hathway, of Freetown, married Dec. 27, 1710.
Daniel Williams and Mercy Dean mar. Feb. 1, 1710–11.
William Hodges and Hannah Tisdale married Feb. 8, 1710–11.
Isaac Hathway and Sarah Makepeace married Feb. 22, 1710–11.
William Manly and Mercy Howin mar. Feb. 22, 1710–11.
Ebenezer Hathway and Hannah Shaw married March 8, 1710–11.
Samuel Myrick and Experience Briggs married March 29, 1711.
Henry Hodges and Sarah Leonard mar. April 5, 1711.
Asaph Lane and Elizabeth Wellman mar. Apr. 17, 1711.
Benjamin Smith and Sarah Maclothlin married May 15, 1711.
John Hackit and Elisabeth Elliot mar. May 18, 1711.
Matthew White and Susana Hall married July 10, 1711.
Samuel Bayley and Elisabeth Caswel mar. Aug. 28, 1711.
Charles Joslen and Dorothy Paul married Oct. 24, 1711.
Stephen Gary and Mercy Gilbert married Nov. 9, 1711.
Mr. Matthew Short and Mrs. Margaret Freeman married Dec. 27, 1711.

John Cleeveland and Martha Simmons married Jan. 1, 1711–12.
Thomas Pain and Susanna Hascall married Feb. 21, 1711–12.
James Hall and Sarah Williams married May 14, 1712.
Samuel Pitts and Rebeckah Williams mar. May 14, 1712.
Joshua Atherton and Elisabeth Leonard married July 23, 1712.
John Forrest and Mary Briggs married July 24, 1712.
William Davis and Keziah Cudworth mar. July 24, 1712.
Seth Smith and Anne Edmister married Nov. 13, 1712.
Josiah White and Margret Leonard mar. Nov. 20, 1712.
Josiah Cane and Damaras Macomber married Dec. 10, 1712.
Seth Leonard and Dorcas White married Dec. 17, 1712.
Thomas Baker and Abigail White married Dec. 17, 1712.
Ebenezer Williams and Judeth King, married Jan. 8, 1712–13.
John Whitman and Rebekah Manley married March 2, 1712–13.
Jeremiah Wetherell and Rachell Basset married March 26, 1713.
Nathaniel Wetherell and Mary White married May 28, 1713.
John Sanford and Abigail Pitts married July 1, 1713.
Ichabod Maxfield and Mary Godfree mar. Aug. 12, 1713.

MARRIAGES, BIRTHS AND DEATHS AT TAUNTON, MASS.

[From the Proprietors' Records. Communicated by EDGAR H. REED, Esq. of Taunton.]

The *Town Records* of Taunton previous to about 1800, were destroyed in the great fire of 1838; and any information, therefore, which can now be obtained of our early families, is exceedingly valuable.

On the *Proprietors' Records*, still existing, are found recorded many Births, Marriages and Deaths, which I have transcribed in the order in which they there appear, and send for publication.

Here followeth the names of those that hath bene maried by Justice Leonard.

George Leonard and Anna Tisdale were married July the fourth, 1695.

Joseph Tucker and Hannah Wilkinson were married Dec. 7, 1695.
Charles Williams and Mary Glading were married Feb. 13, 1695–6.
Joseph Joans and Abigail Caswel were married April the 6th, 1696.
Jacob Staple and Mary Briggs were maried Sept. 15th, 1696.
John Hall and Elizabeth King were married Dec. 17th, 1696.
Samuel Crosman and Mary Sawyer were married Decemb. 22, 1696.
Eleazer Fisher and Hannah Edy were married Decemb. 24, 1696.
Thomas Randall and Rachell Lincoln were married Jan. 20th, 1696–7.
Jacob Hathway and Philip Chase* were married Jan. 28th, 1696–7.
All these were married as above said in Taunton by me.

Thomas Leonard, Justice.

James Bundy, the sone of John Bundy, borne 29 September, 1664; Patiance Bundy, the daughter of John Bundy, dyed 27 March, 1665; Sara Bundy, the daughter of John Bundy, borne the 4th of March, 1668; Samuel Bundy, the son of John Bundy, borne the 4th of October, 1670; John Bundy, the son of John Bundy, borne 6th October, 1677; Joseph Bundy, the son of John Bundy, borne the 1st of Janewary, 1679; Edward Bundy, the son of John Bundy, borne the 13th of August, 1681.

Hana Smith, the daughter of Samuel Smith, borne 17 Sep., 1662; Sarah Smith, the daughter of Samuel Smith, borne 25 Jan., 1664; Sarah, daughter of Samuel Smith, died 18 July, 1665; Samuel, son of Samuel Smith, borne 15 Octo., 1666; Susana, daughter of Samuel Smith, borne 20 July, 1669; Easter, daughter of Samuel Smith, borne 6 Jan'y, 1671; Nathaniel, son of Samuel Smith, borne 26 July, 1675.

Hana Paull, daughter of Mary Paull, born 4th Octo., 1657.

The sons and daughters of Shadrach Wilbore: Mary, born 11th Nov., 1659; Sarah, born 18th M'ch, 1661; Samuel, born 1 Ap'l, 1663;

---

* When we first saw Mr. Reed's transcript from the *Proprietors' Records* of Taunton, several years ago, we thought Mr. R. had mistaken a long and a short *s* united for the letter *p*, and that the name really read *Philiss*; but about four years ago, a record book of Thomas Leonard, who performed the marriage ceremony, was found, and here too the name was recorded *Philip* (*ante*, XIII, 352). Can any of our correspondents furnish us with other instances where this name has been borne by a female ?—ED.

Rebeckah, born 13th Jan'y, 1664; Hana, born 24 Feb'y, 1667; Joseph, born 27 July, 1670; Shadrach, born 5 Sept., 1672; John, born 2 M'ch, 1674 or 5; Eliezer, born 1 July, 1677; Benjamin, born 23 July, 1683.

The sons and daughters of Thomas Caswell: Steven, borne 15 Feb., 1648; Thomas, borne 22 Feb., 1650; Petter, borne last of Octo., 1652; Mara, borne last of Aug., 1654; John, borne (?) last of July, 1656; Sarah, borne (?) last of Nov., 1658; William, borne 15 Sept., 1660; Hana, borne 14 July, 1661; Samuel, borne 26 Jan'y, 1662; Elizabeth, borne 10th Jan'y, 1664; Abigail, borne 27 Octo., 1666; Easter, borne 1 June, 1669.

The sons and daughters of Samuel Hall: Samuel, borne 11 Dec., 1664; John, borne 19 Octo., 1666; Nicklos, borne 23 Jan'y, 1668; Elizabeth, borne 28 Octo., 1670; Mary, borne 3 Octo., 1672; Sarah, borne, 14 Octo., 1674; Ebenezer, borne 19 M'ch, 1677; Sarah, dyed 28 May, 1677; Sarah, borne 2 March, 1679; Goarge, borne 25 Jan'y, 1680.

The names of the children of William Briggs: William, born 25 Jan'y, 1667; Thomas, born 9 Sept., 1669; Sarah, born 10 Sept., 1669; Elizabeth, born 14 M'ch, 1671; Hana, born 4 Nov., 1672; Mary, born 14 Aug., 1674; Mathew, born 5 Feb'y, 1676; John, born 19 M'ch, 1680, Sarah, wife of William Briggs, dyed 20 March, 1680.

The names of the children of Jonathan Brigges: Jonathan, borne 15 M'ch, 1668; David, borne 6 Dec., 1669.

The names of the children of James Leonard, Junior: Unis, borne at Brantry, 25 Nov., 1668; Prudence, 24 Jan., 1669; Hana, borne at Brantrey 2 Octo., 1671; James, borne 1 Feb., 1672; Hana, the wife of James, dyed 25 Feb., 1674; James, the son of James, dyed 30 Dec., 1674; James Leonard, Jun., married to Lidia Culipher of Miltin 29 Octo., 1675; James, son of James, b. 11 May, 1677; Lidia, dr. of James, b. 10 M'ch, 1679; Stephen, son of James, b. 14 Dec., 1680; Abigaill, b. 30 Jan., 1682; Nathaniell, b. 18 M'ch, 1685; Nathaniell, dyed 11 June, 1685; Seth, borne 3 Ap'l, 1686; Sarah, borne 6 Sept., 1688; * Ebenezer, son of James, borne 28 Aug., 1708.

The names of Edward Bobit's children, and their age: Edward, borne 15 July, 1655; Sara, borne 20 M'ch, 1657; Hana, borne 9 M'ch, 1660; Damiras, borne 15 Sep., 1663; Elkana, borne 15 Dec., 1665; Dorkas, borne 20 Jan'y, 1666; Easter, borne 15 Ap'l, 1669; Ruth, borne 7 Aug., 1671; Deliverance, borne 15 Dec., 1673; Dorkas, dyed 9 April, 1674.

The names of James Philipes' children, and their age: James, borne 1 Jan. 1661; Nathaniell, borne 25 M'ch, 1664; Sara, borne 17 M'ch, 1667; William, borne 21 Aug., 1669; Seth, borne 14 Aug., 1671; Danil, borne 9 May, 1673; Ebenezer, borne 16 Jan., 1674.

Israell Woodward maried to Jane Godfree 4 Aug., 1670. Elizabeth, dr. of Israell, borne 15 June, 1670; Israell Woodward died 15 June, 1679; Israell Woodward, son of Israell, borne 18 Sept., 1674.

The names of Joseph Williams' children, and their age: Elizabeth, borne 30 July, 1669; Richard, borne 26 Nov., 1671; Mahitabel, borne 7 June, 1676; Joseph, borne 13 Feb., 1678; Benjamin, borne 15 Octo., 1681; Ebenezer, borne 21 April, 1685; Febe, borne 25 Sept., 1687; Richard dyed 13 July, 1688; Elizabeth dyed by drowning 13 Octo., 1688; Richard, borne 26 M'ch, 1689; Joseph, Sen., dyed 17 Aug., 1692.

---

* In another handwriting.

The names of Joseph Staples' children, and their age: John Staples, borne 28 Jan., 1670; Amy Staples, borne 13 Ap'l, 1674; Mary Staples, borne 26 Jan., 1677; Joseph, 12 M'ch, 1680; Hannah, 17 May, 1682; Nathaniel, 22 M'ch, 1684–5.

The names of the children of Mr. George Shove and Hopestill: Edward, borne Ap'l 28, 1665, buried Aug. 7, 1665; Elizabeth, born Aug. 10, 1666; Seeth, born Dec. 10, 1667; Nathaniel, born Jan. 29, 1668; Samuel, born June 16, 1670; Sarah, born July 30, 1671. Hopestill, wife of Geo. Shove, dyed 7th M'ch, 1673 or 4. George Shove maried to Mrs. Hannah Walley, Feb. 17, 1674–5. Mary, dr. of Geo. Shove, borne Aug. 11, 1676; Johana, dr. of Geo. Shove, borne Sep. 28, 1678. Mrs. Margary Peacock, the mother of Mr. Geo. Shove, buried the 17th day April, 1680. Edward, son of Geo. Shove, borne Octo., 1680; Mercy, dr. of Geo. Shove, borne 7 Nov., 1682. Mr. Geo. Shove married to Mrs. Sarah Farwell Dec. 8, 1686. Mr. Geo. Shove dyed Ap'l 21, 1687; Mrs. Hannah Shove, wife of Geo. Shove, dyed Sept., 1685.

The names of the children of John Smith, Sen.: Elizabeth, borne 7 Sept., 1663; Heniry, borne 27 May, 1666. John Smith, Sen., married Jael Parker of Bridgewater 15 Nov., 1672. Deborah, born 7 M'ch, 1676; Hana, born 22 M'ch, 1676; John, born 6 Dec., 1680.

The names of Samuel Holloway his children: Hana, born 1 M'ch 1667; Samuel, born 14 Sep., 1668; Nathaniel, born 2 July, 1670; Easter, born 14 May, 1673; John, born 24 Feb., 1674.

The names of the children of Jarad Talbut: Jarad, borne 20 March, 1666 or 7; Mary, borne 21 July, 1670; Elizabeth, borne 15 Dec., 1671; Samuel, borne 29 Feb., 1675; Josiah, borne 21 Octo., 1678; Nathaniel, borne 21 Feb., 1679.

John Edy married to Susana Padocke of Dartmouth, 12 Nov., 1665. The names of the children of John Edy: Mary, borne 14 M'ch, 1666 or 67; John, borne 19 Jan'y, 1670; John Edy married to Deliverance of Brantrey, 1 May, 1672; Marcey, dr. of J. Edy, borne 5 July, 1673; Hana, dr. of J. Edy, borne 6 Dec., 1676; Ebenezer, son of J. Edy, borne 16 May, 1679; Elazer, son of J. Edy, borne 16 Oct., 1681; Joseph, son of J. Edy, borne 4 Jan'y, 1683; Jonathan, son of J. Edy, borne 15 Dec., 1689; Susana, dr. of J. Edy, borne 18 Sept., 1692; Patience, dr. of J. Edy, borne 27 June, 1696. Susana, wife of J. Edy, died 14 M'ch, 1670; John Edy, Sen., dyed 27 Nov., 1695.

The names of the children of Richard Briggs: William, borne 21 Nov., 1663; Rebaka, borne 15 Aug., 1665; Richard, borne 7 Ap'l, 1668; John, borne 26 Feb., 1669; Joseph, borne 15 June, 1674; Benjamin, borne 15 Sept., 1677; Richard, borne 12 Jan., 1679; Hana, borne 17 Feb, 1681; Samuel, borne 20 Ap'l, 1683; Mary, borne 1 Jan., 1686; Mahitabel, borne 18 June, 1689.

The names of the children of Samuell Lincon, Senior: Samuell, borne 1 June, 1664; Hana, borne 24 March, 1666; Tamsan, dr., borne 27 Octo., 1667; Elizabeth, borne 24 April, 1669; Ebenezer, borne 15 Octo., 1673; Rachill, borne 16 Sept., 1677; John, borne 15 Sept., 1679; Thomas, borne Sept., 1683.

The sons and daughters of Robert Crossman: John, borne 16 M'ch, 1654; Mary, borne 16 July, 1655; Robert, borne 3 Aug., 1657;

Joseph, borne 25 April, 1659; Nathanill, borne 7 Aug., 1660; Eleazer, borne 16 M'ch, 1663; Elizabeth, borne 2 May, 1665; Samuel, borne 25 July, 1667; Eleazer dyed 26 Octo., 1667; Mercy, borne 20 M'ch, 1669; Thomas, borne 6 Octo., 1671; Susana, borne 14 Feb., 1672.

The names of the children of Jonah Asten, Jr.: Ester, borne 3d Jan., 1662; Mary, borne 12 May, 1663; Sarah, borne 4 Nov., 1665; Jonah, borne 17 Aug., 1667; John, borne 1 July, 1671.

The names of the children of John Lincon: John, borne 11 Octo., 1665; Thomas, borne 15 Sept., 1667.

Farmer Smith step-child, named Nicklos, borne the 21 Feb'y, 1672.

The names of the children of Daniel Fisher: Hana, borne 1 Feb., 1666; John, borne last of Nov., 1667; Samuell, borne 3 Dec., 1669; Eliezer, borne 12 May, 1673; Mary, borne 30 May, 1675; Mary, borne 12 Dec., 1677; Isreall, borne 27 M'ch, 1680; Nathaniel, borne 9 Feb., 1681.

The names of the children of Jabez Hackit: John, borne 26 Dec., 1654; Jabez, borne 12 Sept., 1656; Mary, borne 9 Jan., 1659; Sarah, borne 13 July, 1661; Samuell, borne 29 July, 1664; Hana, borne 25 Jan., 1666. Jabez Hackit, Senior, dyed 4 Nov., 1686.

The names of the sons and daughters of John Richmond: ——, dr., borne at Bridgwatter 2 June, 1654; John, borne at Bridgwatter 6 June, 1656; Thomas, borne at Newport, on Road Iland, 2 Feb., 1658; Susana, borne at Bridgwatter, Nov. 4, 1661; Joseph, borne at Tanton Dec. 8, 1663; Edward, borne at Tanton Feb. 8, 1665; Samuell, borne at Tanton Sep. 23, 1668; Sarah, borne at Tanton Feb. 26, 1670; John, borne at Tanton Dec. 5, 1673; Ebenezer, borne in Newport, R. I., 12 May, 1676; Abigaill, borne 26 Feb., 1678.

The names of the children of James Leonard: Mehitabel, borne 24 Octo., 1691; Elizabeth, borne 19 April, 1694; Mehitabel dyed 10 June, 1695.

The names of the children of John Dean: Samuel, born 24 Jan., 1666; Sarah, born 9 Nov., 1668; John, born 26 July, 1670; Mehitabell, born 9 Oct., 1671; John, born 18 Sept., 1674; Elizabeth, born 15 M'ch, 1676; Mary, born 15 July, 1680; Susana, born 13 Aug., 1683; Israell, born 4 Aug., 1685.

The names of the sons and daughters of Hezakia Hoar: Marcy, borne last Jan'y, 1654; Nathanill, borne last M'ch, 1656; Sarah, borne first April, 1658; Elizabeth, borne 26 May, 1660; Edward, borne 25 Sept., 1663; Lidia, borne 24 March, 1665; Mary, borne 22 Sept., 1669; Hezekiah, borne 10 Nov., 1678.

The names of the children of Joseph Gray: Mahitabell, borne 21 Feb., 1668; Joseph, borne 31 Dec., 1670; Ephraim, borne 20 June, 1673, dyed 21 June, 1675. Rebecka, wife of Joseph, dyed 13 May, 1676.

The names of the children of Thomas Lincon, Jun.: Mary, borne 12 May, 1652; Sarah, borne 25 Sept., 1654; Thomas, borne 21 Ap'l, 1656; Samuell, borne 16 M'ch, 1658; Jonah, borne 7 July, 1660; Hana, borne 15 M'ch, 1663; Constant, borne 16 May, 1665; Marcy, borne 3 April, 1670.

The names of James Bell's children, and their age: Jan, dr., borne 4th Ap'l, 1658; John, borne 15 Aug., 1660; James, borne 15 July, 1663; Nathanill, borne 7 Jan., 1664; Sarah, borne 15 Sep., 1666; Elizabeth, borne 15 Nov., 1668; Mary, borne 7 July, 1669; Joseph, borne 27 June, 1670; Easter, borne 15 Aug, 1672.

The names of the children of Thomas Armsbee: Thomas, borne 23 Feb., 1668; Mary, borne 3 Octo., 1670; Rebecka, borne 26 May, 1672; Juda, dr., borne 8 Jan'y, 1673; Jeremiah, borne 25 Nov., 1678.

The names of the children of John Tisdill, Jr.: Abigall, borne 15 July, 1667; John, borne 10 Aug., 1669; Anna, borne 27 Jan., 1672; Remember, borne 8 July, 1675.

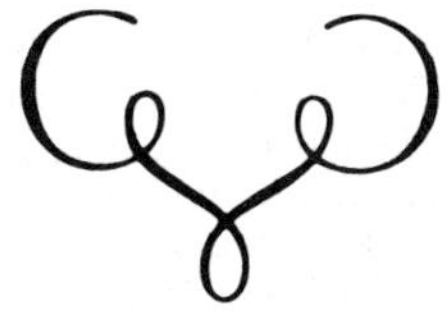

MARRIAGES, BIRTHS AND DEATHS AT TAUNTON, MASS.

[From the Proprietors' Records. Communicated by EDGAR H. REED, Esq. of Taunton.]

The names of the children of Richard Stevins: Richard, borne M'ch. 20, 1667 or 8; Nicklos, borne Feb. 23, 1669; Mary, borne June 8, 1672; Thomas, borne Feb. 3, 1674; Tamsin, borne July 3, 1677; Nathanell, borne July 30, 1680.

William Hack, son of Wm. Hack, borne 28 Nov., 1663.

Anna, dr. of Joseph Wilbore, borne 7 May, 1652; Joseph dyed, 27 Aug., 1691; Anna Wilbore maried Stephen March, 26 Jan'y, 1691.

The names of the sons and daughters of Thomas Joans: Hana, borne 3 Octo., 1657. Lidea, borne 26 July, 1659. Thomas, borne 4 May, 1662. Joseph, borne 5 May, 1664.

The names of the sons and daughters of William Paull: James, borne 7 April, 1657. John, borne 10 July, 1660. Edward, borne 7 Feb., 1664. Mary, borne 8 Feb., 1667. Sarah, borne 5 July, 1668: Abigall, borne 15 May, 1673.

The names of the children of Thomas Dean: Thomas, borne 1 Feb., 1670 ; dyed 26 Feb., 1670. Hanah, borne 14 Jan'y, 1671.

The names of the children of Stephen Caswell: Stephen, borne 11 Dec., 1673. Daborah. Joseph, borne 18 May, 1678.

The names of the children of Austen* Cobb: Elizabeth, borne 10 Feb., 1670. Morgen, borne 29 Dec., 1673. Samuell, borne 9 Nov., 1675. Bethia, borne 5 Ap'l., 1678. Mercey, borne 12 Aug., 1680. Abigaill, borne 28 May, 1684.

James Walker Jr. maried Bershaba Brukes, 23 Dec., 1673. James, son of James, borne 24 Dec., 1674.

John Hall, maried Hanna Penyman, 4 Feb., 1667. John, son of John, borne 27 June, 1672. Joseph, son of John, borne 7 Ap'l., 1674. James, son of John, borne 8 Dec., 1675. Benjamin, son of John, borne 6 Dec., 1677. Jacob, son of John, borne 14 Feb., 1680. Hannah, daughter of John, borne 8 Jan., 1682.

John Polard, son of John Polard, borne 20 M'ch., 1675.

Andrew Smith, the names of his children: Andrew Smith, 30 years, dyed 10 April, 1678. Mary, borne 3 Octo., 1675. Samuell, borne 15 May, 1678. Susana, borne 2 Nov., 1680. Andrew, borne 2 Ap'l., 1683. John, borne 23 Aug., 1685. John, dyed 6 Sep., 1685. Martha, borne 20 Oct., 1686. John, borne 3 June, 1689. Joseph, borne 18 Jan., 1691. Benjamin, 4 Feb., 1695.

John, son of Nathaniel Williams, borne 27 Aug., 1675.

Nathanill French maried Mary Tisdill, 9 Jan , 1676. Sarah, dr. of Nathanill, b. 4 Octo., 1680.

Nicklos White Jun., married to Ursila Macomber of Marshfield, 9 Dec., 1673. Nicklos, borne 3 Feb., 1675. Mathew, borne 25 Octo.,

---

* Probably Augustin.

1676. Ephram, borne 8 Feb., 1678. Dorcas, borne 24 Dec., 1680. John, borne 10 Jan., 1685.

Samuel Philips, maried to the widdow Mary Cob, 15 May, 1676. Mehitabel, dr. Sam., 9 Jan., 1676. Samuell, son of Sam., 29 Aug., 1678.

John Gould, maried to Mary Crossman, 21 Aug., 1673. Mary, dr. of John, 19 June, 1674. Hana, dr. of John, 9 Nov., 1677.

Isack Dean, maried to Hannah Leanard, 24 Jan., 1677. Alice, dr. of Isack, borne 20 Nov., 1678. Abigail, dr. of Isack, borne 16 Nov., 1680. Hannah, dr. of Isack, borne 24 Ap., 1683. Nathaniel, son of Isack, borne 25 Ap., 1685.

Thomas Gilbert, maried at Boston to Anna Black of Milton, 18 Dec., 1676. Hanah, dr. of Thomas, borne 28 Sept., 1677. Sarah and Mary, dr's. Thomas, borne 11 Aug., 1679. Thomas, son of Thomas, borne 11 July, 1681. Nathaniel, son of Thomas, borne 19 July, 1683. Mehitabel, son of Thomas, borne 5 May, 1686. Thomas, son of Thomas, dyed 1 Feb., 1692. Jane Gilbert, the mother of Thomas Gilbert, dyed 1 June, 1691, aged 77 years.

John Cobb, son of John Cobb, borne 31 M'ch., 1678.

The names of the children of John Woodward: John, borne 3 June, 1676. Robert, borne 2 M'ch., 1678. Nathanill, borne 31 July, 1679. Isreall, borne 30 July, 1681. Ebenezer, borne 13 Feb., 1683. Joseph, borne 22 Feb., 1685. Ezekiel, borne 26 Feb., 1687. Mary, borne 26 Feb., 1687. John Woodward Senior, died 10 May, 1688.

William Hoskins, maried to Sarah Caswell, 3 July, 1677. Anna, dr. of William borne 14 Feb., 1678. Sarah, dr. of William, borne last day of Aug., 1679. William, son of William, borne 30 June, 1681. Heniry, son of William, borne last M'ch., 1683; dyed about 15 Dec., 1683. Heniry, son of William, borne 12 Octo., 1686. Josiah son of William, borne 4 Ap'l., 1689. John, son of William, borne 28 Sept., 1690. Jacob, son of William, borne 1 Nov., 1692. Stephen, son of William, borne 2 Sept., 1697.

Edward Rew, dyed 16 July, 1678. Elizabeth Walker, wife of James Walker Sen., dyed 8 July, 1678. James Walker Sen., maried to Sarah Rew, 4 Nov., 1678.

Robert Crossman Jr., maried to Hanah Brooks, 21 July, 1679. Nathaniell, son of Robt., borne M'ch. 10, 1680. Hannah, dr. of Robt., borne Feb. 11, 1681. A son still born of Robt., Octo. 21, 1683. Elizabeth, dr. of Robt., borne Feb'y 20, 1684. Robert, son of Robt., borne Aug. 27, 1686; dyed Apl. 11, 1687. Seth, borne Octo., 1688. Mehitabell, borne June 1, 1694; dyed Feb 25, 1695. Another son dead borne, June 4, 1697. Bethia, borne Aug. 1, 1700; dyed Octo. 6, 1794. Aug. 29, 1717 entred.

Johana, dr. of Nathaniel Thayer, borne 13 Dec., 1665.

Isack Negus, maried to Hannah Andrews, 7th Aprill, 1679.

Benjamin Leonard, maried to Sarah Thrasher, 15 Jan'y, 1678. Sarah, borne 21 May, 1680, Sat. 4 o'clock in the afternoon. Benjamin, borne 25 Jan., 1682. Hannah, borne 8 Nov., 1685 Jerusha, borne 25 June, 1689. Hannah, borne 8 Dec., 1691. Joseph, borne 22 Jan., 1692. Henry, borne 8 Nov., 1695.

Nicholas Stoton, also spelt Stoughton, maried to Elizabeth Knap

17 Feb., 1673. Hanah, dr. of Nicholas, borne 4 July, 1679. Samuell, son of Nicholas, borne 28 Octo., 1690.

Joseph Woode, maried to Heaster Walker, 1 Jan., 1679.

Richard Godfree Jr., maried to Mary Richmond, 1 Jan., 1679. Als, dr. of Richard, borne 20 Aug., 1680. Richard, son of Richard, borne 1 M'ch., 1681. Mary, dr. of Richard, borne 29 May, 1682. Abigail, dr. of Richard, borne 5 Nov., 1684. Joana, dr. of Richard, borne 30 July, 1686. Sarah, dr. of Richard, borne 15 May., 1689. John, son of Richard, borne last day Octo., 1691. Joseph, son of Richard, borne 1 M'ch., 1694 or 5.

Ezra Deane, maried to Bethiah Edson of Bridgewatter, 17 Dec., 16 Bethiah, dr. of Ezra, borne 14 Octo., 1677 ; dyed 27 Nov., 1679. Ezra, son of Ezra, borne 14 Octo., 1680. Samuell, son of Ezra, borne 11 Ap'l, 1681 ; dyed 16 Feb., 1682. Seth, son of Ezra, borne 3 June, 1683.

John White, maried to Hannah Smith, 24 Feb., 1679. John, son of John, borne 16 Aug., 1681. Hannah, dr. of John, borne 19 April, 1683. Josiah, dr. of John, borne 19 April, 1685. Elizabeth, dr. of John, borne 1 Nov., 1687. Samuel, son of John, borne 3 Aug., 1691. Abigail, dr. of John, borne 17 April, 1694. Susana, dr. of John, borne 27 Sept., 1696.

Israel Thrasher, son of Christopher Thrasher, borne 15 Sept., 1648. Israel Thrasher, maried to Mary Caswell, 15 Aug. 1676. Mary, dr. of Israel, borne 7 Aug., 1677.

Heniry Hodges, maried to Easter Gollup, 17 Dec., 1674. Mary, dr. of Heniry, borne 3 Feb., 1675. Easter, dr. of Heniry, borne 17 Feb., 1677. William, son of Heniry, borne 18 M'ch, 1680. Charity, dr. of Heniry, borne 5 Ap'l, 1682.

Samuell Pitts, maried to Sarah Bobit, 25 M'ch., 1680. Sarah, dr. of Samuell, borne 10 M'ch, 1681. Mary, dr. of Samuell, borne 10 M'ch, 1683. Samuel, son of Samuell, borne 12 M'ch, 1685. Henry, son of Samuell, borne 13 July, 1687. Abigail, dr. of Samuell, borne 3 Feb., 1689. Petter, son of Samuell, borne 8 Aug., 1692. Ebenezer, son of Samuell, borne 27 Nov., 1694.

Samuel Rider, maried to Lidia Tildin of Plimouth in Taunton, by James Walker, Sen., 14 June, 168 .

Richard Haskins of Portsmouth, maried to Jane Feuster of Taunton, 2d August, 1686.

Joseph French, the births and deaths of his children. Thomas, borne 12 Dec., 1680 ; dyed 29 Dec., 1680. Ebenezer, borne 27 June, 1682. Nathan, borne 28 June, 1686.

Benjamin Deane, maried to Sarah Williams, 6 Jan., 1681. Naomy, dr. of Benjamin, borne 1 Nov., 1681. Naomy, dr. of Benjamin, dyed 6 Jan., 168$\frac{1}{2}$. Hannah, dr. of Benjamin, borne 26 Dec., 1682. Israell, son of Benjamin, borne Feb. 2, 168$\frac{4}{5}$. Mary, dr. of Benj. borne June 15, 1687. Damaris, son of Benjamin, borne Sep. 4, 1689. Sarah, dr. of Benjamin, borne Aug. 30, 1692. Elizabeth, dr. of Benj. borne M'ch 22, 169$\frac{4}{5}$. Mehitabell, dr. of Benjamin, borne June 9, 1697. Benjamin, son of Benjamin, borne July 31, 1699. Ebenezer, son of Benjamin, borne Feb. 24, 170$\frac{1}{2}$. Lidya, dr. of Benjamin, borne Dec. 11, 1704. Josiah, dr. of Benjamin, borne Octo. 23., 1707 ; dyed M'ch. 22, 170$\frac{9}{10}$.

Joseph Leonard, maried to Mary Black of Milton, 15 Dec., 1679. Mary, dr. of Joseph, borne 2 Octo., 1680. Experiance, dr. of Joseph, borne 18 M'ch, 1682. Joseph, son of Joseph, borne 28 Jan., 1683. Mehitabell, dr. of Joseph, borne 22 Aug., 1685. Edward, son of Joseph, borne 2 Nov., 1688. William, son of Joseph, borne 26 M'ch., 1690. Mary, dr. of Joseph, died 3d June, 1685. Joseph Leonard, Sen., died 19th Octo., 1692.

Edward Cetill, maried to Susana Godfree, 10 July, 1682. Mary, dr. of Edw'd, borne 5 Ap'l, 1683.

John Macomber Jr., maried Anna Euins, 16 July, 1678. Thomas, borne 30 April, 1679. John, borne 18 M'ch, 1681. William, borne 31 Jan., 1683.

William Witherell Jr., maried to Elizabeth Newland, 14 M'ch, 1681.

Anthony Newland, the son of Jeremiah Newland, borne 1 Aug., 1657. Anthony Newland, maried to Easter Austin, 6 Dec., 1682. Jeremiah, son of Anthony, borne 26 Feb, 1683. John, son of Anthony, borne 12 Sep., 1686.

Nathaniel Hoar, maried to Sarah Wilbore, 2 Feb., 1681. Abigal, dr. of Nathaniel, borne 2 Nov., 1682. Samuell, son of Nathaniel, borne 22 M'ch, $168\frac{4}{5}$. William, son of Nathaniel, borne 19 April 1687. Hannah, dr. of Nathaniel, borne 19 M'ch., $168\frac{8}{9}$. Patience, dr. of Nathaniel, borne 12 Octo., 1693.

Hannah Prisberry, dr. of Joseph Prisberry, borne 1 Octo., 1715.

Walter Morey, maried to Martha Cottrill, 17 Jan., 1682.

James Reed, maried to Susana Richmond, 18 April, 1683.

Hugh Brigs, maried to Martha Euerson of Plimouth, 1 M'ch, $168\frac{2}{3}$. Barshaba, dr. of Hugh, borne 11 Jan., 1683. John, son of Hugh, borne 15 Sept., 1686. Mehitabell, dr. of Hugh, borne 15 July, 1687.

The names of the children of Jeremiah Newland. Anthony, borne 1 Aug., 1657. Elizabeth, borne 18 May, 1659. Susana, borne 15 July, 1664. Jeremiah, borne 8 Feb., 1667. John, borne 25 M'ch, 1669. Mary, borne 17 July, 1671. Benjamin, borne 1 Octo., 1673. Mercy, borne 25 M'ch, 1676. Jeremiah Newland, Sen., dyed 25 July, 1681.

Richard Godfree, Sen., maried to the widdow Mary Philips, 26 M'ch, 1684.

Thomas, son of John Bayley, borne 27 Feb., 1683.

Samuel Hall, Jun., maried to Abigaill Prat of Plimouth, 3 Jan., 1683. Jonathan, son of Samuel, borne 22 Aug., 1686.

The names of the children of Thomas Leonard : Mary, borne 2 Aug., 1663. Thomas, borne 22 Jan., 1665. John, borne 18 May, 1668. Goarg, borne 18 April, 1671. Samuell, borne 1 Feb., 1673. Elkanah, borne 15 May, 1677. James, borne 17 Dec., 1679. James, dyed 8 May, 1682. A daughter still born, 10 April, 1681. Seth, borne 28 April, 1682 ; dyed 2 Nov., 1682. Phebe, borne 3d M'ch, 1684 ; dyed 15 July, 1685. Elizabeth, borne 15 July, 1686.

Edward Bobit, maried Abigal Tisdill, 1 Feb., 1683. Edward, son of Edward, borne 14 Feb., 1684.

MARRIAGES, BIRTHS AND DEATHS AT TAUNTON, MASS.

[Copied from the Proprietors' Records, by E. H. Reed, Esq. of Taunton.]

The names of the children of Richard Burt: Abil, borne 5 Dec., 1657. Ester Gollup, dr. of John Gollup, borne 21 July, 1653. Mary Burt, dr. of Richard, borne about 15 May, 1661. Richard, son, borne about 21 June, 1663. Joseph, borne about 15 May, 1666. Ebenezer, borne about 15 May, 1669. John, borne about 21 Aug., 1671. Ephraim, borne 27 Feb., 1674. Abagail, borne 28 Jan., 1676.

The names of the children of Eleazer Gilbert: Elizabeth, borne 9 March, 1683. Mercy, borne 13 Oct., 1684.

Uriah, son of James Leonard, Sen., borne 10 July, 1662.

Uriah Leonard, maried to Elizabeth Caswell, 1 June, 1685. Uriah, son of Uriah, borne 10 April, 1686.

Nathaniell Williams, maried to Elizabeth Rogger of Ducksbery, 17 Nov., 1668. John, son of Nathaniell, borne 27 Aug., 1675. Nathaniel, son of Nathaniell, borne 9 April, 1679. Elizabeth, dr. of Nathaniell, 18 April, 1686.

Benjamin Williams, maried to Rebekah Macey, 12 March, 1689 or 90. Rebekah, dr of Benjamin, borne 27 Nov., 1690. Josiah, son of Benjamin, borne 7 Nov., 1692. Benjamin, son of Benjamin, borne 31 July, 1695. John, son of Benjamin, borne 27 March, 1699.

Samuell Hall, son of Samuell Hall, Sen., maried to Elizabeth Boorn, 7 April, 1686. Elizabeth, dr. of Samuell, borne 20 March, 1687. Remember, dr. of Samuell, borne 15 Feb., 1689. Nicholas, son of Samuell, borne 23 Jan., 1690. Mary, dr. of Samuell, borne last day of Oct., 1692. Nathaniel, son of Samuell, borne 18 May, 1695. Mahitabel, dr. of Samuell, borne 1 Dec., 1697. Enoch, son of Samuell, borne 13 April, 1699.

Abraham Hathaway, maried to Rebekah Wilbore, 28 Aug., 1684. Abraham, son of Abraham, borne 11 Sept., 1685. Thomas, son of Abraham, borne 26 Jan., 1686. Ebenezer, son of Abraham, borne 25 May, 1689.

Joseph White, children's names and age: Lidia, borne 17 Aug., 1682. Joseph, borne 13 Feb., 1683. Edward, borne 27 March, 1686. Mary, borne 19 July, 1688. Susana, borne 8 Aug., 1690. William, borne 28 Oct., 1692. Nathaniel, borne 25 April, 1695. Ebenezer, borne 13 Sept., 1697.

Samuel Bagley, maried to Mary Thayer of Brantrey, 17 May 1686.

Mary Godfree, dr. of Robert Godfree, borne 5 April, 1686.

Mr. Giles Gilbert, maried to Mary Rockit (widow) of Rehoboth, 28 Oct., 1686. John, son of Giles, borne 24 Aug., 1687. John, son of Giles, dyed sometime in March, 1688. Joseph, son of Giles, borne 22 March, 1689.

James Philips, maried to Abigail Hathaway, 9 Dec., 1685. James, son of James, borne 15 Sept., 1686. Sarah, dr. of James, borne 24 Feb., 1687.

The names of the children of James Philips by his wife Elizabeth: Elizabeth, borne 8 March, 1692–3. Mary, borne 7 Nov., 1694. Samuell, borne 10 Feb., 1697. Rebekah, borne last day of Aug., 1700. Experience, borne 8 April, 1702. Nathaniell, borne 11 Feb., 1704. Kezia, borne 18 Nov., 1706. Daniell, borne 23 Oct., 1708.

John Crane, maried to Hannah Leonard, 13 Dec., 1686. Ziporah, dr. of John, borne 13 March, 1688–9. Gershom, son of John, borne 3 Sept., 1692.

William Briggs, son of Richard Briggs, maried to Constant Lincon, 13 July, 1687.

Thomas Braman, maried to Hannah Fisher, 20 Jan., 1685. Thomas, son of Thomas, borne 2 Dec., 1686. Danill, son of Thomas, borne 13 Oct., 1688.

Joseph Woode, maried to Easter Walker, 1 Jan., 1679. Joseph, son of Joseph, borne 4 Aug., 1681. John, son of Joseph, borne 28 Feb., 1683.

Richard Burt, maried to Eunice Leonard, 18 Feb., 1685–6. Jemima, dr. of Richard, borne 12 April, 1687.

Thomas Harvey, Sen., maried to Elizabeth Willis of Bridgwater, 10 Dec., 1679. William, son of Thomas, borne 2 Jan., 1680. Thomas, son of Thomas, borne 17 Sept., 1682. John, son of Thomas, borne 4 Feb., 1683. Jonathan, son of Thomas, borne 30 April, 1685. Joseph, son of Thomas, borne 14 Jan., 1687.

Samuell Thrasher, maried to Bethia Brooks of Rehoboth, 5 Dec., 1683. Samuel, son of Samuell, borne 2 Oct., 1686. Brooks, son of Samuell, borne 11 Sept., 1688. Bezaleel, son of Samuell, borne 28 Oct., 1689. Elnathan, son of Samuel, borne 1 Aug., 1691.

Samuell Wilbore, maried to Sarah Philips, 19 Dec., 1688. Mary, dr. of Samuell, borne 9 Sept., 1689. Sarah, dr. of Samuell, borne 21 March, 1690. Sarah, dr. of Samuell, dyed 31 May, 1690. Anna, dr. of Samuell, borne 16 July, 1692. Samuell, son of Samuell, borne 26 March, 1695. Samuell Wilbore, Sen., dyed 16 Dec., 1695.

Jonathan Pratt, maried to the widow Elizabeth Hall, 3 March, 1689–90.

The names of Thomas Eliot, his children: Joseph, borne 2 March, 1684. Elizabeth, borne 1 Jan., 1686. Benjamin, borne 23 June, 1689. Jane Eliot, wife of Thomas, dyed 9 Nov., 1689.

John Thrasher, borne 8 Dec, 1653; maried to Mercy Crossman, 26 Jan., 1687. Christopher, son of John, borne 9 June, 1689. Mercy, dr. of John, borne 3 April, 1691. John, son of John, borne 2 March, 1693. Damaris, dr. of John, borne 17 April, 1695. Sarah, dr. of John, borne 20 March, 1697. Hannah, dr. of John, borne 14 July, 1701. Israel, son of John, borne 24 Dec., 1703. Catharine, dr. of John, borne 20 Dec., 1707.

John Crossman, maried to Joanna Thayer, 7 Jan., 1689. Abigall, dr. of John, borne 7 Oct., 1690. Sarah, dr. of John, borne 27 Aug., 1692. Joanna, dr. of John, borne 29 March, 1695. Mercy, dr. of John, borne 6 Oct., 1697. Deborah, dr. of John, borne 11 Feb., 1700. John, son of John, borne 27 May, 1702. Jonathan, son of John, borne 27 Jan., 1705. Benjamin, son of John, borne 8 Jan., 1708. Henry, son of John, borne 6 July, 1712.

John Caswell, son of John Caswell, borne 17 July, 1690. Elizabeth, dr. of John, borne 16 Nov., 1691. Samuel, son of John, borne

6 Oct. 1695. Josiah, son of John, borne 1 Jan., 1696. Jedediah, son of John, borne 7 Nov., 1700. Bethiah, son of John, borne 14 June, 1705.

Samuel Hackit's children's birth.

Nathaniel Thayer, Jun., maried to Rebekah Brigs, 11 Feb., 1690. Nathaniel, son of Nathaniel, borne 11 Oct., 1693.

Samuell Smith, maried Rebekah Hoar, 20 Feb., 1690. Samuell, son of Samuell, borne 8 Feb., 1691. Sarah, dr. of Samuell, borne 2 Dec, 1693. Rebekah, wife of Samuell Smith, dyed 30 April, 1694.

Mr. Samuell Danforth, maried ——: Elizabeth, dr. of Samuell, borne 29 July, 1689. Samuell Danforth's twins: the dr. caled Mary, the son lived not to be baptized; both dyed—they were born the first day of June, 1691. James, son of Samuell, borne 11 Nov., 1692.

William Brigs, son of William Brigs, maried to Elizabeth Lincon, 13 Oct., 1693. Sarah, dr. of William, borne 5 July, 1694.

Samuell Crosman's children by his wife Elizabeth: Elizabeth, borne 31 Oct., 1691. Thomas, borne 13 Aug., 1694.

The register of the names of the children of Samuell Crossman by his wife Mary: Joseph and Samuell, borne 22 Aug., 1697. Robert, borne 29 April, 1699. Barnabas, borne 12 March, 1701. Gabriel, borne 6 Nov., 1702. Sarah, borne 15 May, 1704. Phinehas, borne 31 July, 1707. Theophilus, borne 18 March, 1709.

John Hall, son of Samuell Hall (deceased), children's names: Sarah, borne 17 Jan., 1694–5. Susanna, borne 1 Nov., 1696. Seth, borne 7 Sept., 1698. Hezekiah, borne 20 Oct., 1700. Josiah, borne 21 Aug., 1702. Charity, borne 21 July, 1704. Zeporah, borne 4 Aug., 1706. Elizabeth, borne 2 April, 1708.

Elkannah Bobit, maried to Elizabeth Brigs, 25 June, 1609. Elkannah, son of Elkannah, borne 22 April, 1690. Damaris, dr. of Elkannah, borne 18 June, 1691. Dorkas, dr. of Elkannah, borne 12 Aug., 1693. Hopestill, dr. of Elkannah, borne 11 Sept., 1695. Elizabeth, dr. of Elkannah, borne 6 March, 1698. Mercie, dr. of Elkannah, borne 30 Dec., 1699.

Ebenezer Cambel, maried to Hannah Pratt, 29 March, 1694. Othniell, son of Ebenezer, borne 8 Feb., 1695–6. Ebenezer, son of Ebenezer, son of Ebenezer, borne 30 Nov., 1697. Caleb, son of Ebenezer, borne 11 Nov., 1699. Joshua, son of Ebenezer, borne 17 Jan., 1701. Onesimus, son of Ebenezer, borne 10 March, 1704. Nehemiah, son of Ebenezer, borne 15 Feb., 1706. Shuball, son of Ebenezer, borne 28 Sept., 1709. Hannah, dr. of Ebenezer, borne 1 May, 1712.

Thomas Briggs, y[e] son of William Briggs, maried to Abigail Thayer, 24 Oct., 1689. Thomas, son of Thomas, borne 9 Oct., 1690. Sarah, dr. of Thomas, borne 10 Dec., 1693. Nathaniel, son of Thomas, borne 18 June, 1695.

Joseph Tucker, maried to Hannah Wilkinson, 6 Dec., 1695.

Deborah, dr. of Geo. and Lydia Godfrey, borne Oct. 30, 1740; Geo. Godfrey and Bethiah Hodges, maried in Norton, May 9, 1744, by John Godfrey, Justice Peace. Lydia, dr. of Geo. and Bethia, borne May 21, 1745. Joanna, dr. of Geo. and Bethia, borne Nov. 5, 1747. Bethia, dr. of Geo. and Bethia, borne Sept. 22, 1749. Mary, dr. of Geo. and Bethia, borne Nov. 8, 1751. Welthea, dr. of Geo. and

Bethia, borne May 21, 1756. George 2d, son of Geo. and Bethia, borne Sept. 17, 1758. Rufus, son of Geo. and Bethia, borne July 8, 1761. Linday, son of Geo. and Bethia, borne March 1, 1766. All ye aforesd children baptized by ye Rev. Mr. Fisher of Dighton. Departed this life, Bethia Godfrey, wife of said Geo. Godfrey, Esq., Jan 27, 1786. Geo. Godfrey, Esq., and Mrs. Abigail Dean, 2d., was married together at Taunton, Sept. 5, 1786, by the Rev. Mr. Ephraim Judson; her maiden name was Abigail Shaw of Middleboro.

Thos. Caswell, Jun., his children's age: Benjamin, borne 16 Nov., 1675. Thomas, borne 2 Jan., 1677. Mary, borne 16 March, 1679. James, borne 17 May, 1681. John, borne 27 Jan., 1683.

Charles Williams, maried to Mary Glading, 13 Feb., 1695. Chas., son of Charles, borne 27 Oct., 1696.

John Hodges, maried to Elizabeth Macey, 15 May, 1672. John, son of John, borne 5 April, 1673. Nathaniel, son of John, borne 2 April, 1675. Samuell, son of John, borne 20 May, 1678. William, son of John, borne 6 June, 1682. George, son of John, borne 27 Nov., 1685. Ebenezer, son of John, borne 13 March, 1687. Nathan, son of John, borne 23 Oct., 1690.

John, son of Richard and Mary Godfrey, borne Oct. 31, 1691. Joanna Gooding, dr. of Geo. and Deborah Gooding, borne March 13, 1687, being Sabath day. John Godfrey and Joanna Gooding, maried in Dighton, by Henry Hodges, Esq., Feb. 2, 1716. Child of John and Joanna, dead borne, May 19, 1719. Geo. son of John, borne March 19, 1720–1. John, son of John, borne Dec. 24, 1723. John, son of John, dyed Oct 29, 1725. John, son of John, borne Nov. 25, 1728. John, son of John, dyed Nov. 26, 1749. Richard Godfrey, 1st named aforesaid, dyed Aug. 14, 1725. Mary, wife of said Richard, dyed Nov. 5, 1732. John Godfrey, Esq., father of said George, dyed Nov. 4, 1758. Joanna, mother of said George, dyed March 9, 1765.

Ephraim Emerson, maried to Elizabeth Walker, 7 Jan., 1695–6. Theadotia, alias Ephraim, son of Ephraim, borne 24 Dec., 1696.

Geo. Godfrey, 2d, son of Geo. Godfrey, Esq., and Abigail King, dr. of Capt. John King of Raynham, maried 26 Dec., 1782. James, son of Geo., borne April 30, 1784. Samuel Leonard, son of Geo., borne April 7, 1786. Abigail, dr. of Geo., borne April 20, 1788.

John Godfrey, son of Geo. Godfrey, Esq., maried to Jerusha Hodges, dr. of Abijah Hodges, June 3, 1779. John, 2d son of John and Jerusha, borne May 27, 1781. William, son of John, borne May 9, 1783. Charles, son of John, borne March 16, 1785. Geo. 3d, son of John, borne May 13, 1787. Samuel, son of John, borne Oct. 15, 1790.

Samuel Leonard, maried to Katherine Deane, 17 April, 1701. Samuel, son of Samuel, borne 17 May, 1702. Nathan, son of Samuel, borne 5 May, 1704.

Israell Deane, Jun., of Taunton, maried to Catherine Bird of Dorchester, 20 March, 1704–5. The record of the children of Israell Deane, Jun., by Catherine, his wife: Stephen, borne 17 Feb., 1705–6. Stephen, dyed 3 March, 1705–6. Catherine, borne Feb. 10, 1706–7. Silence, borne July 7, 1709. Mehitabell, borne April 10, 1711. Israell, borne Jan. 28, 1712–13. Joshua, borne March 3, 1714–15.

Rufus Godfrey, son of Geo. Godfrey, Esq., and Welthea Crossman, dr. of the wife of Benj. Shores, named Jemima, maried March 9, 1785. Wealthea 2d, dr. of Rufus and Welthea, borne Aug. 17, 1785. Bethiah, dr. of Rufus, borne March 11, 1788. Abigail, dr. of Rufus, borne Sept. 5, 1790.

——, maried to Elizabeth Parker of Bridgwater, 14 Nov., 1665. Thomas Lincon, Sen., maried to Elizabeth Street, viddow, 10 Dec., 1665. Aggnes Smith, wife of Francis Smith, dyed 6 Jan., 1665. William Briges, maried to Sarah Maycomber of Mashfele, 6 Nov., 1666. Samuell Holloway, maried to Jan Braman, 26 March, 1666. Jarad Talbut, maried to Sarah Androwes, 1 April 1664. John Edy, maried to Susana Padack of Dartmouth, the last Nov., 1665. Richard Briges, maried to Rebecka Hoskins of Lackingam, 15 Aug., 1662. John Dean, maried Sarah Edson of Bridgwater, 7 Nov., 1663. Joseph Gray, maried Rebeka Hill, 25 Feb., 1667. Constant Astin, wife of Jonas, Sen., dyed 22 April, 1667. Jonah Asten, Sen., maried Frances Hill of Onckife, 14 Dec., 1667. Timothy, son of Mr. William Poolle, dyed 15 Dec., 1667; he was drowned in a little pond at Wesquabinansit, where it was thought he did swim in after a gose which he had shoote. John Parker, dyed 14 Feb., 1667. Ana, wife of James Burt, dyed 7 Aug., 1665. Elizabeth, w. of Joseph Wilbore, dyed 9 Nov., 1670. John, son of John Deane, dyed 6 Aug., 1670. Thomas Armsbee, maried Mary Fitch of Rehoboth, 11 May, 1667. John Tisdill, Jun., maried Hana Roggers of Ducksbery, 23 Nov., 1664. Goarg Shove, maried Hopestill Numan of Rehoboth, 12 July, 1664. Lidia, wife of John Smith, Sen., dyed 21 July, 1672. Mr. John Pool, maried to Mrs. Elizabeth Brenton, 28 March, 1672. Thomas Dean, maried to Katrin Stephens, 5 Jan., 1669. Stephen Caswell, maried Hana Thrasher, 24 Dec., 1672. John Smith, Sen., maried Jael Parker of Bridgwater, 15 Nov., 1672. Andrew Smith, maried Mary Bundy, 5 Jan., 1673. John Pollard, maried Mary Linard of Bridgwater, 24 Dec., 1673. Mary, dr. of Shadrach Wilbore, dyed 19 June, 1674. Nicklos Stotun, maried Elizabeth Knap, 17 Feb., 1673. Martha, widow of John Bundy, dyed 1 May, 1674. Elias Irish, maried Dorothy Witherell, 26 Aug., 1674. Hannah, dr. of Shadrach Wilbore, dyed 30 Dec., 1675. John Bundy, maried Ruth Gurney of Mendum, 9 Jan. 1676. Jonah Asten 2d, dyed 10 May, 1676. Richard Marshall, maried Easter Bell, 11 Feb., 1676. John Tisdill, Sen., kiled by the Indians, 27 June, 1675. Sarah Tisdill, wife of John Tisdill, Sen., dyed Dec., 1676. John Cobb, maried Jane Woodward, 13 June, 1676. Mrs. Els Pain, dyed 5 Dec., 1682. Jonah Astin, Sen., dyed 30 July, 1683. Mary Wilbore, wife of Shadrach Wilbore, dyed 27 March, 1691. Shadrach Wilbore, maried Hannah Paine of Brantry, 13 Sept., 1692.

Vital Records of Taunton, Mass.: Correction.—In the printed Vital Records of Taunton, vol. 1, p. 365, the father of Anna Richmond, who was baptized 8 July 1764, was Stephen, and not Ephrem, as there given; and on p. 368 the same holds true regarding the father of Wealthy Richmond, baptized 8 July 1764.

Malden, Mass. George Walter Chamberlain.

TISBURY, MASS., VITAL RECORDS,—The following items, copied from a family record in the possession of James F. Luce of West Tisbury, Mass., and now a part of the town records, were received too late for incorporation in the "Vital Records of Tisbury, Mass., to the year 1850," and are given here as supplementing that volume.

John Cleveland born Dec. 2, 1748
" " died Oct. 19, 1825, aged 74 years-10 mo.-13 days.
Catharine Look born April 16, 1758
John Cleveland & Catharine Look married——their Children
Love Cleveland born March 31, 1777
" " died Nov. 18, 1814, aged 36 years-6 mo.-12 days.
James Cleveland born Dec. 24, 1778
Nancy Cleveland born Dec. 3, 1780
John Cleveland born Feb. 14, 1783
" " died Sept. 12, 1801 in Martinique-18 yr.-7 mo.-18 days
George Cleveland born Nov. 13, 1785
" " died Mar. 15, 1809 in Havanah-24 yrs.-4 mo.-26 Days
Aron Cleveland born April 20, 1788
Betsy Cleveland born July 30, 1790
Polly Cleveland born Oct. 2, 1792
" " died Oct. 20, 1792, aged 18 days
David Cleveland born Sept. 2, 1794
" " died Aug. 30, 1834, aged 41 years.
Prudence Luce born July 26, 1781
James Cleveland & Prudence Luce Married Nov. 21, 1802——their Children born—died
Sophronia Cleveland Nov. 6, 1804-Oct. 25, 1819, aged 14 yrs.-11 mo. 20 days
George W. Cleveland Oct. 20, 1806-at Sea in 1851 aged 45 years
Dency L. Cleveland Aug. 4, 1812
A Son July 2, 1815-July 2, 1815
Lorenzo D. Cleveland July 5, 1822

NOTES FROM TISBURY CHURCH RECORDS.—The following memoranda were taken from the Records of the Congregational Church at Tisbury, Mass.:

John Mayhew of Chilmark was the first minister of Tisbury, but not ordained. The time when is unknown. 1673 [*sic*]

Josiah Torrey the first ordained Minister at Tilbury was ordained 1702.

Nathaniel Hancock was ordained 1727.

George Daman was ordained Oct[r]. 1760

Asarelah Morse was installed Dec. 1st. 1784 ["Apr. 5, 1799" written in pencil —evidently date of resignation].

Nymphas Hatch was ordained Oct, 7th. 1801 ["June 26 1819" written in pencil—possibly date of resignation or death]

[In pencil]
Ebenezer Chase June 19, 1835—Dec 25, 1842
John Walker Feb. 15, 1843 May 1847
Henry Van Houton Apr 20 1849 Apr 1850
Lot B. Sullivan Nov. 16, 1851
3 Coll May 1852

In August 1807. there were 196 dwelling houses in Tisbury & 216 Families. 185 dwelling houses in Edgartown & 192 Families. 88 dwelling houses in Chilmark & 101 Families.

In August 1807. there were 32 blacks in Tisbury pure Indians & mix'd, at Gayhead 240 at home & abroad. at Choppoquidoc 65. at Farm neck 10.

The conveyance of this island was from the Earl of Sterling to the Duke of York From the Duke to Sir Francis Lovelace From him to Thomas Mayhew Sen[r].

Boston. ALICE L. WESTGATE.

IMPRESSMENTS AT WAREHAM, MASS., 1741 TO 1748.

By WILLIAM ROOT BLISS, Esq., of Short Hills, N. J.

IN 1741, and again in 1742, the King's snow came up Buzzard's Bay and carried off impressed men. In the following years others were impressed into His Majesty's land service through the agency of Israel Fearing of Wareham (born 1682, died 1754), then a captain of the militia and a justice of the peace. He wrote the names of the impressed men in his account book, from which I copy them, below, exactly as they were written. He also furnished them with some equipments, which he noted in his account book, as follows:

4 halbuds,	£11.00.00
Cullers,	11.09.00
Drum,	3.00.00

And so equipped with drum, flags and halberds, these farmers went from home to fight for the King against French and Indians.

There was plenty of colonial law for impressing these men. The earliest laws of Massachusetts provided for "Impresses" of laborers, cattle, men and merchandize for the King's service; and the way of doing it was regulated by the Great and General Court, from time to time, until the Revolution. Falstaff acknowledged having "misused the King's press most damnably"; and men of authority in the colonies may have done the same thing. But it is probable that Israel Fearing's agency was merely to serve impressment warrants sent to him by superior officers. His record shows that opportunity was given to the impressed men to buy substitutes, to obtain compensation, and even to run away:

April, 1740.—Robert Bese impresed and Nathan Brigg's man; and Nathan Briggs gave Robert Bese fifteen pounds old tener for half a man and Robert Bese went to the Estward.

May ye 15 day 1741 Josiah Cunit Impresed to go on bord ye snow And he Recived ten pounds in mony.

And Edward Bump paid him 5 pounds for his sons.

And John bump ye 3 two pounds.

And After hadawa two pounds for his sun.

And Joseph doty one pound for his sun.

May ye 15 day 1741 Lent to Edward Bump five pounds in mony Lent to Joseph doty one pound In cash.

March 1742 Joshua bese Impresed to go on bord ye sno and Joseph Landers paid 4 pounds for his son to him.

March ye 16 day 1743 Noah bump Imprests for his magests sarvis and Runaway.

June ye 18 day 1744 Jonathan bump Junr Impresed and Samuel peary for his magist sarvis and they both went to the Est frontters.

March 4 day 1745 Oliver Nores impresed and Run away and Joseph doty Jun and Run away Edward bump impresed and Joshua bump And barnabas bates and these 3 went in his magest sarvis to cap britan.

June 13d 1745 Ebenezer peary Jun and Jonathan bump Junr Listed for cap britten and I gave them fouer pounds apeace old tener.

June 17 1745 Jabez bensen was Impresed and went to ye Estward.

In 1745 Joshua Gibbes Jun Impresed and paul Rament and paul Rament Recived twenty pouns old tener and If Either of these are Impresed the other is to Apear and go Into his magestys sarvis or Else to give 20 pounds old tener.

July 23 day 1746 biniamin Chubback Impresed and gave Noah bum twenty pounds old ten to goo half for him.

July 23 day 1746 Samuel peary and Noah bump impresed to go to the Westward frunttery and Samuel peary Received 40 pounds old ten 20 pounds of John bushap for his sonn and ten pounds of Jorg Whit and ten pounds of Joh gibbes ye 20 pounds was for John Whit.

Sepr 26 1746 Jonathan Chubback Jun Impresed for Zeccues Bump At five pounds old ten Joseph Giford Jun prised at five pounds and ten shillings old tener for Edward bump to goo in his magty sarves.

March 1748 Judah Swift and Joseph doty and Edward Rayment Imprest and hired Robart bese for 55 pounds.

CHURCH RECORDS OF WEST YARMOUTH, MASS.

Copied by Florence Conant Howes

Through the courtesy of the Congregational Society of West Yarmouth, Mass., the entries which follow have been copied from the earliest church records of that Society.

In the oldest book the only records of value for reproduction here are baptisms. Those recorded between 17 Dec. 1769 through 2 June 1816 appear in a second recording with additions and variations. Such additional information and variations as appear important have been introduced herewith *between brackets.*

The second book with baptisms, marriages, and deaths contains also a repetition of baptisms from 4 May 1822 through 1849, and notations made from these are incorporated *between parentheses.*

"A Book of Church Records
for the West End of Yarmouth
from Aprill 16th 1729

At which time Thomas Smith was ordained the pastor over it And Before which there is no written account to be obtained. — Hitherto the CC hath had no records.—"

"Thomas Smith was ordained Pastour with the joint concurrence of the whole CC & congregation on the 16th of Aprill 1729

Yarmo. Septr. 15. 1762 — From the time of the Revd. Mr. Smith ceasing to have the oversight of this Church which was in to this time there are no Records —— on which Day Joseph Green Junr. was installed in the Pastoral Office over this Church —

N.B. The Revd. Grindall Rawson was installed in the Pastoral Office & continued the exercise of that office till

But left no Records

If they should be obtained I have left vacancies for them in their proper places. J. Green"

Baptisms Since Aprill 16th 1729

Desire Thatcher
Desire Downs
Joseph Thacher
Moses Hallet
David Jenkins
Steven Taylor
Barnabas Hallet
Elisabeth Bray
Mary Bray
William Homer
Bays Hawse
Jacob Hawse
Anna Hedge
Sarah Hedge
Hannah Hamlen
Hannah Hallet
Three Children of Hannah Lovell: from ye youngest illegitimate. & downwards:—
Thankful Hallet
William ——— Bray
David —— Thatcher
Bethiah Rider
Susannah Godfrey
Josiah Gorham
Desire Thatcher
Elisha Mathews
Barnabas Downs
Benjamin Hallet
Mehetabel Taylor
Jabez Crowell
Moodey Crowell
Barnabas Crowell
Abigail Crowell
[Children of] "Thos."
Ebenezer Tharp
Benjamin Tharp
Mercy Tharp
Eunice Tharp
Deliverance Crowell
Phoebe Hamlen
Desire Thacher
Anthony Thacher
Phoebe Thacher
John Thacher
Thankful Hedge
Benjamin Homer
Isaack Hallet
Eunice Hallet
Jeremiah Joyce
Elisabeth Joyce
M[torn] Joyce
"Tho: Joyces" [children]
Mary Joyce
Dorcas Joyce
Sarah Joyce
Mary Thacher
Thankful Taylor
Esther Rider
James Hawes

Mary
& Twins — Berry
Martha
Ruth Thacher
John Godfree
Hezekiah Gorham
Thankful Hallet
Hannah Downs
Thankful Downs
Mary Oats
John Oats
Peter Oats
James Oats
Thankful Oats
Samuel Oats
Desire Oats
Josiah Thacher
Abigail Taylor
Gershom Cobb
Lemuel Crowell
Timothy Lewes
Martha Lewes
[Children of] "Antipas"
Jabez Parker
Thomas Parker
Hannah Parker
[Children of] "Jacob"
Jabez Lewes
Thankful Lewes
Deborah Lewes
[Children of] "John"
Zealveton Parker
Deborah Parker
Patience Parker
Priscilla Parker
Thankful Parker
Sarah Parker
"Ebenezers" [children]
Sylvanus Merchant
Martha Merchant
Joanna Merchant
Jabez Merchant
"Samll Merchts"
[children]
Daniel Taylour
Lothrop Taylour
"Eben'ers" [children]
James Sears
Mary Sears
Silas Sears
Edward Sears
"Silas" [children]
Hannah Sears
Ebenezer Thacher
Thomas Hawse
Benjamin Parker
Stevens Homer
Elisabeth Hallet
Keziah Taylour
Sarah Hallet
Elisha Thacher
Mary Downs
Moodey Sears
John Hedge
Simeon Crowel
Betty Crowel
"Ephraim Crowels" [children]
Naomi Lewes
Nathaneel Downes
Lydia Rider
Mary Crosbey
Thankful Baxter
Mary Parker
Judah Thatcher
Seth Crowel
Lot Crowel
Thankful Crowel
Naomi Lewes
John Crowel
Shobael Taylour
Thomas Bray
May 18 1735
Mary Smith
Steven and John Gorham
Desire Hawse
Lydia Gorham
Elizabeth Hallet
Elisha Hedge
Mary Hawse
Joshua Hallet
Isaack Hamlen
Thomas Homer
Enoch Hallet
Abner Crowel
Jabez Downs
Eleazar Sears
Shobael Baxter
Temperance Downs
Ruth Thacher
Abram Sturges octobr 24, 1736
Died in Infancy

"Book
belonging to the congregational Church
in Yarmouth, Massachusetts

"This book contains a correct account of the proceedings of the Church, the baptisms,* marriages, and deaths since the ordination of Mr. Nathanael Cogswell."

*These were repetitions of baptisms found in the first book as previously explained on page 84.
(p. 649.)

James Hallet, Son to Timothy: and Joseph Pilcher baptised May 22d. 1737
Lucretia, Daughter to Elisha Thacher Aprill 24: 1737
Hannah, Daughter to Joseph and Desire Hawse May29th. 1737
Stephen, Son to Joseph Crowell June 19th. 1737
Thomas, Son to Deacon Taylour Sarah Daughter to Jonathan Hallet & Hannah Daughter to Ephraim Crowell. Baptizd July 10th. 1737
Desire, Daughter to Philip Vincent July 31 1737
Thomas Sturgis ownd the Covenant August 14th 1737 on the Same Day was baptis'd his Son Prince
Rebecca, Daughter to Jacob Parker baptiz'd September 11: 1737
Ruth, Daughter to Ebenzr Parker Octobr 16. 1737
Benjamin, Son to Elnathan Lewis October 23
Lucretia, Daughter to Saml Sturgis November 20 1737
Peter, Son to Peter Thacher November 27. 1737
Benja — Son to Benjamin Thacher and Elisabeth Daughter to Joseph Hamlen February 12. 1738
Josiah, Son to Thomas Smith Born and Baptis'd February 26, 1738
Experience, Daughter to Antipas Lewis March 19th. 1738
Hannah, Daughter to Thomas Hawse March 26: 1738
Susanna, Daughter to Samll Hallet Aprill 2d. 1738
David Son to Josiah Gorham April 9th. 1738
David, Son to Thomas Bray Aprill 16. 1738
Benj, Son to John Eldridge May 21st. 1738 on wc Day my dwelling house was fired but graciously & wonderfully preserved —
Thankful Crowel, Jo's Daughter Sept. 17, 1738
James — Edward — Temperance and Elisabeth Sturgis, the Children of Edward Sturgis Baptised October 12th. 1738
Hannah, Daughter of Richard & Jane Baxter January 21st 1739
Joshua, Son to Timothy Hallet and Mercy Daughter to Thomas Sturgis March 4, 1738 1739
March 25th. 1739 Children of Ebenzr. Crowel
Elisabeth, Daughter of Silas Sears & Sarah Daughter of Wm Downs Aprill 1 1739
John, Son of John Hall May 13th 1739
The Children of Elisha Wheelden viz Mary—Lydia & Thankful Baptized July 1: 1739
Mercy, Daughter of Shobael & Mercy Taylor July 15, 1739
Samuel, Son of Samuel & Temperance Downs
Nehemiah, Son to Thomas Crowel and
Elisabeth, Daughter to Antipas Lewis July 29 1739
Mary, Daughter of Elnathan Lewis August 19th. 1739
John, Son of Judah & Sarah Thatcher August 26th. 1739
Samuel, Son to Samuel & Mary Mathews Dec. 9. 1739
Joseph, Son to Ebenezer Parker January 6, 1739/40
David & Sarah Wheelden, the children of Mary wife of Jonathan Wheelden Febru. 3d. 1739/40
Abigail, Daughter of Edward & Thankful Sturgis Feb. 10. 1739/40
Rebecca, Daughter of Joseph Hamlen, Aprill 20 1740
Mehetabel, Daughter of Jonathan Hallet May 11 1740
Patience, Daughter of Joseph Crowel June 8th 1740
Mary, Daughter of Thomas & Mary Hedge July 6th
Anne, Daughter of Ephraim & Rose Crowel July 13th 1740
Edmund, Son to Thomas Bray Sept. 21 1740
Joseph, Son to Thomas & Judith Smith born Nov. 22d. 1740 Saturday 3 o'Clock Baptisd 23d day
Isaack Hall, Son to John Hall January 25. 1740/41
Joseph, Son to Capt. Joseph Thatcher Baptisd March 15 1740/41
Edmund, Son to Ebebenezer Crowel—and
Agtha, Daughter to Silas Sears Aprill 26: 1741
Wm, Son to Wm. Downs Aprill: 1741
Prisilla, Daughter to Elisha Wheeldon may 3 1741
Thankful, Daughter to Elnathan Lewis may 24 1741
Ruth, Daugh. to Antipas Lewis June 7th 1741

Dorcas, Daughter to John Eldridge August 9
Saml, Son to Samuel Hallet Sept: 10 1741
Samll. Sturgis, Son to Elisha Thatcher Baptis'd Nov: 18: 1741 —
Shobael, Son to Samuel & Temperance Downs December 27: 1741
Solomon, Ebenezer, Abigail, Thankful & Desire, Children of Sarah Hawse March 4. 1741/2
Lewis, Son to Peter & Anna Thacher Baptisd March 21st. 1741/2
Ann, Daughter of Mathias Gorham March 29. 1742
Thomas, Son of Thomas and Mary Hedge Aprill 11. 1742
Joseph, Son of Joseph Hamlin Isaack, Son of Wm Downs Wm & Josiah, Sons of Saml Hedge all Baptisd June 13th 1742
Ebenezer, Son of Ebenezer Parker & Edward Son of Edward Howse July 11 1742
Thomas, Son To Thomas Smith Born & Bap. July 25: 1742
Isaack, Son to Edward Howse August 8 1742
Robert, Son to Benjamin Homer August 29th 1742
Elisha & Rebecca Taylor, Adults, Baptized upon professing their faith . . . Septem 19 1742 At the same time the other Children of mehetabel Taylor Baptized as Minors their names — Reuben, Simeon, Joseph, Benjamin, Desire, Rhoda
Richard, Son to Richard and Jane Baxter october 10th 1742
Data, Daughter of Ebenezer Crowel octo 31 1742
Desire, Daughter of Jacob Parker Nov: 7. 1742
Samuel, Son to Edward & Thankful Sturgis Dec. 13
Abner, Son to Hezekiah & Mehetable Taylor Dec. 19 1742
Betty, Daughter to Samll & Mercy Hedge Mach 6th
Wm., Son to Judah & Sarah Thacher Aprill 3d. 1743
on the Same Day Edward, Ebenezer. & Lydia, the Children of Ebenezer Rider
Rebecca, Daughter to Thomas Bray & John, Son to John & Betty Eldridge Baptizd April 10 1743
Elisha, Son to Elisha Wheelden May 15 1743
Desire, Daughter of Joseph Hawse June 24 1743
Hannah, Daughter of Thos. Hedge July 24. 1743
Jabez, Son of Antipas Lewis August 21. 1743
Rebecca, Daughter of John Wheelden Sept 13. 1743
Sarah, Daughter of Samll & Susannah Hallet——
Thomas, Son of Eben. Rider Jur December 11. 1743
Enoch, Son of Edward Howse March 18th. 1743/4
Lydia, Daughter of Willm Downs March 25: 1744
Ebenezer, Son of John Airy Aprill 1st. 1744
John, Son of Mathias Gorham Aprill 15th. 1744
Joseph, son to Joseph Thatcher May 27, 1744
Isaack, son to Isaack Mathews June 3. 1744
Hannah, Daughter to Joseph Rider Jur June 10. 1744
Anthony, Son to Elisha Thatcher July 1st. 1744
Desire, Daughter of Richard Baxter July 22
Born 27th Joshua, Son to Thomas Smith & Ephraim, Son to Ephraim Crowel July 29. 1744
Robert, Son to Joseph Crowel Sept 2. 1744
Thankful, Daughter to Peter Thatcher March 10 1744/5
John, Son of John & Susannah Wheelden — Jane, Daughter of Samll & Temperance Downs. Elisabeth, Daughter of John & Betty Eldridge March 24th 1744/5
David, Son of Samll & Mercy Hedge Aprill 21. 1745
Isaac, Son to John Airy June 2d. 1745
Rachel, Daughter to Elisha Wheelden August 4. 1745
Thomas and Ebenezer, Sons of Thomas & Patience Sears October 13th, 1745
Richard & Temperance, Children of Will Taylor
Mary, Daughter to Thomas & Mary Hedge December 1745
Anna, Daughter to Thomas Bray March 2d. 1746
Mehetabel, Daughter to Josiah Smith April 6th. 1746
Clark, Son to Samll Hallet ——
John, Son to Richard Baxter ——
Abigail, Daughter to Ebenezer Rider Jur Baptis'd May 4th 1746

Joseph & Mary, Children of Joseph & Mary Basset May 25 1746
Nathaniel, Son of Thomas & Judith Smith born May 29 & baptized June 1st 1746
Mary, Daughter to Edward Howse June 1746
Mary, Daughter to Matthias Gorham June 1746
Elnathan, Son to Elnathan Lewis July 20 1746
Jacob, Son to Jacob Parker August 1746
Sarah, Daughter of Widow Martha Lewis August 31st 1746
Jonathan, Son of Joseph & Mary Basset octo 12 1746
Hannah, Daughter of Wm. Taylor March 15th. 1747
David, Son of John & Betty Eldridge March 29th. 1747
Henry, Son of Ephraim & Rose Crowel April 5th. 1747
Temperance, Daughter of Joseph Rider April 26th. 1747
Hannah, Daughter of Isaack Mathews May 3d. 1747
Anna, Daugh. to Samll and Mercy Hedge June 7th. 1747
Anna, Daughter to Peter & Anna Thacher July 5th. 1747
Judith, Dau. to Tho. & Judith [?] Nov 1747
Elisha, Son to Jacob Parker March 1748
Gorham, Son to Ebenezer Crowel April 11th. 1748
Sarah, Daughter of Thomas and Mary Hedge May 20th. 1748
David, Son of Eben. & Abigail Rider June 26 1748
The Children of Samuel Merchant Jur Josiah Aug: 7th 1748
Simeon, Son of Leah Baxter illegitimate August 7th 1748
Prince, Son of Richard and Jane Baxter octobr 1748
Daniel Basset & James Merchant, Children of Hezekiah & Elisabeth Merchant Novem 1748
Jonathan, Son of Josiah & Dorothy Smith Feb: 5 1748/9
Simeon, Son of Edward Howse march 26. 1749
Samuel, Son of Joseph Basset March 26th 1749
Children of Jonathan & Elisabeth Rogers May 1749
Sarah, Daughter of Sam Hedge
Sarah, Daughter of Peter & Anna Thacher June 11th. 1749
Barnabas, Son of Isaack Mathews July 9th 1749
Gedeon, Son of John & Betty Eldridge July 16th 1749
Hannah, Daughter of John & Bethiah Dexter Sept 10 1749
Prince, Son of Wm. & Anne Taylor Sept 17 1749
Mercy, Daughter of John & Susannah Wheelden octo 1 1749
Lydia, Daughter of Abram & Mary Hedge Jan 28. 1749/50
Thankful, Daughter of Thomas & Judith Smith March 4th 1749/50
Benjamin, Son of Wm. & Elisabeth Downs and Mathias, Son of Mathias Gorham both March 11th. 1749/50
Rachel, Daughter of Ephraim & Rose Crowel March 25 1749/50
Martha, Daughter of Ebenezer Crowel April 1st. 1750
Hezekiah, Son of Hezekiah & Elisabeth Merchant April 8th
Thomas, Son of Richard & Jane Baxter —
Ensign, Son of Samll Merchant Jur May 27th 1750
Thankful Tobey, Daughter Mercy Tobey
David, Isaack & Hannah, Children of Isaack & Hannah Crowel August 5th 1750
Bethiah, Daughter of Thomas Bray Octobr 28 1750
Thankful, Daughter of Thomas Hedge Feb. 24. 1750/1
Anne, Daughter of Betty Eldridge March 31st
Joseph & Priscilla, The Children of Samuel & Abigail Gorham May 6th 1751
Samuel, Barnabas and Edward, Children of Jasher Taylor Jur June 16th. 1751
A child of Edward Howse
Daughter of Abram Hedge
Isaac, Son of John Dexter October 13th. 1751
Jonathan, Son of John & Susannah Wheelden Nov. 3d. 1751
Lewis, Son of Peter Thacher Novem 24th. 1751
Nathaniel, son of Thomas & Judith Smith born & Baptis'd Feb. 16. 1752
John, Son of William Taylor February 23d. 1752
Elisabeth, Daughter of Ebenezer Crowel July 26 1752
Experience, Daughter of Jasher Taylor Jur July 26. 1752

CHURCH RECORDS OF WEST YARMOUTH, MASS.

Copied by Florence Conant Howes

Elisabeth Wheelden & Prince Wheelden August 23d. 1752
Bethiah, Daughter of Samll Merchant Jur. 1753
Enoch, Son of Ebenezer Rider Jur Sept 23d. 1753
Children of David & Mercy O Killey March 1754
George Thacher, Son of Peter
Abraham Hedge, Son of Abraham
Thomas Hedge, Son of Thomas
Naomi Lewis, Daughter of Elnathan
Mercy Webber, Daughter of Jonathan all April 14. 1754

Baptisms since Septr. 15. 1762.

1762		
Septr.	19th.	Isaiah, Son of Jona. Hallet Junr. & Thankful his Wife
———	26th.	Betty, Dau'ter of Judah & Betty Gage
Octor.	24th.	Isaac, Son of Isaac & Mary Taylor
Novr.	28th.	Thankful, Wife of Joseph Basset
Decr.	5th.	John Beare, Son of Joseph & Thankful Basset
1763		
Jany.	9th.	John Matthews — Ætat: 80:
		John, Son of the Widow Phillippe Dexter
May	1st.	Silvanus, Son of Jonathan & Crowell
July	3d.	Mary, Dau'ter of Isaac & Mary Taylor
———	17th.	The Widow Mary Studley— and Experience Studley
Augut.	7th.	Joseph & Eliza., Children of Prince Hawes Junr. & Eliza. his Wife
———	———	Sarah, Dau'ter of Ezekiel & Ruth Webb
Octor.	16th.	Heman, Matthews, Lot, Willard, Eliza. and Mercy, Children of Lot & Hannah Crowell
———	———	Thankful, Dau'ter of Jasher & Thankful Taylor
———	23d.	Thankful, Dau'ter of Nathan & Hannah Basset
———	30th.	Abigail, Dau'ter of Prince Howes Junr. & Eliza. his Wife
Novr.	6th.	Samll., Barnabas, Enoch & Heman, Children of Enoch & Thankful Hallet
———	27th.	Silvanus, Lemuel, Joseph, Samll., Edward & Sarah, Children of the Widow Mary Studley
———	———	Benja & George, Children of Peter & Lydia Hallet
1764		
April	1st.	Eliza., Dau'ter of Ebenezer & Eliza. Hallet
———	29th.	Abner, Son of Enoch & Thankful Hallet
		Thomas, Son of Judah & Betty Page
July	8th.	Susannah, Dau'ter of Joseph & Thankful Basset
Augst.	26th.	Samll., Son of Samll. & Abigail Gorham
	Septr. 2d. 1764.	Solomon, Son of Solomon & Eliza Cook, Baptiz'd at Prov: Town
1765		
May	19th.	Prince, Son of Peter & Lydia Hallet
———	26th.	Ezekiel, Desire, Judith & Sarah, Children of Thomas Hallet Junr. & Sarah his Wife
June	9th.	Joseph, Son of Samll. & Mehetable Whitney (Indians)
July	14th.	John, Son of Edward & Sarah Howes.
Augst.	4th.	Ruth, Dau'ter of Thos. Hallet Junr. & Sarah his Wife
———	22d.	Ebenezer Gage (Privatim) Ætat: 70.
Septr.	1st.	Josiah, Son of Jonathan Hallet Junr. & Thankful his Wife
Decr.	8th.	Isaiah, Son of Isaac & Mary Taylor

1766		
Feby.	2d.	John, Nathll., Josiah, Atkins, Bethiah & Mary Children of Willm. & Abigail Matthews
March	9th.	Francis, Son of Nathan & Hannah Basset.
May	11th.	David, Son of Enoch & Thankful Hallet.
June	1st.	Sylvia, Daughter of Thomas & Mercy White
———	15th.	Anna, Wife of John Crowell
July	20th.	Henry, Son of John & Anna Crowell
July	27th.	Hannah, Dau'ter of Lot & Hannah Crowell
Novr.	2d.	James, Timothy, Eliza., Mary, Abigail, Phebe & Kezia, Childn. of Moses & Phebe Hallet
———	16th.	William, Son of William & Hannah Bray
Decr.	21st.	The Widow Rebecca Hallet
		Mary Hallet
1767		
Jany.	25th.	Martha, Dau'ter of Joseph & Hannah Green
Feby.	22d.	Eliza. & Abigail (Twins), Dau'ters of Willm. & Abigail Matthews
		Mary, Dau'ter of Joseph Thacher Junr. & Susanna his Wife
March	1st.	Eliza., Wife of Abner Taylor
———	——	Jabez, Son of Edward & Sarah Howes
———	——	Isaac & Desire, Children of Elisha & Mary Hedge
———	22d.	Charles, John & Martha, Children of the Widow Rebecca Hallet
———	——	Lucretia, Desire & Thankful, Children of Jabez & Thankful Crowell
April	12th.	Judah, James, Josiah & Mercy, Children of Josiah & Desire Thacher
———	——	Job, Son of Peter & Lydia Hallet
May	3d.	Benjamin Killey, & Hannah (Wife of Benja.) Matthews
———	10th.	Thankful, Wife of Nathll. Crowell
———	17th.	Reuben, Joseph, Benjamin, Phebe & Dorcas, Children of Benja. and Hannah Matthews
———	24th.	Jeremiah, Son of Isaac & Mary Taylor
———	——	Mayo, Nathll., Jedidah & Bethiah, Children of Nathll. & Thankful Crowell
———	31st.	Manoah, Prince, Rhoda & Jemima, Children of Prince & Desire Crowell
———	——	Desire & Hannah, Children of Joseph & Thankful Griffith
June	14th.	David, Son of David & Abigail Thacher.
———	21st.	Thomas, Son of Joshua & Mary Gray
———	——	Bethiah, Eliza. & Lydia, Children of Joshua & Dorcas Hallet
———	28th.	Isaac, Asa, Samll., Ruth & Susanna, Children of Thankful Hallet (Wife of Stephen) formerly Thankful Taylor — and Mary, Daughter of Stephen & Thankful Hallet
July	5th.	Ebenezer Hallet
———	19th.	Thomas, Elisha, Jeremiah, Mehetable, Prudence & Dorcas, Children of Elisha & Dorcas Taylor.
Augst.	2d.	David, Son of Thankful Hallet (Wife of Stephen) (formerly Taylor)
———	——	Jonathan, Abigail, Susanna, Salome & Mary, Children of Benjamin & Susanna Killey.
Septr.	13.	Sarah, Wife of Jabez Parker.
———	——	Susanna, Wife of John Rider—
———	——	Thomas, Son of Thomas Hallet Junr. & Sarah his Wife
——	27th.	Barnabas, Cornelius, Nathll., David, Jerusha, Hannah, Mary & Thankful, Children of Cornelius & Joanna Baxter.
Octor.	25th.	John, Reuben, Phebe, Desire, Susanna, Mercy, Experience and Ruth (Twins), Children of John & Susanna Rider.
Novr.	8th.	Prince, Barnabas, Jabez, Abigail, Anna, Sarah & Desire, Children of Jabez & Sarah Parker.

CHURCH RECORDS OF WEST YARMOUTH, MASS.

Copied by Florence Conant Howes

Novr.	29th.	Elisha, Son of Elisha & Mary Hedge ——— and Patience & Bethiah, Dau'ters of Eleazar Sears 3d. & Bethiah his wife
Decr.	9th.	Timothy, Samuel, Thaddeus, Martha, Ruth & Priscilla, Children of the Widdow Martha Burges (Privatim)
1768		
Jany.	3d.	Susannah, Dau'ter of Enoch & Thankful Hallet
———	24th.	Lucy, Daughter of Ebenezer & Eliza. Hallet
March	27th.	Anthony Studley
———	———	Thomas, Son of Eleazar Sears 3d. & Bethiah his Wife
April	17th.	Thomas Wheelden
———	———	Andrew, Son of Edward & Sarah Howes
July	3d.	Dorcas, Dau'ter of John & Susannah Rider
———	10th.	Eliza., Dau'ter of Benjamin & Susannah Killey
Augt	7th.	Ezra, Son of Prince & Desire Crowell
———	———	Ruth, Dau'ter of Thomas & Mercy White
———	12th.	Sarah, Dau'ter of Joseph & Thankful Basset (Privatim)
	14th.	Zenas, Son of Jona. Hallet Junr. & Thankful his Wife
		Joshua, Son of Nathan & Hannah Basset
		Hannah, Dau'ter of Joshua & Mary Gray

———	21st.	Lemuel, Silas & Sarah, Children of Silas & Rachel Baker
———	——	Jonathan, Son of Jabez & Sarah Parker
	28th.	Jesse, Son of Thomas & Mehetable Kilbourn — and Ebener., Son of Seth & Mary Nickerson Baptis'd at Provc: Town Pr Jh. Green
September	4th.	Simeon, John, Anthony & Deborah, Children of Anthony & Mary Studly
———	18th.	John, son of John & Thankful Hall
October	30	James, Jeremiah, Isaac, Onan, Howes, Joseph, Rebecca, Sarah, Hannah, Children of Isaac Berry & his Wife
		Ruth, Phebe, children of Eleazar the third & Ruth his Wife —
		James, Son of John & Thankfull Hall
February	12	Mary, Daughter of Nathaniel & Thankful Crowell & Joseph, Son of Joseph & Susannah Thacher
March	19	Desire, Daughter of Josiah & Desire Thatcher
April	2	Susanna, Daughter of Enoch & Thankful Hallet
Augt	20	Susanna, Daughter of Joseph & Thankful Basset
		Levi, Son of Stephen & Thankfull Hallet
		John, Zube, Sarah, Mary, of Simmin & Jegrusha Taylor
Sept	17	Sarah, Daughter of Lot & Hanar Crowell
		Mary, Daughter of Edward & Sarah Howse
Decem.	17	Levi, son of Simeon & Jerusha Taylor
Decem.	24	Josiah, Son of Anthony and Mary Studly
March	25.	Sarah, Daughter of Joseph and Thankfull Griffith [Griffeth]
A.D. 1770		
April	29	Dorcas, Daughter Joshua and Dorcas Hallet
May	13	Joshua, Son of John and Lydia Wheelden [Whilden]
May	20	Judah, Son of Isaac and ——— Berry his Wife [Sarah]
		Uriah Godfree [Godfry]
June	10	Sarah Lewis, wife of Benjamin Lewis
July	8	Mary Taylor, Daughter of Daniel Taylor [Esq. and Elizabeth his wife]
July	15	Mehetabel, Daughter of William and Thankfull Thacher —
August	19	Rebeccah, Daughter of Rebeccah Whilden
Septem	2	Priscilla and Betty, Children of Benjamin and Sarah Lewis
September	9	Lydia, daughter of Eleazer Sears ye third, and Ruth his Wife
October	7	Nathan, son of Edward Hallet and Sarah his Wife
October,	14.	Silvanus and Rebeccah, Children of Elisha and Thankfull Parker
		Priscilla, Daughter of Thomas White and Priscilla his wife
		Marcy [Mercy], Daughter of Josiah Hedge and Thankfull [Molly] his Wife
October	28	Ezra Croel, Son of Prince Croel and Eliza his wife [Prince and Elizabeth Crowell]
Novem	4	Sarah, Daughter of Benjamin Killey & Susannah his wife
		Ansel, Son of Edward Hallet and Sarah his Wife
Decem.	9	Philip, Son of Silas Baker and Rachel his wife
	30	Sarah, Daughter of Joshua Gray and Mary his wife
		Prince & Abigail, Children of Isaac Matthews & Mercy his wife
1771		
January	13	Ebenezer, Son of Jabez and Sarah Parker
		Lothrop, Tamsin [Tamson], Anna, Ruth children of Richard Taylor [& Thankful. N.B. the two first children were children of Ebenezer Taylor her first husband.]
	27	Isaac, Son of Seth Wheelden [Whilden] and Ruth his Wife
February	3	Ebenezer, Son of Ebenezer Hawes & Temperance his wife
April	28	Sarah, Daughter of Peter Hallet and Lydia his Wife
June	23	Anna, Daughter of Josiah Thacher and Desire his Wife
August	18	Ruth and Joseph Hamblen, children of Joseph Hamblen and Susannah

	25	Gideon, Son of Edward and Sarah Howes
September	1	Timothy, Son of the Revd. Timothy Alden and Sarah his Wife
	15	Susanna Haws [Hawes], Daughter of Joseph Thacher and Susanna his Wife
		Thankfull, Daughter of Richard Taylor and Thankfull his Wife
Novem	10	Joseph White [son of Joseph & Rebecca his wife]
	17	Lydia, Zuby [Azubah], Joseph, children of [Deacon] Joseph & Rebecca White
	24	Patience, daughter of Samuel & Mehetebel [Mehitable] Whitney his wife
Decem	29	John and Nancy Gray, Children of Samuel & Lydia Gray
January	19	Daniel White [son of]
1772		
February	23.	Ebenezer, Son of John & Susannah Rider
April	12	Jerusha, daughter of Simeon and Jerusha Taylor
	26	Hannah, Daughter of ye widow hannah Matthews
		Marcy [Mercy], Daughter Isaac Matthews and Marcy [Mercy] his wife
May	3	John & David Hawse [Hawes], children of David & Anna Hawes
		Marcy [Mercy], Daughter of cornelious Baxter and his wife [Joanne]
June	14	Benjamin, Son of Benjamin Lewis and Sarah his wife
June	21	Winthrop, Son of Eleazer Sears junr. and Ruth his wife
July	12	Elizabeth, Daughter of Isaac Berry and his wife [Sarah]
		Isaac Matthews
	26	Mary, Daughter of Joshua and Dorcas Hallet
August	30	Mary and Thankfull, Daughters of Joshua Matthews and [Rebecca] his Wife.
Septem.	13	Ezra, Son of David Hawes and Anna his Wife.
Septem:	27	Isaiah, Son of the Revd. Timothy Alden and Sarah his Wife.
		Benjamin, Isaac, Thankfull, Elizabeth, Anna, children of Isaac & Elizabeth Hallet
October	9	Achsah, Daughter of [Col.] Enoch Hallet and Thankfull his Wife
	11	Gorham, Son of John Hall and his Wife [Thankful]
		Laban, Son of William Thacher and Thankfull his Wife
	18	Obediah [Obadiah], Son of Nathaniel Croel [Crowell] and [Thankful] his wife
	25	Benjamin, Son of Benjamin & Susanah Killey
		Prince, Son of Ebenezer Hawes and Temperance his Wife
November	8	Isaac, Joseph, Daniel, Ezekiel, Sarah, Temperance, children of the Widow Thacher [&] Joseph Thacher deceased and of his
	15	Phebe, Daughter of Joseph Hamblen and Susanah his Wife
Decem:	6	Marcy [Mercy], Daughter of Thomas White and his Wife [Mercy]
January 10–1773		Lydia Hallet, wife of Moses Hallet
February	28	Isaac, Son of Isaac Matthews and his wife [Mercy]
March	28	Hannah, Daughter of Edward Hallet and Sarah his wife
April	4	Mary, Daughter of Joshua Gray and Mary his wife.
May	2	Benjamin, Son of Edward Howes and Sarah his wife
		Elizabeth, Daughter Elisha and Thankfull Parker
		Molly, Daughter of Rachal Baker, wife of Silas Baker
June	4	Seth Wheelden [Whilden] in the Seventy-third year of his Age
July	4	Ebenezer, Sarah, Data, Ansel, Zadok [Zadock], Ezekiel, children of Joseph Croel [Crowell] junr [and Temperance his wife]
		Rhoda, daughter of Peter Hallet and Lydia his wife
	11	Temperance, Daughter of Jabez and Sarah Parker

August	15	Deborah, Daughter of Isaac Hallet and his Wife [Elizabeth]
August	29	Samuel, Son of Samuel Gray and his Wife [Lydia]
		Tabitha, Daughter of Eleazer Sears and his Wife [Ruth]
October	10	Martin, Son of the Revd: Timothy Allen and Sarah his Wife
		Jam[es] & Edward, Sons of Elisha Hedge and Mary his wife
October	17	Molly, Daughter of Seth Wheelden [Whilden] and [Ruth] his wife
December	12	Anah [Anner] Hawes, grandaughter to Es: Judah Thacher
		Richard, Son to Richard Taylor [and Thankful]
January 23–1774		Ebenezer, Son to Joseph Thacher and Susannah his Wife
March	12	Abigail, Daughter of John Eldredge and [Desire] his Wife
April	17	Edmon[d], Son of [Deacn.] Josiah Thacher and Desire his Wife
May	1	Lemuel, Son of Simeon and Jerusha Taylor his Wife
May	8	Sarah, Daughter of Benjamin Lewis and Sarah his Wife
May	15	Ebenezer Matthews, a yongman Son to the widow Dork [Dorcas] Matthews
June	26	Anna, Daughter of David Hawes [and Anner]
July	17	Josiah Hedge, Son of [Deacn.] Josiah and Mary his wife
July	30	Isaiah, Son of William Bray and his wife [Sarah]
August	21	Rebeccah, Daughter of William Matthews and his Wife [Abigail]
		Marcy [Mercy], Daughter of Isaac Matthews and his Wife [Mercy]
Septem	11	Anna, Daughter of Isaac Bery [Berry] and his Wife [Sarah]
October		Kezia, Daughter of Benjamin Killey & Susannah his Wife
	16	Priscilla, Daughter of Hezekiah Croel [Crowell] and his Wife Naomy
	23	Elisabeth, Daughter of Joseph Hamblin and his wife [Susannah]
Novem.	7	Thankfull, Daughter of [Col.] Enoch Hallet and his wife [Thankful]
Decem.	18	Josiah Hawes, Son of Ebenezer Hawes and his Wife [Tempy]
January 10–1775		Rebeccah Croel, aged about 18, Daughter of Joseph Croel [Crowell]
March	12	Oliver, Son of [Revd.] Timothy Alden and Sarah his wife
		John, Son of Isaac Hallet and his Wife [Elizabeth]
March	17	Ellis Pharice [Pharris], wife of Samuel Pharice
March	19	Phebe, Daughter of Joshua Gray and his wife [Mary]
April	30	Samuel, Son of Joshua Matthews and his wife [Rebecca]
		Affia [Aphia], Daughter of Elisha Parker and his wife [Thankful]
May	7	Peter, Son of Peter Hallet and his Wife [Sarah]
May	14	Olive, Daughter of Edward Hallet and his Wife [Sally]
	21	Asa, Son of Silas Baker and his wife [Rachel]
June	4	Patience, Daughter of Joshua Hallet and Wife [Dorcas]
		Thomas, Son of Thomas White and his Wife [Mercy]
	11	Sarah, John, Gideon, Barnabas, Betty and Ruben children of Barnabas Eldredg [Eldridge] and Patience his Wife
	11	Priscilla, Ruth and Abigail, Children of the Widow Hanah Rogers
	18	Molly, Daughter of William Thacher and Thankfull his wife
	25	William, Son of Thomas Hallet and his wife [Sarah]
July	2	Marcy [Mercy], Moody, James, Elisabeth, Prince, Deborah, Martha, Children of Moody Sears and his Wife [Elizabeth]
	9	Sally, Daughter of Eleazer Sears and his Wife [Bethiah]
	16	Molly, Daughter of Samuel Gray and his Wife [Lydia]
Septem	10	Isaac and Rebecah, children of Joseph White & his wife [Rebecca]
		Edward, Son of John Hall and his wife [Thankful]
October	15	Elisabeth, Keziah, Isaac, Seth, children of Isaac Hamblin [and Keziah]
		Prince, Son of Wrichard Taylor and his wife [Richard and Thankful]

october	22	Abraham, son of Elisha Hedge and his Wife [Mary]
october	29	Joseph, Son of Barnabas Eldredg and his Wife [Patience Eldridge]
Novem	2	Ebenezer Wheelden [Whilden, son of Susanna Godfry]
		Thomas, Nehemiah, Barnabas, Azubia [Azuba], Ziza, Abner, Children of Abner Croel [Crowell] and Hanah his Wife
December	10	Ruth, Daughter of John Eldrege [Eldridge] and his wife [Hannah]
January 1776	7	Joshua Hamblin [Hamblen], Son of Isaac Hamblin [Hamblen] and his Wife [Deborah]
	21	Margery, Daughter of Nathaniel Croell [Crowell] and his Wife [Thankful]
March	31	Peter, Son of Peter Thacher and his Wife [Betty]
April	21	Thankfull Godfry [daughter of Uriah Sr.]
May	12	James, Thankfull, children of Peter Thacher and his Wife [Betty]
June	16	Mary, the wife of Josiah Hedge
June	23	Josiah, Son of Josiah Hedge and Mary his Wife
July	7	Susanah, Daughter of Joseph Thacher and Susanah his Wife
	28	Marah Ghorhum and Zipporah, children of Thomas Hedge and Dinah his Wife
Septem	8	Silvester, Son of Samuel [*in the copy* Seth *is written above* Samuel *crossed out*] Baker and his Wife [Prissilla]
October	26	Levet [Leveret], Son of Samuel Gray and his Wife [Lydia]
		Samuel, Son of Samuel Whitny and Mehetebel [Mehitable] his wife
Novem	10	Ruth, Daughter of Benjamin Killy [Killey] and his wife [Susannah]
	17	Rhoda, Daughter of Enoch Hallet and his Wife [Thankful]
		Deborah, Daughter of Hezekiah Croel [Crowell] and his Wife [Naomi]
		Joseph, Son of Seth Wheelden [Whilden] and his Wife [Ruth]
December	1	Marcy [Mercy], Daughter of Isaac Matthews and Phebe his Wife
	22	Sarah Weld, Daughter of Rev. Timothy Alden and Wife [Sarah]

CHURCH RECORDS OF WEST YARMOUTH, MASS.

Copied by Florence Conant Howes

January 1777	9	Mary, Daughter of Isaac Berry and his Wife [Sarah]
	27	Ancel [Ansel], Son of David Hawes and his Wife [Anner]
February	9	Isaiah, Son of Ebenezer Haws and his Wife [Tempy Hawes]
March	9	Hanah, Daughter of William Matthews and his Wife [Abigail]
	23	the Widow Remember Merchent [Remembrance Marchant]
		Henry, Son of Peter Thacher and his wife [Betty]
April	27	Simeon, Son of Simeon Tayler and his Wife [Jerusha Taylor]
May	4	Sarah, Daughter of Abner Croel and his Wife [Hannah Crowell]
	6	the widow Mary Wheelden [Mercy Whilden]
	25	Isaiah, Son of Moody Sears and his Wife [Elizabeth]
July	6	Anna, Daughter of Barnabas Eldredg and his Wife [Patience Eldridge]
	20	Abner, Son of Silas Baker and Rachel his Wife
August	11	Daniel, Son of Jabez Parker and his Wife [Sarah]
	17	Edward, Son of Eleazer Sears and his Wife [Ruth]
Septem	8	Betty, Daughter of Edward Hallet and his Wife [Sarah]
		Susanah, Daugher of Joseph Hamblin and his Wife [Susannah]
October	5	Joshua, Son of Joshua Gray and his Wife [Marcy]
November	9	Hanah, Daughter of Thomas Hedge and Dinah his Wife
Novem	16	Betty, Molly, Azubah, Jabez, Silvanous, Children of Remembrence Marchant [Merchant]
		Mary, Daughter of Peter Hallet and Lydia his Wife
1778 Janu.	5	Molly [Polly], Daughter of Joseph White and his Wife [Rebecca]
	11	Martha Shaw, Daughter of Rev. Timothy Alden and Wife [Sarah]
	31	Hanah Linkhorn, Daughter of John Eldredge [Eldridge] and Wife [Hannah]
March	1	Oliver, Son of Samuel Gray and his Wife [Lydia]
April	12	Sebra [Sabra], Daughter of Eleazer Sears and his Wife [Bethiah]
		Ezekiel, Son of John Hall and his Wife [Thankful]
		Peg Toby [a negro woman]
	15	Thankful, Daughter to William Thacher and his Wife [Thankful]
May	17	Joshua, Son to Joshua Hallet and his Wife [Dorcas]
	24	Mary, Daughter to Elnathan Lewis and his wife [Thankful]

June	7	Rosannah, Daughter of Isaac Hallet and his wife [Elizabeth]
	14	Isaiah Gray, Son of Thomas White and his wife [Mercy]
		Abigail, Daughter of Abner Croel and his wife [Hannah Crowell]
		Susa [Susannah], Daughter of David Lewis and his wife [Phebe]
June	28	Benjamin, Son of Hezekiah Croel [Crowell] and his Wife Naomy
July	5	Henry, Son of Peter Thacher and his Wife [Betty]
	26	Obed, Son of Richard Taylor and his Wife [Thankful]
August	23	Phebe, Daughter of David Lewis and his Wife [Phebe]
October	18	Sarah Leveret, Daughter of Seth Baker and his Wife [Prissilla]
November	29	Elconah [Elkanah] and Betty, Children of Joseph Hallet and Wife [Ruth]
		Joshua, Son of Joshua Matthews and his Wife [Rebeca]
		Deborah, Daughter of Isaac Hamblen and his Wife [Deborah]
1779		
Febry	21	Elizabeth, Daughter of Thomas and Sarah Hallet his wife
		Ezra, Son of David Hawse [Hawes] and his Wife [Anner]
March	14	Patience, Daughter to Barnabas Eldredge [Eldridge] and his Wife [Patience]
		Sarah, Daughter to Benjamin Lewis and his Wife [Sarah]
May	2	Thankfull, Daughter of Elnathan Lewis and his wife [Thankful]
May	23	Olive, Lucia, Anna, Prince, Ruth, Lidia, Ebenezer, children of Ebenezer House [Howes] and Ruth his Wife
	30	Betty, Daughter of Ebenezer Howes and Ruth his Wife
June	20	James, Son of Isaac Matthews and his Wife [Mercy]
August	15	Samuel, Son of Seth Wheelden [Whilden] and Ruth his Wife
	22	John, Son to the Widow Desire Taylor and Leveret her husband
		Desire, Daughter to the Widow [Desire] Taylor
		Temperance, Daughter of Ebenezer Howes and his Wife [Temperance]
Aug.	29.	Nansy [Nancy], Daughter of Jabez Parker and his Wife [Sarah]
		Job, Son of Peter Hallet and his Wife [Eunice]
		Enoch, Son of Moody Sears and his Wife [Elizabeth]
Decem	5	Dinah, Daughter of Thomas Hedge and his Wife [Dinah]
January		Timothy, Son of James Hallet and his Wife [Susannah]
16–1780		Marah [Mary], Daughter of Elisha Hedge and his Wife [Molly]
April	16	Molly, Daughter of John Eldredge [Eldridge] and his Wife [Hannah]
	23	Betty, Daughter of Edward Hallet and his Wife [Sarah]
April	30	Sarah Hallet owned the covenant and was Baptized
May	7	Susanah, Daughter of James Taylor and his Wife [Rachel]
May	14	Pheba [Phebe], Daughter of Joseph Hamblen and his Wife [Susannah]
June	4	Jacob and Hanah, Children of Samuel Gray and his Wife [Lydia]
June	11	Betty Howes, Daughter of Peter Thacher and his Wife [Betty]
		Elijah, Son of Silas Baker and his Wife [Rachel]
	18	Timothy, Son to Abner Crowell and his Wife [Sarah]
		Prissey, Daughter of Seth Baker and his Wife Priscillah
	25	Rebecka, Charlote, Daughters of Charls Hallet and his Wife [Lydia]
July	2	Miller Wheelden and Marcy Wheelden his Wife [Miller and Mercy Whilden, Children of Miller . Abigail Whilden] he owned the covenant
	9	Marcy [Mercy] Hallet
July	23	Ruth Chapman, Daughter of Solomon Hallet [& Ruth]
August	6	Shubel [Shobal] Taylor, aged 18
August	20	Mary, Daughter of John Hall and his wife [Thankful]

CHURCH RECORDS OF WEST YARMOUTH, MASS.

Copied by Florence Conant Howes

September	24	Thankfull, Daughter of Wiliam Thacher and his Wife [Thankfull]
		Lucia, Joshua, Abigail, Children of Joshua Taylor & Wife [Prissilla]
October	22	Samuel, Son of Deacon Isa[a]c Hallet and his Wife [Elizabeth]
Novem.	25	Andrew, Ezekiel, Children of Jonathan Hallet and Wife [Sally]
		Chandler, Son of Joshua Gray and his Wife [Mary]
Decemr.	31	Elizabeth, Daughter of Elisha Hallet and his Wife [Elizabeth]
1781.		
Febry.	25	Joseph, Son of William and Desire Nicols [Nichols], his wife
		Roland Ghorham [Gorham], Son of Joshua Taylor and his Wife [Priscilla]
April	15	Ebenezer, Son of Isaac Matthews and his Wife [Mercy]
May	20	Thomas, Son of Eleazer Sears 3d and his Wife [Sabra]
July	1	Lydia, Daughter of Benjamin Lewis and his Wife [Hannah]
		David, Son of David Lewis and his Wife [Phebe]
		Elnathan, Son of Elnathan Lewis and his Wife [Thankful]
July	29	Anna [Anner], Daughter of David Haws [Hawes] and his Wife [Anner]
August	12	Jerusha Stirges [Sturgis], Daughter of Ebenezer Howes [& Ruth his wife]
Septem	9	Lewis, Son of Peter and his wife [Betty] Thatcher [Thacher]
Septem	23	Nathaniel, Son of Joshua Matthews and his wife [Rebecca]
October	13	John, Benjamin, Mary, children of Elisha Miller & Wife [Mary]
Decem	16	Mercy, Daughter of Joseph Hamblen and his Wife [Susannah]
Decem	31	Sarah, Lot, David, Children of Rebecah [David & Rebecca] Gorham
1782		
January	8	James, Son of James Taylor and his Wife [Rachel]
February	17	Hanah, Daughter of Ebenezer Haws and his Wife [Tempy Hawes]
		Thomas, Son of Thomas Hedge and his Wife
March	24	Edward bangs, Son of Edward Hallet and his Wife [Sarah]
		Jo' [Joseph] Thatcher, Son of Charls Hallet and his Wife [Lydia]
April	14	Thankfull, Daughter of James Hallet and his Wife [Susannah]
June	30	Rebeccah, Daughter of John Eldred [Eldridge] and his Wife [Hannah]
July	14	Edward, Son of Samuel Gray and his Wife [Lydia]
August	4	Isaiah, Elisha, Jacob, Benjamin, Molly: Children of Jacob Parker [& Mary]
Septem	16	Jerusha, Thankful, Rebecah, Daniel, Jeremiah, Joseph, Children of Jeremiah Hallet and his Wife [Hannah]
Octor	13	Anderas [Andrews] Hedge
	20	John, Son of Elisha Hedge and his Wife [Molly]
1783		
February	9	Sally, Daughter of Joshua Taylor and his Wife [Prissilla]
	16	John, Son of John Hall and his Wife [Thankful]
	23	Asia [Asa], Son of Barnabas Eldred [Eldridge] and his Wife [Patience]
March	9	Levina, Daughter of Dea'n. Isaac Hallet and Wife
April	9	Charlote, Daughter of Moody Sears and his Wife [Elizabeth]
May	18	Mary, Daughter of Joshua Gray and his Wife [Mary]
May	18	Elizabeth, Daughter of David Lewis and his Wife [Phebe]

June	8	Jonathan [Jonothan Rawson], Son of the Widow Susanah Thatcher [Thacher]
June	22	Anna, Daughter of Benjamin Killy and his Wife [Susannah]
July	13	Zipporah, Daughter of Abner Crowel and his Wife [Hannah]
August	3	Joseph, Son of Joseph Hallet and his Wife [Ruth]
Septem	6	Richard, Son of Eleazer Sears and his Wife [Sabra]
Septem	13	Thomas & Polly, Children of Thomas Rider & Wife [Bethiah]
October	12	Anner, Daughter of ye Widow Martha Killy
October	26	Billy, Son of James [Thomas] Taylor and his Wife
November	2	Susanah, Daughter of James Hallet and Wife [Susannah]
Novemr	16	Ruth, Daughter of Benjamin Lewis and Wife [Sarah]
Novembr	30	Jonathan, Son of Jonathan Hallet and Wife [Sally]
1784		
February	19	Judah Gage, agd 66
February	23	ye Widow Betty Baker
March	28	Fanne, Daughter of Ebenezer Howes and his Wife [Ruth]
April	4	Lydia Atwood, Daughter of Samuel Gray and his Wife [Lydia]
May	9	James, Son of Thomas Hedge and his Wife [Dinah]
June	6	Rebekah, Daughter of Joshua Matthews and his Wife [Rebecca]
June	20	Benjamin, Son of Joseph Hamlen [Hamblen] and his Wife [Susannah]
		Sally, Daughter of Edward Hallet and his wife [Sarah]
		Sarah Gorham, wife of Joseph Gorham
July	11	Nabby, Nancy, Children of Col. [Enoch] Hallet and Abigail
August	15	George, Son of Charls Hallet and his Wife [Lydia]
Septemr	12	Mary, Daughter of Elisha Miller and his Wife [Mary]
Septemr	19	Judah, Alexander, Sons of Ebenezer Gage and his Wife [Jane]
Septr	26	Fanny, Daughter of Joseph Gorham and his Wife [Sally]
Octor	3	Judah, William, Sons of William Thatcher [Thacher & Thankful]
		William, Thomas, Baxter, Children of Thomas Brag
October	10	Thomas, Son of Jacob Parker and his Wife [Mary]
Novem	14	Daniel, Son of Joseph Thatcher [Thacher] and Wife [Abigail]
Novemr	14	Deborah, Daughter of John Eldrd [Eldridge] and his Wife [Hannah]
1785		
January	3	Polly, Daughter of Ebenezer Gage and his wife [Jane]
		Matha [Martha], Daughter of Joseph Gorham and his wife [Sarah]
March	27	Samuel Clarke, Son of Col. Enoch Hallet and his Wife [Nabby]
April	15	Thomas, Son of David Hawes and Wife [Anner]
June	5	Peregrine, Son of Joseph White and his Wife [Rebecca]
June	26	Polly, Daughter of James Taylor and his Wife [Rachel]
Septem	4	Solomon, Barnabas, Isaac, Children of Barnabas [& Desire] Matthews
Septem	11	Lydia hallet, Barnabas, Isaiah Hallet, Sally, Children of Barnabas Hedge and his Wife [Thankful]
Sept.	18	Elijah, Son of Simeon Taylor and his Wife [Jerusha]
October	2	Joseph, Son of Joseph Basset and his Wife [Mercy]
December	18	Edward, Son of Benjamin Lewis and his Wife [Sarah]
1786		
July	9	Nancy, Daughter of Joseph Gorham and his Wife [Sarah]
August	20	Lowren [Loren], Son of Ebenezer Hows [Howes & Ruth]
August	27	Isaac, Son of Paul Rider Jr. and his Wife [Molly]
		Lucy, Daughter of James Hallet and his Wife [Susannah]
October	15	Gorge, Son of Joshua Taylor and his Wife [Prissilla]
	22	Hanah, Daughter of Thomas Hedge and his Wife [Dinah]
Novem	11	David, Amasa, Children of Joseph Hallet [& Ruth his wife]
	26	Jonathan, Son of Barnabas Hedge and his Wife [Thankful]
January 1787	8	Ebenezer, Son of Ebenezer Gage and his Wife [Ginny]
		Betsy, Daughter of Joseph Thacher and Wife [Abigail]

	15	Ruben Marchant ownd the Covenant, Baptized
February	18	Nancy, Daughter of Edward Hallet [& Sarah]
March	11	Elisha, Son of Dean Isaac Hallet and his Wife
Apr.	8	Lydia, Daughter of John Eldred [Eldridge] and his Wife [Hannah]
May	6	Mehetible, Daughter of William Thacher and Wife [Thankful]
	20	Eunice, Daughter of Charls Hallet and his Wife [Lydia]
		Freman, Patty, Children of John Hallet and Wife [Hannah]
May	27	Josiah, Betsey, Elsie, Lettes [Lettice], Children of Ansel Taylor and Wife [Azubah]
June	10	Jabez, Son of Abner Crowel and Wife [Hannah]
	17	Hannah Miller. ye widow
July	8	Becca [Rebecca], Daughter of Jacob Parker and his Wife [Molly]
July	29	Ebenezer, Son of Ebenezer Sears [& Hannah]
Octor	14	Joseph, Son of Joseph Basset and his Wife
		Elisha, Son of Barnabas Matthews and his Wife [Desire]
October	28	Sally, Daughter of Jonathan Hallet & [Sarah]
Novemr	11	William Inggussel [Ingursel], Son of [Thadeus] Brown and his Wife [Rebecca]
Novmr	25	Elisabeth, Daniel, Robert, Children of Robert Homer [& Jerusha]
		Cynthia, Daughter of Enoch Hallet and his Wife [Mary]
Decembr	9	Olive, Daughter of Ansel Taylor and his Wife [Azubah]
		Nancy, Daughter of Joseph Ghorham [Gorham] and his Wife [Sary]
1788		John, Son of John Hallet and his Wife [Hannah]
	23	Mehetibel, Daughter of Stephen Hallet [& Mercy]
February	2d	Joseph, Son of John Basset and Wife [Elizabeth]
April	30	the Wife, Susanna, and children of Isaac Hall Bethiah, Isaac, Gershom, Susanna, Elisha, Shubeal, Thankfull, Mercy
June	29	Prince, David, Edmond, Desier, Bethiah, Children of David Eldredge [Eldridge] and his Wife [Bethiah]
July	6	Ruben, Son of Ruben Matthews, Deceased [& Sarah]
August	17	Anna, Joseph, Children of Joseph Hawes and Wife [Thankful]
	31	Scotter, Son of Barnabas Hedge and his Wife [Thankful]
Septemr	14	Elisha Miller, Son of Elisha and his Wife [Mary]
October	5	Hannah, Daughter of Pall [Paul] Rider and his wife [Molly]
		Betsey, Daughter of Ebenezer Gage and his Wife
Octobr	26	Timothy, Jeremy [Jeremiah], Phebe, Ezekiel, Children of Jeremy [Jeremiah] Crowel[l] and wife [Molly]
		Lydia, Daughter of James Hallet and his Wife [Susannah]
		Enoch, Son of [Col.] Enoch Hallet and his Wife [Abigail]
Novemr	11	Mary, Naomy, children of Hezekiah Crowel [& Naomi]
November	16	Henry, Son of Thadeous Brown and his Wife [Rebecca]
	23	Nathan, Son of Benjamin Lewis and Wife [Sarah]
Novem	23	Lot, Cate, Ann, Ebenezer, Matthews Crowell, Children of Ebenezer Hallet Jr and his wife [Elizabeth]
Decembr	15	Sarah, Daughter of David Eldredge and his Wife [Bethiah]
1789		
March	15	Charles Hallet, Son of Charles and his Wife
April	12	Rowland [Roland] Rider ownd the covenant and was baptized
	18	Ruben, Freman, Levina, Elisha, Children of Elisha [& Dorcas] Baker
		Isaac, Son of David Hawes and his Wife [Anner]
June	7	Salle, Daughter of Samuel Gray and his Wife [Lydia]
	21	Thankfull, Daughter of Elisha Hallet and his Wife [Betsy]
August	9	Hanah, Daughter of Elisha Miller and his Wife [Mary]
	14	Marcy [Mercy], Seth Taylor, Miller, Children of Miller Wheelden [Whilden & Nabby]
	16	Sophhia, Daughter of Docr Nathaniel Smith and his Wife [Molly]

Septemr	20	Charles, Son of Ebenezer Sears and his Wife [Hannah]
October	11	Elisabeth, Ebenezer, Lydia, Nancy, John, Children of Isaac Berry and his wife Sarah
	25	John, Son of Ebenezer Gage and his Wife [Jane]
November	1	Joseph, Son of Joseph Thatcher and his Wife [Abigail]
	15	Betsy, Daughter of Joseph Gorham and his wife [Sarah]
Decemr	13	John, Son of John Eldred [Eldridge] and his Wife [Hannah]
1790		
February	28	Elisa, Daughter of Ebenezer Hallet and his Wife [Elizabeth]
March	21	Hannah-Hallet, Daughter of John Basset and his Wife [Elizabeth]
	28	Hannah-Griffith, Daughter of John Hallet and his Wife [Hannah]
April	4	Betsy, Daughter of C[ap]t. Lot Crowell and his 2d Wife [Hannah]
April	11	Naomy Baker, wife of Lot Baker
May	9	Wilbur, Son of the Wife of Lot Baker
May	30	Gorham, Son of William Thacher and his Wife [Thankful]
August	1	Rebecca Bray, Wife of William Bray Jun
	15	Marcy [Mercy], Daughter of Isaac Berry and his Wife [Sarah]
		Desiah [Desire], Daughter of Barnabas Matthews and his Wife [Desire]
october	9	Heman, Son of Enoch Hallet and his Wife [Mary]
	16	Mercy Tayler [Taylor daughter of Daniel Esq.]
	23	Hanah [Hannah], Daughter of William Bray 1st Wife
1791		
Januy	16	Worren [Warren], Son of Charles Hallet and his Wife [Lydia]
February	13	Moses, Son of James Hallet and his Wife [Susanna]
	27	David, Son of David Hawes and his Wife [Anner]
March	6	Nathan, Son of Joshua Taylor and his Wife [Prissilla]
	13	Thankfull, Jerusha, Children of James Sears
April	3	Olive, Daughter of David Eldredge [Eldridge] and his Wife [Bethiah]
May	1	Silvanus, Son of Joshua Matthews and his Wife [Rebecca]
	10	Betsy, Daughter of Jacob Parker and his Wife [Mary]
	22	Sam [Samuel] Gorham, Son of Joseph Thacher and his Wife [Abigail]
June	20	Bartlet, Son of Thaddeus Brown and his Wife [Rebecca]
	26	Joseph Nickerson ownd the covenant and was Baptized
July	7	Lothrop Russel, Son of David Thacher and his Wife [Sarah]
		Jeremiah, Hirum, Isaiah, Abigail and Easter [Esther], Children of [David] Chase and Salome his Wife
July	31	Phebe, Daughter of Ebenezer Gage and his Wife [Jane]
August	7	Lott, Son of Lott Crowel [Crowell] and his Wife [Hannah]
		William, Son of Isaac Hall and his Wife [Hannah]
Aug.	14	Sally, Daughter of Joseph Gorham and his Wife [Sarah]
	21	Joshua, Son of Ebenezer Sears and his Wife [Hannah]
	28	Nancy, Daughter of Ansel Tayler and his Wife [Azubah]
Sept.	11	John Welden [Weldin Sr.]
		Polly, Daughter of Jeremiah Crowel [Crowell] and his Wife [Molly]
Sept.	18	Sally, Daughter of Thomas Hedg[e] and his Wife [Dinah]
1792		
May	6	Ruth, Daughter of Samuel Gray and his Wife [Lydia]
June	24	Watson, Son of Edward Hallet and his Wife [Sally]
July	22	Marcy [Mercy], Nancy, Daughters of John Bray and his Wife [Sarah]
August	5	Joshua, Son of John Eldredge [Eldridge] and his Wife [Hannah]

CHURCH RECORDS OF WEST YARMOUTH, MASS.

Copied by Florence Conant Howes

October	14	John, Son of John Basset and his Wife [Elizabeth Bassett]
		Salome, Daughter of David Chase and his Wife [Salome]
October	28	Susanah [Susannah], daughter of Barnabas Matthews and his Wife [Desire]
		Thankfull, daughter of John Hallet and his Wife [Hannah]
Novr.	18	Oliver, Son of Charles Hallet and his Wife [Lydia]
1793		
Jany	20	Polly Sears, Daughter of Enoch Hallet and Mary his Wife
March	24	David, Son of David Thacher and his wife [Eunice]
June	12	Ruben Marchant ownd the Covenant and was baptized — aged 17 years
June	15	Betty, Daughter of James Hallet and his Wife [Susannah]
July	14	Alexander Black
July	27	Sopha, Daughter of Alexander Black and his Wife [Lydia]
		Daniel, Son of Joseph Thacher and his Wife [Nabby]
August	4	Joseph, Son of Joseph Gorham and his Wife [Sarah]
August	18	Lucretia Tayler [Taylor, Daughter of James T. & wife of Samuel]
August	21	Shubel [Shobal], Son of Hezekiah Crowel [Crowell] and his Wife [Naomi]
Septemr	29	Shubal [Shobal], Hannah, Lucy, Jambes [James], Children of Samuel Tayler [Taylor] and Lucrecia [Lucretia] his wife
Octobr	13	David, Jonathan, Eunice, Children of [Eunice] the widow of Jonathan Matthews, decesed
		Harriet, Daughter of Nathan Hallet and his Wife [Azubah]
1794		
January	5	Lorin [Loren], Son of Prince Howes and his Wife [Nabby]
	19	Allen Bangs and Cena Howes, Children of [Capt.] Lot Crowel [Crowell & Hannah his wife]
February	16	Marcy [Mercy], Daughter of Ansel Tayler [Taylor] and his Wife [Azubah]
		Edmond Hall, Son of Thomas Hedge and his wife [Dinah]
April	6	Willard, Son of Ebenezer Sears and his Wife [Hannah]
May	15	Matthews, Joseph, children of Elisha Baker and his wife [Dorcas]
		Betsy, daughter of John Bray and his Wife [Sarah]
June	29	Seleck, Daughter [Son] of Isaac Hedge and his wife [Thankful]
July	13	Sarah Crowell, Daughter of William Webber [& Sarah]
	20	Lucretia, Daughter of Samuel Tayler [Taylor] and his wife [Lucretia]
August	3	Dorcas, Benjamin, Ruben, children of Ruben Rider [& Thankful]
	17	Ruth, Daughter of Zenas Homer and his wife [Experience]
October	5	John, Son of John Eldredge [Eldridge] and his Wife Lucy
	19	Davis, Son of Benjamin Killey and his wife [Molly]
Novembr	9	Arnald [Arnold], Son of David Chase and his Wife [Salome]
Novemr	16	Lucy, Daughter of Nathan Hallet & Wife [Azubah]
	30	Betcy [Betsy], James, Edmond, William, Children of Bithiah Hawes, Widow of Simeon Hawes
Decemr	21	Gorham, Son of John Eldredge [Eldridge] and his Wife [Hannah]
1795		Alexander, Son of Alexander Black and his Wife [Lydia]
January	4	David, Olive, Jonathan, Lucy, Heman, Children of Edward and Mary Sturgis
April	5	Naby Sturges, Daughter of Edward Sturges [Sturgis] and Wife [Mary]

April 12 Henry, Son of John Custis and his Wife [Hannah]
Lucy, Daughter of Ebenezer Hallet Junr and his Wife [Elizabeth]

19 Betsey, Daughter of David Eldredge [Eldridge] and his Wife [Bethiah]
Isaiah, Son of Enoch Hallet and his Wife [Mary]

26 Daniel, Son of John Hallet and his Wife [Hannah]

June 21 Sarah, Wife of Prince Weber [Webber] received to Communion
Serene, Daughter of Isaac Hamblen and Wife [Betty]

July 19 Edward Gorham, Son of Hezekiah [& Abigail], E. T. 14

Octor 11 Ruthe, Daughter of Barnabas Matthews and his Wife [Keziah]

18 Samuel, Son of Joseph Ghorham [Gorham] and his Wife [Sarah]

November 29 Sarah, Daughter of Arving [Arvin] Smith and his Wife Phebe

Decemr 27 Benjamin, Son of Isaac Berry and his Wife [Sarah]

1796

March 6 Henry, Son of Ruben Rider and his Wife [Thankful]

April 3 Molly Tayler, wife of Howes Tayler [Taylor]

17 Dorcas, Daughter of Elisha Baker and his Wife [Dorcas]

24 Edward, Son of Artherton [Atherton] Hall and his Wife [Ruth]

May 17 Sarah, Daughter of John Bray and his Wife [Sarah]
Nancy Chandler, Daughter of John Custis and his wife [Hannah]

June 19 Lydia, Prince, Timothy, William, Sally, Marcy [Mercy], Children of Prince Weber [Webber] and his Wife [Sarah]

June 26 Kezia, Daughter of Isaac Hamblin jur and his Wife [Betty]

July 10 Printis [Prentice], Son of Ezra Crowell and his Wife [Deborah]
Myra, Daughter of Ezra Crowell and his Wife
Phoze, Daughter of Prince Crowell and Wife [Elizabeth]

August 28 Calvin, Ebenezer, Eunice, Reuben, Solomon, Ann, Children of Solomon Crowell and his wife [Lucy]

Octobr 2 Mary Ansel, Daughter of Ansel Tayler [Taylor] and his Wife [Azubah]

16 Barnabas, Naomy, David, Enoch, Edward, Freman, Children of Edward Rider and his Wife [Mercy]

Novemr 27 Davis, Watson, Children of Laben [Laban] Thacher [& Sally]

December 11 Zenas, Son of Zenas Homer and Wife [Experience]

20 Elizabeth, Daughter of Benjamin Tayler [Taylor] aged 19 years

1797

January 22 Polly Thacher, Daughter of Benjamin Killy [Killey] & his Wife [Molly]

24 Mehetabel, Wife of Elish Liniel [Elisha Linnel]

March 5 Samuel, Son of [Hannah] the Widow of John Eldredge [Eldridge]

19 Bradoc [Bradock], Son of Alexander Black and his wife [Lydia]
Temperence Rider

CHURCH RECORDS OF WEST YARMOUTH, MASS.

Copied by Florence Conant Howes

April	9	Sally, Daughter of Joseph Hamblen jur and his Wife [Hannah]
	16	Barnabas, Son of Enoch Hallet and his Wife [Mary]
	23	Higgins, Shubel [Shobal], Silvins [Sylvanus], Joseph, Ebenezer, Abigail, Children of Shubel Crowell and his Wife Abigail
May	21	Nathan, Son of Nathan Hallet and his Wife [Azubah]
June	4	John, Son of Gideon Howes and his Wife [Mary]
	11	Allen, Son of John Hallet and his Wife [Hannah]
		Betsy, Daughter of Samuel Tayler [Taylor] and his Wife [Lucretia]
	12	Prince Weber owned the Covenant and was baptized
July	2	Polly, Daughter of James Hallet and his Wife
		Howard, Son of Prince Crowell and his Wife
July	9	Betsy, Daughter of Edward Rider and his Wife
August	6	Seth, Son of Seth Baker and his Wife
		Betsy, Sally, Jabez, Children of Jabez Howes and his wife
	27	Seth, Son of Lot Crowell and his Wife [Hannah]
		Edward, Son of Jabez Howes and his Wife [Betsy]
Sep.	3	Ezra Crowell, Son of Ezra & his Wife [Deborah]
Novemr	5	Isaac, Son of Joseph Gorham and his Wife [Sarah]
Decembr	3	Laban, Son of Laban Thacher and his Wife [Sally]
1798		
April	15	Ruben, Son of Prince Webber and his Wife [Sarah]
	22	Thankfull, daughter of James Sears and his Wife [Betsy]
April	29	Priscilla, Zenous, Garshom [Gershom], James, Elisabeth, Children of Elisha Whelden [Whilden] and his Wife [Prissilla]
		Davis, Son of Solomon Crowell and his Wife [Lucy]
May	13	Elisabeth, Daughter Shubel [Shobal] Crowell and his Wife [Abigail]
June	17	Susanah, Daughter of David Eldredge and his Wife [Bethiah]
July	1	Hitty, Daughter of Isaiah Sears and his Wife [Anna]
	4	Sollomon Thacher owned the covenant and was babtized.
July	8	Hitty Russel, Daughter of John Custus [Custice] and his Wife [Hannah]
	15	Nabby, Daughter of Joseph Thacher and his Wife [Abigail]
July	23	Zipporah, Daughter of Elisha Baker and his Wife [Dorcas]
	30	Betsy, Daughter of Joseph Hamblen junr and his Wife
August	19	Data, Daughter of John Bray and his Wife [Sarah]
		Temperance, wife of Isaiah Parker
	26	Susanah, Daughter of Benjamin Killey and his Wife [Susannah]
Septemr	16	Benjamin, son of Isaac Hamblen and his Wife [Betty]
		Thankfull Rider, Wife of John
Novembr	11	Lucy, Daughter of Jabez Howes and his Wife [Betsy]
		Keziah Tayler, Rhoda, Daughters of Benjamin Tayler [Taylor & Sarah his wife]
1799		
January	13	Naby Adkines [Atkins], Daughter of Andrras [Andrus] Hows and his Wife [Mercy]
	20	Ruthee, Daughter of Ruben Rider and his Wife [Thankful]
February	10	Desire, Daughter of Abraham Hedge and his Wife [Ruth]
February		Rebecca Matthews, Wife of Isaac Matthews
March	24	Wotson [Watson], Son of Prince Crowell and his Wife [Elizabeth]
	24	Naby, Daughter of Prince Howes and his Wife
April	2	Edward, Son of Laban Thacher and his Wife [Sally]
	21	Randal, Son of Ebenezer Hallet and his Wife [Elizabeth]
June	23	Belinda, Daughter of John Hallet and his Wife [Hannah]

July	7	Sally, Isaac, Matthews, Elisabeth, children of John [Sr] Thacher and Wife [Hannah]
July	21	Joseph, Otis, Children of Joseph White juner and his Wife [Lucy]
	21	Phebe, Daughter of [Thankful] the Widow Rider, wife of John Rider jur
		Susanah, Daughter of [Abiud] Lovejoy and his Wife [Polly]
August	11	William Weber [Webber]
	18	Zuby [Azuby], Daughter of Nathan Hallet and his Wife [Azuby]
		Isaac, Son of Joseph Gorham and his Wife [Sarah]
September	15	Betty Crowell, wife of Silvanus
	22	Freman, Silvanus, Clerissa [Clarissa], Allen, Isaiah, Charloty [Charlotte], Betsey, Elisabeth Parker, Children of Sil-[v]anus Crowell and Wife [Betty]
		Benjamin, Sarah, Anna, Clark [Anne, Clarissa], Children of Benjamin Lewis and his Wife [Hannah]
October	6	Eunice, Daughter of Edward Rider and his Wife [Mercy]
	20	Gorham, Son of Abraham Hedge and his Wife [Ruth]
November	10	James, Son of James Sears and his Wife [Betsy]
Novemr	17	Lydia, Daughter of Elaxander [Alexander] Black and his wife [Lydia]
		Thankfull, Daughter of Enoch Hallet and his Wife [Mercy]

CHURCH RECORDS OF WEST YARMOUTH, MASS.

Copied by Florence Conant Howes

1800		Lucy, Sabra, Children of [Mercy] the widow of Enoch Matthews
February	23	Moody, Son of Isaiah Sears and his Wife [Anna]
April	20	Barnabas, Son of Barnabas Eldredge [Eldridge] and Wife [Zipporah]
May	9	Rebeccah & Mary, twin children of William Bray and his Wife Mary
June	29	Benjamin, Son of Elisha Baker [Jr.] and his Wife [Dorcas]
July	20	Hanah, Daughter of Ebenezer Sears and his Wife [Hannah]
October	20	Printis [Prentice], Son of Joseph White and his Wife [Lucy]
October	30	Ruth Whelden, wife of David Whelden [Whilden]
Novemr	2	Elisha, Son of Jabez Howes and his Wife [Betsy]
	9	John, Son of John Bray and his Wife [Sarah]

November 30	Ruth, Daughter of Silvanus Crowell and his Wife [Betty]
	Nabey [Nabby], Worshington [Washington], Betsey, Children of Jeremiah [and Nabby] Fares [Farris]
December 15	Hanah, Daughter of Isaiah Parker and his Wife [Tempy]
1801	
January 2	Heman Linel [Linnel]
March 29	Isaac, Son of Isaac Hamblen and his Wife [Betty]
April 12	Lucy, Daughter of Solomon Crowell and his Wife [Lucy]
April 19	Edward and Ansel, Children of Ansel Hallet and his Wife [Children of Ansel & Anna Eldridge]
	Stephen, Son of Laban Thacher and his Wife [Sally]
May 10	Betse [Betsy], Olive, William Atkins, Rebecca, Asa Eldridge, Barnabas, Children of Atkins Mathews and his Wife [Sarah]
	Nancy, Daughter of Prince Crowell and his Wife [Elizabeth]
May 24	Gorham, David, George, Children of Gorham Crowell & Wife [Bethiah]
	Bethyah [Bethiah], Daughter of Andrew Howes and his Wife [Mercy]
May 31	Harriat, Desire, Paddoc, Josiah, Childeren of Josiah Thacher Junier and his Wife [Lydia]
	Josiah Tayler, Gorham, Children of Prince Hawes and Wife [Betsy]
June 7	David, Oliver, Noble, Henry, Fredrick, Children of David Thacher and his Wife Eunice
August 30	Anna, Daughter of Ruben Rider and his Wife [Thankful]
	Sarah, Daughter of Ebenezer Hawes junr and Wife [Thankful]
September 6	Nabby, Daughter of Andrew Hedge and his Wife [Mercy]
Sep 23	Lucy, daughter of Prins Weber [Prince Webber] and his Wife [Sarah]
	Arthor [Arthur], Son of David Thacher Esqr and his Wife [Eunice]
	Almira, daughter of Alexander Black and his Wife [Lydia]
	Oliver, Son of Jeremiah Tayler and his Wife [Martha Shaw Taylor]
September 27	Prince, Son of Prince Howes and his Wife [Molly]
November 15	Hirum, Son of Nathan Hallet and his Wife [Azubah]
	Abigail, Daughter of Isaiah Sears and his Wife [Anna]
	Lydia, Daughter of Josiah Thacher junier and his Wife [Lydia]
November 29	Henry, Son of John Hallet and his Wife
Dec.	Patience, Daughter of Atkins Matthews and his wife [Sarah]
1802	
January 3	Marcy [Mercy], Daughter of Edward Rider [and Mercy his wife]
5	Mary, Daughter of Ebenezer Baxter and his Wife [Mercy]
21	Allen, Son of Joseph Gorham and his Wife [Sary]
April 4	Samuel, Son of Benjamin Lewis and his Wife [Hannah]
	Hannah Furnil [Furnel, wife of Benjamin Furnel]
May 16	Susanah, Daughter of Stephen Hallet junr. & Wife [Bethiah
July 4	John, Sukey, Oliver, Children of John Gray and his Wife [Elizabeth]
11	Tempy, Daughter of Isaiah Parker and his Wife [Tempy]
18	Thomas, Phebe, Elisabeth Rider, Thankfull, Joseph, Children of Thomas Matthews, deceased, and Phebe his Widow
	Betey [Betsy], Daughter of Joseph Thacher and his Wife [Abigail]
September 12	Nabby, Daugter of Jeremiah Farres [Farris] and his Wife [Nabby]
September 26	Isaac, Son of Laban Thacher and his Wife [Sally]
	Sally, Daughter of Prince Hawes and his Wife [Betsy]
Septembr 30	Ira, Son of Isaac Hamblen Jur and Wife [Betty]

October	25	Abner, Son of Jabez Howes and his Wife [Betsy]
October	28	John Nikerson [son of James Nickerson]
Novemr	21	Charles, Joshua, Children of Joshua Basset [& Betsy his wife]
1803		
Jany	23	Freman, Son of James Sears & his Wife [Betsy]
		Naby Russel, Daughter of David Thacher & Wife [Eunice]
		Freman, Son of Enoch Hallet & Wife [Marcy]
Febry	6	Anna Clark, Alexander, Nabby, Ruben, Children of Prince Baker and Wife [Mercy]
Feby	13	Thomas, Son of Barnabas Eldredge [Eldridge] and his Wife [Zipporah]
	27	Jane, Wife of Thomas Greenough
		Nabby Russel, Daughter of Esq David Thacher & Wife [This entry omitted from later copy.]
May	8	Polly, Ruth, Sarah, Children of Isaac White
5 June		Bethiah, daughter of Mr John Bray & Wife [Sarah]
August	7	Sally, Daughter of Prince Crowel [Crowell] and his Wife [Elizabeth]
	14	Hannah, Daughter of Elisha Baker and his Wife [Thankful]
August	18	Azuba, Daughter of Nathan Hallet and his Wife [Azuba]
September	4	Rebecca, Polly, Ruth, Richard, Children of Richard Gray and his Wife [Polly]
	11	Henry, Son of Atkins Matthews and his Wife [Sarah] Sally, Daughter of Ebenezer Sears and his Wife [Hannah] Betsey, Daughter of John Custisand his Wife
October	2	Mary, Daughter of Ebenezer Hawes junr and his Wife [Thankful]
	30	Betsey, Joseph Griffith, Children of Benjamin Trip [& Hannah]
Novemr	20	Ruth Berry, wife of Howes Berry
Decemr	4	Gideon, Isaac, Lucy, Sarah, Children of Howes Berry [& Ruth]
Decemr	11	Rosanah, Daughter of Isaiah Sears and his Wife [Anna]
Decemr	18	Joseph, Son of John Gray and his Wife [Elizabeth]
1804		
Febry	12	Mercy, Daughter of Stephen Hallet and wife [Bethiah]
	19	Nabby, Daughter of Joseph Gorham and his Wife [Sarah]
		Isaac, Son of Prince Howes and his Wife [Nabba]
March	12	Polly Thacher, Rachal Thacher, Cloe, Philip, Children of Philip Baker and his Wife Ruth
March	25	John, Son of Joshua Basset and his Wife [Betsy]
April	15	John, Son of Ruben Rider and his Wife [Thankful]
April	29	John, Salley, Children of David Homer and his Wife [Anna]
		Hannah, Daughter of Lot Crowell and his [2d] Wife [Hannah]
May	27	Mary, Daughter of John Hallet and his Wife [Hannah]
Sepr	2	Eben Lewis, Son of Edward Rider and his Wife [Mercy]
Sept.	9	Sam Stirges [Sturgis], Son of Ebenezer Howes jur and his Wife [Patience]
		also Lucia, Daughter of Ebenezer Howes jur [& Patience his Wife]
Sept.	16	Lucia [Lucy] Weld, Daughter of Esqur David Thacher and his Wife Eunice
October	21	Lavina, Daughter of James Sears and his Wife [Betsy]
October	28	Mary Gray, Daughter of Josiah Thacher and his Wife [Lydia]
		Watson, Son of Barnabas Eldredge [Eldridge] and his Wife [Zipporah]
Novemr	25	Mira, Daughter of Isaac White and his Wife [Sarah]
1805		
March	3	Olive, Daughter of Ebenezer Howes and his Wife [Patience]
April	14	Bartlet, Son of William Bray jun and his wife Molly [Polly]
May	19	John, Son of John Custus [Custice] and his Wife [Hannah]

June	9	Howes, Son of Howes Berry and his Wife [Ruth]
June	16	Nethaniel Stirges [Nathaniel Sturgis], Son of Joshua Hallet jur and his wife [Lucy]
		Josiah, Son of Josiah Baker and his Wife [Polly]
June	30	Jacob, Son of Isaiah Parker and his Wife [Tempy]
July	19	Phebe, daugter of John Gray and his Wife [Elizabeth]
	21	Nathan, Son of Ansel Hallet and his Wife [Anna]
August	11	Eliza, Daughter of Joshua Hallet jur and his Wife [Lucy]
September	22	Eliza Jane, Henry Gray, Children Henry Thacher & wife [Betsy]
October	20	Betsy Sears, wife Winthrup [Winthrop]
		Hannah Killy, wife of Sylvanus [deceased]
		Dustin, Ruben, Benjamin, Children of Ruben Eldredge [Reuben Eldridge] and his Wife [Hannah]
Novemr	24	Betsy, Daughter of Ruben Rider and his Wife [Thankful]
		Fredric [Frederick], Son of Prince Matthews and his Wife [Polly]
		Mary Hall, Wife of Isaac Hall [Molly Dauhter of Hezekiah Gorham & wife of Isaac Hall Jr.]
December	15	Polly, Eunice, Joseph, James, Children of James Thacher & wife [Susanna]
	29	Shubal [Shobal], Suky, Nabby, Elisha, Children of Isaac Hall & Wife [Molly]
1806		
January	5	Mercy Hedge, Daughter of Ebenezar Baxter & wife [Mercy]
		Sally, Daughter of Enoch Hallet and his Wife [Mary]
April	20	Thacher, Silvanus, Ebenezer, Children of Silvanus Killey and his Wife [Hannah]
May	18	Ebenezer, Hannah, Children of Ebenezer Tayler & Wife [Thankful Taylor]
		Nancy, Daughter of James Thacher & Wife [Susanna]
June	8	Daniel, Philander, Children of Edmond Crowell Jur and Wife [Catharine]
	15	Sally, Daughter of Thomas Gre[e]nough and his Wife [Ginne]
	22	Betty, Lydia Lewes [Lewis], Children of Hegins [Higgins] Crowell & Wife [Ruth]
July	6	Lydia, Daughter of Isaac White and his Wife [Sarah]
August	3d	Henry, Son of Prince Howes and his Wife [Abigail]
August	17	Thankfull, Wife of William Hedge
Septemr.	14	Henry, Son of Richard Gray and his Wife [Polly]
		Samuel Paddick [Padock], Son of Gideon Howes and his Wife [Mary]
Sepr.	21	Ira, Son of Ruben Eldredge [Eldridge] and his Wife [Hannah]
October	19	Polly, wife of Joshua Hamblen
		Betsy Baker, Daughter of Joshua Basset and his Wife [Betsy]
		Mary, Daughter of Ebenezer Sears and his Wife [Hannah]
Novemr	9	Calven, Son of Calven Tilden and his Wife [Catharine]
		Joseph, Betsy, Deaty [Data], Isaac, Children of Joshua Hamblen and his Wife [Polly]
Novemr	23	Worren [Warren], Son of Laban Thacher and his Wife [Sally]
	30	Debby, Daughter of Isaiah Sears and his Wife [Anne]
Decemr	8	Otis, Son of James Sears and his Wife [Betsy]
	21	Ebenezar, Son of Ebenr. Hawse [Hawes] jr [& Thankful his wife]
1807		
March	22	Francis, Son of Ebenr. Taylor and his Wife [Thankful]
		Benjamin, Son of Benjamin Trip and his Wife [Hannah]
April	19	David Buck and his Wife Susanah
		Molly Godfry, widow of Elisha Godfry
Januy. [April]	11 26]	Eliza, Daughter of Edmon Crowell and his Wife [Catharine]

May	3	Dinah Hall, Daughter of William Bray andhis Wife [Polly]
		Louisa [Loisa] Daughter Barnabas Eldredge [Eldridge] and his Wife [Zipporah]
June	21	Abner, Son of Abner Tayler [Taylor] and his wife [Ruth]
		Mary, Daughter of Jabez Howes and his Wife [Betsy]
		Polly, Eliza, Children of David Buck and his Wife [Susanna]
June	28	Marcy [Mercy], Daughter of Andrew Hedge [Howes] and his Wife [Mercy]
		Ruth, Daughter of Howes Berry and his Wife [Ruth]
		Ruthy, Daughter of Hegins [Thomas] Crowel [Crowell] and his Wife [Molly]
July	12	Thomas, Son of Benjamin Lewis and his Wife [Hannah]
	19	Thankfull, wife of Paul Tayler [Taylor]
July	26	Betcy [Betsy], Daughter of Prince Hawes and his Wife [Betsy]
		Samuel, Son of Paul Taylor and his Wife [Thankful]
August	3	Patience White [Daughter of Daniel White]
Septemb	13	Tempy, Daughter of Isaiah Parker and his Wife [Tempy]

CHURCH RECORDS OF WEST YARMOUTH, MASS.

Copied by Florence Conant Howes

Octr	18	Eliza, Sally, Thacher, Sophia, Josiah, Children of Daniel Taylor & his wife [Desire]
		Jacob Gray, Hannah Gray, Russell, children of Ezekiel Hallet & his Wife [Hannah]
		Job Thacher, Elkanah, Children of Edward Gorham & his wife [Sally]
		Sarah, daughter of Atkins Mathews [Matthews] & his wife [Sarah]
		Prince, Son of Prince Mathews [Matthews] & wife [Polly]
		Winslow, son of Henry Thacher & Wife [Betsy]
Nov.	8th	Joshua, Son of Joshua Hallet Jr. & Wife [Lucy]
Jany	18	Seth, Benjamin, Children of Benjamen Tayler [Taylor] jur. and Wife [Thankful]
1808		
Feby.	5	Lydia, Ansel, Children of Isaac Matthews and his Wife [Rebecca]
	26	Nathan, Son of Ansel Hallet and his Wife [Anna]
March	3	Ruth, Daughter of Prince Howes and his Wife [Nabby]
March	17	Lorin [Loring], Son of Abraham Baker and his Wife [Ruth]
May	15	Joshua, Son of Joshua Hamblen and his Wife [Polly]
June	5	Sally, Daughter of Ruben Rider and his Wife [Thankful]
June	26	Lucy, daughter of Edward Rider and his Wife [Mercy]
July	17	Cinthia, Mary, Children of Uriah Godfry and his Wife [Prissilla]
		Catharine Hichcock, Daughter Calven Tilden and his Wife
		Sally Weld, Daughter of Isaiah Alden and his Wife [Susanna. The two oldest Betsy & Eunice Weld were baptized. the 1st at Nantucket, & 2d at Duxburough.]
August	7	Isaac, Son of Isaac White and his Wife [Sarah]
	28	Samuel, Son of John Gray and his Wife [Elizabeth]
		Jonathan, Content Wedden [Worden], Betsey, Asa Wedden [Worden], Polly Stevens, Children of Jonathan Whelden and Sally his Wife

Seper.	18	Juda [Judah], Son of James Thacher and his Wife [Susannah]
		Nabby, Wife of Lathrop Tayler [Lothrop Taylor]
		Lydia, Wife of Ezekiel Matthews
Sepr.	25	Heman, Sally, Hannah Noles, Children of Solloman Tayler & wife [Solomon Taylor & Hannah]
Octor	2	Freeman, Enoch, David, Sally, Henry, Children of Ezekiel Matthews and his Wife [Lydia]
		Otis, Ruth Eldred [Eldridge], Laban, Nehemiah, Children of Benoney Baker and his Wife [Hannah]
October	9	Molly, Ebenezer, Tempa, Nabby, Ruth, Anna, Children of Lothrop Tayler [Taylor] and his Wife Nabby
	16	Olive, Daughter of Josiah Hedge and his Wife [Dinah]
		Sally Ellis [Wife of Nathaniel] and Rachel Hallet [wid. of Thomas Jr.]
Novemr.	6	Enock, Lucy, Betsy, Sally Butler, Nathaniel, Betsy, Children of Nethaniel Ellis and his Wife [Sally]
		Ebenezer, Son of Ebenezer Baxter and his Wife [Mercy]
	22	Lucinda Baxter, wife of Prince
	29	Henry, Son of Joshua Basset and his Wife [Betsy]
1809		
Jany	14	Elmira [Almira], Elcany, John Miller, Children of Joseph Hallet and his Wife [Polly]
April	9	Thomas, John, Mary, Ichabod, Washburn, Children of Ichabod Shearman [Shermon] and his Wife [Polly]
		Elisha, Son of Abner Tayler [Taylor] and his Wife [Ruth]
April	16	Susa [Susannah] Collins, Daughter of Isaiah Sears and his Wife [Anne]
June	11	Betsy, Daughter of Richard Gray and his Wife [Polly]
		David, Son of David Buck and his Wife [Susanna]
	18	Oliver, Mecy [Mercy] Hedge, Polly, Children of Isaac Tayler [Taylor] and his Wife [Nabby]
	25	Julia Ann, Daughter of Edmond Crowel and his Wife [Catharine]
		Zipporah Hedge, Daughter of Barnabas Eldredge [Eldridge] & Wife [Zipporah]
		Lucy, Daughter of William Bray and his Wife [Polly]
July	12	Alfred, Son of Dr. Calven Tilden and his Wife [Catherine]
	23	Hegen [Higins], Son of Hegen [Higins] Crowell and his Wife [Ruth]
	30	Ruben, Son of Ansel Hallet and his Wife [Anna]
		Anna, Daughter of Ruben Eldredge [Eldridge] and his Wife [Hannah]
		Isaiah, Son of Silvanus Killy [Killey] and his Wife [Hannah]
		Nancy, Daughter of Ezekiel Hallet and his Wife [Hannah]
August	3	Thacher, Watson, Bartlet, Fanny, Frederick, Children of Zenus Hallet and his Wife [Lydia]
August	20	Jane Bradly, wife of Abiod [Abiud]
		Lidia Matthews, daughter of Icabod Shearman [Shermon & Polly his] Wife
October	8	Lidia, Daughter of Jabes Howes and his Wife [Betsy]
Novr.	19	Asa, Elijah, Children of Abiod [Abiud] Bradley and Wife [Jane]
1810		William, Son of Andrew Howes and his Wife [Mercy]
March	8	Paul, Son of Paul Tayler [Taylor] and his Wife [Thankful]
	25	Loisa Jane, Daughter of Abiod [Abiud] Bradly and Wife [Jane]
April	1	Mary Bur [Burr], Daughter of Henry Thacher and Wife [Betsy]
		Jorge [George], Son of Prince Matthews and Wife [Polly]

April	22	Hawes Hallet, Son of Ezekiel Mathews & Wife [Lydia]
		Polly, Daughter of Joshua Hamblin [Hamblen] & wife [Polly]
		Thankfull Tayler [Taylor], Daughter of Nathl. Ellis [& Sally his wife]
May	6	Isaiah, Son of Isaiah Parker & Wife [Tempy]
May	20	Almira, daughter of Mr Edward Rider and his wife [Mercy]
May	27	Solomon, son of Capt. Solomon Taylor & his wife [Hannah]
		Azuba White, Daughter of Alexander Black and his wife [Lydia]
		Onan Berry, Son of David Homer and Wife [Anna]
June	4	Rebeccah, Daughter of Isaac White and his Wife [Sarah]
		Lucy Stirges [Sturgis], Daughter of Joshua Hallet and Wife [Lucy]
June	10	Warren, son of Ebenr. Sears & Wife [Hannah]
		Lydia, Daughter of John Gray & wife [Elizabeth]
June	17	Russel, Son of Josiah Thacher and his Wife [Lydia]
June	24	Joseph, Son of Benony Baker and his wife [Hannah]
July	22nd	Seth, Son of Lydia Hamblin Wid. of Seth
		Debby, Daughter of do do

CHURCH RECORDS OF WEST YARMOUTH, MASS.

Copied by Florence Conant Howes

August	12	Joseph, Son of James Sears and his Wife [Betsy]
	12	Thomas Crowel, ET 78
	19	Phebe Linsey [wife of Jhonothon Lindzy]
Sepr.	2	Clark, Son of Zenus Hallet and his Wife [Lydia]
Sept.	16	Sukey, Daughter of Abraham Baker
	17	Thankfull Merchant, wife of Ensign Merchant [Marchant]
	30	James, son of James Matthews and his Wife [Sally]
Oct.	14	Clarissa, Betsy, Phebe, Greennough, Jane, Jonathan, & Sally, children of Jonathan Lindzee [Lindzy] & Wife [Phebe]
October	21	Susan, Daughter of James Thacher and his Wife [Susannah]
1811		
[Jan. 3–		Weld Noble, son of Isaiah & Susan Alden]
January	25	Edward, son of Edward Gorham and Wife [Sally]
March	3	Hirem [Hirum], son of Richard Gray & Wife [Polly]
March	24	Charlote, Daughter of Icabod Shearmon [Shermon] & Wife [Polly]
April	21	Patte [Patty] Russel, wife of Joshua Matthews jur
April	14	Rebecca, Anna, Loiza, Isaac Mayo, Children of Isaac [Basset] and his Wife [Anna]
		Eleazer, Ruth, Hiram, Alfred, Children of Lewis Sears and his Wife [Ruth]
		Sarah, Ezra, Children of Aron Crowels [Crowells] Widow [Phebe]
April	12	Gideon Eldredg [Eldridge], Son of Ancel [Ansel] Hallet and his wife [Anna]
		Mary, Daughter of Ruben Eldredge [Eldridge] and his wife [Hannah]
		Edmon, Son of Edmon Crowel and his wife [Edmond, son of Edmond Crowell & Catharine his wife]
		Charles, Son of Joshua Matthews jur [& Patty Russel Matthews his wife]
May	19	Susan, Daughter of Joshua Basset and his Wife [Betsy]
		Uriah, Son of Uriah Godfry & Wife [Prissilla]
June	2	Isaac, Son of Isaac Gorham and Wife [Elizabeth]
August	8	Stephen, Betsey, Polly, Barnabas, Marten, Warren, Elizabeth Downs, children of Mr. [Stephen] Bierce
August	25	Susanah Baker, daughter of David Buck and Wife [Susanna]
Septemb	15	Fredrick, Son of Ebenezer Howes and his Wife [Patience]
October	27	Albert, Son of Marten Alden and Mary [Polly] his Wife
November	10	Allen, Son of Josiah Thacher and his Wife [Lydia]
November	17	Maria, Daughter of Jonathan Linsey and his Wife [Phebe]
Dec.	8	Deborah Hallett, Daughter of Joshua Hamblin & wife [Polly]
1812		
April	19	Hanah Thacher, Daughter of Ebenezer Mathews [Jr.] & wife [Elizabeth]
April	26	Elisabeth Parker, Daughter of Abner Tayler [Taylor] & Wife [Ruth]
May	10	Abiod, Son of Abiod [Abiud] Bradly and his Wife [Jane]
June	7	Zipporah Hedge, Daughter of Barnabus Eldredge [Eldridge] & Wife [Zipporah]
		Sally, Daughter of Henry Thacher and his Wife [Betsy]
		Hannah, Daughter of Isaac Tayler [Taylor] and his Wife [Nabby]
July	12	Betsey, Daughter of Joshua Hallet jur and his Wife [Lucy]
August	16	Ebenezer Baxter and Samuel Thacher

August	18	Emela, Daughter of Ezekiel Hallet and his Wife [Hannah]
August	30	Samuel, Son of Samuel Thacher and his Wife [Nancy]
		Sally, Daughter of James Matthew and his Wife [Sally]
		Adaline, Benjamen, Children of Benjamen Rider and Wife [Ruth]
October	11	Lothrop, Son of Edward Gorham & Wife [Sally]
	13	Thomas Worren [Warren], son of Ebenezer Sears & wife [Hannah]
	18	Phebe, Wife of Thomas Bray
		Prince, Son of Prince Mathews [Matthews] and his Wife [Polly]
November	15	Clarry Gage [Clarissa, wid. of Alexander]
	22	Patty Lewes [Lewis], daughter of Isaac Basset and Wife [Anna]
1813		
January	10	Rebecca Bray, a widow of [Capt.] David Bray
January	18	Peter, Mary, Phebe, Achsah, Hall, Lucrecia, Children of Thomas Bray and Phebe his Wife
February	23	Molly Gray, wife of Gidion Gray
April	11	Russel, Son of Richard Gray and his Wife [Polly]
		Betsy, Daughter Hegins Crowel [Higgins Crowell] and his Wife [Ruth]
April	18	Fredick [Frederick], Son of James Thacher and his Wife [Susannah]
		Isaac, Son of Isaac Matthews and his wife [Rebecca]
		Joshua, Son of Joshua Matthews and his Wife [Patty Russel Matthews]
April	25	Ezekiel, Sarah, Barnabas, Edward, Olive, Anner, Isaac, Children of Barnabas Matthews and his Wife [of Barnabas & Milly Thacher]
May	2	William, Son of Icabod Shearman [Shermon] and his Wife [Polly]
May	30	Elisabeth Jane, Daughter of Clarry Gage, Widow [Daughter of Alexander & Clarissa Gage]
May	30	Solomon, Son of Samuel Thacher and Wife [Nancy]
June	20	Polly Nicurson [Nickerson, Daughter of Deborah N.]
		Winslow, Son of Nathaniel Ellice [Ellis] and Wife [Sally]
July	11	Fredric [Frederick], Son of Isaac White & Wife [Sarah]
August	15	Hannah Jarild [Gerald]
Sep.	19	Ebenezer, Son of Ebenezer Rider and Wife [Desire]
	26	Hanner [Hannah], Daughter of Josiah Thacher and Wife [Lydia]
October	10	Isaac, Son of Garshom [Gershum] Hall and his Wife [Thankful]
		Jorge [George] Thacher, Son of Col. Thomas and Wife [Mary]
		Jorge [George] Thacher, Son of Barnabus and his Wife [Barnabas and Molly]
	24	Alven, Son of Stephen Bearse and his Wife [Elizabeth]
		Charlotte, Daughter of Daved Buck & his Wife [Susannah]
November	7	Howes, Son of Isaak Tayler & Wife [Nabby]
1814		
March	7	Samuel, Son of John Gray & his Wife [Elizabeth]
May	15	Caleb Holms [Holmes], Son of Marten Alden and his Wife [Polly]
	24	Sally, Daughter of Nathaniel Matthew and his Wife [Mercy]
	29	Emmaline, Daugter of Joshua Hamblen and Wife [Polly]
June	7	The children of Samuel Matthews and Wife [Sabra] Temperance, Samuel, Sabray, Nathaniel, Richard, Oliver, Bethiah
	19	John, Son of Uriah Godfry and his Wife [Prissilla]
July	10	Ezekiel, Son of Ezekiel Hallet and his Wife [Hannah]
	17	Caroline, Daughter of Barnabas Eldredge [Eldridge] and Wife [Zipporah]
	24	Samuel, Emerey, Susan, Children of Edward Sears and his Wife [Susannah]
	31	Frances, Daughter of William Bray and his Wife [Mary]

August	7	Maria, Daughter of Henry Thacher & Wife [Betsy]
		Sharlotte, Daughter of Prince Matthews & wife [Mary]
October	23	Ollando [Orlando], Son of Icobod Shearman [Shermon] and Wife [Polly]
		Joseph blish, Son of Abiod Bradly and Wife [Jane]
October	30	Sarah Berry, Daughter of Daved Homer and Wife [Anna]
		Rebecca Howes, Daughter of Samuel Matthews [& Sabra his wife]
November	6	Nathan & Edward, Children of James Matthews [& Sally]
1815		
February	13	Ruth, Lydia, Children of Joseph Hallet and Wife [Polly]
April	16	Phebe, daughter Ebenezer Matthews and his Wife [Elizabeth]
		Louisa, dauthter of Edward Gorham and his Wife [Sarah]
		Lucy, daughter of Ebenezer Howes and his Wife [Patience]
July	23	Elisabeth, Daughter of John Gray and his Wife Phebe
	31	Ebon, Barnebus [Eben'., Barnabas], Polly, David Joseph, Children of Eben Bray and his Wife [Phebe]
July	6	Bartlet, Son of Isaac Wite [White] and his Wife [Sarah]
August	29	Eliza, Polley, Thomas, William, Henery, Ruben, Ebenezer, Children of Thomas Gage and his Wife [Hannah]
October	1	Elnathan, Son of Isaac Basset and Wife [Anna]
1816		Lavina, daughter of Hegens Crowel & Wife [Higgins & Ruth Crowell]
May	5	Hannah, daughter of Ruben Eldridge & Wife [Hannah]
June	2d	Susan & Elizabeth Doane, children of Elisha & Susan Doane [Elisha Doane Esqr. & Susannah his wife]
	2d	Susan, daughter of Joshua & Lucy Hallet his wife
July	6	Isaac, Son of Isaac Taylor & Nabby his wife
July	21	Elvira Ann, daughter of Col. Joshua & Polly Hamblen.
August	15	Benjamin Matthews Sr. & Benjamin Matthews Jr., his son.
Sep.	8	Alfred, Son of James Thacher & his wife Susanna
		Joshua, son of Gershom Hall & Thankful his wife
Dec.	8	Watson, son of Deacon Samuel Thacher & Nancy, his wife
Dec.	29	George, son of Henry Thacher & Elizabeth his wife.
		Amanda, daughter of Isaac Mathews & Rebecca his wife.
1817 May	18	Mary Kingman Alden, daughter of Martin Alden & Polly, his wife.
		Susannah White, wife of Joseph White
June	1	Joseph, Frederick, Mary Ann, Eliza Burr, Catherine, children of Cap. Joseph Eldridge & Deborah his wife
Aug.	17	Susan Blossom, daughter of Reuben Chase & Polly his wife.
Aug.	25	David Haws, Sally Lewis, & John, children of John Loring & Anner his wife.
Sep.	14.	Olive, a child of David Buck
Sep.	28	Georgia Anna, a child of Ansil Hallet & Anna his wife
Oct.	12	Mary Ann, daughter of Prince Matthews & Mary his wife.
1818		
March	17.	James Marchant ——
		Bial Marchant } children of James Marchant & his wife Mercy ———
		Crowell, ——— ——— } children of James Marchant & his wife Mercy ———
		James ——— ——— } children of James Marchant & his wife Mercy ———
		Mercy Hallett ——— } children of James Marchant & his wife Mercy ———
1818 Apr	30	Lucy, a child of Joseph White & Susanna his wife
10 May		Phebe, a child of Ebenezer Matthews & Elizabeth, his wife
June	21	Cornelia, a child of Ezekil Hallet & hannah his wife
July	2	Lucy, Nancy, Eliza, Asa, Sally & Edward, children of Cap. John Eldredge & Betty his wife.
July	12	Nabby, John, Lucy, Thacher, Hezekiah, Josiah, Phebe, Oliver, Sukey, children of Hezekiah Gorham & Phebe his wife.
Au.	18.	Olive, daughter of Col. Joshua Hamblin & Polly his wife.
Augt.	30.	Nathaniel, son of Isaac Taylor & Nabby his wife
Oct	11	Sylvanus, son of Samuel Matthews & Sabry his wife

Oc.	19	Temperance, daughter of Ichobod Sherman & Polly his wife
Oc.	19	Adeline, daughter of Ebenezer Hawes & Patience his wife.
Nov.	15	Catharine, daughter of Benjamin Matthews & Serena his wife.
Nov.	29	Printis, son of James Thacher & Susanna his wife.
Dec.	20	Watkins, son of James Matthews & Sally his wife.
1819		
June	6	Maria, daughter of Barnabas Eldridge & Ziporah his wife.
June	20	Joseph & Benjamin, children of Hezekiah Gorham & Phebe, his wife
Aug.	15	Reuben, son of Reuben Chase & Polly his wife
———	29	Timothy, son of Martin Alden & Polly, his wife
———		Thomas, son of Henery Thacher & Betsy his wife.
Sep.	12	Joseph, son of Isaac White & Sarah his wife.
Oct.	17	Alfred, son of Edward Gorham & Sally his wife.
1820		
Apr.	6	Loisa, daughter of Col. Joshua Hamblen & Polly his wife.
May	21	Lauraann, daughter of Ezekiel Hallet & Hannah, his wife.
June	18	Nabby Atkins, daughter of Isaac Taylor & Nabby Atkins, his wife
July	22	Benjamin Lewis, son of Higins Crowell & his wife
Sep.	17	Joseph, Son of Joseph White & Susanna his wife
Oct.	15	Azariah, son of Joseph Eldredge & Deborah his wife.
———		Hannah, daughter of Ichobod Sherman & Polly his wife.
		Joel, Son of Benjamin Matthews & Syrena Matthews his wife
1821		
Ap.	15	Thomas, son of Ansel Hallet & Anne his wife
———		John, son of Ebenezar Hawes & Patience his wife.
July	29.	Elizabeth, Daughter of Ebenezer & Elizabeth Mathews
Aug.	19.	Allen, son of Hezekiah Gorham & his wife —
Septr.	——	Seth, Son of Joshua Hamblen & Wife
1822		
Jany.	4	Charles, Son of Henry Thacher & Betsy his wife
May	(4)	Isaac, child of (Captain) Joseph Eldrige (Eldridge)
June	(16)	Oliver, child of Widow Betty Eldridge
		Nancy, child (Deacon) Samuel Thatcher
		Thomas, Edmond Hawes, George, Reuben, children of Reuben Ryder (Junior)
		Harriet, wife of Reuben Ryder (Junior)
	(30)	Mary, daughter of Ezekiel Hallet
September		(Miss) Sarah Bray
(15)		Isaac, Otis, children of Isaac Ryder
		John, Hiram, children of John Loring
Oct.	(20)	Isaiah, child of Rev. Martin Alden.
December	(8)	Olive, child of (Captain) James Matthews
1823		
February	(23)	Betsey, Christopher, Thankful, Elnathan, Phebe, Edward, Joseph, children of (Captain) Elnathan Lewis
		Bethiha Sears and Reuben Crowel, children of (Capt.) Benjamin Hallet
April	(5)	Metilda, daughter of James Thatcher
June	(15)	Anner, wife of (Capt.) Edward B. Hallet
(Aug.	15)	Bangs, Francis, Gorham, and Susan, children of (Capt.) Edward B. Hallet
		Sarah Ann, child of Randal Hallet
(24 Sep.)		Winthrop, son of Winthrop Crowel
September		Bethiah Gorham, daughter of Joseph Matthews
	(23)	Hannah, wife of Barnabas Crowel
		Mary, wife of Thomas Crowel
		Susannah, wife Sylvanus Crowel
		Polly, wife of Shubal Crowel
		Ruth, wife of Reuben Matthews

		Betsey, wife of Charles Baxter.
		Deborah, wife of Jotham Goodnoo
		Abigail Crowel
		(Martin Luther, son of Rev. Martin Alden)
		Deborah, Anna, Phebe, Ossian, children of Jotham Goodno(o)
Oct.		Charles, son of Charles Baker.
(Oct.	21)	Patia B(aker), Reuben, Hannah, and Heman, children of Reuben Matthews.
		Charles F(reman), Edward, Fanny, children of Charles Baxter.
		Elisabeth, daughter of Thomas Bray.
Nov.	(9)	Edmond B(ray), son of (Col.) Joshua Hamblin.
	(17)	Tempe, daughter of William Hallet
		Lucretia, daughter of Chandler Gray
	(23)	Eliza A(llen), Abner T(aylor) and Velina, children of Ebenezer Crowel
		Pinkham, son of Charles Baker
		Isaiah Freeman, son of Charles Baker
December	(13)	(Mr.) Nathan Crowel
		Lucy E(ldridge), daughter of Nathan Crowel
		Caroline Do Benjamin F(ranklin), Do. Nathan, Do.
1824		
March	(21)	Martha, wife of John Buck
		Patty Lewis, daughter of joice Taylor
		Tabitha Sears, daughter of Joseph Crowell
		(Mr.) John Gorham
April	(18)	Rebekah, wife of Edmond Matthews.
		Dorcas Hawes, daughter of Reuben Ryder
		Cyrus, son of Benjamin Matthews
May	(2)	Daniel H(owes) and Elisha H(owes), children of Daniel Weaver
	(9)	Hope, daughter of Joshua Hallet
		(Polly, daughter of Joshua Hallet)
		William D(eane), Son of John Loring
	(16)	Mercy, daughter of Ebenezer Matthews
Aug.	(28)	Nancy, wife of Isaiah Burgess
(Oct.	17)	Joseph Hamblin, son of Randal Hallet
	(24)	Hannah, Chandler, Thomas, Henry, Lucy, and Mary, children of Chandler Gray.
		Lydia B(aker), daughter of Reuben Matthews
Nov.	(21)	Sylva, daughter of Mrs. Clarissa Hedge (Widow)
December	(12)	Charles, son of Widow Sarah Gorham
		Caroline and Cornelia, children of Henry Thatcher
1825		
January	(9)	Polly, Shelden, Thankful, Abigail P(arker), Hannah T(hatcher), Adaline, and Rodman, children of Shubal Crowel
March	(13)	Elisha, John, Bethiah, children of John Robbins
		Sally, Zabina (Zubia), William, and Nelson, children of john Buck
June.		Samuel and William, children of Chandler Gray.
		Sarah, daughter of Deacon Thatcher.
Aug.	(7)	Betsey G(orham), daughter of Charles (Baker)
1826		
July		Elisabeth A(nner), daughter of john Loring
		Edward, son of (Captain) Edward B. Hallet
Sep.		Benjamin S(ears), son of (Widow) joshua Hamblin
		Oliver, child of Ezekiel Hallet
		Allen T(aylor), son of Freeman Tayler
Nov.		Jabez, son of Daniel Weaver
1827		
May		Ebenezer, son of Ebenezer Matthews
		Capt. Edmond Crowel
		Elisabeth D(oane), daughter of Rev. Nathl. Cogswell
		Ira, son of (Mrs.) Randal Hallet

Ebenezer, son of Reuben Ryder
Mary P(arker), daughter of Otis Crowel
July — Cyrus, son of Capt. Benjamin Matthews
Ruth, wife of Capt. Gorham Eldridge
Abigail L(ydia), daughter of Capt. Gorham Eldridge
(Aug.) — George, son of Joseph White

1828

July — William H(enry), son of Rev. Nathl. Cogswell
George, son of Capt. Freeman Taylor
Erastus, son of Capt. Winthrop Crowel
Sep. — George H(enry), son of John Loring
Dec. — Rebekah, wife of Henry Brown

1829

Aug. — (Miss) Ruth Thatcher
(Mr.) John Buck
child of Otis Crowel
(Sep.) — John B. D., son of Rev. Nathl. Cogswell

1830 — Frederic, son of (Captain) Reuben Eldridge
Mary M(atthews), daughter of (Captain) Gorham Eldridge

1831 — Cornelia, daughter of John Loring
(Oct.) — Susan, daughter of (Captain) Freeman Taylor
Ruth H(owes), Daughter of (Capt.) Franklin Baker
Paulina, daughter of (Captain) Joseph Matthews

1832 — Calvin, son of (Capt.) Winthrop Crowell
Christopher W(illiams), Child of (Capt.) Reuben Eldridge
(Mr.) Ansel Taylor
(Widow) Susannah Crowel
Widow Burgess

1833.

(June) — Cyrus and Ira, children of Reuben Ryder

1834 — son of Deacon Joseph White
Charles, son of (Capt.) Charles Baker
Christopher W(illiams), son of (Capt.) Reuben Eldridge

1835 — George, child of (Capt.) Reuben Eldridge
George H(enry), child of John Loring
Abigail and Nelson, children of Frederic Lewis

1836 — (Capt.) Sylvanus Gage
Zenas, Sally N(ickerson), Isaac B(urgess), Lydia, Mercy, Sylvanus, Eunice M(ariah), children of (Capt.) Sylvanus Gage
Barnabas, child of (widow) Sarah Hallet

CHURCH RECORDS OF WEST YARMOUTH, MASS.

Copied by FLORENCE CONANT HOWES

Sarah, child of (Widow) Sarah Hallet
(May) Freeman, child of (Capt.) Freeman Taylor
Harriet B(arker) and Oliver, children of (Capt.) Freeman Taylor
child of (Capt.) Joice Taylor
(June) Francis, child of (Capt.) Reuben Eldridge
Capt. Solomon Taylor
(Sep.) Capt. Charles Baker
Capt. Franklin Baker
Gerusha (Jerusha), wife of joice Taylor
Alger, son of James Crowel (Esq.)
son of James Crowel
(Nov.) Miss Ruth Taylor
Miss Priscilla Coleman
(Miss Chloe Coleman)
Miss Burgess
1837 Amelia and Annar (Anner Thatcher), children (Capt.) Bangs Hallet
(June) Phebe G(orham), child of Frederick Lewis
Child of Lydia Cotton
(Aug. 8) Nancy D(avis), Caroline G(ibson) and Eliza, children of Samuel H. Burbick
Warren H(edge), Child of John Ryder
Abigail H(allet), child of Vianna Ryder
Franklin, child of (Deacon) Joseph White
Susanna B(aker), child of (Capt.) Joseph Matthews
Caroline W(illis), child of Jeremiah Bray
Eliza, daughter of (Capt.) Reuben Eldridge
Osborn, child of (Capt.) Winthrop Crowel
child of (Capt.) Franklin Baker

		Phebe G(orham), child of (Capt.) Freeman Taylor
		Thomas Coffin, child of John Loring
		Lydia M(atthews), child of William Knowles
		Elisha D(oane), child of Rev. Nathl. Cogswell
(1838		
April)		Charles F(rederick), son of (Capt.) Joice Taylor jur.
1838		
(Oct.	21)	Joseph, son of Samuel H. Burbick
(Nov.	18)	Sarah B(acon), daughter of (Capt.) James B. Crocker
		Elisabeth, Hannah, P(rice) and Joanna (Bacon), children of Daniel Crocker
1839		
(April)		Bangs, son of (Capt.) Bangs Hallet
(June)		Louisa, Joshua, Emely, George W(ashington) and Martha Custis, children of (Capt.) Joshua Eldridge
		Joshua, Ella and Nathaniel, children of (Capt.) Nathaniel Matthews
		Edward, Lothrop and james, children of Edward Gorham
		Elisabeth, daughter of Frederic Lewis
(July	21)	William, son of William Knowles
		Mary and Harriet (Taylor), children of Reuben Ryder
Aug.	(18)	Laura Ann, daughter of john Ryder
		Susan, daughter of Daniel Crocker
		Phebe N(ickerson), daughter of (Capt.) Sylvanus Gage
		(Capt.) Otis Crowel
		(Mr.) Jesse Taylor
		(Mr.) James Hedge Jr.
		(Miss) Eliza Hedge
(Nov.	17)	josiah, son of Jesse Taylor
(Dec.	29)	(Mr.) joice Taylor
		Eliza, daughter of (Capt.) Elisha Baker
1840		
(April	19)	(Capt.) Sylvester Baker
		Veranus, Sylvester, Martha, Russel and Edwin, children of (Capt.) Sylvester Baker
(June	7)	James Crowel (Esq.)
		Jabez Lewis and Rebekah his wife
		(Mrs.) Polly Crowel
		(Mrs.) Lydia Crowel
		(Miss) Catharine Seymour
		William S. [*sic*] (Russel), Prentis, Thankful H(allet), Irene, (Edgar), Lothrop H(owland), children of Jabez Lewis
		Cynthia B(aker), child of Jeremiah Gorham
(1841)		
(June	6)	Ellen, daughter of (Capt.) Reuben Eldridge Jr.
(July	11)	Benjamin G(orham), Lucy Anner, and Mary Anner, children of Frederic Lewis
	(25)	Ichabod, son of William Knowles
1842		Rebekah Hedge
		Frederick Dunbar
		Child of Reuben Eldridge (Jr.)
		James B(acon), Child of (Capt.) James B. Crocker
		(Mr.) Ebenezer Taylor
		Benjamin G(orham), child of Frederic Lewis
		Ichabod, child of William Knowles
		Henry C(hapman), child of (Capt.) Joshua Eldridge
		Mary Anna, child of (Capt.) Bangs Hallet
		Daniel B(acon), child of Daniel Crocker
		Susan Langden, Daughter of Samuel H. Burbick
1848		Edwin, Cyrus, Mary, Samuel, Lawrence, children of Samuel Thatcher jr.

1849			
(May)			Frederic, child of Frederic Dunbar
(July)			Two children of Frederic Lewis
			Baptisms Administered By Rev. A. K. Packard from 1852 to 1859
May	7,	1852	Caroline Matthews
July	17	"	Hannah H. Dunbar
"	"	"	Isaiah & Jane Gould, Children Jeremiah Bray
"	"	"	Emma & Benjamin Hamblin, Children Saml. Thacher Jr.
Aug.	25	"	Oliver Russell, child Oliver & Phebe Matthews
Nov.	7	"	Mrs. Sally Hamblin (wife of Isaac)
"	"	"	Miss Mary B. Lewis
"	"	"	Miss Bethiah Bray
Jany.	2	1853	Caroline C. Packard, child of Pastor
Mch.	6	"	Mrs. Susan H. Dunbar (wife of Fredc.)
Note			Same day in this month By Rev. N. Cogswell on the South Side
			Esther Coffin & John Franklin
			(Children of John Loring Jr.) (pr note of clerk in Records)
Sept.	25	"	Joshua Atkins & (Mercie), Anna Bangs, children of Mrs. Frankn. Matthews
Nov.	9	"	Susan, Almena, children Fredc. & Susan Dunbar
Jany.	1,	1854	Mrs. Mehitable Gorham (wife of Joseph)
"	"	"	Miss Eliza Hall
May	7	"	Mrs. Naomi Lewis (wife of James)
			Miss Mary Ann Long
June	11	"	Sarah Gorham (child of Mrs. Fredc. Lewis)
Oct.	8	"	William, Child of Mrs. Benjn. Matthews Jr.
Apr.	1,	1855	Mrs. Alice Matthews (wife of George)
			Mary, Maria, Alice, & George Prince, children of George and Alice Matthews
June	24	"	Alfred Russell, child of Mrs. Frank Matthews
Sept.	2	"	Edward Wells, Child of John Loring Jr.
Nov.	12	"	Lucinda C., Child of E. B. & Elizabeth Hallet
"	"	"	Benjamin Thacher, Child of Mrs. Benjn. Gorham
"	"	"	Albert, Cyrus, & Thomas, children of Mrs. Thos. Ryder
"	"	"	Joshua Montgomery, child of Mrs. Joshua Sears—Brought after her death, her Husband not a church member
"	"	"	William Carlton, child of the Pastor
March	9,	1856	Henry, James Newell, Wm. Everett, Ruthy Gray, & Edwin, Children Mrs. Jos. Bray
May	18	"	Frederic, Alexander, children Fredc. & Susan Dunbar
June	1	"	Nathan, child of Mrs. Benjn. Matthews Jr.
Oct.	19	"	Sarah Matthews, child of Mrs. Soloman Taylor
March	1,	1857	Mary, Bartlett, Chandler Grey, and Maria Frances, Children of Mrs. Bartlett Bray
"	"	"	Isaac Hamblin, child Mr. & Mrs. S. Thacher Jr.
July	5	"	Zenas Winslow, child of Mrs. Eunice M. Lewis
Nov.	15	"	Susan Thacher, Child of Mrs. Thos. Ryder
"	22	"	Myra Howes, child of Gorham & Bethiah S. Eldridge
Apl.	11,	1858	Anna, child of Mrs. Benjamin Gorham
July	4	"	Edward, Child of A. K. & C. M. Packard
Nov.	3	"	Wallace, Child of Mrs. Soloman Taylor
Jany.	2,	1859	Ensign R. Nixen
			Mrs. Huldah Nixen (wife of E. R.)
Sept.	11	"	Anna, Child of E. B. Hallett
Oct.	23	"	Annie, Child of Mrs. Benjn. Gorham
1861 (Summer)			Child of Soloman Taylor

1861		Baptized By Rev. J. B. Clark
Nov.	3	Lizzie Crocker, child of Sylvester Baker
1862		
Jany.	5	Caroline D. Knowles, wife of Allen H. Knowles
"	"	Ellen Hallet, wife of Edward B. Hallet

Marriages

1822		
August	28	Mr. Barnabas Thacher Jr. to Miss Mary Gray
	28	Mr. Edward Thacher to Miss Lydia T. Gray
Sep.	5	Captain Leonard Smalley to Miss Nabby Thacher
Dec.	29	Mr. Benjamin D. Gorham of Barnstable to Miss Abigal Howland of Yarmouth
1823		
Jan.	7	Mr. David G. Sears of Dennis to Miss Nabby Miller of Yarmouth
	29	Mr. Jonathan Killy of Yarmouth to Miss Elisibeth Killy of Harwich
Feb.	18	Capt. Samuel Nickerson of Dennis to Mrs. Clarissa Gage of Yarmouth
March	24	Mr. Solomon Hallet to Miss Almira Miller
April	10	Mr. Elihu Howes of Dennis to Miss Polly White of Yarmouth
May	29	Mr. Heroy [*sic*] Baker to Miss Mercy Homer
Aug.		Mr. Jabez Lewis to Miss Thankful Hallet
Oct.	9	Mr. Edward Hallet 3d. of Barnstable to Miss Rebeca Hallet of Yarmouth
Nov.	4	Mr. Gorham Eldridge to Miss Ruth Matthews
	20	Mr. John Hawes to Miss Betsey Hawes
Jan.	1824	Mr. Elisha Cash to Miss Ruth Robinson
	23	Mr. Isaac Burgess of Dennis to Miss Eunice Taylor of Yarmouth
Feb.	4	Mr. Gideon Harden of Dennis to Miss Hannah Baker of Yarmouth
March	4	Mr. James Whitemore of Dennis to Miss Loisa Baker of Yarmouth
		Mr. Simeon Croel to Miss Fanny Hallet
April	8	Mr. Winthrop Baker of Dennis to Miss Sally Hawes of Yarmouth
May	17	Mr. Nathanael Simpkins of Boston to Miss Eliza Jane Thatcher of Yarmouth
Sept.	22	Mr. Winthrop Smally to Miss Patience Matthews
Nov.	8	Mr. Eben'er Dunbar of Boston to Miss Betsy Bray of Yarmouth
	21	Mr. Edward W. Crocker of Barnstable to Miss Sally Sears of Yarmouth
	25	Mr. Thomas Sheerman to Miss Lydia Lewis Croel
Dec.	2	Mr. Prentiss White to Miss Nancy Eldridge
	30	Mr. Charles Layman to Miss Nabby Gorham
		Mr. Zenas Wood to Miss Mercy Howes
1825		
Jan.	16	Mr. Simeon Lewis to Miss Polly Baker
		Mr. Richard Gray to Miss Mary Sheerman
	20	Mr. Otis Croel to Miss Sally Hallet
		Mr. Edmond Hallet of Barnstable to Miss Sally L. Buck of Yarmouth
		Mr. Otis Baker to Miss Hannah Snow
Feb.	27	Mr. Dustin G. Eldridge to Miss Bethiah Matthews
March	13	Mr. David Downs of Barnstable to Miss Bethiah Howes of Yarmouth
	17	Mr. Freeman Taylor to Miss Lucy Gorham
	29	Capt. Sylvester Baker of Dennis to Miss Sabra Matthews of Yarmouth

May	26	Mr. Joshua Eldridge to Miss Data Hamblin
June	9	Mr. Barnabas Eldridge Jr. to Miss Lydia Baker
August	5	Mr. John Freeman of Brewster to Miss Ruth Sears of Yarmouth
Oct.		Capt. Baker to Miss Keziah Parker
		Capt. Ebenezer Taylor to Miss Hallet
		Capt. Jabez Howes to Miss Nabby Croel
Dec.	29	Mr. Sears of Dennis to Miss Azubah Croel
1826		
Jan.	19	Mr. Henry J. Colyar of Torringford, Connecticut, to Miss Rhoda Eldridge
		Doctor James Hedge to Widow Mary
Sep.	4	Mr. Abner Baker to Miss Maria Croel
Do.	6	Mr. Warren Lewis to Miss Dyantha Croel
Do.	7	Mr. John Rider to Miss Azubah Hallet
	11	Mr. Joel Crowel to Miss Thankful Baker
Oct.		Capt. John Eldridge 2d to Miss Kesiah Hamblin
		Mr. Benjamin Hamblin to Miss Hannah Sears
		Mr. William Knowles of Chatham to Miss Bial Marchant of Yarmouth
Dec.		Mr. Watson Croel to Miss Temperance Hallet
		Mr. Edward Sears Jun. to Miss Mercy Rider
1827		
Jan.		Mr. Jeremiah Henning to Almira Farris
		Mr. Wilbur Harden of Dennis to Miss Sally Matthews
		Mr. Barnabas Matthews to Miss Elisa Croel
Feb.		Mr. Richard Killey to Miss Betsy Baker
		Capt. Nehemiah Croel Jun. to Miss Anna Basset
		Mr. Levi Nickerson to Miss Myra White
		Mr. Abraham Chapman of Dennis to Miss Eunice Howland of Yarmouth
		Mr. Seth Croel to Mrs. Polly Baker
		Mr. Joseph Baker to Miss Susan Killey
April		Capt. Anthony Chase Sr. to Miss Susanna Studley
June		Mr. Silvanus P. Cottan of Nantucket to Miss Sarah White of Yarmouth
July		Mr. Reuben Worth of Nantucket to Miss Betsey Sears of Yarmouth
		Mr. Allen Berry of Providence to Miss Rosa Baker of Yarmouth
Sep.		Mr. Loring Baker to Miss Susan Homer
Oct.		Capt. Daniel Crowel to Miss Mira Crowel
Nov.		Mr. Luther Hill of Boston to Miss Mercy T. Eldridge
		Mr. James Sears to Miss Rebeca Croel
		Mr. Eben Bray to Mrs. Rebeca Croel
Dec.		Capt. Barnabas Hallet of Barnstable to Miss Sarah Crowel
1828		
Jan.		Capt. Reuben Baker to Miss Louisa Eldridge
		Capt. Crowel of Dennis to Miss Crowell of Yarmouth
		Mr. Hiram Crowel to Miss Betsey Lewis
Feb.		Mr. Elisha Jenkins to Miss Crowel
March		Mr. Matthews Baker to Miss Polly Homer
		Mr. Henry Matthews to Miss Gray
April		Mr. Braddock Baker to Miss Caroline Croel
June		Capt. Benjamin Matthews to Miss Betsey Rider
July		Mr. Orren Crowel to Miss Eliza Crowel
		Mr. Jeremy Gorham to Miss Cynthia Baker
		Mr. James Thatcher to Miss Susannah Hall
		Mr. Ichabot Sherman to Miss Minerva Crowel
Aug.		Mr. Edmond Crowel 3rd. to Miss Sylvia Norris
		Mr. John Caleb to Miss Mary Jenkins both of Barnstable
Sep.		Capt. Samuel E. Killey to Miss Eliza Covil
Oct.		Mr. Matthews C. Hallet to Miss Eliza Taylor

Nov.	Mr. Elkanah Hallet to Miss Marcy Hedge Taylor
Nov.	Mr. Joseph White to Miss Rhesa Crowel
Dec.	Mr. Elbridge Gerry of Boston to Miss Lucy Howland of Yarmouth
Jan. 1829	Mr. Henry Hallet to Miss Gray
	Mr. Philander Crowel to Miss Sally Ryder
	Mr. David Smith of Barnstable to Miss Fanny Baker of Yarmouth
Feb.	Mr. William Chase of Harwich to Miss Lilly Crowell
April	Mr. Arvin Baker to Mrs. Survina Cook
	Mr. Charles Gray of Brewster to Miss Rebecca R. Johnson of Yar.
May	Mr. Gorham Taylor of Yarmouth to Miss Lucy Whorf of Provincetown
July	Capt. Reuben Eldridge to Miss Mary Ann Eldridge
	Mr. Bangs Hallet to Miss Anna Eldridge
	Capt. James Matthews to Mrs. Mary Hedge
Aug.	Mr. Theophilus Basset to Miss Lydia M. Sherman
Aug.	Capt. Gorham Howland to Miss Hannah N. Taylor
	Mr. Ansel Hallet to Miss Charlotte Hallet
Sep.	Mr. Luther Howland to Miss Betsey Custis
Nov.	Mr. Benjamin Blackford of Barnstable to Miss Lydia B. Seymore
Dec.	Mr. Joice Taylor Jr. to Miss Ruth Crowel
1830	
Jan.	Capt. Henry Crowel to Miss Julia Ann Crowel
	Mr. Prince Webber to Miss Polly Buck
	Mr. Allen Hallet to Miss Raleigh Crowel
Feb.	Capt. Timothy Crowel to Miss Lydia Howes
	Mr. Samuel Rider to Miss Sarah Lewis
	Capt. Nathanael Mathews to Miss Hannah T. Mathews
	Mr. Joseph Rider to Miss Crowel
March	Mr. Nathan Baker to Miss Patty Baxter
June	Capt. Higgins Crowel to Mrs. Patia Coleman of Smithf'd, R. I.
Sep.	Mr. Albert Chase to Miss Elisabeth P. Taylor
Sep.	Mr. Clark Hallet to Miss Phebe Bray
Oct.	Mr. James Robertson of Dennis to Miss Patty Cash
	Capt. Abner Howes to Miss Rebekak Baker
1831	
Jan.	Mr. Ames Killey of Dennis to Miss Loira Bassett
	Capt. Joshua Bassett to Miss Belinda Hallet
Feb.	Mr. Henry Hall of Dennis to Mrs. Ruth Turner
March	Captain Laban Baker to Miss Eliza Baker of Falmouth
April	Mr. Timothy Taylor to Mrs. Nancy Montcalm
	Mr. Rhetire Smith to Miss Paulina Buck
May	Mr. William Taylor of Philadelphia to Miss Desieh Nickerson
Oct.	Mr. William Anderson to Miss Hannah Taylor
Nov.	Mr. Elisha Taylor to Miss Sophia Crowel
Dec.	Mr. Sylvanus P. Cotton of Nantucket to Miss Lydia White
Jan. 1832	Mr. Christopher Lewis to Miss Susan Sears
Feb.	Mr. Jonathan Nickerson to Miss Crowel
	Mr. Jesse Taylor to Miss Patia Matthews
March	Mr. Henry Cotton of Nantucket to Miss Elmira Sears
	Mr. Russel Lewis to Miss Mehitable Hallet of Barnstable
	Mr. Francis Hallet to Miss Lucy Gray
April	Mr. John Bray to Mrs. Maria Baker
	Mr. Baxter to Miss Smith
June	Mr. Davis Studley to Miss Mary H. Crowel
Oct.	Mr. Thatcher Gorham to Miss Dinah H. Bray
	Mr. Frederic Lewis to Miss Phebe Gorham

Nov.	Mr. John Brooks to Miss Nancy Pompey
	Mr. Elisha Loring to Charlotte Buck
	Mr. Oliver Taylor to Miss Polly Bray
	Mr. Charles Layman to Miss Patty Lewis Taylor
	Mr. James G. Hallet of Boston to Miss Mary Eldridge
	Mr. Stephen Howes of Dennis to Miss Rebekah White
1833	
Jan.	Mr. Gorham Hallet to Miss Deborah H. Hamblin
	Capt. Ansel Matthews to Miss Susan Thatcher
	Capt. Erastus Chase to Miss Betsey Crowell
	Mr. Zena Baker to Miss Farris
	Capt. Arvin Baker of Falmouth to Miss Jerusha C. Baker
	Mr. Joseph Baker of Falmouth to Miss Cyrene Baker
Feb.	Isaac M. Bassett to Miss Mary Jane Baker
	Mr. Emery Sears to Miss Abagail F. Homer
	Mr. Arvin Smith to Miss Sally Robbins
March	Capt. Richard Nickerson to Miss Hannah Taylor
	Capt. Sylvanus Studley of Dennis to Mrs. Charlotte Berry
	Mr. Samuel Thatcher to Miss Polly Hamblen
	Mr. Thomas Matthews Jr. of Dennis to Miss Elvira Eldridge
April	Mr. Nathan Baker Jr. to Miss Olive Smith
	Mr. Prentiss Lynnet to Miss Polly Webber
July	Mr. Ansel Jones of Barnstable to Miss Eliza Buck
Sep.	Mr. David Buck to Miss Emeline Godfrey
	Mr. Blaney Lewis to Miss Mary Bray
Nov.	Mr. William Howes to Miss Bridjed Baxter
	Mr. William White to Miss Olive Hallet
	Mr. James S. Wilder to Miss Zipporah H. Eldridge
	Capt. Goham Baker to Miss Nabby K. Lewis
	Mr. George Matthews to Miss Alice Hallet
1834	
Jan.	Mr. Samuel Sears to Miss Lavina Hallet
Feb.	Mr. Edmund Crowel Jun. to Miss Mary Norris
	Mr. Washburn Baker to Miss Cordelia Chase
	Mr. Peregrine White to Miss Susan Sears
	Mr. Micajah C. Baker of Lyn to Miss Loisa Crowel
July	Mr. Edmond Gorham to Miss Mercy H. Hallet
Aug.	Mr. Peter Crowel of Dennis to Miss Reliance Colman
	Capt. Henry Bangs of Dennis to Miss Rebekah Matthews
Dec.	Mr. Obed Baker to Miss Mary Jane Studley
1835	
Feb.	Mr. Joshua Hamblin to Miss Olive Rider
	Mr. Reuben Bray jun to Miss Elisabeth Howes
	Mr. Sylvester Robbins of Dennis to Miss Betsey Brown
	Mr. William Kowles to Miss Charlotte Sherman
	Mr. Edward Gorham to Miss Kiziah Lewis
March	Mr. Nathan Hallet to Miss Hannah Eldridge
	Mr. Joseph Hale to Miss Sally Hallet
April	Mr. David Matthews to Miss Emeline Hallet
May	Mr. Benjamin Hallet to Miss Charlotte Matthews
	Mr. Clarke of Ashfield to Miss Lydia Hallet
Aug.	Mr. Edmund Robertson to Miss Mary Ann Chase
	Mr. Stacy Bearse of Barnstable to Miss Mary P. Hallet
Nov.	Capt. Higgins Crowell to Miss Abigail Sears
	Mr. Bartlett Bray to Miss Hannah Gray
Dec.	Capt. Oliver Matthews to Miss Phebe Matthews
	Mr. Chase to Miss Deborah Covil
	Mr. Nelson Chase to Miss Susan Hall
1836	
Jan.	Mr. Alfred White to Miss Almira Crowel
	Mr. David Bray to Miss Huldah Downs

		Mr. William Sears of Dennis to Miss Ruth Berry
		Capt. Isaac Matthews to Miss Hannah Bray
		Mr. Alexander Crowel to Miss Mary Gray
		Mr. Joshua Ellis of Harwich to Mrs. Nancy Fay
April		Mr. Hatsel Crosby of Brewster to Miss Jerusha Homer
		Mr. James T. Leonard of Sandwich to Miss Louisa Newcomb
March		Mr. Sylvanus Bourne to Mrs. Sally Cobb both of Barnstable
May		Mr. John Rider to Mrs. Vianna Tayler
June		Mr. Howes H. Matthews to Miss Basha C. Lewis
		Mr. Joseph Bray to Miss Adaline Rider
Aug.		Mr. Freeman H. Crowel to Miss Phebe Ann Hallet
Oct.		Mr. Simeon Emery to Miss Betsy Adams
		Capt. Benjamin Taylor to Miss Miranda Lane
Dec.		Mr. Samuel P. Anderson of Madison, Con., to Miss Hannah Perkins of Barnstable
Dec.	1	Mr. Allen Farris to Miss Mercy Howes
Dec.	8	Mr. Henry Taylor to Miss Priscilla Coleman
Dec.	8	Mr. Elkanah Sears of Dennis to Miss Sally Berry
Dec.	20	Mr. Oppis Josselyn of Chatham to Miss Fanny Thatcher
		Mr. Robert Crowel to Mrs. Betsey Hallet
		Mr. Joshua Baker to Miss Lois Sears
1837		
Jan.		Mr. Isaac H. Bearse of Barnstable to Miss Elisa A. Crowell
		Mr. Freman Crowell to Miss Tabitha Crowell
Feb.		Mr. Benjamin Bassett of Chatham to Miss Charlotte Brown
March		Mr. Alfred Newcomb to Miss Aurelia Lewis
June	22	Mr. Calvin Hallet to Miss Elisabeth Bray
Aug.	8	Mr. Peleg T. Bassett of Rochester to Miss Susan A. Bray
Sep.		Capt. William Sherman to Miss Harriet W. Norris
[1838]		Mr. Silas Haley of Sandwich to Miss Ann Bangs
Feb.	27	Mr. Isaac Matthews to Miss Hannah Matthews
March	11	Capt. Winslow Gray to Miss Sally Homer
April	29	Mr. Abraham E. Perkins to Miss Charlotte L. Elizabeth of Barnstable
1828 [*sic*]		
June	28	Mr. William H. Davis of Barnstable to Miss Rebecca B. Norris of Barnstable
June	21	Mr. Bartlet Brown to Miss Eliza Crowell
Nov.	11	Mr. Thomas Sherman to Miss Rebekah G. Burgess
Dec.	16	Mr. Strabo Clark of Brewster to Miss Adeline Dunbar of Yarmouth
Dec.	25	Capt. Isaac Downs of Dennis to Miss Mary N. Whelden of Dennis
	27	Mr. Davis Crowel to Miss Jane Crowel
	27	Capt. Hiram Nickerson of Dennis to Miss Fanny Baxter of Yarmouth
		Hallet of Barnstable to Miss
1839		
Jan.	1	Mr. Nathan Nickerson of Dennis to Miss Temperance Sherman of Yarmouth
	22	Mr. Hartson Hallet of Barnstable to Miss Eunice Crowel
	24	Capt. Freeman Baker Jr. of Dennis to Miss Almira Towne of Dennis
March	19	Mr. Eldridge C. Sears of Dennis to Miss Achsah H. Bray
	19	Capt. John E. Baker to Miss Mariah Eldridge
April	10	Mr. Isaiah Chase of Harwich to Miss Rebekah R. Baker
Aug.	29	Mr. Ellery Eldridge to Miss Sally Matthews
Oct.	28	Mr. Reuben Ryder to Mrs. Mary Lewis
Oct.	30	Mr. John Blatchford of Barnstable to Miss Mary A. Howland of Barnstable

CHURCH RECORDS OF WEST YARMOUTH, MASS.

Copied by Florence Conant Howes

Nov.	12	Mr. Jeremiah Coffin of Barnstable to Miss Martha Brewster of Barnstable
Nov.	28	Mr. David Seabury of Dennis to Miss Rebekah C. Matthews
Dec.		Mr. Watson Ryder to Miss Deborah L. Ryder
1840		
Jan.	13	Mr. Nathanael Nickerson of Orleans to Mrs. Rebekah Homer
March	31	Capt. Zenas Howes of Dennis to Mrs. Lydia W. Cotton
April	9	Mr. Wilson Ryder of Barnstable to Miss Betsy Marston
Aug.	9	Mr. John Marser to Miss Mercy Marston
Aug.	27	Caleb S. Hunt Esq. to Miss Sarah Reed
Oct.	11	Capt. William Brown to Miss Polly Berry
Nov.		Capt. Thomas Ryder to Miss Susan Gorham
December	24	Mr. Benjamin Bacon of Barnstable to Miss Olive Buck
1841		Capt. Gorham Eldridge to Miss Bethiah S. Matthews
June	13	Mr. Reuben Hallet to Miss Betsey Hallet
June	24	Mr. Allen Nickerson to Miss Loisa Gorham
Aug.	12	James F. Joy Esq. of Detroit, Michigan, to Miss Martha Reed
Do		Mr. John Lewis to Miss Ruth Taylor
Sep.	7	Capt. Sylvanus Matthews to Miss Eliza Hedge
Sep.	15	Mr. George Brown to Miss Rebecca Salters
Sep.	20	Capt. Reuben Matthews to Miss Frances Bray
Oct.		Mr. Watson Thatcher to Miss Emeline Hamblin
Oct.		Mr. Abner W. Lovell to Miss Olive Crocker

1842		
Jan.	20	Mr. Gorham Bray to Miss Nancy Thatcher
Feb.	7	Rev. D. Rogers to Miss Cornelia Hallet
June	16	Mr. Thomas Long to Miss Nabby A. Taylor
July	17	Isaiah Chase of Harwich to Miss Patty Robertson
Nov.	15	Mr. David Marston of Barnstable to Miss Nabby Hallet
December	10	Mr. John Hall of Dennis to Miss Elisabeth Smalley of Dennis
1843		
Feb.	16	Mr. Elnathan Crowel of Dennis to Miss Elsey Taylor
March	14	Mr. Sidney Studley of Dennis to Miss Mary Crowel of Yarmouth
April	13	Mr. Charles Thatcher to Miss Hannah Thatcher
Aug.		Mr. Robert Homer to Miss Lavina Baker
Sep.		Mr. Thomas Hedge to Miss Elisa B. Eldridge
Sep.		Mr. Edward Lewis to Miss Lucretia Crowell
Oct.		Mr. Zebina Crowel of Dennis to Miss Sarah Bray of Yarmouth
Dec.	6	Mr. Elias B. Harrington of Barnstable to Miss Betsey F. Hallet of Yarmouth
1844		
Feb.	29	Mr. Isaiah P. Matthews to Miss Sally H. Taylor
July		Mr. Oliver Gorham to Miss Eunice T. Hall
1845		
July		Mr. Heman B. Ryder of Dennis to Miss Sally N. Gage
July		Mr. Thomas Isham of Barnstable to Miss Mary Jerrod
Oct.		Mr. James Gibson of Lynn to Miss Sophia Hallet
Dec.		Mr. George Ryder to Miss Sarah N. Hallet
Dec.		Mr. Sylvanus Whilden to Miss Bethiah G. Gorham
1846		
Feb.		Mr. Edward W. Bray to Miss Lucy A. Homer
May		Mr. Edward Wells of Provincetown to Miss Elisabeth A. Loring
1848		
Jan.		Mr. Franklin Matthews to Miss Sarah Matthews
Jan.		Mr. Reuben Ryder to Miss Mary Marston
March		Mr. Mesech Turner to Miss Angelina Bankston
March		Mr. Jeremiah Chase to Miss Martha Robinson
Nov.		Mr. David G. Eldridge to Miss Sarah Thatcher
1849		
March		Mr. Isaac Ryder to Miss Dorcas Ryder
Jan.		Capt. Asa W. Nickerson of Dennis to Miss Ruth A. Nickerson of Dennis
1850		
May		Capt. Jabez Berry of Dennis to Miss Olive Hamblin of Yarmouth
Nov.	28	Mr. Elam S. Mecarta of Harwich to Miss Priscilla Cash of Yarmouth
Nov.	28	Mr. Benjamin Gorham to Miss Clara C. Matthews
Dec.	14	Cap. Heman B. Chase to Martha Crowel
Nov.	21	Charles Hamillen of Nova Scotia to Mrs. Lydia Berry
Dec.	15	Mr. Henry A. Lothrop of Barnstable to Miss Elisabeth Matthews

Deaths

1822		
April	27	Jonathan Whilden, aged 72 years
May	4	Isaac, child of Captain Joseph Eldridge, aged 5 days
July	22	Child of Mr. Joseph White, aged 4 hours
August	3	Widow Mary Gray, aged 77 years
	11	Mr. Reuben Rider, aged 59 years
Sept.	29	Patience, daughter of Azubah Tailor, aged 17 years
Oct.	3	Sally, wife of Captain James Matthews, aged 38 years
	10	Mehitable, wife of Gideon Berry, aged about 25 years
Nov.	13	Widow Elisabeth Parker, aged about 40 years
	29	Mr. Prentiss Hawes, aged about 21 years
Dec.	13	Mr. Howes Berry, aged about 50 years

1823

Jan.	6	Miss Harriot Hallet, aged 30 years
Feb.	4	Child of Capt. Joseph Matthews, aged 3 months
	27	Widow Hannah Taylor, aged 81 years
April	10	Metilda, daughter of Mr. James Thatcher, aged 7 weeks
		Son of Mr. Zenas Hallet
May	15	Son of Capt. Nehemiah Croel, aged about 22 years
June	10	Widow Abigal Croel, aged about 45 years
	8	Russel, son of Mr. Josiah Thatcher, aged 13 years
	Do	Ebenezer B., Son of Mr. Nathanael Adams, aged 12 years
July		Twins of Mr. David Rider
Aug.		Daughter of Zena Killey
		Wife of Anthony Chase
		Child of Heman Chase
		Daughter of Abraham Baker
		Son of Lewis Sears
		Wife of James Hallet
		Child of Capt. Joseph Thatcher
		Mother of Joseph Croel
Oct.		Susannah, wife of James Thatcher
		Child of Nathan Hallet
		Widow Rosa Burgess
		Wife of Prince Gifford
		Child of prince Gifford
Nov.	9	Eunice, daughter of James Thatcher
		Capt. Joseph Thatcher
Dec.		Wife of Benjamin Lane
		Hannah, wife of Reuben Bray
		Son of Widow Miller

1824

Jan.		Sabra, a black woman
		Capt. Eleazer Sears
		Miss Desiah Hallet
		Wife of Capt. Fares
		Mr. Nathan Croel
		Widow Susannah Thatcher
		Widow Thankful Killy
		A black child
		Elihu Baker
		Capt. Thomas Hedge
		Child of Capt. Paddock Thatcher
		Child of Esq. Henry Thatcher
		Wife of Cato Juda
		Mary, daughter of Widow Mary Hallet
		Child of Barnabas Rider
		Widow Ruth Baker
		Wife of Richard Taylor
		Son of Widow Smalley
		Mr. James Hallet
		Mr. Edward Gorham
		Child of Henry Custis

1825

Jan.		Mr. Jabes Croel
		Wife of Mr. Anthony Studley
		Mr. Barnabas Croel
		Mr. William Taylor
		Child of Peleg Coffin
		Wife of Daniel Taylor
		Widow Sally Hallet
		Child of Nathan Croel
		Child of William Farris
		Miss Mary Miller
		Mr. Samuel Ferris

Child of Widow Sally Gorham
Child of Mr. Edward Whelden
Mr. David Baxter
Daughter of Widow Betty Eldridge
Two children of Mr. Joshua Hallet
Mr. Daniel Taylor
Child of Edmond Matthews
A black man
Black child
Child of Ebenezer Croel
Widow Thankful Hedge
Wife of Peter Thatcher
Child of Joseph Croel
Joseph Croel
Lemuel Baker
Widow Elisabeth Hallet
Wife of Sylvanus Studley
Child of Col. Joshua Hamblin
Twins of Mis[tress] Betsey Eldridge
Mr. Asa Croel
Wife of Mr. David Eldridge
Son of Mr. Andrew Hallet
Child of Mr. Asa Coval
Child of Mr. Enoch Rider
Child of Mr. Charles Croel
Child of Mr. ——— Phinney
Child of Mr. Josiah Baker
Wife of Chandler Gray
Child of David Hallet
Mr. Joseph Croel
Child of Kingsley Baker
Child of Mr. Semore
Child of Thomas Croel Jur.
Child of Henry Rider
Son of Capt. Ebenezer Howes
Mrs. Susan Brooks
Wife of John Greenough
Child of John Greenough
Child of Widow Mary Croel
Child of Mr. Richard Gray
Capt. Jonathan Sears
Mr. Jeshap Wing
Mr. Samuel Taylor
Miss Mehitable Howes
Widow Data Bray
Capt. Benjamin Homer
Mr. Thomas Buck
Mr. Prince Baxter
Widow Thankful Howes
Widow Bethiah Croel
Child of Daniel Chase
Child of Jabez Lewis
Child of Benjamin Matthews, Child of Nathan Hallet, Child of Groton Gerald, Child of Sylvester Baker, Mr. William Ferris

1826 Jan. Two children of Mr. John Gage, Wife of Capt. Silas Baker, Mr. John Killey, Child of Lemuel Baker, Widow Anner Hawes, Freeman Rider, Child of John Gage, Child of Laban Baker, Child of Cornelius Baker, Barnabas Rider, Uriah Coffin, Jabez Berry, Child of Capt. Joshua Eldridge, Wife of Capt. Barnabas Eldridge Jun., Wife of Thomas Greenough, Miss Temperance Rider, Miss Sally, daughter of Henry Thatcher Esq., Child of Reuben Rider, Child of James Sears Jun., Wife of James Davis, Child of Henry Thatcher Esq., Widow Patty Russel Matthews, Mr. Berry, Mr. Matthews Croel, Child of Mrs. Mirick, Capt. Reuben Matthews, Child of Andrew Hallet, Child of Enoch Matthews, Child of Edward Thatcher, Child of William Gray, Child of Leonard Berry, Child of Freeman Taylor, Wife of Ezekiel Hallet, Mr. Jothan Goodno, Child of Capt. Paddock Thatcher, Capt. Prince Matthews, Miss Mary Howes, Child of Judah Croel, Child of Isaiah Burgess, Child of John Semore, Child of Gorham Baker, Child of Isaac Buck.

1827 Miss Elisabeth Whelden, Wife of Abner Croel, Wife of Eben Bray, Watson Eldridge, Mr. Robert Croel, Mr. Jeremiah Croel, Child of David Hallet, Child of Capt. Freeman Baker, Child of Timothy Croel, Mr. Joseph Baxter, Mr. Lemuel Baker, Wife of James Sears, Serena, Wife of Capt. Benjamin Mathews, Mr. Otis Sears, Mr. Elisha Cash, Captain John Bray, Wife of Higgins Crowel, Widow Phiney, Child of Jonathan Hallet Jun., Capt. Daniel Baxter, Widow Whelden, Capt. Isaac Matthews, Susan, wife of Joseph White, Joseph, son of James Thatcher, Child of Benjamin Berry, Widow Rebeca White, Son of Widow Berry, Son of Abraham Baker, Child of Groten Gerald, Wife of Deacon Lewis, Widow of Solomon Hallet.

1828 Mr. Jabez Linnet, Child of Elisha Cash, Wife of Jonathan Hallet, Child of Ezekiel Hallet, Ruth, daughter of Capt. Isaac White, Mr. Groton Gerald, Capt. Ebenezer Crowel, Child of Capt. John Eldridge, Child of Mr. Joseph Hallet, Wife of Ebenezer Thatcher, Mr. Nathanael Matthews, Wife of Matthews Croel Hallet, Son of Mr. Nathanael Adams, Child of Mr. Benjamin Berry, Hannah, wife of Capt. Gideon Hardin, Amanda, daughter of Capt. Isaac Matthews, Wife of Mr. Ebenezer Hallet, Child of Richard Gray jun., Child of Thomas Sherman, Daughter of Seth Killey, Son of Capt. James Mathews, Mr. Sylvanus Parker, Widow Ruth Mathews, Mr. Andrew Hedge, Capt. Joshua Gray, Widow Mary Hedge, Wife of David Hallet, Wife of Shubal Crowel, Child of William A. Matthews, Son of widow Custis, Rev. Timothy Alden, Wife of Gorham Baker, Mary Jane, daughter of Col. Gorham Crowel, Wife of Capt. Elisha Baker.

1829 Child of Capt. Ichabot Sherman, Mr. James Wall, Mr. Jeremiah Berry, Capt. Thaddeus Brown, Child of Isaac Nickerson, Child of Daniel Weever, Child of Oliver Studley, Wife of Captain Nathan Hallet, Wife of Obed Taylor, George, the son of widow Rebekah Gray, Samuel, the son of Mr. Chandler Gray, Child of Mr. Crowel, Wife of Mr. Prince Webber, Son of Mr. Joseph Hallet, Child of Mr. Peter Bray, Widow Ruth Hallet, Child of Jeremiah Gorham, Capt. Abner Baker, Son of Mr. Joshua Basset, Mr. Stephen Burse, Wife of Howes Berry, Mr. Edward Crowel, Child of Owen Crowel.

1830 Child of Mr. Isaac Studley, Widow Parker, Wife of Thomas Sherman, Mr. David Homer, Miss Sarah Bray, Widow Bethiah Crowel, Mr. Allen B. Crowel, Capt. Samuel Studley, Wife of Orren Crowel, Child of Daniel Weever, Child of Capt. George Sears, Child of Mr. Edward Crocker, Mr. David Whelden, Child of Samuel B. Seymore, Child of Erving Baker, Miss L Baker, Mr. James Sears, Child of John Loring, Child of Nathanael Cogswell, Mr. Asa Homer.

[1831] Widow Elisabeth Hallet, Child of Doct. James Hedge, Captain Edmond Hawes, Mr. Ebenezer Thatcher, Widow Anner Baker, Mr. Cornelius Baxter, Mr. Calvin Crowel, Child of Mr. Jeremiah Gorham, Hannah, the wife of Mr. Dunbar, Child of Capt. Barnabas Hallet, Wife of Mr. Timothy Reed, Wife of Mr. Randal Hallet, Child of Mr. Timothy Reed, Captain John Gorham, Mr. Prince Webber, Deacon Howes Taylor, Wife of Mr. Richard Nickerson, Child of Mr. Richard Nickerson, Wife of Mr. Perregrine White, Charrissa Hedge, Widow Killey, Mr. Thomas Crowel, Widow Abigail Crowel, Widow Lucinda Baxter, Capt. Timothy Crowel.

1832 Capt. Ansel Hallet, Mr. Randel Hallet, Child of Mr. Edward Crocker, Widow Hannah Crowel, Son of Mr. James Whelden, Child of Mr. John Loring, Widow Anna Merchant, Wife of Mr. Robert Homer, Wife of Capt. Solomon Taylor, Wife of Mr. Jabez Lewis, Widow Burgess, Mr. Joseph Baker, Mr. Simeon Lewis, Mr. Charles Hallet, Mr. Barnabas Thatcher, Mr. Barnabas Hallet, Mr. Ebenezer Hallet, Mr. Joshua Hall, Mr. John Greenough, Son of John Greenough, Mr. Edward Eldridge, Mr. James Thatcher, Widow Temperance Taylor, Mr. Robert Homer, Mr. Timothy Taylor.

1833

Jan. Mr. Henry Thatcher, Captain Elisha Baker, Child of Mr. Daniel Downes, Elnathan, Son of Capt. Elnathan Lewis, Bial, wife of Mr. William Knowles, Child of Mr. William Knowles, Mr. Atkins Matthews, Widow Howland, Henry Thatcher Esq., Capt. Joseph Bassett, Child of Capt. Reuben Eldridge, Widow Thankful Gage, Mr. Peregrine White, Capt. James Welden, Child of Mr. Hiram Crowel, Child of Mr. William Bray, Mr. Henry Hallet, Child of Nabby Gorham.

1834 Mr. Prince Hallet, Child of Henry Crowel, Mr. Winslow E. Thatcher, Son of Chandler Gray, Wife of Capt. Joseph Crowel, Mr. Benjamin Homer, Mr. David Rider, Child of Capt. Isaac Hamblin, Child of Mr. Asa Matthews, Wife of Mr. Lothrop Taylor, Mr. David Killey, Child of Matthews C. Hallet, Child of Capt. Otis Crowel, Child of Mr. John Rider, Mr. David Downes, Widow Mary Gray, Sons of Ichabat Sherman, Dinah, Wife of Mr. Josiah Hedge, Child of Mr. George Matthews, Child of Capt. Reuben Eldridge.

1835 Mr. Joice Taylor, Mr. Stephen Hallet, Child of Benjamin Berry, Widow Lydia Crowel, Widow Dinah Hedge, Child of Thomas Matthews, William Taylor, Child of Capt. Reuben Eldridge, Azubah, wife of Mr. John Rider, Serena, child of Capt. Benjamin Matthews, Child of Capt. Nehemiah Crowel, Isaac White Jun., Miss Mercy Hallet, Widow Priscilla Baker, Mr. Ebenezer Sears, Child of Irving Baker, Mr. John Dunbar, Thomas, son of Mr. Chandler Gray, Lathrop, son of Widow Sally Gorham, Mr. William Hallet, Wife of William Hallet, Mr. Hezekiah Gorham, Child of Mr. Winthrop Smalley, Child of Mr. John Marston, Mr. George Thatcher.

1836 Miss   Godfrey, Miss Phebe Hallet, Child of Capt. John Eldridge, Capt. Isaiah Parker, Mr. Caleb Smith, Mr. John Buck, Mr. Joshua Bassett, Mr. William A. Matthews, Francis, child of Capt. Reuben Eldridge, Capt. Solomon Taylor, Child of Luther Hills, Son of Charles Baxter, Eliza, wife of Mr. Nathanael Sypmkins, Thomas, son of Col.

Isaiah Bray, Lydia, wife of Mr. Josiah Thatcher, Child of Capt. Freeman Taylor, Widow Hannah Crowel, Widow Hannah Hallet, Child of Jabez Lewis, Child of Henry Crowel, Child of Capt. Isaac Hamblin, Child of Capt. Oliver Taylor, Child of Capt. Peregrine White, Child of Patty Fortune [*sic*].

1837 Mr. Thomas Greenough, Child of Capt. Bangs Hallet, Child of Mr. Matthews C. Hallet, Wife of Mr. Heman Linnet, Eliza, child of Capt. Reuben Eldridge, John B. Deane Esq., Miss Mary H. Ryder, Daughter of Mr. Ezekiel Hallet, Capt. Barnabas Eldridge, Child of Mr. Elkanah Gorham, Capt. Jeremiah Crowel, Mr. Abraham Matthews, Mr. Joseph Lewis, Child of Samuel Baker, Child of John Greenough, Wife of James Wall, Mr. Joshua Hall, Mr. Jonathan Hallet.

1838 Widow Lydia Hallet, Lydia Matthews, wife of Mr. Henry Matthews, Widow Mary Hallet, Widow Susannah Crowel, Widow Jerusha Crowel, Child of Freeman Crowel, Child of Zenas Crowel, Grandchild of David Buck, Widow Seymore, Son of Capt. Isaac Bassett, Daughter of Edward Matthews, Thomas Henry, son of John H. Dunbar, Child of Capt. Isaac Hamblin, Child of Henry Matthews, Child of Joshua Hamblin, Child of Benjamin Hamblin, Child of Daniel Crocker, Miss Sally Taylor, Mr. Samuel Sears, Widow Molly Thatcher.

1839 Widow Ruth Taylor, Mr. Shiverick, Wife of Freeman Crowel, Mrs. Tabitha Crowel, Mr. John Seymore, Child of Heman Taylor, Mayo Whelden, Child of Capt. Bangs Hallet, Child of Matthews C. Hallet, Harriet, wife of Mr. Reuben Ryder, Child of Capt. Isaac Hamblin, Child of Samuel Burbick, Child of Capt. Nehemiah Crowel Jr., Wife of Mr. Newcomb, Miss Betsey Bearse, Widow of Mr. David Whelden, Child of Mr. William White, Two children of Capt. John Bray.

1840 Child of Capt. Sylvester Baker, Two children of Capt. Edward Hallet, Wife of Deacon Joseph Hawes, Capt. Isaac M. Bassett, Ruth, wife of Capt. Gorham Eldridge, Polly, wife of Capt. Oliver Taylor, Wife of Mr. Henry Matthews, Wife of Capt. Timothy Hallet, Widow Gere Baxter, Son of James Croel.

1841 Capt. Samuel Taylor, Widow Charlotte Crowel, Child of William Anderson, Mrs. Hannah Matthews and her child, Child of Mr. Prince Matthews, Mr. Isaac Matthews, Capt. Eben Bray, Capt. John Bray, Mr. Peter Bray, Mr. Heman Matthews, Ebenezer, son of Mr. Ebenezer Matthews, Verranus, son of Capt. Sylvester Baker, Son of Enoch Whelden, Son of Edward Whelden, Widow Mary Thatcher, Mr. David Hall and his son, Two children of Mr. Frederic Lewis, Child of Capt. Freman Taylor.

1842 Mrs. Joseph Hamblin, Mrs. Joseph Bassett, Mr. Oliver Hallet, Child of Mr. Lovell, Mother of Mrs. Lovell, Daughter of Widow Nabby F. Sears, Wife of Capt. Sylvanus Gage, Child of Capt. William White, Son of Mr. James Taylor, Capt. Prentiss White.

1843 Mr. Ebenezer Taylor and wife, Child of Capt. Francis Hallet, Child of Capt. Gorham Howland, Child of Joseph Marshal, Wife of Sylvanus Whelden, Wife of John Manser, Child of Isaac Smalley, Child of William Knowles, Wife of Capt. Richard Matthews, Mr. Lewis, Mrs. Thankful Ryder.

INDEX

Abrahams, Eunice 276
William 276
Abrams, Willliam 272
Actkins, Henry 606
Adams, (?) 114, 182, 274, 450, 538
Anna 313
Betsey 127
Betsy 691
Ebenezer B. 694
Edmund 274
Edward 85, 86
Eliashib 99
James 62, 85, 86, 134, 313, 314, 501, 517, 544, 622
James (Cpt.) 123
John 219, 242, 248, 315, 507
Louisa 128
Margaret 314
Martha 621
Martha (Mrs.) 134, 137, 138
Mary 314, 315
Matty (Mrs.) 139
Mayhew 114
Moses 134, 137, 138, 139
Nathanael 694, 696
Reliance (Mrs.) 100
Relyance (Mrs.) 114
Richard 314
Susanna 127
Thankful (Mrs.) 136, 137, 138, 139
William 124, 133, 134, 135, 136, 137, 138, 139, 140, 313
Wm. 125
Adan, Samuel 274
Addey, Webb 501
Adlington, George 274
John 296
Lydia 285
Mary Elizabeth 274
Nancy 296
Advard, Henry 502
Adverd, Elizab. 314
Experience 314
Henry 314
Mary 314
Sarah 314
Ahame, John 71
Airy, Ebenezer 653
Isaac 653
John 653
Rich. 96
Aken, Benjamin 157
Ebenezer 157
Elihu 157
Hannah (Mrs.) 157
James 157
John 157
Judith 157
Susanna 157
Akin, Benjamin (Jr.) 154
Davin (?) 156
Deborah 156
Elizabeth 156
Eunice 154
Hannah 156
John 47, 147, 156
Mary 156
Mary (Mrs.) 154
Susan 156
Susannah 154
Thomas 156
Akin (cont.)
Timothy 156
Akins, (?) 310
Alcocke, Anne 546
Alden, (?) 243, 517, 532
Abigail 12, 20, 576
Albert 678
Anna 12
Betsy 675
Caleb Holmes 679
Caleb Holms 679
Daniel 9
Daniel (Jr.) 12
Eleazer 9
Eunice Weld 675
Ezra 28
Hannah 9
Hannah (Mrs.) 344
Isaac 2, 6, 21
Isaac (II) 27
Isaiah 659, 675, 678, 681
Jemima 11
Jo. 502
John 1, 11, 28, 344, 497, 500, 513, 525, 531, 534
John (Jr.) 502
John (Sr.) 502
Jonathan 20, 245
Lydia 29
Marten 678, 679
Martha Shaw 662
Martin 680, 681
Martin (Rev.) 681, 682
Martin Luther 682
Mary 9, 28
Mary (Mrs.) 678
Mary Kingman 680
Mehitabel 24
Mehitable 8
Mercy 628
Nabby 20
Nathan 14
Nathan (Jr.) 19
Oliver 660
Orpha 584
Polly 584
Polly (Mrs.) 678, 679, 680, 681
Rebecca 16
Sally Weld 675
Sarah 8, 628
Sarah (Mrs.) 659, 660, 661, 662
Sarah Weld 661
Simeon 3
Susan (Mrs.) 678
Susanna 12, 24
Susanna (Mrs.) 675
Timothy 659, 681
Timothy (Rev.) 659, 660, 661, 662, 696
Weld Noble 678
Aldin, Hannah (Mrs.) 346
John 346
Samuel 346
Aldrich, Betesey 583
Catharine 9
Elizabeth 274
Ichabod 274
John 274
Obed 274
Polly (Mrs.) 274
Valentine 274
Aldridge, Elizabeth 274
Ichabod 274
John 274
Aldridge (cont.)
Obed 274
Polly (Mrs.) 274
Valentine 274
Alebat, Mehitable 274
Alexander, (?) 448
George S. (Rev.) 176
Alger, Deliverance 488
Israel 9
John 630
Joseph 9
Alger?, Thomas 545
Allen, (?) 53, 57, 95, 110, 274, 423
(?) (Mrs.) 100, 108, 109, 110, 111
(?) (Sr.) (Mrs.) 100
Abagail 154
Abigail 1, 6, 16, 99, 117
Abigail (Widow) 120, 124
Abigail? 128
Alice 11, 27
Anna 122
Anna (Widow) 118
Asahel 27
Barbara 148
Barza 27, 29
Bathsheba 24, 99
Bathsheba (Mrs.) 119
Bathshebah 103
Benj. 588
Benjamin 11, 99, 107, 274
Bethiah 41, 253, 483, 486
Betsey 127
Betty 15, 26
Beulah 120, 124
Beulah (Mrs.) 120, 123, 134
Bithiah 14
Byram 24
Caleb 43, 274
Catharine (Mrs.) 135, 274
Catherine (Mrs.) 132, 133, 136, 515
Charles Frederick 274
Christian 591
Christopher 90
Christopr. 72
Clarissa (Mrs.) 120, 133, 134, 135, 136, 138
Cynthia (Mrs.) 136, 137, 138
Daniel 57, 274, 591
Danl. 591, 592
David 27, 205, 274
David (Jr.) 274
David Meader 274
Davis 122
Deborah 41, 59
Deborah (Widow) 118
Desire 119
Desire (Jr.) 126
Desire (Mrs.) 118, 122
Eben 100
Ebenezer 6, 74, 144, 154
Edward 274
Eleazer 98, 101, 116
Elisha 6, 12
Elizabeth 52, 99, 149, 587, 592
Elizabeth (Mrs.) 43

Allen (cont.)
Ephm. 122
Ephraim 138, 139, 140, 458, 483
Ephraim (Jr.) 137, 138
Esther 14, 22
Eunice 23, 24, 27, 127
Ezra 15, 119, 120, 134
Francis 503
Frederick 124, 274
Gennet 20
George 122, 148, 274, 503, 515
George (Sr.) 548
Hanna 98, 99
Hannah 23, 29, 128, 154
Hannah (Widow) 12
Hassadyah 59
Henry 124, 128, 135, 136, 137, 139, 515
Hepsibah 129
Howard 274
Huldah 21, 198, 210, 221
Ichabod 100, 105, 113
Increase 72, 89
Increase (Jr.) 145
Isaac 1, 25, 27
Isaac (Jr.) 19
Isaace 42
Isacce 41, 42
Isace 41
Ja. 100, 103
Jacob 15, 24
James 12, 20, 103, 109, 112, 118, 125, 136, 137, 138, 154
James (II) 128
James Henry 274
Jane 99, 128, 622
Japhet 463
Jedidah 117, 120
Jedidiah 197
Jethro 99
Jno. 42
Job 274
John 2, 11, 41, 42, 54, 64, 97, 98, 100, 104, 107, 114, 118, 130, 149, 245, 274, 458, 462, 483, 484, 485, 487, 599, 603
John Nobles 274
Jona. (Jr.) 119
Jonathan 12, 14, 99, 100, 149
Joseph 12, 17, 107, 111, 145, 149
Joshua 98, 99, 103, 114, 483
Josiah 7, 12, 119, 120, 148
Justice 107, 108
Katharine (Mrs.) 41
Katheren (Mrs.) 41
Katherin 97
Katherine 41
Kathren 99, 112
Laben 463
Lois (Mrs.) 119
Love (Mrs.) 119, 130, 131, 274
Lucy (Mrs.) 122, 130, 131
Lydia 145, 483
Lydia (Mrs.) 274
Margaret 119

Allen (cont.)
Mariah 117
Marmaduke 149
Martha 99, 119, 359
Martha (Jr.) 126
Martha (Mrs.) 118
Martin 660
Mary 11, 12, 16, 20, 21, 59, 103, 114, 116, 128, 144, 149, 154, 197, 208
Mary (Mrs.) 100, 107, 109, 118, 130, 149
Mathew 59, 503
Mattheu 135
Matthew 11, 122, 127, 133, 134, 515
Matthew (II) 24
Matthew (Jr.) 11
Mehetabell 600
Mehitabel 6
Micah 12
Mirriam 59
Molly 18, 23, 24
Morrill (Rev.) 451
Moses 100, 109
N. S. 483
Nancy 128, 129
Naomi (Mrs.) 274
Nathan 12
Nathaniel 6, 52, 253
Nehemiah 7, 41
Noah 148, 149
Patience (Mrs.) 122, 133, 134
Paul 274
Peggy 127
Persis 128
Phebe 16
Philip 154
Prudence 128
Prudence (Mrs.) 130, 131, 132, 133, 134, 136
Ralph 515
Raph 503
Rebecah 99
Rebecca 16, 117, 127, 149, 208
Rebecca (Mrs.) 138, 139, 149
Rebeccah 97
Rebekah 108
Reuben 274
Richard 43
Robert 118, 122, 123, 127, 208, 221
Robert (Jr.) 119
Salathiel 122, 130, 131
Sally 26, 124
Saml. 117
Samuel 11, 14, 59, 119, 123, 124, 515
Samuel (Jr.) 6
Samuell 598
Sarah 11, 12, 15, 41, 52, 146, 149, 154, 245, 274
Sarah (Mrs.) 59, 660
Seth 11
Shubael 274
Silvanus 99, 103, 112, 114, 274
Simeon 24
Sophia (Mrs.) 124, 135, 136, 137, 139
Susan 98, 116, 274

Allen (cont.)
Susanna 5, 11, 14, 26, 97, 101
Susanna (Mrs.) 274
Susanna (Widow) 25
Sylvanus 116, 122, 132, 134, 135, 149
Sylvaus 132, 133, 136
Temperance 127, 134
Thomas 107, 503, 504, 591, 598, 599, 600
Timothy 25, 26, 103
Timothy (Rev.) 660
Tristram 120, 127, 133, 134, 135, 136, 138
Unice 103
Walter 274
William 14, 99, 101, 108, 120, 130, 131, 148, 149, 274, 515, 544
William Howard 274
Wm. 119
Zebulon 27, 120, 121, 122, 126, 130, 131, 132, 133, 134, 136, 154
Allene, Christopher 75
Allerton, Bartholomew 497
Isaac 495, 497, 500, 506
John 499
Mary 497
Mary (Mrs.) 497
Remember 497
Sarah 497
Alley, (?) 205, 274
Charles (Cpt.) 274
Eunice (Mrs.) 274
Jacob 274
John 274
Martha (Mrs.) 274
Reuben 274
Richard 274
Allin, Benjamin 143, 257
Caleb 38
Daniel 257, 269
Edward 257, 260
Experience 533
George 533
John 528, 531
John (Cpt.) 517
Joseph 257
Mary 257
Mercy 631
Nathll. 257
Rachel 260
Rebecah 143
Silvanus 257
Thomas 534
Zachariah 74
Zebediah 533
Allyn, Elizabeth 611
Hannah (Mrs.) 611
Samll. 611
Almsburg, (?) (Widow) 487
Alverson, Sarah 492
Ames, (?) (Mrs.) 274
(?) (Widow) 275
Allen 275
Benjamin 274
Daniel 1
Elizabeth 6
Hannah 5, 8
Job 6

Ames (cont.)
John (Jr.) 4
Kezia 2
Mary 2, 9
Nathan 274
Nathanael 480
Nathaniel 7
Noah 5
Polly (Mrs.) 274
Samuel 275
Sarah 1, 5, 7
Thomas 7
Timothy 5
William 6, 9
Amesbury, Caleb 592
Daniel 592
Experience 592
Jacob 591
Jonathan 591, 592
Joshua 592
Mary 592
Mercy 592
Sarah 591
Tho. 592
Amsbury, Jonathan 590
Anable, Samll (Jr.) 94
Samuel (Jr.) 94
Anderson, Rebecca (Mrs.) 449
Samuel P. 691
William 689, 698
Andreus, Thomas 270
Andrew, Frederick 292
Isaac 292
Paul Mitchell 292
Andrewes, Grace 628
Henry 628
Mary 628
Andrews, (?) 77, 449
Abiah 577
Abigail 518, 520, 628
Abraham 275
Alathea (Mrs.) 577
Alfred 577
Asaph 577
Belara 577
Diana 577
Edmund 556
Hannah 547, 639
Henry 72, 82, 88, 518, 520, 537
Henry (Sr.) 518
Isaac 275
Jacob 275
John 557
Joseph 530
Josiah B. (Cpt.) 129
Kezia 583
Mahitabell 629
Mary 518, 520
Mary (Mrs.) 275, 518, 520
Mary (Widow) 88
Phylena 577
Rufus 577
Sally 584
Sarah 518, 520
Walter 577
Andros, Mary (Mrs.) 82
Andross, (?) (Widow) 43
Androwes, Sarah 646
Anegro, Cesar 377
Anger, (?) 395
Angier, (?) 395, 458
Dorothy (Mrs.) 483
J. 17
John 17, 18, 19, 20, 23
Angier (cont.)
John (Rev.) 10, 12, 16, 17, 19, 22, 25
Mary (Mrs.) 16
S. 18, 19, 20, 21, 22, 23, 24
Saml 17
Saml. 17, 18, 19
Samuel 17, 19, 24, 483
Samuel (Rev.) 10, 12, 17, 19, 22, 25
Ann, Mary Frances 427
Sarah 427
Annable, Ann 543
Anthony 504, 509, 528, 543, 623
Desire (Mrs.) 615
Jane 616
John 617
Mary 617
Patience (Mrs.) 616
Samll. 615, 616
Samuel 617
Susannah 623
Annadown, Henery 54
Henry 73
Philip 54, 73
Anniball, (?) 595, 600, 601, 609
Anthony 599, 601
Anthonye 600
Deborah 597
Desyre 600
Esek 600
Samuel 599
Samuell 601
Sarah 602
Annible, Anna 615
Anne (Mrs.) 549
Anthony 546, 548, 549
Hannah 546
Hannah (Mrs.) 548
Jane (Mrs.) 548
Patience 615
Patience (Mrs.) 617
Samll. 615
Samuel 617
Ansell, Mary 603
Anthony, Abraham 148
Alice 79, 80
Daniel 148
Elizabeth 79, 80
Jacob 148
Jno. 38
John 79, 80
John (Sr.) 80
Joseph 79, 80
Richard 148
Ruth (Mrs.) 148
Sarah 148
Susanah 80
Susannah 79
Thomas 148
William 79, 80
Antonia, Joseph 310
Appleton, Mary (Mrs.) 243
Archer, Sarah 620
Arey, Anna (Mrs.) 202
Bulah (Mrs.) 183
Dorra F. 441
Elijah 187, 202, 220
Emeline 218
George W. 218, 275
Lydia 193
Martin 215
Martin (Cpt.) 275
Mary L. 441
Arey (cont.)
Polly 213
Sarah 197
Thomas 183, 197
Thomas (Jr.) (Cpt.) 182
Thos. 185, 188
Armington, Abby 275
Lydia (Mrs.) 275
Armsbee, Jeremiah 637
Juda 637
Mary 637
Rebecka 637
Thomas 637, 646
Armstrong, Gregory 501
William 120, 123
Arnold, (?) 198, 534
(?) (Dr.) 74
Saml. 534
Samuel 250, 503, 543
Samuel (Rev.) 243
Steven 92
William 146
Arnoll, Thomas 516
Arther, Elizabath 266
Arthur, Eunice 261, 270
John 261
Persis 261
Rhoda 261
Ashpot, Cuph 18
Askins, Christopher 11
Aspinwall, William 275
Asten, Ester 636
John 636
Jonah 636
Jonah (II) 646
Jonah (Jr.) 636
Jonah (Sr.) 646
Mary 636
Sarah 636
Astin, Constant (Mrs.) 646
Jonah (Sr.) 646
Jonas (Sr.) 646
Atheaon, Solomon 98
Athearn, Abigail 111
Jabez 110, 111, 222
Jethro 98, 108, 208, 617
John 617
Mary (Mrs.) 617
Mehetable 617
Samuel 127
Sarah 208
Simon 617
Solomon 104, 617
Zerviah 617
Atherton, Joshua 632
Sarah 563
Atkins, Bethia 550
Bethiah (Mrs.) 550
Elizabeth 594
Freeman 550
Henry 501
Isaiah 550
Joseph 550
Joshua 550
Martha 550
Rebecca B. 169
Robert 246, 251
Ruth 550
Ruth (Mrs.) 550
Silas 550
Thankful (Widow) 247
Zerviah 168
Atsat, (?) 177
Atsatt, Thomas 182
Attwood, John 511

Baxter (cont.)
Elisha 305
Fanny 682, 691
Francis 305
Gere (Widow) 698
Hannah 652, 656
Henry 305
Jane (Mrs.) 652, 653, 654
Jerusha 656
Joanna (Mrs.) 656
Joanne (Mrs.) 659
John 653
Joseph 696
Leah 654
Lucinda (Mrs.) 676
Lucinda (Widow) 697
Marcy 659
Mary 656, 672
Mercy 659
Mercy (Mrs.) 672, 674, 676
Mercy Hedge 674
Nathll. 656
Patty 689
Prince 654, 676, 695
Reuben 305
Richard 652, 653, 654
Robert (Cpt.) 305
Shobael 651
Shubael 305
Simeon 654
Thankful 651, 656
Thomas 654
Willm. 267
cornelious 659
willm. 267
Bayes, Ruth 221
Bayley, Hannah 326
John 250, 326, 641
Samuel 628, 631
Thomas 641
Baylie, Benjamin 624
Hannah 624
John 622, 624
Joseph 624
Mary 624
Samuel 624
Sarah 624
William 624
Baylies, Frederick (III) 218
Frederick (Jr.) 217
Baylis, John 620, 622
Beacon, Hannah 341
Mary 340
Mary (Mrs.) 341
Beadle, Joseph 248, 518
Beal, Abigail 20
Andrew 354
Azariah 19
Isaac 478
Japhet 4
Jeremiah 3
Jonathan 21
Perez 478
Polly 27
Rachel 354
Rachel (Mrs.) 354
Seth 479
Therza Hatch 479
Beale, Daniel 14
Elisabeth 14
Sam'l 11
Samuel 10, 12
Beals, Andrew 349
Anne 470
Benjamin 349, 478
Beals (cont.)
Betty 476
Ezra 464, 484
Howland 462, 463, 464, 466, 467, 469, 470, 487
Isaac 462, 473, 474, 476, 477, 478
Isaah 463
Jedudiah 489
John 462, 476, 478
Joshua 3
Luther 477
Lydia 474
Mary 467
Nathan 473
Polly 478
Rachel (Mrs.) 349
Seth 28, 466, 469, 487
Solomon 483, 484
Beamont, John 503
Bean, Lucy (Widow) 427
Lucy Ann 427
Rebecca Cushing 427
William Harper 427
Bearc, Benjamin 612
Ebenezer 612
John 612
Joseph 612
Bearce, Consider 15
Job 21
Shubael 488
Shubial 487
Beard, John 290
John Barrett 277
Ruth 290
William Henry 277
Beare, John 655
Joseph 655
Richard 248, 514
Richd. 530
Thankful (Mrs.) 655
Bearse, Abigail (Jr.) 455
Alven 679
Andrew 11
Asa 453
Austine 504
Betsey 698
Elizabeth (Mrs.) 679
Experience 16
Ford 459, 488
Hannah 459
Hannah (Jr.) 456
Hannah (Widow) 490
Ichabod 454
Isaac H. 691
Jacob 458, 459, 461, 468, 486, 492
Jacob (Jr.) 479, 492
James 457
Job 458
Joseph 613
Josiah 613
Keziah 454
Margaret 16
Mary 479
Obadiah 457
Prince 277
Seth 488
Stacy 690
Stephen 679
Thomas 461, 488
Bearstow, Deborah 345
Lydia (Mrs.) 345
Samll. 345
Beauchamp, William 277
Beauker, Phebe 490
Beck, Isaac (Jr.) 621
Israel 588
Bee, B. F. 445
Nettie M. Rogers (Mrs.) 446
Beebee, Ezra 277
Beecher, Erastus 214
Henry Ward 445
Beers, (?) 277
Henry 277
Beerse, Ebenezer 454
Beerstow, Joseph 318
Susanna 318
Beestow, (?) (Mrs.) 540
William 540
Beetes, Willm. 504
Beetle, Anna 215, 220
Christopher 196, 198, 225
Christopher (Jr.) 220
Eliza 207
Hannah 189
Hannah (Widow) 212
James 185, 187, 193, 194
Jane (Mrs.) 214
John 203
John Thomas 203
Mary 198, 220
Mary (Mrs.) 225
Nabby 196
Phebe (Mrs.) 203, 209
Richard 196
Ruben 202, 212
Sarah 209
Thomas 179, 200, 202, 203, 209
William 214, 215, 216, 220
Wm. 188, 196, 207
Beho, William 53, 57
william 57
Beirce, (?) 597
Abigaile 599
Austen 599, 600
Barnabas 678
Betsey 678
Hannah 600
Hester 600
Joseph 600
Marten 678
Polly 678
Sarah 599
Stephen 678
Warren 678
Belcher, (?) (Cpt.) 105
Ann 18
Deborah 3
Hannah 3
Moses (Jr.) 99
Bell, Easter 637, 646
Elizabeth 628, 636
Ester 629
James 69, 81, 88, 636
Jan 636
John 503, 636
Joseph 637
Mary 637
Nathanill 636
Sarah 636
Benjamin, Joseph 539
Benker, Betty 453
Bennard, Senato 277
Bennet, James 629
Susannah 454
Bennett, (?) 277, 294
Cynthia 277, 286
Hiram 277

Bennett (cont.)
Lucretia 295
Samuel 7
Stephen 277
William 286, 295
William (II) 294
Benny, Lueva 172
Bensen, Jabez 649
Benson, Abiel (Mrs.) 338, 388
Else (Mrs.) 397
Gorham 405
John 8
Joseph 334, 335, 388, 397, 405, 630
Joseph (Jr.) 338
Mary (Mrs.) 335
Sarah Ann 426
Sarah S. 420
Stephen 426
Susan (Mrs.) 444
Thomas 218
William S. 228
Bent, Elizabeth 244
Josiah 242
Benthall, Desire 272
Benum, George 502
Berce, Austen 598
Austin 596, 598
Martha 598
Mary 598
Priscilla 598
Berry, (?) 696
(?) (Widow) 696
Allen 688
Anna 660
Anthony 504
Benjamin 669, 696, 697
Charles A. 440
Charlotte (Mrs.) 690
Desire (Mrs.) 438
Ebenezer 667
Edmond 504
Eleazar (III) 658
Elisabeth 667
Elizabeth 659
Gideon 673, 693
Hannah 658
Howes 658, 673, 674, 675, 693, 696
Isaac 658, 659, 660, 662, 667, 669, 673
Issachour 174
Jabez 695
Jabez (Cpt.) 693
James 658
Jeremiah 658, 696
John 277, 321, 667
Joseph 658
Judah 658
Leonard 696
Lucy 673
Lydia 667
Lydia (Mrs.) 693
Marcy 667
Martha 651
Mary 324, 651, 662
Mehitable (Mrs.) 693
Mercy 667
Nancy 667
Onan 658
Phebe 658
Polly 692
Rebecca 658
Richard 324, 504
Ruth 658, 675, 691
Ruth (Mrs.) 658, 673, 674, 675
Berry (cont.)
Sally 691
Sarah 658, 673
Sarah (Mrs.) 658, 659, 660, 662, 667, 669
Bersto, Benjamin 430
Deborah 323
Hannah 324
Joseph 323, 430
Martha 430
Mary 326
William 324, 325, 326, 430
Berstow, (?) 354
Benjmin 429
Joseph 354
Mary (Mrs.) 354
Rebecca 429
Susanna 621
Berstowe, Abigail 344
Benjamin 348
John 342
John (Jr.) 342
Joseph 357
Lidia (Mrs.) 343
Lydia (Mrs.) 342, 344
Mercy (Mrs.) 348
Samuel 343
Susannah 344
Bery, Anna 660
Isaac 660
Sarah (Mrs.) 660
Besbe, John 326
Martha 326
Besbeach, Elisha 503
Besbee, Elisha 315
Hannah 315
Besbege, Alis 242
Besbetch, (?) 604
Besbitch, (?) 596
Besby, Aron 430
Elijah 430
Elisha 312, 313, 430
Hopestil 339
Hopestill 312
Johannah 327
John 312, 328, 339, 430
Mary 313, 430
Moses 430
Besbye, Elisha 314
Martha 314
Bese, Joshua 649
Robart 649
Robert 649
Bessbetch, (?) 609
Besse, Jonah 25
Bessey, Ann 526
Anthony 526
David 526
Elizabeth 526
Jane (Mrs.) 526
Mary 526
Nehemiah 526
Bessy, Anthony 503
Bestor, (?) 366
Bestow, Abigail 337, 359
Benjamin 328, 354
Benjm. 348, 350, 358, 363, 366
Caleb 354
Elizabeth 348, 429
Elizabeth (Mrs.) 356
James 348
Job 354
Joseph 326, 348, 350, 356, 359, 363
Joshuah 356
Bestow (cont.)
Lydia 377
Lydia (Mrs.) 350, 354, 359, 363, 429
Lydiah 350
Marcy (Mrs.) 354
Margret 363, 377
Margret (Mrs.) 363
Martha 327, 348
Mary 350
Mary (Mrs.) 348, 350, 359
Mercy 358
Mercy (Mrs.) 348, 350, 358, 366
Micael 359
Nathanael 350
Rebecca 328
Saml. 359, 363, 377, 429
Samll. 354
Samuel 350
Susanna 328
Willam 326
William 328
mary (Mrs.) 348, 359
Bestowe, Benjamin 349
Benjm. 349
Mercy (Mrs.) 349
Betts, Alice (Mrs.) 602
Hannah 598
Hope 599
Samuell 598
William 596, 598, 599, 602
Beuker, (?) (Widow) 484
Beckey 473
Benjamin 473, 475, 492
Nelson 459
Phebe (Widow) 460
Rebecca 488
Rebekah 461
Richard 459, 461, 475, 488, 492
Richard Hill 460
Bickford, Deborah 255
Elizabeth 254
Sam. 254
Saml. 255
Bicknel, Jacob (Jr.) 29
Biddle, Joseph 514, 543
Rachel (Mrs.) 543
Bierce, Elizabeth Downs 678
Stephen 678
Billing, Samuel 14
Billings, Nathan 5
Billington, Francis 498, 501
Helen (Mrs.) 498
John 498
John (Jr.) 498
Martha 500, 544
Mary 547
Thomas 530
Bingham, Martha 277
Binks, John 311
Birch, Isaac 515
Bircher, Edward 506
Bird, (?) 610
Ann (Mrs.) 535
Catherine 645
Thomas 529, 535
Birge, (?) 85
John 40, 86
Bisbe, Bathsheba 19
Patience 453
Polly 456

Bisbe (cont.)
Samuel 14
Bisbee, Aaron 458, 484
Abigail (Mrs.) 484
Alimelich 483
Aron 328
Avetus 474
Ebenezer 20
Eleazer 460
Elijah 328
Elisha 328, 515, 535
Gamaliel 458, 470, 471, 472, 473, 476, 478
Gameliel 474
Gammelial 469
Gideon 458, 459, 460, 461, 483, 485
Hannah 19, 485
Huldah 29
John 20, 328, 458, 485, 487, 515, 535
Jonah 458, 460, 483, 485, 488, 492
Jonathan 461, 487
Jotham 458
Louise 470
Lupira 472
Mary 328
Mary (Widow) 487
Moses 328
Orphey 476
Phebe 473
Rebecca 27, 459
Rebecca (Widow) 487
Rizpey 471
Samuel 458
Sarah 458
Sophia 469
Stetson 478
Studley 458
Bisby, Joanna 14
John 331, 347
Martha (Mrs.) 331
Mary (Mrs.) 347
Biscoe, Nathl. 516
Nathl. (Jr.) 516
Bisher, Hannah 621
Bishop, Abigail 347
Abigail (Mrs.) 347, 348, 351
Ann 347
Chas. D. 426
Content 347
Deliverance 347
Dorothy 486
Edward 592
Eliphalet 455
Hudson 355, 452
Hutson 430
Keturah 452
Luke 355
Lusanna 351
Lydia Bowker (Mrs.) 426
Nathanaell 348
Nathaniel 455
Pembroke (Mrs.) 355
Saml. 592
Sarah 453
Stutson 347, 348, 351, 430
Will 591
William 591
Bixby, (?) 437
Bizzel, Abigail (Widow) 277
Nabby (Widow) 277
Bizzel (cont.)
William 277
Black, (?) 72
Alexander 668, 669, 671, 672, 677
Almira 672
Anna 639
Azuba White 677
Betsey (Mrs.) 277
Bradoc 669
Bradock 669
Clovis 277
Elaxander 671
Hannah 245
James W. 218, 219
Ludia (Mrs.) 677
Lydia 671
Lydia (Mrs.) 668, 669, 671, 672
Mary 641
Miles 503
Samuell 44
Sopha 668
Timothy Coffin 277
Blacke, Goodman 526
Sarah 64
Blackford, Benjamin 689
Blackman, Elisabeth 12
Joseph 74
Rebecca 76
Sara 232
Blackmer, Elizabeth 620
William 623
Blackmoor, Phebe 430
Willliam 430
Blackmore, John 244, 319
Peter 318
Phebe 320, 430, 624
William 318, 319, 320, 430, 624
Blackston, Sarah (Mrs.) 549
William 549
Blackwell, Benjamin 277
Hannah (Mrs.) 277
Jane (Mrs.) 277
Joshua 367
Martha 367
Mary 368
Mary (Mrs.) 277, 367, 368
Patience 593
Rowland 277
Saml. 367
Samuel 277, 368
Blagroue, Nathaniel 40, 67
Blagrove, Nath. 40
Blair, (?) (Widow) 111
Bryce 108
Susanna 100, 111
Thomas 100, 109
Blaire, Mary 99
Blak, (?) 73
Blake, Abigail 572
Anna 547
Francis E. 582, 585
Priscilla 630
Samuel 77, 630
Blakemore, John 504
Blanchard, Eli 28
Molly 5
Thomas (Jr.) 24
Blanding, Elizabeth 592
Will 592
Blankenship, Betsey (Mrs.) 277
George (Cpt.) 277
Blankinship, Anne 366
Gordon 366
James 366
Blatchford, John 691
Bleen, Silence 16
Bliffin, Abigail 631
Blifs, Jonathan 47
Blise, Jonathan 513
Mary 513
Nathaniel 513
Thomas 513
Blish, (?) 277
Abraham 277
Bliss, Daniel 590
Elisha 590
Ephraim 590
Jacob 590
John 592
Jonathan 47, 590, 592
Mary 592
Miriam 590
Rachel 546
Saml. 592
Timothy 590
William Root 648
Blood, George 277
Blossom, John 334, 366
Peter P. 228
Samuel 277
Sara (Mrs.) 515
Thankful (Mrs.) 366
Thankfull (Mrs.) 334
Thomas 366, 507, 515
Blossome, Charity (Mrs.) 557
Elijah 557
Elizabeth 602
Levi 557
Sylvanus 557
Thomas 504, 602
Blott, Robert 526
Blower, John 504
Blush, (?) 602
Abraham 504, 539, 598, 599
Joseph 599
Nicholas 504
Sarah 598
Bo---, Elizabeth 245
Boardman, Catherine 119, 126
Elizabeth 119
Jane (Mrs.) 120, 122, 131
Sylvanus 120
Walter 120, 122, 126, 131
Bobbins, Joseph 456
Bobbit, Edward 66
Bobbitts, Elkanah 48
Bobbot, Edward 629
Ester 629
Sarah 630
Bobit, Damaris 644
Damiras 634
Deliverance 634
Dorkas 634, 644
Easter 634
Edward 634, 641
Elizabeth 644
Elkana 634
Elkannah 644
Hana 634
Hopestill 644
Mercie 644
Ruth 634
Sara 634
Sarah 640

Boder, John 195
Bodfish, Elizabeth (Mrs.) 616
Joseph 616, 617
Sarah 617
Boggs, Francis 277
Phebe 277
Boiden, Thomas 595
Boles, Deborah 489
Experiance 630
Samuel 489
Bolton, (?) 485
Abigail 486
Archelaus 560
Elisha 485, 486
Gamaliel 560
Jabesh 486
Jabez 485
John 7
Nelson 560
Sally (Mrs.) 560
Bonne, Lydia 14
Bonnet, Ebenezer 252
Peter 252
Sarah 252
Susanna 252
Bonney, Amy 467
Anne 491
Benjamin 462
Charles 459
Chloe 468
Clarissa 471
Crowell 471
Cynthia Sylvester (Mrs.) 28
David 485
Ebenezer 475, 476, 477, 478, 485, 492
Elizabeth 245, 466
Elizabeth (Widow) 490
Elizabeth Paris 476, 478, 492
Ezekial 475, 476
Ezekiel 458, 460, 461, 473, 477, 478, 490, 491
Ezekiel (Jr.) 485
Ezra 475
Hannah 463, 465, 486
Hervey 472
Ichabod 486
Job 458, 459, 484
Johanna 27
John 484, 489
Jonathan 457, 484
Joseph 464, 465, 466, 467, 468, 469, 470, 471
Judah 476
Lemuel 463, 464, 465, 467, 470, 486
Lemuel (Jr.) 478
Lucy 464, 467, 478, 486
Ludia 478
Luke 459
Luther 465
Lydia 464
Mary 484
Melinda 473
Mercy 462
Nancy 473
Nathaniel 469
Noah 456, 471, 472, 473, 475, 476, 478
Oliver 461
Orphy 470
Rachel 475
Bonney (cont.)
Roland 475, 477, 491
Roxanna 476
Susa 455
Sylvester 460, 470
Thom. 502
William 16, 27, 458, 491
Bonny, Ann 454
Betty 453
Chloe 453
Daniel 454
Ezekiel 459
Ichabod 453
Isaiah 456
James 452
Jonathan 459
Leah 456
Lemuel 453
Lucy 453
Rachel 454
Ruth 452
Bonum, George 540
John 548
Patience 546
Ruth 546
Sarah 548
Bony, Ezekial 458
Job 460
Mary 460
Noah 458
Bonzon, Martin 277
Boorn, Elizabeth 642
Boorne, Hennery 609
Booth, Abraham 624
Benjamin 624
Elizabeth 624
Grace 624
John 624
John (Jr.) 621
Joseph 624
Judith 624
Mary 622, 624
Borden, Abigail 253
Edward 277
Elizabeth (Mrs.) 277
Hannah 253
Mercy 253
Sarah 253
Simon 277
Stephen 253
Susanna 277
Thomas 145
Timothy 253
William 253
Bordman, Thomas 503
Boreman, (?) 504
Thomas 504
Wm Pearse 504
Born, William 143
Borne, Hen. 601
Hennery 595
Henry 504, 515
Borson, Josiah 75
Sampson 75
Zacheus 75
Bosby, Aron 328, 430
Elijah 328, 430
Elisha 328, 430
John 328, 430
Mary 328, 430
Moses 328, 430
Bostan, Reuben 311
Boston, Essex 302
Jane 302
John C. 277
John Lowel 317
Mary 311
Boston (cont.)
Patience 317
Tobias 311
Bosworth, (?) 99
Benjamin 545
Elizabeth (Mrs.) 548
Jonath 50
Nathaniel 545, 548
Boszworth, Hester (Mrs.) 56
Joseph 56
Botefish, Robte. 503
Boty, Mary (Mrs.) 331
Thomas 331
Bouls, Blaney 490
David 490
Joanna 244
Bourage, Lydia 271
Bourden, Edward 277
Elizabeth (Mrs.) 277
Simon 277
Susanna 277
Bourgoin, Lewis 277
Bourn, (?) 363, 382, 387, 395, 399, 400, 429
(?) (Rev.) 368, 369, 370, 371, 374, 387, 401
(?) (Widow) 490
Abel 471, 472, 474, 475, 476, 477, 478, 491
Abigail 241
Abigail (Mrs.) 367, 370, 373
Abigail (Widow) 484
Ann 243
Anne 534
Avice 476
Bethiah 465, 476
David 226
Deborah 238, 461, 477
Deborah (Mrs.) 238
Ebenezar 238
Ebenezer 460, 461, 484
Elizabeth 242, 373, 628
Elizabeth (Mrs.) 248, 250
George 245
Hannah (Mrs.) 238, 594
Isaac 473
James 461, 462, 463, 465, 466, 468, 484, 488
James (Jr.) 472, 473, 474, 476
Jedediah 238, 246
John 249, 367, 370, 373, 534, 536
John Allen 468, 488
Josiah 484, 486, 491
Josiah (Jr.) 483, 484
Lucy 238
Lydia 462, 534
Margaret 534
Martha 534
Mary 631
Mary (Mrs.) 238
Molly 460
Nathaniel 238
Oliver 472, 484
Peter 370
Priscilla 466, 472, 492
Richard 515, 534
Richd. 526

Briant (cont.)
Elijah 399
Elizabeth 82, 324, 430
Elizabeth (Mrs.) 44
Hannah 490
James 395
John 44, 326, 402, 623, 631
John (Jr.) 322, 324, 430
John (Sr.) 430
Joshua 326
Mary (Mrs.) 395
Peleg 395, 401
Rhoda 401
Ruth 485
Saml. 399
Samll. 402
Samuell 326
Stephen 490
William 324, 430
Zine 402
Bridges, Cornelius 321
James 324
John 326
Joseph 321
Mary 324
Brient, Lemuel 584
Briges, Deborah 325
James 321, 620
John 325
Joseph 321
Richard 646
William 646
Brigg, Deborah (Mrs.) 429
Joseph 429
Nathan 649
Nathanael 429
Samuel 510
Sarah 510
Brigges, David 634
Hugh 78
Jonathan 634
Briggs, (?) 277
(?) (Mrs.) 421
(?9 465
Abigail 399
Abigail (Mrs.) 390, 392, 393, 395, 550
Amos 630
Ann 401
Anna 405
Anna (Mrs.) 396
Anne Thomas 473
Avice 467
Barnabas 550
Bathsheba 488, 490
Benj. (Cpt.) 421
Benjamin 635
Betsey (Mrs.) 427
Caroline Otis 421, 427
Cate 550
Catherine 167
Catherine C. 170, 171
Charles 406
Clement 6
Cornelius 345, 367, 620
Cyrus Peirce 277
Deborah 146, 161, 346, 622
Deborah (Mrs.) 332, 345, 346, 350, 429
Deborah C. 420
Deborah Clapp 413
Deborah Thomas 478
Elijah 406
Briggs (cont.)
Elisabeth 406, 412
Elisha 361, 405, 407, 412, 413, 423, 455
Elizabeth 145, 634
Elizabeth Ruggles 427
Elizth. (Mrs.) 418
Enoss 390
Ephraim 466, 467, 468, 470, 471
Eunice 490
Experience 631
Geo. Henry 427
George 26
Hana 634, 635
Hannah 161, 362, 390, 630
Hannah (Mrs.) 331, 337, 351, 353, 354, 357, 361, 362, 367, 372, 390, 393, 395, 406, 428
Hannah Stowel 407
Harriet 421
Henry 421, 427
Hugh 547
Isaac 478
James 331, 348, 351, 353, 354, 357, 361, 362, 367, 372, 390, 393, 396, 400, 423, 428
James (Jr.) 395, 400
James Buffinton 406
Jams. 337
Job 372
John 39, 74, 161, 326, 345, 346, 351, 353, 392, 393, 395, 399, 401, 408, 478, 510, 634, 635
John (Jr.) 456
Jona. 536
Joseph 345, 346, 350, 429, 465, 635
Joseph (Sr.) 332, 361
Joshua 480
Josiah 406
Katherne (Mrs.) 510
Lucy 395, 470, 472
Lucy (Widow) 418
Luther 468
Lydia 412, 471
Mahala 550
Mahitabel 635
Margret 392, 393
Mary 161, 345, 427, 629, 632, 633, 634, 635
Mary (Mrs.) 71
Matthew 634
Matthias 531
Mercy 163, 550
Nathan 649
Nathanael 429
Nathaniel 474, 644
Phebe 165, 558
Rachel 428
Rebaka 635
Rebecah 39
Rebecca (Widow) 73
Remember 71, 72
Richard 39, 73, 546, 635, 643
Ruth 411, 453, 465
Sally 550
Samuel 66, 472, 473, 474, 477, 478, 479,
Briggs (cont.)
635
Samuel (Jr.) 3
Sarah 393, 421, 467, 634, 644
Sarah (Mrs.) 548, 634
Sarah Jacobs 405
Sarah Smith 413
Seneca 477
Seth 357, 390, 550
Susanna 161
Susannah 145
Sylvester 28
Thankful 350
Thomas 47, 66, 88, 161, 634, 644
Thomas (Jr.) 144
Thos. 413
Walter 503, 521, 531
Weston 161
William 39, 418, 545, 548, 628, 634, 635, 643
William (Rev.) 28
William C. 277
Willliam 644
Wm. 66
Bright, Edward 623
Brightman, Henry 30, 57
William 631
Brigs, Abigail 355
Abigail (Mrs.) 392
Barshaba 641
Ceberry 403
Cornelius 403
Deborah (Mrs.) 355
Elisha 416
Elizabeth 348, 644
Hannah 390, 629
Hannah (Mrs.) 351, 353, 358, 370, 390, 428
Hugh 641
James 348, 351, 353, 358, 370, 390, 403, 428
Job 358
John 39, 351, 353, 392, 402, 403, 641
Joseph 355, 402
Joseph Warren 416
Margret 392
Mehitabell 641
Rachel 402, 428
Rebekah 644
Ruth 403
Samuel 629
Sarah 644
Sebre 403
Thomas 628
Thomas Barker 403
William 370, 629, 644
wm. 402
Bringley, Simon 542
Brinsley, (?) 524
Brintnall, Thomas 62
Briton, Mary (Mrs.) 584
Britten, William 629
Britterige, Richard 499
Britton, Robbert Jun 583
William 16
Brittun, Ebenezer 557
Brock, (?) 278
Andrew 270, 278
Aron 328
Barshua 328
Elijah 328
Elisha 328

Brock (cont.)
Eunice (Mrs.) 278
Francis 328
Frederick 278
Grace 328
John 278, 328
Margaret 270
Mary 306, 328
Moses 328
Peleg 278
Priam 278
Thomas (Jr.) 278
William 306
Broks, Abigail (Mrs.) 358
Gilbert 358
Mercy 358
Nath. 402
Nathl. 402
Broocks, Catherine 174
Brook, Abigail (Mrs.) 362
E---m. 338
Elizabeth 313
Gilbert 61, 62, 313, 316, 362
Hannah 312, 316
Johanna 316
Martha 64
Mary 313
Mary (Mrs.) 338, 368, 380
Mehittabel 64
Micael 368
Nathaniel 64, 312
Nathanll. 368
Patience 380
Rachel 61, 313
Ruth 362
Sarah 313
Sarah (Mrs.) 61
Thomas 64
Will. 312
William 313
Willm 313, 316
Wll 312
Wm. 380
mary (Mrs.) 368
Brooke, Batshebah 315
Deborah 314
Gilbert 314, 315
Hanna 430
Nathaniell 430
Phebe 314
Rebecca 315
Thomas 315
William 314, 315
Brooker, Benjamin 412
Brookes, Benjamin 412
Marry 325, 430
Mary 323
Mercy 430
Nathaniell 323, 325
William 325
Brooks, (?) 278, 542
Abigail 367
Abigail (Mrs.) 332, 358, 362, 367, 370, 373, 376, 429
Benjamin 355
Bethia 643
Betsey 419
Charles Stockbridge 373
Charlotte (Mrs.) 421, 427
Charlotte Elizabeth 427
Brooks (cont.)
Deborah (Mrs.) 382, 386
E---m. 338
Ebenezer 357
Elezabeth 57
Elijah 405, 421
Elisabeth 396
Eliz. (Mrs.) 386
Elizabeth 57, 386, 429
Elizabeth (Mrs.) 331, 347, 351
Elizybeth 326
Eunice 419, 426
Experience 370
Gilbert 62, 67, 68, 331, 332, 347, 351, 355, 357, 358, 362, 367, 370, 373, 382, 386, 398, 402, 429
Gilbert (Jr.) 382
Gilferd 376
Hanah 639
Hanna 322, 430
Hannah 382
Hannah (Mrs.) 330, 355, 418
Joanna 327
John 376, 382, 690
John Thaxter 426
Lucy (Mrs.) 419
Lydia 364, 403
Marcy (Widow) 418
Maria (Mrs.) 421
Mary 389, 429
Mary (Mrs.) 331, 338, 354, 356, 358, 364, 368, 371, 373, 378, 382, 384, 389, 396, 397, 429
Mercy 358, 371
Meriam (Mrs.) 382
Methiabel 382
Micael 368
Miriam 314, 386, 620
Miriam (Mrs.) 386, 388
Nat. 331
Nath 427
Nath (Jr.) 403
Nath. 402
Nathan 406
Nathanael 331, 364
Nathanaell 354
Nathaniel 358, 621
Nathaniell 322, 326, 430
Nathanl. 358, 371, 396, 429
Nathanll. 331, 368
Nathl. 373, 402, 421, 427
Nathl. Milton 427
Nathll (Jr.) 410
Nathll. 378
Nathnl. 356
Natll. 386
Noah 356, 388
Rachel 68, 382
Rebekah 629
Ruth 362
Sally 425
Samuel 386
Sarah 384, 427
Seth 388
Simeon 373, 418
Simn. 427
Stephen 378
Susan (Mrs.) 695
Brooks (cont.)
Susanna 393
Susanna (Mrs.) 536
Tailer 354
Tailor 382, 386, 388
Tho. 55
Thomas 57, 326, 327, 330, 621
Timothy (Cpt.) 36
William 278, 314, 347, 384, 388, 399, 406
William (Jr.) 405
Willm (Cpt.) 419
Willm. 399
Wm. 382, 389, 397, 402, 519, 525, 535, 536
Wm. (Cpt.) 426
Wm. (Jr.) (Cpt.) 425
Wm. William 393
mary (Mrs.) 358, 368, 373, 382, 429
methiabel 382
william 388
Broughton, Thomas 516
Broune, John 504
Brown, (?) 39, 50, 51, 54, 72, 73, 84, 86, 457
(?) (Cpt.) 76
(?) (Dr.) 587
Almania 166
Ann 165
Anna (Mrs.) 627
Asa 590
Avery A. 174
Barnabas 230
Bartholomew 29
Bartlet 667, 691
Benjamin 627
Benjamin (Cpt.) 627
Betsey 690
Betsey A. 166
Betty (Widow) 491
Caroline 169
Charles 168, 172
Charlotte 691
Dan. 592
Daniel 626
Danl. 592
David 164, 550
Dorothy (Mrs.) 531, 627
Ebenezer 550
Elijah 230
Elizabeth 311, 592
Enas Ewer 230
Eunice (Mrs.) 550
Ezekiel 172
Foster 164
Francis 272
Francis (Sr.) 299
George 278, 692
George (Jr.) 278
Hannah 170, 531
Hannah (Mrs.) 626
Henry 666, 683
Hezekiah 588
Higgins 164
Ichabod 592
Jabesh 588, 589, 590, 591, 592
Jabish 587
James 84, 531
James (Lt.) 626
James S. 174
Jennet (Widow) 2
Jerusha 589

Buck (cont.)
Ruth 547, 620
Sally 682
Sally L. 687
Sarah 395
Susanah (Mrs.) 674
Susanah Baker 678
Susanna 318
Susanna (Mrs.) 675, 676, 678
Susannah (Mrs.) 679
Thomas 8, 327, 357, 429, 618, 695
William 682
Zabina 682
Zubia 682
john 682
mary (Mrs.) 357, 360, 393
Bucke, Abigail 326
Isaac 326
Margeret 326
Mehitable 621
Buckland, Baruck 589
Benjamin 588
David 591
Deborah 587
James 592
Jonathan 592
Jos. 587, 589
Joseph 41, 587, 588, 590, 591, 592
Joseph (Jr.) 72, 591
Joseph (Sr.) 42
Martha 587
Nehemiah 590
Rachel 589
Sarah 589
Tim. 592
Wm. 531
Bucklen, John 589
Joseph 73, 589
Bucklon, Joseph 73
Bueker, Richard (Jr.) 484
Buitt, George 504
Buker, Benja. 399
Edmund 340
Elisha 399
Elizabeth 340
James 340
Jonathan 399
Lazarus 399
Mary 340
Richard 483
Zebulun 455
Bulkley, Edw. 516
Bulkly, Edward 248
John 248
Bull, Eliza Brown Cartwright 278
John Brown 278
Bullen, Warren 129
Bullock, Richard 514
Richd 538
Richd. 528, 531
Saml1. 84
Samuel 36, 83
Sarah 557
Bump, Abigail 615
Edward 649
Elizabeth 615
Jacob 9
Jane 615
John 615, 649
Jonathan (Jr.) 649
Mary 615
Noah 649
Bump (cont.)
Phebe (Mrs.) 615
Samuel 615
Sarah 7, 615
Thomas 615
Zeccues 649
Bumpas, Benjamin 321
Edward 516
Edward (Sr.) 543
Elizabeth 242
Jacob 322, 430, 543, 620
James 252, 321
John 320, 321
Joseph 252
Mary 252
Mehetabel 252
Penelope 252
Rebekah 252
Samuell 320
Sarah 430
Sarah (Mrs.) 321
Bumpasse, John 319, 320
Mary 319
Bumper, Michael 311
Bumpus, Edward 250
Hannah (Mrs.) 250
Icabod 326
Isaac 430
Jacob 326, 430
Jane 630
Job 324
John 322, 324
Mary 243
Mary (Mrs.) 593
Sarah 242, 430
Zoar 322, 430
Bun, Hannah (Mrs.) 82
Nath. 628
Nathaniel 78
Buncker, Geore. 266
George 266
Bunden, Deborah 535
Bundy, Edward 633
James 633
John 501, 633, 646
Joseph 633
Martha (Mrs.) 646
Mary 646
Patience 633
Samuel 633
Sara 633
Bunker, (?) 279
Abiel 301
Abigail 278
Abigail (Mrs.) 278
Andrew 278
Ann 261, 278
Bachelor 271
Barzillai 278
Benjamin 256, 272, 278
Benjamin (Gen.) 301
Caleb 261, 265, 266, 270, 271, 272
Calib 268
Charles 278
Christopher 270
Daniel 257, 266, 270
David 279
Deborah 270
Dinah 257, 267
Ebenezer 272
Elezabath 269
Elihu 278
Elihu Marshall 278
Elijah 278
Elisha 271
Ellihu S. 279
Bunker (cont.)
Emily A. 278
Eunies 270
Franklin 278
Frederick F. 278
Geore. 266, 267, 269
George 254, 257, 259, 261, 265, 266, 267, 268, 269, 270, 278
George (IV) 278
George C. 278
George F. 279
George M. 278
Gorham 278
Henry C. 279
Hephzibath 268
Isaac 185
Jabez 255
James 278, 285
James Colesworthy 278
Jane 266
John 255, 261, 268, 278, 279
John C. 278
Jonathan 183, 255, 283
Joseph 278
Josephine 278
Joshua 279
Joshua (Cpt.) 290
Judeth 267
Judith 257
Latham 278
Lydia 266, 278
Margaret 290
Martha 255
Mary 289, 301
Matthew 278
Miriam (Mrs.) 279
Nathaniel 278, 279
Nathaniel (Jr.) 279
Obed 279
Owen 278
Peleg 255, 257, 260, 271, 289, 301
Priscilla 279
Prissilla 257, 271
Richard 188, 206
Richard (Cpt.) 279
Robert Folger 279
Ruth 267, 270, 272
Samuel 278, 279
Samuel (Cpt.) 279
Sarah Ann 279
Shubael 278
Shubael (Jr.) 278
Solomon 271
Susan 285
Susanna (Mrs.) 188
Thomas 256, 278, 279
Timothy 278
Uriah 269
William 254, 255, 271, 278, 279
William (Jr.) 279
William B. 227
William Henry 279
William P. 279
Willm. 255, 256
Zephaniah 283
Bunton, Mary 11
Burbick, Caroline G(ibson) 684
Eliza 684
Joseph 685
Nancy D(avis) 684
Samuel 698
Samuel H. 684, 685
Susan Langden 685

Burded, Henry 371
Lydia (Mrs.) 371
Ruth 371
Burden, Deborah (Mrs.) 539
Stephen 629
Wm 539
Wm. 539
Burdet, Elizabeth 360
Francis 366
Henry 360, 364, 366, 371
Joshua 364
Lydia (Mrs.) 360, 364, 371
Ruth 371
Thankful 360
William 360
Burdett, Barzillai 288
Edward 279
Hannah (Mrs.) 279
Reuben 279
William 279
Burgall, Thomas 3
Burges, (?) 279
Cesar 381
Lemuel 279
Martha 657
Martha (Widow) 657
Nathaniel 279
Priscilla 657
Richard 503
Rosilla 279
Ruth 657
Samuel 657
Thaddeus 657
Thomas (Jr.) 503
Thomas (Sr.) 503
Timothy 657
Weston 279
Burgess, (?) 279, 684
(?) (Widow) 123, 683, 697
Abigail 99, 220
Abigail (Widow) 120
Deborah H. 171
Eliza 123
Isaac 687
Isaiah 682, 696
Job 12
Lemuel 279
Nancy (Mrs.) 682
Nathaniel 279
Rebekah G. 691
Rosa (Widow) 694
Rosilla 279
Shubael 123
Thomas 544
Weston 279
Burman, Desire 532
Hannah 532
Hannah (Mrs.) 532
Mary 532
Mehetabel 532
Samuel 532
Thomas 532
Trustrum 532
Burn, John 516
Burnam, Abigail 6
Thomas 546
Burne, Richard 504
Thomas 514
Burnell, Ammiel 287
Barker 287
Daniel 287
Eliza Myrick 279
John 287
Jonathan 279
Burnell (cont.)
Joseph 287
Burnham, Amanda 174
Susanna 7
Burr, Israel 5
Burrage, Jeames 270
Burrel, (?) 399
James 144
Mary 399
Burrell, Deborah Moreton 279
Judith (Mrs.) 279
Samuel 286
Burrige, mary 270
Burrill, John 628
Olive Snow (Mrs.) 443
Burrouges, Jeremy 314
John 314, 430
Burroughes, (?) 524
Jeremiah 315
Jeremy 430
Mary 315
Burroughs, Elizabeth 315
Jeremiah 314
Jeremy 314, 315, 430
John 430
Burrowes, Jeremiah 242, 539
Burrows, James Davis 279
Burse, Stephen 696
Thomas 75
Bursell, James 504
Bursley, (?) 598, 601, 602
Elizabeth 600
Johannah 599
John 504, 529, 599, 600, 601
Mao 600
Mary 598
Bursly, (?) 596
Burstall, John 504
Burt, Abagail 642
Abel 628
Abell 73, 91
Abil 642
Ana (Mrs.) 646
Ebenezer 60, 642
Ephraim 642
James 628, 646
James G. (Rev.) 168
Jemima 643
John 642
Joseph 642
Mary 629, 642
Rachel 628
Richard 78, 628, 642, 643
Richard (Sr.) 48
Burton, (?) 78, 510
Elizabeth 454
Lyman 219
Stephen 38, 43, 80, 243
Burye, Joseph 541
Bush, Anna (Mrs.) 169
Bushap, John 649
Bushop, Richard 501
Butler, (?) 279
(?) (Widow) 178
Abner 178, 200
Anna 188, 222
Anna (Mrs.) 225
Anna (Widow) 200
Anne 197, 209
Arnold 215
Athearn 119, 126, 130, 131
Butler (cont.)
Bartlett 193
Barzillai 191
Bazillai 190
Benj 179, 181
Charles 216
Cornelius 193
Daniel 101, 196, 202, 217
Daniel (Jr.) 221
Danl. 219
Desire (Mrs.) 130, 131
Ebenezer 203, 222
Ebenr. 179, 208
Ebn. 181
Elijah 189
Elijah (Jr.) 187
Elizabeth 123, 184, 191, 369
Elizabeth (Mrs.) 279, 334, 369
Elizabeth (Widow) 118
Elizth. (Mrs.) 373
Ephraim Pease 189
Francis 188, 189, 194
Gamaliel 178, 198, 208, 222
Hannah 208, 220
Hannah (Mrs.) 200, 217
Hannah (Widow) 119
Henry 179, 190, 191, 225
Hepsibah 208
Isaac 179
Israel 111, 334, 369, 373
James 119, 120
Jane 221, 222
Jane (Mrs.) 177
Jean 191
Jedidah 208, 210
John 179, 185, 193, 208, 221
John (Jr.) 188
John Sprague 202
Jonathan 183
Joseph 222
Keziah 197, 220, 221, 222
Lucy (Mrs.) 131
Lydia 200
Mary (Mrs.) 211, 219
Matt 179
Matthew 179, 185, 220
Mercy (Widow) 196
Nathaniel 111
Nicholas 126, 131, 134, 177, 179, 191, 209, 221
Nicholos 131
Oliver 196
Priscilla 197, 209
Prudence 127
Puella 220
Puella (Mrs.) 120
Rebeccah (Mrs.) 213
Rhoda 127
Ruth 191, 209
Saml. 178, 213
Samuel 191
Sarah 220, 373
Sarah (Mrs.) 225
Shubael 454
Silas 183, 187, 189, 208, 211, 216, 279
Silas (Jr.) 193
Simeon 220, 222
Solomon 127

Cobb (cont.)
Lincoln F. 168, 172
Lucindia 165
Lydia (Mrs.) 236
Maria H. 167, 170
Mary 527, 536, 544, 551, 597
Mary (Mrs.) 551
Mary F. 168, 172
Mehetabell 600, 602
Mercey 638
Mercy 163, 436
Morgen 638
Nathan F. 164
Nathaniel 281
Patience 527, 598
Patience (Mrs.) 601
Phebe K. 167, 171
Polly 165
Rebecca H. 167
Reecca H. 172
Reliance 163
Sally 164, 165
Sally (Mrs.) 691
Samuel 532
Samuell 638
Sarah (Mrs.) 597
Scotto 163
Sherebiah 578
Sophia K. 176
Thankful F. 175
Thankful M. 167, 171
Thomas 162, 164
Thomas (II) 165, 169
William 629
William (Jr.) 281
William C. 167, 170
Cobbs, (?) 113, 610
Cocks, Elizabeth Josselyn 468
Enos 466, 479
Ephraim 466
Hetty 474
Isaac 464, 476, 492
Lydia 465, 479
Mary 366
Mary (Mrs.) 366
Nancy 470
Polly 469, 488
Seth 464, 466, 468, 476
Seth (Jr.) 474, 492
William 429, 465, 468, 469, 486, 488, 489, 492
William (Jr.) 464, 465, 468, 470
Wm. 366
william 429
Cod, Coffin 281
Nicholas Coffin 281
Peggy (Mrs.) 281
Codden, Eliz. (Mrs.) 383
George 383
William 383
Codington, (?) 74
Codman, Hepsibah 222
Codomuck, Sue 75
Coffin, (?) 284
Abigail 271
Abigail (Mrs.) 281
Abigaile 257
Abner 272
Absolam 283
Alexander 282
Alexander (Cpt.) 282
Alexander S. 281
Alfred 283
Coffin (cont.)
Andrew Jackson 281
Anna (Mrs.) 281
Asa 284
Avis 304
Avis A. 281
Barnabas 256, 283, 284
Barttlet 267
Barzillai 284
Benj 204
Benja. 193
Benjamin 209, 220, 256, 282, 283
Benjamin F. 281
Benjamin Franklin 284
Betsey (Mrs.) 134
Beulah 184, 210
Brown 274
Bulah 205
Caleb 284
Caleb S. 281
Caroline 282
Charles 217, 282
Charles Frederick 282
Charles G. 284
Charles H. 282
Charles J. 282
Christian 257
Cromwell 282
Daniel 184, 189, 193, 198, 200, 208, 261, 282, 283
Daniel (Cpt.) 282
Danl. 178
David (Cpt.) 282, 283
Deborah 208, 259
Deborah (Mrs.) 282
Delia Maria 282
Desire 208
Dinah 254, 259, 260, 268
Dorcas 257
Ebenezer 255, 260
Eddy (Cpt.) 282
Edward 284
Edy 177, 178, 182
Edy (Jr.) 195
Elenor (Mrs.) 282
Elial 293
Elias 281
Elihu 282
Elijah 284
Elisha 260, 267
Eliza 210, 282, 289
Elizabeth 260
Elizabeth (Mrs.) 204, 282
Elizibath 267
Enoch 177, 181, 188, 190, 191, 198, 199, 202, 210
Enoch (III) 198
Enoch (Jr.) 197, 198, 208, 209, 220
Esther 686
Eunice 209, 258, 268, 276, 285, 296
Eunice (Widow) 200
Eunies 272
Francis 282
Francis (Cpt.) 282, 283
Frederick 215, 282
Frederick Henry 282
Frederick William 282
George 259, 266
George B. 281
George Bunker 284
Coffin (cont.)
George Fearing 283
George Folger 283
George Gardner 283
George Gorham 283, 289
Gideon 283, 284
Gilbert 284
Gorham 284
Grace C. 204
Hannah 184, 283, 288
Hennery 261
Henry 190, 191, 201, 207, 283, 306
Hephzibah 260, 283
Hepsibah 223
Hepsibah (Mrs.) 186, 223
Hezekiah 284
Huldah 220
Huldah (Mrs.) 218
Isaac 273, 274, 281, 285
Isaiah 289
Jacob 283
James 183, 198, 199, 201, 210, 211, 218, 255, 256, 258, 259, 260
James (Jr.) 195, 259, 260
James G. 282
James Josiah 284
James Munroe 284
Jane 220
Jared 283
Jeremiah 692
Jesse 284
Jethro 257, 270, 283, 284
Jno. 177
Job 282, 283
Job B. 284
Job C. 284
John 186, 189, 190, 193, 212, 220, 223, 225, 254, 255, 256, 257, 283, 297, 305
John Foster 281, 282, 283, 284
John Hussey 283
Jonathan 261
Jonathan (Cpt.) 281
Joseph 255, 257, 282, 283
Joshua 260
Joshua (Cpt.) 282
Josia 257
Josiah 267
Josiah (Maj.) 281
Judeth 267
Judith (Mrs.) 283
Kezia 283
Lamuell 256
Latham 282
Lidia 256
Love 191, 220, 255
Lucy 199
Lydia 198, 201, 254, 257, 266, 283
Lydia Beard 283
Margaret 257
Martha 301
Mary 260, 268, 272, 283, 297, 306, 307
Mary (Mrs.) 283
Mary Ann 283
Mary Foster 283
Matilda (Mrs.) 283

Coffin (cont.)
Matthew 127, 134, 283
Mercy 197
Micha 257
Uriah 284
Nathan 260
Nathaniel 256, 283
Nathaniel (Dr.) 282
Nathaniell 257
Nathll. 257
Noah 283
Obadiah 283
Obed 283
Pardon Cook 283
Patience 272
Paul 257, 276, 283, 284
Peggy Pinkham 293
Peleg 271, 694
Peter 190, 204, 217, 254, 255, 256, 258, 271
Peter (Jr.) 256
Peter Fosdick 283
Phebe 283, 285, 293, 298, 303
Philip 282, 288
Polly 188, 198
Polly (Mrs.) 283
Precilla 257
Prince 284
Prissilla 260, 268
Rachel 197, 220
Reuben 283, 284, 285
Reuben Swain 283
Richard 220, 267, 282
Robert 257
Robert Inat 283
Robert Jenkins 284
Rowland C. 284
Sally (Mrs.) 284
Saml (Cpt.) 129
Saml. 207
Samuel 191, 283
Sarah 260, 284
Sarah (Mrs.) 204, 284
Sarah (Widow) 200
Seth 284
Seth (Cpt.) 281
Seth Macy 284
Shubael 281, 283, 284, 293
Shubal 260
Silvanus 282
Silvaus 283
Simeon 190, 191, 203, 209, 283
Solomon 271, 298
Sophia Whitfield 284
Stephen 254, 255, 283, 284, 303
Stephen (Jr.) 260
Stephen (Sr.) 257
Sukey (Mrs.) 218
Susan 284
Susan (Mrs.) 204, 284
Susanna 260, 261, 274
Susanna (Mrs.) 284
Thomas 194, 204, 281, 284, 301
Thomas (Jr.) 284, 307
Thomas C. 284
Thos. 204, 212
Thos. (Cpt.) 193
Timothy 204, 208, 215, 282, 284
Timothy G. 283
Tristram 190, 191,

Coffin (cont.)
256, 284, 285
Uriah 204, 215, 218, 221, 284, 695
Urian 204
Uriel 283, 284
Valentine 284
Valentine Cook 284
William 257, 283, 284
William (Cpt.) 284
William (Jr.) 284
William Allen 284
William Barnard 284
William Henry 284
William P. 284
William Russell 283, 284
Wm. 201
Z. 304
Zaccheus 270
Zenas 284
Zephaniah 260, 283, 284
Zimri 283
Zoraida 215
Zoraide N. 284
mary 268
Coffine, Prince 99
Coffins, Saml. 213
Cofin, Nathan 266
Cogain, Hennery 598
John 598
Cogaine, Hennery 598, 599, 601
Henry 599
Mary 599, 601
Thomas 598
Coggen, Abigail (Mrs.) 515
Henry 504, 515
Thomas 520
Coggeshall, Caleb 284
Gideon 284
James 284
Coggin, (?) 603
Cogswell, Elisabeth D(oane) 682
Elisha D(oane) 685
John B. D. 683
N. (Maj.) 34
N. (Rev.) 686
Nathanael 696
Nathanael (Rev.) 651
Nathl. (Rev.) 682, 683, 685
William H(enry) 683
Cointer, (?) 596
Christopher 596
Colbron, Wm. 526
Colburn, Frederick Riddell 284
Cole, (?) (Mrs.) 410
(?) (Widow) 178
Abagail 459
Abel 458
Alice E. 445
Amaziah 4
Anna 128
Bethiah 163, 175
Betsey 580
Catharine 3
Cephas 465
Cha(n)dler 406
Charles 176, 405, 407, 414
Charles (Sr.) 420
Clara 440
Consider 488

Cole (cont.)
Content 492
Daniel 164, 437, 508
Daniell 504
Deborah (Mrs.) 441
Desire 5
Eleazer 3
Elisabeth 3
Elisha 441, 445
Elkanah 163
Elkanah (Jr.) 174
Emeline 166
Enoch 413
Ephraim 5, 163, 440
Ephraim (Mrs.) 447
Esther 405, 462
Esther (Mrs.) 419
George 464
Hannah 164, 170, 172, 468
Hannah Chandler 406
Henry 503
Heugh 501
Hugh 538
Isaih 461
Jabesh 487
Jabez 458, 462
Jahesh 464
James 72, 393, 395, 401, 410, 413
James (Jr.) 501, 545
James (Sr.) 501
Jane (Mrs.) 462
Jas. (Jr.) 536
Job 504, 508
John 8, 127, 508, 546
Joseph 2, 459, 461, 465, 580, 584
Joshua 166
Joshua (Jr.) 176
Josiah (Jr.) 172
Josiah M. 175, 176
Lydia 171
Martha 465
Mary 2, 166, 170, 437
Mary (Jr.) 545
Mary Clapp 413
Matilda 171, 442, 443
Mehitabel 401
Nancy 414
Nathaniel 163, 174, 469
Noah 462, 463, 464, 465, 467, 470
Patty 27
Paulina 170
Phebe 175
Polly 26
Priscilla 171
Rebecca 4, 470, 508
Rebekah C. 174
Ruth 165, 462
Ruth (Mrs.) 437
Samuel 2
Sarah 393, 463
Sarah (Mrs.) 393
Sophiah 580
Stephen 162
Timothy 162, 165, 170
West 469, 488
William 180, 464, 467
Wm. 178
Zerushah (Mrs.) 580
Zilpah 4
Colebond, Mary 68
Coleborn, Mary 62
Coleman, (?) 286
Abdeel 284

Colman (cont.)
Ruth 270
Zecheriah 621
Colomare, Abigail (Mrs.) 341
Isaac 341
Peter 341
Colt, Sukey 202
Colvin, Abigail 152
Anna 152
Anne 152
Deborah 152
James 152
John 152
Josiah 152
Samuel 152
Stephen 152
Colyar, Henry J. 688
Combe, Francis 542
Comings, Joseph (Cpt.) 170
Commet, Thomas 267
Conant, (?) (Rev.) 593
Abigail 551
Abigail (Mrs.) 551
Bethia 6
Bettey 551
David (Jr.) 12
Hannah 8
John 551
Jonathan 15
Josiah 6
Lydia 8
Mary 9
Nathaniel 9
Rebecca 8
Samuel 551
Sarah 551
Condy, William (Cpt.) 240
Cone, Eliza 285
Congden, James B. 155
Congdon, Caleb 285
James B. 141, 146, 151, 157, 158, 159, 160
Connit, Elizabeth 551
John 551
Kezia (Mrs.) 551
Sarah 551
Converse, Sarah 506
Cook, Ann 547
Anna 548
Barnabas 165
Baty (Mrs.) 551
Bethah 546
Bethiah 164
David 164, 551
Desire (Mrs.) 550
Druzilla D. 172
Ebenezer 550, 551
Edward 551
Elisabeth 550
Elisha 551
Eliza (Mrs.) 655
Elizabeth 545
Elizabeth (Mrs.) 551
Elnathan 550
Experience 162
Experience (Mrs.) 551
Francis 507, 547
Hannah 551
Heman 440
Henry A. 173
Hopestill (Mrs.) 33
Isaac 551
Jabez 550
Jacob 528, 546, 550
Cook (cont.)
James 551
Jane (Mrs.) 551
Jesse 551
John 65, 147, 501, 520, 550, 551
John (Jr.) 164
John Covel 551
Jonathan 551
Joshua 550
Joshua B. 164
Josiah 529, 530
Josias 548
Lemuel 551
Lucy F. 173
Margret 267
Martha 550
Mary 550, 621
Mary (Mrs.) 550, 551
Mercey 65
Oliver 311
Rachel 164
Rebecca 551
Rebecka 551
Rebecka (Mrs.) 550, 551
Ruth S. 163
Samuel 163, 551
Sarah 65, 544, 551
Sarah (Mrs.) 65
Solomon 550, 551, 655
Stephen 551
Survina (Mrs.) 689
Susannah (Mrs.) 551
Sylvanus 453
Zerviah (Mrs.) 550
margret 267
Cooke, Ann 544
Francis 498, 500, 501, 532
Hannah 208
Henry 189, 214
Hester (Mrs.) 500, 532
Jacob 501
Jane (Mrs.) 204
John 208, 223, 498, 500, 501, 532
John (Sr.) 501
Josias 501
Litlton 193
Littleton 194, 196, 214
Mary 220
Mary (Mrs.) 193
Sarah (Mrs.) 65, 538
Temple P. 205
Temple Philip 198, 208
Thomas 213, 454
Thomas (Jr.) 196
Thos. 177, 178, 185, 189, 196, 204, 205, 207
William 207
Cookes, Thomas 185
Coombs, Daniel 285
Daniel Myrick 285
Lydia (Mrs.) 285
Coon, (?) 285
William 285
Cooper, (?) 499, 605, 609
(?) (Mrs.) 607, 609
Humilitie 499
James 588
John 311, 504, 519
Josiah 587
Judah 589
Judith 547
Cooper (cont.)
Martha 591
Mary 311, 589
Mehitabel 590
Nat. 589
Nathaniel 39, 587
Noah 588
Peter 589
Rachell 588
Ruth 590
Saml. 588, 589, 590, 591, 592
Samuel 591
Sarah 591
Sophia (Mrs.) 311
Susannah 587
T. 533
Tho 530
Tho. (Jr.) 588
Tho. (Sr.) 539
Thom. (Jr.) 587
Thomas 39, 516, 517, 531, 533
Thomas (Sr.) 54
Thos. 588
Timothy 631
Copeland, Abigail 1
Ebenezer 400, 411
Ebenr. 406, 408, 418
Elis. (Mrs.) 400
Elisabeth (Mrs.) 391, 396
Eliz. (Mrs.) 376, 385
Elizabeth 376
Elizabeth (Mrs.) 337, 377, 380, 382, 394
Elizth. (Mrs.) 388
Hannah 385, 418
Hannah (Mrs.) 408
Jos. 400
Joseph 337, 376, 377, 380, 382, 385, 388, 391, 394, 396, 399, 402
Lucy (Mrs.) 418
Lydia 391, 418
Mary 14, 382
Rebeckah 402
Rhoda 388
Ruth 380
Sally (Mrs.) 418
Sarah 406
William 399
Wm. (Jr.) 418
Copland, Ebenezer 414
Huldah 414
Coppe, Bethiah 622
Corbet, Betty Robinson 467
Ebenezer 467
Corbett, Agnis 18
Corbison, Mary 629
Corbitt, William 630, 631
Cordner, Abigail 3
Amos 1
Anna 5
Betty 5
Corlew, Bille 412
Jane 414
William 414
Cornelius, (?) 535
Cornell, Elizabeth 146
Lydia (Mrs.) 285
Stephen 146
Thomas 146
William 285
Cornels, Mary 217

Cornet, Peter 6
Cornish, Abigail 366
Joseph 366, 429
Josiah 429
Mary 7
Patience (Mrs.) 366, 429
Ruth 20
Corthel, Levi 384
Mary 387
Mary (Mrs.) 383, 384
Robert 383, 384, 387
Theophilus 625
mary (Mrs.) 383, 384
Corthell, Deborah 625
Cortherill, Jane 410
Cortis, Sarah 489
Cosens, (?) (Widow) 178
Ann Frances 220
Jemimah (Widow) 180
John 180, 210, 220
Sarah 210
Cotle, Shubel 100
Cottan, Silvanus P. 688
Cottel, Edward 254
Lydia 254
Cottell, Edward 254
Judith 254
Cottle, (?) 188
(?) (Widow) 187
Abner 204
Anne 254
Anne (Mrs.) 137, 138
Betsey 128
Cynthia 128
Dorothy 256
Edward 254, 255
Elizabeth 111
Frederick William 285
Hannah 119, 123
Hester 111
James 109
Jane 188
Jeremiah 132
Jerusha 121
Jerusha (Mrs.) 119, 122, 130
John 111, 118, 119, 123, 130, 131, 133, 255
Jonan. 179
Jonathan 181, 183, 191, 208
Katy (Mrs.) 204
Lot 128, 204, 285
Mayhew 128, 136, 137, 138, 139, 140
Polly 127
Rebecca 129
Rebecca (Mrs.) 119, 130, 131, 132, 133
Ruth (Mrs.) 285
Sally (Mrs.) 136, 137, 138, 139, 140
Saml. 177
Sarah 128, 185
Shubael 109, 128, 285
Silas 119, 120, 121, 122, 127, 130
Thos. 185
Truman 140
William 137
Wm. 128, 138
Zerviah (Mrs.) 118
Cottle?, Mayhew 139
Sally (Mrs.) 139
Cottles, John 117
Cotton, (?) 286, 606
Cotton (cont.)
(?) (Dr.) 524
(?) (Rev.) 113
Henry 689
John 286, 539
Josiah 286, 411
Lydia 684
Lydia W. (Mrs.) 692
Rossete 544
Sylvanus P. 689
Cottrill, Martha 641
Couden, (?) (Mrs.) 444
Couell, Ezra 502
Courtis, Anna 314
Elizabeth 313, 314
John 314
Joseph 317
Mary 315
Richard 314, 315
Samuel 319
Thomas 313, 319
William 317, 319
Courtisse, Benjamin 318
Deborah 317
Martha 316
Richard 316, 317
Sarah 317
William 317, 318
Courtney, Barcus 221
Eliza 218, 219
Leonard 219
Love 219
Coval, Asa 695
James 177
Jethro 178
Covel, Anna (Mrs.) 187
Ezra 115
James 222
Jethro 200
Joseph 181, 188
Lydia 205
Mary 222
Obed 286
Rebecca 165
Sarah 188, 198, 225
Wm. 187
Covil, Bulah 190
Deborah 690
Eliza 688
Joseph 189
Judith 189
Cowen, Israel 624
Job (Cpt.) 421
John 623, 624
Joseph 624
Mary 624
Rebecca 624
Cowet, Mary 11
Cowin, Lydia 456
Cowing, Israel 25
Job 376
Mary 376
Cowles, Eliz. 506
Robt. 506
Cox, Benj. 454
Benjamin 459
Edward 459, 460, 461, 484, 485, 488
Elizabeth 461, 485
Hannah 459
Isaac 458, 483
James 454, 459
John 458, 459
Mary 463, 490
Nathaniel 459
Rebecca 459, 461, 484
Rebekah (Mrs.) 485
Ruth 491, 492
Cox (cont.)
Sarah 460
Sarah (Mrs.) 130, 131
Thomas 123, 130, 131, 132, 134
Thomas 458
William 458, 483, 490, 492
William (Jr.) 463
Cozens, John 178
Crackston, John 498
John (Jr.) 498
Cradding, William 509
Craghead, (?) 96, 104
Katheren 96
Katherine 96
Robert 97
Robert (Rev.) 96
Thomas 96
Thomas (Rev.) 97
Crague, Elisabeth 412
Craig, Ruth (Widow) 418
Craighead, Katherine 222
Crandall, Saml. 74
Crandon, John 33
Crane, Caeser 582
Ebenezer 483, 484
Elizabeth 484
Gershom 643
John 78, 628, 643
Lydia 570
Mary 629
Tabitha 483
Ziporah 643
Zipporah 570
Creasy, Edward 275, 285
Elizabeth 285
Creed, James Hatch 551
John 551
Moller (Mrs.) 551
Crips, George 501
Crittenden, Thomas (Dr.) 198
Croad, John 243
Mary 246
Croade, John 237
Priscilla 236
Rachel 236
Rachel (Mrs.) 236, 237
Richd. 516
Thomas 236, 237
Crocker, (?) 281, 596
(?) (Jr.) 610
Abiah (Mrs.) 286
Alexander 230
Alice 614
Alvin 281
Bathsheba 594
Benjamin 229
Blossom 229
Celia 229
Cynthia (Mrs.) 286
Daniel 458, 459, 460, 685, 698
Daniel B(acon) 685
Davis 615
Ebenezer 614
Edward 696, 697
Edward W. 687
Eleazar 600
Elisabeth 685
Elisha 540
Eliza (Mrs.) 203, 207
Elizabeth 598
Elizabeth Jane 230
Ephraim Allen Swift 230
Fear 286

Crocker (cont.)
Francis 504
Hannah 614, 685
Hannah (Mrs.) 611, 613, 615, 616
Hannah P. 228
Henry 228, 229, 230
Henry Robinson 229
Henry S. 228
Isaac 613
Isaiah 286
James 616
James B(acon) 685
James B. (Cpt.) 685
Jane (Mrs.) 594
Joanna 612
Joanna (Bacon) 685
Job 540, 599, 611, 613, 614, 615
John 504, 537, 540, 543, 597, 611
Jonathan 613, 615, 616
Jone (Mrs.) 540
Joseph 286, 540, 613, 616
Joshua 286
Josiah 116, 599, 614
Josias 540
Lemuel 460
Lucy Coffin 203
Lucy Goodspeed 230
Luther 286
Malatiah 614
Margaret 460
Marth 613
Mary 459, 611, 614
Mercy 614
Nailer 286
Nathan 458
Noah 612
Olive 692
P(rice) 685
P. (Rev.) 594
Peter 229
Philander 229
Rebeccah 230
Reliance 614
Remember 616
Rhoda 286
Rhoda (Mrs.) 228, 230
Robinson 286
Russell 227
Samuel 540
Samuell 598
Sarah 613
Sarah B(acon) 685
Seth 286, 614
Silvanus 203, 204, 207
Susan 685
Temperance 612
Temperance (Mrs.) 613, 616
Thankful 613
Thomas 614
Tilden 460
Timothy 286
Unie 229
Willi. 598
William 599, 600, 612
William Henry 230
Willm. 504
Wm 540
Wm. 509, 532
Zeno 286
Croel, Abigail 663
Abigail (Widow) 694
Abner 661, 662, 663, 696
Croel (cont.)
Ansel 659
Asa 695
Azuba 661
Azubah 688
Azubia 661
Barnabas 661, 694
Benjamin 663
Bethiah (Widow) 695
Caroline 688
Charles 695
Data 659
Deborah 661
Dyantha 688
Ebenezer 659, 695
Eliza (Mrs.) 658
Ezekiel 659
Ezra 658
Hanah (Mrs.) 661
Hannah (Mrs.) 663
Hezekiah 660, 661, 663
Jabes 694
James 698
Jeremiah 696
Joseph 660, 694, 695
Joseph (Jr.) 659
Judah 696
Lydia Lewis 687
Margery 661
Maria 688
Mary (Widow) 695
Matthews 696
Nabby 688
Naomi (Mrs.) 661
Naomy (Mrs.) 660, 663
Nathan 694
Nathaniel 659, 661
Nehemiah 661
Nehemiah (Cpt.) 694
Nehemiah (Jr.) (Cpt.) 688
Obadiah 659
Obediah 659
Otis 687
Prince 658
Priscilla 660
Rebeca 688
Rebeca (Mrs.) 688
Rebeccah 660
Robert 696
Sarah 659, 662
Seth 688
Simeon 687
Temperance (Mrs.) 659
Thankful (Mrs.) 659, 661
Thomas 661
Thomas (Jr.) 695
Timothy 696
Watson 688
Zadock 659
Zadok 659
Ziza 661
Crofsman, Robert 61
Croker, Elijah 465
Elizabeth Ramsdell 465
Crook, Thomas 267
Crooker, (?) 453
Abigail (Mrs.) 487
Abner 412
Benjamin 461
Bethany 466
Bethia 456
Bethiah 461, 484
Betty 464
Christopher 250
Daniel 243, 249, 461, 462, 464, 466, 487, 488, 490, 491
Crooker (cont.)
Daniel (Jr.) 466
David (Jr.) 454
Deborah 462
Debrah 454
Deliverance 474
Desire (Jr.) 455
Elijah 466, 486, 488, 491
Elizabeth 245, 454
Ensign 466
Francis 246, 250, 521
Hannah 455
Japhet 454
John 28
Jonathan 245, 250
Lemuel 455, 461
Lydia 453, 456, 466
Mary 487
Mercy 485
Nabby 464
Peniah 490
Salome 491
Sarah 243, 456
Thomas 454
Tilden 456
Ursula (Jr.) 456
Wm. 517
Crosbey, Mary 651
Crosby, (?) 441, 445, 446
(?) (Mrs.) 441
Achsah S. 168, 172
Almond G. 440
Almond Otis 449
Almond S. 441
Caroline 165
Carrie G. 445
Celia H. (Mrs.) 449
Charlotte E. (Mrs.) 286
Clara Snow 440
Clara Snow (Mrs.) 449
Dolly (Mrs.) 207
Edwin E. 440
Eliza N. 172
Elliott E. 442
Frank 445
Freeman G. 447
George L. 286
Hannah N. 176
Harlow 199, 207
Harriet H. 171
Haskel 445
Hatsel 691
Helen M. 444
Isaiah (Jr.) 447
James 212
Jesse 294
John 170, 204, 286
John (Jr.) 209
John F. 441
Joshua 441
Joshua L. 442
Joshua Lewis (Mrs.) 447
Kate 446
Leander 442, 448
Lizzie 442
Lottie 448
Louisa A. 175
Mark 171
Martha 166, 169
Mary 166, 446, 452
Mary (Mrs.) 447
Mary E. 175
Orville W. 446, 449

Crosby (cont.)
Patty (Mrs.) 170
Philander A. 444
Philander Artemus 449
Rebecca (Mrs.) 204
Rollin W. 449
Rosanna S. 173
Sally Freeman (Mrs.) 441
Sarah A. 173
Solomon 440, 448
Susanna 169
Thankful 444
Timothy 169
Vickery N. 441
Warren M. (Mrs.) 440
Wilfred H. 449
Wilfred H. (Mrs.) 449
William (Mrs.) 447
Crosman, (?) (Widow) 44
Elisabeth 631
Elizabeth 644
Elizabeth (Mrs.) 644
Hannah 62, 630
Hannah (Widow) 195
John 211, 629
Joseph 628
Martha 44
Peleg 211
Robert 43, 44, 60, 67, 68, 73, 92
Robt. 44
Samuel 628, 629, 633
Samuell 644
Thomas 644
Wm. 206
Cross, Joseph 53
Crossman, Abiah 558
Abigail 198
Abigall 643
Allice 573
Alvin 578
Anna 558
Annie 573
Anthony 198
Barnabas 644
Barzillai 578
Benjamin 643
Bethia 639
Bradford 578
Cyrus 579
Deborah 643
Eleazer 636
Elizabeth 67, 573, 636, 639
Elkanan 578
Gabriel 558, 573, 578, 644
Hannah 198, 221, 559, 573, 639
Hannah (Mrs.) 221
Henry 643
Joanna 558, 573, 643
Joanna (Mrs.) 558, 573
Joannah (Mrs.) 558
John 67, 91, 635, 643
Jonathan 643
Joseph 1, 636, 644
Keziah 558
Leonard 558, 578
Lydia (Mrs.) 558
Marcey 67
Mary 8, 67, 558, 635, 639
Mary (Mrs.) 644
Mehitabell 639
Mercey 67
Mercy 636, 643
Crossman (cont.)
Nathaniel 630
Nathaniell 639
Nathanill 636
Peleg 198, 216
Phebe 558, 573
Phebe (Mrs.) 558, 573, 578
Phimeas 558
Phineas 558
Phinehas 644
Rachel 558
Robert 61, 62, 67, 91, 558, 635, 639, 644
Robert (Jr.) 639
Robert (Sr.) 43
Robt. 639
Samuel 67, 636
Samuell 644
Sarah 7, 67, 643, 644
Seth 182, 198, 221, 573, 639
Susana 636
Theophilus 558, 644
Thomas 558, 573, 636
Welthea 646
Welthy 558
Zibiah 558
Crow, William 544
Wm 541
Wm. 505, 519
Crowe, Willm. 501
Wm 532
Wm. 510
Yelverton 504
Crowel, (?) 688, 689, 696
(?) (Cpt.) 688
Abigail 682
Abigail (Widow) 697
Abigail P(arker) 682
Abner 651, 665, 666
Abner T(aylor) 682
Adaline 682
Alexander 691
Alger 684
Allen B. 696
Allen Bangs 668
Almira 690
Anne 652
Barnabas 681
Benjamin F(ranklin) 682
Bethian (Widow) 696
Betsy 679
Betty 651
Calvin 697
Caroline 682
Catharine (Mrs.) 676, 678
Cena Howes 668
Charlotte (Widow) 698
Daniel (Cpt.) 688
Data 653
David 654
Davis 691
Ebebenezer 652
Ebenezer 653, 654, 682
Ebenezer (Cpt.) 696
Ebenzr. 652
Edmon 678
Edmond 676
Edmond (Cpt.) 682
Edmond (III) 688
Edmund 652
Edmund (Jr.) 690
Edward 696
Elisabeth 654
Crowel (cont.)
Eliza 688
Eliza A(llen) 682
Elizabeth (Mrs.) 673
Elnathan 693
Ephraim 651, 652, 653, 654
Erastus 683
Eunice 691
Ezekiel 666
Freeman 698
Freeman H. 691
Gorham 654
Gorham (Col.) 696
Hannah 163, 654
Hannah (Mrs.) 654, 665, 666, 667, 668, 681
Hannah (Widow) 697, 698
Hannah T(hatcher) 682
Hegens 680
Hegins 675, 679
Henry 654, 697, 698
Henry (Cpt.) 689
Hezekiah 666, 668
Higgins 679, 680, 696
Higgins (Cpt.) 689
Hiram 688, 697
Isaack 654
Jabez 666
James 684, 685
Jane 691
Jeremiah 666, 667
Jeremiah (Cpt.) 698
Jeremy 666
Jerusha (Widow) 698
Jo 652
Joel 688
John 651
John Buck 683
Jonathan 655
Joseph 652, 653
Joseph (Cpt.) 697
Julia An 689
Julia Ann 676
Lavina 680
Lot 651
Lot (Cpt.) 668
Lott 667
Louisa 690
Lucy E(ldridge) 682
Lydia (Mrs.) 685
Lydia (Widow) 697
Martha 654, 693
Mary 666, 693
Mary (Mrs.) 681
Mary H. 689
Mary Jane 696
Mary P(arker) 683
Minerva 688
Mira 688
Molly (Mrs.) 666, 667, 675
Naomi (Mrs.) 666, 668
Naomy 666
Nathan 682
Nehemiah 652
Nehemiah (Cpt.) 697
Nehemiah (Jr.) (Cpt.) 698
Orren 688, 696
Osborn 684
Otis 683
Otis (Cpt.) 685, 697
Owen 696
Patience 652
Peter 690

Crowel (cont.)
Phebe 666
Philander 689
Polly 667, 682
Polly (Mrs.) 681, 685
Prince 673
Rachel 654
Raleigh 689
Rehesa 689
Robert 653, 691
Rodman 682
Rose (Mrs.) 652, 654
Ruth 689
Ruth (Mrs.) 679, 680
Ruthy 675
Sally 673
Sarah 688
Seth 651
Shelden 682
Shobal 668
Shubal 681, 682, 696
Shubel 668
Silas 652
Silvanus 655
Simeon 651
Sophia 689
Susannah (Mrs.) 681
Susannah (Widow) 683, 698
Sylvanus 681
Tabitha (Mrs.) 698
Thankful 651, 652, 682
Thomas 652, 675, 678, 681, 697
Timothy 666
Timothy (Cpt.) 689, 697
Velina 682
Winthrop 681
Winthrop (Cpt.) 683, 684
Wm 652
Zebina 693
Zenas 698
Zipporah 665
Crowell, (?) 688
Abigail 650, 663, 670
Abigail (Mrs.) 670
Abner 661, 662, 663
Allen 671
Allen Bangs 668
Ann 669
Anna (Mrs.) 656
Ansel 659
Azuba 661
Azubia 661
Barnabas 650, 661
Benjamin 663
Benjamin Lewis 681
Bethiah 656
Bethiah (Mrs.) 672
Betsey 690
Betsy 667, 671, 679
Betty 674
Betty (Mrs.) 671, 672
Calvin 669, 683
Catharine (Mrs.) 674, 678
Cena Howes 668
Charlotte 671
Charloty 671
Chloe S. 228
Christopher 433
Clarissa 671
Clerissa 671
Daniel 674
Data 659
David 672
Crowell (cont.)
Davis 670
Deborah 661
Deborah (Mrs.) 669, 670
Deliverance 650
Desire 656
Desire (Mrs.) 656, 657
Ebenezer 659, 669, 670
Edmon 674, 678
Edmond 678
Edmond (Jr.) 674
Elisa A. 691
Elisabeth 670
Elisabeth Parker 671
Eliza 655, 674, 691
Elizabeth (Mrs.) 658, 669, 670, 672, 673
Ephraim 652
Eunice 669
Ezekiel 659, 666
Ezra 657, 658, 669, 670
Freeman 671
Freman 691
George 672
Gorham 672
Hanah (Mrs.) 661
Hanar (Mrs.) 658
Hannah 652, 656, 673
Hannah (Mrs.) 655, 656, 662, 663, 667, 668, 670, 673
Hegen 676
Hegens 680
Hegins 675, 679
Heman 655
Henry 656
Hezekiah 660, 661, 663, 668
Higgins 670, 679, 680
Higgins (Cpt.) 690
Higins 676, 681
Howard 670
Isaiah 671
Jabez 650, 656
Jedidah 656
Jemima 656
Jeremiah 666, 667
Jeremy 666
John 543, 656
Jonathan 126
Joseph 652, 660, 670, 682
Joseph (Jr.) 659
Lavina 680
Lemuel 651
Lilly 689
Lot 655, 656, 658, 670, 673
Lot (Cpt.) 667, 668
Lott 667
Lucretia 656, 693
Lucy 672
Lucy (Mrs.) 669, 670, 672
Lydia 221
Manoah 656
Margery 661
Mary 658
Mary B. 448
Matthews 655
Mayo 656
Mercie Sears 432
Mercy 655
Molly (Mrs.) 666, 667, 675
Moodey 650
Crowell (cont.)
Myra 669
Nancy 672
Naomi (Mrs.) 661, 668
Naomy (Mrs.) 660, 663
Nathan (Cpt.) 435
Nathaniel 658, 659, 661
Nathll. 656
Nehemiah 661
Obadiah 659
Obediah 659
Paul 93
Phebe 666
Philander 674
Phoze 669
Polly 667
Prentice 669
Prince 656, 657, 658, 669, 670, 672, 673
Printis 669
Priscilla 660
Rebecca (Mrs.) 93
Rebeccah 660
Reuben 669
Rhoda 656
Ruth 672
Ruth (Mrs.) 676, 679, 680
Ruthy 675
Sally 673
Samuel 138
Sarah 551, 658, 659, 662
Sarah (Mrs.) 551, 663
Sarah Adeline (Mrs.) 435
Seth 670
Shobal 668, 670
Shubel 668, 670
Sil(v)anus 671
Silvanus 671, 672
Silvins 670
Solomon 551, 669, 670, 672
Stephen 652
Sylvanus 670
Tabitha 691
Tabitha Sears 682
Temperance 433
Temperance (Mrs.) 659
Thankful 656
Thankful (Mrs.) 551, 656, 658, 659, 661
Thomas 661, 675
Thos. 650
Timothy 663, 666
Watson 670
Willard 655
Winthrop (Cpt.) 683
Wotson 670
Zadock 659
Zadok 659
Ziza 661
Crowells, Aron 678
Ezra 678
Phebe (Mrs.) 678
Sarah 678
Crowels, Aron 678
Ezra 678
Phebe (Mrs.) 678
Sarah 678
Crumwell, (?) (Col.) 607
Cruttenden, Thomas (Dr.) 198
Cu---, Zipporah 412
Cubby, Elizabeth 533
Cuddworth, James 597

Dammon (cont.)
Mehetabel 349
Mehitabel (Mrs.) 351, 356, 359, 362, 368
Mehithabel 331
Mehittable (Mrs.) 429
Mercy 359
Nathaniel 24, 395
Obadiah 374
Rebecca 368
Relief 357
Robert 429
Ruth 395
Samuel 394
Sarah 429
Sarah (Mrs.) 394
Silence 333
Stephen 387
Zachariah (Jr.) 395
Zech. 356
Zechariah 331, 349, 359, 362, 368, 394
Zecheriah 351, 371, 429
mehitabel (Mrs.) 356
Damon, (?) (Widow) 412
Abigail 362
Alvan 423
Amos 399, 402
Anna Lenthal (Mrs.) 396
Barsheba 357
Bathsheba 392
Benjamin 379
Betty 477
Caleb 399
Calvin 411
Clarrissa 404
Daniel 357, 384
Danl. 333, 361, 399
Danniel 392
David 400
Ebenezar 379
Ebenezer 247
Edward 401
Elijah 478
Elijah (Jr.) 475, 476, 477, 479
Elisabeth 402
Eliz (Mrs.) 357
Elizabeth (Mrs.) 359
Gideon Thomas 475
Hannah 402
Ichabod 70
Isaac 397, 403
Jemima 361
Jemima (Mrs.) 333, 357
Jemima (Widow) 397
Jemimah 402
Jemimah (Mrs.) 361
Joanna (Mrs.) 397
John 357, 359
Joseph 337, 397
Joshua 625
Judith (Mrs.) 384, 392
Lidia (Mrs.) 397
Lucinda 404
Lucy 403
Mary 399
Mary (Mrs.) 398, 400
Mehetabel (Mrs.) 396
Mehitabel (Mrs.) 362
Melzar 423
Mercy 359
Nathaniel 479
Relief 357
Robert 398, 399, 400
Samll. 404
Damon (cont.)
Sarah R. 317, 323
Silence 366
Simeon 399
Stephen 399
Susanna 422
William Peaks 476
Wm. 402
Zach 396
Zachariah 396
Zachh. (Jr.) 399
Zech. 401
Zechariah 362, 394
amos 399
Danford, Jonathan 74
Danforth, (?) 78
(?) (Rev.) 565
Elizabeth 644
James 644
Mary 644
Samuel 35, 48, 82
Samuell 45, 644
Danham, Nathan 195
Daniel, Hannah 146
Jeremiah 154
Mercy 146
Reuben 154
Timothy 154
Dannam, Elizabeth 372
Jane (Mrs.) 372
Joseph 372
Darbey, Matthew 543
Darby, John 522
Mary 533
Samuel 15
Darbys, Jonathan 396
Darling, Benjamin 24
John 465
Lydia N. 175
Mercy 454, 466
Rebecca 455
Samuel 465, 466
Thomas 252
Darrow, Ira 217
Dauice, Dollar 598
Ruth 598
Daval, Jeremi'all 147
Dave, John 57
Davenport, William 11
Davice, Margret 270
Mary 44, 603
David, John 527
Davis, (?) 212
(?) (Widow) 207
Abagail 620
Abigail 615
Abraham 164
Amasa 286
Anne 144
Aron 72, 73, 75
Bathshua 613
Benj. 197
Benja. 66
Benjamin 613
Benjm. 189
Benjn. 192, 193
Catharine T. 286
Crocker (Cpt.) 227
Daniel 616
David (Cpt.) 210
Deidamia 126
Dennis 212
Dolar 504
Dollor 616
Dolor 597, 612, 613, 614, 617
Ebenezer 615
Elisha 42
Davis (cont.)
Emaline 227
Emira 227
Experience 613
Experience (Mrs.) 613, 614, 615, 616
Frederick 227
Grace (Mrs.) 367
Hanna 613
Hannah (Mrs.) 597, 612, 613, 614, 616, 617
Isaac 615
Jabez 613, 614, 615, 616
Jacob 616
James 227, 286, 614, 696
James Newton 286
Jedediah 617
Job 617
Job C. 286
John 183, 504, 542, 602, 612, 613, 614, 615, 616, 617
John (Jdg.) 286
John (Jr.) 613
Lathrop 286
Malatiah (Col.) 220
Malt 192
Mary 7, 220
Mary (Mrs.) 52, 615
Melatiah 212, 213
Molly 193
Nathan 613
Nathaniel 613
Nicholas 616
Nicolas 367
Oliver 214, 286
Rebecca (Mrs.) 206
Reuben 613
Robert 504, 537
Rufus 127, 201, 206
S. T. (Dr.) 443
Saml1. 614
Samuel 311
Sanford 194
Shobal 179
Shubael 187
Shubal 614
Simon 37
Sophia 311
Thankfull 614
Timothy 228
Timothy (Rev.) 229, 230
Tristram 620
William 628, 632
William H. 691
Davy, John 58
Dawes, (?) (Widow) 486
Ambross (Jr.) 260
Margaret 11
Mary 486
Robert 12
Samuel 14
Daws, Experience 487
Daye, Edward 590
Priscilla 592
Saml. 590, 592
Dayton, (?) 286
Charles 286
Nehemiah 286
Dean, (?) 586
Abiezer 569
Abigail 558, 559, 579, 582, 591, 630, 639
Abigail (Mrs.) 645

Denneman (cont.)
Mercy 286
Dennis, Bathsheba (Mrs.) 432
Josiah (Rev.) 432
Judith (Mrs.) 522
Mary 529
Phebe (Mrs.) 432
Robert 56, 504, 522
Robt 538
Robt. 529
William 522
Denny, Sarah 80
Derby, John 504
Derrick, John 286
Devell, William 516
Devil, (?) 145
Christopher 152
Jeremiah 146
Jonathan 72
Joseph 152
Lydia 152
Mary 152
Sarah 144
Devil?, Jeremi'all 147
Devol?, Jeremi'all 147
Dewelly, John (Sr.) 327
Dexter, Bethiah (Mrs.) 654
Gideon 286
Hannah 654
Isaac 654
James 246
John 654, 655
Phillippe (Widow) 655
Diatt, Milees 36
Dickarson, John 544
Dickerman, Daniel 4
Dickinson, Thomas 286
Dier, Hannah 163
Dike, Samuel 4
Dill, Abby C. 175
Betsey 175
Columbus 175
Daniel 165
Eldad 163
Eldad A. 175
Elizabeth A. 176
Ezekiel 163
Freeman 167, 171
Hannah A. 168, 172
Hannah D. 165
Hannah H. 169
Hannah T. 175
Harried N. 174
Heman S. 170
Joseph M. 166
Joshua H. 173
Lorenzo Dow 174
Mary H. 171
Mary W. 174
Mehitable 166
Olive D. 175
Sally 164
Sarah D. 166, 169
Tamsin (Mrs.) 175
Tamzin D. 176
Thomas 162, 164
Warren A. 173
William 172
Dillingham, Dorcas 146
Edw. 510, 513
Edward 503, 515, 537
Henry 146, 503, 537
John 537
Rachel 26
Dimack, Thomas 528
Dimmack, Thomas 519
Dimmick, (?) 597, 601, 608
Charles 227
Elijah 227
Joseph 286
Shubeall 599
Timothy 601
Dimmicke, (?) 605
Dimmock, Elisabeth 614
Elizabeth (Mrs.) 613, 614
Hannah 614
Mary 614
Mehetabel 598
Sarah 613
Thomas 504
Timothye 598
Dimock, Benjamir 611
Bethia (Mrs.) 617
Ebenezer 616
Elisabeth (Mrs.) 615
Elizabeth 616
Elizabeth (Mrs.) 616
Joanna 611
Joanna (Mrs.) 611, 612
John 616
Mehetable 611
Nathanll. 611
Sarah (Mrs.) 611
Shubael 611
Shubal 617
Shuball 612
Thankfull 612
Theophilus 615
Timothy 616
Dingley, Abigail 247
Anna (Mrs.) 239
Elizabeth 245
Elizabeth (Mrs.) 251
Ezra 406
Jacob 249, 251
John 239, 248, 504, 518
Mary 242
Nabby (Mrs.) 406
Sarah 242, 245, 247
Thomas 238, 239
Dingly, Hannah 244
Dipple, Grace 623
Ditson, Harry 446
Divis, Rebekah 630
Dixi, John 54
Dixon, Robert 286
Doan, Allice F. 168
Doan?, Ephraim 546
Doane, Abigail 164
Abner 175
Alice 163
Alice F. 166
Anna 164
Barnabas 164
Barnabas (Jr.) 175
Benjamin 173, 175
Bethiah 166
Betsey 167, 171
Betsy 166, 551
Crowell 169, 175
Crowell (Jr.) 165
Curtis 167
Daniel 438
Dorcas 164
Elijah 171
Elisha 438, 551, 680
Eliza 175
Elizabeth 171, 680
Ephraim 551
Esther M. 442
Ezekiel 162
Doane (cont.)
Freeman 164, 176, 445
Gilbert 440
Hannah 163, 164
Hannah (Mrs.) 551
Hannah Knowles 162
Hannah M. 176
Heman 163
Henry 167, 172
Herman 166
Herman (III) (Cpt.) 168
Hezekiah 551
Isaac 171
Isaac (Jr.) 162
James 551
Jeremiah 551
Jesse (Cpt.) 163
John 162, 171, 438
John (II) 176
Jonathan 170
Joseph 437, 438
Joseph (Jr.) 94
Joshua 438, 551
Joshua G. 175
Josiah 163, 164, 167
Julia A. (Mrs.) 448
Knowles 165, 166, 169
Lewis 175
Lidia 551
Lot 163
Louisa 168, 172
Lucindia 167, 171
Lydia 163
Lydia C. S. 173
Mariah 173
Martha 447
Mary 551
Mary (Mrs.) 551
Mary E. 176
Mary K. 174
Mary P. 166, 169
Mary P. (Mrs.) 169
May (Mrs.) 447
Mehitable 170
Mercy 164, 168, 172
Mercy (Mrs.) 94
Mercy Freeman (Mrs.) 448
Myrick 162, 163, 164, 170
Nancy 164
Nehemiah 163, 168
Nemiah 551
Noah 165
Noan 171
Olive C. 445
Olive W. 174
Patina 169
Patty 164, 166, 170
Paulina 166
Phebe 165
Polly 164
Polly F. 163
Prince 164
Priscilla (Mrs.) 174
Priscilla M. 165, 169
Rachel 163, 172
Randal 168
Rebecca 162, 174
Rolin 170
Rowland 176
Russel 169
Russell 166
Ruth 162, 165
Sabra A. 174
Sabrina 164
Samuel 162

Echee, Jno. 78
Eddenden, (?) 512
  Edmond 503, 512
Eddy, Amy 221, 222
  Beulah 210
  Caleb 287
  Deliverance (Mrs.) 66
  John 66, 545, 547, 549
  Samuel 513
  Samuell 501
  Susanna (Mrs.) 549
  Zachariah 79, 544
Edenden, (?) 610
Edes, H. H. 450
Edge, Willm 504
Edgerly, Isaiah D. (Dr.) 227
Edmester, James 628
Edmister, Anne 632
Edmonds, Martha J. 228
Edmunds, (?) (Sir) 62
Edson, Abigail 2
  Abijah 12
  Benjamin 8, 545
  Bethiah 547
  Cyrus 28
  Daniel 3
  David 1, 2
  Ebenezer 2
  Elizabeth 7
  Hannah 12
  Jacob 2
  James 14
  Jesse 2
  Joanna 2
  Joel 25
  John 12, 17, 24
  Joseph 6, 7
  Josiah 4, 7
  Mary 1, 6, 8
  Mehitable 4
  Nathan 5
  Nathanael 15
  Peter 1
  Relief 5
  Samuel 9, 631
  Sarah 2, 546, 646
  Susanna 3
  Timothy 9
  William 2
Edwards, (?) (Mrs.) 449
  Edward 502
  Joseph 287
  Lewis 287
  Samuel 287
  Sarah Perry (Mrs.) 287
Edwon, Bethiah 640
Edy, Bennet 630
  Caleb 630
  Ebenezer 635
  Elazer 635
  Eliezer 630
  Hana 635
  Hannah 629, 633
  J. 635
  John 635, 646
  John (Sr.) 635
  Jonathan 635
  Joseph 635
  Marcey 635
  Mary 635
  Mercy 629
  Patience 635
  Susana 635
  Susana (Mrs.) 635
Eelles, Hannah Schiverick 414
  Mercy 411
Eelles (cont.)
  Nathll. 412
  Nathll. (Jr.) 414
Eells, (?) (Rev.) 394
  Abiah (Mrs.) 372, 373, 378, 385, 386, 388, 391, 395
  Abigail 395
  Anna Lenthal 337, 357
  Benja. Hatch Tower 416
  Benjamin 425
  Desire 386, 387
  Edward 346, 395
  Edward (Rev.) 401
  Edwd. 395
  Frances 330
  Frances (Mrs.) 330
  Hannah 347, 373
  Hannah (Mrs.) 335, 340, 341, 342, 344, 346, 347, 348, 352, 357, 369, 371, 373, 375, 377, 378
  Hannah North 377, 378
  Jerusha (Mrs.) 418
  John 330, 342, 372, 373, 378, 385, 386, 388, 391, 395
  Joseph 391
  Lenthall 388
  Lusanna 385
  Martha Turner 424
  Mary 348
  Nabby (Mrs.) 420
  Nath. (Rev.) 401
  Nathanael 340, 341, 342, 344, 347, 357, 390
  Nathanaell 352
  Nathaneel 416
  Nathaniel 425
  Nathaniel (Rev.) 339, 395
  Nathaniell (Rev.) 326
  Nathanll 348, 415
  Nathl. 420, 424
  Nathll. 346, 395, 412, 416
  Nort(h) 338
  North 337, 352, 386, 387, 390, 393, 394, 395, 396, 399, 401
  Robert Lenthall 371
  Ruth 401
  Ruth (Mrs.) 338, 386, 387, 390, 393, 394, 395, 396
  Saml. 335, 369, 377, 418
  Samll. 373, 416
  Samuel 341, 378, 393
  Samuell 375
  Sarah 340, 373, 386, 402, 424
  Thankful 395
  Thankfull 394
  Waterman 372, 402
  William Witherel 369
  Zilpah Turner 415
Eels, Edward 335
  Hannah 335
Egerton, Abigail (Widow) 21
  Alice G. 444
  Eunice 5
  Hannah 21, 25
  Hezekiah 14
  John 12
Egerton (cont.)
  Ruth 17
Eldedge, Ruth C. 445
Elden, David 252
  John 252, 528
  Priscilla 252
Eldrd, Deborah 665
  Hannah (Mrs.) 665
  John 665
Eldred, Asa 664
  Asia 664
  Barnabas 664
  Bethiah 543
  Elisha 543
  Hannah (Mrs.) 230, 664, 666, 667
  John 664, 666, 667
  Lydia 666
  Patience (Mrs.) 664
  Rebeccah 664
  Reuben 227
  Robte. 501
  Simon 226
  Thomas 229
Eldredg, Anna 662
  Barnabas 660, 661, 662
  Betty 660
  Gideon 660
  John 660
  Joseph 661
  Patience (Mrs.) 660, 661, 662
  Ruben 660
  Sarah 660
Eldredge, Abigail 660
  Abigail (Mrs.) 94
  Anna 676
  Asa 680
  Azariah 681
  Barnabas 663, 671, 673, 675, 676, 678, 679
  Benjamin 674
  Bethiah 666
  Bethiah (Mrs.) 666, 667, 669, 670
  Betsey 669
  Betty (Mrs.) 680
  Caroline 679
  Charles H. 228
  Darcus (Mrs.) 449
  David 94, 666, 667, 669, 670
  Deborah (Mrs.) 681
  Desiah B. 443
  Desier 666
  Desire (Mrs.) 660
  Dustin 674
  Ebenezer 93
  Edmond 666
  Edward 680
  Eliza 680
  Emogene 445
  Gorham 668
  Hanah Linkhorn 662
  Hannah (Mrs.) 662, 663, 667, 668, 674, 676, 678
  Hannah (Widow) 669
  Ira 674
  John 660, 662, 663, 667, 668, 669
  John (Cpt.) 680
  Joseph 681
  Joshua 94, 667
  Loisa 675
  Louisa 675
  Lucy 680

Faunce (cont.)
Hannah 377
Hannah (Mrs.) 373, 381
John 502, 513, 518
Joseph 547
Marcye 545
Mary 545
Mercy? 545
Sarah 545
Thomas 373, 377, 381, 540, 546
Faxon, Asaph 460
Barnabas 460
Benjamin 463
Betty 462
Eliashib 484, 485
Elijah 460, 462, 486
Elisha 458, 459, 461, 463, 484
Elizabeth 458, 484
Priscilla 458
Ruth 459
Ruth (Widow) 488
Samuel 23, 461
Sarah 17, 458
Thomas 458, 459
Faxson, Allen 462
Elisha 462
Fay, Nancy (Mrs.) 691
Faye, (?) 287
Joseph 287
Feake, Henry 503
Fearing, Israel 648
Feeto, Gabriel 581
Hannah (Mrs.) 581
Joseph 581
Philander 581
Fellows, Daniel 206, 207, 211
Daniel (Jr.) 215, 216
Danl. (Jr.) 213
Henry Osborn 213
Hiram 216
Sally 207
William 215
Fennye, John 603
Ferguson, John 120, 124, 198
Mary (Mrs.) 120, 124
William 135
Wm. 132, 133, 134, 135
Fernessyde, John 537
Ferniside, John 514
Ferris, Samuel 694
William 695
Feuster, Jane 640
Ffarefax, Thomas (Sir) 607
Ffish, Elnathan 245
Ffisher, William 243
Ffittsrandolf, Edward 610
Ffobes, goodman 532
Ffolger, Bethiah 254
Ffoord, Elizabeth 245
Samuel 247
Susanna 245
William 247
Fford, Elisha 246
Experience 244
Hannah 247
Margaret 245
Martha 247
Mellicent 242
Mercy 243
Michael 243
William 246
William (Jr.) 242
Ffoster, (?) 604
Edward 609
Elizabeth 243
George 506
John 60
Mary 244
Ffowles, Philip 80
Ffoxwell, (?) 609, 610
Martha 607
Ffreeman, Davide 76
Ffuller, Joanna 247
John 87
Samuel 507
Samuell 506
Ffullinton, John 246
Ficth, Jno. 51
Ficthes, John 50
Fiefield, Abednego 287
Field, (?) 288
Anna 17
Daniel 7
Edward 288
Elizabeth 6
John 6
Lydia 6
Mary 1
Richard 7
Sarah 9
Susanna 1, 3, 4, 9
Fillmore, (?) 288
Daniel 288
Finla, Gunino 116
Finney, (?) 548, 602
Esther 4
John 501, 597
Lurania 4
Mary 559
Robt 538
Robte. 502
Zeruah 487
Finny, John 600
Fish(er), Henry 221
Henry (Sr.) 221
James 220
Fish, (?) (Widow) 187
Alven 594
Asa 288
Benjamin 226
Betsey Freeman 230
Caroline 227
Cecelia (Mrs.) 534
Cinthy (Mrs.) 230
Dan. 194
Daniel 195
Deborah 457
Deborah (Mrs.) 379
Dinah (Mrs.) 186
Easter (Mrs.) 187
Ebenezar 379
Eliza 227
Elizabeth (Mrs.) 594
Ellis 195, 594
Ellis H. 227
Freeman 226
Gamaliel 196
Hannah (Mrs.) 288, 594
Henry 182, 183, 195, 227
Isaack 457
James (Jr.) 188, 189, 195
Jedidah 209
John 148, 198, 209, 503, 534
Jonan. 195
Jonathan 503
Jos. 187
Joseph 222
Fish (cont.)
Lot C. 227
Lucy 228
Lydia (Jr.) 454
Lydia (Mrs.) 196
Mary 379
Mary (Mrs.) 380
Mehitable 146
Mercy 593
Nathan 227, 288
Nathan D. 226
Nathaniel 455
Nathaniell 503
Nathanll. 380
Nathl. 179, 181, 534, 541
Oliff 454
Peggy 195
Reuben 288
Richard 196
Robert 80, 193
Ruth 594
Sally 198
Sally (Mrs.) 195
Saml. 183, 185, 186
Sarah 198, 209, 455
Simeon 288
Stephen 594
Theodore 288
Thomas 191, 209, 244, 456
Timothy 227, 230
W. H. (Rev.) 427
Williams 380
Zacheus 455
Zipporah 226
Fisher, (?) 288
(?) (Mrs.) 218
(?) (Rev.) 645
Abiah 288
Abigail (Widow) 212
Abner 216
Amazh. 201, 213
Amaziah 216
Amaziah (Jr.) 213
Andrew 214, 220
Bartlett 200, 216
Charles 227
Coatny 200
Coffin 201
Daniel 629, 636
Danl. 205
Delia B. 288
Eleazer 633
Eliezer 629, 636
Elizabeth 197
Elizabeth (Mrs.) 216
Francis 205
Frederick 206
Freeborn 213
Gamaliel 206, 217
Hana 636
Hannah 628, 643
Henry 216, 288
Henry (Jr.) 220
Hepsibah (Mrs.) 200
Israell 636
James 207
James Harry 288
John 204, 636
Jonathan 197, 288
Jonathan (Jr.) 218
Joseph 215
Leonard 288
Levy 213
Lydia 209
Lydia (Mrs.) 203
Maltiah 288

Gage (cont.)
685, 698
Thankful (Widow) 697
Thomas 680
Thomas (Gov.) 482
William 680
Zenas 683
Gaishet, Henry 629
Gale, (?) 289
Amory (Dr.) 422
Edmond 289
Patty (Mrs.) 422
Gall, Bryant 280
Peggy 280
Gallagher, John 290
William 290
Gallon, Bethyah Woodard
406
Willm (Jr.) 406
Willm. 431
Gallow, Margaret 413
Willm. 413, 431
Gallup, (?) (Cpt.) 85
Galop, Samuel 93
Gammel, Andrew 2
Ganett, Hanah (Mrs.) 536
Lydia (Mrs.) 536
Matthew 536
Gannatt, Matthew 520
Thomas 520
Gannet, Benjamin 14
Betty 16
Enoch 470
Hannah 21, 618
Jacob 470
Joseph 618
Joseph (Jr.) 12, 618
Lucinda 27
Mary 12
Mary (Mrs.) 618
Matthew 14, 618
Micah 618
Seth 14
Gannett, Armelia 26
Deborah (Mrs.) 19
Hannah 12
Jacob? 469
Jonathan 488
Joseph 412, 469, 547
Joseph (Cpt.) 19
Matthew 23
Mehetable 20
Mehitable 1
Richard 503
Ruth 412
Sarah 2
Thomas 502
Gardiner, Richard 499
Gardner, (?) (Rev.) 242
Abel 259
Abigail 271
Abigail (Mrs.) 290
Abigaile (Mrs.) 259
Albert 290
Alexander (Jr.) 290
Alic (Mrs.) 489
Alice 490
Almira (Mrs.) 311
Amos 486
Andrew 259
Ann Maria 290
Anson 299
Anstrep (Mrs.) 311
Barnabas 267
Benjamin 256, 290
Bethiah 255
Betsey 291
Charity 579
Gardner (cont.)
Charles 290
Charles Lee 290
Charlse 269
Damaris 255
Daniel 290, 311, 468
David 459
Deborah 256
Dinah 272
Dorcas 311
Ealenor 628
Ebenezer 259, 290
Ebinezer 267
Edmund 290
Edward 290
Edward Barnard 290
Edward Pollard 290
Elihu 290
Elijah 290
Eliza 299
Eliza Ann 290
Elizabeth 34, 191,
260, 308
Elizabeth (Mrs.) 290
Elizabeth (Widow) 72
Emmaline Coffin 290
Eunice 208, 290
Francis 290
Franklin 290
Frederick 290
George 290
George C. 290
George Ellis 290
George Washington 311
Gilbert 290
Grafton 290
Grindal 271, 290
Grispus 290
Hannah 259
Henry (III) 290
Henry C. 290
Hephzibah 271
Hephzibath 267
Hope 254, 256
James (Rev.) 245
Jared 290
Jared (Cpt.) 308
Jemima 259
Jesse 290
Jethro 290
John 255, 259, 263,
290
Joseph 254, 255, 256,
290, 468
Joshua 290
Josiah 291
Judith 259
Judith (Mrs.) 290
Lamuel 259
Latham 290
Leah 268
Levi 290
Lidia 256
Love 254
Lucretia (Mrs.) 290
Lydia 271
Lydia Andrews 290
Margaret 259, 271
Margaret (Mrs.) 290
Martha 630
Martha Ann 290
Mary 261, 484
Matthew 259
Mehetable 260
Mehitable 255
Merab (Mrs.) 290
Mercy (Mrs.) 290
Miriam 256
Gardner (cont.)
Nathaniel 259
Nathll. 259
Patience 255
Paul 290
Peleg 259, 290
Peter 290
Prisillah 267
Rachel (Mrs.) 421
Reuben 290
Reuben (Jr.) 309
Rich 264
Richard 254, 255, 256,
290
Richard (Jr.) 255, 256
Robert 57, 259
Rowland 290
Ruth 255, 259, 271
Ruth (Mrs.) 290
Sally 309
Samuel 69, 72, 290
Samuel (Lt.) 72
Sarah 254, 257, 308
Sarah G. 291
Seth 421
Shubael 272, 290
Shubael (Sr.) 290
Shubal 271
Silas 290
Silvanus 290, 300
Simeon 290
Solomon 256
Susanna 459
Susannah 259, 300
Thomas 290
Thomas A. 291
Timothy 290
Timothy (Jr.) 290
Timothy M. 290
Timothy Myrick 290
Tristram 208, 290
Uriah 270, 290
William 290, 291
William Henry 290, 291
Zaccheus 308
Zenas 291
william 267
Gardnr, Samll. 69
Garet, Richard 514
Garey, Mary 490
Garfield, (?) (Pres.)
443
Garnet, Alexander 455
Alice 455
Beersheba (Mrs.) 481
Hannah 454
Huldah 454
James 351
Jams. 351
Jane (Mrs.) 351
Lucee 454
Lydia 453
Nabby 456
Samuel 481
samuel 481
Garnett, Beersheba
(Mrs.) 481
Samuel 481
samuel 481
Garrat, (?) 503
Garret, John 326
Joseph 313, 323
Lidiah 326
Martha 593
Richard 313
Ruth 323
Garrett, Elizabeth
(Mrs.) 541

Garrett (cont.)
John 314
Joseph 324, 620
Mary 315, 324
Nathaniel 314
Richard 314, 315, 515, 621
Garrt, James 165
Gary, Mary 467
Stephen 631
Gaschit, David 630
Gashee, Elijah 582
Samuel 582
Gatchel, Isabel 79, 80
Isabell 79
Mary 56
Priscila 79
Prisilla 80
Gatchell, (?) 144
Mary 56
Priscilla 79
Gates, Andrew 291
Gaunt, Peter 503, 509
Gaut, Elijah 165
Gay, (?) (Mrs.) 493
(?) (Rev.) 379, 381, 395, 401
Ebenezer (Rev.) 493
Gayer, Damaris 255, 257
Dorcas 255, 257, 259
William 255
Willian 255
Willm. 255
Gayns, Hannah 169
Gehton, Samuel 291
Gelston, Betsey 278
Samuel (Dr.) 278
Susanna J. (Mrs.) 295
Genkins, Matthew 257
Thomas 257
Gent, Eliza 165
Geofry, Mol 453
George, Ricd. 92
Gerald, (?) 291
Groten 696
Groton 695, 696
Hannah 679
Timothy 291
Gerrold, James 292
Gerry, Elbridge 689
Ghorham, Joseph 666, 669
Nancy 666
Samuel 669
Sarah (Mrs.) 669
Sary (Mrs.) 666
Gibbes, Joh 649
Joshua (Jr.) 649
Gibbs, Elnathan 291
Hannah (Mrs.) 291
Henry 291
James 291
John 291
Martha (Mrs.) 291
Samuel 291
Silvanus 291
Susanna 99
Susannah 191, 209
Thomas 291, 503
William 291
Gibson, Elizabeth 246
James 693
Gidloo, Annes 144
Gifford, Abigail 158
Abraham 158
Adam 155
Alden 594
Ann (Mrs.) 155
Benjamin 158
Gifford (cont.)
Deborah N. 227
Elizabeth 127
Fear 127
Hananiah 158
Job 158
Keziah 158
Martha 158
Martha (Mrs.) 158
Mary 145, 158
Mary (Mrs.) 158
Mercy (Mrs.) 594
Patience 158
Peace 155
Pricilla 158
Prince 694
Rebecca 146
Robert 291
Rose 126
Rositer 228
Ruth 158
Ruth (Mrs.) 291
Silas 155
Simeon 158
Stephen 147, 158
Susanna 158
Susannah 158
Sylvina N. 228
Thomas 158
William 155
Gifforord, meribah 146
Giford, Joseph (Jr.) 649
Gilbert, Benjamin 350
Daniel 350
Eleazer 642
Elisabeth 630
Elizabeth 642
Giles 35, 36, 44, 642
Gyles 525
Hanah 639
Jane (Mrs.) 639
John 509, 525, 642
John (Sr.) 525
Joseph 525, 642
Judeth (Mrs.) 350
Judith 9
Mary 525, 631, 639
Mary (Mrs.) 49
Mehitabel 639
Mercy 631, 642
Nathaniel 639
Pelatiah 19
Sarah 639
Susana 631
Thomas 66, 78, 83, 504, 525, 547, 639
Winnifred (Mrs.) 525
Gilberte, Giles 36
Giles, David 291
David Upham 291
George Barnard 291
Lurana 290
Mary 291
Paul 291
Gilford, Agatha 352
Eliz. (Mrs.) 350, 363
Elizabeth 363
Elizabeth (Mrs.) 350, 352, 362
John 362
Susannah 350
William 350, 362
Willm. 350
Wm. 352, 363
Gilkey, Grace (Mrs.) 383, 386, 395
Jacob 399
James 383, 386, 395, 399
Gilkey (cont.)
Rachel 383
Gilkie, Grace (Mrs.) 388, 392
Jaames 388
James 392
John 388
Lucresia 392
Gill, Abigail 163
Abijah 173, 174
Amelia 167, 170
Apphia 164
Asa 165
Basset 94
Betsy 164
Caroline 170, 174
Chloe 167
Daniel 165
David 162
Hannah 623
Heman S. 176
Joanna 163
Josiah A. 164
Lewis A. 173
Lidia 163
Mercy 163
Nathan 166
Nathan A. 169
Phebe 163
Rebecca 165
Rebekah 167, 170
Susanna 163
Tabitha M. 166
William 166
Gillmor, Andrew 583
Hannah 582
Isabel 583
Israel 583
James 583
Mercy 583
Gillmore, Lesenda (Mrs.) 584
Gillsonn, (?) 609
Gilmor, Abigail (Mrs.) 560
Andrew 560
Arba 561
Buara 561
Chloe 561
Chloe (Mrs.) 561
Daniel 560
Elisha 560
Hannah 560
James 560
Lemuel 560
Mercy 560
Nabby 561
Ornan 561
Peres 560
Samuel 561
Gilmore, Mary 582
Gilpin, Anthony 520
Gilson, (?) 595
Francis (Mrs.) 509
William 509
Gilsonn, (?) 595
Gingell, John 45
Ginings, (?) 602
Ginkins, Edward 510
Thomas 430
Gladding, Mary 629
Glading, John (Jr.) 76
Mary 633, 645
Glapp, Abigail 412
Glass, Eame 620
Hannah 547, 620
James 518

Gorham (cont.)
678, 679, 681
Sally (Widow) 695, 697
Samll. 655
Samuel 654, 669
Sarah 664
Sarah (Mrs.) 611, 665, 667, 668, 669, 670, 671, 673, 680
Sarah (Widow) 682
Sary (Mrs.) 666, 672
Stephen 612
Steven 651
Sukey 680
Susan 692
Sylvanus 614
Temperance 612
Thacher 680
Thankful 613
Thatcher 689
james 685
Gorton, John 266
Gorum, John 535, 538
Gould, Abigail 173, 441
Alice Roberts 449
Benjamin 442
Bethiah 222
Betsy P. 166
Dan B. 447, 449
Dan B. (Mrs.) 447, 449
Daniel 60
Daniel B. 444, 448, 449
Daniel B. (Mrs.) 448
Dannie B. 446
Dannie B. (Mrs.) 446
Emmeline (Mrs.) 448
Ephraim 488
Ethan 94
Franklin 446
Grace 483
Grace (Widow) 487
Hana 639
Hannah 9, 455, 489
Hannah R. 444
Horace 136
Isaac L. 449
James Alvers 443
John 60, 164, 483, 639
John (Cpt.) 99, 222
Joseph (Mrs.) 446
Josiah 440
Laura A. 175
Lewis A. 173
Lillian Madaline 449
Mary 483, 639
Mary (Mrs.) 67
Mercy 448
Morey 441
Nathaniel 163
Phebe 168, 173
Polly 174
Polly (Mrs.) 136
Rebecca C. 175
Ruth 443
Ruth S. 175
Sally 163, 444
Tamson 166, 169
Thomas 174, 440, 483
Tilson 488
William 483, 487
William (Jr.) 484, 485, 486, 487
Willie F. 446
Goulder, Francis 502
Goumer, Johannah (Mrs.) 237
Priscilla 237
Goumer (cont.)
Rebeckah 237
William 237
Goute, Sally W. 172
Goval, Jethro 0
Gra, Elizabth. 236
Patience (Mrs.) 236
Samuel 236
Graham, James W. 176
Grandison, Harriot 412
Granger, Calvin 291
Elizabeth 514
Grace (Mrs.) 514
John 248, 514
Grant, (?) (Gen.) 444
Gilbert 82
James 291
Graunger, John 521
Thomas 514
Graunt, Hannah 588
Grause, Willm 504
Gray, (?) 196, 688, 689
Betsy 676
Chandler 664, 682, 695, 696, 697
Charles 689
Desire 546
Dezire (Mrs.) 236
Edward 505, 544, 546, 664
Elisabeth 680
Elizabeth 383
Elizabeth (Mrs.) 291, 672, 673, 674, 675, 677, 679
Elizabth. 236
Ephraim 636
Francis 19
Freeman 127
George 375, 696
Gidion 679
Hanah 663
Hannah 657, 682, 690
Henry 674, 682
Hirem 678
Hirum 678
Jacob 663
James 389
John 126, 212, 504, 542, 659, 672, 673, 674, 675, 677, 679, 680, 689
John (Col.) 236
Joseph 35, 196, 546, 636, 646, 673
Joshua 656, 657, 658, 659, 660, 662, 664
Joshua (Cpt.) 696
Leveret 661
Levet 661
Lucretia 682
Lucy 682, 689
Luke 193, 196
Lydia 677
Lydia (Mrs.) 659, 660, 661, 662, 663, 664, 665, 666, 667
Lydia Atwood 665
Lydia T. 687
Mahitabell 636
Marcy (Mrs.) 662
Mary 236, 389, 659, 664, 682, 687, 691
Mary (Mrs.) 656, 657, 658, 659, 660, 664
Mary (Widow) 693, 697
Molly 660
Molly (Mrs.) 679
Gray (cont.)
Nancy 659
Oliver 662, 672
Patience (Mrs.) 236
Phebe 660, 674
Phebe (Mrs.) 680
Polly 673
Polly (Mrs.) 673, 674, 676, 678, 679
Puella (Mrs.) 212
Rebecca 673
Rebecka (Mrs.) 636
Rebekah (Widow) 696
Richard 673, 674, 676, 678, 679, 687, 695
Richard (Jr.) 696
Russel 679
Ruth 667, 673
Salle 666
Samuel 236, 659, 660, 661, 662, 663, 664, 665, 666, 667, 675, 679, 682, 696
Sarah 243, 379, 658
Sarah (Mrs.) 375, 379
Sukey 672
Thomas 236, 375, 379, 501, 548, 656, 682, 697
Thos. 383
William 291, 696
Winslow (Cpt.) 691
Wm. 543
Zenas 167
Zenus 171
Grays, (?) 182
Gre(e)nough, Ginne (Mrs.) 674
Sally 674
Thomas 674
Green, Abisha 229
Abishai 229
Abisher 226
Allen 228
Ana 226
Benjamin 226, 291
Caleb 291
Elizabeth 53
Evelina 229
Hannah 18, 245, 311
Hannah (Mrs.) 131, 656
J. 650
Jno. 55, 57
John 52, 55, 56, 57, 58, 79, 80, 286, 291, 529
John (Maj.) 79
Joseph 71, 129, 656
Joseph (Jr.) 650
Martha 656
Martha M. 174
Rebecca 229
Sarah 246, 286, 337
Sarah G. (Mrs.) 291
Thomas 268, 584
Timothy 131
Greene, John 503
Joseph 502
Greenel, Daniel 74, 79, 80
Jonathan 73
Mary 80
Richard 79
Greenell, Mary (Mrs.) 79
Greenfeild, Thomas 503
Greenhalge, F. T. (Gov.) 448
Greenlaw, Lucy Hall

Greenlaw (cont.)
(Mrs.) 35, 41, 48, 56, 63, 71, 78, 85
Greenleaf, Daniel (Rev.) 451
Greenough, Jane (Mrs.) 673
John 695, 697, 698
Thomas 673, 695, 698
Greens, John 53
Greenwood, Esther 589, 591
Hannah 587
John 587
Noah 588
Greenwoods, (?) 70
Gregory, John 427
Grew, Barzillai 292
Jervis 292
Rebecca 227
Samuel B. 292
Grey, (?) 181
Joseph (Sr.) 78
Grey?, Parmelia 165
Griffeth, Joseph 658
Sarah 658
Thankfull (Mrs.) 658
Griffin, Elisabeth 3
Mary 565
Samll. 411
Simon 2
Griffith, Desire 656
Frederick W. 292
Hannah 656
Joseph 656, 658
Sarah 658
Thankful (Mrs.) 656
Thankfull (Mrs.) 658
Griffth, Wm. 537
Griggs, Mary 631
Nabby 457
Willam 457
Grindey, Martha 267
Grinell, Daniell 32
Grinnell, Benjamin 32
Grome, John 501
Grose, John 625
Gross, Alexander 551
Edmond 397
Edmund 338, 380, 383, 385
Elisabeth (Mrs.) 551
Elish 411
Janne 551
John 380
Micah 551
Oliffe (Mrs.) 383
Olive 385
Olive (Mrs.) 338, 380, 385, 397
Roxana 625
Grosvenor, (?) (Rev.) 595
Grove, Richard 194
Groves, Ephraim 15
Joseph 292
Susa 26
Grozier, Joshua Freeman 551
Martha (Mrs.) 551
William 551
Guild, Lewis A. 173
Gulliford, Henry 251
Gurney, Elisabeth 631
Elisha 2
Ephraim 292
Hannah 21
James (Rev.) 292
Gurney (cont.)
John 4
Mary Jane 292
Micah 3
Molly 25
Ruth 18, 646
Seth 25
Sylvia 29
Zachariah 2
Gurnsey, Elisabeth 2
Gurrell, Hannah (Mrs.) 292
Hannah Mariah 292
John 292
John (Jr.) 292
John (Jr.) (Cpt.) 292
William 292
Gushee, Hannah 567
Gusshee, Silvia (Widow) 583
Gwinn, Zebdial 292
Gwinne, Mehitable 621
H---, Robert 145
Hach, Elizabeth (Mrs.) 342
Lydia 342
Samuel 342
Hack, Mary (Mrs.) 537
William 537, 638
Wm. 638
Hacket, Asael 584
Eleanor 7
Hackit, Hana 636
Hannah 628
Jabez 636
Jabez (Sr.) 636
John 628, 631, 636
Mary 636
Samuel 629, 644
Samuell 636
Sarah 628, 636
Hadawa, After 649
Haden, Deborah 8
Sam. Chanler 502
Wm. 402
Hagadarn, Jacob 292
Mary Dame 292
Haggett, Polly 292
William S. 292
Hailes, Aarthur 62
Hailston, William 519
Hailstone, Willm 504
Wm. 521
Haines, John 7
Hait, (?) 609
Haite, (?) 609
Hale, (?) (Dr.) 524
Joseph 690
Halet, Enoch 661
Rhoda 661
Thankful (Mrs.) 661
Haley, Silas 691
Hall, Abigail 14, 573
Abigail (Mrs.) 561
Adam 247
Adrastus 573
Amariah 583
Amos 562, 572
Anna 582
Artherton 669
Atherton 669
Beniamin 599, 600
Benjamin 601, 638
Bethiah 578, 666
Bezer 573
Brian 573
Charity 541, 644
David 292, 561, 698
Hall (cont.)
Dorothy 456
Ebenezer 573, 630, 634
Edmund 561
Edward 502, 543, 660, 669
Eliphalet 573
Elisabeth 568
Elisha 561, 666, 674
Eliza 686
Elizabeth 562, 628, 629, 634, 642, 644
Elizabeth (Widow) 643
Elkanah 561
Enoch 642
Ester (Mrs.) 543
Eunice T. 693
Ezekiel 662
Garshom 679
Geo. 535
George 520, 530, 541
Gershom 599, 666, 680
Gershum 679
Goarge 634
Gorham 659
Hannah 561, 562, 568, 582, 584, 630, 638
Hannah (Mrs.) 561, 572, 573, 583, 667
Henry 689
Hezekiah 573, 644
Huldah 572
Isaac 530, 666, 667, 674, 679
Isaac (Jr.) 674
Isaack 652
Isaak 583
Jacob 638
James 484, 561, 632, 638, 658
Jemima 572
John 45, 77, 78, 384, 504, 540, 541, 543, 561, 562, 572, 598, 599, 600, 601, 629, 633, 634, 638, 644, 652, 658, 659, 660, 662, 663, 664, 693
John (III) 573
John (Sr.) 55
Jona. 573
Jonathan 561, 562, 572, 573, 641
Jonathan (Jr.) 572
Joseph 541, 561, 598, 638
Joshua 680, 697, 698
Josiah 644
Keziah 454
Laurentia 455
Linus 573
Lois 573
Luther (Mrs.) 449
Lydia 572
Lydia (Mrs.) 572, 573
Macy 561
Mahitabel 642
Mary 561, 629, 634, 642, 663
Mary (Mrs.) 541, 573, 674
Mason 562
Mehetabel 17
Mehitable 558
Mercy 666
Mercy (Mrs.) 593
Molly (Mrs.) 674
Nabby 674

Hamblin (cont.)
Elisabeth 14, 660
Elisha 612
Emeline 692
Europe 462
Experience 612
Hiram 228
Ichabod 612
Isaac 660, 661, 686
Isaac (Cpt.) 697, 698
Isaac (Jr.) 669
Isaac H. (Cpt.) 227
Israel 616
James 504, 612
James (Jr.) 611
Jas (Jr.) 543
Jemima 616
Job 611
John 612
Joseph 612, 660, 662
Joseph (Mrs.) 698
Joshua 661, 677, 678, 690, 698
Joshua (Col.) 680, 682, 695
Joshua (Widow) 682
Kesiah 688
Kezia 669
Keziah 660
Keziah (Mrs.) 660
Louisa 228
Lucretia 227
Lydia (Mrs.) 677
Mary (Mrs.) 611, 612
Mehetabel 612
Mehetable (Mrs.) 612
Mercy 612
Nathan (Cpt.) 227
Olive 680, 693
Patience 612
Polly 677
Polly (Mrs.) 677, 678, 680
Sally (Mrs.) 686
Samll. 612
Sarah (Mrs.) 612
Seth 660, 677
Seth (Cpt.) 227
Susanah 662
Susanna 612
Susanna (Mrs.) 612, 614
Susannah (Mrs.) 660, 662
William 230
Hamedon, Ann 246
Hamet, Robt. 179
Hamillen, Charles 693
Hamilton, (?) 115, 116
Elijah 172
Enoch S. 173
James 96, 110
Mulford 94
Paul 94
Thomas 99
Hamlen, Benjamin 665
Elisabeth 652
Hannah 650
Isaack 651
Joseph 652, 665
Phoebe 650
Rebecca 652
Susannah (Mrs.) 665
Hamlin, (?) 105
Abigail (Mrs.) 615
Abner 458
Asia 468, 487
Cyrus 466
Hamlin (cont.)
David 459
Ebenezer 617
Eleazer 463, 464, 465, 466, 468, 469, 486, 487, 616
Elizabeth (Mrs.) 616, 617
Hannibal 466
Isaac 457, 458, 459, 616, 617
Israel 615
Joseph 615, 653
Lydia 463
Lydia (Mrs.) 486
Mary 1
Mercy (Mrs.) 617
Molly 465
Prudence 615
Reliance 614
Sarah 469
Susan 614
Thankful 615
Hamling, Bartlemew 598
Eliazer 600
Israell 600
James 598, 599, 600, 601
John 599
Sarah 599
Hamlington, mary 268
Hammatt, Benjamin 292
John Howland 426
William 292
Wm. 420, 426
Hammer, John 535, 610
Hammet, (?) 111
Abigail 111
Edward 630
Joseph 190
Robert 199
Robt. 182
Thankful 184
Hammett, Benj. 127
Jane (Mrs.) 190
Joseph 191
Rob. 190
Robert 191
Thankful 191
Hammilton, William 247
Hammon, Agatha 361
Benjm. 361, 378
Elizabeth (Mrs.) 361, 596
Jedidiah 361
John 503
Joseph 243, 361
Sarah 378
Sarah (Mrs.) 378
William 79
Hammond, Aaron 2
Barzillai 292
Benj. 533
Mary 2
Nathaniel 4
Otis G. 265, 268
Rebecca 3
Sarah 3
Thomas 4
Hammot, Hannah 489
Hamond, Benjamin 504
Hampton, Sarah (Mrs.) 35
Thomas 509
Hanard, (?) 448
Hanbury, Peter 503
Wm. 501
Hance, Fredrick 170
Hanckford, Richard 507
Hancock, Betsey 121, 136
Fanny (Mrs.) 138
James 123, 132, 133, 134, 135
John 139, 140
Juliana 129
Nathaniel (Rev.) 647
Philura 129
Saml (Cpt.) 124
Samuel 136, 137, 138
Handcock, (?) 111, 112
Handford, Egglin 602
Lettice 602
Margaret 602
Handy, Rebecca (Widow) 292
Zaccheus 593
Hanford, Egglin 596
Tho. 536
Thomas 502, 512
Hanian, Toney we 631
Hanks, Abigail (Mrs.) 344
Benjamin 246, 344
Elisabeth (Widow) 28
Elizabeth 344
James 457, 484
John 508
Joseph 469, 487
Rachel 28, 469
Sarah 457
Hanlone, Lemuel (Rev.) 166
Hanmer, Abigail 358
Abigail (Mrs.) 358
Benjm. 358
Elizabeth 2
Hannah 316
Jerusha 14
John 15, 316, 610
Joseph 358
Mary 14
Hanmoe, Rebecca 623
Hanmore, John 533
Haray, (?) 263
Hard, David 582
Harden, Deborah 28
Freeman (Jr.) 172
Gideon 687
Hannah 18
Harlow 27
Jacob 20
John 165
John (Jr.) 20, 29
Lydia 12
Nathaniel 8
Perry 455
Rebecca 22
Reuben 22
Samuel 12, 24
Sarah 11
Seth 484
Susanna 484
Wilbur 688
Hardin, Gideon (Cpt.) 696
Hannah (Mrs.) 696
Rebecca 472
Reuben 472
Harding, Abigail 7
Abram 484
Charles L. 175
Chloe 475
Eliza 164
Elizabeth S. 173
Eunice S. 167, 170
Hanry 175
Harlow 469

Harding (cont.)
Henry 169, 446
Isaac 469
Isaiah 94
Joe 476
John 502
Joseph 546
Lucy 172
Martha 507
Mary B. 173
Nathaniel 487, 488, 490
Polly C. 165
Prince 165
Reuben 475, 476, 477, 492
Ruben 489
Salome Barstow 473
Samuel 469, 470, 473, 487
Seth 473
Simeon 230
Simon 226
Sparrow 93
Sylvina 470
Tamzin (Widow) 94
Hardy, Isaac (Jr.) 94
Solomon (Rev.) 168
Harlock, (?) (Mrs.) 113
Bethiah 208
Mary 180, 198
Thomas 208
Thos. 223
Harlow, Joanna 31
Mary 351
Mary (Mrs.) 351, 547
Rebeccah 146
Samll. 351
Samuel 146
William 228, 230, 544, 545, 547, 548
William (Rev.) 229
Wm 540
Wm. 509
mary (Mrs.) 351
Harman, John 501
Harmon, Nathaniel 513
Harney, Mary 445
Harper, Anna 220
Bathsheba 197, 209, 210
Hannah 180
Hannah (Mrs.) 189
John 189, 209, 210, 220, 222, 301
John (Cpt.) 221
Katherine 210
Love 184
Martha 221
Susannah 197, 222
Harps, Eunice (Mrs.) 292
John 292, 293
Nathaniel Chadwick 293
Harrice, Jane 595
Harrington, Elias 229
Elias B. 693
Joseph Henry 229
Josse Hatch 229
Harris, Abiel 4
Abrahm. 425
Abrm. 424
Alice 1
Ann 11
Arthur 11, 12, 21, 502, 528, 532
Benjamin 14
Benjamin (Jr.) 26
David 293
Harris (cont.)
David (Cpt.) 284
Elizabeth 9
Enoch 424
George 293
Isaac 9
James 6
Jane 6
John 27
Jonathan 285
Joseph 293
Mary 8, 311
Patience 311
Polly (Mrs.) 419
Richard 66
Samuel 7, 425
Sarah 19, 284
Seth 4
Stephen 425
Sukey 285
Susanna 285
Susannah 6
William 25
Harry, (?) 263
Elisabeth (Widow) 518
Hart, Archepas 151
Deborah 151
Hannah 151
Hart 151
Lydia 151
Mary 151
Sarah 383
Sarah (Mrs.) 151
Thomas 147
William 147, 151, 383
Hartopp, Wm. 502
Hartshorn, Davis 293
Harvey 293
Hartub, Will 502
Hartwell, Martha 2
Harvey, Elisabeth 12
Experience 7
John 631, 643
Jonathan 643
Joseph 643
Mary 8, 12
Thomas 643
Thomas (Sr.) 67, 643
William 643
Wm. 536
Harvy, Thomas 44
Harwood, Charles E. (Rev.) 449
Hascall, Susanna 632
Hascol, John 253
John (Jr.) 252
Jonathan 253
Sarah 253
Sqier 252
Haskell, Bathsheba (Mrs.) 594
Haskill, Benjamin Franklin 293
Benjamin Worth 293
Sarah (Mrs.) 293
Haskin, Richard 82
Haskins, Richard 628, 640
Samll. 68
Sarah 629
Tho. 540
Zipporah 556
Hassett, Hingham Coney 349
Hat(c)h, Hannah 375
Jeremiah 337
Thomas 375
Zerviah 375
Hatch, (?) 124, 376, 462, 472
(?) (Widow) 312
(?) Turner 414
(Nymphas) (Rev.) 128
Abby D. 176
Abigail 163, 323, 384
Abigail (Mrs.) 525
Adelia 228, 229
Alice 620, 623
Allen 463
Amanda 228
Amos 456
Ann 375, 517, 622
Anna 391
Anne 146, 466, 489
Annie 617
Annie (Mrs.) 617
Anson 406
Antipas 316
Artimissa 405
Benj. 617
Benjamin 226, 356, 617
Bethaia 317
Bethiah 243
Betsey 469, 489
Betsey (Mrs.) 131, 132, 230
Betsy 226
Betty 32
Bezaliel 376
Charlotte 465
Chloe 230
Clarissa 229
Cyrus 127, 131, 132
Daniel 376
David 345, 369, 376, 618
Deborah 358, 419, 464, 472
Deborah (Mrs.) 358, 363
Desire 332
Ebenezer 229, 617
Edmond C. 228
Edy 617
Elijah 405
Elisha 454
Elizabeth 345, 465, 617, 622
Elizabeth (Mrs.) 293, 332, 334, 343, 345, 359, 618
Elizebeth 324
Ellis (Mrs.) 617
Elvira T. 174
Frances (Mrs.) 336, 366
Freeman 164, 173
Freeman Peale 230
George 416
Gibbs 293
Grace 364
Grace (Mrs.) 333, 356, 361, 364, 428, 529
Hanna 312
Hannah 313, 323, 617, 623
Hannah (Mrs.) 345, 346, 371, 380
Hannah (Widow) 410
Harriot N. 229
Harris 456
Henry Y. 174
Hephzibeth 615
Hezekiah 372, 373, 380, 384, 386
Hzekiah 377

Hatch (cont.)
Ibanny 164
Ichabod 617
Isaac 228, 229, 230, 356, 357, 358, 364, 366, 368, 371, 374, 376, 429, 453
Isaace 326
Isaiah 226, 229
Isaiah T. 449
Israel 334, 345, 622
Israel (Jr.) 372
James 465, 466, 467, 469
James (Cpt.) 470, 489, 490
James H. 227
James S. 173, 175
Jane 243, 315, 372, 517
Jane (Mrs.) 517
Jane (Widow) 623
Jedediah 362
Jemima 409
Jeremia 321, 325
Jeremiah 321, 327, 333, 336, 356, 363, 366, 375, 379, 623
Jeremiah (Jr.) 358
Jeremy 316, 317
Jerimya 324
Joannah 321
John 244, 329, 333, 361, 383, 402, 405, 409, 415, 418, 428, 462, 463, 464, 466, 468, 469, 489, 503, 617
John (Jr.) 345, 346, 356, 364, 428
Jonath. 415
Jonath. (Jr.) 405
Jonathan 227, 345, 380
Jonathan (Jr.) 405, 414
Jonth. (Jr.) 406
Joseph 323, 375, 617
Joshua 389
Josia 322
Josiah 358
Judith 454
Keturah 324
Keziah 617
Liddiah 603
Lidia 324, 325
Lidya 345
Lovisa 28
Lucy 122, 226, 412
Lucy (Mrs.) 130, 131, 418
Lucy N. 228
Lurenna 468
Lusannah Ruggles 416
Luther 26
Lydia 315, 453, 537, 617, 621
Lydia (Mrs.) 358, 617
Lydiah 368
M. B. (Mrs.) 230
Macael 393
Malatiah 617
Marah (Mrs.) 322
Margaret 324
Maria (Mrs.) 422
Mark M. 227
Martha 379
Martha (Mrs.) 372, 379, 593

Hatch (cont.)
Mary 14, 20, 314, 316, 323, 327, 361, 371, 429, 462, 465
Mary (Mrs.) 369, 389, 391
Mary B. (Mrs.) 230
Mehetabal 346
Mercy 16, 321, 373
Mercy C. 228
Micael 379, 380, 383, 384, 387, 389, 430
Micah 338, 430
Mical 386
Michael 377, 393, 397, 402, 403
Minerva 176
Molly northy 393
Moses 615
Nathan 366
Nathan M. 175
Nathaniel 226, 228, 470, 489, 617
Nehemiah 372, 379, 389, 391, 393, 398
Nymphas (Rev.) 647
Patience 377
Patience (Mrs.) 372, 373, 376, 377
Penelipa 333
Penelipa (Mrs.) 368
Penelipah (Mrs.) 429
Penellope 364
Penelopa (Mrs.) 374
Penelope 453
Penelope (Mrs.) 364
Penelopia (Mrs.) 371
Penelopy (Mrs.) 376
Phebe 229, 465, 525
Phoebe 314
Priscilla 380
Priscilla (Mrs.) 338, 377, 379, 380, 383, 384, 386, 389, 397
Rachel (Jr.) 226
Rebeca 617
Reiuben 226
Reuben 126, 130, 131
Rhoda 403
Rhoda (Mrs.) 229, 230
Rodolpus 323
Roxanna 227
Ruben 372, 389
Ruth 343, 386, 617
Sally 172
Samll. (Jr.) 343, 359
Samuel 101, 314, 322, 326, 327, 337, 359, 376, 617
Samuel (Jr.) 332
Samuell 323
Sarah 226, 324, 366, 374, 386, 453
Sarah (Jr.) 453
Sarah (Mrs.) 357
Sarah M. 175
Seth 429
Seth R. 230
Shubael 293
Silas 230
Silvanus 226, 229, 230
Simeon 188
Sophronia 229
Southward Potter 229
Stephen 357
Susan 164
Susanna 117
Sylvaus 230

Hatch (cont.)
Tabitha 226, 227, 228
Temperance 227
Thankful 387
Thankfull 384
Thirsa 469
Thirza 28
Thomas 230, 323, 324, 371, 372, 504, 510, 517, 529, 621
Thoms 623
Timothy 230, 617
Timothy M. 176
Tryphena 120, 122
Turner 405
Walter 21, 243, 313, 314, 315, 317, 462, 489, 503, 517, 529, 622
Water 316
William 314, 315, 316, 517, 623
William (Jr.) 525
William (Sr.) 517
William J. 293
Willm. 503
Wll 314
Wm. 516, 537, 622
Zach. 116
Zilpah 453
Hatches, (?) 609, 610
John 416
Hathaway, (?) 232
Abigail 642
Abraham 642
Anna (Mrs.) 293
Anne 146
Apphia 145
Arther 65
Arthur 65, 151, 544
Benjamin 221, 293
Charles 158
Charlotte 158
Daniel 158
Ebenezer 642
Ebenezer (Col.) 231
Ebenr. (Cpt.) 232
Elizabeth 146, 148, 293
Elizabeth (Mrs.) 232, 235
Gilbert 232
Hannah 144
Hannah (Mrs.) 231
Isaac 30, 32, 158, 232, 235
Jacob 32, 235
Jael (Cpt.) 235
Joanna 147, 148, 151
Joannah 144
John 69, 144, 145, 146, 147, 148
Jona. 148
Jonathan 144, 146, 148
Jonathan (Sr.) 148
Josiah (Jr.) 16
Jule 235
Mary 144
Nathaniel 293
Nicholas 158
Osman 158
Patience 221
Paul 148
Polly 583
Richard 144
Russell (Cpt.) 235
Ruth (Mrs.) 158
Sarah 32, 144, 146

Hathaway (cont.)
Sarah (Mrs.) 32
Shadrach 231
Simon 151
Susanna (Mrs.) 148
Thomas 144, 642
Zerviah 158
Hatherley, (?) 596
Timothy 509
Hatherly, (?) 512, 522, 609
Lydia (Mrs.) 536
Timothy 512, 514, 523, 531, 532, 534, 536, 537
Hatherlye, (?) 602
Hatheway, Jael (Cpt.) 235
Rebeckah (Mrs.) 235
Hathway, Abigail 631
Abigaile 628
Abraham 88, 628
Charles 158
Charlotte 158
Daniel 158
Ebenezer 631
Hannah 629
Isaac 158, 628, 631
Isaace 67
Jacob 629, 633
Jno. (Sr.) 78
John 67, 69
Mary 67
Nicholas 158
Osman 158
Rebekah 628
Ruth (Mrs.) 158
Zerviah 158
Hatwell, Nathan 1
Havens, Elizabeth 149
George 149
Joseph 149
Robert 65, 149
Ruth 147, 149
William 149
Haward, John 538
Jonathan 628
Robert 502
Thomas 520
Hawes, Adeline 681
Anah 660
Ances 662
Anna 660, 664, 666
Anna (Mrs.) 659
Anner 660, 664
Anner (Mrs.) 660, 662, 663, 664, 665, 666, 667
Anner (Widow) 695
Ansel 662
Benj. 224
Betcy 668, 675
Betsey 687
Betsy 668, 675
Betsy (Mrs.) 672, 675
Bithiah 668
David 659, 660, 662, 663, 664, 665, 666, 667
Dorcas (Mrs.) 209, 224
Ebenezar 674, 681
Ebeneze 664
Ebenezer 658, 659, 660, 662, 672, 681
Ebenezer (Jr.) 673
Ebenr. (Jr.) 674
Edmond 668
Edmond (Cpt.) 697
Hawes (cont.)
Edmund 522, 529, 537, 538
Eliza 655
Eliza (Mrs.) 655
Elizabeth 222
Ezra 659, 663
Gorham 672
Hanah 664
Isaac 666
Isaiah 662
James 650, 668
James W. 94
John 659, 681, 687
Joseph 655, 666, 698
Josiah 660
Josiah Tayler 672
Mary 623, 673
Patience (Mrs.) 681
Prentiss 693
Prince 659, 672, 675
Prince (Jr.) 655
Sally 672, 687
Sarah 672
Shubael 224
Shubal 117
Simeon (Mrs.) 668
Temperance (Mrs.) 658, 659
Temppy (Mrs.) 662
Tempy (Mrs.) 660, 664
Thankful (Mrs.) 666, 672, 673, 674
Thomas 665
William 668
Hawkes, (?) 125
Fear 128
Sylvia 126
Hawkins, Elizabeth 621
James 68
Job 527
Hawland, John 520
Hawley, Polly (Mrs.) 294
William 294
Zaccheus 294
Haws, Anna 664
Anner 664
Anner (Mrs.) 664
David 664
Ebenezer 662, 664
Hanah 664
Isaiah 662
Tempy (Mrs.) 662, 664
Hawse, Abigail 653
Anna (Mrs.) 659
Anner (Mrs.) 663
Bays 650
David 659, 663
Desire 651, 653
Desire (Mrs.) 652
Ebenezar 674
Ebenezer 653
Ebenr. (Jr.) 674
Ezra 663
Hannah 652
Jacob 650
John 659
Joseph 652, 653
Mary 651
Sarah (Mrs.) 653
Solomon 653
Thankful 653
Thankful (Mrs.) 674
Thomas 651, 652
Haxse, Joseph 59
Sarah (Mrs.) 59
Hayden, (?) 377
Abigail 293
Hayden (cont.)
Ada (Mrs.) 445
Benja. 411
Caleb (Mrs.) 446
Caleb S. 440
Chas. Walter 426
Clifton 446
E. Modena 449
Elisha 416, 425, 426
Eliza F. 444
Emmie Modena 448
Frank M. 443
Freeman H. (Mrs.) 444
Josiah 3
Martha 425
Mary 377
Mary Gorham 293
May S. 442
Morris A. 445
Norris A. 447
Prince 293
Sparrow S. 443
William 416, 425
Zopher 293
Hayford, Abigail 460
Ann 462
Artemisia 464
Arvada 466
Betty 464
Christina 468
Daniel 458, 486
Daniel (Jr.) 458, 459, 460
Deliverance 460, 484, 485
Deliverence 464
Edward 8, 20, 459, 470
Gustavus 467
John 465
Jonathan Bonney 464
Levi 470
Mary 462
Matilda 465
Mercy 465
Mercy Freeman 463
Molly Watterman 466
Nathaniel 460
Priscilla 470
Rebecca 464
Samuel 460, 462, 463, 466, 484, 485
Susanna 485
Thomas 484
Webster 462, 463, 464
William 463, 464, 465, 466, 467, 468, 470
Wm. 453
Hayman, Elizabeth (Mrs.) 67
Nathan 67
Nathan (Cpt.) 66
Hayte, Symeon 595
Hayward, Abel 573
Benjamin 5, 12
Benoni 9
Bethiah 12
Bethya 12
Cary 5
Charlotte 573
Ebenezer 2
Elijah 14, 544
Elisha 7, 9
Elisha (Jr.) 5
Elizabeth (Mrs.) 67
Experience 9
Hannah 8
Hepza 23
Hezikiah 584

Holland (cont.)
Thomas 598
Hollet, Samuell 602
Hollett, John 502, 535, 537
Holley, Eunice 197
Harriet 209
Hepsibah 190
John 190
Joseph (Cpt.) 191
Lucinda 222
Polly (Mrs.) 294
William 294
Zaccheus 294
Hollie, Ann (Widow) 186
John 186
Hollis, Joseph 488
Holloway, Abigail 631
Easter 635
Elisabeth 631
Ester 630
Grace 242
Grace (Widow) 242
Hana 635
John 635
Joseph 33
Malichi 48
Nathaniel 635
Samuel 635
Samuell 646
Sarah 630
Timothy 45
Hollway, Tymothy 504
Willm 504
Holly, Jane (Mrs.) 189
Jos. 189
Joseph 503
Holman, (?) (Col.) 12
Abigail 15
Ann 14
Edward 501
Jane 18
John 11
Mary 12
Peggie 11
Samuel 384
Sarah 14
Holmes, (?) 236
Abiah 464
Abner 465
Abram 249
Allen Gorham 294
Almy (Mrs.) 560
Anna 279
Barnabas 473, 474, 476
Bartlett 294
Bathsheba 243
Benjamin 294
Charles 294
Cynthia 462, 485
D. W. 236
Elizabeth 244
Elizabeth (Mrs.) 249
Hannah 379
Harriot 294
Hezekiah 460, 461, 462, 463, 464, 465, 485, 486
Israel 243, 249
John 237, 245, 246, 501, 544, 545, 560
John (Cpt.) 294
Jonathan Finney 460
Josiah 246, 379
Judith 474
Laurana 463
Lucinda 460
Lydia West 476
Holmes (cont.)
Margaret 527
Mary 242, 294, 527
Melvin 29
Nabby 476
Nancy 473
Nathaniel 545
Orsamus 461
Phebe (Mrs.) 294
Rebecca 307
Robert 294
Samuel 476, 548, 560
Sarah 465, 486, 548
Stetson 459
Thomas 294, 527
Watson 294
William 14, 248, 459, 460
William (Maj.) 527
Willm. 502
Wm 249
Holms, Hannah 379
John 375
Josiah 379
Nathanaell 375
Holway, Ebenezer W. 175
William 294
Homans, Benjamin 294
Homeneck, Esther 270
Homer, (?) 524
Abigail F. 690
Anna (Mrs.) 673, 677
Asa 696
Benjamin 294, 650, 653, 697
Benjamin (Cpt.) 695
Daniel 666
David 673, 677, 696
Elisabeth 666
Experience (Mrs.) 668
Jerusha 691
Jerusha (Mrs.) 666
John 673
Lucy A. 693
Mercy 687
Onan Berry 677
Polly 688
Rebekah (Mrs.) 692
Robert 653, 666, 693, 697
Ruth 668
Salley 673
Sally 691
Stevens 651
Susan 688
Thomas 651
William 650
Zenas 668
Homes, (?) 102
Abra 114
Abraham 317
Agnes 97, 99, 110
Anna (Mrs.) 680
Betty 113
Betty (Mrs.) 112
Daved 680
Elizabeth 97, 99, 110
Elizeb. 317
Experience (Mrs.) 669
Hanna 97
Hannah 118, 122
Isaack 317
Israel 317
Jane 96, 97, 99, 104, 112
John 96, 97, 107, 109, 112, 177, 403
Johnet 96
Homes (cont.)
Josiah 317
Katherin 97
Katherine 197
Kathren 98
Ma(ry?) 98
Margaret 96, 97, 98, 113
Margery 97, 99, 222
Mary 317
Maryan 97
Rebecca 96, 317
Robert 97
Sally Berry 680
Sarah 317, 403
William 96, 97, 114, 271, 317
William (Rev.) 95, 97, 102, 106, 222
Willm. 98
Wllm 317
Zenas 669
Homme, (?) 610
Homsbye, (?) 74
Hoocker, H. B. 230
Hood, Henry 270
Samuel 582
Hooker, Samuel 544
Hooper, Deborah (Widow) 21
Elizabeth 7, 399
Jerusha 20
Ruth 7
Sarah 7, 12, 392
Thomas 9
Hootan, Sarah 294
Hope, Joseph 176
Hopkins, Abba 447
Abba (Mrs.) 445
Abigail 547
Ada 445
Albert 444
Asa 443
Asa (Jr.) 171
Bertie 443
Caleb 171, 443, 446, 498, 501, 512
Clarence S. 442
Constance 498, 512
Curtis 166
Damaris 512
Daniel 441
Davis 445
Deborah 512
Elisa A. 174
Elisha 437
Elisha (Mrs.) 444
Elizabeth 512, 513, 528
Elizabeth (Mrs.) 498
Elkanah 164
Elkanah (Jr.) 174
Ephraim S. 173
Frank W. 446
Giles 498, 500, 509
Gyles 512, 528
Henry Judson 442
J. C. 444
Jean 247
John 164
John N. M. 176
Joshua 437
Josiah (Mrs.) 447
Josiah C. 443
Julia D. (Mrs.) 446
Lillian F. (Mrs.) 444
Lydia 163, 173
Martha A. 442

Hopkins (cont.)
Mary (Mrs.) 437
Mary A. 175
Mary Eliza 449
Mary Foster 446
Mary P. (Mrs.) 175
Nathan (Jr.) 173
Oceanus 498, 499
Phebe 437
Polina 173
Priscilla P. 176
Richard 294
Rosilie 445
Ruth 512
S. Walter 442
Samuel S. 443
Sarah (Mrs.) 443, 449
Stephen 437, 495, 498, 507, 508, 512, 546
Sylvester 449
Sylvester D. 444
Tannie 447
Tempy S. 171
Thankful S. 175
Theophilus 438
Victoria (Mrs.) 443
Hore, John 503
Richard 504
Horffee, Sarah (Mrs.) 59
Horsfield, Timothy 294
Horsford, Joseph 294
Molly (Mrs.) 294
Horskins, Rebeccah 62
Willliam 60
Horssee, Sarah (Mrs.) 59
Horton, Abigail 164
Abram 169
Almira 166, 170
Betsey H. 171
Cushing (Jr.) 168
Eliza A. 173
Eliza F. 170
Freeman 163, 174
Freeman (Jr.) 168
Harriet N. 175
Henry 167, 171
Laura P. 175
Louesa 173
Mary A. 167
Mary H. 176
Mary Jane (Mrs.) 175
Mary P. 173
Maryann 172
Myrick C. 166, 170
Nathan 166
Pamela 167, 170
Percy C. 167
Phebe 175
Polly C. 165
Rachel 167, 171
Rachel A. 168, 173
Samuel 163, 173
Sophia 174
Hosea, Zephamiah 168
Hosier, William Giles 294
Hoskine, Willm. 501
Hoskines, John 45
Hoskins, Anna 639
Elizabeth 545
Heniry 639
Jacob 639
John 78, 536, 639
Joshua 383
Josiah 639
Lydia (Mrs.) 383
Prudence 383
Rebecka 646
Hoskins (cont.)
Rebeckah 546
Sam'l (Sr.) 630
Samuel 628, 629
Sarah 545, 639
Stephen 639
William 78, 520, 547, 639
Wm. 527
Wm. (Jr.) 536
House, Anna 663
Bathsheba 409, 418
David 338, 344, 393
Deborah 358
Ebenezer 663
Elisha 463
Elizabeth 344, 364, 468, 532, 597, 623
Hephzibah 294
Huldah 491
Jacobs 354
James 344, 471
Job 468, 469, 470, 471
John 303, 344, 599, 624
Joseph 344, 356, 358, 362, 364, 624
Joshua 362
Lidia 663
Lucia 663
Lydia 356
Lydia (Mrs.) 358, 362, 364
Lydiah (Mrs.) 356
Mary 345, 470
Moses 455
Olive 663
Prince 663
Rebecca 344, 624
Ruth 663
Ruth (Mrs.) 663
Sally 303
Samll. 332, 345, 347
Samuel 344, 469, 491, 532, 599, 620, 621, 624
Samuell 344, 595, 597, 598
Sarah 338, 347, 393, 598
Sarah (Mrs.) 332, 344, 345, 347
William 294
Hovey, (?) 593
How, (?) (Mrs.) 294
Samuel 294
Howard, Abigail 5
Adam 2
Barnabas 2
Bethia 8
Betty 5, 17
Catherine 3
Damaris 5
Daniel 4
Daniel (III) 29
David 26
David (Jr.) 2
Ebenezer 4
Edward 8
Eliacam 584
Elizabeth 8
James 8
John 8
John (Jr.) 14
Jonathan 9
Martha 2, 3, 6, 8
Mary 2, 3
Robert 2, 526
Howard (cont.)
Sarah 9
Silence 3
Susanna 9
Susannah 7
Thomas 7
Vesta 4
Zephaniah 28
Howdee, (?) (Cpt.) 75
Howe, Mary E. 171
Thomas 504
Howell, Daniel 12
Jeremy 9
Thomas 513
Howes, Abigail 655
Abigail (Mrs.) 433, 674
Abner 432, 673
Abner (Cpt.) 689
Abraham 435
Alexander 434
Amos 432
Andrew 657, 672, 675, 676
Anna 663
Anna (Mrs.) 433
Annar (Mrs.) 433
Anthony 434
Barnabas C. 434
Benjamin 659
Bethiah 687
Bethyah 672
Betsey (Mrs.) 433
Betsy 670
Betsy (Mrs.) 670, 671, 673, 675, 676
Betty 663
Betty (Mrs.) 433
Bety (Mrs.) 434
David 94, 433, 434
Deborah (Mrs.) 433, 434
Dorcas (Mrs.) 432
Eben 435
Eben Foster 434
Ebenezer 433, 663, 664, 665, 673, 678, 680
Ebenezer (Cpt.) 433, 695
Ebenezer (Jr.) 673
Edward 433, 655, 656, 657, 659, 670
Elihu 687
Elisabeth 690
Elisha 432, 671
Eliza. (Mrs.) 655
Elizabeth (Mrs.) 433, 434
Experience (Mrs.) 433
Ezriah 433
Fanne 665
Fannie (Mrs.) 434
Florence Conant 593, 625, 649, 655, 657, 662, 664, 668, 670, 671, 675, 678, 684, 692
Fredrick 678
Gideon 659, 670, 674
Hannah (Mrs.) 432, 433, 434
Henry 434, 674
Hepsy (Mrs.) 435
Huldah (Mrs.) 435
Isaac 433, 434, 673
Isaiah 435
J. C. 432

Johnson (cont.)
Josiah 246, 251
Josiah (Jr.) 23, 26
Margaret 316
Mary 317
Nelson 296
Prudence (Mrs.) 139, 140
Rebecca R. 689
Rhode 15
Samll. 351
Sarah 9
Solomon 25
Susanna 134
Thomas 503
Thomas Jefferson 296
William 20
Jolliff, John 92
Jollop, John 518
Jones, (?) 74
(?) (Cpt.) 495
(?) (Mrs.) 90
Abigail 369, 563
Abigail (Mrs.) 562, 563
Abraham 562
Amy 304
Anna 247, 546
Ansel 690
Asael 583
Barzillai 296
Bathiah (Mrs.) 31
Bathsheba 409, 562
Bathsheba (Mrs.) 562
Benj. 629
Benjamin 90
Bethiah 562
Bethiah (Widow) 186
Betsey 478
Betsey (Mrs.) 420
Betty 381, 402
Catherine (Mrs.) 351
Charles 426, 465, 625
Chloe 584
Cloe 311
Consider 380
Content 374
Cushing 426
Daniel 120, 125, 130, 296
Deborah 463
Dolly 479
Ebenezar 367, 375, 380
Ebenezer 132, 247, 334, 484, 485, 559, 562
Ebenr. 375
Ebenz. 372
Edward 296
Elisha 374, 381
Elizabeth 562
Elizabeth (Mrs.) 562
Elnathan 562
Ephraim 562
Evenr. 369
Ezera 227
Frances 583
George Macy 296
Hannah 359, 367, 466, 468, 487, 562
Hannah (Mrs.) 333, 350, 353, 359, 362, 364, 594
Harriet Ann 296
Hatherly 562, 563
Isaac 344, 350, 353, 359, 362, 364
Isaack 333
Jones (cont.)
Jacob 311
Jane (Mrs.) 334, 367, 369, 372, 375, 380
Jane (Widow) 484
John 244, 402, 409, 414, 562, 594, 625
John (Sr.) 418
Joseph 562, 629
Judith (Jr.) 296
Lucretia (Mrs.) 311
Lurania 478
Lydia 562, 625
Lydia (Mrs.) 33
Mary 76, 311, 353, 559, 562
Mary (Mrs.) 130, 344
Mehitable 227
Miriam (Mrs.) 296
Nathan 562
Nathaniel 464, 478, 479
Nehemiah 562, 584
Noah Nichols 426
Patience 246
Philip 222
Polly (Mrs.) 120
Rebechah 582
Ruth 631
Sally (Mrs.) 296
Samuel 562
Sarah 351, 359, 364
Sarah (Mrs.) 374, 381, 562
Sarah A. 296
Seth 380, 563
Silas (Cpt.) 296
Simeon 29, 372, 463, 464, 465, 466, 468, 478, 487
Solomon 562
Sukey 127
Sukey (Mrs.) 132
Tho. 535
Thomas 311, 414
Thoms. 351
Timothy 562
Willam 296
William 400, 426
Willliam 311
Wm. 400
Jordaine, John 502
Jordan, Eunice (Mrs.) 408, 418
J. 592
James 591
Jedediah 1
John 358, 454
Mary 592
Nath 410
Nathl. 418
Nathll. 408
Patience 358
Patience (Mrs.) 358
Patience (Widow) 397
Jorden, Elizabeth 339
Patience 430
Joseph, Elisabeth 630
Manuel 272
Joslen, Bridget 591
Charles 631
Henry 590, 591
Mary 340
Nathaniel 340
Richard 590
Sarah 590
Joslin, Abigail 321
Abigail (Mrs.) 321
Joslin (cont.)
Abraham 321
Anne 323, 430
Frances (Mrs.) 346
Francis (Mrs.) 348
Henery 321, 323, 430
Henry 349, 356, 361, 620
Isaac 296
Joseph 356
Keziah 349
Mary 346
Nathanaell 348
Nathanll 346
Thomas 361
Joslyn, Henry 412
Joseph 7
Thomas 333
Josselin, Ruth 457
Josselyn, Abigail 460, 474
Abner 469
Abraham 460, 461, 462, 463, 464, 465, 468, 469, 484, 486, 488
Abraham (Jr.) 17, 466, 487
Anna Stockbridge 469
Bethiah 477
Bethiah Thatcher 464
Branch 478
Cela 462
Charles 453
Charles (Jr.) 478
Christiana 475
Debby Hatch 477
Earl 476
Eleanor 478
Eleaxor 463
Eleazer 472, 473, 474, 476, 477, 478
Elisha 478
Emala 478
Ephraim Allen 474
Eunice 466
Francis 472, 473, 474, 476, 489, 491
Frank 478
Hannah 485
Hannah (Jr.) 456
Isaac 465, 474, 475, 476, 477, 478, 486, 492
Isaac Bourn 477
Jemima Lindsey 476
John 456
Joseph 477, 478, 480, 485
Joseph (Jr.) 476
Joseph Barker 466
Lucy 453
Lydia 456, 461, 472
Lyman 476
Mary 456, 476
Nathan 477
Oppis 691
Osen 478
Patience Howland 464
Peter 473
Priscilla 457, 476, 478
Samuel 479
Samuel William 466
Samuel Williams 479
Sarah Hill 478
Sophia 476
Sylvester 456
Tamar 464

Lampham (cont.)
Mary (Mrs.) 161
Landers, Joseph 649
Lane, (?) (Cpt.) 110
(?) Turner 411
Asaph 631
Benja. 404, 405, 406, 414
Benja. (Cpt.) 407, 414
Benja. Turner 404, 406
Benjamin 588, 694
Ebenezer 591
Elisabeth 351
Elizabeth 590
Fanny 406
George 414
Hanah (Mrs.) 351
Isaac 351, 453
Joanna Turner 407
Job 513, 514
John 587, 588, 589, 590, 591
Lucy 405
Maria 414
Melatiah 589
Miranda 691
Sarah 589
Sarah Turner 406
Lanford, Thomas 53
Lang, Nicolas 70
Lange, Nicholas (Jr.) 36
Langford, Thomas 57, 58
Lapham, Abiah (Mrs.) 418
Abiah Joice 406
Abigail 403, 414
Bathsheba 456
Benjamin 424
Caleb 455
Charles 406, 407, 411, 414
Charles Henry 414
Charlotte 407
Elizabeth 516
George 404
Israel 424
Jesse 453
John 141, 146, 152
Joseph 245
Loring Cushing 405
Lyddia King 425
Lydia 413, 516, 536
Mary 152, 455, 490, 516
Mary (Mrs.) 516
Micah 405, 412, 413, 415
Naomi 457
Nicholas 152
Polly 405
Rachel Clap 424
Rebeckah 404
Ruth 404
Sally 421, 424
Sally (Mrs.) 419, 424
Samuel 244
Stephen 403
Temperance 415
Tho. 510
Thomas 141, 145, 419, 425, 503, 516, 536
Thomas (Jr.) 414
Thomas (Sr.) 418
Thoms. 424
Thos. 424, 514
Thos. (Jr.) 404, 405, 406
William 145, 406
Lappam, Abigail (Mrs.) 329
Amos 352, 370
Benjamin 380
David 334, 340, 367, 369, 370, 372, 374, 376, 377, 380
Elisha 374
Elizabeth 342, 376
Hannah 339, 342
Hannah (Mrs.) 329, 342, 344, 346, 348, 352, 363
Joseph 329
Joshua 344
Joshuah 380
Lydia 329, 363
Mary 339
Mary (Mrs.) 380
Mercy 346
Rebecca 372
Rebecca (Mrs.) 367, 369, 370, 372, 374, 376, 377
Rebecka (Mrs.) 334
Samll 340
Samll. 329, 346, 348
Samuel 333, 339, 342, 352, 363, 375, 380
Samuell 344
Stephen 377
Thankful 348
Thomas 329, 367
Lappham, Elizabeth 597
Joseph 313
Rebecca 312
Tho. 312
Thomas 313, 596, 597, 610
Lappum, Israel 401
Ruth 401
Thomas 401
Large, Jervice 601
Larnett, (?) 602
Larry, Abigail (Mrs.) 552
Betty (Mrs.) 552
John 552
Martha 552
Nabby 552
William 552
Lasell, (?) 480
Latham, Alice 23
Allen 27
Anne 8
Betty 12
Chilton 6
Deliverance 12
Galen (Lt.) 29
Hanah 16
Jennet 28
Jerusha (Widow) 26
Leth 28
Lucenda 23
Margaret 210
Mary 16
Nehemiah 29
Rebecca 6
Robert 20
Susanna 8, 24
Thomas 8
Lathan, James 488
Susanna 488
Lathly, Abigail 352
Philip 352
William 352
Lathrop, Abigail 613
Barnabas 537, 611, 612, 614
Bethia 616
Elizabeth 611, 614
Experience 614
Hanna 616
Hannah 611
Isaac (Jr.) 28
James 611
John 8, 509, 611, 612, 613, 616, 617
John (Sr.) 614
Jonathan 611
Joseph 9
Mark 9
Martha 611
Mary 7, 611
Mary (Mrs.) 611, 612
Mehetable (Mrs.) 224
Phebe 617
Samuel 8, 612
Sarah 8
Sarson 121
Susanna (Mrs.) 611, 612
Thankful 611
Thomas 224
Thomas (Cpt.) 123
Zephaniah 5
Lathrop?, John 545
Lathrope, John 504
Lathropp, John 599
Thomas 596
Lathum, Alice (Widow) 12
Anna 12
Arthur 11, 16
Betty 10
Jane 15
Mary 14
Rhoda 12
Susanna 12, 17
Launder, Thomas 503
Launders, William 514
Laurance, Willm. 502
Lavell, Anber 297
Lazarus 297
Lawrence, Betsey G. 297
Charles 297
Ezra 453
Francis S. 297
George 206
George (Jr.) 296
Jedidah 300
Jonathan 3
Judith (Mrs.) 296
Shubael 226
William 297
Winthrop 226
Wm. 128
Lawson, (?) 190, 191, 328
(?) (Rev.) 327
Sarah 1
Thankfull 183
Thomas 184, 191
Thos. 179
Lawton, Robert 79
Layland, William 227
Layman, Charles 687, 690
Laythrope, John 545
Layton, Job 80
Robert 80
Lazel, Isaac 20
Molly 19
Sylvanus 19
Lazell, Abiel 8
Betsey 29
Byram 27

Lettice, Dorothy 546
Elizabeth 544
Thomas 548
Lettis, Thomas 501
Leuerich, Willm. 504
Leveredge, Wm. 515
Leverich, (?) 509
William (Rev.) 450
Leveridge, Wm. 515
Levet, Gad 412
Levit, Israel 351
Mary (Mrs.) 351
Lewes, (?) 347
Antipas 651
Deborah 651
Edward 616
Geo. 622
George 501, 504
Jabez 651
John 503, 616, 651
Martha 651
Mary 622
Naomi 651
Thankful 651
Thomas 111
Timothy 651
Lewice, (?) 610
(?) (Jr.) 600, 609, 610
(?) (Sr.) 609, 610
Ephraim 598
George 597, 598
John 597
Sarah 598
Thomas 603
Lewis, (?) 451, 696, 698
(?) (Sr.) 596
Abigail 683
Anna 671
Anna (Mrs.) 616, 617
Anne 671
Antipas 652, 653
Aurelia 691
Benjamin 652, 658, 659, 660, 663, 664, 665, 666, 671, 672, 675
Benjamin G(orham) 685
Bethany (Mrs.) 230
Betsey 681, 688
Betty 658
Blaney 690
Christopher 681, 689
Clarissa 671
Clark 671
Daniel 480
Daniel (Rev.) 451, 480
David 663, 664
Ebenezer 616
Ebenezr. 617
Edgar 685
Edmund 204
Edward 534, 616, 665, 681, 693
Elijah 411
Elisabeth 652, 685
Elizabeth 617, 664
Elnathan 652, 654, 655, 662, 663, 664, 681, 697
Elnathan (Cpt.) 681, 697
Ephraim 534
Eunice M. (Mrs.) 686
Experience 652
Experience (Mrs.) 615
Fanny 448
Francis 297
Lewis (cont.)
Fredc. 686
Frederic 683, 685, 686, 689, 698
Frederick 176, 684
George 534, 544, 611, 616
George (Sr.) 534
Hannah 617
Hannah (Mrs.) 664, 671, 672, 675
Henry F. 175
Irene 685
Jabez 615, 653, 685, 687, 695, 697, 698
James 534, 616, 686
James (Lt.) 616
James D. 228, 230
Joanna 170
John 140, 147, 509, 534, 615, 616, 617, 692
Joseph 681, 698
Joseph West 297
Judah 652
Kiziah 690
Levi 297
Lothrop H(owland) 685
Lucy Anner 685
Lydia 664
Martha (Widow) 654
Mary 544, 652, 662
Mary (Mrs.) 534, 611, 691
Mary Anner 685
Mary B. 686
Moses 164
Myra 449
Nabby K. 690
Nancy 297
Naomi 655
Naomi (Mrs.) 686
Nathan 666
Nelson 683
Peter 297
Phebe 663, 681
Phebe (Mrs.) 663, 664
Phebe G(orham) 684
Prentis 685
Priscilla 658
Prudence (Mrs.) 617
Rebekah (Mrs.) 685
Robert Barnard 276
Russel 689
Ruth 652, 665
Samll. 410, 617
Samuel 617, 672
Sarah 228, 534, 616, 654, 660, 663, 671, 689
Sarah (Mrs.) 652, 658, 659, 660, 663, 665, 666
Sarah Gorham (Mrs.) 686
Seth Ames (Mrs.) 273, 283, 293, 301
Simeon 687, 697
Susa 663
Susanna 616
Susannah 663
Thankful 652, 681
Thankful (Mrs.) 662, 663, 664
Thankful H(allet) 685
Thankfull 611, 616, 663
Thomas 227, 534, 675
Lewis (cont.)
Warren 688
William S. (Russel) 685
Zenas Winslow 686
Lichfeild, Laurance 504
Lichfield, Josia 323
Judith 622
Nicholas 323
Lillikin, Hannah 629
Linard, Mary 646
Linch, Garvitt 552
Lydia (Mrs.) 552
Rose 552
Lincoln, Abigail 382
Abigail (Mrs.) 337, 381, 382, 387, 391, 392
Abisha 575
Ambrose 575
Benjamin 402
Bethiah (Mrs.) 351
Betsy R. 169
Bridget 582
Constant 628
Content 455
Daniel 354
Dawson 163
Dawson W. 168
Deborah 349, 351, 381
Deborah (Mrs.) 351
Doane 163
Ebenezer 635
Elizabeth 349, 419, 425, 635
Hana 635
Hannah 341, 374, 454, 629
Hannah (Mrs.) 331, 341, 345, 347, 349, 351
Hezekiah 349
Hinckley 175
Huldah 400
Huldah (Mrs.) 398
Ichabod 165
Isaac 174, 337, 347, 381, 382, 384, 387, 392
Isaack 391
Israel 351
Jaac 384
Jacob 392, 625
James 25, 165, 173
Jedediah 351
Jesse 174
Jno. (Jr.) 480
John 635
Joseh 162
Joseph 164
Josh 402
Joshua 338, 345, 374, 377, 379, 381, 385, 398, 400
Joshua W. 168
Josshua 387
Leantes 166, 169
Lois (Mrs.) 575
Margaret 351
Margret (Mrs.) 351
Mart 584
Martha (Mrs.) 354
Mary 387
Mary (Mrs.) 349
Mercy 175, 379
Mercy (Mrs.) 338, 374, 377, 379, 381, 385, 387

Lockwood, Isaac 183, 195, 197
Margaret S. 171
Loe, Margaret 621
Saml. 589
Logan, John 225, 246
Lombard, Eliza. (Mrs.) 593
Lewis 173
Long, John 269
Levi 447
Levi C. 440
Lydia Bangs (Mrs.) 449
Mary 267
Mary Ann 686
Patiance 268
Samuel 266
Thomas 693
Valentine 297
Look, Aaron 139
Catharine 647
Cheney 182
Daniel 128
Elizabeth 255
Experience 254, 260
George 124, 128, 136, 137
Jane 255
Job 132
Lot 131
Persis (Mrs.) 136, 137
Prince 119, 123, 130, 131, 132
Samuel 128
Sarah (Mrs.) 119, 123, 130, 131, 132
Susanna (Mrs.) 131
Thomas 254, 255
Thos. 255
Loper, James 262
Lord, Andrew 614
Hannah (Mrs.) 614
Mary 614
Lorin, Abigail 616
David 616
Elizabeth (Mrs.) 616
Loring, Anner (Mrs.) 680
Benjm. 351
Cornelia 683
David 617
David Haws 680
Deborah 14, 351, 621
Debr. (Mrs.) 351
Edward Wells 686
Elisabeth A(nner) 682
Elisabeth A. 693
Elisha 690
Elizabeth (Mrs.) 617
George H(enry) 683
Hannah 456
Hiram 681
Ignatius 14
James 17, 488
John 27, 680, 681, 682, 683, 685, 696, 697
John (Jr.) 686
Nathl. (Jr.) 454
Priscilla 453
Priscilla (Jr.) 456
Rebecca 15
Ruth (Widow) 17
Sally Lewis 680
Saml. 455
Sarah 454
Solomon 617
Thomas Coffin 685
William D(eane) 682
Lothrop, Anna (Widow) 595
Barbara 519
Barbarah 602
Barshua 615
Bathsua 598
Benjamin 519
Charles B. 168
Elijah (Rev.) 595
Emmersonn 602
Fuller 602
Henry A. 693
Jane 519, 602
John 519, 598, 615
John (Rev.) 595, 610
Lidia 99
Melatiah 599
Samuel 602
Sarah (Widow) 120
Tho. 602
Thomas 519, 599, 602
Lothrope, Benjamin 504
Joseph 504
Nicholas 504
Samuel 504
Thomas 504
Lothropp, (?) 601
Abigaill 597
Bernabas 597
Bethiah 600
Hannah 598
John 597, 602
Joseph 602, 603
Mary 598
Thomas 598, 599, 600
Louden, Jacob 27
Loudon, Richard 245
Lovejoy, Abuid 671
Polly (Mrs.) 671
Susanah 671
Lovel, Andrew 616
Bethiah 98
Hannah (Mrs.) 616
James 14, 614, 616, 617
Lazarus 617
Mary 614
Mary (Mrs.) 616, 617
Mercy 614
Rebecca 616
Thankfull 616
Lovelace, Francis (Sir) 647
Lovell, (?) 698
(?) (Mrs.) 698
Abner W. 692
Andrew 8, 615
Benjamin 297
Hanna (Mrs.) 615
Hannah 650
Jacob 613
James 24, 613, 615
Jane 228
John 517
Martha 615
Mary 613
Mary (Mrs.) 613, 615
Richard L. 297
Low, Anthony 37, 66
Arthur 245
Elezabeth 37
John 37
Samuel 37
Lowden, (?) (Widow) 492
Debby Allen 475
Experience 25
Isaac 471
John 27, 455, 457
Lowden (cont.)
Lucy 456
Nahum 477, 492
Nathaniel 15
Patty 473
Richard 464, 471
Richard (Jr.) 473, 475, 477, 492
Sarah 24
Susanna 25
Lowe, (?) 588
Horace (Mrs.) 162
Rachell 589
Samll. 589
Lowel, Elizabeth 318
John 317, 318
Joseph 317
Phebe 318
Lowell, John 316, 319
Zacheus 319
Lowwell, John 623
Loy, Bethia 319, 430
John 319, 430
Loys, Bethia 430
John 430
Lucas, Jane 365
Mary 365
William 247
Luce, (?) 297
(?) (Widow) 195
Abiah 121
Abigail (Mrs.) 136, 137, 138
Abraham 180
Alsberry 131
Barzillai 204
Benj (Jr.) 127
Benj. 129
Benjn. 207
Christopher 194, 197, 198, 217
Damaris (Mrs.) 129
Daniel 136, 137, 138
David 125, 140, 297
Ebenezer 125, 140
Elijah 297
George 219
Hannah 127, 209
Hannah (Mrs.) 130
Israel 122
Jabez 128
James F. 647
Jane 269
Jasen 193
Jason 194, 201, 213, 221
Jemimah 209
John 209
Love 217
Lydia 179
Obed 297
Prudence 647
Rebecca B. 297
Richard (Cpt.) 129
Ruth (Widow) 219
Sarah 197, 221
Sarah (Mrs.) 131
Shubael 130
Warren 127
Zephaniah 132
Lues, Thomas 111
Luis, Archelaus 151
Elizabeth 151
John 151
Luke, Daniel 100, 113
Lumbar, (?) (Sr.) 598
Beniamin 598
Lumbard, Barnard 504

Macy (cont.)
Judith 282
Margaret B. 297
Mary 254, 297
Nathaniel 297
Obed 297
Paul 297
Paul Bunker 297
Peleg 297
Peter 297
Robert 289
Sally (Mrs.) 297
Sarah 254, 255
Shubael 297
Stephen 297
Susannam 297
Thomas 256
Thomas (Jr.) 255
Thomas W. 297
William W. 297
Zaccheus 297
Maden, Daniel Nicher 298
Deborah C. (Mrs.) 298
John B. 298
Maggoon, Eliab 320
John 320
Magonne, Hannah (Mrs.) 347
John 347
Magoon, Abigail (Mrs.) 377
Hannah 319, 377
Isaac 624
John 247, 319, 352, 377, 624
Magoone, Abigail 372
Abigail (Mrs.) 369, 372, 375
David 340
Elias 340, 342
Hannah (Mrs.) 330, 340
James 343
John 330, 340, 369, 375
John (Jr.) 329, 372
Lusanna 369
Mary 340
Sarah 343
Sarah (Mrs.) 343
Thomas 343
Magoun, Abner 490
Cynthia Briggs 490
Jno. (Cpt.) 481
Lucia 490
Nancy (Mrs.) 419
Mahan, Eliza I. (Mrs.) 446
Walter C. 442
Mahew, Abia 99
Mahurin, Mary 9
Mahyew, Abiah (Mrs.) 122
Betsey 129
Sally 129
Simon 122
Major, Francis 311
Makeny, Daniel 88
Makepeace, (?) (Widow) 78
Anne 628
Mary 628
Sarah 30, 631
Sarah (Mrs.) 32
Thomas 32, 629
William 60
Wm. 628
Makepiace, Hannah 583
Mallard, John W. P. 297
Mallet, Betty 4
Mallet (cont.)
Mary 90
Mary (Mrs.) 89
Thomas 89
Mallett, (?) 75
Thomas 82, 90
Mallus, Mary 383
Mameck, wanack 263
Man, (?) 363
Benjamin 364, 429
Benjm. 429
Betty 456
David 455
Deborah 392
Ebenezer 455
Frances 145
Josia 322
Josiah 392, 393, 394, 624
Martha 333, 364
Martha (Mrs.) 364
Mary 393
Mary (Mrs.) 392, 393
Nathaniel 624
Rebecca 623
Richard 624
Seth 363
Susanna 394
Thomas 41, 322, 624
William 145
Manchester, Job 80
John 53
Thomas 144
Mancrester, John 298
Mandall, Sarah 621
Maning, Rebekah 267
Manle, William 61
Manley, Rebekah 632
William 62, 67, 68
Manly, Olive 3
Thomas 6
William 631
Mann, Bela 411
Experience 8
Priscilla 625
Richard 521
Manning, Betty 255
David 256
Denis 255
Dennis 256
James 256
Phebe 209, 222
Thomas 546
William 222
Manser, John 698
Mansfield, Lyman 298
Manter, Benjamin 298
Deborah 279
Elizabeth (Mrs.) 140
Eunice 209
George 279
George (II) 298
Jeremiah 140
John 110
Lucinda (Mrs.) 298
Reuben 298
Sally (Mrs.) 136
Samuel 124, 135, 136
Seth 298
Manuel, Martin 174
Manwaring, Frances 227
Mao, (?) 604, 605, 606, 608
Elizabeth 600
Hannah 600
Mary 600
Samuel 600
Samuell 597, 600, 607
Marble, Abigail 375
Abigail (Mrs.) 338, 375, 376, 379
David 338, 375, 376, 379
Ephraim 7, 379
Gershom 622
Luther 376
March, Stephen 638
Marchant, (?) 678
(?) (Mrs.) 218
Abisha 188, 200
Abishai 197, 203, 208, 222
Azubah 662
Betty 662
Bial 680, 688
Cornelius 204, 220
Cornelius (Jr.) 194
Corns. 189
Crowell 680
Edgar 204
Elihu 203, 206
Elisa 688
Elizabeth 208, 221, 222
Ephr. 203
Ephraim 196, 199, 215
Gamaliel 190, 191, 206
George 204, 206
Hannah (Mrs.) 194
Henry 190, 217, 218, 219
Huxford 193
Jabez 662
James 680
Jane 221
Jane (Mrs.) 200
Jean 184
John 185, 188, 191, 205, 208, 213, 221, 222
John (Jr.) 191
Lydia 184, 197
Lydia (Widow) 217
Martha 180
Matilda (Mrs.) 208
Mercy (Mrs.) 680
Mercy Hallett 680
Meriam (Widow) 189
Molly 662
Naomi 209, 222
Polly (Mrs.) 196
Rebecca 299
Remember (Widow) 662
Remembrance (Widow) 662
Remembrence 662
Ruben 666, 668
Sarah 213
Seth 220, 221
Silvanous 662
Susanna (Mrs.) 188
Thankful 191, 209, 221
Thankfull (Mrs.) 678
Mare, Hannah 68
Margeson, Edward 499
Marick, (?) 78
Stephen 61, 65, 78, 92
Markelett, John 526
Marlow, Isaack 583
Marrick, Sarah 630
Marser, John 692
Marsh, Dwight W. (Rev.) 482
Roswell 298
Marshal, Daniel F. 169
Joseph 698

Matthews (cont.)
685
Nathaniel (Cpt.) 685
Nathll. 656
Olive 679, 681
Oliver (Cpt.) 690
Oliver Russell 686
Olliver 686
Patia 689
Patia Baker 682
Patience 672, 687
Patte Russel (Mrs.)
678
Patty Russel (Mrs.)
678, 679
Patty Russel (Widow)
696
Paulina 683
Phebe 656, 672, 680,
690
Phebe (Mrs.) 661, 672,
686
Polly (Mrs.) 674, 675,
676, 679
Prince 658, 674, 675,
676, 679, 680, 698
Prince (Cpt.) 696
Rebeca (Mrs.) 663
Rebecca (Mrs.) 659,
660, 664, 665, 667,
670, 675, 679
Rebecca Howes 680
Rebeccah 660
Rebekah 665, 690
Rebekah (Mrs.) 682
Rebekah C. 692
Reuben 656, 681, 682
Reuben (Cpt.) 692, 696
Richard 679
Richard (Cpt.) 698
Ruben 666
Ruth 687
Ruth (Mrs.) 681
Ruthe 669
Sabra 671, 687
Sabra (Mrs.) 679, 680
Sabray 679
Sabry (Mrs.) 680
Sally 676, 688, 691
Sally (Mrs.) 678, 680,
681, 693
Samuel 660, 679, 680
Sarah 675, 679, 693
Sarah (Mrs.) 542, 666,
672, 673, 675
Serena 697
Serena (Mrs.) 681
Sharlotte 680
Silvanus 667
Solomon 665
Susanah 668
Susanna B(aker) 684
Susannah 668
Sylvanus 680
Sylvanus (Cpt.) 692
Syrena (Mrs.) 681
Temperance 679
Thankfull 659, 672
Thomas 672, 697
Thomas (Jr.) 690
Watkins 681
William 298, 660, 662,
686
William A. 696, 697
Willm. 656
Maturin, Elizabeth 558
Maury, Mary 546
Maverick, Moses 497
Mavorick, Moses 542
Maxfeld, Abagail 153
Abraham 153
Dinah (Mrs.) 153
Dorcas 153, 154
Edmund 147, 153
Elizabeth 153
John 153, 154
Lydia 153
Mary 153, 154
Mehitabel (Mrs.) 154
Mehitable 154
Nathaniel 153
Timothy 146, 147, 153
Maxfield, Ichabod 632
Maxy, Isaiah 272
Mary 272
May, Dinah 245
Samuel J. (Rev.) 421
Maycomber, Edith 242
Matthew 541
Sarah 646
Thomas 541
Wm 530
Maycumber, Thomas 243
Wm. 502
Maye, Benj. 592
Elisha 588, 589, 592
Ephraim 591
Hannah 591
Ruth 589
Sarah 588
Mayhen, Zaccheus 225
Mayhew, (?) 124, 193,
196
(?) (Cpt.) 99, 104,
107, 108, 109, 111,
113, 114
(?) (Maj.) 101
(?) (Mrs.) 100, 109,
121
Abia 99
Abiah 105
Abigail 99, 220
Abigail (Mrs.) 118,
130
Abigail (Widow) 131
Abishai 121
Abner 128, 137, 138,
139, 140
Allen 120
Allen (Dr.) 127, 133,
134
Anna 222
Anna (Mrs.) 121
Bathsheba 99
Bathshebah 116
Ben 100
Ben. 101, 103
Benj 131
Benj. 130
Benjamin 103, 131,
132, 134, 135, 136,
137
Bethia 119
Bethiah 99, 101, 105,
122
Betsey (Mrs.) 121,
135, 136, 137, 138
Betsy (Mrs.) 135
Charles 217
Clara 121
Clarissa 127, 129
David 125, 136, 137,
138, 139, 140
Deborah 127, 180
Deborah (Mrs.) 120,
131, 132, 133, 134,
Mayhew (cont.)
135, 136
Dedidah (Mrs.) 131
Dinah 99
Drusilla (Widow) 203
Eleanor 119
Elijah 121
Eliz 99
Elizabeth 107, 184
Elizabeth (Mrs.) 118
Ephraim 121, 124, 130,
131, 132, 133, 137,
139
Ephraim (Jr.) 128
Ethelinda (Mrs.) 138
Eunice 99
Eunice (Mrs.) 120,
133, 134, 136, 137,
138, 139
Experience 100, 103,
106, 107, 108, 109
Fear (Mrs.) 118
Francis 122, 130, 131
Frederick 129, 138
George 129, 140
Hannah 99, 116
Hannah (Mrs.) 123,
131, 133
Harriet 124
Harrison P. 129
Hebron 120, 127, 131,
132, 133, 134, 135,
136
Hilliard 125
James 206
Jane 99, 126
Jane (Mrs.) 121, 207
Jedidah 99, 222
Jedidah (Mrs.) 130,
132, 133, 136, 138
Jedidah (Widow) 121
Jehoiadah 117
Jemimah 99
Jenny 403
Jeremiah 118, 129
Jeremiah (Cpt.) 121,
122, 127
Jerusha 105, 119, 122
Jethro 124
Jno 122, 123
John 96, 105, 107,
118, 121, 131, 133,
134, 647
John (Sr.) 101
Jona. 124
Jonathan 116, 119,
124, 127, 132, 133,
134
Jos. 127
Joseph 136, 138, 139,
140, 216, 217
Josias 123
Lois (Mrs.) 120
Lois (Widow) 123
Luch (Mrs.) 121
Lucinda 117
Lucy 99, 107, 121,
193, 197
Lucy (Mrs.) 138, 139,
140, 195
Lydia 180, 411
Lydia (Mrs.) 131, 132,
134, 136, 137
Malatiah 138
Maltiah 121
Margret (Mrs.) 208
Mark 125
Martha 98

Mayhew (cont.)
Martha (Mrs.) 140
Mary 98, 99, 108, 117, 128, 208, 244
Mary (Mrs.) 96, 123, 130, 131, 132
Matilda 127
Matt. 131
Matthew 96, 108, 109, 118, 119, 129, 130, 133, 209, 222
Matthew (Dr.) 124, 197
Matthew (Jr.) 132
Matthw. 188, 195
Mattw. 212
Matw. 206
Mehitable 118, 122
Melatiah 140
Mercy (Mrs.) 118
Nancy (Mrs.) 119, 217
Nath 403
Nathan 98, 100, 118, 121, 122
Nathan (Cpt.) 123
Nathaniel 108, 129
Nathl 130, 132, 133, 135
Nathl. 131, 134
Oliver 121, 122
Pain 99, 104, 105
Pain (Jr.) 100
Pain (Maj.) 100
Pam (Jr.) 114
Pamela (Mrs.) 130
Parnell 119, 121, 124, 127, 129
Parnell (Mrs.) 120, 124, 130, 131, 132, 133, 134
Patty 124
Patty (Mrs.) 136, 137, 139, 140
Peggy 127, 129
Peggy (Mrs.) 122
Peggy (Widow) 118
Persis 129
Phebe 181
Phebe (Mrs.) 121, 132, 133, 134, 135, 136, 137, 138, 139, 140, 188
Polly 128
Polly (Mrs.) 133, 134, 135, 138
Prudence 119, 126
Prudence (Mrs.) 135, 136, 138, 139
Prudence B. (Mrs.) 137
Rachel 116
Rebecca 120, 121, 127, 129, 132, 210
Rebecca (Mrs.) 119, 129, 131, 133
Reliance 99, 116
Reliance (Mrs.) 105
Ruhamah 120
Ruhamah (Jr.) 127
Ruth 99, 101, 117, 125
Ruth (Mrs.) 118, 130
Samuel 99, 120, 123
Sarah 99, 100, 107, 197, 209
Sarah (Mrs.) 101
Seth 118, 119, 121, 123, 128, 135, 136, 137, 138
Simon 108, 120, 123
Stephen 121

Mayhew (cont.)
Sukey (Mrs.) 137
Susan 129
Susan (Mrs.) 139
Susanna 107, 126
Susanna (Mrs.) 131
Susannah (Mrs.) 137
Symon 103
Thankful 120
Thomas 99, 101, 102, 120, 210, 264
Thomas (Jr.) 214
Thomas (Sr.) 647
Thomas W. 124, 138
Thomas Wade 132
Thos W. 140
Thos Wade 139
Thos. 208
Thos. Wade 130, 131
Tim. 116
Timothy 99, 118, 130
Tristram 124, 212
Wade 138
William 121, 132, 133, 134, 135, 136, 137, 138, 139, 140, 197, 210
William Maning 196
Wilmot 119, 120
Wm. 129, 195, 207
Wm. B. 125, 128, 135, 136, 137, 138, 139, 140
Zaccheus 109, 130, 184, 197, 210
Zaccheus (Cpt.) 107
Zachariah 99, 106
Zachary 101
Zechariah 118
Zechariah (Rev.) 121, 124
Zelinda (Mrs.) 138
Zepaniah 133
Zeph. 100
Zephania 105
Zephaniah 99, 105, 107, 117, 124, 135, 136, 137, 138
Zephh. 108
Zilpha 107
Maynard, John 502, 508
Mayo, Abigail 164, 167
Abigail K. 171
Abijah 167, 171
Alice 172, 437, 447
Alice K. 167
Amariah 440
Barnabas 166
Barnabas K. 170
Benson 94
Bethiah 163, 552
Bethiah C. 167, 172
Betsey 169
Betsy 163
Betsy C. 169
Betty 164, 165
Bety 552
Charlie 442
Clarenton 448
Deborah (Mrs.) 552
Delilah 443
Dora Malana 447
Ebenezer 565
Elisha 552
Elisha Y. 176
Eliza 163
Eliza (Mrs.) 298
Esther 176, 438

Mayo (cont.)
Eunice 162
Freeman 447
Freeman (Mrs.) 446
Freeman D. 166
Gamalel 552
Hannah 164, 530
Hannah (Mrs.) 530
Hannah D. 171
Henry 162, 552
Hitty 163
Jacob W. (Mrs.) 446
James 552
James (Jr.) 163
Jane (Mrs.) 445
Jerusha 552
Joanna 164
John 504
John (Jr.) 162
John (Rev.) 436, 437
Johnnie 443
Jonathan 447
Joseph 447, 552
Joseph C. 169
Joshua Atkins 552
Josiah 164, 165
Judah 436
Lettice 552
Lettis 552
Lettis (Mrs.) 552
Lidia 400
Loui (Mrs.) 440
Louisa Rogers 448
Lucy 163, 164
Lydda 174
Lydia 163, 436
Marcia B. 449
Maria 436
Martha 552
Martha (Mrs.) 442, 552
Mary 436, 546, 552
Mary (Mrs.) 400
Matilda 165
Melissa B. 440
Mercy 162, 165
Molly 400
Naomi 166, 170
Nathan 169
Nathaniel 436, 437, 504, 530, 545
Nathl. 400
Obed (Cpt.) 298
Oliver 174
Overy P. 449
Ovey P. 449
Patty 164
Patty K. 171
Rebecca 165
Rebecca F. 174
Robert 171, 552
Roxanna (Mrs.) 447
Ruth 163, 436
Ruth A. 174
S. E. 445
S. Emery 445
Sally 164
Samuel 162, 163, 530, 552
Samuell 504
Sarah 552
Simeon 164
Solomon 444
Solomon H. 168, 173
Surviah 552
Susan 172, 446
Susanah 164
Susannah (Mrs.) 552
Sylvanus 94

Mayo (cont.)
Tabitha 163
Thankful 162, 163, 552
Theophilus 436, 530
Thomas 176, 436, 530, 552
Timothy 162, 163, 173
Uriah 162
Wallace 442
Walter 449
Warren D. 176
Whitford 552
William 445
William F. 440
Zilla 164
McBride, John 2
McChane, Samll. 411
McClean, Jane 99
McClellan, John 105
McClelland, John 100
McClench, Rebecca 28
McCollm, Archibald 139
Patty (Mrs.) 139
McCollum, (?) 124
Aarchibald 137
Archibald 127, 134, 135, 136, 137, 138, 139
Hanna 124
Patty (Mrs.) 136, 137, 138, 139
Polly (Mrs.) 134, 135
McDaniel, John 490
McFarland, Lydia 455
Rebecca 452
Susanna 455
McGee, Thoma 99
McGill, Joseph 297
McGowan, (?) 110
McKensy, (?) (Cpt.) 217
Phebe (Mrs.) 217
McKenzie, Adeline 221
Daniel (Cpt.) 221
Mary 221
McKinstry, Moses 129
McLelland, James 107
John 107
Mcgoon, Isaack 455
Joseph 455
Lydia 457
Mary 453
Nabby 456
Ruth 454
Sarah 455
Sylvina 454
Mcgown, Joshua 456
Thos. 457
Mclathlin, Robert 453
Mead, William H. 298
Meadbery, Benjamin 54
Hannah 54
Jno. 53, 54
John 54
Nathaniel 54
Nathll. 54
Sarah 54
Sarah (Mrs.) 54
Thomas 54
Meader, Alexander 298
Benjamin 298
Deborah (Mrs.) 298
George 298
Nancy (Mrs.) 305
Rachel Paddock 298
Robert 298
Samuel 298
Mears, (?) (Widow) 178
Garrison 209
Mecarta, Elam S. 693
Medbery, John 49
Sarah (Mrs.) 49
Medcalfe, (?) (Rev.) 109
Meeder, Alexander 298
Benjamin 298
Deborah (Mrs.) 298
George 298
John 269
Rachel Paddock 298
Robert 298
Samuel 298
Meeders, Francis 190
Megoon, Abner 453
Mehuren, Isaac 21
Meigs, Amelia (Mrs.) 298
Joseph 298
Mellus, Mary 383
Mendinghall, Judith 298
Stephen Gardner 298
Merchant, (?) 678
Anna (Widow) 697
Azubah 662
Benjamin 298
Bethiah 655
Betty 662
Cornelius 177, 182, 183
Elisabeth 654
Elizabeth (Mrs.) 654
Ensign 654
Hezekiah 654
Huxford 179
Jabez 651, 662
James 654
Joanna 651
John 178
Josiah 654
Marth 651
Molly 662
Remembrence 662
Samll 651
Samll (Jr.) 654, 655
Samuel (Jr.) 654
Sarah Parr 298
Seth 177
Silas 177, 182
Silvanous 662
Sylvanus 651
Thankful (Mrs.) 678
William 399
Willm. 399
Merchent, Remember (Widow) 662
Remembrance (Widow 662
Merehaw, Elias 144
John 144
Jonathan 144
Thomas 144
Timothy 144
Merick, Stephen 88, 89
Wm. 502
Merino, Francisco 311
Merit, Abigail 355
Abigail (Mrs.) 331, 355
Agatha 355
Aimy 355
Benjamin 371
David 397
Hannah 374
Hannah (Mrs.) 397
Henry 334, 368
Icabod 368, 369, 371
Ichabod 374
Jonathan 336, 375
Joseph 368
Lusanna 368
Merit (cont.)
Margret (Mrs.) 334, 368
Mary 355, 369
Mary (Mrs.) 369, 371, 374
Mehitabel 375
Mehitabel (Mrs.) 336, 375
Simeon 375
Thomas 331, 355
Meritt, Charles 404
Noah 404
Sally (Mrs.) 420
Merrett, (?) 596
Elizabeth (Mrs.) 618
John 618
Nehemiah 618
Merrick, Barbara L. 482, 493
Wm 530
Merricke, Mary 546
Stephen 546
William 547
Merrihew?, Elias 144
John 144
Jonathan 144
Thomas 144
Timothy 144
Merrill, Mary 621
Merrite, Henry 503
John 503
Merritt, (?) 610
Benjamin 406
Consider 406
Henry 519, 622
Joce 406
John 519
Jonathan 621
Joseph 406
Katherine 622
Polly 406
Prissa 406
Roxa 406
Merry, Bathsheba 221
Eliz. 100
Lathrop 128
Mary 208, 222
Rebecca 209
Sam 100
Sam. 112
Samuel 298
Walter 628
Michell, Experience 502, 532, 533
Hannah 141
Hannah (Mrs.) 141
James 141
Middleton, Richard 62
Mighell, (?) (Rev.) 430
Grace 326
Samuell 325
Tho. 326
Thomas 325
Thomas (Rev.) 325
Mighil, (?) (Rev.) 430
Mighill, (?) (Rev.) 243
Mary 324
Thomas 324
Miles, Anna 36
Millard, Samuel 63, 87
Samuell 51
Miller, (?) (Widow) 694
Almira 687
Ann 1
Benjamin 664
Charles H. 298
David 253

Miller (cont.)
Elihu 272
Elisha 664, 665, 666
Elizabeth 590
Faith 242
Francis 252
Hannah 666
Janah 666
Jeremiah 552
John 252, 253, 298, 451, 452, 664
John (Rev.) 451, 452
Josiah 452
Judith 451, 452
Lydia (Mrs.) 451, 452
Mary 664, 665, 694
Mary (Mrs.) 664, 665, 666
Mercy 591
Nabby 687
Nicholas 536
Phebe (Mrs.) 298
Rebecca (Mrs.) 552
Ruth 592
Sally 552
Sarah (Mrs.) 552
Solomon 590, 591, 592
William 552
Millerd, Samll. 50
Samuel 87
Mills, Edward 76
Isaiah 216
John 100, 112
Milton, Thos. 211
Mingo, William 270
Minor, Jared L. 298
Minott, John 62
Mirack, Stephen 629
Mirick, (?) (Mrs.) 696
Mitchel, Alice 15, 25
Ann 18
Celia 21
Cushing 16, 20
Elisabeth 15
Jacob 15, 23, 26
Jno. 453
John 21
Molly 20
Nabby 25
Nathan 18
Oliver 26
Reuben 23
Rotheus 23
Sarah 26, 268
Seth 20
Sylvia 24
Theodore 28
Mitchell, (?) 11, 532
Albert 298
Ariana 298
Bette 148
Bradford (Lt.) 29
Celia 29
Charles 298
David 148, 298
Edward 532
Edward (Jr.) 15
George 298
George Gorham 298, 299
Henry 298
Hephzibah (Mrs.) 298
Isaac 299
Jacob 6, 546
James 298
Jennit 26
Jethro 298
John 532
John R. 298
Mitchell (cont.)
Mary 5, 6, 298, 544
Nahum 27
Paul 277
Pernal (Mrs.) 148
Phebe (Mrs.) 298
Richard 298
Ruth 148
Samuel 298, 299
Sarah (Mrs.) 148
Seth 12, 15, 148, 298
Susa 25
Thomas 1, 6
William 148, 532
William (Jr.) 148
Zenas 28
Mo(?), Rebecca 466
Sylvester 466
Moane, John 311
Modley, Thomas 299
Mohurin, Bathshua (Mrs.) 565
Betty 565
Ebenezer 565
Mary 565
Seth 565
Stephen 565
Molatto, Sylva 452
Monk, Elias 1, 2
Monroe, Benjamin 470, 471
Bennet 460, 479
Bennett 467
Charles Josselyn 479
Cyrus 471
Elizabeth 474
George William 461, 477
Hannah 468
Hannah Josselyn 477
Henry 460, 461, 467, 470
Henry (Jr.) 468, 470, 472, 474
James 472
Joseph 470, 479
Margaret 460
Mary 468
William 479
Monrow, Thomas 629
Montcalm, Moses 304
Nabby 304
Nancy (Mrs.) 689
Sally (Mrs.) 304
Montgomery, Jacob 299
John 4
Sarah 1
Moody, (?) (Rev.) 114
William 299
Mooers, Benjamin 299
Jonathan 299
Robert 299
Samuel 299
William 299
William Coffin 299
Moor, David (Cpt.) 99
John 370, 373
Katherin 98
Lidia 81
Mary 370
Richard 81
Moore, Betty 462, 465, 486
Catharine 15
Ezekiel 463
George 503
Henry 311
Isaac 459
Moore (cont.)
John 458
Mary 458
Mary (Mrs.) 458
Mercy A. 176
Samuel 461
Sarah 466
Sarah (Widow) 12
Sophrona (Mrs.) 311
Theodosius 10
Theofolous 463
Thomas 362, 458, 459, 460, 461, 462, 463, 465, 466, 483, 486
Treat 174
Wm. 362
Moorehead, Arthur 239
John 239
Moores, Treat 163
Moorey, Nicholas 69
More, Mary 489
Thomas 362, 483
Wm. 362
Mores, Mehitable (Mrs.) 174
Moreton, Taber 279
Morey, Nichols (Lt.) 31
Thomas 299
Walter 641
Morgan, Charles West 299
Dudley 299
Morrey, Jonathan 545
Morris, Alexander Gardner 299
Alexander Pollard 299
Charles 299
Eliza (Mrs.) 299
Jacob 299
John P. 299
Jonathan B. 299
Naomi 332
Polly 299
William 299
Morrison, John 3
Robert 2
William 1
Morse, Ammi C. 299
Anna 253
Asarelah 647
David 252
James 299
Jonathan 253
Jonathan (Jr.) 252
Lydia (Mrs.) 299
Solomon 299
Stephen 299
Urian 203
William M. 299
Willliam 299
Morselander, Cornelius 299
Hephzibah (Mrs.) 299
Mary Barnard 299
Zebulon 299
Morslander, Cornelius 299
Hephzibah (Mrs.) 299
Mary Barnard 299
Zebulon 299
Morton, (?) 523
Deborah 540
Eliezer 547
Elizabeth 545
Elizabeth (Mrs.) 141
Eph. 538, 540
Eph. (Lt.) 538
Ephraim 502, 518, 531
George 545, 548

Parker (cont.)
Experience 614
Hanah 672
Hannah 617, 651
Isaac 300
Isaiah 664, 670, 672, 674, 675, 677
Isaiah (Cpt.) 697
Jabez 651, 656, 658, 659, 662, 663
Jacob 651, 652, 653, 654, 664, 665, 666, 667, 674
Jael 635, 646
Jesse 300
John 504, 518, 538, 617, 646
Jonathan 301, 658
Joseph 300, 301, 616, 652
Joshua 346
Joshua H. 300
Judeth 361
Julia Ann 229
Justice 113
Keziah 688
Lydia 300, 315, 620
Martha 313
Mary 313, 340, 538, 621, 651
Mary (Mrs.) 300, 614, 615, 616, 617, 664, 665, 667
Mercy (Mrs.) 616
Miles 315, 341
Miriam 340
Molly 664
Molly (Mrs.) 666
Nancy 663
Nansy 663
Nathan 300
Nathanael 340
Nathaniel 78
Patience 313, 651
Patience (Mrs.) 611
Polly 162
Prince 656
Priscilla 651
Rachel 340
Rachel (Mrs.) 340, 341, 346, 350
Rebecca 615, 652, 666
Rebeccah 658
Robert 611
Robert F. 301
Robt 543
Ruth 346, 652
Samuel 538
Samuel (Rev.) 553
Sarah 651, 656
Sarah (Mrs.) 538, 656, 658, 659, 662, 663
Sarah A. 228
Silas 300, 301
Silvanus 658
Sylvanus 696
Temperance 659
Temperance (Mrs.) 617, 670
Tempy 672, 675
Tempy (Mrs.) 672, 674, 675, 677
Thankful 651
Thankful (Mrs.) 660
Thankfull 615
Thankfull (Mrs.) 658, 659
Thomas 615, 616, 617,

Parker (cont.)
651, 665
William 301, 313, 315, 340, 341, 530, 544, 622
William H. 300
Willm 313
Willm. 502, 504
Wm 532
Wm. 346, 350, 515, 518, 522
Zaelveton 651
Parkers, Willliam 610
Parkman, Mary 256
Samuel 301
Willm. 256
Parlow, Jesse 294
Mary 7
Phebe 294
Parmer, Jane 179
Parris, Josiah 25
Parrottin, Nancy B. (Mrs.) 301
William 301
Parry, Egartha 487
Eleanor 553
Henry 487
Jeremiah 553
Mary (Mrs.) 487
Rebeckah (Mrs.) 553
Richard 553
Parsons, David (Cpt.) 235
Lydia (Mrs.) 419
Mary (Mrs.) 235
Samuel 301
Theodocius 301
Partridge, (?) 508
Bridget 508
Elizabeth 528
Henry 508
John 236, 528
Mary 528
Mary (Mrs.) 236
Patience (Mrs.) 528
Ralph 516
Ralph (Rev.) 528
Robert 528
Pason, Anna 613
Jeremiah 613
Mercy 613
Sarah 613
Patch, Wm. 510
Patingal, Mehetabel 11
Patingale, Sarah (Widow) 16
Patrick, George 502
Patten, Joshua 301
Pauchachux, Sam 75
Paul, Abigail 629
Dorothy 631
Edward 508, 629
John 91, 232, 629
Mary (Mrs.) 232
R. 509
Richard 509
William 78, 232
Paule, Margery (Widow) 521
William 541
Paull, Abigall 638
Edward 638
Hana 633
James 638
John 638
Mary 633, 638
Sarah 638
William 638

Paybody, Annis 537
Francis 537
Isabel (Mrs.) 537
John 537
Thomas 537
William 537
Wm. 502
Payne, Thomas 504
Payton, Mary 167
Peabody, Peleg 127
Peace, (?) (Cpt.) 248
Peacock, Margary (Mrs.) 635
Peafe, Thos. 193
Peak, Nicolas 62
Peakes, Israel 543
Judith (Mrs.) 543
Wm 543
Wm (Sr.) 543
Peaks, William 622
Pearce, Anthony 20
Pearse, Abraham 501, 502
Willm. 504
Wm. 504
Peary, Samuel 649
Peas, (?) (Widow) 178
Abia (Widow) 179
Abigail (Widow) 182
Abraham 178
Barzillai 181
Eph. 178
Hannah 178
Jno. 178
John 178
Jonan. 181
Jonathan 182, 183
Jos. 178
Joseph 179
Lemuel 178
Mel. 181
Obed 178
Peter 182
Prince 179
Sara (Widow) 178
Sarah 268
Stephen 177
Sylvanus 183
Thos. 177, 178
Pease, (?) 180
(?) (Mrs.) 115
Abiah (Mrs.) 188
Abigail 128
Abigail (Mrs.) 223
Abishai 120, 122, 301
Abishai (Jr.) 130
Abner 216
Abraham 301
Alexander 200, 301
Anna 180, 190, 201, 209, 220
Anna (Mrs.) 188
Bart. 207
Bartlett 212
Barzillai 183
Benj 205
Benja. 188
Benja. (Sr.) 187
Benjamin 182, 197, 208, 209, 210, 220
Benjamin (Jr.) 222
Benjamin (Sr.) 222
Benjn. 201, 206
Benjn. (Jr.) 188
Betsey 220
Charles 201
Clement 193
Coffin 301
Daniel 209

Peckham (cont.)
Stephen 153
William 153
Pecks, (?) 36
Peckum, John 593
Pees, James 225
Mrs Abigail 117
Peese, Abigail 98
John 99
Ruth 266
Pegin, Jenny 28
Peirce, Abraham 600
Alice 600
Benjamin 485
Ebenezer W. 233, 234
Ebenezer W. (Gen.) 30
Elizabeth 266
Ephraim 90
Eriakim 90
John 621
Joseph 454
Michael 543
Nehemiah 483, 485
Pensis 543
Persis 621
Ryah 543
Peirse, Micaell 540
Pelham, Elizabeth (Mrs.) 239
Peter (Cpt.) 301
Pell, Benjamin 301
Pelton, Samll. 85
Pemberton, Ebenr. (Rev.) 97
Penfield, Mary 629
Peniman, Daniel 169
Penn, Christian 500
James 527
Pennaman, Daniel 165
Penniman, Betsey (Mrs.) 419
Penny, Christopher 629
Penyman, Hanna 638
Pepper, Abigail 163
Daniel 162
Hannah 163
Mary 163
Mehitable 164
Mercy 162
Sally 162
Zilpha 163
Pequit, Alice (Mrs.) 155
James 155
Lydia 155
Thomas 155
Percival, Augustus 444
Frederick 447
Henry M. 445
Luella (Mrs.) 445
Peren, (?) 50
Abraham 50, 51, 52, 87
Daniel 50
Daniell 50
David 50, 63
Jno. 52
Jno. (Jr.) 51
Jno. (Sr.) 51
John 46, 50
John (Jr.) 49, 50, 51
John (Sr.) 50, 51, 52
Mary 50
Mehetable 49
Mehettabell 50
Noah 50
Samll. 50
Samuel 50
Samuell 50
Sara (Mrs.) 50
Peren (cont.)
Sarah (Mrs.) 46
Sarah (Widow) 49
Susanah 50
Perey, Adam 471
Olive 471
Perin, Abraham 47
Perkins, (?) 401
Abigail 5
Abraham E. 691
Anna 2
Daniel (Rev.) 559, 579
David 6
Dorothy 1
Dorothy (Widow) 2
Elizabeth 15
Hannah 3, 691
Isaac 2
Jemima 2, 4
Jesse 3
Jonathan 12
Josiah 2
Luke 2
Martha (Widow) 11
Mary 3, 4
Nathan 7
Sarah 1
Susanna 5, 11
Thomas 9
William 301
Perrem, Abigail 591
Daniel 592
Danl. 591
Susannah 591
Perren, Abraham 46
Ann 46
John 592
Sarah 46
Perrey, Adam 489
Daniel 471
Henry 462, 463
John 478
Noah 471, 488
Noah (Jr.) 491
Olive 489
Samuel Baker 462
Perrie, Willm. 502
Perrin, Anna 546
Perry, (?) (Widow) 410
Abiel 354
Abigail 328
Abner 338, 356, 387, 390
Adam 459, 470
Alice 453
Amos 328, 334, 356, 360, 363, 364, 368, 370, 373, 376, 382
Barnabas 342, 476
Beniamin 326
Benjamin 332, 346, 348, 367, 389, 397
Benjamin (Jr.) 337
Benjm. 337, 338, 350, 354, 356, 360, 364, 371, 382
Bethiah Barker 476
Christiana 412
David 326, 623
Deacon 591
Deborah (Mrs.) 301
Diman 453, 455
Edward 144
Elizabeth 371, 376, 470
Elizabeth (Mrs.) 327, 340, 374
Elizbeth 371
Perry (cont.)
Elizebeth 324
Elizth. (Mrs.) 376
Hannah 328, 370
Henry 342
Henry (Jr.) 475, 477, 478
Hester 65
Huldah 412
Isaac 328, 332, 364, 376
James 287, 301, 320, 341, 465, 623
Jerimiah 328
Jerusha 328
John 322, 465, 477, 478, 623
Jonathan 301, 382
Joseph 361, 371, 388, 390
Katey 477
Keziah 340
Lewis 478
Louisa 304
Lusanda 390
Lusanna 374, 390
Lydia 369
Lydia (Mrs.) 31
Marriam 271
Mary 321, 341, 363, 468, 623
Mary (Mrs.) 341
Nabby Barker 478
Nat. 592
Nathaniel 475
Noah 467, 468
Patience 591
Peleg 350
Priscilla 360, 398
Rachel (Mrs.) 388
Rhoda 477
Roger 246
Ruth 7, 287, 337, 356, 360, 396, 397
Ruth (Mrs.) 332, 334, 346, 348, 350, 354, 356, 360, 363, 364, 367, 368, 370, 371, 373, 376, 382
Saml. 374, 376
Samuel 8, 59, 287, 346, 459, 489, 491
Samuell 325
Sarah 68, 287
Sarah (Mrs.) 387, 390, 592
Seth 456
Simeon 387, 388
Susana 320
Susanna 623
Susanna (Mrs.) 301
Susannah 327
Tabitha 325, 623
Tho. 320, 321
Tho. (Jr.) 322, 430
Tho. (Sr.) 430
Thomas 319, 320, 322, 325, 326, 620, 623
William 301, 321, 324, 325, 326, 327, 328, 340, 368, 369, 382, 621
Wm. 371
Zillah 367
Pery, Benjm. 382
Ruth (Mrs.) 382
Samuel 47
William 382

Prouty (cont.)
David 359, 400, 411, 416
Deborah 382
Edward 331, 337, 339, 341, 343, 349, 351, 375, 382, 384, 386, 389, 624
Eleanar 370
Elisabeth (Widow) 396
Elisha 349
Eliz. (Mrs.) 343, 359, 369, 372
Elizabeth 339, 363, 382
Elizabeth (Mrs.) 341, 349, 351, 359, 363, 367, 370, 382
Eunice 335
Isaac 359, 363, 367, 372, 400, 403, 624
Issac 369
Jacob 359
James 341, 369, 624
Jemima (Mrs.) 338, 397
Jemimah (Mrs.) 382
Job 359
John 359
Jonathan 382, 402, 624
Lettice (Mrs.) 400
Lusannah 382, 392
Margaret 624
Margret (Mrs.) 380
Mary 351
Nehem. 402, 403
Nehemiah 380, 400
Prisce 403
Priscilla 403
Rebecca 375
Rebecca (Mrs.) 382, 384, 386, 389
Rebecca (Widow) 397
Rebeccah (Mrs.) 375
Richard 343, 382, 624
Ruth 367
Sarah 386
Susannah 389
William 338, 382, 392, 400, 624
Wm. 382, 397
Pryer, (?) 601
Martha 15
Sarah (Mrs.) 10
Pryor, Ann (Widow) 12
Daniel 315, 509
Elizabeth 509
Hannah 9
John 509
Joseph 502, 509
Mary 509
Samuel 509
Sarah 16
Thomas 509
Pullen, John 592
Mary 592
Mich. 592
Willm. 592
Pullin, (?) 66
Pumpely, Apphia 467
Apphia (Mrs.) 467
Barnard 467
Bennet 467
Betty 487
Elizabeth 467
John 467, 487
Reuel 467
Pumpilly, John 468
Samnel 468
Purchas, Oliver 520
Purchase, Oliver 504
Purchis, Oliver 520, 521
Putnam, Rufus (Gen.) 302
Pynchon, Betty 489
Pynson, Thomas 503
Quay, Elisabeth 18
Quill, Joseph Antonio 302
Quinn, Molly 280
Radsford, James 12
Rament, Paul 649
Ramsdale, Abner Turner 464
Noah 26
Simeon 464
Ramsdel, Benjamin 357
Betty 27
Charles 23
Content 354
Gideon 11
Gidion 348
James 24
Jemimah 348
John 23
Joseph 348, 357, 428
Lot 27
Martha (Mrs.) 354
Mary 348, 349
Mary (Mrs.) 349, 357, 428
Matthew 20
Nathaniel 14
Saml1. 349
Samuel 354
Samuell 349
Sarah 348
Sarah (Mrs.) 347, 348
Thomas 347, 348
Ramsdell, Abigail 461
Alderson 468
Alverson 479
Anne (Widow) 491
Bartlett 465, 474
Benjamin 460, 487, 492
Benjamin (Jr.) 468
Betsey 470
Betty 468, 476
Charles 302, 474, 476, 490
Clarinda (Mrs.) 302
Clarissa 475
Content 460, 467
Daniel 81
David 477
Edmund 460
Elijah 476
Elizabeth 486
Eunice (Mrs.) 302
Ezekiel 467
Frederick William 302
George 302
Gersham 469, 470, 475, 476, 477, 478, 479
Gershom 469, 488, 490, 491
Gershum 470
Gideon 468, 469
Gideon (Jr.) 467
James 302
Jemima 490
Job 468
John 461, 474, 475, 476
John S. 302
Joseph 459, 485
Joseph 462
Joseph (Jr.) 460
Ramsdell (cont.)
Joseph Dawes 491
Joseph Marshall 302
Joshua 477
Lazarus 468
Levi 471
Lucy 479
Luther 478
Lydia 467
Lydia (Mrs.) 476
Martin 476
Mary 349, 477, 487, 488, 490, 492
Mary (Mrs.) 349
Mercy Monroe 462
Nathaniel 463, 466
Nehamiah 462
Nehemiah 463, 464, 465, 467, 468, 486
Obed 302
Olive 460
Rebecca 466
Rufus 479
Salome 474
Saml1. 349
Samuel 460, 470, 483, 488
Samuel (Jr.) 461, 471, 476, 477, 486
Samuel (Sr.) 485
Samuell 349
Sarah 469, 477
Sarah Barstow 468
Seth 464, 467
Simeon 459, 461, 462
Thomas 492
William 271, 475
William M. 302
William Myrick 302
Ramsden, Daniel 536
Joseph 454, 502
Luciana 454
Nehemiah 452
Rand, Eliza C. 302
George Clark 302
Isaac (Dr.) 302
Thomas 302
William B. 302
Randal, Abigail 402
Benja. 400
Benja. (Jr.) 399, 402
Benjam. (jr.) 394
Benjamin 370, 384, 397, 399, 428
Benjm. 334, 370, 371, 373, 377, 388
Betty 455
Caleb 339, 368, 373, 377, 379, 383
Daniel 388
Deborah 327, 398
Deborah (Mrs.) 340, 342, 349
Debrah 455
Dorcass (Mrs.) 373
Elijah 370, 411
Elisabeth 401
Elisabeth (Mrs.) 391
Elisha 355, 381, 383, 387, 391
Elizabeth 340, 373, 388
Elizabeth (Mrs.) 388
Ezra 370, 401, 402
Gersh. 401
Gershom 357, 388, 391, 398
Gidion 327, 379

Smallee (cont.)
  Marye Twinnes 599
Smalley, (?) (Widow) 694
  Arnold 227
  Benjamin 555
  Elisabeth 693
  Hannah 545
  Isaac 698
  John 555
  Leonard (Cpt.) 687
  Mary 555
  Mary (Mrs.) 555
  Tailer 555
  Washington 228
  Winthrop 697
Smallwood, James 305
  Martha 305
Smally, Anthony 226
  Mary 226
  Winthrop 687
Smith, (?) 105, 496, 539, 609, 689
  (?) (Cpt.) 105
  (?) (Mrs.) 538
  (?) (Rev.) 401, 650
  (?) (Widow) 188
  Abby S. 176
  Abby Weatherel 305
  Abiah 191
  Abial 374
  Abigail 22, 399, 400, 449, 554, 555, 589, 591, 594, 631
  Abigail (Mrs.) 100, 105, 106, 107, 554
  Abigal 141
  Abner 159
  Abraham 57, 163, 190
  Aggnes (Mrs.) 646
  Albert 167, 171, 305
  Alice 154
  Allan 446
  Allen F. 174
  Allice 403
  Almira 169
  Alvin (Mrs.) 446
  Andrew 638, 646
  Ann 154
  Ann (Widow) 200
  Anna 124, 205, 220
  Anna (Mrs.) 120, 130, 132, 215, 594
  Anne 157
  Anne Lenthll. 625
  Arvin 669, 690
  Arving 669
  Asa (Jr.) 173
  Azanath 163
  Bachuel M. 173
  Barnabas 141, 145
  Bathsheba 166, 472
  Bathshebah 588
  Bathyah 630
  Benaiah 12
  Benj 127
  Benj. 223
  Benja. 205
  Benja. (Jr.) 207
  Benjamin 32, 98, 108, 173, 182, 213, 224, 305, 631, 638
  Benjamin (Cpt.) 191
  Benjn. 202, 215
  Beriah 554
  Bershebe (Mrs.) 93
  Bethiah (Widow) 200
  Betsey 186
  Betsey (Mrs.) 305
Smith (cont.)
  Betsy 166, 169
  Caleb 157, 697
  Caroline 173
  Catharine 157, 451, 456
  Catharine (Mrs.) 207
  Catherine 128, 209
  Charles 402
  Chloe 554
  Christopher 148, 451
  Clarington 170
  Clarissa 166
  Cornelius 188
  Daniel 39, 43, 47, 62, 78, 141, 216, 270, 303, 445, 516, 517, 535, 555, 589
  Daniel (Cpt.) 303
  Daniel (Sr.) 305
  Daniell 47
  Danl. 590, 591, 592
  David 141, 145, 162, 165, 169, 186, 188, 191, 195, 215, 305, 555, 589, 689
  Davis 165
  Dean 164, 174
  Dean S. 175
  Deborah 37, 70, 154, 340, 630, 635
  Deborah (Mrs.) 305
  Deidamia (Mrs.) 139
  Deliuerance 37
  Deliver 587
  Deliverance 37, 43, 70, 147, 154
  Deliverance (Mrs.) 143
  Desire 144
  Dianry B. 176
  Dorcas 4, 209, 600
  Dorothy (Mrs.) 654
  Easter 633
  Easter (Mrs.) 92
  Eben---ezer 601
  Eben. 590, 591
  Ebenezer 184, 191, 207, 209, 554, 599
  Ebenn. 214
  Ebenr. 179, 182, 186, 188, 193, 201, 204
  Ebr. 213
  Edward 305, 451, 513, 516
  Edward Francis 305
  Edwin 446
  Elbridge 555
  Eldridge F. 173
  Eliazar 47
  Eliazer 37
  Eliezer 144, 145
  Eliezers 37
  Elihu 148
  Elijah 118, 121, 127, 186, 199, 200
  Eliphal 144
  Eliphalet 270, 305
  Eliphelit 268
  Elisa. 629
  Elisabeth 12
  Elisabeth (Mrs.) 554, 555
  Elisha 305
  Eliza (Mrs.) 555
  Eliza J. 175
  Elizabeth 141, 144, 145, 148, 157, 587, 635
Smith (cont.)
  Elizabeth (Mrs.) 157, 175
  Elldridge F. 168
  Enock 555
  Ephraim 128, 163, 554, 630
  Esther 592
  Eunice 128, 164, 205
  Evelina 166, 169
  Ezekiel 245
  Fanny 202
  Farmer 636
  Francis 171, 216, 630, 646
  Franklin 170
  Freelove 589
  Freeman 163, 173
  George 143, 154, 159, 311
  Gersham 149
  Gershom 37, 146
  Gideon 157
  Gilbert 216
  Hana 633, 635
  Hannah 6, 37, 70, 141, 163, 450, 546, 554, 559, 630, 640
  Hannah (Mrs.) 118, 121, 594
  Harrison 215
  Hasadiah 146
  Hassadiah 37, 70
  Heman 162, 172
  Heniry 635
  Henry 516, 517, 539, 587
  Henry Thornberry 26
  Hepzibath 269
  Hershom 147
  Hezekiah 37, 147
  Hezeziah 37
  Homes 216
  Hope 143
  Humphrey 141
  Hunt 517
  Isaac 374
  Isaac (Jr.) 176
  Israel 345, 374, 399, 401, 402, 403
  J. F. 443
  James 37, 96, 141, 144, 175, 305, 554, 555, 594
  James (Cpt.) 445
  James G. 166, 168
  Jane (Mrs.) 145, 204
  Jean (Mrs.) 141
  Jedidah (Mrs.) 223
  Jeremi 124
  Jeremiah 141
  Jesse 554, 555
  Joanna F. 174
  Job 305
  Johanna 591
  John 14, 20, 37, 48, 49, 51, 60, 66, 70, 74, 78, 92, 113, 144, 148, 154, 182, 197, 221, 223, 470, 494, 517, 528, 529, 532, 533, 541, 554, 587, 588, 589, 591, 596, 597, 599, 600, 601, 602, 606, 630, 635, 638
  John (Jr.) 201, 203, 216, 544

Smith (cont.)
John (Rev.) 450
John (Sr.) 48, 502, 546, 635, 646
Jonathan 120, 130, 132, 149, 157, 188, 589, 654
Jonathan (Rev.) 118, 594
Jonathan S. 205
Joseph 112, 144, 169, 335, 345, 374, 399, 451, 456, 475, 638, 652
Joseph (Cpt.) 471, 472, 474, 475, 476, 477, 478, 489, 491
Joseph (Jr.) 28
Joseph H. 555
Joshua 47, 374, 451, 476, 491, 587, 653
Joshua (Rev.) 10, 17
Josiah 164, 451, 453, 628, 652, 653, 654
Judah 37, 159
Judith 10, 17, 157, 451, 516, 517
Judith (Mrs.) 517, 652, 654
Judith Miller 474
Kath 116
Katharine 116, 221
Katherin 98
Katherine 490
Kezia 164
Keziah N. 173
Knowles 167, 172
Levi 374
Lewis 167, 170, 555
Lewis G. 168, 172
Lidia (Mrs.) 646
Lois 190
Louisa 169
Love (Mrs.) 215
Lowry 148
Lucia 440, 472
Lucy 401, 471
Lydia 171, 174
Magdalen 517
Margaret 555
Martha 638
Martha (Mrs.) 555
Mary 3, 190, 223, 303, 340, 451, 454, 472, 540, 555, 599, 638, 651
Mary (Mrs.) 147, 148, 223, 553, 555
Mary A. 173
Mary K. 166
Matilda (Mrs.) 121
Mayhew 124, 136, 137, 140
Meahittabell 70
Mehetabel 270, 653
Mehetebel 145
Mehitabell 37
Mehitable 166, 167, 168, 170
Mehittabel 70
Mercy 166, 169
Mical 37
Michael 159
Miribah 159
Molly (Mrs.) 666
Myrick 163
Nat. 591
Nathan 195, 209

Smith (cont.)
Nathaniel 170, 451, 587, 630, 633, 654
Nathaniel (Dr.) 666
Nathl. 538
Nehemiah 163, 171
Nicholas 78
Nicklos 636
Noah 157
Olive 690
Oliver 168, 169, 190
Oliver Reed 468
Pain 165
Pamela 176
Pamela (Mrs.) 168
Patty Young 448
Pedia 163
Peleg 154, 374, 399
Peleg (Jr.) 147, 148
Phebe 170
Phebe (Mrs.) 157, 159, 444, 669
Phebe A. 171
Phebe Ann 167
Phebe Mayhew 221
Philena 172
Philip 190, 209
Phillip 162
Polly 28
Polly A. 166
Polly M. 171
Priscilla (Mrs.) 591
Rachel 3, 374
Rachel (Mrs.) 335, 374
Rachel D. 172
Rebecah 144
Rebecca 147, 148, 157, 220
Rebecca (Mrs.) 141
Rebeccah 145, 173
Rebeckah 554, 587
Rebekah 166, 167
Reuben 228, 442
Reuhamah (Mrs.) 37
Rhetire 689
Rhoda 27
Rhoda (Mrs.) 468
Richard 18, 36, 38, 43, 93, 159, 172, 468, 469, 470, 471, 472
Richard (Jr.) 168
Robe 159
Rufus 93, 94
Ruhamah (Mrs.) 37, 70
Ruth 141, 159, 163, 554
Ruth (Mrs.) 554
Ruth F. 174
S. Newell (Cpt.) 445
Sally 128, 166, 469
Sally (Mrs.) 136, 137, 140
Sally S. 168, 172
Saml. 177, 181, 194, 200, 207
Samuel 78, 92, 115, 180, 197, 220, 554, 555, 633
Samuel (Cpt.) 98, 197
Samuel (Jr.) 180, 184, 197, 209, 210, 221
Samuel (Sr.) 180
Samuel K. 172
Samuell 599, 638, 644
Sarah 37, 70, 164, 173, 197, 209, 267, 547, 554, 555, 599,

Smith (cont.)
633, 644, 669
Sarah (Mrs.) 188
Seth 162, 555, 632
Shubael 107, 139
Shubael (Sr.) 100
Shubaell 600
Shubal (Jr.) 98
Silvanus 166, 471
Simeon 173, 554, 555
Solomon 3, 590
Sophia 666
Stephen 93, 94
Stephen C. 166, 176
Susana 628, 633, 638
Susannah 159, 554, 555
Susannah (Mrs.) 555, 597
Thankful 176, 451, 478, 654
Thankful (Mrs.) 206
Thankful (Widow) 191
Thankful L. Hopkins (Mrs.) 444
Theophilus 165
Thomas 98, 141, 144, 203, 206, 450, 451, 477, 650, 652, 653, 654
Thomas (Rev.) 17, 450, 451, 452
Thos. 179, 213, 214, 594
Timo. 183, 215
Timothy 165, 181, 223
Tumson 450
William 141, 157, 159, 166, 169
William M. 175
Willie 447
Zadoc 157
Zubah 555
Smyth, John 501, 504
Richard 501
Sneal, Thos. 177
Snell, Abigail 2
Amos 6
Anne 7
Charles 5
David 23
Deliverance 16
Ebenezer 3
Ephraim 20
Hannah 1, 5, 14
Jemima 9
John 8
Joseph 8
Lucy 27
Martha 8, 14
Polycarpus 16
Silence 4, 14
Stephen 27
Susanna 4
Thomas 26
Thomas (Jr.) 14
Zebedee 3
Zebedee (Cpt.) 4
Snow, A. 534
A. Lizzie 447
Aaron 305, 446
Abba 443
Abba (Mrs.) 442
Abiah 245
Abigail 12, 243, 442, 449
Abigail (Mrs.) 538
Abner (Jr.) 173
Alice R. 445

Springer, John 305
Rebecca (Mrs.) 305
Sproat, James 305
Mercy 621
Sprout, Abigail 344
Ebenezar 344, 348
Hannah 322, 430
Mary 348
Mercy 317
Robert 322, 327, 430
Robt 317
Thankfull 344
Sproute, Elizabeth 327
Elizabeth (Mrs.) 346
James 346
Robert 346
Sprowel, Hannah 209, 210, 220, 221
Sprowell, Hannah 191, 222
Sprut, Hannah 430
Robert 430
Spur, John 48
Mercy 631
Squire, Stephen 52
Stabuck, Anna 272
Edward 254
Jethro 254, 257
Mary 254
Nathan 254
Nathaniel 254
Stacye, Richard 504
Stanbridge, Elizabeth (Mrs.) 224
John 224
Saml. 224
Standige, (?) (Cpt.) 602
Standish, (?) 512, 513, 517
(?) (Cpt.) 502, 506, 507, 511, 512, 515
(?) (Mrs.) 528
Alexander 502
Allexander 523
Barbara (Mrs.) 522, 523
Charles 523
Hadly 456
Josiah 248
Josias 242, 522, 523
Lora 522
Mary 454
Mary (Mrs.) 248, 522
Miles 497, 500
Miles (Cpt.) 523
Molly 457
Myles 512, 515, 523
Myles (Cpt.) 512, 522
Myles (Sr.) 522
Olive 454
Rose (Mrs.) 497
Thomas 245
Will 453
Standlake, Daniel 509
Standley, (?) 601
(?) (Widow) 413
Mary 324
Richard 324
Standlick, Abigall 323
Lydiah 323
Richard 323
Standly, Abigail 392
Abigail (Mrs.) 392
Deborah (Mrs.) 386
Jabez 386, 392
Stanford, Robert 243
Thomas 305
Stanlake, Joan 515
Stanlake (cont.)
Richard 515
Stanley, Daniel 319
Joanna 317
Richard 317
Staple, Jacob 629, 633
John 71
Mary (Mrs.) 72
Samuel 629
Staples, Amy 635
Elizabeth 344
Elizabeth (Mrs.) 341, 342, 343, 344
Ephraim 630
Hannah 635
John 635
Joseph 635
Joshua 341
Mary 635
Nathaniel 635
Samll. 343, 344
Samuel 7, 16, 342, 343
Samuell 341
Sarah 342
Star, Ruth 480
Ruth (Widow) 481
Starbuck, Abigail 259
Albert Norton 305
Amber A. (Dr.) 274
Anna 259, 305
Benjamin 259
Charles 305, 306
David Joy 305
Dinah (Mrs.) 305
Dorcas 261
Edward 256
Elizabeth 254, 256, 259
Elizabeth Gardner 305
Eunice 255, 261
Frederick 305
Henry 306
Hephsibah 256
Hephzibah 259
Hezekiah 305
Jemima 261
Jethro 259, 260, 261
Joseph Hatch 273
Josiah 306
Judith 310
Lydia 261
Mary 259, 261, 272
Mary (Mrs.) 306
Nathaniel 254
Nathl. 254, 255
Nathll. 256, 259
Nathll. (Jr.) 259
Paul 259
Prissilla 259
Ruth 259
Sarah 260
Susanna 306
Thaddeus 306
Thomas 261, 305
Thomas (II) 306
Trisram 259
William 261
Starbuk, Edward 262
Starr, Comfort 312, 502, 510
Elizabeth 312
John 502
Thomas 312, 504
Starse, Samuel 325
Sarah 325
Steadman, (?) 596
Elizabeth 597
Steaples, Elizabeth
Steaples (cont.)
(Mrs.) 341
Joshua 341
Samuell 341
Stearns, Ezra S. 266
Stedman, (?) 596, 609
Isaack 503
Steel, James 100, 109
Martha 108
Mary 99, 108
Nicolas 525
Susana H. 169
Steele, Mary 444
Norton 449
William (Mrs.) 447
Stephen, (?) 73
Stephens, Ann (Mrs.) 306
Bethiah 246
Calvin 306
Elihu 29
Ester 62
Hanna 246
Joseph 306
Josiah 250
Katrin 646
Nathan 471
Richard 67, 73, 77
Thomas 630
William 246, 306
Wm. (Jr.) 250
Stephenson, Bryant 404
Lusstanos 404
Steples, Elizabeth (Mrs.) 341, 342
Joshua 341
Samuel 342
Samuell 341
Sarah 342
Sterer, Benjm. 385
Ruth (Mrs.) 385
Susanna 385
Sterling, (?) (Earl) 647
Stertevant, Samuell 501
Stetson, (?) 472
Abel 456
Abigail 25, 375, 452, 453
Abijah 339, 369, 372, 375, 377
Abishai 27
Abishar 453
Abner 346
Adam 369
Alice 358
Alpheus 405
Amos 339, 383
Ann (Mrs.) 330, 384, 396
Anna 361, 372
Anna (Mrs.) 333, 351, 358, 361, 369, 374, 428
Anthony 327, 333, 351, 358, 361, 369, 374, 384, 428
Barzillai 306
Bathia 327
Benjamin 472, 473, 475, 490, 621
Benjamin (Cpt.) 326
Benjamin (Jr.) 329, 339
Benjm. 334
Benjn. 418
Bethia 27
C. (Rev.) 422
Caleb 366
Caleb (Rev.) 421

Studley (cont.)
Elizabeth 419
Experience 655
Isaac 696
Joseph 655
Lemuel 655
Mary 15
Mary (Mrs.) 419
Mary (Widow) 655
Mary Jane 690
Oliver 696
Samll. 655
Samuel (Cpt.) 696
Sarah 655
Sidney 693
Silvanus 655
Susanna 688
Sylvanus 695
Sylvanus (Cpt.) 690
Sylvester 473, 490
William 416
William (Sr.) 419
Studly, Abigail 429
Amiel 415
Anthony 658
David William 415
Deborah 658
John 658
Josiah 658
Mary (Mrs.) 658
Simeon 658
Willm. 412
Studson, Abigail 321, 440
Abigail (Mrs.) 321
Benjamin 312, 318, 319, 320, 321, 322, 430
Caleb 320
Cunel 542
Eunice 313
Hanah 322, 430
Hannah 320
Hershom 320
James 319
John 313, 321, 430, 440
Joseph 312, 318
Joshua 322, 430
Lois 314
Mary 321
Matthew 319
Robert 314
Robt 313, 314
Robt. 312, 313, 316
Samuel 313, 320, 322, 430
Samuell 322, 430
Sarah 321, 430
Tho. 321, 430
Thomas 312, 320, 322, 430
Timothy 316
Sturges, Abram 651
Edward 504, 668
John 99, 114, 115
Mary (Mrs.) 668
Naby 668
Nathaniel 616
Samll. 616
Thomas 99
Sturgess, Edward 599
Mary 599
Sturgis, Abigail 652
David 668
Edward 652, 653, 668
Elisabeth 652
Heman 668
Sturgis (cont.)
James 652
John 617
Jonathan 668
Keziah 227
Lucretia 652
Lucy 668
Mary (Mrs.) 542, 668
Mercy 652
Naby 668
Olive 668
Saml. 652
Samll. 653
Samuel 617, 653
Temperance 652
Thankful (Mrs.) 652, 653
Thomas 652
Sturtevant, Ann 545
James 541
John 541, 544, 547
Joseph 541
Josiah 306
Samuel 3, 541
Sturtson, Abigail 430
Barnabas 324
Ben. 323
Beniamin 324
Benjamin 430
Caleb 324
Deborah 323
Elijah 326
Elisha 325
Elizbeth. 323
Eunice 324
Hanah 430
John 324, 430
Joshua 430
Judah 323
Samuel 323, 430
Samuell 430
Sarah 430
Tho. 430
Thomas 324, 325, 326, 430
Stutson, Deborah 412
Ebenezer 568
Eliza 415
Peleg 18
Robert 503
Sudan, Henry 94
Suel, Phillis 24
Sulker, Sarah 565
Sullivan, Lot B. 647
Summerfield, John 306
Summers, John 538
Summerton, Daniel 141
Thomas 141, 145
Summons, Ceasar 311
Cloa (Mrs.) 311
Grace 311
Jeffrey 311
Lettice 311
Noah 311
Sumner, Benjamin 223
Jedidah (Mrs.) 223
John 223, 224
Susannah 224
Susannah (Mrs.) 224
Waitstill 7
Sunderling, John 543
Surrandolfe, Edward Fitts 596
Survash, John 193
Sutlieff, Abraham 531
Sutman, Roger 24
Sutten, John 324, 623
Nathan 324
Suttens, George 610
Sutton, Benjamin 321, 624
Elizab 317
Elizab (Mrs.) 317
Elizabeth 314, 624
Geo 314
Geo. 510, 525
George 313, 503, 536
Hannah 624
Hester 624
John 321, 624
Lydia 313
Mary 624
Nathan 624
Nathaniel 624
Nathaniell 321
Sarah 313, 624
Symon 503, 510
Swain, Abigail 277
Abigail (Mrs.) 306
Abishai (II) 307
Abner 306
Abraham 307
Albert G. 306
Alexander 306
Andrew F. 306
Ann (Mrs.) 307
Anna 272
Barnabas 302, 306
Barzilla Cottle 306
Barzillai 307
Batchelor 277
Benjamin 306
Benjamin (Jr.) 307
Charity 267
Charles 307
Charles (Jr.) 306
Charles Gorham 306
Charles Hussey 306
Christian 269
Daniel 307
David 280, 306
David (II) 306
Edward 306, 307
Edwin 306
Eliakim 266
Elihu 306
Elizabath 267
Elizabeth 255
Eunice D. 306
Frederick 307
Frederick Coffin 307
Frederick Folger 307
Freeman 306
George (Jr.) 307
Grafton 307
Hephzibah 306
Hephzibah (Mrs.) 306
Isaiah 306
James C. 306
Jemima 271
Jerusha (Mrs.) 306
Job 306, 307
John 255
Jonathan 306, 307
Jonathan (II) 307
Joseph 306
Joshua 307
Katharin 267
Laban 307
Lewis 306
Love 306
Margaret (Mrs.) 306
Margret 268
Mary (Mrs.) 306
Mary Lewis 306
Micajah 270, 306

Swain (cont.)
Moses 306
Nabby 277
Nathan 306
Obed B. 307
Peleg 306
Peleg Barrett 306
Peter 267
Polly 280
Priscilla (Mrs.) 307
Prissilla 266
Reuben 307
Richard 307
Rowland 307
Ruth 266
Sally 297
Samuel 306, 307
Samuel L. 307
Samuel Tuck 307
Sarah 307
Sarah W. 307
Shubael 307
Solomon 307
Stephen 268, 269, 307
Susan 307
Susanna (Mrs.) 307
Susanna H. 307
Thaddeus 306
Thomas 297, 306
Timothy 272
Uriah 305
Valentine 306
William 167, 271, 306, 307
William C. 307
William Samuel 307
William Tuck 307
Zaccheus 307
Swaine, Abigail 256
Benjamin 255
Herman 443
Jean (Mrs.) 254
John 254, 255, 258
John (Jr.) 256
Jonathan 256
Joseph 170, 254, 257
Peter 257
Richard 254, 256, 257
Richard (Sr.) 256
Sarah 254
Stephen 254
William 256
Swane, William 172
Swasey, Clarissa 188
Joseph 188, 197, 202, 206, 216, 225
Joseph (Cpt.) 209
Joseph (Jr.) 186, 187
Mary 197
Susanna 225
Susanna (Mrs.) 216, 225
Swazey, David 307
Jonathan 307
Sweet, Elizabeth (Mrs.) 46
Sweeting, (?) 68, 70
Henry 82
Swift, (?) 532
(?) (Rev.) 206
Alexander S. 307
Alexander Swain 307
Chloe P. 227
Elijah 279
Elijah (Jr.) 227
Elizabeth 280
Experience (Mrs.) 367
Ezekiel E. 307
Swift (cont.)
Hannah 533
Hannah (Mrs.) 307
Harriot Frances 229
Henry 307
Jerisha 367
Jethrow 226
Joan (Mrs.) 533
John 226, 229, 367
Joseph 227, 307
Josiah 367
Judah 649
Leml 593
Lucy P. 227
Martha 227
Martha (Mrs.) 230
Paul (Dr.) 280, 307
Rachel (Mrs.) 345
Rebecca (Mrs.) 593
Rosamond 226
Roxanna 227
Sarah Brown 307
Seth 228, 280
Seth F. 307
Thankfull (Mrs.) 367
Thomas 345, 367
Uriah R. 226
William 533
Swyft, Joane (Mrs.) 510
William 510
Willm. 503
Syckles, James 312
Syllice, (?) 610
Hannah 602
Richard 596, 602
Sylvester, Almira 415
Anna 319, 411
Barstow 403
Benjamin 315, 533
Catherine 415
Celia 399, 402
Charles Warren 415
Cloe 409
Deborah 411
Desire 397
Dinah 533
E. 401
Elijah 412
Elisha 396, 398, 403
Elizabeth 533
Eunice 411
Eunice (Mrs.) 396
Fruitfull 410
Gershom 403
Grace (Mrs.) 398
Hannah (Mrs.) 415
Hervey Turner 423
Hester 314, 533
Israel 320, 399, 402, 533
John 319, 533
Joseph 318, 319, 320, 397, 533
Lemuel 403
Lidia (Mrs.) 397
Lucy 409, 414, 416
Lydia 533, 623
Mary 318
Mary (Mrs.) 396, 397
Naomi 313, 319
Naomy 533
Naomy (Mrs.) 533
Nehemiah 403
Rachel 11
Rich 315
Rich. 623
Richard 313, 314, 315, 533
Sylvester (cont.)
Richard (Sr.) 533
Sarah 319
Solomon 320
Thomas 401
Thos. 405
Thos. (Jr.) 404
Tryphine 404
Tryphosy 405
Warren 415, 423
William 397
Wm. (Cpt.) 403
Zachariah 4
Zebulon 396
Symkins, Nicholas 504
Symmes, Elisabeth (Mrs.) 397
Timothy 397
Symmonds, Joseph 17
Symmons, Ebenezar 364
John 318
Joseph 466
Moses 17, 318
Nathaniel 466
Ruben 364
Thomas 503
Symms, Anthony 349, 357
Eliz. (Mrs.) 357
Elizabeth (Mrs.) 332, 345, 349
Elizabth. (Mrs.) 347
Hannah 345
Thomas (Jr.) 335
Timothy 332, 345, 347, 349, 357
Symonds, Aaron 621
Symons, Ebenezar 364
Job 320
Moses 320
Moyses 502
Ruben 364
Thomas 506
Sympkins, Eliza (Mrs.) 697
Nathanael 697
Nicholas 504
Syms, Elizabeth (Mrs.) 345
Hannah 345
Timothy 345
Tabar, Thomas 65
Taber, Abigail 52, 156, 160
Amaziah 154, 156
Benjamin 156
Bethiah 52, 156, 160
Daniel N. 228
Easter 52
Eleanor 159
Eseck 156
Esther 156, 160
Gardner 156
Hester 52
Huldah 158
Jacob 156, 160
James Henry 307
Jesse 158
John 52, 156, 160
John T. 154
Jonathan 154, 156, 160
Joseh 156
Joseph 52, 72, 75, 146, 156, 160
Lidiah 52
Lydia 156, 160
Margaret 156
Mary 52, 156, 160
Meribah 154

Thacher (cont.)
Isaac 659, 671, 672
Isaac Hamblin 686
James 656, 661, 674, 676, 678, 679, 680, 681
John 650
John (Sr.) 671
Jonathan 665
Jonothan Rawson 665
Jorge 679
Joseph 650, 658, 659, 660, 661, 665, 667, 668, 670, 672, 674
Joseph (Jr.) 656
Josiah 651, 656, 658, 660, 672, 673, 677, 678, 679
Josiah (Jr.) 672
Juda 676
Judah 653, 656, 660, 665, 676
Laban 659, 669, 670, 672, 674
Laben 669
Lewis 653, 654, 664
Lothrop Russel 667
Lucia Weld 673
Lucretia 652
Lucy Weld 673
Lydia 672
Lydia (Mrs.) 672, 673, 677, 678, 679
Maria 680
Mary 650, 656
Mary (Mrs.) 679
Mary Bur 676
Mary Burr 676
Mary Gray 673
Matthews 671
Mehetabel 658
Mehetible 666
Mercy 656
Milly 679
Molly 660
Molly (Mrs.) 679
Nabby 670, 687
Nabby (Mrs.) 668
Nabby Russel 673
Naby Russel 673
Nancy 674
Nancy (Mrs.) 679, 680
Noble 672
Oliver 672
Paddoc 672
Peter 528, 652, 653, 654, 655, 661, 662, 663, 664
Phoebe 650
Polly 674
Printis 681
Ralph 60, 528
Russel 677
Ruth 651
S. (Jr.) (Mrs.) 686
Sally 671, 678
Sally (Mrs.) 669, 670, 672, 674
Sam Gorham 667
Saml. (Jr.) 686
Samuel 678, 679, 680
Samuel Gorham 667
Sarah 654, 659
Sarah (Mrs.) 653, 667
Sollomon 670
Solomon 679
Stephen 672
Susan 678

Thacher (cont.)
Susanah 661
Susanah (Mrs.) 661
Susanah (Widow) 665
Susanna (Mrs.) 656, 659, 674, 680, 681
Susanna Hawes 659
Susanna Haws 659
Susannah (Mrs.) 658, 660, 676, 679
Susannnah (Mrs.) 678
Temperance 659
Thankful 662
Thankful (Mrs.) 662, 665, 666, 667
Thankfull 661, 664
Thankfull (Mrs.) 658, 659, 660, 664
Thomas 681
Thomas (Col.) 679
Warren 674
Watson 669, 680
William 658, 659, 660, 662, 664, 665, 666, 667
Winslow 675
Wm. 653
Worren 674
Thacker, Anthony 538
Tharp, Benjamin 650
Ebenezer 650
Eunice 650
Mercy 650
Thatcher, (?) (Mrs.) 105
Abigail 616
Abigail (Mrs.) 665, 667
Anthony 653
B. (Rev.) 165
Barnabas 697
Betty (Mrs.) 664
Caroline 682
Charles 693
Cornelia 682
Cyrus 685
Daniel 665
David 650
Deacon 682
Desire 616, 650, 658
Desire (Mrs.) 616, 658
Dorcas 693
Ebenezer 696, 697
Edward 616, 696
Edwin 685
Elisha 653
Eliza Jane 687
Eunice 694
Fanny 691
George 697
Hannah 693
Henry 682, 694, 696, 697
James 681, 688, 694, 696, 697
John 99, 583, 616, 652
Jonathan 665
Jonathan Rawson 665
Joseph 652, 653, 665, 667, 696
Joseph (Cpt.) 652, 694
Josiah 658, 694, 698
Judah 651, 665
Lawrence 685
Lewis 307, 664
Lydia (Mrs.) 698
Mary 685
Mary (Widow) 698
Mehetable 616

Thatcher (cont.)
Metilda 681, 694
Molly (Widow) 698
Nancy 681, 693
Paddock (Cpt.) 694, 696
Peter 653, 664, 695
Russel 694
Ruth 683
Sally 695
Samuel 681, 685, 690
Samuel (Jr.) 685
Sarah 682, 693
Susan 690
Susanah (Widow) 665
Susannah (Mrs.) 694
Susannah (Widow) 694
Temperance 616
Thankful 653
Thankful (Mrs.) 665
Thomas 616
Watson 692
William 665
Winslow E. 697
Thaxter, (?) 193
(?) (Rev.) 208, 209
Ann (Mrs.) 213
John 140
Jos. 185
Joseph 185, 201, 213
Joseph (Jr.) 206
Joseph (Rev.) 180, 199, 219, 220, 225
Molly (Mrs.) 199
Robert 201
Thayer 219
Thayer, Abigail 628, 644
Abijah 5
Ebenezer 5, 628
Elisabeth 629
Enoch 3
Ephraim 3
Joanna 643
Johana 629, 639
Joseph 27
Mary 5, 628, 642
Nathaniel 39, 639, 644
Nathaniel (Jr.) 644
William 630
Therber, James 84
Thirber, James 587
Jonathan 587
Thirston, Daniel 74
Thistin, Benjamin 269
Benjemin 269
Thomas, (?) 423
A. 244
Abiah (Mrs.) 240
Abigail 247
Abigail (Mrs.) 240
Alice (Mrs.) 240
Ann 240
Anne Cushing 472
Anthony (Col.) 240
Avenic Standish 477
Benjamin 473
Bethiah 253
Betsey 470
Calvin 474, 475, 490
Charles 478
Christopher 456
Daniel 244
Deborah 243, 466, 478
Deborah (Mrs.) 240
Deborah Winslow 26
Dorothy 243, 516, 620
Ebenezer 253
Ebenezer Standish 475

Thomas (cont.)
Edward 253, 458, 459, 460, 470, 484
Edward (Cpt.) 491
Edward (Lt.) 488
Elizabeth 253, 516
Elizth. (Mrs.) 240
Gideon 246
Hannah 252
Ichabod 453
Ichabod (Jr.) 456
Isaac 412, 456, 472, 473, 475, 490
Isaac (II) 478
Isaac (Jr.) 475, 476, 477
Isaac Smith 476
Israel 244
Jacob 252
James 246
Jedediah 253
Jeremiah 253
Jesse 486
John 11, 240, 242, 245, 246, 248, 250, 454, 466, 467, 469, 470, 473
John (Cpt.) 240
John (Sr.) 249, 534
Jonathan 252
Joseph 245, 249, 459, 472, 484
Josiah Cushing 475
Kezie 240
Levi 29
Lucy (Mrs.) 240
Luther 476
Lydia 29, 253
Lydia (Mrs.) 240
Lydia Cushing 473
M. A. 238, 242, 247, 249
March (Mrs.) 240
Mary 253, 472, 516
Mary (Mrs.) 240
Mercy 247
Meriam 253
Nathan 240, 245, 253, 307
Nathaniel 240, 242, 243, 244, 251, 253, 458, 469, 470, 472, 473, 474, 475, 476, 478, 488, 490, 516
Nathaniel Ray 240
Nathl. (Cpt.) 248
Patience 12
Polly 456
Priscilla 23, 253
Rebecca (Mrs.) 307
Ruth 469
Samuel 240, 243, 251
Sarah 243, 246, 247, 253, 460, 467
Sarah (Mrs.) 249
Sarah (Widow) 244
Sophia 440
Susanna 169
Thankful 253
Wealthy 473
William 240, 247, 251, 516, 629
Winslow 26
Zadoc 472
Thompson, Agnes 3
Archibald 15
Barzillai 467
Benjamin 307
Thompson (cont.)
Calvin 468
Cynthia 466
Edward 498, 499
Edward (Rev.) 250
Elizabeth 469
Isaac 307
Isaac C. 307
Isaiah 307
James 16, 307, 464
Jasper 499
John 463, 464, 465, 466, 467, 468, 469, 470, 547
John (Dr.) 307
John Bisbee 463
Mary 5
Peter 463
Robert 619
Sarah 470
Thomas 619
William 307, 465
William (Rev.) 452
Thomson, Ann (Mrs.) 348, 357
Anna (Mrs.) 350
Barnabas 350
John 20, 548
Robert 348, 350, 357
Thomas 357
Thorn, Joseph 348
Rachel 348
Thorne, Joseph 621
Mary 345
Thornton, Robt. 537
Tho. 535, 536
Tho. (Rev.) 537
Thomas 521
Thorp, (?) 245
Joh 507
Thrasher, Bezaleel 643
Brooks 643
Catharine 643
Christopher 640, 643
Damaris 643
Elnathan 643
Hana 646
Hannah 643
Israel 640, 643
John 643
Mary 640
Mercy 643
Samuel 643
Samuell 643
Sarah 547, 639, 643
Thresher, Bethiah 62, 68
Brook 62
Brooks 68
Israel 65, 82, 88, 89
John 44, 78, 91
Marcey (Mrs.) 67
Samll. 43, 68
Samuel 48
Throop, (?) 85
Throope, Dorcas (Mrs.) 35
Thurston, Abigail 12
David 8
John 592
Saml. 592
Thomas 62
Thurstone, Charles 501
Tickner, John 316
William 316, 317
Ticknor, William 620, 622
Tidge, Elizabeth (Mrs.) 528
Tiffany, Nathanl. 369
Tilden, (?) 609
Abigail 318, 328, 354, 624
Alfred 676
Atherton Wales 414
Benjamin 319, 541, 619
Benjm. 372
Betsy 414
Caleb 245, 454
Calven 674, 675
Calven (Dr.) 676
Caroline 421, 425
Catharine (Mrs.) 674
Catharine Hichcock 675
Catherine (Mrs.) 676
David 326, 468, 624
David (Maj.) 469, 470, 488
Desire 356
Desire (Mrs.) 354, 356, 358, 362
Ebenezer 324, 624
Edward Bartlett 415
Elizabeth 318, 541
Elizabeth (Mrs.) 248
Elizebeth 323
Elizth (Mrs.) 541
Ephraim 323, 624
Experience 244
Grace (Mrs.) 372
Hannah 245, 317, 623
Henry 414
Isaac 321, 624
J. 516
Jerusha 247
John 245, 249, 314, 541, 619
Joseph 244, 313, 314, 315, 316, 318, 319, 325, 503, 509, 510, 514, 515, 516, 532, 536, 537, 541, 544, 624
Joshua 246
Judith 319, 510, 624
Julia 415, 421
Lucy Brooks 425
Lucy Turner 414
Luther 414, 415, 416
Luther (Cpt.) 420, 424, 425
Luther Albert 414
Lydia 318, 328, 331, 510, 534, 541, 547, 620, 622
Lydia (Mrs.) 510
Mary 318, 320, 416, 510, 624
Mercy 358, 624
Nathaniel 2, 313, 320, 469, 488, 619, 620, 621
Nathaniel Twynge 470
Nathaniell 321, 323, 325
Nathl 510, 541
Nathl. 534
Peter Thatcher 414
Philenda (Mrs.) 420
Rachel 372
Rebecca 314, 541, 620
Rebeccah 340
Ruth 362, 624
Saml. 334, 362
Samll. 329, 331, 354, 356
Samll. (Jr.) 358

Tilden (cont.)
Samuel 316, 328, 330, 340, 541, 621
Sarah 328, 334, 416, 468, 510
Sarah (Mrs.) 329
Sophia (Mrs.) 421
Stephen 316, 317, 318, 319, 321, 330, 510, 536, 541, 545
Steuen (Sr.) 326
Steven 323, 324, 623
Susanna (Mrs.) 249
Thacher 415
Thatcher 412, 414
Thom. 503
Thomas 242, 248, 249, 510, 543
Wm. Phillips 424
Tildin, Benjamin 345
Desire (Mrs.) 333
Lidia 640
Saml. (Jr.) 333
Samll 329
Samll. 345
Sarah (Mrs.) 329, 345
Tileston, Timothy 620
Tiley, Thomas 502
Till, James 503
Tillden, (?) 602, 609
Wm. 609
Tillding, Steven 620
Tilley, (?) (Mrs.) 498
Edward 498, 499
John 498, 499
Tilly, (?) 509
Heugh 504
Willm. 504
Tillye, (?) (Widow) 602
Tilson, Edmond 502
Edward 529
Elizabeth 544
Ephraim 545
Jane? 545
Jone 545
Mary 545, 547
Rhoda 27
Tilten, John 503
Tilton, (?) 100
(?) (Dr.) 123
(?) (Mrs.) 108
Abiah 124
Abigail (Mrs.) 118, 123
Albert 121, 124
Anna (Mrs.) 139
Asa 128
Bathsheba 124, 126
Bathshebah 99
Beriah 99, 129, 130, 131, 132, 133, 135, 140
Betsey (Mrs.) 122
Beulah (Mrs.) 118
Cornelius 129, 140
Cyrano 122
Cyreno 121
Daniel 125, 127, 132, 133, 134, 135, 137
David 123, 125, 128, 134, 138, 139, 140
Deidamia (Mrs.) 120, 130, 133, 134, 138
Desire 555
Desire (Mrs.) 555
Elijah 119
Elizabeth (Mrs.) 118, 119, 130, 133, 134
Tilton (cont.)
Elizabeth (Widow) 123
Elmira (Mrs.) 140
Eunice 126
Eunice (Mrs.) 119, 121, 131, 132, 133, 134, 136
Experience 555
Ezra 123, 131, 134, 135
Fear (Mrs.) 136, 137, 138, 139
Francis 129, 138, 139
Hannah 127
Hebron 129, 138, 139
Isaac 124, 125, 131, 132
James 555
Jane 98
Jedidah 222
Jedidah (Mrs.) 121, 138, 139, 140
Jemima 119, 127
Jemima (Mrs.) 124, 131, 132
John 117
Joseph 99, 101, 118, 120, 122, 132, 133, 134
Joseph (Jr.) 120, 126, 130, 132
Josiah 118, 119, 121, 129, 139
Josias 140
Lavina (Mrs.) 132, 134, 135, 137
Levina 124
Levina (Mrs.) 133
Levinthia 125
Lucy 126
Lydia 123
Lydia (Mrs.) 129, 130, 131, 132, 133, 135
Marca (Mrs.) 555
Marcy 555
Margaret (Mrs.) 129
Martha B. 129
Mary 117, 127
Mary (III) 126
Mary (Widow) 118, 123
Matthew 119, 124, 128, 130, 131, 132, 133
Matthew (Jr.) 123
Matty (Mrs.) 123, 134
Mercy 551
Moses 125
Nathan 124, 125
Oliver 121, 124, 126, 131, 132, 133, 134, 136
Olivia 127
Pain 125, 130, 139, 140
Pain (Jr.) 129
Paine 138
Parnell 129, 139
Parnell (Mrs.) 138, 139
Peggy 121, 126, 131
Peggy (Mrs.) 121, 130, 132, 133, 134, 135, 136
Persis (Mrs.) 138, 139, 140
Philip 555
Polly (Mrs.) 139
Polly B. 129
Prudence 129
Tilton (cont.)
Prudence (Mrs.) 139
Rachel 120
Rebecca 129
Rebecca (Mrs.) 118, 140
Remember 126
Remember (Mrs.) 121
Reuben 118, 119, 121
Rhoda 555
Rodah 555
Ruhamah 119
Ruth (Mrs.) 101
S--- 121
Salathial 124
Sam (Jr.) 100
Samuel 109, 115, 118, 129, 140
Samuel (Sr.) 100
Sarah 101, 128
Sarah (Mrs.) 119, 124, 130, 131, 132, 133
Serano 138
Stephen 118, 124
Susan (Mrs.) 125
Susanna (Mrs.) 130
Thomas 99, 120, 123, 128, 136, 137, 138, 139
Uriah 121, 222
Ward 122, 130, 133, 134, 139
Ward (Jr.) 129, 139
Will. 109
William 101, 125, 129, 130, 134, 136
William (Jr.) 121
Willliam 555
Wm. 132, 133, 135
Wm. (Jr.) 122, 129, 131, 140
Zelinda 129
Zeno 125
Zilpha (Mrs.) 118
Zilpha (Widow) 124
Timberleg, Mary 52
Tinckham, Ephraim 520
Tingley, Elisab 591
Ephraim 591
Esther (Mrs.) 591
Saml. 591
Tho. 591
Thom. 591
Thomas 591
Timothy 591
Tinker, (?) 499
(?) (Mrs.) 498
Sarah 596
Thomas 498
Tinkham, Ephraim 25, 502
Noah 2
Shubael 245
Tirrel, Saba 455
Tisdail, Abigail 628
Tisdale, Anna 629, 633
Ebenezer 99, 232
Hannah 631
James 232
John 502
Joseph (Jr.) 631
Joshua 628
Mary 631
Mary (Mrs.) 232
Tisdall, Joshua 44
Tisdill, Abigail 641
Abigall 637
Anna 637
John 637

Tuell, Abigail 569
Abigail (Mrs.) 569
Benjamin 349
Castle 349
Joanna (Mrs.) 349
John 569
Tulb, Bethiah 243
Tuper, Thomas 503
Tupper, Charls 368
Deborah 367
Eldad 368
Eliakim 367, 368
Enoch 368
Esther 594
Hannah 594
Hannah (Mrs.) 368
Israel (Jr.) 593
James 200
Joanna (Mrs.) 367, 368
Samuel 368
Silas 594
Tho. 510
Thomas 509
Turn--, Temperance 412
Turner, (?) 383, 416, 421, 499, 595, 596, 609, 610
A. 401
Abel 367
Abial 391
Abiel 341, 381, 383, 386, 388, 395, 398, 399, 407, 421
Abiel (Jr.) 404, 408
Abiell 378
Abigail 327, 328, 370, 386, 388, 425, 619
Abigail (Jr.) 455
Abigail (Mrs.) 333, 338, 341, 367, 370, 372, 381, 387, 390, 394, 395, 397, 429, 619
Abigal (Mrs.) 376, 397
Abner 355, 356, 374
Adam 453
Affee 406
Aimy (Mrs.) 355
Amasa 330, 345, 351, 380, 413
Amos 319, 621
Amos (Col.) 619
An 324
Ann 12, 375, 623
Anna 345, 391
Anna (Mrs.) 330, 345, 351
Anna Eliza 416
Anne 317
Asa 387
Barshua 322, 327
Bartlet 352
Bathsheba 620
Benja. 426
Benjamin 317, 339, 345, 362, 373, 375, 405, 420, 621
Benjm. 337, 369, 373, 376, 379, 383, 388, 391, 429
Benjm. (Jr.) 333, 362
Bethiah 395, 399
Betse (Jr.) 457
Bettsy 405
Betty 381, 453
Caleb 332, 358, 362, 364, 370, 372, 374
Calvin 394
Turner (cont.)
Catherine 375
Charles 329, 340, 347, 373, 404, 405, 406, 408, 413, 426
Charles (Col.) 407, 414, 415
Charles (Jr.) 408, 411, 418
Charles (Rev.) 416
Charls 342, 343, 344, 348, 352, 368, 373, 379, 381, 383, 390, 404
Christina 453
Clarrissa 404
Cloe Stowers 406
Consider 399
Content 358
Daniel 623
Daniell 502
David 9, 320, 375, 400, 401, 619, 623
David (Rev.) 368
David Shirverick 426
Deb. 453
Deb. (Mrs.) 400
Deborah 321, 338, 399, 402, 426
Deborah (Mrs.) 338, 384, 389, 391, 394, 397
Deborah (Widow) 420
Debr. (Widow) 426
Dorothy 369
Edmund 308
Edward 381
Eliab 345, 621
Elijah 394, 404, 405, 410
Elisabeth 1, 391
Elisabeth (Mrs.) 388, 391, 398
Elisabeth (Widow) 396
Elisha 315, 326, 328, 369, 412, 420, 456, 620
Elisha L. 587
Elisth. (Mrs.) 369
Eliz. (Mrs.) 343, 372, 378, 381
Eliza Bailey 405
Elizabeth 315, 327, 328, 343, 347, 372, 377, 381, 428, 620
Elizabeth (Mrs.) 330, 333, 337, 345, 346, 347, 349, 364, 372, 395, 428, 429
Elizth. (Mrs.) 350, 383, 386
Elizth. Robinson 426
Ephraim 343
Eunice 317, 368, 621
Eunice (Mrs.) 368, 373, 379, 381, 383
Ezekiel 358
Ezekiell 313
Fear (Mrs.) 333, 359, 362
Francis 407
George 379
George C. 312
Grace 318, 345, 348, 358, 373, 621
Hanah Jacob 426
Hannah 246, 340, 345, 375
Turner (cont.)
Hannah (Mrs.) 321, 330, 340, 341, 347, 397, 408, 418, 419
Hannah C. (Mrs.) 420
Hannah Cushing 413
Hannah Tolmon 405
Harris 406, 407, 413, 414, 415
Hawkins 334, 339, 366, 369, 373, 375, 377, 381, 383, 387, 391, 397
Humfery 597
Humfrey 503
Humfry 315
Humph 622
Humphrey 503, 515, 544, 622
Ignatius 327
Isaac 324, 345, 347, 353, 355, 358, 362, 388, 397
Isaack 318, 353
Israel 338, 347, 384, 389, 391, 394, 397, 400, 402, 405, 418, 623
Israel (Mrs.) 343
Israell 315
Jacob 320, 328, 394, 623
Jael 428
James 418, 425, 619
James (Cpt.) 619
Jane 12
Japhet 321, 330, 339, 340, 347, 623
Jeffe 339
Jemima 341, 399
Jemymah 322
Jephet 324
Jesse 383, 385, 388, 390, 393, 399, 401, 456
Joanna (Mrs.) 352
Job 347, 402, 455
Johanna 366
John 314, 327, 328, 338, 339, 341, 348, 352, 399, 406, 410, 427, 498, 503, 538, 542
John (Jr.) 315, 316, 317, 318, 320, 622, 623
John (Sr.) 313, 314, 315, 316, 317, 318, 319
Jona. 397, 399
Jonath. 402
Jonatha(n) Star 387
Jonathan 313, 321, 322, 324, 325, 326, 327, 334, 338, 339, 341, 347, 366, 381, 385, 387, 390, 394, 395, 453
Joseph 313, 320, 322, 323, 326, 333, 343, 352, 364, 369, 372, 376, 399, 404, 416, 429, 454, 597
Joshua 324, 372, 391, 428
Joshua (Jr.) 453
Joshua Dauis 406
Josiah 531, 622

Walker (cont.)
Hannah J. 176
Heaster 640
Hester 519
Isaac 245, 456
Jabez 555
Jain 589
James 46, 68, 504, 519, 530, 538, 555, 587, 630, 638
James (Jr.) 638
James (Sr.) 639, 640
Johannah 591
John 169, 242, 248, 536, 628, 647
Lydia 243, 455, 536
Lydia (Mrs.) 536
Margaret (Mrs.) 308
Martha 46, 536, 592
Mary 46, 536, 588
Mary A. 174
Menoy 166
Mercy 169
Nat. 589
Nathan 631
Patience 46
Peter 91, 169
Phebe 162
Philip 46
Phill. 587
Phillip 82, 587, 588, 589, 590
Ruth 166, 592
Ruth A. 169
Ruthie 449
Sally 164
Sam 82
Saml. 47, 592
Samll. 50, 51
Samuel 46, 50, 51
Samuell 46, 50
Sarah 164, 587
Sarah H. 176
Silas 308
Thomas 40
William 545
Wall, James 696, 698
Wallace, Mary (Widow) 308
Wallen, (?) 506
Wallero, Elisabeth 629
Walley, (?) (Rev.) 595
Hannah (Mrs.) 635
John 36, 66
Sarah (Widow) 595
Thomas (Rev.) 595
Wallis, Elizabeth 8
Wamsley, Benjamin 312
Polly (Mrs.) 312
Wanton, Edward 624
Elizabeth 344, 624
George 624
Hannah 624
John 624
Joseph 624
Margaret 624
Michael 624
Philip 624
Sarah 624
Stephen 624
William 624
Ward, (?) (Mrs.) 111
Abigail 166
Abigail M. 169
Ben. 107
Ebenezer 165
Ezekiel 163
George 169
Ward (cont.)
George (Jr.) 166
Hannah (Widow) 185, 199
John 185, 208
Josiah 308
Lydia 166, 170
Rhoda (Mrs.) 308
Ruth 163
Wardall, Vzal 84
Warden, Peter 509
Ware, John 42, 92
Wareham, Jane (Mrs.) 555
Martin 555
William 555
Warren, (?) (Mrs.) 507
Abigail 538
Aimy (Mrs.) 355
Ann 538
Anna 366
Benjamin 308
Ebenezer 1, 4
Elizabeth 538
Elizabeth (Mrs.) 500, 538
Elizabeth (Widow) 549
Eunice 4
Ezra 14, 455
Hannah 5
Jabez 252
James 246, 350, 352
Jane 4
John 350, 352, 355, 358, 366, 516
Joseph 312, 502, 538
Mary 538
Naomi (Mrs.) 358, 366
Naomy 350
Naomy (Mrs.) 350, 352
Nathanael 358
Nathaniel (Sr.) 538
Nathaniell 502
Priscilla 252
Richard 498, 500
Samuel 252
Sarah 5, 500, 538
Sarah (Mrs.) 538
Susanna 4
Warrick, Danah (Mrs.) 491
Joseph 491
Wasbern, Oliver 583
Wasborne, John (Sr.) 502
Washborne, John (Jr.) 502
Phillip 502
Washburn, Abigail 9
Alice 4
Amaziah 308
Anna 15, 28
Benjamin 8, 308
Betty 16
Calvin 565
Cromwell 565
Davis 565
Deliverance 9, 20
Eleazar 12
Eliab 19
Elizabeth 6, 8, 9
Eunice 25
Experience 2
Fanny 565
Hannah 4, 8, 11
Hepzibah 7
Ichabod 247
Isaac 21, 565
Israel 7, 569, 583
Israel (Cpt.) 582
Washburn (cont.)
Jacob 28
James 9
Jane 579
Jean 559
John 8
John (Jr.) 6
John Marshall 565
Leah 569
Lean (Mrs.) 569
Levi 18
Libeus 26
Lysander 565
Mahala 565
Marjoram 6
Mary 9, 29, 569
Nabby 28
Nancy 565
Nehemiah 8, 17, 565, 569, 582
Noah 8
Olive 569
Oliver 21, 569
Polly (Mrs.) 565
Rebecca 9, 16
Sally 28
Samuel 6
Sarah 6
Seth 569, 584
Solomon 18
Southworth 27
Stephen 17
Susanna 29
Susannah 15
Thirza 565
Thomas 7, 8
Waitstill 9
Wealthy 569
William 8
Wason, Ann (Mrs.) 374
Robert 374
Thoms. 374
Wass, Anna 208, 220
Homes 197, 209
John 98, 182
Violet 218
William 193
Wilmot 99, 208
Wasson, Ann (Mrs.) 374
Robert 374
Thoms. 374
Wate, Thomas 144
Waterman, Abigail 247
Anthony 241, 250
Asa 414
Asa Delano 414
Bethiah 245
Charlotte Cushing 414
Deborah 409
Deborah (Jr.) 409
Debr. (Widow) 418
Desire 247
Elizabeth 244, 518
Elizabeth (Widow) 245
Foster 408
Francis. 415
Hannah 404, 485
John 308, 534, 541, 545
Jos. 471
Joseph 241, 245, 250, 534
Joseph (Jr.) 241
Jotham 308
Leml. Cushing 424
Lidia 245
Mary Ann (Mrs.) 308
Nathll. 404

Wheaton, Alice 347
Lydia 354
Obadiah 354
Obediah 347
Robert 63
Sarah (Mrs.) 347, 354
Wheatten, Jerimiah 39
Wheelden, David 652
Ebenezer 661
Elisabeth 655
Elisha 652, 653
Isaac 658
John 653, 654, 658
Jonathan 652, 654
Joseph 661
Joshua 658
Lydia 652
Lydia (Mrs.) 658
Marcy 666
Marcy (Mrs.) 663
Mary (Mrs.) 652
Mary (Widow) 662
Mercy 654, 666
Mercy (Widow) 662
Miller 663, 666
Molly 660
Nabby (Mrs.) 666
Prince 655
Rachel 653
Rebecca 653
Ruth (Mrs.) 658, 660, 661, 663
Samuel 663
Sarah 652
Seth 658, 659, 660, 661, 663
Seth Taylor 666
Susannah (Mrs.) 653, 654
Thankful 652
Thomas 657
Wheeldon, Elisha 652
Prisilla 652
Wheeler, N. G. 228, 229
Wheeller, James 42
Wheelwright, John 384, 391
Sally G. (Mrs.) 309
Samuel 309
Sarah 391
Sarah (Mrs.) 309, 391
Wheildon, Henry 504
Whelden, (?) (Widow) 696
Asa Wedden 675
Asa Worden 675
Betsey 675
Content Wedden 675
Content Worden 675
David 671, 696, 698
Edward 695, 698
Elisabeth 670, 696
Elisha 670
Elizabeth R. 168
Enoch 698
Garshom 670
Gershom 670
James 670, 697
John 202
Jonathan 675
Julia 218
Mary N. 691
Mayo 698
Polly Stevens 675
Priscilla 670
Prissilla (Mrs.) 670
Ruth (Mrs.) 671
Sally (Mrs.) 675
Sylvanus 698
Whelden (cont.)
Zenous 670
Wheldon, Abba 442
Catherine 500
Wheler, Mary 267
Wheleright, John 338
Sarah (Mrs.) 338
Whellen, Jane (Mrs.) 210, 220
Jean (Mrs.) 184
Whetcome, Robt (Sr.) 543
Wheteston, Bathsheba 430
John 430
Whetestone, Abigall 430
John 430
Whetston, Increase 315
John 315, 324, 326, 430
Joseph 324
Mercy 430
Susanna 326
Whetstone, Batsheba 316
Increase 351
John 316, 351
Sarah (Widow) 331
Whettone, Hannah 616
Hannah (Mrs.) 616
John 616
Whight, Benjamin 57
Whilden, David 671
Ebenezer 661
Elisabeth 670
Elisha 670
Garshom 670
Gershom 670
Isaac 658
James 670
John 658
Jonathan 693
Joseph 661
Joshua 658
Lydia (Mrs.) 658
Marcy 666
Mary (Widow) 662
Mercy 666
Mercy (Widow) 662
Miller 666
Molly 660
Nabby (Mrs.) 666
Priscilla 670
Prissilla (Mrs.) 670
Rebeccah 658
Ruth (Mrs.) 660, 661, 663, 671
Samuel 663
Seth 658, 659, 660, 661, 663
Seth Taylor 666
Sylvanus 693
Zenour 670
Whilee, Sybble 583
Whilen, Abigail (Mrs.) 663
Mercy (Mrs.) 663
Miller 663
Whiles, Annah 584
Whipo, Abigail 615
Georg 615
Whipper, James 268
Whippey, Alexander 309
Benjamin 309
Davis 309
Elizabeth 220, 276
Frederick F. 309
George (Sr.) 309
Hannah 288
Henry C. 309
James 285, 309
Whippey (cont.)
Jane 278
John 309
Josiah 309
Kezia (Mrs.) 309
Love 309
Martha (Mrs.) 309
Mary 309
Nathaniel 278, 288, 309
Susanna (Mrs.) 309
Zebulon 276, 309
Whipple, David 76, 163
John 628
Whippo, Abigail 614, 616
Abigail (Mrs.) 615, 617
Elizabeth 617
James 615, 616, 617
Jane 615
Lawrence 614
Margaret 616
Whiston, Abigall 322, 430
Bathsheba 322, 430
John 322, 430
Marcy 430
Sarah 620
Susanna 620
Whistons, John 503
Whit, John 649
Jorg 649
Whitaker, Nathaniel 8
Whitcomb, Catern 622
David 410
James 621
Whitcombe, John 503
White, (?) 593
(?) (Jr.) 248
(?) (Mrs.) 443
Abigail 632, 640
Adeline 570
Alfred 690
Amos 36
Anna 313
Anna (Mrs.) 581
Apollos 581
Ardon 309
Azubah 659
Bartlet 680
Benjamin 245, 251
Benjamin (Jr.) 21
Daniel 243, 251, 581, 582, 659, 675
David 309, 559, 569
Deborah 346
Dorcas 632, 639
Ebenezer 245, 642
Edward 631, 642
Elijah 570, 584
Elijah (Jr.) 570
Eliza 570
Elizabeth 314, 545, 623, 640
Elizabeth (Mrs.) 346, 569, 570, 602
Elvira (Mrs.) 435
Emanuell 504
Ephram 639
Franklin 684
Frederick 679
Fredric 679
George 683
Gideon Thomas 456
Goeing 602
Gowen 502
Gowin 535
Hannah 20, 453, 640

Wood (cont.)
Jno. 89
John 75, 82, 90, 91, 501, 511, 530, 538, 546
John Coffin 310
Jonathan 310
Joseph 60, 75, 89, 90, 91, 629, 630
Josiah 75, 89
Judah 14, 253
Luthan 147, 159
Margaret 76, 89
Martha 151
Mary 159
Mary (Mrs.) 310
Mulborough 159
Obadiah 310
Osman 159
Phebe 151
Rebecah 89
Rebecca 76, 151, 159
Samuel 29
Sarah 4, 75, 89, 159, 521, 538, 546
Sarah (Mrs.) 147, 151, 159
Steephen 501
Stephen 151, 539, 569
Susannah (Mrs.) 159
Thomas 253
Timothy 253
William 35, 60, 72, 75, 82, 89, 90, 628
William (Dr.) 310
William (Sr.) 72
William Fanning 310
Willm. 503
Wm. 89
Zenas 687
Zephaniah 310
Zilpha 151
Woodart, Benjamin 367, 380
Benjm. 357, 361
Bethiah 369, 379
Bethiah (Mrs.) 369
Betty 394
Deborah 380
Deborah (Mrs.) 380
Eben. 369
Hannah 359
James 374, 376, 379, 381, 384, 388, 391, 394
Jesse 367
John 391
Joseph 388
Lydia 374
Mary 357, 384
Mary (Mrs.) 337, 357, 361, 367, 388
Rachel 334
Right 357
Robert 334, 337
Robert (Jr.) 359
Sarah 376, 381
Sarah (Mrs.) 374, 376, 381, 384, 391
Simeon 361
Woodbere, Hugh 81
Woodberree, Hugh 76
Woodbery, (?) 66
Andrew 81
Benjamin 81
Emma (Mrs.) 81
Hugh 60, 80, 81, 90
Isaace 60, 81
Woodbery (cont.)
Isacce 80
Isace 60
Joseph 60, 81
Mary (Mrs.) 80
Nicholas 81
Nicolas 60, 80
Woodbury, Nathaniel 310
Woodcock, John (Sr.) 38, 39
Woode, John 643
Joseph 640, 643
Woodell, Joseph 36
Sarah 79
Woodfield, Ester 543
Hester (Mrs.) 540
John 531, 540
Woodie, Hannah 222
Woods, Charles 310
Daniel 310
David 310
Jera B. 310
John Coffin 310
Jonathan 310
Mary (Mrs.) 310
Obadiah 310
William (Dr.) 310
William Fanning 310
Zephaniah 310
Woodward, Aaron 339
Apollos 579
Aren 339
Beniamin 324
Benjamin 327, 349
Benjm. 349, 351
Bethia (Mrs.) 342
Bethiah 325
Deborah 324, 339
Deborah (Mrs.) 324
Ebenezer 639
Elizabeth 324, 327, 634
Ezekiel 639
Hannah 174
Irana 579
Israel 64, 630
Israell 634
Isreall 639
James 39, 326
Jane 646
Joanna 327
John 351, 428, 639
John (Sr.) 639
Joseph 639
Lydia 342, 418
Mary 327, 639
Mary (Mrs.) 349, 351, 428
Nathaniel 7
Nathanill 639
Ozias 579
Rachel 580
Rachel (Mrs.) 579
Robert 325, 326, 327, 339, 342, 630, 639
Ruth 411
Sarah (Mrs.) 67
Thomas 349
Walter 519
William 579
Woodwart, Abel 428
Benjamin 428
Mary (Mrs.) 428
Woodwis, James Carkis 4
Woodword, Hannah 592
Saml. 592
Woodworth, Abigail 621, 624
Woodworth (cont.)
Ann 428
Benjamin 624
Eamee 624
Ebenezar 428
Ebenezer 624
Elizabeth 624
Hezekiah 622
James 343, 624
Joanna (Mrs.) 428
Joseph 620, 623
Margarett 244
Martha 621
Mary 621
Robert 343
Ruth 624
Sarah 624
Thomas 620, 623, 624
Walter 503, 543
Woolson, (?) 348
(?) (Mrs.) 348
Jonah 348
Worcester, Mark T. 447
Worden, Mehetable (Mrs.) 612
Peter 504, 509
Samll. 612
Wormal, Sarah 7
Wormall, Hester 531, 545
Joseph 531
Josias 531
Mehitable 492
Merriam (Mrs.) 531
Sarah 531
Wormwell, Mary 629
Wormwoll, Elizabeth 366
Wormwool, Elizabeth 366
Worth, (?) 110
Abigail 270
Alexander M. 310
Andrew S. 310
Ann (Mrs.) 224
Benjamin (Cpt.) 310
Benjn. 200, 202
Betty Willm. 257
Charles (II) 310
Charles A. 310
Charles Frederick 310
Cyrus B. (Cpt.) 310
Dorcas 204
Dorcas (Mrs.) 223
Edward 204, 310
Edward Stabuck 310
Eliza Ann (Mrs.) 310
Eunice 272
Frederick 310
George B. 310
Gideon 303
Hagar 257
Henry P. 207
Hiram 200
Jared 196
Jethro 188, 194, 195, 196, 204, 222, 310
Jno. 256
John 194, 195, 199, 201, 209, 223, 224, 254, 256, 271
John (Jr.) 182, 224
John Akins 310
Jonan. 194, 195
Jonathan 207, 256
Joseph 267, 310
Judith 256
Judith (Mrs.) 310
Mary 270
Mary (Mrs.) 188
Nathll. 256

Worth (cont.)
Reuben 688
Richard 256
Sarah 201
Sarah (Mrs.) 195, 224
Seth (Cpt.) 310
Shubael 310
Sophia Folger 310
Susan (Mrs.) 211
Susan Swasey 204
Susanna Clark 310
Thomas 203, 310
Thomas (Cpt.) 216
Thomas Gilbert 203
Thomas S. 310
Thos. 204, 205, 211
Will. 258
William 254, 256, 259, 260, 261, 310
William (II) 310
William Jenkins (Gen.) 184, 209
William Stabuck 310
Willm. 256, 257
Wm. 264
Wm. (Cpt.) 126
Worthelike, Alice 624
Hannah 624
Peter 624
Sarah 624
Wotson, Roberd 266
Wright, Anthony 503
Bristol 312
Christopher 310
Cuffee 5
Daniel 241
David 319
Edward 318, 319, 320, 546
Edwd 318
Elisabeth 2
Fuller 508
Gener 430
Gener (?) 319
Grace 430
Hannah 318
James 405, 412
Jesse 405
Joseph 320
Margaret 318
Mercy 318
Mordeci 547
Nicholas 503
Peter 503
Phillis (Mrs.) 312
Priscilla (Mrs.) 506, 508
Richard 501, 513
Sarah 18
Sarah (Mrs.) 241
Thomas (Cpt.) 310
Will 506
Will. 508
William 508, 547
Zilphah (Mrs.) 310
Wyate, James 518, 520, 521, 529, 530
Wyatt, James (Lt.) 534
Wyborne, Thomas 503
Wyer, Benjamin 310
Caroline Swift 310
Caroline T. 310
Christopher 310
Hannah 119, 123
John 310
Obed (Cpt.) 310
Pernal 310
Yeonge, John 501
Yong, (?) 502
Jo. Brewster 502
York, (?) (Duke) 647
Yost, Mary 594
Youlden, Charles H. 176
Young, Ann P. 173
Ann S. (Mrs.) 444
Anna (Mrs.) 355, 359
David 555
Deborah P. 168
Elijah S. 176
Elisha 404, 405, 410
Elizabeth 319
Eunice 27
Ezekiel 370
George 318, 319, 546, 623
Gracie B. 444
Hannah 197, 317, 318
Hattie 442
Isaac 355
Jennet 23
Joanna (Mrs.) 555
Joanna Walker 555
Johannah 405
John 14, 440, 456
John(?) 448
Jonathan 446
Joseph 355, 359, 370
Joshua 165
Josiah 440
Laura 449
Leonard 173
Lorenzo D. 175
Louisa (Mrs.) 440
Lydia (Mrs.) 370
Marcy (Mrs.) 555
Mary 318, 555
Priscilla F. 172
Richard 93
Robert 19
S. Ada 441
Sally 418
Samuel 555
Thomas 317, 619, 621
Zebediah 440
Zoar, (?) 322